MANAGEMENT
THIRD EDITION

James A. F. Stoner
FORDHAM UNIVERSITY

Charles Wankel
UNIVERSITY OF NEW HAVEN

PRENTICE-HALL, INC., Englewood Cliffs, New Jersey

To our parents

Library of Congress Cataloging-in-Publication Data

Stoner, James Arthur Finch
  Management.

  Includes indexes.
  1. Management.   I. Wankel, Charles.   II. Title.
HD31.S6963 1986   658   85–19313
ISBN 0–13–549783–3

Art Director: Florence Dara Silverman
Development Editor: Steven Anzovin
Production Editor: Eleanor Perz
Book Designer: Jules Perlmutter
Cover Designers: Jules Perlmutter and Florence Dara Silverman
Line Art: Danmark & Michaels, Inc.
Photo Researcher: Eleanor Perz
Manufacturing Buyer: Ray Keating

Printed in the United States of America.

10 9 8 7 6 5 4 3 2 1

ISBN 0-13-549783-3 01

Prentice-Hall International (UK) Limited, *London*
Prentice-Hall of Australia Pty. Limited, *Sydney*
Prentice-Hall Canada Inc., *Toronto*
Prentice-Hall Hispanoamericana, S.A., *Mexico*
Prentice-Hall of India Private Limited, *New Delhi*
Prentice-Hall of Japan, Inc., *Tokyo*
Prentice-Hall of Southeast Asia Pte. Ltd., *Singapore*
Editora Prentice-Hall do Brasil, Ltda., *Rio de Janeiro*
Whitehall Books Limited, *Wellington, New Zealand*

Cover art: Computer-generated image by Turner Whitted and
David Weimer/AT&T Bell Laboratories.

Photo credits: Part one photo (p. 1)—AT&T Communications; part two
photo (p. 83)—Chrysler Corporation; part three photo (p. 231)—Andree
Abecassis; part four photo (p. 415)—Laimute E. Druskis; part five photo
(p. 571)—Chuck Rogers/The New York Times.

CONTENTS

iii

4

5

PART FOUR LEADING   415

15

MOTIVATION, PERFORMANCE, AND SATISFACTION   416

PREFACE

This book is about the job of the manager. It describes how men and women go about managing the people and activities of their organization so that the goals of the organization, as well as their personal goals, will be achieved.

We have attempted in this book to convey the very positive view we have of the manager's job. We believe the job of a manager is among the most exciting, challenging, and rewarding careers a person can have. Individuals can, of course, make great contributions to society on their own. But it is much more likely that major achievements will occur in managed organizations—not only businesses, but also universities, hospitals, research centers, government agencies, and other organizations. Such organizations bring together the talent and resources that great achievements require. A manager working within an organization therefore has a much greater chance to be involved in a significant and far-reaching activity than would an individual working alone.

We also believe that in addition to being fun and rewarding, a managerial career is critically important. The problems our society faces today—and, most likely, the problems it will face in the foreseeable future—require both large- and small-scale solutions that only businesses, governments, and other organizations can provide. How well we learn to manage such problems as pollution, nuclear proliferation, overpopulation, and poverty may help determine whether we survive as nations, cultures, or even as a species. The skill of organization managers will be a vital factor in our ability to meet society's tasks and challenges. The information in this text is designed to help you, the reader, develop these vital managerial skills.

In this text we have chosen to address the reader as a potential manager. At times, in fact, we even adopt a tone that suggests the reader already is a manager. This is done intentionally: We want to encourage the reader to start thinking like a manager as soon as possible. Obviously, the earlier one learns to think like a manager, the sooner one can develop managerial effectiveness. But there is another, more basic reason. All managers, but especially young managers just beginning their careers, are evaluated in large part on how effective they are as subordinates. The more successful an individual is as a subordinate, the more likely it is that his or her career will be successful. And one of the best ways of learning how to be an excellent subordinate is to learn how to think like a manager. Thus, addressing the reader as a manager (or at least as a prospective manager) is meant to be a helpful way of improving the reader's chances for future managerial and career success.

The content of this text has been selected with two objectives in mind: to provide the reader with information that is useful and relevant, and to give the reader an understanding of the management field. Thus, most chapters have practical orientation—for example, how organizational realities affect the ethical behavior of managers (chapter 3); when managers and subordinates should make decisions together (chapter 6); how organizational conflict can be managed (chapter 14); and what organizational realities and career strategies young managers should be aware of in order to manage their careers effectively (chapter 19).

Every attempt has been made to eliminate the excessive use of management jargon, which so often hampers the readability of books on management. Instead, clear and familiar language is used so that the material will be easily accessible to the reader. Where a new term is introduced, it is set off in italics and clearly defined. These terms are also collected in a glossary in the back of the book. The text has also been made more useful to students by referring to various types of organizations—not-for-profit, governmental, and business—in the belief that students will be assuming a wide variety of management positions.

The field of management has grown so rich that it is impossible to describe the work of all management writers and theorists in an introductory text. This text describes the major schools of management thought in one introductory chapter (chapter 2) and refers to major contributors in other chapters when the concepts and research they reported are discussed. The text discusses many of the classical works in the field of management and frequently describes the first research in a new area of inquiry.

This book attempts to integrate the major approaches to the basic introductory management course—the classical, behavioral, and quantitative approaches—and the emerging systems and contingency perspectives. The structure of the book is largely based on the classical approach because (1) managers themselves still seem to find it quite useful; (2) students find it to be a good "handle" and lead-in to the management field; and (3) it provides an excellent organizing framework for all the management approaches. We have specifically noted some of the important differences in the underlying values, assumptions, and action implications of the various approaches.

Organization Features

This book is a revision of the previous editions, which were very well received by professors, students, and managers around the world. In this edition we have retained the strengths of the previous work while taking on the new cargo needed by those going into the world of management in the 1990s. We have reacted to many who have recommended retaining the arrangement of the material in units organized by the four traditional management functions, an approach found helpful in introductory management courses.

The three chapters in part one introduce the field of management and the issues involved in managing (chapter 1), the development of management practice and theory over time (chapter 2), and managerial ethics and the effects on managers of the external environment (chapter 3).

Part two, devoted to planning and decision making, opens with a discussion of the factors involved in doing effective planning (chapter 4). Then, chapter 5 presents an overview of strategy development. A discussion of problem solving and decision making (chapter 6) is followed by explanations of various techniques and aids, including forecasting, that managers can use to improve their decisions and problem solutions (chapter 7). Finally, chapter 8 presents a discussion of the kinds of planning, decisions, and actions that go into managing operations effectively and improving productivity.

We turn to the organizing function in part three, beginning with an overview of the ways in which work is allocated and organizations are structured (chapter 9). Building on that foundation, we examine coordination, organizational design, and the problems associated with rapid growth (chapter 10), and the ways in which managers exercise authority and delegate tasks (chapter 11). We then consider the management of the organization's human resources, including the recent computerized systems now widely used in this area (chapter 12). The management of change at the various levels of the organization is the next subject (chapter 13), followed by a consideration of the sources, consequences, and ways of managing organizational conflicts, including labor negotiation, and the harnessing of organizational creativity (chapter 14).

In part four, the role of the manager as leader is brought into focus. First, we examine ways in which managers interact with subordinates to focus their motivation and ensure job performance (chapter 15). We next look at leadership itself and the factors to be considered in making it effective with individuals (chapter 16) and with groups and committees (chapter 17). In chapter 18, we discuss the communication of information and commands through an organization, including recent technological advances affecting managers. The capstone of this part is a practical guide to the strategies and tactics of career management (chapter 19).

Part five examines the important areas of control, management information and support systems, and international management. First, the designing and implementation of effective control systems are discussed (chapter 20). Then a quick overview of the various financial means of control, including budgeting, is provided (chapter 21). We then examine management information systems, decision support systems, and expert systems—the latest use of artificial intelligence by managers (chapter 22). We complete the text with an entirely new chapter on managing across countries in international organizations (chapter 23).

Although the organization of the book follows a logical sequence, the chapters have been designed to stand on their own, so that instructors can deal with the various topics in whatever order they choose. To make it easier for them to do so, and to show how integrated the management field is, we have included a large number of chapter cross-references.

Each chapter begins with a list of *learning objectives*. These tell the reader specifically what he or she should know after reading the chapter. The student can use this list as a study aid.

A large number of informative *tables, diagrams,* and *other illustrations* have been included. They have been designed to convey information in an attractive and readily comprehensible form. The *boxed inserts* in the text provide interesting supplementary information or summarize important material. In every chapter, one or more *cartoons* provide an amusing sidelight on the topic under discussion.

At the end of each chapter, a *summary* helps students review the material. The summary contains key information, concepts, and definitions. An additional study aid is the list of *review questions*. These questions help students better understand the content of the chapter. They also give students an opportunity to use the management concepts presented in the chapter and to integrate information relating to the topics discussed.

The use of *case studies* has long been recognized as an effective means for helping students acquire and apply management concepts. This text contains a total of 28 cases, many of which have been classroom-tested for effectiveness. The cases describe actual situations in business or nonbusiness organizations; in most cases we give the names of the organizations on which they are based. Each of the five units in the text ends with a major case based on a well-known company or companies that is intended to cover and integrate the important concepts of the entire unit. Each chapter also closes with a short case study or incident that is intended to highlight key concepts of the chapter. Both part and chapter cases are followed by *case questions* to help students focus on their significant aspects.

New to this edition are a *glossary* of key management terms and concepts, which is located at the end of the book, and a new *index of company names* to supplement the *name and subject indexes*.

Supplements

A *Study Guide and Workbook* is available to help students review, understand, and integrate the material in the text. Each chapter in the workbook includes a chapter introduction, chapter objectives, short-answer and discussion questions, self-test questions (with answers), experiential exercises, and one or more brief cases and suggested out-of-class projects that provide practical applications of the chapter material.

The *Instructor's Resource Manual* contains many innovative ideas for supplementing the text. There are lists of such materials as games and simulations, casebooks and readings, and audiovisual resources. For each chapter, there are a chapter organizer overview and a lecture outline with teaching tips and ideas for expansion, including lecture supplement suggestions. Essay questions, with answer guidelines, have been provided for each chapter, as well as answers to the in-text review questions and case questions and analyses of the chapter and part cases. The *Test Item File* contains more than 2,000 questions in both true-false and multiple-choice formats, including 1,000 new questions. These are keyed as either factual or conceptual and are also available in computerized test bank format. One-hundred *Transparency Masters* are free upon adoption, as are 100 *Color Transparencies* and a volume of *Corporate Profiles,* studies of the management practices of major corporations, including companies discussed in the text cases. Also available is *Modern Business Decisions,* a microcomputer decision-making simulation to give students simulated hands-on experience with managerial tasks and problems.

Acknowledgments

One of the most pleasant parts of writing a book is the opportunity to thank those who have contributed to it. Unfortunately, the list of expressions of thanks—no matter how extensive—is always incomplete and inadequate. These acknowledgments are no exception.

Our first thanks must go to the editor of the first edition of this book, Sheldon Czapnik. Sheldon's unflagging patience, constant good humor, and astounding capacity for creative work and long hours made the first edition both possible and successful. Others who contributed greatly to earlier editions include Stuart Whalen, Robert DeFillippi, Peter Pfister, Samuel and Della Dekay, Arthur Mitchell, and Jim McDonald.

In the preparation of this edition, we are grateful for the assistance of George Farris, Jim Clawson, Gary Yunker, and Norman Coates. They were particularly helpful in reviewing and clarifying important sections of the book. We have also been fortunate to have the assistance of many dedicated individuals in completing the extensive research required for this revision. We are especially appreciative of the talents of Monika Advocate, Anna Dadak, Michael Garber, Paul Haffey, Joseph Martyn, Marzenna Politowska, Abraham Schmilowitz, and Rose Sevillano.

The following people also helped immensely with their reviews for this edition: M. Wayne Alexander, Moorhead State University; J. Scott Armstrong, Wharton School of the University of Pennsylvania; Robert M. Ballinger, Siena College; Salvatore J. Bella, University of Notre Dame; Chris A. Betts, California State University, Fresno; Diane B. Birch, Becker Junior College; G. A. Blomquist, Delmar College; Alvin S. Bogart, Upsala College; Robert Z. Bothe, Ferris State College; M. Clinton Cannon, Seattle International University; Steven V. Cates, Valdosta State College; James G. Clawson, University of Virginia; Norman Coates, University of Rhode Island; James A. Croft, University of Pittsburgh; John A. Drexler, Jr., Oregon State University; Guillermo Duenas, Philadelphia College of Textiles & Science; John P. Eberle, Embry-Riddle Aeronautical University; W. Fran Emory, Northern Virginia Community College; Richard N. Farmer, Indiana University; George A. Farris, Rutgers University; Fred Foulkes, Boston University; Ted Gantachi, Bryant College; Claude S. George, University of North Carolina at Chapel Hill; Stephen Globerman, Simon Fraser University; Robert H. Guest, Dartmouth College; Frank Harrison, San Francisco State University; Randy Hlavac, University of Nebraska—Omaha; Marie Hodge, Bowling Green State University; William Jedlicka, William Rainey Harper College; Dewey Johnson, California State University, Fresno; Marvin Karlins, University of South Florida; Olan J. Lehman, West Texas State University; Roy J. Lewicki, Ohio State University; John D. Lunlow, Northern Michigan University; Douglas McCabe, Georgetown University; Joseph McCann, University of Florida; Joyce E. McNally, Aquinas College; Joseph F. Michlitsch, Southern Illinois University; Danny Miller, McGill University; Foster C. Rinefort, Eastern Illinois University; Afife N. Sayin, Howard University; Eugene Siemiatkoski, Central Connecticut State College; Bette Ann Stead, University of Houston; Patricia Sutton, Marshall Hall; Arthur N. Turner, Harvard University; James K. Weeks, University of North Carolina at Greensboro; Charles A. White, Edison Community College; Tilton Willcox, East Carolina University; Robert H. Woodhouse, College of St. Thomas.

Many people at Prentice-Hall have contributed to the development of this revision: Steven Anzovin, development editor; Alison Reeves, business management editor; Eleanor Perz, production editor; Linda Albelli, Noreen Scott, and Asha Rohra, editorial assistants; and Jeff Krames and Mary Franz, marketing managers. We are indebted to Howard Batchelor, Andrew Kimmens, Gian Lombardo, Jim McDonald, Dan Otis, and Jonathan Rogers for their writing ability and professional assistance in the preparation of the manuscript, and to Elaine Luthy for preparation of the index.

Many of our personal colleagues in academia contributed directly and indirectly to this text. Jim's adviser on two theses and early academic mentor, the late Donald G. Marquis, placed his own imprint indelibly and permanently upon him. Jim has frequently drawn heavily on the research and the recalled classes and conversations of Professors George Farris, Thomas Ference, Edgar Schein, and Kirby Warren, and his own interpretations of how they might have thought through problems. Tom was helpful on numerous occasions, and we are very grateful to him and to our colleague Jerome Schnee for allowing us to use their teaching notes and other materials at critical times.

Because this book is about management and about managers, we are indebted to the many outstanding managers and consultants with whom we have worked. These are far too many to list, but a few simply must be credited: Joseph Voci, David Gleicher, Malcolm MacGruer, and the late Victor Milton have all provided profound influence. As consultants, Joe and David can conceptualize and guide the practice of management as well as anyone we have ever met. As practicing managers, Joe, Malcolm, and Victor were always a joy to watch in action.

Finally, in a strictly personal vein, Jim owes thanks for constant stoking of his spirit's furnace to the gentle and lovely Barbara and to his six-year-old, Alexandra, who can lift up a full-grown man with her smile muscles alone. Charlie wishes to thank his family for their psychic kindling in the coldest times and for sharing the warmth of the brightest days.

J.A.F.S.
C.B.W.

PART ONE
INTRODUCTION TO MANAGEMENT

1

MANAGING AND MANAGERS

Upon completing this chapter you should be able to:

1. Define the concept of management and discuss why managers and organizations are needed.
2. List and describe the four basic functions of managers.
3. Describe several additional roles and responsibilities of managers.
4. Discuss excellence in management.
5. Identify what is meant by top, middle, and first-line managers, and functional and general managers, and describe how their work activities differ.
6. Describe what management education can and cannot do for you, and explain why you must be actively involved in learning to become an effective manager.

For most of our lives, we are members of one *organization* or another—a college, a sports team, a musical or theatrical group, a religious or civic association, a branch of the armed forces, or a business. The organizations we belong to will obviously differ from one another in many ways. Some, like the army or a large corporation, may be organized very formally. Others, like a neighborhood basketball team, may be more casually structured. But regardless of how they differ, all the organizations we belong to have several basic things in common.

Perhaps the most obvious common element our organizations will have is a *goal* or purpose. The goals will vary—to win a league championship, to entertain an audience, to sell a product—but without a goal no organization would have any reason to exist. Our organizations will also have some program or method for achieving their goals—to practice playing skills in order to win games, to rehearse a certain number of times before each performance, to manufacture and advertise a product. Without some plan for what it must do, no organization is likely to be very effective. Our organizations must acquire and allocate the resources necessary to achieve their goals—a playing field or rehearsal hall must be available; money must be budgeted for wages. Our organizations are not self-contained, but always exist in an environment with other organizations that they depend on for the resources they need—a team cannot play without the required equipment; most manufacturers must maintain contracts with many different suppliers. Finally, our organizations will all have leaders or managers responsible for helping the organizations achieve their goals. Who the leaders actually are probably will be more obvious in some organizations than in others. But without some manager—a coach, a conductor, a sales executive—the organization is likely to flounder.

This book is about how organizations are managed or, more specifically, how managers can best help their organizations set and achieve their goals. Our emphasis will be on the so-called formal organizations—such as businesses, religious organizations, government agencies, or hospitals—that provide goods or services to their customers or clients and offer career opportunities to their members. It is easier to discuss the management of these organizations, because in such organizations people will usually have various well-defined responsibilities, and the role of the manager will be clear-cut and visible. But regardless of how formal their role is, all managers in all organizations have the same basic responsibility: to help other members of the organization set and reach a series of goals and objectives. Helping you to understand how managers accomplish this task is the subject of this book.

Defining Management

Management has been called "the art of getting things done through people." This definition, by Mary Parker Follett, calls attention to the fact that managers achieve organizational goals by arranging for others to perform whatever tasks may be necessary—not by performing the tasks themselves.

Management is that, and more. So much more, in fact, that no one definition has been universally accepted. Our discussion will start with a somewhat more complex definition, so that we may call attention to additional important aspects of managing:

> **Management is the process of planning, organizing, leading, and controlling the efforts of organization members and of using all other organizational resources to achieve stated organizational goals.**

A process is a systematic way of doing things. We define management as a process because all managers, regardless of their particular aptitudes or skills, engage in certain interrelated activities in order to achieve their desired goals.

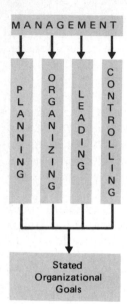

MANAGEMENT

PLANNING
ORGANIZING
LEADING
CONTROLLING

Stated
Organizational
Goals

1. *Planning* implies that managers think through their goals and actions in advance. Their actions are usually based on some method, plan, or logic, rather than on a hunch.
2. *Organizing* means that managers coordinate the human and material resources of the organization. The effectiveness of an organization depends on its ability to marshal its resources to attain its goals. Obviously, the more integrated and coordinated the work of an organization, the more effective it will be. Achieving this coordination is part of the manager's job.
3. *Leading* describes how managers direct and influence subordinates, getting others to perform essential tasks. By establishing the proper atmosphere, they help their subordinates do their best.
4. *Controlling* means that managers attempt to assure that the organization is moving toward its goals. If some part of their organization is on the wrong track, managers try to find out why and set things right.

Our definition also indicates that managers use *all* the resources of the organization—its finances, equipment, and information as well as its people—to attain their goals. People are the most important resource of any organization, but managers would be limiting their achievements if they did not also rely on the other available organizational resources. For example, a manager who wishes to increase sales might try not only to motivate the sales force but also to increase the advertising budget, thus using both human and financial resources to attain the goal.

Finally, our definition says that management involves achieving the organization's "stated goals." This means that managers of any organization—a university, the Internal Revenue Service, or the Washington Redskins—try to attain specific ends. These ends are, of course, unique to each organization. The stated goal of a university might be to give students a well-rounded education in an academic community. The stated goal of a football team might be to win every game in a season. Whatever the stated goals of a particular organization, management is the process by which the goals are achieved.

Why Organizations Are Needed

Almost every day, it seems, headlines like these greet us from the front pages of our daily newspapers:

· "FDIC Puts Up $4.5 Billion to Rescue Failing Illinois Bank"
· "Senator Claims Medicaid System Is Bankrupt"
· "New Orleans World's Fair Loses $1 Million a Week"
· "Federal Deficit at Record Level"

The stories behind these headlines make us wonder whether the organizations of our society have failed. Some Americans feel that government, business, and labor organizations have become too large to keep in touch with people's needs and that their leaders lack high ethical standards.

Criticizing organizations is, of course, a time-honored American custom. However, it is not enough simply to criticize organizations. We must at the same time constantly seek new ways to improve them and make them more effective tools for serving human needs. The reason for this is that organizations, in one form or another, will always be with us. They are a necessary element of civilized life for several reasons: They enable us to accomplish things that we could not do as well— or at all—as individuals; they help provide a continuity of knowledge; and they serve as an important source of careers.

Organizations Accomplish Objectives

Let us consider for a moment how many organizations were involved in bringing us the paper on which this book is printed: loggers, a sawmill, manufacturers of various types of equipment and supplies, truckers, a paper mill, distributors, telephone and electric power companies, fuel producers, the postal service, banks and other financial institutions, and more. Even if an individual acting alone could do all the things those organizations did to produce a ream of paper, which is doubtful, he or she could never do them as well or as quickly.

It is clear, then, that organizations perform this essential function: *By overcoming our limitations as individuals, they enable us to reach goals that would otherwise be much more difficult or even impossible to reach.*

Organizations Preserve Knowledge

We know from history that when recorded knowledge is destroyed on a large scale (as when the museum and library at Alexandria were burned in the third century A.D.) much of it is never regained. We depend on records of past accomplishments, because they provide a foundation of knowledge on which we can build to acquire more learning and achieve greater results. Without such records, science and other fields of knowledge would stand still.

Organizations (such as universities, museums, and corporations) are essential because they store and protect most of the important knowledge that our civilization has gathered and recorded. In this way, they help to make that knowledge a continuous bridge between past, present, and future generations. In addition, organizations themselves add to our knowledge by developing new and more efficient ways of doing things.

Organizations Provide Careers

Organizations are important for still another reason: they provide their employees with a source of livelihood and perhaps even personal satisfaction and self-fulfillment. Many of us tend to associate career opportunities with business corporations, but in fact a variety of other organizations, such as churches, government agencies, schools, hospitals, and so on, also offer rewarding careers.

Thus, we can see that organizations are essential to our society. The question we should be concerned with is not, Do we need so many large organizations? but,

How can we make both large and small organizations more effective in meeting our needs?

The Purpose of This Book

Most readers of this book will spend a good part of their lives working in organizations, either as subordinates or managers or both. The chief purpose of this book is to prepare them for both of these roles. It will help them understand how organizations are managed; that is, what tasks managers must perform to keep their organizations running smoothly and effectively. They will also learn how managers accomplish those tasks, what managers need to know in order to manage effectively, and how they apply their skills and knowledge in order to meet organizational goals (as well as their own).

Usually, when people become employees, their first task is learning to be successful subordinates. The importance of being a good subordinate should not be underestimated. Before they can become managers, most people first have to prove themselves as subordinates. Besides, virtually every member of an organization is subordinate to someone else. Even an organization's president is subordinate to the board of directors, and the board members in turn are, in principle, responsible to the shareholders.

One of the best ways to be an effective subordinate is to understand the job of the boss. This means understanding the demands placed upon the boss by the needs of the organization. Effective subordinates should also be able to view their own role in relation to others in the department or subdivision, the role of the subdivision in relation to the organization, the responsibilities of the subdivision manager, and the goals of the organization as a whole.[1]

The person who has acquired a good basic understanding of how organizations are managed will be able to put this understanding to good use when he or she becomes a member of an organization. For example, by watching various managers in action, an alert, knowledgeable employee can identify the kinds of managerial behavior that seem to be successful (or unsuccessful) in moving the organization toward its goals. The employee can use this learning experience to improve his or her chances of becoming not only a manager but an *effective* manager.

Last but not least, an understanding of management should prove helpful to the reader in many situations and activities outside the formal organization.

What Managers Do

Our working definition describes *managers* as organizational planners, organizers, leaders, and controllers. Actually, every manager—from the program director of a college club to the chief executive of a multinational corporation—takes on a much wider range of roles to move the organization toward its stated objectives. In this discussion of the more detailed aspect of what managers *do*, we will specify more completely what managers *are*.

Managers work with and through other people. The term *people* includes not only subordinates and supervisors but also other managers in the organization. "People" also includes individuals outside the organization—customers, clients, suppliers, union representatives, and so on. These people and others provide goods and services or use the product or service of the organization. Managers, then, work with anyone at any level within or outside their organizations who can help achieve unit or organizational goals.

In addition, managers in any organization work with each other to establish the organization's long-range goals and to plan how to achieve them. They also work together to provide one another with the accurate information needed to perform tasks. Thus, *managers act as channels of communication within the organization.*

Managers are responsible and accountable. Managers are in charge of seeing that specific tasks are done successfully. They are usually evaluated on how well they arrange for these tasks to be accomplished. Managers are responsible also for the actions of their subordinates. The success or failure of subordinates is a direct reflection of managers' success or failure.

All members of an organization, including those who are not managers, are responsible for their particular tasks. The difference is that managers are held responsible, or accountable, not only for their own work but also for the work of others.

Because managers have subordinates and other resources to use in getting a job done, they are able to accomplish more than nonmanagers, who have only their own efforts to rely on. This, of course, means that managers are also *expected* to accomplish more than other members of the organization; that is, they are held accountable for greater achievement. Obviously, there is an element of risk involved here, because the manager's need to get more work done is coupled with the need to rely on others to do that work. Managers, in fact, often feel anxiety because of their responsibility for achieving things beyond their immediate control, and if they have personal financial stakes in the organization—substantial amounts of stock held in the company, for example—even greater anxiety may be felt.

Managers balance competing goals and set priorities. At any given time, every manager faces a number of organizational goals, problems, and needs—all of which compete for the manager's time and resources (both human and material). Because such resources are always limited, each manager must strike a balance between the various goals and needs. Many managers, for example, arrange each day's tasks in order of priority—the most important things are done right away, while the less important tasks are looked at later. In this way managerial time is used more effectively.

Competing Goals

MANAGER

Managers must also decide who is to perform a particular task and must assign work to an appropriate subordinate. Although ideally each person should be given tasks he or she would most like to do, this is not always possible. Sometimes individual ability is the decisive factor, and a task is assigned to the person best able to accomplish it. But sometimes a less able worker is assigned a task as a learning experience. And, at times, limited human or other resources dictate other reasons for making work assignments. Managers are often caught between conflicting human and organizational needs and must identify priorities.

Managers must think analytically and conceptually. To be an analytical thinker, a manager must be able to break a problem down into its components, analyze those components, and then come up with a feasible solution. But even more important, a manager must be a conceptual thinker, able to view the entire task in the abstract and relate it to other tasks. Thinking about a particular task in relation to its larger implications is no simple matter. But it is essential if the manager is to work toward the goals of the organization as a whole as well as toward the goals of an individual unit.

Managers are mediators. Organizations are made up of people, and people disagree or quarrel. Disputes within a unit or organization can lower morale and productivity, and they may become so unpleasant or disruptive that competent employees decide to leave the organization. Such occurrences hinder work toward the goals of the unit or organization; therefore, managers must at times take on the role of mediator and iron out disputes before they get out of hand. Settling quarrels requires skill and tact; managers who are careless in their handling of disputes may be chagrined to find that they have only made matters worse.

Managers are politicians. This does not mean that the organization expects its managers to run for office (unless that is the purpose of the organization!). It means, rather, that managers must build relationships, and use persuasion and compromise to promote organizational goals, just as politicians do to move their programs forward.

Managers should also develop other political skills. All effective managers "play politics" by developing networks of mutual obligations with other managers in the organization. They may also have to build or join alliances and coalitions. Managers draw upon these relationships to win support for proposals or decisions or to gain cooperation in carrying out various activities.[2]

Managers are diplomats. They may serve as official representatives of their work units at organizational meetings. They may represent the entire organization as well as a particular unit in dealing with clients, customers, contractors, government officials, and personnel of other organizations.

Managers are symbols. They personify both for organizational members and for outside observers an organization's successes and failures. Here, too, managers may be held responsible for things over which they have little or no control, and it may be useful for the organization to hold them so responsible. The frequent dismissals of managers of professional sports teams, to take just one type of manager, often have symbolic importance.[3]

Managers make difficult decisions. No organization runs smoothly all the time. There is almost no limit to the number and types of problems that may occur: financial difficulties, problems with employees, or differences of opinion concerning organization policy, to name just a few. Managers are the people who are expected to come up with solutions to difficult problems and to follow through on their decisions even when doing so may be unpopular.

The brief descriptions of these managerial roles show that managers must "change hats" frequently and must be alert to the particular role needed at a given time. The ability to recognize the appropriate role to be played and to change roles readily is a mark of an effective manager.

Managerial and Organizational Performance

How successfully an organization achieves its objectives and meets society's needs depends upon how well the organization's managers do their jobs. If managers do not do their jobs well, the organization will fail to achieve its goals. Just as managers function within the organization, organizations function within the larger society. The performance of its organizations as a group is a key factor in the performance of a society or a nation.

How well managers do their jobs—managerial performance—is the subject of much debate, analysis, and confusion in the United States and in many other countries.[4] How well the organizations of a society do *their* "jobs"—organizational performance—gives rise to an equally lively debate.[5] The chapters that follow discuss a number of criteria and concepts for evaluating managers and organizations.[6] Underlying many of these are two concepts suggested by Peter Drucker, one of the most respected writers on management.[7] Drucker has argued that a manager's performance can be measured in terms of two concepts: efficiency and effectiveness. As he puts it, *efficiency* means "doing things right," and *effectiveness* means "doing the right thing."

Efficiency—that is, the ability to get things done correctly—is an "input-output" concept. An efficient manager is one who achieves outputs, or results, that measure up to the inputs (labor, materials, and time) used to achieve them. Managers who are able to minimize the cost of the resources they use to attain their goals are acting efficiently.

Effectiveness, on the other hand, is the ability to choose appropriate objectives. An effective manager is one who selects the right things to get done. A manager who selects an inappropriate objective—the production only of large cars when demand for small cars is soaring—is an ineffective manager. Such a manager would be ineffective even if the large cars were produced with maximum efficiency. No amount of efficiency can compensate for lack of effectiveness.

A manager's responsibilities require performance that is both efficient and effective, but although efficiency is important, effectiveness is critical. For Drucker, effectiveness is the key to the success of an organization. The manager's need to make the most of opportunities, says Drucker,

> **implies that effectiveness rather than efficiency is essential to business. The pertinent question is not how to do things right, but how to find the right things to do, and to concentrate resources and efforts on them.[8]**

Excellence in Management

A recent study by management consultants Thomas J. Peters and Robert H. Waterman examined the qualities of 43 "excellently managed" U.S. companies, including IBM, Eastman Kodak, 3M, Boeing, Bechtel, Procter & Gamble, and McDonald's.[9] Not only were these firms consistently profitable over a 20-year period but they also were unusually successful in responding to customer needs, providing a challenging and rewarding working environment for their employees, and being good corporate citizens by meeting their social and environmental obligations effectively. Peters and Waterman concluded that these companies were, in their words, "brilliant on the basics." Rather than having some secret strategy or unique market situation, they simply did the most fundamental organizational tasks very well.

From their research Peters and Waterman derived eight attributes that characterize the management style of these excellent companies (see box). The attributes emphasize the critical role played by management at all levels, especially at the top, in creating the values and practices that encourage excellence. In stressing the

1. A bias for action: a preference for doing something—anything—rather than sending a question through cycles and cycles of analyses and committee reports.
2. Staying close to the customer—learning his or her preferences and catering to them.
3. Autonomy and entrepreneurship—breaking the corporation into small companies and encouraging them to think independently and competitively.
4. Productivity through people—creating in *all* employees the awareness that their best efforts are essential and that they will share in the rewards of the company's success.
5. Hands-on, value driven—insisting that executives keep in touch with the firm's essential business.
6. Stick to the knitting—remaining with the business the company knows best.
7. Simple form, lean staff—few administrative layers, few people at the upper levels.
8. Simultaneous loose-tight properties—fostering a climate in which there is dedication to the central values of the company combined with tolerance for all employees who accept those values.

Source: "Eight Basic Principles" from *In Search of Excellence: Lessons from America's Best-Run Companies* by Thomas J. Peters and Robert H. Waterman. Copyright © 1982 by Thomas J. Peters and Robert H. Waterman. Reprinted by permission of Harper & Row, Publishers, Inc.

importance of organizational culture, Peters and Waterman cite such strongly held managerial values as IBM's "respect for the individual" and Frito-Lay's commitment to a "99.5 percent" level of satisfactory service as keys to each company's success.

A danger in labeling any company as "excellently run" is that internal and external conditions can change: A company that embodies excellence one year may founder the next. Peters and Waterman's choices have been no exception. Recently several of the excellent companies have not performed well.[10] In some cases, the difficulties appeared to arise when the companies stopped adhering to one or more of the eight attributes. For example, in the early 1980s Levi Strauss and Company lost close contact with its customers—both the retailers that carried its products and the consumers who wore them. When the jeans market became glutted with suppliers and styles changed, Levi's was slow to sense the changes. It thus lost much of the loyalty of its retailers, many of whom considered the company aloof and unsupportive. Recently Levi's has made a comeback through deliberate efforts to be a more responsive vendor. However, it is not clear that such slippages in performance are caused only when a company loses sight of one or more of the eight attributes: Daniel T. Carroll and others have criticized Peters and Waterman for emphasizing managerial aspects to the exclusion of other factors affecting performance, such as the possession of proprietary technology, differences in national culture, and the restraints on competitiveness created by government regulations.[11]

Even if Peters and Waterman have not discovered the universal prescription for success that managers continue to hope for, their guidelines do make good sense for many organizations. The effort to identify and learn from companies that are doing many things right is an important and positive stimulus to managers seeking to create the conditions for excellence in their own companies.

Types of Managers

We have been using the term *manager* to mean anyone who is responsible for subordinates and other organizational resources. There are many different types of managers, with diverse tasks and responsibilities. Managers can be classified in two ways: by their level in the organization—so-called first-line, middle, and top managers—and by the range of organizational activities for which they are responsible—so-called functional and general managers.

Management Levels

First-Line Managers. The lowest level in an organization at which individuals are responsible for the work of others is called *first-line* or *first-level management*. First-line managers direct operating employees only; they do not supervise other managers. Examples of first-line managers are the "foreman" or production supervisor in a manufacturing plant, the technical supervisor in a research department, and the clerical supervisor in a large office. First-level managers are often called supervisors.

Middle Managers. The term *middle management* can refer to more than one level in an organization. Middle managers direct the activities of other managers and sometimes also those of operating employees. Middle managers' principal responsibilities are to direct the activities that implement their organizations' policies and to balance the demands of their superiors with the capacities of their subordinates. A plant manager in an electronics firm is an example of a middle manager.

Top Managers. Composed of a comparatively small group of executives, *top management* is responsible for the overall management of the organization. It establishes operating policies and guides the organization's interactions with its environment. Typical titles of top managers are "chief executive officer," "president," and "senior vice-president." Actual titles vary from one organization to another and are not always a reliable guide to membership in the highest management classification.

Functional and General Managers

The other major classification of managers depends on the scope of the activities they manage. The *functional manager* is responsible for only one organizational activity, such as production, marketing, sales, *or* finance. The people and activities headed by a functional manager are engaged in a common set of activities. The *general manager,* on the other hand, oversees a complex unit, such as a company, a subsidiary, or an independent operating division. He or she is responsible for all the activities of that unit, such as its production, marketing, sales, *and* finance.[12]

A small company may have only one general manager—its president or executive vice-president—but a large organization may have several, each at the head of a relatively independent division. In a large food company, for example, there might be a grocery products division, a refrigerated products division, and a frozen food products division, with a different general manager responsible for each. Like the

LEVELS OF MANAGEMENT

Top Management

Middle Management

First-Line Management (*also called Supervisor*)

Operatives or Operating Employees

"I've supervised. I've managed. I've directed. I've presided. I've chaired. What else is there?"

Drawing by Vietor; © 1983 The New Yorker Magazine, Inc.

chief executive of a small company, each of these divisional heads would be responsible for all the activities of the unit.

The Management Process

It is easier to understand something as complex as management when it is described as a series of separate parts, or *functions*, that make up a whole process. Descriptions of this kind, known as *models*, have been used by students and practitioners of management for decades. A model is a simplification of the real world used to convey complex relationships in easy-to-understand terms. We, in fact, used a model—without identifying it as such—when we said earlier in this chapter that the major management activities were planning, organizing, leading, and controlling. This model of management was developed at the end of the nineteenth century and, as a glance at our table of contents will indicate, is still in use today.[13]

We have already described briefly these four main management activities. Now that we have acquired some insights into the manager's many roles and responsibilities, we will examine these activities or functions in greater detail.

Planning

Plans give the organization its objectives and set up the best procedure for reaching them. In addition, plans permit (1) the organization to obtain and commit the resources required to reach its objectives, (2) members of the organization to carry on activities consistent with the chosen objectives and procedures, and (3) the progress toward the objectives to be monitored and measured, so that corrective action can be taken if progress is unsatisfactory.

The first step in planning is the selection of goals for the organization. Then objectives are established for the subunits of the organization—its divisions, departments, and so on. Once the objectives are decided upon, programs are established for achieving them in a systematic manner. Of course, in selecting objectives and developing programs, the manager considers their feasibility and whether they will be acceptable to the organization's managers and employees.

Plans made by top management for the organization as a whole may cover periods as long as five or ten years. In a large organization, such as a multinational energy corporation, those plans may involve commitments of billions of dollars. Planning at the lower levels, by middle or first-line managers, covers much shorter periods. Such plans may be for the next day's work, for example, or for a two-hour meeting to take place in a week.

Organizing

Once managers have established objectives and developed plans or programs to reach them, they must design and develop an organization that will be able to carry out those programs successfully. Different objectives will require different kinds of organizations to achieve them. For example, an organization that aims to develop computer software will have to be far different from one that wants to manufacture blue jeans. Producing a standardized product like blue jeans requires efficient assembly-line techniques, whereas writing computer programs requires teams of professionals—systems analysts, software engineers, and operators. Although they must interact effectively, such people cannot be organized on an assembly-line basis. It is clear, then, that managers must have the ability to determine what type of organization will be needed to accomplish a given set of objectives. And they must have the ability to develop (and later to lead) that type of organization.

Staffing is the recruitment, placement, and training of qualified personnel to do the organization's work. We have included staffing in our discussion of the organizing function because the designing of organizations and the placement of people in them are closely related activities.

Leading

After plans have been made, the structure of the organization has been determined, and the staff has been recruited and trained, the next step is to arrange for movement toward the organization's defined objectives. This function can be called by various names: leading, directing, motivating, actuating, and others. But whatever the name used to identify it, this function involves getting the members of the organization to perform in ways that will help it achieve the established objectives.

Whereas planning and organizing deal with the more abstract aspects of the management process, the activity of leading is very concrete; it involves working directly with people.

Controlling

Finally, the manager must ensure that the actions of the organization's members do in fact move the organization toward the stated goals. This is the controlling function of management, and it involves three main elements:

1. **Establishing standards of performance.**
2. **Measuring current performance and comparing it against the established standards.**
3. **Taking action to correct performance that does not meet those standards.**

Through the controlling function, the manager can keep the organization on the right track and not let it stray too far from its goals.

We have presented here a model of the management process. But the relationships described above are interrelated more than our model implies. For example, we saw that standards and benchmarks are used as a means of controlling employees' actions, but, obviously, establishing such standards is also an inherent part of the planning process. And taking corrective action, which we also introduced as a control activity, often involves an adjustment in plans. In practice, the management process does not involve four separate or loosely related sets of activities but a group of interlocking functions.

We should also point out that the four functions do not necessarily occur in the sequence presented in our model (except perhaps when a new organization is being formed). In fact, various combinations of these activities are going on simultaneously in every organization.

In addition, the existence of these distinct management functions does not imply that any manager has complete freedom to perform them whenever he or she wishes. Managers generally are faced with various limitations on their activities, depending on their rank, their role in the organization, and the kind of organization they work for. Some managers, for example, may find that limits are set on their dealings with subordinates—on what they can do to direct, guide, or motivate them—because their leadership style conflicts with the style that prevails in their organization. And a manager may not be able to hire new staff to pursue a new set of objectives, because the organization cannot carry the added expense of their salaries.

In spite of their limitations, models provide a useful approach to learning—as long as we remember their shortcomings and that they are not meant to be exact descriptions of the real world. By analyzing the management process—that is, by separating it into distinct pieces we call "management functions"—this model can improve our understanding of what managers do. And that, after all, is the purpose of this book.

Managerial Skills and Roles

Managers at all levels of an organization need to plan, organize, lead, and control. There are, however, differences among managers in the amount of time they devote to each of these activities. Some of these differences will depend on the kind of organization the manager works for and on the type of job the manager has.

For example, we would expect the manager of a small private clinic to spend his or her time quite differently from the head of a large teaching and research hospital. The clinic manager will probably spend comparatively more time practicing medicine and less time managing the organization than the administrator of a large hospital. Similarly, the technical supervisor of a group of research physicists at AT&T Bell Laboratories will perform activities that are different from those of a production supervisor on the General Motors assembly line—yet both are first-line managers. (Of course, there will also be some similarities in how they spend their time.)

Other differences in how managers spend their time will depend on the level of the individual manager in the organizational hierarchy. In the sections below we discuss how management skills and activities will differ at the various levels of the organization and look at the various roles managers perform.

Management Levels and Managerial Skills

Robert L. Katz, an educator and business executive, has identified three basic types of skills—*technical, human,* and *conceptual*—which he says are needed by all managers.[14]

Technical skill is the ability to use the tools, procedures, and techniques of a specialized field. A surgeon, an engineer, a musician, and an accountant all have technical skill in their respective areas. The manager needs enough technical skill "to accomplish the mechanics of the particular job" he or she is responsible for.

Human skill is the ability to work with, understand, and motivate other people, either as individuals or as groups. Managers need enough of this human relations skill to work with other organization members and to lead their own work groups.

Conceptual skill is the mental ability to coordinate and integrate all of the organization's interests and activities. It involves the manager's ability to see the organization as a whole and to understand how its parts depend on each other. It also involves the manager's ability to understand how a change in any given part can affect the whole organization. A manager needs enough conceptual skill to recognize how the various factors in a given situation are interrelated, so that the actions he or she takes will be in the best interests of the total organization.

Katz suggests that although all three of these skills are essential to effective management, their relative importance to a specific manager depends on his or her rank in the organization. (See fig. 1–1.) Technical skill is most important at the lower levels of management; it becomes less important as we move up the chain of command. A production supervisor in a manufacturing plant, for example, is likely to need more technical skill than the company president, because he or she will have to deal with the day-to-day manufacturing problems that arise.

On the other hand, the importance of conceptual skill increases as we rise in the ranks of management. The higher the manager is in the hierarchy, the more he or she will be involved in the broad, long-term decisions that affect large parts of the organization. For top management, responsible for the entire organization, conceptual skill is probably the most important skill of all.

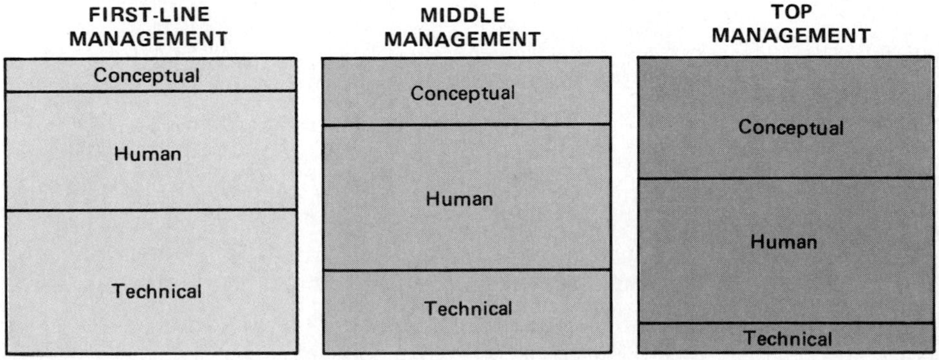

FIGURE 1–1 RELATIVE SKILLS NEEDED FOR EFFECTIVE PERFORMANCE AT DIFFERENT LEVELS OF MANAGEMENT

FIRST-LINE MANAGEMENT	MIDDLE MANAGEMENT	TOP MANAGEMENT
Conceptual	Conceptual	Conceptual
Human	Human	Human
Technical	Technical	Technical

Human skill is very important at every level of the organization. One reason this is so is because managers get their work done through others: high technical or conceptual skills are not very valuable if they cannot be used to inspire and influence other organization members.

Supporting Katz's contention that specific skills are more important at some levels than at others is a study of managerial roles and behavior by Mahoney, Jerdee, and Carroll.[15] More than four hundred managers from all levels of management and a variety of types and sizes of businesses were asked to estimate how much time they spent on eight management tasks: *planning, investigating, coordinating, evaluating, supervising, staffing, negotiating,* and *representing.* Lower- and middle-level managers replied that supervising was their dominant activity, while top managers claimed to spend proportionately more time on planning.

Managerial Roles

Henry Mintzberg offers a view of the job of managing that throws some new light on how managers spend their time and perform their work.[16] Mintzberg made an extensive survey of existing research on this subject and integrated those findings with the results of his own study of the activities of five chief executive officers. The combined survey covered all kinds and levels of managers: factory foremen, sales managers, administrators, presidents, and even street gang leaders.

Mintzberg concluded that there is considerable similarity in the behavior of managers at all levels. All managers, he argued, have formal authority over their own organizational units and derive status from that authority. This status causes all managers to be involved in interpersonal relations with subordinates, peers, and superiors, who in turn provide managers with the information they need to make decisions. These different aspects of a manager's job cause managers at all levels to be involved in a series of interpersonal, informational, and decisional *roles,* which Mintzberg defined as "organized sets of behaviors." (See fig. 1–2.)

The Manager's Interpersonal Roles. Three interpersonal roles help the manager keep the organization running smoothly. Thus, although the duties associated with these roles are often routine, the manager cannot ignore them.

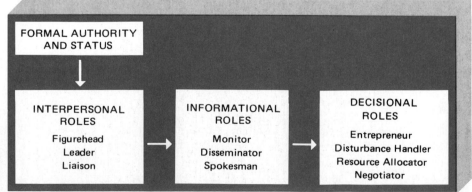

FIGURE 1–2
THE MANAGER'S
ROLES

Source: Reprinted by permission of the *Harvard Business Review.* An exhibit from "The Manager's Job: Folklore and Fact" by Henry Mintzberg (July–August 1975). Copyright © 1975 by the President and Fellows of Harvard College; all rights reserved.

The first interpersonal role is that of *figurehead*. As head of a unit, the manager sometimes acts as a figurehead by performing certain ceremonial duties—greeting visitors, attending a subordinate's wedding, taking a customer to lunch, and so on. Second, the manager adopts the *leader* role—hiring, training, motivating, and encouraging employees. First-line managers, in particular, feel that effectiveness in this role is essential for successful job performance.[17] Finally, the manager must play the interpersonal role of *liaison,* by dealing with people other than subordinates or superiors (such as peers within the organization and suppliers or clients outside of it).

The Manager's Informational Roles. Mintzberg suggests that receiving and communicating information are perhaps the most important aspects of a manager's job.[18] A manager needs information in order to make the right decisions, and others in the manager's unit or organization depend on the information they receive from and transmit through the manager.[19]

There are three informational roles in which managers gather and disseminate information. The first is the *monitor* role. As monitor, the manager constantly looks for information that can be used to advantage. Subordinates are questioned, and unsolicited information is also collected, usually through the manager's system of personal contacts. The monitor role usually enables the manager to be the best-informed member of his or her group. Second, in the *disseminator* role, the manager distributes to subordinates important information that would otherwise be inaccessible to them. Finally, as a *spokesperson,* the manager transmits some of the information he or she has collected to individuals outside the unit—or even outside the organization. Keeping superiors in the organization satisfied by keeping them well informed is one important aspect of the role of spokesperson. Another aspect is communicating outside the organization—when a company president makes a speech before a group of consumer advocates, for example, or when a production manager suggests how a supplier should modify a product.

The Manager's Decisional Roles. So far, we have seen the manager distributing to other people information he or she has taken pains to collect. But, of course, information is also "the basic input to decision making" for managers.

According to Mintzberg, there are four decisional roles the manager adopts. In the role of *entrepreneur,* the manager tries to improve the unit. For example, when the manager receives a good idea, he or she launches a development project to make that idea a reality. As an entrepreneur, the manager initiates change voluntarily. In the role of *disturbance handler,* on the other hand, the manager responds to situations that are beyond his or her control, such as a strike, bankrupt customer, breach of contract, and the like. As a *resource allocator,* the manager is responsible for deciding how and to whom the resources of the organization and the manager's own time will be allocated. In addition, the manager screens all important decisions made by others in the unit before they are put into effect.

The fourth and last decisional role is that of *negotiator:* A company president works out a deal with a consulting firm; a production head draws up a contract with a supplier; an office manager irons out a problem with a union representative. Managers spend a great deal of their time as negotiators, because only they have the information and authority that negotiators require.

Mintzberg's work is particularly interesting because it calls attention to the uncertain, turbulent environment in which the manager operates. Real-life events and situations, he stresses, are only partially predictable and controllable, and the manager often must deal with them as they arise. In his view, managers have neither the time nor the inclination to be reflective thinkers—they are, above all, *doers* coping with a dynamic parade of challenges and surprises.

Thus, Mintzberg's concept of the manager's job offers a useful reminder that our definition of management as a series of functions—planning, organizing, leading, and controlling—is a somewhat idealized but useful overview of what managers try to do. In fact, managers operate in a constantly changing environment. Although they attempt to follow systematic and rational procedures, they are often interrupted in their work.

Management: Art, Science, or Profession?

Follett defined management as an art, but her definition is not universally accepted. It is generally acknowledged that management involves some degree of skill. But beyond that there is an ongoing debate about just how management should be classified: as an art, a science, or a profession?

Is Management an Art or a Science?

In a speech delivered to an international management conference, Luther Gulick, a management educator and author, defined management as a "field of knowledge" that "seeks to systematically understand why and how men work together to accomplish objectives and to make these cooperative systems more useful to mankind."[20] According to Gulick, management meets the requirements for a field of knowledge, because it has been studied for some time and has been organized into a series of theories. (See chapter 2.) Although these theories, he felt, were still too general and subjective, he was optimistic that management was on the way to becoming a science: It was being studied systematically and existing management theories were being tested against experience. The field of management would truly become a science, Gulick held, when theory would be able to guide managers by telling them what to do in a particular situation and enabling them to predict the consequences of their actions.[21]

Henry M. Boettinger, a corporate officer and management lecturer, argues on the other hand that management is an art, "an imposition of order on chaos."[22] In his view, painting or poetry (or any other fine or literary art) requires three components: the artist's vision, knowledge of craft, and successful communication. In these respects management is an art, because it requires the same components. And therefore, just as artistic skill can be developed through training, so can managerial skill be developed in ways similar to those used in training artists.

It seems most likely that, for some time to come, the field of management will more closely resemble art than science. We are learning more about management every day and in many situations can now safely recommend a specific course of action. The use of computers has vastly improved our ability to make valid predictions. But we are at present a long way from possessing the body of theory and accuracy of prediction that belong to science. Indeed, the field of management lags behind the behavioral sciences upon which it draws. A great deal remains to be learned about the interaction of people, about the social structure of organizations, and much more. Until our understanding is more complete, managers will have to rely on their own fallible judgment, their intuition, and often on insufficient information.[23] And so, although some aspects of management have become more scientific, much of management remains an art.

Is Management a Profession?

We have argued that management is part art and part science. Is it a profession? Edgar H. Schein has compared key qualities of professionals with those of managers.[24] In particular, Schein notes three characteristics.

First, professionals base their decisions on general principles. That there are certain reliable management principles is shown by the very existence of management courses and training programs. Although the principles held in common by most managers and management theorists do not apply perfectly in all situations, particular guidelines have high reliability. For example, the simple behavioral guideline, "praise in public and criticize in private," usually works out well, although occasionally it backfires.

Second, professionals achieve professional status through performance, not through favoritism or other factors irrelevant to the work at hand. Unfortunately, in practice managers sometimes achieve managerial positions through their relationships with people in power or by other non-work-related factors. In addition, no agreed-upon body of objective standards exists by which to judge managerial performance. Because of the complexity of factors that enter into the manager's job, it is more difficult to judge managers than, for example, trial lawyers or surgeons.

Finally, professionals must be governed by a strict code of ethics that protects their clients. Because of the professional's expert knowledge in a specific area, clients are dependent upon him or her and, as a result, are in a vulnerable position. Schein argued that no management code of ethics has yet been developed.

Schein concluded that by some criteria management is indeed a profession, but by other criteria it is not. Today we can see many signs that management is working toward increased professionalism, both in business and in nonbusiness organizations.[25] Current social pressures seem to be bringing about a heightened awareness of ethical standards. The growth of formal management training in graduate schools and through executive development programs is spreading a body of accumulated knowledge and teaching the skills that are the hallmark of professionalism.

Borje O. Saxberg has suggested a fourth characteristic of professionalism: dedication and commitment.[26] In any field the true professional combines life and work through personal dedication and commitment. According to this criterion, countless managers are professionals in the best sense of the word.

Training Managers

Although they might disagree about the classification of management as art, science, or profession, Gulick, Boettinger, and Schein appear to agree that at least some managerial skills can be taught.

Most people would agree that the technical, human, and conceptual skills Katz described are important to managers. How effectively can these skills be taught? Katz believes that technical skill is the easiest for a manager to acquire. It is generally well covered in courses at the undergraduate and graduate levels and in company-sponsored training programs; most top managers now have college degrees.

As we might expect, however, human skill is far more difficult to teach or learn than technical skill. Human relations involve many complex emotional elements, and it is difficult to demonstrate that a particular interpersonal approach is more effective than another. Also, even though it may be easy for us to admit that we are ignorant about some technical matter, it is much harder for us to admit that we need to be taught new ways of dealing with people. It is harder still to change our habitual and well-rationalized ways of relating to others.[27] Nevertheless, serious attempts are being made in business schools and company programs to help present and future managers improve their methods of dealing with people. These programs are based on the social sciences of anthropology, sociology, and, most important, psychology. Companies that neglect early training of managerial personnel may later have problems with them as top managers. Large companies such as IBM and GE that have developed a system of careful managerial training and steady advancement, on the other hand, can pick and choose between qualified executives—"a luxury," noted one GE manager, "which most companies don't ever enjoy and one which many just can't afford."[28]

Katz believes that conceptual skill has been difficult to teach, mainly because it involves mental habits that have to be developed early in life. Courses in strategic planning are one method designed to help future managers increase their conceptual skills. Managers who are likely to be promoted to general management are frequently sent to executive development programs to improve this skill.[29]

Management Education Criticized

J. Sterling Livingstone, in an article entitled "The Myth of the Well-Educated Manager," argues that most management training programs neglect to teach people what they must do in order to become fully effective managers.[30] These programs, Livingstone maintains, emphasize only problem solving and decision making. Thus, they help to develop analytical ability but do little to improve other, more important capacities a manager will need.

What managers really should be taught, Livingstone says, is problem finding and opportunity finding. Analytical skills are important, but a manager's success will ultimately depend on his or her ability to anticipate problems long before they arise. Even more important to the manager is the ability to find and take advantage of opportunities. After all, it is not problem solving but making the most of opportunities that helps organizations succeed.[31]

While Livingstone suggests that these abilities can and should be taught, he also maintains that certain characteristics of effective managers are almost impossible to teach. These characteristics are personal qualities, which people develop long before they enter management training programs. According to Livingstone, three such qualities are associated with successful managers:

1. *The need to manage.* Only those people who want to affect the performance of others and who derive satisfaction when they do so are likely to become effective managers.

Need to Manage

Need for Power

Capacity for Empathy

INNATE QUALITIES OF SUCCESSFUL MANAGERS

2. *The need for power.* Good managers have a need to influence others. To do this they do not rely on the authority of their positions but on their superior knowledge and skill.

3. *The capacity for empathy.* The effective manager also needs the ability to understand and cope with the often unexpressed emotional reactions of others in the organization in order to win their cooperation.

With this discussion of the limitations of management education, Livingstone joins Katz and Mintzberg in calling attention to the wide variety of skills and abilities possessed by successful managers. Many of these skills can be and are being taught. But many are qualities of character and style that are difficult to develop in a classroom.[32] Prospective managers will have to look inside themselves to discover whether they have the personal qualities and abilities required of effective managers. If they are truly motivated toward management, they will take the initiative in pursuing the self-development they will eventually need.[33]

Management Learning: Books and Experience

Of course no textbook by itself can teach you how to become an effective manager. Learning how to be an effective manager requires not only knowledge and personal ability but also considerable practice in using the various management skills.

However, a major function of a textbook is to present relevant information in an orderly, systematic way. We say "relevant" because the knowledge in this textbook is based on the experience of managers and on studies by management researchers. You will not be ready to assume all the responsibilities of a manager when you finish this book, but you will know many of the tools you will be using as a manager and you will be more aware of the kinds of problems and opportunities you will be facing.

In order to help you develop your managerial abilities, this book includes case studies that require you to describe and anticipate problems and decide what to do about them. These case studies will provide you with an opportunity to develop your judgment and skill. To the extent that you will work with others in analyzing the cases, you will also be able to practice the human skills Katz described.

Students who have had some working experience, either before returning to management studies or concurrently with them, have the opportunity to observe managers in action. Community service and part-time employment provide a chance to watch managers and organizations at close range. Observe the interactions between levels of management, the characteristics of effective supervisors and leaders, and the qualities that seem to hinder communication and accomplishment. As your study of management progresses, try to find examples in your experience that illustrate the points you will be reading about and discussing.

Put your own management skills to work by assuming leadership roles in extracurricular activities. You might also work in and lead some of the group projects that many schools offer in connection with formal course work. In addition, you can take advantage of whatever skills-oriented courses are available. These courses help develop specific abilities through the use of experiential exercises, unstructured groups, role playing, and other techniques.

The best way to learn to be an effective manager is by working with and observing good managers. Analyze what they do, how they do it, and how things turn out. It is difficult to learn from bad managers—but not impossible. You can notice and analyze what they are doing wrong, and you can develop hypotheses about what you might do instead. In this way, you may learn some things *not* to do.[34] Knowing what not to do is important, but it is far more important to learn what *to do*. For this reason, good managers are easier to learn from—and they are much more enjoyable to work with.

In every career it is inevitable that one will work with both good and bad managers; however, keep in mind that a good manager to work under is one of the most important things to look for in a prospective job.

Summary Organizations are needed in our society because they accomplish things that individuals cannot do, help provide continuity of knowledge, and are a source of careers. The management of organizations involves planning, organizing, leading, and controlling the work of organization members in order to achieve stated goals.

In moving organizations toward their goals, managers adopt a wide range of interpersonal, informational, and decisional roles. The fact that managers need to rely on their fallible judgment in dealing with people and in making decisions suggests that management is still in many ways an art.

Recent attempts have been made to isolate and describe the qualities of managerial excellence in organizations. The effort to identify and learn from organizations that are doing many things right is a positive stimulus to managers seeking to create the conditions of excellence in their own companies.

There are two ways that managers can be classified: by level and by organizational activity. Management levels include first-line, middle and top managers. Functional managers are responsible for only one organizational activity, such as sales. General managers are responsible for all the varied activities in a complex organizational unit.

Managers at different levels of the organization require and use different types of skills. Lower-level managers require and use a greater degree of technical skill than higher-level managers, whereas higher-level managers require and use a greater degree of conceptual skill. Human skill is important at all managerial levels.

Managers work with and through other people; they are responsible and accountable; they must balance competing goals and set priorities; they must be able to think analytically and conceptually; they are mediators, politicians, diplomats, symbols, and decision makers. Above all, managers must be alert to the need to change roles as the occasion arises.

Review Questions

1. How would you define the term *management*?
2. Describe management in terms of the functions of managers. Describe management in terms of what managers do.
3. What are the levels of management discussed in this chapter?
4. How would you distinguish between efficient management and effective management? How can managers achieve excellence in their organizations?
5. Is management an art or a science? Explain your answer.
6. According to Robert L. Katz, what three basic skills do managers need? Discuss each of these skills in terms of management levels.
7. According to Mintzberg, what are the three different roles that a manager may assume in an organization? Briefly discuss each.

Notes

1. A discussion of subordinate/supervisor relations can be found in John J. Gabarro and John P. Kotter, "Managing Your Boss," *Harvard Business Review 58*, no. 1 (January–February 1980):92–100.

2. Politics in business is *per se* neither good nor bad. The importance of political skills in management is becoming increasingly apparent. See Rosabeth Moss Kanter, "Power Failure in Management Circuits," *Harvard Business Review 57*, no. 4 (July–August 1979):65–75; and Graham Astley and

Paramjit S. Sachdeva, "Structural Sources of Intraorganizational Power: A Theoretical Synthesis," *Academy of Management Review* 9, no. 1 (January 1984):104–113.

3. On the symbolic role of managers, see Jeffrey Pfeffer and Gerald R. Salancik, *The External Control of Organizations: A Resource Dependence Perspective* (New York: Harper & Row, 1978), pp. 16–18, 264–265.

4. For a popular critique of American management practice, see Steve Lohr, "Overhauling America's Business Management," *New York Times Magazine*, January 4, 1981, pp. 15ff.

5. For a popular analysis of some of the apparent successes and possible failures of Japanese organizations, see Peter F. Drucker, "Behind Japan's Success," *Harvard Business Review* 59, no. 1 (January–February 1981):83–90.

6. For a discussion of the complexity of evaluating organizational performance, see Terry Connolly, Edward J. Conlon, and Stuart Jay Deutsch, "Organizational Effectiveness: A Multiple-Constituency Approach," *Academy of Management Review* 5, no. 2 (April 1980):211–217.

7. Peter F. Drucker, *The Effective Executive* (New York: Harper & Row, 1967).

8. Peter F. Drucker, *Managing for Results* (New York: Harper & Row, 1964), p. 5. The pressures to focus on efficiency versus effectiveness are great in all organizations. Drucker also observed, in a seminar for federal executives during the Eisenhower administration, that "the greatest temptation is to work on doing better and better what should not be done at all."

9. Thomas J. Peters and Robert H. Waterman, *In Search of Excellence* (New York: Harper & Row, 1982) The themes of *In Search of Excellence* are discussed further in Tom Peters and Nancy Austin, *A Passion for Excellence* (New York: Random House, 1985).

10. "Who's Excellent Now?" *Business Week*, November 5, 1984, pp. 76ff.

11. Daniel T. Carroll, "A Disappointing Search for Excellence," *Harvard Business Review* 61, no. 6 (November–December 1983):78–79ff.

12. Because of their responsibilities for many diverse functions, it is increasingly important for top managers to have broad corporate experience. See W. Walker Lewis, "The CEO and Corporate Strategy in the Eighties: Back to Basics," *Interfaces* 14, no. 1 (January–February 1984):3–9.

13. See also Stephen J. Carroll and Dennis J. Gillen, "The Classical Management Functions: Are They Really Outdated?" *Proceedings of the Forty-Fourth Annual Meeting of the American Academy of Management* (August 1984):132–136.

14. Robert L. Katz, "Skills of an Effective Administrator," *Harvard Business Review* 52, no. 5 (September–October 1974):90–102. Katz's analysis of the manager's job is similar to the views of one of the early pioneers of management theory, Henri Fayol, whose ideas we will examine in chapter 2. See his *Industrial and General Administration*, trans. J. A. Coubrough (Geneva: International Management Institute, 1930).

15. Thomas A. Mahoney, Thomas H. Jerdee, and Stephen J. Carroll, "The Job(s) of Management," *Industrial Relations* 4, no. 2 (February 1965):97–110.

16. Henry Mintzberg, "The Manager's Job: Folklore and Fact," *Harvard Business Review* 53, no. 4 (July–August 1975):49–61 and *The Nature of Managerial Work* (Englewood Cliffs, N.J.: Prentice-Hall, 1973). Important precursors of Mintzberg's work were Sune Carlson, *Executive Behavior: A Study of the Work Load and Working Methods of Managing Directors* (Stockholm, Sweden: Stromberg Aktiebolag, 1951); Rosemary Stewart, *Managers and Their Jobs: A Study of the Similarities and Differences in the Ways Managers Spend Their Time* (London: Macmillan, 1967); and Peter F. Drucker, *The Practice of Management* (New York: Harper & Row, 1954).

17. See Cynthia M. Pavett and Alan W. Lau, "Managerial Work: The Influence of Hierarchical Level and Function Specialty," *Academy of Management Journal* 26, no. 1 (March 1983):170–177.

18. This suggestion has been supported by the work of John P. Kotter. See his *The General Manager* (New York: Free Press, 1982) and "What Effective General Managers Really Do," *Harvard Business Review* 60, no. 6 (November–December 1982):156–167.

19. For examples of how managers spend much of their time talking to accomplish their jobs, see Peter C. Gronn, "Talk as Work: The Accomplishment of School Administration," *Administrative Science Quarterly* 28, no. 1 (March 1983):1–21. Also see William Whitely, "An Exploratory Study of Managers' Reactions to Properties of Verbal Communication," *Personal Psychology* 37, no. 1 (Spring 1984):41–59.

20. Luther Gulick, "Management Is a Science," *Academy of Management Journal* 8, no. 1 (March 1965):7–13.

21. See also Ronald Gribbons and Shelby Hunt, "Is Management a Science?" *Academy of Management Review* 3, no. 1 (January 1978):139–144.

22. Henry M. Boettinger, "Is Management Really an Art?" *Harvard Business Review* 53, no. 1 (January–February 1975):54–64.

23. In highly complex situations, top managers must often use intuition. See Weston H. Agor, "Using Intuition to Manage Organizations in the Future," *Business Horizons* 27, no. 4 (July–August 1984):49–54.

24. Edgar H. Schein, "Organizational Socialization and the Profession of Management," *Industrial Management Review* 9, no. 2 (Winter 1968):1–16.

25. For an example of the spread of managerial professionalism in nonbusiness organizations, see Richard A. Loverd, "Adding More of a Management Thrust to Public Personnel Perspectives," *Policy Studies Journal* 11, no. 2 (December 1982):271–278.

26. Borje O. Saxberg, private communication.

27. See "Does Management Training Work?" *Training* 20, no. 5 (May 1983):82.

28. See Pat Wechsler, "The Long Haul to the Top," *Dun's Business Month* 123, no. 4 (April 1984):52–58ff.

29. See Jeremy Main, "The Executive Yearns to Learn," *Fortune,* May 3, 1982, pp. 234–236ff.

30. See *Harvard Business Review* 49, no. 1 (January–February 1971):79–89.

31. For a good discussion of problem finding, see William F. Pounds, "The Process of Problem Finding," *Industrial Management Review* 11, no. 1 (Fall 1969):1–19.

32. Donald H. Bush and Betty Jo Licata, "The Impact of Skill Learnability on the Effectiveness of Managerial Training and Development," *Journal of Management* 9, no. 1 (Fall 1983):27–39.

33. The importance of the motivation to manage has been studied extensively by John B. Miner; see "The Real Crunch in Managerial Manpower," *Harvard Business Review* 51, no. 6 (November–December 1973):146–158 and *Motivation to Manage* (Atlanta: Organizational Measurement Systems Press, 1977). This topic is also addressed by David McClelland and David H. Burnham in "Power Is the Great Motivator," *Harvard Business Review* 54, no. 2 (March–April 1976):100–110.

34. And see Manfred F. R. Kets de Vries, "Managers Can Drive Their Subordinates Mad," *Harvard Business Review* 57, no. 4 (July–August 1979):125–134.

CASE STUDY: The Vice-President

Tom Brewster, one of the field sales managers of Major Tool Works, Inc., had been promoted to his first headquarters assignment as an assistant product manager for a group of products with which he was relatively unfamiliar. Shortly after he began this new assignment, one of the company's vice-presidents, Nick Smith, called a meeting of product managers and other staff to plan marketing strategies. Brewster's superior, the product manager, was unable to attend, so the director of marketing, Jeff Reynolds, invited Brewster to the meeting to help orient him to his new job.

Because of the large number of people attending, Reynolds was rather brief in introducing Brewster to Smith. After the meeting began, Smith—a crusty veteran with a reputation for bluntness—began asking a series of probing questions, which most of the product managers were able to answer in detail. Suddenly he turned to Brewster and began to question him quite closely about his group of products. Somewhat confused, Brewster confessed that he really did not know the answers.

It was immediately apparent to Reynolds that Smith had forgotten or had failed to understand that Brewster was new to his job, and was attending the meeting more for his own orientation than to contribute to it. He was about to offer a discreet explanation when Smith, visibly annoyed with what he took to be Brewster's lack of preparation, snapped, "Gentlemen, you have just seen an example of sloppy staff work, and there is no excuse for it!"

Reynolds had to make a quick decision. He could interrupt Smith and point out that he had judged Brewster unfairly; but that might embarrass both his superior and his subordinate. Alternatively, he could wait until after the meeting and offer an explanation in private. Inasmuch as Smith quickly became engrossed in another conversation, Reynolds followed the second approach. Glancing at Brewster, Reynolds noted that his expression was one of mixed anger and dismay. After catching his eye, Reynolds winked at Brewster as a discreet reassurance that he understood and that the damage could be repaired.

After an hour, Smith, evidently dissatisfied with what he termed the "inadequate planning" of the marketing department in general, abruptly declared the meeting over. As he did so, he turned to Reynolds and asked him to remain behind for a moment. To Reynold's surprise Smith immediately raised the question of Brewster himself. In fact, it turned out to have been his main reason for asking Reynolds to remain behind. "Look," he said, "I want you to tell me frankly, do you think I was too rough with that kid?" Relieved, Reynolds said, "Yes, you were. I was going to speak to you about it."

Smith explained that the fact that Brewster was new to his job had not registered adequately when they had been introduced, and that it was only some time after his own outburst that the nagging thought began to occur to him that what he had done was inappropriate and unfair. "How well do you know him?" he asked. "Do you think I hurt him?"

For a moment Reynolds took the measure of his superior. Then he replied evenly, "I don't know him very well yet. But, yes, I think you hurt him."

"Damn, that's unforgivable," said Smith. He then telephoned his secretary to call Brewster and ask him to report to his office immediately. A few moments later Brewster returned, looking perplexed and uneasy. As he entered, Smith came out from behind his desk and met him in the middle of the office. Standing face to face with Brewster, who was 20 years and four organization levels his junior, he said, "Look, I've done something stupid and I want to apologize. I had no right to treat you like that. I should have remembered that you were new to your job, but I didn't. I'm sorry."

Brewster was somewhat flustered. He muttered his thanks for the apology.

"As long as you are here, young man," Smith continued, "I want to make a few things clear to you in the presence of your boss's boss. Your job is to make sure that people like myself don't make stupid decisions. Obviously we think you are qualified for your job or we would not have brought you in here. But it takes time to learn any job. Three months from now I will expect you to know the answers to any questions about your products. Until then," he said, thrusting out his hand for the younger man to shake, "you have my complete confidence. And thank you for letting me correct a really dumb mistake."

Source: From *Cases and Problems for Decisions in Management,* by Saul Gellerman. Copyright © 1984 by Random House, Inc. Reprinted by permission of Random House, Inc.

Case Questions   **1.** What do you think was the effect on Brewster and the other managers of Smith's outburst at the meeting?

2. Was Smith right to apologize to Brewster, or should he have left well enough alone?

3. What do you think the apology meant to Brewster?

4. What would it be like to have Nick Smith as a superior? As a subordinate?

5. How does Smith define Brewster's responsibilities as an assistant product manager? How does he define his own role as a top manager?

6. What is the most important aspect of the relations between management levels in this company?

2 THE EVOLUTION OF MANAGEMENT THEORY

Upon completing this chapter you should be able to:

1. Describe the three major schools of management thought and how they evolved.

2. Discuss how each of these schools can contribute to a balanced understanding of and approach to your job as a manager.

3. Identify the models of human nature that underlie each of these schools.

4. Discuss the contributions and limitations of each school.

5. Describe two recently developed approaches to management that attempt to integrate the various schools.

6. Form your own working synthesis of the various management schools.

The theory of relativity helps physicists control the atom. Through the laws of aerodynamics, engineers can predict the effects of a proposed change in airplane design. Similarly, the theories and principles of management make it easier for us to decide what we must do to function most effectively as managers. Without theories, all we have are intuition, hunches, and hope, which are of limited use in today's increasingly complex organizations.

Unfortunately, there is as yet no verified general theory or set of laws for management that we can apply to all situations.[1] As managers, we will have at our disposal many ways of looking at organizations and at the activities, performance, and satisfaction of people in organizations. Each of these ways may be more useful for some problems we will face than for others. For example, a management theory that emphasizes the importance of a good work environment may be more helpful in dealing with a high employee turnover rate than with production delays. Because there is no single, universally accepted management theory, we must be familiar with the major theories that exist.

In this chapter we will focus on three well-established schools of management thought:[2] the *classical school* (which has two branches, *scientific management* and *classical organization theory*), the *behavioral school*, and the *management science school*. Although these schools developed in historical sequence, later ideas have not replaced earlier ones. Instead, each new school has tended to be "layered" on top of the previous ones. At the same time, each has continued to develop. Some merging has also occurred, as later theorists have attempted to integrate the knowledge accumulated.[3] Thus, we will also discuss two recent approaches to management that attempt to integrate the various theories—the *systems approach* and the *contingency approach*.

The Classical Management Theorists

THE THREE SCHOOLS OF MANAGEMENT

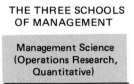

People have been managed in groups and organizations since prehistoric times. Even the simplest of hunting and gathering bands generally recognized and obeyed a leader or a group of decision makers responsible for the welfare of the band. As societies grew larger and more complex, the need for organizations and managers became increasingly apparent. A town government could not, for example, be run by a few individuals. Administrators and bureaucrats were needed to manage the operations of a state or nation.

Attempts to develop *theories* and *principles* of management, however, are relatively recent. In particular, the industrial revolution of the eighteenth and nineteenth centuries gave rise to the need for a systematic approach to management. The development of new technologies at that time concentrated great quantities of raw materials and large numbers of workers in factories. Goods were produced in quantity and had to be distributed widely. That all these elements had to be coordinated called attention to the problems of management.

Forerunners of Scientific Management

Imagine that you live in an English town in the early 1800s. The new factory system has been spreading, and a local entrepreneur has put you in charge of a new plant being built. You will hire employees, assign jobs, and be responsible for setting production goals. What do you think would be foremost in your mind—profits, efficiency, craft? What would you look for in your employees? To what extent would you feel responsible for their welfare? The forerunners of scientific management confronted questions very much like these and had no previous experience to guide them.

Robert Owen (1771–1858). Robert Owen was a manager of several cotton mills at New Lanark, Scotland, during the early 1800s. At that time, working and living conditions for employees were very poor. Child workers 5 or 6 years old were commonplace, and the standard working day was 13 hours long.

Owen conceived of the manager's role as one of *reform*. He built better housing for his workers and operated a company store where goods could be purchased cheaply. He reduced the standard working day to 10½ hours and refused to hire children under the age of 10.

Owen never claimed that he fought for reform on humanitarian grounds alone. Instead, he argued that improving the condition of employees would inevitably lead to increased production and profits. Where other managers concentrated their investments in technical improvements, Owen stressed the fact that a manager's best investment was in the workers, or "vital machines," as he called them.

Aside from making general improvements in working conditions at his mills, Owen instituted a number of specific work procedures that also increased productivity. For example, an employee's work was rated openly on a daily basis. Owen believed that these open ratings not only let the manager know what the problem areas were but also instilled pride and spurred competition. In our organizations today, the practice of posting and publicizing sales and production figures is based on the same psychological principle.

Charles Babbage (1792–1871). A British professor of mathematics, Babbage spent much of his time studying ways to make factory operations more efficient. He became convinced that the application of scientific principles to work processes would both increase productivity and lower expenses.

Babbage was an early advocate of division of labor. He believed that each factory operation should be analyzed so that the various skills involved in the operation could be isolated. Each worker would then be trained in one particular skill and would be responsible only for that part of the total operation (rather than for the whole task). In this way, expensive training time could be reduced, and the constant repetition of each operation would improve the skills and efficiency of workers. Our modern assembly line, in which each worker is responsible for a different repetitive task, is based on many of Babbage's ideas. Contemporary digital computers were anticipated by his invention, at the age of 30, of the world's first practical punch-card mechanical calculator.

Frederick W. Taylor (1856–1915) and Scientific Management

Scientific management arose in part from the need to increase productivity. In the United States especially, skilled labor was in short supply at the beginning of the twentieth century. To expand productivity, ways had to be found to increase the efficiency of workers.

Could some element of the work be eliminated or some parts of the operation combined? Could the sequence of these tasks be improved? Was there "one best way" of doing a job? In his pursuit of answers to such questions, Frederick W. Taylor slowly built the body of principles that constitute the essence of scientific management.

Taylor's ideas grew primarily out of his years of experience and experiment in three companies: Midvale Steel, Simonds Rolling Machine, and Bethlehem Steel.

The Midvale Years. Taylor based his managerial system on his own production-line time studies. This approach marked the true beginning of scientific management. Instead of relying on traditional work methods, Taylor analyzed and timed steel workers' movements on a series of jobs. With time study as his base, Taylor could now break each job down into its components and design the quickest and best methods of operation for each part of the job. He thereby established how much workers should be able to do with the equipment and materials at hand.

At Midvale, Taylor faced the problem that workers were afraid to work fast because they believed their rate of pay would be lowered or they would be laid off if they completed their tasks too quickly. To counter these fears, Taylor encouraged employers to pay more productive workers at a higher rate than others. The increased rate was carefully calculated and was based on the greater profit that would result from increased production. Thus, workers were encouraged to surpass their previous performance standards and earn more pay. Taylor called his plan the *differential rate system*. He believed that workers who met the higher standards ("first-class" workers, as he called them) need not fear layoffs because their companies benefited from the increase in productivity. The higher payments would continue because they were "scientifically correct" rates, set at a level that was best for the company and for the worker. At the same time, no one would be hurt by the differential system. Workers who fell below the standard in productivity would find other work "in a day or two," as he put it, because of the existing labor shortage.

The Consulting Years: Simonds and Bethlehem Steel. By 1893, Taylor decided he could best put his ideas into effect as a private consulting management engineer. He was soon able to report impressive improvements in productivity, quality, worker morale, and wages while working with one client, Simonds Rolling Machine Company. In one operation, Simonds employed 120 women to inspect bicycle ball bearings. The work was tedious, the hours were long, and there seemed little reason to believe improvements could be made. Taylor proved otherwise. First, he studied and timed the movements of the best workers. Then he trained the rest in the methods of their more effective co-workers and transferred or laid off the poorest performers. He also introduced rest periods during the workday, along with his differential pay rate system and other improvements. The results were impressive: Expenses went down, while productivity, quality, earnings, and worker morale went up. (See box.)

In 1898, Bethlehem Steel Company engaged Taylor as a consultant. Taylor set out to make the work of the company yard gang more efficient. The members of the yard gang unloaded raw materials from incoming railcars and loaded the finished product on outgoing cars. Each man earned $1.15 a day for loading an average of

Task:	Inspection of the balls used in bicycle ball bearings. An established operation employing 120 workers who were "old hands" and skilled at their jobs.
Major Changes Made:	Additional training based on study of higher-performing workers. Selection on the basis of appropriate skills, laying off or transferring lower performers. Workday shortened from 10½ to 8½ hours. Rest periods introduced. Efficiency of control system increased (but with no change in inspection standards).
Results Reported:	Thirty-five inspectors did work formerly done by 120. Accuracy improved by two-thirds. Wages received rose by 80 to 100 percent. Apparent improvements in worker morale.

12½ tons. Taylor was told that the workers were habitually slow and that they were not willing to work faster.

After he and a co-worker studied and timed the operations involved in unloading and loading the cars, Taylor concluded that with frequent rest periods, each man could handle about 48 tons a day. Setting 47½ tons as the standard, Taylor worked out a piece rate that would net $1.85 a day to those who met that standard. Thus, the workers were encouraged to adopt Taylor's work methods.

Although Taylor's methods led to dramatic increases in productivity and to higher pay in a number of instances, workers and unions began to oppose his approach. Like the workers at Midvale, they feared that working harder or faster would exhaust whatever work was available and bring about layoffs. The fact that workers had been laid off at Simonds and in other organizations using Taylor's methods encouraged this fear. As Taylor's ideas spread, opposition to them continued to grow. Increasing numbers of workers became convinced that they would lose their jobs if Taylor's methods were adopted.

The Philosophy Behind the Technique. By 1912, resistance to Taylorism had caused a strike at the Watertown Arsenal in Massachusetts, and hostile members of Congress called on Taylor to explain his ideas and techniques. Both in his testimony and in his two books *Shop Management* and *The Principles of Scientific Management,* Taylor outlined his philosophy.[4] It rested, he said, on four basic principles:

1. *The development of a true science of management,* so that, for example, the best method for performing each task could be determined.
2. *The scientific selection of the workers,* so that each worker would be given responsibility for the task for which he or she was best suited.
3. *The scientific education and development of the worker.*
4. *Intimate, friendly cooperation between management and labor.*

Taylor testified, however, that in order for these principles to succeed, "a complete mental revolution" on the part of management and labor was required. Rather than quarrel over whatever profits there were, they should both try to increase production. By so doing, profits would be increased to such an extent that labor and management would no longer have to compete for them. In short, Taylor believed that management and labor had a common interest in increasing productivity.

Other Contributors to Scientific Management

Henry L. Gantt (1861–1919). Henry L. Gantt had worked with Taylor at Midvale, Simonds, and Bethlehem Steel. But after he began to work on his own as a consulting industrial engineer, Gantt reconsidered Taylor's incentive system.

Abandoning the differential rate system as having too little motivational impact, Gantt came up with a new idea. Every worker who finished a day's assigned work load would win a 50¢ bonus for that day. Then he added a second motivation. The *supervisor* would earn a bonus for each worker who reached the daily standard, plus an extra bonus if all the workers reached it. This, Gantt reasoned, would spur a supervisor to train workers to do a better job.

Gantt also built upon Owen's idea of rating an employee's work publicly. Every worker's progress was recorded on individual bar charts—in black on days he or she made the standard, in red when he or she fell below. Going beyond this, Gantt originated a charting system for production scheduling. This system, called the "Gantt chart," is still in use today. (See chapter 7.)

The Gilbreths. Frank B. and Lillian M. Gilbreth (1868–1924 and 1878–1972) made their contribution to the scientific management movement as a husband and wife team. Lillian's doctoral thesis, which later appeared in book form as *The Psychology of Management,* was first published in the magazine *Industrial Engineering* in 1912, under the publisher's condition that the author be listed as L. M. Gilbreth with no indication she was a woman.[5] Although she and Frank collaborated on fatigue and motion studies, Lillian also focused her attention on ways of promoting the welfare of the individual worker. To her, scientific management had one ultimate aim: to help workers reach their full potential as human beings.

Frank Gilbreth began work as an apprentice bricklayer and worked his way up the managerial ladder. Bricklayers, he noticed, used three different sets of motions: one for teaching apprentices, another for working fast, and a third for deliberately holding down the pace. After careful study of the different motions involved, Frank was able to develop a technique that tripled the amount of work a bricklayer could do in a day. His success led him to make motion and fatigue study his lifework.

In Frank Gilbreth's conception, motion and fatigue were intertwined—every motion that was eliminated also reduced fatigue. Using motion picture cameras, he tried to find the most economical motions for each task, thus upgrading performance and reducing fatigue. Both Gilbreths argued that motion study would raise worker morale because of its obvious physical benefits and because it demonstrated management's concern for the worker.

The Gilbreths developed a *three-position plan* of promotion that was intended to serve as an employee development program as well as a morale booster. According to this plan, a worker would do his or her present job, prepare for the next highest one, and train his or her successor, all at the same time. Thus, every worker would always be a doer, a learner, and a teacher and would look forward to new opportunities.

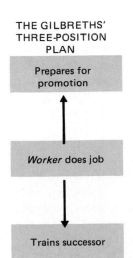

THE GILBRETHS'
THREE-POSITION
PLAN

Prepares for promotion

↑

Worker does job

↓

Trains successor

Contributions and Limitations of Scientific Management

Contributions. A team of people working together, each tending expertly to one or a few tasks, can outproduce the same number of people each performing all of the tasks. The prime example of this is the vastly increased productivity of the modern assembly line, in which conveyor belts bring to each employee the parts needed to do one specific job and then carry the completed work to the next employee on the line. Today's assembly lines pour out their finished products faster than Taylor could ever have imagined. This American production "miracle" is the legacy of scientific management.

The methods of scientific management can be applied to a variety of organizational activities, besides those of industrial organizations. The *efficiency techniques* of scientific management, such as time and motion studies, have made us aware that the tools and physical movements involved in a task can be made more efficient and rational. The stress it placed on *scientific selection and development* of workers has made us recognize the importance of both ability and training in increasing worker effectiveness. Finally, the importance that scientific management gave to *work design* encouraged managers to seek the "one best way" of getting a job done. Thus, scientific management not only developed a rational approach to solving organizational problems but also pointed the way to the professionalization of management.[6]

Limitations. Unfortunately, little if any of the "mental revolution" called for by Taylor came about in practice. While the new technology was readily adopted by management, the philosophy that Taylor espoused was not. Too often, increases in productivity led to layoffs or changes in piece rates that left workers producing more output for the same income. The higher wages and better working conditions enjoyed by today's workers did not result from the voluntary redistribution of increased profits by management. Instead, the tremendous growth of unionism after the depression and the labor shortage in the years following World War II produced many of labor's gains. Today, labor and management frequently are at odds.

Proponents of scientific management were hampered by the notions of human behavior prevalent in Taylor's time. The then-popular model of human behavior was that people were "rational" and thus motivated primarily by a desire for material gain. It was assumed that they would therefore act in a manner best suited to satisfy their *economic* and *physical* needs. Thus, Taylor and his followers overlooked the *social* needs of workers as members of a group and never considered the tensions created when these needs were frustrated. They assumed one had only to tell people exactly what to do to increase their earnings and they would go right ahead and do it, as rational people should.[7] But, as many managers have since discovered, people need to feel important and want a say in the things that matter to them. Financial gain, while significant, is not the only thing that matters to workers.[8]

The proponents of scientific management also overlooked the human desire for job satisfaction. Paradoxically, as the principles of scientific management were successfully applied and affluence spread, there was a growing tendency on the part of workers to question traditional management practices. Thus, workers became more willing to go out on strike over job conditions rather than salary and to leave a job if they were unhappy in it. The result was that the scientific management model of a purely rational worker, interested *only* in higher wages, became increasingly inappropriate.

Henri Fayol (1841–1925) and Classical Organization Theory

Scientific management was concerned with increasing the productivity of the shop and the individual worker. The other branch of classical management—*classical organization theory*—grew out of the need to find guidelines for managing complex organizations, such as factories. We acknowledge Fayol as founder of the classical management school, not because he was the first to investigate managerial behavior but because he was the first to systematize it. Fayol believed that sound managerial practice falls into certain patterns that can be identified and analyzed. From this basic insight, he drew up the blueprint for a cohesive doctrine of management—one that retains much of its force to this day.

Trained as a mining engineer, Fayol made his mark as an industrialist with the French coal and iron combine of Commentry-Fourchambault, where he spent his entire working career. He joined the firm as a junior executive in 1860 and rose quickly through the ranks, retiring as a director of the company in 1918. Fayol always insisted that his success was due not to his personal abilities as a manager but to the methods he used. In fact, he believed that "with scientific forecasting and proper methods of management, satisfactory results were inevitable."

Fayol's insistence that management was not a personal talent but a skill like any other was a major contribution to management thought. It had generally been believed that "managers were born, not made," that practice and experience would be helpful only to those who already had the innate qualities of a manager. Fayol, however, believed that management could be taught, once its underlying principles were understood and a general theory of management was formulated.

Fayol spent much of the later years of his life trying to prove that, when properly applied, his methods and principles would ensure a manager's success. However, widespread recognition of his work came very slowly, partly because his writings were not translated into English until several years after his death. Few, if any, American managers were aware of his work even as late as the 1930s. Yet many of the managerial concepts we take for granted today were first articulated by Fayol.

The Activities of a Business and the Functions of a Manager. In setting out to develop a science of management, Fayol began by dividing business operations into six activities, all of which were closely dependent on one another. These activities were (1) technical—producing and manufacturing products; (2) commercial—buying raw materials and selling products; (3) financial—acquiring and using capital; (4) security—protecting employees and property; (5) accounting—recording and taking stock of costs, profits, and liabilities, keeping balance sheets, and compiling statistics; and (6) managerial.

Fayol's primary focus, of course, was on this last activity, because he felt managerial skills had been the most neglected aspect of business operations. He defined managing in terms of five functions: planning, organizing, commanding, coordinating, and controlling. In this definition, *planning* means devising a course of action that will enable the organization to meet its goals. *Organizing* means mobilizing the material and human resources of the organization to put the plans into effect. *Commanding* means providing direction for employees and getting them to do their work. *Coordinating* means making sure that the resources and activities of the organization are working harmoniously to achieve the desired goals. *Controlling* means monitoring the plans to ensure that they are being carried out properly. (See fig. 2–1.)

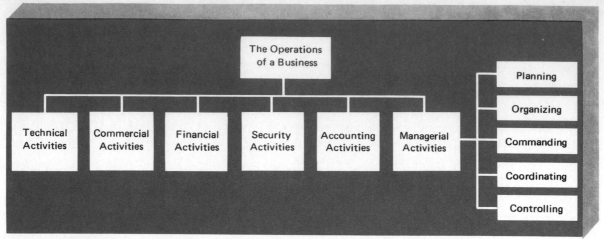

FIGURE 2–1
THE OPERATIONS
OF A BUSINESS AND
THE FUNCTIONS OF
A MANAGER
(FAYOL).

Readers will recognize that Fayol's five management functions are similar to the four functions of planning, organizing, leading, and controlling described in chapter 1. The model of management as a series of functions originated by Fayol remains a keystone of management theory today.

The Abilities of Managers. Fayol observed that the abilities needed by managers in a given organization depend on the managers' position in its hierarchy. For example, in a lower-level job, specific technical skills but very little managerial ability are needed. As we move up the hierarchy, however, managerial abilities become more important as compared to technical skills. Thus the general manager of a firm needs more managerial ability and less technical ability than a lower-level manager. Fayol noted, too, that the need for managerial abilities is also related to the size of the organization. Chief executives in a large business, for example, need a greater measure of managerial skill than chief executives in a small one.

This last point had a strong influence on the development of Fayol's idea that management should be taught. He noted that as the number of large businesses grew, the need for more and better managers increased. Fayol therefore called for the introduction of formal managerial training in schools rather than reliance on the sink-or-swim approach then in use. An added benefit of such managerial training, he suggested, would be that it would help people function better in all areas of life. Fayol always believed managerial ability could be applied to the home, the church, the military, and politics as well as to industry.

The Principles of Management. Fayol carefully chose the term *principles of management* rather than *rules* or *laws*:

> I prefer the word principles in order to avoid any idea of rigidity, as there is nothing rigid or absolute in administrative matters; everything is a question of degree. The same principle is hardly ever applied twice in exactly the same way, because we have to allow for different and changing circumstances, for human beings who are equally different and changeable, and for many other variable elements. The principles, too, are flexible, and can be adapted to meet every need; it is just a question of knowing how to use them.[9]

Fayol listed the 14 principles of management he "most frequently had to apply." (See box.)

FAYOL'S 14 PRINCIPLES OF MANAGEMENT

1. *Division of Labor.* The more people specialize, the more efficiently they can perform their work. This principle is epitomized by the modern assembly line.
2. *Authority.* Managers must give orders so that they can get things done. While their *formal* authority gives them the right to command, managers will not always compel obedience unless they have *personal* authority (such as relevant expertise) as well.
3. *Discipline.* Members in an organization need to respect the rules and agreements that govern the organization. To Fayol, discipline will result from good leadership at all levels of the organization, fair agreements (such as provisions for rewarding superior performance), and judiciously enforced penalties for infractions.
4. *Unity of Command.* Each employee must receive instructions about a particular operation from only one person. Fayol believed that when an employee reported to more than one superior, conflicts in instructions and confusion of authority would result.
5. *Unity of Direction.* Those operations within the organization that have the same objective should be directed by only one manager using one plan. For example, the personnel department in a company should not have two directors, each with a different hiring policy.
6. *Subordination of Individual Interest to the Common Good.* In any undertaking, the interests of employees should not take precedence over the interests of the organization as a whole.
7. *Remuneration.* Compensation for work done should be fair to both employees and employers.
8. *Centralization.* Decreasing the role of subordinates in decision making is centralization; increasing their role is decentralization. Fayol believed that managers should retain final responsibility but also need to give their subordinates enough authority to do their jobs properly. The problem is to find the best amount of centralization in each case.
9. *The Hierarchy.* The line of authority in an organization—often represented today by the neat boxes and lines of the organization chart—runs in order of rank from top management to the lowest level of the enterprise.
10. *Order.* Materials and people should be in the right place at the right time. People in particular should be in the jobs or positions most suited for them.
11. *Equity.* Managers should be both friendly and fair to their subordinates.
12. *Stability of Staff.* A high employee turnover rate is not good for the efficient functioning of an organization.
13. *Initiative.* Subordinates should be given the freedom to conceive and carry out their plans, even though some mistakes may result.
14. *Esprit de Corps.* Promoting team spirit will give the organization a sense of unity. To Fayol, even small factors could help to develop this spirit. He suggested, for example, the use of verbal communication instead of formal, written communication whenever possible.

Contributions and Limitations of Classical Organization Theory

Contributions. Like all theorists, the classical organization theorists were limited by the knowledge that was available to them and the conditions that existed in their time. Nevertheless, much in classical organization theory has endured. For example, the concepts that management skills apply to all types of group activity have, if anything, increased in importance today—in our schools, government, and other institutions. The concept that certain identifiable principles underlie effective managerial behavior and that these principles can be taught also continues to be valid. (For one thing, it is the justification for this book.)

Although classical organization theory has been criticized by members of other schools of management thought, its perspectives have been better received by practicing managers than those of any other school. This may be because classical organization theory helped to isolate major areas of practical concern to the working manager. More than anything else, then, the classical organization school raised issues that are important to managers. It made them aware of basic kinds of problems that they would face in any organization.

Limitations. Classical organization theory has been criticized on the ground that it was more appropriate for the past than for the present. When organizations were in a relatively stable and predictable environment, the classical principles seemed valid. Today, with organizational environments becoming more turbulent, the classical organization guidelines seem less appropriate. For example, it was important to classical theorists that managers maintain their formal authority. Today's better-educated employees, however, are less accepting of formal authority, especially when it is applied arbitrarily. They are also more likely than workers of the past to leave an organization if they are dissatisfied in it.

The principles of classical organization theorists have also been criticized as being too general for today's complex organizations. For example, in modern companies specialization has increased to the point where the lines of authority are sometimes blurred. The maintenance engineer, for instance, may take orders from the plant manager *and* the chief engineer. Here we have a conflict between the classical principles of division of labor and unity of command.[10] Yet classical theory provides little or no guidance for deciding which principle should take precedence over the other.

Transitional Theories: More People-Oriented

Mary Parker Follett, Oliver Sheldon, and Chester Barnard built on the basic framework of the classical school. However, they introduced many new elements, especially in the area of human relations and organizational structure. In this, they anticipated trends that would be further developed by the emerging behavioral and management science approaches.

Mary Parker Follett (1868–1933). Follett was convinced that no one could become a whole person except as a member of a group. Thus, she took for granted Taylor's assertion that labor and management shared a common purpose as members of the same organization. She believed, however, that the artificial distinction between managers and subordinates—order givers and order takers—obscured this natural partnership.[11]

Individual

Needs

of

Employees

ORGANIZATIONAL
SUCCESS

Organization

Goals

Follett argued that in order for management and labor truly to become part of one group, traditional views would have to be abandoned. For example, she believed leadership should not come from the power of formal authority, as was traditional, but from the manager's greater *knowledge* and *expertise*. The manager should simply be the person best equipped to head the group.

Oliver Sheldon (1894–1951). Sheldon spent his entire business career with Rowntree's, the British confectionery company. In his 1923 book he described a "philosophy of management," the first to be so called, that stressed the social responsibility of business in a way more in harmony with the values of the 1980s than those of the 1920s. He believed that business owes a service to society and that "ethics is as essential to management as economics." The goods and services provided by industry "must be furnished at the lowest prices compatible with an adequate standard of quality, and distributed in such a way as directly or indirectly to promote the highest ends of the community."

According to Sheldon, management is generally bound to treat its workers with fairness and honesty, and beyond this each manager must combine the efficient values of scientific management with the ethics of service to the community, according to three principles:

1. **"The policies, conditions, and methods of industry shall conduce to communal well-being."**
2. **"Management shall endeavor to interpret the highest moral sanction of the community as a whole . . . to give practical effect to those ideals of social justice which would generally be accepted by the most unbiased portion of communal opinion."**
3. **"Management shall take the initiative . . . in raising the general ethical standard and conception of social justice."**[12]

Chester I. Barnard (1886–1961). Barnard became president of New Jersey Bell in 1927. He used his work experiences and his extensive readings in sociology and philosophy to formulate his theories on organizational life. According to Barnard, people come together in formal organizations to achieve things they could not achieve working alone. But as they pursue the organization's goals, they must also satisfy their individual needs. And so Barnard arrived at his central thesis: An enterprise can operate efficiently and survive only when both the organization's goals and the aims and needs of the individuals working for it are kept in balance.[13]

For example, to meet their personal goals within the confines of the formal organization, people come together in informal groups, such as cliques. To ensure its survival, the firm must utilize these informal groups effectively, even if they at times work at cross purposes to management's objectives. Recognition of the importance and universality of the "informal organization" was a major contribution to management thought.

The Behavioral School: The Organization Is People

The *behavioral school* emerged in part because managers found that the classical approach did not achieve complete production efficiency and workplace harmony. Managers still encountered difficulties and frustrations because people did not always follow predicted or rational patterns of behavior. Thus, there was increased interest in helping managers deal more effectively with the "people side" of their organizations. Several individuals tried to strengthen classical organization theory with the insights of sociology and psychology.

Hugo Münsterberg (1863–1916) and the Birth of Industrial Psychology

Hugo Münsterberg's major contribution was to apply the tools of psychology to help achieve the same types of productivity objectives sought by other management theories. In his major work, *Psychology and Industrial Efficiency,* he suggested that productivity could be increased in three ways: (1) through finding the best possible person—the worker whose mental qualities single him or her out as best suited for the job; (2) through creating the best possible work—the ideal psychological conditions for maximizing productivity; and (3) through the use of psychological influence, which Münsterberg calls "the best possible effect," to motivate employees.

In each area Münsterberg suggested the use of techniques taken from experimental psychology. For example, psychological testing could be used to help select qualified personnel. Learning research could lead to improved training methods. And the study of human behavior could help formulate psychological techniques for motivating workers to greater effort. The use of modern vocational guidance techniques to identify the skills needed on a job and to measure the skills of candidates for the job are offshoots of Münsterberg's studies.[14]

Elton Mayo and the Human Relations Movement

"Human relations" is frequently used as a general term to describe the ways in which managers interact with their subordinates. When "people management" stimulates more and better work, we have "good" human relations in the organization. When morale and efficiency deteriorate, human relations in the organization are "bad." To create good human relations, managers must know why employees act as they do and what social and psychological factors motivate them.

The Hawthorne Experiments. A famous series of studies of human behavior in work situations was conducted at the Western Electric company from 1924 to 1933. These studies eventually became known as the "Hawthorne Studies" because many of them were performed at Western Electric's Hawthorne plant near Chicago. The studies began as an attempt to investigate the relationship between the level of lighting in the workplace and the productivity of workers—the type of question Frederick Taylor and his colleagues might well have addressed.

In some of the early studies, the Western Electric researchers divided the employees into test groups, which were subjected to deliberate changes in lighting, and control groups, whose lighting remained constant throughout the experiments. The results of the experiments were ambiguous. When the test group's lighting conditions were improved, productivity tended to increase just as expected, although the increases were erratic. But there was a tendency for productivity to continue to increase when the lighting conditions were then made worse. To compound the mystery, the control group's output also tended to rise as the test group's lighting conditions were altered, even though the control group experienced no changes in illumination. Something besides lighting was influencing the workers' performance.

In a new set of experiments, a small group of workers was placed in a separate room and a number of variables were altered: wages were increased; rest periods of varying lengths were introduced; the workday and workweek were shortened. The researchers, who now acted as supervisors, also allowed the groups to choose their own rest periods and to have a say in other suggested changes. Again the results were ambiguous. Performance tended to increase over time, but it also rose and fell erratically. Part way through this set of experiments, Elton Mayo (1880–1949) and some associates from Harvard, including Fritz J. Roethlisberger and William J. Dickson, became involved.

In these and subsequent experiments, Mayo and his associates decided that financial incentives, when these were offered, were not causing the productivity improvements. They believed that a complex chain of attitudes had touched off the productivity increases. Because they had been singled out for special attention, the test and the control groups developed a group pride that motivated them to improve their work performance. Sympathetic supervision had further reinforced their increased motivation. The researchers concluded that employees would work harder if they believed management was concerned about their welfare and supervisors paid special attention to them. This phenomenon was subsequently labeled the *Hawthorne effect*.

The researchers also concluded that informal work groups—the social environment of employees—have a great influence on productivity. Many of the employees found their work dull and meaningless. But their associations and friendship with co-workers, sometimes influenced by a shared antagonism toward the "bosses," imparted some meaning to their working lives and provided a partial means of protection from management. For these reasons, group pressure, rather than management demands, frequently had the strongest influence on how productive workers would be.

To Mayo, then, the concept of "social man"—motivated by social needs, wanting rewarding on-the-job relationships, and responding more to work-group pressures than to management control—had to replace the old concept of "rational man" motivated by personal economic needs.[15]

Contributions and Limitations of the Human Relations Approach

Contributions. By stressing social needs, the human relations movement improved on the classical approach, which treated productivity almost exclusively as an engineering problem. In a sense, Mayo had rediscovered Robert Owen's century-old dictum that a true concern for workers, those "vital machines," paid dividends.

In addition, these researchers spotlighted the importance of a manager's style and thereby revolutionized management training. More and more attention was focused on teaching people-management skills, as opposed to technical skills. Finally, their work led to a new interest in the dynamics of groups. Managers began thinking in terms of group processes and group rewards to supplement their former concentration on the individual worker.

Limitations. Although the Hawthorne experiments profoundly influenced the way managers approached their jobs and the ways research on management was subse-

"Now available for the first time: 'A Treasury of Management Opinions'—a complete collection of management opinions for the past ten years on your choice of L.P. recordings or eight-track tapes. Here's how to order."
Drawing by W. Miller; © 1979 The New Yorker Magazine, Inc.

quently conducted, the research had many weaknesses of design, analysis, and interpretation. Whether Mayo and his colleagues' conclusions are consistent with their data is still the subject of lively debate and considerable confusion.[16]

The concept of "social man" was an important counterweight to the one-sided "rational-economic man" model. But it, too, did not completely describe individuals in the workplace. Many managers and management writers assumed that satisfied workers would be more productive workers. However, attempts to increase output during the 1950s by improving working conditions and employee satisfaction did not result in the dramatic productivity increases that had been expected.

Apparently, the social environment in the workplace is only one of several interacting factors that influence productivity. Salary levels, how interesting work tasks are, organizational structure and culture, and labor–management relations also play a part. Thus, the entire matter of productivity and worker satisfaction has turned out to be more complex than was originally thought.

From Human Relations to the Behavioral Science Approach

Mayo and his colleagues pioneered the use of the scientific method in their studies of people in the work environment. Later researchers were more rigorously trained in the social sciences (psychology, sociology, and anthropology) and used more sophisticated research methods. Thus, these later researchers became known as "behavioral scientists" rather than "human relations theorists."[17]

Mayo and the human relations theorists introduced "social man," motivated by a desire to form relationships with others. Some behavioral scientists, such as Argyris, Maslow, and McGregor, believed that the concept of "self-actualizing man" would more accurately explain human motivations.[18]

According to Abraham Maslow, the needs that people are motivated to satisfy fall into a hierarchy. At the bottom of the hierarchy are physical and safety needs. At the top are ego needs (the need for respect, for example) and self-actualizing needs (such as the need for meaning and personal growth). In general, lower-level needs must be satisfied before higher-level needs are felt. Since many of our lower-level needs have been satisfied in our society, most of us are motivated, at least in part, by the higher-level ego and self-actualizing needs. Being aware of these different needs enables a manager to use different ways to motivate subordinates. (The hierarchy of needs is discussed in greater detail in chapter 15.)

Some later behavioral scientists feel that even this model is inadequate to explain fully what motivates people in the workplace. They argue that not everyone goes predictably from one need level to the next. For some people, work is only a way to meet their lower-level needs. Others are satisfied with nothing less than the fulfillment of their highest-level needs, and may even choose to work in jobs that threaten their safety to attain uniquely personal goals. To these behavioral scientists, the more realistic model of human motivation is "complex man." The effective manager is aware that no two people are exactly alike and tailors his or her attempts to influence people according to their individual needs.

Contributions and Limitations of the Behavioral Science School

Behavioral scientists have made enormous contributions to our understanding of individual motivation, group behavior, interpersonal relationships at work, and the importance of work to human beings. Their findings have caused managers to become much more sensitive and sophisticated in dealing with subordinates. They continue to offer new insights in such important areas as leadership, conflict resolution, the acquisition and use of power, organizational change, and communication.

In spite of the impressive contributions of the behavioral sciences to management, many management writers—including behavioral scientists—believe that the potential of this field has not been fully realized. Managers themselves may resist behavioral scientists' suggestions, because they do not like to admit that they need help in dealing with people. The models and theories proposed by behavioral scientists are seen by many managers as too complicated or abstract to be useful or relevant to their specific problems. The tendency of behavioral scientists to use jargon rather than everyday language in communicating their findings has also inhibited acceptance of their ideas. Finally, because human behavior is so complex, behavioral scientists often differ in their recommendations for a particular problem, making it difficult for managers to decide whose advice to follow.[19]

The Quantitative School: Operations Research and Management Science

At the beginning of World War II, Great Britain was faced with a number of new, complex problems in warfare that it needed desperately to solve. (For example, new tactics in antisubmarine warfare had to be developed.) With their survival at stake, the British formed the first operational research (OR) teams—groups of mathematicians, physicists, and other scientists who were brought together to solve such problems. By pooling the expertise of various specialists in these OR teams, the British were able to achieve significant technological and tactical breakthroughs.

When the Americans entered the war, they formed what they called *operations research* teams, based on the successful British model, to solve similar problems.

When the war was over, the applicability of OR to problems in industry gradually became apparent. New industrial technologies were being put into use. Transportation and communication had become more complicated. These developments brought with them a host of problems that could not be solved easily by conventional means. OR specialists were called on increasingly to help managers come up with new answers to these new problems. With the development of the electronic computer, OR procedures were formalized into what is now called the "management science school."[20]

Today the management science approach to solving a problem begins when a mixed team of specialists from relevant disciplines is called in to analyze the problem and propose a course of action to management. The team constructs a mathematical model to simulate the problem. The model shows, in symbolic terms, all the relevant factors that bear on the problem and how they are interrelated. By changing the values of the variables in the model (such as increasing the cost of raw materials) and analyzing the different equations of the model with a computer, the team can determine what the effects of each change would be. Eventually, the management science team presents management with a rational basis for making a decision.[21]

Contributions and Limitations of the Management Science Approach

The techniques of *management science* are a well-established part of the problem-solving armory of most large organizations, including the civilian and the military branches of government. Management science techniques are used in such activities as capital budgeting and cash flow management, production scheduling, development of product strategies, planning for human resource development programs, maintenance of optimal inventory levels, and aircraft scheduling.

In spite of widespread use for many problems, however, management science has not yet reached the stage where it can effectively deal with the people side of an enterprise. Its contributions to management have been greatest in planning and control activities. But they are still very modest in the areas of organizing, staffing, and leading the organization. Some managers have complained that the concepts and language of management science are too complicated for ready understanding and implementation. Others feel they are not enough involved with management scientists in developing decision-making techniques, with the result that the later, ongoing implementation of these techniques is often unsuccessful.[22] Management scientists, for their part, sometimes feel that they have not achieved their full potential for solving management problems because of their remoteness from and lack of awareness of the problems and constraints actually faced by managers.[23]

The Evolution of Management Theory

We have described the three major schools of management thought in terms of their chronological emergence. All continue to maintain their importance today. The behavioral science and the management science schools both represent vital and energetic approaches to researching, analyzing, and solving management problems. The classical school, too, continues to evolve. It has incorporated much of the research produced by the behavioral sciences, along with the new perspectives of both the behavioral science and the management science schools, and even the newer systems and contingency approaches (which will be discussed below).

Classical theory remains important because it has been able to integrate newer developments into the basic framework of the traditional issues identified by the classical writers. These issues—division of labor, authority and responsibility, initiative—remain important, although in many cases the particular focus has shifted. For example, concern with division of labor has led to speculation about the point at which specialization may become excessive in terms of the values and expectations of today's employees.

As the classical school has evolved, it has become known as the *management process* or the *operational approach*. By whatever name, much of its emphasis and many of its perspectives can still be traced back to the early classical writers. In fact, while the special focus of each remains, the other two major schools also tend to borrow insights and concepts. Indeed, it often seems that the boundaries between the various schools are becoming progressively less distinct.[24]

But the growing similarities should not be exaggerated. Just as there are many individuals who integrate the perspectives of all the schools, so are there many whose training and background are firmly in a single school and who have little or no awareness of other approaches. One benefit of studying the history and perspectives of the three schools is to understand the perspectives of your future colleagues in management and thus be prepared to work effectively with them.

How Will Management Theory Evolve?

There are five possible directions that the evolution of management theory can follow:

1. *Dominance.* One of the major schools could emerge as the most useful. Incorporating some ideas from other schools, the dominant approach would drive the others from the field. This has not been happening. Currently, each approach is recognized as contributing powerful insights, perspectives, and tools to the growing body of management theory.
2. *Divergence.* The major schools could each go off on their own paths, with decreasing cross-fertilization as they show little interest in each other's perspectives. Clearly, this, too, is not happening.
3. *Convergence.* The schools could become more similar, with the boundaries between them tending to blur. This indeed seems to be happening. The convergence is uneven, though. For example, the special tools and mathematically sophisticated models of management science have not been widely accepted by less technically oriented thinkers.[25] In fact, some view the current tendency toward convergence as promising eventual domination by one school over the others.[26]
4. *Synthesis.* Other theorists, however, see the apparent convergence now taking place leading to an integration of the perspectives of the existing schools. This would not be the "layered" buildup of the schools we described earlier. Rather, the integration would be a fresh conceptual approach to the field of manage-

ment. Two candidates for the honor of integration already exist: the systems approach and the contingency approach, to be discussed below.

5. *Proliferation.* As a final possibility, more schools or perspectives may still appear. Again, to some extent this may already be happening. In 1961, in a famous article, "The Management Theory Jungle," Harold Koontz discerned six major schools of management theory.[27] Nearly 20 years later he found 11—almost twice as many—flourishing.[28] However, many of the new approaches seem less to be new schools than specific focuses on a relatively limited set of issues.

The Systems Approach

The *systems approach* to management attempts to view the organization as a unified, purposeful system composed of interrelated parts. Rather than dealing separately with the various parts of an organization, the systems approach gives managers a way of looking at an organization as a whole and as a part of the larger, external environment. (See chapter 3.) In so doing, systems theory tells us that the activity of any part of an organization affects the activity of every other part.[29]

As production managers in a manufacturing plant, for example, we would like to have long uninterrupted production runs of standardized products in order to maintain maximum efficiency and low costs. Marketing managers, on the other hand, would like to offer quick delivery of a wide range of products and therefore may want a flexible manufacturing schedule that can fill special orders on short notice. As systems-oriented production managers, we would make scheduling decisions only after we have identified their impact on other departments and the entire organization. This means that managers cannot function wholly within the confines of the traditional organization chart. To mesh their department with the whole enterprise, managers must communicate with other employees and departments, and frequently with representatives of other organizations as well.[30]

Some Key Concepts. Many of the concepts of general systems theory are finding their way into the language of management. As managers, we should be familiar with the systems vocabulary, so that we can keep pace with current developments.

Subsystems. The parts that make up the whole of a system are called *subsystems*. And each system in turn may be a subsystem of a still larger whole. Thus, a department is a subsystem of a plant, which may be a subsystem of a company, which may be a subsystem of a conglomerate or industry, which is a subsystem of the national economy as a whole, which is a subsystem of the world system.

Synergy. Synergy means that the whole is greater than the sum of its parts. In organizational terms, *synergy* means that as separate departments within an organization cooperate and interact, they become more productive than if each had acted in isolation. For example, it is more efficient for each department in a small firm to deal with one financing department than for each department to have a separate financing department of its own.

Open and Closed Systems. A system is considered an *open system* if it interacts with its environment; it is considered a *closed system* if it does not. All organizations interact with their environment, but the extent to which they do so varies. An automobile plant, for example, is a far more open system than a monastery or a prison.

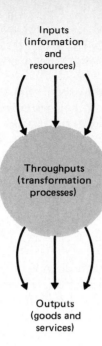

Inputs
(information
and
resources)

Throughputs
(transformation
processes)

Outputs
(goods and
services)

System Boundary. Each system has a boundary that separates it from its environment. In a closed system, the *system boundary* is rigid; in an open system, the boundary is more flexible. The system boundaries of many organizations have become increasingly flexible in recent years. Oil companies that wished to engage in offshore drilling, to cite one example, have increasingly had to consider public reaction to the potential environmental harm.

Flow. A system has flows of information, materials, and energy (including human). These enter the system from the environment as *inputs* (raw materials, for example), undergo transformation processes within the system (operations that alter them), and exit the system as outputs (goods and services).

Feedback. *Feedback* is the key to system controls. As operations of the system proceed, information is fed back to the appropriate people or perhaps to a computer so that the work can be assessed and, if necessary, corrected.[31]

Systems theory calls attention to the dynamic and interrelated nature of organizations and the management task. Thus, systems theory provides a framework within which we can plan actions and anticipate both immediate and far-reaching consequences, and at the same time, it allows us to understand unanticipated consequences as they may develop. With a systems perspective, general managers can more easily maintain a balance between the needs of the various parts of the enterprise and the needs and goals of the firm as a whole.

Systems theory advocates believe that it will absorb concepts of the other management schools until it becomes dominant or that it may eventually develop into a well-defined school by itself. At present, though, it seems most likely to emerge as a perspective that becomes incorporated into the thinking of all the major schools. The systems approach has already permeated management thinking. The concepts just described are an integral part of the thought processes and research designs of both on-the-job managers and academic theorists of all three major schools. Although partisans of this approach hail it as the eventual and long-sought integrating development, only time will tell if the systems approach to management will continue to evolve to the point at which it does absorb, synthesize, and integrate all other approaches.

The Contingency Approach

The well-known international economist Charles Kindleberger was fond of telling his students at MIT that the answer to any really engrossing question in economics is: "It depends." The task of the economist, Kindleberger would continue, is to specify *upon what* it depends, and *in what ways.*

"It depends" is an appropriate response to the important questions in management as well. Management theory attempts to determine the predictable relationships between situations, actions, and outcomes. It is therefore not surprising that a recent approach seeking to integrate the various schools of management thought essentially focuses on the interdependence of the various factors involved in the managerial situation.

The *contingency approach* was developed by managers, consultants, and researchers who tried to apply the concepts of the major schools to real-life situations. They often found that methods that were highly effective in one situation would not work in other situations. They then sought an explanation for these experiences. Why, for example, did an organizational development program work brilliantly in one situation and fail miserably in another? Advocates of the contingency approach had a single and logical answer to such questions: Results differ because situations differ. A technique that works in one case will not necessarily work in all cases.

According to the contingency approach, then, *the task of managers is to identify which technique will, in a particular situation, under particular circumstances, and at a particular time, best contribute to the attainment of management goals.* Where workers need to be encouraged to increase productivity, for example, the classical theorist may prescribe a new work simplification scheme. The behavioral scientist may seek to create a psychologically motivating climate and recommend the opposite: work enrichment. But the manager trained in the contingency approach will ask, "Which method will *work best here*?" If the workers are unskilled and training opportunities and resources are limited, work simplification might be the best solution. With skilled workers, driven by pride in their abilities, a job enrichment program might be more effective.

As we have seen, the systems approach emphasizes the interrelationships between parts of an organization. The contingency approach builds upon this perspective by focusing in detail on the nature of relationships existing between these parts. It seeks to define those factors that are crucial to a specific task or issue and to clarify the functional interactions between related factors. For this reason, advocates of the contingency approach see it as the leading branch of management thought today. In their view, this approach is the long-sought synthesis that brings together the best of all segments of what Harold Koontz has called the "management theory jungle."[32]

The primacy of the contingency approach is challenged, however, by several other theorists.[33] They argue, for one thing, that the contingency approach does not incorporate all aspects of systems theory, and they hold that it has not yet developed to the point at which it can be considered a true theory. Critics also argue that there is really not much that's new about the contingency approach. For example, they point out that even classical theorists such as Fayol cautioned that management principles must be flexibly applied.

To these critics, contingency approach supporters point out that many classical and management process theorists forgot the pragmatic cautions of Fayol and others. Instead, they tried to come up with "universal principles" that could be applied without the "it depends" dimension. Impressed, working managers applied the absolute principles advocated by these theorists—and came smack up against reality with all its shades and complications.

As managers who have studied the contingency approach, then, we would not be satisfied with simply analyzing a particular problem. We would be equally concerned with how well a particular solution fits in with the structure, resources, and goals of our entire organization. Should we try to increase productivity through work simplification or through a job enrichment program? We must take into account more than the needs of the workers. If top management is opposed to increasing specialization of work for policy reasons, then a work simplification program will not gain support. Environmental factors must be considered also. In a depressed economy, for example, job enrichment programs might be too expensive or too uncertain in their outcome. The contingency approach means that we must be aware of the complexity in every situation and that we must take an active role in trying to determine what would work best in each case.

The Approach in This Text

Our approach in this text will include the contributions of all schools and all approaches. Many times our discussion will clearly show its debt to the contingency perspective, which underlies much of the research in management today.

But the formal organization of this text into sections dealing with planning, organizing, leading, and controlling comes directly from the classical-operational perspective. Our discussions, however, will draw on all three of the major schools and both of the newer approaches.

It is important, for several reasons, that you as present or future managers be comfortable with these different viewpoints. First, your awareness of the various perspectives will help you choose what is relevant as you read about management, as you observe managers at work, and as you actually encounter management situations. Even those who favor one particular school will find new ways of incorporating ideas and information once they understand the contributions of the other schools.

Indeed, many of us are more comfortable with one approach than with another. For example, mathematically inclined individuals are frequently attracted to management science. But even so, we may, as managers, come up against situations for which our preferred tools and techniques are not relevant.[34] Furthermore, some managers prefer a combination of approaches. These eclectics need to know all approaches well enough to be able to choose and apply the appropriate response to a given situation.

We started this chapter by noting a prediction that a general theory of management would emerge by the early 1970s. When that did not happen, another forecaster expressed hopes that one would appear by the end of that decade.[35] As we proceed through the 1980s, it seems best to assume that because the tasks of management are a mixture of the simple and the complex, guides to the manager's job will also involve a mixture of simplicity and complexity.[36] The long-awaited general theory may be just around the next corner, but we should not hold our breath. Until it arrives, we will have to use the present, evolving, partial theories.

The eclectic approach is the state of the art in management theory and practice today. It may continue to characterize management in the future. Or it may not. Those who view management theory as a defined, precise, and stable set of perspectives are likely to be confused and buffeted by the flow of ideas to come. But those who are comfortable with the natural evolution of thought and theory can look forward to new concepts with anticipation and excitement. The future promises perspectives that will help us to do our job better. Those new perspectives may also force us to rethink some of our ideas from the past.[37]

Summary Three well-established schools of management thought—classical, behavioral, and quantitative—have contributed to managers' understanding of organizations and to their ability to manage them. Each offers a different perspective for defining management problems and opportunities and for developing ways to deal with them. In their current state of evolution, however, each approach also overlooks or deals inadequately with important aspects of organizational life. The newer systems approach, based on general systems theory, and the contingency approach have already been developed to the point where they offer valuable insights for the practicing manager. Eventually they may lead to the integration of the classical, behavioral, and quantitative schools; or, some new approach not yet perceived on the horizon may accomplish this end.

It is also possible that the theoretical breakthrough may never occur. Managers will then have to continue on their own to select the appropriate perspective or perspectives for each situation. They may, of course, become lost in the management theory jungle. But it is as likely that managers will find such a multiplicity of theories useful.

Review Questions

1. Why is it important for you to understand the various management theories that have developed?

2. What environmental factors enhanced the growth and development of each of the three major schools of thought?

3. What were some of the work methods and tools that Taylor introduced to increase productivity?

4. Was Taylor's assumption that management and labor had a common cause valid? Why or why not?

5. What are the major contributions and limitations of each of the three schools?

6. Which of Fayol's principles and functions of management do you believe still apply today?

7. What was Mayo's principal contribution to management knowledge? What is the Hawthorne effect?

8. Distinguish between the "rational" and "social" models in human relations.

9. What is OR and how does it work?

10. Why is the systems approach more appropriate today than it would have been in Fayol's time?

11. What is the major task of the manager according to the contingency approach?

12. Which approach or school of management thought makes the most sense to you? Why?

Notes

1. In 1963, William C. Frederick (in "The Next Development in Management Science: A General Theory," *Journal of the Academy of Management* 6, no. 3 [September 1963]) was optimistic about the emergence of a general theory within ten years. We are well past that period, but the development of a general theory has turned out to be a more difficult task than he anticipated.

2. Much of the discussion in this chapter on the evolution of management theory is based on Claude S. George, Jr., *The History of Management Thought,* 2nd ed. (Englewood Cliffs, N.J.: Prentice-Hall, 1972), and Daniel A. Wren, *The Evolution of Management Thought,* 2nd ed. (New York: Wiley, 1979).

3. An excellent discussion of this evolutionary process appears in Harold J. Leavitt, "Structure, People, and Information Technology: Some Key Ideas and Where They Come From," *Managerial Psychology,* 4th ed. (Chicago: University of Chicago Press, 1978).

4. Both books, in addition to Taylor's testimony before the Special House Committee, appear in Frederick W. Taylor, *Scientific Management* (New York: Harper & Brothers, 1947). For an assessment of Taylor's impact on contemporary management, see Edwin A. Locke, "The Ideas of Frederick W. Taylor: An Evaluation," *Academy of Management Review* 7, no. 11 (January 1982):14–24.

5. Lillian M. Gilbreth, *The Psychology of Management* (New York: Sturgis and Walton, 1914).

6. Another important contributor to scientific management was Harrington Emerson. See his book *The Twelve Principles of Efficiency,* published in 1913.

7. For a rich discussion of "rational, economic, social, self-actualizing, and complex man," see Edgar H. Schein, *Organizational Psychology,* 3rd ed. (Englewood Cliffs, N.J.: Prentice-Hall, 1980), pp. 52–72 and 93–101.

8. One observer, reporting on an automobile plant, wrote: "Some assembly-line workers are so turned off, managers report in astonishment, that they just walk away in midshift and don't even come back to get their pay for the time they have worked." See Judson Gooding, "Blue Collar Blues on the Assembly Line," *Fortune,* July 1970, pp. 69–70.

9. Henri Fayol, *Industrial and General Administration,* trans. J. A. Coubrough (Geneva: International Management Institute, 1930). Fayol used the word *administration* for what we call *management.*

10. In chapter 8 we will discuss the *matrix* organization, in which individuals have two superiors *by design*—a complete violation of the unity of command principle.

11. See Mary P. Follett, *The New State* (Gloucester, Mass.: Peter Smith, 1918); Henry C. Metcalf and Lyndall Urwick, eds., *Dynamic Administration* (New York: Harper & Brothers, 1941); and L. D. Parker, "Control in Organizational Life: The Contribution of Mary Parker Follett," *Academy of Management Review* 9, no. 4 (October 1984):736–745.

12. See Oliver Sheldon, *The Philosophy of Management* (London: Pitman & Sons, 1924; reprinted, 1965), esp. pp. 81, 284–285.

13. See Chester I. Barnard, *The Functions of the Executive* (Cambridge, Mass.: Harvard University Press, 1938).

14. See Hugo Münsterberg, *Psychology and Industrial Efficiency* (New York: Arno Press, reprint of 1913 edition). An interesting discussion of Münsterberg's work appears in "Measuring Minds for the Job," *Business Week,* January 29, 1966, pp. 60–63.

15. For extensive discussions of Mayo's work, see Elton Mayo, *The Human Problems of an Industrial Civilization* (New York: Macmillan, 1953), and F. J. Roethlisberger and W. J. Dickson, *Management and the Worker* (Cambridge, Mass.: Harvard University Press, 1939). Also see Roethlisberger's autobiography, *The Elusive Phenomena,* ed. by George F. F. Lombard (Boston: Division of Research, Graduate School of Business Administration, Harvard University, 1977). Analysis, criticism, and defense of the Hawthorne studies can be found in George C. Homans, *The Human Group* (New York: Harcourt, Brace, and Co., 1950), pp. 48–155; Alex Carey, "The Hawthorne Studies: A Radical Criticism," *American Sociological Review* 32, no. 3 (June 1967); Henry A. Landsberger, *Hawthorne Revisited* (Ithaca, N.Y.: Cornell University Press, 1958); Jon M. Shepard, "On Carey's Radical Criticism of the Hawthorne Studies," *Academy of Management Journal* 14, no. 1 (March 1971):23–32; and Dana Bramel and Ronald Friend, "Hawthorne, the Myth of the Docile Worker, and Class Bias in Psychology," *American Psychologist* 36, no. 8 (August 1981):867–878.

16. Personal communications with Gary Yunker and a paper by him were particularly helpful in clarifying some of the confusions associated with these experiments. See Gary Yunker, "The Hawthorne Studies: Facts and Myths," *Faculty Working Papers*, Department of Psychology, Jacksonville State University, Summer 1985. One example of the confusions associated with the research focuses on the fact that the Hawthorne effect suffers from many different definitions. Some researchers doubt that it exists at all, and many others feel its power to improve performance is greatly exaggerated. See Berkeley Rice, "The Hawthorne Defect: Persistence of a Flawed Theory," *Psychology Today*, February 1982, pp. 70, 72–74; and John G. Adair, "The Hawthorne Effect: A Reconsideration of the Methodological Artifact," *Journal of Applied Psychology* 69, no. 2 (1984):334–345.

17. See Bernard Berelson and Gary A. Steiner, *Human Behavior: An Inventory of Scientific Findings* (New York: Harcourt, Brace, and World, 1964). Berelson and Steiner define science as a form of inquiry in which procedures are public, definitions are precise, data collection is objective, findings are replicable, the approach is systematic and cumulative, and the purposes are explanation, understanding, and prediction. This is the ideal toward which the behavioral sciences (or any sciences) strive.

18. See Chris Argyris, *Integrating the Individual and the Organization* (New York: Wiley, 1964); Abraham H. Maslow, *Motivation and Personality* (New York: Harper & Row, 1964); and Douglas M. McGregor, *The Human Side of Enterprise* (New York: McGraw-Hill, 1960).

19. See Edgar H. Schein, "Behavioral Sciences for Management," and Edwin B. Flippo, "The Underutilization of Behavioral Science by Management," in Joseph W. McGuire, ed., *Contemporary Management: Issues and Viewpoints* (Englewood Cliffs, N.J.: Prentice-Hall, 1974), pp. 15–32 and pp. 36–41. See also James A. Lee, "Behavioral Theory vs. Reality," *Harvard Business Review* 49, no. 2 (March–April 1971):20–28 passim; and Jay W. Lorsch, "Making Behavioral Science More Useful," *Harvard Business Review* 57, no. 2 (March–April 1979):171–180.

20. Larry M. Austin and James R. Burns, *Management Science* (New York: Macmillan, 1985); Robert J. Thierauf, *Management Science: A Model Formulation Approach with Computer Applications* (Columbus, Ohio: Merrill, 1985); and Kenneth R. Baker and Dean H. Kroop, *Management Science: An Introduction to Decision Models* (New York: Wiley, 1985).

21. The management science approach has been applied to other uses besides industrial problem solving. Jay Forrester and his colleagues, for example, have pioneered attempts to simulate the operations of whole enterprises. He and others have also simulated economic activities of Third World nations and even of the world system as a whole. See Jay W. Forrester, *Industrial Dynamics* (Cambridge, Mass.: MIT Press, 1961) and *World Dynamics,* 2nd ed. (Cambridge, Mass.: MIT Press, 1979); Dennis H. Meadows et al., *The Limits to Growth* (New York: Universe Books, 1972); Dennis H. Meadows, ed., *Alternatives to Growth*—Vol. 1, *A Search for Sustainable Futures* (Cambridge, Mass.: Ballinger, 1977); and Mihajlo Mesarović and Eduard Pestel, *Mankind at the Turning Point* (New York: Dutton, 1975).

22. See James R. Miller and Howard Feldman, "Management Science—Theory, Relevance, and Practice in the 1980s," *Interfaces* 13, no. 5 (October 1983):56–60; and Leonard Adelman, "Involving Users in the Development of Decision-Analytic Aids: The Principal Factor in Successful Implementation," *Journal of the Operational Research Society* 33, no. 4 (1982):333–342.

23. For a discussion of how management science should reorient itself to compete with other approaches, see A. M. Geoffrion, "Can MS/OR Evolve Fast Enough?" *Interfaces* 13, no. 1 (February 1983):10–25.

24. For an example of interaction among the various management theories, see Sang M. Lee, Fred Luthans, and David L. Olson, "A Management Science Approach to Contingency Models of Organizational Structure," *Academy of Management Journal* 25, no. 3 (September 1982):553–566.

25. For an excellent approach to the field of management from the management science perspective, see Martin K. Starr, *Management: A Modern Approach* (New York: Harcourt Brace Jovanovich, 1971).

26. William T. Greenwood ("Future Management Theory: A 'Comparative' Evolution to a General Theory," *Academy of Management Journal* 17, no. 3 [September 1974]:503–511) and Harold Koontz ("The Management Theory Jungle Revisited," *Academy of Management Review* 5, no. 2 [April 1980]:175–187) have also suggested that convergence is occurring around the operational-management process school as other schools adopt and expand its basic concept.

27. Harold Koontz, "The Management Theory Jungle," *Journal of the Academy of Management* 4, no. 3 (December 1961):174–188.

28. Koontz, "The Management Theory Jungle Revisited."

29. See Ludwig von Bertalanffy, Carl G. Hempel, Robert E. Bass, and Hans Jonas, "General System Theory: A New Approach to Unity of Science," I–VI, *Human Biology* 23, no. 4 (December 1951):302–361; and Kenneth E. Boulding, "General Systems Theory—The Skeleton of Science," *Management Science* 2, no. 3 (April 1956):197–208.

30. See Seymour Tilles, "The Manager's Job—A Systems Approach," *Harvard Business Review* 41, no. 1 (January–February 1963):73–81.

31. Fremont E. Kast and James E. Rosenzweig, "General Systems Theory: Applications for Organization and Management," *Academy of Management Journal* 15, no. 4 (December 1972):447–465. See also Arkalgud Ramaprasad, "On the Definition of Feedback," *Behavioral Science* 28, no. 1 (January 1983):4–13.

32. See Fred Luthans, "The Contingency Theory of Management: A Path Out of the Jungle," *Business Horizons* 16, no. 3 (June 1973):62–72; Fred Luthans and Todd I. Stewart, "A General Contingency Theory of Management," *Academy of Management Review* 2, no. 2 (April 1977):181–195; Jon M. Shepard and James G. Hougland, Jr., "Contingency Theory: 'Complex Man' or 'Complex Organization'?" *Academy of Management Review* 3, no. 3 (July 1978):413–427; Fred Luthans and Todd I. Stewart, "The Reality or Illusion of a General Contingency Theory of Management: A Response to the Longenecker and Pringle Critique," *Academy of Management Review* 3, no. 3 (July 1978):683–687; and Jay W. Lorsch, "Making Behavioral Science More Useful," *Harvard Business Review* 52, no. 2 (April 1979):171–180. A recent assessment of contingency theory can be found in Henry L. Tosi, Jr., and John W. Slocum, Jr., "Contingency Theory: Some Suggested Directions," *Journal of Management* 10, no. 1 (1984):9–26.

33. Among the more outspoken critics of contingency theory are Harold Koontz ("The Management Theory Jungle Revisited") and Justin G. Longenecker and Charles D. Pringle ("The Illusion of Contingency Theory as a General Theory," *Academy of Management Review* 3, no. 3 [July 1978]:679–682).

34. Abraham Kaplan has pointed out the human tendency to apply our latest discovery of an idea or technique to any and every situation, whether or not it is relevant. Kaplan, who calls this "the law of the instrument," explains it thus: "Give a small boy a hammer and he will find that everything he encounters needs pounding." See *The Conduct of Inquiry* (San Francisco: Chandler, 1964), p. 28. As managers, when we acquire a new managerial "hammer," we should try to find it a place within our entire tool box of management concepts. This concept was called to our attention by George F. Farris.

35. Greenwood, "Future Management Theory," p. 509.

36. Both *In Search of Excellence* and *A Passion for Excellence* argue that managers can become lost in the complexity of their tasks and organizations. The authors of those books see the "secret" of success in being "brilliant on the basics" and reducing complexity, as in the motto: KISS (Keep It Simple, Stupid).

37. For an excellent treatment of the process of change in theories, see Thomas S. Kuhn, *The Structure of Scientific Revolutions*, 2nd ed., enlarged (Chicago: University of Chicago Press, 1970). See also Richard G. Brandenberg, "The Usefulness of Management Thought for Management," in McGuire, ed., *Contemporary Management*, pp. 99–112.

CASE STUDY: Grandview Morning Press

The *Grandview Morning Press* is published seven days a week in the city of Grandview, an area that undergoes a huge increase in population every summer due to its fine scenery and excellent climate. Normally the paper consists of a single section with occasional advertising supplements. However, in the summer, a second, "Summer Living," section is added, and the number and frequency of advertising inserts increases drastically in an effort to profit as much as possible from the summer trade.

The insertion of the advertising supplements and the collating of the two sections is done by hand. The publishers of the *Morning Press* feel it would be too costly to purchase the necessary machinery when most of the time it would be used only during the summer months. Besides, they feel that hiring a number of vacationing students is a step toward better community relations. Each summer they hire approximately a dozen college students to work in the printing press building each night, usually for between 7 and 14 hours. Because some editions have more advertising "stuffers" than others, the students do not know until they report for work whether that evening's work will be long or short. All time over 8 hours is considered overtime and is paid at time and a half. The normal hourly rate is $4.35.

The summer workers have a code among themselves that no matter what the work load, they will decide exactly how long to work each night. For example, if there seems to be an 8-hour load, the stuffing crew will purposely slow down in order to take 9 hours and thereby get paid overtime. On those occasions when the crew wants to finish early and get to the local disco before the 4 A.M. closing time, an estimated 7- or 8-hour job will be completed in about 6 hours. Newcomers to the crew are made to conform to the group's production norms through verbal abuse for noncompliance.

A member of the stuffing crew for the past two summers, Barbara Warren has supported this code. This summer, however, Warren was asked by the pressroom chief to supervise the work of the stuffing crew. She welcomed the extra 75¢ an hour she would be making and viewed with pride the thought of being able to apply her business school theories to her new "management-level" position.

After the first few nights, she noticed the code was working as it had for untold summers past. But this year she viewed its effects from the "other side." She realized that the slowdown lowered the profits of the paper by raising the labor costs. The drivers were delayed in making their deliveries. On occasion even the janitors had to sit about idle, waiting for the stuffing crew to finish their work.

Warren is puzzled as to what her proper course of action should be. Should she lower the boom and stop the wasteful practice, or should she let it continue? Neither alternative would be satisfactory to everyone concerned.

Source: This case was written by Peter L. Pfister under the direction of James A. F. Stoner.

Case Questions
1. Does Warren have more than the two choices she is considering? If so, what choices?
2. What will be the consequences of her actions, both for herself and for the paper?
3. How would the situation differ if these were full-time employees on a regular job?
4. Why does the *Morning Press* management permit the code to operate?
5. How would you handle the code?

3 ETHICS, SOCIAL RESPONSIBILITY, AND THE EXTERNAL ENVIRONMENT OF ORGANIZATIONS

Upon completing this chapter you should be able to:

1. Define and discuss the concept of corporate social responsibility.
2. Describe the stakeholders of an organization and how they relate to the organization's external environment.
3. Identify the direct-action and indirect-action environments of organizations and explain why managers must be concerned about them.
4. Describe the ways you as a manager can keep abreast of changes in the environment.
5. Describe how concepts of managerial and organizational responsibility have been changing.
6. Discuss how the values of managers have changed and how your own values are likely to affect your actions as a manager.
7. Describe the barriers to increased social responsibility by organizations.

The classical, behavioral, and quantitative schools of management focused on aspects of the organization that managers could influence directly. These schools advised managers on how many subordinates they should have, why working conditions should be improved, and how the computer could be used in decision making. But in their concern with the *internal environment* of organizations, they underestimated the importance of the *external environment*. The political climate of society and how people outside the organization felt about its business practices were never the main concerns of the three management schools.

This was not necessarily bad. When an organization operates in a stable and predictable external environment, its managers need to pay only moderate attention to external conditions. In our time, however, the external environment has undergone rapid changes that have had far-reaching effects on organizations and their management strategies. The ups and downs of the economy, the changing attitudes of customers, the requirements of government agencies, the inflated costs of energy, materials, and labor—all these affect the organization and its management. Indeed, an organization's responsiveness to its environment may be critical to its survival.

Once it was enough for organizations to maximize profits; managers were judged according to whether they furthered the financial interests of the *stockholders*. Now, organizations must consider the effects of their actions on the quality of life, holding themselves responsible not only to their stockholders but also to the larger and more disparate community of *stakeholders*—those groups or individuals who are affected directly or indirectly by the organization's pursuit of its goals. There are two categories of stakeholders: internal stakeholders, including owners, employees, and stockholders, and external stakeholders, such as unions, suppliers, competitors, public interest associations, protest groups, and government agencies. Figure 3–1 depicts the relationship between the organization and typical categories of internal and external stakeholders.

The importance of the external environment and the influence of stakeholders have been increased by the social issues and problems of the 1960s and 1970s, which gave rise to demands for high levels of *corporate social responsibility*—the idea that corporations have an obligation to act for the good of society at large, even when by doing so they may lower their profits. The debate on the role of business in society has created an agenda of social problems that includes environmental pollution, equal employment opportunity for women and minority workers, consumer safety, and many other concerns reflecting the moral and social aims of stakeholders. While some stakeholders are able to influence a corporation by purchasing its stock, others are able to change its policies by exerting political pressure, as is the case with religious and civil rights groups who oppose investment in South Africa, or the aggressive marketing of infant formula in the Third World.[1]

In responding effectively to the external environment, the "systems" and "contingency" approaches discussed in chapter 2 come into their own. Both take explicit account of the total environment within which an organization operates. And both emphasize specifically the adjustments needed as managers attempt to dominate, control, neutralize, or adapt to that environment.[2]

With the systems and contingency approaches as guides, we will focus first on the

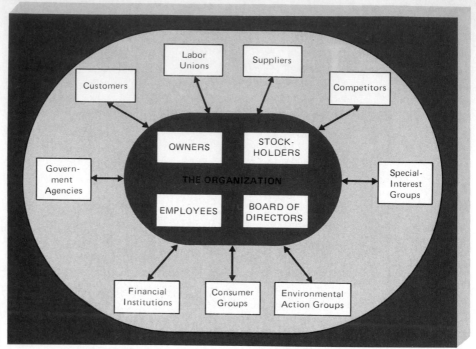

FIGURE 3–1
INTERNAL
AND EXTERNAL
STAKEHOLDERS
OF AN
ORGANIZATION

Note: Categories of stakeholders may differ from organization to organization and vary during the lifetime of an organization.

direct-action environments of organizations—that is, on those elements of the total environment that directly affect and are affected by the organization's major operations. Then we will consider the indirect-action environments—those that do not directly influence the work of the organization but that can, nonetheless, influence decisions made by its managers. Next we will discuss how managers relate their organizations to the external environment. Finally, we will examine the changes in standards and expectations concerning managerial ethics and corporate social responsibility.

The External Environment

The external environment consists of elements outside an organization that are relevant to its operations. Organizations are neither self-sufficient nor self-contained. They exchange resources with the environment and depend on it for their survival. Raw materials, money, labor, and energy are external environment *inputs* that organizations acquire and transform into products or services, which they then provide as *outputs* to the external environment.

   The external environment has both *direct-action* and *indirect-action* elements.[3] Examples of direct-action elements are consumers, government agencies, competitors, labor unions, suppliers, and financial institutions; these are all stakeholders of the organization as well. (See fig. 3–1.)

Indirect-action elements include the technology, economy, and politics of the society. Indirect-action elements affect the climate in which the organization operates and have the potential for becoming direct-action elements. When changes in public expectations concerning corporate behavior lead to new governmental regulatory agencies, as has happened often during the twentieth century in the United States, indirect-action elements become direct-action elements.[4]

Depending on their practical impact, nonstakeholder elements of the indirect-action environment of one organization might also be direct-action stakeholders of another organization. For example, the actions of labor unions might have only a small, indirect impact on a firm in a nonunionized industry, such as book publishing, but a major and direct impact on a firm in a heavily unionized industry, such as automobile manufacturing. Thus, labor unions would be among the stakeholders of the automaker but not among those of the book publisher.

Direct-Action Components of the External Environment

The major direct-action components of the external environment include such stakeholders as suppliers, customers, competitors, labor unions, financial institutions, shareholders, and government agencies. These will be specific to a given organization (U.S. Steel will interact often with the Occupational Safety and Health Administration [OSHA] but rarely with the Food and Drug Administration [FDA]), and they will change in composition over time (some customers will be lost and new ones acquired).

Suppliers. Every organization takes in raw materials, services, energy, equipment, and labor from the environment and uses them to produce its output. Every organization is therefore dependent upon its suppliers of materials and labor.

Organizations usually deal with suppliers of materials, services, and energy through a purchasing manager or agent. The purchasing manager has relationships with several competing suppliers and may sometimes pay a higher unit price to some in order to keep the organization from becoming overly dependent on a single supplier. By dividing purchases among various vendors, the purchasing agent takes advantage of competition among suppliers to obtain lower prices, better quality work, and faster deliveries.

Labor Supply. Labor supply is dealt with in a similar fashion, through personnel or human resources specialists (or other managers who may have specific hiring and negotiating responsibilities). Organizations require workers whose skills and types of experience vary; therefore, they use many channels for locating workers. When an organization employs labor union members, union and management will normally engage in some form of *collective bargaining* to negotiate wages, working conditions, working hours, and other aspects of the work situation.

Customers. Selling tactics vary according to customer and market situation. Usually, a marketing manager analyzes the potential customers and the market conditions and directs a marketing campaign based on that analysis. A company's customer may be an institution, such as a school, hospital, or government agency; it may be another firm, such as a contractor, distributor, or manufacturer; or it may be an individual consumer.

The customer market may be highly competitive, with large numbers of potential buyers and sellers seeking the best deal. In such markets, managers must be especially concerned about price, quality, service, and product availability if they want to keep old customers and attract new ones.

Competitors. Closely linked to the customer environment are the type, number, and behaviors of the organization's competitors. To increase its share of the market, the firm must take business away from somebody else. This means it must provide superior customer satisfaction. To achieve that satisfaction, managers must analyze the competition and establish a clearly defined marketing strategy.[5]

Firms like General Motors, Ford, Chrysler, American Motors, and their foreign counterparts are clearly competitors in the American automobile market. But competition can also come from organizations that provide substitute products or services. In Chicago, for example, the public transit network competes with the automobile. The world petroleum crisis that started in the 1970s drew attention to the competitive interrelationships in the energy industry. Thus, while Texaco, Mobil, and Exxon compete in the sale of petroleum, together they face the competition of energy-producing substitutes from the coal, nuclear, solar, and geothermal industries.

In an oligopolistic market, relatively few sellers confront large numbers of buyers. Price and market share may be determined by tacit or informal industry agreement under the leadership of the dominant company. Oligopoly is a very common market situation, but there are other types. In a monopoly, every customer must buy from one available source, such as an electric utility. In that case, relations with government regulators are very often a major concern. Sometimes a firm enjoys a temporary monopoly, as was the case with Xerox when it introduced the electrostatic copier.

Financial Institutions. Organizations depend on a variety of financial institutions, such as commercial banks, investment banks, and insurance companies, to maintain and expand their activities. Both new and well-established business firms may borrow on a short-term basis to finance current operations or on a long-term basis to build new facilities or acquire new equipment.

Because effective working relationships with financial institutions are so important, establishing and maintaining such relationships is normally the joint responsibility of both the chief financial officer and the chief operating officer of the organization.

Government Agencies. Organizations have become extensively involved with government agencies. Of course, when the federal government appears in the role of customer (as with the defense industry), such involvement is welcomed. More controversial is an organization's relation to regulatory agencies, such as the Federal Communications Commission (FCC) and OSHA. These agencies establish and enforce ground rules within which an industry must operate.

For many years, the role of government in business has been the subject of debate between those who believe that government intervention in business has placed stifling restraints on free enterprise and those who maintain that the government should protect the public and the natural environment from the effects of business competition. This debate became even more heated when the Reagan administration began its attempts to reform regulatory law in 1981. Supporters of the Reagan administration's proposals accepted the claim that deregulation would result in savings of $150 billion by 1990;[6] its opponents doubted that savings projection and argued that deregulation was a return to the law of the jungle.[7] Those who advocate reform point out that regulations have not always achieved their goals of protecting the food supply, improving conditions in the workplace, or preventing environmental pollution, and that when the costs of regulation are balanced against the benefits, it often appears that the task of creating a cleaner, safer society is better left to free enterprise.[8]

In the 1980s, business opposition to government regulation became more active. A recent example of business resistance to federal regulation occurred in 1984, when the government's efforts to revise and tighten controls on the export of high-technology products in the interests of national security were blocked by counterproposals advocating self-regulation by corporations. If the concept of corporate social responsibility continues to gain ground, agreements and compromises between corporations and stakeholders may reduce the pressure for government intervention.

Shareholders and Boards of Directors. The governing structure of large public corporations suggests that shareholders, by exercising their voting rights, can influence *boards of directors* and thus affect the actions of organizations. In practice, however, this is frequently not what happens. Many shareholders buy and sell their stock according to short-run market opportunities, and have little or no interest in influencing corporations' actions.

Even when shareholders actively attempt to influence corporations, barriers exist. A Securities and Exchange Commission ruling of 1983 has made it more difficult for social activists who purchase small quantities of stock to force votes on controversial issues, such as investment in South Africa, at annual corporate meetings.[9]

The social activism of the 1960s gave rise to criticisms of the passive role of most board members, who, it was felt, did little more than collect their fees and approve the decisions of chief executive officers. With demands for greater corporate social responsibility during the 1970s came proposals for increasing the independence and authority of boards, who are well-placed to guide the ethical conduct of corporations. Ralph Nader has suggested that board members should:

1. Devote more time to their duties.
2. Maintain a full-time staff to report on working conditions in the company.
3. Specialize in specific aspects of corporate activity.[10]

John Diebold, a management consultant, takes these suggestions one step further by recommending that:

1. No more than 25 percent of the board should consist of former officers of the corporation.
2. No director should have a business relationship with the company.
3. Board members should meet regularly with the company's auditors and legal staff and with outside lawyers.[11]

Indirect-Action Components of the External Environment

The indirect-action components of the external environment affect organizations in two ways. First, outside groups that are not stakeholders may influence an organization indirectly through one or more elements of its direct-action environment. Second, indirect-action elements create a climate—rapidly changing technology, economic growth or decline, changes in attitudes toward work—in which the organization exists and to which it may ultimately have to respond. For example, today's computer technology makes possible the acquisition, storage, coordination, and transfer of large amounts of information about individuals. Banks and other business firms use this technology to maintain, store, process, and exchange information about the credit status of potential borrowers. Many people worry about misuse of such data, invasion of personal privacy, and errors. Concerned individuals may decide to form a special-interest pressure group to seek voluntary changes in business practices on the part of banks and other organizations. This group, if especially effective, may enter the direct-action environment of its target organization if, for example, it organizes a successful boycott of a certain bank. The group then becomes, if only briefly, a stakeholder of the bank.

These complex interactions can be grouped into broad factors that influence the organization and must be considered by its managers. These factors are the technological, economic, sociocultural, political-legal, and international variables present in the external environment. Figure 3–2 depicts the interrelationship of the indirect-action and the direct-action environments and the organization.

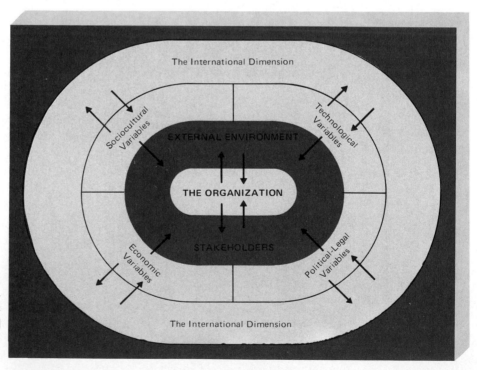

FIGURE 3–2
THE DIRECT-
ACTION AND INDI-
RECT-ACTION
ENVIRONMENTS OF
AN ORGANIZATION

■ Direct-Action Environment   □ Indirect-Action Environment

Technological Variables. In any society or industry, the level of technology plays a significant role in determining what products and services will be produced, what equipment will be used, and how various operations will be managed. For example, some feel that continued advances in technology will lower the demand for middle managers. Many companies now use computers for operating forecasts and production scheduling, activities that were frequently performed or supervised by middle managers. Although some jobs may have been eliminated in these activities, human beings are still needed to develop, interpret, and act on the data that go into and come out of the computers. If the enhanced capacity of computers leads to much more data being collected, analyzed, and acted on, new jobs may be created to replace some of the old ones that were lost.

Changes in technology may frequently affect the actions of competitors, presenting an example of how an indirect-action aspect of the environment may become part of the direct-action arena. For many years, the Polaroid company was able to compete against Eastman Kodak because it had a unique product protected by a network of exclusive patents. When Kodak finally developed an alternative technology, Polaroid's unique market position was threatened. Polaroid responded with an extensive series of lawsuits and the development of new products.

Technological breakthroughs can also lead to new competitive positions in different industries. By installing on-line computer services to their principal customers, for example, some manufacturing companies have succeeded in reducing ordering costs and becoming more responsive to demand.[12]

Economic Variables. Managers will always have to take into account the major costs—such as labor and raw materials—that their organizations incur. Since such costs vary over time, they must also assess prospects for price stability or inflation. In much of the post-World War II period, it seemed possible for most developed and some underdeveloped countries to achieve fairly steady rates of economic growth while holding the line on inflation. But the 1970s and 1980s have shown that controlling inflation is a more difficult task, with a higher societal cost, than economists had realized.

The prices set by competitors and suppliers, as well as the government's fiscal and monetary policies, significantly influence the costs of producing products or offering services and the market conditions under which those products or services are sold. Thus, business managers must devote considerable time and resources to forecasting the economy and to anticipating changes in prices.

Sociocultural Variables. The values and customs of a society establish guidelines that determine how most organizations and managers will operate. Sometimes the guidelines will be relatively narrow—like the restrictions on black workers in South Africa, who are denied both by law and by custom the right to managerial positions where they might have to supervise whites. Or, as in most countries, social barriers are raised against women who seek managerial careers, although a few do make it to the top against all the odds and at the cost of considerable personal sacrifice.[13]

In other areas, the guidelines may be quite broad—like the wide latitude of acceptable boss-subordinate relationships in a single city or even in the same organization. In some cases, the normal relationship may be very formal, with a great show of outward respect by the subordinate for those above him or her in the hierarchy. In other organizations, there may be little evidence of differences in rank.

The values and customs of society are also reflected in a firm's organizational structure. In Japan, for example, where employees may work for the same company all their lives, lower-level workers participate in policy and decision making more freely than American workers do. French companies, operating in a society where relationships are somewhat formal, tend to be more rigidly structured than their American and Japanese counterparts.

Location affects the kinds of pressure groups that form and the issues with which they are concerned. For example, people living in the vicinity of Love Canal near Buffalo, New York, or Three Mile Island, near Harrisburg, Pennsylvania, have had good reason to form groups resisting chemical pollution of ground water and the existence of nuclear power plants. Such groups gain power when their causes are taken up by groups in other parts of the country.[14]

Perhaps most important, the values and customs of a society influence how individuals feel about organizations and how they feel about work. The changes in attitudes toward work itself that have occurred in our own society have complicated the task of managers enormously. Whereas employee participation in managerial decision making was once seen as a means of improving worker morale and productivity, it is now regarded by some observers as an ethical imperative.[15]

Political-Legal Variables. Will a government agency adopt a hard or a soft stance in its relations with management? Will antitrust laws be rigidly enforced or ignored? Will government policy curb or enhance management's freedom to act? The answers to such questions depend in large part on the political and legal climate of the time.

In the United States, the political climate has ranged from strong support of corporate autonomy—epitomized in President Coolidge's dictum that "the business of America is business"—to the deep suspicion and distrust of business and government that began in the 1960s and has continued ever since.

Government involvement in the affairs of business and nonprofit organizations has steadily increased during this century. Usually, increased regulation (or interference, depending on one's point of view) has followed a major economic or social disruption. For example, the depression of the 1930s and the civil rights movement of the 1960s both led to the passage of much legislation and the formation of new regulatory agencies. This trend increases when people call upon government to protect the consumer, preserve the environment, and put an end to discrimination in employment, education, and housing. And these pressures are reinforced by those— many managers among them—who call for adherence to high ethical principles in the conduct of business and the professions.

Many people deplore the constraints placed upon organizations by our laws and regulatory agencies. But the opportunities thus created have too often been overlooked. Antipollution laws, for example, stimulated the growth of the pollution-control industry to the point where at one time its securities were counted among the Wall Street "glamour stocks." And as the Office of Economic Opportunity (OEO) enforced its antidiscrimination regulations, it created a demand for training and consulting services, which, in turn, led to the formation of some profitable new companies.

Government has also opened up new opportunities by channeling resources into priority areas like defense and highway construction. But shifts in priorities have transformed attractive investment opportunities into problems for companies that suddenly found themselves struggling with reduced budgets when government funding was reduced.

The International Dimension. The international component of the external environment also presents opportunities and challenges and has the potential for moving from an indirect- to a direct-action factor. For example, many American companies find it profitable to perform assembling and manufacturing operations on the Mexican side of the U.S.-Mexico border, while wholesale and retail businesses have been established on the American side of the Rio Grande to serve the needs of visiting Mexicans. When, in 1984, the Mexican government devalued the peso and instituted currency controls to prevent capital leaving the country, manufacturing operations on the Mexican side of the border tended to benefit, while many of the wholesale and retail businesses on the American side of the border were virtually devastated. This example dramatizes the need for companies involved in foreign trade to include assessments of political and economic risks in their strategies.[16]

In another development, the Foreign Corrupt Practices Act of 1977, a law prohibiting the payment of bribes or fees to agents of foreign governments or businesses, made company officers personally liable for their company's actions. This has led to the strengthening of corporate codes of conduct by businesses.[17]

Firms that engage in foreign production and sales quickly learn that success or failure often depends on accurate knowledge of the laws, customs, ethics, economic systems, and methods of management in the countries where they do business. The multinational giants, which establish production facilities in ten or 20 different countries and sell in 50 or more, have had to accumulate a vast store of knowledge of these variables in the countries in which they operate. (The management of international business operations is discussed in chapter 23.)

The international environment is an important factor in the day-to-day business situations even of managers whose primary responsibilities are devoted to domestic transactions and concerns. Even companies that restrict themselves to domestic operations may have to become aware of how people in other countries operate because they find themselves facing foreign competitors. Companies with no foreign customers or competitors may depend on foreign suppliers for raw materials or production equipment. Just the simple act of arranging payment for imported goods requires some knowledge of foreign exchange markets and of trends in foreign exchange rates.

Trends in the External Environment. In recent years, the public has become a particularly demanding component of the external environment. The media, with access to more information than ever before, have created a mass audience of well-informed consumers. Feelings about authority have changed, and people are less likely to be acquiescent. The work force, as a subgroup of the public, has also become more vocal in asserting itself.

Difficulties in dealing with complex and sometimes conflicting regulations and directives from the government have led to increasing pressure for reduced government involvement in the business world. Fewer regulations may ease some of the manager's tasks, but may also require new initiatives by managers to achieve the same socially desirable ends the regulations were attempting to achieve.

Relating the Organization to the Environment

The extent to which the external environment influences managers varies with the type and purpose of the organization. It differs among the positions and functions within an organization and even between the hierarchical levels inside the organization. Thus, managers at Exxon may be more influenced by factors in the external environment than managers at A&P, pollution control engineers more than sales division managers, and executives more than clerical workers.

Because of their greater power and broader perspective, managers at the higher levels in organizations bear greater responsibility for managing relations with the external environment than do lower-level managers. Top managers play a key role in guiding their organizations' adjustments to new regulations, in supervising the redesign of products and the workplace to meet high standards of quality, safety, and health, and in achieving equal work and career opportunities for employees.

Managers and their organizations respond to the external environment both by attempting to influence the direct-action environment and by forecasting and adjusting to trends in the indirect-action environment.

Influencing the Direct-Action Environment. To deal effectively with the direct-action environment, managers must concentrate their efforts on the key aspects of the environment, those relevant to a particular goal of the organization. If they were to consider equally each and every component, they would expend time and energy in unproductive ways. But by focusing on key factors, managers can target their attempts to influence the environment.

The direct-action environment is a known quantity with which the organization has regular and established patterns of interaction. Many techniques have been developed for influencing it. Managers influence consumer preferences through advertising. They establish cooperative relations and negotiate with suppliers to ensure prompt delivery of needed materials at acceptable prices. They provide certain amenities as well as competitive pay scales to attract and hold workers and enter into agreements with unions to stabilize labor market conditions. And they lobby in their state capitals and in Washington to gain passage of favorable legislation and forestall the passage of undesirable laws and regulations.

Forecasting and the Indirect-Action Environment. Often, change in the indirect-action environment is the first sign of a later impact on an organization's activities. Managers resort to a variety of expedients to keep abreast of such developments. They may monitor environmental trends continually, hoping by this means to develop a usable understanding of the external environment. For example, a downward trend in consumer spending in general might alert a manufacturer of luxury items to reduce production before sales to established customers begin to decline.

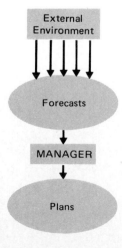

Information about the indirect-action environment comes from many sources: an industry's grapevine, managers in other organizations, the data generated by the organization's own activities, government reports and statistics, trade journals, general financial and business publications, on-line computer data-bank services, and more. Hints, predictions, statistics, gossip—any of these may alert a manager to a trend that should be monitored. Research can be done to clarify the developments that can be expected. By using *forecasting* techniques, managers can anticipate changes in government regulations, public attitudes, suppliers' costs, availability of raw materials, actions of competitors, and so on and be prepared with alternative courses of action and concrete plans for future actions.

Planning, Organizational Design, and the Environment. The most important way managers adjust to the external environment is through the development and implementation of plans for their organizations. These plans may be simple, short-range, and restricted in scope, or they may be sophisticated, long-range, and encompassing. The potentially most sophisticated and encompassing plans embody the basic concept of the organization and the strategies it will follow to achieve its objectives. These strategic plans not only guide the organization's adaptation to the direct and indirect external environment but also guide its attempts to influence the behavior of agents in the direct-action environment.[18]

A special type of managerial adjustment to the environment involves changes in the organization's formal structure—its work flows, authority patterns, reporting relationships among managers, and the like. This form of adjustment to the environment is often called "organizational design"—implying a conscious structuring of the organization so it will best meet the demands of the environment at a given time. While few organizations are designed quite so rationally, many are regularly reorganized and restructured in accord with environmental dictates. We will describe this process in part three of this book.

Changing Concepts of Managerial and Organizational Responsibility

Our century has seen significant changes in what society expects of its institutions and in what managers believe is their proper role in organizations. The depression of the 1930s and the activist movements of the 1960s and 1970s stimulated in different ways a mounting criticism of business behavior. This criticism was directed against the view that business should pursue profit single-mindedly, with little or no consideration of social needs.

In the 1980s, it is quite clear that the far-reaching changes accomplished in this century were, for the most part, necessary. We have seen the gradual erosion of the traditional ethic of *caveat emptor* (let the buyer beware) as a new contract between business and society has evolved. Many people, including many managers, believe that managers have a responsibility to society in addition to their responsibility toward the organizations they serve. But where does such responsibility begin and where does it end? What rules of conduct should govern the exercise of executive authority? Should a firm place stockholders' interests before those of society or the environment? Should a firm be held responsible for the social consequences of its operations? When is regulation necessary and when is it an excessive burden?

Concepts of Organizational Responsibility

The changed external environment has created a new set of values and expectations. More is expected of organizations and their managers, but there is no consensus as to exactly what the priorities should be. Although the debate over priorities and expectations applies to all organizations, much of it has focused on business firms.

The Role of Business. One leading business group, the Committee for Economic Development (CED), has published a pamphlet entitled *Social Responsibilities of Business Corporations* that urges management to involve itself actively in such social causes as aid to education, urban renewal, opening up better job opportunities to minorities and women, training the disadvantaged, controlling environmental pollution, and much more.

While ethical and social demands on business have increased steadily, direct government support for social programs declined in the early 1980s, reflecting public discontent with the performance of many programs and with the levels of federal spending for social services. The Reagan administration, acknowledging that such spending is aimed at real social problems, has expressed the hope that voluntary contributions by business organizations will take up the shortfall in federal spending. Despite widespread acceptance of the view that corporations should take an active role in forecasting and meeting social needs, it is doubtful that corporate action could ever take over the social responsibilities of government entirely.[19]

The most prominent opponent of the concept of broad corporate social responsibilities is Milton Friedman, who won the Nobel Prize in economics in 1976. "There is one and only one social responsibility of business," says Friedman: "to use its resources and energy in activities designed to increase its profits so long as it stays within the rules of the game . . . engages in open and free competition, without deception and fraud. . . . Few trends could so thoroughly undermine the very foundations of our free society as the acceptance by corporate officials of a social responsibility other than to make as much money for their stockholders as possible. . . . Can self-selected individuals decide what the social interest is? Can they decide how great a burden they are justified in placing on themselves and their stockholders to serve that interest?"[20] Managers who devote corporate resources to pursue their own, perhaps misguided notions of social good, Friedman goes on to say, are unfairly taxing their own shareholders, employees, and customers. In short, businesses should produce goods and services efficiently and leave the solution of social problems to government agencies and concerned individuals.

More recently, Friedman has argued that government intervention is frequently undesirable as well. He alleges that it has failed to achieve intended social objectives.[21] Those responsible for implementing programs, he charges, have little incentive to economize in spending the allocated funds and are not sensitive to the real needs of recipients. Friedman favors eliminating many social security and government benefits and adopting instead a limited set of government actions to influence national income. Citing growing productivity problems, he believes that our present system is a disincentive to work and calls for a renewal of the business system so individuals would have greater freedom to make their own economic decisions in the absence of government controls. Friedman believes this freedom would lead to less waste and greater productivity.

Friedman's views are generally considered to represent one extreme of a continuum that recognizes some division of social responsibility among the various segments of society, including government and the business community. Because business and government are the two most powerful institutions in the country, their sheer dominance and size oblige them to attack problems of public concern. Corporations are dependent on acceptance by the society of which they are a part, and for them to ignore social problems might in the long run be self-destructive. If business does not amend its public image voluntarily, it will almost inevitably be subject to increased government regulation. Keith Davis has said that there is "an iron law of responsibility which states that in the long run those who do not use power in a manner that society considers responsible will tend to lose it."[22] Procter & Gamble's quick action in voluntarily removing from the market a tampon that

"Why should I be worried about fish contaminated with dioxin? Won't the acid rain kill them?"

Reprinted by permission of Tribune Media Services, Inc.

may have been responsible for toxic shock syndrome is an example of one company's awareness of this law.[23]

Levels of Business Activism: How Companies Respond. Major corporations have taken various approaches to social responsibilities. Some provide a variety of social services for their employees, following the example of Kaiser Aluminum, which instituted a pioneering health maintenance plan in the late 1930s. Some companies have invited the community to participate in some corporate decisions affecting the region, while others contribute to local urban renewal or antipollution programs.

But there are still many examples on the negative side. For instance, some mining companies routinely submit data to the government to show that implementing safety standards would be too costly and unreasonable. Yet, in some foreign countries the dangers of cave-ins and explosions have largely been eliminated, thanks to the same safety technology available to American mining companies.

R. Joseph Monsen has suggested a four-level hierarchy of business activism. At the base are managers who feel that society is well served as long as the firm *obeys the law*. At the next level are managers who go beyond the legal minimum, accepting the need to *cater to public expectations* also and responding to public opinion. At the third level, managers *anticipate public expectations;* while at the fourth and highest level are managers who themselves *create new public expectations* by voluntarily setting and following idealistic standards of moral and social responsibility.[24]

A 1970 survey found that most organizations were at the first two levels. A few years later, however, studies were showing increased business activism at the two higher levels; and indications are that this trend has continued.[25]

Robert Ackerman has described three phases through which companies pass in developing a response to social issues. (See table 3–1.) In phase 1, top managers

Create
Public
Expectations

Anticipate
Public Expectations

Cater to
Public Expectations

Obey the Law

HIERARCHY OF
BUSINESS
ACTIVISM

TABLE 3–1 ACKERMAN'S THREE STAGES OF SOCIAL RESPONSIBILITY

Organizational Level	Phases of Organizational Involvement		
	Phase 1	Phase 2	Phase 3
Chief Executive	Issue: Corporate obligation Action: Write and communicate policy Outcome: Enriched purpose, increased awareness	Obtain knowledge Add staff specialists	Obtain organizational commitment Change performance expectations
Staff Specialists		Issue: Technical problem Action: Design data system and interpret environment Outcome: Technical and informational groundwork	Provoke response from operating units Apply data system to performance measurement
Division Management			Issue: Management problem Action: Commit resources and modify procedures Outcome: Increased responsiveness

Source: Reprinted by permission of the *Harvard Business Review.* An exhibit from "How Companies Respond to Social Demands" by Robert W. Ackerman (July–August 1973). Copyright © 1973 by the President and Fellows of Harvard College; all rights reserved.

within a corporation become aware of existing social concerns. Although pressures are not directed at the organization itself, the chief executive officer will acknowledge the situation by making either a written or an oral statement communicating the company's policy toward it. In phase 2, staff specialists are hired or experts consulted to study the situation and design ways to cope with it. So far, actions still are restricted largely to intentions and plans. But in phase 3, the implementation stage, the company's policy toward the problem is integrated into corporate operations. Unfortunately, implementation frequently lags until government or other sanctions appear likely.[26]

The Role of Profits

Before an organization can devote resources to socially desirable objectives, it must make enough profit to maintain the confidence and support of its shareholders and creditors. Resources allocated to social action serve an organization's self-interest when they prevent conflict with stakeholders and enhance the organization's public image. But when the financial costs of social activism run too high, there may be tension between economic and social goals.

Generally, social programs add costs that can be borne by organizations in four major ways: increased efficiency, higher prices, lowered wages, or reduced profits. The first and most fortunate one occurs when the socially responsible action is actually more profitable for the firm than doing business as usual. Kellogg and Control Data, two companies that have pursued a policy of building manufacturing plants in depressed inner-city neighborhoods with the cooperation of local community leaders, have succeeded in reconciling the social aim of providing employment in ghetto areas with their own economic objectives. And even the interests of oil companies and environmentalists can coincide, as when Texaco designed its oil well protection barriers to also provide vital wildlife refuges.[27]

But most corporate social policies will raise costs without providing a compensating competitive or other gain. In this situation, companies pass the costs along to consumers in higher prices, to workers by holding the line on wage increases, or to shareholders through reduced profits and lower dividends.

The claim that someone must eventually bear the costs of social responsibility is the crux of Friedman's argument that managers should focus on what they know best: how to make a profit. The same consideration also leads many business managers to criticize the growing constraints and pressures placed on business by government agencies and consumer and environmental advocates.

The pressure for business to devote more of its resources, and profits, to social programs might be reduced if average corporate profit levels were better understood. Most people outside business believe that corporate profits are higher and corporate taxes lower than they are in reality. For example, a Gallup poll of college students found that they estimated corporate profits at 45 percent of sales, when in reality profits average about 5 percent.[28]

Organizational Social Performance

Attempts to develop a systematic measure of an organization's social impact go back to at least the 1940s, but there still is no agreed measure. Although Friedman argues that profits provide the answer, other management experts are struggling to define a broader and more sophisticated approach to measuring the effects of business on society.

The problem of defining social performance is similar to the problem of defining organizational effectiveness in general. One difficulty in both cases results from the fact that every organization has a broad constituency of stakeholders, who have different desires and so judge the corporation by different, and often conflicting, criteria. In a study of organizational effectiveness, Friedlander and Pickle studied 97 small businesses in a variety of product and service areas and identified seven key constituencies.[29] Figure 3–3 shows the seven constituencies and examples of their differing criteria.

Measuring Social Performance. One systematic measure of an organization's social impact is the *corporate social audit*. This is, according to Archie B. Carroll and George W. Beiler, "a managerial effort to develop a calculus for gauging the firm's socially oriented contributions. That is, it is an attempt to measure, monitor, and

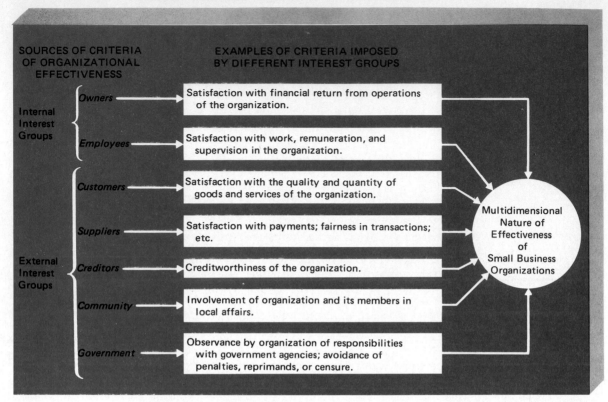

Source: Adapted from Frank Friedlander and Hal Pickle "Components of Effectiveness in Small Organizations," *Administrative Science Quarterly*, September 1968, in Robert H. Miles, *Macro Organizational Behavior* (1980), p. 365.

evaluate the organization's performance with respect to its social programs and social objectives."[30]

One approach to the social audit analyzes the costs and benefits of the organization's major interactions with its environment. Obviously, only the major effects can be evaluated, and the values attached to the transactions can only be approximations. The best-known example of this approach is the one used by Abt Associates, a Massachusetts consulting firm. This firm's social audit, which looks somewhat like a profit and loss statement, has been included in the company's annual report in all years except one, since 1972.

A second and more common approach is based on the major social programs engaged in by the particular organization. Individual audits vary, but most include an inventory of the social programs, a determination of their original purpose, an evaluation of the resources devoted to them, and an attempt to measure how well they met their original objectives or new ones that may have evolved since their initiation. This approach has the advantage of focusing on specific programs that can be directly altered in response to audit findings.

At present, many problems and ambiguities plague the social audit movement. Questions have been raised about what such audits should accomplish, how a manager's resistance to being "audited" can be overcome, and how and to whom the results should be reported. It seems likely, though, that as pressure for social responsibility increases, the social audit concept will be further developed and more widely adopted.

Barriers to Improved Social Performance

Efforts to achieve greater social responsibility encounter barriers at every level of the organization. By becoming aware of these barriers, we can work to overcome them.

The Individual Manager. The individual manager is the person who is ultimately responsible for the social action programs of any organization. The manager can initiate, advocate, and execute programs, and also prevent programs from being planned or carried out. Almost all managers in business are employees. Their careers may be in jeopardy if they consistently advocate actions of which their supervisors disapprove or if they make unprofitable trade-offs. For this reason, most managers are cautious about proposing significant changes.

Public criticism of an organization's shortcomings by its employees, known as "whistle blowing," usually embarrasses management and can be done with impunity only when the whistle blower is leaving the organization voluntarily.[31] Managers who want to "blow the whistle" must make hard choices between socially responsible behavior and their own careers. To the extent that top managers encourage ethical and socially responsible behavior in their subordinates, the need for whistle blowing is reduced.[32]

The Division. Like the organization of which it is a part, a division must try to maintain itself as a profit center. Any socially responsible decision that reduces the level of profits might threaten the division's viability. Thus, most divisions are slow to initiate socially responsible programs until they receive clear instructions to do so from top management.

The head of a division may obtain approval for such programs if he or she can demonstrate that they will not be too costly or will benefit the organization in other ways—for example, by improving the organization's public relations. Sometimes top management will try such programs as an experiment and publicize them if they succeed.

The Organization. At the organizational level, the greatest barrier is the focus on profits. Social action projects must always be evaluated in terms of net cost. Shareholders want current profits distributed in dividends or reinvested to increase future profits. Employees want better working conditions and higher salaries or wages. Against these competing claims, social programs may have little chance.

A company's social responsibility may even affect its competitive position. A company that decides not to purchase raw materials from a nation whose internal policies are repressive risks having to pay higher prices elsewhere. Meanwhile a less conscientious competitor gets a bargain.

In such situations, top management is faced with a truly difficult choice. It must weigh the short-term needs of the organization, as well as its stockholders and employees, against the unpredictable long-term needs of the organization and often ambiguous standards of right and wrong.

The Industry. Obviously, the danger of a competitor taking advantage of one company's socially responsible actions is lessened if an entire industry adopts a similar policy. The motion picture code is a well-known example of an industry's attempt to police itself. But there are barriers that can prevent industries from acting in a unified way. Companies that regard each other as competitors may be reluctant to enter into an industry-wide agreement. In an environment where business is already suspect, any industry-wide action would be viewed with skepticism and might even create antitrust problems. Finally, a decision made by an American industry would not be binding on foreign companies. Thus, the domestic industry might lose its competitive position internationally. For example, a major justification for American arms sales abroad is that "if we don't do it, others will." In this case, it is argued that to forgo revenues (and political influence) from foreign arms sales would achieve little, since the purchasing countries could obtain similar weapons elsewhere.

Changing Views of the Manager's Role

We would expect that our present view of the manager's role would differ from that of earlier periods. One interesting way of describing how our concepts of proper managerial behavior have evolved is the one presented by Robert Hay and Ed Gray.[33] They suggest that three distinct phases of management responsibility can be identified.

Phase I, *profit-maximizing management,* derives from Adam Smith's *Wealth of Nations.* Writing in 1776, when poverty was the common lot of humanity, Smith opened on a paradoxical note. Do we want to promote the welfare of *all*? If so, we must cater to the selfish desires of a *few*.

Entrepreneurs produce what people want only when they can earn a profit by doing so. If society allows entrepreneurs to give full rein to their desire for profits, then their own self-interest will cause them to increase production. This will make more goods available to all. Of course, in a competitive market, entrepreneurs would not be able to increase prices at will, because other entrepreneurs would enter the business and drive prices down. But within the limitations of the competition, Smith believed that entrepreneurs should be allowed to pursue their own self-interest for the benefit of all.

For many years, Smith's philosophy prevailed and was associated with the increasing availability of goods and services in America and most Western countries. The attitude "What's good for me is good for my country" became common and perhaps was justifiable. But there was a negative side to the way his ideas were used. As nineteenth-century railroad tycoon William Henry Vanderbilt once said, "The public? The public be damned!"

Phase II, *trusteeship management,* began with the diffusion of corporate ownership as thousands of stockholders shared ownership in a single enterprise. Where once the owners of a business personally supervised its operations, operating control came to rest in the hands of hired professional managers. Managers were expected not only to maximize profits but also to serve as trustees who mediated the opposing claims of employees, stockholders, suppliers, customers, and the public at large.

This trusteeship concept was a product of the depression-ridden 1930s, when business came under severe attack because of widespread unemployment. The trusteeship notion was an attractive and altruistic one, implying that manager/trustees were dedicated, not to their own enrichment, but to the welfare of the many diverse groups in the organization's environment. This type of management implied a concern for the interests of others as well as one's own. "What's good for me . . . " had changed subtly into "What's good for General Motors is good for the country."

Phase III, *quality-of-life management,* came upon the scene in the 1960s, just about the time when the silent generation was giving way to the committed one. The free speech movement activist whose sign proclaimed—"I am a U.C. student. Please don't bend, fold, spindle, or mutilate!"—articulated a disillusionment and discontent with what was seen as a remote and faceless corporate world. As this new mood permeated the ranks of managers, pressures were generated for active corporate involvement in social progress.

The values of quality-of-life managers contrast sharply with both the profit maximizer and the trustee manager. Now the essential equation becomes "What's good for society is good for our company." While accepting profit as essential, the quality-of-life manager would neither produce nor sell unsafe or shoddy goods. And where the other management types inveigh against government in business, the phase III manager recognizes government as a partner in a joint effort to solve society's problems.

The Values and Ethics of Managers

In a given culture at a given time, there is broad agreement on major values. Most people agree on what is good (for example, the right to vote) and what is bad (for example, corruption in government). Not all hold the same values, but those of the majority will affect the beliefs and behaviors of society.

The actions of managers are influenced by their personal values.[34] For example, managers who are motivated by economic values will tend to stress the importance of growth for their companies. Managers who are motivated more by social values, on the other hand, might be willing to sacrifice some company growth to improve conditions for their employees. Of course, values are not the only factors that will influence a manager's decisions; the specific situation a manager faces will have great influence on, or even dominate, how a manager behaves.[35]

The Ethics of Managers. Managers' ethics influence a wide range of organizational decisions and actions. A recent study of the values and ethics of managers by Barry Posner and Warren Schmidt found that:

· **The foremost goal of managers is to make their organizations effective.**
· **Profit maximization and stockholders' interest were not the central goals of the managers studied.**
· **Attending to customers was seen as important.**
· **Integrity was the characteristic most highly rated by managers at all levels.**
· **Pressure to conform to organizational standards was seen as high.**
· **Spouses are important in helping their mates grapple with ethical dilemmas.**
· **Most managers seek the advice of others in handling ethical dilemmas.[36]**

Factors in Making Ethical Decisions. Robert J. Mockler has identified five factors that affect decisions on ethical problems.[37] Some simplify the problems; others complicate them.

Law

Government Regulations

Industry and Company Ethical Code

Social Pressures

Tension between Personal Standards and Organization Needs

FACTORS AFFECTING ETHICAL DECISIONS

The law is a simplifying factor since it defines minimum ethical standards in a given area of practice. For example, deceptive advertising is defined as illegal. Violations of this law are clearly defined, and violators risk substantial fines and court-ordered corrective measures as well as the loss of goodwill. However, there are many gray areas, such as padding expense accounts, pirating employees from competing companies, and disparaging competitors. Some of these may not actually be illegal or may be illegal in some jurisdictions but not in others.

Government regulations also simplify the issue by mandating what is acceptable and what is not. Rulings on such matters as unfair competition, price discrimination, and unsafe products set guidelines for the manager. Sometimes the government may enforce the standards with a cease and desist order or even a criminal charge. Usually a firm or industry will comply voluntarily with an agency finding. But a positive response at home to a government ruling does not always resolve the ethical issue. In 1969, the FDA banned the use of cyclamates in food on the grounds that these artificial sweeteners were carcinogenic (cancer-causing). Over the next 16 months, a major food packer sold some 300,000 cases of cyclamate-sweetened food to overseas customers.[38]

Industry and company ethical codes can also be seen as simplifying factors, because they expressly spell out the ethical standards a manager should follow. In most industries, there are some standard practices that are observed by virtually all managers. But many industry-wide codes are unwritten, and those that are set down in black and white seldom include enforcement procedures. Generally, written codes clarify the ethical issues but they do leave the resolution to an individual's conscience. A proposed "Ten Commandments of Corporate Social Responsibility" by Larry D. Alexander and William F. Matthews appears on the opposite page.

Social pressures complicate the matter because the ethics of one group are imposed upon another. In recent years, for example, the Nestlé company faced a consumer boycott organized to protest its aggressive efforts to sell infant formula in underdeveloped countries. Some observers concluded that many cases of infant illness and death by starvation occurred because impoverished and uneducated mothers mixed the formula with unsterilized water, overdiluted the formula when money ran out, and could no longer produce milk themselves. Nestlé, which had pioneered modern agricultural methods in Latin America and Africa, felt it was unjustly criticized. Nevertheless, it undertook extensive changes in its marketing techniques that eventually resulted in the lifting of the boycott. Nestlé was able to reestablish credibility and remove the accusation of causing a "commerciogenic disease" by endorsing the World Health Organization's Code of Marketing for Breast Milk Substitutes, setting up an independent watchdog panel, and making efforts to open its affairs to the scrutiny of pressure groups and journalists.[39]

The Nestlé case is only one in which pressure groups have tried to make business management more responsive to social concerns through picketing, publicity in the press and on television, political lobbying, and consumer boycotts. Such efforts may alter managerial behavior in some cases and provoke stubborn resistance in others.

Tension between personal standards and the needs of the organization complicate a manager's task enormously. As a member of management, the manager has a clear-cut mission: produce more, sell more, make more profit. As a citizen, however, the same person has an obligation to advance the welfare of the community. Often the two aims clash. Managers are understandably more willing to attend to kinds of

THE TEN COMMANDMENTS OF CORPORATE SOCIAL RESPONSIBILITY

1. Thou shall take corrective action before it is required.
2. Thou shall work with affected constituents to resolve mutual problems.
3. Thou shall work to establish industry-wide standards and self-regulation.
4. Thou shall publicly admit your mistakes.
5. Thou shall get involved in appropriate social programs.
6. Thou shall help correct environmental problems.
7. Thou shall monitor the changing social environment.
8. Thou shall establish and enforce a corporate code of conduct.
9. Thou shall take needed public stands on social issues.
10. Thou shall strive to make profits on an ongoing basis.

Source: Reprinted by permission from *Business and Society Review,* Summer 1984. Copyright © 1984, Warren, Gorham and Lamont Inc. 210 South Street, Boston, Mass. All rights reserved.

unethical behavior that reduce profits, such as conflict of interest and embezzlement, than they are to amend questionable practices that are both profitable and legal, such as aggressively marketing sugary products to children.[40]

Barriers to Exposing Unethical Behavior

Concerned employees who are aware of unethical behavior on the part of their superiors and/or colleagues are often perplexed as to how to handle their situations. James A. Waters has described a series of "organizational blocks" that make it difficult to call attention to shady practices.[41] The three types that most often get in the way involve the chain of command, group membership, and ambiguous priorities.

Chain of command. An employee may become aware of or unknowingly involved in some illegal or unethical activities on the part of an associate or superior. If the superior is involved or does not take action after the problem is revealed, the individual has no place to turn. To expose the situation to the superior's boss is a violation of the chain-of-command structure, and the well-intentioned employee may be labeled disloyal, or worse. The punishment could be quite severe if the employee has misunderstood the situation and no unethical or illegal actions have occurred. Furthermore, according to the chain of command, the superior, in turn, may be acting on orders from his or her superior. To whom does a conscientious employee report the unethical behavior then?

Group membership. A group of individuals who work together—or even those who meet for lunch or travel together to or from work—develops its own code of behavior. Feelings of loyalty exist in such groups, and a group member who reports unethical behavior by other members will be ostracized for blowing the whistle. Disloyalty to the group will be countered by pressure on nonconforming members to stay in line.

Ambiguous priorities. Executives are faced with contradictory and unclear policies within their organizations more often than they like to admit. Sometimes a stated policy is designed to be ignored: A directive to solicit bids from suppliers openly, for example, is often overlooked as the same supplier wins time after time. Managers who advocate buying from a new supplier might be taking a bigger career risk than they suspect. Ambiguous policies with respect to exposing unethical or illegal behavior can leave employees wondering if they will be heroes or heels if they act according to the dictates of their conscience.

Possible Solutions. Honest and conscientious organization members need a great deal of courage to expose wrongdoing. They may risk their jobs, be responsible for another person's termination, or destroy friendships and working relationships.

The single most important factor in improving the climate for ethical behavior in organizations is the actions taken by top-level managers. In addition to setting examples by their own behavior, there are a number of steps that can be taken:

· **Top management** *should establish clear policies that encourage ethical behavior.* **For example, goal-setting programs should yield realistic goals so no employee is pressured to do something unethical to meet impossible objectives.**
· **Management must** *assume responsibility for disciplining wrongdoers.* **Inaction sets a poor example for the rest of the organization and can even induce other employees to behave unethically. A company policy of dismissing violators of its ethical code, and of totally cooperating with law enforcement authorities in criminal situations, will deter most potential violators.**
· **Companies can** *provide a mechanism for whistle blowing as a matter of policy.* **All employees who observe or become aware of criminal practices or unethical behavior should be encouraged to report the incident to their superiors, to a higher level of management, or to an appropriate unit of the organization, such as an audit committee. Formalized procedures for complaining can encourage honest employees to report questionable incidents. However, careful verification then becomes necessary to guard against use of such means to get even with other employees.**

Management training seminars and orientation meetings that include discussions of actual situations can alert employees to potential ethical conflicts and serve to communicate the organization's code of ethics. By offering courses in business ethics, colleges and universities can also play a part in creating conscientious managers with a morally responsible approach to business. The need for responsible managers is all the more acute since questions of business ethics cannot be wholly determined by law or government regulation, but must primarily remain the concern of individual managers.

Summary Organizations are increasingly being influenced by their external environment. The stakeholders of an organization, who include its managers, employees, and shareholders as well as direct-action components of the external environment such as customers, suppliers, financial institutions, competitors, labor unions, and government agencies, interact with the organization directly and on a continual basis. Indirect-action components, which include technological, economic, sociocultural, political-legal, and international variables, affect the organization occasionally or irregularly. However, the indirect-action components have the potential for moving into the direct-action sphere, as in the case of active consumer or environmental action groups that may directly affect day-to-day operations by picketing, boycotting, lobbying for new laws, and so forth.

Changes in the external environment require managers to try to anticipate future changes and to monitor them on a continuing basis. More effective managers plan for potential changes in the environment, using forecasting techniques and strategic planning. Other managers respond to changes as they occur, and their effectiveness varies accordingly. At higher organizational levels, managers have greater exposure to external factors and greater responsibility for dealing with them.

Public concern, expressed by the pressures of various interest groups and government regulation, is greater today than ever before, due to higher education levels in our society and sophisticated media that keep the community well informed. Many organizations have been forced by such pressures to improve the quality and safety of their products, to reduce pollution, and to guard the health and safety of their workers. Companies have been required to modify their hiring practices to give equal opportunity to minorities, women, and the disadvantaged.

In the 1980s, managers are increasingly pressed to adhere to society's legal and ethical standards. At the same time, unprecedented attention has been focused on the organization's response to social issues. This has had two major consequences. First, many organizations now find it wise to go beyond their primary mission and take into account the needs of the community. Second, better measures of social performance are now being devised to help organizations determine how well they are doing in this regard and also to make them more accountable for the effects of their behavior. How managers choose to deal with the issues raised in this chapter will, of course, reflect their personal ethics, their organization's policies, and the social values that prevail at the time.

Review Questions
1. Define "external environment" relative to organizations.
2. Who are the stakeholders of an organization?
3. Distinguish between direct-action and indirect-action elements, giving examples of each.
4. What are the four major variables that constitute the environment of organizations? Give examples of elements that might be found in each.
5. How do business firms respond to public demands for socially responsible actions? Specifically, how do firms convert social responsiveness from policy to action?
6. What factors may affect the ethics of decision making by managers? Give an example of each of these factors.
7. What are the barriers, as discussed in the text, to exposing unethical behavior?

Notes
1. Stakeholder influence on corporate policy is discussed in R. Edward Freeman and David L. Reed, "Stockholders and Stakeholders: A New Perspective on Corporate Governance," *California Management Review* 25, no. 3 (Spring 1983):88–106; and R. Edward Freeman, *Strategic Management: A Stakeholder Approach* (Boston: Pitman, 1984). Corporations can also attempt to control the power of stakeholders or adapt to pressure by including representatives of special-interest groups in the decision-making process. See Liam Fahey and Richard E. Wokutch, "Business and Society Exchanges: A Framework for Analysis," *California Management Review* 25, no. 4 (Summer 1983):128–142.

2. Jeffrey Pfeffer, *Organizations and Organization Theory,* (Boston: Pitman, 1982) p. 198. For an account of the benefits of analyzing the external environment, see John Diffenbach, "Corporate Environmental Analysis in Large U.S. Corporations," *Long Range Planning* 16, no. 3 (June 1983):107–116.

3. See Alvar O. Elbing, "On the Applicability of Environmental Models," in Joseph W. McGuire, ed., *Contemporary Management: Issues and Viewpoints* (Englewood Cliffs, N.J.: Prentice-Hall, 1974), pp. 283–289.

4. Direct-action environment members can also be removed. Budget pressures and public disappointment with the performance of some regulatory agencies led to the closing of some agencies and to curtailment of the activities of others in the late 1970s and early 1980s.

5. See Lyn S. Wilson, "Managing in the Competitive Environment," *Long Range Planning* 17, no. 1 (February 1983):59–64.

6. Henry Eason, "Deregulation: Dream Deferred," *Nation's Business*, February 1984, pp. 24–26.

7. Susan J. Tolchin and Martin Tolchin, *Dismantling America: The Rush to Deregulate* (Boston: Houghton Mifflin, 1983).

8. See Robert A. Leone, "Examining Deregulation," *Harvard Business Review* 62, no. 4 (July–August 1984):56–58.

9. See Richard L. Hudson, "SEC Tightens Annual Meeting Proposal Rules," *Wall Street Journal,* August 17, 1983, p. 4. The evolution and effects of shareholder activism are discussed in David Vogel, "Trends in Shareholder Activism: 1970–1982," *California Management Review* 25, no. 3 (Spring 1983):68–87.

10. Ralph Nader, "Reforming Corporate Governance," *California Management Review* 26, no. 4 (Summer 1984): 126–132.

11. John Diebold, *The Role of Business in Society* (New York: Amacom, 1982).

12. F. Warren McFarlan, "Information Technology Changes the Way You Compete," *Harvard Business Review* 62, no. 3 (May–June 1984):98.

13. Frank Taylor, "Women Grab Management Power," *International Management* 39, no. 2 (February 1984):24, 25ff.

14. For a discussion of almost two decades of battle between the Consolidated Edison Company of New York and environmentalists over the proposed Storm King plant, see Duane Windsor, George Greanias, and Jesse H. Jones, "Long-Range Planning in a Politicized Environment," *Long Range Planning* 16, no. 3 (June, 1983):82–91.

15. Marshall Sashkin, "Participative Management Is an Ethical Imperative," *Organizational Dynamics* 12, no. 4 (Spring 1984):5–22.

16. See Stephen Kobrin, *Managing Political Risk Assessment* (Berkeley: University of California Press, 1982).

17. See Steven J. Root, "Foreign Corrupt Practices Act: Where Do We Go from Here?" *Internal Auditor* 40, no. 2 (April 1983):28–30; and William B. Johnston, "All in Favor of Bribery, Please Stand Up," *Across the Board* 21, no. 6 (June 1984):3–5.

18. A useful discussion of how managers respond to the challenges of the environment is found in Rosemary Stewart, "Managerial Agendas—Reactive or Proactive?" *Organizational Dynamics* 8, no. 2 (Autumn 1979):34–47. According to Stewart, *reactive* managers respond to events after they have taken place, while *proactive* managers provide for future eventualities in their plans and programs.

19. See William G. Frederick, "Corporate Social Responsibility in the Reagan Era and Beyond," *California Management Review* 25, no. 3 (Spring 1983):145–157.

20. Milton Friedman, *Capitalism and Freedom* (Chicago: University of Chicago Press, 1963), p. 133. See also "The Social Responsibility of Business Is to Increase Its Profits," *New York Times Magazine,* September 13, 1970, pp. 33ff.

21. Milton Friedman and Rose Friedman, *Free to Choose* (New York: Harcourt Brace Jovanovich, 1980).

22. Keith Davis, "The Meaning and Scope of Social Responsibility," in McGuire, ed., *Contemporary Management,* p. 631.

23. Susan B. Foote, "Corporate Responsibility in a Changing Legal Environment," *California Management Review* 26, 3 (Spring 1984):217–228.

24. In McGuire, ed., *Contemporary Management,* pp. 615–629.

25. See, for example, David C. Aaker and George S. Day, "Corporate Responses to Consumerism Pressures," *Harvard Business Review* 50, no. 6 (November–December 1972):114–124; Henry Eilbert and Robert Parket, "The Current Status of Social Responsibility," *Business Horizons* 16, no. 4 (August 1973):5–14; and Vernon M. Buehler and Y. K. Shetty, "Managerial Response to Social Responsibility Challenge," *Academy of Management Journal* 19, no. 1 (March 1976):66–78.

26. Robert W. Ackerman, "How Companies Respond to Social Demands," *Harvard Business Review* 51, no. 4 (July–August 1973):88–98. Also see Sandra L. Holmes, "Adapting Corporate Structure for Social Responsiveness," *California Management Review* 21, no. 1 (Fall 1978):45–54.

27. See Stuart Diamond, "Oilmen Join with Ecologists: Texaco Aids Gulf Wetlands," *New York Times,* November 27, 1984, pp. D1, D4.

28. Reported in James J. Kilpatrick, "Why Students Are Hostile to Free Enterprise," *Nation's Business,* July 1975, pp. 11–12.

29. Frank Friedlander and Hal Pickle, "Components of Effectiveness in Small Organizations," *Administrative Science Quarterly* 13, no. 2 (September 1968):289–304.

30. Archie B. Carroll and George W. Beiler, "Landmarks in the Evolution of the Social Audit," *Academy of Management Journal* 18, no. 3 (September 1975):589–599. For a discussion of criteria for appraising corporate social involvement, see Robert J. DeFillippi, "Conceptual Frameworks and Strategies for Corporate Social Involvement Research," *Research in Corporate Social Performance* 4 (1982):35–56.

31. See the case of the $7,622 coffeepot reported in the *New York Times,* September 20, 1984, p. A27.

32. See Alan F. Westin, *Whistle Blowing: Loyalty and Dissent in the Corporation* (New York: McGraw-Hill, 1980); and David W. Ewing, *Do It My Way or You're Fired: Employee Rights and the Changing Role of Management Prerogatives* (New York: Wiley, 1983).

33. Robert Hay and Ed Gray, "Social Responsibilities of Business Managers," *Academy of Management Journal* 18, no. 1 (March 1974):135–143.

34. William D. Guth and Renato Tagiuri, "Personal Values and Corporate Strategy," *Harvard Business Review* 44, no. 5 (September–October 1965):123–132.

35. See George W. England, "Personal Value Systems of American Managers," *Academy of Management Journal* 10, no. 1 (March 1967):53–68.

36. Barry Z. Posner and Warren H. Schmidt, "Values and the American Manager: An Update," *California Management Review* 26, no. 3 (Spring 1984):202–216. A recent Gallup poll has shown that company executives have higher ethical standards than the general public. See the *Wall Street Journal,* November 3, 1983, p. 33.

37. Robert J. Mockler, *Business and Society* (New York: Harper & Row, 1975).

38. Stanford N. Sessor, "Beating the Ban," *Wall Street Journal,* February 11, 1971, pp. 1, 17.

39. See James E. Post, "Assessing the Nestlé Boycott: Corporate Accountability and Human Rights," *California Management Review* 27, no. 2 (Winter 1985):113–131; Joani Nelson-Hochler, "Fighting a Boycott, Swiss Style," *Industry Week,* January 23, 1984, pp. 54–55; and "Nestlé Boycott Being Suspended," *New York Times,* January 27, 1984, p. A1.

40. Donald R. Cressey and Charles A. Moore, "Managerial Values and Corporate Codes of Ethics," *California Management Review* 25, no. 4 (Summer 1983):71.

41. James A. Waters, "Catch 20.5: Corporate Morality as an Organizational Phenomenon," *Organizational Dynamics* 6, no. 4 (Spring 1978):3–15. This section draws freely on Waters's ideas.

CASE STUDY: Aftermath of a Tragedy

Shortly after midnight on December 3, 1984, outside Bhopal, India, a cloud of deadly methyl isocyanate gas leaked from a pesticide plant owned by the Indian subsidiary of Union Carbide. The choking gas covered the town, quickly killing hundreds—including many children, who were less resistant to the gas than adults—and forcing Bhopal's 670,000 inhabitants to flee in panic. By the end of the week more than 2,000 people had died from inhaling the gas, and 150,000 more had to be hospitalized for respiratory and eye damage, making Bhopal's "night of death" the worst industrial disaster in history. Images of stunned families burying or burning their dead and blaming Union Carbide for their agony were broadcast worldwide.

There were immediate repercussions for Union Carbide and for the chemical industry as well. The Indian government accused the plant management of failing to take adequate safety precautions and indicated that it held the parent company ultimately responsible. Lawsuits brought by American lawyers on behalf of the victims asked for billions of dollars in compensatory and punitive damages and threatened to send the company into bankruptcy. Union Carbide's stock price plummeted; it halted production of methyl isocyanate at the one West Virginia plant that produced the chemical in the United States.

Officials in the United States and India called for increased regulation and inspection of chemical processing plants. Many U.S. localities considered passing "right-to-know" laws that would require chemical companies to provide detailed information about hazardous materials to the employees who make them and to residents living near the plants. Several companies countered with voluntary right-to-know programs to head off public sentiment for government regulation. In the wake of protests against Union Carbide in other parts of the world, some multinational corporations claimed that the Bhopal disaster had chilled the international climate for U.S. business.

Union Carbide, which had earned an above-average record on industrial safety over the decade preceding the disaster, appeared paralyzed by the magnitude of Bhopal's suffering. Corporate chairman Warren Anderson rushed to India to inspect the site and was briefly arrested by Indian authorities. Union Carbide's one hundred thousand employees observed a moment of silence for the dead and injured; many donated money for disaster relief. Top management spent sleepless nights grappling with the company's crushing problems and its uncertain future. Morale at the company was low; production at many plants temporarily dropped. However, while expressing profound sympathy for the Bhopal victims and promising to make a fair restitution, Union Carbide maintained its essential innocence. "There's no criminal responsibility here," said Anderson.

Sources: This case was based on material from the following articles: Pico Iyer, "India's Night of Death," *Time,* December 17, 1984, pp. 22–31; Judith Dobrzynski, William Glaberson, Rosa King, William Powell, Jr., and Leslie Helm, "Union Carbide Fights for Its Life," *Business Week,* December 24, 1984, pp. 52–56; and Maria Recio and Vicky Cahan, "Bhopal Has Americans Demanding the 'Right to Know,' " *Business Week,* February 18, 1985, pp. 36–37.

Case Questions
1. What are the key issues in this case?
2. If you were a manager of Union Carbide, what effect would the news of the disaster have on you? What would you tell your subordinates?
3. What responsibilities does Union Carbide have to the victims of the Bhopal disaster?
4. What do you think the long-term effects of the disaster will be on the company?
5. Should government require that corporations make public information on hazardous materials or processes even if that would harm their businesses? What effects would such "right-to-know" laws have?

CASE ON INTRODUCTION TO MANAGEMENT

Weirton Steel

The Weirton Steel division of National Steel Corporation, with more than 7,000 workers, was the largest single-location employer in West Virginia. Located in Weirton, a one-industry town of 26,000 in the north panhandle of the state on the east bank of the Ohio River, the company has been for decades the linchpin of the area's economy.

Pioneering industrialist Ernest T. Weir moved his steelmaking plant from Clarksburg to the then-tiny town in 1909. He dreamed of establishing a fully integrated steel company, one that owned its own mines as well as its mills; he also imagined himself as the benevolent patriarch of a company town in which workers and managers were also friends and neighbors. To keep the aggressive United Steelworkers Union from organizing his workers, Weir set up an in-house union and consistently paid significantly higher wages than the industry average. Weirton workers have always been more than satisfied with this arrangement: their last strike occurred in 1933. By the end of the 1970s, Weirton employees were the highest-paid steelworkers in the world. Incomes of $35,000 per year were common, and some specialized workers might earn double that figure. Even nonemployees benefited indirectly from the high wages: In 1980, the Weirton area could boast the fourth-highest average pay in the United States. The town had grown insular in its prosperity, "shut off," as a local clergyman said later, "from the way much of the rest of America lives."

But the hard times besetting the domestic steel industry soon overtook the company and the town. In March 1982, National Steel (the integrated company formed by E. T. Weir in 1929) announced from its offices in Pittsburgh, 30 miles to the east of Weirton, that it could no longer afford to invest in its subsidiary. The parent company had been backing away from steel for some time, using Weirton's profits to diversify into banking, insurance, and real estate, and was now determined to make a 20 percent return on each of its holdings. No U.S. steel operation could come close to such a return, but National believed its shareholders would not be satisfied with less. National proposed turning the Weirton works into a finishing mill, scaling back the work force to about 1,500 employees. Weirton workers and townspeople, caught in the middle of the worst national recession in five decades, faced total economic devastation. They were the main stakeholders in Weirton's continued success, and they nearly all believed that the absentee management of National—never a popular operation as far as they were concerned—intended, in one worker's words, "to dump the plant."

National offered but one ray of hope: The workers and plant managers could buy the mill themselves under an employee stock ownership plan (ESOP), a scheme adopted by Congress in 1978. Under it, an independent Weirton Steel would issue stock to employees in return for tax benefits that would pay off loans and fund capital investment. Such a deal might save Weirton, but in the short run would benefit National far more, bringing in a great deal of ready cash and, especially, enabling the conglomerate to avoid closure costs—pension liabilities and severance payments—that might run as high as $800 million. The scheme seemed attractive to many in Weirton. At best, it would create an autonomous enterprise, free of National's onerous control, and foster creativity and a spirit of entrepreneurship in a disgruntled work force.

A joint committee of managers and workers was formed at Weirton almost immediately to consider an ESOP as a solution to their dilemma. A nationally known consulting firm carried out a feasibility study, which found that at least $1 billion would have to be spent to make the company competitive and that all employees would have to take a 32 percent cut in pay and benefits. If these twin goals could be met, the ESOP might work. Encouraged, the joint committee then moved to hire more outside assistance, engaging the services of a law firm and an investment bank, both experienced in setting up ESOPs, both from New York, and both, as the consulting firm had been, very expensive. The union strike fund and executives' contributions were insufficient to cover these outsiders' fees, and so the committee called on the community for help. With sock hops, bake sales, rallies, and a telethon on the local cable television station, enthusiastic townspeople were able within a few months to raise nearly half the $1 million needed to pay the lawyers' and bankers' fees, which often topped $250 an hour.

In March 1983, a year after National's bombshell and after months of tense negotiations, the Weirton joint committee announced agreement in principle on an ESOP. The Weirton workers would pay National $66 million for the plant and equipment—a figure that represented 22 percent of the operation's depreciated book value. Payment of the principal would run from the sixth to the fifteenth year, and no payment of the 10 percent interest from various bank loans would be required until the new company attained a net worth of $100 million. For the company's current assets—accounts receivable and inventory—National would receive $200 million: $75 million at the time of closing and the remainder spread out over up to 28 years. For its part, National would retain responsibility for all existing pension liabilities, and would be liable for almost all costs if the new company failed within five years. Weirton's president, who confessed that he had received many letters accusing him and his colleagues of fostering socialism, saw the ESOP quite differently: "The idea is to establish capitalists. We fervently hope to add 7,000 capitalists to the rolls." After a summer of informed debate, 85 percent of the employees voted to adopt the ESOP, and Weirton became the largest employee-owned company in the country.

Few of the new owners were under any illusion that the ESOP would transform Weirton Steel into a workers' democracy. No rank-and-file worker would sit on the board of directors, workers' total givebacks even exceeded the 32 percent initially forecast, and they could receive no wage increases for six years. Yet most were impressed by the possible future benefits: 6.65 million shares of Weirton common stock would be put in a trust for the workers, who would be allocated shares in the trust each year based on their rate of pay. Although distribution of these trust shares could not begin for five years, their value after ten years, if the company prospered, might climb to an average of $100,000 per worker. A pride of accomplishment was evident throughout the community, a feeling summed up by one veteran Weirton worker: "We felt deep in our hearts that we didn't need National Steel, and if it takes a pay cut to rebuild this mill for ourselves and our community, we'll do it."

One of the company's greatest intangible assets was the universally recognized high quality of its two principal steel products: tinplate for cans and sheet for the car industry. The tinplate market has been in a steady decline for more than a decade, and Weirton's 48-inch mill was unable to manufacture sheet steel wide enough to meet the preferences of some major automakers. Yet the new company was able to recruit its own sales force—in the past it had had to rely on National's. The new sales managers quickly decided to offer customers the best service in the industry. In its first year of independence, the company added nearly 200 new sheet steel customers. It was also advancing on its goal of garnering 25 percent of the declining tinplate market, up from its 20 percent average over recent years. Most important, Weirton's profitability in its first year of operation was the industry's highest. The wage cuts reduced costs by 10 percent, which amounted to about $50 a ton. This produced an operating profit of about $45 a ton in 1984, sharply higher than the industry average of about $5 a ton. Up to $700 million will be spent on retooling and capital improvements over the first decade of the company's existence, relining blast furnaces, replacing coke ovens, and installing new, modern continuous-casting machines. This raw steelmaking end of the mill had been for years almost totally neglected by National. Weirton intends eventually to cast all its own steel, thus further improving quality and cutting costs.

But proving that employee ownership could work on the shop floor was the most urgent order of business for the new top management. A new chairman and chief executive officer, Robert L. Loughhead, was recruited. Loughhead had considerable experience in companies that had adopted ESOPs and knew that improving morale, and therefore productivity, involved more than simply outlining the change of ownership. Workers still were bitter over what they saw as the hard-nosed attitude of National's managers and needed to be convinced that they would indeed have new say in management in the plant. To increase productivity in such a situation, he had to demonstrate a respect for the individual worker. To this end, he immediately moved to involve union officials in day-to-day decision making, meeting regularly with them and leaders of the nonunion salaried workers to review company performance. Each week he also scheduled meetings with different small groups of workers on the shop floor to answer their questions and discuss problems of every kind. He set up dozens of small employee participation groups, in which workers make suggestions, voice complaints, and generally try to raise morale, cut costs, and improve quality and productivity. Shop-floor supervisors are being trained to allow more worker participation in decision making. These initiatives have led to a spirit of change that, according to both workers and managers, can be felt throughout the mill. One labor-relations expert who has observed closely the changing atmosphere at Weirton remarked, "There's more upward communication going on in this company than any steel company I've seen."

Many observers of American industry regard employee ownership as the wave of the future. They believe that the traditional separation of ownership and responsibility—based on the differing aims and interests of stockholders and employees—has proved dangerous for many industrial sectors, sharply reducing or even eliminating profits and closing companies in the face of stiff foreign competition. Weirton Steel seems to have succeeded in effecting a turnaround under its ESOP and in preserving the community's way of life. Yet the flexibility with which both town and company met their crisis may be exceptional. Other industries, even other steel companies, might not be able to perform nearly as well.

Sources: This case was prepared by Andrew Kimmens and drew upon the following articles: "Town Meets to Save Its Steel Plant," *New York Times*, July 4, 1982, p. 12; Kenneth Labich, "A Steel Town's Bid to Save Itself," *Fortune*, April 18, 1983, pp. 103–107; William Serrin, "Steelworkers Approve Plan to Buy Their Own Plant," *New York Times*, September 24, 1983, p. 9; Jonathan Rowe, "Buying Out the Bosses," *Washington Monthly*, January 1984, pp. 34–36; "Making Money—and History—At Weirton," *Business Week*, November 12, 1984, pp. 136–140; Steven Greenhouse, "Employees Make a Go of Weirton," *New York Times*, January 6, 1985, p. F4.

Questions

1. What changes in the external environment of Weirton Steel forced changes in its management? Describe this process.
2. In threatening to abandon the mill, did National neglect its social responsibility to the workers and their community?
3. Does the new mill represent a fulfillment of the views of its founder, E. T. Weir?
4. Have the definition and role of managers changed at the plant since the takeover? How might they change in the future?
5. Does Weirton now show some of the characteristics of an "excellently managed" company? Explain.

PART TWO
PLANNING AND DECISION MAKING

4

MAKING PLANNING EFFECTIVE

Upon completing this chapter you should be able to:

1. Describe the basic steps in the planning process.
2. Identify and describe the different types of plans and discuss where in the organizational hierarchy each type is most likely to be used.
3. Explain how the functions of planning and controlling are linked.
4. Describe the barriers to effective planning and explain how they can be reduced or eliminated.
5. Identify the common elements of effective management by objectives (MBO) programs.
6. State the strengths and weaknesses of management by objectives and describe how the weaknesses can be overcome.

ndividuals and organizations both need to plan. Whether we plan for a party, a vacation, the next step in a career, or a new sales program, *planning* is the basic process we use to select our goals and determine how to achieve them.

In the overview of management in part one of this text, the function of planning was noted several times. In chapter 1 we saw that a major task for managers is to plan the efforts of organization members and the use of other resources to achieve stated organizational goals. Chapter 1 also described the activities of managers in ways that implied the central importance of planning. For example, Peter Drucker's distinction between *effectiveness*—doing the right things—and *efficiency*—doing things right—is paralleled in the steps of selecting goals and then determining how to achieve them.

Chapter 2 examined the evolution of management thought, which was caused in part by changing views of organizational goals. For example, F. W. Taylor emphasized productivity as a goal, while Elton Mayo stressed employee satisfaction. Management thought also changed in response to new notions about how goals could be achieved; for example, Taylor's use of economic incentives versus Mayo's small group and social interaction approaches.

In chapter 3, we became aware of the increasing difficulty of management in a progressively more turbulent external environment and the importance of strategic planning as a response. We saw how, in the changing environments of the 1980s, planning must rely more heavily on systematic and rational procedures and less on hunches and intuition.

In part two of this book we will focus on the specific elements of the planning process and the closely related processes of problem solving and decision making. The present chapter introduces the concept of planning and suggests approaches to make planning of all types effective. Chapter 5 deals with strategy and methods of developing a strategic plan. In chapter 6, the relationship between problem solving and decision making is discussed; the two processes are described, and suggestions are given for improving their effectiveness. Chapter 7 examines management science approaches and forecasting techniques used in planning and decision making. Chapter 8 discusses production and operations management, one of the organizational activities in which planning and decision-making methods are particularly important.

In this chapter, our consideration of ways to ensure effective planning begins with a survey of the purposes and processes of the planning function. We will look at the major types of plans (strategic and operational) used by organizations, discuss some barriers to effective planning and how to overcome them, and conclude with a detailed analysis of one system frequently used to make planning more effective, management by objectives (MBO).

Planning and the Management Process

Before managers can organize, lead, or control, they must make the plans that give purpose and direction to the organization, deciding *what* needs to be done, *when* and *how* it needs to be done, and *who* is to do it.

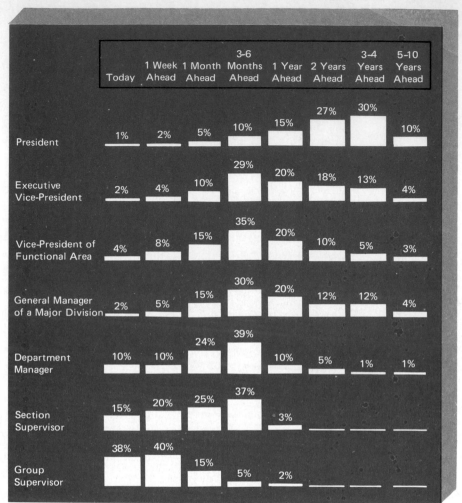

	Today	1 Week Ahead	1 Month Ahead	3-6 Months Ahead	1 Year Ahead	2 Years Ahead	3-4 Years Ahead	5-10 Years Ahead
President	1%	2%	5%	10%	15%	27%	30%	10%
Executive Vice-President	2%	4%	10%	29%	20%	18%	13%	4%
Vice-President of Functional Area	4%	8%	15%	35%	20%	10%	5%	3%
General Manager of a Major Division	2%	5%	15%	30%	20%	12%	12%	4%
Department Manager	10%	10%	24%	39%	10%	5%	1%	1%
Section Supervisor	15%	20%	25%	37%	3%			
Group Supervisor	38%	40%	15%	5%	2%			

FIGURE 4–1
"IDEAL" ALLOCATIONS OF TIME FOR PLANNING IN THE "AVERAGE" COMPANY

Source: Reprinted with permission of The Free Press, a division of Macmillan Inc., from *Top Management Planning* by George A. Steiner. Copyright © 1969 by The Trustees of Columbia University in the City of New York.

We noted in chapter 1 that the need for planning exists at all levels and actually increases at higher levels, where it has the greatest potential impact on the organization's success. Upper-level managers generally devote most of their planning time to the distant future and the strategies of the entire organization. Managers at lower levels plan mainly for their own subunits and for the shorter term. Figure 4–1 suggests how planning time might be spent at different company levels under ideal conditions.

Variations in planning responsibilities also depend on the organization's size and purpose and on the manager's specific function or activity. Thus a multinational company would be more concerned with planning for the distant future than would a local retailer. Some organizations, such as oil or mining companies, airlines, or the

Department of Defense, must make long-range commitments because of their particular purposes and objectives. A home video rental store or a bookstore might concentrate on seasonal or annual goals. Still other types of organizations must strike a balance between short- and long-term planning responsibilities. Dress manufacturers, for example, because of frequently changing styles, might make only short-range plans in design and purchasing, but they would still need long-term planning for personnel selection and improvement of production techniques and capacity. It is important, therefore, for managers to understand the roles of both long-range and short-term planning in the overall planning scheme.

Plans and Decision Making

Managers who develop plans but do not commit themselves to action are simply wasting time. Ideas that are not accompanied by definite ways to utilize them have no practical effect. Planning is a process that does not end when a plan is agreed upon; plans must be implemented. At any time during the implementation and control process, plans may require modification to avoid becoming useless or even damaging. "Replanning" can sometimes be the key factor leading to ultimate success.

An important aspect of planning is *decision making*, the process of developing and selecting a course of action to solve a specific problem. Decisions must be made at many points in the planning process. Managers must decide which predictions in such areas as the economy and the actions of competitors are likely to be most accurate. They must analyze organizational resources and decide how to allocate them to achieve their goals most effectively. Because decision making is such an important part of planning, it will be discussed at length in chapter 6.

The Need for Flexibility

Organizations that have operated for a long time in a stable environment tend to lose flexibility and find change difficult or impossible. An excellent example of this truism is the seeming paralysis afflicting the U.S. automobile industry when faced with the urgent need to increase the fuel efficiency of its products. Changes in organization or environment can cause chaos unless appropriate "change-responsive behaviors" are developed to minimize any disruption.[1]

Managers must continually monitor relevant environmental factors so that the organization can adapt to new situations as quickly as possible. They should begin to manage surprises before they occur.[2] To do this, managers must establish ongoing processes to collect data on the organization's internal functioning, in order to always have fresh information on its efficiency and the attitudes of its personnel. Whatever information comes from these data-collecting processes must be regularly compared with previously established standards or benchmarks of performance. Serious divergences from these benchmarks should raise an alarm so that corrective action can be taken.

The Four Basic Steps in Planning

Planning is quite straightforward and can be condensed into four basic steps. (See fig. 4–2.) These four planning steps can be adapted to all planning activities, at all organizational levels.

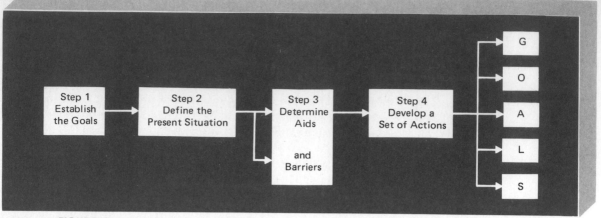

FIGURE 4-2
THE FOUR BASIC
STEPS IN PLANNING

Step 1: Establish a goal or set of goals. Planning begins with decisions about what the organization or subunit wants or needs. Without a clear definition of goals, organizations spread their resources too broadly. Identifying priorities and being specific about their aims enable organizations to focus their resources effectively.

Step 2: Define the present situation. How far is the organization or the subunit from its goals? What resources are available for reaching the goals? Only after the current state of affairs is analyzed can plans be drawn up to chart further progress. Open lines of communication within the organization and between its subunits provide the information—especially financial and statistical data—necessary for this second stage.

Step 3: Identify the aids and barriers to the goals. What factors in the internal and external environments can help the organization reach its goals? What factors might create problems? It is comparatively easy to see what is taking place now, but the future is never clear. Although difficult to do, anticipating future situations, problems, and opportunities is an essential part of planning. (The vital role of forecasting will be discussed in greater detail in chapter 7.)

Step 4: Develop a plan or set of actions for reaching the goal(s). The final step in the planning process involves developing various alternative courses of action for reaching the desired goal or goals, evaluating these alternatives, and choosing from among them the most suitable (or, at least, a satisfactory) alternative for reaching the goal. This is the step in which decisions about future actions are made and where the guidelines for effective decision making (to be discussed in chapter 6) are most relevant.

This fourth step in planning is not necessary if the manager, after examining current trends, predicts that the plan already in effect will carry the organization or subunit to its desired goal. In such a case, the manager usually watches (that is, controls) progress under the old plan very closely and is ready to react quickly if it deviates from expectations. Most of the time, however, we engage in planning because present conditions are not meeting goals and expectations. In such cases a new plan has to be developed.

Operational Plans

Within an organization, plans are arranged in a hierarchy that parallels the organization's structure. At each level, plans serve two functions: They provide the objectives to be met by plans at the lower level; and they in turn provide the means for achieving the objectives set in the plans of the next higher level.

There are two main types of plans: (1) *strategic plans*, designed to meet the broad objectives of the organization—to implement the mission that provides the unique reason for the organization's existence; and (2) *operational plans*, providing the details of how the strategic plans will be accomplished.

There are two main types of operational plans. *Single-use plans* are developed to achieve specific purposes and dissolved when these have been accomplished; *standing plans* are standardized approaches for handling recurrent and predictable situations. (See fig. 4–3.) We will discuss strategic plans in detail in chapter 5; now we will focus our attention on the single-use and standing plans that translate the broad objectives of strategic plans into day-to-day decisions and actions of organization members.[3]

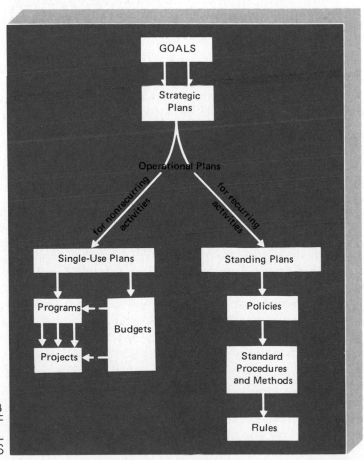

FIGURE 4–3
THE HIERARCHY OF
ORGANIZATIONAL
PLANS

Single-Use Plans

Single-use plans are detailed courses of action that probably will not be repeated in the same form in the future. For example, a firm planning to set up a new warehouse because it is expanding rapidly will need a specific single-use plan for that project, even though it has established a number of other warehouses in the past. It will not be able to use an existing warehouse plan, because the projected warehouse presents unique requirements of location, construction costs, labor availability, zoning restrictions, and so forth. The major types of single-use plans are programs, projects, and budgets.

Programs. A *program* covers a relatively large set of activities. The program shows (1) the major steps required to reach an objective, (2) the organization unit or member responsible for each step, and (3) the order and timing of each step. The program may be accompanied by a budget or a set of budgets for the activities required.

A program may be as large in scope as placing a person on the moon or as comparatively small as improving the reading level of fourth-grade students in a school district. Whatever its scope, it will specify many activities and allocations of resources within an overall scheme that may include other single-use plans as projects and budgets.

Projects. *Projects* are the smaller and separate portions of programs. Each project has limited scope and distinct directives concerning assignments and time. In the warehouse example, typical projects might include the preparation of layouts, a report on labor availability, and recommendations for transferring stock from existing facilities to the new installation. Each project will become the responsibility of designated personnel who will be given specific resources and deadlines.

Budgets. *Budgets* are statements of financial resources set aside for specific activities in a given period of time. They are primarily devices to control an organization's activities and so are important components of programs and projects. Budgets itemize income as well as expenditures and thus provide targets for such activities as sales, departmental expenses, or new investments.

Managers often use budget development as *the process by which decisions are made to commit resources to various alternative courses of action*. In this sense, budgets can be considered single-use plans in their own right. If the allocation of resources during the budgeting process does not take strategic objectives into account, the organization's strategy can have only a limited effect on its actual activities. Thus, budgeting often becomes the key planning process by which other activities are chosen and coordinated.

Standing Plans

Whenever organizational activities occur repeatedly, a single decision or set of decisions can effectively guide those activities. Once established, *standing plans* allow managers to conserve time used for planning and decision making because similar situations are handled in a predetermined, consistent manner. For example, a bank can more easily approve or reject loan requests if criteria are established in advance to evaluate credit ratings, collateral assets, and related applicant information. In some cases, though, standing plans can be disadvantageous because they commit managers to past decisions that may no longer be appropriate. For this reason, it is particularly important that standing plans be interpreted and used in flexible ways.

The major types of standing plans are policies, procedures, and rules.

Policies. A *policy* is a general guideline for decision making. It sets up boundaries around decisions, including those that can be made and shutting out those that cannot. In this way it channels the thinking of organization members so that it is consistent with organizational objectives. Some policies deal with very important matters, like those requiring strict sanitary conditions where food or drugs are produced or packaged. Others may be concerned with relatively minor issues, such as the way employees dress.

Policies are usually established formally and deliberately by top managers of the organization. These managers may set a policy because (1) they feel it will improve the effectiveness of the organization; (2) they want some aspect of the organization to reflect their personal values (for example, dress codes); or (3) they need to clear up some conflict or confusion that has occurred at a lower level in the organization.

Policies may also emerge informally and at lower levels in the organization from a seemingly consistent set of decisions on the same subject made over a period of time. For example, if office space is repeatedly assigned on the basis of seniority, that may become organization policy. In recent years policy has also been set by factors in the external environment—such as government agencies that issue guidelines for the organization's activities (such as requiring certain safety procedures).

Standard Procedures. Policies are carried out by means of more detailed guidelines called "standard procedures" or "standard methods." A *procedure* provides a detailed set of instructions for performing a sequence of actions that occurs often or regularly. For example, the refund department of a large discount store may have a policy of "refunds made, with a smile, on all merchandise returned within seven days of purchase." The procedure for all clerks who handle merchandise returned under that policy might then be a series of steps like these: (1) Smile at customer. (2) Check receipt for purchase date. (3) Check condition of merchandise . . . and so on. Such detailed instructions guide the employees who perform these tasks and help insure a consistent approach to a specific situation.

Rules. *Rules* are statements that a specific action must or must not be taken in a given situation. They are the most explicit of standing plans and are not guides to thinking or decision making. Rather, they are substitutes for them. The only choice a rule leaves is whether or not to apply it to a particular set of circumstances. In an office where the rule requires all employees to work until five o'clock, the manager may decide to suspend the rule in order to dismiss the staff earlier on a hot day if the air-conditioning system breaks down. The proliferation of rules can often adversely affect employee morale.[4]

The Link between Planning and Controlling

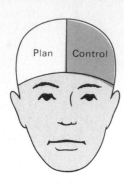

We have described planning as an analytic and decision-making process that ends when a specific plan is developed. Plans are implemented through detailed actions aimed at realizing specified objectives. It is at this action-taking stage that planning moves into another management function, controlling.

Controlling can be simply defined as the process of ensuring that actions conform to plans. This definition shows the close relationship between planning and controlling. Controlling cannot take place unless a plan exists, and a plan has little chance of success unless some efforts are made to monitor its progress.

Control compares information about what is really happening during a plan's implementation *(actual data)* with the budgets, programs, standards, and so on called for and predicted during the planning stages *(planned data)*.[5] If the actual and the predicted events diverge too much, one or more of three types of adjustment may be necessary:

1. **Alter activities in some way so that results will approach those called for in the plan.**
2. **Reconsider and perhaps revise the plan.**
3. **Reevaluate the controls to be sure they are appropriate for the plan and its objectives.**

Types of Controls

Budgeting is the most common link between planning and controlling. A budget is almost always a key part of the planning process because it guides decisions about allocating resources toward the attainment of goals. A well-planned budget harmonizes an organization's strategy and structure, its management and personnel, and the tasks it needs to accomplish.[6] Overrunning a budget is frequently an early signal that activities are not proceeding as planned. Excessive expenditures may be due to inadequate planning or changed conditions or other unforeseen and unplanned-for events. When budget overruns become too large, the entire plan may need to be revised.

In some organizations, planning and controlling are also linked together by the process of employee participation in planning. When employees participate in establishing goals, they are more likely to control their own activities to make sure the goals are met. For example, if sales force members develop the form and target submission dates for sales reports, they might voluntarily work longer hours to make sure the reports are completed on time.

Although planning and controlling are linked, there are advantages in keeping the two functions formally separated. Separation emphasizes the importance of each. It encourages employees to take control seriously and to ensure that relevant activities are not neglected or performed haphazardly. Such separation may on occasion lead to disputes between planners and controllers over how well the control system is functioning.[7] In any event, a strong controller plays a key role in maintaining the integrity of the system.[8]

Overcoming Barriers to Effective Planning

There are two major barriers to developing effective plans. The first is the would-be planner's internal resistance to establishing goals and making plans to achieve them. In other words, the individual is unwilling or unable to engage in meaningful goal-oriented activities.

The second barrier, which exists not within but outside the planner, is the general reluctance of organization members to accept planning and plans because of the changes they bring. This is not a rejection of planning but only of the new activities and goals it imposes on those who must implement the plan. Both types of obstacles to effective planning are discussed below.

Reluctance to Establish Goals

Because goal setting is the essential first step in planning, managers who are unable to set meaningful goals will be unable to make effective plans. There are a number of reasons why some managers hesitate—or fail entirely—to set goals for their organizations or subunits.[9]

· *Unwillingness to give up alternative goals.* The decision to establish new goals and commit resources to their achievement requires that other choices be forgone. Each of us at times will find it difficult to accept the fact that we cannot achieve all of the things that are important to us. As a result we may be reluctant to make a firm commitment to one goal because it is too painful to give up desirable alternatives.

· *Fear of failure.* A person who sets a definite, clear-cut goal takes the risk of failing to achieve it. Managers are as likely as anyone else to see failure as a threat to their self-esteem, to the respect others have for them, and even to their job security. Thus, the fear of failure keeps some managers from taking necessary risks and establishing specific goals.

· *Lack of organizational knowledge.* Managers cannot establish meaningful objectives for their subunits without having a good working knowledge of the subunit and the organization as a whole. Part of each manager's job is keeping his or her own subunits' plans consistent with those of top management. A new or uninformed manager may well hesitate to set objectives if he or she senses that they may conflict with those already set at higher levels. Similarly, the manager must be aware of other subunits' objectives, to avoid conflict or duplication. A manager whose information network is undeveloped or faulty may try to avoid making new plans altogether and instead fall back on already established goals.

· *Lack of knowledge of the environment.* In addition to understanding the organization's internal environment, the manager needs to understand the external environment—the competition, clients or customers, suppliers, government agencies, and the general public. Without knowledge of the external environment, managers are apt to become confused about which direction to take and are reluctant to set definite goals.

· *Lack of confidence.* To commit themselves to goals, managers must feel that they and the subunit or organization have the ability to achieve those goals. Obviously, if managers lack confidence in themselves or the organization, they will hesitate to establish challenging goals.

Resistance to Change

Resistance to change and ways of overcoming it are such important and widespread facts of organizational life that we will discuss them in detail in chapter 13. In brief, there are three major reasons why organizational members may resist change:[10]

· **Uncertainty about the causes and effects of change**
· **Unwillingness to give up existing benefits**
· **Awareness of weaknesses in the changes proposed**

Thus, most people have some fear of the unknown, as well as some interest in preserving the status quo if it has proved workable in the past. And, on some occasions, they quite accurately perceive important errors in the plan.

Overcoming the Barriers

As managers of others, we can best help them overcome planning barriers by creating an organizational system that facilitates goal setting instead of hampering it. We must remember, too, that planning and goal setting are not reserved for top managers only. Lower-level managers also make plans, and nonmanagerial employees plan their own work.

Helping Individuals Establish Goals. What can be done to help an individual overcome the impediments to effective goal setting? Some of the answers are implied by the problems themselves. Managers who lack knowledge of the organization or its external environment need assistance in developing a viable information system. This assistance can be given in a variety of ways. For example, one of the important benefits of in-company management development programs is that they help participants establish informal contacts with people from different departments, divisions, and locations. These contacts help managers find things out and get things done. This, in turn, raises their confidence in others and in themselves.[11]

The barriers due to fear of failure and unwillingness to give up attractive alternative goals are reduced in companies that have effective and well-communicated systems for planning. Where planning is a well-understood process, it is easier for each individual to develop his or her own goals—and to obtain help in developing plans to achieve those goals. Where effective decision-making techniques are widely used, it is easier to determine which are the more attractive alternatives and to recognize the necessity of forgoing some alternatives in order to achieve others.

Fear of failure and lack of confidence are also reduced by setting realistic goals and achieving them. The individual's immediate superior plays a key role in creating a climate in which difficult but attainable goals will be set. Providing training and guidance in ways to achieve such goals is one important step. Recognition and reward for successful goal achievement is a second step; and providing constructive and supportive responses when targets are occasionally missed is a vital third step.

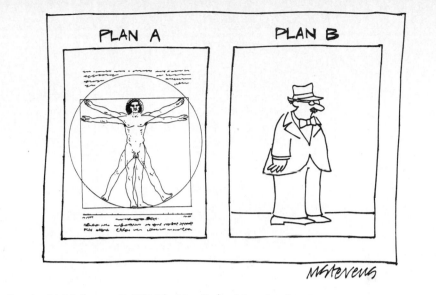

PLAN A | PLAN B

Drawing by M. Stevens; © 1983 The New Yorker Magazine, Inc.

Overcoming Resistance to Change. Planning implies change, and implementing and managing change are important parts of a manager's job. There are a number of ways for managers to reduce or eliminate resistance to planned changes:

· Involve employees and other concerned groups, including stakeholders, in the planning process.[12]
· Provide more information to employees about plans and their probable consequences so that they will understand the need for change, the expected benefits, and what is required for effective implementation.
· Develop a pattern of effective planning and effective implementation. A successful track record encourages confidence in the planners and acceptance of new plans.
· Be aware of the impact of proposed changes on organization members and minimize unnecessary disruptions. If introduction of a new manufacturing process led to sizable layoffs in the past, it can be expected that implementation of a new process in the future will meet with suspicion and resistance. In this case, employment guarantees would be one step in allaying suspicion.

Management by Objectives

The term *management by objectives (MBO)* was popularized as an approach to planning by Peter Drucker in 1954 in his book *The Practice of Management*.[13] Since that time, MBO has spurred a great deal of discussion, evaluation, and research. Many similar programs have been developed, including "management by

Theory X 1. The average human being has an inherent dislike of work and will avoid it whenever possible.

2. Most people must be coerced, controlled, directed, or even threatened with punishment to get them to put forth adequate effort toward the achievement of organizational goals.

3. The average human being is lazy, prefers to be directed, wishes to avoid responsibility, has relatively little ambition, and wants security above all.

Theory Y 1. The expenditure of physical and mental effort in work is as natural as at play or rest.

2. Commitment to objectives is a function of the rewards associated with their achievement.

3. Human beings will exercise self-direction and self-control in the service of objectives to which they are committed.

4. The average individual learns, under proper conditions, not only to accept but also to seek responsibility.

5. The capacity for imagination, ingenuity, and creativity in the solution of organizational problems is widely distributed in the population.

6. Under the conditions of modern industrial life, the intellectual potentialities of the average human being are only partially utilized.

Source: Adapted from Douglas McGregor, *The Human Side of Enterprise* (New York: McGraw-Hill, 1960), pp. 33–34, 47–48. Used with the permission of McGraw-Hill Book Company.

results," "goals management," "work planning and review," "goals and controls," and others. Despite differences in name, these programs are similar. Not only for use in business, they may be found increasingly in nonbusiness environments, such as educational, health, religious, and government organizations.[14]

MBO refers to a formal, or moderately formal, set of procedures that begins with goal setting and continues through performance review. The key to MBO is that it is a participative process, actively involving managers and staff members at every organizational level. By building on the link between the planning and controlling functions, MBO helps to overcome many of the barriers to planning.

The starting point for MBO is a very positive philosophy about people and what makes them want to work. According to Douglas McGregor, there are two sets of assumptions about how people are motivated to work (see box). In the traditional view, people regard work only as necessary for survival and will avoid it whenever possible. According to this view, known as Theory X, managers have to be strict and authoritarian because subordinates would otherwise accomplish little.

MBO advocates, on the other hand, are likely to hold a much more optimistic attitude toward human nature, known as Theory Y: People want and are eager to work, derive a great deal of satisfaction from work under the right circumstances, and can do a good job of it, too. MBO aims to take advantage of this willingness and ability to work by showing managers how to provide a climate that will bring out the best in all staff members and give them room for personal improvement.

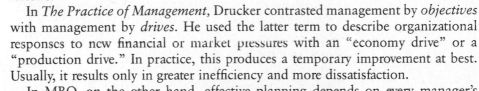
The essence of an MBO system lies in the establishment of common goals by managers and their subordinates acting together. Each person's major areas of responsibility are clearly defined in terms of measurable expected results (objectives). These objectives are used by subordinates in planning their work and by both subordinates and their superiors for monitoring progress. Performance appraisals are conducted jointly on a continuing basis, with provisions for regular periodic reviews.

In *The Practice of Management*, Drucker contrasted management by *objectives* with management by *drives*. He used the latter term to describe organizational responses to new financial or market pressures with an "economy drive" or a "production drive." In practice, this produces a temporary improvement at best. Usually, it results only in greater inefficiency and more dissatisfaction.

In MBO, on the other hand, effective planning depends on every manager's having clearly defined objectives that apply specifically to his or her individual functions within the company. Each manager's objectives must also contribute to those of higher management and of the company as a whole. This set of integrated objectives provides a sharp focus for all managerial activities.

How these objectives are arrived at is of crucial importance. As Drucker pointed out, managers must either set their own objectives or, at the very least, be actively involved in the objective-setting process. The imposition of predetermined objectives on managers runs the very real risks that they will either refuse to cooperate or make only halfhearted efforts to implement "someone else's" objectives.

In addition, Drucker suggested that managers at every level should participate in setting objectives for levels higher than their own. In this way, they will better understand the broader objectives of the company and how their own specific objectives relate to the overall picture.

For Drucker, the relationship of each individual's objectives to the common goal is of primary importance. The main purpose of implementing MBO is to achieve an efficient operation of the total organization through the efficient operation and integration of its parts.

Douglas McGregor, on the other hand, favored MBO because of its value as a performance planning and appraisal system. He recommends that individual managers, after agreeing on their basic job responsibilities with their immediate superiors, set their own performance objectives for a short-term period, such as six months.[15] Thus, they are also responsible for making specific plans to achieve their own objectives. At the end of the period, each manager carries out a self-appraisal that is then discussed with the superior, and new objectives are set for the next period. In this way, ambiguities and tensions that often accompany other types of appraisal programs are reduced.

MBO in Action. More than 30 years have passed since Drucker introduced the concept of MBO. In recent years, many management writers have enlarged upon his theme.[16] But has MBO become an established approach with American companies?

The acceptance of MBO was highlighted in a professional journal, which noted that in a national survey conducted by four independent consulting firms, MBO was

one of the 13 most popula⟨...⟩s in
widespread favor included ⟨...⟩tion
systems, organizational dev⟨...⟩

A 1974 survey found tha⟨...⟩yed
reported using some form ⟨...⟩ had "highly
successful applications."[18] ⟨...⟩ many companies
with successful MBO progr⟨...⟩erstood what MBO was supposed to do or how it shoul⟨...⟩lied.

In a later study, 41 percent of hospitals surveyed were using MBO and another 33 percent were planning to start in the near future. The great majority of respondents reported that MBO had improved performance in such areas as planning, coordination, control, and communications.[19]

The Formal MBO System

MBO programs can vary enormously. Some are designed for use in a subunit, while others are used for the organization as a whole. The particular methods and approaches that managers use in an MBO program will differ. There also may be wide differences in emphasis. In the United Kingdom, for example, MBO is known chiefly as a system for corporate planning or strategy development. The emphasis is on efficiency in reaching company objectives. In the United States, individual motivation is more often the focus of attention. Managers concentrate on human needs and on increasing subordinate participation in goal setting rather than on strategy. Nevertheless, in most effective MBO systems, the following common elements exist.[20]

Commitment to the Program. At every organizational level, managers' commitment to achieving personal and organizational objectives and to the MBO process is required for an effective program. Much time and energy are required to implement a successful MBO program. Managers must meet with subordinates first to set objectives and then to review progress toward these objectives. There are no easy shortcuts. If objectives are set but not reviewed periodically, they are not likely to be achieved. If subordinates' progress is reviewed in an overly judgmental way, resentment and impaired functioning will result.

Top-Level Goal Setting. Effective planning programs usually start with top managers, who set preliminary goals after consulting with other organization members. Goals should be stated in specific, measurable terms—"a 5 percent increase in sales next quarter," "no increase in overhead costs this year," and so on. In this way, managers and subordinates will have a clearer idea of what top management hopes to accomplish, and they can see how their own work directly relates to achievement of the organization's goals.

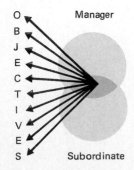

O
B
J
E
C
T
I
V
E
S

Manager

Subordinate

Individual Goals. In an effective MBO program, each manager and subordinate has clearly defined job responsibilities and objectives; for example: "The manager of Subunit A will be responsible for increasing sales 15 percent over a 12-month period." The purpose of setting *objectives* in specific terms at every level is to help employees understand clearly just what they are expected to accomplish. This helps each individual plan effectively to achieve his or her targeted goals.

Although emphasis and methods vary considerably, most effective MBO programs include the following elements:

1. Commitment to the approach at all levels of the organization.
2. Effective goal setting and planning by top management.
3. Setting of individual goals related to the organization's goals by managers and subordinates.
4. Considerable autonomy in developing and selecting means for achieving objectives.
5. Regular review of performance in relation to objectives.

Objectives for each individual should be set in consultation between that individual and his or her supervisor. In such joint consultations, subordinates help managers develop realistic objectives since they know best what they are capable of achieving. Managers help subordinates "raise their sights" toward higher objectives by showing willingness to help them overcome obstacles and confidence in subordinates' abilities.

Participation. The degree of subordinate participation in setting objectives can vary enormously. At one extreme, subordinates may participate only by being present when objectives are laid down by management. At the other extreme, subordinates may be completely free to set their own objectives and methods for achieving them. Neither of these extremes is likely to be effective. Managers sometimes set objectives without full knowledge of the practical constraints under which their subordinates must operate; subordinates may possibly select objectives that are inconsistent with the organization's goals. As a general rule, the greater the participation of both managers and subordinates in the setting of goals, the more likely it is that the goals will be achieved.

Autonomy in Implementation of Plans. Once the objectives have been set and agreed upon, the individual has a wide range of discretion in choosing the means for achieving the objectives. Within the normal constraints of organization policies, managers should be free to develop and implement programs to achieve their goals without being second-guessed by their immediate superiors. This aspect of MBO programs is particularly appreciated by managers.

Review of Performance. Managers and subordinates periodically meet to review progress toward the objectives. During the review, they decide what problems, if any, exist and what they can each do to resolve them. If necessary, objectives may be modified for the next review period.

To be fair and meaningful, review should be based on measurable performance results rather than on subjective criteria, such as attitude or ability. Rather than attempting to assess how energetic a salesperson has been in the field, for example, a manager should emphasize actual sales figures achieved and detailed knowledge of specific accounts.

Evaluation of MBO

Do MBO concepts really work? Stephen J. Carroll and Henry L. Tosi reviewed the research on three key concepts—specific goal setting, feedback on performance, and participation—to determine if optimism about MBO was justified.[21]

Goal Setting. The evidence clearly showed that, when it comes to goal setting, nothing succeeded like success. Individuals who determine their own goals tend to aim for an improvement on past performance. If they achieve this improvement, they again set themselves a higher goal. If they fail to reach their target, however, they tend to set more conservative levels of aspiration for the next period.

The research also suggests that when employees are given specific goals, they reach a significantly higher performance level than those who are merely asked to do their best.[22] However, if employees feel that goals are impossible rather than challenging, performance is likely to decrease.

Although most of the research Carroll and Tosi reviewed was not performed in organizations with established MBO programs, the research does indicate that MBO should improve performance if the goals are realistic and accepted by the employees involved.[23] The actual degree of improvement, however, depends on many factors, such as the individual employee's past experience with success or failure in reaching goals and how difficult the actual goals are.[24]

Feedback on Performance. There was also clear evidence that providing feedback on performance to employees generally led to better performance. In addition, the periodic review process was found to have positive effects on employees' attitudes, creating feelings of friendliness, confidence in management, and a more tolerant acceptance of criticism.[25]

Several studies showed a relationship between the quality of the feedback and the degree of improvement: The more specific and timely the feedback, the more positive the effect. The manner in which the feedback is provided also affects performance. The feedback should be given in a tactful manner, particularly if it conveys a failure to meet objectives. Otherwise, hostility and reduced performance can result. (The effects of various management communication styles will be further examined in chapter 18.)

Participation. Most research studies on participation indicate that subordinates who set or participate in setting their own goals are likely to show higher performance levels than those who have goals set for them. In one well-known study conducted at General Electric, subordinates who had more influence in setting objectives showed more favorable attitudes and higher levels of achievement. On the other hand, subordinates who had little influence showed defensive behavior and, in some cases, lower levels of performance.[26]

The research suggests that there are at least two ways in which participating in setting goals can lead to higher performance. First, participation can lead to a great likelihood that goals will be accepted, and accepted goals are more likely to be achieved. Second, participation can lead to the setting of higher goals, and higher goals lead to higher performance.[27]

Carroll and Tosi also concluded that, in addition to its impact on performance, the very process of participation leads to increased communication and understanding between managers and subordinates.[28]

Studies of MBO Programs in Organizations. As Carroll and Tosi reported, only a few studies on MBO programs in organizations have been produced. Research conducted at General Electric, Purex, the University of Kentucky, and elsewhere focused on specific aspects of MBO: performance review, superior-subordinate relationships, program implementation problems, and methods of program introduction. This research indicated generally that MBO can improve managerial planning and performance, but that successful implementation required much time and effort. Generally, active support and continued attention to program requirements by managers were also necessary to introduce MBO techniques effectively.

Problems in Evaluating MBO Programs. The major reason for the lack of studies of entire MBO programs is the difficulty of conducting such research. To be most useful, a study should be set up as a controlled field experiment, in which the performance of similar groups differing in respect to a limited number of variables could be compared. It is a very unusual manager who would permit an outsider to perform any form of experiment in his or her organization or would have the time and patience to participate in one. Even if such support could be obtained, it would still be difficult to control even the most important variables that could affect the results of the experiment. Because considerable time may have to elapse before improvements from MBO implementation become visible, the problems of controlling key variables becomes more severe and the chance that other changes and events will influence the results increases.[29]

Strengths of MBO

In a survey of managers, Tosi and Carroll note these major advantages of MBO programs in order of importance:[30]

1. It lets individuals know what is expected of them.
2. It aids in planning by making managers establish goals and target dates.
3. It improves communication between managers and subordinates.
4. It makes individuals more aware of the organization's goals.
5. It makes the evaluation process more equitable by focusing on specific accomplishments. It also lets subordinates know how well they are doing in relation to the organization's goals.

From this and other analyses, it seems clear that MBO has major advantages to offer to the individual as well as to the organization. For individuals, perhaps the main advantage is the increased sense of involvement and understanding of the organization's goals. This allows efforts to be concentrated where they are most needed and most likely to be rewarded. In addition, individuals know they will be evaluated, not on personal traits or a superior's biases, but on how well they accomplish the objectives they themselves have helped to establish. As a result, individuals in an MBO process are more likely than others to carry out their responsibilities willingly and successfully.

All these individual benefits, at least indirectly, benefit the organization as well. In addition, there are advantages to a successfully implemented MBO program that apply directly to the organization. Since all levels of the organization help in setting objectives, the organization's goals and objectives are more realistic. Also, the improved communication that results from MBO can help the organization achieve its goals more easily, since its activities will be better coordinated. Finally, the entire organization has an increased sense of unity: Lower-level employees are more aware of top management's expectations and, in turn, assist in establishing attainable objectives.

Weaknesses of MBO

MBO does not, of course, solve all an organization's problems. Appraisal of subordinates is a particularly difficult area, because it involves status, salaries, and promotions. Even in the best MBO program, the review process might well cause tension and resentment. Not all accomplishments can be quantified or measured. Even if achievements (or their lack) are measurable—such as the total number of sales in a subordinate's area—the subordinate may not be responsible for them. For example, sales may drop despite the subordinate's best efforts because of some unexpected move by a competitor. The changes MBO requires in a manager's behavior may also cause problems. In the MBO process, the emphasis is shifted from judging subordinates to helping them. This is a difficult shift for many managers to make.

Most of the problems are recurring ones faced by organization members whether or not they have an MBO program. However, two categories of weaknesses are unique to organizations having formal MBO programs. In the first category are weaknesses inherent in the MBO process. These include the considerable time and effort involved in learning to use MBO techniques properly and the paperwork usually required.[31] In the second category are weaknesses that theoretically should not exist but that frequently seem to develop in even properly implemented MBO programs.

This second category includes several key problems that must be controlled if the program is to be successful:[32]

1. *Management style and support.* If top managers prefer a strong authoritarian approach and centralized decision making, they will require considerable reeducation before they can implement an MBO program.
2. *Adaptation and change.* MBO may require many changes in organizational structure, authority patterns, and control procedures. Managers must support these changes. Those who participate only because they are forced to go along with the organization may easily doom the program to failure.
3. *Interpersonal skills.* The manager-subordinate goal-setting and review process requires a high level of skill in interpersonal relations. Many managers have neither previous experience nor natural ability in these areas. Training in counseling and interviewing may be required.
4. *Job descriptions.* Framing a specific list of individual objectives and responsibilities is difficult and time-consuming. In addition, job descriptions must be reviewed and revised as conditions within the organization change. This is particularly critical during the implementation stages, when the impact of the MBO system itself may cause changes in duties and responsibilities at every level.

5. *Setting and coordinating objectives.* Setting challenging, yet realistic, objectives is frequently a source of confusion for managers. There may be problems in making the objectives measurable, in finding a happy medium between targets that are too easy and those that are impossible, and in describing the objectives clearly and precisely. In addition, it may be difficult to coordinate the overall objectives of the organization with the personal needs and objectives of individuals.[33]

6. *Control of goal achievement methods.* Considerable frustration can result if one manager's efforts to achieve goals are dependent on the achievement of others within the organization. For example, production-line managers cannot be expected to meet a target of assembling 100 units per day if their department is being supplied with parts for only 90 units. Group goal setting and flexibility are needed to solve this type of problem.

7. *Conflict between creativity and MBO.* Tying performance evaluation, promotion, and compensation to the achievement of objectives may be counterproductive if it tends to discourage innovation. If managers fail to try something new and possibly risky because their energies are devoted to their specific MBO objectives, some opportunities may be lost. To guard against this danger, Odiorne argues that a commitment to innovation and change should be part of the process of establishing goals.[34]

Making MBO Effective

MBO should not be considered a panacea for an organization's planning, motivation, evaluation, and control needs. And it is certainly not a simple process that can be quickly and easily implemented. However, many organizations use some form of MBO. Recognition is growing of the advantages of having some mechanism for managerial goal setting and evaluation and for the integration of personal goals with those of the organization.[35]

Because many of us will encounter some kind of formal objective-setting program in our organizations, we should review some of the elements required for MBO effectiveness. These can be seen as the key steps required of the highest-level manager involved in the program:[36]

1. *Demonstrate continuing top-level commitment.* Initial acceptance and enthusiasm among employees for an MBO program may quickly disappear unless top management makes concerted efforts to keep the system alive and fully functioning. Managers who find it difficult to set and review objectives may revert to more traditional and authoritarian approaches. Top managers must be aware of these tendencies and provide continuing support to keep the program a vital part of the organization's operating procedures.[37]

2. *Educate and train managers.* For MBO to succeed, managers must understand it and have the appropriate skills. They must be educated concerning the procedures and advantages of the system, the skills required, and the benefits MBO provides to the organization and their own careers. If managers remain resistant, an MBO program will not succeed.

3. *Formulate objectives clearly.* Managers and subordinates must be satisfied that

objectives are realistic and clearly understood, and that they will be used to evaluate performance. It may be necessary to train managers in the skills of setting useful, measurable goals and communicating them effectively.

4. *Make feedback effective.* An MBO system depends on participants who know where they stand in relation to their objectives. Setting goals is not a sufficient incentive; regular performance review and feedback of results are necessary.

5. *Encourage participation.* Managers must realize that participation by subordinates in goal setting may imply some reallocation of power. Managers must be willing to relinquish some direct control over their subordinates and encourage subordinates to take more active roles in defining and achieving their own objectives. Some managers are very uncomfortable with this seeming loss of power, but an MBO program can be effective only if they give up some control. (In part five, we will discuss why this apparent decrease of control may be more illusory than real.)

Some Speculations on MBO Success and Failure. Up to this point, we have tried to restrict our observations and conclusions on MBO to statements based on research and the views of experienced managers. Now we will try to go beyond the data and speculate about the key factor in MBO success.

In the long run, the key to effective MBO programs probably lies in the assumptions, beliefs, and attitudes of managers and subordinates. MBO techniques work well when managers hold *Theory Y* assumptions and subordinates' actions and attitudes are consistent with those assumptions. Theory Y managers and subordinates are an ideal combination for MBO.

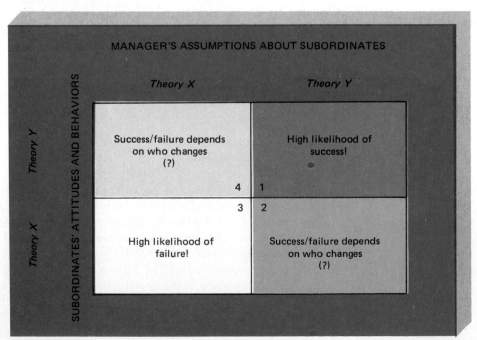

FIGURE 4–4
LIKELIHOOD OF
SUCCESS OF MBO
PROGRAMS

However, as figure 4–4 indicates, there are other combinations of managers and subordinates. If managers accept and subordinates fit the *Theory X* assumptions, successful MBO implementation is very unlikely. Managers may try to use the techniques, but their belief that they won't work will be bolstered by the subordinates' discomfort with the new procedures.

In the other two boxes of figure 4–4, the outcome probably depends on who changes. The MBO procedures and the manager's positive view of subordinates expressed in box no. 2 may help Theory X-style subordinates develop to the point where they fit Theory Y assumptions. In that case, an MBO program would have a good chance of success. In the situation described in box no. 4, success can result if the manager conscientiously applies MBO techniques, even though he or she believes they won't work. Positive reactions of subordinates might then cause the manager to reevaluate some basic assumptions. The shading in figure 4–4 reflects our estimate that managers are more likely to cause changes in subordinates than vice versa. (The reason for this judgment will become clearer when we discuss the self-fulfilling prophecy concept in chapter 18).

Summary

Planning is the first step in managing an organization and can be seen as the manager's most fundamental responsibility at all levels. Planning involves four basic steps: (1) establishing goals, (2) defining the present situation, (3) determining aids and barriers to goal achievement, and (4) developing courses of action.

Single-use plans are established for unique situations; standing plans provide standardized responses to recurring situations. Single-use plans include programs, projects, and budgets. Standing plans include policies, procedures, and rules.

Planning and controlling are closely linked; without planning there can be no controlling. To ensure that performance conforms to plans, progress must be monitored and corrective action taken when necessary.

Two barriers to effective planning are the reluctance to establish goals and resistance to change.

Management by objectives (MBO) is one approach to planning that helps to overcome some of these barriers. Essentially, MBO involves managers and subordinates in jointly establishing specific objectives and periodically reviewing progress toward meeting those targets. MBO is based on Theory Y assumptions that, given the proper conditions, people will find satisfaction in work and will accept responsibility for their own performance.

The basic elements of effective MBO programs include (1) the commitment of top managers to the MBO system, (2) subordinate participation in setting objectives, (3) autonomy in implementing plans, and (4) periodic review of performance. MBO-type programs have achieved considerable acceptance, even though they require a great deal of time and energy, because they appear to result in improved performance and higher morale.

Review Questions

1. Why is flexibility a characteristic of a good plan?
2. Describe the basic steps in the planning process. Why is each step important?
3. What are the main types of operational plans? Under what conditions is each type of plan appropriate?
4. Justify the use of standing plans.
5. How are planning and controlling linked? Why is it important for you as a manager to keep these two management functions formally separated?

6. One barrier to effective planning is the would-be planner's resistance to establishing goals. Why might managers be reluctant to establish goals?

7. How does management by objectives differ from management by drives?

8. Describe the five elements of an effective MBO program.

9. How can an individual be helped to overcome difficulties in setting goals?

10. MBO may be said to be a participative process. What does this mean?

11. What are the strengths and weaknesses of MBO?

Notes

1. See William R. Boulton, *Business Policy: The Art of Strategic Management* (New York: Macmillan, 1984), pp. 204–205.

2. See David W. Fischer, "Strategies Toward Political Pressures: A Typology of Firm Responses," *Academy of Management Review* 8, no. 1 (January 1983):71–78.

3. Our discussion draws upon the classification and description of plans in William H. Newman, *Administrative Action: The Techniques of Organization and Management,* 2nd ed. (Englewood Cliffs, N.J.: Prentice-Hall, 1963), pp. 13–54. The types of plans we include in the classification and our specific interpretation of their use differ somewhat from Newman's version.

4. See Lloyd L. Byars, *Concepts of Strategic Management: Planning and Implementation* (New York: Harper & Row, 1984), p. 212.

5. Robert N. Anthony, John Dearden, and Norton M. Bedford, *Management Control Systems,* 5th ed. (Homewood, Ill.: Irwin, 1984), pp. 12–13.

6. See Neil C. Churchill, "Budget Choice: Planning vs. Control," *Harvard Business Review* 62, no. 4 (July–August 1984):150–164.

7. See Peter Lorange and Declan Murphy, "Considerations in Implementing Strategic Control," *Journal of Business Strategy* 4, no. 4 (Spring 1984):27–35.

8. See Vijay Sathe, "The Controller's Role in Management," *Organizational Dynamics* 11, no. 3 (Winter 1983):31–48.

9. See David A. Kolb, Irwin M. Rubin, and James M. McIntyre, *Organizational Psychology: An Experiential Approach to Organizational Behavior,* 4th ed. (Englewood Cliffs, N.J.: Prentice-Hall, 1984), p. 102. The authors discuss why individuals are reluctant to set personal goals regarding their careers, but their reasons are also applicable to the reluctance of managers to commit themselves to setting organizational goals. Similarly, the solutions that the authors offer can be applied to improving a manager's effectiveness in goal setting.

10. Paul R. Lawrence, "How to Deal with Resistance to Change," *Harvard Business Review* 47, no. 1 (January–February 1969):4–12.

11. See Rosabeth Moss Kanter, "Power Failure in Management Circuits," *Harvard Business Review* 57, no. 4 (July–August 1979):65–75; and John P. Kotter, "Power, Dependence, and Effective Management," *Harvard Business Review* 55, no. 4 (July–August 1977):125–136. These two articles stress the importance of such contacts for accomplishment of some managerial jobs.

12. Some plans may have unavoidable adverse effects on specific employees. In such cases, their participation in the planning process may increase rather than decrease resistance. See chapter 6 for a discussion of the extent to which employees should be involved in decision making and planning.

13. Peter F. Drucker, *The Practice of Management* (New York: Harper & Brothers, 1954).

14. See Dale D. McConkey, *How to Manage by Results,* 4th ed. (New York: American Management Associations, 1983), p. 3. See also Stephen J. Carroll, Jr., and Henry L. Tosi, Jr., *Management by Objectives: Applications and Research* (New York: Macmillan, 1973), p. 3.

15. Douglas McGregor, "An Uneasy Look at Performance Appraisal," *Harvard Business Review* 35, no. 3 (May–June 1957):89–94. See also George A. Goens, "Myths about Evaluation," *Phi Delta Kappan* 63, no. 6 (February 1982):411, 420.

16. Notable among these are George S. Odiorne, a major proponent of and contributor to the development of MBO, and Heinz Weihrich, an author of many articles on the application of MBO to a variety of situations. See especially Odiorne's *MBO II: A System of Managerial Leadership for the 80's* (Belmont, Calif.: Fearon Pitman, 1979) and *The Effective Executive's Guide to Successful Goal Setting* (Westfield, Mass.: MBO, Inc., 1980); and Weihrich's "Goal Setting by the OK MBO Boss," *S.A.M. Advanced Management Journal* 42, no. 4 (Fall 1977):4–13 and "Getting Action into MBO," *Journal of Systems Management* 28, no. 11 (November 1977):10–13.

17. "EDP Leads the Thirteen 'Most Popular' Management Techniques," *Administrative Management* 34, no. 6 (June 1973):26–29, 64–65.

18. Fred E. Schuster and Alva F. Kindall, "Management by Objectives: Where We Stand—A Survey of the Fortune 500," *Human Resource Management* 13, no. 1 (Spring 1974):8–11.

19. Fred Luthans and Jerry L. Sellentin, "MBO in Hospitals: A Step Toward Accountability," *Personnel Administrator* 21, no. 7 (October 1976):42–45. See also Merle O'Donnell and Robert J. O'Donnell, "MBO—Is It Passé?" *Hospital and Health Services Administration* 28, no. 5 (September–October 1983):46–58. A contrasting view is reported by Charles H. Ford in "MBO: An Idea Whose Time Has Gone," *Business Horizons* 22, no. 6 (December 1979):48–55.

20. See W. J. Reddin, *Effective Management by Objectives: The 3-D Method of MBO* (New York: McGraw-Hill, 1971), pp. 13–19; and Odiorne, *MBO II*, pp. 127–140, 161–165, and 320–321.

21. Carroll and Tosi, *Management by Objectives*, pp. 1–19.

22. John M. Ivancevich, "Different Goal-Setting Treatments and Their Effects on Performance and Satisfaction," *Academy of Management Journal* 20, no. 3 (September 1977):406–419. See also Gary P. Latham and Timothy P. Steele, "The Motivational Effects of Participation versus Goal Setting on Performance," *Academy of Management Journal* 26, no. 3 (September 1983):406–417.

23. Gary P. Latham and Edwin A. Locke, "Goal Setting—A Motivational Technique that Works," *Organizational Dynamics* 8, no. 2 (Autumn 1979):68–80. Latham and Locke reach the conclusion that goal setting increases performance whether goals are set unilaterally by the supervisor or with the participation of the employees—as long as the goals are *accepted* by the employees.

24. A thorough review of the effects of goal setting on performance is provided in Gary P. Latham and Gary A. Yukl, "A Review of Research on the Application of Goal Setting in Organizations," *Academy of Management Journal* 18, no. 4 (December 1975):824–845.

25. See Jay S. Kim, "Effect of Behavior plus Outcome Goal Setting and Feedback on Employee Satisfaction and Performance," *Academy of Management Journal* 27, no. 1 (March 1984):139–149.

26. See Herbert H. Meyer, Emmanuel Kay, and John R. P. French, Jr., "Split Roles in Performance Appraisal," *Harvard Business Review* 43, no. 1 (January–February 1965):123–129.

27. For a thorough discussion of the literature on participation, and the ambiguities in much of the research, see Edwin A. Locke and E. M. Schweiger, "Participation in Decision-Making: One More Look," in Barry M. Staw, ed., *Research in Organizational Behavior*, Vol. 1 (Greenwich, Conn.: JAI Press, 1979), pp. 265–339.

28. For a discussion of how satisfaction is related to setting objectives, see Thomas I. Chacko, "An Examination of the Affective Consequences of Assigned and Self-Set Goals," *Human Relations* 35, no. 9 (September 1982):771–726.

29. For a well-designed attempt to study an MBO program under "experimental conditions," see Jan P. Muczyk, "A Controlled Field Experiment Measuring the Impact of MBO on Performance Data," *Journal of Management Studies*, 15, no. 3 (October 1978), 318–329.

30. Henry L. Tosi and Stephen J. Carroll, "Managerial Reaction to Management by Objectives," *Academy of Management Journal* 11, no. 4 (December 1968):415–426.

31. Odiorne notes that paperwork can, and should, be controlled. Managers who get caught up in report writing may do so to avoid the face-to-face requirements of the system. See Odiorne *MBO II*, p. 326.

32. This discussion is based in part on an article by Bruce D. Jamieson, "Behavioral Problems with Management by Objectives," *Academy of Management Journal* 16, no. 3 (September 1973):496–505.

33. See Harry Levinson, "Management by Whose Objectives?" *Harvard Business Review* 48, no. 4 (July–August 1970):125–134.

34. Odiorne, *MBO II*, pp. 127–140. Odiorne also argues that there should be three types of goals: routine, creative, and personal development. For a discussion of personal development goals (which can be of special importance to younger employees), see pp. 174–175.

35. See, for example, Edwin A. Locke, "The Ubiquity of the Techniques of Goal Setting in Theories of and Approaches to Employee Motivation," *Academy of Management Review* 3, no. 3 (July 1978):594–601.

36. See Tosi and Carroll, "Managerial Reaction to Management by Objectives," pp. 424–426.

37. The importance of top management support of MBO programs is discussed by John M. Ivancevich, J. Timothy McMahon, J. William Streidl, and Andrew D. Szilagyi, Jr., "Goal Setting: The Tenneco Approach to Personnel Development and Management Effectiveness," *Organizational Dynamics* 16, no. 3 (Winter 1978):58–80.

CASE STUDY: The Dashman Company

The Dashman Company was a large concern making many types of equipment for the armed forces of the United States. It had over 20 plants, located in the central part of the country, whose purchasing procedures had never been completely coordinated. In fact, the head office of the company had encouraged each of the plant managers to operate with their staffs as independent units in most matters. . . . When it began to appear that the company would face increasing difficulty in securing certain essential raw materials, Mr. Manson, the company's president, appointed an experienced purchasing executive, Mr. Post, as vice-president in charge of purchasing, a position especially created for him. Mr. Manson gave Mr. Post wide latitude in organizing his job, and he assigned Mr. Larson as Mr. Post's assistant. Mr. Larson had served the company in a variety of capacities for many years, and knew most of the plant executives personally. Mr. Post's appointment was announced through the formal channels usual in the company, including a notice in the house organ published by the company.

One of Mr. Post's first decisions was to begin immediately to centralize the company's purchasing procedures. As a first step, he decided that he would require each of the executives who handled purchasing in the individual plants to clear with the head office all purchase contracts that they made in excess of $10,000. He felt that if the head office was to do any coordinating in a way that would be helpful to each plant and to the company as a whole, he must be notified that the contracts were being prepared at least a week before they were to be signed. He talked his proposal over with Mr. Manson, who presented it to his board of directors. They approved the plan.

Although the company made purchases throughout the year, the beginning of its peak buying season was only three weeks away at the time this new plan was adopted. Mr. Post prepared the following letter to send to the 20 purchasing executives of the company:

Dear_____:

The board of directors of our company has recently authorized a change in our purchasing procedures. Hereafter, each of the purchasing executives in the several plants of the company will notify the vice-president in charge of purchasing of all contracts in excess of $10,000 that they are negotiating at least a week in advance of the date on which they are to be signed.

I am sure that you will understand that this step is necessary to coordinate the purchasing requirements of the company in these times when we are facing increasing difficulty in securing essential supplies. This procedure should give us in the central office the information we need to see that each plant secures the optimum supply of materials. In this way the interests of each plant and of the company as a whole will be best served.

Yours very truly,

Mr. Post showed the letter to Mr. Larson and invited his comments. Mr. Larson thought the letter an excellent one, but suggested that, since Mr. Post had not met more than a few of the purchasing executives, he might like to visit all of them and take the matter up with each of them personally. Mr. Post dismissed the idea at once because, as he said, he had so many things to do at the head office that he could not get away for a trip. Consequently he had the letters sent out over his signature.

During the following two weeks replies came in from all except a few plants. Although a few executives wrote at greater length, the following reply was typical:

> Dear Mr. Post:
>   Your recent communication in regard to notifying the head office a week in advance of our intention to sign contracts has been received. This suggestion seems a most practical one. We want to assure you that you can count on our cooperation.
>
>   Yours very truly,

During the next six weeks the head office received no notices from any plant that contracts were being negotiated. Executives in other departments who made frequent trips to the plants reported that the plants were busy, and the usual routines for that time of year were being followed.

Source: This case was prepared by George F. F. Lombard as the basis for class discussion rather than to illustrate either effective or ineffective handling of an administrative situation. Reprinted by permission of the Harvard Business School. Copyright © 1942 by the President and Fellows of Harvard College.

Case Questions
1. How would you evaluate the goal(s) of the new purchasing program?
2. How would you evaluate the control process that Mr. Post has established?
3. Might the problems—if any—with the purchasing procedures be symptomatic of a larger problem in the company?
4. What would you have done if you were Mr. Post?
5. What would you have done if you were Mr. Larson?
6. Mr. Manson, president of the Dashman Company, has hired you as an outside consultant to advise him about the purchasing policy. What model would you use to aid you in determining your recommendations?

5 STRATEGIC PLANNING

Upon completing this chapter you should be able to:

1. Explain what a strategy is and how it differs from normal planning.
2. Identify and describe the three modes of strategy making and discuss which mode is most effective for a particular organization.
3. State the advantages and disadvantages of strategic planning.
4. Identify the three levels of strategy, and describe the differences in strategy between these levels.
5. Describe how strategic planning takes place in large organizations.
6. Identify and describe the nine steps in the formal strategic planning approach at the business unit level.
7. Describe how managers can devise an effective strategy for their organizations.
8. Identify obstacles to effective strategic planning and means of overcoming them.

I n the last chapter, we discussed ways of planning effectively. We looked at the major types of plans, described some obstacles to effective planning, and outlined ways of overcoming them. In this chapter, we discuss *strategic planning*, the process by which top management establishes an organization's goals and selects the means for achieving them.

The Concept of Strategy

What Is Strategy?

Strategy can be defined from at least two different perspectives: from the perspective of what an organization intends to do, and also from what an organization eventually does, whether or not its actions were originally intended.

From the first perspective, strategy is "the broad program for defining and achieving an organization's objectives and implementing its missions."[1] The word "program" in this definition implies an active, conscious, and rational role played by managers in formulating the organization's strategy.

From the second perspective, strategy is "the pattern of the organization's responses to its environment over time." In this definition, every organization has a strategy—although not necessarily an effective one—even if that strategy has never been explicitly formulated. That is, every organization has a relationship with its environment that can be examined and described. This view of strategy includes organizations whose managers' behavior is reactive—who respond and adjust to the environment as the need arises.

Our discussion of strategy will use both definitions, but we will emphasize the active role. The active formulation of a strategy is known as *strategic planning,* which takes a broad and usually long-range focus. Before we discuss strategy in detail, we must examine a vital component: *organizational goals.*

Organizational Goals

The goals of an organization provide its basic sense of direction. We will use the word "goals" to include the organization's purpose, mission, and objectives—terms we define below. We will try to use these terms in a consistent manner throughout this book, but there is some overlapping and discrepancy in the use of these terms in the management literature. Many authors and managers, for example, use the words "goal" and "objective" interchangeably. It is therefore more important to understand the concepts behind the terms than to distinguish between them.[2]

The *purpose* of an organization is its primary role in society, a broadly defined aim—such as manufacturing electronic equipment—that it may share with many other organizations of its type. The *mission* of an organization is the unique reason for its existence that sets it apart from all others. Although the terms "purpose" and "mission" are often used interchangeably, to distinguish between them may help in understanding organizational goals.

Within the broad limits of its purpose, each organization chooses a mission that can be described in terms of products and markets, services and clients. The Sony Corporation, for example, has recently decided to redefine its mission, shifting the emphasis of its operations away from consumer electronics to manufacturing products for business markets.[3] An organization's mission is translated into the various *objectives* that it must reach in order to achieve its goals. These may be described by the gross sales of the organization, the productivity of its subunits, or a variety of other ways. A strategy creates a unified direction for the organization in terms of its many objectives, and it guides the deployment of the resources used to move the organization toward those objectives.

Characteristics of Strategy

Robert H. Hayes and Steven C. Wheelwright have identified five major characteristics of strategy that distinguish it from the general types of planning discussed in chapter 4:[4]

1. *Time horizon.* Generally, the word *strategy* is used to describe activities that involve an extended time horizon, with regard to both the time it takes to carry out such activities and the time it takes to observe their impact.
2. *Impact.* Although the consequences of pursuing a given strategy may not become apparent for a long time, their eventual impact will be significant.
3. *Concentration of effort.* An effective strategy usually requires concentrating one's activity, effort, or attention on a fairly narrow range of pursuits. Focusing on these chosen activities implicitly reduces the resources available for other activities.
4. *Pattern of decisions.* Although some companies need to make only a few major decisions in order to implement their chosen strategy, most strategies require that a series of certain types of decision be made over time. These decisions must be supportive of one another, in that they follow a consistent pattern.
5. *Pervasiveness.* A strategy embraces a wide spectrum of activities ranging from resource allocation processes to day-to-day operations. In addition, the need for consistency over time in these activities requires that all levels of an organization act, almost instinctively, in ways that reinforce the strategy.

These five characteristics clearly indicate that an organization's strategy is the central hub around which other major organizational activities revolve. Strategy is long-term and wide-ranging; it pervades and controls important organizational actions, and is an important determinant of an organization's success or failure over time.

Approaches to Developing a Strategy

In the 1920s, General Robert E. Wood was president of the giant mail-order house Sears, Roebuck & Co. Wood realized that the growing popularity of the automobile would allow increasing numbers of people access to urban areas. And a population no longer confined to the countryside, he reasoned, would abandon the mail-order catalog in favor of the retail store. So Sears embarked on the long-range strategy of converting to a retail chain. According to Wood, the company "made every mistake in the book" at first, but its carefully laid plans spelled success in the end. "Business is like war in one respect," the general wrote. "If its grand strategy is correct, any number of tactical errors can be made and yet the enterprise proves successful."[5]

Developing that "grand strategy" is the focus of the rest of this chapter.

The Three Modes of Strategy Making

In this section, we will look briefly at the various strategy-making styles. Mintzberg has described three modes of strategy making: entrepreneurial, adaptive, and planning.[6]

In the *entrepreneurial mode,* one strong leader, usually the founder of the business, makes bold, risk-taking decisions more or less intuitively; that is, he or she relies on personal judgment formed by experience. With power centralized in the chief executive's hands, the entrepreneurial organization is motivated essentially by one overriding goal: constant growth. Strategy making is dominated by an active search for new opportunities with choices guided not by charted rule but by the chief's personal plan of attack. (See fig. 5–1.)

The *adaptive mode* has been called "the science of muddling through."[7] Whereas the entrepreneur confronts the environment as a force to be controlled, the adaptive manager reacts to each situation as it arises. Whereas strategy in the entrepreneurial organization consists typically of dramatic leaps forward in the face of uncertainty, the adaptive organization moves ahead timidly in a series of small, disjointed steps. And whereas the entrepreneur constantly seeks to beat competition to the punch, the adaptive manager tends to react defensively to the actions of competitors.

The difference stems from the lack of a central source of power. Caught in a web of conflicting demands by stakeholders, management cannot always negotiate a clear statement of objectives. The result, oddly enough, may be a reactive, fragmented strategy making, which adds a flexibility that accounts largely for the organization's ability to muddle through.[8]

The third mode of strategy making Mintzberg terms the *planning mode.* It provides the guiding framework and strong sense of direction the other modes lack. In this mode, top-level planners follow a systematic procedure that requires them to analyze the environment and the organization so they can develop a plan to move into the future. While planners must also make risk-taking decisions, their choices

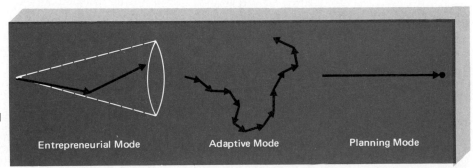

FIGURE 5–1
PATHS OF THE
THREE MODES OF
STRATEGY MAKING

Entrepreneurial Mode   Adaptive Mode   Planning Mode

Source: Reprinted by permission from *California Management Review*, vol. 16, no. 2, p. 49. Copyright © 1973 by the Regents of the University of California.

are systematic and structured; that is, they are based on a rational estimate of opportunities and threats in the environment and are tailored to fit the overall mission and capabilities of the organization.

Considerations in Selecting the Approach

No one approach to strategy making will work best for all organizations and in all situations. Indeed, the same organization may benefit from using different approaches at particular stages in its evolution or for particular issues.

A small, relatively young organization with a strong chief executive who likes the quick, bold stroke is made to order for the entrepreneurial mode. The organization can plunge ahead boldly with little to lose and much to gain from every risk-taking action. This entrepreneurial behavior may also suit an organization in trouble, when the bold stroke may be the only hope of salvation. Even in these special situations, however, some systematic attempt on the part of the entrepreneur to formulate strategy can provide a useful framework for intuitive decisions.

The adaptive mode may be the only choice open to organizations committed to irreversible investments and having a management structure of competing groups holding one another in check. Many universities, hospitals, and government agencies fit this description, as do some large corporations. These conditions restrict flexibility of action and effective planning.

In practice, most organizations combine the three modes according to the needs of a project or organizational unit or the personalities and styles of their managers. Thus, a research and development department might be in the entrepreneurial mode, while the marketing department might be in the planning mode—and both could be reporting to a strictly adaptive-style top-level manager. In some cases, managers may prefer to follow the planning approach but be forced into the adaptive mode because of lack of power.

Logical Incrementalism. In some instances, organizations follow an approach called *logical incrementalism* that is a synthesis of the planning, adaptive, and, to a lesser extent, entrepreneurial modes of strategy making.[9] In this approach, top management has a clear idea of the organization's objectives and begins informally to move the organization in the desired direction. Top management then supports those activities that reinforce and advance the organization's objectives and institutes more formal planning in that direction. When the organization moves in undesired or unexpected directions, management has the options of pushing harder in the desired direction, backing off temporarily, adapting to the new situation, or initiating new activities. In this way, management uses the mode of strategy making—planning, adaptive, or entrepreneurial—that is best suited in a particular situation to move the organization incrementally (by steps) toward its goals.

What Is Strategic Planning?

Strategic planning is the process of selecting an organization's goals, determining the policies and programs necessary to achieve specific objectives en route to the goals, and establishing the methods necessary to assure that the policies and strategic programs are implemented.[10] This comprehensive definition might be

1. Basic Questions
2. Framework for Day-to-Day Decisions
3. Long Time Frame
4. Focuses Energies and Resources
5. Top-Level Involvement

distilled into a shorter one: *Strategic planning is the formalized, long-range planning process used to define and achieve organizational goals.*

Characteristics of Strategic Planning

There is no universally accepted definition of strategic planning, and many authors and managers would not fully agree with the one just offered. Different writers also use different terms for the same concepts, as students of management rapidly discover. "Comprehensive planning" and "long-range planning" are often used in place of "strategic planning." However, there would probably be more agreement on five important attributes of strategic planning, attributes that reflect in part the five characteristics of strategy discussed earlier.

1. **It deals with basic questions.** Strategic planning provides answers to such questions as, "What business are we in and what business ought we to be in?" "Who are our customers and who should they be?"
2. **It provides a framework for more detailed planning and for day-to-day decisions.** Faced with such decisions, a manager can ask, "Which of the available courses of action will be most consistent with our strategy?"
3. **It involves a longer time frame than other types of planning.**
4. **It helps focus an organization's energies and resources on high-priority activities.**
5. **It is a top-level activity in the sense that top management must be actively involved.** This is because only top management, from its high vantage point, has the vision necessary to consider all aspects of the organization, and because commitment from top management is necessary to generate and support commitment at lower levels.

Strategic versus Operational Planning

Strategic planning is the planning activity of an organization in which top management's role is most crucial. Planning done at lower levels is called operational planning, as we saw in chapter 4. To distinguish the two types of planning, remember that strategic planning focuses on doing the right things (effectiveness), while operational planning focuses on doing those things right (efficiency).

Because strategic planning provides guidance and boundaries for operational management, the two types of planning overlap. Both are necessary. Effective management must have a strategy *and* must operate on the day-to-day level to achieve it.

The Importance of Strategic Planning

The importance of strategic planning for managers and organizations has grown in recent years. Strategic planning provides a framework for organizational activity that can lead to improved organizational functioning and responsiveness. In this section we will discuss why strategic planning is important, its advantages and disadvantages, and the evidence that strategic planning does indeed pay off.

Why Strategic Planning Is Important

Most organizations now recognize the importance of strategic planning to their long-range growth and health. Managers have found that by specifically defining the mission of their organization they are better able to give it direction and focus its activities. Organizations function better as a result and become more responsive to a changing environment.

Improved Functioning. As an example of how the introduction of strategic planning can result in an organization's working better, consider the international car rental firm of Avis, which operated at a loss for many years. Then Robert Townsend stepped in as president, gave Avis a sorely needed sense of direction, and in three years made it number two in its field. In Townsend's words, defining the firm's purpose, "let us . . . stop considering the acquisition of related businesses like motels, hotels, airlines, and travel agencies. It also showed us we had to get rid of some limousine and sightseeing companies we already had."

Townsend then went on to formulate long-range objectives. "It took us six months," he wrote, "to define one objective: 'We want to become the fastest-growing company with the highest profit margins in the business of renting and leasing vehicles without drivers,' . . . I used to keep a sign where I couldn't miss it: 'Is what I'm doing or about to be doing getting us closer to our objective?'" That one sign, he concluded, kept him from expending his energy in a lot of unproductive activity.[11]

Strategic planning, then, helps us develop a clear-cut concept of our organization. This, in turn, makes it possible to formulate the plans and activities that will bring our organization closer to its goals.

Responsiveness to a Changing Environment. Another reason strategic planning has become important for managers is that it enables them to prepare for and deal with the rapidly changing environment in which their organizations operate. When the pace of change was slower, managers could operate on the assumption that the future would be similar to the past. They could establish goals and plans simply by extrapolating from past experiences. Today, events move too rapidly for experience always to be a reliable guide, and managers must develop new strategies suited to the unique problems and opportunities of the future.

Since World War II, the dramatic increase in the rate of technological change and the growing complexity of the external environment have vastly complicated the manager's job. To cope with the pace of change, managers must look farther ahead than ever before. This means a longer lead time between current decisions and their future results. But the consequences of taking a short-term perspective can be severe. The U.S. automobile industry lost a large share of the market (24 percent in 1984) to imported cars because of an earlier failure to focus on the long-term need to develop fuel-efficient, well-built vehicles. Short-term planning on the part of American machine-tool producers led to insufficient capacity to supply the domestic market; again, foreign firms stepped in.

Advantages and Disadvantages of Strategic Planning

It should be clear by now that strategic planning will vary with the organization and the situation in degree of sophistication, in costs and completeness, in the use of quantitative methods, and in formality. Formal planning is not always possible, especially in small businesses and smaller not-for-profit organizations, where resources may be too limited to mount an extensive, formal strategic planning process and the benefits of such a program may not outweigh the costs. In other organizations, managerial commitment to formal strategic planning may be lacking. In such cases, significant benefits may still be obtained by top managers who utilize strategic concepts informally on an ongoing basis but do not try to implement a formal system.[12]

The Advantages. Strategic planning provides consistent guidelines for the organization's activities. By using strategic planning, managers give their organizations clearly defined objectives and methods for achieving them. In addition, the planning process helps managers anticipate problems before they arise and deal with problems before they become severe.

Another important advantage of strategic planning is that it helps managers recognize risky and safe opportunities and choose between them. The careful analysis provided by strategic planning gives managers more of the information they need to make good decisions.

Strategic planning also minimizes the chance of mistakes and unpleasant surprises, because goals, objectives, and strategies are subjected to careful scrutiny. They are therefore less likely to be faulty or unworkable. The advantages provided by strategic planning are particularly important in organizations where a long time passes between a manager's decision and its results. For example, in a manufacturing company, years of research and development may separate the initial decision to manufacture a product and the moment the first unit rolls off the assembly line. Many events can occur during this intervening period to nullify the effectiveness of the manager's original decision. Through strategic planning, managers can increase their chances of making decisions that will stand the test of time.

The Disadvantages. The major disadvantage of formal strategic planning is the danger of creating a large bureaucracy of planners that may lose contact with the business's products and customers. According to a recent *Business Week* study, in their efforts to develop effective strategic planning systems some companies have invested heavily in consultants, planning staffs, and sophisticated models and planning programs. These planning staffs can usurp the initiative and power of operating managers. From their ivory towers, staff planners may make decisions based on abstract concepts rather than on close familiarity with the real needs of the business.[13]

The considerable investment in time, money, and people that a formal planning system requires may take years to pay off. Until the strategic planning process begins to function smoothly, the organization may move slowly and uncertainly on important decisions. This can result in lost opportunities. A further disadvantage is that strategic planning sometimes tends to restrict the organization to the most rational and risk-free option. Managers learn to develop only those strategies and objectives that can survive the detailed analysis of the planning process, and may avoid attractive opportunities that involve high degrees of uncertainty or are difficult to analyze and communicate.[14]

Evidence for the Effectiveness of Strategic Planning. A number of research studies have compared organizations that use formal strategic planning with those that do not. J. Scott Armstrong reviewed these studies—some of which are summarized below—and concluded that formalized strategic planning pays off.[15] Although most studies have been limited to large companies, it is likely that this conclusion is valid for small organizations as well.

Most organizations do not face a choice between no planning and a complete, full-blown, finely tuned strategic planning system. Instead, the choice is often between no explicitly stated strategy and a conscientious attempt to develop one. In an organization already accustomed to sophisticated operational planning, the choice may be between a very rough, informal process of developing a strategy and a somewhat more formalized process. In other words, the practical option open to most organizations is to move toward more formality in strategy making.

An early study by Stanley S. Thune and Robert J. House found that firms with formal, long-range planning procedures consistently outperformed those that confined themselves to informal planning.[16] The advantage of formal strategic planning was most evident in industries in a rapidly changing environment (such as the drug or computer industries). Managers in such industries had to chart their course carefully to help their organizations survive and grow. A follow-up study supported this conclusion.[17]

A more recent analysis of 38 chemical/drug, electronics, and machinery firms found that on nine out of 13 financial measures (sales volume, earnings per share, net income, and so on) "formal, integrated long-range planners" far outperformed "informal planners."[18] A study of large U.S. banks[19] also confirmed the advantages of formal planning in a service industry.[20]

The research just cited focuses on the presence or lack of formal strategic planning systems. Other studies have related performance to the presence or lack of a formal strategy. Not surprisingly, the findings are similar. For example, of 100 firms drawn from four industries, those with clear, well-defined strategies generally outperformed companies that had informal, unclear strategies. The "winners" in this study identified their distinctive areas of competence and took advantage of them through planning. The "losers" more often simply reacted to the external environment. The only case in which this reactive approach seemed to work was in the air transport industry, which was heavily regulated and protected at the time of the study and subject to very little uncertainty.[21]

The Formal Strategic Planning Process

Most organizations, we have observed, can profit from some form of strategic planning. In this section we will describe the formal approach to developing strategic plans and explain how managers carry it out.

To a great extent, the nature and size of an organization determine the kind of formal strategic planning process it employs. For example, the planning process

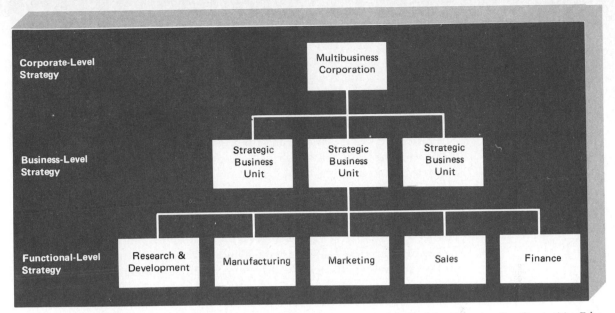

FIGURE 5–2
THREE LEVELS OF
STRATEGY

Source: Adapted from Robert H. Hayes and Steven C. Wheelwright, *Restoring Our Competitive Edge: Competing Through Manufacturing*, p. 28. Copyright 1984 by John Wiley & Sons, Inc.

used in a diversified corporation will usually be different from the strategic planning adopted in a single-business company. Since it markets many different products in diverse locations, the diversified corporation has to consider many more variables in its external environment, as well as the competing demands of units within the organization. Also, by contrast, the single-business company faces a less complex situation and can afford to employ less-formal strategic planning procedures.

The Three Levels of Strategy

Arthur A. Thompson and A. J. Strickland describe three levels of strategy: corporate, line of business or business unit, and functional area.[22] (See fig. 5–2.)

1. *Corporate-level strategy.* Corporate strategy is formulated by top management to oversee the interests and operations of organizations that contain more than one line of business. The two major questions at this level are: What kind of businesses should the company be engaged in? And how should resources be allocated among those businesses? To answer these basic questions, corporate strategic planners, usually top management, must address a further series of questions, such as: What businesses should we get into, and which should we get out of? Which customers should the organization serve? What new technologies should it use? How do we manage the range of our activities, and how do we acquire and allocate resources for the activities we choose to pursue? Corporate-level strategy addresses the actions the total organization is taking and should take, and attempts to determine the roles each business activity is playing and should play in the organization.

2. *Business unit strategy.* Business unit strategy is concerned with managing the interests and operations of a particular business. It deals with such questions as: How will the business compete within its market? What products/services

should it offer? Which customers does it seek to serve? How will the various functions—manufacturing, marketing, finance, and so on—be managed in order to meet market goals? How will resources be distributed within the business? Business unit strategy attempts to determine what approach the business should take to its market and how the business should conduct itself, given its resources and the conditions of the market.

Many corporations have extensive interests in different businesses. Top managers of these companies have difficulty organizing their corporations' complex and varied activities. One approach to dealing with this problem is the creation of strategic business units. A *strategic business unit (SBU)* groups together all business activities within a multibusiness corporation that produce a particular type of product or service and treats them as a single business unit. The corporate level provides a set of guidelines for the SBUs, which then develop their own strategies on the business unit level. The corporate level then reviews the SBU plans and negotiates changes if necessary. Single-business corporations use business-unit-level strategy making unless they are contemplating expanding into other types of business. At that point, strategic planning on the corporate level becomes necessary.

3. *Functional-level strategy.* Functional-level strategy creates the framework for the management of functions—such as finance, research and development, and marketing—so that they conform to the business-unit-level strategy. For example, if the business unit strategy calls for the development of a new product, the R&D department will create plans on how it will develop that product.

As we move from corporate to business to functional-level strategies, the plans become more detailed and specific. In the rest of this chapter we will discuss in detail how to develop corporate and business-unit-level strategies.

Corporate-Level Strategy

Steven C. Wheelwright has identified two major approaches managers can take to developing corporate strategy:[23]

1. *The values-based approach.* In this approach, the beliefs and convictions (values) of managers and workers about how the firm should conduct its business are the key to setting the organization's long-term direction. Values-based strategies develop gradually and incrementally and provide general guidance rather than a narrowly focused plan. Consensus by organizational members is important; often there is a "company way" of doing things that determines what strategies will be pursued. Major strategic decisions evolve over time and are confirmed by the entire organization. Firms such as S. C. Johnson and Hewlett Packard, as well as many Japanese companies, take this approach.

2. *The corporate portfolio approach.* In this approach, top management evaluates each of the corporation's various business units with respect to the marketplace and the corporation's internal makeup. When all business units have been evaluated, an appropriate strategic role is developed for each unit to improve the overall performance of the organization. The corporate portfolio approach is rational and analytical, is guided primarily by market opportunities, and tends to be initiated and controlled by top management only. Texas Instruments is one company that has used the corporate portfolio approach extensively.

The BCG Matrix. One widely used portfolio management method, the BCG matrix, was devised by the Boston Consulting Group in the 1970s. The BCG approach focuses on three aspects of a particular business unit: its sales, the growth of its market, and whether it absorbs or produces cash in its operations. The approach seeks to develop a balance among business units that use up cash and those that supply cash.

Figure 5–3 shows a four-square BCG matrix in which business units can be plotted according to the rate of growth of their market segment and their relative market share. Each cell in the matrix has its own significance. A business unit in the "question mark" category (a business with a small relative market share in a rapidly growing market), for instance, can be an uncertain and expensive venture. The rapid growth of the market may force it to invest heavily simply to maintain its low share of the market, even though that low market share may yield low or even negative profits and cash flow. Increasing the question mark's market share relative to the market leader would require still larger investments. Yet the rapid growth of the market segment offers exciting opportunities if the proper business strategy—and the funds to implement it—can be found.

A business in the "star" category—high relative market share in a rapidly growing market—should be quite profitable. However, the need to keep investing to keep up with the market's rapid growth may use up more cash than is currently being earned. The "cash cow"—high relative market share in a slowly growing market—is both profitable and a source of excess cash from its operations: The slow

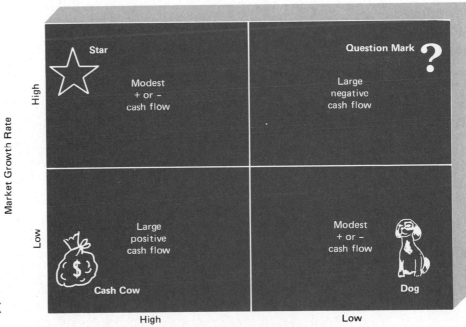

FIGURE 5–3
THE BCG MATRIX

Source: Reprinted by permission of Arnoldo C. Hax and Nicolas S. Majluf, "The Use of the Growth-Share Matrix in Strategic Planning," *Interfaces* 13, no. 1 (February 1983). Copyright © 1983, The Institute of Management Sciences.

growth of the market does not require large investments to maintain market position. Finally, the "dog"—low relative market share in a slowly growing or stagnant market—is seen as a moderate user or supplier of cash.

A "success sequence" in the BCG matrix involves investing excess cash from cash cows and the more successful dogs in selected question marks to enable them to become stars by increasing their relative market shares. When the rate of market growth slows, the stars will become cash cows, generating excess cash in their turn to invest in the next generation of promising question marks.

Critiques of the BCG Matrix. The BCG matrix approach has been the most widely used corporate portfolio approach in the 1970s and 1980s.[24] However, it has received its share of criticism[25]—not the least of which is associated with the clever and colorful names of the business units in the matrix's various cells. With the dividing line in figure 5–3 between high and low market growth typically being chosen at 10 percent per year in physical units, and with only the single market share leader being classified as "high" in market share, about 60 to 70 percent of business units would be classified as "dogs." However misleading, that label encourages managers to look negatively on the prospects and opportunities those businesses possess.[26] Similarly, the name and concept underlying "cash cow" encourage it to be "milked"—used to supply funds for other businesses—when it may actually be an excellent candidate for further investment. Obviously, skillful analysis can avoid dangers such as these, but like many potentially useful concepts, the BCG approach's simplicity and abstractness can encourage simplistic approaches to complex problems and situations.

Business Unit Strategy

In this section we will describe the formal approach to strategic business unit (SBU) planning and explain how managers carry it out. Our description of the process (as shown in fig. 5–4) combines the planning steps suggested by several writers.[27] Although generally applicable to any type of organization, our model best describes the planning process as it would be conducted in a medium-size, single-product-line business.

Figure 5–4 looks formidable, but it is surprisingly straightforward and easy to understand if we translate each step into a simple question or statement. The following list shows the various steps of figure 5–4 as a series of basic questions or statements that could be used to develop a strategy for an organization (or to develop a personal career strategy).

· **What do we want? (Step 1)**
· **What are we now doing to get what we want? (Step 2)**
· **What's "out there" that needs doing? (Step 3)**
· **What are we able to do? (Step 4)**
· **What can we do that needs doing? (Step 5)**
· **Will continuing to do what we are now doing take us where we want to go? (Step 6)**
· **This is what we'll do to get what we want. (Step 7)**
· **Do it. (Step 8)**
· **Check frequently to make sure we're doing it right. (Step 9)**

Now let's consider each of these nine steps in more detail:

Values of Managers

GOAL FORMULATION

Define the Organization's Mission

Establish the Organization's Objectives

Step 1: Goal Formulation. Setting the goals of the organization is the most essential step in the business unit strategic planning process. Because the goals chosen will take up a large amount of the business's resources and will govern many of its activities, goal formulation is a key responsibility of upper-level managers.

As we defined goal formulation at the beginning of this chapter, it includes reviewing and understanding the organization's purpose, defining its mission, and establishing the objectives that translate the mission into concrete terms. The key step in goal formulation is defining the mission of the organization. Identifying the organization's mission can take managers a long way toward selecting objectives. For example, AT&T's visionary mission some 80 years ago was described by a former chairman in this way: "The dream of good, cheap, fast, worldwide telephone service . . . is not a speculation. It is a perfectly clear statement that you're going to do something."[28] Faced with its recent divestiture, AT&T has since altered its mission; the company now aims to be "a major factor in the worldwide movement and management of information."[29] Most observers would probably agree that this mission statement does not have the clarity and potential for excitement that the earlier one possessed. Before deciding what their objectives are going to be, managers must know the purpose and mission of their organization.[30] This includes knowing which businesses to stay out of as well as which to pursue.

Figure 5–4 indicates that the values held by managers will affect the kinds of goals they select. As we noted in chapter 3, these values may be social or ethical, or they may involve practical matters, such as the size that managers would like their organization to be, the kind of product or service they would like to produce, or simply the way they prefer to operate. Peters and Waterman, Pascale and Athos, and other researchers have concluded that many excellently managed companies are "value-driven"; that is, organizational values actually guide many managers' actions. An early leader of a value-driven organization, often the founder, is usually seen as playing a key role in creating these values.[31] Such organizations would be good candidates for the value-based approach to strategic planning described earlier in this chapter.

Step 2: Identification of Current Objectives and Strategy. Once the organization's mission has been defined and translated into concrete objectives, managers are ready for the next stage in the process. Steps 2 through 6 provide the basis for determining what must be done differently to achieve those objectives. The first step in this series is to identify the organization's existing objectives and strategy. Sometimes the newly defined mission and objectives will be quite similar to the mission and objectives on which the existing strategy is based. Sometimes, however, the goal formulation process yields a substantial change in mission and objectives; this is especially true if the organization has been failing to meet key objectives.[32]

The existing objectives and strategy may be well defined and clearly communicated throughout the organization. This optimal situation usually follows earlier formal strategic planning or informal but explicit strategy making by a strong organizational leader. All too often, though, step 2 uncovers no explicit strategy; managers then face the task of inferring from its day-to-day actions what the organization's top leadership is attempting to accomplish. Managers in small businesses and not-for-profit organizations often face this situation because such organizations have rarely developed formal strategic plans.

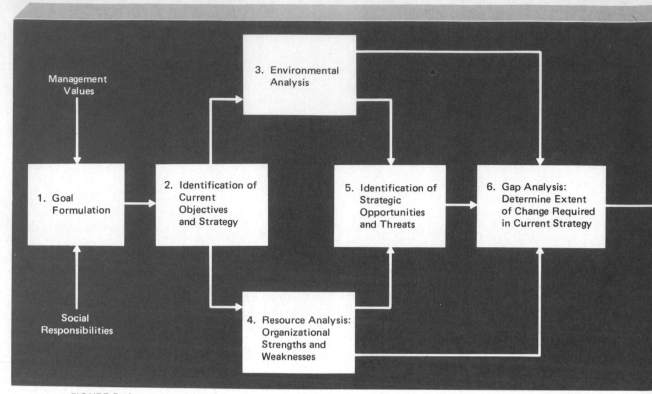

FIGURE 5–4
STEPS IN THE FORMULATION AND IMPLEMENTATION OF STRATEGY

Source: This figure draws heavily upon the concepts of Andrews in *The Concept of Corporate Strategy* as interpreted by Hofer in *Strategy Formulation*. Hofer's model has been modified for this figure. Copyright © 1986 by West Publishing Company. All rights reserved.

Many managers determine their organization's current strategy by asking themselves such questions as, What is our business and what should it be? Who are our customers and who should they be? Where are we heading? What major competitive advantages do we enjoy? In what areas of competence do we excel?

Step 3: Environmental Analysis. Knowledge of the organization's goals and existing strategy provide a framework for defining which aspects of the environment will have the greatest influence on the organization's ability to achieve its objectives. The purpose of environmental analysis is to identify the ways in which changes in an organization's economic, technological, sociocultural, and political/legal environments can indirectly influence the organization and the ways competitors, suppliers, customers, government agencies, and others can directly influence it (see chapter 3).[33] For example, a manufacturer of steel shelving might find the usual market for its product reduced in a recession. Careful analysis, however, would show that while industrial users may purchase less shelving, individual consumers are likely to buy more, since steel shelving costs less than wood shelving. In response, the company might make its product line more attractive for home use—and thus beat the recession.

It is important in this planning step to develop a list of only those factors judged

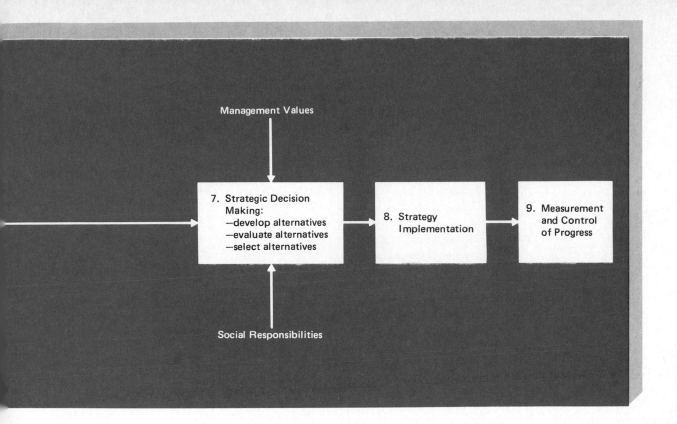

to be truly crucial. No list is likely to identify all potentially relevant factors; yet a serious effort to do so can aid in planning. Useful sources of information include customers and suppliers, trade publications and exhibitions, and technical meetings.

Forecasting and management science methods for analyzing the environment are discussed in chapter 7. As James M. Utterback has noted, one key to successful environmental analysis for strategy formulation is the early detection of changes. Late identification of changes in the environment often increases an organization's vulnerability to competitors.[34] Although forecasts rarely predict with complete accuracy, environmental analysis helps the organization adjust to changes in the indirect-action environment and anticipate and influence activity in the direct-action environment.

Strategic anticipation of the reactions of stakeholders to the implementation of a strategy is becoming increasingly important. Strategic anticipation can be rather subtle. For example, Ian C. MacMillan has reported that one firm delayed launching a new product until the marketing manager of its main competitor had departed for an extended business trip and vacation. The company established a dominant position in the market while its competitor was paralyzed as the absent manager's stand-in slowly grappled with this new threat and eventually acted too late.[35] This illustrates the value of systematically gathering information on competitors, a technique that, according to a recent study, is too little used in American business.[36]

FOUR STEPS TO RESOURCE ANALYSIS

1. Profile skills and resources.

2. Determine key success requirement of market.

3. Compare resource profile to key success requirement.

4. Compare organization strengths and weaknesses with those of competitors.

Step 4: Resource Analysis. The organization's goals and existing strategy also provide a framework for analyzing its resources. This analysis is necessary to identify the organization's competitive advantages and disadvantages. Competitive advantages and disadvantages are the strengths and weaknesses of the organization relative to its present and likely future competitors.

The question is not "What do we do well or poorly?" but rather, "What are we doing better or worse than anyone else?" If all the universities in an area provide excellent teaching, then University X does not gain a competitive advantage in attracting students because its faculty performed well in the classroom. On the other hand, if University X offers only good, but not excellent, teaching while the other universities do a poor job, then it would have a competitive advantage in this dimension.

Furthermore, relative strength also depends on what an organization is trying to do. A strong sales force will be of little or no use to a firm that plans to shift its operations to direct-mail selling.

Hofer and Schendel offer four steps for analyzing resources.[37]

1. **Develop a profile of the organization's principal resources and skills in three broad areas: financial; physical, organizational, and human; and technological.**
2. **Determine the key success requirement of the product/market segments in which the organization competes or might compete.**
3. **Compare the resource profile to the key success requirements to determine the major strengths on which an effective strategy can be based and the major weaknesses to be overcome.**
4. **Compare the organization's strengths and weaknesses with those of its major competitors to identify which of its resources and skills are sufficient to yield competitive advantages in the marketplace.[38]**

Step 5: Identification of Strategic Opportunities and Threats. Identifying strategy, analyzing the environment, and analyzing the organization's resources (steps 2, 3, and 4) come together in the fifth step: determining the opportunities available to the organization and the threats it faces. Opportunities and threats may arise from many factors: Land purchased for farming activities by a large agribusiness corporation may become so valuable that the company considers forming or acquiring a housing development division. In this instance, changed market conditions present a new opportunity.

In the 1960s, organizations owing their success to expertise in designing and manufacturing complex electromechanical products, such as cash registers, found that advances in electronic technology rapidly made both their skills and their plants and equipment obsolete. Here, technological changes were a clear threat. But firms that could move ahead rapidly with the new technology had the opportunity to do so. Thus, the same environment that posed a threat to some organizations offered opportunities to others.

Existing Strategy

PERFORMANCE GAP

New Goals and Objectives

Step 6: Determination of Extent of Strategic Change Required. After resources and the environment have been analyzed, the results of the existing strategy can be forecast. The longer that strategy has been in place and the more stable the environment, the easier it will be to make this prediction. Then managers can decide whether or not to modify that strategy or its implementation. This decision should be based on whether *performance gaps* can be identified. A performance gap is the difference between the objectives established in the goal formulation process and the results likely to be achieved if the existing strategy is continued. Performance gaps can result from choosing more difficult objectives or from the failure of past performance to meet expectations because of effective responses by competitors, changes in the environment, loss of resources—or because the strategy itself had not been well thought out. The greater the gap, the greater the change in strategy is likely to be.

Step 7: Strategic Decision Making. If a change in strategy appears necessary to close the performance gap, the next step involves identifying, evaluating, and selecting alternative strategic approaches. The process of decision making is discussed in detail in chapter 6; our discussion here highlights those aspects that concern strategic alternatives.

Identification of Strategic Alternatives. In a given instance, a variety of alternatives for closing the performance gap probably exist. New markets may be entered; key products may be redesigned to enhance quality or reduce cost; new investments may be undertaken or old ones terminated.

If only a minor change in the existing strategy is needed, the logical alternatives may be few. If, for example, a lag in new-product introduction has been identified as a major cause of dwindling sales, a program to improve the performance of the research and development department may be the obvious choice. But if a significant change in the strategic approach is required, more alternatives must be identified and greater care will be needed later to avoid attempting to blend incompatible options into a new strategic approach.

Evaluation of Strategic Alternatives. Richard P. Rumelt has described four criteria for evaluating strategic alternatives:[39]

1. **The strategy and its component parts should have consistent goals, objectives, and policies.**
2. **It should focus resources and efforts on the critical issues identified in the strategy formulation process and separate them from unimportant issues.**
3. **It should deal with subproblems capable of solution, given the organization's resources and skills. [For example, he has noted that "A strategy for competing in the electric typewriter market . . . by creating a radically cheap yet durable machine defines a subproblem (inventing the machine) that is probably no more amenable to attack than the original strategic problem."]**
4. **Finally, the strategy should be capable of producing the intended results—that is, it should show promise of actually working.**

In evaluating alternatives it is also important to focus on a particular product or service and on those competitors who are direct rivals in offering them. A strategy that does not create or exploit a particular advantage of the organization over its rivals should be rejected.

Selection of Strategic Alternatives. In choosing among the available possibilities, managers should select the alternatives that are best suited to the organization's capabilities. Successful strategic plans utilize the existing strengths of the organization. New capabilities can be acquired only through investment in human resources and/or equipment and cannot be built up quickly. Therefore, it is seldom advisable to embark on a strategic plan requiring resources or skills that are weak or nonexistent. Instead, recognized strengths should be fully exploited.

Step 8: Strategy Implementation. Once the strategy has been determined, it must be incorporated into the daily operations of the organization. Even the most sophisticated and creative strategy will not benefit the organization unless it is carried out. Whether the strategy is recorded in a formal and detailed strategic plan or not, it must be translated into the appropriate tactical plans, programs, and budgets.

Let us assume our strategic plan calls for the introduction of a new line of products in five years. The personnel department might have to develop a short-term hiring program. The marketing department might have to make up a short-term budget for the first year of the plan, perhaps to cover preliminary market testing for new product concepts. The research and development department might set forth preliminary plans for the entire period of the new strategy. The production department may work up preliminary cost estimates during the early stage of the strategic plan, becoming more actively involved as the new products achieve final form in the research and development department.

Step 9: Measurement and Control of Progress. As implementation proceeds, managers must check progress against the strategic plan at periodic or critical stages to assess whether the organization is moving toward its strategic objectives. Company controllers often play an important role in designing systems of *strategic control* (as this process is generally known). The two main questions in strategic control are: (1) Is the strategy being implemented as planned? and (2) Is the strategy achieving the intended results?[40]

Approaches to Formal Strategic Planning

Arthur A. Thompson and A. J. Strickland have described four basic approaches to formal strategic planning:[41]

1. *Bottom-up approach:* Initiatives in formulating strategy are taken by the various units or divisions of an organization and then passed upward for aggregation at the corporate level. Corporate strategy will then be a composite of these plans. The weakness of this approach is that corporate strategy may end up as an incoherent muddle that merely reflects the objectives of the divisions before the planning attempt was made.
2. *Top-down approach:* Initiative is taken by the upper-level executives of the organization, who formulate a unified, coordinated strategy, usually with the advice of lower-level managers. This overall strategy is then used to establish objectives and evaluate the performance of each business unit.
3. *Interactive approach:* In this approach, a compromise between the bottom-up and top-down methods, corporate executives and lower-level managers develop strategy in consultation with each other, making a link between wider corporate objectives and the managers' detailed knowledge of specific situations.
4. *Dual-level approach:* Strategy is independently formulated at both the corporate and business levels. All units form plans to suit their particular situations, and these plans are regularly reviewed by corporate management. At the corporate level, strategic planning is continuous and focuses on the larger goals of the organization: when to acquire and when to divest businesses; how to react to competition and the external environment; what priorities to attach to the organization's various units.

The Role of Planning Staffs in Large Organizations

As organizations grow, they often find that a formally staffed planning department becomes a necessity. Strategic planning in large organizations is often too complex for their managers to handle without the help of a planning staff. In addition, large organizations tend to be involved in long-term projects that require a considerable investment of time and resources. Finally, they have the stability and resources needed to set up a planning staff.[42]

Historically, the planning staff helps top managers formulate their strategies and objectives by acquiring data through surveys and research. The planning staff monitors and forecasts the changing needs of the organization's customers, the shifts in the organization's economic environment, advances in technology that can affect the organization, and the development of new market opportunities for the organization. In light of the information it gathers, the planning staff recommends appropriate strategies and objectives to top managers. It may also evaluate the strategies and objectives that top managers propose.

In recent years, the role of professional planning staffs has changed. Where planning staffs once played a centralized, dominant role in directing the creation of strategic plans in some large organizations, their function now is more to support and assist line managers in strategic planning—acting as catalysts for change rather than imposing plans from corporate headquarters. The role of chief executive officers has also changed. Many of them, foreseeing an end to the rapid growth of the economy and anticipating a more competitive marketplace, are now taking a more active part in planning instead of leaving much of this function to a staff of specialists.[43]

Strategic Planning in Small Business Organizations

The size of an organization can make a big difference to its planning (and other) procedures. Th. P. van Hoorn has observed that small organizations differ from large ones in the following respects:[44]

- They create relatively few products or services.
- Their resources and capabilities are comparatively limited.
- They generally do not have formal procedures to monitor the environment, make forecasts, or evaluate and control strategies in progress. As a result, information necessary for implementation or revision of strategic plans is unavailable or unreliable.
- Most management and staff personnel have been trained on the job. They tend to rely on experience as a guide, rather than on systematic, specified procedures.
- Management positions and large blocks of shares are often held by relatives of the founder(s).

Because of these differences, strategic planning in small companies generally differs from the formal procedures used in large organizations. The planning process itself will be less systematized and explicit—less formal. The nine-step strategic planning model presented above is a useful guideline, but in small companies analyses tend to be less detailed and complex.

For all these reasons, then, it is important for managers in small organizations to realize two things: First, strategic planning does not have to be expensive, complex, quantitative, or even very formal. It can be managed on a modest scale, with its focus only on those steps relevant to the particular organization and its needs. Frank F. Gilmore has argued that, in smaller companies, "strategy should be formulated by the top management team at the conference table. Judgment, experience, intuition, and well-guided discussions are the key to success, not staff work and mathematical models."[45]

Second, strategic planning is a learning process. Over time, the organization's members will learn progressively more about the organization's capabilities and limitations, about the threats and opportunities in its environment, and about the process of strategic planning itself. As skills in strategic planning are developed, the process—and the resulting plans—can become more formal and more sophisticated.[46]

Steiner has noted that one of the biggest obstacles to strategic planning in smaller organizations is often the top manager's doubts that it is useful at all.[47] These doubts may well arise in part from lack of understanding of the two points discussed above. They also overlook the fact that strategic planning is frequently easier to accomplish in small companies. And once developed, strategies can be communicated clearly and rapidly to all personnel, making it easier to ensure that all employees understand and implement those strategies.[48]

Strategic Planning in Not-for-Profit Organizations

Just as small businesses differ from large businesses, not-for-profit organizations differ from profit-making ones—and they differ from each other as well.[49] These differences, as we will see, account for the fact that the top managers of not-for-profit organizations are less likely than other managers to engage in formal or even informal strategic planning. These differences also affect the type of planning not-for-profit organizations actually do.

The range of not-for-profit organizations is suggested by their names; for example, the Stanford Research Institute (a not-for-profit consulting organization), the Boston Food Coop, Brigham Young University, the Teamsters Union, the Republican Party, and the local United Fund. Because of the differences among them, strategic planning techniques will be more useful for some not-for-profit organizations than for others.

In spite of their great diversity, many not-for-profit organizations share characteristics that distinguish them from profit-oriented firms. William H. Newman and Harvey W. Wallender III have listed six characteristics that are fairly common in not-for-profit organizations:[50]

1. The service they provide is intangible and hard to measure.
2. Customer influence may be weak.
3. Strong employee commitment to professions or to a cause may weaken their allegiance to the organization.
4. Resource contributors may intrude into internal management.
5. Restraints on the use of rewards and punishments result from 1, 3, and 4 above.
6. Charismatic leaders and/or the "mystique" of the enterprise may be important means of resolving conflict in objectives and overcoming restraints.

Newman and Wallender have noted that, although some business firms may possess these characteristics to a greater or lesser extent, they are more frequently found in not-for-profit organizations.

Because strategic planning techniques have developed out of the experiences and situations of large business organizations, they have not been easy to apply in not-for-profit situations. At the same time, the diversity among not-for-profits makes it difficult to determine which formal planning experiences and problems of one type of not-for-profit might prove relevant to others.

Given these and other problems, it is not surprising that Max S. Wortman found that not-for-profit organizations tended to be "managed much more in a short-term operations sense than in a strategic sense."[51] As Hofer and Schendel have noted: "There is some evidence that some of these organizations have no strategies at all. Rather, they seem motivated more by short-term budget cycles and personal goals than by any interest in reexamining their purpose or mission in light of altered environmental circumstances."[52]

In spite of the barriers, strategic planning efforts appear to be increasing in not-for-profit organizations. Pressures created by cutbacks in federal funding and the presence of business persons on the boards of trustees of not-for-profits have encouraged many of these organizations to develop more formal strategies. The rapid changes in environmental factors that have led business organizations to undertake strategic planning have also had direct impact on not-for-profit organizations. Reports of strategic planning efforts in colleges, hospitals, libraries, local governments, and churches now appear regularly, but because the use of strategic planning by not-for-profits is still in its infancy, it is too soon to predict with confidence how these procedures will eventually differ from those used in business.[53]

Many observers believe that strategic planning is more difficult in not-for-profit organizations than in profit-making businesses. However, not-for-profits may even have some underused planning advantages; for example, the level of employee commitment to the mission of a not-for-profit organization can be utilized in formulating and implementing strategy. Although strategic planning methods derived from business situations may need modification for not-for-profit use, they offer promise for these organizations and a framework for satisfying the requirements of stakeholders.[54]

Overcoming Barriers to Formal Strategic Planning

In the previous section we saw how formal strategic planning can be applied in various types of organizations. Even if the most appropriate method of formal planning is chosen, however, there are still two types of problems that may stand in the way of its use or effective implementation. First, specific characteristics of the formal strategic planning process may discourage *development* of formal strategies. And second, managers may not fully understand the process and may *implement* the plans ineffectively. These problems may prevent formal planning from occurring; they may sidetrack and sabotage planning efforts; and they may interfere with translating the plan into action.

Factors that Discourage Developing Formal Plans. The five factors that may discourage some organizations from developing formal strategic plans are:[55]

1. Conflict between the formal planning process and management style
2. Inappropriateness of formal planning for small organizations
3. Expense of the process
4. Overemphasis on quantitative aspects
5. Vulnerability of formal planning to unexpected events

These objections can usually be overcome by selecting a level of formality appropriate to the organization, by eliminating unnecessary and expensive frills such as outside consultants and elaborate reports, and by emphasizing strategic flexibility. It should be kept in mind that *any* degree of formality in making and communicating strategy will result in many of the advantages of a formal planning system.

Obstacles to Effective Implementation of Formal Plans. Kjell Ringbakk has identified ten major reasons why organizations can fail in their strategic planning efforts:[56]

1. Formal planning is not accepted by all managers.
2. Some aspects of formal planning are not understood by planners.
3. Managers at some levels are not included in planning activities.
4. Primary responsibility for planning is surrendered to staff.
5. Long-range plans are considered unchangeable.
6. An elaborate and expensive planning system is chosen.
7. Good plans are simply ignored.
8. Forecasting and budgeting are confused with planning.
9. Available information is inadequate.
10. Managers get bogged down in details.

These obstacles involve errors in perception, education, and implementation. In many cases they can be effectively addressed by teaching all managers about the planning process and involving them in it and by always keeping the overall goals of strategic planning in mind.

Organizations that start off on the wrong foot when developing a formal strategic planning process frequently evolve more effective methods as they gain experience. For example, the *Business Week* study cited above found that many companies developed elaborate planning departments staffed with experts who were not always familiar with the businesses they were planning for. These experts took an "ivory tower" approach to planning that was frequently unsuccessful. The efforts of the planning staff and, in some cases, planning departments were then scrapped as line management properly reassumed the task of strategic planning. In other cases, planning staff was retained to instruct and aid line management in complex aspects of planning.

Factors Favoring the Spread of Formal Planning. Despite the obstacles described above, the use of formal strategic planning is expanding. The process itself is becoming better understood, and managers are more skilled than ever before in determining which approaches and systems are appropriate for different situations. They are also more skilled at developing and implementing such systems.

"These projected figures are a figment of our imagination. We hope you like them."
Drawing by Weber; © 1982 The New Yorker Magazine, Inc.

In addition, the concept of organizational strategy making is becoming accepted as the starting point for understanding and managing an organization. Managers are now less likely to ask, "Should we engage in formal strategic planning?" Rather, the question now is, "When, how, and with whose help should we develop our strategic planning system—and just how formal should it be?"

Summary

Strategic planning has become increasingly important to managers in recent years. Defining fundamental goals and objectives in specific terms, and determining the means to achieve them, provides a basic, long-range framework into which other forms of planning can fit. Strategic planning can strongly influence the survival and growth of an organization in the contemporary, frequently volatile environment.

Three modes of strategy making are the entrepreneurial, adaptive, and formal planning modes. Each has usefulness in some situations and some organizations, but studies have indicated that the formal planning mode is the most effective. Some organizations use an approach to strategy making (logical incrementalism) that synthesizes aspects of the three modes of strategy making.

Strategy is defined at three levels: corporate, business unit, and functional area. On the corporate level, managers are concerned with developing a strategy for their organization's varied business interests. In doing their strategic planning, some organizations take a values-based approach—one rooted in the values, culture, and philosophy of the organization. Others use corporate portfolio management. The BCG matrix is one popular corporate portfolio management model. On the business-unit level, managers deal with the particular concerns of one line of business. On the functional level, managers administer corporate and business-level strategies in functional areas—manufacturing, marketing, and so on.

To devise an appropriate strategy, managers must determine their organization's purpose, mission, and goals. What should the business of the organization be? Who are its customers, and who should they be? Where is the organization heading? By answering such fundamental questions, managers can determine the true capabilities of their organizations and devise the most effective strategies to utilize these capabilities.

In the formal strategic planning process, managers (1) formulate organizational goals; (2) assess their organization's current objectives and strategy; (3) analyze the environment; (4) analyze the organization's resources; (5) identify strategic opportunities and threats; (6) determine the extent of change required in the current strategy; (7) identify, evaluate, and select the best strategic alternatives; (8) implement the strategy; and (9) measure and control the process of implementation.

These basic steps in the formal planning approach are handled differently in various types of organizations. Large organizations are likely to use a specialized planning staff to formulate objectives and strategies and to coordinate the strategic planning process. Small organizations, which usually do not have a planning staff and may not formalize the planning process, will nevertheless benefit by following its key concepts. Not-for-profit organizations, which differ in many respects from the business organizations that pioneered strategic planning and toward which it is oriented, nevertheless can also apply these principles with positive results.

Managers also need to be aware of obstacles to the development and implementation of formal strategic planning and the means of overcoming these obstacles.

Review Questions

1. Why do you think it would be important for you as a junior manager to understand strategic planning?

2. Why has strategic planning become even more important to managers and their organizations?

3. What are the entrepreneurial, adaptive, and planning modes of strategy making? Under what conditions might each mode be used? Which mode is most appealing to you?

4. What is logical incrementalism? How is it used in strategy making?

5. How is strategic planning different from operational planning?

6. Name three advantages and three disadvantages of strategic planning.

7. What are the three levels of strategy? How do they differ from one another? How do they complement one another?

8. Why might managers perform corporate portfolio analysis? How is this done? When might managers choose to use a "values-based" corporate-level planning process?

9. What are the nine steps in the formal planning approach?

10. How do you see your own values influencing the kinds of objectives you might select for your organization?

11. What factors might influence the way an organization structures its planning activities?

12. Outline the possible responsibilities of a planning staff.

13. What are three significant differences in strategic planning in small business organizations?

14. What are three characteristics of strategic planning in not-for-profit organizations?

15. What are the barriers to effective strategic planning? How can these barriers be overcome?

Notes

1. For a history of the concept of strategy, see Roger Evered, "So What *Is* Strategy?" *Long Range Planning* 16, no. 3 (June 1983):57–72. Recent research is contributing to our understanding of organizational strategy. See Ari Ginsberg, "Operationalizing Organizational Strategy: Toward an Integrative Framework," *Academy of Management Review* 9, no. 3 (July 1984):548–557; and James W. Fredrickson, "Strategic Process Research: Questions and Recommendations," *Academy of Management Review* 8, no. 4 (October 1983):565–575.

2. Our discussion of organizational goals in this chapter draws upon William H. Newman's classification and description of plans in *Administrative Action: The Technique of Organization and Management*, 2nd ed. (Englewood Cliffs, N.J.: Prentice-Hall, 1963). However, our classification and interpretations differ somewhat from his.

3. E. S. Browning, "Japan's Sony, Famous for Consumer Electronics, Decides that the Future Lies in Sales to Business," *Wall Street Journal*, October 9, 1984, p. 33.

4. Quoted from Robert H. Hayes and Steven C. Wheelwright, *Restoring Our Competitive Edge: Competing Through Manufacturing* (New York: Wiley, 1984), pp. 27–28.

5. Quoted in Alfred D. Chandler, Jr., *Strategy and Structure* (Cambridge, Mass.: MIT Press, 1962), p. 325.

6. Henry Mintzberg, "Strategy-Making in Three Modes," *California Management Review* 16, no. 2 (Winter 1973):44–53.

7. Charles E. Lindblom, "The Science of 'Muddling Through,'" *Public Administration Review* 19, no. 2 (Spring 1959):79–88.

8. The need for strategies to deal with the diverse interests of multiple stakeholders is discussed in R. Edward Freeman, *Strategic Management: A Stakeholder Approach* (Boston: Pitman, 1984).

9. For a discussion of logical incrementalism, see James B. Quinn, *Strategies for Change: Logical Incrementalism* (Homewood, Ill.: Irwin, 1980).

10. This definition borrows, with a shift in terminology, from that given in George A. Steiner, John B. Miner, and Edmund R. Gray, *Management Policy and Strategy* (New York: Macmillan, 1982), pp. 155–156.

11. Robert Townsend, *Further Up the Organization* (New York: Knopf, 1984), pp. 155–156.

12. Techniques to determine the capability of an organization to undertake strategic action are given in R. T. Lenz, "Strategic Capability: A Concept and a Framework for Analysis," *Academy of Management Review* 5, no. 2 (April 1980):225–234.

13. "The New Breed of Strategic Planner," *Business Week*, September 17, 1984, pp. 62–68.

14. See Richard B. Robinson, Jr., and John A. Pearce II, "The Impact of Formalized Strategic Planning on Financial Performance in Small Organizations," *Strategic Management Journal* 4, no. 3 (July–September 1983):197–207. Some recent best-selling management books suggest that we should be wary of rational plans that suppress managers' entrepreneurial impulses. See Thomas H. Peters and Robert S. Waterman, *In Search of Excellence* (New York: Warner Books, 1982); Tom Peters and Nancy Austin, *A Passion for Excellence: The Leadership Difference* (New York: Random House, 1985); and Rosabeth M. Kanter, *The Changemasters* (New York: Simon & Schuster, 1983).

15. J. Scott Armstrong, "The Value of Formal Planning for Strategic Decisions: Review of Empirical Research," *Strategic Management Journal* 3, no. 3 (July–September 1982):197–211.

16. Stanley S. Thune and Robert J. House, "Where Long-Range Planning Pays Off," *Business Horizons* 13, no. 4 (August 1970):81–87.

17. David M. Herold, "Long-Range Planning and Organizational Performance," *Academy of Management Journal* 15, no. 1 (March 1972):91–102.

18. Zafar A. Malik and Delmar W. Karger, "Does Long-Range Planning Improve Company Performance?" *Management Review* 64, no. 9 (September 1975):27–31.

19. D. Robley Wood, Jr., and R. Lawrence LaForge, "The Impact of Comprehensive Planning on Financial Performance," *Academy of Management Journal* 22, no. 3 (September 1979):516–526.

20. In contrast, no positive relationship was found in the service sector by two other investigators: Robert M. Fulmer and Leslie W. Rue, "The Practice and Profitability of Long-Range Planning," *Managerial Planning* 22, no. 6 (May–June 1974):1–7. This may be because many of the service organizations studied had begun their planning activities too recently for the systems to begin to have an effect.

21. Charles C. Snow and Lawrence G. Hrebiniak, "Strategy, Distinctive Competence, and Organizational Performance," *Administrative Science Quarterly* 25, no. 2 (June 1980):317–336. For a review of studies relating strategy, structure, and organizational performance, see Jay R. Galbraith and Daniel A.

Nathanson, *Strategy Implementation: The Role of Structure and Process*, 2nd ed. (St. Paul, Minn.: West Publishing, 1986). The accuracy of some studies is questioned in Alfred Rappaport, "Corporate Performance Standards and Shareholder Value," *Journal of Business Strategy* 3, no. 4 (Spring 1983):4–8, 26.

22. The discussions on levels of strategy and on corporate-level strategy are drawn largely from Arthur A. Thompson, Jr., and A. J. Strickland III, *Strategy Formulation and Implementation: Tasks of the General Manager*, rev. ed. (Plano, Texas: Business Publications 1983). Thompson and Strickland also note a fourth level of strategy—operating-level strategy, which regulates the day-to-day activities of departmental and supervisory managers.

23. Steven C. Wheelwright, "Strategy, Management, and Strategic Planning Approaches," *Interfaces* 14, no. 1 (January–February 1984):19–33. Our terminology differs slightly from his.

24. A survey of U.S. companies by Phillipe Haspeslagh (*Harvard Business Review* 60, no. 1 [January–February 1982]:58–73) concluded that by 1979, 36 percent of *Fortune* 1000 and 45 percent of *Fortune* 500 industrial companies had introduced this approach.

25. For a detailed discussion of the BCG matrix, see Barry Hedley, "A Fundamental Approach to Strategy Development," *Long Range Planning* 9, no. 6 (December 1976):2–11. For a critique, see Thompson and Strickland, *Strategy Formulation and Implementation*.

26. For example, "dogs" are frequently seen as providing only minimal cash flow, if any. However, recent research has concluded that the average dog has enough positive cash flow to finance one question mark. Donald C. Hambrick, Ian C. MacMillan, and Diane L. Day, "Strategic Attributes and Performance in the BCG Matrix—A PIMS-Based Analysis of Industrial Product Businesses," *Academy of Management Journal* 25, no. 3 (September 1982):510–531.

27. Figure 5–4 and our discussion are based mainly on Charles W. Hofer, *Strategy Formulation: Issues and Concepts*, 2nd ed. (St. Paul, Minn.: West Publishing, 1986); Dan E. Schendel and Charles W. Hofer, eds., *Strategic Management: A New View of Business Policy and Planning* (Boston: Little, Brown, 1978); Kenneth R. Andrews, *The Concept of Corporate Strategy* (Homewood, Ill.: Dow Jones-Irwin, 1971); and J. Kalman Cohen and Richard M. Cyert, "Strategy: Formulation, Implementation, and Monitoring," *Journal of Business* 46, no. 3 (July 1973):349–367. See also Max Richards, *Setting Strategic Goals and Objectives* (St. Paul, Minn.: West Publishing, 1986); and Glenn Boseman, Arvind Phatak, and Robert Schellenberger, *Strategic Management* (New York: Wiley, 1986).

28. Quoted in Charles H. Granger, "The Hierarchy of Objectives," *Harvard Business Review* 42, no. 3 (May–June 1964):63–74.

29. Jeremy Main, "Waking Up AT&T: There's Life After Culture Shock," *Fortune,* December 24, 1984, pp. 66–74.

30. Our definition of organizational purpose (see p. 111) suggests that managers must understand the relationship of their organization to society. This perspective, while essentially accurate, does not emphasize the active debate concerning the proper societal roles (purposes) of business, government, and other types of organizations, and it minimizes both the ambiguity of their roles and the role changes that continue to take place today.

31. Peters and Waterman, *In Search of Excellence;* and Richard Tanner Pascale and Anthony G. Athos, *The Art of Japanese Management: Applications for American Executives* (New York: Simon & Schuster, 1981).

32. Our model of the formal strategic planning process starts with the goal formulation process, but other approaches are also used. For example, the process can start by focusing on current strategies and organizational strengths. The preexisting objectives are accepted with little or no further scrutiny. See Steven C. Wheelwright, "Strategic Planning in the Small Business," *Business Horizons* 14, no. 4 (August 1971):51–58; and Michael B. McCaskey, "A Contingency Approach to Planning: Planning with Goals and Planning without Goals," *Academy of Management Journal* 17, no. 2 (June 1974):281–291.

33. Hofer, *Strategy Formulation*.

34. James M. Utterback, "Environmental Analysis and Forecasting," in Schendel and Hofer, eds., *Strategic Management*, p. 135. See also Utterback's article, pp. 134–144, and Harold E. Klein's commentary on it, pp. 144–151, for discussions on the use of environmental analysis in strategy formulation.

35. Ian C. MacMillan, "Commentary," in Schendel and Hofer, eds., *Strategic Management*, p. 171.

36. See William L. Sammon, Mark A. Kurland, and Robert Spitalnic, *Business Competitor Intelligence* (New York: Wiley, 1984); and Liam Fahey and V. K. Narayanah, *Environmental Analysis* (St. Paul, Minn.: West Publishing, 1986).

37. Hofer, *Strategy Formulation*. The author combines our second and third steps, analysis of existing strategy and environment, into a single step.

38. Strengths and weaknesses may also be related to the structure of organizations. See Ian C. MacMillan and Patricia E. Jones, "Designing Organizations to Compete," *Journal of Business Strategy* 4, no. 4 (Spring 1984):11–26.

39. Richard P. Rumelt, "Evaluation of Strategy: Theory and Models," in Schendel and Hofer, eds., *Strategic Management,* pp. 196–212.

40. See David A. Aaker, "How to Select a Business Strategy," *California Management Review* 26, no. 3 (Spring 1984):167–175. Aaker has suggested that the accuracy of a strategy's evaluation can be increased by including factors beyond sales and profit forecasts, such as judgments of its flexibility, feasibility, consistency with the firm's mission, and responsiveness to the environment.

41. Adapted from Thompson and Strickland, *Strategy Formulation and Implementation* pp. 98–101.

42. See Erwin von Allman, "Setting Up Corporate Planning," in Bernard Taylor and Kevin Hawkins, eds., *A Handbook of Strategic Planning* (London: Longman, 1972), pp. 34–47.

43. See C. Don Burnett, Dennis P. Yeskey, and David Richardson, "New Roles for Corporate Planners in the 1980s," *Journal of Business Strategy* 4, no. 1 (Summer 1983):64–68.

44. Th. P. van Hoorn, "Strategic Planning in Small and Medium-Sized Companies," *Long Range Planning* 12, no. 2 (April 1979):84–91.

45. Frank F. Gilmore, "Formulating Strategies in Smaller Companies," *Harvard Business Review* 49, no. 3 (May–June 1971):81.

46. Richard B. Robinson, Jr., and John W. Pearce II, "Research Thrusts in Small Firm Strategic Planning," *Academy of Management Review* 9, no. 1 (January 1984):128–137.

47. George A. Steiner, "Approaches to Long-Range Planning for Small Businesses," *California Management Review* 10, no. 1 (Fall 1967):3–16.

48. See George H. Rice, Jr., "Strategic Decision Making in Small Business," *Journal of General Management* 9, no. 1 (Autumn 1983):58–65.

49. Differences between not-for-profit and profit-making organizations are discussed by Paul C. Nutt, "A Strategic Planning Network for Nonprofit Organizations," *Strategic Management Journal* 5, no. 1 (January–March 1984):57–75.

50. William H. Newman and Harvey W. Wallender III, "Managing Not-for-Profit Enterprises," *Academy of Management Review* 3, no. 1 (January 1978):26.

51. Max S. Wortman, Jr., quoted in Schendel and Hofer, eds., *Strategic Management,* p. 314.

52. Ibid., p. 314.

53. Ellen Greenberg, in "Competing for Scarce Resources," *Journal of Business Strategy* 2, no. 3 (Winter 1982):81–86, presents a model that not-for-profit organizations can use to analyze their ability to compete for resources. See also Ellen Earle Chaffee, "Successful Strategic Management in Small Private Colleges," *Journal of Higher Education* 55, no. 2 (March–April 1984):212–241.

54. See Steiner, Miner, and Gray, *Management Policy and Strategy* pp. 515–527.

55. Derived from discussion in E. Kirby Warren, *Long-Range Planning: The Executive Viewpoint* (Englewood Cliffs, N.J.: Prentice-Hall, 1966); George A. Steiner, *Top Management Planning* (New York: Macmillan, 1969); and Bernard Taylor, "Strategies for Planning," *Long Range Planning* 8, no. 4 (August 1975):27–40.

56. Derived from discussion in Kjell Ringbakk, "Why Planning Fails," *European Business,* Spring 1971, pp. 16–24.

CASE STUDY: Grafting a Team onto an Idea

"Occasionally," confides Stuart Evans, "I have this awful nightmare. It takes place in Santa Clara, California, or Tokyo, Japan, and it features a little guy in his garage frantically working away on an identical system to our coded tag."

All but the most foolishly cocksure entrepreneurs admit to these fears. But Evans, who has turned his back on a successful career in consulting and risked his house and surplus equity to invest and take over the reins at Cotag International, actually spends more time thinking about new strategies to crack the marketplace than looking over his shoulder for competitors galloping from behind.

Cotag is a typical example of a small technology-led business that, by grafting on marketing and commercial skills, now aims to become a substantial company in the worldwide information technology field. Its latest product—the Cotag—is a system based on miniature identification tags containing a custom-built chip programmed with a unique code or identity. The tag is designed to be attached to a person, animal, or object. When it passes within range of a reading device, this code is read and validated, and the information transferred to a computer for action or storage. The system can be used in production automation, materials handling, vehicle and personnel identification, and agricultural applications such as the management of livestock, among other fields. According to Evans, it can be used "in situations where immediate knowledge of the location and identity of a moving or stationary object can reduce costs and/or improve service levels, control, and safety."

While Evans and his colleagues are confident that they have a significant technological lead on the competition, they recognize that the major challenge is to get the idea out into the marketplace and quickly build up sales.

Formed in 1978 after electronics engineer John Falck and two small businessmen thought up the idea in their sailing club, Cotag initially specialized in the design and manufacture of active radio frequency (RF) transponder systems. The company soon developed its first product, an antishoplifting device that combined good detection and a low incidence of false alarms, and has since shipped 1,000 complete systems itself.

By late 1982, when field trials were being started to test the newly developed coded tag, Falck and his colleagues realized that they lacked the marketing capability to cash in on their obvious technical skills. In a surprisingly bold move for a small firm, they hired Evans, a Harvard MBA who was then a management consultant but whose previous experience included selling with IBM, as managing director. Within a year he was made chief executive officer.

Evans's first major contribution was to redefine the company's market strategy. He saw that the company would do better not to provide entire systems, but would prosper instead as a low-cost provider of parts of larger systems. This process led to the lucrative sale of the marketing rights for the security retailing system. This helped clean up a greatly overstretched balance sheet and finance further development of the company, but it was clear that extra financing would be required for a major marketing push.

In search of cash, Evans gave a presentation before a hard-to-satisfy audience of venture capitalists at a financial forum organized by the British Venture Capital Association, among others. From three serious contenders, Evans chose a London-based syndicate comprising a bank, an investment firm, and an insurance company. "Businessmen should see money just like any other commodity," says Evans. "You should get it as cheaply as possible but also take account of the people who are providing it." Of the three syndicates prepared to offer a deal, he says, one was "too stodgy," and another "wanted to get too closely involved for our liking." Evans and Falck favored the syndicate they eventually selected because it had the same strong market orientation that they possessed.

How can Cotag avoid the fate of so many small electronics groups that are knocked out of the market by a major multinational seizing the market opportunity itself? Says Evans, "The key to marketing will be the establishment of partnerships with other sub-system suppliers and systems integrators in order to provide customers with a total package. The aim is to remain a highly efficient specialist supplier making a small bit of technology that sits on the edge of a network."

Source: Adapted from Tim Dickson, "Grafting a Team onto an Idea," *Financial Times of London,* October 2, 1984, p. 9. Used with permission.

Case Questions
1. Why did John Falck look for a new direction for Cotag International?
2. How did Evans change Cotag's strategy? Why?
3. What market challenges does Cotag face?
4. Outline a future strategy for the company.

6

PROBLEM SOLVING AND DECISION MAKING

Upon completing this chapter you should be able to:

1. Identify the different types of decisions made by managers.
2. Describe the various conditions under which managers make decisions.
3. Explain why managers often settle for a satisfactory decision, rather than trying to make the ideal decision.
4. Explain why an important part of a manager's job is to find the right problem to work on.
5. Explain why it is important for managers to be aware of their own values and backgrounds when they work on problems.
6. Describe the formal problem-solving process and explain why it is preferable to informal methods of problem solving.
7. Describe ways in which managers can improve their decisions and make them more acceptable to subordinates.

People at all levels in an organization must constantly make decisions and solve problems. For managers, the decision-making and problem-solving tasks are particularly important parts of their jobs. How should profits be invested? Which employee should be assigned a particular task? Large problem or small, it is usually the manager who must confront it and decide what action to take. Managers' decisions provide the framework within which other organization members make their decisions and act.

Decision making is thus a key part of a manager's activities. It plays a particularly important role, however, when the manager is engaged in *planning*. Planning involves the most significant and far-reaching decisions a manager can make. In the planning process, managers decide such matters as what goals or opportunities their organization will pursue, what resources will be used, and who will perform each required task. The entire planning process involves managers in a continual series of decision-making situations. How good their decisions are plays a large role in determining how effective their plans will be.

Decision making describes the process by which a course of action is selected as the way to deal with a specific problem. George P. Huber distinguishes decision making from *choice making* and *problem solving*. According to Huber, choice making refers to the narrow set of activities involved in choosing one option from a set of alternative options. So, choice making is one part of decision making. Problem solving refers to the broad set of activities involved in finding *and implementing* a course of action to correct an unsatisfactory situation.[1] Many authors and managers use the terms *decision making* and *problem solving* interchangeably, but in this

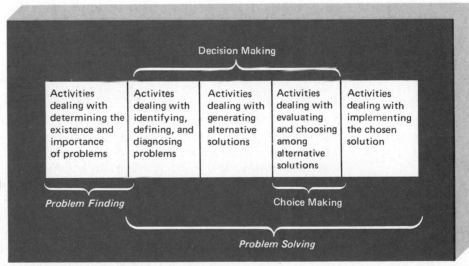

FIGURE 6–1
PROBLEM FINDING, CHOICE MAKING, DECISION MAKING, AND PROBLEM SOLVING

Note: Huber includes "problem identification," which is similar in some respects to problem finding, in the problem-solving process. We have separated problem finding from problem solving to emphasize the importance of making explicit and careful decisions about the problems to work on.

Source: Adapted from *Managerial Decision Making* by George P. Huber. Copyright © 1980 Scott, Foresman and Company. Reprinted by permission.

chapter we will attempt to use them the way Huber does. Figure 6–1 indicates the various types of activities included in each of these categories.

Before problems can be solved they must be found. That is, individuals must determine which situations represent problems and which of these problems should be solved. We will use the term *problem finding* to refer to this process of identifying problems and making the decision to attempt to solve them.[2] In this chapter we will look at problem finding as the basis for effective managerial decisions. We will emphasize the formal decision-making process—how managers systematically go about reaching reasoned and intelligent decisions that can best meet their goals. Implementing and monitoring decisions—the remaining parts of the problem-solving process—are discussed in other parts of the book, so we will not emphasize them in this chapter. Our analysis will conclude in the next chapter with a discussion of several sophisticated methods to improve the effectiveness of problem solving and decision making.

Types of Problems and Decisions

As managers, we will make different types of decisions under different circumstances. When deciding whether or not to add a new wing to the administration building or where to build a new plant, extensive investigation of alternatives and other considerations are necessary. When deciding what salary to pay a new employee, less intensive analysis is involved.

Similarly, the amount of information available to us when making a decision will vary. When a supplier is chosen on the basis of price and past performance, then we can be reasonably confident that the selected supplier will meet our expectations. When deciding to enter a new market, however, there is much less certainty about the outcome. For this reason, we will have to be particularly careful in making decisions when there is little past experience or information to guide us.

Programmed and Nonprogrammed Decisions

Managers have to vary their approach to decision making, depending on the particular situation. It is useful to distinguish between situations that call for programmed decisions and those that call for nonprogrammed decisions.[3]

Programmed decisions are those made in accordance with some habit, rule, or procedure. Every organization has written or unwritten policies that simplify decision making in recurring situations by limiting or excluding alternatives. For example, we would not usually have to worry about what to pay a newly hired employee; organizations generally have an established salary scale for all positions. Routine procedures exist for dealing with routine problems.[4]

Routine problems are not necessarily simple ones; programmed decisions are used for dealing with complex as well as with uncomplicated issues. If a problem recurs, and if its component elements can be defined, predicted, and analyzed, then it may be a candidate for programmed decision making. For example, decisions about how much inventory to maintain on a given product can involve a great deal of fact-finding and forecasting; however, careful analysis of the separate elements in the problem may yield a series of routine, programmed decisions.

To some extent, of course, programmed decisions limit our freedom, because the organization rather than the individual decides what to do. However, programmed decisions are intended to be liberating. The policies, rules, or procedures by which we make programmed decisions free us of the time needed to work out new solutions to old problems, thus allowing us to devote attention to other, more important activities. For example, deciding how to handle customer complaints on an individual basis would be time-consuming and costly, but a policy stating "exchanges will be permitted on all purchases within 14 days" simplifies matters considerably.

We should note, however, that effective managers lean on policy to save time but remain alert for exceptional cases. For example, company policy may put a ceiling on the advertising budget for each product. A particular product, however, may need an extensive advertising campaign to counter the newly aggressive marketing strategy of a competitor. A programmed decision—that is, a decision to advertise the product in accordance with budget guidelines—might be a mistake in this case. Ultimately, managers must use their own judgment in deciding whether a situation calls for a programmed decision.

Nonprogrammed decisions, on the other hand, are those that deal with unusual or exceptional problems. If a problem has not come up often enough to be covered by a policy or is so important that it deserves special treatment, it must be handled by a nonprogrammed decision. Such problems as how to allocate an organization's resources, what to do about a failing product line, how community relations should be improved—in fact, most of the significant problems a manager will face—will usually require nonprogrammed decisions. As one moves up in the organizational hierarchy, the ability to make nonprogrammed decisions becomes more important because progressively more of the decisions made are nonprogrammed.

For this reason, most management development programs try to improve managers' abilities to make nonprogrammed decisions—usually by trying to teach them to analyze problems systematically and to make logical decisions. The decision-making process we describe in this chapter is used mainly for nonprogrammed decisions.

Tools for Making Decisions. Traditional and modern techniques of making both programmed and nonprogrammed decisions are listed in table 6–1. As this table suggests, traditional decision making is giving way to methods using the computer. Computer simulation and data processing now provide rapid means of analyzing recurrent situations. Programmed decisions can be entered into a computer program, and even the means for carrying out the decisions often becomes part of the program as well.

Progress in developing and using the operations research tools referred to in table 6–1 has been rapid in the last 40 years. As the techniques have developed, the efficiency of solving programmed problems and the quality of the solutions have also improved. And many previously nonprogrammed problems have become programmed ones.

In 1962, in an early application of heuristic problem-solving techniques, Geoffrey Clarkson described computer software developed to simulate the complex nonprogrammed decision-making processes used by a bank trust officer to select stocks for a client's portfolio. Detailed information about the general economy, the client's investment objectives, specific industries, and individual companies was entered

TABLE 6–1
TRADITIONAL AND
MODERN
TECHNIQUES OF
DECISION MAKING

Types of Decisions	Decision-Making Techniques	
	Traditional	**Modern**
Programmed: Routine, repetitive decisions Organization develops specific processes for handling them	1. Habit 2. Clerical routine: Standard operating procedures 3. Organization structure: Common expectations A system of subgoals Well-defined informational channels	1. Operations research: Mathematical analysis Models Computer simulation 2. Data processing
Nonprogrammed: One-shot, ill-structured, novel policy decisions Handled by general problem-solving processes	1. Judgment, intuition, and creativity 2. Rules of thumb 3. Selection and training of executives	Heuristic problem-solving technique applied to: a. Training human decision makers b. Constructing heuristic computer programs

Source: Herbert A. Simon, *The New Science of Management Decision,* Revised Edition, p. 48. Copyright 1977. Reprinted by permission of Prentice-Hall, Inc., Englewood Cliffs, N.J.

into the computer's memory. This information became the basis for selecting stocks suitable for investment in specific situations.[5]

Although Clarkson's work was conducted a quarter century ago, progress on heuristic or empirical problem-solving techniques for nonprogrammed decision making has not been as rapid as progress on techniques for programmed decisions. However, as we will discuss in chapter 22, progress on these techniques has accelerated in the last few years.

Decision Support Systems. The *decision support system (DSS),* a computerized information and analysis system, is one application of computer technology that can aid managers in decision making.[6] Recent advances in flexible, user-friendly software for desktop computers are making these systems accessible to nearly all managers regardless of their computer knowledge.[7] These systems have significant advantages over *management information systems (MIS),* which require the manager to work through the organization's centralized data processing system. A DSS combines a separate data base or direct access to information in the organization's data processing system with the ability to analyze that information. The fact that a DSS can be used for on-line data manipulation as well as data retrieval is a major advantage. For example, a marketing research DSS might contain data covering products, prices, sales histories, and other factors that constitute a typical market model. A manager could then use the model to estimate the results of using different prices, advertising expenditures, and so on.

Currently, the heaviest application of DSS is in financial modeling. At TRW, for example, a DSS permits managers to perform in ten minutes financial analyses that formerly took half a day; and managers at Holiday Inns have used DSS to analyze a wide range of situations, from the effects of a rules change on blackjack odds to the effects of a gas crisis on hotel rates.[8] One recent development of DSS is the *group decision support system (GDSS)*. Through the use of GDSS in meetings, decision makers can make more efficient use of information for group decisions.[9]

John Dearden has argued that the effects of computers on the middle manager and small business owner have been pervasive, but less so on top managers who still rely heavily on information passed to them by subordinates.[10] Also, as we shall see later in this chapter, most of the problems forwarded to top managers require nonprogrammed decisions, and, as we just noted, available computer-based techniques for these types of problems are currently few in number. (We will discuss management information, decision support, and related systems more extensively in chapter 22.)

Certainty, Risk, and Uncertainty

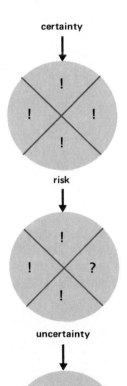

Managers make decisions in the present for actions that will be taken and goals they hope to achieve in the future. All important decision-making situations contain some aspects that are unknowable and very difficult to predict: a specific competitor's reaction, interest rates in three years, the reliability of a new supplier using a promising but unproven technology. Although uncertainty exists in many situations, the amount of uncertainty varies greatly.

In deciding how to attack a problem, managers frequently find it useful to locate the problem on a continuum ranging from predictable situations to situations extremely difficult to predict. Three words to describe different positions on this continuum are: "certainty," "risk," and "uncertainty."[11]

Under conditions of *certainty*, we know what will happen in the future. Under *risk* we know what the probability of each possible outcome is. Under *uncertainty* we do not know the probabilities—and maybe not even the possible outcomes.

Under conditions of certainty, there is accurate, measurable, reliable information available on which to base decisions. The future in this case is highly predictable. Diamond merchants, for example, can be so confident of their relationship with one another, even across international boundaries, that they customarily seal multi-million dollar transactions with a handshake. They can act in complete confidence that their agreements will be honored, informal though those agreements may be.[12]

Where predictability is lower, a condition of risk exists. Complete information is unavailable, but we have a good idea of the probability of particular outcomes. Oil companies, for example, may not know if any particular well will produce oil; but in a drilling program involving a great many wells, good estimates can be made of the number of wells that will be successful.

Under conditions of uncertainty, however, very little is known. For example, managers engaged in international business may face for the first time cultural customs radically different from their own and for which they may have no preparation. In some parts of the world, a written contract does not carry the binding force we associate with it but merely signals the start of a new round of negotiations. Decisions made under these conditions lead to sleepless nights. At the same time, conditions of uncertainty generally accompany our most crucial—and most interesting—decisions.

But managers do have tools at their disposal to make the unknown future a little more comfortable to anticipate and deal with. Although few management situations are likely to fit precisely the definitions of certainty and risk, it is frequently useful for managers to analyze some situations as though they did. The methodology of management science, discussed in the next chapter, is particularly well suited to making viable decisions under these conditions.

The Nature of Managerial Problem Solving

The idea that managers are decision makers may conjure up an image of managers sitting behind their desks, calmly deciding what to do about every problem that arises. In fact, effective managers do not try to solve every problem thrust upon them by subordinates, superiors, and peers; they conserve their time and energy for those problems that really require their decision-making ability. Minor problems are handled by quick judgments or assigned to a subordinate.

Problem and Opportunity Finding

Some problems come to managers, but others must be found. Managers try to anticipate problems, deciding how to prevent them or what to do if they occur. In addition, managers actively seek opportunities, deciding first which opportunities to pursue and then what to do to make them a reality. Since organizations face a great number of problems and opportunities, a critically important skill for managers is the ability to select the right problem or opportunity.

As Guth and Tagiuri have noted, the types of problems and opportunities managers choose to work on are influenced by their values and backgrounds.[13] If managers are motivated primarily by economic values, they usually want to make decisions on practical matters, such as those involving marketing, production, or profits. If they have a more theoretical orientation, they may be concerned with the long-term prospects of their organization. If their orientation is political, they may be more concerned with competing with other organizations or with their own personal advancement.

The backgrounds and expertise of managers will also influence what they see as problems and opportunities. A study of executives by De Witt C. Dearborn and Herbert A. Simon found that managers from different departments will define the same problem in different terms.[14] In this study, a group of executives were presented with a complex business case and asked to describe what they saw as the most important problem facing the company. Each executive tended to be sensitive to those parts of the case that related to his or her department, defining opportunities and problems from his or her particular perspective. For example, marketing managers want inventory to be high and view low inventory as a problem situation. Finance managers, on the other hand, view a high inventory situation as a problem, preferring low inventory in most situations.[15]

Managers' particular sensitivities to certain types of problems and opportunities can sometimes be an advantage, as they may be aware of possibilities that others ignore. But it can also work to the organization's disadvantage, because experts in one area may not see problems and opportunities in other areas. Clarifying their

"Then again, gentlemen, we're in complete agreement in the sense that nobody knows the answer to any of the questions that have been raised."

Drawing by Stan Hunt; © 1983 The New Yorker Magazine, Inc.

own values and being conscious of the blinders imposed by past experiences, training, and successes can help managers guard against seeing only a few of the problems and opportunities facing their organizations.

The Problem-Finding Process

William Pounds has described four situations that alert managers to possible problems: when there is a deviation from past experience, when there is a deviation from a set plan, when other people present problems to the manager, and when competitors outperform the manager's organization.[16]

When there is a *deviation from past experience*, a previous pattern of performance in the organization is broken. This year's sales are falling behind last year's; expenses have suddenly increased; employee turnover has increased. Events such as these are signals to the manager that a problem has developed.

When there is a *deviation from the plan*, the manager's projections or expectations are not being met. Profit levels are lower than anticipated; a department is exceeding its budget; a project is off schedule. Such events tell the manager that something must be done to get the plan back on course.

Other people often bring problems to the manager. Customers complain about late deliveries; higher-level managers set new performance standards for the manager's department; subordinates resign. Many decisions that managers make daily involve problems presented by others.

The *performance of competitors* can also create problem-solving situations for the manager. When other companies develop new processes or improvements in operating procedures, the manager may have to reevaluate processes or procedures in his or her own organization. Competitors within the same organization may also pose problems for the manager. If a company has many plants, for example, top management may compare the performance of each plant. The manager of a plant that is performing below average will have to decide what can be done to bring the plant's performance up to par.

Pounds suggests that management science techniques can also be used to help managers locate problems in addition to solving them. However, such techniques are difficult for many present managers to learn.[17] Pounds found that problem finding is informal and intuitive. Therefore, the four methods described are likely to be those most often used in the years ahead.

A study by Marjorie A. Lyles and Ian I. Mitroff supports Pounds's view that the problem-finding process is informal and intuitive. Lyles and Mitroff collected case histories from upper-level managers of major organizations. Eighty percent of these managers said they had become aware of the existence of a major problem before it showed up on financial statements or as a result of other formal indicators—and even before it was presented to them by superiors or subordinates. "Informal communication and intuition" were described as the sources of their information.[18]

Problem finding is not always straightforward. Sara Kiesler and Lee Sproull have identified some of the more common errors made by managers in sensing problems; these common errors are outlined in the box on the opposite page. Kiesler and Sproull describe three main categories of pitfalls that managers may encounter: false association of events, false expectation of events, and false self-perceptions and social image. For example, under the category of false expectations might be listed the belief among managers of mainframe computer manufacturing companies during the 1960s and early 1970s that a significant demand for personal computers did not and probably would not exist. The idea of a market for personal computers did not fit their expectations.[19]

Opportunity Finding

It is not always clear whether a situation a manager faces presents a problem or an opportunity. For example, missed opportunities create problems for organizations, and opportunities are often found while exploring problems.[20] David B. Gleicher, a management consultant, provides a useful distinction between the two terms. He defines a problem as something that endangers the organization's ability to *reach* its objectives, while an opportunity is something that offers the chance to *exceed* objectives.[21]

False Association of Events	• Wrongly assuming that events are connected because they are similar.
	• Wrongly assuming that events are important causes because they are the focus of attention.
False Expectations of Events	• Wrongly assuming that events did not occur, that in fact did, because they did not fit the expected pattern of events.
	• Wrongly assuming that events have occurred, when they haven't, because they were expected to occur.
	• Failing to take into account surprising or extreme events that contradict expectations.
False Self-Perception and Social Image	• Preferring ambiguous information to hard facts that might reflect badly on previous decisions.
	• Focusing on successful actions while ignoring bad decisions.

Source: Adapted from Sara Kiesler and Lee Sproull, "Managerial Response to Changing Environments: Perspectives on Problem Sensing from Social Cognition," *Administrative Science Quarterly* 27, no. 4 (December 1982): 560.

Henry A. Mintzberg, Duru Raisingham, and André Théorêt distinguish between crises, problems, and opportunities. Their research indicates that crisis decisions are usually triggered by a sudden, single event (a fire or bankruptcy of a key supplier, for example) that requires immediate attention. Problems become apparent through a stream of ambiguous and frequently verbal data stimulated by the accumulation of multiple events. Opportunities, on the other hand, are often evoked by an idea or a single (noncrisis) event. When dealing with problems and opportunities, managers accumulate and process information until a certain threshold is reached. When the threshold is reached, the manager is ready to make a decision. The threshold varies among managers and with the nature of the decision to be made.[22]

The *dialectical inquiry method* is useful in problem solving and opportunity finding.[23] In this method, the decision maker determines possible solutions and the assumptions they are based on, considers the negation, or opposite, of all of his or her assumptions, and then develops counter solutions based on the negative assumptions. This process, in turn, may generate more useful alternative solutions as well as bringing to the forefront any hitherto unnoticed opportunity.

An enormous amount of research has been devoted to problem solving, whereas a very small amount concerns problem finding, and even less concerns opportunity finding. Yet, as Peter Drucker makes clear, opportunities rather than problems are the key to organizational and managerial success. Drucker observes that solving a problem merely restores normality, but results "must come from the exploitation of opportunities." Drucker links exploitation of opportunities to finding "the right things to do, and . . . [concentrating] resources and efforts on them."[24]

Deciding to Decide

refer few problems to a superior

Managers should

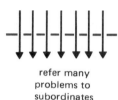

refer many problems to subordinates

As we have seen, some problems come to managers, and some they must locate for themselves. But no manager can possibly handle every problem that arises in the daily course of business. It is important to learn how to establish priorities for problems and to delegate to subordinates responsibility for taking care of the minor ones.

Thus, when managers are presented with a problem, they should ask themselves the following questions:

1. *Is the problem easy to deal with?* Some problems are difficult and expensive to deal with, others are not. Questions such as whether to acquire a subsidiary obviously require extensive consideration. Most problems, however, require only a small amount of the manager's attention. A quick decision is justified in resolving insignificant problems. Even if the decision turns out to be wrong, correcting it will be relatively speedy and inexpensive. To avoid getting bogged down in trivial details, effective and efficient managers reserve formal decision-making techniques for problems that require them. A manager who gives the same level of attention to every problem will get very little work done.

2. *Might the problem resolve itself?* The classic illustration of this principle concerns Napoleon, who was reputed to have let incoming mail pile up on his desk for three weeks or more. When he finally read the accumulated mail, he was pleased to find that most matters had been resolved in the interim. In like manner, managers find that an amazing number of time-wasting problems can be eliminated if they are simply ignored. Therefore, when establishing priorities for dealing with several problems, managers should rank them in order of importance. Those at the bottom of the list usually take care of themselves or can be dealt with by others. If one of these problems worsens, it moves to a higher priority level on the list.

3. *Is this my decision to make?* When confronted with an important problem requiring a decision, a manager must determine if he or she is responsible for making the decision. Here is a general rule that can be of help: The closer to the origin of the problem the decision is made, the better. This rule has two corollaries: (a) Pass as few decisions as possible to those higher up, and (b) pass as many as possible to those lower down. Usually, those who are closest to a problem are in the best position to decide what to do about it.

When managers refer an issue to someone higher up for a decision, they have to be sure they are not simply passing the buck instead of being properly cautious. (Referring a matter to a subordinate is not passing the buck, because the manager still retains ultimate responsibility.) Managers are usually closer to the problem than their superiors, but they must pass along all decisions that would be better or more appropriately made by someone else. How can they decide when they should pass a problem on to a superior? If our basic rule and its corollaries do not supply the answer, managers can supplement them with a few other questions:

· Does the issue affect other departments?
· Will it have a major impact on the superior's area of responsibility?
· Does it require information available only at a higher level?
· Does it involve a serious breach of our departmental budget?
· Is this problem outside my area of responsibility or authority?

A "yes" answer to any of these questions is an indication that the issue should probably be referred to a superior.

The Rational Problem-Solving Process

If a manager is faced with an unusually difficult problem or issue, if it is an important problem that will not resolve itself, and if the manager is the person who must decide what to do about it, then he or she is in a problem-solving situation.[25] Many managers rely on informal problem-solving methods. They may, for example, rely on tradition and make the same decisions that were made when similar problems or opportunities arose in the past. They may also appeal to authority and make a decision based on suggestions from an expert or a higher-level manager. Finally, they may use what philosophers call *a priori reasoning:* They assume that the most superficially logical or obvious solution to a problem is the correct one.[26]

These three methods may be useful in some cases. In others, however, they will lead the manager to make the wrong decision. For example, one company was plagued by a serious quality problem: Too many of the parts it was making were returned because of defects. The obvious management decision was to tighten up quality control procedures. However, this did not solve the problem. Further investigation revealed that the real culprit was excess worker fatigue caused by a faulty ventilation system. In this case, the most obvious solution to the problem was not the correct one.

No approach to decision making can guarantee that a manager will always make the right decision. However, managers who use a rational, intelligent, and systematic approach are more likely than other managers to come up with high-quality solutions to the problems they face.

The basic process of rational decision making is similar to the process of formal strategic planning discussed in chapter 5. It involves diagnosing, defining, and determining the sources of the problem, gathering and analyzing the facts relevant to the problem, developing and evaluating alternative solutions to the problem, selecting the most satisfactory alternative, and converting this alternative into action. The model of this process that we shall use consists of four major stages. (See fig. 6–2.)[27]

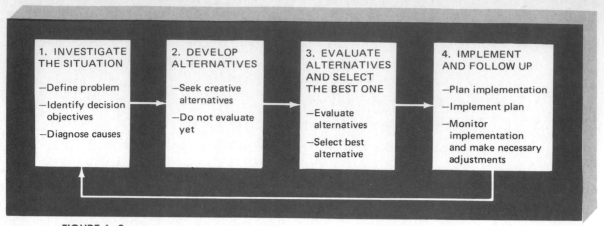

FIGURE 6–2
THE RATIONAL
PROBLEM-SOLVING
PROCESS

Stage 1: Investigate the Situation

The problem-solving process begins when the problem has been identified for action. The manager's first task is to search for all the factors that may have created the problem or may be incorporated into the eventual solution. A thorough investigation has three aspects: problem definition, identification of objectives, and diagnosis.

Define the Problem. Confusions in problem definition arise in part because the events or issues that attract the manager's attention may be symptoms of another, more fundamental and pervasive difficulty. A manager may be concerned about an upsurge in employee resignations, but the increase in employee turnover is not a problem unless it interferes with the achievement of organizational objectives. If the individuals resigning are relatively low performers and more qualified people can be readily found to replace them, the resignations may represent an opportunity rather than a problem. Curing the turnover problem, then, may be the last thing the manager should do. Defining the problem in terms of the organizational objectives that are being blocked helps to avoid confusing symptoms and problems.

Identify the Decision Objectives. Once the problem has been defined, the next step is to decide what would constitute an effective solution. How will things be different when the problem has been solved? As part of this process, managers should begin to determine which parts of the problem they *must* solve and which they *should* try to solve. Most problems consist of several elements, and a manager is unlikely to find one solution that will work for all of them. Managers therefore need to distinguish between their "musts" and their "shoulds" so that they will have a basis for proposing and evaluating alternative solutions. For example, if we have a staffing problem, we *must* hire someone who can do a good job in a difficult position at a certain salary. And we *should* hire someone who has had some experience and who will fit in well with others in the organization. We can eliminate all candidates who do not meet our "musts" criteria; and we will evaluate all the other candidates by how well they meet our "shoulds."

If our solution enables us to achieve our organizational objectives, it is a successful one. More ambitious objectives, however, may be appropriate. The immediate problem may be an indicator of future difficulties that we can prevent by taking early action. Or the problem may offer the opportunity to improve, rather than merely restore, organizational performance.

Diagnose the Causes. When managers have found a satisfactory solution, they must determine the actions that will achieve it. But first, they must obtain a solid understanding of all the sources of the problem so they can formulate hypotheses about the causes. They should ask such questions as: What changes inside or outside the organization may have contributed to the problem? What people are most involved with the problem situation? Do they have insights or perspectives that may clarify the problem? Do their actions contribute to the problem?

Causes, unlike symptoms, are seldom apparent, and managers have to rely on intuition to ferret them out. Different individuals, whose views of the situation are inevitably colored by their own experiences and responsibilities, may perceive very different causes for the same problem. It is up to the manager to put all the pieces together and come up with as clear a picture as possible.

Stage 2: Develop Alternatives

The temptation to accept the first feasible alternative too often prevents managers from achieving the best solutions to their problems. Developing a number of alternatives allows them to resist the temptation to solve their problems too quickly and makes reaching an effective decision more likely.

No major decision should be made until several alternatives have been developed. Problem solving at this stage frequently requires finding creative and imaginative alternatives. (Chapter 14 offers some techniques managers can use to uncover original and unusual alternative solutions for complex problems.)

Another temptation often interferes with the development of an adequate number of alternatives: the inclination to appraise alternatives as they are developed. This temptation, too, should be resisted. Evaluation at this stage is premature, preventing managers from generating other viable alternatives.

Stage 3: Evaluate Alternatives and Select the Best One

Once managers have developed a set of alternatives, they must evaluate them to see how effective each would be. Effectiveness can be measured by two criteria: how realistic the alternative is in terms of the goals and resources of the organization, and how well the alternative will help solve the problem.

Each alternative must be judged in light of the goals and resources of the organization. An alternative may seem logical, but if it cannot be implemented, it is useless. For example, if sales are high but profits are declining, we may want to reduce overhead costs. If costs have already been cut sharply, however, or if further cuts would reduce the quality of the product, this alternative may not be feasible.

In addition, each alternative must be judged as to its consequences for the organization. Will new problems arise when a particular course of action is followed? Managers must determine how willing their subordinates will be to carry out a decision and what might happen if the decision is not implemented wholeheartedly. Practical problems may be involved in implementing the decision, such as the need to obtain additional funding. Other departments in the organization that would be affected by the decision must be consulted.[28] Competitors may be affected by the decision, and their reactions will have to be taken into account.

Each alternative must also be evaluated in terms of how well it will achieve the "musts" and "shoulds" of the problem. In some cases managers may be able to experiment with possible solutions by trying one or more of the alternatives in different parts of their organization to see which is most effective. In other cases, they may use simulation techniques to explore the possible outcomes of alternative solutions. But usually they will simply use their knowledge, judgment, and experience to decide which alternatives are most attractive.

The selected alternative will be based on the amount of information available to the managers and their imperfect judgment. More likely than not, the selected alternative will also represent a compromise among the various factors that have been considered. (Some modern tools to help managers evaluate and choose among alternatives are described in chapter 7.)

Stage 4: Implement the Decision and Follow Up on It

Once the best available alternative has been selected, managers must make plans to cope with the requirements and problems that may be encountered in putting it into effect.[29]

Implementing a decision involves more than giving appropriate orders. Resources must be acquired and allocated as necessary. Managers set up budgets and schedules for the actions they have decided upon. This allows them to measure progress in specific terms. Next, they assign responsibility for the specific tasks involved. They also set up a procedure for progress reports and prepare to make corrections if new problems should arise.

Potential risks and uncertainties have been identified during the earlier evaluation-of-alternatives stage, and these must be kept in mind. There is a human tendency to forget possible risks and uncertainties once a decision is made. (In the *theory of cognitive dissonance,* this process is known as *dissonance reduction.*) By taking extra time to reexamine their decision at this point and to develop detailed plans for dealing with these risks and uncertainties, managers can counteract this tendency.[30]

After managers have taken whatever steps are possible to deal with adverse consequences if they arise, actual implementation can begin. Ultimately, a decision (or a solution) is no better than the actions taken to make it a reality. A frequent error of managers is to assume that once they make a decision, action on it will automatically follow. If the decision is a good one, but subordinates are unwilling or unable to carry it out, then that decision will not be effective.

Actions taken to implement a decision must be monitored. Are things working according to plan? What is happening in the internal and external environments as a result of the decision? Are subordinates performing according to expectations? What is the competition doing in response? Decision making is a continual process for managers—and a continual challenge.

Improving the Effectiveness of Managerial Problem Solving

Norman Maier has isolated two criteria by which a decision's potential effectiveness can be appraised. The first is the *objective quality* of the decision, and the second is the *acceptance* by those who must execute it.[31]

The objective quality of the decision is determined by how well the formal decision-making process is carried out. The manager has a choice of making decisions alone or with the help of others. However, there is little choice when it comes to implementation. A number of people are almost always involved in implementing decisions; gaining their acceptance and cooperation is essential.

Improving Individual Problem Solving

Most managers realize that an apparently excellent decision—that is, one based on information that has been gathered, analyzed, and evaluated effectively—may turn out poorly because of an unforeseeable event. Conversely, an unlikely and unpredictable event may turn a bad or illogical decision into a fortunate choice. Even if a decision works as well as predicted, a manager can never be completely sure another one would not have been equally effective or even better.

Most managers also agree that decisions should be evaluated on the basis of the situation at the time they were made, rather than second-guessed after the results are in. However, bosses, peers, and subordinates tend to be blessed with 20/20 hindsight, and the temptation to second-guess a manager's decision is difficult to resist, especially if the results are disappointing.

For these and other reasons, most managers experience some tension in deciding how to go about solving a problem and then implementing the solution. They know they will frequently be evaluated according to the success or failure of their solution, and they know that almost all second-guessing will be aimed at their less successful decisions. It is not unusual for people in such situations to set up barriers to problem solving or to devote time and energy to developing justifications for avoiding difficult problems that confront them. To make effective decisions, managers must first overcome the barriers that discourage them from recognizing and attacking emerging problems in their organizations.

Barriers to Managerial Problem Solving. Irving L. Janis and Leon Mann have identified four defective problem-recognition and problem-solving approaches that can hinder people who must make important decisions.[32] (See fig. 6–3.)

1. *Relaxed avoidance:* The manager decides not to decide or act after noting that the consequences of inaction will not be very great. This might be the attitude of a manager who has been informed by a superior that a promotion will depend on improved performance. Learning through the grapevine that the superior may be dismissed, the manager does nothing. But if she or he did not know of the superior's shaky position, that same manager would eagerly work harder and put in longer hours.

2. *Relaxed change:* The manager decides to take some action, noting that the consequences of doing nothing will be serious. However, rather than analyzing the situation, the manager takes the first available alternative that appears, on the surface, to involve low risk. Careful analysis is avoided.

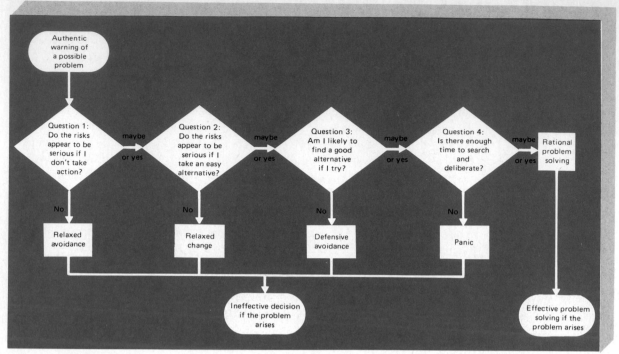

FIGURE 6-3
EFFECTIVE AND
INEFFECTIVE
PROBLEM-SOLVING
APPROACHES

3. *Defensive avoidance:* Faced with a problem and unable to find a good solution based on past experience, this manager seeks a way out. He or she may put off considering the consequences or may try buck passing. He or she may let someone else make the decision (and suffer the consequences) or simply ignore the risks and choose the most obvious solution. This resigned posture may prevent consideration of more viable alternatives.

4. *Panic:* The manager feels pressured not only by the problem itself but by time. This produces a high level of stress that may manifest itself in sleeplessness, irritability, nightmares, and other forms of agitation. In extreme form, physical illness may result. In the panic state the individual may be so agitated that he or she is unable to appraise the situation realistically or accept help from subordinates. And given inappropriate handling, the situation is likely to deteriorate.

Managers who react to problems in the above ways often opt for a simplistic approach to decisions. A frequent method is *incremental adjustment,* choosing an alternative that represents only a minor change from existing policies.[33] In many instances this is indeed the most sensible approach, because it avoids extensive investigation of the problem and thus saves time and money. It presents the manager with familiar, nonspeculative, and relatively stable and predictable data for analysis. But such an approach often results in inferior solutions because it is a substitute for gathering new information and for innovative thinking. When managers use incremental adjustment, it is highly unlikely that new ideas will be considered; and it is quite likely that long-run advantages will be sacrificed to short-term gains.

Limitations of Rational Problem Solving. Even when managers attempt to use a rational problem-solving approach, mistakes still arise from limitations in their ability to acquire and use information. Information in any situation is almost always incomplete. Time and cost may prevent acquisition of certain data; other data, especially those relating to the future, may simply not exist.

Most complex decisions involve too many variables for one person to be able to examine them all fully. And individuals give differing weights to the facts they do possess. In organizational life, managers act within what Herbert Simon has called *bounded rationality*; that is, they make the most logical decisions they can, limited by their inadequate information and by their ability to utilize that information. Rather than seeking the best or ideal decision, managers frequently settle for a decision that will adequately serve their purposes. In Simon's terms, they *satisfice*, or accept the first satisfactory decision they uncover, rather than *maximize*, or search until they find the optimal decision.[34]

As managers, we will rarely have the mental ability, time, or information we need to make perfect decisions. Moreover, some problems, perhaps most problems, simply cannot be solved to perfection. This does not mean, of course, that managers must give up trying to make the best possible decisions. It simply means they must recognize that at some point it will become too expensive, time-consuming, or difficult to acquire additional information or attempt to analyze it, and that the consequences of decisions cannot always be foreseen.[35]

Overcoming Barriers to Individual Problem Solving. Familiarity with the rational problem-solving process described earlier gives managers confidence in their ability to understand and deal with difficult situations. This confidence is important for two reasons. First, it increases the likelihood that managers will actively try to locate problems, and opportunities, in their organizations. And second, it increases the likelihood that they will, in fact, find good solutions to the problems they confront.

In addition to using the rational problem-solving process, there are other specific ways individuals can manage their decision making more effectively.

1. *Set priorities.* Managers are faced with numerous problems and tasks daily. Sometimes the sheer quantity of the workload is overwhelming. To avoid being snowed under by tasks and unfinished business, managers should review the priorities of their workload daily. After setting, or resetting, priorities, they should allocate time according to those priorities. (Some effective managers review their priorities and replan their work a number of times a day.)[36]

2. *Acquire relevant information.* George P. Huber has defined specific categories of information relevant in decision making.[37] *Basic information* provides the essential structure of the decision situation and is derived in the course of identifying the problem and developing alternatives. Basic information includes the alternatives that can be identified and the likely consequences of choosing each alternative; the relevant events that may occur in the future (the management scientist calls these future conditions "states of nature"); and the possible criteria that can be used to evaluate the eventual decisions and solutions.

Elaborating information focuses the basic information and helps us evaluate alternatives. One of its two components includes the probabilities of future states of nature and the likelihood that the anticipated consequence of each alternative will actually occur. The other component is the relative importance of each criterion in achieving the organization's objectives.

Performance information is the outcome, or payoff, for the organization of various courses of action. One component is the gain or loss for the organization deriving from the various alternatives. The most frequently discussed criterion for determining gains and losses in businesses is, of course, profit, but many other candidates exist. The second component is the constraints that a solution must meet: a maximum budget figure or a minimum sales level, for example. These are the "musts" we described above—just as the gain or loss criteria can be thought of as "shoulds." (Some criteria may be both: For example, profit *should* be as high as feasible, but it *must* be at least $500,000.)

Not all of these kinds of information are equally relevant to a given problem, but all are important in some situations and most come into play when a major or complex decision must be made.

3. *Proceed methodically and carefully.* Many forms of the rational problem-solving model outlined above exist, but none of them work well if they are not used well. In following a rational problem-solving model (see pp. 151–154), managers should keep in mind some common mistakes. For example, in stage 1 many people tend to define a problem in terms of only one possible solution, to focus on lower priority goals, or to diagnose the problem in terms of its symptoms but not its underlying causes. In stage 2, when alternatives are being developed, there is a tendency to evaluate them right away; this prevents creation of a sufficient number of alternatives. In stage 3, evaluating alternatives, people fail to use information systematically, and tend to proceed in hit-or-miss fashion. Finally (in stage 4), mistakes crop up during implementation. Managers may not motivate staff members or give them clear instructions; they sometimes do not gain acceptance of the decision, allocate appropriate resources, or provide in advance the information needed to monitor the solution program.[38] By knowing these common pitfalls, we can avoid them as we make and follow through on decisions.

Deciding Who Decides

Managers make decisions as individuals, and managers involve other individuals in the decision-making process. The first decision a manager must make is: Who will decide? In making this decision, Maier's concepts of objective quality and acceptance are useful guidelines.

As we noted earlier (see p. 155), the objective quality of the decision is determined by how well the manager carries out some form of the rational problem-solving process. In doing so, the manager may work alone or may be involved with many other individuals. If the problem is properly defined and diagnosed, facts gathered and evaluated carefully, attractive alternatives developed and well evaluated, then the resulting decision should have high objective quality. Maier suggests that where the problem is largely a technical one, a quality decision may be enough to solve it.

If people are involved in the problem, however, then a quality decision may not be sufficient, according to Maier. The acceptance of the people involved may also be required to make it effective. A difficulty arises for managers if "quality" considerations conflict with "acceptance" considerations. The decision that objectively would work best may not be acceptable to the people affected. On the other hand, the decision most favored by subordinates may not be the best one for the organization.

Involving Others: Quality and Acceptance. Traditionally, the final responsibility for making decisions belongs to managers, who may have to persuade or compel subordinates to obey. But this approach is not always appropriate. Sometimes subordinates have excellent reasons for resisting a decision. Perhaps they are aware, for example, of alternatives or relevant factors that were not considered in the original analysis. In such cases, a managerial decision may fail because the manager is unable to convince subordinates to carry it out willingly. In other cases, subordinates may implement a decision loyally even though they disagree with it, but the results will be poor because the decision was poor.

Maier recommends that managers evaluate each problem to see how important quality and acceptance are in its solution. Managers can then increase their effectiveness by tailoring their decision procedures to the particular problem. In some problems, quality is very important but acceptance is not. High quality/low acceptance problems tend to involve technical details such as those concerned in purchasing, engineering, and finance—areas where the manager's specialized knowledge is important. If the manager has all of the knowledge and skills required, these problems can be solved effectively by the individual manager working alone.

With some problems, however, high acceptance is a crucial factor and quality is relatively unimportant. These can best be solved through group decision making, because a solution that is not accepted by those involved is likely to fail. A problem concerning the work conditions of subordinates, such as the rearrangement of office space, may be a high acceptance/low quality decision.

Finally, some decisions must have both high quality and high acceptance. For these problems, group decision making is also frequently the most effective approach. The skills of the manager and subordinates in handling group processes is a key factor in determining both the quality and acceptance of the resulting decisions. There is strong evidence that commitment to decisions is usually increased when employees are involved in the decision-making process. (See chapters 13 and 15.)

When subordinates are given the responsibility for dealing with a problem, their self-esteem increases and they take pride in their demonstrated value to the organization. Of course, there are disadvantages as well as advantages to involving a number of individuals in the problem-solving process. Because individuals' time is valuable, we should involve them when the benefits—quality, acceptance, morale, development—are greater than the likely costs in time, money, or the frustration of employees who feel they should not be involved.

When to Involve Subordinates: A Model

In an extension of Maier's work, Victor Vroom and Philip Yetton have developed a method to help managers decide when and to what extent they should involve subordinates in solving a particular problem.[39] First, Vroom and Yetton isolated five styles of decision making that represent a continuum from authoritarian decision-making approaches (AI, AII) to consultative (CI, CII), to a fully participative one (GII). (See box and fig. 6–4 on following pages.)

AI Managers solve the problem or make the decision themselves, using information available at that time.

AII Managers obtain the necessary information from subordinate(s), then decide on the solution to the problem themselves. They may or may not tell subordinates what the problem is when they request information. The role played by subordinates in making the decision is clearly one of providing the necessary information to managers, rather than generating or evaluating alternative solutions.

CI Managers share the problem with relevant subordinates individually, getting their ideas and suggestions without bringing them together as a group. Then managers make the decision that may or may not reflect subordinates' influence.

CII Managers share the problem with subordinates as a group, collectively obtaining their ideas and suggestions. Then they make the decision that may or may not reflect subordinates' influence.

GII Managers share a problem with subordinates as a group. Managers and subordinates together generate and evaluate alternatives and attempt to reach agreement (consensus) on a solution. Managers do not try to influence the group to adopt their preferred solution, and they accept and implement any solution that has the support of the entire group.

Source: Adapted, by permission of the publisher, from "A New Look at Managerial Decision Making," by Victor H. Vroom, *Organizational Dynamics,* Spring 1973, p. 67. © 1973 by AMACOM, a division of American Management Associations, New York. All rights reserved.

The authors then suggest several questions that managers can ask themselves to help determine which decision-making style to use for the particular problem they are facing:

· **Do we have enough information or skill to solve the problem on our own?** If not, then AI, where we make the decision ourselves, would be inappropriate.

· **Do we need to make a high-quality decision that our subordinates are likely to disagree with?** If so, GII, where we seek the consensus of the group, would not be appropriate. In this case, giving up our authority to make the final decision would probably mean that the decision would not have the objective quality the problem requires.

· **Is the problem structured?** That is, do we know what information we need and where to get it? If not, then CII and GII, which allow for the greatest group interaction, would be preferable. The other styles would either keep us from getting the information we need or supply us with information in an inefficient manner.

FIGURE 6-4 DECISION MODEL SHOWING FEASIBLE SET OF ALTERNATIVES

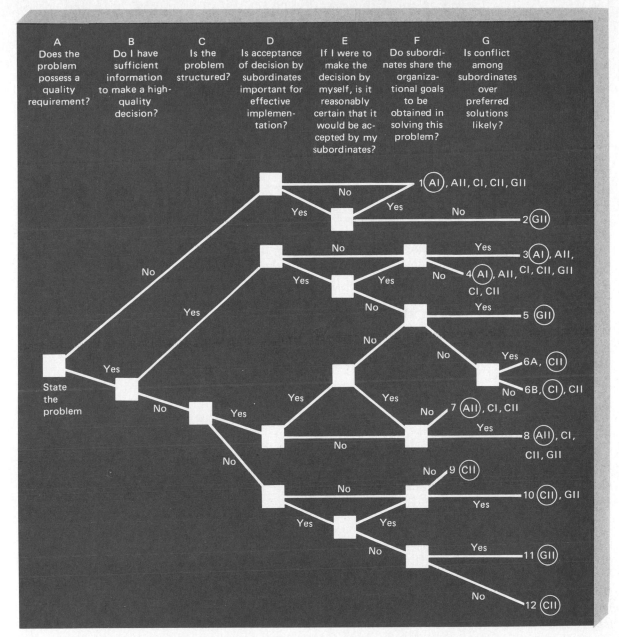

This model shows the preferred management styles for various types of problems. The most "time-efficient" feasible alternative for each problem is circled. (See also the box on the opposite page.)

Source: Adapted, by permission of the publisher, from "A New Look at Managerial Decision Making," by Victor H. Vroom, *Organizational Dynamics*, Summer 1973, p. 70. Copyright © 1973 by AMACOM, a division of American Management Associations, New York. All rights reserved.

- Is the acceptance of the group critical for the success of the decision? If so, then styles AI and AII, which involve subordinates the least, might not be appropriate.
- If acceptance of the decision is important, are our subordinates likely to disagree among themselves about which is the best solution? If so, then styles CII and GII, which involve group decision making, are preferable. Only within the group can differences between subordinates be discussed openly and ultimately resolved. The other styles might leave some subordinates dissatisfied with the decision.

Depending on the nature of the problem, more than one decision-making style may be suitable, or feasible. Vroom and Yetton call this suitable group the "feasible set of alternatives." (See fig. 6–4.) Where there are feasible choices, the manager may freely choose among them because both decision quality and acceptance have been taken into account. As guidance for choosing within a feasible set, Vroom and Yetton suggest two criteria:

1. When decisions must be made quickly or time must be saved, managers should choose authoritarian decision styles ("time-efficient" ones). The payoffs for these choices will occur in the short run, in the form of quicker, more efficient decisions. (Figure 6–4 indicates the approaches that may be feasible in a given problem-solving situation. The most time-efficient solutions are circled.)
2. When managers wish to develop their subordinates' knowledge and decision-making skills, the more participative styles ("time-investment") should be selected. The payoffs for these choices will occur in the longer run, in the form of more effective subordinates and perhaps better working relationships. (In figure 6–4, the most participative style is the last one in each feasible set.)

Vroom and others have conducted research and concluded that decisions consistent with this model tend to be successful, and those inconsistent with the model's recommendation are generally unsuccessful. In addition, subordinates appear to prefer their managers' making decisions consistent with the model.[40] Perhaps the strongest contribution of the Vroom and Yetton approach is the fact that it moves the debate about whether or not to use participative approaches out of the "always" or "never" arena. Their approach, an example of the contingency approaches we discussed in chapter 1, provides guidelines concerning *when* authoritarian or participative approaches should be used and *how much* involvement by subordinates is desirable. Figure 6–4 shows that group problem solving is sometimes the recommended alternative. Because the management of group problem solving is so important to the management of today's organizations, we will be examining it closely in chapter 17.

Summary

Managers must solve problems and make decisions. The types of problems and the conditions under which they must be solved vary. Decision-making approaches, therefore, must be tailor-made to fit particular circumstances.

Programmed decisions are those that are made by habit or policy. Nonprogrammed decisions, on the other hand, are made under new or unusual conditions and require creative thinking and rational consideration. This chapter is concerned with nonprogrammed decision making.

Managers make decisions with varying amounts of information. Therefore, it is frequently useful for managers to approach decisions as though they were being made under conditions of certainty, risk, or uncertainty. Under conditions of certainty, managers assume they know precisely the results of each of the available alternatives. Under conditions of risk, they act as though they know the probabilities of the outcomes of each alternative. Under conditions of uncertainty, the outcome probabilities are assumed not to be known. Decision support systems (DSS) are increasingly important in providing managers with adequate information and analysis on which to base decisions.

Effective managers do not merely wait for problems to arise; they actively look for problems and opportunities. One of the more significant responsibilities of managers is deciding which problems and opportunities should receive their full attention. Opportunity finding, problem finding, and problem solving are all important managerial activities. Although opportunity finding is the most important of these three processes, it is the least understood.

It is often useful for managers to follow formal and rational procedures for solving problems. One model of that process can be described in four stages: (1) define, diagnose, and find the sources of the problem; (2) develop alternatives; (3) evaluate the alternatives and select the best one; and (4) implement the selected alternative and follow up on the implementation.

Although managers are presented with many problem situations in the course of their daily activities, not all of them require the formal problem-solving process. Ranking problems in the order of importance, or setting priorities and making daily schedules, helps managers decide which ones should receive their immediate and full attention.

In opportunity and problem finding and in problem solving, managers should rely heavily on the insights and energies of subordinates. This is especially important if the subordinates' acceptance of the decision is necessary for it to succeed and if they play a major role in its implementation. The extent to which managers and subordinates should jointly make decisions depends on the type of problem and the conditions under which the decision is being made.

Review Questions

1. What is the difference between planning, choice making, and decision making?
2. Contrast programmed and nonprogrammed decisions.
3. What are the differences between decisions made under conditions of uncertainty, certainty, and risk? Why do managers try to assess probabilities before reaching a decision?
4. What are some decision-making techniques useful for resolving programmed and non-programmed decisions?
5. What is the principal difference between problem finding and opportunity finding?
6. What are three questions managers should ask when they are presented with a problem?
7. Describe the four basic stages in the rational problem-solving process.
8. What does Norman R. F. Maier suggest for improving the effectiveness of managerial problem solving?
9. Describe the limitations of rational problem solving suggested by Herbert Simon.
10. What are the five styles of managerial decision making suggested by Vroom and Yetton? Which style appeals to you most?

Notes

1. George P. Huber, *Managerial Decision Making* (Glenview, Ill.: Scott, Foresman, 1980), pp. 8, 9.
2. See William F. Pounds, "The Process of Problem Finding," *Industrial Management Review* 11, no. 1 (Fall 1969):1–19.
3. These terms are from the computer field. A program provides the computer with a sequence of

coded instructions for carrying out tasks. See Herbert A. Simon, *The Shape of Automation* (New York: Harper & Row, 1965), pp. 58–67.

4. See also Herbert A. Simon, *The New Science of Management Decision,* rev. ed. (Englewood Cliffs, N.J.: Prentice-Hall, 1977), pp. 45–49.

5. See Geoffrey P. E. Clarkson, *Portfolio Selection: A Simulation of Trust Investment* (Englewood Cliffs, N.J.: Prentice-Hall, 1962), and "A Model of the Trust Investment Process," in Edward A. Feigenbaum and Julian Feldman, eds., *Computers and Thought* (New York: McGraw-Hill, 1963), pp. 347–371. Simon (note 4 above) also describes how modern management techniques, and especially data processing, have been able to transfer complex problems from the area of nonprogrammed decision making to the area of programmed decision making.

6. For more information on the range of DSS applications, see Ernest A. Kallman and Leon Reinharth, *Information Systems for Planning and Decision Making* (New York: Van Nostrand Reinhold, 1984).

7. The following discussion and examples of DSS are derived from "Fourth-Generation Languages Make DSS Feasible for All Managers," *Management Review* 73, no. 4 (April 1984):4–5.

8. "Sometimes You Must Learn Decision Support Pitfalls the Hard Way," *Infosystems* 31, no. 6 (June 1984):12.

9. See George P. Huber, "Issues in the Design of Group Decision Support Systems," *MIS Quarterly* 8, no. 3 (September 1984):195–204.

10. John Dearden, "Will the Computer Change the Job of Top Management?" *Sloan Management Review* 25, no. 1 (Fall 1983):57–60.

11. See F. H. Knight, *Risk, Uncertainty, and Profit* (New York: Harper & Brothers, 1920); and Stephen A. Archer, "The Structure of Management Decision Theory," *Academy of Management Journal* 7, no. 4 (December 1964):269–287.

12. Murray Schumach, *The Diamond People* (New York: Norton, 1981).

13. See William D. Guth and Renato Tagiuri, "Personal Values and Corporate Strategy," *Harvard Business Review* 37, no. 5 (September–October 1965):123–132.

14. De Witt C. Dearborn and Herbert A. Simon, "Selective Perception: A Note on the Departmental Identification of Executives," *Sociometry* 21, no. 2 (June 1958):140–144.

15. Robert J. Graham, "'Give the Kid a Number': An Essay on the Folly and Consequences of Trusting Your Data," *Interfaces* 12, no. 2 (June 1982):41.

16. Pounds, "The Process of Problem Finding." See also Peter F. Drucker, *The Practice of Management* (New York: Harper & Brothers, 1954), pp. 351–354.

17. A useful model of how problems are recognized and dealt with by organizations is provided by Thomas P. Ference, "Organizational Communications Systems and the Decision Process," *Management Science* 17, no. 2 (October 1970):B83–B96.

18. Marjorie A. Lyles and Ian I. Mitroff, "Organizational Problem Formulation: An Empirical Study," *Administrative Science Quarterly* 25, no. 1 (March 1980):102–119. For a discussion of the use of intuition by managers, see Thomas S. Isaack, "Intuition: An Ignored Dimension of Management," *Academy of Management Review* 3, no. 4 (October 1978):917–922; and W. H. Agor, "Tomorrow's Intuitive Leaders," *Futurist,* August 1983, pp. 49–53.

19. Sara Kiesler and Lee Sproull, "Managerial Response to Changing Environments," *Administrative Science Quarterly* 27, no. 4 (December 1982):548–570.

20. The author uses the phrase "the Pollyanna theory of management" to describe the belief that every problem has an opportunity embedded in it. Robert J. Graham uses the maxim that "problems are merely opportunities in disguise" in "Problem and Opportunity Identification in Management Science," *Interfaces* 6, no. 4 (August 1976):79–82.

21. Personal communication.

22. Henry A. Mintzberg, Duru Raisingham, and André Théorêt, "The Structure of 'Unstructured' Decision Processes," *Administrative Science Quarterly* 21, no. 2 (June 1976):246–275.

23. For a discussion of dialectical inquiry, see Richard A. Cosier, "Approaches to the Experimental Examination of the Dialectic," *Strategic Management Journal* 4, no. 1 (January–March 1983):79–84; and Lyle Sussman and Richard Herden, "Dialectical Problem Solving," *Business Horizons,* January–February 1982, pp. 66–71.

24. Peter F. Drucker, *Managing for Results* (New York: Harper & Row, 1964), p. 5. See also J. Sterling Livingston, "Myth of the Well-Educated Manager," *Harvard Business Review* 49, no. 1 (January–February 1971): 79–89.

25. In this section we will use the terms *problem solving* and *decision making* more or less interchangeably because most of our discussion focuses on the decision-making portion of the total process.

26. Francis J. Bridges, Kenneth W. Olm, and J. Allison Barnhill, *Management Decisions and Organizational Policy* (Boston: Allyn and Bacon, 1971).

27. The discussion that follows is based on John Dewey, *How We Think* (Boston: Heath, 1933), pp. 102–118; Drucker, *The Practice of Management,* pp. 354–365; Charles H. Kepner and Benjamin B. Tregoe, *The Rational Manager: A Systematic Approach to Problem Solving and Decision Making* (New York: McGraw-Hill, 1965); and Ernest R. Archer, "How to Make a Business Decision: An Analysis of Theory and Practice," *Management Review* 69, no. 2 (February 1980):43–47. We have adapted and modified Archer's approach for our basic model.

28. A "corporate devil's advocate" who would specifically search for the flaws in solutions has been suggested by Theodore T. Herbert and Ralph W. Estes in "Improving Executive Decisions by Formalizing Dissent: The Corporate Devil's Advocate," *Academy of Management Review* 2, no. 4 (October 1977):662–667.

29. Charles H. Kepner and Benjamin B. Tregoe, *The Rational Manager: A Systematic Approach to Problem Solving and Decision Making* (New York: McGraw-Hill, 1965), pp. 190–194.

30. Leon Festinger, *Conflict, Decision, and Dissonance* (Stanford, Calif.: Stanford University Press, 1964), p. 182.

31. Norman R. F. Maier, *Problem-Solving Discussions and Conferences: Leadership Methods and Skills* (New York: McGraw-Hill, 1963).

32. Irving L. Janis and Leon Mann, *Decision Making: A Psychological Analysis of Conflict, Choice, and Commitment* (New York: Free Press, 1977). We have used a somewhat different terminology for their four approaches.

33. Charles E. Lindblom, *The Intelligence of Democracy* (New York: Free Press, 1965), pp. 143–145.

34. Herbert A. Simon, *Models of Man: Social and Rational* (New York: Wiley, 1957). See also James G. March and Herbert A. Simon, *Organizations* (New York: Wiley, 1958); Herbert A. Simon, *Administrative Behavior,* 3rd ed. (New York: Free Press, 1976); Herbert A. Simon, *Reason in Human Affairs* (Stanford, Calif.: Stanford University Press, 1983), pp. 12–23; and Anna Grandori, "A Prescriptive Contingency View of Organizational Decision Making," *Administrative Science Quarterly* 29, no. 2 (June 1984):192–209.

35. Paul Shrivastava and Ian I. Mitroff have noted that managers have not adopted many of the sophisticated decision-making methods devised by academics because such approaches rarely work in the unstructured situations that managers face; see "Enhancing Operational Research Utilization: The Role of Decision Makers' Assumptions," *Academy of Management Review* 9, no. 1 (January 1984):18–26.

36. This process is known as time management, and it may be the single most important way for managers to improve their overall efficiency. Some useful books are Kenneth Blanchard and Spencer Johnson, *The One-Minute Manager* (New York: Morrow, 1982), which emphasizes a process for establishing and remaining focused on a limited set of priorities ("one-minute goal-setting"); and Peter Turla and Katherine Hawkins, *Time Management Made Easy* (New York: Dutton, 1984).

37. Huber, *Managerial Decision Making,* pp. 30–40.

38. Ibid., pp. 11–12.

39. Victor H. Vroom and Philip W. Yetton, *Leadership and Decision Making* (Pittsburgh: University of Pittsburgh Press, 1973). This model has been subsequently refined by Vroom and Art Jago. We will refer to it throughout the text as the Vroom-Yetton model since this is now its standard title. Also see Victor H. Vroom, "Reflections on Leadership and Decision-Making," *Journal of General Management* 9, no. 3 (Spring 1984):18–36.

40. Vroom, "Reflections on Leadership and Decision-Making." Supporters of the model and challengers have studied it extensively. See, for example, Arthur Jago, "A Test of Spuriousness in Descriptive Models of Participative Leader Behavior," *Journal of Applied Psychology* 63, no. 3 (June 1978):383–387; R. H. Field, "A Critique of the Vroom-Yetton Contingency Model of Leadership Behavior," *Academy of Management Review* 4, no. 2 (April 1979):249–257; and Victor H. Vroom and Arthur C. Jago, "An Evaluation of Two Alternatives to the Vroom-Yetton Normative Model," *Academy of Management Journal* 23, no. 2 (June 1980):347–355. In support of the model, also see Richard M. Steers, "Individual Differences in Participative Decision-Making," *Human Relations* 30, no. 9 (September 1977):837–847.

CASE STUDY: Three Managerial Decisions

1. You are a manufacturing manager in a large electronics plant. At considerable expense, the company's management has recently installed new robotic assembly equipment, trimmed the work force, and put in a new simplified work system. To the surprise of everyone, however, yourself included, the expected increase in production has not materialized. In fact, production has begun to drop, overall quality has fallen off, and the number of voluntary employee separations has risen.

You do not believe there is anything wrong with the robots. Reports from other companies using them confirm this opinion, and representatives from the firm that built them have inspected them and report that they are working at peak efficiency. The robot-made assemblies are of uniform high quality.

You suspect that the new work system may be responsible for the change. But this view is not shared by your immediate subordinates, who are four first-line supervisors, each in charge of a section, and your supply manager. They variously attribute the drop in production to poor retraining of the operators, lack of adequate financial incentives, or poor morale due to fear of increasing automation. Clearly, this is an issue about which there is considerable depth of feeling within individuals and potential disagreement among your subordinates.

This morning you received a phone call from your division manager. She had just received your production figures for the last six months and was calling to express her concern. She indicated that the problem was yours to solve as you thought best, but that she would like to know within a week what steps you plan to take.

You share your division manager's concern over the falling productivity and know that your workers do too. The problem is to decide what steps to take to rectify the situation.

2. You are a general supervisor in charge of a construction team laying a coal slurry pipeline and have to estimate your rate of progress in order to schedule materials deliveries to the next field site.

You know the nature of the terrain you will be crossing and have the historical data needed to compute the mean and variance in the rate of speed over that type of terrain. Given these two variables, it is a simple matter to calculate the earliest and latest times at which materials and support facilities will be needed at the next site. It is important that your estimate be reasonably accurate. Underestimates result in idle supervisors and workers, and overestimates result in tying up materials for a period of time before they are to be used.

Progress has been good, and your five supervisors and other members of the team stand to receive substantial bonuses if the project is completed ahead of schedule.

3. You are supervising the work of 12 chemical engineers. Their formal training and work experience are very similar, permitting you to use them interchangeably on projects. Yesterday, your manager informed you that a request had been received from a Middle Eastern affiliate for four engineers to go abroad on extended loan for a period of six to eight months. For a number of reasons, he argued and you agreed that this request should be met from your group.

All your engineers are capable of handling this assignment and, from the standpoint of present and future projects, there is no particular reason why anyone should be retained over any other. The problem is somewhat complicated by the fact that the overseas assignment is in what is generally regarded as an undesirable location.

Case Questions Three managerial decision-making situations have been described. Using the five decision-making styles outlined in the box on page 160, answer the following questions for each of the decision-making situations.

1. After reading the three situations, and before analyzing them, decide which of the decision-making style alternatives (AI, AII, CI, CII, GII) you would *personally* prefer to use in making each decision. Then answer the remaining questions.
2. Which is more important in the situation, quality or acceptance of the decision?
3. How critical is time in making a decision?
4. Does the manager have the information necessary to make the decision?
5. Is the decision-making situation highly structured?
6. Choose the best decision-making style (AI, AII, CI, CII, GII) and give the reason for your choice.
7. Did your choice of the "best" style in question 6 differ from the style you would personally have chosen in question 1? If so, why do you think they differed?

7 AIDS FOR PLANNING AND PROBLEM SOLVING

Upon completing this chapter you should be able to:

1. Describe the major features of a management science (MS) program.

2. Identify and describe the five major steps in the management science approach to problem solving.

3. Describe the most popular MS techniques, and discuss the problems to which they are best applied.

4. Discuss the advantages and limitations of MS.

5. Discuss the barriers to effective implementation of MS and how these barriers can be overcome.

6. Discuss why forecasting is an important part of planning and decision making.

7. Explain how and why Gantt charts, milestone schedules, and PERT and CPM networks are developed.

I n recent years, the operations of organizations have become more complex and costly. It has therefore become more difficult and more important for managers to make effective plans and decisions. To help managers improve their planning and problem solving, a variety of techniques and tools have been developed. We describe these managerial aids in this chapter.

Specifically, we will focus on management science/operations research techniques. The terms *management science (MS)* and *operations research (OR)* are, in general, used interchangeably in the United States. Management science seeks to describe, understand, and predict the behavior of complex systems of human beings and equipment. The goal of management science is to provide accurate information on which decisions can be based. To do this, mathematical and scientific techniques are used to construct models that forecast changes in the environment, predict the outcomes of various actions, and evaluate those outcomes.

Our concern here will not be with the technical details of MS techniques. Instead, we will focus on their underlying assumptions, capabilities, and limitations. This chapter attempts to answer such questions as: How can knowledge of MS sharpen a manager's judgment? For what problems are specific techniques best suited? What difficulties can arise in employing them?

Management science techniques can be classified in different ways. Our approach in this chapter emphasizes the ways in which they are used by managers.[1] We begin with an overview of the entire field, discuss briefly several widely used methods, and then consider problems and guidelines for using the methods effectively. We include forecasting—a planning-related activity—in this chapter because of the close link between planning and problem solving, the similarities of management science and forecasting techniques, and the important role of forecasting in many MS projects.

We conclude the chapter with a detailed discussion of the Program Evaluation and Review Technique (PERT) and the Critical Path Method (CPM), which are useful in planning and controlling large projects and are easy to grasp and to use. These techniques demonstrate that one does not have to be an expert to use the basic concepts of the techniques.

The Use of Management Science

The use of management science techniques in industry, government, and the not-for-profit sector has grown rapidly since World War II. Criminal justice, health care, and educational systems employ management science. So do traffic studies, engineering design projects, airports, and supermarkets. The growing use of MS has been closely linked to the increasing availability of high-speed computers and increasing expertise in their use.[2]

Given the range of techniques and the complexity of some of them, choosing and applying an appropriate one is not a simple matter. Managers must themselves be sufficiently knowledgeable about management science to choose the right approach for their organizations—or to communicate with the staff professionals who will make this choice. These are relatively new technologies, and we have to learn how (and sometimes how not) to use them.

"Even a small kingdom, Your Highness, can make effective use of modern management techniques."

Drawing by P. Steiner; © 1982 The New Yorker Magazine, Inc.

A Historical Perspective

Rick Hesse has described the alternating phases of optimism and pessimism associated with the process of learning how to use management science techniques effectively.[3] When management science techniques were first developed in England and then in the United States to deal with the large-scale tactical and strategic problems of World War II, they were frequently very useful. After the war, the techniques were applied with great expectations to an expanding array of industries. However, problems of implementation soon became apparent. These problems were most severe when the MS proponents became enamored with the esoteric aspects of the new technology.[4] For some, the methodology became an end in itself, and they forgot that MS techniques were meant to help managers solve problems. Management scientists and managers often found themselves working at cross purposes, and pessimism replaced the early optimism.

Today, a balanced realism is emerging. Management scientists have proved the usefulness of their techniques for solving many important problems: inventory control, working capital management, product-mix decisions in petroleum refining, equipment scheduling for airlines, and so on. They have also adopted an appropriate modesty about the types of problems in which MS techniques have not yet been able to make major contributions: complex strategic decisions, crises requiring immediate action, situations with minimal and ambiguous data.

In a further development, the advent of the desktop microcomputer and inexpensive personal decision support system (DSS) software has made it possible for managers to do many more routine MS applications themselves. (See chapters 6 and 22 for discussions of DSS.) Bayard Wynne suggests that DSS will supplant MS in the management of recurrent, routine tasks, and that the usefulness of DSS will increase as advances in artificial intelligence and the design of *expert systems* make computers better able to supplement human judgment.[5]

Characteristics of Management Science

Management scientists approach problems with various degrees of rigor and thoroughness. Some problems are complex and important enough to require a full-scale project; others are more limited in scope and significance. The skilled management scientist can help improve managerial decision making by recognizing that some situations require only a scaled-down approach.

Keeping this qualification in mind, we will describe the seven major features of a full-scale management science project:

1. *A decision-making focus.* The end result of MS should be information that directly helps managers reach a decision. Moreover, the MS proposal should not suggest something managers or their organizations would find impossible to do.
2. *Use of the scientific method.* MS employs the scientific approach to problem solving. This involves defining the problem, learning the behavior of the system containing the problem, and developing possible solutions that are subjected to experimental tests as the basis for acceptance or rejection.
3. *Economic effectiveness.* The cost of an action suggested by MS should be justified by increased savings or revenues. A suggestion that would solve the problem but that would be too expensive to implement is not effective. Some problems are not sufficiently important to warrant a full-blown MS project: The probable savings would be less than the cost of the study.[6] Other studies, when completed, are unable to produce solutions that will result in savings greater than the cost of implementing the solution.
4. *Use of a mathematical model.* A model, by definition, is a representation of reality. MS reduces the elements of a complex problem to their mathematical equivalents. These are then used to construct a model on which experiments can be made. That is, elements of the model are changed and manipulated, and the results recorded. It is assumed that these results would occur in the real situation if it were similarly manipulated.
5. *Reliance on a computer.* A computer is usually necessary to process the model, since the computations involved are often too complex or tedious for human beings to handle efficiently. Of course, a computer cannot think for itself; if it is given improper data, such as bogus information, it will not yield meaningful solutions. (In the computer field, this is known as GIGO—garbage in, garbage out.) For this reason, managers must clarify their assumptions and objectives beforehand so that the information given to the computer will accurately describe their problem.

A Team Approach

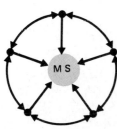

6. *A team approach.* The problems that MS addresses are frequently too complex for one person to solve alone. The skills and knowledge of a number of specialists—such as statisticians, economists, and industrial psychologists—are often required. The exact composition of an MS team will vary with the problem, but in general the team members will represent a number of disciplines. In addition, managers who are neither specialists in MS nor experts in a discipline but who will be involved in implementation of the project are often included to provide knowledge of the problem situation and to minimize barriers when implementation occurs.
7. *A systems orientation.* MS considers what is best for the organization as a whole, not for a department or a division. A special difficulty arises when the

MS process must mediate differences not only between the parts and the whole but also between the parts. A traffic manager, for example, may seek to minimize freight costs. But the sales manager may insist on fast customer service. These objectives clash: Faster deliveries cost more, but if the traffic manager minimizes costs, customers may turn to other sources for faster delivery. The MS analysis will take both cost and service into account, seeking a balance that advances the overall interests of the enterprise even though the special interests of the two managers are not fully satisfied.

Steps in a Management Science Project

The procedures of management science closely resemble those of the rational problem-solving approach discussed in chapter 6. There are three key differences, however. First, the decision-making process relies on logic, while MS usually relies on a formal mathematical model. Second, individual managers apply the decision-making process themselves; MS, however, is usually carried out by a team of specialists. (A single person may well wrestle with a small-scale problem alone, but larger ones are generally attacked by interdisciplinary teams.) Finally, managers are already sold on a decision once they have made it themselves; MS professionals may have to "sell" their solutions to the managers responsible for implementing them.

The management science approach to problem solving has five basic steps:[7]

1. Diagnosis of the problem
2. Formulation of the problem
3. Model building
4. Analysis of the model
5. Implementation of findings

THE MS PROCESS

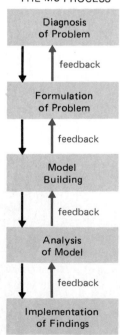

Diagnosis of Problem

feedback

Formulation of Problem

feedback

Model Building

feedback

Analysis of Model

feedback

Implementation of Findings

Diagnosis of the Problem. Before problem solving can begin, the major elements of the problem must be identified. The MS team will try to obtain at least preliminary answers to such questions as: What are the central parts of the problem situation? Will the likely benefits of an MS solution justify the costs of the study? Should an optimum solution be the goal, or will compromise solutions be acceptable or necessary? Seasoned MS personnel will try to approach the problem from the same viewpoint as the manager, who must eventually accept or reject their findings.

Formulation of the Problem. Once the problem's major elements have been identified, the MS team must begin to formulate the problem in specific terms. In particular, the team must define what criteria the proposed solution must meet and what aspects of the problem are outside the manager's control.

For example, as managers we might want to find the most efficient inventory level for a given product. We can contract or expand our storage facilities by a simple rearrangement of floor and shelf space. The storage arrangement is a *controllable variable* in the problem: It is something we—and the MS team—can manipulate as part of the solution-finding process. However, our source for the product can supply us with only a certain maximum quantity. The product supply is the *uncontrollable variable;* it defines the limits within which the solution must be confined. An inventory level that calls for larger deliveries than our supplier is capable of handling would not be feasible.

Model Building. As the major elements of the problem are isolated, the problem variables defined, and the objectives and constraints of the solution identified, the full dimensions of the problem will begin to emerge. To determine the best solution, various possibilities must be tested. Because conditions in the real world cannot be manipulated experimentally within a reasonable period of time or at a reasonable cost, the MS team constructs a mathematical model that symbolically incorporates the elements of the problem. Appropriate MS specialists devise mathematical formulas that describe the interrelationships between elements of the problem (or of a part of the problem). Within the model, the values of the controllable variables can be changed at will without interfering with the work of the organization.

Analysis of the Model. Once the basic model has been constructed, a solution to the problem must be derived. As the values of the controllable variables are changed, the model is analyzed by computer. The combination of values that best meets the objectives will represent the solution to the defined problem.

Implementation of Findings. The MS staff can only advise; it is the manager who must apply (or file) the findings. And because managers are typically more at home with practice than with theory, they may dismiss MS recommendations as the product of "ivory-tower theorizing." This hurdle can best be surmounted by securing the manager's active cooperation from the very beginning of the project, to make sure the MS team clearly understands what objectives the manager has in mind. (See figure 7–1 for the results of a study on how management participation in one aspect

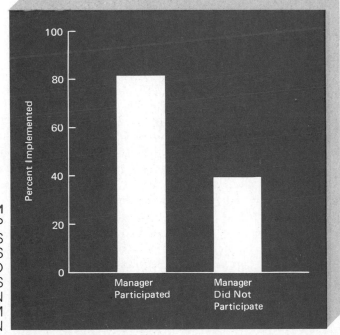

FIGURE 7–1
RELATIONSHIP BETWEEN MS PROPOSALS IMPLEMENTED AND MANAGER'S PARTICIPATION IN PROBLEM DEFINITION

Source: Lars Lonnstedt, "Factors Related to the Implementation of Operations Research Solutions," *Interfaces* 5, no. 2, part 1 (February 1975):24. Copyright © 1975 by The Institute of Management Sciences. Reprinted by permission.

of the MS process—problem definition—affects the implementation of MS solutions.)

Types of Models and Management Science Techniques

As we have noted, most MS projects lean heavily upon precise mathematical models. A mathematical model requires that all important elements and cause-and-effect relationships of the problem be specified. The models developed in MS must mirror reality closely. Otherwise they may yield misleading conclusions.

There are a number of ways of classifying the models used in MS.[8] A useful distinction we can make is between normative and descriptive models. A *normative model* describes what *ought* to be done. It is used to present managers with the best or optimum solution. A normative model—probably of the linear programming type (see description below)—could be used to determine the ideal size of a sales force. A *descriptive model* portrays things *as they are*. It provides managers with information they need to make decisions—that is, it does not supply solutions to problems but suggests what would happen if problem variables were changed. To anticipate the effect of a price increase, the MS staff would use a descriptive model to find the answer—perhaps a simulation model, described below.

To illustrate the variety of management science models, we will describe four that offer quite distinct approaches to solving the kinds of organizational problems most managers face.

Linear Programming Models. *Linear programming models* are widely used to determine the best way to allocate limited resources to achieve some desired end. (Because they seek optimum solutions, linear programming models are considered normative.) The problems for which linear programming might be used are those that can be expressed in terms of linear—that is, directly proportional—relationships.

Linear programming models can be applied to those business and industrial operations where some maximum or minimum value can be derived—establishing maximum machine output, ideal inventory levels, best product mix, and the like. Many businesses, from airlines to crude oil shippers, use linear programming to maximize the efficiency and lower the cost of systems with many variables, such as, in the case of airlines, dozens of destinations, hundreds of planes with varying passenger capacities, and differing numbers of flights needed at different times of day and different days of the week. But some scheduling and organization problems are so complex that they have resisted linear programming solutions. For example, AT&T and other carriers of long-distance telephone service must instantaneously route hundreds of thousands of calls to tens of thousands of locations while allowing for the differing volume of calls to different areas at certain times of day and week and the varying capacities of telephone equipment at each location. No successful application of linear programming to the long-distance telephone system as a whole has yet been made. However, recent improvements in linear programming methods may make even such large-scale problems soluble.[9]

Queuing or Waiting-Line Models. *Queuing* or *waiting-line models* are developed to help managers decide how long a waiting line would be most preferable. If trucks arrive at a loading platform at the rate of approximately three per hour, and it takes approximately 20 minutes to load each truck, a queue or waiting line will form when trucks arrive late or when the loading pace slows down. There are costs associated with such a waiting line, and these costs increase as the line grows—gasoline expenses if engines are idling, truck driver wages, and traffic congestion, to name a few. There would also be costs associated with a more efficient loading operation—for example, it may require many extra workers to load every truck within ten minutes. Similarly, if customers wait too long at a supermarket checkout counter, they may take their business elsewhere. But it might be too expensive to keep a sufficiently large number of checkout counters operating to assure quick service to everyone who wants it.

Game Theory. *Game theory* attempts to predict how rational people will behave in competitive situations. By so doing, it helps people who are competing to develop strategies that will combine high gains with low costs. While game theory is most widely used in military strategy, it is also used in industries where individual firms must adjust their actions to the likely actions of their competitors. Game theorists may, for example, attempt to describe how competitors will respond to a price increase, the introduction of a new product, or a new advertising campaign. If, for instance, a price reduction would quickly be matched by competitors, there would be little immediate advantage in lowering prices.

By analyzing what competitors are likely to do in certain situations, game theorists can help managers develop effective strategies. Unfortunately, most competitive situations are extremely complex and involve many possible variables. Game theory has not yet developed to the point where it provides strong guidance for any but the simplest problems in planning and strategy.

Simulation Models. In one sense, all models use the process of simulation in that they imitate reality. *Simulation models*, however, are specifically designed to be used for problems that are too complex to be described or solved by standard mathematical equations (such as those used in linear programming). They try to replicate a part of an organization's operations in order to see what will happen to that part over time, or to experiment with that part by changing certain variables. (Thus, simulation models are descriptive rather than normative.)

For example, simulation models are used to train space shuttle astronauts. Computers present the astronauts with every imaginable simulated contingency, to which they must react as they would in the real situation. The computers are programmed to respond realistically, so that a serious mistake by an astronaut will result in an automatic abort. A recent ruling by the FAA allows experienced 747 pilots to learn to fly the next generation of aircraft—757s and 767s—entirely in sophisticated flight simulators.[10]

Simulation models have a variety of uses, including the testing of machine systems and large-scale operations such as airports. Like all models, they permit experimentation to take place without interfering with actual operations. Another major advantage of simulation models is that they can be speeded up (through the computer) to indicate within minutes what would occur in the real world over a period of years.

Application of MS Techniques

Management problems tend to include a variety of overlapping elements—they do not fall neatly into one category or another.[11] Nevertheless, it is convenient to consider each type of problem separately and see which MS technique is best suited for it.[12] We will look at seven types of practical problems for which MS techniques are most frequently applied: inventory, allocation, queuing, sequencing, routing, replacement, and competition.

Inventory Problems. Inventory problems are among those best approached through MS techniques because they involve the balancing of conflicting objectives. Unit costs of products tend to go down as the quantity ordered (or made in-house) goes up. Large inventories might therefore seem desirable. On the other hand, large inventories tie up capital that could otherwise be invested, and they require greater expenditures for storage and insurance. Similarly, the need for sufficient inventory to meet customer demand conflicts with the need to prevent excessive stockpiling.

As managers, we might have to decide how much inventory to carry and when inventory needs to be replenished. To help us decide, the MS team will try to balance these conflicting cost tendencies so as to find an optimal solution. That is, they will propose an inventory program that will balance the need to satisfy customer demands against the need to maintain low ordering and carrying costs. Linear programming models might well be used for such problems. In more complex cases, simulation models may be required.

Allocation Problems. There are two common types of allocation problems, both of which are best solved through linear programming. In the first type, a given set of resources can be combined in different ways to perform a particular job. For example, in an assembly plant, the same number of products could be produced by many employees and a few machines, or more machines and fewer employees. Assuming managers have the resources to buy the machines or hire new employees, their allocation problem is to find the best mix of machines and employees—that is, the mix that will minimize their costs.

The other type of allocation problem appears when there are not enough resources available to do all the jobs that managers would like to have done. On an individual and organizational level, managers solve one kind of allocation problem when they make up a budget. A more complex example of this type of problem can be found in organizations that can produce many different kinds of products but only several kinds at the same time (a container manufacturing company, for example). The allocation problem is to find the most profitable product mix.

Queuing (Waiting-Line) Problems. Queuing problems involve designing facilities to meet a demand for services. Such problems may arise in gas stations, telephone and telegraph switching operations, checkout counters, and airline booking practices.[13] Usually, queuing models are used to solve waiting-line problems, but in some complex cases simulation techniques may be required.

Sequencing Problems. Sequencing problems arise when we have to decide in what order the parts of a job are to be performed. For example, in a factory assembly line, a product must pass through several work stations before it is completed. On a poorly planned line, some stations will be idle while others are overburdened. The problem is to sequence the work stations in such a way that idle time is minimized and working time at all stations is roughly equalized. Solutions to sequencing

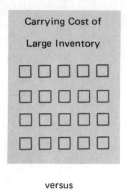

Carrying Cost of

Large Inventory

versus

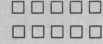

Unit Cost of

Small Inventory

problems are usually found through simulation, which allows the efficiency of different sequences to be tested.

Routing (or Scheduling) Problems. Routing problems arise if we have to decide *when* (rather than in what order) parts of a job are to be done. For example, freight may have to be shipped from point A to point B via a number of intermediate points. Which is the quickest, least expensive schedule? Similarly, a salesperson may have a number of clients or locations to visit. Which route or schedule would allow him or her to make all necessary visits in the shortest possible time (or at the lowest possible cost)? Complex routing problems may be handled by linear programming, queuing models, or some combination of the two.

Replacement Problems. Some expensive items in an organization will deteriorate over time or become obsolete—machinery and trucks are obvious examples. If they are kept for too long a period of time, they become inefficient and increasingly expensive to operate. (They may require increased maintenance, for example.) But replacing them may also involve considerable cost. One type of problem, then, is to decide exactly when such items must be replaced.

Another type of replacement problem involves large numbers of inexpensive items, such as light bulbs, which tend to operate consistently until they suddenly fail. The manager's problem is to decide whether to have each item replaced as it fails or to wait until a set number fail and then have several items replaced simultaneously. Developing a replacement schedule for the bulbs on a bridge or at an airport is a typical example. These types of problems are usually solved through linear programming, which can suggest the least expensive replacement schedule.

Competition Problems. Competition problems develop when two or more organizations are trying to achieve inherently conflicting objectives—such as each trying to increase its market share when an increase for some will obviously mean a decrease for others. Since the decisions made by one competitor can affect and are affected by the decisions of other competitors, the problem becomes finding those strategies and decisions that will maximize one's gains and minimize one's losses. For example, when the managers of store A are considering new price and advertising policies to attract more customers, they have to take into account what store B is doing now and may do in retaliation. Similarly, in competitive bidding for a contract, each bidder must reckon with the actions and reactions of other bidders. Game theory offers guidelines to help managers in competitive situations select the most effective—or least risky—strategies and decisions.

Effective Use of Management Science

When selected and applied with care, management science techniques are often useful. Accordingly, the number of businesses and not-for-profit organizations that employ them and the range of MS applications have grown steadily. MS techniques are not intended to replace managerial judgment but to give it a sturdier foundation. Managers should be able to recognize situations that call for MS and be able to work with the specialists who apply its techniques.

Advantages and Limitations of Management Science Approaches

Advantages. MS techniques have but one purpose: to help managers make better decisions. They can fulfill this purpose because they have three major advantages. First, they make it possible to break down a complex, large-scale problem into smaller parts that can be more easily diagnosed and manipulated. Second, in building and analyzing MS models, researchers have to pay close attention to details and follow logical, systematic procedures. This increases the likelihood of a good decision. Errors creep in more easily when decisions are made solely on the basis of subjective judgment, past experience, or rules of thumb. Third, MS is helpful in assessing alternatives. If managers are more aware of the risks and opportunities inherent in the alternatives available, they will be more likely to make the right choice.

Limitations. As might be expected, MS projects are frequently costly. The expense of the MS specialist's time alone often makes the techniques too expensive. For this reason, each MS study should be subjected to its own cost-benefit analysis before the decision to do the study is made.

Another disadvantage of MS is that it cannot be effectively applied in many situations. Some problems are altogether too complex to be handled by the mathematical tools now available. Managers' intuitive judgments will still be required. In crisis situations, there will be no time for the extended analysis of MS; managers will have to respond quickly on their own. Similarly, there are many situations where the available information is inadequate for an MS study. This is particularly true in situations involving human qualities and interpersonal relationships that cannot yet be quantified.

Perhaps the greatest drawback of MS is that it can easily become a technique divorced from reality—either because of defects in the initial assumptions about a problem or because certain crucial variables are ignored. An MS analysis cannot be more sound than the information it is based upon. Accounting records, for example, are far from exact; they include estimates and approximations. If an MS analysis relies on such records for figures on manufacturing costs and profits, it may turn out to be faulty. Another great danger in using MS is that researchers may ignore important aspects of a problem simply because they are not measurable. Again, MS can provide guidance on a problem; it is never a substitute for managerial judgment.

Using Management Science

John Anderson and Thomas Hoffman distinguish three dimensions of an MS effort: installation, implementation, and internalization. In *installation*, a full mathematical model has been developed and put into use with actual data. This model generates information for managers to use in making decisions. *Implementation* occurs when concepts or methods developed during an MS effort are used by managers to solve problems. Implementation can take place whether or not the relevant model is installed. In *internalization*, the concepts and perhaps methodology of MS have become part of the thinking of managers so that they are able to recognize when these techniques might be appropriate and perhaps use them to solve other problems.[14]

Ideally, all three dimensions are realized; that is, a model can be installed and implemented, with the MS perspective internalized by managers. However, implementation and internalization can both usefully take place without model installation. Indeed, several combinations of these dimensions can occur. For example, installation of a mathematical model is not always practical. Real data may exist only in a form that would require redesign of the organization's information system. Gathering new data and making it compatible with the existing system may represent an enormous expenditure in people and money, or may seem superfluous once a basic understanding of the model has been developed. For such reasons, models are often not installed. But if managers use the concepts derived during the model-making process (implementation), then a successful outcome is possible. Similarly, the ability of managers to understand the methodology of MS and incorporate it in their approach to ongoing work (internalization) in itself can raise their effectiveness. Thus, implementation and internalization can take place, separately or in combination, even if installation is never completed.

The Effect of Management Styles. James McKenney and Peter Keen suggest that managers differ from management scientists in their information-gathering and problem-solving styles, and these differences can affect how fully managers will accept MS recommendations.[15] Methods of information gathering can be either preceptive or receptive. *Preceptive* individuals bring preconceived notions to a situation; they note how various items relate to each other and whether they conform to or deviate from expectations. *Receptive* individuals are not swayed by preconceptions; they reach conclusions by examining evidence carefully and objectively.

McKenney and Keen also describe two problem-solving styles. *Intuitive* individuals prefer to use trial-and-error methods, readily switch from one problem-solving approach to another and tend to jump to conclusions. *Systematic* individuals, on the other hand, formally structure a problem and analyze its elements to find a solution.

Many types of managerial jobs (such as those in marketing and production) are suited to preceptive-intuitive styles. However, MS specialists are likely to have systematic-receptive styles.

McKenney and Keen hypothesize that managers whose own styles are systematic are more likely to be comfortable with MS specialists and to find MS helpful. Intuitive managers are less likely to find MS helpful or to feel comfortable working with MS specialists. To learn to accept MS, say McKenney and Keen, such managers should interact informally with MS specialists and experiment with using the simpler MS techniques on some of their problems.

The Keys to Effective Use

Wagner has suggested that the most beneficial MS programs contain the following eight elements:[16]

1. *Sponsorship by top management.* Without the support of top management, an MS program will be less likely to have a manager's cooperation. It is also top management's job to make sure an MS program serves the needs of the entire organization, rather than only one part.

2. *Managerial responsibility for the program.* If managers have the ultimate responsibility for the success of an MS project, they are more likely to become actively involved in it. When responsibility for the program is left to the MS staff, it is easier for managers to ignore MS's findings.

3. *Manager participation.* If managers participate in establishing program objectives, the MS models will be much more realistic. In turn, the solutions suggested by MS studies will be more useful.

4. *Use of managerial judgment.* A manager's advice must be obtained at carefully chosen points in the MS process. Such a procedure will prevent an MS project from derailing and also make managers more open to the solutions offered by MS.

5. *Technical aspects not permitted to dominate.* The mathematical and technical procedures of MS must, of course, be performed competently if the technique is to have any value. However, MS personnel must take into account the less measurable aspects of a problem. They should be particularly aware of how people affect and are affected by the solutions they suggest.

6. *Rapid data collection.* A long, extended process of information gathering will not be helpful to the manager who needs to make decisions as soon as possible. Collecting data quickly and efficiently will shorten the MS process and thus make it more useful.

7. *Preparation for initial difficulties.* When a new MS system is being tested and installed, temporary difficulties are to be expected. If managers anticipate problems and prepare for them, the effectiveness of the system will not be hindered. For example, to prevent resentment when an MS program is begun, managers can work with their subordinates in developing ideas and suggestions to make the program work.

8. *Accurate recordkeeping.* As an MS program progresses, the assumptions and facts that originally went into the models may become outdated. The organization itself may change over time, or the MS team may have to refine the models as it collects additional information. Instead of building new models each time the situation changes, an effective MS team will periodically bring the original models up to date, saving both time and expense. Keeping MS models current will also make it easier to use the models to solve similar problems in the future.

Models for Forecasting the Environment

Some writers consider forecasting models to be MS techniques (although others do not) for a number of reasons: Many forecasting methods employ sophisticated mathematical MS techniques; forecasting is needed as input to other models; and forecasts are key aids to planning and problem solving. In fact, forecasts are used not only as input to MS problem-solving models but also to establish the very premises on which plans and controls are developed. Both uses will be discussed below.[17]

Purposes of Forecasts

An observation popular with many forecasters is that "the only certain thing about a forecast is that it will be wrong." Beyond its irony, this observation touches on an important point: Forecasts do not have to be right to be useful. They simply have to predict future events closely enough to guide present actions in a valid and purposeful way. The fact that many forecasts made by meteorologists, economists, politicians, and managers prove inaccurate may make us forget how widespread and important forecasts really are. Most daily actions people take, as individuals or managers, are based on some type of forecast. Forecasts are necessary; without them, individuals as well as organizations are at the mercy of future events.

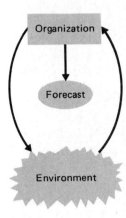

Forecasts as Planning Premises. The most important use of forecasts is as premises for planning. When managers assess the alternatives available to them, they try to forecast how events within and outside the organization will affect each alternative and what the outcome of each alternative will be. These forecasts are the *premises*, or basic assumptions, upon which planning and decision making are based.[18]

Two broad types of forecasts are used as planning premises: (1) forecasts of events that will not be influenced by the organization, and (2) forecasts of events that will be influenced, at least in part, by the organization's behavior.

Certain basic economic and social variables are unaffected by any one organization's behavior. Thus, managers need not take their organization's possible actions into account when making predictions about such variables. Instead, they will look to leading broad-based indicators—such as Department of Commerce statistics—in finding the information they need. For example, if administrators want to decide whether to expand their college's facilities, federal statistics can give them some idea of long-term college enrollment trends.

Forecasts affected by an organization's behavior are more difficult, because they require assumptions about the organization's actions as well as assumptions about events outside the organization's control. A sales forecast, for example, starts initially as a company objective. In the planning process, managers' analyses of anticipated company actions and probable competitor responses—together with their projections of the economic environment—may indicate that the sales objective will not be realized if existing programs and policies are left unchanged. In such a case, as described in chapter 4, a planning gap is said to exist. Accordingly, the managers will rework the decisions previously adopted until analysis indicates that the planning gap for the sales forecast has been closed—that is, until forecasted sales under the new program and the sales objectives are the same. Once the planning gap has been closed, the sales forecast becomes a premise for subsequent parts of the planning process; for example, to help establish production plans and schedules.

Forecasts for Problem Solving. Forecasts focus attention on factors that are normally outside our control but can nevertheless be key factors—even the main factors—to consider. Two such factors are the state of the economy and the rate of inflation. Such factors play key roles in the systems that MS models seek to describe. Forecasts of their influence are therefore vital parts of the MS problem-solving process.

Forecasting Techniques for Economic and Sales Information

Because of the importance of predicting future economic and sales trends, our discussion of forecasting techniques will focus on these areas. The same techniques can, of course, be used for forecasting other variables (such as the anticipated

TABLE 7–1 TYPES OF FORECASTS

Qualitative	Quantitative
Judgmental Methods	**Extrapolation Methods**

Use intentions and opinions as data
1. Intentions studies—how people say they will act
2. Surveys of opinions
   —jury of executive opinion
   —sales force composite
   —Delphi technique (queries to panel of experts; each reviews others' opinions and works toward consensus)
Caution: Allows bias to creep in, e.g., in selecting judges and posing questions
	Project past and/or current trends into future; "naive" method (looks at only one key variable)
	1. Time series analysis—used to detect seasonal or annual trends and patterns
	Caution: Often changes in trend are key

	Causal Models

Projective Methods (Technological Forecasting)	Deal with relationships between several variables (dependent and independent)
	1. Econometric methods
	   —use statistical regression techniques to measure economic data
	   —equations express known relationships among key variables
	2. Segmentation methods
	   —equations work with groupings or classes or related variables that do not respond identically in all respects
	Caution: Often expensive

Start with informed ideas and build on them
1. Brainstorming
   —groups focus intensively on given problem
   —generates many new ideas/alternatives rapidly
   —no evaluation until idea generation is completed
2. Scenario construction
   —builds logical, hypothetical sequences of events (stories)
   —answers question "If ... then ..."
Caution: Little research on efficacy	

Bootstrapping Methods	
Develop an explicit model from the judgmental forecast of an individual to attain more consistent performance. Caution: Difficult to wean people away from strictly judgmental methods	

Source: Adapted from discussion in J. Scott Armstrong, *Long-Range Forecasting: From Crystal Ball to Computer*, 2nd ed. (New York: Wiley-Interscience, 1985). Copyright 1985 by John Wiley & Sons.

number of job applicants in a town where the company may open a plant or the number of votes a political candidate will receive). J. Scott Armstrong has discussed the two main techniques used in these areas—qualitative forecasting and quantitative forecasting—and has raised some cautions about their use.[19] (See table 7–1.)

Qualitative Forecasting. *Qualitative forecasting* is appropriate when hard data are scarce or difficult to use. For instance, when a new product or technology is introduced, past experience is not a reliable guide for estimating what the near-term effects will be. This forecasting involves the use of subjective judgments and rating schemes to transform qualitative information into quantitative estimates. Examples of qualitative forecasting include the jury of executive opinion, sales force composite, and the Delphi technique.

Quantitative Forecasting. *Quantitative forecasting* extrapolates from the past or is used when there is sufficient "hard" or statistical data to specify relationships between key variables. Extrapolation forecasting, such as time series analysis, uses past or current trends to project future events. Sales records of the past several years, for example, could be used to extend the sales pattern into the coming year. Causal models are used where good data exist for a number of related variables and where the relationships between variables can be clearly expressed. The computer is invaluable for handling the complex mathematical formulas and the values assigned to variables in quantitative forecasting.[20]

Qualitative forecasting does not demand numerical or statistical data in the same way that quantitative forecasting does. Quantitative forecasting can be used if information exists about the past, if this information can be specified numerically, and if it can be assumed that the pattern of the past will continue. Inputs to qualitative forecasts are mainly the results of intuitive thinking, judgment, and accumulated knowledge. Specialists from a variety of fields are sometimes called upon to provide such input. Qualitative techniques may be used alone or in combination with quantitative methods. Most (although not all) studies comparing the two forecasting techniques, however, find that quantitative methods are generally more accurate than qualitative ones.[21] Table 7–1 outlines several subcategories of qualitative and quantitative forecasting and lists the main drawback of each.

Forecasting Technological Change

The rapid pace of technological change has led many firms, hospitals, government agencies, and other institutions to recognize the importance of predicting future technological developments. Discoveries in such areas as lasers, jet aircraft, energy, data communications, biotechnology, and advanced plastics have drastically affected many organizations.[22] As managers, we may often have to ascertain what technological developments are likely to occur to prepare our organization for change.

The forecasting techniques described in the preceding pages carry the implication that the future will be similar to the past. But where technological change is concerned, we can often anticipate that the future will be quite different from what has gone before. The consequences of new developments may be subtle, or massive. Often even the most knowledgeable observers have under- or overestimated the effects of a key development. For nearly 30 years, for example, the computer industry has outstripped predictions of its impact on society and the individual; computing power has grown faster and costs declined more rapidly than nearly anyone imagined. On the other hand, early predictions of the impact of atomic energy indicated that energy would be so inexpensive it would virtually be given away. But this inexhaustible, cheap, safe energy supply has not materialized.

These and numerous similar examples make it necessary to ask three key questions when technological change (as opposed to technological stability) is being considered:

1. **Will there be a major change in an existing body of technology within a specific period?**
2. **What will be the nature of this change?**
3. **What will be the consequences?**

"This survey indicates you can fool seventeen per cent of the people a hundred per cent of the time, thirty-four per cent of the people fifty-one per cent of the time, and a hundred per cent of the people twelve per cent of the time."

Drawing by Stevenson; © 1977 The New Yorker Magazine, Inc.

Because the consequences of technological change and its impact on people, organizations, and industries are unpredictable by the mathematical methods described above, forecasters depend on creative techniques that let them predict discontinuities and complex new relationships.

Qualitative methods such as brainstorming (see chapter 14), scenario construction, and the Delphi technique are especially favored in technological forecasting.[23] These methods allow managers to make predictions when there is comparatively little information available to them.

Scenario construction, employed by "think tanks" such as the Rand Corporation, builds a logical, hypothetical description of events—a scenario. In constructing the scenario, its architects explore the details and dynamics of alternative events, rather than only isolated specific elements of change.[24]

The *Delphi method* is a survey of expert opinion in which the experts also review one another's ideas. It may yield some "hard" quantitative data, but is not really expected to do so. There are disadvantages to this approach: Would a different group of experts reach the same conclusions? Would a smaller group of top experts give equal or better results than a larger but less skilled group?[25]

One study of manufacturing firms found that 80 percent of those surveyed used technological forecasting, and over 50 percent felt that technological forecasting was very important currently or would be very important within a few years.[26] Technological forecasting is especially useful—even crucial—in firms that make high-technology, capital-intensive products.[27]

Choosing the Appropriate Forecasting Technique

No single method of forecasting can satisfy the requirements of all types of managers and organizations. The method a manager selects depends on such factors as the type of decisions to be made, the amount of information available, the level of accuracy required, the time period to be forecast, the time available to complete the analysis, and the value of the forecast to the organization. (See box.)

There are two important prerequisites for selecting a method. First, the persons doing the selecting must be familiar with the available methods; and second, some kind of systematic procedure should be used to compare the strengths and weaknesses of the various methods. Several writers have offered guidelines to aid in the selection process.[28] Armstrong, saying that "there is safety in numbers," points out the advantages of "amalgamated forecasts" in averaging the findings of a number of judges for qualitative forecasts or in using the combined forecasts from several quantitative forecasts.[29]

One survey has suggested that organizations generally adapt an *evolutionary approach* to forecasting—using simpler methods in limited areas first and then proceeding to more complex techniques and wider applications once forecasting proves its worth.[30] Although many companies have concluded that increased sophistication in forecasting is worth the added costs, recent research on forecasting concludes that simple forecasting methods, such as extrapolation forecasting, are at least as accurate as, and much less expensive than, more sophisticated ones.[31]

CRITERIA FOR SELECTING A FORECASTING METHOD

Factor 1: **Manager's Technical Ability**	—Level of forecasting sophistication	—Understanding of the method —Formal training in forecasting
Factor 2: **Cost**	—Manager's time —Preparer's time	—Computer time —Data collection
Factor 3: **Problem-Specific Characteristics**	—Time horizon to be forecast —Length of each time period —Functional area involved	—Degree of top management support —Manager-forecaster relationship
Factor 4: **Method Characteristics Desired**	—Accuracy —Statistics available	

Source: Reprinted by permission of the *Harvard Business Review*. An exhibit from "Corporate Forecasting: Promise and Reality" by Steven C. Wheelwright and Darral G. Clarke (November–December 1976). Copyright © 1976 by the President and Fellows of Harvard College; all rights reserved.

PERT and CPM:
Models for Planning and Control

We conclude our discussion of aids for planning and decision making with a description of PERT and CPM, closely related techniques that are useful for planning, controlling, and making decisions about large, complex projects. They illustrate how quickly some MS concepts can be grasped and how useful they can be, even for nonexperts. They also illustrate how a contribution by a scientific management pioneer has evolved into two sophisticated management science techniques.

The Gantt Chart

One of the earliest and best-known approaches to project management was developed by Henry L. Gantt. (See chapter 2.) A *Gantt chart* (fig. 7–2) is a graphic planning and control method. A project is broken down into separate tasks. For each task, estimates are made of the amount of time required and of the termination date necessary to meet the specified completion date for the project. This information is shown as a pair of brackets, one of which indicates the starting date and the other the end date, for each task. The Gantt chart enables a manager to make commitments based on the planned completion times, to acquire extra resources to shorten some of the times, and so on. In addition, filling in the brackets ("accomplishment" in fig. 7–2) enables the manager to see immediately what tasks are behind (or ahead of) schedule, and how far. (In figure 7–2, shipping of product B is slightly behind schedule.) Extra effort can be applied to lagging parts of an operation before the overall completion date is threatened.

Milestone Scheduling

If you select a date when a certain accomplishment, decision, or event is to take place and indicate that date on the horizontal bar of a chart, you have created a *milestone*.[32] The milestone may be the date when a decision is to be made concerning outside financing, when announcement of the project to the trade press is planned, when a thorough project progress review is scheduled, or whatever. *Milestone scheduling* indicates selected dates by which the various phases of the entire project are to be completed. Milestones thus add detail to the Gantt chart. They serve as formal review points where costs, progress, and the need for replanning or schedule modification can be reviewed. In figure 7–2, milestones appear on the bars for product C to indicate (1) mailing of final purchase orders and (2) completion of the first quality inspection. Gantt charts show the relationship between milestones *within the same task* but not within different tasks. Modifying a Gantt chart to overcome this limitation leads to the formation of a network.[33]

Network-Based Scheduling Techniques

Gantt charts are appropriate for scheduling a series of unrelated activities, such as separate production runs in a job shop operation. Milestone scheduling can be used to divide a major project into subactivities so that managers can achieve greater

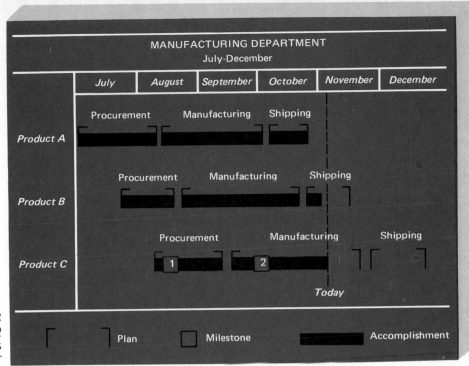

FIGURE 7–2
GANTT CHART FOR
MANUFACTURING
DEPARTMENT

control. Neither approach, however, can adequately deal with the interrelationships between activities or events that characterize more complex projects and programs. In such situations, some form of *network analysis* is necessary.

The two major network techniques are *PERT*, which stands for *Program Evaluation and Review Technique,* and *CPM,* the *Critical Path Method.* Both systems were independently developed around 1957–58. PERT was developed by the U.S. Navy's Special Projects Office with Lockheed and Booz, Allen & Hamilton to help coordinate the more than 3,000 contractors and agencies working on the Polaris missile–nuclear submarine program. Faced with the problem of predicting with certainty the completion time for many interrelated project tasks that had never been attempted before, the planners developed PERT as a method of estimating and controlling scheduling needs.[34] The use of PERT is credited with trimming two years from the Polaris program. CPM was developed by Du Pont to facilitate its control of large, complex industrial projects.

The two systems are essentially similar, but can be used to best advantage in somewhat different situations. CPM is better suited to repetitive processes in which tasks are of fixed duration and the completion time is known, while PERT can best handle nonrepetitive processes in which the duration and completion time of tasks can be only roughly estimated.

The use of PERT and CPM is widespread and has significant impact on the planning and control of projects and programs. Formerly, establishing a PERT or CPM system was generally too time-consuming and expensive for all but the most complex, time-critical projects, such as highway construction, shipbuilding, or the installation of a large-scale data processing system.[35] Now, network analysis software for desktop microcomputers has made PERT and CPM accessible to managers who did not have the technical background or the resources to use them before. Such software enables managers to apply these methods to much smaller projects; managers can now quickly develop and frequently update schedules and rapidly check the effects of "what-if" factors, such as a supplier's possible delay in shipping a crucial component, on the progress of the project.[36]

Developing the Network. There are a number of PERT and CPM techniques with different names and slight variations of methods. All, however, are essentially systems for planning projects and implementing those plans. Their approach is to divide the project into separate operations and then chart the order in which the operations should be carried out, when each should be started and completed, and when the entire project should be completed. Since PERT and CPM are basically similar in technique, we will discuss them together, pointing out the differences between them whenever appropriate.

There are four requirements for translating a program into a PERT or CPM network:[37]

1. **The activity must be broken down into individual tasks. These tasks will then be put into the network in the form of events and activities. Events are usually indicated in circles on the chart; they represent those parts of the tasks to be accomplished at specific points in time. Activities represent the time or the resources required to progress from one event to another. They are usually indicated by arrows on the chart. For example, the official start of a design project would represent the chart's first event; the five weeks necessary to prepare preliminary blueprints would represent the chart's first activity.**

2. **Events and activities are placed in the chart in a logical, sequential, and integrated way. For example, each activity is preceded and followed by the appropriate events; no activity may start until its preceding event (or events) has been completed.**

3. **The length of time required for each activity is estimated and written in on the network. In CPM, a single time estimate is established for each activity. In PERT, however, each activity may be assigned four time estimates: an "optimistic" estimate for the length of time the activity would require under ideal conditions; a "most probable" estimate of the normal time such an activity should take; a "pessimistic" estimate taking into account the possibility that just about everything will go wrong; and an "expected" time estimate based on a probability analysis of the other three estimates.**

   The times are shown on the network diagram as:

   $$\frac{\text{optimistic, most probable, pessimistic}}{\text{expected}}$$

4. **A critical path through the network must be determined. This requirement will be discussed in the next section.**

Events
and
Activities

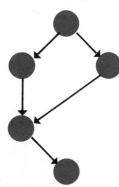

TABLE 7–2 ACTIVITY LIST AND TIME ESTIMATES FOR CORDLESS VACUUM CLEANER PROJECT, IN WEEKS

Activity	Description	Immediate Predecessors	Optimistic Time Estimate	Most Probable Time Estimate	Pessimistic Time Estimate	Expected Time
A	R & D product design	—	4	5	12	6
B	Plan market research	—	1	1.5	5	2
C	Routing (manufacturing engineering)	A	2	3	4	3
D	Build prototype model	A	3	4	11	5
E	Prepare marketing brochure	A	2	3	4	3
F	Cost estimates (industrial engineering)	C	1.5	2	2.5	2
G	Preliminary product testing	D	1.5	3	4.5	3
H	Market survey	B, E	2.5	3.5	7.5	4
I	Pricing and forecast report	H	1.5	2	2.5	2
J	Final report	F, G, I	1	2	3	2
					Total	32

We can illustrate the construction of a network, using as an example the development of a new cordless vacuum cleaner.[38] The major activities (tasks) in this job and their immediate predecessors are listed in table 7–2. For example, preliminary product testing, task G, cannot begin until task D, construction of a prototype model, is completed. Also included in the table are a range of estimates for the duration (in weeks) of each task: optimistic time, most probable time, pessimistic time, and the expected time of completion. In this case, since it is not possible to make accurate time estimates, the PERT system will be used. If accurate estimates based on ample prior experience were available, the CPM system would be more applicable.

From the information in the table, we can construct the network shown in figure 7–3. This network illustrates which tasks can be performed simultaneously and which must wait for predecessors to be completed. Once the cordless vacuum cleaner has been designed, for example, construction and testing of the prototype, routing (manufacturing engineering), and cost estimation can go on at the same time. But the market survey cannot be started until the market research plan and the marketing brochure have been completed.

Determining the Critical Path. The *critical path* is simply the longest route through the network in terms of time. It is determined by totaling the amount of time required for each sequence of tasks (as opposed to tasks that are performed simultaneously). The task chain with the longest time is the critical path. In figure 7–3, the critical path is marked with the thicker arrows. For example, once the path reaches 2, there are three possible routes to 8. Since we are looking for the longest

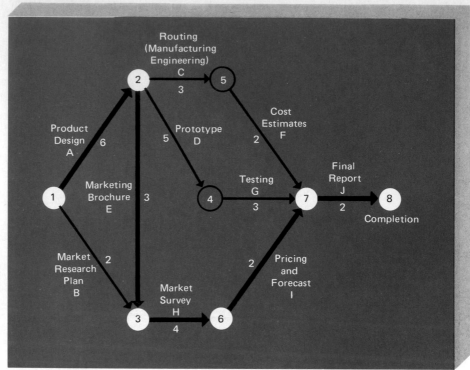

FIGURE 7–3
PERT CHART FOR
CORDLESS
VACUUM CLEANER
PROJECT WITH
EXPECTED
ACTIVITY TIMES (IN
WEEKS)

route, the critical path will follow 2, 3, 6, 7, 8, since that will add the most weeks (9) to the total.

The significance of the critical path is that it determines the total length of time, or completion date, of the entire project. If an event on the critical path is delayed, the entire project will be delayed.

Paths other than the critical path are called *subcritical.* These contain some slack since the total time for their completion is less than that of the critical path. One of the ways PERT and CPM can reduce project completion time is to indicate resources that can be transferred from activities on subcritical paths to activities on the critical path. For example, transferring staff from F, cost estimates, to I, pricing and forecast report, might increase the time for F on the subcritical path by a week, but the time required for I might be reduced by a week. Since I is on the critical path, this would reduce completion time for the whole project by a week.

Extension of PERT and CPM Techniques. The main function of PERT and CPM is to determine and control the time required to complete a project. The main benefit to be gained from these techniques is time saved through the initial scheduling of tasks and as the project progresses. Since time and cost are closely related, saving time usually leads to savings in costs.

In addition, both PERT and CPM have been adapted and applied explicitly to costs. They can, for example, be used to develop an optimum cost-efficiency schedule. This can help managers determine the savings and costs involved in achieving a shorter production schedule. Using extra labor to reduce the duration of an activity, for instance, may cost more than would a bonus for early completion. Various extensions of PERT and CPM significantly enhance their usefulness.[39]

Advantages and Limitations of PERT and CPM

The increasing use of PERT and CPM indicates that managers can gain significant advantages from them. These advantages include:

1. *Illustrating task relationships.* By providing a graphic representation of how the performance of each task is dependent on others, networks offer a distinct advantage over simpler graphs such as bar charts.
2. *Encouraging effective planning.* Drawing up a network requires that the project manager plan the project from start to finish in considerable detail.
3. *Pinpointing problem areas.* Bottlenecks and potential trouble spots are discovered early enough for preventive measures or corrective action to be taken.
4. *Improving communication.* The network diagram provides a common frame of reference for all parties involved in a project, such as designers, managers, contractors, and other employees.
5. *Comparing alternative actions.* Managers are provided with an opportunity to compare the impact on time and cost of different methods for reaching the project goal.
6. *Allowing concentration on key jobs.* By identifying critical tasks, CPM and PERT allow managers to apply their attention where it is most needed. At the same time, the network will indicate when other tasks are falling behind schedule. This will allow managers to take immediate action.[40]
7. *Creating flexibility.* In a complex project, the critical path may change a number of times, as time estimates prove inaccurate. PERT and CPM provide managers with the ability to identify the current critical path on a continuing basis.

PERT and CPM also have limitations. The cost of setting up such systems on a large scale, especially in terms of computer time, should obviously be considered before adopting them. More important, PERT and CPM will certainly not help managers solve all their problems. Manager-subordinate relationships, relations with suppliers, difficulties with quality control—all the day-to-day pressures that make up the manager's job—will not be relieved by PERT and CPM. Moreover, the accuracy of scheduling with CPM and PERT depends on the ability of the staff making the estimates and the accuracy of the methods they use.

Nor will these systems substitute for managerial planning and control. In fact, the reverse is true. In order for the systems to be effective, they must be carefully planned and tightly controlled throughout a project. When unforeseen events occur—as they often do—managers will have to respond. Network schedules should always be regarded as tentative. They are never a substitute for effective management. When properly constructed and used, however, PERT and CPM can provide valuable aids for planning and control.

Summary

Management science or operations research techniques help managers improve the quality of their problem solving. Management science seeks to describe, understand, and predict the behavior of complex systems of human beings and equipment. Its goal is to provide managers with accurate information on which decisions can be based.

Management science projects are undertaken to help managers make more effective decisions. They are conducted by teams of specialists, who diagnose the problem, formulate the problem in more specific terms, build an appropriate mathematical model, perform computer analysis of the model, and advise the manager(s) on implementation of the findings.

Management science (MS) relies heavily on models that represent aspects of a real situation. Some widely used MS tools are linear programming models, queuing or waiting-line models, game theory, and simulation models. Some of these tools, such as linear programming, are normative in that they suggest a best solution. Others, such as simulation models, are descriptive in that they suggest what will happen if a particular solution is adopted. Each MS tool is best suited for certain types of problems.

Implementation of MS findings can be viewed as having three dimensions. Installation occurs when a full mathematical model has been developed and put into use with actual data. Implementation can take place without full installation, if managers use the concepts or methods developed during the MS effort to solve their problems. Internalization, which can also take place independently of the other two dimensions, occurs when managers understand MS concepts and methodology so well that they can recognize other problem situations for which these approaches might be useful and can apply the techniques.

Forecasting techniques for economic and sales information include qualitative forecasting (such as a jury of executive opinion) and quantitative forecasting (such as time series analysis). Tools for forecasting technological change include the Delphi method and scenario construction. Mathematical models are used when quantifiable data exist from which future events can be predicted.

Management science techniques for project planning and control include Gantt charts, milestone scheduling, PERT, and CPM. The Gantt chart graphically indicates the tasks involved in each project and the time it will take to complete them. Milestones on a Gantt chart indicate important dates in a project—usually when a certain phase of the project is to be completed. PERT and CPM networks illustrate the tasks involved in a project, the time it will take to complete them, and the interrelationships between those tasks.

MS techniques are powerful aids for planning and problem solving. They are not meant to replace managerial judgment but to place it on a sturdier footing. Managers need not become professional statisticians, but they should be able to spot situations where MS can help and should be able to interact effectively with those MS specialists.

Review Questions

1. What is the goal of management science (MS)?

2. Why is it important for a manager to be acquainted with MS techniques?

3. What are the seven major features of a full-scale MS project?

4. What are the key differences between the procedures of MS and the rational problem-solving approach of chapter 6?

5. Describe the five basic steps in the MS approach to problem solving.

6. What is the difference between normative and descriptive models?

7. What are linear programming models, queuing models, game theory, and simulation models? For which of the eight types of problems discussed in the chapter can each MS technique be used?

8. How does managerial style affect decision making?

9. What are the major defects and limitations of MS, and how can they be overcome?

10. Why do you think forecasts do not have to be completely accurate to be meaningful?

11. Why is forecasting an important part of the planning or decision-making process? What are the two types of forecasts that serve as planning premises?

12. Describe and give examples of quantitative and qualitative forecasting.

13. Briefly describe the principal characteristics of Gantt charts, milestone scheduling, and network analysis, including PERT and CPM.

Notes

1. Our discussion draws upon Elwood S. Buffa and James S. Dyer in *Essentials of Management Science/Operations Research*, rev. ed. (New York: Wiley, 1981); Efrain Turban and Jack R. Meredith, *Fundamentals of Management Science*, rev. ed. (Plano, Texas: Business Publications, 1981); and Robert J. Thierauf, *Management Science: A Model Formulation Approach with Computer Applications* (Columbus, Ohio: Merrill, 1985).

2. Two recent texts emphasizing the use of computers in MS applications are Warren J. Erikson and Owen P. Hall, *Computer Models for Management Science*, 2nd ed. (Reading, Mass.: Addison-Wesley, 1986); and Sang M. Lee and Jung Shim, *Micro Management Science* (Dubuque, Iowa: Brown, 1986).

3. Rick Hesse, "Management Science or Management/Science?" *Interfaces* 10, no. 1 (February 1980):104–109. For examples of how MS techniques can clarify murky situations for managers, see also Allen F. Grum and Rick Hesse, "It's the Process Not the Product (Most of the Time)," *Interfaces* 13, no. 5 (October 1983):89–93.

4. For a recent, rather harsh critique of MS along these lines, see Tony Lowe and Tony Tinker, "One-Dimensional Management Science: The Making of a Technocratic Consciousness," *Interfaces* 14, no. 2 (March–April 1984):40–56.

5. Bayard E. Wynne, "A Domination Sequence—MS/OR; DSS; and the Fifth Generation," *Interfaces* 14, no. 3 (May–June 1984):51–58.

6. Surprises are, however, possible. Some apparently "unimportant" problems turn out, under investigation, to be symptoms of a substantially different, and major, problem. Subsequent study of that problem may yield great savings or improvements. See Russell L. Ackoff, *Redesigning the Future: A Systems Approach to Societal Problems* (New York: Wiley, 1974), pp. 20–22.

7. See K. Roscoe Davis, Patrick G. McKeown, and Terry Rakes, *Management Science*, 2nd ed. (Reading, Mass.: Addison-Wesley, 1986); and Bernard W. Taylor III, *Introduction to Management Science*, 2nd ed. (Dubuque, Iowa: Brown, 1986).

8. For alternative classifications of MS approaches, see John M. Wilson, "Classification of Models in Operational Research," *Journal of the Operational Research Society* 36, no. 3 (March 1985):253–256.

9. A new method of linear programming modeling is described in James Gleick, "Breakthrough in Problem Solving," *New York Times*, November 19, 1984, p. Al.

10. Jonathan B. Tucker, "Visual Simulation Takes Flight," *High Technology* 4, no. 12 (December 1984):34–47.

11. Russell L. Ackoff has observed that every problem exists in association with related problems, which he refers to as a "system of problems," or, for want of a more suitable word, a "mess." See his book about "mess management," *Redesigning the Future*, especially chapter 2.

12. See Russell L. Ackoff and Patrick Rivett, *A Manager's Guide to Operations Research* (New York: Wiley, 1963). See also Ronald L. Gue and Michael E. Thomas, *Mathematical Models in Operations Research* (New York: Macmillan, 1968), pp. 8–12.

13. See Marvin Rothstein, "OR and the Airline Overbooking Problem," *Operations Research* 33, no. 2 (March–April 1985):237–248.

14. This discussion draws on John C. Anderson and Thomas R. Hoffman, "A Perspective on the Implementation of Management Science," *Academy of Management Review* 3, no. 3 (July 1978):563–571.

15. James L. McKenney and Peter G. W. Keen, "How Managers' Minds Work," *Harvard Business Review* 52, no. 3 (May–June 1974):79–90.

16. Harvey M. Wagner, *Principles of Operations Research*, 2nd ed. (Englewood Cliffs, N.J.: Prentice-Hall, 1975), pp. 943–951. Lars Lonnstedt (in "Factors Related to the Implementation of Operations Research Solutions," *Interfaces* 5, no. 2, part 1 [February 1975]:23–50) adds one more element: problem scope. He found that MS findings were more likely to be implemented if they were not limited to a small part of the problem. See also Geoff Lockett and Eileen Polding, "Model Choice in Production—Optimization?" *Interfaces* 13, no. 5 (October 1983):94–100.

17. Buffa and Dyer, *Essentials of Management Science/Operations Research*. See also James Morrell, ed., *Management Decisions and the Role of Forecasting* (Baltimore: Penguin Books, 1972).

18. See George A. Steiner, *Strategic Planning: What Every Manager Must Know* (New York: Free Press, 1979), pp. 18–20 and 122–148.

19. Our discussion of forecasting techniques is heavily indebted to J. Scott Armstrong, *Long-Range Forecasting: From Crystal Ball to Computer* (New York: Wiley, 1978). See also Spyros Makridakis and Steven C. Wheelwright, eds., *The Handbook of Forecasting* (New York: Wiley, 1982).

20. M. J. Lawrence, "An Exploration of Some Practical Issues in the Use of Quantitative Forecasting Models," *Journal of Forecasting* 2, no. 2 (April–June 1983):169–179.

21. See Essam Mahmoud, "Accuracy in Forecasting: A Survey," *Journal of Forecasting* 3, no. 2 (1984):139–159; and Joseph P. Martino, *Technological Forecasting for Decision Making*, 2nd ed. (New York: North Holland, 1983).

22. See Daniel D. Roman, "Technological Forecasting in the Decision Process," *Academy of Management Journal* 13, no. 2 (June 1970):127–138.

23. For a survey of the popularity of such forecasting methods, see R. Balachandra, "Perceived Usefulness of Technological Forecasting Techniques," *Technological Forecasting and Social Change* 16, no. 2 (February 1980):155–166.

24. Howard S. Becker, "Scenarios: A Tool of Growing Importance to Policy Analysts in Government and Industry," *Technological Forecasting and Social Change* 23, no. 2 (February 1983):95–120.

25. Frederick J. Parente, Janet K. Anderson, Patrick Myers, and Thomas O'Brien, "An Examination of Factors Contributing to Delphi Accuracy," *Journal of Forecasting* 3, no. 2 (1984):173–182; and Teri Spinelli, "The Delphi Decision-Making Process," *Journal of Psychology* 113, no. 1 (January 1983): 73–80.

26. R. Balachandra, "Technological Forecasting: Who Does It and How Useful Is It?" *Technological Forecasting and Social Change* 16, no. 1 (January 1980):75–85.

27. J. P. Martino, *Technological Forecasting for Decision-Making* (New York: Elsevier, 1983).

28. See Armstrong, *Long-Range Forecasting*, pp. 67–72; Makridakis and Wheelwright, *The Handbook of Forecasting*; and Buffa and Dyer, *Essentials of Management Science/Operations Research*, pp. 135–136.

29. Armstrong, *Long-Range Forecasting*. Chapters 5 through 10 each have a section on amalgamated forecasts. Armstrong also gives some basic rules for combining methods of forecasting on pp. 248–251 and 268.

30. Steven C. Wheelwright and Darral G. Clarke, "Corporate Forecasting: Promise and Reality," *Harvard Business Review* 54, no. 6 (November–December 1976):60. An excellent discussion of the successful implementation of forecasting can be found in Randall L. Schultz, "The Implementation of Forecasting Models," *Journal of Forecasting* 3, no. 1 (1984):43–55.

31. Mahmoud, "Accuracy in Forecasting."

32. See James L. Riggs and Charles O. Heath, *Guide to Cost Reduction through Critical Path Scheduling* (Englewood Cliffs, N.J.: Prentice-Hall, 1966).

33. See Robert J. Thierauf and Richard A. Grosse, *Decision Making through Operations Research* (New York: Wiley, 1970); and Robert W. Miller, *Schedule, Cost, and Profit Control with PERT* (New York: McGraw-Hill, 1963).

34. See James B. Dilworth, *Production and Operations Management: Manufacturing and Non-manufacturing*, 3d ed. (New York: Random House, 1986).

35. See Riggs and Heath, *Guide to Cost Reduction through Critical Path Scheduling*, pp. 16–20; and Richard J. Schonberger, "Custom Tailored PERT/CPM Systems," *Business Horizons* 15, no. 6 (December 1972):64–66.

36. For an overview of recent project management software, see Andrew Pollack, "Software Aids Small Projects," *New York Times*, October 25, 1984, p. D2. Typical microcomputer project management programs are *Pro-Ject* 6 (Clearwater, Fla.: SoftCorp, 1984); *Project Scheduler 5000* (Sunnyvale, Calif.: Scitor Corp., 1985); and *Pertmaster* (Palo Alto, Calif.: Westminster Software, 1985).

37. Robert W. Miller, "How to Plan and Control with PERT," *Harvard Business Review* 40, no. 2 (March–April 1962):93–104. See also Miller, *Schedule, Cost, and Profit Control with PERT*, pp. 32–38.

38. This example is taken from David R. Anderson, Dennis J. Sweeney, and Thomas A. Williams, *Quantitative Methods for Business* (New York: West Publishing, 1983).

39. See Riggs and Heath, *Guide to Cost Reduction through Critical Path Scheduling*; and T. M. McCann and H. W. Lanford, "Effective Planning and Control of Large Projects—Using Work Breakdown Structure," *Long Range Planning* 16, no. 2 (April 1983):38–50.

40. These six points are from Joseph Horowitz, *Critical Path Scheduling* (New York: Ronald Press, 1967), pp. 10–12.

CASE STUDY: Building a Custom Sports Car

The Maser is a new custom-designed sports car. An analysis of the task of building the Maser reveals the following list of relevant activities, their immediate predecessors, and their duration.

Job Letter	Description	Immediate Predecessors	Normal Time (Days)
A	Start		0
B	Design	A	8
C	Order special accessories	B	0.1
D	Build frame	B	1
E	Build doors	B	1
F	Attach axles, wheels, gas tank	D	1
G	Build body shell	B	2
H	Build transmission and drive train	B	3
I	Fit doors to body shell	G, E	1
J	Build engine	B	4
K	Bench-test engine	J	2
L	Assemble chassis	F, H, K	1
M	Road-test chassis	L	0.5
N	Paint body	I	2
O	Install wiring	N	1
P	Install interior	N	1.5
Q	Accept delivery of special accessories	C	5
R	Mount body and accessories on chassis	M, O, P, Q	1
S	Road-test car	R	0.5
T	Attach exterior trim	S	1
U	Finish	T	0

Source: The authors are indebted to Peter L. Pfister for the material on which this case is based.

Case Questions

1. Draw an arrow diagram of the project "Building the Maser."
2. Mark the critical path and state its length.
3. If the Maser had to be completed two days earlier, would it help to:
   a. Buy preassembled transmissions and drive trains?
   b. Install robots to halve engine-building time?
   c. Speed delivery of special accessories by three days?
4. How might resources be borrowed from activities on the subcritical paths to speed activities on the critical path?

8

OPERATIONS MANAGEMENT AND PRODUCTIVITY

Upon completing this chapter you should be able to:

1. Explain why production/operations management is important to society, the organization, and the individual.
2. Describe the major features of an operations system.
3. Identify the six decision areas that go into the design of an operations system.
4. Name the three key objectives of operations planning and explain why it is important to strike a balance among them.
5. Explain the significance of productivity and describe the way in which it is commonly expressed.
6. Identify factors that affect productivity on the national level and in individual organizations.

ystems for the production and delivery of goods and services have always been an essential part of civilization. They have existed, in various degrees of sophistication, from the days when our prehistoric ancestors went out on hunting and gathering trips through every stage of history up to and including the establishment of today's tribal meeting place, the suburban shopping mall.

In every modern society, resources are limited. Efficient utilization of resources is necessary if we are to meet educational, health care, and other service and material needs and demands. In addition, the survival of any individual organization depends on how efficiently it produces its goods and/or services. The quality and cost of a product are determined largely by the effectiveness and efficiency of the production system used to produce it. And finally, our standard of living and work satisfaction are determined in no small part by the nature of the production systems of our society.[1]

Changing Views of Production and Operations

Since the industrial revolution, a substantial body of knowledge has accumulated on the use of mathematics, computers, industrial engineering, and behavioral science techniques in manufacturing environments. Successful use of these methods in the first half of the twentieth century helped make the U.S. economy the most productive in the world. From the early 1950s until recently, however, the importance of maintaining leadership in productive activities was largely ignored by American managers in their quest for dynamic marketing approaches and ever more sophisticated financial arrangements. Today, manufacturing production systems in the United States need revitalization to remain competitive in the international environment. Production systems, the majority of which were developed several decades ago, also require adaptation to the most recent social, economic, and technological changes.

Because of the need to revitalize production systems, the management of *production* and *operations* has reemerged as an exciting and challenging aspect of organizational life. Three trends are becoming evident that, compared to the approaches of the last few decades, can almost be called revolutionary:

1. **Greater worker involvement and participation at all levels of the organization.**
2. **Significant changes in production process design. For example, increasingly effective methods for integrating design with production requirements have great potential for improving both quality and manufacturability.**
3. **A growing recognition that a focus on high quality is often associated with high productivity. Productivity and quality are, in fact, now seen as complementary rather than competing goals.**

This chapter is based in part on information and research provided by James K. Weeks, University of North Carolina at Greensboro.

"We could never have done it without him."
Drawing by Chas. Addams; © 1957, 1985 The New Yorker Magazine, Inc.

Trends such as these acquire a revolutionary character when contrasted with the traditional view that production/operations management was limited to manufacturing. It was, in fact, originally known as *manufacturing management*, and was oriented primarily toward the production of physical goods in large quantities at the lowest possible cost. Production/operations systems, however, exist in service as well as manufacturing organizations, as implied by the newer term, *operations management*, which we use in this book.

Operations management typically entails: (1) planning the production/operations system; (2) organizing the necessary human and capital resources; (3) directing operations and personnel; and (4) monitoring the system's performance to be sure it meets organizational objectives. In recent decades, operations management has received particular attention in such areas as retailing, health, transportation, and government.[2]

This chapter will examine the ways in which organizations manage their productive systems, how these systems can be designed and improved, and how managers can increase the overall productivity of their organizations. In the process we shall attempt to convey some of the excitement of the new developments in operations management, developments that may go a long way toward rejuvenating U.S. industry.

Characteristics of Production/Operations Systems

In this section we will describe how production/operations systems work. For simplicity's sake, we will use the term *operations system* to denote both manufacturing and service systems.

An organization that produces goods and/or services may be viewed as a *system,* a set of related and interacting components that perform functions and have goals pertaining to the whole. (See chapter 2.) These related components are called subsystems, and operations is one of them. Decisions made regarding one subsystem usually affect the other subsystems. If, for example, the personnel subsystem declares a six-month moratorium on hiring, the operations subsystem will certainly feel the effects when terminated employees are not replaced.

The Operations System: A Model

The operations subsystem can be defined as a "set of components whose function is to transform a set of inputs into some desired output."[3] The input (workers, equipment, and technical knowledge) provides the resources and energies needed to produce the output. Output includes the desired goods and/or services of the organization as well as undesirable by-products, such as atmospheric pollution or toxic waste.[4]

The processes of transformation or conversion from input to output are varied. *Physical* transformations occur in manufacturing, *locational* in transportation, and *exchange* in retailing. In warehousing the transformation is merely *storage,* while in a legal firm it is *informational,* in medicine *physiological,* and in entertainment the transformation results in *gratification.*

The external environment includes such factors as government regulations, inflation, economic policies, labor supply and negotiations, weather, international relations, suppliers, vendors, or any other influence on resources and operations. (See chapter 3.) The feedback loop (see fig. 8–1) reflects the information gained during the entire process. This information makes it possible to decide whether changes are required.

Any operations system can be described or analyzed with this model. For example, in the case of a hospital some components might be:[5]

· *Input:* patients, nurses, doctors, medical supplies, equipment
· *Transformation:* health-care treatment
· *Output:* treated patients
· *Feedback:* hospital costs, number of patients treated, quality of care
· *Environment:* government regulations, insurance charges, inflation, labor problems, accidents

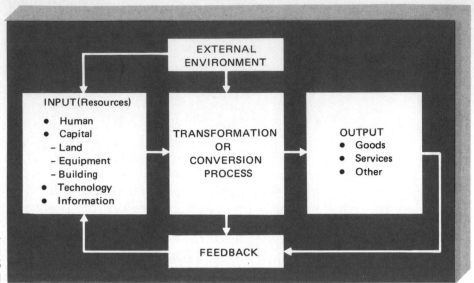

FIGURE 8–1
CONCEPTUAL
MODEL OF AN
OPERATIONS
SYSTEM

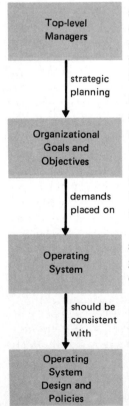

Operations management activities include both decisions related to the design of the operations system and decisions related to the operation and control of the system. In the first category are decisions on product design, process design, job design, capacity planning, layout planning, and site selection. These are long-term, strategic decisions. Operation and control decisions affect such matters as production and inventory planning and control, purchasing, and quality control. Decisions in these areas have to be made frequently and continually to keep the system going.

Operations Management and Strategic Planning. Because the effectiveness of the operations system is so important to the success of the organization, it should be designed to be compatible with the strategies of the organization. (See chapter 5.) Conversely, existing and future operations systems capabilities should be considered in formulating organizational strategy. The hazards of failing to view operations as an important component of strategy development have been emphasized by U.S. companies' recent competitive problems in worldwide manufacturing industries such as automobiles, machine tools, and consumer electronics.

The operations system operates within the larger framework of organizational strategy. The strategic plan of the organization should serve as a clear, consistent guide to operations policies. Figure 8–2 charts the path of decisions involved in developing a typical operations strategy.

The demands placed upon the operations system to meet organizational strategy should be consistent with the design and operating policies of the operations system. Wickham Skinner has termed this top-down approach a "manufacturing focus."[6] This focus starts with an explicit statement of the organization's objectives and strategies, which is then translated into a set of operations system decisions and policies. For example, an operations system that cannot be readily modified to produce new products would be inconsistent with an organizational strategy of a firm that is adapting to rapidly changing customer demand.

Some students of management—and some managers—have tended to look on production or operations as the backwater of corporate activity, removed from the real challenge and action. But this has never been true. Many organizations have in fact prospered precisely because they used their production capabilities as a strategic weapon that gave them a competitive edge over other firms that did not share this philosophy. The success of many Japanese firms, for example, can be traced in part to the effectiveness with which they have achieved attractive design, high quality, and low cost in their operating systems.

Continuous and Assembly-Line Production and Job-Shop Production. Operations systems can be categorized using a scale that has *continuous and assembly-line production* at one end and *job-shop production* at the other.[7] Continuous and assembly-line systems produce standardized output of their own design, frequently in large volumes. Examples are oil refineries, automobile assembly lines, and fast-

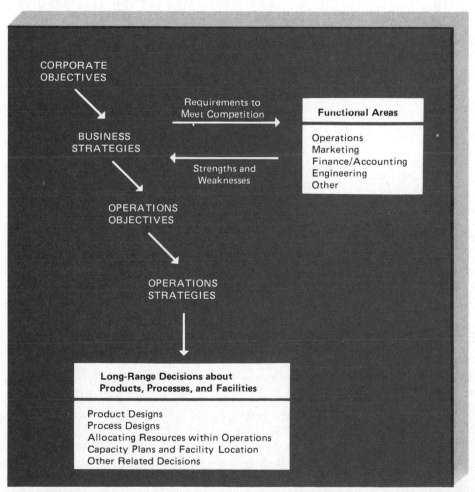

FIGURE 8–2
DECISIONS
INVOLVED IN
OPERATIONS
STRATEGY

Source: From *Production and Operations Management*, Second Edition, by Norman Gaither. Copyright © 1984 CBS College Publishing. Reprinted by permission of The Dryden Press, CBS College Publishing.

food chains. In contrast, job-shop systems make small amounts of custom-tailored products after receiving contracts to do so. A custom furniture maker is an example of a job shop; so is an automotive repair center.

In planning, the type of system selected—continuous or job shop—should be consistent with the nature of the organization's product or service and with the organization's strategic goals. And since products have life cycles, it is necessary for an organization to plan new products from time to time to continue to meet its objectives of growth and efficiency.

Designing Production/Operations Systems

Designing a production/operations system involves making decisions about *what, how many, how, where,* and *who.* This section will deal with each of those decisions in turn. For simplicity's sake, we will continue to use the term *operations system* to denote both manufacturing and service systems.

Product/Service Planning and Design

The first design decision affecting the operations system is planning *what* output is to be produced. This decision influences, and is in turn influenced by, the technology available and the operations structure within the organization.

Planning products and services is a strategic task involving marketing, finance, human resources, and operations. After some preliminary analysis of potential products and services has been carried out by marketing and engineering, the operations manager often becomes involved in this design decision.

The product/service design process consists of three basic steps:

1. *Research:* Generate the product/service ideas.
2. *Selection:* From among the research-generated ideas, choose those that are technologically feasible, marketable, and compatible with organizational strategy.
3. *Design:* Develop design specifications for the product/service. Final specifications should be optimal in terms of reliability, quality, and cost (which can be kept low by such means as component compatibility, interchangeability, and design simplicity).

CAD. Technological advances have recently made it possible for product design and drafting to be performed interactively on a computer, a process known as *computer-aided design* (CAD).[8] For example, General Motors now uses CAD to design the metal-stamping dies for its new cars. Car bodies are made from sheet metal that is stamped in large presses into the correct shape. Different dies are inserted into the press to give each stamping (a hood or fender) its form; the dies must be carefully designed to prevent wrinkling or tearing the sheet metal during the process. With CAD, GM designers can create computer models of proposed stamping forms early in the designing procedure and avoid later manufacturing difficulties. Previously, it took about 27 months to create the tooling for new car models. GM officials estimate that the use of CAD could reduce that time by up to seven months.[9]

Once decided upon, the product or service design becomes a key source of information for planning the required input and the transformation process for the operations system.

Capacity Planning

The second decision in designing the operations system is *how many* products—or *how much* service—is to be produced. This is called *capacity planning*.

"Capacity" refers to "the maximum theoretical rate of productive or conversion capability for an existing product mix of an organization's operations."[10] Capacity planning is a complex process that involves the following steps:[11]

· **Predicting future demand, including, insofar as possible, the likely impact of technology, competition, and other events.**
· **Translating these predictions into actual physical capacity requirements.**
· **Generating alternative capacity plans to meet the requirements.**
· **Analyzing and comparing the economic effects of the alternative plans.**
· **Identifying and comparing the risks and strategic effects of the alternative plans.**
· **Deciding on a plan for implementation.**

Long-range technological forecasting—which can extend five or ten years into the future depending on the industry—may be needed to anticipate or predict future capacity demands. Unforeseeable events—new technological discoveries, wars, recessions, embargoes, and the effects of an unknown inflation rate—cannot always be factored into forecasting equations. Although planning demand well into the future is complicated and risky, organizations often properly expend considerable effort in doing so. (See chapter 7.)

Completed forecasts must then be translated into capacity requirements. This implies that existing capacity must be measured. In some cases, measuring capacity is easy enough; for example, gauging the number of tons of steel produced by a steel mill. For a system with a diverse and less readily classified product or service—such as a legal office—measuring capacity is less straightforward. Input measures are generally used for such systems; that is, capacity may be defined as the number of lawyers in the legal office.

The physical capacity requirements that are forecast may compel the organization to change its operations system in order to meet the future demand. Capacity changes may be brought about by short-run and/or long-run modifications. *Short-run capacity changes* include overtime work, shifting existing personnel, sub-contracting, and using inventories or back orders. *Long-run capacity changes* involve adding or removing physical capacity by physical facility expansion (more press hammers, more lawyers) or contraction (fewer press hammers, fewer lawyers).

Alternative capacity plans, each of which fits the required demand but through different means (more press hammers, subcontracting), should be analyzed. The costs of each and all of their strategic effects should be weighed and compared. The alternative with the lowest cost could turn out to result in lost sales and market-share losses, which may (or may not) be inconsistent with organizational strategy. (A subcontracting slowdown may cause delays in delivery and thus loss of market to a competitor.) Costs, risks, and strategic effects must be thoughtfully weighed by managers.

TABLE 8–1 PROCESS CHOICES: BASIC HARDWARE MANUFACTURING PROCESSES

Casting and Molding	Machining	Metal Working	Assembly	Finishing
Sand casting	Turning	Forging	Soldering	Cleaning
Shell casting	Drilling	Extruding	Brazing	Blasting
Investment casting	Milling	Punching	Welding	Deburring
Die casting	Shaping	Trimming	Mechanical fastening	Painting
Permanent mold casting	Cutting	Drawing	Gluing	Plating
Powered metal molding	Broaching	Rolling	Press fitting	Heat treating
Compression molding	Grinding	Forming	Shrink fitting	Buffing
Transfer	Honing	Coining		Polishing
Extrusion	Etching	Swaging		Hardening
Injection molding		Spinning		
Laminating				

Source: Adapted from Donald F. Eary and Gerald E. Johnson, *Process Engineering for Manufacturing* (Englewood Cliffs, N.J.: Prentice-Hall, 1962), p. 3. Adapted by permission of Prentice-Hall.

Process Selection

Process selection, the third design decision, determines *how* the product or service will be produced. According to Richard Chase and Nicholas Aquilano, process selection involves four technological decisions:[12]

1. *Major Technological Choice.* Does technology exist to produce the product? Are there competing technologies among which we should choose? Should innovations be licensed from elsewhere, such as foreign countries, or should an internal effort be made to develop the needed technology?[13] The importance of the major technological choice phase is highlighted by such recent developments as microchips and gene splicing. Although the major technical choice is largely the province of engineers, chemists, biogeneticists, and other technical specialists, top managers should comprehend as fully as possible the technology, its likely evolution, and the alternatives.

2. *Minor Technological Choice.* What transformation processes will be used? Once the major technological choice is made, there may be a number of minor technological *process alternatives* available. The operations manager should be involved in evaluating alternatives for costs and for consistency with the desired product and capacity plans. Should the process be continuous? A continuous process, which is carried out 24 hours a day in order to avoid expensive startups and shutdowns, is used by the steel and chemical industries, among others. An assembly-line process, on the other hand, follows the same series of steps to mass-produce each item but need not run 24 hours a day; examples are the automobile and ready-to-wear clothing industries. Job-shop processes produce items in small lots, perhaps custom-made for a given market or customer; examples are lumber yards and aircraft manufacturers.

Even if the continuous job-shop choice can be easily made, the alternatives do not end there. For example, in a factory, the fabrication, joining together, and finishing of two pieces of metal may represent only a minuscule part of creating a finished product. There may be numerous ways of casting and molding, several ways of cutting, forming, assembling, and finishing. (See table 8–1.) A simple hardware operation could thus involve choices among 46 process alternatives and numerous combinations. Deciding on the best combination of processes in terms of costs and the total operations process can be difficult.

3. *Specific Component Choice.* What types of equipment (and degree of automation) should be used? Should the equipment be specific-purpose (tying it to this product), or general-purpose (leaving open the possibility of using the equipment to make other products)? To what degree should machines be used to replace human labor in performing and automatically controlling the work? *Computer-aided manufacturing (CAM)* and industrial robots are being used increasingly in many manufacturing systems.

CAM involves the use of a computer to help monitor and control processing equipment through the various phases of production. When CAD and CAM are linked in *computer integrated manufacturing (CIM)*—which is also called CAD/CAM—new product designs can be manufactured immediately and automatically in the factory. Computers in the plant retool production machinery and initiate assembly operations according to instructions provided by the CAD system; in turn, the CAD system works within the limits of the CAM's retooling and production capabilities. Such totally integrated design and manufacturing facilities are currently being developed and tested. (See fig. 8–3.)

Most industrial robots are basically computer-controlled mechanical arms that can be equipped with grippers, tools, or vacuum cups. More sophisticated robots may also be equipped with video imaging systems that allow them to "see" their work and with built-in computers that allow them to sort items or perform other complicated tasks on their own. In some industries, notably automotive manufacturing, robots are already performing simple assemblies. They are automated, flexible, and more reliable than human labor—though, of course, far more limited—and are especially suited for use in dangerous environments.

4. *Process Flow Choice.* How should the product or service flow through the operations system? The final process-selection step determines how materials and products will move through the system. Assembly drawings, assembly charts, route sheets, and flow process charts are used to analyze process flow. Analysis may lead to resequencing, combining, or eliminating operations in order to reduce materials handling and storage costs. In general, the less storage and delay involved in the process, the better.

In recent years, increasing use has been made of Automated Guided Vehicle Systems (AGVS). These systems employ driverless battery-operated vehicles that move back and forth between pickup and delivery points. Currently, this is achieved by placing a wire guide path in the floor that can be sensed by the vehicles' antennas. Research is now in progress to do away with the wire and to combine AGVS with robotics to create mobile robots.[14]

The four phases of process selection are closely interrelated. In each phase, choices should be made to minimize the process operations costs.

In service systems, process selection depends on the nature of the system. Service systems with low customer contact, such as the check-clearing operation of a bank, can carry out process selection by following the four phases outlined above. In systems with high customer contact, such as retail establishments, the processes or procedures for interacting with the customer must also be selected. For a standardized service, these processes can be specific and allow for little variability—for example, the cash-dispensing function of an automated teller machine (ATM) at a

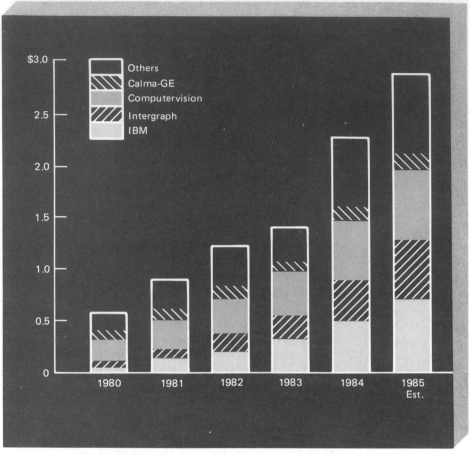

Total sales of major CAD/CAM systems manufacturers in billions of dollars.
Source: Eric N. Berg, "CAD/CAM's Pioneer Bets It All," *New York Times*, March 24, 1985, p. F4.
Copyright © 1985 by The New York Times Company. Reprinted by permission.

bank. For customized services, variable procedures must be designed—for example, the evaluation of a personal loan application at the same bank.

Facility Location Planning

Choosing where the production facility will be located is one of the most important design decisions. "The more aggregate a facility's planning mistake—for example, a factory, a department, a machine—the more costly it will be, the less likely that it will be changed, and the longer it will affect the operation."[15]

The objective of location planning is to position the capacity of the system so as to minimize total production and distribution costs. *Fixed capital costs* for construction, land, and equipment are incurred for new or additional facilities. *Variable operations costs* such as wages, taxes, energy and materials acquisition, and distribution are also incurred. In addition, qualitative factors such as labor availability, union activity, quality of life, and community attitudes should be evaluated. The location decision requires balancing all of these costs, effects on potential revenues, and qualitative factors.

Location analysis proceeds by determining location requirements and then evaluating alternative regions, communities, and specific sites. Traditional financial models, linear programming, statistical models, computer simulation models, and location factor rating models are used to evaluate the alternative locations. For many manufacturing firms, resource considerations are primary in selecting a location. For many service organizations—particularly convenience services—nearness to the customer often dominates the selection process because the location strongly affects demand and revenue.[16]

Layout Planning

Layout planning involves decisions about *how* to arrange the physical facilities spatially. This is the integrative phase of designing the operations system. In layout planning, the process and equipment decisions are translated into physical arrangements for production.

Space must be provided for:

- *Productive facilities,* such as work stations and materials-handling equipment.
- *Nonproductive facilities,* such as storage areas and maintenance facilities.
- *Support facilities,* such as offices, restrooms, waiting rooms, cafeterias, and parking lots.

Space must also be provided for materials and additional capacity. Any location-related requirements, such as docking facilities or heating units, must also be planned.

A good layout minimizes materials handling, maximizes worker and equipment efficiency, and satisfies a host of other factors. (See box for characteristics of a good layout.) Layouts can be characterized either by work flow or by function of the operations system.

Work-flow layouts include:

- *Product layouts,* arranged for the sequential steps in producing the product or rendering the service. Such a layout is appropriate for continuous or repetitive operations, such as mass-producing air conditioners or serving food in a cafeteria. (Figure 8–4 depicts a simple product layout in a small factory.)
- *Process layouts,* arranged according to task. Such a layout is appropriate for job-shop operations systems, such as universities and automotive repair shops, where there is no one route through the system for all products or services.
- *Fixed-position layouts,* where a large or heavy product itself—such as a ship— stays in one location, with people, tools, materials and equipment moved to the product as needed.

Function layouts include:

- *Storage layouts,* designed to minimize inventory and storage costs, as in warehouses.
- *Marketing layouts,* designed to maximize product exposure and sales instead of minimizing work flow. Supermarkets are an example.
- *Project layouts,* established to build projects or one-of-a-kind products, such as dams or buildings. This differs from the fixed-position layout described earlier in that the latter is designed to turn out more than one unit of a large product.

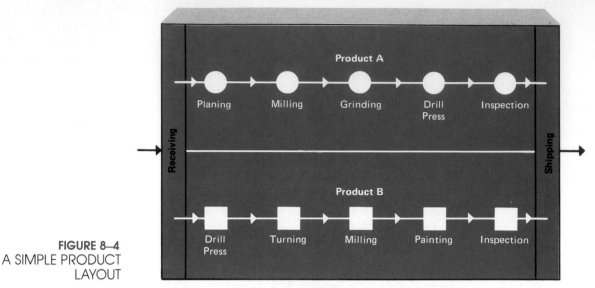

Source: *Production and Operations Management,* Third Edition, by Arthur C. Laufer, published by South-Western Publishing Co., Cincinnati, Ohio.

FIGURE 8–4
A SIMPLE PRODUCT
LAYOUT

In practice, most operations systems use a combination of layouts appropriate to the needs of different stages of product or service creation.

Job Design

The final decision in designing the operations system concerns the structure of individual jobs—*how* will the work be done and *who* will do it? Job design specifies the content and methods of work by individuals and groups in the operations system. Because job design is reflected in labor costs, it affects the ultimate cost of the product or service.

Job design consists of three activities: specifying individual work tasks, specifying the method of performing the work tasks, and combining work tasks into jobs for assignment to individuals (job content). (Considerations in the design of jobs are discussed in chapter 9).

Work methods analysis attempts to find the best way of performing the tasks in a given job. Time and motion studies, principles of motion economy, and other industrial engineering tools have been applied to determine optimal work arrangements. These techniques are used to study such factors as the rhythm of work, the use of the hands and tools, and ways to avoid fatigue on the job. Such environmental factors as temperature, air flow, humidity, noise, and lighting levels should be controlled to ease task performance and increase job satisfaction. Job design must also take into account health and safety requirements and regulations as set forth in the Occupational Safety and Health Act of 1970 (OSHA) and subsequent federal, state, and local regulations.

Once job design has been completed, job or work production standards are then developed using work measurement techniques. Such standards are established as a basis for comparison when measuring and judging output. A standard can be

THE MARKS OF A GOOD PLANT LAYOUT

1. Planned activity interrelationships
2. Planned materials flow pattern
3. Straight-line flow
4. Minimum backtracking
5. Auxiliary flow lines
6. Straight aisles
7. Minimum handling between operations
8. Planned materials-handling methods
9. Minimum handling distances
10. Processing combined with materials handling
11. Movement progresses from receiving toward shipping
12. First operations near receiving
13. Last operations near shipping
14. Point-of-use storage where appropriate
15. Layout adaptable to changing conditions
16. Planned for orderly expansion
17. Minimum goods in process
18. Minimum materials in process
19. Maximum use of all plant levels
20. Adequate storage space
21. Adequate spacing between facilities
22. Building constructed around planned layout
23. Materials delivered to employees and removed from work areas
24. Minimum walking by production operators
25. Proper locations of production and employee service facilities
26. Mechanical handling installed where practicable
27. Adequate employee service functions
28. Planned control of noise, dirt, fumes, dust, humidity, etc.
29. Maximum processing time to overall production time
30. Minimum manual handling
31. Minimum re-handling
32. Partitions don't impede material flow
33. Minimum handling by direct labor
34. Planned scrap removal
35. Receiving and shipping in logical locations

Source: James M. Apple, *Plant Layout and Materials Handling*, 3d ed., pp. 18–19. Copyright © 1977 by John Wiley & Sons, Inc. Used by permission.

established for various product attributes, such as quantity, quality, or cost. Production standards indicate what an average worker or group of workers can produce under average job conditions. They are usually developed using a combination of informal rules of thumb, historical performance studies, stopwatch studies, predetermined time studies, and statistical approaches to work sampling.

Standards form the basis for comparison to be used in planning and controlling the operations system—the subject of the next section.

Planning and Control Decisions

Even when the operations system has been successfully designed and placed into actual operation, much of the managerial challenge still remains. This is because decisions on a shorter-term basis—month to month, day to day, and even hour to hour—must be made as to how the system will be operated and controlled.

FIGURE 8–5
MODEL OF
OPERATIONS
PLANNING AND
CONTROL SYSTEM

Operations planning and control decisions involve scheduling and control of labor, materials, and capital input to produce the desired quantity and quality of output most efficiently. (See fig. 8–5.)

Operations planning and control are based on forecasts of future demand for the

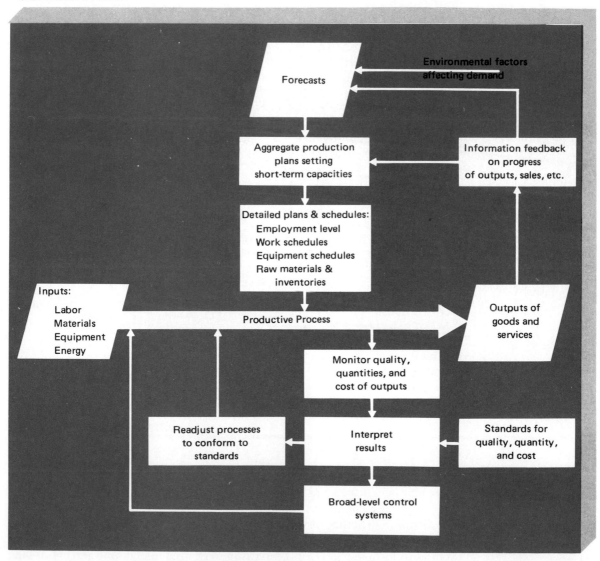

Source: Adapted from Elwood S. Buffa, *Modern Production/Operations Management*, 6th ed., p. 159. Copyright © 1980 by John Wiley & Sons. Used by permission.

output of the system. Even with the best possible forecasting and the most finely tuned operations system, however, demand cannot always be met with existing system capacity in a given time period. Unexpected market trends, new-product developments, or whatever, can throw the forecasts off, and problems in the operations system can reduce capacity. Ultimately shorter-term managerial decisions must be made to allocate system capacity in order to meet demands in a given time period.

Operations Planning and Control

Operations managers typically formulate plans that range from daily or weekly to yearly in outlook. The objectives of operations planning and control are to maximize customer service, minimize inventory investment, and maximize system operating efficiency. Often these three objectives conflict, and plans must be made to obtain the best balance among them. For example, if we as operations managers focus too rigidly on minimizing inventory investment, a sudden pickup in sales will find us unable to meet customer service requirements.

To some extent, completely meeting any one of the objectives means sacrificing the other two. Our system may operate with the greatest efficiency when it is put into operation only after sufficient orders have been received to require a large batch of output. In meeting the third objective, then, we will definitely have failed to meet the first, since we have been unable to serve customers for some time. The second objective has also been slighted since our large-batch philosophy demands a large available stock of input materials in inventory. However, if in addition to maintaining a large input inventory we also keep enough output in inventory to satisfy a certain number of customer orders, at the expense of further failing at the second objective, we could in fact meet the first and also our large-batch (third) objective. And so it goes. In this "what if" manner, the trade-off calculations are endless. Achieving a balance in operations objectives is one of the most delicate jobs within an organization.

Production Plans. Production plans are based on forecasts. First, overall plans are made for a six- to 18-month period. These aggregate production plans specify how operations system capacity will be used to meet anticipated output demands. The variables in the operations system that can be controlled are aggregate production rates, employment levels, and inventory levels. Next, the aggregate operations plans must be translated into master production schedules that specify the quantity and short-term timing of specific end products.

Detailed Scheduling. Detailed or short-term scheduling specifies the quantity and type of items to be produced and how, when, and where they should be produced for the next day or week. Detailed scheduling involves the following processes:

· **Allocating orders, equipment, and labor to work centers**
· **Establishing a sequence for the work**
· **Developing work schedules**
· **Initiating work performance**
· **Updating the status of the work**
· **Revising schedules**

The scheduling techniques employed to do this depend on the nature of the operations system.

Materials Requirements Planning. The master production schedule is the basis of the materials requirements planning (MRP) system. End products are analyzed or "exploded" to determine the materials and parts needed to produce the product. The required quantity is then adjusted for materials and parts already on hand. Order time for the materials and parts still needed is calculated, incorporating the lead time necessary to order the materials and receive them in ample time before production begins.

Since the proliferation of microcomputers in the corporate world, many managers have come to rely on their decision support systems (see chapter 6) for MRP. Product design specifications in the form of bills of materials (BOM) are supplied on an input file. This BOM file identifies the parts needed to produce the end product. Inventory records files (from the inventory planning and control system, described below) are used to keep account of the materials on hand. The MRP program reads both the BOM and inventory files to compute the quantities needed for each item.[17]

Inventory Planning and Control System

Maximize customer service

Minimize inventory investment

Maximize system operating efficiency

Inventory includes raw materials, work in process, finished goods, and supplies. An inventory planning and control system is a set of policies and decision-making rules for maintaining these items at desired levels.[18] Inventory decision rules specify when to order materials and how to order them.

Inventories serve many functions. They make a rational production system possible, since materials often cannot be relied upon to arrive exactly when they are needed. Inventories can absorb uncertainties in materials supply or customer demand by acting as a safety buffer. In addition, inventories are one method for creating a smooth flow of production. With adequate supplies of finished products in inventory, the operations system does not have to gear up suddenly to meet new demands.

However, inventories also have their associated costs. Inventories incur storage, breakage, investment, theft, and other carrying costs. Ordering materials or products from inventory involves clerical and perhaps transport costs. Insufficient inventories also result in shortages and lost sales. To minimize these costs and maintain inventories at optimal levels, numerous mathematical and computer-based inventory models have been developed to help operations managers decide when and how much to order.[19]

Just-in-Time Inventory. Inventories are also associated with an entirely different problem: They allow weaknesses in operations systems to remain hidden and uncorrected. In the mid-1970s, the world began to take notice of the Japanese *kanban*, or *just-in-time inventory system*. *Kanban* strives toward an ideal state in which production quantities are equal to delivery quantities. In other words, carrying costs are minimized by eliminating as much as possible the amount of inactive inventory kept on hand. Materials are bought more frequently and in smaller amounts, "just in time" to be used, and finished goods are produced and delivered "just in time" to be sold.[20] In striving toward ever smaller inventories of work in process, problems in the operations system are revealed. Correcting the problems can improve productivity and quality dramatically.

The possibility of improving *both* productivity *and* quality is one of the more exciting aspects of just-in-time and other modern approaches to operations management. In its 1985 annual report, Intel Corporation—a leading manufacturer of microprocessors—reported improvements in both quality and productivity from installing just-in-time and related systems. For example, as figure 8–6 shows, defects per million parts on a microcomputer product dropped by more than tenfold in a three-year period, and the rework rate in an assembly operation showed similar improvements. Not only are these types of improvements leading managers to rethink the quality/productivity trade-offs long taken for granted, but they are also raising questions about the need to sacrifice one or more of the operations planning and control objectives of maximizing customer service, minimizing inventory investment, and maximizing system operating efficiency.

In its dishwasher assembly factory in Louisville, Kentucky, GE has achieved similar results by combining the just-in-time method with a "use a part, make a part" system, in which machines manufacture parts right next to the assembly line.[21] (See the chapter case for a fuller discussion of GE's productivity experiment.)

FIGURE 8–6 IMPACTS OF MODERN OPERATIONS METHODS AT THE INTEL CORPORATION

Quality Control. According to David Garvin of Harvard University, "quality is the competitive issue of the '80s."[22] With Americans no longer seeing *quality control* as a mere inspection task, it is now being viewed as an integral part of company strategy. One result is that quality control is being practiced increasingly at each

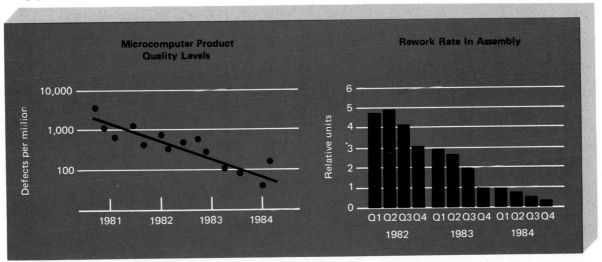

Note: Q1, Q2, Q3, and Q4 represent the first quarter, second quarter, third quarter, and fourth quarter, respectively.

Source: *Intel Corporation—First Quarter Report,* March 30, 1985, and *Annual Stockholders Meeting Report,* March 26, 1985. Courtesy Intel Corporation.

stage of the manufacturing process, making early corrections possible, instead of coming into play only at an end-of-line inspection where faulty products are discarded or reworked.

Changes are also apparent in the means companies are adopting to improve product quality. Many recent quality-improvement efforts encourage worker involvement and management participation that cut across functions and levels.[23]

Recognizing that the trade-off between productivity and quality, once thought of as inevitable, does not seem to exist in many cases, Lee Iacocca turned the phrase "quality and productivity—they go together" into one of his reform measures when he assumed the helm of the troubled Chrysler Corporation in 1978.[24] He foresaw that improving quality meant lower repair, inspection, scrap, and product warranty costs. More reliable automobiles also meant greater customer loyalty and increased sales. (See the part two case on pp. 227–230.)

Managers make two kinds of quality-control decisions: strategic decisions and tactical decisions.[25] Strategic decisions set the level of quality for the output of the organization. They influence product design, training of personnel, selection and maintenance programs for equipment, reward systems, and so on. Tactical, day-to-day decisions on quality control are concerned with such matters as when output should be inspected, how much of the output should be inspected, what should cause output to be rejected, and when corrective actions should be taken regarding the production process or personnel.

Statistical quality-control procedures fall into two categories. *Acceptance sampling procedures* determine if the completed product conforms to design specifications. (Does it work as it should?) *Process control procedures* monitor quality while the product is actually being produced or while the service is actually being rendered. (Are design specifications being met?) Process control also can detect shifts at some point in the process that may signal future quality problems in output.

The "control" part of quality control takes place when output that does not conform to specifications is identified and corrective action is taken: A new supplier might be located, a worn machine overhauled, or an incompetent worker retrained or replaced.

In some Japanese companies, statistical quality control has been used very successfully to motivate workers to produce high-quality products. This approach has also been used successfully by some U.S. firms, such as Motorola.[26] One of the mechanisms used is the *quality circle*, which consists of a group of labor and management personnel belonging to a single department that meets at regular intervals to solve quality-control problems. Quality circles provide a future-oriented approach, seeking high-quality products in the current production run and in the future.[27] (Japanese management methods are discussed in detail in chapter 23.)

Productivity

"The chief means whereby humankind can raise itself out of poverty to a condition of relative material affluence is by increasing productivity."[28] This should be obvious: The main way to increase output *per capita* (which normally translates directly into the standard of living) is by increasing productivity.

Productivity is the measure of how well an operations system functions. The importance of productivity to our economic well-being as a nation and to the survival of individual organizations is demonstrated by the wide discussion this topic is currently receiving. Such indicators of national economic health as inflation, economic growth, and the balance of payments are related to the level of productivity and changes in this level. For example, increases in productivity save scarce resources, since the resource requirement is less per unit of output. Productivity increases help mitigate inflation by counteracting the escalating costs of labor, materials, energy, and other expenses. Productivity improvements also strengthen the competitive position of a firm—or a country—in the important international market.

For the individual manager, productivity is vital because it indicates the level of efficiency and competitiveness of his or her firm or department.

What Is Productivity?

John Kendrick defines productivity as "the relationship between output of goods and services (O) and the inputs (I) of resources, human and nonhuman, used in the production process; the relationship is usually expressed in ratio form O/I." That is, productivity is the ratio of output to input. The higher the numerical value of this ratio, the greater the productivity.

For example, assume that a legal clinic with eight lawyers (the input) produces output consisting of 100 client consultations per day. Productivity would equal 100/8 or 12.50. Assume that a second legal clinic next door has 15 lawyers handling 125 consultations per day. The productivity ratio would be 125/15 or 8.33. The smaller firm has a higher productivity ratio on a quantitative basis. (Whether this is due to the greater skill or experience of its associates or to their lower standards of performance is reflected in the *quality* of their output, an issue that is not factored into this productivity ratio.)

Both the level of a productivity ratio for a given period and the comparison with other ratios over time are important measures. The level at any given time measures the efficiency of the operations at that time. Comparisons of the ratios over time measure the gain or loss in productivity.

There are two types of productivity ratios:[29]

· **Total productivity** relates all output to all input with the ratio Total Output/Total Input.
· **Partial productivity** relates all output to major categories of input with the ratio Total Output/Partial Input.

One familiar example of a partial productivity ratio is the labor productivity index or output per work-hour ratio. (The legal clinic example above was such a partial productivity ratio.) Most productivity measures quoted by economists and business executives are, in fact, labor productivity indexes. This partial productivity measure may be appropriate for the national economy, but its use is questionable in gauging the productivity of an individual organization.[30]

Improving Productivity in Organizations

Productivity and the means to increase it have become a major focus of managerial attention today. The possible actions that may be taken to improve productivity in an organization are many. For example:[31]

1. **The introduction of management decision support systems**
2. **Opening a central warehouse with automatic storage and retrieval**
3. **Smoothing work flow to cut down on the number of employees needed at peak times**
4. **Providing computer facilities in user areas**
5. **Training**
6. **Incentive programs based on increases in long-term productivity**

Attempts to increase productivity have been classified by Jon English and Anthony R. Marchione as either *big bang approaches* or *incremental approaches*.[32]

Subscribers to the "big bang" method attempt to boost productivity by large one-time investments in capital equipment. Although this approach is often effective, improvements in technology and equipment do not automatically lead to higher productivity. As English and Marchione have noted, for example, the airline industry learned a painful lesson when it invested in jumbo jets in 1966. Productivity was hardly improved by operating scores of high-priced planes with more empty seats than passengers inside.

The incremental approach seeks to improve productivity by making small changes in equipment, training, and procedures. This recognizes the fact that no matter how new or technologically advanced its equipment, an organization cannot be truly efficient unless its people, processes, and structure are efficiently coordinated.

Productivity Improvements in One Industry. One type of business that has been relatively successful in improving productivity is the retail clothing store. The average annual improvement in the productivity of labor in retail stores over the past 16 years has been 2.9 percent in retail clothing, compared with 1.2 percent for all nonfarm businesses.[33]

There are several apparent reasons for this success. One is the increase in the ratio of chain stores to unaffiliated independents. This results in an overall increase in productivity for the industry because chain stores have greater sales per employee than the independents. The latter emphasize personal service and are consequently far more labor-intensive. Another contributing factor is the proliferation of discount clothing stores. These stores employ such features as self-selection and central checkout, which raise the productivity levels.[34]

Technological advances have greatly contributed to the increased efficiency of retail stores in general. Point-of-sale computers have facilitated the monitoring of stock levels and made for speedier reordering. The computerization of customer billing and accounts payable has reduced the amount of time spent on bookkeeping. More effective security and antishoplifting systems have contributed by lowering theft costs.

Because of investment cost, computerization had been largely confined to chain stores until recently. As the price of microcomputers and specialized retailing software continues to fall, however, more and more small independent retail shops are taking advantage of that technology to narrow the productivity gap between themselves and chain stores. Some managers are now calling on computers for help in analyzing various staffing patterns and their associated costs. For example, a manager might devise alternative staffing plans based on his or her own experience, and then use a spreadsheet program to determine the comparative costs of each approach.[35]

Productivity through People

Workers' attitudes are of great importance to productivity. In recent years, much concern has been expressed about the apparent decline of the vaunted U.S. work ethic—the American commitment to hard work and personal achievement. A study by Daniel Yankelovich and John Immerwahr for the Public Agenda Foundation[36] has demonstrated the alarming lack of commitment of many Americans to their jobs, but does not attribute that lack of commitment to the loss of the old work ethic. This study found that the work ethic was still alive and healthy; yet only 23 percent of workers surveyed reported that they are performing at their full capacity, almost half (44 percent) said they do not put a great deal of effort into their jobs over and above what is required, and 62 percent of workers, managers, and labor union leaders believed people are not working as hard as they used to. Yankelovich and Immerwahr attribute much of this lack of effort on the job to management's failure to reward hard work and high performance. For example, almost one-half of the managers surveyed said there was no relationship between how good a job they do and how much they are paid.

Faced with the task of improving productivity, many managers concentrate on updating equipment rather than on developing employees. Experience has shown this approach to be limited in effectiveness. According to one set of estimates, since 1929 less than one-fifth of American productivity improvement has been due to increasing the amount of capital per worker. More than 75 percent has been due to improving worker training and knowledge, health care, and the allocation of tasks.[37]

Peters and Waterman (see chapter 1) revealed that the excellently managed companies they studied see the average employee "as the root source of quality and productivity gain." Such companies do not look to "capital investment as the fundamental source of efficiency improvement." Instead, employees are considered the source of ideas for improvement. Keys to the excellent companies' success in achieving high productivity are having high expectations for their employees' performance, "respecting them as individuals," trusting them, and "treating them as adults."[38]

Improving Worker Productivity. Don Nightingale has concluded that *profit sharing* has led to productivity improvement in thousands of firms.[39] Company-wide profit-sharing plans can be particularly effective in situations where supervising and evaluating individual performance is not viable. Additionally, profit sharing can lower internal resistance to technological change and foster teamwork between employees.

The use of *financial incentives* to motivate performance has been a part of management theory for quite some time. For example, Frederick W. Taylor (see chapter 2) wrote in 1911 that "the best type of management in ordinary use . . . [is] the management of 'initiative and incentive.' "[40] (We will discuss the use of rewards more thoroughly in chapter 15.)

Many companies are finding that offering financial or merchandise awards to employees for productivity improvement ideas can pay off quite effectively. Employees of Stanley Air Tools, which implemented a program offering prizes such as video recorders, generated 18,000 ideas, of which 4,000 were found to be usable.[41] The amount that companies award for successful ideas is generally related to the value of the suggestions. For example, a company might give a certain percentage of the amount saved by implementing a suggestion or offer a set dollar amount for ideas leading to less measurable improvements, such as increased safety or worker attendance.

The concept of *white-collar productivity* is growing in importance as the ratio of white-collar to blue-collar workers continues to rise. The need for improvement in this area is accentuated by the estimates of some experts that most office employees waste 45 percent of the day.[42] Furthermore, some predict that by the turn of the century, the percentage of all wage earners represented by white-collar workers might rise from the current number of slightly more than half to as much as 90 percent.[43]

Factors Influencing Productivity

The role of management in influencing productivity gains is clear. However, many other interrelated factors also affect productivity. Their complexity is clear when we look at the following considerations.

1. *Work Force.* The makeup of the work force is very important to productivity. For example, some observers feel that the large influx of untrained teenagers and women returning to work during the 1970s may have contributed to the decline in U.S. productivity rates during that decade.

2. *Energy Costs.* The costs of oil, gas, and electricity have a significant effect on productivity. Spiraling energy costs and shortages were regarded by many observers as the biggest factors in slowing productivity growth during the 1970s.

3. *Condition of Facilities and Investment in New Plants and Equipment.* Other nations, starting from a nonindustrial base or rebuilding after wartime destruction, have modern, efficient production facilities. On the other hand, U.S. industry, especially heavy industries such as steel, has been hampered by old facilities and outdated equipment.

4. *Level of Research and Development Spending.* The early 1980s have seen a significant improvement in industry support for basic research at universities.[44] This follows a decade or so of reduced investment in research and development by both government and private industry. The research on manufacturing that was carried out during the 1970s tended to concentrate on saving energy and reducing pollution rather than focusing on improving worker performance and productivity processes. The result was that, in many cases, productivity improvements lagged.

5. *Growth of the Less Productive Service Sector.* In 1970, 20 million people were

employed in the service sector; by 1983, however, the figure had increased to 31 million. Much of the increase was in jobs that pay below-average wages, such as fast-food-chain attendants and nursing-home aides. At the same time, those employed in manufacturing have decreased slightly, from 20.7 million in 1970 to 19.9 million in 1983, and agricultural workers have remained about the same.[45]

6. *Changes in Family Structure.* With over half of married women at work, the increased divorce rate, the attraction of alternative life-styles, and the increase in single-parent families, added financial and emotional pressure on many workers may produce negative effects on work performance.

7. *Increased Use of Alcohol and Drugs.* This is a difficult factor to evaluate, but alcohol and drug abuse, more frequent now than a few decades ago, has been estimated to cost employers billions of dollars annually.

8. *A Shift in Worker Attitudes and Motivation.* As we noted earlier, some employers and social critics contend that workers today no longer have the traditional work ethic: that is, that they no longer work as hard as they used to. Other observers believe the work ethic is strong but that management practices discourage workers from doing their best on the job.

9. *Cost to Industry of Government Regulation.* Many industries must comply with strict government regulations concerning pollution control and other measures to improve health and safety on the job. Productivity is affected because the cost of the equipment and paperwork involved has to be absorbed by the business organizations affected. The 1980s have seen a decrease of regulation in some areas.

10. *Inflation.* In recent years inflation has been minimal. When it is high, however, it may affect productivity growth by making it difficult to anticipate and control production costs and by discouraging additional investment.

11. *Tax Policies.* Outdated tax laws have frequently penalized new investment by ignoring inflation. Deductions for depreciation have been spread over too long a period to provide for replacement costs of outdated equipment, and rising prices can create illusory profits on which real taxes must still be paid.

The impact of the factors just discussed (as well as of others) upon future productivity growth is varied. Some factors may be temporary and their effects already absorbed by the economy. For example, the work force expansion during the 1970s has slowed down and is not likely to retard future productivity gains. The 1981 tax bill was designed to encourage business investment, and subsequent tax reform efforts could have a variety of effects. Other factors, such as drug abuse and changes in family structure, are social problems affecting all levels of national life. But some must be addressed by managers if productivity gains—necessary to counter inflation and improve the quality of life for all—are to be realized. In this latter category are such factors as new facility investment and research and development programs. Figure 8–7 shows that, despite many factors adversely affecting U.S. productivity, sales per employee have grown in several key industries over the last decade.

Productivity in Japan: Theory Z

After the 1970s, many observers were struck by the contrast between the slowing of American productivity gains and the remarkable growth of the Japanese economy

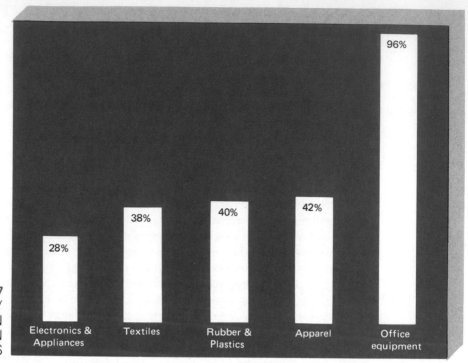

FIGURE 8–7
PRODUCTIVITY
GROWTH IN
CERTAIN
INDUSTRIES

Percentage change in sales growth per employee by industry (1973–1983).
Source: Peter Nulty, "The Princes of Productivity," *Fortune*, April 30, 1983, p. 254. Used by permission.

and the high quality of Japanese products. Among those who looked to the Japanese model for answers to the American problem was William G. Ouchi, whose studies of Japanese business organizations led him to describe a *Theory Z* management style. Reaching a conclusion similar to that reached a few years later by Peters and Waterman, Ouchi observed that "the Theory Z approach to management suggests that involved workers are the key to increased productivity."[46] We will discuss Japanese management in more detail in our international business chapter.

Productivity Management. In an attempt to improve productivity, some organizations have set up systematic and coordinated productivity improvement programs.[47] Chase and Aquilano observe that methods to improve productivity fall into four general categories:

1. **Product and process improvements**
2. **Work and job improvements**
3. **Employee motivation methods**
4. **Organizational change**

We will be exploring aspects of these topics in many of the remaining chapters of this book. Work and job improvements are discussed in chapter 9, the need for change and ways to effect it in chapters 13 and 14, and employee motivation in chapter 15. Chapters 20, 21, and 22 examine ways that managers can keep abreast of productivity in their organizations, and chapter 23 discusses productivity in the light of international management practices.

Summary   Production management or operations management is a key job in an organization and is important as well to our society and to us as individuals. How well production systems function is closely tied both to organizational health and to our standard of living. Once thought of solely as manufacturing management, production management is now recognized as a necessity for service industries also, and hence this chapter uses the newer term "operations management." Recently, operations management has been undergoing major changes, with greater worker involvement, improvements in production process design, and achievement of both high quality and high productivity being the most important aspects.

Operations systems can be studied as a "set of components whose function is to transform a set of inputs into some desired output." The input—workers, technology, know-how—is transformed by means of a particular process into output—the finished products or services. Operations managers have a twofold job: supervising design of the operations system and supervising the performance of the system. Both functions should be carried out in a manner that implements organizational strategy; and conversely, an organization's strategy should be formulated with its operations system in mind.

Design of an operations system means deciding upon (1) the product or service to produce; (2) the quantity or amount of it to produce—capacity planning; (3) the processes to employ to produce it; (4) the location at which to produce it; (5) the layout of facilities; and (6) how the jobs will be structured and assigned.

The second operations management function—supervising the performance of the system—becomes important once the system has been designed. Ultimately, managerial operations decisions are made month by month, day by day, and even hour by hour. Managers must strike a balance among three key objectives: to maximize customer service, minimize inventory investment, and maximize system operating efficiency. Various types of specialized planning and control techniques play key roles in operations management, such as materials requirements planning, inventory planning and control, detailed scheduling, and quality control.

The measure of how well an operations system functions is called productivity. Productivity is measured as the ratio of output to input. Productivity figures, imprecise at best, indicate an improving or deteriorating competitive situation when compared over time. On a national scale, productivity influences the standard of living, inflation, economic growth, and balance of payments. At the level of the individual firm, it is one of the keys to survival.

Much attention has been paid recently to increasing productivity. Improvements have focused on changes in capital equipment, employee policies, and organizational procedures and structure. Although new technologies like CIM (CAD/CAM) systems play important roles in increasing productivity in some industries, many observers still see the key to productivity gains in the way people are treated and managed.

Review Questions

1. What do the terms *production management* and *operations management* mean?
2. How do the authors define the operations subsystem within the organization?
3. What are the five elements of a system as the authors define them?

4. The authors further define operations systems as continuous and assembly-line systems or job-shop systems. Discuss the characteristics and give an example of each.

5. Discuss the basic steps in the product/service design process.

6. What is meant by capacity planning?

7. The third major decision in design is process selection, or how the product or service will be produced. Chase and Aquilano suggest that this is a four-part decision. What are those parts?

8. Distinguish between facility location planning and layout planning.

9. The final decision in designing an operations system is the structure of individual jobs, or job design. Specifically what is meant by the term *job design*?

10. What are the objectives of operations planning and control, and how are they related?

11. What do the acronyms MRP and BOM mean?

12. Inventories are an integral or important part of many production systems. What are the major opposing costs associated with inventories?

13. What is a productivity ratio, and what does it measure?

14. Describe the just-in-time concept of inventory control.

15. What is the difference between a "big bang" approach and an incremental approach to improving productivity?

16. What changes have recently occurred in the way managers view quality control?

17. What benefits does computerization offer to the manager of a retail store?

Notes

1. John O. McClain and L. Joseph Thomas, *Operations Management: Production of Goods and Services,* 2nd ed. (Englewood Cliffs, N.J.: Prentice-Hall, 1985), p. 6.

2. This discussion is based on Everett E. Adam, Jr., and Ronald J. Ebert, *Production and Operations Management: Concepts, Models, and Behavior,* 2nd ed. (Englewood Cliffs, N.J.: Prentice-Hall, 1981), pp. 18, 25; and James B. Dilworth, *Production and Operations Management: Manufacturing and Nonmanufacturing,* 2nd ed. (New York: Random House, 1983), p. 14.

3. Richard B. Chase and Nicholas J. Aquilano, *Production and Operations Management: A Life Cycle Approach,* 3rd ed. (Homewood, Ill.: Irwin, 1981), p. 11. Many other discussions in this chapter are based on this text.

4. This description of the model is based on Elwood S. Buffa, *Modern Production/Operations Management,* 6th ed. (New York: Wiley, 1980), pp. 4, 8–9.

5. Chase and Aquilano, *Production and Operations Management,* p. 11, contains the basis for this example and gives other examples as well.

6. Wickham Skinner, *Manufacturing in the Corporate Strategy* (New York: Wiley, 1978), p. 406.

7. Dilworth, *Production and Operations Management,* pp. 10–11.

8. James R. Evans, David R. Anderson, Dennis J. Sweeney, and Thomas A. Williams, *Applied Production and Operations Management* (St. Paul, Minn.: West Publishing, 1984), p. 49. See also Stan Kolodziej, "Micro-Based CAD Systems—From Plain Vanilla to Thirty Flavors," *Computerworld Focus,* June 19, 1985, pp. 39–40.

9. John Holusha, "Metal Forming By Computer," *New York Times,* November 22, 1984, p. D2.

10. Adam and Ebert, *Production and Operations Management,* p. 157.

11. Buffa, *Modern Production/Operations Management,* p. 85.

12. Chase and Aquilano, *Production and Operations Management,* p. 34. Our discussion of process selection is based in part on their discussion, pp. 34–41.

13. For a detailed analysis of this subject, see Bela Gold, "Managerial Considerations in Evaluating the Role of Licensing in Technological Development Strategies," *Managerial and Decision Economics* 3, no. 4 (1982):213–217.

14. Gunnar K. Lofgren, "Automatic Guide Vehicle Systems," *Production and Inventory Management Review* 3, no. 2 (February 1983):28–29.

15. Philip E. Hicks and Areen M. Kumtha, "One Way to Tighten Up Plant Location Decisions," *Industrial Engineering* 3, no. 4 (April 1971):19–23.

16. For a survey of the current state of the art of retail store location selection, see C. Samuel Craig, Avijit Ghosh, and Sara McLafferty, "Models of the Retail Location Process: a Review," *Journal of Retailing* 60, no. 1 (Spring 1984):5–36.

17. For a detailed description of MRP systems, see Joseph Orlicky, *Materials Requirements Planning* (New York: McGraw-Hill, 1975). Typical MRP DSS software include *Myte Myke Manufacturing* (Orchard Park, N.Y.: MDS Assoc., 1985); *Twin Oaks mrp 2* (Cottage Grove, Minn.: Twin Oaks, Inc., 1985); and *MCBA Manufacturing System* (Southfield, Mich.: MDM Systems, 1985).

18. Much of our discussion of inventory planning and control is based on Chase and Aquilano, *Production and Operations Management*, pp. 461–466. See also George W. Plossl and Oliver W. Wright, *Production and Inventory Control: Principles and Techniques*, 2nd ed. (Englewood Cliffs, N.J.: Prentice-Hall, 1985).

19. For a brief but excellent discussion of the innovative approach to minimizing inventories used by some Japanese companies, see Robert H. Hayes, "Why Japanese Factories Work," *Harvard Business Review* 59, no. 4 (July–August 1981):59.

20. For an excellent discussion of JIT systems, see Richard J. Schonberger, *Japanese Manufacturing Techniques: Nine Hidden Lessons in Simplicity* (New York: Free Press, 1982).

21. Gene Bylinsky, "America's Best-Managed Factories," *Fortune,* May 28, 1984, p. 23.

22. Quoted in Sandra Blakeslee, "Restoring Quality in Quality Control," *New York Times* Careers '85 Special Supplement, October 14, 1985, p. 34. See also Bradley T. Gale and Richard Klavans, "Formulating a Quality Improvement Strategy," *Journal of Business Strategy* 5, no. 3 (Winter 1985):21–32; and Madhev H. Sinha, *Essentials of Quality Assurance Management* (New York: Wiley, 1986).

23. Frank S. Leonard and W. Earl Sasser, "The Incline of Quality," *Harvard Business Review* 60, no. 5 (September–October 1982):168.

24. Al Fleming, "Chrysler Quality & Productivity VP George Butts," *Automotive News,* February 28, 1983, p. E10.

25. For an analysis of the advantages of strategic-operations decisions, see Steven C. Wheelwright, "Japan—Where Operations Really Are Strategic," *Harvard Business Review* 59, no. 4 (July–August 1981):67–74; and Robert H. Hayes and Steven C. Wheelwright, *Restoring Our Competitive Edge: Competing through Manufacturing* (New York: Wiley, 1984).

26. See Francesca Lunzer, "Does Your Car Have a Fan Belt?" *Forbes,* December 3, 1984, p. 222. See also J. M. Juran, *Quality Control Handbook* (New York: McGraw-Hill, 1974).

27. For an evaluation of American companies' experience with quality circles, see Robert Wood, Frank Hull, and Koya Azumi, "Evaluating Quality Circles: The American Application," *California Management Review* 26, no. 1 (Fall 1983):37–52.

28. The following discussion is drawn from John W. Kendrick, *Understanding Productivity: An Introduction to the Dynamics of Productivity Change* (Baltimore: Johns Hopkins, 1977), pp. 1, 14.

29. Charles E. Craig and R. Clark Harris, "Total Productivity Measurement at the Firm Level," *Sloan Management Review* 14, no. 3 (Spring 1973):13–29.

30. Donald J. Wait, "Productivity Measurement: A Management Accounting Challenge," *Management Accounting* 16, no. 11 (May 1980):25.

31. For these and other examples, see K. L. Brookfield, "Dimensions of Productivity Improvement," *Journal of Systems Management* 34, no. 12 (December 1983):26–29; and Robert C. Holland, "Strategic Planning: Some New Directions," *Journal of Accountancy* 156, no. 3 (September 1983):132.

32. Jon English and Anthony R. Marchione, "Productivity: A New Perspective," *California Management Review* 25, no. 2 (January 1983):58.

33. Brian Friedman, "Apparel Stores Display Above-Average Productivity," *Monthly Labor Review* 107, no. 10 (October 1984):37.

34. Shoppers who desire personal attention from salespeople might argue that some of these "productivity" improvements are overstated because the decrease of quality implicit in decreased personal service has not been taken into account.

35. F. Warren Benton, *EXECUCOMP—Maximum Management with the New Computers* (New York: Wiley, 1983), p. 167.

36. Daniel Yankelovich and John Immerwahr, *Putting the Work Ethic to Work: A Public Agenda Report on Restoring America's Competitive Vitality* (New York: Public Agenda Foundation, 1983).

37. Thomas R. Horton, "Training: A Key to Productivity Growth," *Management Review* 72, no. 9 (September 1983):2.

38. Thomas J. Peters and Robert H. Waterman, Jr., *In Search of Excellence: Lessons from America's Best-Run Companies* (New York: Warner Books, 1982), pp. 14–15, 260–277.

39. Don Nightingale, "Profit Sharing: New Nectar for the Worker Bees," *Canadian Business Review* 11, no. 1 (Spring 1984):11.

40. Frederick W. Taylor, *The Principles of Scientific Management* (New York: Norton, 1947; originally published in 1911), p. 34.

41. Bruce A. Jacobs, "Prizes for Productivity Ideas," *Industry Week,* July 11, 1983, p. 66.

42. Merrill Douglass and Donna Douglass, "Improve White-Collar Productivity," *Personnel Administrator* 27, no. 2 (December 1982):12.

43. Edmund Fitzgerald, "Telecommunications Seen as the Missing Link in the Productivity of Managers," *Communications News* 20, no. 12 (December 1983):100–101.

44. Donald R. Fowler, "University-Industry Research Relationships," *Research Management* 27, no. 1 (January–February 1984):35.

45. *Statistical Abstract of the United States: 1985,* 105th ed. (Washington, D.C.: Bureau of the Census, 1984), p. 404.

46. William G. Ouchi, *Theory Z: How American Business Can Meet the Japanese Challenge* (Reading, Mass.: Addison-Wesley, 1981), p. 4.

47. For a survey of the emerging productivity management staff function, see Marta Mooney, *Organizing for Productivity* (New York: Conference Board, 1981).

CASE STUDY: GE Turns Old into New in Kentucky

"In this plant," says Ray Rissler, "we have proved that it is possible to take a 30-year-old facility and transform it into a competitive new unit; and we have also shown that you can take a labor force with a strong union that resisted change and convince it that change is necessary."

Rissler is manager of the modernization project at General Electric's dishwasher plant in Louisville, Kentucky. All around him, one of the showpieces of modern-day U.S. factory engineering is humming away to the smooth rhythms of a largely automated production line. It is a rhythm that is currently tapping out dollars in abundance for GE, as the combination of increased market share and an expanding domestic economy bring back memories of the industry's peak year in 1973.

Like several other U.S. factories that have recently arisen on the foundations of the mature old manufacturing industries, the plant represents a renaissance in U.S. methods and productivity. Its startup has been accompanied by a quantum leap in productivity and what amounts to a revolution in quality. With the same number of workers as before the changeover, the plant now produces 25 percent more units in a year, giving GE about 30 percent of the market. As far as quality is concerned, Rissler says the plant has delivered virtually a tenfold improvement as measured by customer complaints in the first year of warranty.

The change in the plant goes back to 1979, when GE, faced with intense pressure on profit margins generally in household appliances, was asking itself if it wanted to continue at all in that sector. Unlike Westinghouse, however, GE decided to stay. "Our name on household appliances is a pervasive reminder of the company in virtually every household in America," says Rissler. GE also saw that to survive as an effective force it had to improve both quality and productivity. These objectives were partly prompted by the market environment, which had become steadily tougher. But they also derived indirectly from the threat of Japanese competition. The market had been educated by Japanese products to demand better quality; and GE had good reason to believe that after the highly successful foray of the Japanese electrical companies into television and audio, they were lining up kitchen products as well.

Because the dishwasher division is a relatively small one, it was able to go for a radical—and risky—method of reorganizing, involving the production workers in the design of the product line and the production process. The reorganization got off to a good start when the normally militant work force came into the discussions early and threw its weight behind the plan. The project has thus been much less bothered by disputes than others in the past—strikes at the entire Louisville complex, which embraces a variety of products, have fallen from 400,000 people-hours a year to less than 50,000.

On the production side, engineers solved a problem that had baffled them for two decades. Because of the large range of machines manufactured by the company, the assembly process was necessarily complex and required a degree of dexterity apparently beyond the reach of automation. The solution occurred in a flash one day when a GE team was visiting a plant in Japan and noticed that all the manufacturing processes that introduced elements—usually decorative trim and electronic controls—to differentiate products from one another had been pushed to the end of the line. Using this principle, GE was able to go back and redesign the entire plant and the whole product range so that only in the last few steps is individualized assembly needed on each washer.

The revamp was helped by the use of a GE-developed weight-bearing plastic, Permatuf, that virtually did away with steel and porcelain in the construction of the central washing tub and provided the base for the new dishwasher design. It also created a concept around which to organize the plant, since it led the GE engineers toward standardization of the basic washtub. By simplifying the design at this point, the company was able to automate a major part of the manufacturing process.

As a result, manufacturing has been enormously accelerated. The tubs are manufactured at the beginning of the three-mile-long production line, then meander around the plant on robolized assembly lines to emerge as finished machines on an average of 18 hours. Before the change, the machines were much heavier, were made of more parts, and took six days to make. In addition, virtually all plastic and metal parts are now made at the point of use, reducing inventory costs from around $9.5 million to $3.9 million despite the higher rate of output.

GE uses a variety of computerized optical devices, including laser bar-code readers, to track units on the production line and automatically divert washers in need of repair or testing to a special holding area. An optical alignment system installs the dishwasher doors to tolerances of a few thousandths of an inch.

GE admits that the impressive results of these changes have not been exposed to the criteria of Japanese competition, now regarded as the iron test of U.S. technology. But GE's next step will be a $200 million investment in the refrigeration business, where its ability will be directly measured against the Japanese. Sanyo has established a plant in California, and GE believes that the Japanese company has sufficient experience in the Japanese refrigerator market to make it a tough competitor. "In dishwashers we did what we had to do to remain ahead even though we did not absolutely need to do it," says Roger Schipke, senior vice-president. "But in refrigerators we know that we have to be competitive on a world-class basis because the Japanese competitors market their products worldwide. We believe at the moment that we can go into the lead."

Source: Adapted from Terry Dodsworth, "Turning the Old into the Dynamic New," *Financial Times*, September 10, 1984, p. 19.

Case Questions

1. Why did GE revamp its dishwasher plant?
2. What changes were made, and how did they increase productivity?
3. How has Japanese competition influenced GE's operations strategy in household appliances?
4. In your opinion, are foreign-made goods of higher quality than American-made goods? Support your opinion with specific examples.

CASE ON PLANNING AND DECISION MAKING

Chrysler's Turnaround Strategy

For the Chrysler Corporation, the 1970s was a decade of deepening crisis. The third-largest automaker in the United States, as well as the country's tenth-largest corporation, Chrysler was more and more out of step with market demand.

· In 1971, Chrysler began extensive retooling to emphasize a new corporate strategy: to build and sell primarily full-size family cars. The larger, heavier, and more powerful Plymouths, Dodges, and Chryslers became available in 1973, just weeks before the OPEC oil embargo gave a violent shock to the American car-buying public. Chrysler was completely unprepared to meet the sudden, huge demand for smaller, fuel-efficient cars.

· After two more years of costly retooling, the compact-size Plymouth Volare and Dodge Aspen were introduced in late 1975. Sales fell considerably short of expectations because of a temporarily slackening demand for small cars. Relative to its main domestic competitors, General Motors and Ford, Chrysler was cash-poor, yet had chosen to offer a full product line equal to theirs.

· In the summer and early fall of 1978, Chrysler invested heavily in advertising to promote its new smaller luxury models, the Newport, New Yorker, and St. Regis. Many customers were attracted to dealers' showrooms, but various manufacturing problems prevented the delivery of any of the luxury models until late November. By then, customers had bought the cars of other manufacturers.

· In 1979, Chrysler introduced a new line of front-wheel-drive cars, the Plymouth Horizon and Dodge Omni. Critical and popular response to the new models was enthusiastic, but the company discovered it would have no more than 300,000 units to sell that year, because it had no power to increase the number of engines contracted for, engines that were being supplied by a foreign competitor, Volkswagen.

On November 2, 1978, Chrysler made two announcements: the company suffered a record loss of $158.5 million in the third quarter; and Lee J. Iacocca, the recently dismissed president of Ford, would first become Chrysler's president and then, within a year, its chairman and chief executive officer. Iacocca was a controversial figure, a consummate salesman with political savvy and a blunt sense of humor. During his nearly three decades with Ford he had developed some of the company's flashiest and most successful models, among them the Mustang and the Maverick. But at the time of his dismissal, he left Ford in serious financial trouble, with sales falling because of the company's reputation for building poorly made and unsafe cars—a reputation due, according to some industry observers, to Iacocca's preference for style and rhetoric over substance.

In his tough-talking book, *Iacocca*, a kind of business autobiography, the new president described some critical first impressions of Chrysler:

- **"I noticed a couple of seemingly insignificant details that gave me pause. The first was that the office of the president . . . was being used as a thoroughfare to get from one office to another. I watched with amazement as executives with coffee cups in their hands kept opening the door and walking right through the president's office. Right away I knew the place was in a state of anarchy."**

- **"I'll never forget visiting the Michigan State Fairgrounds, jammed with thousands of unsold Chryslers, Dodges, and Plymouths, vivid evidence of the company's structural weakness. The volume would vary, but the number of cars was usually far above what we could hope to sell. . . . At a time when our cash was dwindling away and interest rates were high, the costs of carrying this inventory were astronomical. But even worse, the cars were just sitting there in the great outdoors and slowly deteriorating."**

- **"All through the company, people were scared and despondent. Nobody was doing anything right. I had never seen anything like it. The vice-presidents were all square pegs in round holes. [The former president] and his people had taken guys who had performed well enough in one area and had moved them around at will. . . . After a few years of being shuffled around, everybody at Chrysler was doing something he wasn't trained for. And believe me, it showed."**

Iacocca moved on several fronts to assert managerial control.

- **He replaced virtually all senior managers, largely with former colleagues of his from Ford.**
- **He ordered monthly meetings between his sales department and dealers, to determine dealers' needs for the next two months and to build production schedules based on those needs.**
- **He abolished the sales bank, taking heavy losses to sell off Chrysler's huge and deliberately created backlog of inventory.**
- **He became the company's spokesman in most advertising—in effect, the symbol of Chrysler's struggle to turn itself around.**

The company's most serious problem, by all accounts, was its lack of cash. Iacocca became the chief lobbyist in a long struggle to persuade Congress to approve loan guarantees covering $1.5 billion of Chrysler's borrowings. The only alternative to federal help, Iacocca always maintained, was bankruptcy. The special bill, hotly opposed by free marketers, was finally passed in December 1979. As the price for its cooperation, Congress insisted on Chrysler's winning on its own about

$2 billion in concessions from unions, suppliers, and others, whittling itself down to a leaner and more viable core.

Iacocca then initiated a strategy involving severe retrenchment and divestiture; it aimed to reduce operating expenses and to improve productivity, profit margins, and cash flow.

Salaried expense dropped markedly as half the work force, both white and blue collar, was laid off. Unions acceded not only to the layoffs, but even to wage cuts of 13 percent and to major give-backs in fringe benefits. Fixed plant costs also fell, as the company closed 20 of 60 plants, sold extensive foreign operations, and terminated about a quarter of domestic dealerships.

Chrysler modernized the remaining 40 plants to make them more productive and cost-efficient. The company was among the first domestic automakers to introduce robot welding and computerized quality control. Great savings in inventory came from reducing the number of different parts required throughout the manufacturing system from 75,000 to 40,000.

These and other cuts ultimately halved Chrysler's break-even point. By 1982, the company needed to sell just 1.2 million vehicles before it could start to show a profit, half the unit sales required in 1979.

The loan guarantees in themselves provided no overnight cure for Chrysler's problems. From 1978 through 1981, the company lost a staggering $3.5 billion. In 1982, there was a modest profit of $170 million, resulting not from the sales of cars but from selling off the company's Michigan-based tank division to General Dynamics for $349 million. Yet, with the national economy moving strongly out of its 1981–82 recession, Chrysler's profitability, based on its newly streamlined structure, rose impressively. Earnings were $701 million in 1983, and in 1984 reached a record $2.38 billion.

Cash flow improved markedly. On July 13, 1983, Iacocca announced that Chrysler had repaid all outstanding guaranteed loans, seven years ahead of the federally imposed 1990 deadline. In addition to its great value as a public-relations move, retiring the long-term debt saved the company about $350 million in interest payments over the period. On February 14, 1985, announcing the record earnings for 1984, Iacocca offered a $500 "voluntary, thank-you" payment to each of Chrysler's 100,000 employees. "Our people and their families have earned this payment," the chairman said. "They earned it in work, in worry, in sacrifice. They were part of the action, so now they're getting a little piece of the action."

Most analysts of the automotive industry agree that Chrysler's newly refound success can continue, but only if the company can avoid several serious pitfalls:

- **Collapse in demand for new cars. Americans buy lots of cars when the economy is strong, but far fewer in a recession. Chrysler's $6.6-billion, five-year production program needs a growing economy to succeed.**
- **Elimination of voluntary restraints on exports by the Japanese. The lifting of restrictions in early 1985 was expected to increase the Japanese share of the auto market, likely at the expense of Chrysler.**

- Loss of patience by the work force. The nearly $1 billion given up by Chrysler's unsalaried employees has not yet been recovered, and they continue to be paid wages lower than their counterparts in other car companies.

- A serious, long-term softening in the price of oil. Chrysler has a lot riding on its cars' superior fuel economy—ahead of federal guidelines and substantially better than GM or Ford—but a rollback in gasoline prices could create renewed demand for heavier, more powerful cars, a demand the company would be unable to meet.

- Need for improving product quality. *Consumer Reports* in April 1984 listed 92 recommended used cars by price; none of them was an American-made Chrysler product. The magazine also rated 1982 and 1983 cars for incidence of repair; of American-made Chrysler products, 4 were rated average, 9 worse than average, and 5 much worse than average. By way of contrast, 16 of 17 Toyota models were rated much better than average.

Sources: This case is based on material in the following articles and books: James K. Glassman, "The Iacocca Mystique," *New Republic*, July 16–23, 1984, pp. 20–23; Lee Iacocca with William Novak, *Iacocca* (New York: Bantam Books, 1984); Lee Iacocca, "The Rescue and Resuscitation of Chrysler," *Journal of Business Strategy* 4, no. 1 (Summer 1983):67–69; Alexander L. Taylor III, "Iacocca's Tightrope Act," *Time,* March 21, 1983, pp. 50–61; and Michael Schwartz and Glenn Yago, "What's Good for Chrysler Is Bad for Us," *Nation,* September 12, 1981, pp. 200–203.

Questions

1. Describe Chrysler's internal problems and strategic planning errors. How did the company's problems relate to external threats and opportunities?
2. Characterize Lee Iacocca's management style.
3. What do you think was the most difficult problem he had to solve at Chrysler?
4. Outline Chrysler's turnaround strategy. Why did it work so well?
5. What did Chrysler do to improve productivity?
6. Iacocca has written, "Chrysler is ready to compete and is planning to outrun the best of them in the next few years." Given the difficult problems the company still faces, what strategy would you suggest Chrysler pursue?

PART THREE
ORGANIZING FOR STABILITY AND CHANGE

9 DIVISION OF WORK AND ORGANIZATIONAL STRUCTURE

Upon completing this chapter you should be able to:

1. Describe the organizing process and explain why it is important for organizations.
2. Explain the relationship between strategy and organizational structure.
3. Describe the relationship between specialization and job satisfaction.
4. Define and describe job enlargement and job enrichment.
5. Define the formal structure of the organization, and identify the various ways an organization can be structured.
6. State what is shown on an organization chart.
7. Describe functional, product/market, and matrix structures, and identify the advantages and disadvantages of each.

The word *organization* has two common meanings. The first meaning signifies an *institution* or functional group; for example, we refer to a business, a hospital, a government agency, or a basketball team as an organization. We discussed the importance of organizations in this sense in chapter 1. The second meaning refers to the process of organizing—the way work is arranged and allocated among members of the organization so that the goals of the organization can be efficiently achieved. We will be dealing with various aspects of the organizing process in this section of the text (chapters 9–14).

Our discussion begins by defining the five steps in the organizing process and examining their importance. The organizing process involves balancing a company's needs for both stability and change. On the one hand, an organization's structure gives stability and reliability to the actions of its members. Stability and reliability are required for an organization to move coherently toward its goals. On the other hand, altering an organization's structure can be a means of adapting to and bringing about change, or it can be a source of resistance to change.

Thus, the first group of chapters in part three emphasizes the stabilizing aspects of organizational structure. In them we will see how managers create predictability of organizational behavior through the ways they structure the organization and define tasks, responsibilities, and relationships in the workplace. Then, in chapter 12 we will consider the selection, training, and development of the organization's members. In the remaining two chapters of part three, our attention will turn to organizing in the face of change and to managing conflict and creativity within the organization.

The Importance of Organizing

THE ORGANIZING PROCESS

Ernest Dale describes organizing as a multistep process:[1]

1. *Detailing all the work that must be done to attain the organization's goals.* Every organization is created with a set of purposes—hospitals are created to care for the sick, basketball teams are created to win games, businesses are created to sell goods and services. Each of these purposes will obviously be accomplished in a different way. For the organization's goals to be achieved, therefore, the tasks of the organization as a whole must first be determined. For example, before the organizers of a hospital can help the sick, they will have to purchase equipment, hire physicians and other professional and nonprofessional personnel, set up various specialized medical departments, arrange for accreditation with professional organizations, coordinate with various agencies in the community, and so on.

2. *Dividing the total work load into activities that can logically and comfortably be performed by one person or by a group of individuals.* Organizations are created because the work they are meant to accomplish cannot be performed by one person alone. Thus, the work of the organization must be appropriately divided among its members. By "appropriate" we mean, first, that individuals will be assigned to tasks on the basis of their qualifications for those tasks and, second,

that no individual will be charged with carrying too heavy or too light a work load.

3. *Combining the work of the organization's members in a logical and efficient manner.* As an organization expands in size and hires more people to perform various activities, it becomes necessary to group individuals whose assigned tasks are related. Sales, human resources, production, accounting, and marketing are some typical departments in manufacturing organizations. In a given department are workers with a number of different skills and levels of expertise, whose interactions with one another are governed by established procedures. This aggregation of work is generally referred to as departmentalization.

4. *Setting up a mechanism to coordinate the work of organization members into a unified, harmonious whole.* As individuals and departments carry out their specialized activities, the overall goals of the organization may become submerged or conflicts between organization members may develop. For example, marketing managers in a manufacturing company may press for larger advertising budgets to stimulate demand, even though the larger interests of the company may be best served by investment in more automated equipment to lower costs. In a university, various schools or departments may compete aggressively for limited funds. Coordinating mechanisms enable members of the organization to keep sight of the organization's goals and reduce inefficiency and harmful conflicts.

5. *Monitoring the effectiveness of the organization and making adjustments to maintain or increase effectiveness.* Because organizing is an ongoing process, periodic reassessment of the four preceding steps is necessary. As organizations grow and situations change, the organization's structure must be reevaluated to be sure it is consistent with effective and efficient operation to meet present needs.

Many organizations evolve haphazardly, making additions to and changes in their structure from time to time as tactical expedients to meet specific ends. A number of specific factors determine an organization's actual structure. Among those factors are the technology it uses, the environment in which it operates, and the values of its members. There is no "one best way" for all organizations to be designed. The most desirable structure is an individual matter that will vary from one organization to the next and within one organization over time.

As we saw in part two, the planning process results in a schedule of tasks for managers to accomplish. Strategic planning helps managers focus on the long-range goals of the organization. In part three we will be examining how the managerial tasks defined in the planning stages can be divided and reintegrated to achieve the organization's objectives.

We will focus in this chapter on two major aspects of organizational structure: division of work and departmentalization. *Division of work* is the breakdown of a work task so that each individual in the organization is responsible for and performs a limited set of activities rather than the entire task. *Departmentalization* is the grouping of work activities so that similar and logically related activities occur together. It represents the formal structure of the organization as it might be represented on an organization chart. Both concepts engaged the attention of the earliest management writers and continue to interest writers and managers today. The subject of an individual's work tasks—how specialized or varied they should be—was one of the earliest concerns in management and is still a major subject of debate and research.

Division of Work

Many businesses as well as departments within companies start out small. A single entrepreneur or individual may be able to handle the entire operation. As the work load of the business or department grows, however, the entrepreneur or individual becomes a manager as assistants are added and work is divided among them. With further expansion, it becomes necessary for the manager to group employees into departments.

Our discussion of the allocation of work starts with the individual worker and his or her job. We will examine such questions as: What are the advantages of job specialization? What effect has such specialization on worker morale? To what extent can job dissatisfaction be eliminated without simultaneously sacrificing the benefits of specialization? Then we will look at the ways in which work is specialized and aggregated in the organization as a whole.

Advantages of Job Specialization

The advantages of specialization have long been recognized. In fact, the rise of civilization can be attributed to the division of labor. The greater productivity resulting from *job specialization* gave humanity the resources needed for art, science, and education.

Adam Smith's *Wealth of Nations* opens with a famous passage describing the minute specialization of labor in the manufacture of pins. Describing the work in a pin factory, Smith wrote: "One man draws the wire, another straights it, a third cuts it, a fourth points it, a fifth grinds it at the top for receiving the head. . . . " Ten men working in this fashion, he said, made 48,000 pins in one day. "But if they had all wrought separately and independently," each might at best have produced 20 pins a day. As Smith observed, the great advantage of the division of labor was that in breaking down the total job into small, simple, and separate operations in which each worker could specialize, total productivity multiplied geometrically.[2]

Why does division of work result in a dramatic increase in productivity? (We use the more modern phrase "division of work" rather than the classic "division of labor" because the latter term implies that only routine tasks are specialized; in fact, specialization applies to all types of work activities, including those of managers and other professionals, as the cartoon on page 236 suggests.) The answer is that no one person is physically able to perform all the operations in most complex tasks, nor can any one person acquire all the skills needed to perform the various tasks that make up a complex operation. Thus, to carry out tasks requiring a number of steps, it is necessary to parcel out the various parts of the task among a number of people. Such specialized division of work allows people to learn skills and become expert at their individual job functions. Simplified tasks can be learned in a relatively short

"Let's switch. I'll make the policy, you implement it, and he'll explain it."
Drawing by Stevenson; © 1981 The New Yorker Magazine, Inc.

time and be completed quickly. Also, the availability of a variety of jobs makes it possible for people to choose, or be assigned to, positions they will enjoy and for which they are well suited.

Early Concerns about Specialization

The advantages of specialization in terms of increased productivity received the greatest attention of management writers up to the beginning of the twentieth century. Some writers, however, raised strong questions about the impact of job specialization on the worker. Karl Marx and Friedrich Engels, writing in the middle of the nineteenth century, saw even the most general division of work as a source of alienation and entrapment for the individual:

> **The division of labor offers us the first example of how . . . man's own deed becomes an alien power opposed to him which enslaves him instead of being controlled by him. For as soon as the distribution of labor comes into being, each man has a particular, exclusive activity . . . from which he cannot escape. He is a hunter, a fisherman, a shepherd . . . and must remain so if he does not want to lose his means of livelihood.[3]**

And Émile Durkheim, the French sociologist, writing before the extreme job specialization of assembly-line production became widespread, also raised questions about its effects. He believed that both the individual and society would be damaged by the demoralizing impact of dull and repetitive jobs.[4]

These apprehensions became more widespread with the development of the assembly line, which became the symbol of dehumanizing jobs and alienation of the individual from the workplace. Perhaps the best-known exposition of this theme occurs in Charlie Chaplin's film *Modern Times,* in which Chaplin as the little tramp is driven to distraction as he mindlessly repeats the same task over and over again while the assembly line moves at top speed.

Job Design

Before going on to discuss more modern views of the relationships between specialization, satisfaction, and productivity, we will examine two ways of looking at how specialized a given job actually is. The concepts of job depth and job scope were early attempts to describe aspects of job specialization.

By *job depth* we mean the extent to which an individual can control his or her work. When management sets rigid standards, organizes the work to the last detail, prescribes methods, and supervises the work closely, job depth is low. But if, after objectives and general rules are set, employees are free to set their own pace and do the job as they think best, then job depth is high.

JOB DEPTH

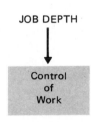

By *job scope* we mean the number of different operations a particular job requires and the frequency with which the job cycle must be repeated. The lower the number of operations and the greater the number of repetitions, the lower the scope. For example, a hospital nurse who checks temperatures, dispenses medicines, and takes blood samples has more scope than the technician who only analyzes the blood samples.

JOB SCOPE

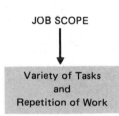

Of course, different portions of the same job may vary in either depth or scope or both. For example, a university professor who is also a department head may have tasks that run the gamut of possible combinations. He or she chooses and designs a research project (high depth, high scope); teaches three sections of the same course (high depth, low scope); performs numerous routine administrative tasks (low depth, high scope); and grades a large number of multiple-choice exams (low depth, low scope).

The overall amount of depth and scope indicates how specialized a given job is. Overall, the lower the depth of the job and the more limited its scope, the more specialized it is likely to be. The job of a university department head is clearly far from specialized; that of a sign maker is much more so.

Job Characteristics. J. Richard Hackman and others[5] have extended their observations beyond job depth and scope and have come up with five core job dimensions: skill variety, task identity, task significance, autonomy, and feedback. Table 9–1 describes these dimensions and gives examples.

Jobs of broad scope are likely to require greater skill variety and perhaps will encompass more task identity. Job depth is directly related to autonomy and may encompass skill variety, task identity, and feedback, too. The university department head ranks high on all these counts; but the job of a professor in that department will have less scope and less depth, since it limits skill variety and autonomy.

Hackman has observed that meaningfulness, responsibility, and an understand-

TABLE 9–1 TASK CHARACTERISTICS

Characteristic	Description	High Degree	Low Degree
Skill variety—the extent to which a variety of skills and talents are required to accomplish the assigned tasks.	Perform different tasks that challenge the intellect and develop skills in coordination.	Dress designer	Messenger
Task identity—the extent to which the job involves completion of an identifiable unit, project, or other piece of work.	Handle an entire job function from start to finish and be able to show a tangible piece of work as the outcome.	Software designer	Assembly-line worker
Task significance—the extent to which the task affects the work or lives of others, inside or outside the organization.	Be involved in a job function that is important for the well-being, safety, and perhaps survival of others.	Air traffic controller	House painter
Autonomy—the extent of the individual's freedom on the job and discretion to schedule tasks and determine procedures for carrying them out.	Be responsible for the success or failure of a job function and be able to plan work schedule, control quality, etc.	Project manager	Cashier in a department store
Feedback—the extent to which the individual receives specific information (praise, blame, or other comment) about the effectiveness with which his or her tasks are performed.	Learn about the effectiveness of one's job performance through clear and direct evaluation from a supervisor or colleagues or the results of the work itself.	Professional athlete	Security guard

ing of the results of work contribute to motivation and job satisfaction.[6] Individuals whose jobs involve high levels of skill variety, task identity, and task significance experience work as highly meaningful. A high level of autonomy leads to a greater sense of responsibility and accountability. And where feedback is provided, workers develop a useful understanding of their specific roles and functions. Thus, the greater the extent of all five task characteristics in a job, the more likely it is that the jobholder will be highly motivated and experience job satisfaction. (See fig. 9–1.)

More recently, Gerald Salancik and Jeffrey Pfeffer[7] have developed a social information processing model of the task design process. This model emphasizes the effect of social influences on how a person values the various dimensions of his or her job.[8] It has been shown, for example, that the extent to which a supervisor engages in "small talk" and offers advice on how to do a job affects the extent to which employees feel autonomous.[9]

Work Simplification. When scientific management theorists such as Taylor and the Gilbreths (see chapter 2) looked at job design, they were concerned with increasing productivity and efficiency. To that end they devised ways to break jobs down into their component tasks. The theoretical notion that a worker repeatedly performing the same few tasks would become highly efficient at the work became the guiding principle of the assembly line. The same principle has been applied in other kinds of

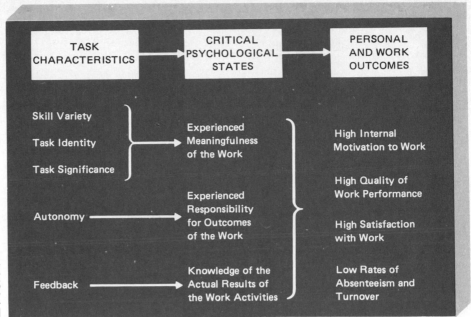

FIGURE 9–1
TASK
CHARACTERISTICS
AND WORK
MOTIVATION

Source: Adapted from J. Richard Hackman, "Work Design," in Hackman and Suttle, eds., *Improving Life at Work* (Santa Monica, Calif.: Goodyear, 1977), figure 3–4, p. 129. Used with permission.

work. Companies can now reduce training costs by using computers that provide "menus" of simple instructions on how to proceed with tasks. A computer used by loan officers, for example, might tell them what questions to ask, analyze the answers received, propose follow-up questions, and ultimately recommend credit decisions.[10] Many firms now use preprogrammed system control of jobs to improve quality and efficiency and reduce the uncertainty stemming from employee control. In the process, they may make jobs routine, undemanding, and nearly automatic.[11]

Work simplification, then, reduces both job depth and job scope. It also affects most of the task characteristics described above. Skill variety, task identity, and autonomy are sharply reduced, and feedback is often minimized. Only task significance is unaffected, since this term refers to the ultimate end-product of the work—not to the significance of the individual worker's activities.

Specialization-Satisfaction-Productivity Trade-offs

By 1960, modern management writers like Chris Argyris,[12] Frederick Herzberg,[13] and Douglas McGregor[14] had all called attention to the problems that extreme work simplification was causing individuals. They pointed out that when jobs become highly specialized or fragmented, workers find their tasks unpleasantly monotonous and unsatisfying. Thus, employees lose their sense of autonomy and challenge and become powerless and dependent. These writers do not claim that all forms of specialization are undesirable. But they do suggest that specialization in some areas has reached the point where its potential advantages in efficiency and productivity are not achieved because of the human disadvantages.

For example, we might design a group of jobs so that employees are taken from very unspecialized tasks and transferred to a department in which they will perform more specialized functions. (The unspecialized tasks are considered high in job depth and scope, whereas the specialized ones are of low depth and scope.) At first the transferred employees will probably show interest in their new assignment; productivity will increase as the advantages of specialization come into play. These workers are likely to take new pride in themselves and their jobs because they have the opportunity to develop and learn a few skills in depth, improve their work status, and presumably increase their earnings. However, once they have met the challenges of the new situation and are able to perform their new skills by rote, they may begin to feel dissatisfied. Productivity may flag as workers, no longer challenged by their jobs, lose interest in and commitment to the work. At some point dissatisfaction may become so great, and the work itself so meaningless, that absenteeism, careless performance, and even sabotage become rampant.[15] These losses will overtake any increased technical advantages from additional specialization. If the employees can insist upon increased financial payment to compensate for their reduced enjoyment, the combination of poorer work performance and higher wages may make increased specialization more costly than less specialization.

These arguments sound persuasive. However, research indicates that the relationship between specialization and job satisfaction does not hold in all situations.[16] In their review of the research on this subject, Charles L. Hulin and Milton R. Blood concluded that employee satisfaction or dissatisfaction with specialized jobs depends to a great extent on the attitudes of the workers being studied.[17] Those employees who believe in the "Protestant work ethic"—that is, who see work as important, meaningful, and leading to success—are likely to become dissatisfied in jobs that are too specialized. Hulin and Blood suggest, however, that employees who feel alienated in their work may even prefer narrower, more restricted jobs because such work is easier and requires little attention or commitment. Hackman, who has drawn similar conclusions, refers to a "growth need" instead of the Protestant work ethic. According to his studies, individuals with high growth needs will be more satisfied in expanded and challenging jobs than will individuals with low growth needs.[18]

Job Enlargement and Job Enrichment

Some research supports Hackman's and Hulin and Blood's conclusions,[19] but some does not.[20] It does appear, however, that for many workers highly specialized jobs cause dissatisfaction. For this reason considerable attention has been given to finding ways to make routine jobs more rewarding. These attempts fall into two broad categories: job enlargement and job enrichment. The first stems from the thinking of industrial engineers, the second from motivational theory.

Job Enlargement. *Job enlargement* tackles dissatisfaction by increasing job scope. Various work functions from a horizontal slice of an organizational unit are combined, thereby giving workers more operations to perform. For example, two or more jobs may be aggregated into a single one, thereby restoring some sense of the wholeness of the job. Or a system of job rotation may be initiated, so that workers move from one job to a completely different one. By giving workers the opportunity to develop different skills, job rotation offers challenge and motivates achievement. In both instances, workers are relieved of some of the monotony of a restricted routine and work cycle.

Job Enrichment. *Job enrichment* tries to deal with dissatisfaction by increasing job depth. Work activities from a vertical slice of the organizational unit are combined in one job so that employees experience greater job autonomy. Individual employees may be given responsibility for setting their own work pace, for correcting their own errors, and/or for deciding on the best way to perform a particular task. They may also help make decisions that affect their particular subunits. As work becomes more challenging and worker responsibility increases, motivation and enthusiasm also increase.[21]

Job Satisfaction and Alternative Work Schedules. Many companies are finding that alternative work schedules reduce worker frustration. Unlike job enlargement and job enrichment approaches, which are intended to make the work itself more meaningful, these specially designed time arrangements make work hours more convenient for employees and enhance the quality of nonwork time. Two versions of alternative work schedules that are being increasingly incorporated into organizational structures today are the compressed workweek and flextime.

Employees following a compressed workweek schedule usually exchange the traditional five-day week for a four- or even a three-day week. Instead of working eight hours a day for five days (5/40), they may work ten hours a day for four days (4/40) or twelve hours a day for three (3/36). Such work arrangements make it possible for employees to share household responsibilities equally with a spouse, to attend school, or to pursue other activities.[22]

In some instances, compressed workweeks have been initiated by employers to reduce costs of overtime, overhead, and personal leave time. Small manufacturing or service operations are frequently well suited to such schedules, especially where there is little or no physical work and where worker fatigue will not result in occupational injuries. Young or newly hired employees are particularly receptive to the compressed workweek because they can adapt their life-styles to the extra leisure time offered. Workers who are used to the traditional routine generally take longer to adjust or resist such changes altogether. They may not be able to alter their life-styles, which may be more tied to other family members' schedules.

Flextime, which has become more widespread in Europe than in the United States, permits employees to arrange their work hours to suit their personal needs and life styles. An especially attractive aspect of flextime is the possibility of avoiding rush-hour travel. It is particularly suited to situations with fluctuating work loads. Flextime employees are responsible for coordinating their functions with other employees and thereby have more responsibility and autonomy. Companies depending on assembly-line operations, however, are usually not suited to individualized time arrangements.[23]

Typical flextime arrangements require employees to be on the job during a core period, often about four hours in the middle of the day, but allow them to choose their own starting and ending times.

TABLE 9–2 JOB ENRICHMENT GUIDELINES

Principle	Method
1. Form natural work units.	Apportion tasks on the basis of: • levels of workers' training/experience • meaningfulness and importance to workers
2. Combine tasks.	Encourage development of several skills by combining a number of specialized functions into one whole task.
3. Establish client relationships.	Create opportunities for workers to interact with clients (product or service users). Workers will benefit by: • direct feedback (both positive and negative) on their work output • development of interpersonal skills and increased self-confidence • increased responsibility for managing relationships with clients
4. Increase employees' autonomy (vertical loading).	Give workers more responsibility and control by allowing them to: • decide on work methods • advise and train workers with less experience • schedule overtime • assign work priorities • manage their own crises instead of relying on a supervisor • control budgetary aspects of their own projects
5. Open feedback channels.	Give workers feedback while they are performing their tasks, instead of after the fact. Job-provided feedback can come from: • direct client relationships • workers' responsibility for quality-control inspections • frequent and standard reports on individual performance

Source: J. Richard Hackman, "Work Design," in J. Richard Hackman and J. Lloyd Suttle, eds., *Improving Life at Work* (Santa Monica, Calif.: Goodyear, 1977), pp. 136–140. Used with permission.

Using Job Redesign Effectively

There is not yet enough research evidence for us to be able to reach firm conclusions about the effects of job enlargement and job enrichment. Most studies suggest that such programs will increase employee satisfaction, lower absenteeism and turnover rates, and improve the accuracy and quality of the work that is done.[24] In some cases, however, it has been shown that such programs do not increase productivity. This is not surprising, since job enlargement and enrichment programs are meant to counteract the psychological and emotional effects of job specialization; they are not usually intended to increase productivity unless job specialization has been carried so far that productivity has suffered.

Job enlargement and job enrichment are relatively new approaches to work redesign, and a variety of approaches have been used in designing and implementing programs. Therefore, some of the apparent inconsistencies in results from different programs can probably be attributed to differences in development and implementation. As with any new technology, we will need more experience with these tools to learn how best to apply them. (Table 9–2 offers guidelines for enriching the work environment.)

Job enlargement and job enrichment programs can be expensive to design and install. Therefore, management must carefully weigh the pros and cons before undertaking them. If it can be determined that company losses due to poor worker performance, absenteeism, and turnover are higher than the cost of a corrective program, then it may be worthwhile to begin one.

Organizing and Organizational Structure

Although we have been using the terms "organizing" and "organizational structure" throughout this chapter, we have not yet defined or discussed them in detail. In its broadest sense, *organizing* can be thought of as *the process of making the organization's structure fit with its objectives, its resources, its environment. Organizational structure* can be defined as *the arrangement and interrelationship of the component parts and positions of a company.* An organization's structure specifies its division of work activities and shows how different functions or activities are linked; to some extent it also shows the level of specialization of work activities. It also indicates the organization's hierarchy and authority structure, and shows its reporting relationships.[25] It provides the stability and continuity that allow the organization to survive the comings and goings of individuals and to coordinate its dealings with its environment.

Elements of Organizational Structure

It is useful to analyze organizational structure in terms of the following five elements:

1. Specialization of activities
2. Standardization of activities
3. Coordination of activities
4. Centralization and decentralization of decision making
5. Size of the work unit

Specialization of activities refers to the specification of individual and group work tasks throughout the organization (division of work) and the aggregation of these tasks into work units (departmentalization).

Standardization of activities refers to the procedures used by the organization to ensure the predictability of its activities. Many of these procedures (such as the organization chart that will be discussed in this chapter) are established by formalizing the activities of and relationships within the organization.

To standardize is to make uniform and consistent. Managers use job descriptions, operating instructions, rules, and regulations to standardize the jobs of their subordinates. They use formalized selection, orientation, and training programs to standardize the skills of their work force. Through formal planning and control systems, managers attempt to standardize the output of their organizations.

Coordination of activities refers to the procedures that integrate the functions of subunits within the organization. According to Henry Mintzberg, standardization mechanisms make it easier to coordinate activities, especially in organizations with uncomplicated work patterns.[26] However, as work becomes more complex and specialization increases, standardization is no longer sufficient to coordinate activities. New mechanisms must be developed to integrate the work of interdependent units.

Centralization and decentralization of decision making refers to the location of decision-making power. In a centralized organizational structure, decisions are made at a high level by top managers or even by a single individual. In a decentralized structure, the decision-making power is dispersed among more individuals at middle and lower management levels. Mintzberg distinguishes between vertical and horizontal decentralization. "The dispersal of formal power down the chain of command . . . [is] *vertical decentralization. Horizontal decentralization* . . . [is] the extent to which nonmanagers control decision processes."

Size of the work unit refers to the number of employees in a work group.[27]

Determinants of Organizational Structure

Managers organize the total organization and its subunits to be congruent with its objectives, resources, and environments, both internal and external. Our discussion here will prepare the reader for the more extensive coverage of the factors that influence the design of organizational structures in chapter 10. Four major determinants of organizational structure are: strategy, or plans for achieving the company's objectives; the technology used to carry out the strategy; the people employed at all levels and their functions; and the size of the total organization.

Strategy and organizational structure: When management writers such as Alfred D. Chandler use the phrase "structure follows strategy," they mean that the mission and overall goals of an organization will help shape its design.[28]

Strategy will determine how the lines of authority and channels of communication are set up between various managers and subunits. It will influence the information that flows along those lines, as well as the mechanisms for planning and decision making. The close relationship between organizational strategy and structure was demonstrated by Chandler in a classic study. After analyzing the administrative histories of such companies as Du Pont, General Motors, Standard Oil, and Sears, Roebuck, Chandler concluded that changes in corporate strategy precede and lead to changes in organizational design.

Technology as a determinant of structure: The nature of the technology used in an organization to create its products (or the methods by which it offers its services) also influences the way the organization is set up. For example, the mass production technologies in industries such as automobile manufacturing involve high degrees of standardization and specialization of work activities. Technology also influences the coordination mechanisms, the level at which decisions are made, and the size of organizational units. Technologies for creating products to meet rapidly changing customer preferences, such as in the high-fashion clothing industry, are associated with lower levels of standardization and specialization.

People as a determinant of structure: The people involved in the organization's activities affect its structure. Managers make decisions relating to the lines of communication and authority and the relationships between work units. In making these decisions, managers are influenced by their own needs and preferred work environments. The abilities and attitudes of subordinates, including their need to work with each other in specific ways, must also be taken into account when work units are set up and tasks allocated. In addition, people outside the organization influence its structure, which must provide for regular interactions with clients or customers, suppliers, and others in the external environment.

Size and structure: Both the overall size of an organization and the size of its subunits influence its structure. Larger organizations tend to have greater specialization of activities and more formalized procedures (greater standardization). Chandler has suggested that as organizations increase in size, a point is reached at which they are forced to decentralize and to develop a greater variety of formal mechanisms to coordinate their activities.

Departmentalization

The job functions of employees need to be divided among them and combined in logical ways. Workers with related functions usually share a common work area and constitute a work unit. Efficiency of work flow depends on the successful integration of various units within the organization. Division of work and logical combinations of tasks should lead to logical department and subunit structures.

An Early Reorganization

An example of the importance of establishing an effective division of work and a sound organizational structure appears in Exodus 18:13–26. Following the departure of the Israelites from Egypt, Moses found himself the sole judge of the disputes that arose among the people. Consequently, the people "stood by Moses from the morning unto the evening," waiting for him to make decisions. When Jethro, Moses' father-in-law, saw what was happening, he realized that little could be done with such an unwieldy organization. He offered his advice, thereby becoming the first recorded management consultant. If we translate the language of Exodus into modern management jargon, we find that Jethro's advice to Moses has a decidedly contemporary ring:

> And thou shalt teach them ordinances and laws, and shalt show them the way wherein they must walk, and the work that they must do. [Establish policies and standard practices, conduct job training, and prepare job descriptions.] Moreover thou shalt provide out of all the people able men . . . and place such over them, to be rulers of thousands, and rulers of hundreds, rulers of fifties, and rulers of tens. [Appoint individuals with supervisory ability and establish a chain of command.] And let them judge the people at all seasons; and it shall be, that every great matter they shall bring unto thee, but every small matter they shall judge. [Delegate authority and work tasks and follow the *exception principle*—that is, allow routine problems to be handled at lower levels and settle only the big, exceptional problems yourself.]

The obvious effect of this proposed reorganization (which Moses adopted) was to save Moses time and effort. This in itself was no small accomplishment; increased efficiency is one of the desired benefits of the organizing process. However, Jethro's suggestions in fact accomplished a great deal more; they permitted Moses and the Israelites to achieve their goals. Moses' main aim was to lead his people to the Promised Land; yet he was spending all his time settling disputes. The Israelites' main aims were to carry out God's commandments and follow Moses; yet they were spending all their time awaiting Moses' rulings. Under Jethro's reorganization plan, an Israelite who, after hearing the law explained, still needed a ruling could quickly obtain one from a supervisor. Moses, freed of minor but time-consuming tasks, was able to concentrate on his major responsibilities. And he and the people were able to move more rapidly toward the Promised Land.

The Organization Chart

As a company grows, the number of work units and subunits increases, and layers of supervision are added. Managers and subordinates alike become further removed from the eventual results of their actions. They need a clear understanding of how their activities fit into the larger picture of what the organization is and does. Most organizational structures are too complex to be conveyed verbally. To show the organization's structure, managers customarily draw up an *organization chart,* which diagrams the functions, departments, or positions of the organization and shows how they are related. The separate units of the organization usually appear in boxes, which are connected to each other by solid lines that indicate the *chain of command* and official channels of communication. (See figures 9–2 to 9–6 on pages 248–253 for examples of organization charts.)

Not every organization welcomes such charts. For example, Robert Townsend, the former president of Avis, suggested that organization charts are demoralizing, because they reinforce the idea that all authority and ability rest at the top of the organization.[29] Most organizations, however, do develop these charts and find them helpful in defining managerial authority, responsibility, and accountability.

The organization chart illustrates five major aspects of an organization's structure. In doing so, it also displays some information about the elements of structure described above.

1. *The division of work.* Each box represents an individual or subunit responsible for a given part of the organization's work load.
2. *Managers and subordinates.* The solid lines indicate the chain of command (who reports to whom).
3. *The type of work being performed.* Labels or descriptions for the boxes indicate the organization's different work tasks or areas of responsibility.
4. *The grouping of work segments.* The entire chart indicates on what basis the organization's activities have been divided—on a functional or regional basis, for example.
5. *The levels of management.* A chart indicates not only individual managers and subordinates but also the entire management hierarchy. All people who report to the same individual are on the same management level, regardless of where they may appear on the chart.

The extent to which work in the organization is specialized can be estimated by reading the labels that indicate different work tasks and seeing how the tasks are grouped. The lines showing the chain of command indicate one of the key means of coordination in any organization. It may even be possible to judge the size of the organization from a chart of its structure. But while the organization chart contains some useful clues, it is possible to derive an inaccurate picture without additional information.[30]

The advantages and disadvantages of organization charts have long been a subject of debate among management writers.[31] One advantage is that employees and others are given a picture of how the organization is structured. Managers, subordinates, and responsibilities are delineated. In addition, if someone is needed to handle a specific problem, the chart indicates where that person may be found. Finally, the process of making up the chart enables managers to pinpoint organizational defects—such as potential sources of conflict or areas where unnecessary duplication exists.

A major disadvantage of charts is that there are many things they obscure or do not show. They do not, for example, indicate who has the greater degree of responsibility and authority at each managerial level. Nor do they indicate the organization's informal relationships and channels of communication, without which the organization could not function efficiently. Also, people often read into charts things they are not intended to show. For example, employees may infer status and power on the basis of distance from the chief executive's box. These disadvantages can be minimized if charts are used only for their intended purpose—revealing the basic framework of the organization.

The Formal Organizational Structure

An organization's departments can be formally structured in three major ways: by function, by product/market, or in matrix form. While these three forms of structure are most frequently cited in discussing business organizations, they can be used in organizations of any type.

Organization by *function* brings together in one department all those engaged in one activity or several related activities. For example, the organization divided by function might have separate manufacturing, marketing, and sales departments. A sales manager in such an organization would be responsible for the sale of *all* products manufactured by the firm.

Product or *market* organization, often referred to as organization by division, brings together in one work unit all those involved in the production and marketing of a product or related group of products, all those in a certain geographic area, or all those dealing with a certain type of customer. For example, the organization might include separate chemical, detergent, and cosmetic divisions. Each division head would be responsible for the manufacturing, marketing, and sales activities of his or her entire unit.

In *matrix* organization, two types of design exist simultaneously. Permanent functional departments have authority for the performance and professional standards of their units, while project teams are created as needed to carry out specific programs. Team members are drawn from various functional departments and report to a project manager, who is responsible for the outcome of the team's work. The matrix structure is found much less frequently in organizations than are the functional and product market structures.[32]

As we shall see, all three types of organization design have advantages and disadvantages. Few organizations rely on any one type exclusively.

FIGURE 9–2 FUNCTIONAL ORGANIZATION CHART FOR A MANUFACTURING COMPANY

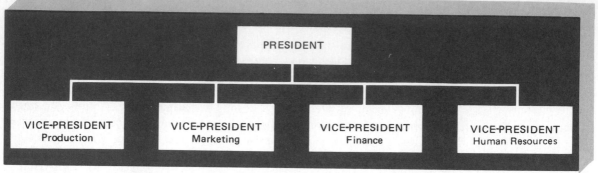

Each vice-president is in charge of a major organizational function.

Functional Organization

Functional organization is perhaps the most logical and basic form of departmentalization. (See fig. 9–2.) It is used mainly (but not only) by smaller firms that offer a limited line of products, because it makes efficient use of specialized resources. Another major advantage of a functionalized structure is that it makes supervision easier, since each manager must be expert in only a narrow range of skills. In addition, a functionalized structure makes it easier to mobilize specialized skills and bring them to bear where they are most needed. (See box.)

As an organization grows, either by expanding geographically or by broadening its product line, some of the disadvantages of the functional structure begin to become apparent. It becomes more difficult to get quick decisions or action on a problem because functional managers have to report to central headquarters and

---

CHARACTERISTICS OF FUNCTIONAL STRUCTURE

Advantages
1. Suited to a stable environment.
2. Fosters development of expertise.
3. Offers colleagues for specialists.
4. Requires little internal coordination.
5. Requires fewer interpersonal skills.

Disadvantages
1. Slows response time in large organizations.
2. Causes bottlenecks due to sequential task performance.
3. Does not encourage innovation; has narrow perspective.
4. Fosters conflicts over product priorities.
5. Does not foster development of general managers.
6. Obscures responsibility for the overall task.

Source: Arthur A. Thompson, Jr., and A. J. Strickland III, *Strategy Formulation and Implementation*, p. 324. Copyright © 1983 by Business Publications, Inc. Used with permission.

may have to wait a long time before a request for help is acted on. In addition, it is often harder to determine accountability and judge performance in a functional structure. If a new product fails, who is to blame—research and development, production, or marketing? Finally, coordinating the functions of members of the entire organization may become a problem for top managers. Members of each department may feel isolated from (or superior to) those in other departments. It therefore becomes more difficult for employees to work in a unified manner to achieve the organization's goals. For example, the manufacturing department may concentrate on meeting cost standards and delivery dates and neglect quality control. As a result, the service department may become flooded with complaints.

Top managers who wish to use a functional structure or add a functional department to an existing structure must weigh potential benefits against expected costs. The economic savings brought about by a functional structure may be outweighed by the additional managerial and staff salaries and other overhead costs that are required. Top managers also have to consider how often they expect to use the special skills of a functional department. In a small firm, for example, it may be more economical to retain outside legal services whenever necessary, rather than set up an in-house legal department.

Product/Market Organization

Most large, multiproduct companies, such as General Motors, are organized according to a *product* or *market organization* structure. At some point, sheer size and diversity of products make servicing by functional departments too unwieldy. When a company's departmentalization becomes too complex for the functional structure, top managers will generally create semiautonomous divisions, each of which designs, produces, and markets its own products.

A product or market organization can follow one of three major patterns:

1. In *division by product,* each department is responsible for a product or related family of products. For example, General Foods has a different division for each of its major types of food products. Product divisionalization is the logical pattern to follow when a product type calls for manufacturing technology and marketing methods that differ greatly from those used in the rest of the organization. (See fig. 9–3.)
2. *Division by geography* brings together in one department all activities performed in the region where the unit conducts its business. This arrangement follows logically when a plant must be located as close as possible to (a) its sources of raw materials, as with mining and oil-producing companies; (b) its major markets, as with a division selling most of its output overseas that must locate abroad; or (c) its major sources of specialized labor, as with diamond-cutting operations in New York, Tel-Aviv, and Amsterdam. (See fig. 9–4.) Service, financial, and other nonmanufacturing firms are generally organized on a geographic basis.
3. *Division by customer* occurs when a division sells most or all of its products to a particular class of customer. An electronics firm, for example, might have separate divisions for military, industrial, and consumer customers. As a general rule, manufacturing firms with a highly diversified line of products tend to be organized by customer or by product. (See fig. 9–5.)

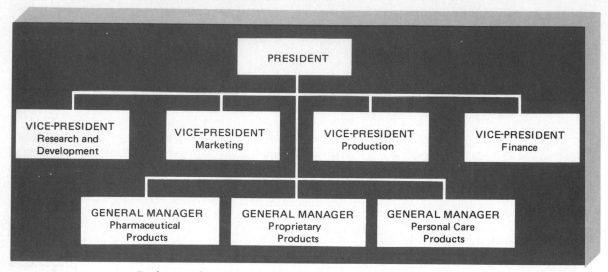

Each general manager is in charge of a major category of products, and the vice-presidents of the functional areas provide supporting services to the general managers.

FIGURE 9–4 PRODUCT/MARKET ORGANIZATION CHART FOR A MANUFACTURING
COMPANY: DIVISION BY GEOGRAPHY

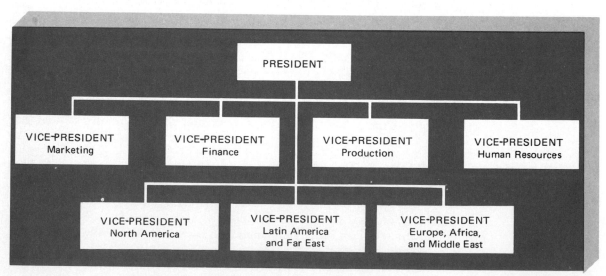

Each area vice-president is in charge of the company's business in one geographic area. The functional vice-presidents provide supporting services and coordination assistance for their areas of responsibility.

FIGURE 9–5
PRODUCT/MARKET
ORGANIZATION
CHART FOR A
MANUFACTURING
COMPANY:
DIVISION BY
CUSTOMER

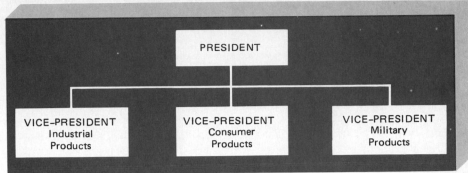

Each vice-president is in charge of a set of products grouped according to the type of customer to whom they will be marketed.

Unlike a functional department, a division resembles a separate business. The division head focuses primarily on the operations of his or her division, is accountable for profit or loss, and may even compete with other units of the same firm. But a division is unlike a separate business in one crucial aspect: It is not an independent entity; that is, the division manager cannot make decisions as freely as the owner of a truly separate enterprise, because he or she must still report to central headquarters. As a rule, a division head's authority will end at the point where his or her decisions have a significant effect on the workings of other divisions.

Pros and Cons of Product/Market Organization. Organization by division has several advantages. Because all the activities, skills, and expertise required to produce and market particular products are grouped in one place under a single head, a whole job can be more easily coordinated and high work performance maintained. In addition, both the quality and the speed of decision making are enhanced, because decisions made at the divisional level are closer to the scene of action. Conversely, the burden on central management is eased because divisional managers have greater authority. Perhaps most important, accountability is clear. The performance of divisional management can be measured in terms of that division's profit or loss.

There are, however, some disadvantages to the divisional structure. The interests of the division may be placed ahead of the needs and goals of the total organization. For example, because they are vulnerable to profit and loss performance reviews, division heads may take short-term gains at the expense of long-range profitability. In addition, administrative expenses tend to increase. Each division, for example, has its own staff members and specialists, leading to costly duplication of skills. (See box on p. 252.)

Matrix Organization

Neither of the two types of structures we have discussed meets all the needs of every organization. In a functional structure, specialized skills may become increasingly sophisticated—but coordinated production of goods may be difficult to achieve. In a

CHARACTERISTICS OF PRODUCT/MARKET STRUCTURE

Advantages
1. Suited to fast change.
2. Allows for high product visibility.
3. Allows full-time concentration on tasks.
4. Clearly defines responsibilities.
5. Permits parallel processing of multiple tasks.
6. Facilitates the training of general managers.

Disadvantages
1. Fosters politics in resource allocation.
2. Does not foster coordination of activities among divisions.
3. Encourages neglect of long-term priorities.
4. Permits in-depth competencies to decline.
5. Creates conflicts between divisional tasks and corporate priorities.

divisional structure, various products may flourish while the overall technological expertise of the organization remains undeveloped. The matrix structure attempts to combine the benefits of both types of designs while avoiding their drawbacks.[33]

In a *matrix organization,* employees have in effect two bosses—that is, they are under dual authority. One chain of command is functional or divisional, diagrammed vertically in the preceding charts. The second is shown horizontally in figure 9–6. This lateral chain depicts a project team, led by a project or group manager who is expert in the team's assigned area of specialization. For this reason, matrix structure is often referred to as a "multiple command system." (In mathematics, a matrix is an array of vertical columns and horizontal rows; hence the name is applied to this two-directional organizational structure.)

Matrix organizations were first developed in the aerospace industry by firms such as TRW. The initial impetus was a government demand for a single contact manager for each program or project who would be responsible to the government for the project's progress and performance. To meet this need for a single coordination point, a project leader was established, sharing authority with the leaders of the preexisting technical or functional departments. This temporary arrangement then evolved into formal matrix organizations. Now matrix organization is used in the units of many major companies, in management consulting firms, and in advertising agencies, among many other types of businesses. In some companies the matrix structure is found at all levels, while in others it is used only in certain departments.

Few organizations are able to make a sudden and effective transition from functional or divisional organization to a fully functioning matrix structure. When considering such a changeover, management must realize that much time and effort is required to make the matrix work.

Davis and Lawrence outline four phases of matrix evolution: phase I, the *traditional pyramid,* in which command is unified at the top level; phase II, *temporary overlay,* in which project teams are created only for special and immediate needs; phase III, *permanent overlay,* in which project teams are continued for ongoing

FIGURE 9–6 MATRIX ORGANIZATION (AEROSPACE DIVISION)

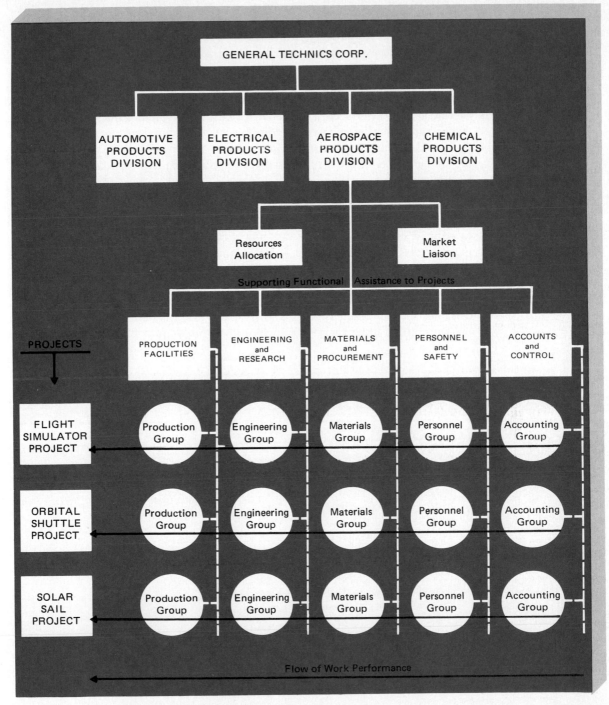

Source: Adapted from John F. Mee, "Matrix Organizations," *Business Horizons* 7, no. 2 (Summer 1964):70–72. Copyright 1964 by the Foundation for the School of Business at Indiana University. Reprinted by permission.

purposes; and phase IV, a *mature matrix*, in which both dimensions of structure are permanent and balanced, with power held equally by both a functional and a project manager.[34]

Not everyone adapts well to the matrix system. An effective matrix structure requires flexibility and cooperation from the people at all levels of the organization. The complexity of the structure requires open and direct lines of communication throughout both dimensions. Special training in new job skills or interpersonal relationships may be necessary for managers and subordinates when a matrix overlay is first introduced, or when a temporary overlay becomes permanent. To protect individuals who have functioned well in traditional structures but who have difficulty adjusting to a matrix structure, many companies make special efforts to retrain personnel before they are assigned to project teams, or select only volunteers for the teams.

Advantages and Disadvantages of Matrix Organizations. The matrix structure is often an efficient means for bringing together the diverse specialized skills required to solve a complex problem. (See box.) The problem of coordination—which plagues most functional designs—is minimized here, because the most important personnel for a project work together as a group. This in itself produces a side benefit—by working together, people come to understand the demands faced by those who have different areas of responsibility. A report from AT&T Bell Labs, for example, indicated that systems engineers and systems developers overcame their preconceptions about each other's jobs and acquired more realistic attitudes about

CHARACTERISTICS OF MATRIX STRUCTURE

Advantages
1. Gives flexibility to organization.
2. Stimulates interdisciplinary cooperation.
3. Involves and challenges people.
4. Develops employee skills.
5. Frees top management for planning.
6. Motivates people to identify with end product.
7. Allows experts to be moved to crucial areas as needed.

Disadvantages
1. Risks creating a feeling of anarchy.
2. Encourages power struggles.
3. May lead to more discussion than action.
4. Requires high interpersonal skills.
5. Is costly to implement.
6. Risks duplication of effort by project teams.
7. Affects morale when personnel are rearranged.

Source: Some of the material in this box is from Harold Kerzner, "Matrix Implementation: Obstacles, Problems, Questions, and Answers," in David I. Cleland, ed., *Matrix Management Systems Handbook* (New York: Van Nostrand Reinhold, 1984), pp. 307–329; and William Jerkovsky, "Functional Management in Matrix Organizations," *IEEE Transactions on Engineering Management* 30, no. 2 (May 1983):89–97.

each other after working together as a project team. (This was not, however, in a pure matrix structure.) Indeed, the exposure to workers in other areas was so effective that some systems developers decided to move into full-time systems engineering.[35] (See chapter 14 for a related discussion on overcoming conflict between groups.) Another advantage of the matrix structure is that it gives the organization a great deal of cost-saving flexibility; each project is assigned only the number of people it needs, thus avoiding unnecessary duplication.

A disadvantage is that team members require more than the usual skill in interpersonal relations to deal intensively with other team members and to get the help they need from functional departments. In addition, morale can be adversely affected by personnel rearrangements when projects are completed and new ones are begun.[36]

Matrix structures will probably become more commonplace in the future. When organized and operating properly, they are an excellent mechanism for undertaking and accomplishing complex projects. For example, a major New York bank instituted matrix organization to enable it to expand the number of services it could offer. By creating project teams to handle special groups of accounts (such as physicians, lawyers, and professional athletes), the bank was able to supply a high level of expertise to the specific estate-planning, loan, and investment needs of these client groups.[37]

The Informal Organization

Relationships within an organization are certainly not restricted to those official ones outlined in formal organization charts. Managers have always realized that an *informal organization* exists side by side with the formal one. This informal organization grows inevitably out of the personal needs and group needs of company members. It has been described by Herbert A. Simon[38] as "the interpersonal relationships in the organization that affect decisions within it but either are omitted from the formal scheme or are not consistent with it."

Among the first to recognize the constructive possibilities of the informal organization was Chester Barnard, whom we discussed in chapter 2. Barnard suggested that strict adherence to the formal structure—that is, always "going through channels"—could be detrimental. In emergencies, for example, an informal communication network makes faster decisions possible. Informal relationships also smooth the flow of personnel and materials across the lines of authority, and these relationships promote cooperation among departments that have only indirect points of contact on the organization chart. The informal relationships that develop in an organization not only help organization members satisfy their social needs but also assist them in getting things done.

Barnard, however, overlooked the fact that informal organization may also arise among employees as a protective device against management. In such cases, the aims of the informal organization may well run counter to the objectives of the enterprise. For instance, the informal group may set work norms well below the standards prescribed by management and enforce a slowdown in various ways, ranging from persuasion to violence.

Choosing the Right Structure

The structure that will work best for a specific organization will likely vary over time. In chapter 10, we will expand our discussion of strategy as one key determinant of structure and of the need for structure to fit with the organization's people, technology, informal structure, management practices, and so on. As these variables evolve, the most appropriate structure may also change. Peter Drucker has suggested several criteria that managers should consider in judging the appropriateness of a specific organizational structure:[39]

- *Clarity,* as opposed to simplicity. The Gothic cathedral is not a simple design, but your position inside it is clear, you know where to stand and where to go. A modern office building is exceedingly simple in design, but it is very easy to get lost in one; it is not clear.
- *Economy* of effort to maintain control and minimize friction.
- *Direction of vision* toward the product rather than the process, the result rather than the effort.[40]
- *Understanding* by each individual of his or her own task as well as that of the organization as a whole.
- *Decision making* that focuses on the right issues, is action-oriented, and is carried out at the lowest possible level of management.
- *Stability,* as opposed to rigidity, to survive turmoil, and *adaptability* to learn from it.
- *Perpetuation and self-renewal,* which require that an organization be able to produce tomorrow's leaders from within, helping each person develop continuously; the structure must also be open to new ideas.

Summary

For a company or any other organization, the organizing process involves determining the work that must be done in order for the company's goals to be achieved, appropriately dividing the work among company members, and setting up a mechanism to coordinate the company's activities. One result of this process will be an organizational structure, which represents the formal procedures through which the company is managed. A company's organizational structure will depend to a large extent on its purpose and strategy at a given period in time.

Departmentalization is the grouping together of similar or logically related work activities. Employees assigned to specialized departmental tasks develop skills and proficiency in their particular functions but may find that the day-to-day routine results in a loss of incentive and challenge. Job specialization increases efficiency of operations and expands productivity, but it may also lead to employee boredom and dissatisfaction.

Job depth refers to the degree of control an individual has over his or her work assignment. Job scope refers to the variety of tasks and the number of skills required for job performance. Research has shown that many, but not all, people demonstrate more interest in their work and feel a sense of pride and self-worth when job depth and job scope are high.

Work assignments can also be viewed in terms of five task characteristics: skill variety, task identity, task significance, employee autonomy, and feedback on worker performance. Job enrichment and job enlargement are ways to alter jobs to enhance these task characteristics and thus to heighten work involvement and commitment.

The formal structure of a company can be shown on an organization chart, which identifies the division of work, managers and subordinates, the types of work performed, the grouping of work, and the levels of management. There are three types of formal organization structure: A functional structure is organized by kinds of work activity; authority tends to be centralized, and specialized skills can be developed and maintained. In product/market organization, different activities related to a single market or set of products are grouped; there is greater coordination of activities and accountability, but duplication of human resources is likely. The matrix organization tries to avoid the disadvantages of both of these structures by overlaying functional departments with project teams. Employees report to both a functional and a project manager. Although complex in design and implementation, the matrix organizational structure is proving effective for handling complex projects.

The informal organization coexists with the formal one. It consists of the interpersonal relationships and lines of communication that inevitably develop when people work together. All of the various aspects of the organization—its strategy, people, technology, and so on—must be considered in choosing the right organizational structure.

Review Questions

1. Describe and diagram the five principal steps that constitute the organizing process.
2. Describe the main difference between division of work and departmentalization.
3. What are two advantages of job specialization? Why do you think specialization developed?
4. What is involved in the process of work simplification? What are its advantages and disadvantages?
5. What is the purpose of job enlargement and job enrichment?
6. How have Hackman and others described job characteristics?
7. What are the trade-offs with specialization, satisfaction, and productivity?
8. What do the terms *job scope* and *job depth* mean?
9. What are five key elements of organizational structure?
10. What does the statement "structure follows strategy" mean?
11. What are four determinants of organizational structure?
12. What does an organization chart illustrate? What are the major advantages and disadvantages of an organization chart? How do you think you might be affected by seeing your name or position on an organization chart?
13. How would you decide whether the functional organization would be appropriate for a company?
14. What are the different ways a product/market organization can be organized? What are the advantages and disadvantages of a product/market form of organization?
15. Under what conditions would a matrix structure be most suitable? What are its advantages and disadvantages? What happens to team members when they have completed their project?
16. What are the positive and sometimes negative aspects of the informal organization?
17. What criteria should managers consider in judging the appropriateness of their organization's structure?

Notes

1. Ernest Dale, *Organization* (New York: American Management Associations, 1967), p. 9. Our sequence of five steps is an elaboration of the three-step process described by Dale.

2. Adam Smith, *Wealth of Nations* (New York: Modern Library, 1937; originally published in 1776), pp. 3–4.

3. Karl Marx and Friedrich Engels, *The German Ideology,* Part I, edited by C. J. Arthur (New York: International Publishers, 1970; originally published in 1846), p. 53.

4. Émile Durkheim, *The Division of Labor in Society* (New York: Macmillan, 1933; originally published in 1893).

5. J. Richard Hackman and Edward E. Lawler, "Employee Reactions to Job Characteristics," *Journal of Applied Psychology Monograph 55* (1971):269–286; J. Richard Hackman and Greg R. Oldham, "Development of the Job Diagnostic Survey," *Journal of Applied Psychology 60,* no. 2 (April 1975):159–170; and J. Richard Hackman and J. Lloyd Suttle, eds., *Improving Life at Work* (Santa Monica, Calif.: Goodyear, 1977), pp. 130–131.

6. J. Richard Hackman, "Work Design," in Hackman and Suttle, eds., *Improving Life at Work,* pp. 128–130.

7. Gerald R. Salancik and Jeffrey A. Pfeffer, "A Social Information Processing Approach to Job Attitudes and Task Design," *Administrative Science Quarterly 23,* no. 2 (June 1978):224–253.

8. Joe Thomas and Ricky Griffin, "The Social Information Processing Model of Task Design," *Academy of Management Review 8,* no. 4 (October 1983):672–682.

9. Gerald R. Ferris, "The Influence of Leadership on Perceptions of Job Autonomy," *Journal of Psychology 114,* no. 2 (July 1983):253–258.

10. Norman D. Kurland, "Training on a Chip," *PC,* November 13, 1984, p. 91.

11. Jon L. Pierce, "Job Design and Technology: A Sociotechnical Systems Perspective," *Journal of Occupational Behavior 5,* no. 2 (April 1984):147–154.

12. Chris Argyris, *Personality and Organization* (New York: Harper & Brothers, 1957).

13. Frederick Herzberg, Bernard Mausner, and Barbara Snyderman, *The Motivation to Work,* 2nd ed. (New York: Wiley, 1959).

14. Douglas McGregor, *The Human Side of Enterprise* (New York: McGraw-Hill, 1960).

15. See Vida Scarpello and John P. Campbell, "Job Satisfaction and the Fit between Individual Needs and Organizational Rewards," *Journal of Occupational Psychology 56,* no. 4 (1983):315–328; Melvin Blumberg and Donald Gerwin, "Coping with Advanced Manufacturing Technology," *Journal of Occupational Behavior 5,* no. 2 (April 1984):113–130; and Paul S. Goodman, Robert S. Atkin, and Associates, *Absenteeism: New Approaches to Understanding, Measuring, and Managing Employee Absence* (San Francisco: Jossey-Bass, 1984).

16. Studies and reviews of the literature on the relationship between employee satisfaction and job specialization include: Jon L. Pierce and Randall B. Dunham, "Task Design: A Literature Review," *Academy of Management Review 1,* no. 4 (October 1976):83–97; Jon M. Shepard, "Technology, Alienation, and Job Satisfaction," *Annual Review of Sociology 3* (1977):1–21; J. Kenneth White, "Individual Differences and the Job Quality–Worker Response Relationship: Review, Integration, and Comments," *Academy of Management Review 3,* no. 3 (April 1978):267–280; and Robert P. Vecchio, "Individual Differences as a Moderator of the Job Quality–Job Satisfaction Relationship: Evidence from a National Sample," *Organizational Behavior and Human Performance 26,* no. 3 (December 1980):305–325. For a broad survey of this subject, see also *Work in America: Report of a Special Task Force to the Secretary of Health, Education, and Welfare* (Cambridge, Mass.: MIT Press, 1973).

17. Charles L. Hulin and Milton R. Blood, "Job Enlargement, Individual Differences, and Worker Responses," *Psychological Bulletin 69,* no. 1 (1968):41–53.

18. See Hackman, "Work Design," p. 118.

19. See Pierce and Dunham, "Task Design: A Literature Review," and Vecchio, "Individual Differences as a Moderator of the Job Quality–Job Satisfaction Relationship." Vecchio, however, finds that while individual differences do influence reactions to job specialization, the influence is not all that great.

20. For example, see John E. Oliver, "Job Satisfaction and Locus of Control in Two Job Types," *Psychological Reports 52,* no. 2 (April 1983):425–426; Jiing-Lih Farh and W. E. Scott, Jr., "The Experimental Effects of 'Autonomy' on Performance and Self-Reports of Satisfaction," *Organizational Behavior and Human Performance 31,* no. 2 (April 1983):203–222; and Gordon E. O'Brien, "Skill-Utilization, Skill Variety and the Job Characteristics Model," *Australian Journal of Psychology 35,* no. 3 (December 1983):461–468.

21. A paper by Robert N. Ford, "Job Enrichment Lessons from AT&T," *Harvard Business Review 51,* no. 1 (January–February 1973):96–106, describes some of the techniques used by AT&T to redesign white- and blue-collar jobs in one of the most extensive job-enrichment programs in American industry.

22. Riva Poor, *Four Days, Forty Hours* (Cambridge, Mass.: Bursk and Poor, 1970).

23. "Flextime in the Utilities Industry," *Personnel* 61, no. 2 (March–April 1984):42–44.

24. Frank Friedlander and L. Dave Brown, "Organization Development," in Mark Rosenzweig and Lyman W. Porter, eds., *Annual Review of Psychology* 25 (1974):313–341; and John M. Nicholas, "The Comparative Impact of Organization Development Interventions on Hard Criteria Measures," *Academy of Management Review* 1, no. 4 (October 1982): 531–542.

25. Robert H. Miles, *Macro Organizational Behavior* (Santa Monica, Calif.: Goodyear, 1980), p. 17.

26. Henry Mintzberg, *The Structuring of Organizations* (Englewood Cliffs, N.J.: Prentice-Hall, 1979), pp. 7, 185–186.

27. Organizational structure can also be specified by other sets of components. Henry Mintzberg, for example, identifies eight elements, some of which duplicate and some of which differ from those listed. See his "Organization Design: Fashion or Fit?" *Harvard Business Review* 59, no. 11 (January–February 1981):116.

28. Much of the following discussion is based on Alfred D. Chandler, Jr., *Strategy and Structure: Chapters in the History of the American Industrial Enterprise* (Cambridge, Mass.: MIT Press, 1962), pp. 14, 223, 383–396.

29. Robert Townsend, *Further Up the Organization* (New York: Knopf, 1984), p. 159.

30. Harold Stieglitz, "What's Not on an Organization Chart," *Conference Board Record* 1, no. 11 (November 1964):7–10.

31. See Dale, *Organization*, p. 238; Stieglitz, "What's Not on an Organization Chart," pp. 8–10; and Karol K. White, *Understanding the Company Organization Chart* (New York: American Management Associations, 1963), pp. 13–19.

32. Robert A. Pitts and John D. Daniels, "Aftermath of the Matrix Mania," *Columbia Journal of World Business* 19, no. 2 (Summer 1984):48–54; and John R. Adams and Nicki S. Kirchof, "The Practice of Matrix Management," in David I. Cleland, ed., *Matrix Management Systems Handbook* (New York: Van Nostrand Reinhold, 1984), pp. 13–30.

33. See John F. Mee, "Matrix Organizations," *Business Horizons* 7, no. 2 (Summer 1964):70–72; Jay R. Galbraith, "Matrix Organization Designs," *Business Horizons* 14, no. 1 (February 1971):29–40; Stanley M. Davis and Paul R. Lawrence, *Matrix* (Reading, Mass.: Addison-Wesley, 1977); and Harvey F. Kolodny, "Evolution to a Matrix Organization," *Academy of Management Review* 4, no. 4 (1979):543–553.

34. Davis and Lawrence, *Matrix*, pp. 39–45.

35. R. F. Grantges, V. L. Fahrmann, T. A. Gibson, and L. M. Brown, "Central Office Equipment Reports for Stored Program Control Systems," *Bell System Technical Journal* 62, no. 7 (September 1983):2365–2395.

36. See Harold Kerzner, "Matrix Implementation: Obstacles, Problems, Questions, and Answers," in Cleland, ed., *Matrix Management Systems Handbook*, pp. 307–329; and William Jerkovsky, "Functional Management in Matrix Organizations," *IEEE Transactions on Engineering Management* 30, no. 2 (May 1983):89–97.

37. Martyn E. Gossen, "California Bank Personal Finance Group," case no. 9–478–055 (Cambridge, Mass.: Harvard Business Case Services, 1978). "California Bank" in a pseudonym for a well-known New York-based bank. For an example of successful use of a matrix structure in the public sector, see Mary E. Simon, "Matrix Management at the U.S. Consumer Product Safety Commission," *Public Administration Review* 43, no. 4 (July–August 1983):357–361.

38. Herbert A. Simon, *Administrative Behavior*, 3d ed. (New York: Macmillan, 1976). For other rich discussions of informal groups, see Chester I. Barnard, *The Functions of the Executive* (Cambridge, Mass.: Harvard University Press, 1938); F. J. Roethlisberger and William J. Dickson, *Management and the Worker* (Cambridge, Mass.: Harvard University Press, 1947); and Charles Perrow, *Complex Organizations*, 3d ed. (New York: Random House, 1986).

39. Quoted from Peter F. Drucker, "New Templates for Today's Organizations," *Harvard Business Review* 52, no. 1 (January–February 1974):51.

40. Rather than putting the focus on the *product*, as Drucker does, we might prefer to put it on the *customer*. This change of emphasis would be consistent with much of Drucker's other writing and also with the analyses of Peters and Waterman (see chapter 1).

CASE STUDY: Canadian Marconi Company

Keith Glegg had worked his way up through the technical arm of Canadian Marconi to become Chief Engineer and then General Manager of the Avionics Division. (See exhibit 1.) He was an important inventor and innovator in basic frequency-modulated continuous wave (FM-CW) Doppler radar technology. This FM-CW technology gave Avionics a world leadership position in Doppler radar equipment design and production. All Avionics equipment designs were state of the art at the time of their design, a result of the importance Glegg attached to the role of innovative research and development engineering for the department's future.

EXHIBIT 1 CANADIAN MARCONI COMPANY—AVIONICS DIVISION

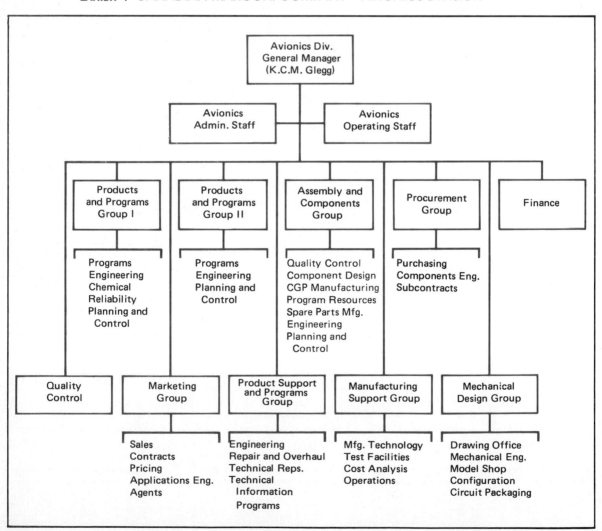

EXHIBIT 2 AVIONICS DIVISION—TYPICAL PROGRAM ORGANIZATION

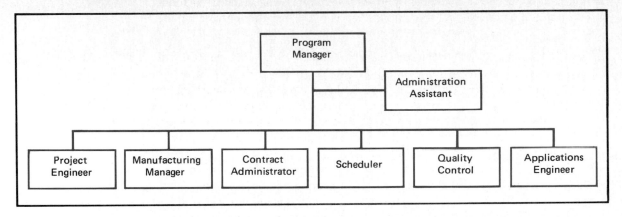

Doppler radars were used in airborne navigation systems to determine aircraft velocity and distance by bouncing microwave signals off the terrain and calculating the desired parameters from the Doppler effect of returning signals. A typical Doppler system was composed of several "black boxes" of electronic and electromechanical equipment. The Doppler systems in the Avionics product line sold for prices that ranged between $20,000 and $80,000 per system.

As the division grew and Avionics's success with Doppler systems brought large increases in sales, Glegg's preoccupations became considerably more managerial than technical. He began to reassess some of his own thinking about organizations. The organization appeared too weak, both structurally and managerially, to cope with the increasing complexity of his division's activities.

Glegg was finding it impossible to cope with the number of major decisions that had to be made. Six major programs and several minor ones were in different stages of design and/or production. (See exhibit 2.) All had different customers, sometimes in different countries. Every program's product, although they were all Doppler radar systems, was significantly different from every other one, particularly in its technology. Nevertheless the programs had to share manufacturing facilities, major items of capital equipment, and specialized functions. Glegg felt he had to find some way to force the whole decision process down to some level below his own.

Source: Stanley M. Davis and Paul R. Lawrence, *Matrix*, pp. 59–62, including figures 3.1 and 3.2. Copyright 1977, Addison-Wesley, Reading, Mass. Reprinted with permission.

Case Questions
1. What is the principal problem with Canadian Marconi's existing organizational structure?
2. How can the matrix form of organization assist Keith Glegg?
3. As a management consultant, what specific recommendations do you have that can help relieve Keith Glegg of some of his current problems?

10 COORDINATION AND ORGANIZATIONAL DESIGN

Upon completing this chapter you should be able to:

1. Explain why the activities and objectives of an organization must be coordinated.
2. Describe the three basic approaches to achieving effective coordination.
3. Define span of management and explain the factors that must be considered in selecting an appropriate span.
4. Describe the classical and neoclassical approaches to organizational design and identify their limitations.
5. Identify the key variables in the contingency approach to organizational design and explain how each can affect organizational structure.
6. Discuss the four stages of the integrative model of organizational growth and evaluation.
7. Describe the special problems encountered by rapidly expanding organizations.
8. Discuss recent thinking on characteristics relevant to organizational decline.

In the preceding chapter we discussed two aspects of the organizing process, division of work and departmentalization. In this chapter we will consider other aspects of the organizing process—coordination, span of management, and organizational design.

If work activities are divided and departmentalized, it is necessary for managers to coordinate these activities to achieve organizational goals. Managers must communicate to each unit the organization's goals, translated into appropriate unit objectives. They must also keep each unit informed about the activities of other units so that the various parts of the organization can work together smoothly.

The ability of managers to achieve effective coordination depends in part on the number of subordinates reporting to them and to other managers in the organization. That number is known as the "span of management." An organization's choice of span of management can be crucial in influencing its productivity, costs, and efficiency.

Organizational design—choosing the best type of organizational structure for a given situation—has long been an important consideration for managers in all types and sizes of organizations. For example, recent U.S. presidents, claiming that the federal bureaucracy is wasteful and inefficient, have attempted to restructure it to better meet its goals. In the private sector, an inappropriate structure can lead to high costs and even the failure of an entire organization. When the Pennsylvania Railroad merged with the New York Central to form Penn Central, for example, the opportunities for a larger, more efficient operation seemed promising. However, the two companies did not merge their organizations into one sound structure. The result was rivalry and costly duplication of effort—both of which contributed to the financial collapse of Penn Central in the early 1970s.[1] Following large losses by creditors and shareholders, the Penn Central emerged from bankruptcy in 1980 with a very different organizational structure and strategy.

In this chapter, then, we will deal with three major topics: how to achieve effective organizational coordination, how to choose the most appropriate span of management, and how to design an organizational structure that is appropriate to the environment and that is capable of evolving as the organization and its environment change.

Coordination

Managers divide work into specialized functions or departments to increase the productivity and efficiency of their organizations. At the same time, though, they create the need for coordinating these divided work activities. *Coordination* is the process of integrating the objectives and activities of the separate units (departments or functional areas) of an organization in order to achieve organizational goals efficiently.[2] Without coordination, individuals and departments would lose sight of their roles within the organization. They would begin to pursue their own specialized interests, often at the expense of the larger organizational goals.

The Need for Coordination

The activities of organizational units differ in the extent to which they need to be integrated with the activities of other units. The need for coordination depends on the nature and communication requirements of the tasks performed and the degree of interdependence of the various units performing them.[3] When these tasks require or can benefit from information flow between units, then a high degree of coordination is best. However, if there is no such requirement or benefit, the work might be better completed if less time were spent in interaction with members of other units. A high degree of coordination is likely to be beneficial for work that is nonroutine and unpredictable, for work in which factors in the environment are changing, and for work in which task interdependence is high (for example, if one unit cannot function without receiving information or a product component from another unit). A high level of coordination is also needed in organizations that set high performance objectives.

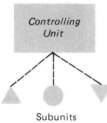

POOLED
INTERDEPENDENCE

According to James D. Thompson, there are three varieties of interdependence among organizational units:[4] *Pooled interdependence* exists when organizational units do not depend upon one another to carry out their day-to-day work but do depend on the adequate performance of each unit for ultimate survival. Each part renders a separate contribution to the whole and is supported by the whole. For example, the seven national branches of a New York law firm may have little communication with one another. The Palm Beach branch will function in complete independence of the Seattle and Houston branches. Yet good performance by each is required for the survival of all.

In *sequential interdependence,* one organizational unit must act before the next can. For example, fertilizer and insecticides from the Midland, Michigan, operation of an organization may be used to raise turf in Clare; until the turf has grown, the Lansing distributor will have nothing to distribute.

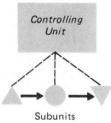

SEQUENTIAL
INTERDEPENDENCE

Reciprocal interdependence involves give-and-take relationships between units. Take the case of a trucking firm with units located outside major cities. For long-distance shipping, one unit fills a truck and drives it to another unit, where the truck is unloaded and local shipping of the contents is arranged. Each unit "produces" filled trucks that it sends out; in turn, each unit needs a steady supply of empty trucks to fill, and their supply is assured by the arrival of other units' trucks to be emptied.

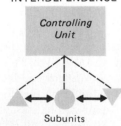

RECIPROCAL
INTERDEPENDENCE

Problems in Achieving Effective Coordination

The need for coordination of organizational activities is least with pooled interdependence, greater with sequential interdependence, and greatest with reciprocal interdependence. As the need for coordination increases, so does the difficulty of achieving it effectively. Similarly, increased specialization also increases the need for coordination. But the greater the degree of specialization, the more difficult it is for managers to coordinate the specialized activities of different units. Paul R. Lawrence and Jay W. Lorsch have pointed out that people in specialized units tend to develop their own sense of the organization's goals and how to pursue them.[5]

Lawrence and Lorsch have noted that division of work involves more than a difference in precise activities, such as tightening a bolt or writing advertising copy.

It also influences how we perceive the organization, how we perceive our role in it, and how we relate to each other. These differences are desirable because they enable the organization to match individuals' talents, skills, and perspectives to the specialized needs of different tasks and activities.

The researchers also identified four types of differences in attitudes and working style that tend to arise among the various individuals and departments in organizations. These differences—which they call *differentiation*—complicate the task of effectively coordinating an organization's activities:

1. *Differences in orientation toward particular goals.* Members of different departments develop their own views about how best to advance the interests of the organization. To salespeople, product variety may take precedence over product quality. Accountants may see cost control as most important to the organization's success, while marketing managers may regard product design as most essential.

2. *Differences in time orientation.* Some members of an organization, such as production managers, will be more concerned with problems that have to be solved immediately. Others, like members of a research and development team, may be preoccupied with problems that will take years to solve.

3. *Differences in interpersonal orientation.* In some organizational activities, such as production, there may be relatively abrupt ways of communicating. Decisions may be made in a quick, "let's-get-on-with-it" manner in order to keep things moving. In other activities, such as R&D, the style of communication may be much more easygoing. Everyone may be encouraged to discuss their ideas with others.

4. *Differences in formality of structure.* Each type of unit in the organization may have different methods and standards for evaluating progress toward objectives and for rewarding employees. In a production department, for example, the standards may be quite explicitly defined in terms of cost, quality, and schedule, and a control system may exist for precise measurement of these criteria. In the personnel department, however, standards of performance may be quite broadly defined—such as "upgrading the quality of field personnel"; the control system for measuring progress against such standards will be correspondingly less precise.

In place of the term *coordination*, Lawrence and Lorsch use *integration* to designate the degree to which members of various departments worked together in a unified manner. Departments should cooperate and their tasks be integrated where necessary, without reducing the differences that contribute to task accomplishment. It may be useful for the sales department to give advice on advertisements to the graphic artists who will prepare them; however, if salespeople view themselves as adjuncts of the advertising department, then the functioning of both sales and advertising units will be impaired. Division of work and specialization help the organization use its resources most efficiently, even though they increase the coordination burden of managers.

Differentiation encourages conflict among individuals and organizational units. Various members of the organization present their viewpoints, argue them openly, and in general make certain that they get heard. In this way they force managers to consider the special needs and knowledge of individual departments when problems exist. Constructively resolved conflict is healthy for an organization's operations. A recent study of managers in eight nations and four national groupings found that most managers appeared to be rewarded more for noncooperativeness, *within reasonable limits,* than for cooperativeness. Exceptions included Japan and the Scandinavian countries, where cooperativeness was more rewarded.[6] Constructive conflict is seen as so important that modern management writers regard the absence of a reasonable level of conflict as a danger signal. (Creative uses of conflict will be dealt with more extensively in chapter 14.)

Approaches to Achieving Effective Coordination

Communication is the key to effective coordination. Coordination is directly dependent upon the acquisition, transmission, and processing of information. The greater the uncertainty of the tasks to be coordinated, the greater the need for information. For this reason, it is useful to think of coordination as essentially an *information processing* task.[7]

In this section we will examine three approaches to achieving effective coordination: using basic management techniques, increasing the potential for coordination, and reducing the need for coordination. (See fig. 10–1.)

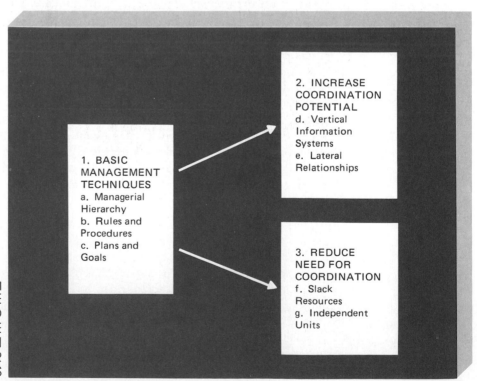

FIGURE 10–1
THREE APPROACHES TO EFFECTIVE COORDINATION METHODS FOR MANAGERS

1. **BASIC MANAGEMENT TECHNIQUES**
   a. Managerial Hierarchy
   b. Rules and Procedures
   c. Plans and Goals

2. **INCREASE COORDINATION POTENTIAL**
   d. Vertical Information Systems
   e. Lateral Relationships

3. **REDUCE NEED FOR COORDINATION**
   f. Slack Resources
   g. Independent Units

Source: Adapted from Jay R. Galbraith, "Organization Design: An Information Processing View," *Interfaces* 4, no. 3 (May 1974). Copyright © 1974 by The Institute of Management Sciences. Reprinted by permission.

Basic Management Techniques. The problems of organizations with relatively modest coordination requirements can often be resolved through the use of the basic managerial mechanisms for achieving control. These mechanisms are discussed at length in other chapters, so we will mention them only briefly here.

· *The managerial hierarchy.* The organization's chain of command specifies relationships among its members and the units they oversee, thereby facilitating the flow of information and work between units.
· *Rules and procedures.* An organization's rules and procedures are designed to handle routine events before they arise. If they are regularly followed, subordinates can take action quickly and independently, leaving more time for managers to devote to new or unique events.
· *Plans and goals.* Plans and goals achieve coordination by assuring that all units direct their efforts toward the same broad targets.

Increasing Coordination Potential. When an organization's various units become more interdependent or expand in size or function, more information is necessary for the organization to achieve its objectives, and thus its coordination potential must also be increased. When the basic management techniques just described are insufficient, additional mechanisms may be desirable. Coordination potential may be increased in two directions, vertically and laterally.

Vertical Information Systems. A *vertical information system* is the means by which data are transmitted up and down the levels of the organization. The communication may occur within or outside of the chain of command. Management information systems have been developed in such activities as marketing, finance, production, and international operations to increase the information available for planning, coordination, and control.[8] (We will examine management information systems in detail in chapter 22.)

Lateral Relationships. Cutting across the chain of command, *lateral relationships* permit information to be exchanged and decisions to be made at the level where the needed information actually exists. There are several kinds of lateral relationships; our discussion will begin with relatively simple ones and move toward more complex ones that require a greater investment of time and effort.

The simplest form of lateral relationship is *direct contact* between the individuals who must deal with the same situation or problem. This avoids the necessity for referring problems upward to division managers for resolution.

Boundary-spanning roles also facilitate lateral relationships. When the number of contacts between departments increases dramatically, it may be best to create explicit boundary-spanning roles and appoint unit members to them. The employees chosen for such roles should be well acquainted not only with their own units but also with the responsibilities and concerns of the units they are dealing with as liaisons. Members of the engineering and marketing departments, for example, can almost be said to speak different languages. Boundary-spanning individuals must be fluent in the other unit's "language" if they hope to function well as a channel for communication.

Committees and task forces are in many cases an effective means of pooling the expertise of different members of an organization and channeling their efforts toward a common goal. *Committees* are usually formally organized groups with a designated membership and chairperson and regularly scheduled meetings. Generally long-lasting or permanent parts of an organization's structure, they deal with recurring problems and decisions. *Task forces,* on the other hand, are formed as needed to deal with special problems. Each of the units concerned with the problem contributes one or more members. Once a solution is reached, the task force is dissolved. The distinctions between committees and task forces and their effective use are discussed more fully in chapter 17.

Integrating roles are roles established when a specific product, service, or project that spans several departments requires continuing coordination and attention from a single individual not in the departments in question. Integrators act like diplomats, speaking the languages of each department or group (for example, computer programmers and line supervisors). They can maintain neutrality when the groups to be integrated are excited and distrustful, and they can attempt to balance power differences between departments—restraining the more powerful ones and bolstering the less powerful.

Managerial linking roles may be called for if the integrating position described above does not coordinate a particular task effectively. A linking manager has *formal authority* over all the units involved in a project. This authority often takes the form of control over the budgets of all units to assure that they work together toward the goals of the organization as a whole.

A *matrix organization* has characteristics of both the managerial linking role and the task force. In a matrix structure (see chapter 9), the managers of two areas supervise a group of employees that is responsible to them both, so the requirements of both areas are routinely taken into account. Like a task force, a particular matrix structure may be dissolved when a project has been completed.

Reducing the Need for Coordination. When basic management techniques are insufficient, coordination can be increased with the above methods. When the need for coordination is so great that even these are ineffective, the best approach is to reduce the need for tight coordination. Galbraith describes two ways to reduce the need for coordination: creating slack resources and creating independent units.[9]

Creating Slack Resources. Providing slack (additional) resources gives units leeway in meeting each other's requirements.[10] Suppose, for example, that Mercedes-Benz anticipates that it will sell 10,000 cars in a given region of the United States over a three-month period beginning January 1. The manufacturer might establish a production quota of 12,000 cars, in case demand is larger than anticipated, and a production deadline of October 1 of the previous year to give itself a three-month safety margin should production or transportation difficulties arise.

Creating Independent Units. Another way to reduce the need for coordination is to create units that can perform all the necessary aspects of a task internally. A company that builds a variety of kitchen appliances, for example, could form an independent unit that designs, manufactures, and markets all of its food processors, thereby eliminating the need for continual consultations with centralized engineering, manufacturing, and marketing staffs.

Selecting the Appropriate Coordination Mechanisms

The key consideration in selecting the best approach to coordination is to match the organization's *capacity* for coordination with its *need* for coordination. How much

TABLE 10–1
COMPARISON OF
COORDINATING
MECHANISMS

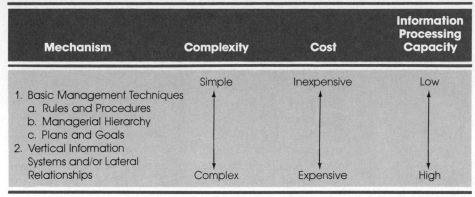

Mechanism	Complexity	Cost	Information Processing Capacity

1. Basic Management Techniques
  a. Rules and Procedures
  b. Managerial Hierarchy
  c. Plans and Goals
2. Vertical Information
  Systems and/or Lateral
  Relationships
	Simple ↕ Complex	Inexpensive ↕ Expensive	Low ↕ High

Source: Adapted from Michael L. Tushman and David A. Nadler, "Information Processing as an Integrating Concept in Organizational Design," *Academy of Management Review* 3, no. 3 (July 1978), figure 2, p. 618.

information does the organization need to perform its operations? How much information is it capable of processing? If the need is greater than the ability, the organization must make a choice: It can either increase its coordination potential (by improving its performance of the basic management techniques, by introducing or expanding vertical information systems and lateral relationships, or both), *or* reduce the need (by appropriating slack resources or creating independent units). Table 10–1 indicates one of the trade-offs involved in introducing or expanding coordinating mechanisms: As information processing capacity increases, both complexity and cost increase as well.

In selecting appropriate coordinating mechanisms, managers in the 1980s need to recognize that organizational coordination capabilities are improving rapidly due to electronic information processing systems, which are simple, readily available, and increasingly inexpensive. It is practical and cost-effective for even small organizations to purchase information systems that reduce bottlenecks in information processing and that can grow and change with the organization and its needs. As we discuss in chapter 22, failure to bring information processing capabilities in line with needs can endanger an organization's viability.

Span of Management

Span of management (also called *span of control*) can be simply defined as the number of subordinates who report directly to a given manager. This aspect of organization has interested managers since ancient times. Both the Roman legions and the Chinese civil service, for example, had to address span of management questions (although neither explicitly recognized the concept as such).[11]

The modern approach to the subject began with the industrial revolution. In the nineteenth and first half of the twentieth centuries, various writers attempted to determine the maximum number of subordinates one manager could supervise. Many concluded that the universal maximum was six. The idea that a manager can control only a certain number of subordinates regardless of circumstances seems odd today, but the earlier writers must be given credit for recognizing that there is an optimal number of subordinates and also that there is a number beyond which supervision becomes less effective.[12]

There are two major reasons why the choice of the appropriate span may be important: First, span of management may affect the efficient utilization of managers and the effective performance of their subordinates. Too wide a span may mean that managers are overextending themselves and that their subordinates are receiving too little guidance or control. Too narrow a span of management may mean that managers are underutilized.

Second, there is a relationship between span of management throughout the organization and organizational structure. Narrow spans of management result in "tall" organizational structures with many supervisory levels between top management and the lowest levels. Wide spans, for the same number of employees, mean fewer management levels between top and bottom. Either structure may influence the effectiveness of managers at any level.

Selecting the Appropriate Span

If too wide or too narrow a span of management can influence productivity and costs, selecting the appropriate span may offer the opportunity to increase organizational performance. Rather than searching for the universally correct span, contemporary researchers have sought to determine the span of management most appropriate to a given situation.

Span of Management Studies. Attempts to find a relationship between span of management and organizational performance have reached varying conclusions. After thoroughly reviewing past studies and conducting their own, David D. Van Fleet and Arthur G. Bedeian concluded that there may be no connection between span of management and managerial or organizational effectiveness.[13] On the other hand, in an early study the managers of Lockheed Missile and Space Company found that significant savings could be achieved by altering the span of middle managers. We shall review that study in detail because it shows an interesting attempt by managers and researchers to translate management theory into action.

Harold Stieglitz and C. W. Barkdull have each described how analysts at Lockheed developed their own contingency approach for selecting the appropriate management span for specific situations.[14] The Lockheed analysts first identified seven factors that most affect the choice of span. (See box.) They then tried to rank the factors in order of importance. For example, it seems reasonable that the more time managers spend in planning, the less time they will have for supervision; their span will thus become narrower. Similarly, the more complex the functions that managers are responsible for, the more difficult their supervisory task becomes; again, the span will narrow. But which of these factors—planning or complexity—will most affect the width of the span? By using their common sense and experience, and doing some experiments, the analysts were able to make judgments on such questions and arrive at a ranking for the seven factors.

Each factor was then assigned a point value based on its rank; the more critical the factor in selecting a management span, the higher its point value. The various managerial positions in the company were then analyzed to determine their total point value. For each point total (or position), a "suggested span of management" was established. For example, the positions with the highest point value—that is, the positions with a high proportion of critical factors affecting choice of span—had a suggested narrow span of 4–5 subordinates. Positions with the lowest point values

Lockheed's analysts selected and defined seven factors that they felt influenced the span of management:

1. *Similarity of functions supervised:* the degree to which the functions or subordinate tasks for which the manager is responsible are alike or different.
2. *Geographic contiguity of functions supervised:* how closely located to the manager the functions or subordinates are.
3. *Complexity of functions supervised:* the nature of the functions or tasks for which the manager is responsible.
4. *Direction and control needed by subordinates:* the degree of supervision that subordinates require.
5. *Coordination required of the supervisor:* the degree to which the manager must try to integrate functions or tasks within the subunit or between the subunit and other parts of the organization.
6. *Planning required of the supervisor:* the degree to which the manager will have to program and review the activities of his or her subunit.
7. *Organizational assistance received by the supervisor:* how much help in terms of assistants and other support personnel the manager can rely on.

Source: Quoted and adapted from C. W. Barkdull, "Span of Control—A Method of Evaluation," *Michigan Business Review* 15, no. 3 (May 1963): 27–29. Reprinted by permission of the *Michigan Business Review,* published by the Graduate School of Business Administration, The University of Michigan.

(such as some first-line supervisors with subordinates performing routine tasks) had spans as wide as 16–22 subordinates.

Lockheed's managers decided to reorganize several units of their company along these guidelines. For example, the average span for middle managers was increased from 3.9 to 5.9, and the number of management levels was reduced from seven to five, resulting in improved coordination and communication. Economic savings, though not a primary goal of the program, were significant. The payroll was reduced by an estimated $280,000 annually. An additional amount was saved through the elimination of secretarial assistance, office space, and supplies.

Jon G. Udell surveyed the marketing and sales divisions of 67 manufacturing companies to confirm whether the factors suggested by Lockheed's (and other) analysts actually did affect management span.[15] He found that some of the factors were related to the span chosen by managers in those firms, particularly the availability of organizational assistance, the similarity of functions supervised, and the length of experience of subordinates. Other factors appeared to have little impact on the choice of span.

Udell's most significant finding was related to the geographic dispersion of subordinates. Most writers have assumed that geographic separation would make supervision more difficult and therefore would narrow the span of management. Udell found the opposite to be true: Geographic dispersion was associated with a wider rather than a narrower span of management. One possible explanation is that the geographic variable might be related to other important ones. For example, geographically separated subordinates frequently have similar functions and work relatively independently, requiring less supervision and therefore making a wider span possible.

Guidelines for Selecting the Appropriate Span. As these cases demonstrate, the appropriate span of management cannot be calculated from any single formula or rule of thumb. There are, however, some guidelines that indicate whether a span should be relatively broad or relatively narrow. The guidelines include factors relating to the situation, subordinates, and the manager.

Some of these factors imply that the optimal span of management may not always be the same, even for the same manager and subordinates. For example, as a manager and subordinates improve in their work, the optimal span would increase. A change in the nature or quantity of work may require narrowing the span if closer supervision is required.

If the span of management appears to be inappropriate, either the span itself or the factors that influence it can be adjusted. For example, if "supervisors are harassed and subordinates are frustrated"—a symptom of too large a span—some subordinates and their work might be transferred to other supervisors. Alternatively, additional training for lower-level managers and subordinates, adding supervisory assistants, or arranging assistance with nonsupervisory tasks might be tried. By understanding the relationships between the variables, we can identify the most promising factors to adjust.

Organizational Design

We have been discussing specific aspects of organization—coordination and span of management—that help knit an organization together and influence the efficiency of its operations. In this section we look at the topic of *organizational design* as a whole. Our discussion emphasizes the key role of strategy in determining an appropriate organizational structure and also the importance of designing a structure that is appropriate to the people, technology, and tasks of the organization.

The process we describe may sound neat, rational, and precise, but in practice it rarely is. Designing an organization is, first of all, a continuing process because environments, organizations, and strategies inevitably change over time. Thus, large changes in organizational structure may be required occasionally and smaller changes may be needed frequently. Second, changes in structure usually involve many trial-and-error attempts, accidents, and accommodations to political realities, rather than a purely rational approach. For example, it may seem logical to cut back a particular department, but if the head of that department has strong allies elsewhere in the organization or perhaps even on the board of directors, the cutback may not be effected. In other words, like many complex managerial issues, the problem of organizational design may never be permanently resolved in any particular organization. And it is not always possible to implement what appears at the time to be the best design.

Early Approaches to Organizational Design

Early management writers attempted to find the "one best way" or the "universal" approach to designing organizations. They tried to establish a set of principles that would yield an organizational structure that was efficient and effective in all situations. Such an approach implied that organizational structure was affected by neither the organization's environment nor its strategy—that a sound structure would succeed regardless of external conditions and internal objectives.

Today, management writers have moved from a "one-best-way" approach to a contingency approach. They argue that an organization is highly interdependent with its environment and that different situations require different structures. Managers, then, must identify the variables that affect their organization so that they can design it appropriately. Before discussing these key variables, we will briefly review the early management approaches to the organizing process. We will then look at more recent perspectives on how an organization should be designed.[16]

The Classical Approach to Organizational Design

The sociologist Max Weber[17] and management writers Frederick Taylor and Henri Fayol were major contributors to the so-called classical approach to organizational design. They believed that the most efficient and effective organizations had a hierarchical structure based on a legalized formal authority. (Weber called an organization with such a structure a *bureaucracy*.) Members of the organization were guided in their actions by a sense of duty to the organization and by a set of rational rules and regulations. When fully developed, according to Weber, such organizations were characterized by specialization of tasks, appointment by merit, provision of career opportunities for members, routinization of activities, and a rational, impersonal organizational climate.

Today the word "bureaucracy" has many negative connotations. The early management writers, however, found much to commend in bureaucracy as an organizational design. Weber in particular praised its rationality, its establishment of rules for decision making, its clear chain of command, and its promotion of people on the basis of ability and experience rather than favoritism or whim. He also admired the clear specification of authority and responsibility, which he believed made it easier to evaluate and reward performance.

Of course, Weber, Taylor, and Fayol developed their theories at a time when organizations that resembled their bureaucratic model were among the more modern and efficient ones. It soon became evident, however, that some of the major advantages of the bureaucratic structure could become disadvantages. For example, the safeguards against favoritism and bias could be too rigidly imposed by adhering excessively to rules and procedures—resulting in the depersonalization of managers and subordinates.

Criticisms of the Classical Approach. The classical approach has been criticized from two major perspectives. First, it has been criticized as a theory that may not have a basis in reality. Have organizations like those described by Weber and the others ever existed? And, if they existed, did they achieve the predicted results?[18]

Second, it has been criticized as a prescription for managers—one that claims organizations designed and managed according to bureaucratic principles will enjoy the predicted benefits. These critics argue that the world does not currently fit the assumptions in Weber's model (if it ever did), and so a bureaucracy is not likely to yield the results he describes.

In addition, because the word "bureaucracy" has come to imply large size, some criticisms of bureaucracies are more nearly criticisms of bigness *per se* rather than of a particular structure or of classical theory.

The second group of criticisms is more important for managers. Critics from this group claim the bureaucratic model will not yield an effective organization because:

1. It neglects the human aspects of organization members, assuming they are motivated only by economic concerns. As educational levels, affluence, and work expectations have risen, this criticism has become more severe.
2. It does not suit rapidly changing and uncertain environments. Formalized bureaucratic organizations have difficulty in changing their established procedures.
3. It assumes that upper-level managers will be respected and obeyed by subordinates because of their superior knowledge and skills. Therefore, they can guide the work of subordinates effectively. But as the organization increases in size, top-level managers lose touch with lower levels. And in periods of rapid technological change, young newcomers frequently have relevant knowledge and skills not possessed by managers above them.
4. As organizational procedures become more formalized and individuals more specialized, means often become confused with ends. Specialists, for example, may concentrate on their own finely tuned goals and forget that their goals are a means for reaching the broader goals of the organization.
5. The bureaucratic structure has also been criticized for encouraging what Victor Thompson calls "bureaupathology."[19] Because managers compete for advancement, are held accountable for mistakes, and direct subordinates who may have superior technical knowledge, they may feel insecure. Thompson believes that bureaucratic structures permit counterproductive personal insecurities to flourish and that some managers try to protect their authority and position by aloof, ritualistic behavior. This is "pathological," according to Thompson, because it can prevent the organization from meeting its goals.

The Neoclassical Approach

Early human relations researchers and behavioral scientists attempted to deal with what they saw as the major inadequacy of the classical bureaucratic model: neglect of the human element within the organization. They argued that an industrial organization has two objectives: economic effectiveness *and* employee satisfaction.

As we saw in chapter 2, the initial impetus for this point of view was provided by the Hawthorne studies, which were interpreted as implying that when management showed concern for employees, increased productivity resulted. Human relations researchers and behavioral scientists argued that the bureaucratic structure could be improved by making it less formal and by permitting more participation of subordinates in decision making. Because they did not reject the classical model, but only tried to improve it, these researchers are sometimes called neoclassicists. Among them are Douglas McGregor,[20] Chris Argyris,[21] and Rensis Likert,[22] whose work we describe below.

Douglas McGregor. McGregor believed that the vertical division of labor that characterized organizations under the bureaucratic system was based in part on a set of negative assumptions about workers. In vertical division of labor, activities are specialized by levels in the management hierarchy. Planning and decision making

Drawing by Chas. Addams; © 1976 The New Yorker Magazine, Inc.

take place at upper levels of management, while implementation of the decisions is done by people at lower levels. Although this separation has always existed to some extent, it was increased by the application of scientific management techniques.

As we saw in chapter 4, McGregor believed that many managers accept Theory X assumptions about lower-level employees (see chapter 4 for a discussion of Theory X and Theory Y). These include the belief that most people have little ambition, that they desire security above all, and that they avoid work unless coerced into it. In this view, a rigid, formal organizational hierarchy is necessary to maintain managers' authority over subordinates. Organizations structured around Theory Y assumptions, McGregor claimed, would better meet their members' needs and use their potential more effectively. Theory Y assumes that people can find satisfaction in work, that they desire achievement, and that they seek responsibility. Such organizations permit employees more independence, a larger role in decision making, and greater openness in communication with their managers and with each other.

Chris Argyris. Argyris was also concerned that in a bureaucratic organization managers had near-total responsibility for planning, controlling, and evaluating the work of their subordinates. Argyris argued that such domination of the workplace by managers can cause subordinates to become passive and dependent, as well as decrease their sense of responsibility and self-control.

To Argyris, such conditions were incompatible with the human needs for self-reliance, self-expression, and accomplishment. Members of the organization, particularly at lower levels, will become dissatisfied and frustrated in their work as these needs are blocked. The result, he suggested, is not only increased unhappiness among organization members but also increased problems in meeting organizational goals. For example, dissatisfied workers may change jobs frequently, increasing staffing costs, or do their work carelessly, increasing production costs. Employees may also insist on higher wages because their work is so psychologically unrewarding.

As an alternative, Argyris argued for an organizational design that would better meet human needs and increase the satisfaction of organization members. Like McGregor, he favored allowing subordinates much more independence and decision-making power and creating a more informal organizational culture.

Rensis Likert. Likert shared the perspectives of McGregor and Argyris. In his research on effective group performance, he found that traditional authoritarian managers were less able to motivate their subordinates to high standards of achievement than managers who actively supported their subordinates' feelings of self-worth and importance. Based on these findings, Likert created a model to describe different organizational designs and their effectiveness.

In Likert's model, organizational structure can be based on one of four systems. (See chapter 16 for a fuller discussion of Likert's model.) In *System 1*, the traditional organizational structure, power and authority are distributed strictly according to the manager-subordinate relationship. Managers at one level tell members at lower levels what to do, and so on down the chain of command. *Systems 2* and *3* are intermediate stages. *System 4* organizations represent Likert's view of how an organization should ideally be designed and managed. At this stage, there is extensive group participation in supervision and decision making. The System 4 manager's primary task is to build a group that can make decisions and carry them out. To reach System 4, Likert says, organizations should (1) accept that managers and work activities should enhance individual members' personal sense of worth and importance; (2) use group decision making where appropriate; and (3) set high performance goals.

Criticisms of the Neoclassical Approach. The neoclassical approach to organizational design compensates for some limitations in the traditional classical model, but it, too, has been criticized.

1. **The neoclassicists share the classical assumption that there is "one best way" to design an organization. They overlook environmental, technological, and other variables that might affect an organization's design.**
2. **Theory X and Theory Y oversimplify human motivation. Not everyone is motivated by the nonmonetary aspects of work, nor can all work be made intrinsically challenging and rewarding.**
3. **The coordination of decentralized, fragmented groups to achieve organizational goals may be more difficult than the neoclassicists suggest, particularly when the objectives of lower-level employees are not consistent with the goals of upper-level managers.**

Contingency Approaches to Organizational Design

As we have already suggested, the research and writing of today's management theorists express doubt that there is a single, ideal way to design organizations. According to the current contingency approaches, the most appropriate structure for an organization depends on the particular circumstances of that organization at a given time.

The key variables that affect the organization and thus influence its structure are its strategy, the environment in which it operates, the technology it uses to carry out its activities, and the characteristics of its members. The manager's job, in the contingency view, is to establish an effective "fit" between the organization's structure and those variables.[23]

Strategy and Structure

The close relationship between organizational strategy and structure was first demonstrated by Chandler in his study of large American industrial enterprises.[24] After analyzing the histories of such companies as Du Pont, General Motors, Standard Oil, and Sears, Roebuck, Chandler concluded that changes in corporate strategy precede and lead to changes in organizational design.

In their initial stages, each company Chandler studied had a centralized structure that was appropriate for its limited product line. As population, national income, and rate of technological innovation increased, however, these companies introduced new products, entered new markets, and increased output. The resulting complexity made a highly centralized structure inefficient and impractical. The entry into new product markets in particular required more independence at lower levels to ensure quick response to those evolving markets. Some centralized control was (and still is) maintained; but, in general, these companies had to shift to a decentralized structure, with several near-autonomous divisions, in order to remain successful.

In selecting a strategy—and the structure to implement it—managers must consider how the external environment will affect the organization. The relationship between strategy, structure, and environment can be viewed from two major perspectives. (See fig. 10–2.) In the first perspective, the organization is *reactive* to its environment: The strategy formulation process must consider the environment in which the organization operates at present and will be operating in the future. In the second perspective, the organization is *proactive* because the strategy formulation process involves choosing the environment in which the organization will operate in the longer run.

Most organizations are not large enough to influence major parts of the external environment in which they operate; in this sense they must adjust to their environment. However, through their strategies they can and do choose those parts of the external environment with which they will interact the most and which, therefore, will exert the most influence.

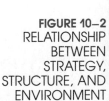

FIGURE 10–2
RELATIONSHIP
BETWEEN
STRATEGY,
STRUCTURE, AND
ENVIRONMENT

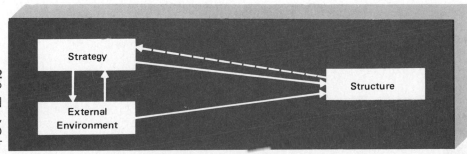

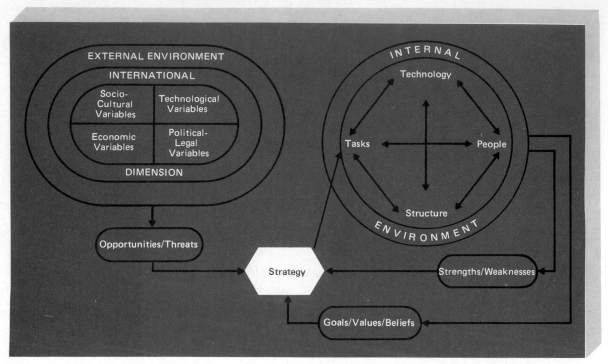

As we saw in chapter 5, an organization's strategy will be influenced by the opportunities and threats in its external environment; the goals, values, and beliefs of its members (especially top management); and its strengths and weaknesses—which are embodied in its members and derived from its history (see fig. 10–3).[25] This strategy, in turn, has three consistent and augmenting impacts on an organization's structure:

1. Strategy determines organizational tasks, which are the ultimate basis for design of the organization. (Highly technical and creative tasks, for example, may require a matrix type of organizational design.)
2. Strategy influences the choice of technology and people appropriate for accomplishment of those tasks—and these, in turn, influence structure.
3. Strategy determines the specific environment within which the organization will operate; this too influences structure.

The key to a successful organizational structure is its fit, or agreement, not only with the strategy and external environment but also with the enterprise's internal environment. In turn, each of those components must be in harmony with each other and with the structure.[26]

Our discussion so far has been conducted as though the formulation of strategy and the design of structure were occurring in an organization with no preexisting strategy or structure. In most cases, of course, an organization will have both structure and strategy already in place. Their existence greatly influences the formulation of a new strategy and structure. (This is identified most clearly in the strengths/weaknesses feedback loop in figure 10–3.) Obviously, the constraints will be greater for short-term than for long-term planning, but managers must always consider the present state of the organization when redesigning its strategy and structure.

External Environment and Structure

In examining the effects of the environment on organizational design in greater detail, it is useful to distinguish between three types of environments: stable, changing, and turbulent.[27]

The Stable Environment. A stable environment is one with little or no unexpected or sudden change. Product changes occur infrequently and modifications can be planned well in advance. Market demand has only minor and predictable fluctuations. Laws that affect the particular organization or product have remained the same for an extended period and are unlikely to change abruptly. New technological developments are unlikely to occur, so research budgets are either minimal or nonexistent.

Stable environment

Because of the increasing rate of technological change, stable organizational environments are hard to find. Still, they do exist. For example, E. E. Dickinson, the major distiller of witch hazel, a topical astringent, has been operating in essentially the same way since 1866. The product, the process, and the company's way of doing business have remained viable despite the passage of more than a century.[28]

Changing environment

The Changing Environment. Environmental changes can occur in any or all of the previously mentioned areas—product, market, law, or technology. Such changes however, are unlikely to take the top managers of the organization completely by surprise. Trends are likely to be apparent and predictable, and organizations are easily able to adjust. For example, a law firm like the Wall Street law firm of Willkie, Farr & Gallagher is in a changing environment because its lawyers must acquaint themselves with each new law. However, the basic body of law changes very gradually. Other organizations in a changing environment include many service, construction, and appliance industries.

Turbulent environment

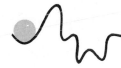

The Turbulent Environment. When competitors launch new, unexpected products, when laws are passed without appreciable warning, and when technological breakthroughs suddenly revolutionize product design or production methods, the organization is in a turbulent environment.

Few organizations face a continuously turbulent environment. If a rapid and radical change does occur, organizations usually pass through only a temporary period of turbulence before making an adjustment. For example, hospitals had to adjust to a sudden increase in demand for their services when Medicaid legislation was passed. Similarly, new pollution-control laws and the energy crisis created a turbulent environment for some time. Some firms, however, experience almost constant turbulence—computer companies, for example, have been dealing with a rapid rate of technological and market change for three decades.

Matching the Structure to the Environment. Tom Burns and G. M. Stalker have distinguished between two organizational systems: mechanistic and organic.[29] In a *mechanistic* system, the activities of the organization are broken down into separate, specialized tasks. Objectives and authority for each individual and unit are precisely defined by higher-level managers. Power in such organizations follows the classical bureaucratic chain of command described earlier.

In an *organic* system, individuals are more likely to work in a group setting than alone. There is less emphasis on taking orders from a superior or giving orders to subordinates. Instead, members communicate across all levels of the organization to obtain information and advice.

After studying a variety of companies, Burns and Stalker concluded that the mechanistic system was best suited to a stable environment, whereas organic systems were best suited to a turbulent one. Organizations in changing environments would probably use some combination of the two systems.

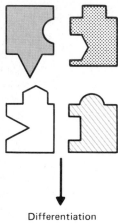

Differences in Functional Orientation

Differentiation

In a stable environment, organization members have little need for a flexible array of skills, since each is likely to continue performing the same task. Thus, skill specialization is appropriate. In turbulent environments, however, jobs must be constantly redefined to cope with the ever-changing needs of the organization. Organization members must be skilled at solving a variety of problems, not at repetitively performing a set of specialized activities. In addition, the creative problem solving and decision making required in turbulent environments are best carried out in groups in which members can communicate openly. Thus, for turbulent environments, an organic system is appropriate.

The findings of Burns and Stalker were supported and extended by the research of Paul Lawrence and Jay Lorsch discussed earlier in this chapter.[30] They examined ten companies, measuring the degree of differentiation and integration these companies exhibited in relation to the type of external environment in which they operated.

Lawrence and Lorsch hypothesized that departments in organizations such as plastics manufacturing companies, which were operating in unstable environments, would be more differentiated than departments in organizations operating in stable environments, such as container manufacturing companies. They further reasoned that not all departments would be affected to the same extent by an unstable environment; therefore, different types of structures might be appropriate for different departments in the same organization. Last, they predicted that high-performing organizations in each type of environment would have a greater degree of integration than low-performing companies: Effective cooperation and coordination within an organization would make it more successful.

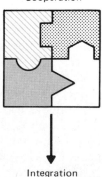

Functional Cooperation

Integration

The results of their study confirmed their hypotheses. Of the companies studied, those operating in an unstable environment were the most highly differentiated, whereas those operating in a stable environment were least differentiated. In addition, high-performing organizations in both types of environments had a higher degree of integration than the low-performing organizations. Those successful organizations with a high degree of differentiation integrated their operations effectively by using a variety of integrating mechanisms such as committees and task forces. The Lawrence and Lorsch study supports the importance of an organization's internal structure being appropriate for its environment.

John J. Morse and Jay W. Lorsch extended this line of research by comparing the *effectiveness* of departments that matched or failed to match their environments.[31] In their study, four departments of a large company were evaluated. Two of these departments, which manufactured containers, operated in a comparatively stable environment. Two other departments were in the unstable environment associated with communications research. In each pair, one department had been evaluated as highly effective and the other as less effective. They found that the most effective manufacturing department was structured in a mechanistic fashion, with clearly defined roles and duties, while the most effective research department was structured in an organic fashion, with roles and duties loosely defined. On the other hand, the less effective manufacturing department was structured in an organic way, while the less effective research department was mechanistically structured. In short, the structures of the most effective departments fit their environments, while the structures of the less effective departments did not.

Task-Technology and Structure

A number of research studies have confirmed that an organization's task-technology is also a major determinant of its structure. Some of the most influential studies in this area were the South Essex studies of Joan Woodward and her colleagues in the mid-1960s.[32] The purpose of these studies was to find out if the classical principles of management taught in British schools were actually practiced by managers and if application of these principles had any effect on an organization's success. The 100 manufacturing firms studied ranged in size from 11 to about 40,000 employees, although most had fewer than 1,000 employees.

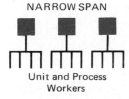

NARROW SPAN

Unit and Process Workers

A preliminary analysis by Woodward and her co-researchers had shown no relationship between the success of a firm and the degree to which it adhered to classical principles. Managers in some successful firms, for example, appeared to violate the classical span of management principle by having very large numbers of subordinates reporting to them; whereas managers in some unsuccessful firms did not violate this principle.

Puzzled by this lack of consistency, the researchers decided to examine the relationship between a firm's technology and its structure to see if this could in some way account for a firm's performance. They divided the firms into three groups according to their task-technology: (1) unit and small batch production, (2) large batch and mass production, and (3) process production. (These terms are equivalent to the terms "job shop," "assembly-line," and "continuous" production methods we used in chapter 8.)

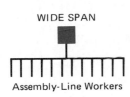

WIDE SPAN

Assembly-Line Workers

Unit production refers to the production of individual items tailored to a customer's specifications. Custom-made clothes, for example, are produced in single units. The technology used in unit production is the least complex of all groups, because the items are produced largely by individual craftsmen. *Small batch production* refers to products made in small quantities in separate stages, such as machine parts that are later assembled. *Large batch* and *mass production* refer to the manufacture of large quantities of products, sometimes on an assembly line (as with automobiles). *Process production* refers to the production of materials that are

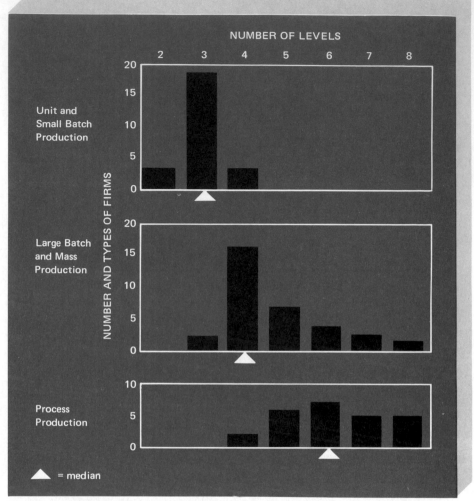

FIGURE 10–4
TECHNOLOGICAL
COMPLEXITY AND
MANAGEMENT
LEVELS

Source: Joan Woodward, *Industrial Organization.* Copyright© 1965. By permission of Oxford University Press.

sold by weight or volume, such as chemicals or drugs. These materials are usually produced with highly complex equipment that operates in a continuous flow.

When Woodward reanalyzed the firms in her study, she found a number of relationships between technological processes and organizational structure:

1. *The more complex the technology—from unit to process production—the greater is the number of managers and management levels.* In other words, complex technologies lead to tall organizational structures and require a greater degree of supervision and coordination. (See fig. 10–4.)

2. *The span of management of first-line managers increases from unit to mass production and then decreases from mass to process production.* Lower-level employees in both unit and process production firms tend to do highly skilled work. As a result, they tend to form small work groups, making a narrow span

inevitable. Assembly-line workers, on the other hand, usually perform similar types of unskilled tasks. Large numbers of such workers can be supervised by one manager.

3. *The greater the technological complexity of the firm, the larger are the clerical and administrative staffs.* The larger number of managers in technologically complex firms require supportive services—to do the additional paperwork, for example, or to handle nonproduction-related work, such as human resource administration. In addition, complex equipment requires more attention in terms of maintenance and production scheduling to keep it in operation a high proportion of the time.

Woodward found that the successful firms in each category had in fact similar structural characteristics, which tended to cluster around the median value for those characteristics at each technological level. For example, if the median span of management in process firms was five, the successful process firms would have spans near that number. Less successful firms, on the other hand, would have structural characteristics well above or below the median in each category.

The significance of this finding is that *for each type of technology there were specific aspects of organizational structure that were associated with more successful performance.* In other words, the successful firms were those with the appropriate structure for their level of technology. For mass production firms, the appropriate structure conformed to the classical management principles. In the other two types of firms, however, the appropriate structure did *not* conform to classical guidelines.

Woodward's studies provide impressive evidence of the influence of technology on organizational structure. Other research has suggested that the impact of technology on structure is strongest in small firms (which the firms studied by Woodward tended to be). For large firms, the impact of technology seems to be felt mainly at the lowest levels of the organization.[33]

People and Structure

The attitudes, experiences, and values of organization members are also related to the structure of the organization. We will discuss this topic in terms of the two categories of people in an organization: managers and employees in general.

Managers and Structure. We have already mentioned the importance of managerial values in determining the strategy of an organization. The organization's managers—especially the top managers—influence the choice of strategy directly through their preferences for certain goals and certain ways of getting things done. Their selection of strategy will, in turn, affect the kind of structure that emerges in the organization.

Organizational structure is also influenced directly by managers' personal preferences for specific types of organization, for ways of relating to subordinates, customers, and other managers, and for ways of attacking problems. These preferences translate directly into various types of organizational structures. For example, a manager with strong Theory X assumptions will prefer a more mechanistic organizational structure, while a manager with Theory Y assumptions may prefer a more organic system.

Other important influences on structure may result from managers' personal attitudes toward authority, their regard or disregard for formality, and their past experiences (positive or negative) with different types of organizational design. Some writers believe that growing dissatisfaction with the depersonalized, mechanistic concept of organizational authority could cause managers to choose a structure with less emphasis on career competition and individual rewards and greater emphasis on collaboration and personal growth.[34]

Employees and Structure. Such factors as employees' level of education, background, degree of interest in work, and availability of work alternatives outside the organization are important determinants of organizational structure. For example, highly educated individuals who have excellent outside alternatives and enjoy their work are appropriately organized in an organic structure. Individuals with low levels of education performing boring and repetitive jobs might be better managed in a more mechanistic structure.

Many companies are taking active steps and experimenting with new ideas to provide a more rewarding environment for their employees. Programs for job enrichment and job enlargement are examples of attempts to alter the organizational structure and work processes to meet individual needs. Although the best known of these programs have been carried out by Volvo and other Swedish firms, they have also been a feature of some American companies (AT&T, Texas Instruments, and IBM, for example).[35]

Organizational Growth, Change, and Decline

The Burns Electronics Company has been a successful, diversified organization for many years. It is structured along product lines, with a separate management hierarchy responsible for each family of products. Overall direction for the company is still provided by top managers at corporate headquarters. In recent years, the efforts by top managers to improve coordination and control throughout the company have aroused resentment among division managers. They feel they are getting bogged down in a mountain of reports and in endless meetings.

Jayne Crucillo has chaired the county school board for four years. Twenty-five years ago the county embarked on a major building program and reorganization of the school system. A group of modern and well-equipped primary and secondary schools was established, each relatively autonomous and headed by a strong and well-qualified principal. However, by the time Jayne was elected, a decade of low birth rates and slow growth in the county had reduced the school-age population by 30 percent. No new teachers have been hired in five years, and a recent bond referendum to renovate the science labs failed to pass. This week Jayne learned that state aid for a series of special programs would be reduced and that a consultant would recommend consolidating four elementary schools into two to save on administrative and teacher salaries. Principals and parents are likely to oppose the recommendation strongly.

We have seen that an organization's structure must fit with its strategy, environment, technology, and employees. As the above examples suggest, however, such factors change over time. The structure that suits an organization during one stage in its life cycle may not be suitable at another. Managers have to alter the organizational structure periodically to fit the changing needs and circumstances of their organizations.

The Emphasis on Growth

Most management research and training has emphasized the importance of understanding and managing organization growth. Historically, this emphasis has been appropriate: In the decades following World War II, organizations throughout the world grew phenomenally. During the 1970s, however, expansion of the world economy, and the organizations that play such a key role in it, faltered. A scarcity of resources, inflation, problems in international cooperation, and changing life-styles and attitudes caused serious problems for many large and small organizations. In the 1980s, American firms faced increased competition from abroad.

Of course, organizations have always experienced growth, stability, and decline. Now, however, after a period of sustained growth, it appears that the number of organizations reaching stability or experiencing decline is rising considerably faster than the number of growing organizations. Management writers, once concerned primarily with organizational growth, are beginning to pay more attention to the problems of organizational maturity, stagnation, and decline.[36]

In the final part of this chapter, we will discuss organizational growth and change, and then we will look at some of these recent perspectives on organizational decline.

Organizational Life Cycles

A number of life-cycle models of organizations have been devised. These models assume that the changes that occur in organizations follow a predictable pattern that can be characterized as a series of developmental stages. The stages in an *organizational life cycle* described by various authors have several characteristics in common. First, they are sequential in nature—one stage is followed by another. Second, the stages occur in a progression that is difficult to reverse. Once an organization has advanced to a later stage, it generally cannot return to an earlier one. Third, the stages influence a broad range of organizational activities and structures, from the way decisions are made to the array of products produced or services provided.

Robert E. Quinn and Kim Cameron have integrated nine life-cycle models into one summary model.[37] (It is from their report that most of this discussion is drawn.[38]) They found that the models they examined had four stages in common. (See table 10–2.) The first is an *entrepreneurial* stage, which emphasizes innovation, creativity, and the acquisition of necessary resources. The second, *collectivity*, emphasizes cohesiveness, commitment, cooperation, and a personal form of leadership. During the third stage, *formalization and control*, the organization becomes more conservative; the emphasis is on efficiency and developing rules and procedures to enhance stability and control. In the final stage, *structural elaboration and adaptation*, the organization focuses more of its energies on monitoring and adjusting to the external environment and strives to renew itself, expand its domain, or both. At this stage, the structure is decentralized and a balance between differentiation and integration is needed. The model does not include as a final stage—organizational decline and death. This omission might be due to the relative unpredictability of organizational actions at this point, and perhaps to the possibility that organizational death can be continually deferred.

This summary model is potentially useful to managers because it emphasizes that organizations develop in accordance with a consistent pattern and that certain characteristics are typical of each stage of development. It also suggests that some managerial theories may be more appropriate for some stages than for others. However, the model offers little or no guidance for the important task of predicting a particular organizational shift from one stage to another. Nor does it specify what factors influence how long the various stages will last.[39]

The Creation of Organizations. One life cycle issue that has received relatively little research attention is the founding and development of new businesses.[40] This is unfortunate because about a quarter of all American businesses are less than a year old. Although the median age for all businesses is about seven years, only 54 percent survive past 18 months and only 25 percent survive longer than six years.[41] One of the reasons relatively few businesses survive for long may be that early decisions are often made without much thought for their long-term strategic significance and consequences. Decisions made by the managers of a young organization concerning its structure, governance, expertise, and domain can put it on a course that is difficult to change. Even among companies that do succeed in establishing them-

TABLE 10–2 AN INTEGRATIVE MODEL OF ORGANIZATIONAL LIFE CYCLES

Stages and Their Characteristics			
1. Entrepreneurial	**2. Collectivity**	**3. Formalization and Control**	**4. Elaboration of Structure**
—Resources are marshaled. —Ideas abound. —Entrepreneurial activities are undertaken. —Little planning and coordination are needed. —A niche is formed. —A "prime mover" has power.	—Structure and communication are informal. —There is a sense of being a collective whole. —Employees work long hours. —Employees have a sense of mission. —Innovation continues. —Employees are highly committed.	—Rules are formalized. —Structure is stable. —Emphasis is on efficiency and maintenance. —Organization becomes more conservative. —Procedures are institutionalized.	—Structure is elaborated. —Decentralization takes place. —Domain is expanded. —Adaptations are made. —The organization renews itself.

Source: Reprinted by permission of Robert E. Quinn and Kim Cameron, "Organizational Life Cycles and Shifting Criteria of Effectiveness: Some Preliminary Evidence," *Management Science* 29, no. 1 (January 1983). Copyright © 1983, The Institute of Management Sciences.

selves, however, change is often necessary. The circumstances that allowed them to start growing may evolve, and then the initially successful strategy must be altered as well. Some firms, such as Apple Computer, have attempted to maintain the organizational culture of a small new firm after they have become large and established. After a number of years of carefully nurtured informality and flexibility, Apple was forced to restructure in more formal and less flexible ways.

Problems of Very Rapid Growth

An organization that manages to overcome its initial obstacles may not fall into the usual pattern if its growth is very rapid. John Kotter and Vijay Sathe have identified some of the problems arising from rapid growth and have discussed how they influence the management of the organization's human resources.[42]

Kotter and Sathe have reported that in rapidly growing organizations, relative to other organizations:

· Decisions need to be made faster.
· Individuals' job demands expand faster.
· Large recruiting and training needs have to be met.
· Individuals must cope with constant change.
· Financial and human resources are severely strained.

To deal with these problems, Kotter and Sathe have recommended:

· Careful screening and selectivity in hiring to obtain well-qualified workers who have the capacity for hard work and growth in responsibility and who will require less training.
· Use of team or matrix structures.
· Creation of an organizational philosophy or culture that emphasizes open communication, a shared vision of the organization's future, and a sense that it "cares."
· Projection of future staffing needs and ongoing planning and monitoring to match human resources and organizational needs.
· Organization and staffing of an effective human resources department for recruiting, training, organizing team-building projects, and assisting employees in adapting to the stresses and strains of a rapidly growing company.
· Sensitivity of top management to the human needs of company members and toughness to deal with unpleasant problems when necessary.

Some Perspectives on Organizational Decline

The life cycle of an organization can be compared with that of a human.[43] Both experience birth, growth, maturity, setbacks, and periods of revitalization. For both, conditions during birth and early infancy have a significant effect on later development. Furthermore, controversy exists about the extent of environmental impact on their respective behaviors.

Although similarities exist, there are at least two major differences between the life cycles of organizations and people: (1) death is inevitable for humans, but an organization could (theoretically) live forever or even be reborn; (2) the developmental stages of human life are relatively predictable, whereas the timing of the organizational stages has so far eluded prediction.

David Whetten has suggested some perspectives that can help us gain insight into the nature of organizational decline.[44]

Decline as Stagnation or Cutback. Whetten argues that it is useful to distinguish between two types of decline: stagnation and cutback. In *stagnation*, losses occur because of poor managerial performance in an attractive market (environment), or poor managerial judgment in entering or remaining too long in an unattractive one. In *cutback*, on the other hand, a previously attractive market that management had successfully penetrated is no longer as attractive, and management consciously withdraws resources as a successful organizational adaptation to environmental changes beyond its control.

Importance of Acknowledging Decline and Its Causes. The way management identifies the problem and its causes determines what responses will be considered. Managers must be willing to recognize the declining situation and deal with it, as the new top managers of Pullman Company and Westinghouse did when they took over leadership of companies in severe trouble. The previous leaders had ignored and denied the increasing problems.[45]

Chris Argyris has used the terms "single" and "double loop learning" to distinguish between identifying and addressing the day-to-day operational problems in an organization and identifying and addressing the more fundamental and strategic problems for which apparent operational problems are sometimes merely symptoms.[46] In situations of decline, the problems are frequently fundamental and strategic, and so "double loop learning" is required. In crises and stages of decline, middle managers may hesitate to confront their superiors with the facts, and top managers may deny or ignore the seriousness of the facts when they do emerge. As a result, repeated attempts to apply corrective actions at the operational level merely waste resources and allow the problems to become steadily worse.

Decline and Personal Stress. In a situation of decline, managers are frequently under strong pressure to improve performance immediately. The stress that results may lead them to repeat previously successful approaches, rather than take the time to search out new and appropriate solutions. Problem solving in groups tends to be forgotten as top managers cope in isolation; this results in poor coordination and actually increases the momentum toward decline. High personal stress is one of the factors that make double loop learning less likely. Just as Kotter and Sathe recommended special assistance for individuals experiencing high stress in very rapidly growing organizations, top management should arrange for such assistance in declining ones.

Decline as a Cause of Conflict. The tension, problems, time pressure, and opposing views that accompany a decline often lead to increased conflict between units and individuals. As we will see in chapter 14, conflict ideally should be managed to result in constructive change and growth. However, it is particularly difficult to manage conflict effectively in a declining situation where all alternatives are likely to be unattractive and incapable of achieving organizational objectives. The absence of a "good solution" allows the conflict to worsen.

Structural Responses to Decline. Each of the preceding points has implications for ways to manage and structure an organization in decline. For example, conflicts and lack of integration can be dealt with through the introduction of new coordinating mechanisms. Whatever the problem, the organization must react to it, for failure to adapt leads to organizational death. Older, well-established organizations are more likely to survive than younger ones, but they are far from immortal. William Starbuck reports that only 2 percent of all corporations created reach the age of 50 years, and even in this stable group a full 30 percent can be expected to disappear within ten more years.[47] Some organizations facing crises can determine where the problem lies, replace their top managers if necessary, reorient, and survive. Frequently, however, they cannot make the needed adjustments, and as a result they die.[48]

Survival of the Fittest. A more recent perspective on organizations portrays them as members of a group rather than as individual entities. This perspective studies a "population" of a certain kind of organization, such as private schools, fast-food restaurants, or software development firms. According to this "population perspective," the individual organizations in a species compete for scarce resources.[49] Some organizations, as a result of an accidental "mutation," will prove to be more competitive, and as a result they will survive. Those that are poorly adapted will fail. The novel aspect of this "survival-of-the-fittest" model is that it downplays the role of managers, focusing instead on the role of chance in developing strategic advantages.

Summary

Coordination is the process of integrating the objectives and activities of separate units of an organization to achieve organizational goals. The need for coordination varies according to the degree of interdependence between units. It is especially difficult for reciprocally interdependent units to achieve good coordination.

Coordination is essentially an information processing task. There are three basic approaches to achieving effective coordination. The first involves basic management techniques, such as using the managerial hierarchy to facilitate the flow of information, establishing rules and procedures, and developing plans and goals. The second approach is to increase the coordination potential vertically, laterally, or in both directions. Lateral relationships can be established through such mechanisms as boundary-spanning roles and the use of committees and task forces. The third approach is to reduce the need for coordination through such means as creating slack resources and developing independent units. In practice, combinations of approaches are often used. A key consideration for managers is to match the organization's capacity for coordination with its need for coordination.

Span of management is the number of subordinates who report directly to a given manager. Early writers attempted to establish a universal rule concerning how many subordinates a manager could supervise, but today we recognize that the optimal number of subordinates varies with the situation. An inappropriate span of management may adversely influence productivity, costs, and efficiency, although the research results on this possibility are inconsistent. The guidelines for choosing the most appropriate span take into account factors related to the situation, subordinates, and the manager. Alterations can make an inappropriate span of management more workable.

The design of an effective organizational structure is a continuous process because environments and strategies inevitably change. Classical management writers tried to find the "one best way" of designing an organization. They tended to favor a bureaucratic, hierarchical structure based on legalized formal authority and characterized by task specialization. However, such a structure is relatively inflexible and neglects the human and environmental factors that can affect the organization.

Neoclassicists tried to improve the classical model. McGregor suggested that organizational structure based on Theory Y values would increase the effectiveness and satisfaction of organization members. Argyris argued that there was a need for a more informal organizational design that would give members greater independence and power. Likert favored what he called a System 4 organizational structure, which would permit greater group participation in supervision and decision making. Although these approaches enriched the classical model, they also overlooked technological and environmental variables that can affect the organization, and they simplified the complexity of human motivation.

Contingency approaches to organizational design stress the need to fit an organization's structure to its strategy, environment, task-technology, and people. An organization's strategy affects its structure because strategy determines the types of tasks that employees perform and the specific environment in which the organization operates. The external environment of an organization also affects its structure. Mechanistic designs tend to be most appropriate in stable environments, whereas organic designs tend to be most appropriate in turbulent environments. Tasks and technology affect structure because some structures are more appropriate for a given technology and set of tasks than are others. Organizational design is also influenced by employees' level of education, work involvement, and other characteristics. Managers' attitudes and values directly influence structure since managers have the ultimate responsibility for designing the organization. The increasing demand of employees for greater job satisfaction and participation is also likely to have an effect on structure.

Life cycle models assume that organizations develop in a predictable sequence of stages. Quinn and Cameron's integrative life-cycle model suggests that there are four stages: an entrepreneurial stage, a collectivity stage, a formalization and control stage, and a structural elaboration and adaptation stage.

Relatively little research attention has been devoted to the beginnings of organizations, which is unfortunate because many businesses are young and decisions made at an early stage can have long-term significance. Fast-growing companies face special problems. Organizational decline has also received relatively little research attention. It is important that managers acknowledge stages of decline when they occur and take steps to respond to them.

Review Questions

1. What is coordination?
2. What types of differences in attitude and working style can develop in the various departments in an organization? How do such differences make coordination more difficult? How do organizations benefit from such differences?
3. What are the three types of coordinating mechanisms that managers can use?
4. Describe three approaches to achieving effective coordination and give examples of each.
5. What is span of management, and why is it important?
6. What factors did Lockheed's analysts select as significant in choosing a span of management? Which factors were confirmed by subsequent research? Which factor was found to have an effect opposite to that suggested by Lockheed's analysts?
7. What are the three basic categories of factors that managers should consider in attempting to choose an appropriate span of management?
8. What are the advantages and disadvantages of the classical bureaucratic model of organizational design?
9. According to McGregor, how would an organization structure based on Theory Y assumptions differ from an organization based on Theory X assumptions?

10. According to Likert, what are the differences between a System 1 and a System 4 organization?

11. What are the four key variables that influence an organization and hence its structure?

12. What are three ways that strategy influences structure?

13. According to Burns and Stalker, what form of organizational system is best suited to a stable environment? To a turbulent environment?

14. What were the relationships Woodward found between the technological process a firm used and its structure?

15. How can the attitudes and values of managers influence an organization's structure?

16. What are the characteristics associated with the four stages in Quinn and Cameron's integrative life-cycle model of organizational development?

17. What are some problems related to very rapid organizational growth?

18. What is the difference between organizational decline due to stagnation and decline due to cutback?

Notes

1. Joseph R. Daughen and Peter Binzen, *The Wreck of the Penn Central* (Boston: Little, Brown, 1971).

2. James Mooney defines coordination as "the orderly arrangement of group effort, to provide unity of action in the pursuit of a common purpose." See *The Principles of Organization,* rev. ed. (New York: Harper & Brothers, 1947), p. 5.

3. See Joseph L. C. Cheng, "Interdependence and Coordination in Organizations: A Role System Analysis," *Academy of Management Journal* 26, no. 1 (March 1983):156–162.

4. James D. Thompson, *Organizations in Action: Social Science Bases of Administrative Theory* (New York: McGraw-Hill, 1967), pp. 54–60.

5. Paul R. Lawrence and Jay W. Lorsch, *Organization and Environment: Managing Differentiation and Integration* (Homewood, Ill.: Irwin, 1967), p. 9.

6. Eliezer Rosenstein, "Cooperativeness and Advancement of Managers: An International Perspective," *Human Relations* 38, no. 1 (January 1985):1–21.

7. Our discussion of coordination is based to a large extent on Jay R. Galbraith, "Organization Design: An Information Processing View," *Interfaces* 4, no. 3 (May 1974):28–36; Jay R. Galbraith, *Organization Design* (Reading, Mass.: Addison-Wesley, 1977); and Michael L. Tushman and David A. Nadler, "Information Processing as an Integrating Concept in Organizational Design," *Academy of Management Review* 3, no. 3 (July 1978):613–624.

8. See Richard L. Daft and Robert H. Lengel, "Information Richness: A New Approach to Managerial Behavior and Organization Design," in *Research in Organizational Behavior*, vol. 6 (Greenwich, Conn.: JAI Press, 1984), pp. 191–233.

9. Galbraith, *Organization Design,* pp. 50–52. Galbraith also offers a third method: managing the organization's relationship with the environment so as to reduce uncertainty and the need for tight coordination. We do not discuss this as a separate method, preferring to consider it part of the basic task of relating the organization to the environment through its strategy-making and planning/control systems. However, Galbraith's discussion calls attention to the open nature of the organization as a system: It can reduce the need for internal capacity by altering the ways in which it deals with the external environment.

10. See Kenneth E. Marino and David R. Lange, "Measuring Organizational Slack: A Note on the Convergence and Divergence of Alternative Operational Definitions," *Journal of Management* 9, no. 1 (Fall 1983):81–92.

11. David D. Van Fleet and Arthur G. Bedeian, "A History of the Span of Management," *Academy of Management Review* 2, no. 3 (July 1977):356–372.

12. Some early writers did, however, consider situational factors. Early in this century, for instance, F. R. Mason referred to variables that affected the span of management in *Business Principles and Organization* (Chicago: Cree Publishing, 1909). Considerably later, Lyndall F. Urwick emphasized the

interdependence of the work of subordinates, and Luther Gulick mentioned a variety of important factors, such as the type of work and the variety of tasks performed. See Lyndall F. Urwick, "The Manager's Span of Control," *Harvard Business Review* 34, no. 3 (May–June 1956):39–47; and Luther Gulick, "Notes on the Theory of Organization," in Luther Gulick and L. Urwick, eds., *Papers on the Science of Administration* (New York: Institute of Public Administration, Columbia University, 1937), pp. 1–46.

13. Van Fleet and Bedeian, "A History of the Span of Management"; David D. Van Fleet and Arthur G. Bedeian, "Conceptual Developments in the Span of Management," *Akron Business and Economic Review* 9, no. 1 (Spring 1978):25–30; David D. Van Fleet, "Span of Management Research and Issues," *Academy of Management Review* 26, no. 3 (September 1983):546–552; and David D. Van Fleet, "Empirically Testing Span of Management Hypotheses," *International Journal of Management* 2, no. 2 (June 1984) 5–10.

14. Harold Stieglitz, "Optimizing the Span of Control," *Management Record*, September 1962, pp. 25–29; and C. W. Barkdull, "Span of Control—A Method of Evaluation," *Michigan Business Review* 15, no. 3 (May 1963):25–32.

15. Jon G. Udell, "An Empirical Test of Hypotheses Relating to Span of Control," *Administrative Science Quarterly* 12, no. 3 (December 1967):420–439. In addition to most of the factors identified by Lockheed, Udell's study included competence of the supervisor, competence of the subordinates, formalization of job relationships, and time available for supervision.

16. For the overall perspective in this section, the authors are indebted to Kenneth N. Wexley and Gary A. Yukl, *Organizational Behavior and Personnel Psychology*, rev. ed. (Homewood, Ill.: Irwin, 1984); Y. K. Shetty and Howard M. Carlisle, "A Contingency Model of Organizational Design," *California Management Review* 15, no. 1 (Fall 1972):38–45; and Jay R. Galbraith and Daniel A. Nathanson, "The Role of Organizational Structure and Process in Strategy Implementation," in Dan E. Schendel and Charles W. Hofer, *Strategic Management: A New View of Business Policy and Planning* (Boston: Little, Brown, 1979), pp. 249–283. See also Daniel Robey, *Designing Organizations*, 2nd ed. (Homewood, Ill.: Irwin, 1986).

17. Max Weber, *Economy and Society: An Outline of Interpretative Sociology* (New York: Bedminster Press, 1968; originally published in 1925), pp. 956–958.

18. Weber addressed this criticism by defining a hypothetical "ideal" organization that incorporated every one of the characteristics of bureaucracy. He believed that the closer an actual institution approached this ideal one, the more fully it would enjoy the benefits of bureaucracy.

19. Victor A. Thompson, *Modern Organization* (New York: Knopf, 1961), p. 152.

20. Douglas McGregor, *The Human Side of Enterprise* (New York: McGraw-Hill, 1960) and *The Professional Manager* (New York: McGraw-Hill, 1967).

21. Chris Argyris, *Personality and Organization* (New York: Harper & Brothers, 1957) and *Integrating the Individual and the Organization* (New York: Wiley, 1964).

22. Rensis Likert, *New Patterns of Management* (New York: McGraw-Hill, 1961) and *The Human Organization* (New York: McGraw-Hill, 1967); and Rensis Likert and Jane Gibson Likert, *New Ways of Managing Conflict* (New York: McGraw-Hill, 1976).

23. For a discussion of the need to clarify the concepts of contingency theory and suggestions for future research, see Henry L. Tosi, Jr., and John W. Slocum, Jr., "Contingency Theory: Some Suggested Directions," *Journal of Management* 10, no. 1 (Fall 1984):9–26; and Andrew Van de Ven and R. Drazin, "The Concept of Fit in Contingency Theory," in L. Cummings and Barry Staw, eds., *Research in Organizational Behavior*, vol. 7 (Greenwich, Conn.: JAI Press, 1985), pp. 333–365.

24. See Alfred D. Chandler, Jr., *Strategy and Structure: Chapters in the History of the American Industrial Enterprise* (Cambridge, Mass.: MIT Press, 1962), pp. 383–396. Also see Alfred D. Chandler, Jr., and Herman Daems, eds., *Managerial Hierarchies: Comparative Perspectives on the Rise of the Modern Industrial Enterprise* (Cambridge, Mass.: Harvard University Press, 1980).

25. The authors are indebted to Professor Thomas P. Ference and his colleagues at Columbia University's Graduate School of Business for the basic form of this figure. See also Harold J. Leavitt, "Applied Organizational Change in Industry," in W. W. Cooper, H. J. Leavitt, and M. W. Shelly II, eds., *New Perspectives in Organizational Research* (New York: Wiley, 1964), pp. 53–71.

26. See Raymond E. Miles and Charles C. Snow, "Fit, Failure and the Hall of Fame," *California Management Review* 26, no. 3 (Spring 1984):10–28; and W. Alan Randolph and Gregory G. Dess, "The Congruence Perspective of Organization Design: A Conceptual Model and Multivariate Research Approach," *Academy of Management Review* 9, no. 1 (January 1984):114–127.

27. Ross A. Webber, Marilyn A. Morgan, and Paul C. Browne, *Management* (Homewood, Ill.: Irwin,

1985), pp. 433–436; Fred E. Emery and E. L. Trist, "The Causal Texture of Organizational Environments," *Human Relations* 18, no. 1 (February 1965):21–31; Shirley Terreberry, "The Evolution of Organizational Environments," *Administrative Science Quarterly* 12, no. 4 (March 1968):590–613; Michael C. White, Michael D. Crino, and Ben L. Kedia, "Environmental Turbulence: A Reappraisal of Emery and Trist," *Administration and Society* 16, no. 1 (May 1984):97–116; and Gareth Morgan, "Rethinking Corporate Strategy: A Cybernetic Perspective," *Human Relations* 36, no. 4 (April 1983):345–360.

28. Peter Kerr, "Witch Hazel Still Made in Old-Fashioned Way," *New York Times*, May 11, 1985, pp. 27–28.

29. Tom Burns and G. M. Stalker, *The Management of Innovation* (London: Tavistock, 1961).

30. Lawrence and Lorsch, *Organization and Environment*.

31. John J. Morse and Jay W. Lorsch, "Beyond Theory Y," *Harvard Business Review* 48, no. 3 (May–June 1970):61–68. See also Robert Duncan, "What Is the Right Organization Structure? Decision Tree Analysis Provides the Answer," *Organizational Dynamics* 7, no. 3 (Winter 1979):59–80. Duncan has classified environments in terms of their complexity and rate of change and offers guidelines for selecting between several forms of functional and divisional structures that vary according to the requirements of the environment.

32. Joan Woodward, *Industrial Organization* (London: Oxford University Press, 1965). See also Karl O. Magnusen, "A Comparative Analysis of Organizations," *Organizational Dynamics* 2, no. 1 (Summer 1973):16–31; James D. Thompson, *Organizations in Action* (New York: McGraw-Hill, 1967); and Charles Perrow, *Complex Organizations: A Critical Essay*, 2nd ed. (Glenview, Ill.: Scott, Foresman, 1979).

33. See, for example, David J. Hickson, D. S. Pugh, and Diana C. Pheysey, "Operations Technology and Organization Structure: A Critical Reappraisal," *Administrative Science Quarterly* 14, no. 3 (September 1969):378–397.

34. See Warren G. Bennis, "Organizational Developments and the Fate of Bureaucracy," *Industrial Management Review* 7, no. 2 (Spring 1966):41–55. For a later, less optimistic perspective, see Warren G. Bennis, "A Funny Thing Happened on the Way to the Future," *American Psychologist* 25, no. 7 (July 1970):595–608.

35. For a discussion of the very successful structural and managerial approaches of some American companies—and their similarity to many Japanese companies—see William G. Ouchi, *Theory Z: How American Business Can Meet the Japanese Challenge* (Reading, Mass.: Addison-Wesley, 1981); and Richard Tanner Pascale and Anthony G. Athos, *The Art of Japanese Management: Applications for American Executives* (New York: Simon & Schuster, 1981).

36. See David A. Whetten, "Organizational Decline: A Neglected Topic in Organizational Science," *Academy of Management Review* 5, no. 4 (October 1980):577–588.

37. These included Ichak Adizes, "Organizational Passages: Diagnosing and Treating Life Cycle Problems in Organizations," *Organizational Dynamics* 8, no. 1 (Summer 1979):3–24; Anthony Downs, "The Life Cycle of Bureaus," in Anthony Downs, *Inside Bureaucracy* (Boston: Little, Brown, 1967), pp. 296–309; Larry E. Greiner, "Evolution and Revolution as Organizations Grow," *Harvard Business Review* 52, no. 4 (July–August 1972):37–46; John R. Kimberly, "Issues in the Creation of Organizations: Initiation, Innovation, and Institutionalization," *Academy of Management Journal* 22, no. 3 (September 1979):437–457; Dina Lavoie and Samuel A. Culbert, "Stages in Organization and Development," *Human Relations* 31, no. 5 (May 1978):417–438; and Robert H. Miles, "The Role of Organizational Learning in the Early Creation and Development of Organizations," in John R. Kimberly, Robert H. Miles et al., *The Organizational Life Cycle: Issues in the Creation, Transformation, and Decline of Organizations* (San Francisco: Jossey-Bass, 1980).

38. Robert E. Quinn and Kim Cameron, "Organizational Life Cycles and Shifting Criteria of Effectiveness: Some Preliminary Evidence," *Management Science* 29, no. 1 (January 1983):33–51.

39. John A. Murray, "A Concept of Entrepreneurial Strategy," *Strategic Management Journal* 5, no. 1 (January–March 1984):1–13.

40. Andrew H. Van de Ven, Roger Hudson, and Dean M. Schroeder, "Designing New Business Startups: Entrepreneurial, Organizational, and Ecological Considerations," *Journal of Management* 10, no. 1 (Fall 1984):87–107. See also Dennis N. T. Perkins, Veronica F. Nieva, and Edward E. Lawler III, *Managing Creation: The Challenge of Building a New Organization* (New York: Wiley, 1983). For an extensive case study examination of the creation and growth of an organization, see John R. Kimberly, "Organizations: A Biographical Approach," in Jay W. Lorsch, ed., *Handbook of Organizational Behavior* (Englewood Cliffs, N.J.: Prentice-Hall, 1986).

41. Van de Ven et al., "Designing New Business Startups," p. 87.

42. John Kotter and Vijay Sathe, "Problems of Human Resource Management in Rapidly Growing Companies," *California Management Review* 21, no. 2 (Winter 1978):29–36.

43. Mason Haire, "Biological Models and Empirical Histories of the Growth of Organizations," in Mason Haire, ed., *Modern Organization Theory* (New York: Wiley, 1959), pp. 272–306; and Kimberly, Miles et al., *The Organizational Life Cycle*, pp. 6–13.

44. Whetten, "Organizational Decline," pp. 582–584.

45. John R. Kimberly, "The Anatomy of Organizational Design," *Journal of Management* 10, no. 1 (Fall 1984):109–126.

46. Chris Argyris, *Reasoning, Learning, and Action: Individual and Organizational* (San Francisco: Jossey-Bass, 1982), pp. 104–106.

47. William H. Starbuck, "Organizations as Action Generators," *American Sociological Review* 48, no. 1 (February 1983):91–102.

48. Recent articles on managing organizational decline include Karen Seashore Louis and Ronald G. Corwin, "Organizational Decline: How State Agencies Adapt," *Education and Urban Society* 16, no. 2 (February 1984):165–188; and Daniel R. Longo and Gary A. Chase, "Structural Determinants of Hospital Closure," *Medical Care* 22, no. 5 (May 1984):388–402. For one of the "early" contributions, see Kathryn R. Harrigan, *Strategies for Declining Businesses* (Lexington, Mass: Lexington Books, 1980).

49. See Howard Aldrich, Bill McKelvey, and Dave Ulrich, "Design Strategy from the Population Perspective," *Journal of Management* 10, no. 1 (Fall 1984):67–86. See also William R. Rosengren, "Environmental Conditions and Organizational Change: Rational versus Natural Systems," *Human Organization* 43, no. 1 (Spring 1984):54–61.

CASE STUDY: Problems in Plant Democracy

General Foods Corporation had experienced productivity and morale problems among blue-collar workers in one of its traditionally organized pet food plants. To prevent these problems from arising in the new Topeka, Kansas, plant it built in the early 1970s, the company organized the plant so that workers would perform many of the tasks formerly assigned to management—making job assignments, supervising, and even deciding pay raises. Work responsibility for each phase of the new plant's operations was assigned to worker teams, who were under the direction of a "coach" rather than a supervisor. Team members handled a variety of tasks, such as manufacturing, equipment maintenance, and quality control, thereby increasing the span of management and eliminating the need for many managerial personnel. Status differences between managers and workers were blurred—for example, managers no longer had reserved parking spaces.

The new system was regarded by GF management as a model for the future. Costs and turnover were lower than in traditionally organized plants, and some employees stated the plant was the best place they had ever worked in. However, major problems soon developed at the plant. Many managers and technical personnel resented the system, because they felt their own authority and expertise were being challenged. Competition between teams and team leaders developed and coordination suffered. Workers felt uncomfortable about deciding pay raises for their co-workers. As a result of such pressures, some aspects of the plant system were changed: The number of management positions was increased, supervision was stiffened, and several plant functions were returned to managers.

When GF opened another plant in 1976 next to the Topeka plant, it did so without implementing some of the elements in the Topeka system. As a result, according to one observer, members of the Topeka plant came to feel that GF's management was not fully committed to the changes it had made at the Topeka plant. In addition, GF seemed reluctant to give Topeka employees bonuses as a reward for the system's financial success, because of possible resentment at other GF plants. Morale problems at the plant reportedly increased. Managers also seemed to have suffered, since they felt GF was unprepared to promote innovative managers who had been involved in and supported the system at Topeka. By 1977, the system still seemed productive and desirable but appeared to some observers to be declining.

Source: Case based on an article in the March 28, 1977 issue of *Business Week*, pp. 78–82.

Case Questions

1. Why did GF try a new organizational design for its first Topeka plant? Which school of organizational design did it most closely approach?
2. What coordination problems were experienced in the plant? Why?
3. Will GF be successful in operating two closely situated plants with different organizational designs?
4. How could GF stop the decline of its Topeka operations?
5. What predictions would you make about the status and performance of the Topeka plant this year?

11 AUTHORITY, DELEGATION, AND DECENTRALIZATION

Upon completing this chapter you should be able to:

1. Define power, influence, and authority and explain their importance in organizational life.

2. Distinguish between the "classical" and the "acceptance" views of formal authority.

3. Identify and describe the sources of managerial power and informal power in organizations.

4. Distinguish between line and staff authority, and describe the various types of personal, specialized, and functional staffs.

5. Explain the importance of delegation in organizations and describe how delegation can be made effective.

6. Identify and describe the factors that influence the amount of centralization and decentralization in organizations.

I n the seventeenth century, European traders, soldiers, and missionaries who came across some Indian groups in the western Great Lakes region commented on their unusual social organization: Several Central Algonkian tribes were living harmoniously in the area without a formal leadership system. In fact, the Indians appeared to "carry out their subsistence, religious, administrative, and military activities in the virtual absence of any sort of recognizable authority!"[1]

Not only did the Indians appear to lack a formal system of authority, but they also deeply resented any efforts to control their actions. All members of the tribe knew what was required of them by lifelong familiarity with the tasks of the community. These tasks tended to be simple and repetitive, since the Algonkians's rate of social change was slow. Thus, although subgroups such as warriors had acknowledged leaders, no real authority was required. Rather than issuing direct orders (which were considered insulting), members of the tribe would arouse others to action by persuasion, flattery, and example.

It would be difficult, if not impossible, to implement such a system in our own society. Most of us have grown up under one authority or another for as long as we can remember. Our parents, our teachers, our bosses, our government, all have the acknowledged right under certain conditions to tell us what to do. The concept of authority is so much a part of our culture that it is hard for us to imagine a workable society without it. How, for example, could federal budgets and programs be maintained without the authority vested in the Internal Revenue Service to collect taxes? We have been culturally disposed to rely on authority to get things done and would probably be uncomfortable with or incompetent at using the Algonkian methods of flattery and persuasion on a large scale.

Of course, the major reason why the Algonkian system would be inadequate for us is that our society is too large and complex. The vast number of tasks that various members of our society have to perform—often under tight time and resource limitations—could not be handled by the Algonkian system. Projects as comparatively small as reorganizing an accounting department or as large as launching a space shuttle would result in chaos if clear lines of authority and accountability did not exist. In modern organizations, the formal authority system is necessary to achieve organizational objectives.

For an organization to function efficiently, however, a formal authority system must be supplemented by informal bases of power and influence. Managers use more than their official authority to obtain the cooperation of their subordinates. They also rely on their knowledge, their experience, and their leadership abilities. In fact, although authority is obviously a part of every manager-subordinate interaction, effective managers rarely have to resort to their formal authority to influence employees. They may even rely on the Algonkian methods of persuasion, flattery, and example.

In this chapter, we first discuss the formal and informal methods of influence that managers use to achieve their personal and organizational goals. We then examine the line and staff structure through which authority is exercised. Next, the theory and practice of delegating authority effectively are reviewed before we conclude with a discussion of decentralization.

Influence, Power, and Authority

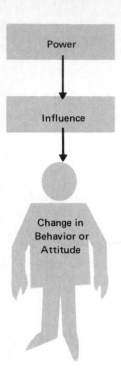

Power

↓

Influence

↓

Change in Behavior or Attitude

Writers on management have defined and used the terms *influence, power,* and *authority* in a variety of ways and have not always been in agreement.[2] We will define *influence* as *actions or examples that, either directly or indirectly, cause a change in behavior or attitude of another person or group.* For example, a hard-working person may, by setting an example, influence others to increase their productivity. This definition takes into account also those types of influence that do not lead to more intangible changes. For example, managers may use their influence to improve morale. This influence would not necessarily change behavior; it might simply bring about a change in attitude.

We will define *power* as *the ability to exert influence.* To have power is to be able to change the behavior or attitudes of other individuals. In the example above, the hard-working person would be more likely to have power to influence the work group if he or she were popular than if he or she were disliked. In general, those persons who can exert influence over others in an organization are called stakeholders, as we mentioned in chapter 3. We will focus on internal stakeholders—specifically, employees and volunteers within an organization—in this chapter.

Formal authority is one type of power. It is based on the recognition of the legitimacy or lawfulness of the attempt to exert influence. The individuals or groups attempting to exert influence are seen as having the right to do so within recognized boundaries. This right arises from their formal position in an organization.

The Basis of Formal Authority: Two Views

"What gives you the right to tell me what to do?" This familiar question bluntly suggests that before we comply with an instruction, we must be satisfied that the person issuing it has the right to do so. It is unlikely that we would ask this question of a superior in our organization, since we assume that a superior does have the right to issue instructions to us. But why is this so? Where do managers get the right to direct subordinates' activities?

There are two major views on the origin of formal authority in organizations: the classical view and the acceptance view. The *classical view* supposes that authority originates at some very high level of society and then is lawfully passed down from level to level. At the top of this high level may be God, the bureaucracy (in the form of a king, a dictator, or an elected president), or the collective will of the people.[3]

In the classical view of formal authority in American organizations, management has a right to give lawful orders and subordinates have an obligation to obey. This obligation is, in effect, self-imposed. Members of our society, in agreeing to abide by the Constitution, accept the rights of others to own private property and to own and control a business. By entering and remaining in an organization, subordinates in the United States accept the authority of owners or superiors and therefore have a duty to obey lawful directives.

This view is *normative* and partially *descriptive.* It expresses the way individuals should—and most often do—behave and implies that disobedience of lawful and legitimate orders of managers is wrong and indefensible. That we are all willing to conform to a considerable range of lawful directives is shown by our acceptance of

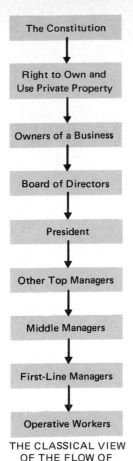

The Constitution

↓

Right to Own and
Use Private Property

↓

Owners of a Business

↓

Board of Directors

↓

President

↓

Other Top Managers

↓

Middle Managers

↓

First-Line Managers

↓

Operative Workers

THE CLASSICAL VIEW
OF THE FLOW OF
AUTHORITY

"no smoking" signs, for example, and requests to report to the boss right away. Willingness to perceive these types of formal authority as legitimate is widespread, even when no explicit reward or punishment is likely to follow compliance or refusal.

The classical view, however, is not fully descriptive. It does not account for the fact that many laws are disregarded and that others are obeyed for reasons other than acceptance of authority, such as fear or habit. The classical view also offers only one explanation of how authority is obtained.

The second perspective on the origin of formal authority, the *acceptance view*, finds the basis of authority in the *influencee* rather than in the *influencer*. This view starts with the observation that not all legitimate laws or commands are obeyed in all circumstances. Some are accepted by the subordinate or receiver of the order, and some are not. The key point is that it is the *receiver* who decides whether or not to comply. In the acceptance viewpoint, therefore, whether or not authority is present in any particular law or order is determined by the receiver, not the person issuing the order. For example, if a supervisor storms along an assembly line shouting at everyone to work harder, the subordinates may not question the supervisor's right to do so but, through anger or indifference, may choose not to comply with the order. The authority of the order will then be nullified.

This view should not suggest that insubordination and chaos are the norm in organizations; most formal authority is, in fact, accepted by the members of an organization. Chester I. Barnard, a strong proponent of the acceptance view (see chapter 2), has defined the conditions under which a person will comply with higher authority:[4]

A person can and will accept a communication as authoritative only when four conditions simultaneously obtain: (a) he can and does understand the communication; (b) *at the time of his decision* **he believes that it is not inconsistent with the purpose of the organization; (c)** *at the time of his decision* **he believes it to be compatible with his personal interest as a whole; and (d) he is able mentally and physically to comply with it.**

In addition to these conditions, cooperation in accepting authority is fostered by what Barnard calls the "zone of indifference" and Herbert A. Simon refers to, perhaps more descriptively, as the "area of acceptance."[5] Both expressions refer to the inclination of individuals to accept most orders given to them by their superiors, provided the orders fall within a "normal" range. Most of us, for example, will accept the need for periodic progress reports on our work and will usually not stop to consider whether or not to comply with a request for such reports from our superiors.

The Sources of Power

Power does not simply derive from an individual's level in the organizational hierarchy. John French and Bertram Raven have identified five sources or bases of power.[6] Each may occur at all levels.

Reward power is based on one person (the influencer) having the ability to reward another person (the influencee) for carrying out orders or meeting other requirements. One example is the power of a supervisor to assign work tasks to subordinates. The greater the attractiveness of a particular task in the eyes of the influencee, the greater the reward power of the influencer. However, rewards are best used to reinforce the desirable actions of subordinates and not as "bribes" to carry out tasks.[7]

Coercive power, based on the influencer's ability to punish the influencee for not meeting requirements, is the negative side of reward power. Punishment may range from loss of a minor privilege to loss of a job. Coercive power is usually used to maintain a minimum standard of performance or conformity among subordinates.

Legitimate power, which corresponds to our term *authority* (see above), exists when a subordinate or influencee acknowledges that the influencer has a "right" or is lawfully entitled to exert influence—within certain bounds. It is also implied that the influencee has an obligation to accept this power. The right of a manager to establish reasonable work schedules is an example of "downward" legitimate power. A plant guard may have the "upward" authority to require even the company president to present an identification card before being allowed onto the premises.

Expert power is based on the perception or belief that the influencer has some relevant expertise or special knowledge that the influencee does not. When we do what our doctors tell us, we are acknowledging their expert power. Expert power is usually applied to a specific, limited subject area. Although we may accept the advertising advice of our company's marketing specialists, we may discount their recommendations on how to lower production costs.

Referent power, which may be held by a person or a group, is based on the influencee's desire to identify with or imitate the influencer. For example, popular, conscientious managers will have referent power if subordinates are motivated to emulate their work habits. Referent power also functions at peer level—charismatic colleagues may sway us to their sides in department meetings. The strength of referent power is directly related to such factors as the amount of prestige and admiration the influencee confers upon the influencer.

These are potential sources of power only. They are the ways in which one person can influence another person. Possession of some or all of them does not guarantee the ability to influence particular individuals in specific ways. For example, we may have their respect and admiration as an expert in our field, but we still may be unable to influence them to be more creative on the job or even to get to work on time. Thus, the role of the influencee in accepting or rejecting the attempted influence remains the key one.

Normally, each of the five power bases is potentially inherent in a manager's position. A specific degree of legitimate power always accompanies a manager's job and is especially important because it shapes the hierarchical relationships within which the other forms of influence and power occur. Subordinates are assumed to accept a manager's formal authority and will generally obey him or her within reasonable limits. Managers usually have the power to reward subordinates with money, privileges, or promotions and to punish them by withholding or removing these rewards. Also, managers are assumed to possess some degree of expertise, at least until they prove otherwise. Since referent power so obviously depends on an individual's style and personality, it is least likely to be an expected part of a manager's position. Many examples of it, however, exist in organizations, for instance in the tendency of subordinates to model themselves after successful senior executives.

LEGITIMATE COMMANDS

ACCEPTANCE OF COMMANDS

Possible Noncompliance

Used area of Acceptance

Unused area of Acceptance

POWER

| Coercive | Reward | Legitimate | Referent | Expert |

The Five Bases of Power

Power in Organizations

The concept of power is a difficult one for Americans to deal with objectively—perhaps because the United States was founded in opposition to an authoritarian regime and peopled by successive waves of immigrants who were seeking to avoid oppressive governments throughout the world. A distrust of excessive power is reflected in the United States Constitution, which, while establishing the powers of the federal government, clearly limits those powers as well, reserving a great deal of authority to the states. The Constitution's specific system of checks and balances was designed to give each of the three branches of government—legislative, executive, and judicial—the means of preventing the others from accumulating too much power. In addition, the Bill of Rights and subsequent amendments were enacted to protect the rights of individuals.

Most Americans, then, have ambivalent feelings about power. They may covet it but are reluctant to admit this openly. They may both admire and resent power in others. This uneasiness about power perhaps explains why management writers have neglected it in the past, even though the exercise of power is an obvious part of a manager's job.

In recent years, power and political processes in organizations have become major concerns of management writers.[8] Both our realistic understanding of the role of these factors and our understanding of how they can be used constructively have been increasing rapidly. For example, David McClelland has described "two faces of power"—a negative face and a positive one.[9] The negative face is usually expressed in terms of dominance-submission: If I win, you lose. To have power implies having power over another, who is less well off for it. Leadership based on the negative face of power regards people as little more than pawns to be used or sacrificed as the need arises. This is self-defeating, since people who feel they are pawns tend either to resist leadership or to become passive. In either case, their value to the manager is severely limited.

The positive face of power is best characterized by a concern for group goals—for helping to formulate and achieve such goals. It involves exerting influence on behalf of rather than over others. Managers who exercise their power positively encourage group members to develop the strength and competence they need to succeed as people and as members of the organization.

McClelland and David H. Burnham report that successful managers have a greater need to influence others for the benefit of the organization than for self-aggrandizement.[10] Managers who use their power with self-control will be more effective than those who wield power to satisfy a need to dominate others or those who neglect to use their power out of a strong need to be liked. When a manager continually eases rules and changes procedures to accommodate subordinates, they will suspect that he or she is not flexible but weak and indecisive. McClelland concluded that good managers exercise power with restraint on behalf of others. Such managers encourage team spirit, support subordinates, and reward their achievements, thereby raising morale.

Characteristics of Successful Power Users. But just what do good managers do with their power? What specific techniques and styles are most effective? John Kotter developed a list of characteristics that he found to be common to managers who used their power successfully.[11]

1. Effective managers are sensitive to the source of their power and are careful to keep their actions consistent with people's expectations. For example, specialists with expert power in one field might lose credibility if they tried to influence actions in a different area.
2. Good managers understand—at least intuitively—the five bases of power and recognize which to draw on in different situations and with different people. They are aware of the costs, risks, and benefits of using each kind of power.
3. Effective managers recognize that all bases of power have merit in certain circumstances. They try to develop their skills and credibility so they can use whatever method is needed. Thus, they establish useful alliances with others in the organization, develop expertise, and generally display confidence at all times.
4. Successful managers have career goals that will allow them to develop and use power. They seek jobs that will build skills, which in turn will make others dependent on them. They also seek jobs that demand a type of power they feel comfortable using.
5. Effective managers temper power with maturity and self-control. They avoid impulsive or egotistical displays of their power and shun tactics that are unnecessarily harsh on others around them.
6. Successful managers know that power is necessary to get things done. They feel comfortable in the use of power and accept the fact that they must be able to influence the behavior of others to achieve goals.

The successful manager recognizes just which tactics are effective in given situations and which are likely to be counterproductive.

Power at Lower Levels. Kotter's analysis concentrates on the use of power by managers, but our earlier discussion of Barnard's acceptance perspective reminds us that power is not possessed only by managers. David Mechanic points out that lower-level members of an organization often have a great deal of informal power. [12] This power may be based on their information or knowledge about the organization, the skills they possess, and the resources they control and can supply to others. For example, new doctors in a hospital may have to rely on nurses to "teach them the ropes," and this dependence will give the nurses power to influence the doctors' actions. Similarly, low-level employees with control over special equipment (such as the copying machine) will often have the power to impede or improve a manager's work flow. In addition, peer regulation of behavior in highly cohesive groups of subordinates may reduce the power that managers can exert in monitoring individuals within the group.[13]

Power, then, is an important fact of organizational life; it cannot be ignored. As managers we must not only accept and understand power as an integral part of our jobs, but we must learn how to use, and not abuse, it to further our own and our organization's goals.[14]

Line and Staff Authority

Formal authority, the legitimate power associated with an organizational position, derives from subordinates' accepting that it is appropriate and desirable to follow orders from superiors in the organizational hierarchy. Another usage of the word

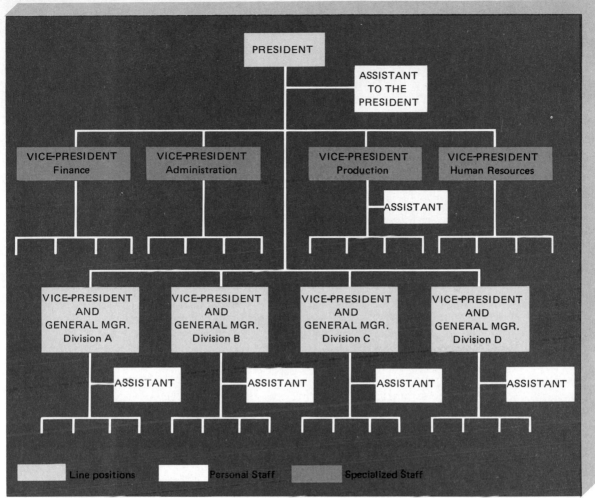

FIGURE 11-1
LINE AND STAFF
POSITIONS

"authority" occurs in distinguishing between what are frequently called *line* authority and *staff* authority.

Not all authors agree that the line/staff distinction is meaningful.[15] Line and staff authority are, however, such pervasive and often confusing elements in organizations that they need to be examined and understood. In this section, we will review the elements of line and staff functions in light of the increasing complexity of organizations, which tends to blur the distinctions between them. We will then examine the roles of staff members and the differences between personal and specialized staff, and conclude by discussing functional authority and line–staff interaction. (See fig. 11–1.)

Line Positions

Every organization exists to achieve specific goals. Line managers may be defined as those in the organization directly responsible for achieving these goals. Line authority is represented by the standard chain of command, starting with the board of directors and extending down through the various levels in the hierarchy to the point where the basic activities of the organization are carried out.

Since line activities are identified in terms of the company's goals, the activities classified as line will differ with each organization. For example, a manufacturing company may limit line functions to production and sales, while a department store, in which buying is a key element, will include the purchasing department as well as the sales department in its line activities.

When an organization is small, all positions may be line roles; staff roles are added as the organization grows and it becomes useful to hire specialists to assist the line members in doing their primary jobs.[16]

Staff Positions

Staff includes individuals or groups in an organization who provide services and advice to line. The concept of staff includes all elements of the organization that are not classified as line.

The concept and use of advisory staffs is not a recent development. Advisory staffs have been used by decision makers from emperors and kings to parliamentary governments and dictatorships over the course of recorded history. The staffs of kings often included court jesters and fools.[17]

Staff provides managers with varied types of expert help and advice. Staff can offer line managers planning advice through research, analysis, and options development. Staff can also assist in policy implementation, monitoring, and control, in legal and financial matters, and in the design and operation of data-processing systems.[18]

The distinction between line and staff can often be made with reasonable ease and accuracy. Sometimes, however, clarity is lacking: Line managers seem to be performing staff functions, and staff members seem to have some line responsibilities. Staff personnel, however, will devote most of their time to providing services and advice to line members, while line managers will tend to focus their efforts directly on producing the organization's products or services.

Staff positions differ from line in their sources of power. Line managers have formal authority (legitimate power) to tell others what to do. They also have a great deal of reward and coercive power because of their hierarchical relationships to subordinates.

Staff members do not have formal authority to give orders in most of their activities, and they are not supposed to have reward and coercive power. Instead, they give advice and counsel, thereby exerting primarily expert power.

In spite of this emphasis on expert power, the staff service and advisory roles have a considerable amount of potential reward and coercive power because effective or timely performance can be provided or withheld. Staff is not supposed to exercise this potential power, but it frequently does.

Personal Staff and Specialized Staff

It is useful to make a distinction between personal staff and specialized staff. The *personal staff* reports to the manager and assists him or her in carrying out a variety of activities. The manager continues to perform and be responsible for those activities, despite the aid of the personal staff. The *specialized staff* performs work requiring skills or objectivity that the line does not possess. Since the work of the specialized staff usually cannot be performed by the line, it may be completely delegated to the staff without involving a line manager. The specialized staff, not the line manager, is responsible for accomplishing this work.

The personal staff provides a wide range of services but concentrates on assisting one department or individual. The specialized staff, on the other hand, concentrates on one specific area of expertise, but normally makes its services and advice widely available.

Functional Staff Authority

The role of staff members to provide advice and service to line members implies that staff lacks independent, formal authority. In reality, staff departments, especially those responsible for audit functions, may have formal authority over line members within the limits of their functions. The right to control activities of other departments as they relate to specific staff responsibilities is known as *functional authority*.

In figure 11–2, the finance manager of Division A reports through the chain of command to the general manager of Division A. The finance manager, however, is also responsible to the vice-president at the corporate level in a "dotted-line" relationship representing the functional authority between specialized staff and line managers.

The need for functional authority is very real. It arises from the need for a degree of uniformity and an unhindered application of expertise in carrying out many organizational activities. For this reason, functional authority is common in organizations. The skills required to manage functional authority relationships (and the problems arising from them) are similar to those required in the dual-boss relationships in matrix organizations.

FIGURE 11–2
FUNCTIONAL AUTHORITY AND "DOTTED-LINE" RELATIONSHIPS

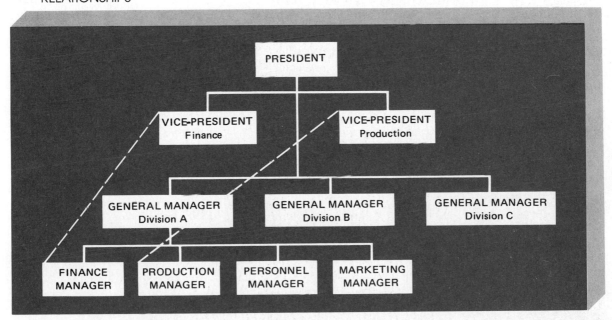

"Miss Roth, send someone in here to roll up our sleeves."
Drawing by Leo Cullum; © 1982 The New Yorker Magazine, Inc.

Delegation

We may define *delegation* as the assignment to another person of formal authority and responsibility for carrying out specific activities. The delegation of authority by superiors to subordinates is obviously necessary for the efficient functioning of any organization, since no superior can personally accomplish or completely supervise all the organization's tasks.

Although delegation is the transfer of legitimate power, it relates to the other power bases as well. When formal authority is conferred, the power to reward and punish goes with it to some extent. Expert power can also be indirectly conveyed by delegation: The subordinate who now acts in place of the superior will acquire expert power to the extent that he or she develops the necessary skills to perform the task.

The extent to which managers delegate authority is influenced by such factors as the culture of the organization, the specific situation involved, and the relationships, personalities, and capabilities of the people in that situation.[19] While there are many contingency factors that managers will have to take into account in deciding what and how much to delegate, there are also some basic guidelines that apply to most situations.

Classical Guidelines for Effective Delegation

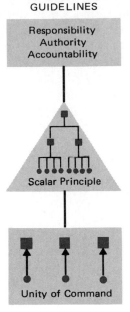

Responsibility
Authority
Accountability

Scalar Principle

Unity of Command

Delegation was an important subject of the early management writers, and their basic considerations remain valid today. Many of the guidelines for effective delegation are therefore based on classical principles.[20]

Responsibility, Authority, and Accountability. As we have indicated in previous chapters on the organizing process, every position in an organization has, or should have, specified tasks and the responsibility for carrying them out. For the organization to make efficient use of its resources, *responsibility for specified tasks is assigned to the lowest organizational level at which there exists sufficient ability and information to carry them out competently.* For example, it would be a waste of a company president's time—which should be spent in directing achievement of the overall goals of the organization—to check personally the time cards of lower-level employees. Such a task can be performed most efficiently by lower-level supervisors.

A corollary of this rule is that *for individuals in the organization to perform their assigned tasks effectively, they must be delegated sufficient authority to do so.* For example, as sales managers, we would be responsible for a certain standard of performance in our sales department. But if we did not have the formal authority to assign territories, reward the most effective salespeople, and fire incompetents, we would not be able to fulfill our obligations. Through delegation of authority, then, members of the organization are given the power they need to carry out their assigned responsibilities.

A necessary part of the delegation of responsibility and authority is *accountability*—being held answerable for results. By accepting responsibility and authority, individuals in the organization also agree to accept credit or blame for the way in which they carry out their assignments. For managers, the concept of accountability has an added dimension: Not only are managers held accountable for their own performance, but they are also held accountable for the performance of their subordinates. In fact, accountability for the actions of subordinates is one of the defining characteristics of a managerial position.

The Scalar Principle. For delegation to work effectively, members of the organization should know where they stand in the chain of command. Otherwise, they could neither accept nor assign responsibility with any confidence. The *scalar principle* suggests that there must be a clear line of authority running step by step from the highest to the lowest level of the organization. This clear line of authority will make it easier for organization members to understand (1) to whom they can delegate, (2) who can delegate to them, and (3) to whom they are accountable.

When establishing the line of authority, *completeness of delegation* is required; that is, all necessary tasks in the organization should be assigned. Unassigned tasks, called *gaps,* have to be avoided, because otherwise it is likely that the tasks will remain unperformed—or the people who voluntarily perform those tasks will resent their extra burden. For example, we should not assume that our purchasing manager will also take care of inventory control. Either we will clearly define the inventory tasks as his or her responsibility or we will delegate the task to someone else. Similarly, there should be no *overlaps* (responsibility for the same task assigned to more than one individual) and no *splits* (responsibility for the same task assigned to more than one organizational unit). Otherwise, confusion of authority and accountability will result.

Unity of Command. The *unity of command* principle states that each person in the organization should report to only one superior. Reporting to more than one superior makes it difficult for an individual to know to whom he or she is accountable and whose instructions he or she must follow. For example, a computer graphics designer who must report to several managers will frequently receive conflicting orders about whose proposal or presentation has priority. The designer is then likely to feel confused and bullied. Reporting to more than one superior also encourages individuals to avoid responsibility, since they can easily blame poor performance on the fact that with several bosses they have too much to do.

Limitations of the Classical Guidelines

The guidelines we have been discussing are representative of the classical "top to bottom" view of authority in organizations. While they remain quite useful in many situations, they do have some limitations.

One problem with the guidelines is that they overlook the fundamental point made earlier in this chapter—namely, that the acceptance of legitimacy of managers by subordinates determines whether those managers can exercise authority effectively. Managers may have the formal right to delegate tasks, but if subordinates do not accept that right, the delegation process breaks down. As we shall see, managers often must seek the support of subordinates in order to make delegation effective.

Another problem arises from the complexity of many modern organizational structures. The unity of command principle, for example, is explicitly violated in matrix organizations. The matrix structure exists because, in some situations, the advantages of the dual reporting system exceed the disadvantages, even though some of the disadvantages arise precisely from this violation.[21]

The utility of the classical guidelines also depends on the ability of a boss to define precisely the tasks to be done. In a dynamic organizational environment, task definition is an ongoing activity, with responsibility and authority frequently being reallocated. In such a situation, flexibility on the part of both subordinates and managers is essential. In dealing with gaps and splits, cooperation and initiative are generally more effective than spending valuable time seeking precise authority/ responsibility allocations that may have to be reallocated after a short time.

The classical guidelines for delegation are useful in many cases and, when overlooked, will often lead to predictable types of problems. However, when the situation requires it, managers may have to violate these guidelines in order to achieve specific objectives.

The Advantages of Effective Delegation

When used properly, delegation has several important advantages. The first and most obvious is that the more tasks managers are able to delegate, the more opportunity they have to seek and accept increased responsibilities from higher-level managers. Thus, as managers we will try to delegate not only routine matters but also tasks requiring thought and initative, so that we can be free to function with

DEGREES OF DELEGATION

Harvey Sherman has listed the following as typical degrees of delegation:

1. Take action—no futher contact with me is needed.
2. Take action—let me know what you did.
3. Look into this problem—let me know what you intend to do; do it unless I say not to.
4. Look into this problem—let me know what you intend to do; delay action until I give approval.
5. Look into this problem—let me know alternative actions available with pros and cons and recommend one for my approval.
6. Look into this problem—give me all the facts; I will decide what to do.

Source: Quoted from Harvey Sherman , *It All Depends: A Pragmatic Approach to Organizations* (University, Ala.: University of Alabama Press, 1966), pp. 83–84. © 1966 by the University of Alabama Press. Used by permission.

maximum effectiveness for our organizations. (See box for a description of the degrees of delegation a manager can use.)

Another advantage of delegation is that it frequently leads to better decisions, since subordinates closest to the "firing line" are likely to have a clearer view of the facts. For example, the West Coast sales manager will be in a better position than the vice-president of sales to allocate the California sales territories.

In addition, effective delegation speeds up decision making. Valuable time is lost when subordinates must check with their superiors (who then may have to check with *their* superiors) before making a decision. This delay is eliminated when subordinates are authorized to make the necessary decision on the spot. Finally, delegation causes subordinates to accept responsibility and exercise judgment. This not only helps train subordinates—an important advantage of delegation—but also improves their self-confidence and willingness to take initiative.

Barriers to Effective Delegation

In spite of the advantages, many managers are reluctant to delegate authority and many subordinates are reluctant to accept it. Both these barriers hinder effective delegation.

Reluctance to Delegate. There are a number of reasons that managers commonly offer to explain why they do not delegate: "I can do it better myself"; "My subordinates just aren't capable enough"; "It takes too much time to explain what I want done." These reasons are often excuses that managers use to hide the real reasons they avoid delegation.

Insecurity may be a major cause of reluctance to delegate. Managers are accountable for the actions of subordinates, and this may make them reluctant to "take chances" and delegate tasks. Or the manager may fear a loss of power if the subordinate does too good a job.

Reluctance
to Delegate

↕

BARRIERS
TO
EFFECTIVE
DELEGATION

↕

Reluctance
to Accept
Delegation

An additional cause of reluctance to delegate is a manager's lack of ability. Some managers may simply be too disorganized or inflexible to plan ahead and decide which tasks should be delegated to whom or to set up a control system so that subordinates' actions can be monitored.

Lack of confidence in subordinates is a third major reason why managers avoid delegation. In the short run, this lack of confidence may be justified if subordinates lack knowledge and skill. In the long run, there is no justification for failing to train subordinates. Managers who lack confidence in their subordinates—perhaps because of an inflated sense of their own worth—will severely limit their subordinates' freedom to act and their opportunity to grow.

Reluctance to Accept Delegation. Insecurity can also be a barrier to the acceptance of delegation. Some subordinates want to avoid responsibility and risks, and so would like their bosses to make all the decisions. Similarly, subordinates who fear criticism or dismissal for mistakes are frequently reluctant to accept delegation.

Another common reason for reluctance is that subordinates may not be given sufficient incentive for assuming extra responsibility. Accepting delegation frequently means they will have to work harder under greater pressure. Without appropriate compensation, subordinates may be unwilling to do so. (See chapter 15 for a discussion of ways to increase subordinates' motivation to work.)

Overcoming the Barriers

The most basic prerequisite to effective delegation is the willingness of managers to give their subordinates real freedom to accomplish delegated tasks. Managers have to accept the fact that there are usually several ways to solve a problem and that subordinates may legitimately choose a path different from their own. And, subordinates will make errors in carrying out their tasks. But they must be allowed to develop their own solutions to problems and to learn from their mistakes. The solution to subordinates' mistakes is not for the manager to delegate less but to train or otherwise support subordinates more.

Improved communication between managers and subordinates will increase mutual understanding and thus help to make delegation more effective. Managers who know the abilities of their subordinates can more realistically decide which tasks can be delegated to whom. Subordinates who are encouraged to use their abilities and who feel their managers will back them up will in turn be more likely to accept responsibility.[22]

A useful method for overcoming barriers to delegation is to increase the complexity of delegated assignments and the degree of delegation over time. Thus, a manager can delegate successively more work and subordinates will accept more responsibility for particular tasks. If there is no progress within a planned period, then some problem in the superior-subordinate relationship is indicated (such as inadequate training, lack of mutual confidence, or poor communication).

In a humorous article, William Oncken, Jr., and Donald L. Wass described how some subordinates cleverly "delegate upward" to their bosses or laterally to their peers by casually transferring responsibility for a task from themselves to their bosses or co-workers.[23] They shift the "monkey" from their own to the other person's back by asking for decisions, opinions, or information that they themselves should make or obtain. Then they check with the boss or peer periodically to see what progress is being made in the "assignment."

To overcome inappropriate upward delegation, Oncken and Wass remind managers to make certain that subordinates have and retain the initiative for solving their own problems. Ways to do so include being clear and explicit about the degree of delegation associated with each problem, keeping the focus on what the subordinate will do about the problem, and setting appointments for progress reports by subordinates.

Decentralization

The delegation of authority by individual managers is closely related to an organization's decentralization of authority. Delegation is the process of assigning authority from one level of management down to the next. The concepts of decentralization and centralization refer to the extent to which authority has been passed down to lower levels (*decentralization*) or has been retained at the top of the organization (*centralization*). This terminology derives from a perspective, held in many countries, of the organization as a series of concentric circles. The chief executive of the organization is situated in the very center and a "web" of authority radiates out from him or her. The greater the amount of authority delegated throughout the organization, the more decentralized the organization is. For example, to the extent that lower-level managers can expend significant sums for equipment or supplies without first checking with higher-level managers, the organization is more decentralized.

Considerable confusion often arises between the terms *decentralization* and *divisionalization*. Part of the confusion is because of the tendency to refer to divisionalized firms as decentralized and to functionally structured firms as centralized. After all, the most obvious example of an increase in decentralization is an organization that moves from a centralized functional structure to a decentralized divisional structure. Furthermore, many of the advantages of divisionalization, as discussed in chapter 9, also apply to decentralization. The two, however, are not the same and should not be regarded as such. Any divisionalized organization may be relatively centralized or decentralized in its operations.

The advantages of decentralization are similar to the advantages of delegation: unburdening of top managers; improved decision making because decisions are made closer to the scene of action; better training, morale, and initiative at lower levels; and more flexibility and faster decision making in rapidly changing environments. These advantages are so compelling it is tempting to think of decentralization as "good" and centralization as "bad."

But total decentralization, with no coordination and leadership from the top, would clearly be undesirable. The very purpose of organization—efficient integration of subunits for the good of the whole—would be defeated without some centralized control. For this reason, the question for managers is not whether an organization should be decentralized but to what extent it should be decentralized.

As we shall see, the appropriate amount of decentralization for an organization will vary with time and circumstances. It will also vary for the different subunits of the organization. For example, production and sales departments have gained a high degree of decentralization in many companies, whereas financial departments have tended to remain comparatively centralized.

Factors Influencing Decentralization

Decentralization has value only to the extent that it assists an organization to achieve its objectives efficiently. In determining the amount of decentralization appropriate for an organization, the following factors are usually considered.[24]

1. **Influences from the business environment outside the organization, such as market characteristics, competitive pressures, and availability of materials.**
2. **Size and growth rate of the organization.**
3. **Characteristics of the organization, such as costliness of given decisions, top management preferences, the organization's culture, and abilities of lower-level managers.**

The first two factors help to determine the logical degree of decentralization—that is, they suggest what top managers *should* do. The last factor suggests what managers are *likely* to do. For example, a particular supermarket chain might be better off if each store manager had some discretion in adapting purchasing and pricing policies to local conditions. An autocratic top management might be unwilling to delegate this authority. But it will have to either change its attitude or accept the fact that the organization will suffer losses in some areas at the hands of competitors.

Strategy and the Organization's Environment. The strategy of an organization will influence the types of markets, technological environment, and competition with which the organization must contend. These factors will, in turn, influence the degree of decentralization that the firm finds appropriate. Alfred Chandler, for example, found that firms such as Westinghouse and General Electric that developed new products through a strategy of research and development leading to product diversification chose a decentralized structure. Other companies, operating in industries in which markets were more predictable, production processes less dynamic technologically, and competitive relationships more stable, tended to remain or become more centralized. United States Steel, for example, became more, rather than less, centralized in the first half of this century.[25]

Size and Rate of Growth. It is virtually impossible to run a large organization efficiently while vesting all decision-making authority in one or a few top managers. This is almost certainly the strongest single force for delegation and, hence, for decentralization.

As an organization continues to grow in size and complexity, decentralization tends to increase. The faster the rate of growth, the more likely it is that upper management, bearing the weight of an ever-increasing work load, will be forced to accelerate the delegation of authority to lower levels. When the growth rate slows, however, upper management may attempt to regain decision-making authority under the guise of "tightening things up" and protecting profits.

Characteristics of the Organization. The extent to which decision-making authority is centralized is also likely to be influenced by such internal characteristics of the company as:

1. *The cost and risk associated with the decision.* Managers may be wary of delegating authority for decisions that could have a heavy impact on the performance of their own subunits or of the organization as a whole. This caution is out of consideration not only for the company's welfare but for their own as well, since the responsibility for the results remains with the delegator.

2. *An individual manager's preference for a high degree of involvement in detail and confidence in subordinates.* Some managers pride themselves on their detailed knowledge of everything that happens within their area of responsibility. (This is known as "the good manager runs a tight ship" approach.) Others take equal pride in confidently delegating everything possible to their subordinates in order to avoid getting bogged down in petty details and to save their own expertise for the unit's major objectives.

3. *The organizational culture.* The shared norms, values, and understandings (culture) of members of some organizations support tight control at the top. The culture of other organizations support the opposite. The history of an organization helps to create its current culture. A firm that has had slow growth under a strong-willed leader may have a very centralized structure. In contrast, a firm that has grown rapidly through acquisitions will have learned to live with the greater independence of the acquired companies. (See chapter 13 for a further discussion of corporate culture.)

4. *The abilities of lower-level managers.* This dimension is, in part, circular. If authority is not delegated because of lack of faith in the talent below, the talent will not have much opportunity to develop. In addition, the lack of internal training will make it more difficult to find and hold talented and ambitious people. This, in turn, will make it more difficult to decentralize.

Trends in Decentralization

The period from the end of World War II to the early 1970s was a time of great economic growth. On balance, decentralization probably increased during this period. In the 1970s to mid-1980s, low rates of economic growth, pressure from foreign competition, and eventually the competitive disadvantages arising from the strength of the U.S. dollar encouraged centralization; many companies sought ways to increase productivity by eliminating costly duplication of functions.

Changes in attitude and education may be currently influencing the degree of decentralization. In this country and elsewhere there is a trend toward higher education levels among organization members; an increased desire for worker autonomy, participation, and industrial democracy; and a growing reluctance to bow to established authority. Recent advances in technology also provide management with increasing possibilities for decentralization. Such innovations as computer software that instruct beginning users with easy-to-use menus of choices and procedures make it possible for managers to relegate formerly very complicated activities to lower levels for decision making. Managerial decision support systems (DSS), for example, also offer line managers the ability to understand and second-guess staff specialists and, in some instances, enable them to do their tasks through DSS without recourse to specialists at all. If these trends continue through the 1980s, we can anticipate pressures on top management from below for more decision-making power at lower levels. These pressures, in turn, may lead to increased decentralization.

However, there might be a counter trend toward greater centralization brought on by advances over the next decade in expert systems (ES) using artificial intelligence. With the next generations of computers and intelligent software, upper levels of management will be able to process more data and make more decisions than were previously thought possible. A greatly increased ability to evaluate information may give top management more direct control of their organizations' activities and reduce its reliance on expert staff and middle managers. (See chapters 6 and 22 for discussions of DSS and expert systems.)

Summary

Power, influence, and authority are necessary elements of organizational life. From a classical viewpoint, formal authority is a legitimate managerial right that subordinates are obligated to recognize. From an "acceptance" viewpoint, formal authority is legitimized by subordinates.

There are five sources or bases of power: reward, coercive, legitimate, expert, and referent. In exercising their power, managers may take a dominance-submission approach toward subordinates, or they may use a more positive style based on concern for group goals and the encouragement and support of subordinates. The latter approach seems to work better, and effective managers learn to temper their use of power with maturity and self-control.

Line positions can be defined as those directly responsible for achieving the organization's goals. *Staff positions* provide expert advice and service to the line.

Effective delegation helps an organization use its resources efficiently—it frees managers for important tasks, improves decision making, and encourages initiative. Classical guidelines for effective delegation include the need to give subordinates authority and responsibility and the need to follow the scalar principle and the principle of unity of command. These guidelines, however, will not apply to all situations.

Barriers to effective delegation usually involve the reluctance of managers to delegate or the reluctance of subordinates to accept delegation. To overcome these barriers, managers can clearly specify subordinates' responsibilities, motivate and train subordinates, and set up a system of controls.

Delegation is closely related to decentralization in the sense that the greater the amount of delegation, the more decentralized the organization. The appropriate amount of decentralization for a particular organization will depend on external environmental forces, the organization's size and growth, and its culture. Current trends toward increased worker participation and higher education levels may lead to increased decentralization in our organizations, as may the widespread use of decision support systems. On the other hand, computers may also increase the decision power of top management and thus lead to increased centralization.

Review Questions

1. What are the two major views of authority? How do you think each view would affect a manager's attitude and behavior toward subordinates?

2. What is the "zone of indifference"?

3. What are the five bases of power described by French and Raven? Give one example of a manager's exercise of each type of power.

4. What are the "two faces of power" described by David McClelland?

5. What are the characteristics of successful power users?

6. What is the difference between line positions and staff positions? Is the difference always clear in organizations?

7. Describe the difference between personal staff and specialized staff. What does the phrase "functional staff authority" mean?

8. What are the advantages of delegation? Describe the classical guidelines to effective delegation. What are the limitations of these guidelines?

9. What are the barriers to effective delegation, and how can they be overcome? Do you think it will be difficult for you to delegate?

10. How are decentralization and delegation related?

11. What factors influence the extent to which an organization is decentralized?

12. Do you believe there will be a trend toward centralization or decentralization over the next several years? Why?

Notes   1. Walter B. Miller, "Two Concepts of Authority," in Harold J. Leavitt and Louis R. Pondy, eds., *Readings in Managerial Psychology* (Chicago: University of Chicago Press, 1964), pp. 557–576.

2. See, for example, Dennis H. Wrong, "Some Problems in Defining Social Power," *American Journal of Sociology* 73, no. 6 (May 1968):673–681.

3. See Max Weber, "The Three Types of Managerial Rule," *Berkeley Journal of Sociology* 4 (1953):1–11 (orig. 1925); and Cyril O'Donnell, "The Source of Managerial Authority," *Political Science Quarterly* 67, no. 4 (December 1952):573–588.

4. Chester I. Barnard, *The Functions of the Executive*, 30th anniversary ed. (Cambridge, Mass.: Harvard University Press, 1968), p. 165.

5. Herbert A. Simon, *Administrative Behavior*, 3d ed. (New York: Macmillan, 1976), pp. 12, 18.

6. John R. P. French and Bertram Raven, "The Bases of Social Power," in Dorwin Cartwright, ed., *Studies in Social Power* (Ann Arbor: University of Michigan Press, 1959), pp. 150–167.

7. Gary Yukl and Tom Taber, "The Effective Use of Managerial Power," *Personnel* 60, no. 2 (March–April 1983):37–44.

8. Jeffrey Pfeffer has explored the basis for the unease about power and politics and has concluded that power processees are often ubiquitous and generally beneficial rather than harmful to organizations and the people who work in them. See Jeffrey Pfeffer, *Power in Organizations* (Marshfield, Mass.: Pitman, 1981); and Henry Mintzberg, *Power in and Around Organizations* (Englewood Cliffs, N.J.: Prentice-Hall, 1983).

9. David C. McClelland, "The Two Faces of Power," *Journal of International Affairs* 24, no. 1 (1970):29–47.

10. David C. McClelland and David H. Burnham, "Power Is the Great Motivator," *Harvard Business Review* 54, no. 2 (March–April 1976):100–110.

11. John P. Kotter, "Power, Dependence and Effective Management," *Harvard Business Review* 55, no. 4 (July–August 1977):135–136.

12. David Mechanic, "Sources of Power of Lower Participants in Complex Organizations," *Administrative Science Quarterly* 7, no. 3 (December 1962):349–364. For a discussion of the factors that tend to increase or mitigate the power of one organizational group—computer staffs—see Henry C. Lucas, Jr., "Organizational Power and the Information Services Department," *Communications of the ACM* 27, no. 1 (January 1984):58–65.

13. See Mechanic, "Sources of Power of Lower Participants in Complex Organizations"; and Ahmed Sakr Ashour and Gary Johns, "Leader Influence Through Operant Principles: A Theoretical and Methodological Framework," *Human Relations* 36, no. 7 (July 1983):618.

14. A key concern of current research is the integration of the various theories of power into a unified theory. See W. Graham Astley and Paramjit S. Sachdeva, "Structural Sources of Intraorganizational Power: A Theoretical Synthesis," *Academy of Management Review* 9, no. 1 (January 1984):104–113; and Anthony T. Cobb, "An Episodic Model of Power: Toward an Integration of Theory and Research," *Academy of Management Review* 9, no. 3 (July 1984):482–493.

15. See, for example, Gerald G. Fisch, "Line-Staff Is Obsolete," *Harvard Business Review* 39, no. 5 (September–October 1961):67–79; and Vivian Nossiter, "A New Approach Toward Resolving the Line and Staff Dilemma," *Academy of Management Review* 4, no. 1 (January 1979):103–106.

16. For a discussion of the various ways staff activities are integrated in the organizational structure, see Harold Stieglitz, "On Concepts of Corporate Structure: Economic Determinants of Organization," *Conference Board Review,* February 1974, pp. 148–150.

17. Alfred Kieser, "Advisory Staffs for Rulers: Can They Increase Rationality of Decisions?"

Unpublished paper delivered at the seminar on "Improvement of Top-Level Decision-Making" at the Institute for Advanced Study, Berlin, February 1983.

18. For an early discussion of ways in which staff members can support line managers, see Louis A. Allen, "The Line-Staff Relationship," *Management Record* 17, no. 9 (September 1955):346–349ff.

19. See Gerald G. Fisch, "Toward Effective Delegation," *CPA Journal* 46, no. 7 (July 1976):66–67.

20. Our discussion in this section is based on James D. Mooney and Alan C. Reiley, *The Principles of Organization* (New York: Harper & Brothers, 1939), pp. 14–19, 23–24; and S. Avery Raub, *Company Organization Charts* (New York: National Industrial Conference Board, 1964).

21. John R. Adams and Nicki S. Kirchof, "The Practice of Matrix Management," in David I. Cleland, ed., *Matrix Management Systems Handbook* (New York: Van Nostrand Reinhold, 1984), pp. 13–30.

22. See Fisch, "Toward Effective Delegation," p. 67; and William Newman, "Overcoming Obstacles to Effective Delegation," *Management Review* 45, no. 1 (January 1956):36–41.

23. William Oncken, Jr., and Donald L. Wass, "Management Time: Who's Got the Monkey?" *Harvard Business Review* 52, no. 6 (November–December 1974):75–80.

24. See Ernest Dale, *Organization* (New York: American Management Associations, 1967), pp. 114–130.

25. Alfred D. Chandler, Jr., *Strategy and Structure: Chapters in the History of the American Industrial Enterprise* (Cambridge, Mass.: MIT Press, 1962).

CASE STUDY: The National Sales Manager

1. Pat McDill, formerly a regional sales manager of Century Soap Company, had recently been promoted to national sales manager. Derek Arnott, McDill's immediate superior, had told him when he began his new job that his primary task would be to bring up all four national sales regions to a set sales quota while pursuing a new strategy of rapidly capitalizing on emerging regional market trends. But McDill anticipated problems with one regional sales manager, Ken Blackwell. Although he liked the man personally, he felt that Blackwell exerted excessive control over operations in his region and that the result was a lack of initiative on the part of the district sales managers who reported to Blackwell and the salespeople themselves.

While still a regional manager, McDill had often pointed out to Blackwell what he regarded as the advantages of delegation. He had noted that when a regional manager insists on approving all key decisions by his or her district managers, and countermanding decisions made without his explicit consent, his or her subordinates tend to protect themselves by taking no risks and deferring even minor decisions until they can be cleared by the regional manager. The result, McDill predicted, would be a less flexible response to market pressures and a reduced share of the market.

However, Blackwell had not taken these comments seriously; he believed in making sure that every subordinate knew that he or she was under firm control. "I have learned the hard way," he liked to say, "that if you do not make sure that every salesperson is doing the job right, some of them won't do their job right."

2. At the time of his promotion, McDill resolved to put his biases aside and give Blackwell a fair, unprejudiced chance. In his visits to Blackwell's region, however, McDill was distressed to find that many of his fears seemed to be borne out. Salespeople were reluctant to make decisions that might have improved the market position of the company's products without the approval of their district manager, who in turn was often reluctant to grant that approval without checking with Blackwell. The result was a conservative and mostly uniform approach to an

increasingly volatile and segmented market with, at best, sluggish adaptation to local circumstances. Thus, Blackwell's region was falling behind the others in meeting the new sales quotas.

Even so, McDill clung to his resolve to keep his preconceived feelings from affecting his judgment. He felt that as differences in managerial style were to some degree a matter of taste, it would be unfair to insist that all his managers operate his way. He was also aware of the informal grapevine between the four regional managers, and he feared that if he made an issue over what was essentially a philosophical difference between him and one of his subordinates, the others might hear of it and lose some of their respect for him.

At a monthly meeting with Arnott, McDill confessed that the deviations between forecasted and actual sales were due almost entirely to the inability of one region—Blackwell's—to keep pace with the records of the other three. In fact, under the new strategy, sales had even begun to decline in Blackwell's region. Arnott said that McDill's initial reluctance to insist on a change in management style was perhaps understandable, but as more than a year had now passed since McDill had assumed his new job, his continued inaction could hardly be justified. "You should not have waited until the tide began to run against us in that region," said Arnott. He accused McDill of bending over backward in order to preserve his image of himself as a fair and judicious person. Arnott did not, however, specify the action he wanted McDill to take.

3. McDill then called in Blackwell for a private meeting. Blackwell interpreted the situation entirely in terms of fortuitous problems—a "streak of bad luck," as he put it—and the ineptness of a district manager whom he proposed to fire. McDill noted that the sales decline was roughly uniform in all districts of Blackwell's region and that whatever the district manager's faults might be, she could not be blamed for the region's poor showing. He then asked Blackwell to attempt a sharp and sustained change of approach, delegating broadly to his district managers and encouraging them to do likewise. Although Blackwell was skeptical, he agreed to try.

During the next several weeks, the sales decline was arrested in this region, although virtually none of the lost market share was recovered. Blackwell went to some lengths to assure McDill of the extent to which he had delegated decisions. However, he also reported that the policy was working no better than he thought it would, because the district managers continued to seek his "advice."

At this point, McDill recognized that abrupt changes in the behavior of the district managers were most unlikely, especially as they had been selected by Blackwell himself on the basis of their compatibility with his management style. McDill's real problem was to decide whether he could accept at best a gradual change in the way this region operated or whether he would have to take more drastic action.

Source: Adapted by permission of Random House, Inc. from *Cases and Problems for Decisions in Management* by Saul Gellerman. Copyright © 1984 by Random House, Inc.

Case Questions 1. What are the issues in this case?

2. Contrast McDill's and Blackwell's attitudes toward authority and delegation. Which is more effective?

3. Was Arnott remiss in not giving McDill specific instructions for dealing with Blackwell? Why or why not?

4. What should McDill do now?

12 STAFFING AND HUMAN RESOURCE MANAGEMENT

Upon completing this chapter you should be able to:

1. Explain why staffing is an essential management function.

2. Describe the staffing process.

3. State why human resource planning is important, what the aims of human resource planning are, and how the process of human resource planning is carried out.

4. Describe the process of recruitment both within and outside the organization.

5. Describe each step in the selection procedure.

6. Indicate how early job experiences have an effect on new employees' eventual success.

7. Describe the various types of training and management development programs.

8. Identify the four basic appraisal approaches and how appraisal can be managed so as to lead to improved employee performance.

The most important resources of an organization are its human resources—the people who supply the organization with their work, talent, creativity, and drive. Thus, among the most critical tasks of a manager are the selection, training, and development of people who will best help the organization meet its goals. Without competent people, at the managerial level and indeed at all levels, organizations will either pursue inappropriate goals or find it difficult to achieve appropriate goals once they have been set.

Staffing is the management function that deals with the recruitment, placement, training, and development of organization members. In this chapter we will examine how organizations determine what human resources they need now and in the future; how managers recruit and select people with the best potential for each position; how managers train people so that they will perform effectively; and finally, what types of development programs will best assure a constant flow of managerial talent from lower to higher levels of the organization.

Raymond E. Miles and Charles C. Snow have argued that two phenomena have recently caused top management to focus renewed attention on the staffing function and to give it added status. First, efficient foreign competition has led many American firms to seek to improve human resource management systems as a means to improve organizational performance. And second, the growing high-technology, service-based economy is making human resource management even more crucial for organizational success.[1]

In this chapter we will be taking a "top-down" view of staffing and the human resource function—that is, our emphasis will be on how managers recruit, select, train, and appraise lower-level managerial and nonmanagerial employees.[2] In chapter 19, "Organizational Careers and Individual Development," we will be taking a more "bottom-up" view by describing how individuals can manage their own careers as they start and move up the organizational ladder.

The Staffing Process

As figure 12–1 suggests, the composition of an organization's work force changes over time. Managers in organizations do not stay in their positions permanently. Successful managers are usually promoted; many of those who are not promoted seek better jobs elsewhere. Unsuccessful managers are, in many cases, transferred or replaced. The same is true of nonmanagerial staff. Thus, the organization and its managers must accommodate themselves to a constant change of personnel over time.

The staffing process can be seen as a continuing step-by-step procedure to keep the organization supplied with the right people in the right positions at the right time. The steps in this process include:

1. *Human Resource Planning. Human resource planning* is designed to ensure that the personnel needs of the organization will be constantly and appropriately met. Such planning is accomplished through analysis of (1) internal factors, such as current and expected skill needs, vacancies, and departmental expansions and

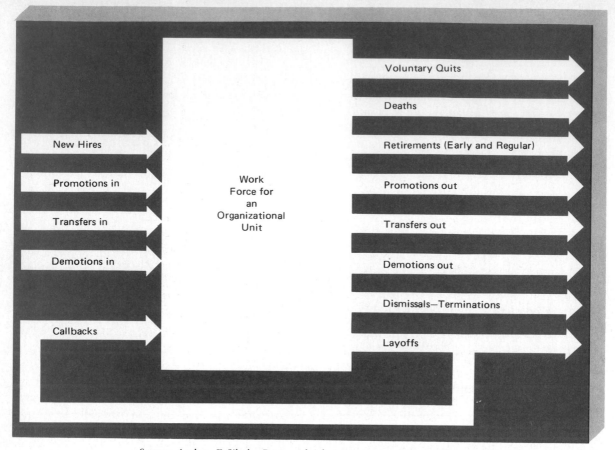

Source: Andrew F. Sikula, *Personnel Administration and Human Resource Management* (New York: Wiley, 1976), p. 158. Used by permission.

reductions; and (2) factors in the external environment, such as the labor market. As a result of this analysis, plans are developed for executing the other steps in the staffing process. Human resource planning usually covers a period from six months to five years in the future.

2. *Recruitment. Recruitment* is concerned with developing a pool of job candidates, in line with the human resource plan. The candidates are usually located through newspaper and professional journal advertisements, employment agencies, word of mouth, and visits to college and university campuses.

3. *Selection. Selection* involves evaluating and choosing among job candidates. Application forms, résumés, interviews, employment and skills tests, and reference checks are the most commonly used aids in the selection process.

4. *Induction and Orientation. Induction* and *orientation* are designed to help the selected individuals fit smoothly into the organization. Newcomers are introduced to their colleagues, acquainted with their responsibilities, and informed about the organization's policies and goals.

5. *Training and Development.* The process of training and development aims at increasing the ability of individuals and groups to contribute to organizational effectiveness. *Training* is designed to improve skills in the present job; for example, employees might be instructed in new decision-making techniques or the capabilities of data processing systems. *Development* programs are designed to educate employees beyond the requirements of their present position so that they will be prepared for promotion and able to take a broader view of their role in the organization.

6. *Performance Appraisal.* *Performance appraisal* compares an individual's job performance against standards or objectives developed for the individual's position. If performance is high, the individual is likely to be rewarded (by a bonus, for example, or by more challenging work assignments). If performance is low, some corrective action (such as additional training) might be arranged to bring the performance back in line with desired standards.

7. *Transfers.* A *transfer* is a shift of a person from one job, organizational level, or location to another. Two common types of transfers are *promotion*—a shift to a higher position in the hierarchy, usually with added salary, status, and authority—and *lateral* moves—a shift from one position to another at the same level. The third type of transfer is *demotion*—a shift to a lower position in the hierarchy.

8. *Separations.* A *separation* may be a resignation, layoff, discharge, or retirement. Analysis of the type and quantity of separations can provide insights into the managerial effectiveness of the organization. For example, too many resignations might signify a noncompetitive pay scale; recurrent layoffs sometimes result from poor integration of production with market demand; and too many discharges might indicate poor selection or training procedures. (Figure 12–2 illustrates the staffing process.)

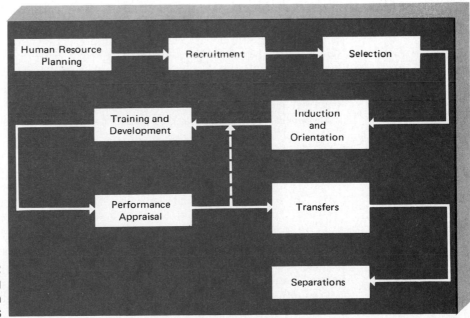

FIGURE 12–2
The Staffing
Process in
Organizations

Human Resource Planning

The need for human resource planning may not be readily apparent. After all, one might ask, if an organization needs new people, why doesn't it simply hire them? In fact, an organization's human resource needs can hardly ever be met as quickly or as easily as this question implies. An organization that does not plan for its human resources will often find that it is not meeting either its personnel requirements or its overall goals effectively.

For example, a manufacturing company may hope to increase productivity with new automated equipment, but if the company has not started to hire and train people to operate the equipment before installation is begun, it may remain idle for weeks or months. Similarly, an all-male, all-white organization that does not plan to add women and minority group members to its staff is likely to become the defendant in a civil rights lawsuit.

Planning Steps

There are four basic steps in human resource planning.[3]

1. *Planning for future needs.* How many people with what abilities will the organization need to remain in operation for the foreseeable future?
2. *Planning for future balance.* How many people presently employed can be expected to stay with the organization? The difference between this number and the number the organization will need leads to the next step.
3. *Planning for recruiting and selecting or for laying off.* How can the organization bring in the number of people it will need?
4. *Planning for development.* How should the training and movement of individuals within the organization be managed so that the organization will be assured of a continuing supply of experienced and capable personnel?

To accomplish these steps, the managers of a human resource planning program must consider a number of factors. The primary factor is the organization's strategic plan. (See chapter 5.) The organization's basic strategy and the detailed goals, objectives, and tactics for making that strategy a reality will define the personnel needs of the organization. For example, a strategy based on internal growth will mean that additional personnel will have to be hired. A strategy based on acquiring other companies will suggest the need to hire managers who have had experience with the types of firms being acquired.

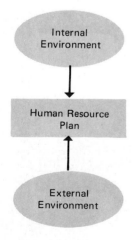

Internal Environment

Human Resource Plan

External Environment

Another factor to be considered by managers is potential change in the external environment of the organization. As we saw in chapter 3, this may mean a change in the market, the availability of financing, or the labor force. In a booming economy, for example, an organization might want to expand, and so its personnel needs will increase. At the same time, however, there may be fewer job candidates available because unemployment will be low. In a depressed economy, many organizations cut back on the number of employees; however, an organization that wishes to expand is likely to have an increased number of candidates available because of unemployment. There is a variety of other external changes that can affect the staffing function: Technological changes, for instance, may increase the number of specialized personnel an organization will require; changes in union demands may affect layoff policies; and changes in government regulations can affect all personnel actions, from recruitment to separation.

In sum, the organization's internal environment (as exemplified by its strategic plan), as well as its external environment, will broadly define for managers the limits within which their human resource plan must operate. Once these broad limits have been established, managers can begin to compare their future personnel needs against the existing personnel situation in order to determine what recruitment, training, and development procedures they will need to follow. Because the internal and external environments of an organization change, managers must monitor these environments to keep their human resource plans up to date.[4]

Forecasting and the Human Resource Audit

The central elements in human resource planning are forecasting and the human resource audit. *Forecasting* attempts to assess the future personnel needs of the organization. The *human resource audit* assesses the organization's current human resources. These two elements give managers the information they need to plan the other steps in the staffing process, such as recruiting and training.

Forecasting. Human resource forecasting attempts to determine what personnel the organization will need to maintain its growth and exploit future opportunities. Thus, forecasters try to predict the number, type, and quality of people needed in the future; specify the range of responsibilities that will have to be met; and establish what skills and knowledge organization members will need.[5]

The use of computerized decision support systems (DSSs) can facilitate human resource forecasting and scheduling and make them more accurate. Such forecasts are usually short-range, covering a period of six months to a year, and are often tied to the human resource needs of a specific project, such as the opening of a new production facility. In addition, forecasts of terminations, retirements, and effects of management successions can be easily made using a DSS. (See chapter 7 for a discussion of forecasting techniques.)[6]

Human Resource Audit. Once the forecasts are completed, the next step is to obtain information about the organization's present personnel. Two kinds of information are needed: Do organization members have the appropriate skills for their jobs? Are they performing effectively? The answers to these questions will enable planners to match the organization's personnel strengths and weaknesses against future requirements. Particular emphasis should be placed on locating existing skills and potential within the organization, since it is usually more economical to promote from within than to recruit, hire, and train people from outside.

In a human resource audit, the skills and performance of each individual in the organization are appraised. Within each department, individuals are ranked according to the quality of their work. The information thus obtained will give upper-level managers an idea of the effectiveness of staff in each department. More detailed audits may, in addition to performance appraisal, take into account the age and education of each individual, his or her likely promotability, and what additional training is necessary.

For higher levels of management, the next step in the auditing process may be to develop a detailed succession plan or replacement chart. The *replacement chart* shows the positions in the organization, present incumbents in those positions, likely future candidates for those positions, and the readiness of those candidates to take over those positions. (See fig. 12–3 for a detailed example.) Replacement charts with this much detail are usually developed only for upper-level managers. However, the need to compare existing human resources with future requirements exists at all levels of the organization.

Recruitment

The purpose of recruitment is to provide a large enough group of candidates so that the organization will be able to select the qualified employees it needs. *General recruiting,* which is most appropriate for operative employees, takes place when the organization needs a group of workers of a certain kind—for example, typists or salespeople. It follows comparatively simple, standardized procedures. *Specialized recruiting,* which is used mainly for higher-level executives or specialists, occurs when the organization desires a particular type of individual. In specialized recruiting, candidates receive personalized attention over an extended period.[7]

The recruiting of college and MBA graduates falls somewhere between these two extremes. It resembles general recruiting in the sense that many candidates are screened for a given group of openings and many may be hired with only a vague idea about their initial jobs—especially if the first "job" is in a management training program. On occasion, internships may be offered to students before graduation so that both sides may approach the employment decision with more information.[8]

Position Description

An important part of the recruiting process is developing a written statement of the content and location (on the organization chart) of each job. At the operative level, this statement is called the *job description;* at the managerial level, the statement is called a *position description.* Each box on the organization chart will be linked to a description that lists the title, duties, and responsibilities for that position. For example, a brief position description might read as follows: "Sales Manager: Duties include hiring, training, and supervising small sales staff and administration of sales department; responsible for performance of department; reports to Division Manager."

Once the position description has been determined, an accompanying hiring or job specification is developed. The *hiring specification* defines the background, experience, and personal characteristics an individual must have in order to perform effectively in the position. The hiring specification for Sales Manager might read: "Position requires BBA degree; five years' experience in sales and two years' supervisory experience; energetic, motivated individual with well-developed interpersonal skills."

Sources for Recruitment

Recruitment takes place within a *labor market*—that is, people available with the skills needed to fill the positions open in the organization. The labor market changes over time in response to environmental factors.

FIGURE 12–3 MANAGEMENT REPLACEMENT CHART

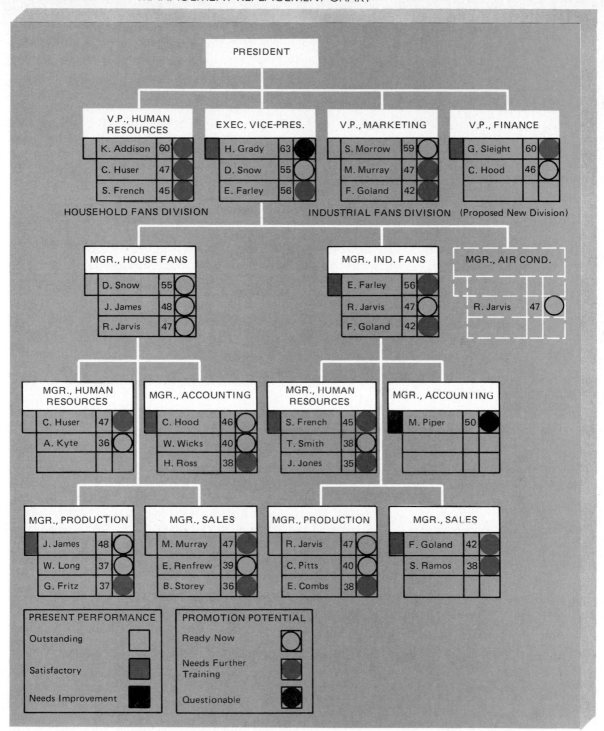

Source: From *Developing Managerial Competence* by Walter S. Wikstrom. Copyright © 1964 The Conference Board.

The sources to which human resources departments turn to meet their recruitment needs depend on the availability of the right kinds of people in the local labor pool, as well as on the nature of the positions to be filled. An organization's ability to recruit employees often depends as much on the organization's reputation and the attractiveness of its location as on the attractiveness of the specific job offer. If the people with the appropriate skills are not available in the organization itself or in the local labor pool, they may have to be recruited from competing organizations and/or from some distance away.

For many types of jobs at every level, private employment agencies and newspaper "Help Wanted" advertisements are important sources for letting the local job market know an opening exists. "Employment Opportunities" advertisements in trade and professional journals, as well as communication directly with social and professional organizations, are important sources of recruitment of middle- and upper-level people.

Of all methods of locating potential employees, the most often used and the most successful is word of mouth. In most organizations, more workers at every level are introduced to the firm through a personal contact. In any individual career, more employment opportunities are likely to have been found through personal recommendation and referral. For the individual, developing a wide range of personal contacts and "networking" may be the most useful career planning activities. (See chapter 19 for a discussion of career planning.)

Outside Recruitment for Managers and Professionals. For most large companies, college and graduate school campuses are a major source of new managerial and professional talent. Almost all schools have a placement office; the company representative will usually work with the placement office to set up an interview schedule and to have company brochures distributed. A disadvantage of campus recruiting is that it tends to be quite expensive. Ten to 15 interviews may be conducted for every candidate hired. In addition, a large proportion of those hired will not remain with the organization for more than two or three years.

Competition for middle management and professional talent is often no less vigorous than competition for market share. This competition is particularly intense in areas where top-quality ability is in short supply, as in advertising or investment analysis. Recruiters in such areas may buy large, expensive ads in newspapers and in national publications. Professional and middle management candidates may also be recruited by word of mouth and through placement agencies.

A top-level vacancy often poses a complicated problem for an organization because the right person for the position is usually not in the job market. He or she must be located in the upper reaches of some other firm, often a competitor, and induced to switch. Corporate managements frequently turn to outside executive search firms. These professional recruiters are expected to locate three or four carefully sifted prospects who not only are highly qualified but can be enticed from their present positions by the right offer.

Recruitment from Within. Many firms, such as IBM, General Foods, and Procter & Gamble, have a policy of recruiting or promoting from within the organization except in very exceptional circumstances. There are three major advantages of this policy. First, individuals recruited from within will already be familiar with the organization; therefore they are likely to succeed because of their knowledge of the

Drawing by Chas. Addams; © 1982 The New Yorker Magazine, Inc.

organization and its members. Second, a promotion-from-within policy helps to foster loyalty and inspire greater effort among organization members. Finally, it is usually less expensive to recruit or promote from within than to hire from outside the organization. The major disadvantages of this policy are that it limits the pool of talent available to the organization; it reduces the chance for a fresh viewpoint to enter the organization; and it may encourage complacency because employees may assume that their seniority will assure their promotion.

Equal Employment Opportunity and Affirmative Action

In the early 1960s, the growing civil rights and women's movements called national attention to the discriminatory effects of existing human resource practices. Responses to these efforts began with the Equal Pay Act of 1963 and the Civil Rights Act of 1964. These were expanded by the courts and most state legislatures and through various amendments and executive orders. The implications of such legislation for human resource policies and practices are still evolving and being clarified by court decisions and administrative interpretations. Some of the changes in the employment patterns of women are illustrated in figure 12–4 and table 12–1. They show both change and stability. The median annual earnings of women at work have increased significantly since 1960, yet the ratio of women's to men's wages has stayed relatively constant, averaging about 61 percent over the years. The increase of women employed in some of the higher-status, higher-paid occupations is dramatic, yet the proportion of women in those occupations is still low. "For example," as Janet L. Norwood, U.S. Commissioner of Labor Statistics, noted, "the number of

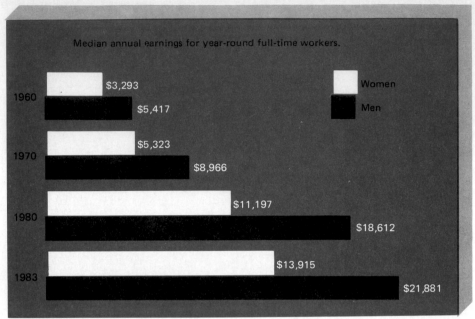

FIGURE 12–4
WOMEN AT
WORK—WHAT
THEY EARN

Source: William Serrin, "Experts Say Job Bias Against Women Persists," *New York Times,* November 25, 1984, pp. A1, A32. Copyright © 1984 by The New York Times Company. Reprinted by permission.

TABLE 12–1
WOMEN AT
WORK—THEIR
JOBS

Job Category	1972 (nos. in thousands)	1984 (nos. in thousands)	Percent change
Professional, technical, and managerial:	6,054	11,856	+ 95.8
Executive, administrative, and managerial	1,433	3,889	+171.4
Professional specialty	3,881	6,440	+ 65.9
Technician and related support	740	1,527	+106.4
Sales occupations	3,473	6,032	+ 73.7
Administrative support, including clerical	9,845	13,361	+ 35.7
Service occupations	6,614	8,607	+ 30.1
Precision production, craft, and repair	493	1,112	+125.6
Operators, fabricators, and laborers	4,183	4,385	+ 4.8
Farming, forestry, and fishing	593	562	− 5.2
Total	31,257	45,915	+ 46.9%

Sources: William Serrin, "Experts Say Job Bias Against Women Persists," *New York Times,* November 25, 1984, pp. A1, A32; and U.S. Bureau of Labor Statistics, *Employment and Earnings* 32, no. 1 (January 1985):174.

TABLE 12–2 SOME DIFFERENCES BETWEEN EEO (NONDISCRIMINATION) AND AA

	EEO	Affirmative Action
Who is affected?	Virtually everyone is covered by law	Legally applies only to certain organizations
What is required?	Employment neutrality Nondiscrimination	Systematic plan
What are the sanctions?	Legal charges can be filed Possible court action	Withdrawal of contracts or funds if noncompliant
What are some examples of compliance?	Not barring female, minorities, or handicapped persons from employment Selecting, promoting, and paying people solely on the basis of bona fide job-related qualifications	Actively recruiting and hiring female, veteran, minority, or handicapped persons Validating tests; rigorously examining company practices in selection, promotion, and benefits to eliminate non-job-related qualifications that discriminate against protected persons

Source: *The Management of Affirmatiave Action* by Francine S. Hall and Maryann H. Albrecht. Copyright © 1979 by Scott, Foresman and Company. Reprinted by permission.

women lawyers increased more than fivefold over the last decade, but there are still less than 100,000 in the legal profession, and they make up only 15 percent of the total."[9]

The Law. The key legislation is Title VII of the Civil Rights Act of 1964, amended in 1972, which prohibits employment discrimination on the basis of race, sex, age, religion, color, or national origin. These requirements for nondiscriminatory treatment are called *equal employment opportunity (EEO)* requirements. They apply to virtually all private and public organizations. Executive orders of 1965 and 1968 (amended in 1977) required, in addition, that firms doing business with the federal government make special efforts to recruit, hire, and promote women and members of minority groups. These requirements are called *affirmative action (AA)*. The differences between equal employment opportunity and affirmative action are summarized in table 12–2.

Employment rights of persons 40 to 70 years old were protected in the Age Discrimination in Employment Act of 1967, while the Vocational Rehabilitation Act of 1973 (amended in 1974) added protection for the physically and mentally handicapped if they were qualified to perform job tasks with reasonable accommodation by the employer. The Vietnam-era Veterans' Readjustment Act of 1974 requires those doing business with the federal government to extend affirmative action programs to veterans of that period and to disabled veterans generally.

Sexual harassment (unwanted sexual requests or advances) when related to hiring or promotion decisions or the work environment violates Title VII.[10] A 1978 amendment to Title VII, the Pregnancy Discrimination Act, prohibits dismissal of women because of pregnancy alone and protects their job security during maternity leaves.[11] In various states, legislation extends these employment rights to employees of very small firms and to specific groups not mentioned in federal legislation as yet, such as homosexuals and former prison inmates.[12]

This mass of legislation and subsequent legal decisions has attempted to deal with two kinds of discrimination of concern to managers. *Access discrimination* refers to hiring considerations and practices (different qualifying tests, lower starting salaries) that are not related in any way to an employee's present or future job performance but are based on the employee's membership in a particular population subgroup. *Treatment discrimination* involves practices unrelated to job performance (less favorable work assignments, slower promotion rates) that treat subgroup members differently from others once they are in the work force.[13]

It has not been easy for organizations to make the rapid changes required by EEO and AA legislation and decisions. In one study, managers reported problems in:[14]

1. **Developing, updating, and monitoring the affirmative action plan**
2. **Recruiting, selecting, and placing qualified women and minorities**
3. **Determining job placement, salary, and fringe benefits**
4. **Designing and implementing training and development procedures**
5. **Planning promotion and transfer systems**
6. **Developing positive attitudes toward affirmative action**
7. **Developing discipline and grievance procedures**
8. **Developing organization-wide support**

Managers received practical assistance in implementing their responses to equal employment opportunity legislation in 1978 when the Uniform Guidelines on Employee Selection Procedures were issued. Under these guidelines, organization practices or policies that adversely affect employment opportunities for any race, sex, or ethnic group are prohibited unless the restriction is a justifiable job requirement. Thus, courts have found height and weight requirements illegal when they prevented employment of women and people of Hispanic origin and were not shown to be job-related.

In a landmark decision on employment discrimination in 1982, the Supreme Court departed from the policy of the previous two decades and ruled that the fact that a seniority system at American Tobacco Company has a discriminatory impact is not in itself enough to make it illegal: actual intent to discriminate must be proved.[15] Since 1981, the Justice Department has appeared to favor seniority systems over affirmative action programs.

In 1985, legislation was introduced in Congress to prohibit discrimination against individuals with histories of cancer who can perform acceptably at work. Some states, including California, already had such laws. Research by the Metropolitan Life Insurance Company and American Telephone and Telegraph found comparable performance, absenteeism, and turnover for individuals with and without a history of cancer.[16]

Implications for Managers. In the recruitment process, the human resources department normally has prime responsibility for assuring compliance with equal employment opportunity and affirmative action provisions. Ultimately, however, all managers are affected because these provisions determine the pool of applicants for available positions and influence the procedures that must be used in managing and developing the individuals who are recruited. The human resources department must instruct and educate other organization members in the implications of compliance for their respective departments. Even job titles can be sexist and reflect *de facto* discrimination. For example, the job titles *foreman* and *salesman* are now outmoded; they should be replaced by *supervisor* and *sales worker* or *salesperson,* respectively. Managers must realize that neither they as individuals nor the organization as a whole have completely free choice in the recruiting, hiring, training, and promotion of human resources. Individuals and organizations failing to comply may be reported to the Equal Employment Opportunities Commission (EEOC) for investigation, or become defendants in class-action or specific lawsuits. In one widely reported class-action suit, several thousand female flight attendants won $52.5 million from Northwest Airlines when the company's employment practices were found to be discriminatory. Female employees elsewhere, including clerical workers who struck at Yale University in 1984, have demanded equal pay for jobs deemed by the employer to be of comparable worth. The Reagan administration, however, has not favored the idea of comparable worth as a means of correcting employment discrimination. And, in June 1985, the Equal Employment Opportunity Commission ruled in a case involving the Housing Authority of Rockford, Illinois, that employers are not required by federal law to provide equal pay for different jobs of comparable worth.[17]

Managers in general, and human resources administrators in particular, must keep aware of the many fair employment laws as they are approved and amended. They must periodically review their firms' policies and practices, making sure that all employees are recruited, selected, rewarded, and generally treated appropriately on the basis of job performance criteria alone. Everyone involved in human resource management should strive above all for consistency and evenhandedness, and should maintain careful documentation of each significant action. Using computer simulation technology, managers may also consider the effects over time of various human resource policies on their organizations.[18]

Selection

The selection process involves mutual decision making. The organization decides whether or not to make a job offer and how attractive the offer should be. The job candidate decides whether the organization and the job offer will fit his or her needs and goals. However, when the job market is extremely tight, the selection process in practice will be more one-sided. Several candidates will be applying for each position, and the organization will, on the basis of a series of screening devices, hire the candidate it feels is most suitable. The process is also one-sided when the candidate is a highly qualified executive or professional who is being courted by several organizations.

Steps in the Selection Process

The standard hiring sequence follows a seven-step procedure diagrammed in figure 12–5. In practice, the actual selection process will vary with organizations and between levels in the same organization. For example, the selection interview for lower-level employees may be quite perfunctory; heavy emphasis may be placed instead on the initial screening interview or on tests. In selecting middle- or upper-level managers, on the other hand, the interviewing may be extensive—sometimes lasting eight or more hours—and there may be little or no formal testing. Instead of initially filling out an application, the candidate may submit a résumé. Completion

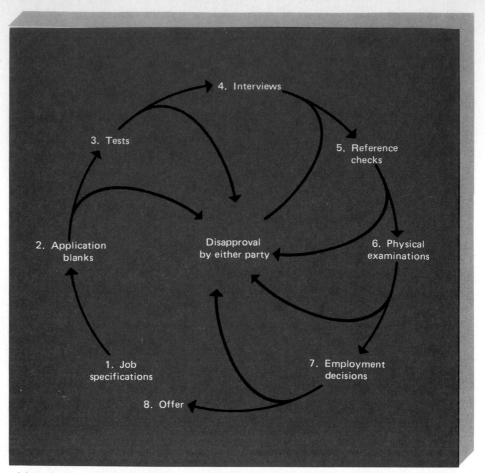

FIGURE 12–5
THE STANDARD
SELECTION
PROCESS

Although this chapter focuses on the selection of employees, the term "employment decisions" is used in this illustration, since both parties are making a decision in the process.

Source: *The Personnel Management Process.* Fifth Edition, by Wendell L. French, p. 238. Copyright © 1982 by Houghton Mifflin Company. Used by permission.

of the formal application may be delayed until after the job offer has been accepted. Some organizations omit the physical examination (step 6 in fig. 12–5).

1. The *application form* serves three purposes. First, it formally indicates that the applicant desires a position. Second, it provides the interviewer with the basic information he or she needs to conduct an interview. Third, it becomes a part of the organization's personnel information if the applicant is hired. Legally, the application form can request only information that has been shown to predict success in the job for which the candidate is applying. (It is illegal, for example, to request information on race or religion.)[19]

2. The *initial screening interview* is used to make a quick evaluation of the applicant's suitability for the particular job. In effect, the initial interview determines for both the applicant and the interviewer whether the selection process should proceed. The applicant may be asked questions on his or her experience, salary expectations, willingness to relocate, and the like.

3. Through *testing,* an organization attempts to measure a candidate's relevant job skills and ability to learn on the job. Most written tests in current use are graded by computer, and testing companies have taken care to eliminate from them cultural and gender biases. Complete testing packages are available to organizations; they may include a computer, a scanner for scoring, and test-generating software. Some organizations are currently employing unusual and even controversial testing procedures, including handwriting analysis (graphology) and lie-detector tests (polygraphy). IBM even announced in 1985 that it would begin routinely administering urinalysis to all prospective employees in an effort to weed out drug users.[20]

4. In a *background investigation,* the truthfulness of a candidate's résumé or application form will be checked, and further information will be sought from one or more of the candidate's references or previous employers. Such an investigation is useful, since studies have shown that as many as half of the applications submitted contain false or erroneous material. Usually, the manager or interviewer will simply call the applicant's previous supervisor (with the applicant's permission), confirm the information the applicant has supplied, and ask the supervisor to rate the applicant's skills and abilities. However, many companies, such as the Southmark Corporation in Dallas, prohibit their managers from giving outsiders any evaluative information on former employees to avoid lawsuits. This concern is real, though addressing it can be complicated. For instance, in 1985 the Minnesota Court of Appeals upheld a damage award of more than a million dollars to three former employees of the Equitable Life Assurance Society, agreeing that the company defamed them by not giving information on the circumstances of their discharges from the firm.[21]

5. The *in-depth selection interview* is designed to fill in gaps on the candidate's application or résumé, find out more about the applicant as an individual, and, in general, obtain information of interest to the interviewer so that the suitability of the candidate for the job and the organization can be determined. Unlike the screening interview, which is usually conducted by a member of the human resources department, the in-depth interview is usually conducted by the manager to whom the candidate would report if hired. (Because the in-depth interview is probably the most important part of the selection process, we discuss it in greater detail below.)

6. The *physical examination* will be one of the last steps in the selection process, unless the job involves heavy physical labor or stress. Physical examinations are designed to ensure that the candidate can perform effectively in the position for which he or she is applying, to protect other employees against contagious diseases, to establish a health record for the applicant, and to protect the organization against unjust workers' compensation claims.

7. If an applicant successfully passes through these selection stages and continues to indicate a desire for employment, a *job offer* may be made. Although other factors such as benefit packages, maternity leave, or job security may also be considered, for many people money is the paramount consideration. The salary offered should be competitive with salaries for similar jobs in other organizations and be compatible with the organization's existing salary structure. Too low an offer, if accepted, will cause the new employee to feel disgruntled when he or she finds out what others are being paid. Too high an offer, on the other hand, may cause problems with existing employees.

Interviewing

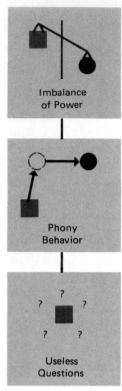

Imbalance
of Power

Phony
Behavior

Useless
Questions

For many positions, particularly in management, the in-depth interview is probably the most important factor in the organization's decision on whether or not to make a job offer and in the individual's decision on whether or not to accept the offer. The most effective interviews—that is, those that are best able to predict the eventual performance of applicants—are usually planned carefully and the same questions are usually asked of all candidates for the same position.[22] Most interviews, however, tend to be far less structured and deliberate.

Inadequate interviews can lead to poor employment decisions. Richard Nehrbass has identified three common defects in interviewing that may produce inaccurate information about job applicants.[23] The first defect is the imbalance of power in the interview situation. The interviewer is likely to be experienced and at ease. The interviewee, on the other hand, who is probably inexperienced in the interview situation and to whom the job may represent a livelihood, a career, and an important part of his or her self-image, is likely to feel ill at ease. The interviewee may therefore behave in an uncharacteristically tense manner.

The second defect of interviews is that they may cause the job candidate to adopt "phony" behavior. The applicant feels compelled to project an image that he or she thinks will be acceptable to the interviewer. Sometimes the "act" put on by a qualified applicant is obviously false or projects an image that is contrary to the organization's style. In such cases, a less qualified candidate who projects a realistic image may be offered the position.

A third defect is the tendency of interviewers to ask questions that have no useful answers, such as "Tell me about yourself" or "What would you say is your greatest weakness?" Applicants are likely to sense the lack of skill and preparation of the interviewer who asks such open-ended questions. They may feel uneasy and give superficial answers, or they may try to second-guess the interviewer and go off on a lengthy tangent. As Nehrbass asserts, interviews that focus on the requirements of the job and the actual skills and abilities of candidates will provide interviewers with more useful information and be better predictors of performance.

The interview process may also prove unreliable because of the differing objectives of the interviewer and interviewee. The prospective employer wants to sell the organization as a good place to work and so may exaggerate the organization's strengths. The prospective employee wants to be hired and so may exaggerate his or her qualities. Some organizations have attempted to reduce this problem through the *realistic job interview,* in which candidates are exposed to the unattractive as well as the attractive aspects of the job. (See chapter 19.)[24]

Manager Selection

The most important hiring decisions made in organizations involve the selection of managers, because they play a critical role in organizational success. The task of selecting managers is, however, a difficult one because of the complexity of the manager's job. Because managers are required to utilize a wide variety of skills and abilities, their selection depends on accurate assessment of candidates' proven or potential skills and abilities.

Selecting Experienced Managers. Organizations may seek to hire experienced managers for a variety of reasons. A newly created post may require a manager with experience not available within the organization; an established post may exist and the talent to fill it is unavailable within the organization; a key position might suddenly open and there is no time to train a replacement; or a top performer in a competing organization is sought to improve the organization's own competitive position.

Past performance is generally expected to predict future performance. Experienced managerial candidates will therefore be assessed to the greatest possible extent on their performance record. It is often difficult, however, to obtain verifiable data on a manager's past performance. Moreover, even when results are available, it is difficult for interviewers to judge how much of that performance is due to the manager's ability. The manager may have had unusually able subordinates, may simply have been lucky, or may have sacrificed long-term results to achieve short-term, temporary profits. In short, the manager's apparent past performance may or may not predict the manager's future performance with the organization. For these reasons, interviewers must frequently rely on other assessment tools.

The most important of these tools, as we have already observed, is the interview process; testing is not widely used to assess experienced managers. Experienced managers typically go through several interviews. Their interviewers are almost always higher-level managers in the organization because members of the human resource department do not have close personal experience with the detailed skills and abilities that the available position requires.

The interviewers attempt to assess the candidate's suitability and past performance. Particular emphasis is placed on personal qualities; interviewers will try to determine how well the candidate seems to fit their idea of what a good manager should be. Desirable qualities cannot always be judged in the interview process. Interviewers look, though, for indications of such qualities as *emotional stability*—levelheadedness and ability to operate effectively under pressure; *self-confidence*—an air of assurance and self-esteem; and *interpersonal skill*—the ability to get along with and motivate others. The interviewers also attempt to assess how compatible the candidate's personality, past experience, personal values, and style of operating are with the organization.

Selecting Potential Managers. Potential managers usually enter the organization after graduating from college. They will typically take entry-level positions—a research job or a staff job, or a position in a training program. Their performance in these entry-level positions will have a strong influence on the type of managerial job they eventually will receive.

Assessing an individual's potential for managerial performance is difficult because the future manager must be judged on things he or she has not yet done. However, such an assessment is also extremely important, since the potential managers selected may well determine the future success of the organization.

Most assessments of prospective managers begin with a review of school grades. However, except for technical positions, school performance does not seem to be strongly associated with managerial performance. Other aspects of the school record, however, can provide some insights into nonacademic abilities, such as interpersonal skills, leadership qualities, and ability to assume responsibility. For this reason, many organizations look for evidence of extracurricular managerial interest or experience—working on a campus journal, for example, or directing part of a community project.[25] Finally, like experienced managers, the prospective managers may be interviewed extensively to determine whether they have what the interviewers consider to be the appropriate personal styles for managers.

In general, the likelihood of making good candidate choices is improved when several managers interview each candidate. The multiplicity of viewpoints made available through this approach lessens the possibility that effective managers will be lost to the organization because of one interviewer's bias or point of view.

Assessment Centers

Another method that has proven effective in selecting qualified candidates is the assessment center. Assessment centers were originally used during World War II as a means of selecting OSS (Office of Strategic Services) agents. Assessment centers have since been used with considerable success as devices for predicting the future management performance of both experienced and potential managers.[26] In the assessment center approach, candidates are asked to participate in a wide range of simulation exercises while trained observers note and assess the candidates' behavior. One common exercise is the *in-basket*. In this simulation, the candidate is informed that he or she has just been promoted to a newly vacant position and will have to leave town soon to attend an important meeting. The candidate is given one hour to deal with the memos, letters, reports, telephone messages, and other materials in the previous incumbent's in-basket. The candidate must handle each item in the most appropriate manner and in many cases will have an opportunity to explain or discuss his or her decisions in a follow-up interview.

In the *leaderless group discussion* exercise, the participants are given a problem requiring a group decision. The way the candidates handle themselves in this situation helps to reveal their leadership qualities and interpersonal skills. Candidates may also participate in *management games* geared to the level of the job being filled, make oral presentations, and take any number of tests probing mental ability, general knowledge, and personality.

Assessment centers are not only excellent predictors of management potential but also can serve as part of a management development program. In fact, some graduate schools of business use some of the techniques to guide an individual's self-development program. However, the assessment center approach is so costly that it is restricted to a few relatively large, successful organizations. An assessment typically involves a number of assessors working with a small group of candidates over a period of several days.[27]

Assessment centers have also come under criticism on other grounds. Richard Klimoski, for example, has pointed out that the tests focus on maximum performance under certain conditions rather than typical performance. They prove that a person *can* perform well without evidence that he or she *will* perform well.[28]

Induction and Orientation

Induction and orientation are designed to provide a new employee with the information he or she needs in order to function comfortably and effectively in the organization. Typically, induction and orientation will convey three types of information: (1) general information about the daily work routine; (2) a review of the organization's history, purpose, operations, and products or services, and how the employee's job contributes to the organization's needs; and (3) a detailed presentation, perhaps in a brochure, of the organization's policies, work rules, and employee benefits.

Many studies have shown that employees feel anxiety when they enter an organization. They worry about how well they will perform in the job; they feel inadequate compared to more experienced employees; and they are concerned about how well they will get along with their co-workers. For these reasons, effective induction and orientation programs are deliberately aimed at reducing the anxiety of new employees. Information on the job environment and on supervisors is provided, co-workers are introduced, and questions by new employees are encouraged.[29]

The Effects of Early Job Experiences

Early job experiences appear to play a critical role in the individual's career with the organization. It is during these experiences that the individual's expectations and the organization's expectations confront each other. If these are not compatible, dissatisfaction will result. As might be expected, employee turnover rates are almost always highest among the organization's new employees.

David E. Berlew and Douglas T. Hall found that for management trainees, the amount of challenge in the individual's first job correlated significantly with the individual's subsequent career progress in the organization. Individuals who were initially given demanding tasks internalized high standards of performance and were better prepared for future assignments. Individuals who were given easy assignments appeared less motivated to perform at a high level. After five years, those who were given demanding assignments when they entered the organization were, as a group, higher in the organizational hierarchy than new employees who were not given challenging assignments.[30]

James A. F. Stoner, John D. Aram, and Irwin M. Rubin found a similar relationship between early job experiences and subsequent job performance. The individuals in this study were young MBAs and lawyers who had been given technical-assistance assignments in Africa. The initial reaction of the technical assistants to their jobs was assessed from informal letters that they sent back to the administrators of the assistance program within their first two weeks on the job. These initial reactions correlated significantly with how well the job worked out for both employee and employer for the duration of the one- or two-year assignment.[31]

Training and Development

Training programs are directed toward maintaining and improving *current* job performance, while *development programs* seek to develop skills for *future* jobs. Both managers and nonmanagers may receive help from training and development programs, but the mix of experiences is likely to vary. Nonmanagers are much more likely to be trained in the technical skills required for their current jobs, while managers frequently receive assistance in developing the skills—particularly conceptual and human relations skills—required in future jobs. In our discussion of training and development, we will cover training briefly and then focus on management development.

Training Programs

The need to train new or recently promoted employees is self-evident: Such employees need to learn new skills, and since their motivation is likely to be high, they can be acquainted relatively easily with the skills and behavior expected in their new position. On the other hand, training experienced employees to make their performance more effective can be problematic. The training needs of such employees are not always easy to determine, and when they are determined, the individuals involved may resent being asked to change their established ways of doing their jobs.

There are four procedures that managers can use to determine the training needs of individuals in their organization or subunit:

1. *Performance appraisal*—each employee's work is measured against the performance standards or objectives established for his or her job.
2. *Analysis of job requirements*—the skills or knowledge specified in the appropriate job description are examined. Those employees without necessary skills or knowledge become candidates for a training program.
3. *Organizational analysis*—the effectiveness of the organization and its success in meeting its goals are analyzed to determine where differences exist. For example, members of a department with a high turnover rate or a low performance record might require additional training.
4. *Survey of human resources*—managers as well as nonmanagers are asked to describe what problems they are experiencing in their work and what actions they believe need to be taken to solve them.

Once the organization's training needs have been identified, managers must initiate the appropriate training effort. There are a variety of training approaches that managers can use. The most common of these approaches are *on-the-job training* methods. These include *job rotation,* in which the employee, over a period of time, works on a series of jobs, thereby learning a broad variety of skills; *internship,* in which job training is combined with related classroom instruction; and *apprenticeship,* in which the employee is trained under the guidance of a highly skilled co-worker.

Off-the-job training takes place outside the actual workplace but attempts to simulate actual working conditions. This type of training includes *vestibule training,* in which employees work on the actual equipment and in a realistic job setting but in a different room from the one in which they will be working. The object is to avoid the on-the-job pressures that might interfere with the learning process. In *behaviorally experienced training,* some of the methods used in assessment centers—business games, in-basket simulation, problem-centered cases, and so on—are employed so that the trainee can learn the behavior appropriate for the job through *role playing.* Off-the-job training may focus on the *classroom,* with seminars, lectures, and films, or it may be undertaken by means of *computer-assisted instruction* (CAI), which can both reduce the time needed for training and provide more help for individual trainees.[32]

Management Development Programs

Management development, as we have already suggested, is designed to improve the overall effectiveness of managers in their present positions and to prepare them for greater responsibility when they are promoted. Management development programs have become more prevalent in recent years because of the increasingly complex demands being made of managers and because letting experience alone train managers is a time-consuming and unreliable process. The investment of many companies in management development can be quite large. For example, for years a minimum of 40 hours of human resource management training has been required by IBM for all new managers,[33] and similar levels of training are continued after this initial involvement.

Early management development activities were program-centered; that is, a program would be designed and administered to managers regardless of their individual differences. However, it is being increasingly recognized that managers differ in ability, experience, and personality. Thus, management development programs are becoming more *manager-centered*—tailored to fit the unique developmental requirements of the managers attending. Before a program is selected, a *needs analysis* is made to identify the particular needs and problems of the manager or group of managers. The appropriate training activities are then recommended.[34]

As in other training programs, there are a number of on-the-job and off-the-job management development approaches.[35]

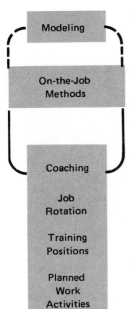

On-the-Job Methods. On-the-job methods are usually preferred in management development programs. The training is far more likely than off-the-job training to be tailored to the individual, job-related, and conveniently located.

Modeling (or imitation), a central part of all behavioral learning, is an informal but important on-the-job way to learn. Imitating the behavior of an outstanding manager is one of the easiest and best ways to learn good managerial habits. (Watching a poor manager, on the other hand, can teach one a few things to avoid doing but not what should be done.) When the manager does more than simply set a good example or act as a role model and takes an active part in his or her subordinate's development, then the training becomes even more effective.

There are four major formal on-the-job development methods:

1. *Coaching*—the training of a subordinate by his or her immediate superior—is by far the most effective management development technique. Unfortunately, many managers are either unable or unwilling to coach their subordinates. To be meaningful, on-the-job coaching must be tempered by considerable restraint—subordinates cannot develop unless they are allowed to work out their problems in their own way. Managers too often feel compelled to tell their subordinates exactly what to do, thereby negating the effectiveness of coaching. In addition, some managers feel threatened by the idea of coaching their subordinates, for fear of creating a rival. In reality, it is the manager who has much to gain from coaching subordinates, since a manager frequently will not be promoted unless there is a successor available to take his or her place.

Many firms, particularly those with MBO programs (see chapter 4), make a point of training their managers in the fine art of coaching. Conscientious managers often keep a "development file" for each subordinate, indicating the training the subordinate is receiving, the skills the subordinate is acquiring, and how well the subordinate is performing. A record of *critical incidents*—situations in which a subordinate displayed desirable or undesirable behavior—may also be included. In discussing these incidents with the subordinate, managers can reinforce good habits ("You really handled that customer's complaint well"), gently point out bad habits ("Do you think you should be firmer with the supplier?"), and identify the areas in which the subordinate needs further development.

2. *Job rotation* involves shifting managers from position to position so that they may broaden their experience and familiarize themselves with various aspects of the firm's operations.

3. *Training positions* are a third method used to develop managers. Trainees are given staff posts immediately under a manager, often with the title of "assistant to." Such assignments give trainees a chance to work with and model themselves after outstanding managers who might otherwise have little contact with them.

4. Finally, *planned work activities* involve giving trainees important work assignments to develop their experience and ability. Trainees may be asked to head a task force or participate in an important committee meeting. Such experiences help them gain insight into how organizations operate and also improve their human relations skills.

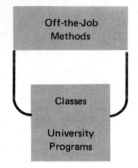

Off-the-Job Methods. Off-the-job development techniques remove individuals from the stresses and ongoing demands of the workplace, enabling them to focus fully on the learning experience. In addition, they provide opportunities for meeting people from other departments or organizations. Thus, they will be exposed to useful new ideas and experiences and will make contacts that may be useful to them when they return to their jobs. The most common off-the-job development methods include in-house classroom instruction and management development programs sponsored by universities and other organizations, such as the American Management Associations.

Almost every management development program includes some form of *classroom instruction*. Specialists from inside or outside the organization are asked to teach trainees a particular subject. To counteract possible passivity and boredom, classroom instruction may be supplemented with case studies, role playing, and business games or simulations. For example, managers may be asked to play roles on both sides in a simulated labor–management dispute.

Some organizations send selected employees to *university-sponsored management development programs*. Many major universities have such programs, which range in length from about a week to three months or more. Some universities (such as MIT and Stanford) also have one-year, full-time study programs for middle-level managers. These managers usually have been slated for promotion; their organizations send them to these university programs to broaden their perspectives and prepare them for movement into general (as opposed to functional) management. University programs will often combine classroom instruction with case studies, role playing, and simulation.

Large corporations are increasingly assuming many of the functions of universities with regard to advanced off-the-job training of employees. U.S. business now spends an estimated $60 billion each year on in-house education, a figure comparable with that spent by the nation's colleges and universities. Some organizations, such as the Rand Corporation, now offer Ph.D. degrees, while Arthur D. Little,

Wang Laboratories, and Northrop Corporation offer master's degrees. By 1988, more than two dozen corporations and industry associations are expected to be offering advanced, accredited academic degrees. Xerox, RCA, and Holiday Inns have each acquired educational facilities that closely resemble university campuses, while IBM, Westinghouse, and Digital Equipment Company have established the National Technological University. The latter is an example of a "satellite university," where high-level continuing education is transmitted via satellite to classrooms throughout the country and abroad.[36]

Conditions for Effective Management Development Programs. One of the greatest challenges to the development program takes place when the trainee returns to his or her job. If the on-the-job environment does not encourage or support the new managerial skills and knowledge, they will quickly disappear. In fact, an individual's performance sometimes actually declines compared with his or her performance before the development program. This has been observed following human relations training, where individuals are taught to use more democratic, participative management styles. Those individuals whose supervisors do not favor such a style may become even more autocratic than they were before the training. For this reason, the support of top management and the trainees' supervisors is important in making a training program effective.

Jack W. Taylor has identified a number of other mistakes that organizations should avoid in order to make their development programs more useful.[37] These mistakes include:

1. *Placing the prime responsibility for training on staff.* Although staff departments can play a major role in developing and executing training programs, they should not be held accountable for developing an organization's human resources. It remains the line managers' responsibility to develop their human resources.
2. *Failing to equip managers for their training role.* Managers who are expected to develop or train their subordinates must be given training themselves in the appropriate developmental skills.
3. *Making a hasty needs analysis.* For the training program to be properly tailored to the individual, the needs analysis must be thorough.
4. *Substituting training for selection.* Training cannot create potential; it can only help to develop it. Managers need to select individuals who can benefit from a development program.
5. *Limiting training to the classroom.* Some experience in the work environment is necessary to make training successful.
6. *Trying to modify the trainee's personality.* Training can be used to change some dysfunctional behaviors, but using training to try to change a person's personality is both unproductive and unethical.

Performance Appraisal

Performance appraisal is one of the most important tasks any manager has, yet it is one that most managers freely admit they have difficulty in handling adequately. It is not always easy to judge a subordinate's performance accurately, and it is often even more difficult to convey that judgment to the subordinate in a constructive and painless manner.

Informal and Formal Appraisal

We will use the term *performance appraisal* to mean the continuous process of feeding back to subordinates information about how well they are doing their work for the organization. This process occurs both informally and systematically. *Informal appraisal* is conducted on a day-to-day basis. The manager spontaneously mentions that a particular piece of work was performed well or poorly; or, the subordinate stops by the manager's office to find out how a particular piece of work was received. Because of the close connection between the behavior and the feedback on it, informal appraisal quickly encourages desirable performance and discourages undesirable performance before it becomes ingrained. An organization's employees must perceive informal appraisal not merely as a casual occurrence but as an important activity, an integral part of the organization's culture.[38]

Systematic appraisal occurs semiannually or annually on a formalized basis. Such appraisal has four major purposes: (1) It lets subordinates know formally how their current performance is being rated; (2) it identifies those subordinates who deserve merit raises; (3) it locates those subordinates who require additional training; and (4) it plays an important role in identifying those subordinates who are candidates for promotion.

It is important for managers to differentiate between the current performance and the promotability (potential performance) of subordinates. Managers in many organizations fail to make this distinction; they assume that a person with the skills and ability to perform well in one job will automatically perform well in a different or more responsible position. For this reason people are often promoted to positions in which they cannot perform adequately.[39]

Formal Appraisal Approaches

Who is responsible for formal performance appraisals? In answer to this question, four basic appraisal approaches have evolved in organizations.

The first approach, *a superior's rating of subordinates,* is by far the most common. However, other approaches are becoming more popular and can be a valuable supplement to appraisal by a single superior.

A group of superiors rating subordinates is the second most frequently used appraisal approach. Subordinates are rated by a managerial committee or by a series of managers who fill out separate rating forms. This approach, because it relies on the views of a number of people, is often more effective than appraisal by a single superior. However, it is time-consuming and often dilutes subordinates' feelings of accountability to their immediate superior.

The third appraisal approach is *a group of peers rating a colleague.* The individual is rated separately and on paper by his or her co-workers on the same organizational level. This approach is least common in business organizations because of the difficulty of asking employees to make appraisals on which raise or promotion decisions can be based. It is used mainly in the military, particularly in military academies, to identify leadership potential.

In the fourth approach, *subordinates' rating of bosses,* subordinates evaluate their superior's performance. This approach has a common analog in colleges, where students are often asked to evaluate their teacher on a number of performance measures. Although not widely used in business organizations, this approach is becoming a more common method of evaluating managers and helping them improve their performance.[40]

Traditionally, appraisals have concentrated on such personal characteristics as intelligence, decisiveness, creativity, and ability to get along with others. Today, however, appraisals are increasingly based on the individual's performance—that is, on how well the subordinate is helping the organization achieve its goals. MBO (see chapter 4) is an example of a performance-based appraisal approach that involves establishing specific objectives and comparing performance against those objectives. The box below lists and defines the major current approaches to performance appraisal.

Problems of Appraisal

Probably the most influential study of performance appraisal was conducted at the General Electric Company in the early 1960s by Herbert Meyer and his associates.[41] They found that formal appraisals by managers are often ineffective in improving the performance of subordinates. Individuals who were formally criticized about their job performance once or twice a year tended to become defensive and resentful. Their performance after the appraisal interview tended to decline.

DEFINITIONS OF PERFORMANCE APPRAISAL APPROACHES

Graphic rating	Assessing performance by a graph or line representing the range of a personal trait or dimension of the job.
Behavioral Rating	Assessing performance by specific descriptions of work behavior.
Work standards approach	Comparing actual performance against expected levels of performance.
Essay	Writing a commentary discussing an individual's strengths, weaknesses, and so forth.
Management by objectives (MBO) approach	Setting of future objectives and action plans jointly by subordinate and supervisor and then measuring outcome against goals.
Objectives-based approach	Setting of future objectives (without action plans) jointly by subordinate and supervisor and then measuring outcome against goals.
Forced distribution systems	Rating employees on scales with a set percentage of employees assigned for each scale point.

Source: Adapted, by permission of the publisher, from "Strategic Issues in Performance Appraisal: Theory and Practiace," by Charles J. Fombrun and Robert L. Laud, *Personnel*, November–December 1983, p. 25. Copyright © 1983 Periodicals Division, American Management Associations, New York. All rights reserved.

Meyer and his colleagues suggest that the goal of appraisal should be to improve the future performance of subordinates and that this goal is difficult to achieve if managers act in their traditional role of judge. Instead, Meyer and his colleagues argue, a manager and an individual subordinate should set performance goals together and then evaluate progress toward those goals. Participatory appraisal, they found, leads to both greater satisfaction and higher performance on the job. Meyer and his co-workers also suggest that the appraisal process should be a continuous one; that is, it should become part of the day-to-day interaction between managers and subordinates rather than be imposed on subordinates once or twice a year.

Aside from the tendency to judge subordinates, there are a number of other pitfalls managers must avoid in order to make their formal and informal appraisal programs effective:

1. *Shifting standards.* Some managers rate each subordinate by different standards and expectations. A low-performing but motivated employee, for example, might be rated higher than a top-performing but seemingly indifferent employee. To be effective, the appraisal method must be perceived by subordinates as based on uniform, fair standards.[42]

2. *Rater bias.* Some managers allow their personal biases to distort the ratings they give subordinates. These biases may be gross prejudices regarding not only sex, color, race, or religion but also other personal characteristics, such as age, style of clothing, or political viewpoint. An increasing number of organizations try to deal with this problem by requiring documentation or explanations for rating reports.

3. *Different rater patterns.* Managers (like teachers) differ in their rating styles. Some managers rate harshly, others rate easily. The lack of uniform rating standards is unfair to employees, who can become confused about where they stand; it is also unfair to the organization, since it becomes difficult to decide which employees should be rewarded. Differences in rating patterns can be reduced through precise definitions of each item on the rating form.

4. *The halo effect.* There is a common tendency, known as the halo effect, to rate subordinates high or low on all performance measures based on one of their characteristics. For example, an employee who works late constantly might be rated high on productivity and quality of output as well as on motivation. Similarly, an attractive or popular employee might be given a high overall rating. Rating employees separately on each of a number of performance measures and encouraging raters to guard against the halo effect are two ways the halo effect can be reduced.

Approximately two decades after the original study by Meyer and his colleagues, a research team headed by Edward E. Lawler, Allan M. Mohrman, and Susan M. Resnick conducted a followup study at GE. Their study supported many of the original findings and led to the following additional recommendations:[43]

1. **Top management should take care to integrate performance appraisal into the overall organizational culture and human resource strategy, to emphasize its importance, and to evaluate it continually.**

2. **The nature of an employee's job, as well as the performance expectations attached to it and the ways in which performance will be measured, should all be made clear at the outset of employment.**

3. Discussions about the bases for pay increases and the relationship between pay and performance should be a natural and important part of the appraisal process.
4. In a *separate* process, well integrated into the overall human resource management system, a manager should discuss an employee's career development opportunities and outline that employee's developmental needs to reach his or her potential.
5. The employee should be an equal and active partner with the manager throughout the appraisal process.

Promotions, Transfers, Demotions, and Separations

The movement of personnel within an organization—their promotion, transfer, demotion, and separation—is a major aspect of human resource management. The actual decisions about whom to promote and whom to fire can also be among the most difficult, and most important, a manager has to make.

Promotions

Because the possibility of advancement serves as a major incentive for superior managerial performance, it is extremely important that promotions be fair—that is, based on merit and untainted by favoritism. Promotions are the most significant way to recognize superior performance; however, no manager should be promoted to a position in which his or her strengths cannot be applied. For example, a district manager who functions best in a post that requires independent judgment and quick decision making might be out of place in a higher-level staff post where final decisions would be the line manager's responsibility.

Even when promotions are fair and appropriate, they can still create a number of problems. One major problem is that organization members bypassed for promotion frequently feel resentful, which may affect their morale and productivity. Many organizations compound this resentment by turning the promotion process into a top-secret affair, thereby creating unrealistic expectations among all the lower-level members of the subunit. Making it clearer who the favored candidate is (if seniority is not a giveaway) and explaining the promotion once it is made will help subordinates accept the authority of the newly promoted manager.

Another major problem in promotions is discrimination. Most people accept the need or at least the legal obligation to avoid racial, sex, or age discrimination in the hiring process. However, less attention has been paid to discrimination against women, the aged, and minority groups in promotion decisions. Despite laws such as the Civil Rights Act of 1964 and the Age Discrimination Employment Act, women and minority groups are still underrepresented in upper-level management positions, and older employees are sometimes passed over for promotion because of their age. Affirmative action programs, which seek to ensure that members of groups that have been discriminated against are groomed for advancement, have become more widespread. They are one means of overcoming the effects of past discrimination.

Transfers

Transfers serve a number of purposes. They are used to give people broader job experiences as part of their development and to fill vacancies as they occur. Transfers are also used to keep promotion ladders open and to keep individuals interested in the work. For example, if an individual is doing a good job in one position but is not considered promotable, he or she may be blocking the progress of those at a lower-level. In a large firm, such an individual might be transferred to a job outside the major channels of promotion. Similarly, many middle managers reach a plateau simply because there is no room for all of them at the top. Such managers may be shifted to other positions to keep their job motivation and interest high. Finally, inadequately performing employees may be transferred to other jobs simply because a higher-level manager is reluctant to demote or separate them.

Demotions and Separations

If a manager proves ineffective in a given position, that manager may be transferred, asked to go for retraining or further development, or be fired. The transfer may be a demotion, a shift to another same-level position, or even a "promotion" to a position with a more impressive title but with less responsibility. Demotion is an infrequently used option, since in most cases the demoted manager and his or her former peers and subordinates find their continuing relationships difficult to handle.

Where demotion or other transfer is not feasible, it is usually better to separate than to let the poor performer stay on the job. It is helpful to keep in mind that poor performance does not necessarily mean incompetence. The corporate environment, the personality of the poor performer's superior, the lack of further advancement opportunities, the conviction that one has been treated unfairly can all contribute to lackluster performance. A surprising number of times, a man or woman dismissed from one firm becomes a solid success in another. Thus, no matter how agonizing separation decisions may be, the logic of human resource planning and management development frequently requires that they be made. When handled properly, separation can work out in the best interests of the individual, who may reach his or her full potential in a different environment, as well as ensuring more effective management for the organization. Some companies, in order to assist separated employees, provide *outplacement* services to help them find new and more suitable employment.

Evaluating the Effectiveness of Human Resources Departments

The effectiveness of a human resources department is measured by the extent to which it meets the needs and demands of all those who have a stake in the organization. It is therefore positively related to the organization's productivity and growth, as well as to job satisfaction and productivity in the work force and the quality, strength, and professionalism of managers.[44] The criteria of effectiveness have traditionally included such factors as turnover rate, morale, number of grievances, and accident rate. Meeting the expectations of the various governmental regulatory agencies is now an additional and important area of concern.[45]

Human Resource Information Systems. The *human resource information system (HRIS)* represents for many organizations an effective management tool. A HRIS is an information system for the collection, storage, maintenance, retrieval, and validation of all data relating to an organization's personnel. In addition to facilitating many routine administrative chores, a computer-oriented HRIS, properly designed and operated, can greatly increase the timely and practical use of human resource information.[46] Specialized software is widely available to simplify such tasks as recruiting, job analysis, government reporting, compensation, and succession planning.[47] (See the discussion of decision support systems [DSS] and management information systems [MIS] in chapters 6 and 22.)

Summary

The staffing process includes (1) human resource planning, (2) recruitment, (3) selection, (4) induction and orientation, (5) training and development, (6) performance appraisal, (7) transfer, promotion, and demotion, and (8) separation.

Human resource planning includes planning for the future personnel needs of the organization, planning what the future balance of the organization's personnel will be, planning a recruitment–selection or layoff program, and planning a development program. Human resource plans are based on forecasting, often computer-assisted, and the human resource audit, in which the skills and performance of organization members are appraised. To be meaningful, human resource plans have to take into consideration the strategic plan and the external environment of the organization.

General and specialized recruitment are designed to supply the organization with a sufficiently large pool of job candidates. Job recruits can be drawn from within or outside the organization. However, before recruitment can take place, a job analysis, consisting of the position description and job specification, must be made.

Successive federal and state legislation, executive orders, and legal decisions since the early 1960s have mandated equal employment opportunity (EEO) regardless of race, sex, age, color, religion, or ethnic group membership. EEO legislation also covers Vietnam-era and disabled veterans and the physically and mentally handicapped. Nondiscriminatory procedures must provide equal access to jobs, training, and promotion, and equal treatment in the work environment. Firms doing business with the federal government are subject to affirmative action (AA) programs to add and develop women and minority group members.

The selection process follows a seven-step procedure: completed job application, initial screening interview, testing, background investigation, in-depth selection interview, physical examination, and job offer. For managerial positions, the in-depth interview is probably the most important step. Ideally, it should be realistic and factually based. Assessment centers may also be used to select managers.

Induction and orientation help the new employee and the organization accommodate to each other. Giving new employees challenging assignments has been shown to correlate with future success.

Training programs seek to maintain and improve current job performance, while development programs are designed to impart skills needed in future jobs. The need for training may be determined through performance appraisal, job requirements, organizational analysis, and human resource surveys. Both training and development methods can be classified as on-the-job or off-the-job. Coaching is the most important formal on-the-job development method. Other development methods include job rotation and classroom teaching. Both training and development should be reinforced in the work situation.

Performance appraisal may be informal or systematic. To improve performance, appraisal should be based on goals jointly set by managers and subordinates. Problems of appraisal include shifting standards, rater bias, different rater patterns, and the halo effect.

To be useful as employee incentives, promotions must be fair. Discrimination in promotion, though illegal, has still not disappeared.

Transfers are used to broaden a manager's experience, to fill vacant positions, and to relocate employees whom the organization does not want to demote, promote, or fire. Demotions are an infrequently used option in dealing with ineffective managers. Separations, though painful, are more widely used and frequently prove beneficial to the individual as well as to the organization.

The performance of a human resources department is positively related to the productivity and growth of an organization. Computer-oriented human resource information systems (HRIS) are useful tools for managing organizational human resources.

Review Questions

1. What are the steps in the staffing process? Are managers likely to be engaged in more than one step at a time? Why or why not?

2. Why is human resource planning necessary? Name the four steps in human resource planning. What factors must managers of a human resource planning program consider?

3. What methods of recruitment can managers use? What are the advantages and disadvantages of recruitment from within?

4. What changes have occurred in EEO and affirmative action in recent years? What are the implications for managers?

5. What is the standard, seven-step hiring sequence? Is this sequence the same under all conditions? Why or why not?

6. What are the defects of in-depth interviews? How can these defects be minimized?

7. What information is induction and orientation designed to provide?

8. What is the difference between training and development?

9. What development approaches and methods can managers use? Which method is most effective?

10. What are the basic differences between systematic and informal appraisal? What are the four basic appraisal approaches? How may formal appraisals be made more effective in leading to improved performance? What appraisal pitfalls do managers need to avoid?

11. What are the problems associated with promotions? How may these problems be overcome?

12. When are transfers used in organizations?

13. What is the best way to evaluate the effectiveness of a human resource management system?

Notes

1. Raymond E. Miles and Charles C. Snow, "Designing Strategic Human Resource Systems," *Organizational Dynamics* 13, no. 1 (Summer 1984):36.

2. The following books, from which we have drawn some of the material in this chapter, treat the staffing function in detail: George T. Milkovich and William F. Glueck, *Personnel: Human Resources Management,* 4th ed. (Plano, Tex.: Business Publications, 1985); Randall S. Schuler and Stuart Youngblood, *Effective Personnel Management,* 2nd ed. (St. Paul, Minn.: West Publishing, 1986); and Frederick E. Schuster, *Human Resource Management,* 2nd ed. (Reston, Va.: Reston, 1985). See also Wendell L. French, *Managing Human Resources* (Boston: Houghton Mifflin, 1986); and Douglas T. Hall and James G. Goodale, *Human Resource Management* (Glenview, Ill.: Scott, Foresman, 1986).

3. See Edwin L. Miller, Elmer H. Burack, and Maryann H. Albrecht, *Management of Human Resources* (Englewood Cliffs, N.J.: Prentice-Hall, 1980); and Burckhardt Wenzel, "Planning for Manpower Utilization," *Personnel Administrator* 15, no. 3 (May–June 1970):36–40.

4. Jennifer McQueen, "Integrating Human Resource Planning with Strategic Planning," *Canadian Public Administration* 27, no. 1 (Spring 1984):1–13; Judy D. Olian and Sara L. Rynes, "Organizational Staffing: Integrating Practice with Strategy," *Industrial Relations* 23, no. 2 (Spring 1984):170–183; and Randall S. Schuler and Ian C. MacMillan, "Gaining Competitive Advantage through Human Resource Management Practices," *Human Resource Management* 23, no. 3 (Fall 1984):241–255.

5. For a survey of recent advances in task analysis, see Kenneth N. Wexley, "Personnel Training," *Annual Review of Psychology* 35 (1984):522–525.

6. K. H. Chan, "Decision Support System for Human Resource Management," *Journal of Systems Management* 35, no. 4 (April 1984):17–25. See also Sheldon Zedeck and Wayne F. Cascio, "Psychological Issues in Personnel Decisions," *Annual Review of Psychology* 35 (1984):461–518.

7. See John B. Miner and Mary G. Miner, *Personnel and Industrial Relations,* 3d ed. (New York: Macmillan, 1977); Richard M. Coffina, "Management Recruitment Is a Two-Way Street," *Personnel Journal* 58, no. 2 (February 1979):86–89; and John P. Wanous, *Organizational Entry: Recruitment, Selection, and Socialization of Newcomers* (Reading, Mass.: Addison-Wesley, 1980).

8. See Jarice Hanson, "Internships and the Individual: Suggestions for Implementing (or Improving) an Internship Program," *Communication Education* 33, no. 1 (January 1984):53–61.

9. William Serrin, "Experts Say Job Bias Against Women Persists," *New York Times,* November 25, 1984, pp. A1, A32.

10. Our discussion of equal employment opportunity and affirmative action issues derives from Terry L. Leap, William H. Holley, Jr., and Hubert S. Feild, "Equal Employment Opportunity and Its Implications for Personnel Practices in the 1980s," *Labor Law Journal* 31, no. 11 (November 1980):669–682; and Francine S. Hall and Maryann H. Albrecht, *The Management of Affirmative Action* (Santa Monica, Calif.: Goodyear, 1979), pp. 1–23. See also David P. Twomey, *A Concise Guide to Employment Law* (Cincinnati: South-Western, 1986).

11. Leap, Holley, and Feild, "Equal Employment Opportunity," pp. 677–679. See also Bette Ann Stead, *Women in Management* (Englewood Cliffs, N.J.: Prentice-Hall, 1978). Attitudes toward women in an organization might be assessed using the MATWES scale in Peter Dubno, John Costas, Hugh Cannon, Charles Wankel, and Hussein Emin, "An Empirically Keyed Scale for Measuring Managerial Attitudes Toward Women Executives," *Psychology of Women Quarterly* 3, no. 4 (Summer 1979):357–364.

12. Leap, Holley, and Feild, "Equal Employment Opportunity," p. 671. See also Richard A. Fear and James F. Ross, *Jobs, Dollars, and EEO* (New York: McGraw-Hill, 1983).

13. Hall and Albrecht, *The Management of Affirmative Action,* pp. 9–10.

14. Ibid., p. 19.

15. The case was *American Tobacco* v. *Patterson,* cited in Karen Paul and George Sullivan, "Equal Employment Opportunity vs. Seniority Rights: The Emergence of a Changing Social Policy," *Business and Society* 23, no. 1 (Spring 1984):8–14. See also Philip Shenon, "U.S. Acts to Stop Quotas on Hiring It Once Supported," *New York Times,* April 30, 1985, pp. A1, A22.

16. Birch Bayh, "Unfair Treatment of Cancer Victims," *New York Times,* June 22, 1985, p. 27.

17. See Lionel C. Skaggs, Reita Hall Bomar, Roger S. McCullough, Ann Ward, and Fred Rogan, "Good Sense Management: The Economics of EEO/AA Training," *Journal of the College and University Personnel Association* 34, no. 4 (Winter 1983):1–9; William L. Kandel, "Current Developments in EEO: Insurance and EEO," *Employee Relations Law Journal* 9, no. 1 (1983):136–144; David A. Pierson, Karen S. Koziara, and Russell E. Johannesson, "Equal Pay for Jobs of Comparable Worth: A Quantified Job Content Approach," *Public Personnel Management Journal* 12, no. 4 (Winter 1983):445–460; and Robert Pear, "Equal Pay Is Not Needed for Jobs of Comparable Worth, U.S. Says," *New York Times,* June 18, 1985, p. A12.

18. James Ledvinka and W. Bartley Hildreth, "Integrating Planned-Change Intervention and Computer Simulation Technology: The Case of Affirmative Action," *Journal of Applied Behavioral Science* 20, no. 2 (1984):125–140.

19. See, for example, Robert Hershey, "The Application Form," *Personnel* 48, no. 1 (January–February 1971):38; and Irwin L. Goldstein, "The Application Blank: How Honest Are the Responses?" *Journal of Applied Psychology* 55, no. 5 (October 1971):491.

20. David Tuller, "What's New in Employment Testing?" *New York Times,* February 24, 1985, p. F17.

21. Kirk Johnson, "Why References Aren't 'Available on Request,'" *New York Times,* June 9, 1985, pp. F8–F9.

22. See Robert E. Carlson, Donald P. Schwab, and Herbert G. Heneman III, "Agreement among Selection Interview Styles," *Journal of Industrial Psychology* 5, no. 1 (March 1970):8–17.

23. Richard G. Nehrbass, "Psychological Barriers to Effective Employment Interviewing," *Personnel Journal* 56, no. 2 (February 1977):60–64.

24. See Wanous, *Organizational Entry.*

25. See Frank Malinowski, "Job Selection Using Task Analysis," *Personnel Journal* 60, no. 4 (April 1981):288–291.

26. See Larry D. Alexander, "An Exploratory Study of the Utilization of Assessment Center Results," *Academy of Management Journal* 22, no. 1 (March 1979):152–157. An excellent description of the well-known AT&T assessment center can be found in Douglas W. Bray, Richard J. Campbell, and Donald Grant, *Formative Years in Business* (New York: Wiley, 1974).

27. For additional information on assessment centers, see Marilee S. Niehoff, "Assessment Centers: Decision-Making Information from Non-Test-Based Methods," *Small Group Behavior* 14, no. 3 (August 1983):353–358; and Clive A. Fletcher and Victor Dulewicz, "An Empirical Study of a U.K.-Based Assessment Centre," *Journal of Management Studies* 21, no. 1 (1984):83–97.

28. Richard Klimoski, quoted in Barbara Lovenheim, "A Test to Uncover Managerial Skills: Hopefuls Try Out, Watched by Assessors," *New York Times,* January 21, 1979, pp. D1, D4.

29. See, for example, Earl R. Gomersall and M. Scott Myers, "Breakthrough in On-the-Job Training," *Harvard Business Review* 44, no. 4 (July–August 1966):62–72. See also Gareth R. Jones, "Organizational Socialization as Information Processing Activity: A Life History Analysis," *Human Organization* 42, no. 4 (1983):314–320.

30. David E. Berlew and Douglas T. Hall, "The Socialization of Managers," *Administrative Science Quarterly* 11, no. 2 (September 1966):207–223.

31. James A. F. Stoner, John D. Aram, and Irwin M. Rubin, "Factors Associated with Effective Performance in Overseas Work Assignments," *Personnel Psychology* 25, no. 2 (Summer 1972):303–318.

32. Dennis L. Dossett and Patti R. Hulvershorn, "Increasing Technical Training Efficiency: Peer Training via Computer-Assisted Instruction," *Journal of Applied Psychology* 68, no. 4 (November 1983):552–558; Stephen Schwade, "Is It Time to Consider Computer-Based Training?" *Personnel Administrator* 30, no. 2 (February 1985):25–28; and William C. Heck, "Computer-Based Training—The Choice Is Yours," *Personnel Administrator* 30, no. 2 (February 1985):39–48.

33. Milkovich and Glueck, *Personnel,* pp. 72–73.

34. On needs analysis, see F. L. Ulschak, *Human Resource Development: The Theory and Practice of Need Assessment* (Reston, Va.: Reston, 1983).

35. Lynn S. Summers, "Out of the Ivory Tower: A Demand-Side Look at the Future of Management Development," *Training and Development Journal* 38, no. 1 (January 1984):97–101; and Jan Asplind, Håkan Behrendtz, and Frank Jernberg, "The Norwegian Savings Banks Case: Implementation and Consequences of a Broadly Scoped, Long-Term, System-Driven Program for Management Development," *Journal of Applied Behavioral Science* 19, no. 3 (1983):381–394.

36. Edward B. Fiske, "Booming Corporate Education Efforts Rival College Programs, Study Says," *New York Times,* January 28, 1985, p. A10.

37. Jack W. Taylor, "Ten Serious Mistakes in Management Training/Development," *Personnel Journal* 53, no. 5 (May 1974):357–362.

38. Edward E. Lawler III, Allan M. Mohrman, Jr., and Susan M. Resnick, "Performance Appraisal Revisited," *Organizational Dynamics* 13, no. 1 (Summer 1984):20–35; and Roy Serpa, "Why Many Organizations—Despite Good Intentions—Often Fail to Give Employees Fair and Useful Performance Review," *Management Review* 73, no. 7 (July 1984):41–45.

39. See Laurence J. Peter and Raymond Hull, *The Peter Principle* (New York: Morrow, 1969).

40. In a fifth approach, the training and development section of the human resources department appraises performance and assists line managers in implementing any of the four approaches already described. See R. Bruce McAfee, "Performance Appraisal: Whose Function?" *Personnel Journal* 60, no. 4 (April 1981):298–299.

41. Herbert H. Meyer, Emanual Kay, and John R. P. French, "Split Roles in Performance Appraisal," *Harvard Business Review* 43, no. 1 (January–February 1965):123–129. See also Douglas M. McGregor, "An Uneasy Look at Performance Appraisal," *Harvard Business Review* 35, no. 3 (May–June 1957):89–94.

42. See Ed Yager, "A Critique of Performance Appraisal Systems," *Personnel Journal* 60, no. 4 (February 1981):129–133.

43. See Lawler, Mohrman, and Resnick, "Performance Appraisal Revisited," pp. 31–34. See also Charles J. Fombrun and Robert L. Laud, "Strategic Issues in Performance Appraisal: Theory and Practice," *Personnel* 60, no. 6 (November–December 1983):23–31; and Donald L. Kirkpatrick, "Two Ways to Evaluate Your Performance Appraisal System," *Training and Development Journal* 38, no. 8 (August 1984):38–40.

44. Harish C. Jain, "Management of Human Resources and Productivity," *Journal of Business Ethics* 2, no. 4 (November 1983):273–289.

45. Anne Tsui, "Personnel Department Effectiveness," *Industrial Relations* 23, no. 2 (Spring 1984):184–197.

46. See Milkovich and Glueck, *Personnel,* pp. 634–650; Randall S. Schuler, *Personnel and Human Resource Management* (St. Paul, Minn.: West Publishing, 1984), p. 46; Lee White, "Keeping Track of Human Resources," *Computerworld Focus,* May 8, 1985, pp. 39–43; and Ren Nardoni, "The Building Blocks of a Successful Microcomputer System," *Personnel Journal* 64, no. 1 (January 1985):28–34.

47. The following are representative examples of human resource management software: *Executrak: Microcomputer Succession Planning System* (Fairfield, Iowa: Corporate Education Resources, 1984); *Human Resource System* (Walnut Creek, Calif.: Integral Systems, 1985); and *Decision Support Services and Tools for Human Resource Management* (Los Altos, Calif.: SCOPOS, 1983).

CASE STUDY: Employee Testing at Toy City

Toy City, Inc., one of the nation's largest toy retailers, has been plagued with a variety of personnel problems that are hurting its operations and, in some cases, its reputation with its customers.

Toy City has adopted the strategy of becoming the single largest toy retailer in each geographic region. Rather than clustering several smaller stores in an area, it opens one large store and depends on its very complete stock of the latest toys to attract distant customers. More than two-thirds of Toy City's work force is under 25 years old, including many assistant managers and some supervisors, who are always promoted from within. There is relatively little lateral transfer of personnel among the different stores. High employee turnover, theft by employees (especially of expensive electronic games and home computers), and drug use in the stock areas are endemic.

Toy City's director of human resources, Judith Abrams, recently purchased a computerized employee testing system that she believed would help identify troublesome employees and more effectively screen prospective hires. Over the space of several weeks, all employees were given a standardized computer test that asked them, among other questions, whether they had a criminal record or had ever used drugs. While taking the test, they were hooked up to a lie detector.

Abrams was astonished to discover that nearly 40 percent of Toy City's employees, including a surprisingly high number of supervisors, were unable to pass some part of the test. She now faces a difficult problem. In a labor-intensive retail operation like Toy City's, simply firing such a high proportion of employees would cause massive dislocation. And many prospective employees are also unable to pass the test, making it difficult to fill the ranks. In addition, more minority than white employees failed the test. Hiring and firing on the basis of the test results might be seen as an act of discrimination with legal ramifications. At the same time, current personnel problems are eroding Toy City's profitability and cannot be allowed to continue.

Source: This case was prepared by Jonathan Rogers.

Case Questions
1. What is the essential problem in this case?
2. Was employee testing the right solution to Toy City's personnel problems?
3. Should Abrams ditch the testing program? Would training and/or management development programs be more effective?
4. Has human resource planning been neglected at Toy City?

13 MANAGING ORGANIZATIONAL CHANGE AND DEVELOPMENT

Upon completing this chapter you should be able to:

1. Identify two constructive responses to change pressures and suggest when each approach is appropriate.
2. Describe internal and external forces for organizational change.
3. Summarize the six phases of the organizational change process.
4. Identify the sources of resistance to change and the ways this resistance can be overcome.
5. Describe the three major approaches to change.
6. Describe a model of individual change.
7. Describe the organizational development approach to change and the assumptions and values upon which this approach is based.
8. Discuss the effect of organizational culture on change.

n chapter 10 we saw how organizations can be designed to fit the environments in which they operate. Even if an organization's design is appropriate for its environment at a given time, the managers must anticipate changes in the environment that will require future adjustments in the organization's design. Managing such change effectively is not only a challenge but also a necessity for organizational survival.

This chapter will focus on systematic programs to bring about planned change in organizations or their subunits. The forces that create the need for organizational change, when to recognize that the time for change has come, and how to overcome resistance to change will be discussed in turn. Approaches to planned change, with an emphasis on the technique known as organizational development (OD), the assumptions and values on which it is based, and the role of organizational culture will complete our discussion.

Forces for Change

As we saw in chapter 3, organizations depend on and must interact with their external environment in order to survive. Any factor in the external environment that interferes with the organization's ability to attract the human and material resources it needs, or to produce and market its services or products, becomes a force for change. Any factor in the internal environment that affects the way the organization carries out its activities is also a force for change.

External Forces

There are numerous specific types of external forces for change. Increasing costs and scarcity of natural resources, worker safety and antipollution regulations, consumer boycotts, higher levels of education in the labor market, high interest rates—the list of environmental factors that have changed our lives as workers and consumers in recent years goes on. A fatal leak of toxic chemicals from the Union Carbide plant in Bhopal, India, intensified worldwide public concern about safeguards and standards in the chemical industry. Reduced government spending for the arts has led many cultural institutions to restrict their activities and increase their search for funds from other sources. An enormous variety of external forces, from technological advances to competitive actions, can pressure organizations to modify their structure, goals, and methods of operation.

Internal Forces

Pressures for change may also arise from a number of sources within the organization, particularly from new strategies, technologies, and employee attitudes and behavior. For example, a top manager's decision to seek a higher rate of long-term growth will affect the goals of many departments and may even lead to some reorganization. The introduction of automated equipment to perform tasks that previously required human labor may call for a complete change in work routines, training programs, and compensation arrangements. Worker dissatisfaction, as manifested in high turnover rates or strikes, may lead to changes in management policies and practices.

External and internal forces for change are often linked. The link is particularly strong when changes in values and attitudes are involved. Persons with new attitudes enter the organization and cause it to change from within. Many of the changes described in earlier chapters—such as job enrichment programs and the trend toward greater subordinate participation in decision making—represent in part a response to changes in people's attitudes toward authority and expectations of work satisfaction.

Managerial Responses to Pressures for Change

Managers can respond to pressures for change in ways that are ultimately destructive—for example, by denying that they exist, resisting them, or avoiding them. Companies that have lost millions of dollars in lawsuits because of flagrant violations of toxic waste disposal laws are paying the price for denying or resisting change in social values and government regulations. Businesses that were suddenly forced to close down early in 1977 because of natural gas shortages—even though those shortages had been predicted for years—clearly had avoided responding in an adaptive or constructive way to changes in the environment.

To deal with change, managers use two major approaches. First, they *react* to the signs that changes are needed, making piecemeal modifications to deal with particular problems as they arise. Second, they develop a *program of planned change*, making significant investments of time and other resources to alter the ways their organizations operate. In the latter case, they deal not only with present difficulties but with anticipated problems not yet clearly observable.

The first response—which is simpler and less expensive than the second—is necessary for the small, day-to-day adjustments integral to the manager's job. Examples of such adjustments are easy to find: A sales form is modified because the old layout led to errors in specifying quantity and price; young managers are having difficulty with tasks involving financial analysis, so a two-week seminar on financial analysis is arranged; two managers, working together on a high-priority project, temporarily move into adjoining offices until the project is completed. These small changes require minimal planning because they can and should be handled in a quick and routine manner. We will not deal with this type of reactive response in this chapter, since we deal with it throughout the book in descriptions of the daily problems and decisions that managers confront.

The second response, a program of planned change, has been defined by John M. Thomas and Warren G. Bennis as "the deliberate design and implementation of a structural innovation, a new policy or goal, or a change in operating philosophy, climate, and style."[1] Such a response is appropriate when the entire organization, or a major portion of it, must prepare for or adapt to change.

Planned change is greater in scope and magnitude than reactive change. It is a means of dealing with those changes that may be crucial for survival. It involves a greater commitment of time and resources, requires more skills and knowledge for successful implementation, and can lead to more problems if implementation is

"We ought to consider taking Freedley off crisis management."
Drawing by Stevenson; © 1981 The New Yorker Magazine, Inc.

unsuccessful. Because planned change has become so important to many organizations in today's world, it is the subject of the remainder of this chapter.

The Role of the Change Agent

The *change agent* is the individual who is responsible for taking a leadership role in managing the process of change. The individual, group, or organization that is the target of the change attempt is called the *client system*. Change agents can be members of the organization or they can be consultants brought in from outside. For complex and lengthy change programs, it is often desirable that an outside change agent manage the process, since specialized expertise and skills may be required, freedom from distraction by day-to-day operating responsibilities may be essential, and the prestige of being an outsider can be helpful. Outsiders with no vested interests in the organization are often more likely to be confided in, listened to, and able to form objective judgments.[2]

Models of the Change Process

Although organizations are beset by many forces for change, it is important to recognize that other forces act to keep an organization in a state of equilibrium. Forces opposing change are also forces supporting stability or the *status quo*.

To understand how pressures for change and pressures for stability interact, we will present a model that describes how the level of behavior or performance in any organization is influenced by forces that push in opposing directions. Other models will show how an organization, department, or individual can be helped to change, and whether an organization is likely to mobilize the energies necessary for successful change.

Forces for Stability

According to the "force-field" theory of Kurt Lewin, any behavior is the result of an equilibrium between *driving* and *restraining* forces.[3] The driving forces push one way, the restraining forces push the other. The performance that emerges is a reconciliation of the two sets of forces. An increase in the driving forces might increase performance, but it might also increase the restraining forces. For example, a manager may believe that he or she can get improved results by telling subordinates that there will be absolutely no time off until productivity increases. But the likely response of hostility, distrust, and greater resistance may cause additional declines in productivity, even though the formal prohibition against taking time off is observed.

The natural tendency for most of us, if we want change, is to push. However, the equally natural tendency of whomever or whatever is being pushed is to push back: Driving forces activate their own restraining forces. Decreasing the restraining forces, therefore, is normally a more effective way to encourage change than by increasing the driving forces. In the productivity example, the manager would be more likely to get results by identifying pointless bureaucratic bottlenecks and eliminating them.

Lewin's model (see fig. 13–1) reminds us to look for multiple causes of behavior rather than a single cause. It is applicable to our purposes because it is generalized: The forces can be of many types, and the behavior or performance can be that of an individual, group, or entire organization. The equilibrium concept also suggests that organizations have forces that keep performance from falling too low, as well as forces that keep it from rising too high.

Programs of planned change are directed toward removing or weakening the restraining forces and toward creating or strengthening the driving forces that exist in organizations.

The Process of Change

Lewin also studied the process of bringing about effective change. He noted that individuals experience two major obstacles to change. First, they are unwilling (or unable) to alter long-established attitudes and behavior. A manager told that he or she needs to learn a new analytic technique may accept this information with little or no difficulty. But if that same manager is told that he or she is too aggressive and abrasive in dealing with others, the manager is much more likely to resent and reject the information. Suggesting the need to make a change in managerial style or attitude is perceived as a violation of one's self-image and an indication of inadequacy.

The second major obstacle noted by Lewin was that change frequently lasts only a short time. After a brief period of trying to do things differently, individuals often return to their traditional pattern of behavior.

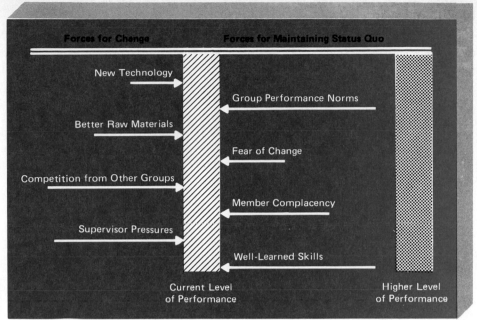

FIGURE 13–1
FORCE-FIELD
DIAGRAM

Note: Length of arrow is equal to amount of force.

Source: Adapted from Edgar F. Huse and Thomas G. Cummings, *Organization Development and Change,* 3d ed. p. 73. Copyright © 1985 by West Publishing Company. All rights reserved.

To overcome obstacles of this sort, Lewin developed a three-step sequential model of the change process. The model, later elaborated by Edgar H. Schein and others, is equally applicable to individuals, groups, or entire organizations.[4] It involves "unfreezing" the present behavior pattern, "changing" or developing a new behavior pattern, and then "refreezing" or reinforcing the new behavior.

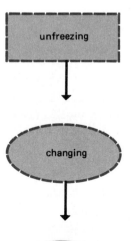

1. *Unfreezing* involves making the need for change so obvious that the individual, group, or organization can readily see and accept it.
2. *Changing* requires a trained change agent to foster new values, attitudes, and behavior through the processes of *identification* and *internalization.* Organization members identify with the change agent's values, attitudes, and behavior, internalizing them once they perceive their effectiveness in performance.
3. *Refreezing* means locking the new behavior pattern into place by means of supporting or reinforcing mechanisms, so that it becomes the new norm.

The System's Readiness for Change

The Lewin-Schein change model implies that planned change efforts may fail because too much energy is needed to move the system to the point where change is desired or because those seeking change do not put enough energy into attempts to bring it about. If the unfreezing step is too difficult, the change effort will fail.

David B. Gleicher has proposed a simple, general formula to help managers determine whether an organizational change effort is likely to be successful:

$$C = (A \times B \times D) > X$$

where C = change; A = level of dissatisfaction with the status quo; B = clearly identified desired state: D = practical first steps toward the desired state; X = cost of the change (in terms of energy, emotions, financial costs, etc.); and the $\times$'s indicate multiplication of A times B times D.

In other words, change takes place when the cost of the change is not too high. The cost of change will be too high unless dissatisfaction with the status quo (A) is quite strong, unless the desired state (B) is clearly evident, and unless practical steps can be taken toward the desired state (D). The multiplication signs indicate that if any of the factors A, B, or D is zero, there will be no change. For example, if we are *satisfied* with the status quo (A), we are not likely to change even if we can envision a more desirable state (B) and we can see practical steps to move toward it (D).

In addition to diagnosing how ready the system is for change and predicting how likely it is that change will take place, the formula can also suggest ways to make the system more ready for change. For example, if dissatisfaction with the current state of affairs is strong on everyone's part, but there is no concrete notion of how things could be better, then a vision of a future ideal state needs to be created and communicated.[5]

Resistance to Change

A major obstacle to the implementation of new policies, goals, or methods of operation is the resistance of organization members to change.

Sources of Resistance to Change

That an outside change agent is often necessary for the success of change programs is an indication of how strong such resistance can be. There are three general sources of resistance to change:[6]

1. *Uncertainty about the causes and effects of change.* Organization members may resist change because they are worried about how their work and lives will be affected by the proposed change. Even if they have some appreciable dissatisfaction with their present work, they may still worry that things will be worse when the proposed changes are implemented. When the change is initiated by someone else, they may feel manipulated and wonder what is the "real" intention behind the change.
2. *Unwillingness to give up existing benefits.* Appropriate change should benefit the organization as a whole, but for some individuals, the cost of change in terms of lost power, prestige, salary, quality of work, or other benefits will not be sufficiently offset by the rewards of change.
3. *Awareness of weaknesses in the changes proposed.* Organization members may resist change because they are aware of potential problems that have apparently been overlooked by the change initiators. Different assessments of the situation represent a type of desirable conflict (see chapter 14) that managers should recognize and use to make their change proposals more effective.

TABLE 13–1 METHODS FOR DEALING WITH RESISTANCE TO CHANGE

Approach	Commonly used when ...	Advantages	Disadvantages
1. Education + communication	There is a lack of information or inaccurate information and analysis.	Once persuaded, people will often help implement the change.	Can be very time-consuming if many people are involved.
2. Participation + involvement	The initiators do not have all the information they need to design the change, and others have considerable power to resist.	People who participate will be committed to implementing change, and any relevant information they have will be integrated into the change plan.	Can be very time-consuming if participators design an inappropriate change.
3. Facilitation + support	People are resisting because of adjustment problems.	No other approach works as well with adjustment problems.	Can be time-consuming, expensive, and still fail.
4. Negotiation + agreement	Some person or group with considerable power to resist will clearly lose out in a change.	Sometimes it is a relatively easy way to avoid major resistance.	Can be too expensive if it alerts others to negotiate for compliance.
5. Manipulation + co-optation	Other tactics will not work, or are too expensive.	It can be a relatively quick and inexpensive solution to resistance problems.	Can lead to future problems if people feel manipulated.
6. Explicit + implicit coercion	Speed is essential, and the change initiators possess considerable power.	It is speedy and can overcome any kind of resistance.	Can be risky if it leaves people angry with the initiators.

Source: Reprinted by permission of the *Harvard Business Review*. An exhibit from "Choosing Strategies for Change" by John P. Kotter and Leonard A. Schlesinger (March–April 1979). Copyright © 1979 by the President and Fellows of Harvard College; all rights reserved.

Overcoming Resistance to Change

Resistance to a change proposal is a signal to managers that something is wrong with the proposal or that mistakes have been made in its presentation. Managers, therefore, must determine the actual causes of resistance and then remain flexible enough to overcome them in an appropriate manner.

Kotter and Schlesinger offer six ways of overcoming resistance to change.[7] Highly situation-dependent, these techniques are discussed below and summarized in table 13–1. More than one of these techniques may be used in any given situation.

1. *Education and communication.* If the need for and logic of the change are explained early—whether individually to subordinates, to groups in meetings, or to entire organizations through elaborate audiovisual education campaigns— the road to successful change may be smoother.
2. *Participation and involvement.* According to a classic study by Lester Coch and John French, resistance to change can be reduced or eliminated by having those involved participate in the design of the change.[8] Paul Lawrence came to similar conclusions, suggesting that in order to avoid resistance, managers should take into account what he called the social effects of change.[9]

3. *Facilitation and support.* Easing the change process and providing support for those caught up in it is another way managers can deal with resistance. Retraining programs, allowing time off after a difficult period, and offering emotional support and understanding may help.

4. *Negotiation and agreement.* It is sometimes necessary for a manager to negotiate with avowed or potential resisters to change, and even to obtain written letters of understanding from the heads of organizational subunits that would be affected by the change.

5. *Manipulation and co-optation.* Sometimes managers covertly steer individuals or groups away from resistance to change, or they may co-opt an individual, perhaps a key person within a group, by giving him or her a desirable role in designing or carrying out the change process.

6. *Explicit and implicit coercion.* Managers may force people to go along with a change by explicit or implicit threats involving loss or transfer of jobs, lack of promotion, and the like. Such methods, though not uncommon, risk making it more difficult to gain support for future change efforts.

Approaches to Planned Change

In the previous sections, we described how the impetus for change develops in an organization and how the change process can be carried out. In this section, we will discuss the various elements of the organization to which the change process can be applied. Specifically, we will try to answer the question: What aspects of the organization can be changed?

Harold J. Leavitt states that an organization can be changed by altering its structure, its technology, and/or its people.[10] Changing the organization's *structure* involves rearranging its internal systems, such as its lines of communication, work flow, or managerial hierarchy. Changing the organization's *technology* means altering its equipment, engineering processes, research techniques, or production methods. Changing the organization's *people* involves changing the selection, training, relationships, attitudes, or roles of organization members. Because we have already dealt with structure and technology to some extent in earlier chapters of this unit, we will deal with them only briefly here. Our main focus will be on change efforts aimed at the people in the organization; in particular, we will emphasize organizational development (OD) programs, which attempt to change the ways people work together to achieve the organization's and their own objectives.

Interdependence of the Three Approaches

Organizations are made up of interacting, interdependent elements under the influence of common forces; that is, organizations are systems. The three elements above—structure, technology, and people—are therefore highly interdependent. A change in one is likely to affect the other elements as well.[11] (See fig. 13–2.) Thus, an effective change program is likely to be one that acknowledges the interaction of these three elements and attempts to change all three, as necessary.

Normally, the greater the amount of change managers desire, the higher the likelihood that the change efforts will have to involve all three elements in order to

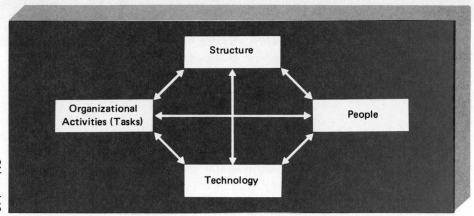

FIGURE 13–2
INTERDEPENDENT
ORGANIZATIONAL
ELEMENTS

Source: Adapted from Harold J. Leavitt, "Applied Organization Change in Industry: Structural, Technical, and Human Approaches," in W. W. Cooper, H. J. Leavitt, and M. W. Shelly II, eds., *New Perspectives in Organization Research* (New York: Wiley, 1964), p. 56. Used by permission.

be effective. For example, let us assume we are managers in a large company and wish to increase sales in two product categories: proprietary drugs and personal care products. To achieve our goal, we might conclude that a major structural change will be required. The sales force will have to be divided into two separate units so that the efforts of salespeople are more focused on each product line and accountability is easier to determine. Such a structural change may well involve technological changes. For example, new computer programs may have to be used to transfer the old marketing and sales information into more appropriate formats; or new sales techniques and procedures may be developed to increase the professionalism of the sales force. In addition, people changes are also likely to be required. Some new sales personnel may have to be hired and trained, and previously hired personnel will have to be retrained or reassigned. Individuals who are unable to adjust to the new circumstances may have to be transferred or even replaced.

Structural Approaches

Leavitt divides structural efforts to bring about organizational change into three areas. *Classical organizational design* seeks to improve organizational performance by carefully defining the job responsibilities of organization members and by creating appropriate divisions of labor and lines of authority. Managers can still improve the performance of their organizations by changing management spans, job descriptions, areas of responsibility, reporting relationships, and the like.

Decentralization creates smaller, self-contained organizational units that increase the motivation and performance of the members of those units and help them to focus their attention on the highest-priority activities. Decentralization also permits each unit to adapt its own structure and technology to the tasks it performs and to its external environment.

Modifying the *flow of work* in the organization and careful grouping of specialties may also lead directly to an improvement in productivity and to higher morale and work satisfaction.[12]

Technological Approaches

Frederick Taylor, through "scientific management" (see chapter 2), attempted to analyze and refine the interactions between workers and machines to increase efficiency in the workplace. Through time and motion studies, setting piece rates, and other efforts to redesign work operations and reward systems, Taylor and later industrial engineers tried to improve organizational performance.

Technological changes are often difficult to implement successfully and may prove incompatible with an organization's structure. For example, Trist and Bamforth found that decreased satisfaction and performance followed the introduction of technological innovations in a mining operation.[13] The miners, who had performed a variety of tasks in small, closely knit work groups, were forced to work on more specialized tasks in a much larger, less cohesive group when the technical changes were implemented. The result was low productivity, more accidents, and a high turnover rate.

Combining Technological and Structural Approaches. *Technostructural* approaches to change attempt to improve performance by changing some aspects of both an organization's structure and its technology. For example, in the mining operation mentioned above, many of the original small work groups were eventually reintroduced in ways that would be compatible with the new mining machinery and led to dramatic improvements in morale and productivity.

Job enlargement and job enrichment programs are other examples of technostructural approaches to change (see chapter 9). In these programs, the tasks that make up a job, the ways the tasks are performed, and employee relationships are altered to improve employee satisfaction and perhaps to increase productivity. In *job enrichment*, some activities from a vertical slice of the organization are combined in one job to make it more challenging (thereby stimulating the jobholder's sense of responsibility). Under *job enlargement*, various tasks at the same level of the organization are combined to provide employees with greater variety on the job and increase their sense of work involvement.

People Approaches

Both the technical and structural approaches attempt to improve organizational performance by changing the work situation, which should cause employee behavior to become more productive. The people approaches, on the other hand, attempt to change the behavior of employees directly by focusing on their skills, attitudes, perceptions, and expectations. Improvements in these may lead to more effective job performance and to employee-initiated changes in the organization's structure and technology.

Figure 13–3 summarizes the three approaches to change.

Efforts to change people's behavior and attitudes can be directed at individuals, groups, or the organization as a whole. Many but not all such efforts are known as organizational development (OD) techniques. Non-OD approaches for changing people include management development (see chapter 12), behavior modification (described in chapter 16), and management by objectives (see chapter 4).

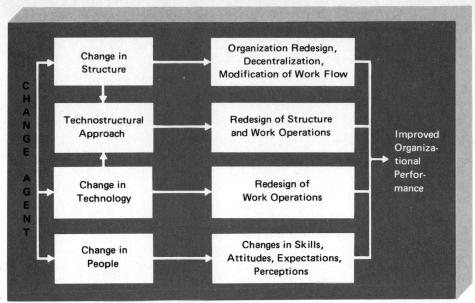

FIGURE 13–3
THE THREE CHANGE
APPROACHES

The Organizational Development Approach

The approaches to change just discussed are particularly appropriate for solving immediate and specific problems. Organizational development (OD), on the other hand, is a longer-term, more encompassing change approach meant to move the entire organization to a higher level of functioning while greatly improving the performance and satisfaction of organization members. Although OD frequently includes structural and technological changes, its primary focus is on changing people and the nature and quality of their working relationships.

As a formal concept OD is new, and "the term 'organizational development' itself remains inconsistently defined, being primarily a convenient label for a variety of activities."[14] We will use a definition that stresses certain aspects of and approaches to managing organizational change or development. However, no definition is sacred. Many activities quite different from the ones we describe are legitimately called OD by their practitioners and users. The field is also changing so rapidly, as we will see, that in a few years the label OD may well be applied to a somewhat different set of activities.

Organizational development has been defined by Wendell French and Cecil Bell as

> a top-management-supported, long-range effort to improve an organization's problem-solving and renewal processes, particularly through a more effective and collaborative diagnosis and management of organization culture—with special emphasis on formal work team, temporary team, and intergroup culture—with the assistance of a consultant-facilitator and the use of the theory and technology of applied behavioral science, including action research.[15]

In this definition, *problem-solving process* refers to the organization's methods of dealing with the threats and opportunities in its environment. For example, managers might choose to solve the organization's problems on their own, or they might participate with subordinates in problem solving and decision making.

Through a *renewal process*, the organization's managers can adapt their problem-solving style and goals to suit the changing demands of the organization's environment. Thus, one aim of OD is to improve an organization's self-renewal process so that managers can more quickly adopt a management style that will be appropriate for the new problems they face.

Collaborative management means management through subordinate participation and power sharing, rather than through the hierarchical imposition of authority.

The term *culture* refers to prevalent patterns of activities, interactions, norms, values, attitudes, and feelings. Culture includes the informal aspects of organizational life as well as the formal—the "covert" attitudes that form the submerged part of the iceberg shown in figure 13–4. Organizational culture will be discussed in greater detail at the end of this chapter.

Action research refers to the way OD change agents go about learning what aspects of the organization need to be improved and how the organization can be

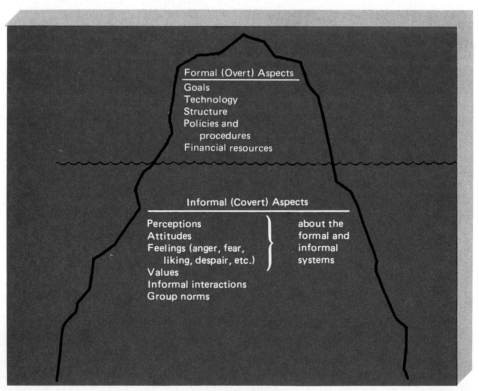

FIGURE 13–4
THE
ORGANIZATIONAL
ICEBERG

Source: Adapted from Stanley N. Herman, "TRW Systems Group," in Wendell L. French and Cecil H. Bell, Jr., *Organization Development: Behavioral Science Interventions for Organization Improvement*, (3rd ed.), p. 19. © 1984. Used by permission of Prentice-Hall, Inc., Englewood Cliffs, N.J.

helped to make these improvements. Briefly, action research involves (1) a preliminary diagnosis of the problem by OD change agents; (2) data gathering to support (or disprove) the diagnosis; (3) feedback of the data to organization members; (4) exploration of the data by organization members; (5) planning of appropriate action; and (6) taking appropriate action.

OD Assumptions and Values

Most practitioners of OD as defined above share certain assumptions about people's needs and aspirations as individuals, as group members, as group leaders, and as members of organizations.

People as Individuals. Two basic assumptions upon which OD is based are that people have a natural desire for personal development and growth and that most people have not only the potential to make a greater contribution to the organization but also the desire to do so. OD aims to overcome those organizational factors that do not encourage or allow members to grow and to contribute more toward the achievement of organizational goals.

People as Group Members and as Leaders. OD practitioners assume that it is important for people to be accepted by their work group and that the climate in most groups and organizations does not encourage open expression of feelings. The necessity of hiding feelings, OD practitioners believe, has a negative effect not only on group members' willingness and ability to solve problems constructively but also on job satisfaction and performance. Encouraging openness can be difficult and risky, but it can also lead to greater job satisfaction and more effective group performance.

People as Members of Organizations. OD practitioners assume the way work groups are linked has a strong influence on how effective they are. For example, if communication between work groups is limited to their managers, coordination and cooperation are likely to be less effective than if all group members can interact. A second assumption is that the policies and methods of managers of large groups (particularly upper-level managers) will have an effect on the way smaller groups operate. And a third assumption is that win–lose conflict strategies—those based on one group or department winning at the expense of another—have little chance of leading to long-term organizational success. It is more desirable to find an approach acceptable to all the groups involved. (See chapter 14.)

Values of OD Change Agents. The values held by OD change agents influence the kinds of changes they suggest. Three widely shared values are that:

1. **Satisfying human needs and aspirations is an important purpose of organizational life. Change agents are therefore directly concerned with self-fulfillment of people in organizations.**
2. **Encouraging the awareness and development of feelings as an integral part of organizational life will improve organizational performance.**
3. **Equalization of power within the organization is not only desirable but also necessary for long-run organizational health.**

In most situations, power equalization involves increasing the opportunities for subordinates to influence their bosses and their organization's activities. In some organizations, however, such as certain universities, hospitals, and city administrations, lower-level participants may have too much power, and the need is to enhance the power of top-level administrators who need that power to operate effectively.

Types of OD Activities

Change agents have many techniques and intervention approaches available to them, not all of which will be used in a given change program. One useful way of classifying these techniques is in terms of the target groups with which they might be employed. The techniques can be used to improve the effectiveness of individuals, the working relationship between two or three individuals, the functioning of groups, the relationship between groups, or the effectiveness of the total organization.[16] Some techniques described here are applicable to more than one target group.

1. *OD for the individual. Sensitivity training* was an early and fairly widespread OD technique. In "T" ("training") groups, about ten participants are guided by a trained leader to increase their sensitivity to and skills in handling interpersonal relationships. Sensitivity training is now less frequently used by organizations, and participants are usually screened to make certain that they can withstand the anxiety raised by a T-group. Precautions are also taken to assure that attendance is truly voluntary.[17]

2. *OD for two or three people. Transactional analysis* (T.A.) concentrates on styles and content of communication (transactions or messages) between people. It teaches people to send messages that are clear and responsible and to give responses that are natural and reasonable. Transactional analysis attempts to reduce destructive communication habits or "games," in which the intent or full meaning of messages is obscured.[18]

3. *OD for teams or groups.* In *process consultation,* a consultant works with organization members to help them understand the dynamics of their working relationships in group or team situations. The consultant helps the group members to change the ways they work together and to develop the diagnostic and problem-solving skills they need for more effective problem solving.[19]

   Team building, a related approach, analyzes the activities, resource allocations, and relationships of a group or team to improve its effectiveness. This technique can be used, for example, to develop a sense of unity among members of a new committee. Team building is described in more detail later in this chapter.[20]

4. *OD for intergroup relations.* To permit an organization to assess its own health and to set up plans of action for improving it, the *confrontation meeting* may be used. This is a one-day meeting of all of an organization's managers in which they discuss problems, analyze the underlying causes, and plan remedial actions. The confrontation meeting is typically used after a major organizational change, such as a merger or the introduction of a new technology.[21]

5. *OD for the total organization.* The *survey feedback* technique can be used to improve the total organization's operations. It involves conducting attitude and other surveys and systematically reporting the results to organization members.

Members then determine what actions need to be taken to solve the problems and exploit the opportunities uncovered in the surveys.

Grid OD is a multipart program that uses many OD techniques. It generally uses questionnaires to gather information on how the organization is functioning and to provide feedback to managers and subordinates. Grid OD is based on the idea that two variables are fundamental to organizations—concern for production and concern for people—and that a high score on both is desirable. Survey feedback and grid OD are examined in more detail in the next section.

OD Techniques in Closeup

We will take a more detailed look at three widely used OD techniques—survey feedback, team building, and Grid OD—each for specific reasons. Survey feedback exemplifies the action research concept, and research suggests it is particularly effective. Team building is employed in many large-scale OD programs; it was chosen for a closer look because OD has historically had a group focus and has stressed the importance of the small group. Grid OD, also widely used, is a well-developed, large-scale, integrated technique designed to change an entire organization.

Survey Feedback. Survey feedback uses a familiar tool—the questionnaire—but does more than simply collect data. The collected data are returned to managers and subordinates so that the survey results can be employed as a basis for change. The survey feedback process, which is summarized and contrasted to traditional questionnaire use in table 13–2, has been described by French and Bell as consisting of five steps:

· *Step 1:* Organization members at the top of the hierarchy are involved in the preliminary planning.
· *Step 2:* Data are collected from all organization members.
· *Step 3:* Data are fed back to the top executive team and then down through the hierarchy in functional teams. . . .
· *Step 4:* Each superior presides at a meeting with his or her subordinates in which the data are discussed and in which (a) subordinates are asked to help interpret the data, (b) plans are made for making constructive changes, and (c) plans are made for the introduction of the data at the next lower level.
· *Step 5:* Most feedback meetings include a consultant who has helped prepare the superior for the meeting and who serves as a resource person.

Team Building. A fundamental unit of an organization, the team or working group, can be a logical focus for improving the effectiveness of the organization.[22] OD team-building activities can improve the performance of teams and the sense of participation among members. *Team building* can be directed at two different types of teams or working groups: first, an existing or permanent team made up of a manager and his or her subordinates, often called a *family group*; and second, a new group that may have been created through a merger or other structural change in the organization or formed to solve a specific problem, which we will call the *special group*.

TABLE 13–2
SURVEY FEEDBACK
vs. TRADITIONAL
SURVEY
APPROACH

	Traditional Approach	Survey Feedback Approach
Data collected from:	Rank and file, and maybe manager	Everyone in the system or subsystem
Data reported to:	Top management, department heads, and perhaps to employees through newspaper	Everyone who participated
Implications of data are worked on by:	Top management (maybe)	Everyone in work teams, with workshops starting at the top (all superiors with their subordinates)
Third-party intervention strategy:	Design and administration of questionnaire, development of report	Obtaining concurrence on total strategy, design and administration of questionnaire, design of workshops, appropriate interventions in workshops
Action planning done by:	Top management only	Teams at all levels
Probable extent of change and improvement:	Low	High

Source: Wendell L. French and Cecil H. Bell, Jr., *Organization Development: Behavioral Science Interventions for Organization Improvement*, 3rd ed., p. 182. © 1984. Reprinted by permission of Prentice-Hall, Inc., Englewood Cliffs, N.J.

For both kinds of groups, team-building activities aim at diagnosing barriers to effective team performance, improving task accomplishment, improving relationships between team members, and improving processes operative in the team, such as communication and task assignment. Table 13–3 summarizes these activities for both family and special groups.

TABLE 13–3 TEAM-BUILDING ACTIVITIES

Activity	Family Groups	Special Groups
Diagnosis	Diagnostic meetings: "How are we doing?"	Diagnostic meetings: "Where would we like to go?"
Task accomplishment	Problem solving, decision making, role clarification, goal setting, etc.	Special problems, role and goal clarification, resource utilization, etc.
Building and maintaining relationships	Focus on effective interpersonal relationships, including boss–subordinate and peer	Focus on interpersonal or interunit conflict and underutilization of other team members as resources
Management of group processes	Focus on understanding group processes and group culture	Focus on communication, decision making, and task allocations
Role analysis and role negotiation	Techniques used for role clarification and definition	Techniques used for role clarification and definition

Source: Adapted from Wendell L. French and Cecil H. Bell, Jr., *Organization Development: Behavioral Science Interventions for Organization Improvement*, p. 104. © 1984. Used by permission of Prentice-Hall, Inc., Englewood Cliffs, N.J.

FIGURE 13–5 THE MANAGERIAL GRID

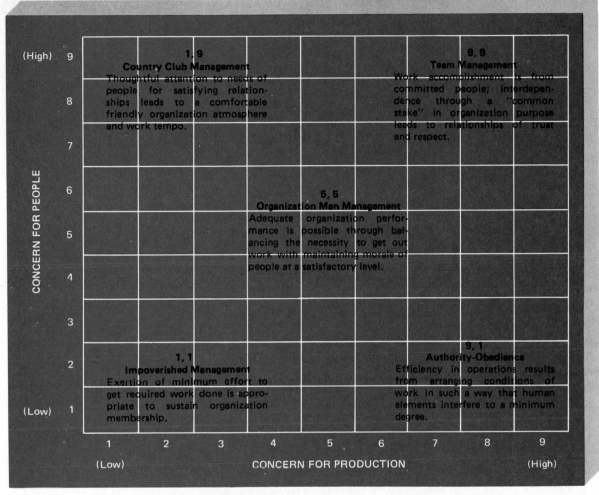

Source: *The Managerial Grid III,* by Robert R. Blake and Jane Srygley Mouton (Houston: Gulf Publishing Company), p. 12. Copyright © 1985. Reproduced by permission.

Diagnostic meetings may involve the total group or several subgroups and require only a brief time—a day or less—to identify strengths and problem areas. Actual team building requires a subsequent longer meeting, ideally held away from the workplace. The consultant interviews participants beforehand and organizes the meeting around common themes. The group proceeds to examine the issues, rank them in order of importance, study their underlying dynamics, and decide on a course of action to bring about those changes perceived as necessary. A follow-up meeting at a later time may then evaluate the success of the action steps.

Grid® OD. Grid OD is based on the Managerial Grid developed by Robert Blake and Jane Mouton.[23] The Managerial Grid identifies combinations of concern for *production* and concern for *people* and attempts to increase attention to both variables. The combinations, as shown in figure 13–5, range from a 1.1 management style—low concern for both production and people—to a 9.9 management style—high concern for both. Blake and Mouton believe the most effective style is the latter one, in which managers build cohesive, committed work groups distinguished by both high productivity and high satisfaction.

A Grid OD program commonly has six phases:

GRID OD

Training

Team Development

Intergroup Development

Organizational Goal Setting

Goal Attainment

Stabilization

- *Phase 1: Training.* Key managers learn about grid concepts, assess their own managerial styles, and work on improving such skills as team development, group problem solving, and communication.
- *Phase 2: Team Development.* The trained managers bring their new understanding to the work situation. Emphasis is placed on improving both manager-subordinate relationships and team effectiveness.
- *Phase 3: Intergroup Development.* This phase focuses on the relationship between the organization's work groups to improve coordination and cooperation, relieve tensions, and solve problems jointly.
- *Phase 4: Organizational Goal Setting.* Top managers together create an ideal model of the organization and set goals to be tested, evaluated, and refined.
- *Phase 5: Goal Attainment.* Organization members seek to make the ideal model a reality.
- *Phase 6: Stabilization.* The results of all the phases are finally evaluated to determine which areas of the organization still need improvement or alteration. Efforts are made to stabilize positive changes and to identify new areas of opportunity for the organization.

Evaluating OD

Evaluation of programs like Grid OD is difficult because of their complexity, scope, and long-term nature. Even more limited activities, like a team development project, may be difficult to evaluate because of inability to prevent changes in membership and to control related organizational activities. In addition, a variety of approaches to team development may be used, so evaluation of one type of team development effort may not tell much about how a different approach will work.

A special problem in evaluating OD programs is the existence of organizational politics that can make objective assessment difficult. The individuals with the greatest commitment to the program may also have to play a leading role in the evaluation. And, as in any change in an organization, the results following an OD program may be due to other causes—for example, when changes in the economy lead to changes in the turnover rate. For these reasons, efforts to evaluate OD programs frequently yield ambiguous results.[24]

Conditions for Successful OD Programs

Although it is difficult to evaluate the total impact of a specific OD program or to compare different types of OD activities, it is sometimes obvious that a particular program has failed. When a clear failure is analyzed, it is not unusual to conclude—with 20/20 hindsight—that the failure was almost inevitable: The program was undertaken in an organizational environment that did not have the prerequisite conditions for success, or it was executed in ways that contributed to its failure. French and Bell have identified a set of conditions they believe are necessary for an OD program to succeed:[25]

1. *Recognition by top or other managers that the organization has problems.* Without this, it is highly unlikely that the necessary time, effort, and money will be invested in OD.
2. *Use of an outside behavioral scientist as a consultant.* Internal change agents are unlikely to have, or to be seen as having, the experience, objectivity, expertise, or freedom required to implement a major change program.
3. *Initial support and involvement of top-level managers.* Top managers play a key role in overcoming initial resistance to change. Lack of involvement and support from them would signal to lower-level managers that the activity is not considered important.
4. *Involvement of work group leaders.* Activities to improve the effectiveness of existing work groups are frequently an important part of OD programs. To be successful, such programs require active support and involvement by the manager of the work group.
5. *Achieving early successes with the OD effort.* When the first OD changes are made and prove successful, organization members are motivated to continue the process and to attempt larger-scale changes. Early failures may destroy the credibility of the change agents and may weaken the commitment of top-level supporters.
6. *Education of organization members about OD.* People are likely to feel manipulated if they do not understand the reasons for changes and, to some extent, the theories on which OD change programs are based.
7. *Acknowledgment of managers' strengths.* Managers who are already using good management techniques are likely to resent an OD change agent who overplays the "expert" or "teacher" role. The things managers do well need to be acknowledged and reinforced.
8. *Involvement with managers of human resource departments.* The expertise and support of managers in the human resource department are essential in designing and implementing changes in such areas as employee evaluation, development, and reward policies.
9. *Development of internal OD resources.* Internal change agent expertise must be developed, and the organization's line managers must acquire many of the change agent skills.
10. *Effective management of the OD program.* Failure by change agents and clients to coordinate and control the OD program may result in loss of impetus and isolation from the felt needs of the organization members.
11. *Measurement of results.* The success of the organization in meeting its organizational and human goals must be monitored. Data on results provide change agents and managers with important feedback on the organization's change efforts.

Organizational Culture

Culture, according to Vijay Sathe, is "the set of important understandings (often unstated) that members of a community share in common."[26] These shared understandings consist of norms, values, attitudes, and beliefs, and the community in question may be as wide as a society or industry, or as narrow as a company,

Shared Things

1. Shirt sleeves.
2. One-company town.
3. Open offices.

Shared Sayings

4. "Get out there" to understand the customer. (Belief in travel)
5. "We cannot rely on systems" to meet customer needs. (Highly responsive customer service)
6. "We don't stand on rank." (No parking privileges)

Shared Actions

7. Participate in lots of meetings.
8. Make sure organization is detail-oriented to provide quality customer service.
9. Engage in personal relationships and communications.
10. Rally to meet customer needs in a crisis.
11. Expedite jobs to deliver highly responsive service.
12. Maintain close relationship with union.

Shared Feelings

13. The company is good to me.
14. We like this place.
15. We care about this company because it cares about us as individuals.

Shared Cultural Understandings

A. Provide highly responsive, quality customer service (4, 8, 11).
B. Get things done well and quickly ("expediting") (4, 7, 10, 11).
C. Operate informally (1, 6, 9, 12).
D. Perceive company as part of the family (2, 12, 13, 14, 15).
E. Encourage constructive disagreement (3, 7).

FIGURE 13–6
HOW SHARED THINGS, SAYINGS, ACTIONS, AND FEELINGS SUGGEST SHARED CULTURAL UNDERSTANDINGS

Source: Adapted from Vijay Sathe, "Implications of Corporate Culture: A Manager's Guide to Action," *Organizational Dynamics* 12, no. 2 (Autumn 1983):9.

department, or particular work unit. Corporate culture is an integral part of organizational life, and has important implications for managerial action.

The culture of a particular organization may be inferred from the things, sayings, doings, and feelings held in common. For example, the formality of a company's operations may be gauged by the existence of warm personal relationships within it and by its employees' style of dress. For a schematic look at such inferences for one hypothetical corporation, see figure 13–6.

A strong, widely recognized corporate culture is frequently cited as a reason for the success of such companies as IBM and Procter & Gamble. The ceremonies, rewards, decor, and other symbolic forms of communication found in such a company as Mary Kay Cosmetics have established a corporate culture that guides the actions of organization members. Apple Computer, a company that grew relatively quickly to eminence in its industry, worked hard to maintain the informality and personal relationships characteristic of a small company, even positioning itself in its marketing as the small-company alternative to IBM and other industry giants.

A company's predominant culture may change quite rapidly, or be forced by competition into change. For example, in the U.S. banking industry, pressures unleashed by deregulation have produced a marked change in attitude among established banks from what one banker called "the old bureaucratic 'your books balance at the end of the day' culture" to a culture that is more entrepreneurial, more oriented to sales and attuned to competition.[27] Peters and Waterman (see chapter 1) make the point that companies with strong cultures that are focused externally— that is, centered on service to the customer—may, in fact, be more sensitive to environmental changes and more quickly able to adapt to them than companies without strong cultures.[28]

A manager who desires to change his or her organization's culture must proceed cautiously, realizing that culture change is more difficult to effect than behavior change, and usually takes longer as well. Sathe has shown that culture's durability and efficiency represent both an asset and a liability for an organization, and a smart manager must learn when to stop perpetuating a culture that is unresponsive to the needs of the business. Often only the chief executive has the power and influence to institute a change in overall organizational culture, which involves not merely structural and technological change, but also change in shared symbols, rituals, and beliefs.[29]

Summary

Organizational change is bound to occur, given the variety of forces for change that exist both within and outside of an organization. There are two constructive ways that managers can deal with change: react to it, and plan for it. The former approach is appropriate for the day-to-day decisions a manager must make. The latter approach is necessary when a major part or all of the organization needs to change. An outside change agent can be particularly valuable to managers in planned change programs.

Kurt Lewin developed a three-step model of planned change: (1) "unfreezing" the present behavior pattern; (2) "changing," or developing a new behavior pattern; and (3) "refreezing" the new behavior pattern. This model recognizes that many organizations and individuals are not ready for change. Pressures for equilibrium or stability may counteract those for change. To determine whether pressures for stability can be overcome, it is useful to consider the level of dissatisfaction with the status quo and the availability of both a clear concept of a more desirable future state and practical steps to get there.

Resistance to change may be based on uncertainty about its causes and effects, unwillingness to give up existing benefits, and awareness of weaknesses in the proposed change. Much of the resistance can be overcome by including subordinates in change decisions.

Organizational change can involve structure, technology, and/or people. Structural changes may be made by application of classical management principles, decentralization, or changes in work flow. Technological changes may require redesign of work operations. Technostructural changes combine technological and structural elements. People changes attempt to improve the attitudes, skills, and knowledge of organization members.

Many of the efforts to change people are referred to as organizational development (OD) techniques. OD applies the principles of behavioral science to improve the effectiveness of individuals, groups, or the entire organization. Survey feedback techniques employ attitude and other surveys and systematically report the results as a basis for change. Team building is aimed at improving group effectiveness by improving task performance and relationships between team members. Grid OD, a six-phase program based on the concept of the Managerial Grid, uses a variety of OD activities to bring about a high level of concern for people and production in the organization as a whole.

Organizational culture, the shared understandings—norms, values, attitudes, and beliefs—of an organization, can foster or impede change.

Review Questions

1. What are some external and internal sources of change in organizations?

2. What are some nonconstructive responses to change pressures? Can you think of some examples of these nonconstructive responses in any of our society's political, business, or not-for-profit organizations?

3. What are the two major approaches managers use to deal with change? When is each approach likely to be used?

4. What were the two major obstacles to change noted by Lewin? According to the model developed by Lewin and elaborated by Schein, what are the two mechanisms through which individuals learn new attitudes?

5. What are the three categories of resistance to change? Which type of resistance should be encouraged? How may resistance to change be overcome?

6. What are the three structural approaches to change?

7. What do technostructural approaches to change attempt to do? Why were these approaches to change developed? What are some approaches to technostructural change?

8. How does the assumption underlying the people approach to change differ from the assumption underlying the structural and technical approaches?

9. What is a good working definition of OD?

10. What assumptions about people do most OD practitioners make? Do you also hold these assumptions?

11. What are the values upon which OD is based? Which of these values do you share?

12. What are three widely used OD techniques?

13. What are the five types of managerial styles indicated on the Managerial Grid?

14. What are the six phases of Grid OD?

15. According to French and Bell, what conditions are required for a successful OD program?

16. What is organizational culture? How does it affect an organization's ability to change?

Notes

1. John M. Thomas and Warren G. Bennis, eds., *The Management of Change and Conflict* (Baltimore: Penguin, 1972), p. 209.

2. For a review of the various types of change agents, see Richard N. Ottaway, "The Change Agent: A Taxonomy in Relation to the Change Process," *Human Relations* 36, no. 4 (April 1983):361–392. On the use of political skills by change agents, see Newton Margulies and Anthony P. Raia, "The Politics of Organization Development," *Training and Development Journal* 38, no. 8 (August 1984):20–23.

3. Kurt Lewin, *Field Theory in Social Science: Selected Theoretical Papers* (New York: Harper & Brothers, 1951).

4. Kurt Lewin, "Frontiers in Group Dynamics: Concept, Method, and Reality in Social Science," *Human Relations* 1, no. 1 (1947):5–41. See also Edgar H. Schein, *Organizational Psychology,* 3d ed. (Englewood Cliffs, N.J.: Prentice-Hall, 1980), pp. 243–247; and Edgar F. Huse and Thomas G. Cummings, *Organization Development and Change,* 3d ed. (St. Paul, Minn.: West Publishing, 1985), p. 20; William J. McGuire, "Attitudes and Attitude Change," in Gardner Lindzey and Elliot Aronson, eds., *Handbook of Social Psychology,* 3d ed., vol. 2 (New York: Random House, 1985), chapter 6; and Joel Cooper and Robert T. Croyle, "Attitudes and Attitude Change," *Annual Review of Psychology* 35 (1984):395–426.

5. Gleicher's model is described in Richard Beckhard and Reuben T. Harris, *Organizational Transitions: Managing Complex Change* (Reading, Mass.: Addison-Wesley, 1977), pp. 25–27.

6. See Paul R. Lawrence, "How to Deal with Resistance to Change," *Harvard Business Review* 47, no. 1 (January–February 1969); John P. Kotter and Leonard A. Schlesinger, "Choosing Strategies for Change," *Harvard Business Review* 57, no. 2 (March–April 1979):107–109; and Herbert Kaufman, *The Limits of Organizational Change* (University, Ala.: University of Alabama Press, 1971).

7. Kotter and Schlesinger, "Choosing Strategies for Change," pp. 109–112.

8. Lester Coch and John R. P. French, Jr., "Overcoming Resistance to Change," *Human Relations* 1, no. 4 (1948):512–532. See also Stanley R. Hinckley, Jr., "A Closer Look at Participation," *Organizational Dynamics* 13, no. 3 (Winter 1985):57–67.

9. Lawrence, "How to Deal with Resistance to Change," pp. 4–12ff.

10. Harold J. Leavitt, "Applied Organization Change in Industry: Structural, Technical, and Human Approaches," in W. W. Cooper, H. J. Leavitt, and M. W. Shelly II, eds., *New Perspectives in Organization Research* (New York: Wiley, 1964). pp. 55–71. For an amplification of such a model, see David A. Nadler, "Managing Organizational Change: An Integrative Perspective," *Journal of Applied Behavioral Science* 17, no. 2 (April–May–June 1981):191–211.

11. For a more detailed description of system element interdependence, see Wendell L. French and Cecil H. Bell, Jr., *Organization Development: Behavioral Science Interventions for Organization Improvement*, 3rd ed. (Englewood Cliffs, N.J.: Prentice-Hall, 1984), pp. 54–62.

12. See, for example, Eliot D. Chapple and Leonard R. Sayles, *The Measure of Management* (New York: Macmillan, 1961).

13. Eric L. Trist and K. W. Bamforth, "Some Social and Psychological Consequences of the Long-Wall Method of Coal-Getting," *Human Relations* 4, no. 1 (February 1951):3–38.

14. Robert L. Kahn, "Organizational Development: Some Problems and Proposals," *Journal of Applied Behavioral Science* 10, no. 4 (July–August–September 1974):485.

15. French and Bell, *Organization Development*, p. 17.

16. Ibid., p. 131. French and Bell also discuss other ways of classifying OD techniques and describe many of the techniques in detail.

17. Morton A. Lieberman, Irvin D. Yalom, and Matthew B. Miles, *Encounter Groups: First Facts* (New York: Basic Books, 1973).

18. See Eric Berne, *Games People Play* (New York: Ballantine, 1978); and Abe Wagner, *The Transactional Manager: How to Solve People Problems with Transactional Analysis* (Englewood Cliffs, N.J.: Prentice-Hall, 1981).

19. See Edgar H. Schein, *Process Consultation: Its Role in Organization Development* (Reading, Mass.: Addison-Wesley, 1969); and Larry Hirshhorn and James Krantz, "Unconscious Planning in a Natural Work Group: A Case Study in Process Consultation," *Human Relations* 33, no. 10 (October 1982):805–844.

20. Examples of team-building efforts in a broadcast system and a university administration can be found in William G. Dyer, *Team Building: Issues and Alternatives* (Reading, Mass.: Addison-Wesley, 1977), pp. 64–67 and 82–83, respectively. An experiment in which this technique did not improve performance but did generate a perceptible increase in participation is reported in Richard W. Woodman and John J. Sherwood, "Effects of Team Development Intervention: A Field Experiment," *Journal of Applied Behavioral Science* 16, no. 1 (April–May–June 1980):211–227.

21. See Richard Beckhard, "The Confrontation Meeting," *Harvard Business Review* 45, no. 2 (March–April 1967):149–155.

22. See French and Bell, *Organization Development*, pp. 138–154.

23. See Robert R. Blake and Jane S. Mouton, *The Managerial Grid III* (Houston: Gulf Publishing, 1985), and *Building a Dynamic Organization through Grid Organization Development* (Reading, Mass.: Addison-Wesley, 1969). Note that the word Grid is a registered service mark of Scientific Methods, Inc. and is used by permission.

24. For discussions of efforts to evaluate OD programs, see Warren R. Nielsen (Chairperson), John R. Kimberly, Larry E. Pate, Robert T. Golembiewski, Robert M. Frame, John J. Wakefield, and Richard E. Ault, "Seminar on Organization Development Assessment: Theory, Research, and Applications," *Midwest Academy of Management Proceedings*, April 1977, pp. 407–416; Jerry I. Porras and Per Olaf Berg, "Evaluation Methodology in Organization Development: An Analysis and Critique," *Journal of Applied Behavioral Science* 14, no. 2 (April–May–June 1978):151–173; and John M. Nicholas, "Evaluation Research in Organizational Change Interventions: Considerations and Some Suggestions," *Journal of Applied Behavioral Science* 15, no. 1 (January–February–March 1979):23–40.

25. French and Bell, *Organization Development*, pp. 215–228.

26. Vijay Sathe, "Implications of Corporate Culture: A Manager's Guide to Action," *Organizational Dynamics* 12, no. 2 (Autumn 1983):5–23. Several books published in the early 1980s aroused great interest in corporate cultures. On the culture of Japanese organizations, see William G. Ouchi, *Theory Z: How American Business Can Meet the Japanese Challenge* (Reading, Mass.: Addison-Wesley, 1981); and Richard Tanner Pascale and Anthony G. Athos, *The Art of Japanese Management* (New York: Simon & Schuster, 1981). For discussions of successful companies and the cultures they have generated, see Thomas J. Peters and Robert H. Waterman, Jr., *In Search of Excellence* (New York: Harper & Row, 1982); and Terrence E. Deal and Allan A. Kennedy, *Corporate Cultures: The Rites and Rituals of Corporate Life* (Reading, Mass.: Addison-Wesley, 1982). Recent books exploring the concept in depth include Edgar H. Schein, *Organizational Culture and Leadership* (San Francisco: Jossey-Bass, 1985); Stanley M. Davis, *Managing Corporate Culture* (Hagerstown, Md.: Ballinger, 1985); and Ralph H. Kilman, Mary Jane Saxton, and Ray Serpa, eds., *Gaining Control of Corporate Cultures* (San Francisco: Josssey-Bass, 1985).

27. Raoul D. Edwards et al., "Marketing in a Deregulated Environment," *U.S. Banker 95*, no. 4 (April 1984):34–36ff.

28. Peters and Waterman, *In Search of Excellence,* pp. 77–78.

29. Bro Uttal, "The Corporate Culture Vultures," *Fortune,* October 17, 1983, pp. 66–72.

CASE STUDY: Progress on Purpose

Carl Bolling is a participant in the company's training program titled Systems and Procedures Studies. The participants meet once weekly for two hours over an eight-month period. The program is staffed by a local college professor.

As part of the requirements of the program, each participant is required to undertake a work-study project of his own choosing with the idea of critically analyzing the work activities observed and suggesting improvement for them through the application of techniques and ideas learned in the program. It was stressed by the professor at the beginning of the program that the "human element" was one of the prime factors to pay attention to when undertaking such a study.

Carl Bolling has the title of Planning Engineer. In this capacity, he engages in coordinating activities between the operating, production, and engineering departments. His selected work-study project for the training program deals with the purchase and order of heavy equipment for installation in new plants being constructed by the company. It concerns specifically the control of costs associated with purchased equipment that sometimes sits crated on a new plant location for weeks before it is ready for installation. Carl Bolling had analyzed the scheduling procedures of the construction department and the purchasing procedures of the operating department plus the required specifications and design of equipment by the engineering department. It was his opinion that thousands of dollars yearly could be saved by the company if the construction and operating departments would adopt the formal planning and purchasing procedures that he proposed. He felt convinced that his analysis of the problem was sound and his analysis of potential cost savings accurate.

Upon submitting his work-study project to fellow participants in the training program, he felt pleased that the group and the professor endorsed this project as "sound" and "well done." Upon submitting his proposal to his immediate boss, the vice-president of engineering, he was gratified to know that the vice-president planned to propose the introduction of his new procedures at the next meeting of the executive management committee.

Two weeks later the vice-president of engineering called Bolling to his office and told him his suggested planning and purchasing procedures had been presented to the executive management committee. The reaction had been violent! They resented a mere planning engineer crossing functional lines and making recommendations in areas other than his own. They disliked the implication that their activities were costing the company thousands of dollars yearly, and they told the vice-president of engineering that, in the future, he (Bolling) would be considered *persona non grata* in their departments.

The vice-president of engineering suggested to Bolling that maybe it would be best if he were transferred to another division in the company. At least he would not run the risk of meeting these executives personally.

Source: From Kenneth W. Olm, F. J. Brewerton, Susan R. Whisnant, and Francis J. Bridges, *Management Decisions and Organizational Policy,* Third Edition. Copyright © 1981 by Allyn and Bacon, Inc. Reprinted with permission.

Case Questions

1. Could Bolling have avoided the problem brought about by his proposal? How?
2. How should the vice-president of engineering have handled Bolling's proposal?
3. What do you think of the vice-president's suggestion that Bolling should transfer to another division?
4. What do you think Bolling should do now?

14 MANAGING ORGANIZATIONAL CONFLICT AND CREATIVITY

Upon completing this chapter you should be able to:

1. Identify two views of organizational conflict.
2. Distinguish between functional and dysfunctional conflict.
3. Describe the sources of the various types of conflict.
4. Identify the consequences of organizational conflict.
5. Describe the sources and approaches to line–staff and management–labor conflict.
6. Identify and describe methods for stimulating, reducing, and resolving conflict.
7. Describe the creative process in individuals and in organizations.
8. Explain how creativity can be stimulated and encouraged in organizations.

The vice-president of a large midwestern oil refinery met one morning with senior managers in the engineering department. The purpose of the meeting was to draft a proposal for the creation of a committee to plan the company's plant operations and capital expenditures for the coming year. It was no secret that the proposal was the vice-president's pet project.

To start the ball rolling, the vice-president circulated a first draft of the proposal. Most of the ensuing discussion centered on the wording of the draft. One manager, however, was apparently unsure that there was a real need for such a committee. He kept raising a series of questions about why the committee was being created and how it would affect senior department head responsibilities. After a short while the vice-president, visibly impatient with these questions, remarked, "I don't see why you're so worried about all this. I strongly believe the committee will benefit our company, and I expect reasonable people will have no problem adjusting to it." The manager hesitated, then quickly replied, "My objections could be resolved just by changing a few words in the draft." The vice-president agreed to make these minor changes in the proposal, then looked up and said, "I take it there is common agreement now." No one dissented.

At first glance, it would seem that nothing unusual or harmful occurred at this meeting. Most members of the group obviously wanted to avoid clashing with a powerful superior. When disagreement surfaced, the vice-president moved quickly to suppress it. After the new committee had been in operation for several months, however, it became clear that the dissenting manager had raised valid questions. The committee took up a great deal of time, its decisions seemed mediocre and unpopular, and department heads resented the loss of power to plan their own operations and expenditures. By discouraging conflict at the meeting, the vice-president lost the opportunity to determine the weaknesses in the proposal and to develop improvements.

In this chapter we will discuss how conflict can be managed effectively in organizations and how innovation and creativity can be encouraged. As we discuss conflict and creativity, we will see that the two are frequently connected. Too much or too little conflict can inhibit creativity. Poorly managed conflict can do the same. But when conflict is well managed, problems can be resolved effectively, and the solutions are more likely to be fresh and innovative.

Conflict, Competition, and Cooperation

The subject of conflict has been confused by different definitions and conceptions of the term. We will define conflict in a way that will allow us to discuss its constructive, functional aspects.

Organizational conflict is a disagreement between two or more organization members or groups arising from the fact that they must share scarce resources or work activities and/or from the fact that they have different statuses, goals, values, or perceptions. Organization members or subunits in disagreement attempt to have their own cause or point of view prevail over that of others.

This definition is intentionally broad. It does not specify how severe the disagreement is, in what manner the conflicting parties seek to prevail, how the conflict is managed, or what the outcomes are. In each case, these factors determine whether the conflict is functional or dysfunctional for the organization and to what extent.

One of the many semantic difficulties relating to organizational conflict is the distinction between conflict and competition. We can distinguish between these concepts on the basis of whether one party is able to keep the other from attaining its goals. *Competition* exists when the goals of the parties involved are incompatible but the parties cannot interfere with each other. For example, two production teams may compete with each other to be the first to meet a quota. (Obviously, both teams cannot come in first.) If there is no opportunity to interfere with the other party's goal attainment, a competitive situation exists; however, if the opportunity for interference exists, and if that opportunity is acted upon, then the situation is one of conflict.

Cooperation occurs when two or more parties work together to achieve mutual goals. It is possible for conflict and cooperation to coexist. The opposite of cooperation is not conflict but lack of cooperation. For example, two parties may agree on goals but disagree strongly on how to attain those goals. When we speak of managing conflict, we mean that managers should try to find ways to balance conflict and cooperation.

Changing Views of Conflict

Attitudes toward conflict in organizations have changed considerably in the last 30 years. Stephen P. Robbins has traced this evolution, emphasizing the difference between the traditional view of conflict and the current one, which he calls the *interactionist* view.[1]

The *traditional* view of conflict was that it was unnecessary and harmful. Early managers and management writers generally thought that the appearance of conflict was a clear signal that there was something wrong with the organization. They believed that conflict would develop only if managers failed to apply sound management principles in directing the organization or if managers failed to communicate to employees the common interests that bind management and employees together. If these failures were corrected, according to the traditional view, the organization should operate as a smoothly functioning, integrated whole. For example, Frederick Taylor believed that if the principles of scientific management were applied, the age-old conflict between labor and management would disappear.

The traditional view of conflict started to change as behavioral science researchers and management writers began to identify causes of organizational conflict independent of management error and as the advantages of effectively managed conflict started to be recognized. The current view is that conflict in organizations is inevitable and even necessary, no matter how organizations are designed and operated. This view still suggests that much conflict is, in fact, dysfunctional: it can harm individuals and impede the attainment of organizational goals. But some conflict can also be functional because it may make organizations

TABLE 14–1 OLD AND CURRENT VIEWS OF CONFLICT

Old View	Current View
Conflict is avoidable.	Conflict is inevitable.
Conflict is caused by management errors in designing and managing organizations or by troublemakers.	Conflict arises from many causes, including organizational structure, unavoidable differences in goals, differences in perceptions and values of specialized personnel, and so on.
Conflict disrupts the organization and prevents optimal performance.	Conflict contributes to and detracts from organizational performance in varying degrees.
The task of management is to eliminate conflict.	The task of management is to manage the level of conflict and its resolution for optimal organizational performance.
Optimal organizational performance requires the removal of conflict.	Optimal organizational performance requires a moderate level of conflict.

more effective. Conflict can lead to a search for solutions. Thus, it is often an instrument of organizational innovation and change. (See table 14–1.)

From this perspective, the task of managers is not to suppress or resolve all conflict but to manage it, so as to minimize its harmful aspects and maximize its beneficial aspects.[2] Such management may even include the stimulation of conflict in situations where its absence or suppression (as in our chapter opening example) may hamper the organization's effectiveness, creativity, or innovation.

Functional and Dysfunctional Conflict

Conflict, as we have defined it, is inherently neither functional nor dysfunctional. It simply has the potential for improving or impairing organizational performance, depending on how it is managed. For example, managers in a company may be in conflict over how the annual budget is to be divided among their divisions. Properly handled, such conflict could lead to new sharing arrangements that might benefit the entire organization. For instance, more money might be allocated to the divisions in the fastest-growing markets. (In such a case, the managers who would receive less money than usual might feel that the conflict was dysfunctional; but, overall, the organization would benefit.) Other functional outcomes might be that (1) the managers find a way to use the money they receive more effectively; (2) they find a better way to cut down on expenses; or (3) they improve the whole unit's performance so that additional funds become available to all of them. It is also possible, however, that the outcome of the conflict will be dysfunctional. For example, cooperation between the managers may break down, making it difficult to coordinate the organization's activities.

The relationship between organizational conflict and performance is illustrated in figure 14–1. There is an optimal, highly functional level of conflict at which performance is at a maximum. When the level of conflict is too low, the organization changes too slowly to meet the new demands being made upon it, and its survival is

FIGURE 14–1 ORGANIZATIONAL CONFLICT AND ORGANIZATIONAL PERFORMANCE

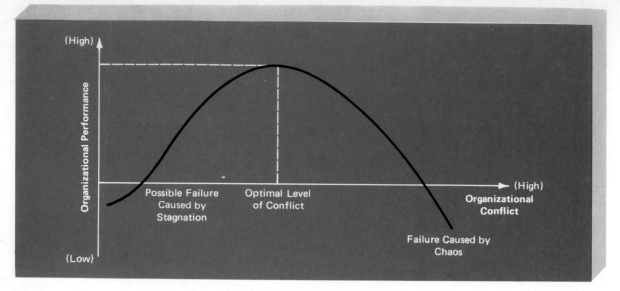

threatened. When the level of conflict is too high, chaos and disruption also endanger the organization's chances for survival.

Types of Conflict. There are five types of conflict possible in organizational life:

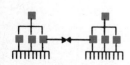

1. *Conflict within the individual* occurs when an individual is uncertain about what work he or she is expected to perform, when some demands of the work conflict with other demands, or when the individual is expected to do more than he or she feels capable of doing. This type of conflict often influences how an individual responds to other types of organizational conflict. (We will discuss this type of conflict in more detail in chapter 19.)

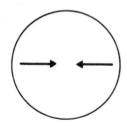

2. *Conflict between individuals* in the same organization is frequently seen as being caused by personality differences. More often, such conflicts erupt from role-related pressures (as between managers and subordinates) or from the manner in which people personalize conflict between groups.

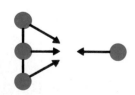

3. *Conflict between individuals and groups* is frequently related to the way individuals deal with the pressures for conformity imposed on them by their work group. For example, an individual may be punished by his or her work group for exceeding or falling behind the group's productivity norms.

4. *Conflict between groups in the same organization* is the type of conflict with which we will be most concerned in this chapter. Line–staff and labor–management conflicts, discussed below, are two common areas of intergroup conflict.

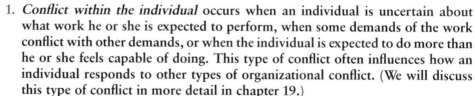

5. *Conflict between organizations* in the economic sphere has been considered an inherent and desirable form of conflict in the United States and many other countries; usually this type of conflict is called competition. Such conflict has been recognized to lead to the development of new products, technologies, and services, lower prices, and more efficient utilization of resources.[3] Government

laws and regulatory agencies attempt to promote functional conflict (through antitrust legislation, for example) and manage the dysfunctional aspects of such conflict (such as false advertising and industrial espionage). One controversial trend of the 1980s has been to deregulate heavily regulated industries (airlines, banks, and railroads, for example) to spur economic competition in those industries.

Sources of Organizational Conflict

The sources of organizational conflict discussed here are related most clearly to intergroup conflict. However, they also apply to conflict between individuals and between individuals and groups. The major sources of organizational conflict include: the need to share scarce resources; differences in goals between organization units; the interdependence of work activities in the organization; and differences in values or perceptions among organization units.[4]

Shared Resources. If every unit in an organization had access to unlimited workers, money, materials, equipment, and space, the problem of how to share these resources would hardly arise. The potential for conflict exists because these vital resources are limited. They must be allocated, so some groups inevitably will get less than they want or need. Conflict or loss of cooperation can result as organizational groups compete for the greatest possible share of available resources.

Differences in Goals. As we have seen, organization subunits tend to become specialized or differentiated as they develop dissimilar goals, tasks, and personnel. Such differentiation frequently leads to conflicts of interest or priorities, even when the overall goals of the organization are agreed upon. The sales department, for example, might want low prices to attract more customers, while the production department might want higher prices to meet manufacturing costs. Because members of each department develop different goals and points of view, they often find it difficult to agree on programs of action.

Interdependence of Work Activities. Work interdependence exists when two or more subunits depend on each other to complete their respective tasks. In such a case, the potential for a high degree of conflict or cooperation exists, depending on how the situation is managed. Sometimes conflict arises when all the groups involved are given too much to do. Tension among the various group members will increase, and they may then accuse each other of shirking their responsibilities. Conflict may also flare up if the work is evenly distributed but the rewards are dissimilar. Potential for conflict is greatest when one unit is unable to begin its work until the other unit completes its job. ("How can we meet our production quota if your people don't get those parts to us on time?")

Differences in Values or Perceptions. The differences in goals among the members of the various units in the organization are frequently accompanied by differences in attitudes, values, and perceptions that can also lead to conflict. For example, first-line supervisors who must get shipments out quickly may give in to union shop stewards on some issues rather than risk a slowdown. Higher-level managers, concerned with long-range management–union considerations, might want to avoid setting precedents on those issues and may try to restrict the flexibility of first-

"Wilson is our idea factory."

Drawing by Weber; © 1982 The New Yorker Magazine, Inc.

line supervisors. Members of the engineering department might value quality products, sophisticated design, and durability, while members of the manufacturing department might value simplicity of design and low manufacturing costs. Such incompatibility of values can lead to conflict. ("It is too expensive to do it your way." "But we'll lose our reputation for quality if we do it your way.")

Other Sources of Conflict: Individual Styles and Organizational Ambiguities. Some people enjoy conflict, debate, and argument; and when kept under control, mild discord can stimulate organization members and improve their performance. Some individuals, however, escalate their conflicts, debates, and arguments into full-scale battles. People who are highly authoritarian, for example, or low in self-esteem may frequently anger their colleagues by overreacting to mild disagreements. In general, the potential for intergroup conflict is highest when group members differ markedly in such characteristics as work attitudes, age, and education.

In addition to conflicts created by erratic individuals, intergroup conflict can also result from ambiguously defined work responsibilities and unclear goals. One manager may try to expand the role of his or her subunit; this effort will usually stimulate other managers to "defend their turf." Also, if members of different groups know little about each other's jobs, they may unwittingly make unreasonable demands on each other. These demands may, in turn, trigger conflict.

Ambiguous communications can also cause intergroup conflict, as when the same phrase has different meanings for different groups. In one case, when the management of a large mining corporation modernized its equipment, the union was told that no employees would lose their jobs. A few months later, when a group of former rock crushers were transferred to warehouse jobs, the union struck. It had interpreted "job" to mean "task responsibility," whereas management had used "job" to mean "employment."

Dynamics and Consequences of Organizational Conflict

In a classic study of intergroup conflict, Muzafer and Carolyn Sherif and their colleagues divided a boys' camp into two groups, stimulated intense conflict between the groups, and observed the changes in group behavior that occurred.[5] Their study indicated that groups who have been placed in a conflict situation change in predictable ways.

1. *Increased cohesion.* As a rule, group members in an intergroup conflict situation close ranks and put aside former disagreements. ("We've got to pull together!") The rise in cohesion stimulates greater efforts that may translate into action to resolve problems or to take advantage of opportunities, but the pressures toward conformity that develop may discourage creativity and fresh approaches to problems.[6]
2. *Rise of leaders.* When conflict becomes intense, those individuals who can most contribute to victory become more important. The more aggressive, able, or articulate group members are given increased power by the group. Rivalry for leadership decreases, and the group works harder to overcome "the enemy."
3. *Distorted perceptions.* Group members' perceptions of their own and the opposing groups become distorted. They regard their own skills and performance as superior and rationalize or dismiss their own shortcomings while emphasizing those of competitors. (You're all greedy," thinks the management representative at the outset of collective bargaining. "You're all cheap," thinks the union official.)
4. *Increase in negative stereotypes.* As each side belittles the other's ideas, the differences between the groups are seen as *greater* than they actually are, while the differences *within* each group are seen as *less* than they actually are.
5. *Selection of strong representatives.* To deal with the other side, each group selects representatives that it believes will not cave in to pressure from the other group. Each group perceives its own representatives in a highly positive way and opposing representatives in a negative way.
6. *Development of blind spots.* Competitive struggle adversely affects the rivals' ability to grasp and think accurately about their respective positions. Strong group identification, heightened by fear of defeat or sellout, blinds both sides to the similarities in their proposals that, if recognized, could make a settlement possible.

The Conflict Dynamic: Disagreement to Antagonism

Despite their diverse sources, controversies in organizations develop in remarkably similar ways. The Sherifs's research looks at the development of conflict in terms of its effects on the opposing groups. A different perspective—a view of the "battle"

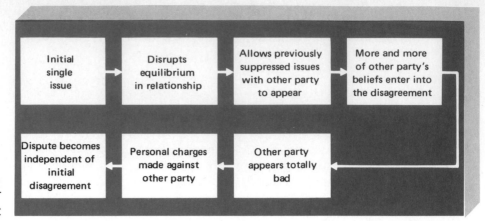

FIGURE 14–2
THE CONFLICT
DYNAMIC

Source: Adapted from James S. Coleman, *Community Conflict*, p. 11. © 1957 by the Free Press, a Corporation.

itself—is presented in James S. Coleman's model of the dynamics of a conflict incident. (See fig. 14–2.)[7] If the conflict is badly managed, the specific issue that led to the conflict may give way to more general issues. ("Not only do I disagree with what you propose to do in this case, but I think your entire approach is wrong.")

As the conflict intensifies, new issues often unrelated to the initial problem are brought up. Subjects that had been suppressed are brought to the surface and new issues are raised to convince those as yet uncommitted to join the fray. ("While I'm at it, I might as well tell you . . . .")

Once started, a conflict can continue even after the original issue has been resolved. What begins as a disagreement on a single point may end in mutual dislike because of our tendency to seek consistency in our attitudes; we want to see people as either entirely good or entirely bad.

Functional and Dysfunctional Consequences

Once the conflict is over, there are different consequences for winners and losers.[8] Leaders of the winning group normally strengthen their hold over the group. Winners may rest on their laurels, resisting any change in their ways of doing things.[9] Conversely, defeated groups tend to split into factions as old leaders are challenged by new aspirants to leadership. Losers also become more amenable to new ways of behaving and operating. For both winners and losers, the negative stereotypes engendered by win–lose conflict can become so severe as to make future intergroup cooperation extremely difficult.

Less intense conflict can have a more constructive impact. New, more effective leaders may emerge. Modified goals may help the organization adjust to change. And conflict management may become institutionalized so that disagreements can be expressed without damaging the organization. In many organizations, for example, managers freely air their differences in committee meetings but abide by committee decisions once they are made.

Three factors determine whether the net result of a given dispute will be a *functional conflict* or a *dysfunctional conflict*: the level of conflict, the organizational structure and culture, and the way in which the conflict is managed.

The Level of Conflict. Moderate levels of conflict have far greater potential for desirable outcomes than high levels. With moderate conflict, the rival groups are more likely to learn to interact in constructive, problem-solving ways. As the level of conflict rises, however, so does the temptation to engage in destructive acts toward the rival group. David Mechanic describes a case in a mental hospital where ward attendants agreed to take on some of the administrative duties of the ward physicians in exchange for inclusion in the decision-making machinery.[10] When the physicians reneged on their part of the agreement, conflict escalated until the attendants disobeyed orders and deliberately withheld information essential to the physicians. Such high levels of conflict are almost always destructive to the organization.

Organizational Structure and Culture. Conflict can call attention to the problem areas of an organization and can lead to more effective achievement of organizational goals. However, if an organization rigidly resists change, the conflict situations may never be relieved. Tensions will continue to mount, and each new conflict will split organization subunits further apart. In general, the more rigid the structure and culture of the organization, the less beneficial conflict is likely to be.

Unresolved conflict can also adversely affect informally structured organizations, where subunits depend a great deal on each other for information (rather than receiving most of their information from higher up). In a conflict situation, communication between subunits can break down, leaving each subunit unable to reach sound decisions.[11]

Methods for Managing Conflict

In this section we discuss three forms of conflict management: (1) stimulating conflict in units or organizations whose performance is lagging because the level of conflict is too low; (2) reducing or suppressing conflict when its level is too high or counterproductive; and (3) resolving conflict.

Conflict Stimulation Methods

Most of us have been taught since childhood to avoid conflict or even disagreement. "Stop fighting!" we are told, or "It's better to turn the other cheek," or "Why don't you be nice and give in?" However, the tendency in our culture to paper over dissension is not always productive, as Elise Boulding has demonstrated.[12] In an experiment, Boulding formed a series of groups to tackle a problem. Some groups contained a planted member prepared to challenge the majority view; some groups did not. Without fail, those groups that harbored a conflict-stimulator analyzed the problem more perceptively and came up with better solutions than the others. Yet when the groups were instructed to drop one member, every group that had a planted dissident chose that dissident to be dropped. Such resistance to conflict, in themselves and in others, is one of the obstacles that managers have to overcome in stimulating productive conflict.

Situations in which conflict is too low generally involve people who are afraid to "rock the boat." Rather than trying to find new and better ways of getting things done, they passively accept things the way they are. Events, behavior, and information that could stir up people to do a better job are ignored; group members tolerate each other's weaknesses and lack of performance. Managers of such groups who become alarmed that their units seem to be drifting often find that stimulating competition and conflict can have a galvanizing effect.[13]

Suggestions for Stimulating Conflict. The attitude of top managers is of critical importance in encouraging and controlling conflict. Openly stating that conflict is desirable—"I'd like to see you two take the time to fight these things out between yourselves until you reach a decision you like, rather than just smoothing things over"—will encourage organization members to bring up disagreements they might otherwise suppress. Openly stating the rules of conflict—"If you're completely deadlocked, call in a third party for help before you come to me"—will help keep conflict at functional levels.

Conflict stimulation methods include:[14]

1. *Bringing in outsiders.* A frequently used method of "shaking up" a stagnant unit or organization is to bring in managers whose backgrounds, values, and styles vary significantly from the norms. Edmund G. Brown, Jr., former governor of California, resorted to this method in 1977 when he put consumer representatives on state regulatory boards, which had long been dominated by individuals connected with the industries being regulated.

2. *Going against the book.* Excluding individuals or groups from communications that they normally receive, or adding new groups to the information network, may redistribute power and thus stimulate conflict. For example, a nursing home administrator concerned about the passivity of his patients provided them with regular information about their own conditions. They then felt more confident about disagreeing with their doctors about their treatment and took a more active role in improving their own health.

3. *Restructuring the organization.* Breaking up old work teams and departments and reorganizing them so that they have new members or responsibilities will create a period of uncertainty and readjustment. Conflict that arises during this period may lead to improved methods of operation as members adjust to new circumstances. A more open climate may also lead to conflict as organization members are encouraged to air their views.

4. *Encouraging competition.* Offering bonuses, incentive pay, and citations for outstanding performance will foster competition. If competition is maintained at a high level, it may lead to productive conflict as groups struggle to outdo each other.

5. *Selecting appropriate managers.* Authoritarian managers who do not allow opposing viewpoints to be raised often make their work groups passive. Other groups may need an active manager to shake them out of their lethargy. Finding the right manager for the particular group can encourage useful conflict where none exists.

Conflict Reduction Methods

Usually managers are more concerned with reducing rather than stimulating conflict. Conflict reduction methods reduce the antagonism aroused by conflict. Thus, these methods manage the level of conflict by "cooling things down" but do not deal with the issues that gave rise to the original conflict.[15]

The Sherifs and their colleagues, in the study cited earlier, stimulated conflict by encouraging rivalry between groups at a boys' camp. When the conflict had become very intense and disruptive, they experimented with a variety of ways of restoring harmony. First, they tried three methods that proved ineffective:

1. **They provided each group with favorable information about the other group. However, this information was so at odds with the negative impressions induced by the conflict that the boys rejected it.**
2. **They increased pleasant social contacts between the groups by having them eat together and watch movies together. But friction increased as the rivals jostled and shoved each other and called each other names.**
3. **They asked the group leaders to negotiate and provide their respective groups with favorable information about the other. But the leaders felt they might be dethroned if they tried to reconcile their differences. Even in adult intergroup conflict, agreements worked out between representatives can be limited by group members' suspicions that the agreements are "sellouts."**

Two methods that were tried did work. In the first effective approach, the researchers substituted superordinate (superior) goals that both groups accepted for the competitive goals that had kept them apart. For example, the boys were told the camp could "not afford" to rent a movie all had requested. Both groups then joined in a fund-raising drive to pay for the rental. This joint effort effectively lowered the level of conflict.

The second effective method was to unite the group to meet a common "threat" or "enemy." For example, a camp truck was rigged to break down on the way to a campout. Neither group could tow the truck in for repairs on its own; working together, they were able to do so. Such common acts eventually stimulated cooperation and friendship between group members.

In the boys' camp study, because the original sources of conflict had been artificially created by the researchers, the combination of diverting attention from their disagreements and providing shared experiences of successful cooperation were effective means of removing conflict. In normal situations, however, where conflict is not artificially created, diverting the groups' attention is likely to be more difficult to accomplish. Furthermore, the sources of the unresolved conflict will remain once the diversions have been exhausted. For these reasons, conflict reduction methods may be unsatisfying ways of dealing with conflict in organizations.

Conflict Resolution Methods

Our discussion of conflict resolution methods will focus on actions managers can take to deal directly with the conflicting parties. Other possible methods for resolving conflict include changes in organization structure—so that, for example, conflicting members or units are separated or a grievance agency is set up. In addition, some of the coordinating mechanisms we discussed in chapter 10—such as liaison individuals and committees—can also be used to resolve conflict.

The three conflict resolution methods most frequently used are dominance or suppression, compromise, and integrative problem solving. These methods differ in the extent to which they yield effective and creative solutions to conflict. They also differ in the extent to which they leave parties in the conflict able to deal with future conflict situations.

Dominance and Suppression. Dominance and suppression methods usually have two things in common: (1) They repress conflict, rather than settle it, by forcing it underground; and (2) they create a win–lose situation in which the loser, forced to give way to higher authority or greater power, usually winds up disappointed and hostile. Suppression and dominance can occur in the following ways:

Forcing. When the person in authority says, in effect, "Cut it out—I'm the boss and you've got to do it my way," argument is snuffed out. Such autocratic suppression may lead to indirect but nonetheless destructive expressions of conflict, such as malicious obedience. When, for example, a supervisor suggested delaying a shipment until a quality audit could identify suspected deficiencies, the production manager snapped: "Keep your nose out of things until I tell you otherwise." A few mornings later, when a cutting machine broke down in the supervisor's unit, machine and operator spent an idle day before the production manager found out about it. "Why didn't you call the maintenance crew?" the manager asked the supervisor. "You told me to keep my nose out of things until I heard from you," the subordinate shot back. Malicious obedience is merely one of many forms of conflict that can fester where conflict suppression is the rule.

Smoothing. In smoothing, a more diplomatic way of suppressing conflict, the manager minimizes the extent and importance of the disagreement and tries to talk one side into giving in. Where the manager has more information than the other parties and is making a reasonable suggestion, this method can be effective. But if the manager is seen as favoring one side or failing to understand the issue, the losing side is likely to feel resentful.

Avoidance. If quarreling groups come to a manager for a decision but the manager avoids taking a position, no one is likely to be satisfied. Pretending to be unaware that conflict exists is a frequent form of avoidance. Another form is refusal to deal with conflict by stalling and repeatedly postponing action "until more information is available."

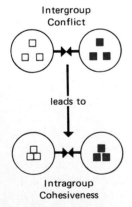

Intergroup
Conflict

leads to

Intragroup
Cohesiveness

Majority rule. Trying to resolve group conflict by a majority vote can be effective if members regard the procedure as fair. But if one voting bloc consistently outvotes the other, the losing side will feel powerless and frustrated.

Compromise. Through compromise, managers try to resolve conflict by convincing each party in the dispute to sacrifice some objectives in order to gain others. Decisions reached by compromise are not likely to leave conflicting parties feeling frustrated or hostile. From an organizational point of view, however, compromise is a weak conflict resolution method because it does not usually lead to a solution that can best help the organization achieve its goals. Instead, the solution reached will simply be one that both parties in the conflict can live with.

Forms of compromise include *separation,* in which opposing parties are kept apart until they agree to a solution; *arbitration,* in which conflicting parties submit to the judgment of a third party (usually, but not always, the manager);[16] *settling by chance,* in which some random event such as the toss of a coin determines the outcome; *resort to rules,* in which the deadlocked rivals agree to "go by the book" and let the organization's rules decide the conflict outcome; and *bribing,* in which one party accepts some compensation in exchange for ending the conflict. None of these methods is likely to leave the parties to the conflict fully satisfied or to yield creative solutions.

Integrative Problem Solving. With this method, intergroup conflict is converted into a joint problem-solving situation that can be dealt with through problem-solving techniques. Together, parties to the conflict try to solve the problem that has arisen between them. Instead of suppressing conflict or trying to find a compromise, the parties openly try to find a solution they all can accept. Managers who give subordinates the feeling that all members and groups are working together for a common goal, who encourage the free exchange of ideas, and who stress the benefits of finding the optimum solution in a conflict situation are more likely to achieve integrative solutions.

There are three types of integrative conflict resolution methods: consensus, confrontation, and the use of superordinate goals.

In *consensus,* the conflicting parties meet together to find the best solution to their problem, rather than trying to achieve a victory for either side. Group consensus will often yield a more effective solution than that offered by any one individual. However, it is important to prevent a premature consensus, in which the selected solution reflects the desire to end the conflict quickly instead of finding the *best* solution. The Labatt Brewing Company of Toronto hired a full-time "resident iconoclast" to generate innovation by keeping management flexible and providing ideas alien to the corporate culture.[17] (See chapter 17 for a detailed discussion of group problem-solving processes.)

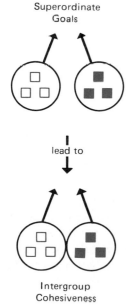

Superordinate Goals

lead to

Intergroup Cohesiveness

In *confrontation,* the opposing parties state their respective views directly to each other. The reasons for the conflict are examined and methods of resolving it are sought. With skilled leadership and willingness to accept the associated stress by all sides, a rational solution can frequently be found.

We noted earlier that appeal to a higher-level goal can be an effective conflict reduction method by distracting the attention of the parties in conflict from their separate and competing goals. The establishment of *superordinate goals* can also be a conflict resolution method if the higher-level goal that is mutually agreed upon incorporates the conflicting parties' lower-level goals.[18] For example, two academic departments in a university had been engaged in a lengthy and destructive conflict over their relative shares of grants from a university research fund. The animosity continued for years until a group of young faculty members from each department submitted a joint proposal for a large grant from a government agency. When the proposal was accepted, the two departments started to turn their attention to increasing grants from outside agencies and reduced their competition for the university research funds. Striving for a superordinate goal (outside grants) not only resolved the major conflict between the two departments but also fostered *intergroup cohesiveness;* faculty from each discipline exchanged more information and initiated more interdepartmental projects.

Line and Staff Conflict

A common form of organizational conflict is the conflict between line and staff members. Because of its frequency, and because of the importance of achieving effective line–staff collaboration in modern organizations, we will discuss this type of conflict here.

Line and staff members, like members of the other differentiated units in the organization, have different time horizons, goals, interpersonal orientations, and approaches to problems. (See chapter 10.) These differences enable line and staff members to accomplish their respective tasks effectively, but the differences also increase the potential for conflict between them.[19]

The View from the Line

Line members frequently believe that staff members are prone to four major failings:

1. *Staff oversteps its authority.* Because line managers bear ultimate responsibility for results, they tend to resent staff intrusion on their prerogatives.
2. *Staff does not give sound advice.* Staff members may be cut off from the day-to-day operational realities that line members confront. Their suggestions may therefore lack applicability. Some staff members contribute to this stereotype by recommending ideas that worked well in other organizations but may not be suitable for their own organization.
3. *Staff steals credit from line.* Staff members frequently have greater access to top managers than do line members, and may take advantage of that access to take credit or avoid blame. ("When things go wrong, we get the blame. But when things go right, they take the bows.")
4. *Staff has narrow perspectives.* Staff members tend to be specialists—industrial engineers, labor relations experts, and so on. As such, say line managers, they have a limited perspective and fail to relate their suggestions to the organization's overall needs and goals.

The View from the Staff

For their part, staff members have analogous complaints about the failings of line members:

1. *Line does not use staff properly.* Line managers resist calling in a staff expert, because they like to retain authority over their subunit or because they fear admitting openly that they need help. As a result, staff may be called in only when the situation has completely deteriorated.
2. *Line resists new ideas.* Staff members are usually the first to be aware of useful innovations in their area of expertise. Line managers, however, may resist making changes. They are therefore seen by staff members as overly cautious and rigid.
3. *Line gives staff too little authority.* Staff members often feel that they have the best solutions to problems in their specialty. They therefore resent it when their suggestions are not supported and implemented by line managers.

Other Line–Staff Differences

Differences in style and other characteristics often exacerbate conflicts between line and staff. For example, Melville Dalton found that staff members tend to be younger, better educated, more ambitious, more individualistic, and more concerned with their dress than are line members.[20] Alvin W. Gouldner has classified organization personnel in terms of what he called "cosmopolitans" and "locals."[21] His two categories correspond roughly to the "staff" and "line" distinction. "Cosmopolitan" staff members are committed to their work for its intrinsic qualities; they are likely to feel closer to specialists in similar activities outside the organization than to other members of their own organization. "Local" line members identify themselves and their career aspirations more closely with their organizations and are less committed to specialized job skills and outside reference groups. Such differences may be seen as "lack of loyalty" by line members and "provincialism" by staff members.

Reducing Line–Staff Conflict

Edward C. Schleh and other management writers have suggested ways in which the dysfunctional aspects of line–staff conflict can be reduced:[22]

- *Spell out line and staff responsibilities clearly.* In general, line members should remain responsible for the operating decisions of the organization; in other words, they should be free to accept, modify, or reject staff recommendations. On the other hand, staff members should be free to give advice when they feel it is needed—not only when line members request it.
- *Integrate staff and line activities.* Staff suggestions would be more realistically based if staff members consulted line members early in the process of developing their suggestions. Such staff–line consultation would also make line members more willing to implement staff ideas.
- *Educate line to use staff properly.* Line managers will make more effective use of staff expertise when they know what the specialist can do for them. Schleh suggests that staff members describe their functions to line in conferences or brief line members individually.
- *Hold staff accountable for results.* Line members would be more amenable to staff suggestions if staff members were held liable for the failure of those suggestions. Accountability would also increase the likelihood that staff members would develop their suggestions more carefully.

Management–Labor Conflict

Another important, and classic, form of organizational conflict is that between management and labor. The potential for conflict here always exists, but escalates especially when a management–union labor contract is about to expire, thus requiring renegotiation.[23]

Workers and Unions

Although declining in size, unions still represent a major source of potential conflict with which managers have to deal. Approximately 22 million workers in the United States belong to unions, representing under 20 percent of the eligible, non-agricultural work force in 1984 as opposed to 35 percent in 1950, and the percentage of eligible unionized workers may decline still further.[24] Workers join unions to protect a variety of job interests they feel management does not adequately guarantee:

1. *Economic*—the right to a livable wage.
2. *Job safety*—job security, freedom from arbitrary actions by management.
3. *Social affiliation*—a need to belong and to be accepted by peers.
4. *Self-esteem*—being able to have a voice in the "system."
5. *Status and self-fulfillment*—the exercise of leadership or other abilities through union service.

Of these, safety, social affiliation, and self-esteem are the major reasons why workers join unions today. Social pressure (the urgings of unionized co-workers) and job requirements ("union shops" requiring union membership as a condition of employment) also motivate workers to join unions.

In recent years, the intensification of price and technological competition, deregulation, and public-sector budget cutbacks has led managers to seek more efficient use of their organizations' work force. Efforts to improve efficiency frequently disrupt established work routines or threaten job security (for example, combining worker tasks, restricting overtime or weekend work, and laying off workers). Unions, in turn, have made work rule and job security issues a high priority. This situation, which is the source of conflict in many current management–labor interactions, shows no sign of abating and is likely to continue through this decade.

Approaches to Management–Labor Relations

There are six basic approaches that management and unions can take to each other when beginning negotiations:

1. *Outright conflict:* Both management and union refuse to compromise on any issue, indulge in negative stereotyping of each other, and seek to undermine each other's position in any way possible.
2. *Armed truce:* Both management and union acknowledge that they will always be at odds. Management adheres to labor law and bargains only on the basis of what issues the law covers, trying to limit the union's field of interest as much as possible.
3. *Power bargaining:* Management accepts the reality of the union and uses its power to bargain against the union's power (posing strength against weakness) in an attempt to achieve a "balance of power."
4. *Accommodation:* Management and union have settled into a livable day-to-day routine and have developed means of resolving differences by meeting each other halfway.
5. *Cooperation:* The union is an active partner with management in company

operations and deals with personnel and production problems together with management. Management not only accepts and supports the union, but finds union participation desirable.

6. *Collusion:* Management and union leadership protect their mutual interests through unethical and illegal actions, such as bribery.

As with any relationship, the type of management–labor relations in a particular company depends on the actions of both parties. If the union maintains a belligerent attitude toward management, management is likely to take a belligerent attitude in return. In such a situation, conflict is maximized, and both parties are likely to suffer. But outright hostility between management and union is now relatively rare. Currently, accommodation typifies the management–labor relations of most companies in the United States.

Minimizing Negotiation Conflict

Successful management–labor negotiations depend a good deal on thorough preparation. The typical union contract is far too complex to leave until the last minute. It is now common, and necessary, to prepare for negotiations at least six months to a year before they are to commence.

In planning for negotiations, the manager first lists all the issues that have surfaced in previous negotiations, gathering information for this from past contracts, and then determines the overall priorities of these issues in terms of the company's financial, administrative, and productivity objectives. Next he or she reviews reports from line and staff on problem areas of the last contract, grievance statistics, morale problems, and any insights into the union climate and bargaining issues. Using this information, the manager can determine in advance the most and least preferable settlements on all of the bargaining issues. Computer modeling and analysis of financial data can be a tremendous aid in calculating the costs of various possible settlements in advance and during actual negotiations. In this way, once issue priorities and settlement ranges are set, management can then gauge its, and the union's, strengths and weaknesses. Decision support system (DSS) software is available to help prepare for negotiations. One such program, *The Negotiating Edge,*[25] can be used by managers—or union leaders—to size up opponents and identify their areas of vulnerability.

Traditionally, the union presents the company its proposed contractual changes to open the negotiations. The company replies with a counterproposal. Before the negotiation process, management should be clear on its stance toward the union, its objectives and priorities on each bargaining issue, and its bargaining behavior.

Reed C. Richardson has observed that most labor–management negotiations follow four stages:[26]

1. *Setting-in:* Both sides familiarize themselves with each other's position and the climate of the negotiations.
2. *Consolidation:* The negotiators progress to more substantive discussions of the bargaining issues and resolve issues of minor importance.
3. *Finalization:* Higher-priority issues are tackled, and both parties push and pull to reach a final agreement.
4. *Mopping-up:* The final agreement is written in language checked and approved by both sides.

- Have set, *clear objectives* on every bargaining item and understand the context upon which the objectives are established.
- *Do not hurry.*
- When in doubt, *caucus.*
- Be *well prepared* with firm data support for clearly defined objectives.
- Maintain *flexibility* in your position.
- *Find out the motivations* for what the other party does.
- *Do not get bogged down.* If there is no progress on a certain item, move on to another and come back to it later. Build the momentum for agreement.
- Respect the importance of *face-saving* for the other party.
- Be a good *listener.*
- Build a reputation for being *fair* but *firm.*
- Control your *emotions.*
- Be sure as you make each bargaining move that you know its *relationship* to all other moves.
- *Measure each move* against your *objectives.*
- Pay close attention to the *wording* of each clause negotiated.
- Remember that negotiating is by its nature a *compromise* process.
- Learn to *understand* people—it may pay off during negotiations.
- Consider the *impact of present negotiations* on *future* ones.

Source: Adapted from Reed C. Richardson, *Collective Bargaining by Objectives: A Positive Approach* (Englewood Cliffs, N.J.: Prentice-Hall, 1985), pp. 168–169.

Upon entering negotiations, either management or labor, or both, may present a proposal that contains excessive demands. Such a proposal may be a negotiating ploy to obtain leverage for later trade-offs, or it may be a smoke screen to conceal the bargainer's real position. Excessive demands by unions might also reflect the pet concerns of the rank and file or of influential officials. As the negotiations move into the consolidation and finalization stages, flexibility in negotiation takes on greater and greater importance. For progress to be made in the negotiations, each side needs to be able to back away from initial positions and excessive demands, make trade-offs, and introduce alternative solutions. See the box for 17 guidelines for conducting successful negotiations.

In the end, it is the strike deadline that often motivates the progress of the negotiations. Management may not be able to afford a strike; the union may risk losing valuable demands if it strikes. The threat of a strike can bring both parties back to reality and grant them the opportunity to reassess their positions. Each side will make major concessions in order to avert a strike that is not in their best interests.

Although the number of strikes has decreased in the past 20 years, they still do occur. Negotiations on occasion do reach an impasse, and no other alternative may be viable for the union to reach its goals. In some instances, union members may reject a negotiated agreement, or the union may feel it needs to strike to air its grievances. Some companies might welcome a strike in order to reduce excessive inventories.

Managing Organizational Creativity

Time ⟶

Creativity has become an important part of organizational life. When functional conflict is well managed, it enables the organization to find new and better ways—and more creative ways—of accomplishing its work. In this age of tough competition, resource scarcity, and high labor and equipment costs, anything that leads to more efficient and effective operations increases an organization's chances to survive and succeed. Creativity also enables the organization to anticipate change. This has become very important as new technologies, products, and methods of operation make old ones obsolete.

Like functional conflict, creativity flourishes best in a dynamic, tolerant atmosphere. Creative people can be bothersome; they question how things are done, they upset routine, and their ideas require checking and shaping. To encourage and manage creativity, managers must understand the creative process, know how to select people with creative ability, be able to stimulate creative behavior, and provide an organizational climate that nurtures creativity.

Creativity and Innovation

Some management writers distinguish between creativity and innovation. They define *creativity* as the generation of a new idea and *innovation* as the translation of such an idea into a new product, service, or method of production. In Lawrence B. Mohr's words, creativity implies "bringing something new into being; innovation implies bringing something new into use."[27]

Such a distinction can be meaningful in organizational life. The skills required to generate new ideas are not the same as those required to make these ideas a reality. To make full use of its ideas, the organization may need both creative and innovative personnel. In addition, creativity alone contributes little or nothing to organizational effectiveness unless the creative ideas can in some way be used or implemented. Thus, in organizations, the creative process must include both creative and innovative elements: A new idea must indeed be created, but it must also be capable of implementation and must actually be implemented for the organization to benefit from it.

Steps in the Creative Process

We will examine the creative process as it takes place within the individual before we describe the process by which managers manage the creativity of individuals and groups.

It is convenient to divide the creative process into the following five steps:[28]

1. *Problem finding or sensing.* The individual selects a problem to work on or, more likely, becomes aware that a problem or disturbance exists. ("I'm getting bogged down in these monthly reports. Isn't there a better way to do this?")
2. *Immersion or preparation.* The individual concentrates on the problem and becomes immersed in it, recalling and collecting information that seems relevant and dreaming up hypotheses without evaluating them. ("Other companies must do this differently. Perhaps they only require bimonthly reports.")
3. *Incubation or gestation.* After assembling the available information, the individual relaxes and lets his or her subconscious mull over the material. In this little-understood but crucial step, the individual often appears to be idle or daydreaming, but his or her subconscious is in fact trying to arrange the facts into a new pattern.
4. *Insight or illumination.* Often when least expected—while eating, or falling asleep, or walking—the new, integrative idea will flash into the individual's mind. ("A preprinted checklist! That way I can give my boss the right information without wasting time.") Such inspirations must be recorded quickly, because the conscious mind may forget them in the course of other activities.
5. *Verification and application.* The individual sets out to prove by logic or experiment that the idea can solve the problem and can be implemented. Tenacity may be required at this point, since new ideas may be initially rejected as fallacious and impractical, only to be vindicated later.

Individual Creativity

Individuals differ in their ability to be creative. Highly creative people tend to be more original than less creative people. If asked to suggest possible uses for automobile tires, noncreative people might say "buoys" and "tree swings"; creative people might say such things as "eyeglass frames for an elephant" or "halos for big robots." Creative people also tend to be more flexible than noncreative people—they are able and willing to shift from one approach to another when tackling a problem. They prefer complexity to simplicity and tend to be more independent than less creative people, sticking to their guns stubbornly when their ideas are challenged. Creative people also question authority quite readily and are apt to disobey orders that make no sense to them. For this reason they may be somewhat difficult to manage in most organizations. Motivated more by an interesting problem than by material reward, they will work long and hard on something that intrigues them.

There are a number of tests for measuring creative ability.[29] These tests offer organizations some guidance for selecting individuals who will be most effective in situations that require creativity—new-product development, research, and advertising, for example. However, there are practical difficulties associated with administering tests for creativity, because it is hard to predict from such tests which people will actually act creatively. It is generally more practical to manage people so that their creative *actions* are increased, regardless of their initial creative *ability,* rather than attempting to select especially creative people.

Stimulating Individual and Group Creativity

The methods of stimulating creativity discussed here—brainstorming, nominal group process, synectics, and creative decision making—are designed to be used in groups. However, the principles that underlie these methods can also help individuals improve their creativity.[30]

Brainstorming. We discussed brainstorming in chapter 7 in connection with forecasting. However, the technique was developed originally by Alex F. Osborn to generate ideas for advertising campaigns.[31] And it is still most often used in advertising and new-product development and to develop possible solutions for complex problems.

Brainstorming encourages the free flow of ideas without inhibition by prejudgment or criticism. In group brainstorming, group members are assembled, presented with the problem, and urged to produce as many ideas or solutions as they can. No evaluation is permitted. Quantity is preferred to quality, and rapid-fire contributions are sought. Even impractical suggestions are well received and recorded, since they may stimulate more useful recommendations. In individual brainstorming, the individual freely produces ideas, again without criticizing or evaluating them.

Donald W. Taylor, Paul C. Berry, and Clifford H. Block compared the effectiveness of groups and individuals who used the brainstorming technique. They found that individuals working alone usually developed more and better ideas than the same number of people working together in a group. The authors concluded that, despite the free atmosphere of brainstorming sessions, group members still inhibit one another's creativity and thus limit the range of ideas that are produced.[32]

The fact that brainstorming group sessions, as opposed to individual sessions, are still used in organizations may be because managers are unaware of studies like those of Taylor and his colleagues. It may also be easier for managers to arrange group sessions, which generally are fun and stimulating for the participants, than to induce individuals to brainstorm on their own. In addition, the fun of working together may provide additional advantages, such as building team spirit, mobilizing enough commitment for implementing some of the ideas, and increasing communication among members.[33]

Nominal Group Process. An extension and modification of the brainstorming approach, called the nominal group process, removes the vocal interaction that may inhibit some individuals. Group members work alone but in the same room, developing ideas. They then share their lists of ideas, one item at a time in round-robin fashion. This approach appears to yield more ideas than brainstorming, yet keeps some of the advantages of that technique.[34]

Synectics (the Gordon Technique). This technique was developed by William J. Gordon when he was a member of Arthur D. Little, Inc., a well-known research and consulting firm.[35] It was designed to help the firm invent new products for its clients. While the object of a brainstorming session is to generate as many ideas as possible, synectics aims for only one radically new idea focused on a specific problem area.

In synectics, only the group leader knows the exact nature of the problem. In this way, quick, easy solutions are avoided, and participants do not have a chance to become overly enamored of their own ideas. Group discussion is organized around a subject that is related to the problem but that does not reveal what the problem actually is. For example, if the problem is to produce a new toy, the leader might suggest play or enjoyment as the discussion area. The session might open with give-and-take on the meaning of play and what types of play lead to the greatest enjoyment. Eventually, under the careful direction of the leader, the discussion might start to focus on what kinds of new toys children would find most enjoyable.

Creative Group Decision Making. Creative group decision making is appropriate when there is no apparent or agreed-upon method of solving a problem. According to André L. Delbecq, creative decision-making groups should be composed of competent personnel from a variety of backgrounds and should be directed by a leader who can stimulate creative behavior.[36] The group problem-solving process is somewhat akin to brainstorming in that discussion is spontaneous, all group members participate, and the evaluation of ideas is suspended at the beginning of the session. But while brainstorming *avoids* decision making, *reaching* a decision is the aim of the creative decision-making group.

Organizational Creativity and Innovation

Just as individuals differ in their ability to translate their creative talents into results, so organizations differ in their ability to translate the talents of their members into new products, processes, or services. To enable their organizations to use creativity most effectively, managers need to be aware of the process of innovation in organizations and to take steps to encourage this process. (See figure 14–3 for an outline of the process of idea evaluation developed by Eastman Kodak's Office of Innovation.) The creative process in organizations involves three steps: idea generation, problem solving or idea development, and implementation.[37]

Generation of Ideas. The generation of ideas in an organization depends first and foremost on the flow of people and information between the firm and its environment. For example, the vast majority of technological innovations have been made in response to conditions in the marketplace. If organization managers are unaware that there is potential demand for a new product, or that there is dissatisfaction with already existing products, they are not likely to seek innovations.

Outside consultants and experts are important sources of information for managers, because they are frequently aware of new products, processes, or service developments in their fields. New employees may have knowledge of alternative approaches or technologies used by suppliers and competitors. Among the organization's regular members, those who constantly expose themselves to information outside their immediate work setting are valuable sources of new ideas. These people, called "technological gatekeepers" by Thomas Allen, can play a particularly important role in stimulating creativity and innovation in research and development labs.[38]

Idea Development. Unlike idea generation, which is greatly stimulated by external contacts, idea development is dependent on the organizational culture and processes within the organization. Organizational characteristics, values, and processes

FIGURE 14–3 EASTMAN KODAK'S INNOVATION/IDEA EVALUATION SYSTEM

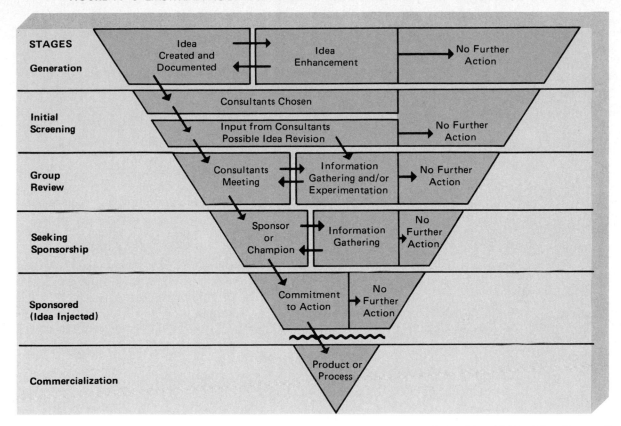

Source: Robert Rosenfeld and Jenny C. Servo, "Business and Creativity: Making Ideas Connect," *Futurist* 18, no. 4 (August 1984): 24.

can support or inhibit the development and use of creative ideas. Commitment to the rational problem-solving approaches discussed in chapter 6 increases the likelihood that high-quality and creative ideas will be recognized and developed fully.

The organizational structure also plays an important role. Rigidly structured organizations that inhibit communication between departments will often keep potentially helpful people from knowing that a problem exists. By creating barriers to communication, such organizations may also prevent problem solutions from reaching managers who need them. Management information systems (MISs), decision support systems (DSSs), and expert systems store and retrieve generated ideas and aid managers in idea development.[39] Recent advances in networking of such systems are especially helpful for integrative problem solving. (See chapters 6 and 22 for discussions of expert systems, DSS, and MIS.)

Implementation. The implementation stage of the creative process in organizations consists of those steps that bring a solution or invention to the marketplace. For manufactured goods, these steps include engineering, tooling, manufacturing, test marketing, and promotion. While a high rate of innovation often reduces short-term profitability, it is necessary for long-term growth. For example, the Swiss watch industry, which operates by traditional practices and old-fashioned individual craftsmanship, has been in decline since the mid-1970s, when more innovative competitors introduced new products, such as digital watches, into the market.[40] When Swiss watchmakers recently introduced new products, such as the popular, inexpensive Swatch wristwatch, they were able to regain part of a market that had appeared to be lost to them.

For innovation to be successful, a high degree of integration is required among the various units of the organization. Technical specialists, responsible for the engineering side of the new product, must work with administrative and financial specialists responsible for keeping the cost of innovation within practical limits. Production managers, helping to refine the specifications of the new product, must work with marketing managers, who are responsible for test marketing, advertising, and promoting it. Proper integration of all these groups is necessary for a quality innovation to be produced on time, on budget, and for a viable market. Organizations that are too rigidly structured may have a difficult time integrating their activities. In contrast, frequent and informal communication across an organization has been shown to have positive effects on innovation.[41] For this reason, task forces (to be discussed in chapter 17) and matrix-type organizational structures (chapter 9), which encourage interdepartmental communication and integration, are particularly suited for generating, developing, and implementing creative ideas and approaches.

Establishing a Climate for Organizational Creativity

As we have seen, creativity is best nurtured in a permissive climate, one that encourages the exploration of new ideas and new ways of doing things. Such a climate is difficult for many managers to accept. They may be uncomfortable with the continuing process of change, which is a necessary accompaniment of creativity. They may also be concerned that in a permissive atmosphere, discipline or cost control may break down.

How can managers take these real feelings and concerns into account and yet create a climate that will encourage creativity? The steps listed below suggest a possible answer:[42]

1. *Develop an acceptance of change.* Organization members must believe that change will benefit them and the organization. This belief is more likely to arise if members participate with their managers in making decisions and if issues like job security are carefully handled when changes are planned and implemented. (See our discussion on overcoming resistance to change in chapter 13.)
2. *Encourage new ideas.* The managers in the organization, from top managers to lower-level supervisors, must make it clear in word and deed that they welcome new approaches. To encourage creativity, managers must be willing to listen to subordinates' suggestions, implementing promising ones, or conveying them to higher-level managers.
3. *Permit more interaction.* A permissive, creative climate is fostered if individuals have the opportunity to interact with members of their own and other work

groups. Such interaction encourages the exchange of useful information, the free flow of ideas, and fresh perspectives on problems.

4. *Tolerate failure.* Many new ideas prove impractical or useless. Effective managers accept and allow for the fact that time and resources will be invested in experimenting with new ideas that may not work out.

5. *Provide clear objectives and freedom to achieve them.* Organization members must have a purpose and direction for their creativity. Supplying guidelines and reasonable constraints will also give managers some control over the time and money invested in creative behavior.

6. *Offer recognition.* Creative individuals are motivated to work hard on tasks that interest them. But, like all individuals, they enjoy being rewarded for a task well done. By offering recognition in such tangible forms as bonuses and salary increases, managers demonstrate that creative behavior is valued in their organizations.

Summary

Views of conflict have changed in the last three decades. In the traditional view, all conflict is seen as a harmful result of the failure to apply management principles. The current view is that conflict is not only inevitable but sometimes even necessary for the organization to survive.

There are various types of conflict. Conflict between groups in the same organization may be caused by their need to share scarce resources, by the interdependence of work activities, and by their differences in goals, values, or perceptions. Individual style differences, as well as organizational ambiguities and communication problems, may also contribute to group conflict.

Effects of conflict include a rise in group cohesion, selection of strong leaders and group representatives, and the development of distorted perceptions about one's own group and the opposing group. Whether or not these and other consequences will prove functional or dysfunctional for the organization will depend on the level of conflict, the organizational structure and culture, and how the conflict is managed.

The management of conflict may include conflict stimulation, reduction, or resolution. Conflict stimulation methods include bringing outsiders into the organization, encouraging competition, restructuring the organization, and redistributing power among the organization work groups. Conflict reduction methods include establishing superordinate goals and uniting the conflicting groups to meet a common threat.

Undesirable or ineffective conflict resolution methods include compromise and the suppression of conflict. Integrative problem solving, on the other hand, allows managers to resolve conflict in a way that most benefits the organization and does the least harm to conflicting individuals or groups.

Line–staff conflict and management–labor conflict are common examples of organizational conflict. Disputes between line and staff tend to derive from functional and personal differences between the two groups. Management–labor conflict tends to be more adversarial in nature. There are six approaches that unions and management can take in their relations: outright conflict, armed truce, power bargaining, accommodation (the most widespread), cooperation, and collusion. Conflict between management and unions is heightened during labor contract negotiations; successful negotiations usually require thorough preparation, the setting of clear goals and priorities, and flexibility in demands by both parties.

The management of organizational creativity requires an understanding of the creative process and how it can be stimulated. In individuals, the creative process can be divided into five steps: problem finding or sensing, immersion, incubation, insight, and application. Individual or group creativity can be stimulated through brainstorming, nominal group process, synectics, and creative group decision making.

Effective organizational creativity and innovation follow a three-step procedure: idea generation, idea development, and implementation. This procedure is facilitated by an organizational structure and climate that encourage (1) the free flow of communication between the organization and its environment; (2) the free flow of communication among organization members; and (3) the integration of organizational activities.

Review Questions

1. What is the difference between conflict and competition?

2. What are the traditional and interactionist views of conflict? With which view do you agree? Why?

3. What are the five types of conflict possible in organizations? Under what conditions will each type of conflict arise?

4. Why does differentiation of organization groups often lead to conflict?

5. What are the effects of organizational conflict on group attitudes and behavior? What factors determine whether these effects will be functional or dysfunctional?

6. What are the consequences of a very low level of organizational conflict? What methods of conflict stimulation can managers use?

7. In the Sherifs's conflict reduction experiment, what two methods proved effective? Why might these methods be ineffective in organizations?

8. What are three types of conflict resolution methods? In what ways can these methods be manifested? Which method is usually best? Why?

9. How do line and staff members view each other and their role in the organization? How can line and staff conflict be reduced?

10. What are the six approaches that management and unions can take toward one another? How might these affect management–labor negotiations?

11. Why do you think creativity is important in organizational life?

12. What is the difference between creativity and innovation?

13. What are the steps in the creative process in individuals?

14. What techniques can be used to stimulate individual or group creativity?

15. What are the three steps in the organizational creativity process? How can each step be facilitated or inhibited?

16. How can managers establish an organizational climate that encourages creativity?

Notes

1. Stephen P. Robbins, *Managing Organizational Conflict* (Englewood Cliffs, N.J.: Prentice-Hall, 1974).

2. See M. Afzalur Rahim, "A Strategy for Managing Conflict in Complex Organizations," *Human Relations* 38, no. 1 (January 1985):81–89.

3. See, for example, William E. Rothschild, *How to Gain (and Maintain) the Competitive Advantage in Business* (New York: McGraw-Hill, 1984).

4. See James G. March and Herbert A. Simon, *Organizations* (New York: Wiley, 1958); Richard E. Walton and John M. Dutton, "The Management of Interdepartmental Conflict," *Administrative Science Quarterly* 14, no. 1 (March 1969):73–84; M. Afzalur Rahim, "Measurement of Organizational Conflict," *Journal of General Psychology* 109, no. 2 (October 1983):189–199; and Walter G. Stephan, "Intergroup Relations," in Gardner Lindzey and Elliot Aronson, eds., *Handbook of Social Psychology*, vol. 2, 3d ed. (New York: Random House, 1985), chapter 11.

5. A short summary of the research is found in Muzafer Sherif, "Experiments in Group Conflict," *Scientific American*, November 1956, pp. 54–58. See also Muzafer Sherif and Carolyn W. Sherif, *Groups in Harmony and Tension* (New York: Octagon, 1966); and Andrew Tyerman and Christopher Spence, "A Critical Test of the Sherifs' Robber's Cave Experiments: Intergroup Competition and Cooperation Between Groups of Well-Acquainted Individuals," *Small Group Behavior* 14, no. 4 (November 1983):515–531.

6. One factor frequently associated with high cohesion is consistency of perceptions. A study of top

managers' perceptions of their organizations found that agreement on strategic strengths and weaknesses was positively related to performance. See Lawrence G. Hrebiniak and Charles C. Snow, "Top-Management Agreement and Organizational Performance," *Human Relations* 35, no. 12 (December 1982):1139–1158.

7. James S. Coleman, *Community Conflict* (New York: Free Press, 1957), pp. 9–11; and Samuel F. Dworkin, Thomas P. Ference, and Donald B. Giddon, "The Nature of Conflict," in *Behavioral Science and Dental Practice* (St. Louis: Mosby, 1978), pp. 154–155.

8. See, for example, Robert R. Blake and Jane S. Mouton, "Reactions to Intergroup Conflict Under Win–Lose Conditions," *Management Science* 7, no. 4 (July 1961):420–435.

9. For a discussion of how the dysfunctional consequences of winning had to be overcome to create the Boston Celtics basketball "dynasty," see Bill Russell and Taylor Branch, *Second Wind* (New York: Random House, 1979), pp. 119–170.

10. David Mechanic, "Sources of Power of Lower Participants in Complex Organizations," *Administrative Science Quarterly* 7, no. 3 (December 1961):349–364.

11. See Joseph A. Litterer, "Conflict in Organization: A Re-examination," *Academy of Management Journal* 9, no. 3 (September 1966):178–186; and Robert H. Miles, *Macro Organizational Behavior* (Santa Monica, Calif.: Goodyear, 1980), chapter 5.

12. Elise Boulding, "Further Reflections on Conflict Management," in Robert L. Kahn and Elise Boulding, eds., *Power and Conflict in Organizations* (New York: Basic Books, 1964), pp. 146–150.

13. The skillful handling of the Cuban missile crisis in 1962 by John F. Kennedy has been attributed to systematic attempts to avoid what we called "groupthink" in chapter 12. Kennedy was careful to include individuals with differing points of view among his advisors, encouraged all to express their disagreements forcefully and openly, and kept his own position ambiguous to discourage his advisors from agreeing with him. See Irving L. Janis, *Groupthink: Psychological Studies of Policy Decisions*, 2nd ed. (Boston: Houghton Mifflin, 1982).

14. Robbins, *Managing Organizational Conflict*, chapter 9.

15. Bertram H. Raven and Jeffrey Z. Rubin, *Social Psychology: People in Groups*, 2nd ed. (New York: Wiley, 1983), chapter 15.

16. Blair H. Sheppard, "Third Party Conflict Intervention: A Procedural Framework," in *Research in Organizational Behavior*, vol. 6 (Greenwich, Conn.: JAI Press, 1984), pp. 141–190.

17. Shona McKay, "A Boardroom Iconoclast," *McLeans*, September 19, 1983, p. 58. Also see Charles R. Schwenk, "Devil's Advocacy in Managerial Decision-making," *Journal of Management Studies* 21, no. 2 (April 1984):153–168.

18. Roy J. Lewicki and Joseph A. Litterer, *Negotiation* (Homewood, Ill.: Irwin, 1985), pp. 279–311.

19. Louis A. Allen, "The Line–Staff Relationship," *Management Record* 17, no. 9 (September 1955):346–349ff.

20. Melville Dalton, "Conflicts between Staff and Line Managerial Officers," *American Sociological Review* 15, no. 3 (June 1950):342–351.

21. Alvin W. Gouldner, "Cosmopolitans and Locals: Toward an Analysis of Latent Social Roles—I," *Administrative Science Quarterly* 2, no. 3 (December 1957):281–306.

22. Edward C. Schleh, "Using Central Staff to Boost Line Initiative," *Management Review* 65, no. 5 (May 1976):17–23. See also Allen, "The Line–Staff Relationship," pp. 375–376. Using staff effectively is similar to using a consultant effectively. For some guidelines, see Robert R. Blake and Jane Srygley Mouton, *Solving Costly Organizational Conflicts: Achieving Intergroup Trust, Cooperation, and Teamwork* (San Francisco: Jossey-Bass, 1984), chapters 4 and 5.

23. Labor–management negotiation is just one type of bargaining that managers must be engaged in. For negotiating strategies of a more general type, see John Winkler, *Bargaining for Results* (New York: Facts on File Publications, 1984); Earl Brooks and George S. Odiorne, *Managing by Negotiations* (New York: Van Nostrand Reinhold, 1984); and Edward Levin, *Negotiating Tactics* (New York: Fawcett, 1985).

24. The bulk of the discussion in this section on labor negotiations is drawn from Arthur A. Sloane and Fred Witney, *Labor Relations*, 5th ed. (Englewood Cliffs, N.J.: Prentice-Hall, 1985), chapters 1, 2, and 5. For an analysis of current changes in management–labor relations, see George Strauss, "Industrial Relations: Time of Change," *Industrial Relations* 23, no. 1 (Winter 1984):1–15.

25. *The Negotiating Edge* (Palo Alto: Human Edge Software, 1985). Another program for preparing for negotiations is *The Art of Negotiating* (Berkeley, Calif.: Experience in Software, 1985).

26. Reed C. Richardson, *Collective Bargaining by Objectives: A Positive Approach*, 2nd ed. (Englewood Cliffs, N.J.: Prentice-Hall, 1985), pp. 165–168.

27. Lawrence B. Mohr, "Determinants of Innovation in Organizations," *American Political Science Review* 63, no. 1 (March 1969):112. See also Teresa M. Amabile, "The Social Psychology of Creativity: A Componential Conceptualization," *Journal of Personality and Social Psychology* 45, no. 2 (August 1983):357–376.

28. See John F. Mee, "The Creative Thinking Process," *Indiana Business Review* 31, no. 2 (February 1956):4–9; and Frederic D. Randall, "Stimulate Your Executives to Think Creatively," *Harvard Business Review* 33, no. 4 (July–August 1955):121–128.

29. See, for example, J. P. Guilford, "Creativity: Its Measurement and Development," in Sidney J. Parnes and Harold F. Harding, eds., *A Source Book for Creative Thinking* (New York: Scribner's, 1962), pp. 151–168; and Jim G. Gillis, "Creativity, Problem-Solving, and Decision-Making," *Journal of Systems Management* 34, no. 9 (September 1983):40–42.

30. See Charles S. Whiting, "Operational Techniques of Creative Thinking," *Advanced Management* 20, no. 10 (October 1955):24–30. See also J. Geoffrey Rawlison, *Creative Thinking and Brainstorming* (New York: Halsted Press, 1981); and Roger von Oech, *A Whack on the Side of the Head: How to Unlock Your Mind for Innovation* (New York: Warner Books, 1983).

31. Alex F. Osborn, *Applied Imagination* (New York: Scribner's, 1953).

32. Donald W. Taylor, Paul C. Berry, and Clifford H. Block, "Does Group Participation When Using Brainstorming Techniques Facilitate or Inhibit Creative Thinking?" *Administrative Science Quarterly* 3, no. 1 (June 1958): 23–47. See also T. Rickards and B. L. Freedman, "Procedures for Managers in Idea-Deficient Situations: An Examination of Brainstorming Approaches," *Journal of Management Studies* 15, no. 1 (February 1978): 43–55.

33. Some support for these possibilities can be found in the following two articles. Mark E. Comadena found that individuals who provided more new ideas in brainstorming groups preferred to work in such groups: "Brainstorming Groups: Ambiguity, Tolerance, Communication, Apprehension, Task Attraction, and Individual Productivity," *Small Group Behavior* 15, no. 2 (May 1984):251–264. Robert Kerwin, a manager at Hughes Aircraft, reports enthusiastically on the use of brainstorming techniques to achieve some of these broader objectives: "Brainstorming as a Flexible Management Tool," *Personnel Journal* 62, no. 5 (May 1983):414ff.

34. Jeff T. Casey, Charles F. Gettys, Rebecca M. Pliske, and Tom Mehle, "A Partition of Small Group Predecision Performance into Informational and Social Components," *Organizational Behavior and Human Performance* 34, no. 1 (August 1984):112–139; and André L. Delbecq and Andrew H. Van de Ven, "A Group Process Model for Problem Identification and Program Planning," *Journal of Applied Behavioral Science* 7, no. 4 (July–August 1971):466–492.

35. See William J. Gordon, *Synectics* (New York: Collier Books, 1968). Synectics is also described at length in Eugene Raudsepp, *How to Create New Ideas: For Fun and Profit* (Englewood Cliffs, N.J.: Prentice-Hall, 1982).

36. André L. Delbecq distinguishes between routine decisions, compromises or negotiated decisions, and creative decisions; the decision-making approach is different for each. See "The Management of Decision-Making within the Firm: Three Strategies for Three Types of Decision-Making," *Academy of Management Journal* 10, no. 4 (December 1967):329–339.

37. James M. Utterback, "Innovation in Industry and the Diffusion of Technology," *Science*, February 15, 1974, pp. 620–626.

38. Thomas J. Allen and Stephen I. Cohen, "Information Flow in Research and Development Laboratories," *Administrative Science Quarterly* 14, no. 1 (March 1969):12–19; and Lewis A. Myers, Jr., "Information Systems in Research and Development: The Technological Gatekeeper Reconsidered," *R&D Management* 13, no. 4 (July 1983):199–206.

39. Stephen G. Green, Alden S. Bean, and B. Kay Snavely, "Idea Management in R&D as a Human Information Processing Analog," *Human Systems Management* 4, no. 2 (1983):98–112.

40. R. W. Roetheli, H. U. Balthasar, and R. R. Niederer, "Productivity Increase and Innovation," an unpublished paper delivered at the TIMS/ORSA Conference, Dallas, October 17, 1984.

41. Yar M. Ebadi and James M. Utterback, "The Effects of Communication on Technological Innovation," *Management Science* 30, no. 5 (May 1984):572–585.

42. See Richard E. Dutton, "Creative Use of Creative People," *Personnel Journal* 51, no. 11 (November 1972):818–822ff.; H. Joseph Reitz, *Behavior in Organizations*, rev. ed. (Homewood, Ill.: Irwin, 1981), pp. 214–220, 242–249; and Augustus Abbey and John W. Dickson, "R&D Work Climate and Innovation in Semiconductors," *Academy of Management Journal* 26, no. 2 (June 1983):362–368.

CASE STUDY: Chiefland Memorial Hospital

Mr. James A. Grover, retired land developer and financier, is the current president of Chiefland Memorial Hospital's board of trustees. Chiefland Memorial is a 200-bed voluntary short-term general hospital serving an area of approximately 50,000 persons. Mr. Grover has just begun a meeting with the administrator of the hospital, Mr. Edward M. Hoffman. The purpose of the meeting is to seek an acceptable solution to an apparent conflict-of-authority problem within the hospital between Mr. Hoffman and the Chief of Surgery, Dr. Lacy Young.

The problem was brought to Mr. Grover's attention by Dr. Young during a golf match between the two men. Dr. Young had challenged Mr. Grover to the golf match at the Chiefland Golf and Country Club; but it turned out that this was only an excuse for Dr. Young to discuss a hospital problem with Mr. Grover.

The problem that concerned Dr. Young involved the operating room supervisor, Geraldine Werther, R.N. Ms. Werther schedules the hospital's operating suite in accordance with policies that she "believes" to have been established by the hospital's administration. One source of irritation to the surgeons is her attitude that maximum utilization must be made of the hospital's operating rooms if hospital costs are to be reduced. She therefore schedules in such a way that operating room idle time is minimized. Surgeons complain that the operating schedule often does not permit them sufficient time to complete a surgical procedure in the manner they think desirable. More often than not, insufficient time is allowed between operations for effective preparation of the operating room for the next procedure. Such scheduling, the surgical staff maintains, contributes to low-quality patient care. Furthermore, some of the surgeons have complained that Ms. Werther shows favoritism in her scheduling, allowing some doctors more use of the operating suite than others.

The situation reached a crisis when Dr. Young, following an explosive confrontation with Ms. Werther, told her he was firing her. Ms. Werther then made an appeal to the hospital administrator, who in turn informed Dr. Young that discharging nurses was an administrative prerogative. In effect, Dr. Young was told he did not have authority to fire Ms. Werther. Dr. Young asserted that he did have authority over any issue affecting medical practice and good patient care in Chiefland Hospital. He considered this a medical problem and threatened to take the matter to the hospital's board of trustees.

As the meeting between Mr. Grover and Mr. Hoffman began, Mr. Hoffman explained his position on the problem. He stressed the point that a hospital administrator is legally responsible for patient care in the hospital. He also contended that quality patient care cannot be achieved unless the board of trustees authorized the administrator to make decisions, develop programs, formulate policies, and implement procedures. While listening to Mr. Hoffman, Mr. Grover recalled the position belligerently taken by Dr. Young, who had contended that surgical and medical doctors holding staff privileges at Chiefland would never allow a "layman" to make decisions impinging on medical practice. Dr. Young also had said that Mr. Hoffman should be told to restrict his activities to fund raising, financing, maintenance, housekeeping—administrative problems rather than medical problems. Dr. Young had then requested that Mr. Grover clarify in a definitive manner the lines of authority at Chiefland Memorial.

As Mr. Grover ended his meeting with Mr. Hoffman, the severity of the problem was unmistakably clear to him, but the solution remained quite unclear. Mr. Grover knew a decision was required—and soon.

Source: Case reprinted with permission from John M. Champion and John H. James, *Critical Incidents in Management*, 4th ed., pp. 40–41. Copyright © 1980. Used by permission of Richard D. Irwin, Inc.

Case Questions
1. Why do you think conflict has developed at Chiefland Memorial?
2. Would establishing clear lines of authority solve all the problems described in the case? Why or why not?
3. What should Mr. Grover do?

CASE ON ORGANIZING FOR STABILITY AND CHANGE

The Breaking Up of AT&T

When the U.S. government reached out and touched Ma Bell, more than its fingers did the walking. On January 1, 1984, the world's largest corporation was split apart.

For the more than one million employees of American Telephone & Telegraph, who were steeped in a tradition of company loyalty and unquestioned faith in the security of their jobs, the future was filled with uncertainties. Despite assurances by the company, many still feared the change.

The most resounding cut of the government's ax was the splitting away from AT&T of the local telephone companies. These were grouped into seven regional holding companies, all operating independently. The "new" AT&T was also reorganized into AT&T Communications and AT&T Technologies. (See exhibit.) AT&T Technologies was, in turn, divided into five divisions: Bell Laboratories, Network Systems, Technology Systems, International, and Information Systems.

Prior to divestiture, AT&T had been structured along functional lines. Bell Labs researched, Western Electric manufactured, and so on. Each division carried out its own function and responded to its own inner needs. As part of a new emphasis on sales, necessitated by the cruel realities of the competitive marketplace, the company now divided up its functional units to conform to its lines of business. Product managers were assigned to oversee a product through development, production, marketing, and sales, instead of letting the different divisions work independently (and sometimes jealously) on their parts of the job.

A major change also occurred in the company's status, changing it abruptly from a regulated monopoly to a large corporation thrust into the competitive hustle of the open marketplace. Public reaction was varied. Some regarded it, with a nostalgic sigh, as the end of an era of inexpensive phone service. Others, aware of AT&T's awesome resources, agreed with *Time* magazine that the stage was set for a telecommunications revolution in the areas of technology and marketing.

AT&T's breakup came almost exactly two years after the company struck a deal with the U.S. Justice Department, ending an antitrust suit that had been going on since 1974. Some observers felt that AT&T had given in to the government too easily. AT&T chairman Charles Brown, however, believing that sooner or later the breakup was inevitable, opted for sooner. "Time was not on our side," he said. "The government's determination to restructure the Bell System would have gone on for years, draining our energy and preventing us from planning our own future."

There was also widespread suspicion in technological towers that AT&T was impatient to join in the communications revolution that was increasingly combining the functional properties of telephones and computers. Previously, as a regulated monopoly, it had been unable to enter the data processing business.

The task of overhauling the company's structure and culture was an undertaking of gargantuan proportions. AT&T was an organization with deeply rooted traditions and rituals. No longer sheltered by a noncompetitive market, everything from AT&T's corporate philosophy—to provide universal phone service of high quality at a reasonable price—to its managerial structure and paternalistic attitude toward its employees had suddenly become obsolete. To complicate matters further, AT&T also had to contend with current economic uncertainties and increasing competition in the marketplace. Meanwhile, top management was so busy dealing with the Federal Communications Commission, the Justice Department, and Congress that it had little time left to worry about internal matters.

Some debate appeared in the executive and managerial ranks as to the extent to which the company's legendary "measurements and practices"—volumes of detailed written instructions issued by corporate headquarters on how to perform every task—should be restructured or even abolished. Some executives were wary of abandoning a system that they felt had served the company well for many years. In opposition, many managers expressed the need for more flexibility in their decision making and a desire to see success valued more highly than procedure.

Eventually the "abolitionists" prevailed, and AT&T adopted a new policy of encouraging greater initiative and responsiveness in its employees, rather than having them react primarily to orders from above. In addition, from corporate headquarters on down, the company cut back on the level of supervision and simplified the chain of command.

Some middle managers welcomed the management opportunities created by this and other new AT&T policies designed to emphasize competition, initiative, and cooperation. However, there were a number of older managers who, rather than bend with the wind of change, decided on early retirement, an option AT&T was offering as a means of reducing its payrolls. Explained one retiree: "All of us took a certain pride in where we had come from. It doesn't give you satisfaction tearing it apart."

Significant psychological trauma and stress were experienced throughout the company's ranks. There was a tendency to view the divestiture not only as an unwanted process thrust upon the company by the government but also as a personal assault on employees' rights and values. AT&T had a history of guaranteeing lifetime employment and promoting from within, policies that guaranteed a high proportion of loyal, veteran employees. One AT&T employee likened the feelings aroused by the breakup to having been "through a divorce that neither my wife nor my children wanted. . . . It was like waking up in familiar surroundings, but your family and all that you held dear were missing."

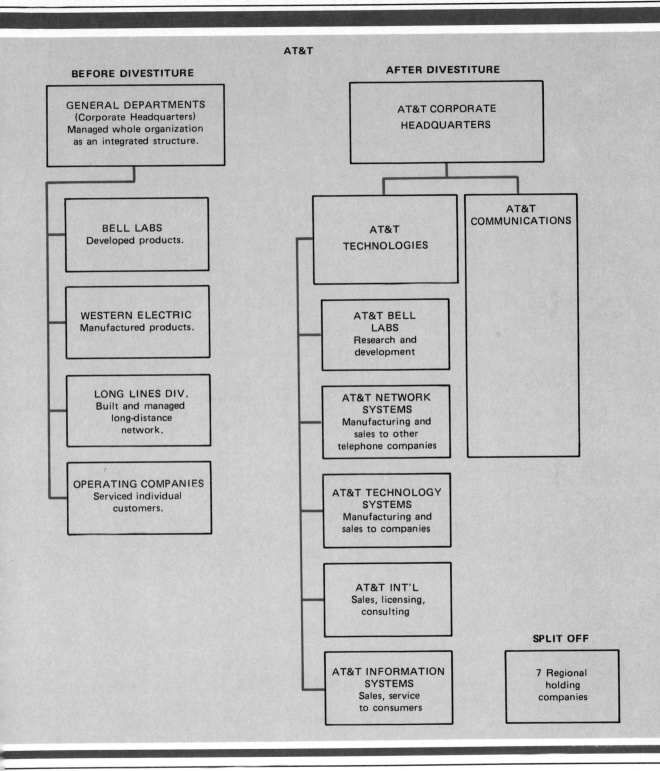

AT&T

BEFORE DIVESTITURE

GENERAL DEPARTMENTS
(Corporate Headquarters)
Managed whole organization
as an integrated structure.

BELL LABS
Developed products.

WESTERN ELECTRIC
Manufactured products.

LONG LINES DIV.
Built and managed
long-distance
network.

OPERATING COMPANIES
Serviced individual
customers.

AFTER DIVESTITURE

**AT&T CORPORATE
HEADQUARTERS**

**AT&T
TECHNOLOGIES**

**AT&T
COMMUNICATIONS**

**AT&T BELL
LABS**
Research and
development

**AT&T NETWORK
SYSTEMS**
Manufacturing and
sales to other
telephone companies

**AT&T TECHNOLOGY
SYSTEMS**
Manufacturing and
sales to companies

AT&T INT'L
Sales, licensing,
consulting

**AT&T INFORMATION
SYSTEMS**
Sales, service
to consumers

SPLIT OFF

7 Regional
holding
companies

411

Also contributing to employees' anxiety was uncertainty over job security. In the course of the reorganization, there were plant closings and reductions in the work force. Many employees who had had their future promotions clearly mapped out and taken for granted found themselves in a new and volatile situation, making them understandably less confident about the future.

AT&T employees were not the only people who were unhappy following the breakup. Many business customers, used to the company's outstandingly reliable customer service, became frustrated during the first half year by the delays encountered in obtaining services, particularly in the installation of private lines, custom-made phone lines that are important not only for person-to-person voice communication but also for transmitting computer data.

This enormous backlog of new private-line installation occurred for several reasons. AT&T Communications' monthly orders total jumped from 18,000 to 60,000 following divestiture due to the inheritance of some services (such as toll-free 800 lines and low-cost WATS lines) from the local operating companies. The new workers the division acquired to handle this increase were put on the job with almost no training in the new procedures. Therefore clerical work was initially slow and error-prone.

In addition, the installation of these lines is a process that needs to be partially carried out by a local operating company. The failure, therefore, of AT&T and the 22 operating companies to agree on a common order form created further delay and confusion.

With respect to the operating companies, AT&T found itself dealing with a loss of authority. In the past, when a problem such as the private lines backlog arose, AT&T had the authority, which it often exercised, to lean on an operating company to give precedence to the "corporate" problem. Now each operating company has the independence to set its own work priorities and procedures—such as the design of the order form.

Many of the problems that led to the backlog were remedied within several months, but AT&T by that time had already lost a certain amount of stature in the eyes of its business customers. To its credit, however, the company's disruptions occurred only in new services. Existing ones continued as smoothly as ever.

The most visible results of divestiture to the average residential customer were a more confusing phone bill and a drop in the cost of long-distance services and telephone equipment. This initial saving will be gradually offset over the next few years, though, as local companies raise their rates to cover their full costs. Prior to the breakup, low residential rates were subsidized by higher rates on other services provided by AT&T.

AT&T will continue to feel the effects of divestiture for years to come. There will be many new challenges to face, such as the one posed by "equal access." Under this provision, callers choose their long-distance carrier by dialing just one extra digit.

This removes what had been an advantage for AT&T over competitors like MCI and GTE's Sprint, whose customers had to enter a multidigit code to gain access to those systems. In Charleston, West Virginia, the first "equal access" city, MCI grabbed 15 percent of the long-distance market and Sprint took 6 percent.

AT&T is also debating with the government over the rapidity with which the company should be freed from regulation. One aspect of the continuing regulations governing AT&T is that it is not allowed to reduce long-distance rates without regulatory approval, although its competitors may do so. Since it is now part of the competitive market, AT&T feels it should have the same freedom as its competitors to set long-distance rates. Competitors have been arguing that if AT&T is released from regulation too quickly, it will still have the size and resources to pull the plug on them.

In the summer of 1985, the competitive situation took a new turn when IBM bought a stake in MCI. As part of the deal, IBM agreed to sell MCI its 60 percent share of Satellite Business Systems, a joint venture with Aetna Life and Casualty. Previously, IBM had purchased the Rolm Corporation, a leading manufacturer of PBXs (private branch exchanges that connect telephones within a building). Following IBM's move, Randall L. Tobias, chairman and CEO of AT&T's long-distance unit, told the press: "This announcement should put to rest any remaining questions about the strength of the competition in the telecommunication business."

AT&T is also experiencing increased competition in providing international long-distance service. While AT&T controls about 97 percent of the $5 billion market, its rivals are targeting their discounted service on this lucrative area. Howard A. Neckowitz, director of Spring International, said, "We have determined that our customers desire connectivity to as many countries as possible." And Seth D. Blumenthal, president of MCI International, said, "We realized that if a company is serious about being a full-service provider, it had to expand internationally."

Chairman Brown described his company's new mission as: "to be a major factor in the worldwide movement and management of information. . . . It involves the universalizing of the information age," a declaration that *Fortune* magazine described as "less than a clarion call." AT&T's major task is still to redefine its new corporate philosophy in a manner that adapts to the changes in the marketplace and inspires confidence in and loyalty from its employees.

Sources: This case was prepared by Jim McDonald and is based on material in the following articles: John S. DeMott, "Click! Ma Is Ringing Off," *Time*, November 21, 1983, pp. 60–74; "Culture Shock Is Shaking the Bell System," *Business Week*, September 26, 1983, pp. 112–118; Jeremy Main, "Waking Up AT&T: There's Life After Culture Shock," *Fortune*, December 24, 1984, pp. 66–74; Brian O'Reilly, "AT&T: What Was It We Were Trying to Fix?" *Fortune*, June 11, 1984, pp. 30–36; Mark D. Maremont, "Did It Make Sense to Break Up AT&T?" *Business Week*, December 3, 1984, pp. 86–89; Eric N. Berg, "MCI Sees Big Lift from IBM," *New York Times*, June 26, 1985, pp. D1ff.; Andrew Pollack, "The Battle of the Titans: II," *New York Times*, June 30, 1985, pp. F1ff.; and Eric N. Berg, "AT&T's Rivals Go Abroad," *New York Times*, July 8, 1985, pp. D1ff.

Questions
1. How would you characterize AT&T before the breakup? What kind of organization did it aim to become?
2. What structural changes were forced on the company? What advantages and problems have these changes created?
3. What effects have changes in company culture had on AT&T's employees? On AT&T's customers?
4. What external threats and new opportunities does the company now face?
5. How might MCI's relationship with IBM affect its ability to compete with AT&T? And what should the government do about the pace at which it removes its regulatory control over AT&T?
6. What factors will govern AT&T's success or failure in the marketplace?

PART FOUR
LEADING

15 MOTIVATION, PERFORMANCE, AND SATISFACTION

Upon completing this chapter you should be able to:

1. Identify and describe three theoretical approaches to motivation.
2. State how views of motivation in organizations have evolved.
3. Explain the systems view of motivation in organizations.
4. Describe the contributions of various theorists on motivation, and state how their work is related to motivation in organizations.
5. Explain the behavior modification approach to influencing behavior in organizations.
6. Describe two integrative approaches to motivation.
7. Discuss the implications for managers of current theories of motivation.

O f all management functions, leadership involves managers most directly with subordinates. Thus, leading is a central part of the manager's role, which involves working with and through others to achieve organizational goals. To a large extent, a manager's leadership ability—that is, a manager's ability to motivate, influence, direct, and communicate with subordinates—will determine the manager's effectiveness.

This chapter is concerned with how managers can motivate subordinates so that their performance and satisfaction will be increased. We start a unit on leadership with a chapter on motivation because managers cannot lead unless subordinates are motivated to follow them. In chapter 16 we will examine the leadership styles available to managers and trends for the future. Chapter 17 discusses groups and committees and how to lead them; chapter 18 focuses on the importance of effective communication in organizations. Chapter 19 is designed to help prospective managers plan their careers and to tell them what they can expect as they enter and rise in the organizational hierarchy.

The Importance of Motivation

Motivation—that which causes, channels, and sustains people's behavior—has always been important for managers to understand. Managers, by definition, work with and through people, but people are complex and sometimes irrational in their behavior. Their motivations are not always easy to discern. Many theories exist about motivation, and most differ in what they implicitly suggest managers should do to obtain the most effective performance from their employees. Most successful managers, however, have learned by experience that people are very responsive to praise and encouragement—expressed not only in words but also in actions—and need to feel successful in their work to give their best effort to the organization. IBM, for example, deliberately sets its sales quotas low enough to be attainable by the majority of its salespeople. Most people are also strongly self-motivated and seek the freedom and autonomy to perform their jobs in their own way. Managers who find the key to their employees' inner motivations can tap an immense source of productive energy.[1]

In the following discussion, we will cover both old and new theoretical perspectives in order to understand current knowledge about motivation and its relationship to work behavior and satisfaction.[2] In considering these theories, it is important to keep in mind that motivation is not the only influence on a person's performance level. Also involved are the individual's *abilities* and his or her understanding of what behaviors are necessary to achieve high performance (and high satisfaction); this factor is called *role perception*. Motivation, abilities, and role perceptions are all interrelated. Thus if *any* one factor discourages or inhibits high performance, the performance level is likely to be low, even if the other factors encourage performance.

Early Views of Motivation in Organizations

As we saw in chapter 2, management theories have changed over time to accommodate changes in the nature of managers' jobs. Early managers, for example, dealt with subordinates performing relatively uncomplicated tasks, whereas many, if not most, of today's managers deal with individuals performing complicated work. We also noted that understanding of effective and ineffective managerial approaches and the importance of social forces in the workplace grew over time. These factors also affected the development of management thought.

At different stages in the evolution of management thought, managers subscribed to different models or theories of motivation. We will look at three of them in the order in which they evolved: the traditional model, the human relations model, and the human resources model. As we shall see, the beliefs that managers have about motivation are important determinants of how they attempt to manage people.

The Traditional Model

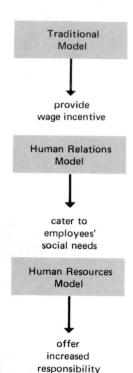

Traditional Model

↓

provide wage incentive

Human Relations Model

↓

cater to employees' social needs

Human Resources Model

↓

offer increased responsibility

The traditional model of motivation is associated with Frederick Taylor and the scientific management school. This school held that an important aspect of the manager's job was to make sure that workers perform their boring, repetitive tasks in the most efficient way. Managers determined how the jobs should be done and used a system of wage incentives to motivate workers—the more they produced, the more they earned.

This perspective assumed that workers were essentially lazy and that managers understood the workers' jobs better than the workers did. Workers could only be motivated by financial reward and had little to contribute beyond their labor. In many situations this approach was effective. As efficiency improved, fewer workers were needed for a specific task. Over time, managers reduced the size of the wage incentive. Layoffs became common, and workers sought job security rather than only temporary and minor wage increases.

The Human Relations Model

Eventually it became apparent that the traditional approach to motivation was no longer adequate. Elton Mayo and other human relations researchers found that the social contacts employees had at work were also important and that the boredom and repetitiveness of tasks were themselves factors in reducing motivation. Mayo and others also believed that managers could motivate employees by acknowledging their social needs and by making them feel useful and important.

As a result, employees were given some freedom to make their own decisions on the job. Greater attention was paid to the organization's informal work groups. More information was provided to employees about managers' intentions and about the operations of the organization.

In the traditional model, workers had been expected to accept management's authority in return for high wages made possible by the efficient system designed by management and implemented by the workers. In the human relations model, workers were expected to accept management's authority because supervisors treated them with consideration and were attentive to their needs. The intent of managers, however, remained the same—to have workers accept the work situation as established by managers.

The Human Resources Model

Later theorists such as McGregor and Maslow, and researchers such as Argyris and Likert, criticized the human relations model as being simply a more sophisticated approach to the manipulation of employees. These theorists suggested that employees were motivated by many factors—not only money, or the desire for satisfaction, but also the need for achievement and meaningful work. They argued that most people are already motivated to do a good job and that they do not automatically see work as undesirable. They suggested that employees are likely to derive satisfaction from good performance (rather than performing well because they are satisfied, as in the human relations model). Thus, employees can be given far more responsibility for making decisions and carrying out their tasks.

From a human resources perspective, then, managers should not induce workers to comply with managerial objectives by bribing them with high wages, as in the traditional model, or manipulate them with considerate treatment, as in the human relations model. Instead, managers should share responsibility for achieving organizational and individual objectives, with each person contributing on the basis of his or her interests and abilities. (See table 15–1 for a description of all three approaches.)

One study found that contemporary managers tend to believe in two models of motivation simultaneously. With their subordinates, managers tend to operate according to the human relations model: They try to reduce subordinates' resistance by improving morale and satisfaction. For themselves, however, managers prefer the human resources model: They feel their own talents are underutilized, and they seek greater responsibility from their superiors.[3]

Ways of Looking at Motivation

It is useful to review some of the major classifications of motivation theories, since each theoretical perspective will shed light on how motivation influences work performance. Distinctions are made on the basis of *content theories,* which focus on the "what" of motivation, and *process theories,* which focus on the "how" of motivation. *Reinforcement theories,* a third approach, emphasize the ways in which behavior is learned.

Content Theories

The content approach is associated with such names as Maslow, McGregor, Herzberg, Atkinson, and McClelland. Some of these are familiar to managers because these authors have strongly influenced the management field and have affected the thoughts and actions of practicing managers.

The content perspective stresses understanding the factors within individuals that cause them to act in a certain way. It attempts to answer such questions as: What needs do people try to satisfy? What impels them to action? In this view, individuals

TABLE 15–1 GENERAL PATTERNS OF MANAGERIAL APPROACHES TO MOTIVATION

Traditional Model	Human Relations Model	Human Resources Model
Assumptions		
1. Work is inherently distasteful to most people. 2. What they do is less important than what they earn for doing it. 3. Few want or can handle work that requires creativity, self-direction, or self-control.	1. People want to feel useful and important. 2. People want to belong and to be recognized as individuals. 3. These needs are more important than money in motivating people to work.	1. Work is not inherently distasteful. People want to contribute to meaningful goals that they have helped establish. 2. Most people can exercise far more creativity, self-direction, and self-control than their present jobs demand.
Policies		
1. The manager should closely supervise and control subordinates. 2. He or she must break down tasks into simple, repetitive, easily learned operations. 3. He or she must establish detailed work routines and procedures, and enforce these fairly but firmly.	1. The manager should make each worker feel useful and important. 2. He or she should keep subordinates informed and listen to their objections to his or her plans. 3. The manager should allow subordinates to exercise some self-direction and self-control on routine matters.	1. The manager should make use of underutilized human resources. 2. He or she must create an environment in which all members may contribute to the limits of their ability. 3. He or she must encourage full participation in important matters, continually broadening subordinate self-direction and self-control.
Expectations		
1. People can tolerate work if the pay is decent and the boss is fair. 2. If tasks are simple enough and people are closely controlled, they will produce up to standard.	1. Sharing information with subordinates and involving them in routine decisions will satisfy their basic needs to belong and to feel important. 2. Satisfying these needs will improve morale and reduce resistance to formal authority—subordinates will "willingly cooperate."	1. Expanding subordinate influence, self-direction, and self-control will lead to direct improvements in operating efficiency. 2. Work satisfaction may improve as a "by-product" of subordinates' making full use of their resources.

Source: Adapted from Richard M. Steers and Lyman W. Porter, eds., *Motivation and Work Behavior*, 3d ed. (New York: McGraw-Hill, 1983), p. 14. Copyright 1983 by McGraw-Hill Book Company. Used with permission of the publisher.

have inner needs that they are motivated to reduce or fulfill. That is, individuals will act or behave in ways that will lead to the satisfaction of their needs. (See fig. 15–1.) For example, an employee who has a strong need to achieve may be motivated to work extra hours to complete a difficult task on time; an employee with a strong need for self-esteem may be motivated to work very carefully to produce high-quality work.

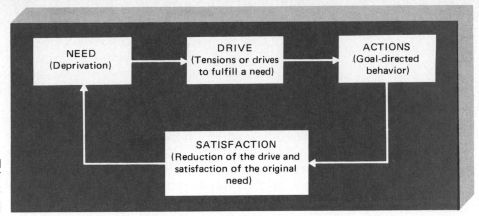

FIGURE 15–1
A CONTENT
THEORY MODEL OF
MOTIVATION

At first glance, this approach seems simple: It suggests that managers can determine subordinates' needs by observing their actions and that managers can predict subordinates' actions by becoming aware of their needs. In practice, however, motivation is far more complicated. There are several reasons for this complexity.

First, needs differ considerably among individuals and will change over time. Furthermore, individual differences complicate a manager's motivational task enormously. Many ambitious managers, highly motivated to achieve power and status, find it hard to understand that not all people have the same values and drives they have. As a result, such managers find that trying to motivate subordinates is a frustrating and discouraging experience.

Second, the ways in which needs are eventually translated into actions also vary considerably among individuals. Someone with a strong need for security may play it safe and avoid accepting responsibility for fear of failing and being fired. Another person with the same security need may seek out responsibility for fear of being fired for poor performance.

Third, people do not always act on their needs consistently, and the needs that motivate them may vary. One day a subordinate may outperform our highest expectations, while at another time that same subordinate will perform a similar task in a mediocre manner.

Finally, the reactions of individuals to need fulfillment or lack of fulfillment will differ. Some individuals with a high security need who fail to attain their goal (say, achieving a sales objective) may become frustrated and give up trying. Others may be motivated to redouble their efforts (say, by prospecting for new customers and making additional calls on existing ones).

The more we get to know the people around us (and ourselves), the better able we will be to understand their needs and what will motivate them. However, human behavior depends on so many complexities and alternatives that we are bound to make incorrect predictions a fair number of times.

Process Theories

Rather than emphasizing the content of needs and the driving nature of those needs, the process approach emphasizes how and by what goals individuals are motivated.

In this view, needs are just one element in the process by which individuals decide how to behave. For example, individuals may see the strong possibility of receiving some reward (say, a salary increase) if they act in a certain way (say, by working hard). This reward will become an incentive or motive for their behavior.

Basic to process theories of motivation is the notion of expectancy—that is, what a person anticipates is likely to occur as a result of his or her behavior. For example, if a person expects that meeting deadlines will earn praise from superiors and that not meeting deadlines will earn disapproval, and if that person prefers praise, then he or she will be motivated to meet deadlines. Conversely, if this person expects that meeting deadlines will not earn praise, he or she may not be as motivated to do so.

An additional factor in motivation is the valence or strength of an individual's preference for the expected outcome. For example, if an individual expects that exceeding production quotas will lead to promotion to supervisor and if the individual strongly desires to be promoted, then he or she will be strongly motivated to exceed production quotas.

Reinforcement Theories

Reinforcement theories, associated with B. F. Skinner and others, are also often called *behavior modification* or *operant conditioning*. These theories do not utilize the concept of a motive or a process of motivation. Instead, they deal with how the consequences of a past action influence future actions in a cyclical learning process. In this view, people behave the way they do because, in the past, they learned that certain behaviors were associated with pleasant outcomes and that other behaviors were associated with unpleasant outcomes. Because people generally prefer pleasant outcomes, they are likely to avoid behaviors with unpleasant consequences. For example, individuals may be likely to obey the law—and a manager's legitimate instructions—because they have learned at home and at school that disobedience leads to punishment.

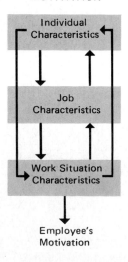

A SYSTEMS VIEW OF MOTIVATION

A Systems View of Motivation in Organizations

With so many different views of motivation, how can managers utilize current knowledge to improve their understanding of how individuals behave in organizations? Lyman Porter and Raymond Miles have suggested that a systems perspective of motivation will be most useful to managers.[4] By systems perspective they mean that the entire set, or system, of forces operating on the employee must be considered before the employee's motivation and behavior can be adequately understood. They believe that system consists of three sets of variables affecting motivation in organizations: individual characteristics, job characteristics, and work situation characteristics. (See table 15–2.)

Individual characteristics are the interests, attitudes, and needs a person brings to the work situation. Obviously, people differ in these characteristics, and their motivations will therefore differ. For example, one person may desire prestige, and so may be motivated by a job with an impressive title. Another may desire money, and so may be motivated to earn a high salary.

TABLE 15–2 VARIABLES AFFECTING MOTIVATION IN ORGANIZATIONAL SETTINGS

Individual Characteristics	Job Characteristics	Work Situation Characteristics
1. Interests 2. Attitudes (examples): —Toward self —Toward job —Toward aspects of the work situation 3. Needs (examples): —Security —Social —Achievement	Examples: —Types of intrinsic rewards —Degree of autonomy —Amount of direct performance feedback —Degree of variety in tasks	1. Immediate Work Environment a. Peers b. Supervisor(s) 2. Organizational Actions a. Reward practices (1) System-wide rewards (2) Individual rewards b. Organizational culture

Note: These lists are not intended to be exhaustive; they are meant to indicate some of the more important variables influencing employee motivation.

Source: Lyman W. Porter and Raymond E. Miles, "Motivation and Management," in Joseph W. McGuire, ed., *Contemporary Management: Issues and Viewpoints*, p. 547. © 1974. Adapted by permission of Prentice-Hall, Inc., Englewood Cliffs, N.J.

Job characteristics are the attributes of the employee's tasks and include the amount of responsibility, the variety of tasks, and the extent to which the job itself has characteristics that people find satisfying. A job that is intrinsically satisfying will be more motivating for many people than a job that is not.

Work situation characteristics are factors in the work environment of the individual. Do colleagues encourage the individual to perform to a high standard, or do they encourage low productivity? Do superiors reward high performance, or do they ignore it? Does the organization's culture foster concern for members of the organization—or does it encourage cold and indifferent formality?

Characteristics of the Individual

Each individual brings his or her own interests, attitudes, and needs to the work situation. In this section, we will discuss some contributions to our understanding of human needs and motivation.

The Hierarchy of Human Needs. Maslow's hierarchy of needs has probably received more attention from managers than any other theory of motivation. This is because Maslow's theory not only classifies human needs in a convenient way but also has direct implications for managing human behavior in organizations.[5]

Maslow viewed human motivation as a hierarchy of five needs:

1. *Physiological*—includes the need for air, water, food, and sex.
2. *Security*—includes the need for safety, order, and freedom from fear or threat.
3. *Belongingness and love (or social needs)*—include the need for love, affection, feelings of belonging, and human contact.
4. *Esteem*—includes the need for self-respect, self-esteem, achievement, and respect from others.
5. *Self-actualization*—includes the need to grow, to feel fulfilled, to realize one's potential.

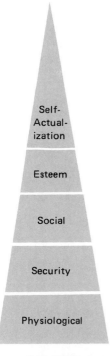

Self-Actualization

Esteem

Social

Security

Physiological

MASLOW'S HIERARCHY OF NEEDS

According to Maslow, individuals will be motivated to fulfill whichever need is prepotent, or most powerful, for them at a given time. The prepotency of a need depends on the individual's current situation and recent experiences. Starting with the physical needs, which are most basic, each need must be at least partially satisfied before the individual desires to satisfy a need at the next higher level.

The practical implications of this theory for motivation in organizations are many. The basic, physiological needs of employees must be satisfied by a wage sufficient to feed, shelter, and protect them and their families satisfactorily, and a safe working environment must be provided before managers offer incentives designed to provide employees with esteem, feelings of belonging, or opportunities to grow. Security needs require job security, freedom from coercion or feelings of arbitrary treatment, and clearly defined regulations.

In the modern organization, both physiological and security needs are usually (but not always) met satisfactorily. The need to belong and be loved, most strongly felt in relation to one's family, can also be satisfied in social contexts through friendship and being "one of the gang" at work. The work environment is a social environment, and unless employees feel that they are an integral part of the organization, they will be frustrated by an unmet need to belong and will be unlikely to respond to higher-order opportunities or incentives.

Maslow described two types of esteem needs—the desire for achievement and competence and the desire for status and recognition. In organizational terms, people want to be good at their jobs; they also want to feel that they are achieving something important when they perform their jobs. As managers, we have many ways of fulfilling both types of esteem needs in subordinates by providing challenging work assignments, performance feedback, performance recognition, and personal encouragement and by involving subordinates in goal setting and decision making.

When all other needs have been adequately met, according to Maslow, employees will become motivated by the need for self-actualization. They will look for meaning and personal growth in their work and will actively seek out new responsibilities. Maslow stresses that individual differences are greatest at this level. For some individuals, producing work of high quality may be a means for self-actualization, while for others, developing creative, useful ideas serves the same need. By being aware of the different self-actualization needs of subordinates, managers can use a variety of approaches to enable subordinates to achieve personal as well as organizational goals.[6]

The Urge to Achieve and Entrepreneurial Behavior. John W. Atkinson and others hold that all healthy adults have a reservoir of potential energy. How this energy is released and used depends on the strength of the individual's motivational drives and the situations and opportunities presented. An individual's striving for a particular goal results from (1) the strength of the basic motive or need involved, (2) his or her expectation of succeeding, and (3) the incentive value attached to the goal.[7]

Atkinson's model related behavior and performance to three basic drives, which vary significantly among individuals: the need for achievement, the need for power, and the need for affiliation or close association with others. For example, an individual might be motivated by a high need for affiliation. If he or she is in a work environment where considerable interaction with other employees takes place, the individual's potential energy for affiliation will be released, and work enjoyment might be high. On the other hand, if the work environment is unfriendly or the individual must work alone, then the individual's affiliation need will not be met in the workplace, and so motivation to come to work might be low.

David C. McClelland related these concepts directly to business drive and management. (We have already discussed, in chapter 11, the relationship between the need for power and management success.) McClelland's research indicated that a strong need for achievement was related to how well individuals were motivated to perform their work tasks.[8]

The need for achievement can be defined as a desire to excel or to succeed in competitive situations.[9] In his research, McClelland found that people with a high need for achievement have several characteristics of interest to managers:

1. **They like taking responsibility for solving problems.**
2. **They tend to set moderately difficult goals for themselves and to take calculated risks to achieve their goals.**
3. **They place great importance on feedback on how well they are doing.**

Thus, those with high achievement needs tend to be highly motivated by challenging and competitive work situations. Conversely, people with low achievement needs tend to perform poorly in competitive or challenging work situations.[10]

There is considerable evidence of the correlation between high achievement needs and high performance. McClelland himself, for example, found that people who succeeded in competitive occupations were well above average in achievement motivation. Successful managers, who presumably operated in one of the most competitive of all environments, had a higher achievement need than other professionals.[11] McClelland later reported considerable success in teaching adults to increase their achievement motivation and, in turn, to improve their work performance.[12]

For managers, these findings highlight the importance of matching the individual and the job. Employees with high achievement needs thrive on work that is challenging, satisfying, stimulating, and complex. They welcome autonomy, variety, and frequent feedback from supervisors. Employees with low achievement needs prefer situations of stability, security, and predictability. They respond better to considerate than to impersonal high-pressure supervision and look to the workplace and coworkers for social satisfaction. McClelland's research also suggests that managers can, to some extent, raise the achievement-need level of subordinates by creating the proper work environment—permitting their subordinates a measure of independence, increasing responsibility and autonomy, gradually making tasks more challenging, and praising and rewarding high performance.

High achievement needs can also be fueled by an individual's *fear of failure*.[13] Managers may be strongly motivated to take action by their fear of failing to meet personal or organizational goals and by the fear of possible public embarrassment when these failures are recognized. Conversely, for some individuals, *fear of success* can be a motive.[14] Such people fear the stress and burden of their success and the envy and dislike it may awaken in others.

Characteristics of the Job Task

The characteristics of the job and its associated tasks, the second variable influencing motivation in organizations, is the one on which managers have the greatest potential impact. Researchers have tried to discover how a particular job will affect an individual's desire to perform that job well. The fact that routine, assembly-line types of jobs were shown to reduce employee motivation and to add to dissatisfaction was a major reason why interest in this area developed. Understanding of the relationship between job characteristics and motivation increased when Frederick Herzberg introduced his two-factor theory. Herzberg's work generated a great deal of interest in the role of motivation in the daily operations of organizations.

A Two-Factor Approach to Work Motivation. In the late 1950s, Herzberg and his associates conducted a study of the job attitudes of two hundred engineers and accountants.[15] Subjects were asked to recall times when they felt exceptionally good about their jobs and times when they felt bad. From his research, Herzberg concluded that job satisfaction and job dissatisfaction come from two separate sets of factors, which he called *satisfiers* (motivating factors) and *dissatisfiers* ("hygiene" factors).

The satisfiers included achievement, recognition, responsibility, and advancement. The satisfiers are related to the nature of the work (the job *content*) and to rewards that result directly from performance of the work tasks. The dissatisfiers included salary, working conditions, and company policy. They come from the individual's relationship to the organization's environment (the job *context*) in which the work is being done. The most important of these factors is company policy, which is judged by many individuals to be a major cause of inefficiency and ineffectiveness. Positive ratings for these factors did not lead to job satisfaction but merely to the absence of dissatisfaction.

Herzberg's work has been criticized for his method of collecting data, which assumed that people will report their satisfying and dissatisfying experiences accurately.[16] Subsequent research indicates that the two-factor theory oversimplifies the relationship between satisfaction and motivation, and that the same factors may result in job satisfaction for one person and job dissatisfaction for another.[17]

Nevertheless, Herzberg's theory is still regarded as an important contribution to our understanding of the effects of job characteristics on satisfaction, motivation, and performance. Job enrichment programs, for example, which we discussed in chapter 9, were strongly influenced by the work of Herzberg and his colleagues.

Characteristics of the Work Situation

The work situation, the third set of variables that can affect job motivation, consists of two categories: the actions, policies, and culture of the organization as a whole and the immediate work environment.

Organizational Policies, Reward Systems, and Culture. The overall personnel policies of the organization, its methods for rewarding individual employees, and the organization's culture all translate into organizational actions that influence and motivate workers.

Personnel policies, such as wage scales and employee benefits (vacations, pensions, and the like), generally have little impact on individual performance. But

"It has come to my attention that somebody in here is only going through the motions."
Drawing by Stevenson; © 1982 The New Yorker Magazine, Inc.

these policies do affect the desire of employees to remain with or leave the organization and its ability to attract new employees.

The *reward system* of the organization guides the actions that generally have the greatest impact on the motivation and performance of individual employees. Salary increases, bonuses, and promotions can be strong motivators of individual performance, provided they are effectively administered. The reward or compensation must justify, in the employee's mind, the extra effort improved performance requires; the reward must be directly associated with that improved performance so that it is clear why the reward has been given; and it must be seen as fair by others in the work group so that they will not feel resentful and retaliate by lowering their own performance levels.

The organization's *culture*—the shared norms, values, and beliefs of its members—can enhance or decrease an individual's performance. Employees whose personalities do not mesh with the culture of their organization—for example, a creative, unconventional individual with low respect for authority working in a conservative accounting firm—will not be as highly motivated as employees who "fit" the culture. In addition, certain types of cultures are likely to be more successful in motivating employees than are others. Cultures that foster respect for employees, that integrate them into the decision-making process, and that give them autonomy in planning and executing tasks encourage better performance than cold, uncaring, and highly regimented cultures. (See chapter 13 for a fuller discussion of organizational culture.)

As managers, we want to motivate employees to high levels of performance, to loyalty and commitment to the organization, and to stability on the job. Money is the most obvious and frequently used incentive, but it is not the only means of motivating workers. In fact, assuming they perceive their compensation as fair, today's workers are responsive to such nonmonetary incentives as extra vacation days, flextime arrangements, day care for their children, recreation facilities at the workplace, and company-sponsored local transportation. Financial incentives other than salary or bonuses also have a place in an incentive system and might include pension plans with early vesting, company shareholding, company contributions to further education, and auto or home loans.

In spite of the advantages of linking pay to performance, many organization do not attempt to use extra compensation as a motivating factor. It can be difficult to measure the performance of individuals accurately, especially when they hold jobs that are not as directly quantifiable as many production and sales jobs are. In addition, when managers do not feel capable of determining differences in individual performance, they may prefer to keep employees performing the same type of task at about the same salary level, in order to avoid creating resentment about hard to justify pay differences.

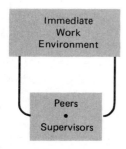

The Immediate Work Environment. The immediate work environment includes attitudes and actions of peers and supervisors and the "climate" they create. Numerous studies have found that peer groups in the work situation can have an enormous influence on people's motivation and performance. Most people desire the friendship and approval of peers, and will behave in accordance with the norms and values of the peer group. If the group has an "us-versus-them" approach to management and regards high producers as "rate-busters," its members will not be motivated to perform at their best level and may even be motivated to perform poorly.

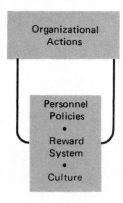

Immediate supervisors strongly influence the motivation and performance of employees by example and instruction and through rewards and penalties ranging from praise, salary increases, and promotions to criticism, demotions, and dismissals. They also strongly affect job design and are important transmitters of the organizational culture, especially to new employees. Terrence E. Deal and Allan A. Kennedy point out that corporate "heroes" and "heroines"—managers who embody the values of the culture—provide "a pantheon of role models for managers and employees."[18] Supervisors who emulate the behavior of the organization's heroes and heroines will, in turn, transmit cultural values to their subordinates.

The Impact of Past Consequences on Behavior

An influential—and controversial—approach to influencing human behavior is based on the observation that the consequences of an individual's behavior in one situation influence that individual's behavior in future, similar situations. Techniques based on this principle have been developed to change people's behavior. Such techniques, known usually as "behavior modification" or "operant conditioning," have been advocated by B. F. Skinner, among others.[19] Their implication that individual behaviors can be predicted from a person's past experiences and present environment is disturbing to some of the individuals who strongly believe that people freely choose how to behave.

However, one does not have to agree with all the underlying assumptions of these techniques to see that they are a part of daily life within and outside organizations. Rewarding a child for obedience, smiling at someone we like, frowning at something with which we disagree, grading papers, and raising the salary of a highly productive employee are familiar acts that modify behavior. We assume that the receivers of these actions will behave in the desired ways.

Work behaviors are learned. Individuals learn to be good managers or poor managers. They learn to perform a job well or poorly. They learn to be prompt, cooperative, agreeable to co-workers, and so on. Behavior modification in organizations focuses on establishing work situations—such as reward and recognition policies—that help subordinates learn work habits that are satisfying to them and that aid in the achievement of organizational goals.[20]

Behavior Modification

The behavior modification, or learning, approach to behavior is based on the law of effect, which states that behavior that has a rewarding consequence is likely to be repeated, whereas behavior that leads to a negative, or punishing, consequence tends not to be repeated.[21] In an organization, the frequency of various behaviors can be seen as depending on the immediate consequences of those behaviors. If, for example, employees work hard to achieve organizational objectives and are directly rewarded with bonuses or privileges, they will tend to repeat their efforts when new objectives are set.

The behavior modification process may be expressed as follows:

$$\text{Stimulus} \rightarrow \text{Response} \rightarrow \text{Consequences} \rightarrow \text{Future Response}$$

That is, the individual's own voluntary behavior (response) to a situation or event (stimulus) is the cause of specific consequences. If those consequences are positive, the individual will in the future tend to have similar responses in similar situations, but if those consequences are unpleasant, the individual will tend to change his or her behavior in order to avoid them.

This suggests that if managers wish to change the behavior of a subordinate, they must change the consequences of the behavior. A person who is frequently late, for example, might be motivated to come in on time (a behavior change) if the manager expresses strong approval for each on-time or early appearance (change of consequences), rather than shrugging the matter off. Lateness also may be stopped by expressing strong disapproval of the late arrival time. However, as we shall see, researchers believe that it is generally more effective to reward desired behavior than to punish undesired behavior.

For the consequences to influence a person's behavior, it is important that they be clearly related to that behavior. One reason managers often fail to motivate subordinates is that the reinforcements they offer are far removed from the subordinate's actions. For example, informing subordinates during the annual salary review that they have done a good job is probably less motivating than praising them when they perform a task particularly well.

Methods of Behavior Modification

Four techniques that managers can use to modify the behavior of subordinates are positive reinforcement, avoidance learning, extinction, and punishment.

Positive Reinforcement. A consequence that encourages repetition of a given behavior is a *positive reinforcement*. Reinforcers may be either primary or secondary. Primary reinforcers, such as water and food, satisfy biological needs. Secondary reinforcers are rewarding because of positive past associations for the individual. Common secondary reinforcers are praise, promotion, and money; most individuals regard these as pleasant and are therefore likely to repeat behaviors that earn these rewards. Because positive reinforcers differ among individuals, managers must either develop a reward system that is appropriate for all the members of their work group or tailor their rewards to suit each individual.

Avoidance Learning. *Avoidance learning* takes place when individuals learn to avoid or escape from unpleasant consequences. Much lawful behavior in our society is based on avoidance learning; for example, people learn to drive carefully to avoid accidents. In the workplace, avoidance learning usually occurs when peers or supervisors criticize an individual's actions ("That report you did was really sloppy," or "When are you going to start carrying your share of the work load?"). The individual may try to avoid future criticism by improving his or her performance.

Extinction. Extinction and punishment are designed to reduce undesired behavior, rather than reinforce desired behavior. *Extinction* is the absence of reinforcement following undesired behavior; behavior that is ignored eventually disappears or becomes "extinct." For example, teachers often use extinction to control disruptive behavior in the classroom. By ignoring the disruptive students (rather than giving them extra attention in the form of frowns or comments), teachers avoid rewarding the disruptive behavior; eventually the students may try another type of behavior. In the workplace, extinction is commonly used to deal with overly inquisitive or moderately disruptive employees.

Punishment. Through punishment, managers try to correct improper behavior of subordinates by providing negative consequences. Giving harsh criticism, docking pay, denying privileges, demoting, and reducing an individual's freedom to do his or her job are common forms of punishment in the workplace.[22]

Although most ethical criticisms of behavior modification techniques focus on punishment, Skinner and other behaviorists advocate the use of positive reinforcement rather than punishment to change behavior. Punishment, by definition, only tells the individual what should *not* be done rather than what *should* be done. Thus, one mistake may be followed by a new one as the individual seeks to find, by trial and error, behavior that will not be punished. In addition, punishment causes resentment, which is usually counterproductive. For most organization members who are mature and willing to be productive, positive reinforcement (combined with extinction if necessary) is more effective and humane.

Learning Theory in Practice

Whether they realize it or not, managers are constantly influencing the behavior of their subordinates through the ways they withhold or offer rewards. In order to make their influence more effective, managers need to be aware of how reinforcement can best be applied.

Perhaps the first general rule which managers should know is that what is rewarding for one individual is not necessarily so for another. For example, many employees are influenced to work longer hours by the promise of more money, but others may place a higher value on time off. It has been found, too, that in some situations rewards may be counterproductive; for example, financial incentives may actually undermine the performance of intrinsically interesting tasks.[23] Offering extra money for high job performance tends to reduce a worker's intrinsic motivation to do a competent job on his or her own.[24] However, recent American and Japanese studies find that praising job performance increases a worker's intrinsic motivation.[25]

Another rule to keep in mind is that managers should not always accept the reasons which individuals themselves give for their actions. This is especially true when success and failure are involved. Lee Ross has described the "fundamental attribution error," which is the tendency for people to attribute success to their own efforts but failure to the actions of others or to the nature of the situation.[26]

Managers should also be aware that some schedules of reinforcement are more effective than others. Under a *continuous reinforcement* schedule, the individual is immediately rewarded each time he or she manifests the desired behavior; for example, the individual is praised each time the work task is properly completed. Under a *partial reinforcement* schedule, rewards are provided intermittently—for example, through occasional praise for good performance and regular praise for exceptionally fine work. Continuous reinforcement has been found to lead to faster initial learning. Partial reinforcement, however, leads to a more permanent change in behavior.

Rules for Modifying Behavior. W. Clay Hamner has identified six rules (see box) for using behavior modification, or learning theory, techniques. He points out that even though these rules make obvious sense, managers often violate them.[27]

Fred Luthans and Robert Kreitner have described a systematic five-step procedure for using the learning theory approach to manage organizational behavior.[28] (See fig. 15–2.)

Step 1, *identification*, involves specifying the behaviors the manager considers undesirable.

In step 2, *measurement*, the manager charts the frequency of the behavior over time. This allows the manager to determine his or her success in changing the subordinate's behavior. It may also provide insight into the circumstances associated with the behavior.

FIGURE 15–2 STEPS IN ORGANIZATIONAL BEHAVIOR MODIFICATION

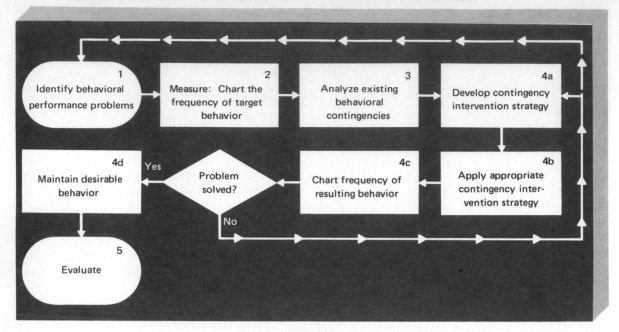

Source: Adapted, by permission of the publisher, from "The Management of Behavioral Contingencies," by Fred Luthans and Robert Kreitner, *Personnel*, July–August 1974, p. 13. Copyright © 1974 AMACOM, a division of American Management Associations, New York. All rights reserved.

In step 3, *analysis,* the manager attempts to ascertain what is causing the behavior to continue.

Step 4, *intervention,* involves (a) developing a strategy for changing the behavior, (b) implementing the strategy, and (c) measuring the frequency of the resulting behavior. The key to changing behavior is to alter the *consequences* of the subordinate's behavior. Analysis is likely to show that undesired behavior has been rewarded in the past and desired behavior has been ignored (or possibly punished). The new strategy should reward desired behavior and ignore (or punish, if necessary) undesired behavior. A record is kept of how often the problem behavior is repeated. If a behavior change has occurred in the desired direction, the manager selects a reinforcement schedule that will maintain the desired behavior—step 4d.

In step 5, *evaluation,* the manager decides how effective the entire procedure has been. Ineffective strategies are analyzed to see why they did not work or whether there are other types of individuals or circumstances for which they might be appropriate. Effective strategies are kept in mind for possible future use.

Encouraging results have been reported in a number of studies of the effectiveness of behavior modification techniques. Fred Luthans and David Lyman, for example, found that supervisors trained in the five-step behavior modification procedure were able to improve the performance of workers in their department.[29] And a survey of ten major corporations, including Emery Air Freight, Michigan Bell, Standard Oil, and General Electric, found that positive reinforcement techniques resulted in major gains in efficiency, cost savings, attendance, or productivity.[30]

RULES FOR USING BEHAVIOR MODIFICATION TECHNIQUES

Rule 1: *Don't reward all individuals equally.* To be effective behavior reinforcers, rewards should be based on performance. Rewarding everyone equally in effect reinforces poor or average performance and ignores high performance.

Rule 2: *Be aware that failure to respond can also modify behavior.* Managers influence their subordinates by what they do not do as well as by what they do. For example, failing to praise a deserving subordinate may cause that subordinate to perform poorly the next time.

Rule 3: *Be sure to tell individuals what they can do to get reinforcement.* Setting a performance standard lets individuals know what they should do to be rewarded; they can then adjust their work pattern accordingly.

Rule 4: *Be sure to tell individuals what they are doing wrong.* If a manager withholds rewards from a subordinate without indicating why the subordinate is not being rewarded, the subordinate may be confused about what behavior the manager finds undesirable. The subordinate may also feel that he or she is being manipulated.

Rule 5: *Don't punish in front of others.* Reprimanding a subordinate might sometimes be a useful way of eliminating an undesirable behavior. Public reprimand, however, humiliates the subordinate and may cause all the members of the work group to resent the manager.

Rule 6: *Be fair.* The consequences of a behavior should be appropriate. Subordinates should be given the rewards they deserve. Failure to reward subordinates properly or overrewarding undeserving subordinates reduces the reinforcing effect of rewards.

Source: Based on W. Clay Hamner, "Reinforcement Theory and Contingency Management in Organizational Settings," in Henry L. Tosi and W. Clay Hamner, eds., *Organizational Behavior and Management: A Contingency Approach.* rev. ed. (New York: Wiley, 1977). Copyright 1977 by John Wiley & Sons, Inc.

Integrative Approaches

Each of the approaches to motivation that we have discussed so far concentrates on one of the three sets of variables illustrated in the systems table at the beginning of the chapter (table 15–2). Integrative approaches include two or more sets of variables in their analysis of motivation. One in particular, the *expectancy approach* (also called the expectancy/valence approach), has received considerable support from research. For this reason, and because of the generality of its applications, it has significant implications for managers. This approach attempts to overcome criticisms sometimes directed at other motivational theories: namely, that they assume all employees are alike, that all situations are alike, and that there is one best way of motivating employees. The expectancy approach attempts to account for differences between individuals and between situations.

Expectations, Outcomes, and Work Behavior

According to David Nadler and Edward Lawler, the expectancy approach is based on four assumptions about behavior in organizations.[31]

1. *Behavior is determined by a combination of forces in the individual and in the environment.* People have different needs and expectations, formed by past experiences, that influence their response to the work environment. Different types of work environments usually make people behave in different ways.
2. *Individuals make conscious decisions about their own behavior in organizations.* These decisions may be about (a) *membership behavior*—coming to work, staying at work, being a member of the organization; or (b) *effort behavior*—how hard to work in performing their jobs.
3. *Individuals have different needs, desires, and goals.* Individuals are satisfied or rewarded by different outcomes. Understanding individual needs leads to an understanding of how each individual can be best motivated and rewarded.
4. *Individuals decide among alternative behaviors based on their expectation that a given behavior will lead to a desired outcome.* People tend to behave in ways that they believe will lead to rewards and to avoid behavior that may lead to undesirable consequences.

These assumptions are summarized in the so-called expectancy model, which has three major components: performance-outcome expectancy, valence, and effort-performance expectancy.

Performance-Outcome Expectancy. Individuals engaged in or contemplating a certain behavior expect certain consequences. For example, a worker who is thinking about doubling his or her output may expect that doubling the output will result in praise, more pay, or perhaps no reward at all. The worker may even expect hostility from other workers. Each expected outcome will affect the individual's decision on whether or not to proceed with the contemplated behavior.

Valence. The outcome of a particular behavior has a specific *valence* (motivating power or value) for each specific individual. For example, the possibility of transfer to a higher-paying position in another location may have a high valence for individuals who value money or who enjoy the stimulation of a new environment; it may have a low valence for individuals who have strong ties to their neighborhood, friends, or work group. Valence is determined by the individual and is not an objective quality of the outcome itself; for a given situation, valence differs from one person to the next.

Effort-Performance Expectancy. People's expectations of how difficult it will be to perform successfully will also affect their decision on whether or not to proceed. For example, an individual may be told that increasing sales by 50 percent will lead to a much-desired salary increase. Before deciding whether or not to pursue the sales increase, the individual must estimate the probability of achieving it.

Given a choice, then, an individual will tend to select the level of performance that seems to have the best chance of achieving a valued outcome. The individual asks, in effect, "Can I do it?" and "If I do it, what will it bring me?" and "Is what it will bring me worth the effort of doing it?"

FIGURE 15–3 THE EXPECTANCY MODEL OF MOTIVATION

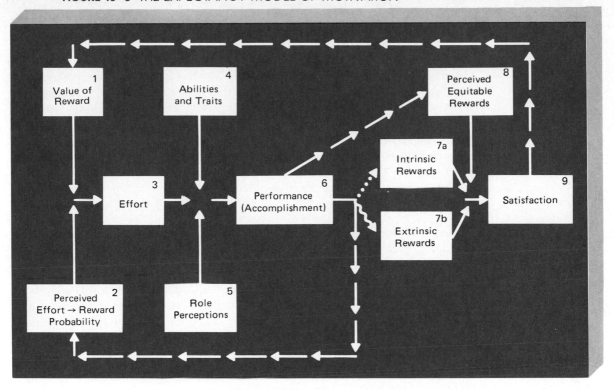

Source: Lyman W. Porter and Edward E. Lawler III, *Managerial Attitudes and Performance*, p. 165. Copyright © 1968. Used by permission of Richard D. Irwin, Inc.

The answers to these questions for the individual will depend to some extent on the types of outcomes expected. *Intrinsic* outcomes are experienced directly by the individual as a result of successful task performance. They include feelings of accomplishment, increased self-esteem, and the development of new skills. *Extrinsic* outcomes, such as bonuses, praise, or promotion, are provided by an outside agent, such as the supervisor or work group. A single level of performance may be associated with several outcomes, each having its own valence. (If I perform better, I will receive higher pay, be noticed by my supervisor, be loved more by my spouse, and feel better about myself.) Some of these outcomes may even have valence because of the individual's expectation that they will lead to other outcomes. (If my supervisor notices the quality of my work, I may get a promotion.)

Figure 15–3 illustrates the theoretical working of the expectancy model. The value of the expected reward to the individual (1) combines with the individual's perception of the effort involved in attaining the reward and the probability of achieving the reward (2) to produce a certain level of effort (3). (The probability that a given level of effort will achieve the reward [2] is composed of two probabilities: first, the probability that a given level of effort will yield successful task accomplishment; and second, the probability that successful task accomplishment will be followed by the anticipated reward.) This effort combines with the individual's abilities and traits (4) and the way he or she does the task (5) to yield a specific performance level (6). This resulting level of performance leads to intrinsic rewards (or perhaps negative consequences, if the performance level is lower than expected), which are inherent in the task accomplishment (7a), and perhaps to extrinsic rewards (7b). The wavy line in the model leading to the extrinsic rewards indicates that those rewards are not guaranteed, since they depend on how the supervisor and perhaps others assess the individual's performance and on the willingness of the organization to reward that performance. The individual has his or her own idea about the appropriateness of the total set of rewards received (8), which, when measured against the rewards actually received, results in the level of satisfaction experienced by the individual (9). The individual's experience will then be applied to his or her future assessments of the values of rewards for further task accomplishment.[32]

Implications for Managers. The expectancy model presents managers with a number of clear implications on how to motivate subordinates. As outlined by Nadler and Lawler, these include:

1. *Determine the rewards valued by each subordinate.* If rewards are to be motivators, they must be suitable for the individual. Managers can determine what rewards their subordinates seek by observing their reactions in different situations and by asking them what rewards they desire.
2. *Determine the performance you desire.* Managers must identify what performance level or behavior they want so that they can tell subordinates what they must do to be rewarded.
3. *Make the performance level attainable.* If subordinates feel that the goal they are asked to pursue is too difficult or impossible, their motivation will be low.
4. *Link rewards to performance.* To maintain motivation, the appropriate reward must be clearly associated within a short period of time with successful performance.
5. *Analyze what factors might counteract the effectiveness of the reward.* Conflicts between the manager's reward system and other influences in the work situation may require the manager to make some adjustments in the reward. For example, if the subordinate's work group favors low productivity, an above-average reward may be required to motivate a subordinate to high productivity.
6. *Make sure the reward is adequate.* Minor rewards will be minor motivators.[33]

Implications for Organizations. The expectancy model of motivation also has a number of implications for organizations. As outlined by Nadler and Lawler, these include:

1. *Organizations usually get what they reward, not what they want.* The organization's reward system must be designed to motivate the behaviors desired. Seniority benefits, for example, reward the duration of one's employment in the organization, not the quality of one's performance.
2. *The job itself can be made intrinsically rewarding.* If jobs are designed to fulfill some of the higher needs of employees (such as independence or creativity), they can be motivating in themselves. This implication is obviously the basis of many

job enrichment programs. However, those individuals who do not desire enriched jobs should not be made to take them.[34]

3. *The immediate supervisor has an important role in the motivation process.* The supervisor is in the best position to define clear goals and to provide appropriate rewards for his or her various subordinates. The supervisor should therefore be trained in the motivation process and be given enough authority to administer rewards.[35]

Perceptions of Equitable Treatment and Work Behavior

Another approach to job motivation, known as *equity theory* or *inequity theory,* is based on the thesis that a major factor in job motivation, performance, and satisfaction is the individual's evaluation of the equity or fairness of the reward received. Equity can be defined as a ratio between the individual's job inputs (such as effort or skill) and the job rewards (such as pay or promotion) *compared with the rewards others are receiving for similar job inputs.* Equity theory holds that an individual's motivation, performance, and satisfaction depend on his or her subjective evaluation of the relationships between his or her effort/reward ratio and the effort/reward ratio of others in similar situations.[36]

Most discussion and research on equity theory center on money as the reward considered most significant in the workplace. People compare what they are being paid for their efforts with what others in similar situations receive for theirs. When they feel that inequity exists, a state of tension develops within them. People try to resolve this tension by appropriately adjusting their behavior. A worker who perceives that he or she is being underpaid, for example, may try to reduce the inequity by exerting less effort. Overpaid workers, on the other hand (also in a state of tension through perceived inequity), may work harder.

Recent studies have shown that an individual's reaction to inequity is dependent on the history of his or her experience of inequity. Richard A. Cosier and Dan R. Dalton point out that work relationships are not static and that inequities usually do not exist as isolated or one-time events.[37] They suggest that there is a threshold up to which an individual will tolerate a series of unfair events. However, once the "straw that broke the camel's back" (that is, a relatively minor injustice that pushes the individual beyond his or her limit of tolerance) is added, an extreme and seemingly inappropriate reaction will result. For example, an outstanding worker who is denied an afternoon off for no compelling reason may suddenly become enraged if he or she has experienced a string of similar petty decisions in the past.

Individuals differ, and their methods of reducing inequity will also differ. Some will rationalize that their efforts were greater or less than they originally perceived them to be, or that the rewards are more or less valuable. For example, one person failing to receive a promotion may "decide" that the previously desired job actually involved too much responsibility. Others may try to make the co-workers with whom they are comparing themselves change their behavior; work team members receiving the same pay but exerting less effort, for example, may be persuaded to work harder, or high-performance workers may be discouraged from "making the rest of us look bad." For managers, equity theory has several implications, the most important of which being that, for most individuals, rewards must be perceived as fair in order to be motivating.

Guidelines for Effective Motivation

There is a discrepancy between the practice of motivating employees in most organizations and the findings of recent theories. This may be because the newer theories are unknown to many managers and ignored by others. Managers may often prefer the older theories of motivation, such as Herzberg's, because they have long been familiar with them and because these theories are easier to apply to large numbers of employees. The newer findings put a premium on understanding subordinates, carefully planning what to do, and being consistent and patient in carrying out those plans. All of these actions require some hard work and self-control.[38] In addition, increased automation and computerization may cause some managers to feel that employees can do little to improve the performance of productive systems. (See chapter 8 for a refutation of this idea.)

Richard M. Steers and Lyman W. Porter suggest some implications of current theories of work motivation for managers:[39]

1. **Managers must actively and intentionally motivate their subordinates.**
2. **Managers should understand their own strengths and limitations before attempting to modify those of others.**
3. **Managers must recognize that employees have different motives and abilities.**
4. **Rewards should be related to performance, not to seniority or other non-merit-based considerations.**
5. **Jobs should be designed to offer challenge and variety. Subordinates must clearly understand what is expected of them.**
6. **Management should foster an organizational culture oriented to performance.**
7. **Managers should stay close to employees and remedy problems as they arise.**
8. **The active cooperation of employees should be sought in improving the organization's output; employees are, after all, also stakeholders in the organization.**

Summary

Motivation is very important for managers to understand, since managers must channel people's motivation so they will achieve personal and organizational goals. However, people's abilities and role perceptions are also important factors in how well they will perform.

Theories of motivation can be characterized as content, process, or reinforcement. Content theories stress the importance of drives or needs within the individual as motives for the individual's actions. Process theories emphasize how and by what goals individuals are motivated. Reinforcement theories focus on how the consequences of an individual's actions in the past affect his or her behavior in the future. These motivational theories have evolved from the traditional model, which suggested that people are motivated by economic necessity, through the human relations model, which emphasized job satisfaction as a motivator, to the human resources model, which suggests that high performance leads to satisfaction. According to the latter model, individuals perform best when they can achieve personal as well as organizational goals.

The systems perspective on motivation identifies three variables that affect motivation in the workplace: individual characteristics, which include the interests, attitudes, and needs of the individual; job characteristics, which are the attributes inherent in the task; and work situation characteristics, which include the organization's personnel and reward policies, organizational culture, and the attitudes and actions of peers and supervisors.

Maslow theorized that individuals are motivated to fulfill a hierarchy of needs, with the need for self-actualization at the top. McClelland found that the need for achievement is closely associated with successful performance in the workplace. Herzberg developed a two-factor approach to work motivation in which job satisfaction was attributed to factors related to job content and to job context.

Characteristics of the work situation, particularly the actions of managers, have a strong impact on motivation. Proper application of behavior modification techniques, which are based on operant conditioning principles, has been found effective in improving employee performance and satisfaction. Behavior modification, or learning theory, suggests that behavior that is followed directly by reward is reinforced and tends to be repeated, while unrewarded or punished behavior tends not to be repeated. Managers may use a variety of reinforcement techniques, such as positive reinforcement, avoidance learning, extinction, or punishment. The most effective technique, in terms of performance and satisfaction, has been found to be positive reinforcement combined with extinction. The positive reinforcement should, however, be tailored to fit individual preferences.

Integrative approaches to motivation include the expectancy approach and equity theory. The expectancy model bases motivation, performance, and satisfaction on what the individual expects from the proposed performance, how much effort the individual expects the proposed performance will require, and the valence, or value, the anticipated rewards have for the individual. Equity theory suggests that an individual's motivation, performance, and satisfaction depend on the individual's comparison of his or her contributions and rewards with those of others in similar situations.

Many managers have not applied the findings of recent motivation theories to their own organizations; properly used, however, these theories can lead to more effective worker performance.

Review Questions

1. What is motivation and why is it important? What other factors influence a person's performance?
2. How have views of motivation in organizations evolved? How might each view affect the ways in which managers behave toward subordinates?
3. According to content theories, what motivates people? What theorists advocated this approach? Why are content theories difficult to apply?
4. What aspects of motivation do process theories emphasize? How do process theories relate the concepts of expectancy and valence to motivation?
5. How do reinforcement theories explain behavior? Why do you think the concept of motives should not be used in the reinforcement approach?
6. In the systems perspective, what three variables affect motivation in the workplace?
7. How is Maslow's hierarchy of needs related to motivation in organizations?
8. According to Atkinson, what determines the strength of an individual's motivational drive? How did McClelland relate Atkinson's work to management? What are the implications of his findings for managers?
9. What is Herzberg's two-factor approach to job satisfaction and dissatisfaction? Why has the approach been criticized?
10. How may an organization's culture and its personnel and reward policies affect motivation?
11. Why is behavior modification controversial? What do you think of behavior modification techniques? Do you unknowingly use them yourself?
12. How does behavior modification work? What does this suggest managers should do if they wish to change the behavior of subordinates?
13. What types of reinforcement techniques can managers use? Which technique is most effective? Least effective? Why?
14. What is the systematic procedure described by Luthans and Kreitner for using the learning theory approach to manage behavior?

15. Upon what assumptions is the expectancy approach based?

16. Define performance-outcome expectancy, valence, and effort-performance expectancy. How do they affect a worker's level of performance?

17. What implications does the expectancy model have for managers and organizations?

18. What does equity theory suggest about the motivation, performance, and satisfaction of individuals in the organization?

19. List the implications for managers of recent motivation theories.

Notes

1. See Thomas J. Peters and Robert H. Waterman, *In Search of Excellence* (New York: Harper & Row, 1982), pp. 55–57, 80–81.

2. For a major part of our discussion on motivation, we are deeply indebted to Richard M. Steers and Lyman W. Porter, eds., *Motivation and Work Behavior,* 3d ed. (New York: McGraw-Hill, 1983); and to Lyman W. Porter and Raymond E. Miles, "Motivation and Management," in Joseph W. McGuire, ed., *Contemporary Management: Issues and Viewpoints* (Englewood Cliffs, N.J.: Prentice-Hall, 1974), pp. 545–570.

3. Raymond E. Miles, "Human Relations or Human Resources," *Harvard Business Review* 43, no. 4 (July–August 1965):148–163.

4. Porter and Miles, "Motivation and Management," pp. 546–550.

5. See Abraham H. Maslow, *Motivation and Personality,* 2nd ed. (New York: Harper & Row, 1970), pp. 35–58.

6. See Ellen L. Betz, "Two Tests of Maslow's Theory of Need Fulfillment," *Journal of Vocational Behavior* 24, no. 2 (April 1984):204–220; and Howard S. Schwartz, "Maslow and the Hierarchical Enactment of Organizational Reality," *Human Relations* 36, no. 10 (October 1983):933–956.

7. John W. Atkinson and David Birch, *An Introduction to Motivation,* rev. ed. (New York: Van Nostrand Reinhold, 1978), pp. 346–348; and John W. Atkinson, *Personality, Motivation, and Action: Selected Papers* (New York: Praeger, 1983), pp. 174–188.

8. David C. McClelland, *The Achieving Society* (Princeton, N.J.: Van Nostrand, 1961), and "Business Drive and National Achievement," *Harvard Business Review* 40, no. 4 (July–August 1962):99–112. Also see John G. Nicholls, "Achievement Motivation: Conceptions of Ability, Subjective Experience, Task Choice, and Performance," *Psychological Review* 91, no. 3 (July 1984):328–346.

9. For a good discussion of achievement motivation in work situations, see Edward E. Lawler III, *Motivation in Work Organizations* (Monterey, Calif.: Brooks/Cole, 1973), pp. 20–23.

10. Danny Miller, "The Correlates of Entrepreneurship in Three Types of Firms," *Management Science* 29, no. 7 (July 1983):770–791.

11. See McClelland, "Business Drive and National Achievement," pp. 99–112; and Michael J. Stahl, "Achievement, Power and Managerial Motivation: Selecting Managerial Talent with the Job Choice Exercise," *Personnel Psychology* 36, no. 4 (Winter 1983):775–789.

12. David C. McClelland, "Toward a Theory of Motive Acquisition," *American Psychologist* 20, no. 5 (May 1965):321–333. Also see the interview with David C. McClelland in "As I See It," *Forbes,* June 1, 1969, pp. 53–57.

13. See Leonard H. Chusmir, "Personnel Administrators' Perception of Sex Differences in Motivation of Managers: Research-Based or Stereotyped?" *International Journal of Women's Studies* 7, no. 1 (January–February 1984):17–23; and Heinz Heckhausen, Heinz-Dieter Schmalt, and Klaus Schneider, *Achievement Motivation in Perspective* (Orlando, Fla.: Academic Press, 1985).

14. Maureen Kearney, "A Comparison of Motivation to Avoid Success in Males and Females," *Journal of Clinical Psychology* 4, no. 4 (July 1984):1005–1007.

15. Frederick Herzberg, Bernard Mausner, and Barbara Snyderman, *The Motivation to Work* (New York: Wiley, 1959). See also Frederick Herzberg, *Work and the Nature of Man* (New York: World Publishing, 1966); and "One More Time: How Do You Motivate Employees?" *Harvard Business Review* 46, no. 1 (January–February 1968):53–62. For a critique of this and other models, see James A. Lee, *The Gold and Garbage in Management Theories* (Athens: Ohio University Press, 1980).

16. Victor Vroom, *Work and Motivation* (New York: Wiley, 1964).

17. Robert J. House and Lawrence A. Wigdor, "Herzberg's Dual-Factor Theory of Job Satisfaction and Motivation," *Personnel Psychology* 20, no. 4 (Winter 1967):369–389.

18. Terrence E. Deal and Allan A. Kennedy, "Culture: A New Look Through Old Lenses," *Journal of Applied Behavioral Science* 19, no. 4 (1983):498–505.

19. See, for example, B. F. Skinner, *Beyond Freedom and Dignity* (New York: Knopf, 1971).

20. Our discussion is based on W. Clay Hamner, "Reinforcement Theory and Contingency Management in Organizational Settings," in Henry L. Tosi and W. Clay Hamner, eds., *Organizational Behavior and Management: A Contingency Approach* (Chicago: St. Clair Press, 1974); Donald Sanzotta, *Motivational Theories and Applications for Managers* (New York: American Management Associations, 1977); and Fred Luthans and Robert Kreitner, "A Social Learning Approach to Behavioral Management: Radical Behaviorists 'Mellowing Out,' " *Organizational Dynamics* 13, no. 12 (August 1984):47–63.

21. The original formulation of the law of effect was based on years of animal experiments by Edward L. Thorndike and appeared in *Animal Intelligence* (New York: Macmillan, 1911), p. 244.

22. See Richard D. Arvey and John M. Ivancevich, "Punishment in Organizations: A Review, Propositions, and Research Suggestions," *Academy of Management Review* 5, no. 1 (January 1980):123–132; and Henry P. Sims, Jr., "Further Thoughts on Punishment in Organizations," *Academy of Management Review* 5, no. 1 (January 1980):133–138.

23. Thomas L. Daniel and James K. Esser, "Intrinsic Motivation as Influenced by Rewards, Task Interest, and Task Structure," *Journal of Applied Psychology,* 65, no. 5 (October 1980):566–573.

24. Edward L. Deci, "Work—Who Does Not Like It and Why," *Psychology Today,* August 1972, pp. 57–58ff.

25. Katsuhisa Hashiguchi, "The Effects of Extrinsic Rewards and Positive Feedback on Intrinsic Motivation," *Japanese Journal of Psychology* 55, no. 4 (1984):228–234 (in Japanese; all statistical tables and summary in English); and Louis P. Cusclla, "The Effects of Feedback Source, Message and Receiver Characteristics on Intrinsic Motivation," *Communication Quarterly* 32, no. 3 (Spring 1984):211–221.

26. Lee Ross, "The Intuitive Psychologist and His Shortcomings," in *Advances in Experimental Social Psychology,* vol. 10, ed. Leonard Berkowitz (New York: Academic Press, 1977), pp. 173–220. See also Michael Ross, "Attributions and Social Perception, " in Gardner Lindzey and Elliot Aronson, eds., *Handbook of Social Psychology,* vol. 2, 3d ed. (New York: Random House, 1985), chapter 2.

27. Hamner, "Reinforcement Theory and Contingency Management in Organizational Settings," pp. 96–98.

28. Fred Luthans and Robert Kreitner, *Organizational Behavior Modification and Beyond: An Operant and Social Learning Approach* (Glenview, Ill.: Scott, Foresman, 1985).

29. Fred Luthans and David Lyman, "Training Supervisors to Use Organizational Modification," *Personnel* 50, no. 5 (September–October 1973):38–44.

30. W. Clay Hamner and Ellen P. Hamner, "Behavior Modification on the Bottom Line," *Organizational Dynamics* 4, no. 4 (Spring 1976):2–21.

31. David A. Nadler and Edward E. Lawler III, "Motivation—A Diagnostic Approach," in J. Richard Hackman, Edward E. Lawler III, and Lyman W. Porter, eds., *Perspectives on Behavior in Organizations* (New York: McGraw-Hill, 1977), p. 27.

32. Lyman W. Porter and Edward E. Lawler III, *Managerial Attitudes and Performance* (Homewood, Ill.: Irwin, 1968). See also Cynthia M. Pavett, "Evaluation of the Impact of Feedback on Performance and Motivation," *Human Relations* 36, no. 7 (July 1983):641–654; and Vida Scarpello and John P. Campbell, "Job Satisfaction and the Fit between Individual Needs and Organizational Rewards," *Journal of Occupational Psychology* 56, no. 4 (1983):315–328.

33. Philip M. Podsakoff, William D. Tudor, Richard A. Grover, and Vandra L. Huber, "Situational Moderators of Leader Reward and Punishment Behaviors: Fact or Fiction?" *Organizational Behavior and Human Performance* 34, no. 1 (August 1984):21–63.

34. See J. Richard Hackman, Greg Oldham, Robert Janson, and Kenneth Purdy, "A New Strategy for Job Enrichment," *California Management Review* 17, no. 4 (Summer 1975):57–71.

35. James C. Naylor and Daniel R. Ilgen, "Goal Setting: A Theoretical Analysis of a Motivational Technology," *Research in Organizational Behavior* 6 (1984):95–140.

36. J. Stacey Adams, "Toward an Understanding of Inequity," *Journal of Abnormal and Social Psychology* 67, no. 5 (November 1963):422–436. See also Robert P. Vecchio, "Models of Psychological Inequity," *Organizational Behavior and Human Performance* 34, no. 2 (October 1984):266–282.

37. Richard A. Cosier and Dan R. Dalton, "Equity Theory and Time: A Reformulation," *Academy of Management Review* 8, no. 2 (April 1983):311–319.

38. Benjamin Schneider, "Organizational Behavior," in Mark R. Rosenzweig and Lyman W. Porter, eds., *Annual Review of Psychology* (Palo Alto, Calif.: Annual Reviews, 1985), pp. 573–611.

39. Steers and Porter, *Motivation and Work Behavior,* pp. 642–643.

After three days of interviewing for the job of director of the Center City YWCA, Harriet Bowen was having lunch with Margaret Pierce, the retiring director. When Pierce offered her the position, Bowen hesitated.

"You still aren't sure?" Pierce asked. "Tell me what's bothering you."

"As I've told you," Bowen replied, "I'm looking for a job with a challenge. I would expect the YW to face financial difficulties—in today's economy, every nonprofit agency has these problems. But despite all the ideas and energy you have—not to mention the wide diversity of programs—the staff seems uninspired and worn out."

Pierce smiled. "That's true. You've hit on one of our biggest problems. As I've told you, the YWCA has undergone major changes in goals and programs over the past few decades. We no longer serve as a dormitory for young women when they first move to the city. Nor are we simply a place for a quick swim after work. At the National Convention, the YWs declared our major targets to be relevant programs for women, youth, and minorities. And yet our image in Center City—and even for some of our staff—is clearly that of a community recreation center, not a powerful force in the women's movement."

Bowen became animated. "I can see the types of programs you have: bilingual activities for Hispanics, creative skills classes, the Women's Center, the Rape Crisis Center, a battered wives program, youth programs, a nursery, as well as a health club for women, men, and children, and a small residence. The building is in pretty good shape. Where's the problem?"

Pierce paused. "As you know, a lot of our staff in the sixties and seventies started as volunteers and became paid staff when we got federal funding. But the fervor of the social movement has waned at the same time that government grants, including CETA programs, were cut back. Although the neighborhood is much safer, thanks to urban renewal, many of our traditional big contributors have moved to the suburbs. Membership has not really increased substantially. So we've had to cut some programs, lose staff, and freeze wages. As a result, we don't have enough people to maintain the building or keep up the records, let alone reach out into the community."

"But surely you must still have some idealists around," Bowen commented.

"Yes, we do. But many have left, and most of our staff does just the minimum work required, for barely adequate wages." Pierce continued, "The morale problem is more complex. In the seventies we adopted the strong affirmative action program of the National YWCA; as a result, our staff today reflects the racial composition of Center City—half white, half minority. This wasn't easy. Qualified minority professionals are difficult to recruit. We lost some board members and long-term volunteers because of affirmative action. And some of the staff complained that less qualified people were being hired to meet quotas. Further, we lost many white members who resisted integration. Therefore, some of our programs are unintentionally segregated. But with our limited finances it's hard to create new programs and recruit really talented staff."

Bowen listened carefully as Pierce added, "It's very frustrating. We have the facilities and some good programs—but I haven't been able to communicate this to the staff *or* the community. I don't have time to institute better record-keeping and an organized system of promotion and raises. So you see, we have a lot of the basic resources, but also a lot of problems."

Bowen smiled and sat back. "I think I understand the situation. It won't be easy to communicate my enthusiasm, but I'd like to try. I'll take the job."

"I'm very pleased," responded Pierce. "And remember, I intend to stay a member of the YW, so you can always call on me for help. Good luck."

Source: This case was written by Ellen Greenberg of the Columbia University Graduate School of Business. It is based on a real organization, but facts have been altered to enhance the teaching value of the material. Preparation of the case was supported by the Institute for Not-for-Profit Management of Columbia University. Parts of this case are adapted from an earlier case. © 1981 by The Institute for Not-for-Profit Management, Columbia University. All rights reserved.

Case Questions
1. What are the major problems facing Harriet Bowen?
2. If you were Herzberg, how would you advise Harriet Bowen to manage the YWCA?
3. What would Nadler and Lawler tell Harriet Bowen to assist her in leading her staff?
4. How might reinforcement theory apply to this case?

16 LEADERSHIP

Upon completing this chapter you should be able to:

1. Define and explain the leadership process.
2. Describe three major approaches to the study of leadership.
3. Distinguish between the two major leadership styles.
4. Summarize the situational factors that affect leadership effectiveness.
5. Describe three contingency approaches to leadership.

What makes a leader effective? Most people, when asked this question, would probably reply that effective leaders have certain desirable traits or qualities—for example, charisma, foresight, persuasiveness, and intensity. And indeed, when we think of heroic leaders such as Napoleon, Washington, Lincoln, Roosevelt, and Churchill, we recognize that such traits were natural to them and necessary for what they accomplished. However, as we shall see, hundreds of studies of leaders and leadership—some dating back to the nineteenth century—have failed to demonstrate that any trait or quality is consistently associated with effective leadership.[1]

Although research has not yielded a set of traits possessed by effective leaders, it does seem clear that leaders play a critical role in helping groups, organizations, or societies achieve their goals. For example, it is generally accepted that England might well have lost World War II had Neville Chamberlain remained as Prime Minister. Instead, the determined and inspiring leadership of Winston Churchill probably saved England and perhaps the rest of the world as well. Managers are seldom called on to be leaders in the heroic mold of a Churchill or a Lincoln. Nevertheless, leadership abilities and skill in directing are important factors in managers' effectiveness. Many business organizations that appeared to be floundering have achieved new vigor when their presidents were replaced. If we could identify the qualities associated with leadership, our ability to select effective leaders would be increased. And if we could identify effective leadership behaviors and techniques, we would presumably be able to *learn* and *teach* these behaviors and techniques—thereby improving our personal and organizational effectiveness.

Defining Leadership

Ralph M. Stogdill, in his survey of leadership theories and research, has pointed out that "there are almost as many different definitions of leadership as there are persons who have attempted to define the concept."[2] We will define managerial *leadership* as the process of directing and influencing the task-related activities of group members. There are three important implications of our definition.

First, leadership must involve *other people*—subordinates or followers. By their willingness to accept directions from the leader, group members help define the leader's status and make the leadership process possible. Without subordinates, all the leadership qualities of a manager would be irrelevant.

Second, leadership involves an unequal distribution of *power* among leaders and group members. Leaders have the authority to direct some of the activities of group members, who cannot similarly direct the leader's activities. Nonetheless, group members will obviously affect those activities in a number of ways.

Third, in addition to being legitimately able to give their subordinates or followers orders or directions, leaders can also *influence* subordinates in a variety of other ways as we discuss below.

The Nature of Leadership

Why do subordinates accept directions from a manager? What are the sources of a leader's power and influence? We partially answered this question in chapter 11 when we discussed the five bases of a manager's power: *reward power, coercive power, legitimate power, referent power,* and *expert power.*[3] The greater the number of these power sources available to the manager, the greater will be his or her potential for effective leadership. It is, for example, a commonly observed fact of organizational life that managers at the same level in the organizational hierarchy may differ widely in their ability to influence, motivate, and direct the work of subordinates. Although managers at the same level may have the same legitimate power, they are simply not equal in terms of the exercise of reward, coercive, referent, or expert power.

In this chapter, we will attempt to extend further our understanding of leader effectiveness by discussing three major approaches to the study of leadership. The first approach views leadership as growing out of a combination of *traits.* The second approach attempts to identify the personal *behaviors* associated with effective leadership. Common to both these approaches is the assumption that individuals who possess appropriate traits or display appropriate behaviors will emerge as leaders in whatever group situations they find themselves.

Current thinking and research lean toward a third approach, the *situational* perspective on leadership. This perspective assumes that the conditions that determine leader effectiveness vary with the situation—the tasks to be accomplished, the skills and expectations of subordinates, the organizational environment, the past experiences of leader and subordinates, and so on. An individual who is an effective leader in one situation might do very poorly in another. This perspective has given rise to *contingency* approaches to leadership, which attempt to specify the situational factors that determine how effective a particular style will be. We examine the contributions of all these approaches below.

The Search for Leadership Traits

The first systematic effort by psychologists and other researchers to understand leadership was the attempt to identify the personal characteristics of leaders. This view of leadership—that leaders are born, not made—is in fact still popular (though not among researchers). After a lifetime of reading popular novels and viewing films and television shows, perhaps most of us believe that there are individuals who have a predisposition to leadership—that they are naturally braver, more aggressive, more decisive, and more articulate than other people.

This view has certain practical implications as well. If leadership traits could be identified, then nations and organizations would become far more sophisticated in selecting leaders. Only those people who possessed the designated leadership traits would become politicians, officers, and managers. Presumably, organizations and societies would then operate more effectively.

In searching for measurable leadership traits, researchers took two approaches: (1) They attempted to compare the traits of those who emerged as leaders with the traits of those who did not; and (2) they attempted to compare the traits of effective leaders with those of ineffective leaders.

Most studies on leadership traits are in the first category; and these studies have failed to uncover any traits that clearly and consistently distinguish leaders from followers.[4] Leaders as a group have been found to be somewhat taller, brighter, more extroverted, and more self-confident than nonleaders. However, millions of people have these traits, but most of them obviously will never attain a leadership position.

"Want something that projects reason and reciprocity, quiet, confident leadership, and understated yet unmistakable power."

Drawing by D. Reilly; © 1980 The New Yorker Magazine, Inc.

In addition, many established leaders did not and do not have these traits. (Napoleon, for example, was quite short, and Lincoln was moody and introverted.) It is also possible that individuals become more assertive and self-confident once they occupy a leadership position, and so even these traits may be results, rather than causes, of leadership ability. Although personality measurements may one day become more exact, and certain traits may in fact become identified with leadership ability, the evidence thus far suggests that individuals who emerge as leaders possess no single constellation of traits that clearly distinguish them from nonleaders.

Attempts to compare the characteristics of effective and ineffective leaders—the second category of leadership trait studies—are more recent and fewer in number. But these studies, too, have generally failed to isolate traits that are strongly associated with successful leadership. One study did find that traits such as intelligence, initiative, and self-assurance were associated with high managerial levels and performance.[5] However, this study also found that the most important factor related to managerial level and performance was the manager's supervisory ability—that is, his or her skill in using supervisory methods appropriate to the particular situation. Most other studies in this area also have found that effective leadership did not depend on a particular set of traits but on how well the leader's traits matched the requirements of the situation he or she was facing.[6]

Recent studies have found that women are still less likely than men to emerge as leaders, but that they are just as effective when they do. Persistent, often unconscious sexual stereotyping continues to hamper the recognition of women as potential leaders, even though an increasing number of people believe in equality of ability and opportunity. When women do become leaders, however, they perform as well as male leaders and generally are perceived as equally effective by their subordinates.[7]

The Behavior of Leaders

When it became evident that effective leaders did not seem to have any distinguishing traits or characteristics, researchers tried to isolate the behaviors that made leaders effective. In other words, rather than try to figure out what effective leaders *were,* researchers tried to determine what effective leaders *did*—how they delegated tasks, how they communicated with and tried to motivate their subordinates, how they carried out their tasks, and so on. Unlike traits, behaviors can be learned; it followed, therefore, that individuals trained in the appropriate leadership behaviors would be able to lead more effectively.

Research showed, nevertheless, that leadership behaviors appropriate in one situation were not necessarily appropriate in another. For example, an executive skilled at motivating creative individuals might be very successful in a consumer goods company in a highly competitive industry. Such a firm may depend on flamboyant marketing techniques, and so the executive's ability to manage creative people (like artists and copywriters) would be most useful. In an electronics company manufacturing specialized, high-quality components, such a manager might be less useful and perhaps even counterproductive. This is because the company's success would probably depend on its ability to maintain product quality and service rather than on its marketing approach.

Nevertheless, despite growing evidence that effective leadership behaviors depend at least partially on the leader's situation, some researchers have reached the conclusion that certain management behaviors are more effective than others in a wide variety of circumstances. These researchers have focused on two aspects of leadership behavior: *leadership functions* and *leadership styles.*

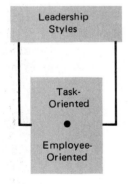

Leadership Functions and Styles. This first aspect of the behavioral approach to leadership shifted the focus from the individual leader to the functions that leaders performed within their group. It appeared that in order for a group to operate effectively, *someone* has to perform two major functions: "task-related" or problem-solving functions and "group maintenance" or social functions. Task-related functions might include suggesting solutions and offering information and opinions. Group maintenance functions include anything that helps the group operate more smoothly—agreeing with or complimenting another group member, for example, mediating group disagreements, or even taking notes on group discussions.

Studies in this area have found that most effective groups have some form of shared leadership in which one person (usually the manager or formal leader) performs the task function, while another group member performs the social function.[8] This leadership specialization occurs because an individual may have the temperament or skill to play only one role or because an individual will be preoccupied with one role at the expense of the other. For example, a manager focusing on the task function may present his or her ideas forcefully and encourage the group to make rapid decisions. The group maintenance function, on the other hand, requires that the individual remain responsive to the ideas and feelings of the other group members. An individual who is able to perform both roles successfully would obviously be an especially effective leader.

The second perspective on leadership behavior focuses on the style a leader uses in dealing with subordinates. Researchers have identified two leadership styles: a task-oriented style and an employee-oriented style. *Task-oriented* managers direct

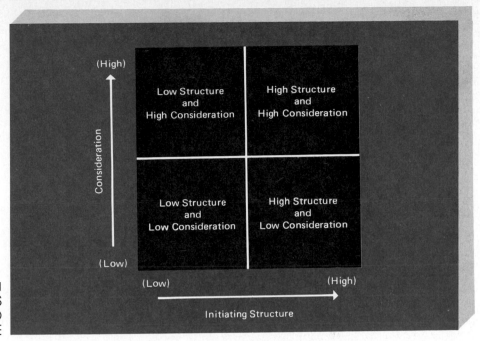

FIGURE 16–1
LEADERSHIP STYLES
STUDIED AT OHIO
STATE

and closely supervise subordinates to ensure that the task is performed to their satisfaction. A manager with this leadership style is more concerned with getting the job done than with the development and growth of subordinates. *Employee-oriented* managers try to motivate rather than control subordinates. They encourage group members to perform tasks by allowing group members to participate in decisions that affect them and by forming friendly, trusting, and respectful relationships with group members.

The Ohio State and University of Michigan Studies. Research has tried to determine which of these two leadership styles leads to the most effective group performance. At Ohio State University, researchers studied the effectiveness of what they called "initiating structure" (task-oriented) and "consideration" (employee-oriented) leadership behaviors. They found, as might be expected, that employee turnover rates were lowest and employee satisfaction highest under leaders who were rated high in consideration. Conversely, leaders who were rated low in consideration and high in initiating structure had high grievance and turnover rates among their employees. (Figure 16–1 diagrams the leadership styles studied at Ohio State.)

The researchers also found, however, that subordinates' ratings of their leaders' effectiveness did not depend on the particular style of the leader but on the situation in which the style was used. For example, Air Force commanders who rated high on consideration were rated as less effective than task-oriented commanders. It is possible that the more authoritarian environment of the military, coupled with the air crews' belief that quick, hard decisions are essential in combat situations, would cause people-oriented leaders to be rated less effective. On the other hand, non-production supervisors and managers in large companies were rated more effective if they ranked high in consideration.[9]

Similarly, researchers at the University of Michigan distinguished between production-centered and employee-centered managers. Production-centered managers set rigid work standards, organized tasks down to the last detail, prescribed the work methods to be followed, and closely supervised their subordinates' work. Employee-centered managers encouraged subordinate participation in goal setting and in other work decisions and helped ensure high performance by inspiring trust and respect. The Michigan studies found that the most productive work groups tended to have leaders who were employee-centered rather than production-centered. They also found that the most effective leaders were those who had supportive relationships with their subordinates, tended to use group rather than individual decision making, and encouraged their subordinates to set and achieve high performance goals.

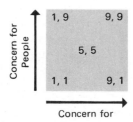

The Managerial Grid and System 4 Management. These two management styles underlie two approaches to effective management described in earlier chapters: Blake and Mouton's Managerial Grid (chapter 13) and Likert's System 4 (chapter 10).

The Managerial Grid identifies a range of management behaviors based on the various ways that task-oriented and employee-oriented styles (each expressed as a continuum on a scale of 1 to 9) can interact with each other.[10] (See fig. 13–5 in chapter 13.) Thus, style 1,1 management, at the lower left-hand corner of the grid, is *impoverished management*—low concern for people and low concern for tasks or production. This style is sometimes called *laissez-faire* management, because the leader abdicates his or her leadership role.

Style 1,9 management is *country club management*—high concern for employees but low concern for production. Style 9,1 management is *task* or *authoritarian management*—high concern for production and efficiency but low concern for employees. Style 5,5 is *middle-of-the-road management*—an intermediate amount of concern for both production and employee satisfaction.

Style 9,9 management is *team* or *democratic management*—a high concern for both production and employee morale and satisfaction. Blake and Mouton argue strongly that the 9,9 management style is the most effective type of leadership behavior. They believe this approach will, in almost all situations, result in improved performance, low absenteeism and turnover, and high employee satisfaction. The Blake and Mouton Managerial Grid is widely used as a training device.

Rensis Likert, again incorporating the basic style categories of task orientation and employee orientation, devised a four-level model of management effectiveness.[11] System 1 managers make all the work-related decisions and order their subordinates to carry them out. Standards and methods of performance are also rigidly set by managers. Failure to meet the managers' goals results in threats or punishment. The managers feel little trust or confidence in subordinates, and subordinates, in turn, fear the managers and feel that they have little in common with them.

System 2 managers still issue orders, but subordinates have some freedom to comment on those orders. Subordinates are also given some flexibility to carry out their tasks but within carefully prescribed limits and procedures. Subordinates who meet or exceed the managers' goals may be rewarded. In general, managers have a condescending attitude toward their subordinates, and subordinates are cautious when dealing with their managers.

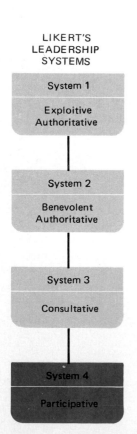

System 3 managers set goals and issue general orders after discussing them with subordinates. Subordinates can make their own decisions about how to carry out their tasks, since only broad, major decisions are made by higher-level managers. Rewards, rather than the threat of punishment, are used to motivate subordinates. Subordinates feel free to discuss most work-related matters with their managers, who, in turn, feel that to a large extent subordinates can be trusted to carry out their tasks properly.

System 4 is Likert's ideal system toward which organizations should work. Goals are set and work-related decisions are made by the group. If managers formally reach a decision, they do so after incorporating the suggestions and opinions of the other group members. Thus, the goal they set or the decision they reach may not always be the one they personally favor. To motivate subordinates, managers not only use economic rewards but also try to give their subordinates feelings of worth and importance. Performance standards exist to permit self-appraisal by subordinates, rather than to provide managers with a tool to control subordinates. Interaction between managers and subordinates is frank, friendly, and trusting.

Influences on Choice of Leadership Style. Robert Tannenbaum and Warren H. Schmidt were among the first theorists to describe various factors that they believe should influence a manager's choice of leadership style.[12] While personally favoring the democratic style, they acknowledge that managers need to take certain practical considerations into account before deciding how to manage. They suggest that a manager should consider three sets of "forces" before choosing a leadership style: forces in the manager, forces in subordinates, and forces in the situation. This approach sees the most effective managers as flexible, able to select leadership behaviors needed in a given time and place.

How a manager leads will primarily be influenced by his or her background, knowledge, values, and experience (*forces in the manager*). For example, a manager who believes that the needs of the individual must come second to the needs of the organization may take a very directive role in his or her subordinates' activities. (See fig. 16–2.)

Characteristics of *subordinates* also must be considered before managers can choose an appropriate leadership style. According to Tannenbaum and Schmidt, a manager can allow greater participation and freedom when subordinates:

· **Crave independence and freedom of action.**
· **Want to have decision-making responsibility.**
· **Identify with the organization's goals.**
· **Are knowledgeable and experienced enough to deal with the problem efficiently.**
· **Have experience with previous managers that leads them to expect participative management.**

Where these conditions are lacking, managers may have to lean toward the authoritarian style. They can, however, vary their behavior once subordinates gain self-confidence in working with them.

Finally, a manager's choice of leadership style must reckon with such *situational* forces as the organization's preferred style, the specific work group, the nature of the group's work tasks, the pressures of time, and even environmental factors, which may affect organization members' attitudes toward authority.

FIGURE 16–2 CONTINUUM OF LEADERSHIP BEHAVIOR

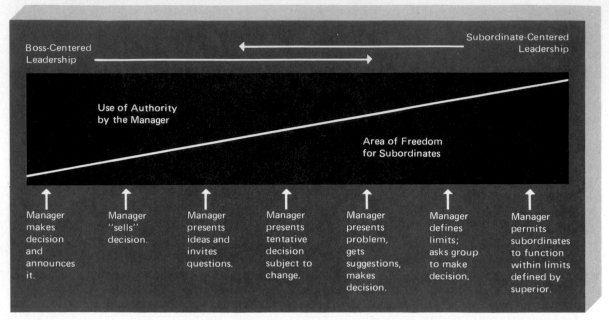

Boss-Centered
Leadership

Subordinate-Centered
Leadership

Use of Authority
by the Manager

Area of Freedom
for Subordinates

| Manager makes decision and announces it. | Manager "sells" decision. | Manager presents ideas and invites questions. | Manager presents tentative decision subject to change. | Manager presents problem, gets suggestions, makes decision. | Manager defines limits; asks group to make decision. | Manager permits subordinates to function within limits defined by superior. |

Source: Reprinted by permission of the *Harvard Business Review*. An exhibit from "How to Choose a Leadership Pattern" by Robert Tannenbaum and Warren Schmidt (May–June 1973). Copyright © 1973 by the President and Fellows of Harvard College; all rights reserved.

Most managers, for example, will move toward the leadership style favored by the organization's hierarchy. If top management emphasizes human relations skills, the manager will incline toward an employee-centered style. If a decisive, take-charge style seems favored, the manager will tend to be task- rather than employee-oriented.

The specific work group also affects the choice of style. A group that works well together may respond more to a free and open atmosphere than to close supervision. So will a group confident of its ability to solve problems as a unit. But if a work group is too large or too widely dispersed geographically, a participative management style may be difficult to use.

The nature of the problem and time pressures are other situational factors that may influence the choice of managerial style. For example, a complex problem requiring highly specialized skills and knowledge that only the manager possesses may make direct instructions and close supervision necessary. Similarly, in situations where quick decisions are essential (as in emergencies), even democratic managers may revert to an authoritative leadership style.

Factors in Leadership Effectiveness

The trait and behavioral approaches produced research showing that effective leadership seemed to depend on a number of variables, such as organizational culture, the nature of the tasks and work activities, and managerial values and experience. No one trait was common to all effective leaders; no one style was most effective in all situations.

Researchers then took the next logical step: They tried to identify the factors in the situation that influence the effectiveness of a particular leadership style. Since the early work of Tannenbaum and Schmidt, many researchers have added to and elaborated on the situational factors that affect the leadership style a manager selects and how effective a particular style is.

How the work situation affects a manager will depend on his or her perception of the situation. Managers who misperceive a situation may only gradually come to understand its true dimensions. For example, a manager who believes that his or her subordinates are lazy and low in ability will manage them on that basis for a prolonged period, even if the subordinates are actually eager to work and have excellent skills. In order for the manager's leadership style to change to one that is more appropriate to the situation, the manager's perception of the situation will first have to change.

Factors that influence leader effectiveness include the leader's personality, past experience, and expectations; the superior's expectations and behavior; the subordinates' characteristics, expectations, and behavior; the requirements of the task; the organizational culture and policies; and the expectations and behavior of peers.[13] (See fig. 16–3.) These factors also influence the leader in return. The influence process is *reciprocal*—leaders and group members, for example, influence each other and affect the effectiveness of the group as a whole.

The Leader's Personality, Past Experiences, and Expectations. As we have observed, the manager's values, background, and experiences will affect his or her choice of style. A manager who has had success in exercising little supervision, for example,

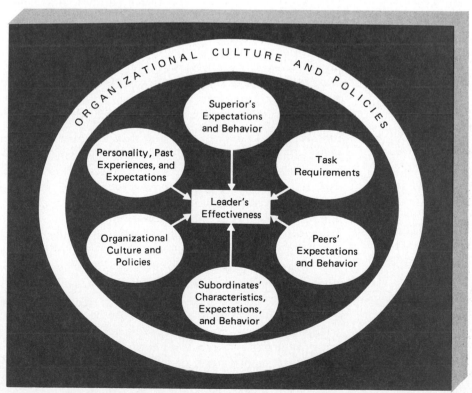

FIGURE 16–3
PERSONALITY AND SITUATIONAL FACTORS THAT INFLUENCE EFFECTIVE LEADERSHIP

or who values the self-fulfillment needs of subordinates may adopt an employee-oriented style of leadership; a manager who distrusts subordinates or who simply likes to manage all work activities directly may adopt a more authoritarian role. In general, managers develop the leadership style with which they are most comfortable.

The fact that a manager's personality or past experience helps form his or her leadership style does not mean that the style is unchangeable. Managers learn that some styles work better for them than others; if a style proves inappropriate, they can alter it. However, it is important to note that managers who attempt to adopt a style that is very inconsistent with their basic personality are unlikely to use that style effectively.

A manager's expectations are still another component. Evidence has shown that, for a variety of reasons, situations tend to work out the way we expect them to; this is sometimes referred to as *self-fulfilling prophecy*. In fact, one study found that new leaders who were told that their subordinates were low performers managed in a much more authoritative manner than new leaders who were told that their subordinates were high performers.[14] Managers' expectations of what style would be necessary to get subordinates to work effectively led to their choice of style.

The Expectations and Behavior of Superiors. The leadership style that a manager's superiors approve is very important in determining the orientation a manager will select. For example, a superior who clearly favors a task-oriented style ("You really run a tight ship—keep it up") may cause the manager to adopt that type of leadership. A superior who favors an employee-oriented style ("You really seem to get to know your subordinates—I think that's an important thing for a manager to do") encourages the manager to adopt a more employee-centered orientation.

Because of their power to dispense organizational rewards, such as bonuses and promotions, superiors clearly will affect the behavior of lower-level managers. In addition, lower-level managers tend naturally to model themselves after their superiors. One study found that supervisors who learned new behaviors in a human relations training program tended to give up those behaviors quickly if they were not consistent with their immediate superior's leadership style.[15]

Subordinates' Characteristics, Expectations, and Behavior. Subordinates play a critical role in influencing the manager's leadership style. They are, after all, the people whom that style is supposed to affect. Ultimately, the response of subordinates to the manager's leadership determines how effective the manager will be.

The characteristics of subordinates affect the manager's leadership style in a number of ways. First, the skills and training of subordinates influence the manager's choice of style: Highly capable employees will normally require a less directive approach. Second, the attitudes of subordinates will also be an influential factor: Some types of employees (such as military police) may prefer an authoritarian leader, while others (such as research scientists) may prefer to be given total responsibility for their own work.

The expectations of subordinates is another factor in determining how appropriate a particular style will be. Subordinates who have had employee-centered managers in the past may expect a new manager to have a similar style and may react negatively to authoritarian leadership. Similarly, highly skilled and motivated workers may expect the manager not to "meddle." Employees faced with new and challenging tasks, on the other hand, may expect the manager's directives and may be upset if they are not forthcoming.

The reactions of subordinates to a manager's leadership style will usually signal to the manager how effective his or her style is. For example, the subordinates' confusion or resentment that often accompanies an inappropriate style will usually suggest to the manager that a change in style is required. Sometimes, however, a new manager may feel that changing the subordinates' expectations would be better than changing his or her own style—for example, the manager may be very reluctant to adopt an authoritarian approach. In such situations, it will normally require a great deal of time and patience on the manager's part before subordinates accept the new manager's style.

Task Requirements. The nature of subordinates' job responsibilities will also affect the type of leadership style a manager will use. For example, jobs that require precise instructions (such as testing printed circuits) demand a more task-oriented style than jobs (such as university teaching) whose operating procedures can be left largely to the individual employees. Similarly, where much cooperation and teamwork are involved, as in new-product development, employees generally prefer people-centered supervision, whereas those working in isolation—truck drivers, for example—prefer more task-oriented direction.

Organizational Culture and Policies. The culture of an organization shapes both the leader's behavior and the expectations of subordinates. The stated policies of the organization also affect a manager's leadership style. For example, in organizations where climate and policies encourage strict accountability for expenses and results, managers usually supervise and control subordinates closely.

Peers' Expectations and Behavior. One's fellow managers are an important reference group. Managers form friendships with their colleagues in the organization, and the opinions of these colleagues matter to them. In addition, the attitude of a manager's peers can often affect how effectively the manager performs; hostile colleagues may compete aggressively for organization resources, harm the manager's reputation, and prove uncooperative in other ways. In many ways, the behavior of managers affects and influences that of their associates. A manager who is comparatively lenient, for example, may well become more autocratic if others comment negatively. ("You're letting your subordinates leave too early. My people are starting to complain." Or, "You're only giving two tests a term? Most instructors give four.") Whatever their own inclinations, managers tend, to some extent, to imitate the management style of their peers.

Contingency Approaches to Leadership

The situational perspective on leadership identified various factors that can influence leadership behavior. The *contingency* approaches to leadership attempt (1) to identify which of these factors is most important under a given set of circumstances and (2) to predict the leadership style that will be most effective under those circumstances. In the sections below, we will review three of the more recent and well-known contingency models of leadership.

Leadership Style and the Work Situation: The Fiedler Model

The most thoroughly researched of the three contingency models we will discuss was developed by Fred E. Fiedler. Fiedler's basic assumption is that it is quite difficult for managers to alter the management styles that have helped them develop successful careers. For this reason, he believes that trying to change a manager's style to fit the situation is inefficient or useless. Since styles are relatively inflexible, and since no one style is appropriate for every situation, effective group performance can be achieved by matching the manager to the situation or by changing the situation to fit the manager. For example, a comparatively authoritarian manager can be selected to fill a post that requires a directive leader; or a job can be changed to give an authoritarian manager more formal authority over subordinates.

The leadership styles that Fiedler contrasts are similar to the employee-centered and task-oriented styles discussed above. What differentiates his model from the others is the measuring instrument he used. Fiedler measured leadership style on a simple scale that indicated "the degree to which a man described favorably or unfavorably his least preferred co-worker (LPC)"—the employee with whom the person could work least well. It is this measure that locates an individual on the leadership style continuum. According to Fiedler's findings, " . . . a person who describes his least preferred co-worker in a relatively favorable manner tends to be permissive, human relations-oriented, and considerate of the feelings of his men. But a person who describes his least preferred co-worker in an unfavorable manner—who has what we have come to call a low LPC rating—tends to be managing, task-controlling, and less concerned with the human relations aspects of the job."[16]

According to Fiedler, then, high LPC managers want to have warm personal relations with their co-workers. They will regard close ties with subordinates as important to their overall effectiveness. Low LPC managers, on the other hand, want to get the job done; the reactions of subordinates to their leadership style is of far lower priority than the need to maintain production. Low LPC managers who feel that a harsh style is necessary to maintain production will not hesitate to use it.

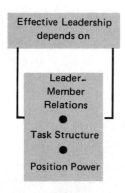

Effective Leadership depends on

Leader-Member Relations

•

Task Structure

•

Position Power

Leadership Situations. Fiedler has identified three elements in the work situation that help determine which leadership style will be effective: leader-member relations, the task structure, and the leader's position power. Fiedler's studies did not include such other situational variables as employee motivation and the values and experiences of leaders and group members.

The quality of *leader-member relations* is the most important influence on the manager's power and effectiveness, according to Fiedler. If the manager gets along well with the rest of the group, if group members respect the manager for reasons of personality, character, or ability, then the manager may not have to rely on formal rank or authority. On the other hand, a manager who is disliked or distrusted may be less able to lead informally and may have to rely on directives to accomplish group tasks.

Task structure is the second most important variable in the work situation. A highly structured task is one in which step-by-step procedures or instructions for the task are available; group members therefore have a very clear idea of what they are expected to do. Managers in such situations automatically have a great deal of authority: There are clear guidelines by which to measure worker performance, and the manager can back up his or her instructions by referring to a rulebook or manual. When tasks are unstructured, on the other hand, as in committee meetings,

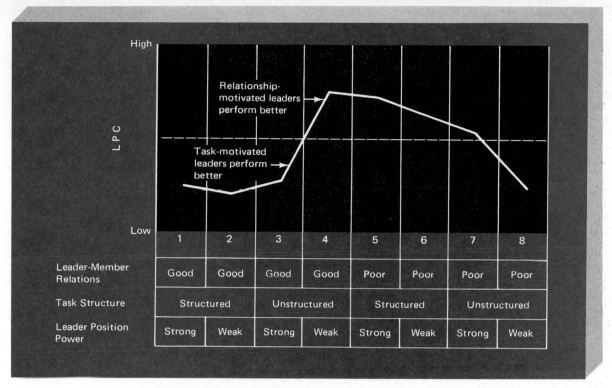

Source: Fred E. Fiedler and Martin M. Chemers. *Leadership and Effective Management* (Glenview, Ill.: Scott, Foresman, 1974), p. 80. Copyright © 1974 by Scott, Foresman and Company. Reprinted by permission.

group member roles are more ambiguous, because there are no clear guidelines on how to proceed. The manager's power is diminished, since group members can more easily disagree with or question the manager's instructions.

The leader's *position power* is the final situational variable identified by Fiedler. Some positions, such as the presidency of a firm, carry a great deal of power and authority. The chairperson of a fund-raising drive, on the other hand, has little power over volunteer workers. Thus, high position power simplifies a leader's task of influencing subordinates, while low position power makes a leader's task more difficult.

Matching the Situation to the Leader. There are eight possible combinations of these three variables in the work situation: Leader-member relations can be good or bad; tasks may be structured or unstructured; and position power may be strong or weak.

Using these eight categories of leadership situations and his two types of leaders—high and low LPC—Fiedler reviewed studies of over eight hundred groups to see which type of leader was most effective in each situation. (Among the groups studied were basketball teams, executive training workshops, and Air Force and tank combat crews. A well-liked leader of a bomber crew, for example, would be in category 1 of figure 16-4, while a disliked temporary committee chairperson would be in category 8.) He found that low LPC leaders—those who were task-oriented or authoritarian—were most effective in extreme situations where the leader either had a great deal of power and influence or had very little power and influence. High LPC leaders—those who were employee-oriented—were most effective in situations where the leader had moderate power and influence.

For example, a respected head of a research team would have only moderate influence over team members; this influence would be based largely on the fact that the team respects the leader. Research tasks are relatively unstructured, and so the leader would have little influence over the way the work would be organized and performed. In addition, the leader's position power is low, because team members would regard themselves as colleagues rather than subordinates (category 4). An authoritarian style would therefore be ineffective; team members would resent it, and it would stifle the flow of research ideas. A supportive style, on the other hand, would encourage high performance by the group.

Fiedler's model, then, suggests that an appropriate match of the leader's style (as measured by the LPC score) and the situation (as determined by the interaction of these three variables) leads to effective managerial performance. This model has been used with some success as the basis of a training program in which managers are shown how to alter the situational variables to match their leadership styles, rather than modifying their styles to fit the situation.[17]

Although the validity of Fiedler's model has been questioned,[18] it is widely agreed that he has made a significant contribution to our understanding of how leaders and situations can be matched for effective performance.

A Path-Goal Approach to Leadership

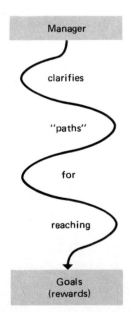

Manager

clarifies

"paths"

for

reaching

Goals
(rewards)

Like other contingency approaches, the *path-goal model* of leadership tries to help us understand and predict leadership effectiveness in different situations. The model, formulated by Martin G. Evans[19] and Robert J. House,[20] represents a new and evolving approach.

The path-goal approach is based on the expectancy model (described in the previous chapter), which states that an individual's motivation depends on his or her expectation of reward and the valence, or attractiveness, of the reward. The path-goal approach focuses on the leader as a source of rewards. It attempts to predict how different types of rewards and different leadership styles affect the motivation, performance, and satisfaction of subordinates.

Managers have at their disposal a number of ways to influence subordinates. According to Evans, the most important are the manager's ability to provide rewards and to clarify what subordinates must do to earn them. Thus, managers determine the availability of "goals" (rewards) and make clear the "paths" to be taken to reach them.

Evans suggests that a manager's leadership style influences which rewards will be available to subordinates, as well as subordinates' perceptions of what they have to do to earn those rewards. An employee-centered manager, for example, will offer a wide range of rewards to subordinates—not only pay and promotion, but also support, encouragement, security, and respect. In addition, that manager will be sensitive to individual differences between subordinates and will tailor rewards to the individual needs and desires of subordinates. A task-oriented manager, on the other hand, will offer a narrower, less individualized set of rewards. However, according to Evans, such a manager will usually be much better at linking subordinate performance to rewards than an employee-centered manager. Subordinates of a task-oriented manager will know exactly what productivity or performance level they have to attain in order to gain bonuses, salary increases, or promotions. Evans believes that the leadership style that will most motivate subordinates will depend on the types of rewards they most desire.

Path-Goal Contingency Variables. House and his colleagues have attempted to expand the path-goal theory by identifying the contingency variables that help determine the most effective leadership style. The two variables they identify are the *personal characteristics of subordinates* and the *environmental pressures and demands in the workplace* with which subordinates must cope.

The leadership style subordinates favor will, according to House, be partially determined by their personal characteristics. He cites studies suggesting that individuals who believe their behavior affects the environment favor a participatory leadership style. Individuals who believe events occur because of luck or fate tend to find an authoritarian style more congenial.

Subordinates' evaluation of their own ability will also influence subordinate style preference. Those who feel highly skilled and capable may resent an overly controlling manager, whose directives will be seen as counterproductive rather than rewarding. Subordinates who feel less skilled or able, on the other hand, may prefer a manager whose more directive behavior will be seen as enabling them to carry out their tasks properly and therefore making it possible for them to earn organizational rewards.

House identifies three environmental factors that help determine the leadership style subordinates prefer:

1. *The nature of subordinates' tasks* will affect leadership style in a number of ways. For example, an individual performing a structured task, such as equipment maintenance, or a repetitive task, such as truck loading, is likely to find an overly directive style redundant, since it is already clear exactly what needs to be done. Similarly, where the task itself is already highly satisfying, consideration shown by the manager will have little effect on a subordinate's motivation. If the task is unpleasant, however, a display of support by the leader may add to the subordinate's satisfaction and motivation.
2. *The organization's formal authority system* usually clarifies for subordinates which actions are likely to be met with disapproval (exceeding the budget, for example) and which are likely to lead to rewards (coming in under budget).
3. *The subordinates' work group* also affects the nature of leadership style in several ways. For groups that are not very cohesive, for example, a supportive, understanding style may be more effective. As a general rule, the leader's style will motivate subordinates to the extent that it compensates for what they see as deficiencies in the task, authority system, or work group.

The path-goal theory of leadership is considered highly promising, especially because it attempts to explain *why* a particular leadership style is more effective in one situation than in another. Some research has already appeared supporting the validity of path-goal theory predictions.[21]

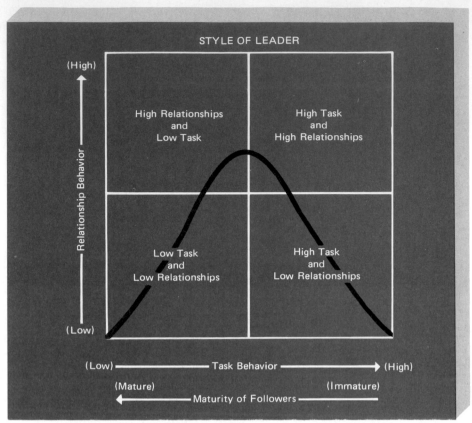

STYLE OF LEADER

(High)

High Relationships
and
Low Task

High Task
and
High Relationships

Low Task
and
Low Relationships

High Task
and
Low Relationships

(Low)

Relationship Behavior

(Low) —————— Task Behavior —————→ (High)

(Mature)　　　　　　　　　　　(Immature)

← ———— Maturity of Followers ———— →

FIGURE 16–5
THE SITUATIONAL
THEORY OF
LEADERSHIP

Source: Adapted from Paul Hersey and Kenneth H. Blanchard, *Management of Organizational Behavior: Utilizing Human Resources*, 4th ed., p. 152. Copyright © 1982. Reprinted by permission of Prentice-Hall, Inc., Englewood Cliffs, N.J.

Situational Theory of Leadership

The third major contingency approach to leadership is Paul Hersey's and Kenneth H. Blanchard's *situational leadership theory*,[22] which holds that the most effective leadership style varies with the "maturity" of subordinates. Hersey and Blanchard define maturity not as age or emotional stability but as desire for achievement, willingness to accept responsibility, and task-related ability and experience.

Hersey and Blanchard believe that the relationship between a manager and subordinates moves through four phases—a kind of life cycle—as subordinates develop and "mature" and that managers need to vary their leadership style with each phase. (See fig. 16–5.) In the initial phase—when subordinates first enter the organization—a high task orientation by the manager is most appropriate. Subordinates have to be instructed in their tasks and familiarized with the organization's rules and procedures. At this stage, a nondirective manager causes anxiety and confusion among new employees. However, a participatory employee relationship approach would also be inappropriate at this stage, according to Hersey and Blanchard, because subordinates cannot yet be regarded as colleagues.

As subordinates begin to learn their tasks, task-oriented management remains essential, because subordinates are not yet willing or able to accept full responsibility. However, the manager's trust in and support of subordinates can increase as the manager becomes familiar with subordinates and wishes to encourage further efforts on their part. Thus, the manager can start to use employee-oriented behaviors.

In the third phase, the subordinates' ability and achievement motivation are increased, and subordinates actively begin to seek greater responsibility. The manager will no longer need to be directive (indeed, close direction might be resented). However, the manager will continue to be supportive and considerate in order to strengthen the subordinates' resolve for greater responsibility.

As subordinates gradually become more confident, self-directing, and experienced, the manager can reduce the amount of support and encouragement. Subordinates are then "on their own" and no longer need or expect a directive relationship with their manager.

The situational leadership theory has generated interest because it recommends a leadership type that is dynamic and flexible rather than static. The motivation, ability, and experience of subordinates must constantly be assessed in order to determine which style combination would be most appropriate. If the style is appropriate, according to Hersey and Blanchard, it will not only motivate subordinates but also help them move toward maturity. Thus, the manager who develops subordinates, increases their confidence, and helps them learn their work will constantly be shifting style.[23]

How Flexible Are Leadership Styles?

One of the major issues raised by the contingency perspective—which is currently favored by leadership theorists and researchers—is the extent to which managers actually are able to choose among leadership styles in different situations. The issue is important because it can affect a wide range of management selection, placement, and promotion activities. If managers are flexible in leadership style, or if they can be trained to vary their style, then presumably they will be effective in a variety of leadership situations. If, on the other hand, managers are relatively inflexible in leadership style, then they will operate effectively only in those situations that best match their style or can be adjusted to match their style. Such inflexibility would not only hamper the careers of individual managers but would also complicate enormously the organization's task of filling its management positions effectively.

Fred Fiedler, as noted above, believes that leadership styles are quite inflexible. He is also very pessimistic about the possibility of training individuals to use different styles.[24] He suggests that managers be *matched* to the situation or that the situation be changed to suit the manager. An inappropriately authoritarian manager, for example, could be given subordinates who preferred a directive style. If this were impractical, the work situation or the manager's position power might be altered to make it more appropriate.

Victor H. Vroom and Philip W. Yetton are more optimistic about the ability of managers to select a style appropriate for each situation.[25] They have developed a model (see chapter 6) that managers can use for selecting the proper amount of group involvement in a variety of problem-solving and decision-making situations:

The amount of subordinate participation should depend on how much information or skill the manager possesses, whether a high-quality decision is required, the extent to which the problem is structured, and whether acceptance by the group is critical for successful implementation. Thus, Vroom and Yetton suggest that managers can be flexible and adopt a number of styles, from making the decision solely on their own through various degrees of group participation in accordance with their analysis of the needs of the situation. They have designed a training program to help managers recognize how much group participation they normally use, to show them how to determine the most appropriate approach in a given situation, and to help them select the optimum amount of participation for future situations.

Obviously, some people find it easier than others to adjust to different life situations. Several studies on leadership imply that managers actually do have a great deal of *potential* flexibility in responding to situational influences on their leadership style.[26] No reasonably alert manager, for example, whose subordinates are clearly uncooperative and whose group's performance is declining will persist in using a specific leadership style without at least questioning its effectiveness. Thus, it is possible that individuals can learn how to diagnose a leadership situation and can alter their style, at least to some extent, to make their leadership more effective.

The Importance of Flexibility. In organizations, as elsewhere in life, flexibility is desirable. It helps us respond appropriately to people and situations and to make adjustments when things don't turn out as anticipated. As managers, we should be aware of the variety of leadership styles available. Knowledge of the theories described in this chapter will help us to identify leadership behaviors as we encounter them. And we should also use our own observations to learn about leadership in actual situations. Finally, we should experiment with different approaches and learn through analysis of the results. As managers, our leadership behaviors will be learned on the job as we interact with our subordinates and their tasks.

The Future of Leadership Theory

In the future, some integration of present leadership theories can be expected, perhaps under the contingency perspective as the models are expanded to incorporate more variables such as intelligence, training, and experience.[27] Several newer or alternative approaches should become more prominent. Three candidates for increased attention are social-learning/behavior-modification approaches, leadership of self-managed groups, and "transformational" or "charismatic" leadership. We will discuss the first two briefly and the third one at some length.

Social-Learning/Behavior-Modification Approaches. There is increasing interest in the implications of operant conditioning (discussed in chapter 15) for leadership practice. The operant conditioning approach—now frequently called the social-learning or behavior-modification approach—focuses on the way leaders influence the behavior of subordinates by giving rewards, administering punishment, and creating situations that lead to desirable or undesirable actions by subordinates. According to this model, important constraints on the influence of leaders are limits on time and resources, the requirements of the task, and the conditioning power of the leader's own superiors.[28]

One of the more commercially successful management books of the mid-1980s, *The One-Minute Manager,* was based in part on operant conditioning perspectives.[29] *The One-Minute Manager* provides simple and very quick (one-minute) procedures for providing performance feedback to subordinates and similar guidelines for setting and sticking to goals. Although many leadership researchers are uncomfortable with the book's guidelines and perspectives, managers were attracted by its message.[30]

Self-Managed Groups. Another new area of leadership theory is concerned with self-managed groups, those in which employees are highly autonomous and self-directed. Joseph Finkelstein and David Newman have argued that such major high-technology "change agents" as microcomputers, computer-integrated manufacturing, global telecommunications, genetic engineering, and the like have changed methods of production and operations so dramatically that previously successful methods of management are now inadequate.[31] In this new managerial context, they believe one of the keys to productivity is the ability of groups to manage their own work. For the design of new products and processes, the need to bring together "knowledge workers" from a variety of specializations to work on complex projects in a rapidly changing technological and market environment requires different types of management skills than have traditionally been required.

Even where the task is not as complex and sophisticated as new-product or process development, the growth of participative management has been rapid, and such management involves increased work-group autonomy and self-control. Early studies of self-managed groups, such as those by Charles C. Manz and Henry P. Sims, Jr.,[32] suggest that the less formal and traditional leadership roles of facilitator, collaborator, and coordinator are more effective than the more formal and traditional role of order-giver. Manz and Sims have referred to this new type of leadership as "unleadership." Unleading involves helping groups to lead themselves in making decisions and allocating resources. As Manz and Sims speculate, "The leader of the future may be the person who, rather than providing subordinates with specific directions, can best help others find their own way."[33]

Transformational or Charismatic Leadership. A third area of growing interest focuses on individuals who have exceptional impact on their organizations. These individuals may be called *charismatic*[34] or *transformational*[35] *leaders*. The recent interest in such transformational leaders seems to stem from at least two sources. First, many large companies—including some historically very successful ones such as AT&T, IBM, and GM[36]—have recently embarked on programs involving large amounts of change that must be accomplished in short periods of time. These changes are so large and pervasive that they are often called "transformations," and it has been argued that transformational leaders are necessary to bring these companies through successfully.[37]

A second factor encouraging the growth of interest in transformational leadership is a sense that leadership theory is losing sight of the leader. As the focus of leadership theory has moved from the attempt to identify the inborn traits of leaders, to the study of the roles and behaviors of leaders and managers, to the analysis of the leadership situation, work tasks, and followers, the leader—as a person—has become a progressively less salient part of the theory. The public visibility of a business leader like Lee Iacocca of Chrysler or a military leader like General

Douglas MacArthur reminds us that some leaders seem to have personal characteristics that do make a difference in their organizations and are not fully captured by our existing theories.

In his explorations of the concept of transformational leadership, Bernard M. Bass has contrasted two types of leadership behaviors: *transactional* and *transformational*. Transactional leaders determine what subordinates need to do to achieve their own and organizational objectives, classify those requirements, and help subordinates become confident that they can reach their objectives by expending the necessary efforts. Transformational leaders, in contrast, "motivate us to do more than we originally expected to do" by raising our sense of the importance and value of our tasks, "getting us to transcend our own self-interests for the sake of the team, organization, or larger polity," and by raising our need level to the higher-order needs, such as self-actualization.[38]

Much of the leadership theory we have discussed in this chapter fits Bass's transactional category reasonably well. And Bass argues that such theory is useful and helpful, as far as it goes. However, to be fully effective, and to have a major impact on their organizations, leaders need to use their personal vision and energy to inspire their followers.

Although the transformational leadership concept dates back at least to Max Weber's discussions of charismatic leaders in the first decades of the century,[39] the concept has, until recently, received relatively little research attention. One of the more notable contributions to systematic analysis of the subject is Robert J. House's theory of charismatic leadership.[40]

In chapter 11 we discussed the referent power some managers possess. House's theory suggests that charismatic leaders have very high levels of referent power and that some of that power comes from the leaders' need to influence others, "extremely high levels of self-confidence, dominance, and a strong conviction in the moral righteousness of his/her beliefs"—or at least the ability to convince followers that he or she possesses such confidence and conviction.[41]

House suggests that charismatic leaders communicate a vision or higher-level ("transcendent") goal that captures the commitment and energies of followers. They are careful to create an image of success and competence and to set examples, by their own behavior, of the values they espouse. They also communicate high expectations for the performance of their followers and confidence that their followers will perform up to those expectations.

House's theory has not yet been extensively researched, but we can expect increasing attention to be directed toward it in the near future. One aspect likely to receive careful attention is the type of vision transformational leaders and their followers pursue. As stirring as the names Winston Churchill, Mahatma Gandhi, and Martin Luther King are for many, House and others are well aware that the ability to inspire great commitment, sacrifice, and energy from followers is no guarantee that the cause or vision is a worthwhile one. Adolf Hitler and the Reverend Jim Jones of Jonestown were also known for their charisma—and for the tragedies their leadership brought. Transformational leaders may possess great potential for revitalizing declining institutions and helping individuals find meaning and excitement in their work and lives. But they also can pose great dangers if their goals and values run counter to the basic tenets of civilized society.

Summary Leadership is an important subject for managers because of the critical role played by leaders in group and organizational effectiveness. Leadership may be defined as the process of influencing and directing the task-related activities of group members.

Three approaches to the study of leadership have been identified: the trait, behavior, and contingency approaches. The trait approach has not proved useful, since no one combination of traits consistently distinguishes leaders from nonleaders or effective leaders from ineffective leaders.

The behavior approach has focused on leadership functions and styles. Studies have found that both task-related functions and group maintenance functions have to be performed by one or more group members in order for a group to function effectively. Studies of leadership styles have distinguished between a task-oriented, authoritarian, or initiating structure and an employee-centered, democratic, or participative style. Some studies suggest that the effectiveness of a particular style depends on the circumstances in which it is used. Tannenbaum and Schmidt, for example, maintain that a manager's choice of leadership style should be influenced by various forces in the manager, in subordinates, and in the work situation.

The difficulty of isolating universally effective leadership traits or behaviors caused researchers to try to determine the situational variables that will cause one leadership style to be more effective than another. The major situational variables they identified include: the leader's personality and past experience; the expectations and behavior of superiors; the characteristics, expectations, and behavior of subordinates; task requirements; organizational culture and policies; and the expectations and behavior of peers.

The contingency approach to leadership attempts to identify which of these situational factors is most important and to predict which leadership style will be most effective in a given situation. According to the Fiedler model, leader-member relations, task structure, and the leader's position power are the most important situational variables. This model predicts which types of leaders (high LPC or low LPC) will be most effective in the eight possible combinations of these variables.

The path-goal approach focuses on managers' abilities to dispense rewards. The leadership style a manager uses will affect the types of rewards offered and subordinates' perceptions of what they must do to earn those rewards. The personal characteristics of subordinates, as well as the environmental pressures and demands to which they are subjected, will affect which leadership style subordinates actually or potentially find rewarding.

The situational theory of leadership suggests that leadership style should vary with the maturity of subordinates. The manager–subordinate relationship moves through four phases as subordinates develop achievement motivation and experience; a different leadership style is appropriate for each phase.

Fiedler suggests that leadership styles are relatively inflexible and that therefore leaders should be matched to an appropriate situation, or the situation changed to match the leader. Others, however, believe that managers have a great deal of potential flexibility in their leadership styles and can therefore learn to be effective in a variety of situations.

Review Questions

1. How is leadership defined in this chapter? Discuss three implications of this definition.
2. Why was the trait approach a logical attempt to understand leadership? What two approaches did the trait researchers take? What did the leadership trait studies reveal?
3. Describe the two basic leadership functions needed for effective group performance. Must the leader perform both of these functions?
4. What are the two basic leadership styles identified by the Ohio State and University of Michigan studies? Which style was thought to be more effective?

5. Outline the basic theory of the Managerial Grid. Which leadership style in the Grid do Blake and Mouton feel is most effective?

6. List Likert's four management systems. Which of these systems does Likert believe is most effective?

7. Outline the basic idea of the Tannenbaum and Schmidt model. What factors should influence a manager's style, according to Tannenbaum and Schmidt? What are some of the practical considerations that they suggest managers must take into account in selecting a style?

8. What basic assumptions underlie the Fiedler model? What is the LPC Scale? What are the basic elements in the work situation that determine which leadership style will be most effective? In what situation is a high LPC leader effective? In what situations is a low LPC leader effective?

9. Describe the path-goal model. On what theory of motivation is the model based? According to this model, how do managers with different leadership styles differ in their ability to influence or reward subordinates? What variables, according to this theory, help determine the most effective leadership style? Why?

10. What is the "situational leadership theory"? How should the manager's style vary in each of the four phases?

11. In what ways, if any, have your views on leaders and leadership changed as a result of reading this chapter? Which leadership style do you feel is best suited to you? Which style would you be most likely to use? How flexible in leadership style do you believe you are? Do you think your answers to these questions will affect your career choice(s)?

Notes

1. Gary A. Yukl, *Leadership in Organizations* (Englewood Cliffs, N.J.: Prentice-Hall, 1981), p. 90.

2. Bernard M. Bass, *Stogdill's Handbook of Leadership: A Survey of Theory and Research,* rev. ed. (New York: Free Press, 1981), p. 7.

3. John R. P. French and Bertram Raven, "The Bases of Social Power," in Dorwin Cartwright, ed., *Studies in Social Power* (Ann Arbor, Mich.: University of Michigan, 1959), pp. 150–167. See also Dennis A. Gioia and Henry P. Sims, Jr., "Perceptions of Managerial Power as a Consequence of Managerial Behavior and Reputation," *Journal of Management* 9, no. 1 (Fall 1983):7–26; and Edwin P. Hollander, "Leadership and Power," in Gardner Lindzey and Elliot Aronson, eds., *Handbook of Social Psychology,* 3d ed. (New York: Random House, 1985), chapter 9.

4. Robert J. House and Mary L. Baetz, "Leadership: Some Empirical Generalizations and New Research Directions," in Barry M. Staw, ed., *Research in Organizational Behavior,* vol. 1 (Greenwich, Conn.: JAI Press, 1979), pp. 348–354; David A. Kenny and Stephen J. Zaccaro, "An Estimate of Variance Due to Traits in Leadership," *Journal of Applied Psychology* 68, no. 4 (November 1983):678–685; Ralph M. Stogdill, "Personal Factors Associated with Leadership: A Survey of the Literature," *Journal of Psychology* 25, no. 1 (January 1948):35–71; R. D. Mann, "A Review of the Relationships between Personality and Performance in Small Groups," *Psychological Bulletin* 56, no. 4 (July 1959):241–270; and Howard M. Weiss and Seymour Adler, "Personality and Organizational Behavior," *Research in Organizational Behavior* 6 (1984):1–50.

5. See Edwin E. Ghiselli, *Explorations in Managerial Talent* (Pacific Palisades, Calif.: Goodyear, 1971), pp. 39–56.

6. See Dorwin Cartwright and Alvin Zander, eds., *Group Dynamics,* 3rd ed. (New York: Harper & Row, 1968).

7. Natalie Porter, Florence Lindauer Geis, and Joyce Jennings, "Are Women Invisible Leaders?" *Sex Roles* 9, no. 10 (October 1983):1035–1049; Robert W. Rice, Debra Instone, and Jerome Adams, "Leader Sex, Leader Success, and Leadership Process: Two Field Studies," *Journal of Applied Psychology* 69, no. 1 (February 1984):12–31; and Susan M. Donnell and Jay Hall, "Men and Women as Managers: A Significant Case of No Significant Difference," *Organizational Dynamics* 8, no. 4 (Spring 1980):60–77.

8. See Robert F. Bales, *Interaction Process Analysis* (Reading, Mass.: Addison-Wesley, 1951). A

recent study finding contrary evidence is C. Roger Rees and Mady Wechsler Segal, "Role Differentiation in Groups: The Relationship Between Instrumental and Expressive Leadership," *Small Group Behavior* 15, no. 1 (February 1984):109–123.

9. See Victor H. Vroom, "Leadership," in Marvin D. Dunnette, ed., *Handbook of Industrial and Organizational Psychology* (New York: Wiley, 1983), pp. 1527–1551.

10. Robert R. Blake and Jane S. Mouton, *The New Managerial Grid III* (Houston: Gulf Publishing, 1984). For an early classification of leadership styles into authoritarian, *laissez-faire,* and democratic leadership, see Kurt Lewin, Ronald Lippitt, and Ralph K. White, "Patterns of Aggressive Behavior in Experimentally Created Social Climates," *Journal of Social Psychology* 10, no. 2 (May 1939):271–299.

11. See Rensis Likert, *New Patterns of Management* (New York: McGraw-Hill, 1961), and *The Human Organization* (New York: McGraw-Hill, 1967).

12. Robert Tannenbaum and Warren H. Schmidt, "How to Choose a Leadership Pattern," *Harvard Business Review* 51, no. 3 (May–June 1973):162–164ff. (Reprint of March–April 1958 article.)

13. See, for example, Martin M. Chemers, "The Social, Organizational, and Cultural Context of Effective Leadership," in Barbara Kellerman, ed., *Leadership: Multidisciplinary Perspectives* (Englewood Cliffs, N.J.: Prentice-Hall, 1985), pp. 91–112.

14. George F. Farris and Francis G. Lim, Jr., "Effects of Performance on Leadership, Cohesiveness, Satisfaction, and Subsequent Performance," *Journal of Applied Psychology* 53, no. 6 (December 1969):490–497. See also Dov Eden, "Self-Fulfilling Prophecy as a Management Tool: Harnessing Pygmalion," *Academy of Management Review* 9, no. 1 (January 1984):64–73.

15. E. A. Fleishman, "Leadership Climate, Human Relations Training, and Supervisory Behavior," *Personnel Psychology* 6, no. 2 (Summer 1953):205–222.

16. Fred E. Fiedler, "Engineer the Job to Fit the Manager," *Harvard Business Review* 43, no. 5 (September–October 1965):116. See also Fred E. Fiedler, "The Contingency Model," in Harold Proshansky and Bernard Seidenberg, eds., *Basic Studies in Social Psychology* (New York: Holt, Rinehart & Winston, 1965), pp. 538–551, and "Validation and Extension of the Contingency Model of Leadership Effectiveness," *Psychological Bulletin* 76, no. 2 (August 1971):128–148.

17. Fred E. Fiedler and Linda Mahar, "A Field Experiment Validating Contingency Model Leadership Training," *Journal of Applied Psychology* 64, no. 3 (June 1979):247–254.

18. See, for example, John E. Stinson and Lane Tracy, "The Stability and Interpretation of the LPC Score," *Proceedings of the Academy of Management* 32 (1972): 182–184; George Graen, James B. Orris, and Kenneth Alvares, "Contingency Model of Leadership Effectiveness: Some Experimental Results," *Journal of Applied Psychology* 55, no. 3 (June 1971):196–201; and Walter Bungard, "Sense and Nonsense of the LPC Scale: Criticism of Fiedler's Contingency Model," *Gruppendynamik* 15, no. 1 (1984):59–74. (In German.)

19. Martin G. Evans, "Leadership and Motivation: A Core Concept," *Academy of Management Journal* 13, no. 1 (March 1970):91–102.

20. See Robert J. House, "A Path-Goal Theory of Leader Effectiveness," *Administrative Science Quarterly* 16, no. 5 (September 1971):321–328; and Robert J. House and Terence R. Mitchell, "Path-Goal Theory of Leadership," *Journal of Contemporary Business* 3, no. 4 (Autumn 1974):81–97.

21. Chester A. Schriesheim and Angelo S. DeNisi, "Task Dimensions as Moderators of the Effects of Instrumental Leader Behavior: A Path-Goal Approach," *Proceedings of the Academy of Management* 39 (1979):103–106.

22. Paul Hersey and Kenneth H. Blanchard, *Management of Organizational Behavior*, 4th ed. (Englewood Cliffs, N.J.: Prentice-Hall, 1982). See also William J. Reddin, "The 3-D Management Style Theory," *Training and Development Journal* 21, no. 4 (April 1967):8–17, on which Hersey and Blanchard base much of their work.

23. The theory has been criticized for its inability to handle some actual management situations logically. See Claude L. Graeff, "The Situational Leadership Theory: A Critical View," *Academy of Management Review* 8, no. 2 (April 1983):285–291. Blake and Mouton also critique the situational theory and argue for the universal superiority of the 9,9 style in "A Comparative Analysis of Situationalism and 9,9 Management by Principle," *Organizational Dynamics* 10, no. 4 (Spring 1982):20–43.

24. See Fred E. Fiedler, "The Trouble with Leadership Training Is that It Doesn't Train Leaders," *Psychology Today*, February 1973, pp. 23ff.

25. See Victor H. Vroom, "Can Leaders Learn to Lead?" in J. Richard Hackman, Edward E. Lawler III, and Lyman W. Porter, eds., *Perspectives on Behavior in Organizations* (New York: McGraw-Hill, 1977), pp. 398–408.

26. See Farris and Lim, "Effects of Performance on Leadership, Cohesiveness, Satisfaction, and Subsequent Performance." See also Lawrence R. James and John F. White III, "Cross-situational Specificity in Managers' Perceptions of Subordinate Performance, Attributions, and Leader Behaviors," *Personnel Psychology* 36, no. 4 (Winter 1983):809–856.

27. Robert W. Rice and Denise R. Kastenbaum, "The Contingency Model of Leadership: Some Current Issues," *Basic and Applied Social Psychology* 4, no. 4 (December 1983):373–392. See also Rick Roskin, "Management Style and Achievement: A Model Synthesis," *Personnel Review* 12, no. 3 (1983):9–13; and James G. Hunt, "Organizational Leadership: The Contingency Paradigm and Its Challenges," in Kellerman, *Leadership,* pp. 113–138..

28. Ahmed Sakr Ashour and Gary Johns, "Leader Influence Through Operant Principles: A Theoretical and Methodological Framework," *Human Relations* 36, no. 7 (July 1983):603–626.

29. Kenneth Blanchard and Spencer Johnson, *The One-Minute Manager* (New York: Morrow, 1982). See also Kenneth H. Blanchard, *Putting the One-Minute Manager to Work* (New York: Morrow, 1984).

30. Recent descriptions of the progress in applying operant conditioning principles to management and in integrating them with other perspectives can be found in Fred Luthans and Robert Kreitner, *Organizational Behavior Modification and Beyond* (Glenview, Ill.: Scott Foresman, 1985); and Fred Luthans and Robert Kreitner, "A Social Learning Approach to Behavioral Management: Radical Behaviorists 'Mellowing Out,' " *Organizational Dynamics* 13, no. 2 (Autumn 1984):47–63.

31. Joseph Finkelstein and David A. H. Newman, "The Third Industrial Revolution: A Special Challenge to Managers," *Organizational Dynamics* 13, no. 1 (Summer 1984):53–65.

32. Charles C. Manz and Henry P. Sims, Jr., "Searching for the 'Unleader': Organizational Members' Views on Leading Self-Managed Groups," *Human Relations* 37, no. 5 (May 1984):409–424; and Charles C. Manz, *The Art of Self-Leadership* (Englewood Cliffs, N.J.: Prentice-Hall, 1983).

33. Manz and Sims, "Searching for the 'Unleader,' " p. 441.

34. Max Weber, *Economy and Society: An Outline of Interpretative Sociology* (New York: Bedminster Press, 1968; originally published in 1925), pp. 241–254; and Robert J. House, "A 1976 Theory of Charismatic Leadership," in James G. Hunt and Lars L. Larson, eds, *Leadership: The Cutting Edge* (Carbondale, Ill.: Southern Illinois University Press, 1976), pp. 189–207.

35. Bernard M. Bass, "Leadership: Good, Better, Best," *Organizational Dynamics* 13, no. 3 (Winter 1985):26–40; and Noel M. Tichy and David O. Ulrich, "The Leadership Challenge—A Call for the Transformational Leader," *Sloan Management Review* 26, no. 1 (Fall 1984):59–68.

36. See Jeremy Main, Waking Up AT&T: There's Life After Culture Shock," *Fortune,* December 24, 1984, pp. 66ff.; David E. Sanger, "The Changing Image of IBM," *New York Times Magazine,* July 7, 1985, pp. 13ff.; and Cary Reich, "The Innovator: The Creative Mind of GM Chairman Roger Smith," *New York Times Magazine,* April 21, 1985, pp. 29ff.

37. See Tichy and Ulrich "The Leadership Challenge." Tichy and Ulrich list the following additional companies as ones undergoing major transformations: Honeywell, Ford, Burroughs, Chase Manhattan Bank, Citibank, U.S. Steel, Union Carbide, Texas Instruments, and Control Data.

38. Bass, "Leadership: Good, Better, Best," pp. 27–28, 31.

39. Weber, *Economy and Society,* pp. 241–254.

40. House, "A 1976 Theory of Charismatic Leadership," pp. 189–207.

41. Ibid., p. 193.

CASE STUDY: Leadership at the Top

The Executive Committee of the Board of Directors had made an exhaustive search to find the "right" person to become President of Metro Mortgage and Finance Company. None of the persons under consideration had the exact profile desired by the Executive Committee. As a last minute recommendation, the committee received the nomination of Grover Stable, a nephew of Warren Stable, the largest shareholder in the company. Warren Stable had recommended his nephew because, as he put it to the Executive Committee, "You've wasted three months and a lot of money coming up with nothing. Right under your nose is a bright, energetic young man with an M.B.A. degree, five years' experience with the company, and motivation to spare. Grover's experience may be limited, but he has vision and toughness that will give the company great leadership for years to come."

The committee, embarrassed by their failure to find an acceptable candidate for the presidency, decided to recommend Grover Stable for President to the full Board of Directors. Upon receiving the nomination, the Board voted to appoint Grover Stable as President, effective immediately.

During the first week of Grover's tenure as President, he called a meeting of the management team and stated his personal philosophy of management:

> . . . effective immediately I shall solicit your support of my administration. I expect to maximize the development of each of you and organize this company to bring about extreme efficiency and new records in performance. Each of you will have an opportunity to comment on the standards of excellence that will be set for you, and each of you can demonstrate your loyalty to the organization by accepting my philosophy as a reflection of your own. It is nice for employees to act as individual thinkers, but when you're in management, you represent the company and much of your thinking is done by those above.
>
> Let's solidify our efforts and get behind my new administration with all our capabilities. The success of this company will depend upon my leadership ability and your willingness to execute top-management decisions.

Source: Adapted from Francis J. Bridges and James E. Chapman, *Critical Incidents in Organizational Behavior and Administration* (Englewood Cliffs, N.J.: Prentice-Hall, 1977), p. 157. Reprinted by permission of the authors.

Case Questions
1. Describe Warren Stable's concept of the "best" leadership style using the Managerial Grid theory of leadership.

2. Describe Grover Stable's perception of the "best" leadership style using the "situational" theory of leadership.

3. What do you think of Grover Stable's leadership style in terms of appropriateness for Metro Mortgage and Finance Company?

17 GROUPS AND COMMITTEES

Upon completing this chapter you should be able to:

1. Describe the characteristics of formal and informal groups.
2. State why groups are an important part of organizational life.
3. Explain how group leaders, group norms, and group cohesiveness develop.
4. Identify the factors that can affect group performance.
5. Identify the assets and liabilities of group problem solving and describe how group performance can be improved.
6. State the roles of task forces and committees in organizations.
7. Describe the advantages and disadvantages of committees and task forces and how they can be made effective.

Winter Survival: A Test

You have just crash-landed in the woods of northern Minnesota and southern Manitoba. It is 11:32 A.M. in mid-January. The light plane in which you were traveling crashed on a lake. The pilot and copilot were killed. Shortly after the crash the plane sank completely into the lake with the pilot's and copilot's bodies inside. None of you who survived are seriously injured and you are all dry.

The crash came suddenly, before the pilot had time to radio for help or inform anyone of your position. Since your pilot was trying to avoid a storm, you know the plane was considerably off course. The pilot announced shortly before the crash that you were 20 miles northwest of a small town that is the nearest known habitation.

You are in a wilderness area made up of thick woods broken by many lakes and streams. The snow depth varies from above the ankles in windswept areas to knee-deep where it has drifted. The last weather report indicated that the temperature would reach $-25°$ in the daytime and $-40°$ at night. There is plenty of dead wood and twigs in the immediate area. You are dressed in winter clothing appropriate for city wear—suits, pantsuits, street shoes, and overcoats.

You may assume that the number of passengers is the same as the number of persons in your group and that the group has agreed to stick together. While escaping from the plane, several members of your group salvaged 12 items. Your task is to rank these items according to their importance to your survival, starting with *1* for the most important item and ending with *12* for the least important one.

____ Ball of steel wool
____ Newspapers (one per person)
____ Compass
____ Hand ax
____ Cigarette lighter (without fluid)
____ Loaded .45-caliber pistol
____ Sectional air map made of plastic

____ Piece of heavy-duty canvas 20 by 20 feet
____ Extra shirt and pants for each survivor
____ Can of shortening
____ Quart of 100-proof whiskey
____ Family-size chocolate bars (one per person)[1]

What do you think? In this life-and-death situation, would you and the group have a better chance to survive if you made the important decisions for the group by yourself or if you and the other survivors jointly decided what to do? For example, if all of you decided to rank the 12 items as a group, would the group's ranking be superior to your own? And how could you improve the quality of the solutions offered by your group?

Many people are likely to conclude that they would be better off making these survival decisions on their own. Working through groups is often a frustrating experience, and the idea that groups actually can be managed to outperform individuals may be difficult to accept. For example, the authors have frequently been asked by students how they could chart a management career that would avoid the inefficiency and frustration they see as inherent in group work. But such an attempt to escape group work is an unpromising approach for anyone who desires a challenging and mobile managerial career. Groups are an inevitable and useful feature of organizational life, and a considerable part of a manager's job is devoted to group and committee work. As managers, our task will be to manage organizational groups in such a way as to make them more productive and satisfying to their members.[2]

In this chapter we will describe the various types of groups that exist in organizations. We will also describe how group problem solving can be managed and improved. First, though, try the "Winter Survival" test: Work with no more than five other students, each of whom should rank the 12 items alone, without looking at each other's answers. When you have completed your individual rankings, discuss the problem together as a group, sharing your individual solutions until you reach a consensus. Finally, check both your individual and group answers against the rankings given by survival experts—which are given in your teacher's Instructor's Manual. This exercise will show you in a practical way the relative merits of individual versus group problem solving. It may also give you some insight into the kinds of problems in human relationships that managers of groups may face.

Types of Groups

A *group* may be defined as two or more people who interact with and influence each other toward a common purpose.[3] Three types of groups commonly exist in organizations: (1) *command groups,* composed of managers and their subordinates; (2) *committees* and *task forces,* formed to carry out specific organizational activities; and (3) *informal groups,* which emerge in the organization whether or not managers desire or encourage them. The first two types are *formal groups.* Managers determine their membership and direct them in order to achieve specific objectives.

Command groups will be described briefly in this chapter but are primarily dealt with elsewhere in this book, particularly in the extended discussion of leadership. In this chapter we will take a close look at committees and task forces and how they function.

Managers should be aware that there are other types of groups as well. For example, *reference groups* are made up of those persons with whom specific individuals identify and compare themselves. A manager's reference group might be the other managers at his or her level within the organization or even within the industry. If the manager strongly desires promotion, his or her reference group is likely to be higher-level managers. In private life, the manager's other reference groups might include members of his or her club or community.

Such groups can affect an individual's attitudes and behavior, since people tend to model themselves after the members of their reference group. Reference groups, therefore, can be an important influence in organizational life, since the members frequently adopt the performance standards and expectations of their reference groups.[4]

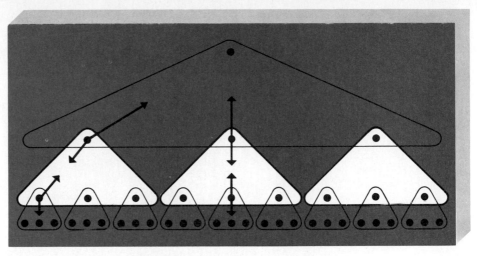

FIGURE 17–1
THE LINKING PIN

Note: The arrows indicate the linking pin function.

Source: Rensis Likert, *New Patterns of Management* (New York: McGraw-Hill, 1961), p. 113. Copyright © 1961 by McGraw-Hill Inc. Used with permission of McGraw-Hill Book Co.

Formal Groups

Formal groups are created deliberately by managers and charged with carrying out specific tasks to help the organization achieve its goals.[5] (Informal groups, as we shall see, may sometimes have objectives that run counter to organizational goals.)

The most prevalent type of formal group in organizations is the command group, which includes a manager and his or her subordinates. The formal structure of organizations consists of a series of overlapping command groups. Managers belong to command groups composed of themselves and their subordinates, and they simultaneously belong to command groups composed of their fellow managers and their own higher-level manager. In Rensis Likert's terminology, managers are the "linking pins" between the various formal work groups in their organizations.[6] (See fig. 17–1.)

Permanent formal groups include command groups and permanent committees. (A planning committee is a common example of a permanent formal group.) *Temporary formal groups* include task forces and project groups that are created to deal with a particular problem and are disbanded once the problem is solved. We will discuss task forces and committees in detail later in this chapter.

Informal Groups

Informal groups emerge whenever people come together and interact regularly. Such groups develop within the formal organizational structure. (See fig. 17–2.) Members of informal groups tend to subordinate some of their individual needs to those of the group as a whole. In return, the group supports and protects them. Informal groups may further the interests of the organization—Saturday morning softball games, for example, may strengthen the players' ties to the organization. They may also oppose organizational objectives, such as high performance standards, when these are considered harmful to the group.

FIGURE 17–2 SOME INFORMAL GROUPS WITHIN AN ORGANIZATION

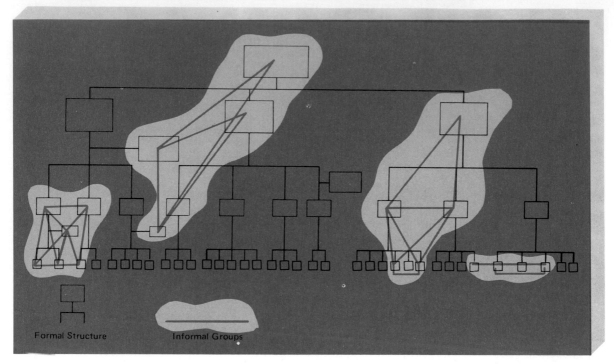

Formal Structure   Informal Groups

Advantages of Informal Groups. Informal groups serve four major functions:[7]

1. *They perpetuate commonly held social and cultural values.* Members of the same informal group are likely to share certain norms and values. In their day-to-day interactions, these norms and values guide behavior and are further reinforced.

2. *They provide social satisfaction, status, and security.* In a large corporation many individuals may feel they are just anonymous workers to their employers. Within their informal groups, however, these same employees are personal friends who share jokes and gripes, eat together, and perhaps socialize after work. Informal groups satisfy human needs for friendship and support. They recognize individuality. They help people confirm their identity and define the status and self-esteem associated with that identity. Security is also enhanced by the "strength in numbers" of the group and the psychological advantages of knowing that others are in the same situation.

3. *They help their members communicate.* To stay informed about matters that may affect them, informal group members develop their own channels of communication alongside the formal channels established by management. In fact, managers often use the informal network to convey information "unofficially"—for example, to squelch rumors about a possible takeover by another company.

4. *They help to solve problems.* Concerns and problems of group members can be handled by the group. A sick or tired employee may be given help, information

vital to job or group interests may be gathered, or games may be devised to counteract boredom. This group problem-solving function can work to the organization's advantage, as when lazy or careless employees are told to "shape up" by their co-workers, or when the group aids an individual whose personal problems are interfering with work. Alternatively, this function may work to the detriment of the organization, as when enthusiastic new employees are persuaded to reduce their efforts to the time-tested lower standards of the group.

Possible Disadvantages of Informal Groups. Each of the above advantages has a negative aspect as well:

1. *Conformity.* Informal groups usually act as reference groups, encouraging conformity among their members. This is good up to a point: Shared norms and values can smooth a group member's day-to-day activities and even free his or her creative energics for finding new ways to approach the work. But excess conformity can also make group members reluctant to act differently, creatively, or assertively, for fear of losing group approval. In that case, the organization suffers because its members show less initiative and innovation.

2. *Conflict.* Providing social satisfaction may enhance the work environment, but it may also conflict with management's needs. For example, many people believe that a coffee break increases productivity. But if the informal group stretches it out for an extra 15 or 20 minutes every morning, the members' gain in social satisfaction may be at the expense of lost production for the company.

3. *Rumor.* Every organization must come to grips with the grapevine—the informal group's communication system that dispenses true and false rumors with equal dispatch. When employees are not kept informed on matters that directly affect them, they may spread incorrect information that undermines morale or leads people to make poor decisions.

4. *Resistance to change.* Perpetuating shared values preserves the integrity of the group and adds stability to the work situation. When carried too far, however, such stability can become a barrier to change. For example, minority-group employees just hired by an organization may have a difficult time being accepted by existing informal groups.

Characteristics of Groups in Organizations

Managers who deal with groups must (1) determine when and how groups can be utilized most effectively to achieve organizational goals, (2) manage groups so they perform at a high level, and (3) overcome the disadvantages that may be associated with groups. To do all this, managers must be aware of some special characteristics of groups that may aid or hinder them.

Informal Leadership

The formal leader of a group is, of course, appointed or elected to head the group. Informal leaders, on the other hand, tend to emerge gradually as group members interact. The man or woman who speaks up more than the others, who offers more and better suggestions than anyone else, or who gives direction to the group's

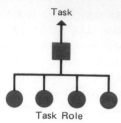

Task

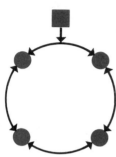

Task Role

Maintenance
Role

activities usually becomes the informal leader. Even in formal groups, such self-confident, assertive individuals often develop into rivals of the formally chosen leaders, thereby weakening the leader's hold on the group members.[8]

As we discussed in chapter 16, both formal and informal leaders play two basic roles. In the *task role*, the leader directs the group toward completion of the activities it is seeking to accomplish. As a sales manager, for example, our task role would include hiring and firing personnel, assigning territories, and supervising the training of new sales force members. In the *group building and maintenance role*, the leader is concerned with fulfilling the group's social needs by encouraging feelings of solidarity. For example, if as sales managers we help settle some non-work-related dispute between salespeople, we are acting in a maintenance role. Proper exercise of this role enables the leader to keep members attached to the group over extended periods of time.

Ideally, the group leader can play both roles, enabling the group to perform with a high degree of effectiveness. In practice, however, a single leader will often be unable to perform both roles equally well; in such cases, a second person can close the gap by taking over the neglected function (usually the maintenance role).

Group Norms and Conformity

Over time, group members form expectations about how they and the other members of the group will behave and exert pressure on one another to ensure that these expectations are met. For example, an executive who comes to work in running shoes when all the other executives are wearing dress shoes will, at the very least, be questioned about the unusual attire; perhaps he or she will even be ridiculed gently for this violation of group norms. The anticipation of rejection by the group is usually enough to ensure that members conform to their group's expectations in advance—so it is unlikely that the executive will come to work in running shoes even once.

When an individual does not conform to group norms, the other members of the group will initially try to persuade the deviant to conform.[9] They will try to reason with the deviant or make pointed jokes at his or her expense. If this approach fails, they are likely to escalate the pressure. If the norm being violated is considered important, they will use criticism, sarcasm, ridicule, and finally ostracism—total rejection of the individual through the "silent treatment." In some kinds of groups, where the deviant behavior touches on a truly sensitive area—as with the rate-buster who exceeds the group's output norms—the deviant may even be physically harassed.

Such enforced conformity clearly has its negative side: It may stifle initiative and innovation and reduce performance. Executives, of course, have more important matters to occupy their minds than footwear, but the conformity pressures of small, informal groups can be very powerful for important as well as trivial decisions and actions. A classic series of experiments by Solomon Asch demonstrated the power of small groups in pressuring individuals to yield to a majority opinion that could be clearly discerned as false.[10] Subsequent experiments have found specific factors that cause individuals to succumb to group pressure and other factors that reduce conformity.[11] Disturbingly, some studies indicate that many individuals will conform to illegitimate demands of persons in apparent authority. For example, Stanley

Milgram found his subjects willing to obey authority to the point of administering what they believed to be (but were not) dangerous, high-voltage electric shocks to a victim.[12] In another experiment, student guards and prisoners in a mock prison conformed to expectations about guard and prisoner behavior in troubling and even frightening ways.[13]

So group pressures, like many other forces, have positive and negative sides. They maintain predictable patterns of work, nurture teamwork, and defend group and individual interests. But they may also suppress new ideas, restrict individual choices, and even encourage undesirable actions. For managers, the problem has never been to prevent group pressures—which are inevitable—but to channel them in constructive directions.

Group Cohesiveness

Group cohesiveness, or solidarity, is an important indicator of how much influence the group as a whole has over individual members. The more cohesive the group—that is, the more positive individuals feel about their membership in the group—the greater the potential influence of the group. Individual group members are not likely to violate the norms of a group to which they are strongly attached.

Group cohesiveness tends to develop in a circular fashion: Individuals will join groups whose members they admire or identify with. Once they become members of a group and learn to know and like the other members, individuals will tend to feel an even closer sense of identification with the group; cohesiveness increases. As we saw in chapter 14, conflict with outside individuals or other groups increases ingroup cohesiveness still further. Highly cohesive groups often have less tension, misunderstandings, and hostility than noncohesive groups. For this reason, they are potentially more productive than noncohesive groups.[14]

Group cohesiveness can be a problem when it hampers communication or cooperation between groups within an organization. When intergroup cooperation are especially important—for example, when the organization is involved in strategic planning—managers should take steps to de-emphasize the importance of group membership.[15]

Group Performance

Two aspects of group *performance* that are frequently important to managers are: (1) the relationship between group cohesiveness and performance, which is especially important when managers work with informal groups, and (2) the differences between group and individual problem solving and decision making, which are especially important when managers work with task forces and committees.

Group Cohesiveness and Group Performance

As we have already seen, group norms may encourage either high or low performance by group members. There have been many studies of informal work groups (such as bricklayers, assembly-line workers, and typists) whose individual members'

Cohesive Group

Uniform Output

Less Cohesive Group

Less Uniform Output

output can be accurately measured. These studies have found that the output of members of cohesive groups tends to be more *uniform* than that of members of less cohesive groups. That is, in cohesive groups, individual productivity will stay within a narrow range. Groups with low cohesion will have a much wider range of output among their members, reflecting the groups' weaker social control.

A corollary of this finding is that if their norms favor high output, cohesive groups will be uniformly high producers. On the other hand, if their norms favor low output, cohesive groups will be low producers. For noncohesive groups, where the pressure to conform is not so strong, the relationship between norms and output is usually much more ambiguous.[16]

For managers, these findings are important because cohesive groups commonly set their own production standards. If the group is antagonistic to management, it will restrict output to a level well below management standards. In factories, this sort of restriction often occurs in a work group assigned to a job for which piece rates have been established. Members of such groups often believe that if management standards are reached or surpassed, a higher standard or lower piece rate will be forthcoming; they therefore restrict their output. The group members may also feel that if their actual output stays below the set level, management may offer a more favorable rate as an inducement to increase productivity.[17]

Managers' success or failure in meeting organizational objectives may therefore depend on how well they manage the cohesive groups with which they must deal. One way to encourage group norms that support high output is to minimize employee–management antagonism deliberately, perhaps by involving employees more in the decision-making process. Informal group members may then come to see themselves as part of the larger organization. Managers may also want to encourage increased cohesiveness in groups that have—or are likely to acquire—high-output norms.

One way to increase group solidarity is to give group members greater choice in selecting co-workers. A study of Chicago-area construction workers found that once they were given such a choice, turnover dropped significantly and output increased, with the construction firm recording a 5 percent saving in total production costs.[18]

Individual versus Group Problem Solving

Many studies have shown that group solutions to problems tend to be somewhat better than the average solutions of individuals. (The *best* individual solutions, however, are often superior to group solutions.)[19] For example, the "Winter Survival" test at the start of this chapter has been given to individuals and to groups; group solutions tend to be closer than individual solutions to those of survival experts. Part of the improved performance by groups results from the greater chances that errors will be caught, since more people are considering the proposed solutions. Moreover, group members bring new information to the problem and also generate more alternative solutions.

Despite the tendency for groups to perform well in problem-solving activities, managers will often choose to make decisions on their own. Group decisions usually take longer—meetings and discussions are time-consuming—and are usually more expensive because of the greater number of employee-hours involved. Effective managers take the cost of making decisions into account in selecting a

"That's settled, then. We'll all go back to our respective divisions and act busy."

Drawing by Weber; © 1983 The New Yorker Magazine, Inc.

decision-making approach. Thus, they may opt for an acceptable one-person decision quickly rather than seek a somewhat better group decision later. This is especially true for simple problems, and even for technical ones in which the manager has an adequate amount of information.[20]

For more difficult problems, such as new-product development, group decision making may be necessary. Such problems can be solved only if a great amount of information is applied to them; and large quantities of information can be efficiently gathered and evaluated only by a group. In addition, there are problems for which acceptance by the group is particularly important for effective implementation. For example, a manager who tries to set up a work schedule without consulting subordinates is likely to encounter resistance to the schedule. Such problems require that managers and subordinates participate in seeking solutions as a group.

In chapter 6 we discussed how managers can decide whether to make decisions alone or in a group. We will now examine ways for managers to improve the process of group decision making. The manager or group leader plays a critical role in this process. Indeed, when the formal leader is not skilled in group leadership, decision quality may be sacrificed to gain acceptance—or acceptance sacrificed to improve decision quality. And many times, both acceptance and quality suffer.[21]

Problem Solving in Groups

Every group brings assets and liabilities to the problem-solving task. It also brings some factors that, depending on the skills of its members and leader, can be either assets or liabilities. Our discussion of such factors will apply to all types of problem-solving groups, whether they are *ad hoc* groups or formal committees and task forces. It will, however, draw most heavily on the considerable research that has been done on problem solving in small *ad hoc* groups.[22]

Advantages of Group Problem Solving

A study of the group problem-solving process shows that group problem solving has four major advantages:

1. *Greater knowledge and information.* No matter how much knowledge any one individual brings to the task, the total information possessed by all the members is bound to be greater. Thus, a design engineer might best be able to develop the blueprint for a new machine, but an assembly-line worker would have a better idea of how co-workers might react to it.
2. *More approaches to a problem.* There is no way of knowing beforehand which approach to a complex problem will best achieve the desired result. The more approaches considered, the better is the chance of finding the best solution. Obviously five or ten people in a group will generate many more approaches than any one person could.
3. *Increased acceptance of solutions.* As we saw in chapter 6, a decision will not be effective unless those who must implement it accept the decision and make it work. Many studies have shown that when people participate in solving a problem, they see the solution as "their own" and acquire a psychological stake in its success.
4. *Better comprehension of the decision.* When a manager makes a decision individually, he or she must relay it to those who have to carry it out. Failure to implement decisions effectively can often be traced to garbled communication. When those who must execute the decision have participated in making it, the chance of communication failure is reduced.

Disadvantages of Group Problem Solving

Studies of the group problem-solving process have also turned up four major disadvantages:

1. *Premature decisions.* Most problem-solving groups suggest a number of solutions, each of which receives some support and some criticism. Frequently, the first solution to gain appreciable support is adopted—even though winning support may be due more to skillful presentation than to objective quality. Hoffman has noted that groups seem to react in the same way as individuals: Uncomfortable when presented with a situation with no obvious solution, they immediately search for one. Solutions that fall in line with traditional ways of thinking are more readily accepted than new approaches.[23] Once an acceptable alternative has been found, better solutions that may be subsequently introduced rarely receive full consideration.
2. *Individual domination.* A formal (or informal) leader may dominate group discussion and strongly influence the outcome, even though his or her problem-solving ability may be poor. Extroverted and socially assertive persons tend to be more active than other participants and thus more influential. Group members with high self-confidence based on past success or favorable relations with

management will also tend to dominate discussions.[24] Often, one or more participants simply babble on, thinking they are scoring points with the group leader. If such monologues are not checked, others may become frustrated and "tune out"—or start playing the same game. Domination from any quarter can put a damper on the group's best problem solvers.

3. *Conflicting alternative solutions.* When a group sets out to tackle a problem, everyone generally agrees on the major goal: finding the best possible solution. But as alternative solutions are proposed, group members may start to view and defend their own from a "win or lose" standpoint, instead of considering objectively the merits of each. When people care more about winning the battle than about finding the best solution, even a superior synthesis of available alternatives may be viewed as a personal defeat instead of being recognized for its quality.

4. *Prior commitment.* Some group members may have a prior commitment to a particular solution. Instead of open-mindedly seeking the best possible decision, they may argue early and forcibly for their choice and fail to consider alternatives. This can occur in any type of group but is most likely to happen in formal groups. Prior commitments may be due to ties to persons outside the group, "empire building" attempts, or belief that a decision will have a significant personal impact. Once the decision has been made, groups tend to increase their commitment to it, even if evidence emerges that the decision was a bad one.[25]

Factors That Can Be Assets or Liabilities

The following five factors can be assets or liabilities, depending on how the group leader handles the situation:

1. *Disagreement.* The clash of ideas that develops in a group can foster creativity and innovation, or it can breed resentment and hurt feelings. Skillful group leaders use disagreements to generate creative solutions ("Both ideas look good; how about a solution that incorporates both?") When disagreements threaten to become harmful, skillful leaders put a stop to them.

2. *Conflicting interests.* Group members often disagree on solutions because they approach the problem from different perspectives and with different goals in mind. For example, a group may consider ways to reverse a poor profit situation for a particular product line. The sales manager sees the situation as a failure to break into specific markets and suggests more aggressive sales and promotion tactics. The controller, on the other hand, thinks costs have gotten out of hand; perhaps commissions should be cut. The group leader must organize the discussion in such a way that group members can agree on the essence of the problem and the desired goals before solutions are proposed.

3. *Taking risks.* It is popularly assumed that groups are more "conservative" and cautious than individuals. Considerable evidence shows, however, that in some situations groups make riskier decisions than individuals.[26] As management writers put it, in those situations group solutions tend to represent "risky shifts" from solutions that might be offered by individual group members. For example, in dealing with a hypothetical case in which an individual must decide whether to stay in a secure job or leave for one that is less secure but offers a

higher salary, groups have been more likely than individuals to recommend the riskier option.[27]

4. *Time requirements.* Group decisions take longer and are more expensive than individual decisions. But, in many cases, group decisions are more effective than individual decisions. Thus, time can be an asset for group decision making because it yields better decisions and facilitates implementation, and it can be a liability because it results in increased decision-making costs. The skillful group leader will reduce costs and increase effectiveness by preventing irrelevant discussion and focusing on the major tasks to be accomplished.

5. *Changing minds.* Rarely, if ever, do all group members start with the same possible solution to a problem. To reach agreement, some group members must change the position they started with. This can be an asset or a liability, depending on whose mind is changed. If those with the most creative ideas are induced to change, the group winds up with a mediocre decision. But if those with the least constructive ideas are led to change their minds, the final decision is improved. The leader can get group members to keep an open mind by being ambiguous about his or her own position, so that they will not align themselves with it. The leader can also help a consensus emerge by encouraging the group to focus on ways around barriers rather than being blocked by them.[28]

Improved Problem Solving: Effective Leadership

Norman Maier has described how he believes leaders should behave in order to get the best performance from their groups.[29] His conclusions are based on his extensive research over a number of years into group problem solving.

Maier distinguishes between problem-solving activity and persuasion. *Problem-solving activity* represents group interaction at its best: Each member serves as a sounding board for the ideas of others. All group members participate in proposing and evaluating suggestions. *Persuasion* follows a different pattern: Each group member has a fixed point of view that he or she tries to "sell," closing his or her ears and mind to opposing views. Competition replaces cooperation; domination by a few articulate or aggressive individuals replaces participation by all.

From this perspective, a leader has one major task: to manage discussion so that the group engages in true problem solving. Maier feels that leaders should focus entirely on this task and virtually give up the attempt to make substantive contributions themselves. True leaders, according to Maier, must forgo the temptation to sell their own solutions during group sessions and rely instead on the resources of the entire group (including their own nondominating suggestions). In this way initiative is encouraged, and group members regard themselves as a working team. (See table 17–1.)

The authors have seen and participated in groups led by managers who perform the leadership role as described by Maier. Those groups usually did outstanding work, and most of their members were highly satisfied. Two things, however, stand in the way of the universal application of Maier's ideas: Managers do not easily accept the self-restraint such a role demands; and they do not always command the high level of interpersonal skill that must go with this role. As Anthony Jay has observed, "It is the chairman's self-indulgence that is the greatest single barrier to

TABLE 17–1
EFFECTIVE AND
INEFFECTIVE
GROUP BEHAVIORS

Effective: Problem-Solving Activity	Ineffective: Persuasion
Trying out ideas on each other	Selling preformed opinions
Listening to understand	Listening to refute—or not listening at all
Willingness to change one's position	Defending one's position to the end
All members generally participating in discussion	A few members dominating the discussion
Finding stimulation in disagreement	Reacting unfavorably to disagreement
Interacting and reaching consensus	Converting others through one-to-one inter- action

the success of a meeting. His first duty, then, is to be aware of the temptation and of the dangers of yielding to it. The clearest of the danger signals is hearing himself talk a lot during a discussion."[30]

Task Forces and Committees

Comments and jokes about the time-wasting proclivities of committee work have always been popular among managers, who generally pride themselves on their individualism. Opponents of task forces and committees feel they have inflicted a crushing blow when they say something like, "No committee ever painted a Mona Lisa or sculpted a Pietà." In reality, however, a committee or task force is frequently the best means for pooling the expertise of different members of the organization and for channeling their efforts toward effective problem solving and decision making.

The need for committees has long been widely recognized in organizations. As long ago as 1960, Rollie Tillman concluded from a survey that "94 percent of the firms with more than 10,000 employees reported having formal committees."[31] It is probable that the number and types of groups active in organizations have grown considerably since that time. The greater complexity and rate of change in organizations today require the kind of information pooling and problem evaluation that committees and task forces are designed to provide.

Types of Formal Working Groups

Organizations have three main types of committees and formal task groups: task forces, standing committees, and boards or commissions.[32]

Task Forces. *Task forces* or project teams are formed to deal with a specific problem or task. They continue in existence only until the task is completed or the problem solved. Task forces are usually formed to deal with complex problems or tasks that involve several organization subunits. For example, assume a computer firm develops a new storage device that cannot be manufactured by existing facilities. A special task force may be created to determine what new manufacturing equipment will be needed, how it can be best obtained, and what changes it will require in

Drawing by Stevenson; © 1981 The New Yorker Magazine, Inc.

the firm's work patterns. Task forces usually include representatives (or key decision makers) from subunits, plus whatever technical experts the problem or task requires.

Task forces may achieve their results in one of three ways:

1. **By making recommendations to the executive to whom they are responsible.**
2. **By reaching decisions in the group when the appropriate executive is the formal leader.**
3. **By the individual representatives of the various units committing their units to take specific actions in accord with the group's conclusions.**[33]

Standing Committees. *Standing*, or permanent, *committees* remain in existence to meet a continuing organizational need. Typical standing committees might be the finance committee or new-products review committee in a company, or an admissions committee in a college. Usually such committees either make formal recommendations to a higher-level manager or have the authority to make their own decisions for a limited organizational activity.

Boards and Commissions. *Boards* are made up of individuals who are appointed or elected to manage a public or private organization. School board members, for example, are elected by their community to set school policy, raise revenues, hire a principal, and perhaps even select textbooks. The board of directors of a corporation is selected by stockholders to oversee the management of the assets of the company, set company policies and goals, hire company officers to carry out those policies, and review the progress of the company toward those goals. Members of *commissions* are usually appointed by government officials to carry out administrative, legislative, or regulatory duties (the Federal Trade Commission and the Securities and Exchange Commission, for example).

Whereas the other formal groups we have discussed are concerned with the internal needs of the organization, these groups represent the interests of people outside the organization. School board members, for example, are responsible to the community; commission members are generally responsible to the public; board members are responsible to their stockholders and, increasingly, to the society of which they are a part.

Some Differences between Task Forces and Committees

In many instances, committees and task forces are managed in similar ways. Some differences in procedure, however, stem from the way they are formed and the tasks they undertake. Although much of this chapter applies to both categories of formal working groups, we should note some key distinctions between them. (See table 17–2.)

Committees are generally long-lasting and perhaps permanent parts of an organization's structure. They are formed to deal with recurrent problems and decisions, to give or withhold approval, or to exchange information regularly for coordination purposes. For example, a loan approval committee in a bank might meet every week to vote on recommendations by lending officers.[34]

Committees are also characterized by stability of membership. Turnover may be quite low, and there may be no formal procedure for evaluating the appropriateness and performance of committee members. Members may be chosen because of their title or position instead of individual qualifications. Committees frequently play only a passive role in task identification. Tasks are assigned through normal organizational channels, and normally only those tasks deemed appropriate for the committee reach it.

TABLE 17–2 SOME DIFFERENCES BETWEEN COMMITTEES AND TASK FORCES	Committees	Task Forces
Duration	*Long-term:* Ends if reorganization of organization's structure terminates committee.	*Short-term:* Ends when task is completed.
Basis of Membership	*Organizational Roles and Position:* Based primarily on organizational role or hierarchical position.	*Expertise and Skills:* Role and hierarchical position are important, but particular skills and expertise may be equally or more important.
Stability of Membership	*Stable:* Members are appointed and remain on committee.	*Fluid:* Members are added and dropped as current activities require.
Identification of Tasks, Problems, and Opportunities	*Passive:* Tasks, problems, and opportunities are usually referred to committee by other parts of the organization on basis of committee's area of responsibility.	*Active:* Initial task is basis of task force formation; problem and opportunity finding are integral parts of task accomplishment.

FIGURE 17–3 SURVEY OF EXECUTIVE COMMITTEE MEMBERSHIP

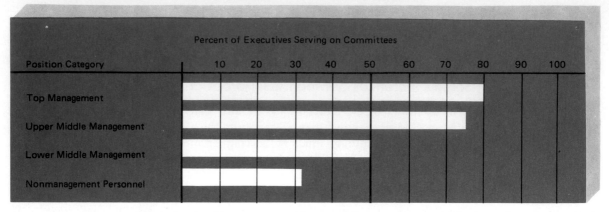

Source: Reprinted by permission of the *Harvard Business Review*. Exhibit from "Committees on Trial" by Rollie Tillman, Jr., (May–June 1960). Copyright © 1960 by the President and Fellows of Harvard College; all rights reserved.

Task forces contrast with committees in each attribute just described. Task forces are impermanent: They are formed to solve a problem, and when that is done they are dissolved (although solution of a complex problem may require years). Their membership is fluid and consists of those persons best able to carry out the current part of the task. Members tend to be chosen for their skills and expertise. Task forces also tend to be more active than committees in searching out related problems and opportunities that might affect the larger task.

As a rule, committee and task force membership (and the proportion of time spent working in them) is greater for managers at the top level than at the lower levels of the organization. (See fig. 17–3.) One reason for this is that only top-level managers have the authority to make policy decisions for the organization. In addition, the higher a manager's level, the larger the number of organizational subunits he or she affects. Higher-level managers, therefore, have a greater need than lower-level managers to coordinate their own work activities with those of other subunits. This need for close coordination between higher-level managers and other subunits is often met through committees and task forces made up of individuals from the various parts of the organization.

Possible Advantages of Committees and Task Forces

Committees and task forces have some of the same advantages and disadvantages as other types of groups. However, because they are a formal part of the organization's structure and work processes, they have some unique advantages and disadvantages as well.[35]

As our earlier discussion of groups in general implied, the two most important advantages of committees and task forces are:

1. *Better quality decisions.*
2. *Enhanced likelihood of implementation.*

In addition, other major advantages include:

3. *Improved coordination.* During committee discussions, members learn how the activities of their units affect the work of other units. This awareness leads to a new willingness and ability to coordinate the work of all units to achieve the overall goals of the organization.

4. *Training managers.* Organizations are constantly in need of new executive talent. Committees serve as a training ground for young executives, who, freed from the parochial concerns of their individual units, learn to think in terms of wider issues that may one day confront them. In the meetings, lower-level managers have the opportunity to learn how upper-level managers perceive and deal with problems and opportunities; higher-level managers also have opportunities to evaluate the styles and abilities of less-experienced associates.

5. *Dispersion of power.* Many things can be done faster and with fewer complications under the direction of a single authority. However, too much authority concentrated in any one person's hands may lead to abuse of power, favoritism, and unwise decisions. By spreading responsibility among its members, a committee reduces the chance that excessive power will be concentrated in any one individual. It also reduces the possibility that those adversely affected by a committee decision (such as a choice among investment projects) can complain of favoritism or bias.

Possible Disadvantages of Committees and Task Forces

The status and power realities in committees and task forces increase the likelihood that some of the potential disadvantages of groups in general become serious problems. These include:

1. *Premature agreements and mediocre compromises.* Committee members with prior commitment to one point of view may defend it to the exclusion of others; and committee members with no prior commitment may accept an alternative proposed by a more powerful associate during a meeting. In such groups, *political pressures* for compromise can be strong, as when executives go along with a watered-down "solution" to an issue they do not view as crucial, in order to gain approval of their own pet project. In addition, as Irving Janis has noted, *psychological pressures* in a cohesive group can lead to "groupthink" (the word was coined by George Orwell in his novel *1984*), in which the drive for consensus and compromise inhibits a potential dissenter or critic. Because of the decreased objectivity and individual judgment that characterizes groupthink, members may abdicate their responsibility for critically scrutinizing the pros and cons of alternative solutions. For example, Janis attributed President John F. Kennedy's decisions on the disastrous Bay of Pigs invasion to groupthink pressures. On the other hand, he also believes that a conscious attempt to understand what went wrong in the Bay of Pigs decision and to avoid its repetition led Kennedy and his advisers to handle the Cuban missile crisis much more successfully.[36]

2. *Individual domination.* In any group, individual domination may be counterproductive. Because committees are run by formal leaders who are usually the superiors of the other members, they are particularly in danger of being

dominated by the leader. Domination (as opposed to leadership) may limit the committee's effectiveness. "Hidden agendas" may emerge as committee members, conscious of rank and status, worry more about creating favorable impressions than about the business of the committee.[37]

3. *Lack of responsibility.* Because no one committee member feels solely responsible for the committee's ultimate decision, members may be less careful than if they bore individual responsibility. In addition, if the committee's decision should go wrong in application, members may not work as hard to overcome the difficulty as they would if they were held individually accountable.

4. *Waste of time and money.* The cost of committee meetings is high. The time that eight people spend in a two-hour meeting, for example, is two person-days of work, excluding preparation and follow-up time. If meetings are poorly handled, exorbitant amounts of both time and money may be wasted. Yet there is another side to the story, as Alan Filley, Robert House, and Steven Kerr have noted.[38] Time can be saved when a manager communicates with a number of subordinates at a meeting, instead of on a one-to-one basis. In addition, problems may be solved faster and more effectively with all of the relevant people in the same room at the same time.

Making Formal Groups Effective

Since formal groups play a necessary role in organizations, managers must learn to use them effectively. (We will use the term *committees* to refer to all formal groups, explicitly mentioning task forces only when they should be so distinguished.) Earlier we discussed some guidelines Maier suggested on how to improve group performance in general. Here we will provide additional guidelines for committee meetings, leaders, and members.

Because committees differ greatly in their functions and activities, these guidelines will not be appropriate for all cases. For example, a highly directive committee responsible for communicating instructions from top management to subordinates should be managed differently from a committee whose major task is to solve complex managerial problems. The following suggestions apply to problem-solving committees, which must be managed flexibly if the skills of members are to be used most effectively.

Formal Procedures. Several formal procedures are useful in helping committees operate effectively.[39]

· The committee's goals should be clearly defined, preferably in writing. This will focus the committee's activities and reduce discussion of what the committee is supposed to do.

· The committee's authority should be specified. Can the committee merely investigate, advise, and recommend, or is it authorized to implement decisions?

· The optimum size of the committee should be determined. With fewer than five members, the advantages of group work may be diminished. Potential resources increase as group size increases. While size will vary with the circumstances, the ideal number of committee members for many tasks seems to range from five to ten. With more than ten to 15, a committee may become unwieldy, and it may be difficult for each member to enter and influence the work.[40]

· A chairperson should be selected on the basis of his or her ability to run an efficient meeting—that is, the ability to encourage the participation of all committee members, to keep the committee meetings from getting bogged down in irrelevancies, and to see that the necessary paperwork gets done.

· Appointing a permanent secretary to handle communications is often useful.

· The agenda and all supporting material for the meeting should be distributed before the meeting. When members can prepare in advance, they are more likely to stick to the point and to be ready with informed contributions.

· Meetings should start and end on time. The time when they will end should be announced at the outset.

Guidelines for Leaders. Committee leadership is a key factor in the successful outcome of the committee's work. The leader is responsible for the membership of the committee, for the satisfactory completion of its assigned tasks, and for his or her own leadership behavior.

The leader should control not only the size of the committee but also the qualifications of its members. Are they the right people for this committee's work? Do they have the needed skills? If not, can others be added? Are some members unnecessary? Can time be saved by removing them? In many committee situations the membership is fixed, and the chairperson may have little control over membership; even then, however, it may be possible to bring in special people with needed skills to provide assistance.

The leader must also screen the work assigned to the committee. Many committees are ineffective because they try to grapple with problems for which they do not have the expertise, organizational power, required information, or responsibility. The leader can save time and concentrate the committee's efforts by detecting inappropriate work at the outset and avoiding it.

A committee leader should be aware of the decision-making style with which he or she is most comfortable and which is most suitable for the committee's task. Leaders should make certain that the two types of leadership roles—task and maintenance—noted earlier in this chapter, are provided either by themselves or by other committee members.

To manage discussions effectively, the leader should begin by making clear what the meeting should accomplish.[41] Was it called to stimulate thinking, or to draft a specific proposal? The leader should then make certain that all members understand the issue and why they are meeting to discuss it. A brief summary of the situation by the leader or another informed person is usually sufficient. As discussion proceeds, the leader should clarify misunderstandings when they occur. For example, two people may employ the same term but mean different things by it, and a third party can often spot and rectify such miscommunication. Finally, the leader should terminate the discussion at an appropriate time. This may come when agreement has been reached, when more information is needed, or whatever. The leader should recognize a logical ending point when it arrives and close the discussion swiftly.

Jay recommends that leaders follow these seven rules:[42]

1. Control the garrulous.
2. Draw out the silent.
3. Protect the weak.
4. Encourage the clash of ideas.
5. Watch out for the suggestion-squashing reflex.
6. Come to the most senior people last.
7. Close on a note of achievement.

Guidelines for Members. For Jay Hall, the group decision process has one basic aim: to resolve conflicts creatively by reaching a consensus. He defines consensus not as unanimity but as a condition in which each member accepts the group's decisions because they seem most logical and feasible. Hall offers five guidelines to help group members achieve consensus.[43]

1. State your position as clearly and logically as you can—but do not argue for it. Listen to and ponder the other members' reactions before you push your point.
2. If discussion between some members gets bogged down on any one point, do not treat it as a win-or-lose proposition. Instead, seek out the next most acceptable alternative.
3. Do not yield on any point just for the sake of harmony. Accept a solution only when it is based on sound logic.
4. Shun techniques that bypass logic for the sake of reducing conflict (such as majority vote, flipping a coin, bargaining, and averaging). When a dissenting member finally goes along with the group, don't make up for this by letting the yielder have his or her own way on some other point.
5. Root out differences of opinion and pull everyone into the discussion. Only by airing the widest possible range of opinions and drawing in all available information can the group come up with high-quality solutions.

Working with college students and with management executives, Hall found that groups trained to apply this five-point process did consistently better in solving problems than untrained groups. A trained group frequently outperformed even its best individual member—an outcome he described as "synergy." (*Synergy* may be defined as "a condition in which the whole is greater than the sum of its parts.") Hall's guidelines encourage the maximum participation of group members and the search for the best possible problem solutions. They are most useful for committees working on a task that requires an ingenious or creative solution.

Special Procedures for Task Forces

Although the above guidelines for committee and task force leaders and members are applicable to running a task force, the formal procedures (on pp. 488–489) are less appropriate. Figure 17–4 summarizes a method of task force management that emphasizes the use of task force meeting time for work planning and control.[44] Most of the work is *not* done at meetings. The group time is used to define problems and opportunities and to arrange for the right people to work on them outside of the meeting.

FIGURE 17–4 TASK FORCE WORK FLOW

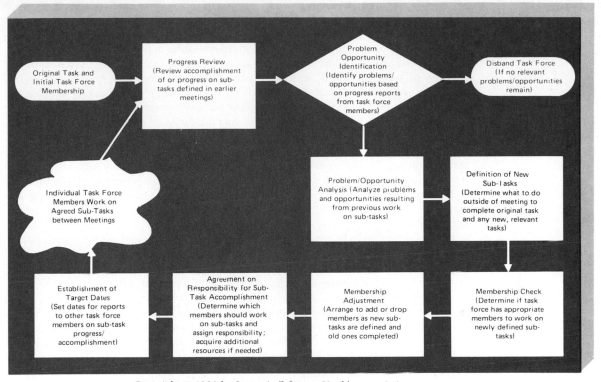

Copyright © 1982 by James A. F. Stoner. Used by permission.

Figure 17–4 indicates the work flow of a task force meeting. Past progress is briefly reviewed, and then the current situation is described and analyzed in terms of its problems and opportunities. Based on this analysis, new outside-the-meeting sub-tasks are defined. Next, the task force membership is reviewed for its appropriateness to the current roster of sub-tasks, and arrangements are made to add or drop members as needed. Finally, sub-task responsibility is allocated among task force members, and target dates are established for sub-task completion.

This task force management procedure is well suited to complex, ambiguous problems of major scale, such as reorganizing the entire sales force of a company or developing a new generation of computer terminals. There are, however, a number of other ways to manage task forces and their work.[45]

Although many of the skills required for task force and committee management are the same, a frequent problem is the failure to see how task forces differ from committees and to use their special flexibilities effectively. For example, a committee that encounters a new problem outside of its original scope of operations may be accused of power-grabbing or empire building if it tries to bring that problem into its domain. Task forces, on the other hand, routinely encounter new problems in the pursuit of their original objective, and it is quite legitimate for a task force to seek solutions to new problems so that work can move forward on their prime objective.

Summary Groups are an inevitable part of organizational life. The manager's job is to use them effectively at appropriate times.

There are both formal and informal groups in organizations. Informal groups develop whenever people come into contact regularly. They emerge with or without the encouragement of management. Informal groups share certain values and provide social satisfaction, status, and security. They can further or frustrate the achievement of organizational objectives. Group members provide each other with support and protection. In turn, they expect each other to conform to group norms. Members who violate group norms may be subjected to a variety of pressures, ranging from attempts at persuasion to physical assault. Some level of conformity to group norms can free creative energies for more important tasks; too much conformity, however, can stultify innovation.

Formal groups include command groups (managers and their subordinates), task forces, and committees. Task forces are formed to deal with a specific problem or task; once the task is successfully accomplished, the group is dissolved and personnel reassigned. Committees, on the other hand, remain in existence to meet continuing organizational needs. These stable groups deal with recurrent types of problems or decisions (although sometimes they outlive any useful function).

Groups are generally better at problem solving than the average individual. This is because they bring a greater amount of information and expertise to bear on a problem, generate more alternative solutions, catch mistakes, and make it more likely that the solution will be understood, accepted, and implemented. However, group problem solving is also more time-consuming and costly than individual problem solving.

Formal groups in organizations improve coordination, develop managerial talent, and avoid excessive concentration of power in a single individual. They also run the risks of reaching decisions prematurely, discouraging individual responsibility, and being dominated by individuals who do not necessarily have the most to offer.

Managerial skill in guiding, but not dominating, group activities is an important factor in achieving success in group work. Suggestions for effective results include formal procedures for meetings, guidelines for group leaders, and guidelines for group members. For task forces, a special set of recommendations applies.

Review Questions

1. What are the three basic types of groups in organizations? Which type of group do you think is most important? Why?

2. What are reference groups? Why is it important for managers to be aware of them? Can you identify your own reference groups?

3. Why do you think informal groups emerge in organizations? What organizational needs do they serve? What member needs do they serve?

4. How do informal leaders emerge in informal and formal work groups?

5. What are the two leadership roles of formal and informal group leaders?

6. How do group members try to enforce conformity?

7. What is the relationship between group cohesiveness and group performance? How can group cohesiveness be increased?

8. On what bases would a manager decide whether to use individual or group problem solving?

9. What are the possible advantages and disadvantages of group decision making and problem solving?

10. What is the "risky shift"?

11. According to Maier, how can the manager improve the effectiveness of a group's problem-solving activities?

12. What is a task force? What are the different types of committees and their functions?

13. What are the advantages and disadvantages of task forces and committees?

14. What formal procedures will help make committees effective? How can committee leaders and members help make committees effective?

Notes

1. This material is adapted from David W. Johnson and Frank P. Johnson, *Joining Together: Group Theory and Group Skills,* 2nd ed. (Englewood Cliffs, N.J.: Prentice-Hall, 1982).

2. See Dorwin Cartwright and Ronald Lippitt, "Group Dynamics and the Individual," *International Journal of Group Psychotherapy* 7, no. 1 (January 1957):86–102; and Linda N. Jewell and H. Joseph Reitz, *Group Effectiveness in Organizations* (Glenview, Ill.: Scott, Foresman, 1981).

3. See Marvin E. Shaw, *Group Dynamics,* 3rd ed. (New York: McGraw-Hill, 1981).

4. See Dorwin Cartwright and Alvin Zander, eds., *Group Dynamics: Research and Theory,* 3rd ed. (New York: Harper & Row, 1968), p. 53; and Harold H. Kelley, "Two Functions of Reference Groups," in Guy E. Swanson, Theodore Newcomb, and Eugene J. Hartley, eds., *Readings in Social Psychology,* rev. ed. (New York: Holt, 1952), pp. 410–414.

5. See Edgar H. Schein, *Organizational Psychology,* 3rd ed. (Englewood Cliffs, N.J.: Prentice-Hall, 1980), pp. 146–153.

6. Rensis Likert, *New Patterns of Management* (New York: McGraw-Hill, 1961).

7. Keith Davis, *Human Relations at Work,* 2nd ed. (New York: McGraw-Hill, 1962), pp. 235–257, and *Human Behavior at Work: Organizational Behavior,* 6th ed. (New York: McGraw-Hill, 1981), pp. 331–332; and Schein, *Organizational Psychology,* pp. 150–152.

8. David O. Sears, Jonathan L. Freedman, and Letitia A. Peplau, *Social Psychology* (Englewood Cliffs, N.J.: Prentice-Hall, 1985), pp. 367–368.

9. See David C. Feldman, "The Development and Enforcement of Group Norms," *Academy of Management Review* 9, no. 2 (January 1984):47–53.

10. Solomon E. Asch, "Studies of Independence and Conformity: A Minority of One Against a Unanimous Majority," *Psychological Monographs* 70, no. 9 (September 1956).

11. Sarah Tanford and Steven Penrod, "Social Influence Model: A Formal Integration of Research on Majority and Minority Influence Processes," *Psychological Bulletin* 95, no. 2 (March 1984):189–225; and Serge Moscovici, "Social Influence and Conformity," in Gardner Lindzey and Elliot Aronson, eds., *Handbook of Social Psychology,* vol. 2, 3d ed. (New York: Random House, 1985), chapter 7.

12. See Stanley Milgram, "Some Conditions of Obedience and Disobedience to Authority," *Human Relations* 18, no. 1 (January 1965):57–76, and *Obedience to Authority: An Experimental View* (New York: Harper & Row, 1974).

13. Philip G. Zimbardo, Curtis Banks, Craig Haney, and David Jaffe, "A Pirandellian Prison," *New York Times Magazine,* April 8, 1973; and Craig Haney, Curtis Banks, and Philip G. Zimbardo, "Interpersonal Dynamics in a Simulated Prison," *International Journal of Criminology and Penology* 1, no. 1 (February 1973):69–97. The fact that these experiments were even conducted is troubling to many; and a number of social psychologists have challenged the ethics of such experiments. For a discussion of recent unethical uses of attitude change techniques, see Philip Zimbardo, "Mind Control in 1984," *Psychology Today,* January 1984, pp. 68ff.

14. Sears, Freedman, and Peplau, *Social Psychology,* pp. 356–357. See also Robert S. Feldman, *Social Psychology: Theories, Research, and Applications* (New York: McGraw-Hill, 1985); and Steven Penrod, *Social Psychology,* 2nd ed. (Englewood Cliffs, N.J.: Prentice-Hall, 1986).

15. John C. Whitney and Ruth A. Smith, "Effects of Group Cohesiveness on Attitude Polarization and the Acquisition of Knowledge in a Strategic Planning Context," *Journal of Marketing Research* 20, no. 2 (May 1983):167–176.

16. For a discussion of this topic and numerous supporting studies, see Bertram H. Raven and Jeffrey Z. Rubin, *Social Psychology: People in Groups,* 2nd ed. (New York: Wiley, 1983), p. 454.

17. Lester Coch and John R. P. French, Jr., "Overcoming Resistance to Change," *Human Relations* 1, no. 4 (August 1948):512–532.

18. Raymond H. Van Zelst, "Sociometrically Selected Work Teams Increase Production," *Personnel Psychology* 5, no. 3 (Autumn 1952):175–185.

19. See, for example, Frederick C. Miner, "Group versus Individual Decision Making: An Investigation of Performance Measures, Decision Strategies, and Process Losses/Gains," *Organizational Behavior and Human Performance* 33, no. 1 (February 1984):112–124.

20. See Edward H. Bowman, "Management Decision-Making: Some Research," *Industrial Management Review* 3, no. 1 (Fall 1961):56–63.

21. L. Richard Hoffman, "Applying Experimental Research on Group Problem Solving to Organizations," *Journal of Applied Behavioral Science* 15, no. 3 (July–August–September 1979):377.

22. See, for example, Normal R. F. Maier, "Assets and Liabilities in Group Problem Solving," *Psychological Review* 74, no. 4 (July 1967):239–249; Hoffman, "Applying Experimental Research on Group Problem Solving to Organizations"; L. Richard Hoffman, ed., *The Group Problem-Solving Process: Studies of a Valence Model* (New York: Praeger, 1979); and Shaw, *Group Dynamics*.

23. Hoffman, "Applying Experimental Research on Group Problem Solving to Organizations," p. 382.

24. Ibid., pp. 377–378; Donal E. Carlston, "Effects of Pooling Order on Social Influence in Decision-Making Groups," *Sociometry* 40, no. 2 (June 1977):115–123; and Godfrey M. Hochbaum, "The Relation Between Group Members' Self-Confidence and Their Reactions to Group Pressures to Uniformity," *American Sociological Review* 19, no. 6 (December 1954):678–687.

25. Max H. Bazerman, Toni Giuliano, and Alan Appelman, "Escalation of Commitment in Individual and Group Decision Making," *Organizational Behavior and Human Performance* 33, no. 2 (April 1984):141–152. See also Hoffman, "Applying Experimental Research on Group Problem Solving to Organizations," p. 378.

26. Dorwin Cartwright, "Risk Taking by Individuals and Groups: An Assessment of Research Employing Choice Dilemmas," *Journal of Personality and Social Psychology* 20, no. 3 (December 1971):361–378, and "Determinants of Scientific Progress: The Case of Research on the Risky Shift," *American Psychologist* 28, no. 3 (March 1973):222–231.

27. See James A. F. Stoner, "A Comparison of Individual and Group Decisions Involving Risk" (Master's thesis, Massachusetts Institute of Technology, School of Industrial Management, 1961). There have been hundreds of studies published since the first "risky shifts" were demonstrated by Stoner in 1961. In spite of these extensive research efforts, the types of situations in which the phenomenon occurs and the cause and nature of the phenomenon are still unclear and remain a source of lively debate and research. See also James A. F. Stoner, "Risky and Cautious Shifts in Group Decisions: The Influence of Widely Held Values," *Journal of Experimental Social Psychology* 4, no. 4 (October 1968):442–459; and Russell D. Clark, "Group-Induced Shift toward Risk: A Critical Appraisal," *Psychological Bulletin* 76 no. 4 (October 1971):251–270.

28. See Richard Tanner Pascale, "Zen and the Art of Management," *Harvard Business Review* 56, no. 2 (March–April 1978):153–162.

29. Maier, "Assets and Liabilities in Group Problem Solving," pp. 244–247.

30. Anthony Jay, "How to Run a Meeting," *Harvard Business Review* 54, no. 2 (March–April 1976):43–57. See also Andrew S. Grove, "How (and Why) to Run a Meeting," *Fortune,* July 11, 1983, pp. 132ff.

31. Rollie Tillman, Jr., "Committees on Trial," *Harvard Business Review* 48, no. 4 (May–June 1960):6–7ff.

32. A fourth type of committee is the plural executive or general management committee, a formal committee that functions as a chief executive and is responsible for the overall management of the organization in the same way that an organization president would be. See William H. Mylander, "Management by the Executive Committee," *Harvard Business Review* 33, no. 4 (May–June 1955):51–58.

33. Note that in matrix organizations, discussed in chapter 9, the project team may have its own budget and enjoy a great deal of autonomy in implementing solutions and decisions.

34. This tendency toward permanence offers the opportunity to achieve effective, predictable, and stable committee performance. However, it also runs the danger that the committee will remain in existence after the need for it has ended. Anthony Jay has observed that "many long-established committees are little more than memorials to dead problems." See "How to Run a Meeting," p. 43.

35. The discussion is based on Ernest Dale, *Planning and Developing the Company Structure* (New York: American Management Associations, 1952) and *Organization* (New York: American Management Associations, 1967); and Hoffman, "Applying Experimental Research on Group Problem Solving to Organizations."

36. Irving Janis, *Groupthink: Psychological Studies of Policy Decisions,* 2nd ed. (Boston: Houghton Mifflin, 1982); and Jeanne Longley and Dean G. Pruitt, "Groupthink: A Critique of Janis's Theory," in Ladd Wheeler, ed., *Review of Personality and Social Psychology,* vol. 1 (Beverly Hills: Sage Publications, 1980), pp. 74–93.

37. See E. Paul Torrance, "Some Consequences of Power Differences on Decision Making in Permanent and Temporary Three-Man Groups," in A. Paul Hare, Edgar F. Borgatta, and Robert Bales, eds., *Small Groups* (New York: Knopf, 1955), pp. 482–492.

38. Alan C. Filley, Robert J. House, and Steven Kerr, *Managerial Process and Organizational Behavior* (Glenview, Ill.: Scott, Foresman, 1976).

39. Cyril O'Donnell, "Ground Rules for Using Committees," *Management Review* 50, no. 10 (October 1961): 63–67. See also Jay, "How to Run a Meeting."

40. L. Richard Hoffman and M. Clark, "Participation and Influence in Problem-Solving Groups," in Hoffman, ed., *The Group Problem-Solving Process*. See also Philip Yetton and Preston Bottger, "The Relationship among Group Size, Member Ability, Social Decision Schemes, and Performance," *Organizational Behavior and Human Performance* 32, no. 2 (October 1983): 145–149.

41. Most of the remaining leadership guidelines in this section are taken from Jay, "How to Run a Meeting."

42. Ibid., pp. 56–57.

43. Jay Hall, "Decisions, Decisions, Decisions," *Psychology Today*, November 1971, p. 54.

44. The author wishes to thank David B. Gleicher and Malcolm S. MacGruer for helping him to understand this approach.

45. See, for example, Lawrence W. Bass, *Management by Task Forces* (Mount Airy, Md.: Lomond Books, 1975).

CASE STUDY: The Sales Meeting

Progressive Packaging Corporation (PPC) had traditionally held a meeting of its sales force each January at pleasant southern resorts. These meetings had three basic purposes: to reward the salespeople after a hard year's work, to inspire them with laudatory speeches, and to announce new products and strategies for the coming year.

But the last year had been particularly unfortunate. Due to an economic recession, sales were down, and the company had actually suffered a loss of market share, due to the aggressive introduction of new products by a competitor for which PPC had, as yet, no equivalent. Thus, many salespeople had failed to meet their yearly sales quotas. Their traditionally fat commissions had been comparatively slender.

Another blow to their morale was the resignation of their well-liked national sales manager, "Big Bob" Bailey, a forceful and colorful individual with an inspirational style of speaking who had tried unsuccessfully to champion the cause of sales with top management. A month after his departure, it was learned that he had joined a major competitor as vice-president of sales.

His replacement as national sales manager, Susan Evans, was a comparatively young woman who had risen rapidly through the ranks. Although she was respected for her capacity for hard work and ability to analyze sales problems, Evans lacked the charisma and showmanship of her predecessor, and additionally faced the problem that many of the sales staff were men who were older and more experienced than she was. She realized that she would be the subject of unfavorable comparison with Bailey unless she could quickly establish herself as an effective leader.

However, more than her personal prestige was involved. Evans was convinced that the confidence of the salespeople in their company was strongly influenced by their perceptions of their top sales executives. If their observations led them to believe that PPC was in retreat, they might try harder to protect "safe" business than to acquire new customers. If they felt PPC was on the verge of a rout, they might defect to more successful companies, especially the one that Bailey had joined. Her task, therefore, was not merely to develop a strategy for reversing the company's fortunes but also to convince the salespeople that they were capably led.

Evans's immediate problem was to cope with rumors that members of top management wanted to cancel the annual sales meeting. She announced that the meeting would be held on schedule and at a more glamorous resort than the ones usually used for this purpose. This was taken as a brave gesture, but, in itself, it did little to lighten the gloomy feelings among the salespeople.

At a party the night before the first general session, Elmer Detweiler, a veteran regional manager, expressed the opinion that Evans had erred in holding the meeting at all. Coming to a sales meeting under these circumstances, he said, was "like being invited to your own funeral." The remark seemed to catch the prevailing mood of futility, and by morning, everyone had heard it.

Evans briefly addressed the group that morning; her speech was delivered without flamboyance but with obvious sincerity. She began by explaining her reasons for holding the meeting: First, because they deserved it, having done what she considered a superb job against severe odds; second, as a clear demonstration that the company had not lost confidence in its salespeople; and third, and most important, to plan the strategies with which to restore a favorable sales trend. Instead of the customary lengthy review of the preceding year, she confined herself to saying, "It's over."

Next, she announced the immediate formation of "Management Advisory Boards." These ten-person panels, made up of field and headquarters managers and salespeople, would develop approaches to specific problems. She would define the problem for each board and indicate the financial and policy limits within which a solution would be acceptable. Evans promised to commit herself in advance to accept their recommendations, provided they were unanimous.

Then she announced the formation of three boards: one to devise strategies to counter the inroads of new competitive products, one to develop new applications for existing products, and another to maximize the effectiveness of the limited sales promotion budget. About half of the people attending the meeting were assigned to boards. She directed the boards to present their conclusions to the group the next morning. Then, to everyone's astonishment, she adjourned the general meeting until the next day. Those not assigned to boards were free to enjoy themselves, but with the understanding that they would be sitting on other boards in their turn.

The immediate reaction was very much in contrast to the cheering and elation that used to follow Bailey's speeches. After a moment of surprise, the salespeople became serious and thoughtful. Even those not chosen found themselves discussing the problems that had been presented to the boards. Many had half expected to be castigated for the year's poor performance, and they were relieved at Evans's positive approach.

But their primary reaction was not to her but to the problems she had posed. As they debated the intricacies of these problems, they began to see that tradeoffs were involved and that a long-range view had to be taken. Unanimous agreement was reached on only a few matters by the boards, but Evans was as good as her word: She put the recommendations into full effect.

The aftermath of the meeting was subtle. The salespeople were not particularly enthusiastic, as they had usually been after a meeting conducted by Bailey. But neither were they depressed and pessimistic, as they had been before the meeting. Their problems still seemed difficult, but no longer impossible.

During that year the sales force gradually reversed the losing trend, and as they did so, they began to regard Evans with increased admiration. Detweiler—a man known for his quotable remarks—summed up the eventual effects of the meeting by saying: "When we went down there we were writing our own obituaries. But she made us into live salespeople and managers again."

Source: Adapted by permission of Random House, Inc. from *Cases and Problems for Decisions in Management* by Saul W. Gellerman. Copyright © 1984 by Random House, Inc.

Case Questions
1. What adverse factors were affecting the performance of the sales force?
2. Would a leadership style such as Bailey's have been effective in solving these problems?
3. What did Evans aim to accomplish with her creation of Management Advisory Boards?
4. Why was a group problem-solving approach effective in this case?

18 INTERPERSONAL AND ORGANIZATIONAL COMMUNICATION

Upon completing this chapter you should be able to:

1. Define communication and state why it is important to managers.
2. Describe a model of the communication process.
3. Distinguish between one-way and two-way communication.
4. Summarize the barriers to interpersonal communication and explain how they can be overcome.
5. Distinguish between defensive and supportive communication.
6. Describe the factors that influence the effectiveness of organizational communication.
7. Explain the role of the grapevine in organizations.
8. State how the barriers to effective organizational communication can be overcome.
9. Discuss how the use of advanced information technology might affect interpersonal relations and other organizational activities.

The following exchange took place between a supervisor and her subordinate via their company's electronic mail system:

To Eric / From Jane / Re Quarterly Report

As you know, your quarterly report is due in two weeks. I must emphasize how important it is that you get the report in on time. Division headquarters cannot proceed with its review unless reports from all district managers are in. However, you seem to be busy with the new marketing campaign. If you are unable to complete the report by the due date, you may take an extension. I will have to explain to headquarters why quarterly reports for my department are incomplete.

To Jane / From Eric / Re Your Message

What you say comes as a big shock to me. Frankly, you don't seem to appreciate the amount of work this new marketing campaign requires. I've been working late *and* on weekends so that we can make the new products a success. I was going to ask for an extension for the quarterly report, but if the report is so very important I'll make sure it's on time. Just don't expect the report and the marketing campaign to be as good as they should be.

The above exchange—by no means atypical—is an example of poor communication. Jane obviously had not clarified in her own mind what she wanted her memo to accomplish. On the one hand, she clearly wanted Eric's report to be in on time. On the other hand, she was aware that he was tied up with the marketing campaign and felt the need to offer him an extension. Her unresolved conflict resulted in a stiff, confusing memo that must have frustrated Eric. His memo, in turn, expressed his angry reaction and suggested that he would accomplish both his tasks on time by sacrificing their quality. The result was that neither the individuals involved nor the organization got what they needed.

The Importance of Communication

Planning

Organizing

Leading

Controlling

Communication

THE FOUNDATION
OF THE
MANAGEMENT
FUNCTIONS

Effective communication is important for managers for two reasons. First, communication is the process by which the management functions of planning, organizing, leading, and controlling are accomplished. Second, communication is the activity to which managers devote an overwhelming proportion of their time.

The *process* of communication makes it possible for managers to carry out their task responsibilities. Information must be communicated to managers so that they will have a basis for planning; the plans must be communicated to others to be carried out. Organizing requires communicating with people about their job assignments. Leading requires managers to communicate with subordinates so that group goals can be achieved. Oral, written, and, increasingly, electronic communications are an essential part of controlling. Managers can carry out their management functions only by interacting with and communicating with others. The communication process is thus the foundation for the management functions.[1]

A large share of managerial time is devoted to the *activity* of communication. Rarely are managers alone at their desks thinking, planning, or contemplating alternatives. In fact, managerial time is spent largely in face-to-face, electronic, or telephone communication with subordinates, peers, supervisors, suppliers, or customers. When not conferring with others in person or on the telephone, managers may be writing or dictating memos, letters, or reports—or perhaps reading memos, letters, or reports sent to them. Even in those few periods when managers are alone, they are frequently interrupted by communications. For example, one study of middle and top managers found that they could work uninterruptedly for a half hour or more only once every two days.[2]

Henry Mintzberg, whose work we discussed in chapter 1, has described the manager's job in terms of three types of roles.[3] Communication plays a vital part in each:

1. In their *interpersonal roles,* managers act as the figurehead and leader of their organizational unit, interacting with subordinates, customers, suppliers, and peers in the organization. Mintzberg cited studies indicating that managers spend about 45 percent of their contact time with peers, about 45 percent with people outside their units, and only about 10 percent with superiors.
2. In their *informational roles,* managers seek information from peers, subordinates, and other personal contacts about anything that may affect their job and responsibilities. They also disseminate interesting or important information in return. In addition, they provide suppliers, peers, and relevant groups outside the organization with information about their unit as a whole.
3. In their *decisional roles,* managers implement new projects, handle disturbances, and allocate resources to their unit's members and departments. Some of the decisions that managers make will be reached in private, but they will be based on information that has been communicated to the managers. The managers, in turn, will have to communicate those decisions to others.

Managers have traditionally favored the immediacy of oral communications, but since the advent of electronic mail this situation has changed somewhat. Electronic mail is used in an increasing number of organizations because it can be transmitted greater distances nearly instantaneously in a storable and confidential form and permits one to contact and solicit responses from a number of individuals simultaneously.

In this chapter we deal with communication in organizations. First, we present a model of interpersonal communication, describe the barriers to effective interpersonal communication, and suggest ways these barriers can be overcome. Second, we show how the different types of communication channels in organizations will influence variables such as group performance, leader emergence, and group member motivation and satisfaction. We then discuss problems of communication up and down the organization's chain of command and the informal channels of communication that develop in organizations. Finally, we deal with means for overcoming organizational (rather than interpersonal) barriers to effective communication.

Before we begin our discussion, we should note that one of the major difficulties surrounding communication as a subject of study is in defining exactly what it is. One researcher uncovered as many as 95 definitions, none of them widely accepted.[4] For our purposes, we will define *communication* as the process by which people attempt to share meaning via the transmission of symbolic messages.

Interpersonal Communication

Our definition of communication above calls attention to three essential points: (1) that communication, as we are using the term, involves *people,* and that understanding communication therefore involves trying to understand how people relate to each other; (2) that communication involves *shared meaning,* which suggests that in order for people to communicate, they must agree on the definitions of the terms they are using; and (3) that communication is *symbolic*—gestures, sounds, letters, numbers, and words can only represent or approximate the ideas they are meant to communicate.[5]

The Communication Process

The simplest model of the communication process is as follows:

$$\text{Sender} \rightarrow \text{Message} \rightarrow \text{Receiver}$$

This model indicates three essential elements of communication; obviously, if one of the elements is missing, no communication can take place. For example, we can send a message, but if it is not heard or received by someone, no communication has occurred.

Unfortunately, this simple model does not begin to suggest the complexity of the communication process. Most of us, for example, are familiar with the game of "telephone," in which one person whispers a message into the ear of another. That person whispers the message to another, and so on. Inevitably, when the last person says the message out loud, it is quite different from what had first been whispered. "Telephone" illustrates one complexity in the communication process: The sender may send a message, but the receivers may "hear" or receive a message the sender did not intend.

Figure 18–1 illustrates a far more sophisticated model of the communication process. In our discussion below, we will describe each of the major elements of this model.[6]

FIGURE 18–1 A MODEL OF THE COMMUNICATION PROCESS

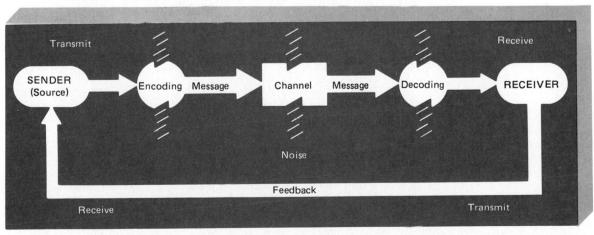

Sender (Source). The *sender*, or source of the message, initiates the communication. In an organization, the sender will be a person with information, needs, or desires and a purpose for communicating them to one or more other people. A manager wishes to communicate information about an important production deadline for the purpose of motivating other members of the department. A production-line worker speaks to the shop supervisor for the purpose of requesting additional help with a project. Without a reason, purpose, or desire, the sender has no need to send.

Encoding. *Encoding* takes place when the sender translates the information to be transmitted into a series of symbols. Encoding is necessary because information can only be transferred from one person to another through representations or symbols. Since communication is the object of encoding, the sender attempts to establish "mutuality" of meaning with the receiver by choosing symbols, usually in the form of words and gestures, that the sender believes to have the same meaning for the receiver. Lack of mutuality is one of the most common causes of misunderstanding or lack of communication. In Bulgaria and some parts of India, for example, "yes" is indicated with a side-to-side shake of the head, while "no" is indicated with a nod. Visiting foreigners who do not share these symbols can quickly experience or cause bewilderment when they talk with citizens of these areas. Misunderstandings may also result from subtler differences in mutuality. A manager who asks a number of subordinates to "work late" may cause a good deal of confusion as each employee decides independently what "late" means.

Gestures, too, may be subject to different interpretations. A worker in a noisy factory may convey to a co-worker that he wants a machine to be shut off by drawing his hand, palm down, across his neck in a "cutthroat" gesture.[7] If one walked up to a police officer and made the same gesture, a different reaction might result. Even raising one's eyebrows can have varying meanings, expressing surprise in one context and skepticism in another.

Message. The *message* is the physical form into which the sender encodes the information. The message may be in any form that can be experienced and understood by one or more of the senses of the receiver. Speech may be heard; written words may be read; gestures may be seen or felt. A touch of the hand may communicate messages ranging from comfort to menace. A wave of the hand can communicate widely diverse messages depending on the number of fingers extended. Nonverbal messages are an extremely important form of communication, since they are often more honest or meaningful than oral or written messages. For example, a manager who frowns while saying "Good morning" to a late-arriving subordinate is clearly communicating something more than a polite greeting.

Channel. The *channel* is the method of transmission from one person to another (such as air for spoken words and paper for letters); it is often inseparable from the message. For communication to be effective and efficient, the channel must be appropriate for the message. A phone conversation would be an unsuitable channel for transmitting a complex engineering diagram;[8] overnight express mail might be more appropriate. The needs and requirements of the receiver must also be considered in selecting a channel. An extremely complicated message, for example, should be transmitted in a channel that permits the receiver to refer to it repeatedly.

Although managers have a broad array of channels available to them, they may not always use the one that is most effective. Their choices may be guided by habit or personal preference. One person may use the telephone because he or she dislikes writing; another may continue to use handwritten memos when electronic mail would be much more efficient. Both modes are appropriate in certain circumstances, so the manager must make individual decisions for each situation.

How does one choose the best channel? Written and graphic communications, such as memos, letters, reports, and blueprints, are clear and precise and provide a permanent record. The telephone and face-to-face oral communication offer the advantage of immediate feedback. In choosing the appropriate channel, then, managers must decide whether clarity or feedback is more important. Many different factors are involved in the communication process, so no single technique is always preferable to the alternatives.[9]

Receiver. The *receiver* is the person whose senses perceive the sender's message. There may be a large number of receivers, as when a memo is addressed to all the members of an organization, or there may be just one, as when one discusses something privately with a colleague. The message must be crafted with the receiver's background in mind. An engineer in a microchip manufacturing company, for example, might have to avoid using technical terms in a communication with someone in the company's advertising department; by the same token, the person in advertising might find engineers unreceptive to communications about demographics. If the message does not reach a receiver, communication has not taken place. The situation is not much improved if the message reaches a receiver but the receiver doesn't understand it.

Decoding. *Decoding* is the process by which the receiver interprets the message and translates it into meaningful information. It is a two-step process: The receiver must first perceive the message, then interpret it.[10] Decoding is affected by the receiver's past experience, personal assessments of the symbols and gestures used, expectations (people tend to hear what they want to hear), and mutuality of meaning with the sender. In general, *the more the receiver's decoding matches the sender's intended message, the more effective the communication has been.*

One decoding problem occurred when a manager asked a subordinate if she would like to work overtime on a weekend. There were a number of other employees available to do the work, but the supervisor thought the one he singled out would appreciate an opportunity to earn extra income. The subordinate had made special plans for Saturday, but she interpreted the manager's offer as a demand, canceled her plans, and spent the weekend working. As a result of poor communication, she interpreted the manager's message differently than he intended.[11]

Noise. *Noise* is any factor that disturbs, confuses, or otherwise interferes with communication. It may be internal (as when a receiver is not paying attention) or external (as when the message is distorted by other sounds in the environment). Noise can occur at any stage of the communication process. It may occur during passage through the channel—for example, a radio signal may be distorted by bad weather—but most interference arises in the encoding or decoding stage.[12]

The urge to make sense of a communication is so strong that a puzzling or even nonsensical communication is often decoded by the receiver into a sensible statement that may have an entirely different meaning from the originally encoded message. For example, unclear instructions on how to perform a task may cause employees to "hear" different and incorrect instructions.

Since noise can interfere with understanding, managers should attempt to restrict it to a level that permits effective communication. It can be very tiring to listen to a subordinate who speaks softly on a noisy assembly line or to try to conduct a conversation over telephone static.[13] Physical discomfort such as hunger, pain, or exhaustion can also be considered a form of noise and can interfere with effective communication. The problems are made worse, of course, by a message that is excessively complex or unclear to begin with. A clear message expressed in a straightforward fashion ("Turn off that radio!"), however, can be conveyed even in an extremely "noisy" environment.

EFFECTIVE
COMMUNICATION

Intended Message

↓

Encoding

↓

Decoding

↓

Intended Message

Feedback. *Feedback* is a reversal of the communication process in which a reaction to the sender's communication is expressed. Since the receiver has become the sender, feedback goes through the same steps as the original communication. Organizational feedback may be in a variety of forms, ranging from direct feedback, such as a simple spoken acknowledgment that the message has been received, to indirect feedback, expressed through actions or documentation. For example, a straightforward request for a faster rate of production may be met directly with an assenting nod of the head or indirectly with record-breaking output or a union strike.

As the dotted lines in figure 18–1 suggest, feedback is optional and may exist in any degree (from minimal to complete) in any given situation. In most organizational communications, the greater the feedback, the more effective the communication process is likely to be. For example, early feedback will enable managers to know if their instructions have been understood and accepted. Without such feedback, a manager might not know (until too late) whether the instructions were accurately received and carried out.

One-Way and Two-Way Communication

As our description of the communication process implies, communication may be one-way or two-way. In *one-way communication*, the sender communicates without expecting or getting feedback from the receiver. Policy statements from top managers are usually examples of one-way communication. *Two-way communication* exists when the receiver provides feedback to the sender. Making a suggestion to a subordinate and receiving a question or countersuggestion is an example of two-way communication.

Harold Leavitt and Ronald Mueller conducted early experiments on the effects and effectiveness of one-way and two-way communication.[14] In these experiments, individuals were asked to describe an arrangement of geometric shapes to groups of listeners. They were to use words only. The listeners were asked to reproduce the diagrams from the verbal descriptions. The experiments were conducted under conditions of one-way communication and two-way communication. In the one-way communication, the sender could not see or hear the listeners. In the two-way experiment, descriptions were still limited to words, but the sender was allowed to face the listeners and the listeners could question or comment freely. The results of the experiments were as follows:

1. **One-way communication takes considerably less time than two-way communication.**

2. Two-way communication is more accurate than one-way communication. (That is, the diagrams were more accurately reproduced when two-way communication was used.) The feedback allows the sender to refine his or her communication for the receivers so that it becomes more precise and accurate.

3. Receivers are more sure of themselves and of their judgments when two-way communication is used. The very fact that they are permitted to ask questions probably increases the receivers' self-confidence. In addition, they can use questions to clarify any doubts they may have.

4. Senders can easily feel attacked when two-way communication is used, because receivers will call attention to the senders' ambiguities and mistakes.

5. Although it is less accurate, one-way communication appears much more orderly than two-way communication, which often appears noisy and chaotic.

As Leavitt has pointed out,[15] these results can provide guidelines for communication in organizations. If communication must be fast and accuracy is easy to achieve (as when informing employees about a minor change in the company's health plan), one-way communication is both more economical and more efficient. If orderliness is considered vital—as in a large, public meeting—one-way communication might also be more appropriate. One-way communication also has political benefits: It reduces the chance that the sender's mistakes will be publicly revealed and challenged.

Where accuracy of communication is important, however (as in instructions for carrying out complex tasks), the two-way method is almost essential. Without feedback from the receiver, the sender has little basis for judging the accuracy of the communication or the degree of understanding and comprehension experienced by the receiver.

In most situations, managers will have to create the most efficient mix of one-way and two-way communication. Some categories of managerial communications, such as straightforward statements of company rules and policies, require little or no feedback to assure clarity. In many other cases, such as the formulation of organizational objectives or the implementation of a new sales strategy, two-way communication is usually essential.

Barriers to Effective Communication

Any factor that impedes the exchange of information between a sender and a receiver is a barrier to communication.[16] Such barriers are extremely common in everyday life, and they appear in an almost unlimited variety of forms. Some are obvious problems with obvious solutions. If you are talking to a colleague and a jackhammer starts up on the sidewalk outside your window, you can wait for the jackhammer to stop or you can move to where the noise won't bother you. Other barriers are much more subtle; one must be quite perceptive even to recognize them. An older manager, for example, may feel threatened by an aggressive younger employee and as a result tend to dismiss the younger manager's most carefully thought out suggestions, perhaps without even realizing that he or she is doing so. Although less overt, barriers of this sort have as much potential for causing problems as do the more conspicuous problems of the jackhammer variety. Indeed, one could argue that the hidden problems are likely to be more damaging because they are often related to individuals' vulnerabilities and defenses and so cannot be fixed the way a broken telephone can. Their resolution may require great tact, self-awareness, and maturity on the part of everyone involved.

Whatever their source, barriers to effective communication interfere with the receiver's understanding of the intended meaning of the sender's message. As we have already noted, managers spend most of their time communicating, and a good manager should be able to identify and understand the communication barriers that can occur in different situations—from peer to peer, subordinate to superior, superior to subordinate, and employee to customer. Understanding the general characteristics of communication barriers will help managers improve their own communications and solve communication problems with others.[17]

Communication barriers vary in their imperviousness and their significance. Rarely are they total blocks—some part of the intended message is generally able to filter through. In some cases, it is sufficient that the gist of the message be communicated. A mailroom clerk who understood relatively little English might be able to function adequately most of the time if he or she clearly understood the difference between "first class" and "express mail." If the clerk failed to grasp the important part of a message and mistakenly sent a package to MIT rather than IBM, however, there might be serious consequences. Barriers often occur in groups. The clerk, for example, might avoid answering the telephone because of his or her difficulty in understanding what people were saying. He or she might consistently deliver John Jonson's mail to John Jenson. Removing one barrier—by enrolling the clerk in a program of instruction in English, perhaps—might remove a whole series of barriers to effective communication throughout the organization.

The following are some of the most common barriers to effective communication:

Differing Perceptions. One of the most common sources of communication barriers is individual variation. People who have different backgrounds of knowledge and experience often perceive the same phenomenon from different perspectives. Suppose that a new supervisor compliments an assembly-line worker for his or her efficiency and high-quality work. The supervisor genuinely appreciates the worker's efforts and at the same time wants to encourage the other employees to emulate his or her example. Others on the assembly line, however, may regard the worker's being singled out for praise as a sign that he or she has been "buttering up the boss"; they may react by teasing or being openly hostile. The event is the same, but individuals' perspectives on it differ radically.

The way a communication is perceived is influenced by the environment in which it occurs. A disagreement between colleagues during a planning session for a major project might be regarded by others as acceptable or even healthy. If the same disagreement broke out during the chief executive officer's annual address to employees, it would be regarded somewhat differently. Events that are considered appropriate in some circumstances are inappropriate in others.

Language Differences. Language differences are often closely related to differences in individual perceptions. For a message to be properly communicated, the words used must mean the same thing to sender and receiver. The same symbolic meaning must be shared. Suppose that different departments of a company receive a memo stating that a new product is to be developed in "a short time." To people in research

BARRIERS TO COMMUNICATION

Differing perceptions

Language differences

Noise

Emotionality

Inconsistent communication

Distrust

"Confound it, Merriwell! Do you mean that all this time you've been talking micro while we've been talking macro?"
Drawing by Lorenz; © 1982 The New Yorker Magazine, Inc.

and development, "a short time" might mean two or three years. To people in the finance department, on the other hand, "a short time" might be three to six months, whereas the sales department might think of "a short time" as a few weeks. Since many different meanings can be assigned to some words—the 500 most common English words have an average of 28 definitions *each*[18]—great care must be taken to ensure that the receiver gets the message that the sender intended.

Further barriers to communication may result from the use of jargon. People who have special interests or knowledge, such as software designers or behavioral psychologists, are often unaware that not everyone is familiar with their specialized terms. Sometimes people use jargon to exclude others or to create an impression of superiority—both of which make communication difficult.

Because words often have strong symbolic significance, using them as labels should be avoided. If we label certain people "slow" or "unreliable," for example, we begin to see them that way. Worse still, such labels can become self-fulfilling prophecies: People so labeled may themselves begin to believe the labels and act accordingly. As we discussed in chapter 17, the self-fulfilling aspect of labels or beliefs is sometimes called "the Rosenthal effect" or "the Pygmalion effect."[19]

Noise. As we have already explained, noise is any factor that disturbs, confuses, or otherwise interferes with communication. Little communication occurs in totally noise-free environments, of course. Individuals learn to screen out many of the irrelevant messages they receive. Sometimes, however, the relevant information is also screened out. A person talking on the phone in a busy office may not hear the message her secretary is giving her from across the room. The "boy who cried wolf" was eventually correct, but his previous messages had been given so often that they had come to be dismissed as noise. Similarly, a manager who labels every order "urgent" may find that subordinates are slow to respond when a real emergency develops.

Emotionality. Emotional reactions—anger, love, defensiveness, hate, jealousy, fear, embarrassment—influence how we understand others' messages and how we influence others with our own messages. If, for example, we are in an atmosphere where we feel threatened with loss of power or prestige, we may lose the ability to gauge the meanings of the messages we receive and will respond defensively or aggressively. The best approach is to learn to accept emotions as part of the communication process and attempt to understand them when they cause problems. If you are confronted with a subordinate behaving aggressively, try to empathize. Get the person to talk about his or her concerns, and pay careful attention to what is said. Once you understand the person's reactions, you may be able to improve the situation by modifying your own behavior. In general, it is best to cultivate an atmosphere of rationality, openness, and trust, encouraging subordinates to talk freely about themselves and their interests. Subordinates who are met with an emotional or hostile response whenever they have a problem or make a mistake may distort messages or avoid communicating altogether.[20]

Inconsistent Verbal and Nonverbal Communication. We think of language as the primary medium of communication, but the messages we send and receive are strongly influenced by such nonverbal factors as body movements, clothing, the distance we stand from the person we're talking to, our posture, gestures, facial expression, eye movements, and body contact. Even when our message is as simple as "Good morning," we can convey different intents by our nonverbal communication. A busy manager who does not want to be disturbed might respond to a subordinate's greeting without looking up from his or her work, for example. A supervisor who usually wears a scowl will likely be unpopular with subordinates, despite his or her best attempts to treat employees kindly and fairly, if they react to his nonverbal cues rather than his verbal ones.

Distrust. The credibility of a message is, to a large extent, a function of the credibility of the sender in the mind of the receiver. A sender's credibility is, in turn, determined by a variety of factors. In some cases, the fact that a message comes from a manager will enhance its credibility, but it can also have the opposite effect. In negotiations between labor and management, for example, labor often regards the claims of managers with some suspicion. In this situation, as in others, the perceived character or honesty of the sender is important. A person's education about and experience with the subject of a communication are also influential. Another important factor is the rapport of the receiver with the sender; a subordinate and a manager who have a long history of amicable relations are more likely to deal with one another effectively than are two individuals who are constantly arguing. In general, a manager's credibility will be high if he or she is perceived by others as knowledgeable, trustworthy, and sincerely concerned about the welfare of others.[21]

Overcoming Barriers to Interpersonal Communication

Overcoming barriers is a two-step process. First, one must learn to recognize the various types of barriers that can occur. Second, one must act to overcome the barriers.[22] We describe below some of the techniques that can be used to overcome the specific barriers described above.

Overcoming differing perceptions. To overcome differing perceptions, the message should be explained so that it can be understood by those with different views and experiences. Whenever possible, we should learn about the background of those with whom we will be communicating. Empathizing and seeing the situation from the other person's point of view and delaying reactions until the relevant information is weighed helps to reduce ambiguous messages. When the subject is unclear, asking questions is critical.[23]

Overcoming differences in language. To overcome language differences, the meanings of unconventional or technical terms should be explained. Simple, direct, natural language should be used. To ensure that all important concepts have been understood, asking the receiver to confirm or restate the main points of the message is particularly helpful. In some cases, when all members of an organization or group are going to be dealing with a new terminology, it may be worthwhile to develop a training course of instruction to acquaint members with the new topic. Receivers can be encouraged to ask questions and to seek clarification of points that are unclear or may be misunderstood.[24]

It is also helpful to remain sensitive to the various alternative interpretations possible for a message. Messages can often be restated in different terms. Sometimes even a minor change can have beneficial effects. If, for example, we are replacing an unpopular sales quota system with a new system in which reaching sales objectives is only one measure of productivity, we might do well to avoid the word "quota" entirely because of its negative association with the old system.

Overcoming noise. Noise is best dealt with by eliminating it. If noise from a machine makes talking difficult, turn off the machine or move to a new location. If you notice that your receiver is not listening closely, try to regain his or her attention. Avoid distracting environments. Alternately, when noise is unavoidable, increase the clarity and strength of the message.

Overcoming emotionality. The first step in overcoming the negative effects of emotionality is to increase one's awareness of them. Being sensitive to one's own moods and being aware of how they might influence others before communicating an important message to them is helpful. Trying to understand the emotional reactions of others and preparing oneself beforehand for dealing with emotional encounters are also useful approaches.

On a more general level, steps can be taken to create an atmosphere in which destructive emotionality is unlikely. Fostering a supportive environment in which new or different approaches are given serious consideration reduces emotions. Employees should be given constructive feedback. If done properly, evaluations of employees can lead to improved trust and respect. The development of trust, confidence, and openness results in a secure, nonthreatening communication environment, and such an environment is less likely to engender emotionality and defensiveness.

Overcoming inconsistent verbal and nonverbal communication. The keys to eliminating inconsistencies in communication are being aware of them and not attempting to send false messages. Gestures, clothes, posture, facial expression, and other powerful nonverbal communications should agree with the message. Analyzing the nonverbal communication of other people and applying what one learns to oneself and to one's dealings with others is helpful.

Overcoming distrust. Overcoming distrust is to a large extent the process of creating trust. Credibility is the result of a long-term process in which a person's honesty, fairmindedness, and good intentions are recognized by others. There are few shortcuts to creating a trusting atmosphere; a good rapport with the people one communicates with can only be developed through consistent performance.

Two additional approaches are generally useful in getting one's message across. The first is *redundancy*—repeating the message or restating it in a different form. Redundancy counteracts noise by reducing the uncertainty in the transmission of the message.[25] The optimal level of redundancy varies with the circumstances. If a message is sent in a permanent form—on paper, a tape, or a disk, for example—then little redundancy within the communication is called for. On the other hand, if the message is extremely complex, it may be useful to repeat key points in several different forms even in a written communication. Redundancy is also more important in oral and other "perishable" forms of communication. If someone is giving us a phone number and we don't have a pencil and paper, we are more likely to remember it if it is repeated several times.

Like other techniques, redundancy can be overused. If we hear the same message too many times, we may become bored or angry. Eventually, a receiver will come to treat such a message as noise. Furthermore, in some situations, storage of the redundant information can be a problem. Many libraries would like to have two copies of every book they buy, for example, but two copies cost twice as much, take up twice as much space, and take almost twice as long to catalog. The money, space, and time might better be devoted to another book.

The second general approach is one that we have already mentioned: encouraging the development of an environment, or organizational culture, that supports giving and receiving feedback. Feedback is most useful when it focuses on things that the person who receives it has the power to change. Feedback on a spoken presentation, for example, can help the speaker improve his or her wording, delivery, and use of gestures; comments should emphasize these areas. The timbre of the speaker's voice cannot be significantly changed, however, so there would be little point in commenting on this dimension of a performance.[26]

Providing feedback helps both sender and receiver. In the telephone number example above, the most useful action is to repeat the number back to the sender. This step not only helps in remembering it, but it also enables the sender to confirm the accuracy of the transmission.

Often, all that is necessary to obtain feedback is to ask if the listener understands what is meant. Nonverbal clues can also be useful in assessing a person's reaction. For example, one can give a speaker nonverbal encouragement by nodding one's head every few moments and maintaining direct eye contact.[27] The manner in which feedback is given can be used by managers to strengthen mutual respect.

Moving from Defensive to Supportive Communication. One important approach to overcoming communication barriers is described by Jack R. Gibb.[28] Gibb has suggested that the type of behavior or attitudes people manifest affects the way they communicate. Certain types of behavior will cause individuals to react defensively and will inhibit communication, while other types will cause people to feel they are supported—thereby facilitating communication. The two categories of behavior identified by Gibb are listed in table 18–1. Behavior characterized by any of the qualities in the left column causes defensiveness in the receiver; those in the right column are seen as supportive and hence act to reduce defensiveness. We will briefly discuss each of the six pairs of behaviors.

Evaluation—Description. If the speaker's manner, expression, tone, or choice of phrase is interpreted as a judgment about or an evaluation of the listener, then the listener may become defensive. This reaction is not unrealistic, since much com-

TABLE 18–1
CATEGORIES OF
DEFENSIVE AND
SUPPORTIVE
COMMUNICATION
BEHAVIORS

Defensive Behaviors	Supportive Behaviors
1. Evaluation	1. Description
2. Control	2. Problem Orientation
3. Strategy	3. Spontaneity
4. Neutrality	4. Empathy
5. Superiority	5. Equality
6. Certainty	6. Provisionalism

Source: Jack R. Gibb, "Defensive Communication," *Journal of Communication* 11, no. 13 (September 1961): 143. Used by permission of the International Communication Association and the author.

munication is, in fact, evaluative. As managers, we will often find it difficult not to pass judgment on subordinates automatically. Conscious effort is sometimes needed to avoid this defense-provoking behavior. Senders should pay careful attention to objectivity in communication ("description"). Receivers can test the quality of their understanding through the instructive suggestion of Carl Rogers:

> The next time you get into an argument . . . just stop the discussion for a moment and, for an experiment, institute this rule: "Each person can speak up for himself only *after* he has first restated the ideas and feelings of the previous speaker accurately and to that speaker's satisfaction."[29]

This technique inhibits the tendency that most of us have to formulate our reply mentally while the other person is speaking, instead of concentrating on listening to what the speaker is actually saying.

Control—Problem Orientation. Statements, orders, or simple observations that seemingly attempt to control other persons imply that the speaker has better judgment and therefore that the listeners are inferior. Methods of communicating an attempt to control may range from a threat-backed command to a simple disapproving frown. Since these imply that the receiver is not capable of making a wise decision without direction, they create defensiveness even if the control is accepted. When the sender makes it clear, however, that he or she is trying to join with the receiver in defining and solving a problem, a supportive climate results and an improvement in communication is almost inevitable.

Strategy—Spontaneity. If we think someone is "playing games" with us, rather than acting spontaneously, our usual reaction is resistance. Deceit and manipulation can "turn us off" to anyone from a potential date to a candidate for governor. Managers who have been superficially involved in sensitivity or human relations training frequently attempt to act spontaneously; the listener often senses an underlying insincerity. Genuine and honest communication, however, usually creates a genuine and honest response.

Neutrality—Empathy. Communication that demonstrates empathy for the listener will produce highly favorable reactions. Conversely, a cold, clinical attitude will be seen as indifference and will lead to stiff, formal, less satisfying interchanges.

Superiority—Equality. As we all know from experience, individuals who act superior do not usually get cooperative and friendly responses. Those who lecture and admonish will be received coldly. Those who talk as equals, on the other hand, and who indicate they trust and respect their listeners, will usually receive honest and forthright replies. Managers who want two-way communication with their subordinates must work hard to keep their rank from getting in the way.

Certainty—Provisionalism. When we try to impress others that we know all the answers and that nothing will shake us from our convictions, our listeners are likely to become defensively argumentative or sullenly acquiescent. If, on the other hand, we indicate that we want to hear other perspectives and consider new information, a supportive and cooperative attitude is engendered and open communication is encouraged. People usually are willing to be flexible in their positions in response to a flexible position.

Communication in Organizations

> Because Christmas Eve falls on a Thursday, the day has been designated a Saturday for work purposes. Factories will close all day, with stores open a half day only. Friday, December 25, has been designated a Sunday, with both factories and stores open all day. Monday, December 28, will be a Wednesday for work purposes. Wednesday, December 30, will be a business Friday. Saturday, January 2, will be a Sunday, and Sunday, January 3, will be a Monday.—*From an Associated Press report on a Prague government edict.*

All the factors that we have discussed in relation to interpersonal communication also apply to communication within organizations. Effective communication in organizations, like effective communication anywhere, still involves getting an accurate message from one person to another (or perhaps to several people). As in the example above, unclear organizational communication can make a complex idea or process completely unintelligible. However, several factors unique to organizations influence the effectiveness of communication. In this section we will deal specifically with how the realities of formal organizations can affect the communication process.

Raymond V. Lesikar has described four factors that influence the effectiveness of organizational communication: the formal channels of communication, the organization's authority structure, job specialization, and what Lesikar calls "information ownership."[30]

The *formal channels of communication* influence communication effectiveness in two ways. First, the formal channels cover an ever-widening distance as organizations develop and grow. For example, effective communication is usually far more difficult to achieve in a large retail organization with widely dispersed branches than in a small department store. Second, the formal channels of communication inhibit the free flow of information between organizational levels. An assembly-line worker, for example, will almost always communicate problems to a supervisor rather than to the plant manager. While this accepted restriction in the channels of communication has its advantages (such as keeping higher-level managers from getting bogged down in information), it also has its disadvantages (such as keeping higher-level managers from receiving information they should sometimes have).

The organization's *authority structure* has a similar influence on communication effectiveness. Status and power differences in the organization help determine who will communicate comfortably with whom. The content and accuracy of the communication will also be affected by authority differences among individuals. For example, conversation between a company president and a clerical worker may well be characterized by somewhat strained politeness and formality; neither party is likely to say much of importance.

Job specialization usually facilitates communication *within* differentiated groups. Members of the same work group are likely to share the same jargon, time horizons, goals, tasks, and personal styles. Communication *between* highly differentiated groups, however, is likely to be inhibited.

The term *information ownership* means that individuals possess unique information and knowledge about their jobs. A darkroom employee, for example, may have found a particularly efficient way to develop photoprints; a department head may have a particularly effective way of handling conflict among subordinates; a salesperson may know who the key decision makers are in his or her major accounts. Such information is a form of power for the individuals who possess it; they are able to function more effectively than their peers. Many individuals with such skills and knowledge are unwilling to share this information with others. As a result, completely open communication within the organization does not take place.

In the following sections we will discuss in some detail the effects of the organization's formal communication channels and authority structure on communication effectiveness. In addition, we will discuss the organization's informal communication system (the grapevine), which supplements the organization's formal communications network.

Communication Networks within the Organization

Some very interesting research has been carried out on communication channels in organizations and their effects on communication accuracy, task performance, and group member satisfaction. This research is particularly important because managers have some influence over how communication channels develop in their units. For example, the formal authority structure that managers establish will help determine who will interact with whom. Thus, managers can design their work units to facilitate effective communication.

Organizations can design their *communication networks* or structures in a variety of ways. Some communication networks may be rigidly designed. For example, employees can be discouraged from talking with anyone except their immediate supervisor. Such a network is usually intended to keep higher-level managers from being overburdened with unnecessary information and to maintain the higher-level managers' power and status. Other networks may be more loosely designed: Individuals may be encouraged to communicate with anyone at any level. Such networks may be used wherever a free flow of information is highly desirable, as in a research department.

To test the effect of various communication structures, a series of experiments have been performed.[31] In a representative study in this series, five subjects were seated at a table and asked to solve different types of problems. The subjects were separated by partitions and could communicate with each other to solve the problems along communication lines controlled entirely by the researchers.

Figure 18–2 illustrates four communication networks the researchers tested. In the "circle" network, for example, subject B could communicate (through the partitions) only with subjects A and C. To communicate with subject E, subject B would have to go through subject A or through subjects C and D. Subject C in the "star" pattern, on the other hand, could communicate directly with A, B, D, and E,

FIGURE 18–2 TYPES OF COMMUNICATION NETWORKS

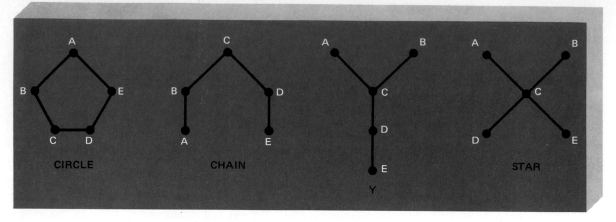

although these subjects could not communicate directly with each other. Each of these networks can represent a real network in an organization. The "star" pattern, for example, might represent four salespeople (A, B, D, E) reporting to a district manager (C); the "chain" pattern might represent two subordinates (A and E) reporting to supervisors (B and D, respectively), who in turn report to the same supervisor (C).

The subjects in the experiments were given both simple and complex problems to solve. The series of studies demonstrated that network centrality was the critical feature that determined whether a particular communication network was effective and/or satisfying to its members on a particular type of task. Some networks, such as the "Y" and "star," are highly centralized, with subject C at the central position. But the "circle" and "chain" networks are decentralized, with no one member able to communicate with all the other members.

In most tests, centralized networks performed faster and more accurately than decentralized networks, *provided the tasks were comparatively simple.* For *complex* tasks, however, the decentralized networks were comparatively quicker and more accurate.

The centrality of the networks also affected leader emergence and group member satisfaction. For both simple and complex tasks, centralized groups tended to agree that person C, occupying the central position, was the leader. Obviously, C emerged as the leader in centralized networks because the other group members were so completely dependent on C for their information. In decentralized networks, however, no one position in the network emerged as the leadership position.

Group member satisfaction, on the other hand, tended to be higher in decentralized networks for all types of tasks. In fact, satisfaction was highest in the "circle," next highest in the "chain," and then in the "Y." The least satisfied group members were in the "star" network. The reason for the greater satisfaction in the decentralized networks was that members of those networks could participate in finding problem solutions. The only highly satisfied member of the centralized networks was the person at position "C," who played an active leadership role.

These experiments have many implications for the relationships between organizational structure and communication. For example, an organization with mostly routine, simple tasks would seem to work most efficiently with a formally centralized communication network, whereas more complicated tasks seem to call for decentralization. Also, the emergence of the person in the most centralized position as the leader reinforces the idea that access to information is an important source of power in organizations.

Vertical Communication

Vertical communication consists of communication up and down the organization's chain of command. Downward communication starts with top management and flows down through management levels to line workers and nonsupervisory personnel. The major purposes of downward communication are to advise, inform, direct, instruct, and evaluate subordinates and to provide organization members with information about organizational goals and policies.

The main function of upward communication is to supply information to the upper levels about what is happening at the lower levels. This type of communication includes progress reports, suggestions, explanations, and requests for aid or decisions.[32]

Problems of Vertical Communication. Downward communication is likely to be filtered, modified, or halted at each level as managers decide what should be passed down to their subordinates. Upward communication is likely to be filtered, condensed, or altered by middle managers who see it as part of their job to protect upper management from nonessential data originating at the lower levels.[33] In addition, middle managers may keep information that would reflect unfavorably on them from reaching their superiors. Thus, vertical communication is often at least partially inaccurate or incomplete.

The importance to an organization of vertical communication was emphasized by a survey of research conducted by Lyman W. Porter and Karlene H. Roberts, who reported that two-thirds of a manager's communication takes place with superiors and subordinates.[34] The studies reviewed by Porter and Roberts also found that the accuracy of vertical communication was aided by similarities in thinking between superior and subordinate. But it was limited by status and power differences between manager and subordinate, by a subordinate's desire for upward mobility, and by a lack of trust between manager and subordinate. For example, some studies suggest that communication is likely to be less open and accurate the higher the subordinates' aspirations for upward mobility. Such subordinates are likely to be ambitious, strongly opinionated, forceful, and aggressive, and consequently are more concerned with defending their self-image than in reaching an agreement or an objectively accurate appraisal of a situation. They are also less likely to communicate reports that may be interpreted as negative comments on their performance or ability. Subordinates are also more likely to screen out problems, disagreements, or complaints when they feel that their superior has the power to punish them.

Even unambitious subordinates will be guarded in their communications if an atmosphere of trust does not exist between them and their superiors. Subordinates conceal or distort information if they feel that their superiors cannot be trusted to be fair or that they may use the information against them. The net result of these communication problems is that higher-level managers frequently make decisions based on faulty or inadequate information.

Problems in downward communication exist when managers do not provide subordinates with the information they need to carry out their tasks effectively. Managers are often overly optimistic about the accuracy and completeness of their downward communication; in fact, they frequently fail to pass on important information (such as a higher-level change in policy) or to instruct subordinates adequately on how to perform their duties. This lack of communication is sometimes deliberate, as when managers withhold information to keep subordinates dependent on them. The net effect of incomplete downward communication is that subordinates may feel confused, uninformed, or powerless and may fail to carry out their tasks properly.

Lateral and Informal Communication

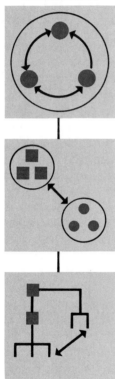

Lateral Communication

Lateral communication usually follows the pattern of work flow in an organization, occurring between members of work groups, between one work group and another, between members of different departments, and between line and staff. The main purpose of lateral communication is to provide a direct channel for organizational coordination and problem solving. In this way, it avoids the much slower procedure of directing communications through a common superior.[35] An added benefit of lateral communication is that it enables organization members to form relationships with their peers. These relationships are an important part of employee satisfaction.[36]

A significant amount of lateral communication occurs outside the chain of command. Such lateral communication often occurs with the knowledge, approval, and encouragement of superiors who understand that lateral communication often relieves their communication burden and also reduces inaccuracy by putting relevant people in direct contact with each other.[37]

Another type of *informal communication*, not officially sanctioned, is the grapevine. The grapevine in organizations is made up of several informal communication networks that overlap and intersect at a number of points—that is, some well-informed individuals are likely to belong to more than one informal network. Grapevines show admirable disregard for rank or authority and may link organization members in any combination of directions—horizontal, vertical, and diagonal. As Keith Davis puts it, the grapevine "flows around water coolers, down hallways, through lunch rooms, and wherever people get together in groups."[38] The grapevine should not be confused with legitimate information that management seeks to transmit by word of mouth. However, when such information is transmitted by word of mouth, people at the lowest level of the organization are least likely to receive it accurately. For this reason, managers who wish to ensure that the lowest-level employees receive certain information often communicate in writing.

In addition to its social and informal communication functions, the grapevine has several work-related functions as well. For example, although the grapevine is hard to control with any precision, it is often much faster in operation than formal communication channels. Managers may use it to distribute information through planned "leaks" or judiciously placed "just-between-you-and-me" remarks.

Keith Davis, who has extensively studied grapevines in organizations, has identified four possible types of *grapevine chains*.[39] (See fig. 18–3.) In the "single-strand" chain, person A tells something to person B, who tells it to person C, and so on down the line. This chain is least accurate at passing on information. (It is the

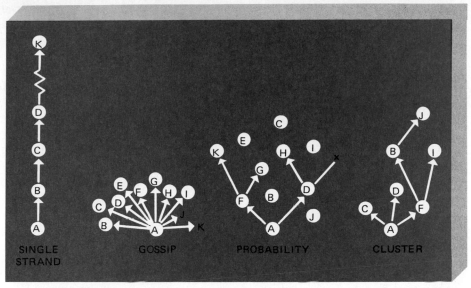

FIGURE 18–3
TYPES OF
GRAPEVINE
CHAINS

SINGLE STRAND   GOSSIP   PROBABILITY   CLUSTER

Source: Reprinted by permission of the *Harvard Business Review*. An exhibit from "Management Communication and the Grapevine" by Keith Davis (September–October 1953). Copyright © 1953 by the President and Fellows of Harvard College; all rights reserved.

equivalent of the chain in the "telephone" game we described at the beginning of the chapter.) In the "gossip" chain, one person seeks out and tells everyone the information he or she has obtained. This chain is often used when information of an interesting but non-job-related nature is being conveyed. In the "probability" chain, individuals are indifferent about whom they offer information to; they tell people at random, and those people in turn tell others at random. This chain is likely to be used when the information is mildly interesting but insignificant. In the "cluster" chain, person A conveys the information to a few selected individuals; some of those individuals then inform a few selected others.

Davis believes that the cluster chain is the dominant grapevine pattern in organizations: Usually, only a few individuals, called "liaison individuals," pass on the information they have obtained; and they are likely to do so only to individuals they trust or from whom they would like favors. They are most likely to pass on information that is interesting to them, job-related, and, above all, timely. People do not pass on old information for fear of advertising the fact that they are uninformed.

Overcoming Organizational Barriers to Communication

In order to deal with the barriers to organizational communication, we must first recognize that communication is an inherently complex process. For one thing, the verbal and visual symbols we use to describe reality are far from precise. A simple word like "job," for example, can be applied to anything from a child's newspaper route to the presidency of the United States. Words like "achievement," "effectiveness," and "responsibility" are even more vague. This imprecision of language (and gestures) is one reason that perfect communication is difficult, if not impossible, to achieve.

Another reason that communication is inherently difficult is that human beings perceive and interpret reality based on their individual backgrounds, needs, emotions, values, and experiences. A production manager's memo to supervisors asking for figures on absenteeism will be seen as a legitimate request by one supervisor and as unnecessary meddling by another; a manager's instructions may seem coldly formal to some subordinates and appropriately polite to others; a quarterly report may be clear to one superior and confusing to another. Some writers, in fact, believe that most organizational barriers to communication are based on differences in the way people interpret the communications they receive.[40]

Comprehending the innate barriers to communication and taking steps to minimize them are therefore the first steps toward improving a manager's ability to communicate effectively. For example, making explicit as many relevant aspects of a situation as possible will probably lead to a more effective and meaningful communication: A memo to members of the quality control department about the need to adjust inspection standards, for example, will usually be better received if it states the practical reasons for the changes (such as an increased marketing emphasis on the organization's ability to deliver high-quality products). Such a memo will sound less like an autocratic directive and more like a frank request from one person to another. Similarly, the manager should not assume that information left out of a communication will be known to the receiver. For example, a manager providing instructions should first check to see if the subordinates understand the specialized terms likely to be used. The manager should also remember that some words may have meanings to the receiver different from those the manager intends. A memo asking employees to be more careful in their work, for example, may be interpreted by employees as a statement that they have been sloppy. Communications asking for improved employee performance must be carefully and positively phrased to avoid causing hurt feelings and resentment. Decision support system software, such as *The Communication Edge* by Human Edge Software of Palo Alto, is now available to help managers achieve their communication goals when dealing with others in the organization.

The American Management Associations (AMA) has codified a number of communication principles into what it calls the "Ten Commandments of Good Communication." These "commandments," designed to improve the effectiveness of organizational communication, are listed and summarized in the accompanying box.

The AMA principles provide us with useful guidelines on how the communication of individual managers can be improved. Management by objectives (discussed in chapter 4) and organizational development (discussed in chapter 13) can help improve communication in organizations as a whole. MBO emphasizes joint goal setting, performance feedback, and joint problem solving. Thus, MBO programs are particularly useful for improving downward communication in organizations and for creating an atmosphere of trust between managers and subordinates. OD approaches attempt to change an organization's culture. Bringing about this change affects the organization's communication system. Successfully applied, OD will establish open, objective, and authentic communication between individuals and managers at all levels of the organization.

In recent years, the idea that the physical layout of the workplace can influence an organization's communication patterns, and in turn its culture and policies, has attracted increasing interest. An open office layout, in which everyone has direct

TEN COMMANDMENTS OF GOOD COMMUNICATION

1. *Seek to clarify your ideas before communicating.* The more systematically we analyze the problem or idea to be communicated, the clearer it becomes. . . .

2. *Examine the true purpose of each communication.* Before you communicate, ask yourself what you really want to accomplish with your message—obtain information, initiate action, change another person's attitude? Identify your most important goal and then adapt your language, tone, and total approach to serve that specific objective.

3. *Consider the total physical and human setting whenever you communicate.* Meaning and intent are conveyed by more than words alone. . . . Consider, for example, your *sense of timing*—i.e., the circumstances under which you make an announcement or render a decision; the *physical setting*— whether you communicate in private, for example, or otherwise; the *social climate* that pervades work relationships within the company or a department and sets the tone of its communications; . . .

4. *Consult with others, where appropriate, in planning communications.* . . . Such consultation often helps to lend additional insight and objectivity to your message. Moreover, those who have helped you plan your communication will give it their active support.

5. *Be mindful, while you communicate, of the overtones as well as the basic content of your message.* Your tone of voice, your expression, your apparent receptiveness to the responses of others— all have tremendous impact on those you wish to reach.

6. *Take the opportunity, when it arises, to convey something of help or value to the receiver.* Consideration of the other person's interests and needs—the habit of trying to look at things from his or her point of view—will frequently point up opportunities to convey something of immediate benefit or long-range value to him or her.

7. *Follow up your communication.* This you can do by asking questions, by encouraging the receiver to express his reactions, by follow-up contacts, by subsequent review of performance. Make certain that every important communication has a "feedback" so that complete understanding and appropriate action result.

8. *Communicate for tomorrow as well as today.* While communications may be aimed primarily at meeting the demands of an immediate situation, they must [also] be consistent with long-range interest and goals. For example, it is not easy to communicate frankly on such matters as poor performance or the shortcomings of a loyal subordinate—but postponing disagreeable communications makes them more difficult in the long run and is actually unfair to your subordinates and your company.

9. *Be sure your actions support your communications.* In the final analysis, the most persuasive kind of communication is not what you say but what you do. . . . For every manager this means that good supervisory practices—such as clear assignment of responsibility and authority, fair rewards for effort, and sound policy enforcement—serve to communicate more than all the gifts of oratory.

10. *Seek not only to be understood but to understand—be a good listener.* When we start talking we often cease to listen—in that larger sense of being attuned to the other person's unspoken reactions and attitudes. . . . [Listening] demands that we concentrate not only on the explicit meanings another person is expressing, but on the implicit meanings, unspoken words, and undertones that may be far more significant.

Source: Reprinted, by permission of the publisher, from *Management Review,* October 1955. Copyright © 1955 American Management Associations, Inc. All rights reserved.

access to everyone else, will result in one type of interpersonal interaction; linear corridors of rooms will result in a different type. Thus, the design of a company's work spaces can be used to foster or inhibit such characteristics as creativity, privacy, and direct face-to-face interactions.[41]

Communication and Advanced Information Technology

The growing use of computers has dramatically altered many aspects of organizational activity. Innovations such as corporate electronic mail and teleconferencing are not yet the norm in all offices, but it appears that computer-mediated techniques will soon be used routinely for communication both within and between organizations.[42]

Increasingly, computers are used not just to gather, store, and process data but also to serve as communication centers for distributing numerical data and textual information throughout an organization.[43] In industry, a number of organizations have begun to provide economic forecasts, competitive information, facts on different types of markets, and other data; as a result, managers sitting at their desks now have access to enormous amounts of information from thousands of sources around the world.[44] By using *electronic mail*, people studying the same subject on opposite sides of the country can communicate with each other. *Video conferencing* allows people who are miles (or continents) apart to be in visual contact. At Aetna, for example, a systems development group located seven miles from its users permits face-to-face communication over a two-way video-conferencing connection. Foremost McKesson, a distribution company, revolutionized its whole approach to business by the efficient use of computers to keep track of inventory and by integrating its computer system with its customers', thereby allowing them to enter orders directly and receive products more quickly.[45] Already, people in some occupations are *telecommuting*—using computers connected by telephone to send and receive work that they do at home.[46]

How does the computer revolution in communications affect organizations and their managers? One consequence is that the form, content, size, and frequency of messages have changed. This has had a strong influence on how individuals and departments interact with one another. Because employees working on easy-to-use computers can complete their tasks without much help from others, they are spending less time in direct interpersonal communication. This is especially true among lower-level workers, but managers using decision support systems (see chapters 6 and 22) to perform managerial analyses are also affected. It is now sometimes less necessary for managers or subordinates to interact with others to get information—they can call it up on their screens in seconds.

This development has an important implication for supervisors: If computer workers become too isolated, the organization may lose valuable training and knowledge-sharing advantages that come from informal social contact at work. Therefore, special efforts must be made to encourage computer workers to interact with others. This can be done in several ways. Work breaks can be scheduled more frequently. Jobs can be designed so that employees do not spend all day at their terminals. Tasks can be organized so that employees must work in cooperative groups to complete them.[47] Other problems will probably arise as computers continue to proliferate in the workplace. For example, how can a supervisor manage telecommuting employees whom he or she rarely or never sees? Before introducing new technology, managers should try to understand exactly what they want it to do for their communications. They should also try to anticipate problems the new system may cause and eliminate them before they arise, rather than waiting until the system is in place and attempting to deal with difficulties as they crop up.[48]

Summary

Communication may be defined as the process by which people attempt to share meanings through symbolic messages. The process of communication is important to managers because it enables them to carry on their management functions. The activity of communication, particularly oral communication, takes up a large portion of a manager's work time.

Elements of the proposed model of communication include the sender, encoding, message, channel, receiver, decoding, noise, and feedback. Encoding is the process by which the sender converts the information to be transmitted into the appropriate symbols or gestures. Decoding is the process by which the receiver interprets the message. If the decoding matches the sender's encoding, the communication has been effective. Noise is that which interferes with the communication. Types of noise include distractions and environmental noise. Feedback is the receiver's reaction to the sender's message; thus, it repeats the communication process with the sender and receiver roles reversed.

Communication may be one-way or two-way. In two-way communication, unlike one-way communication, feedback is provided to the sender. One-way communication is faster than two-way and better protects the authority of the sender. Two-way communication, however, is more accurate and leads to greater receiver confidence. For complex organizational tasks, two-way communication is much preferred.

Barriers to communication include such factors as differing perceptions, language differences, noise, emotionality, inconsistent verbal and nonverbal communications, and distrust. Many of these barriers can be overcome by using simple, direct language, attempting to empathize with the receiver, avoiding distractions, being aware of one's own emotionality and nonverbal behavior, and being honest and trustworthy. Encouraging feedback and repeating one's message may also be helpful. Honest and meaningful communication can be encouraged through the use of supportive behaviors that reduce defensive reactions.

The effectiveness of organizational communication is influenced by the organization's formal channels of communication and authority structure, by job specialization, and by information ownership. The formal channels may be rigid and highly centralized, with individuals able to communicate with only a few persons; or, they may be loose and decentralized, with individuals able to communicate with each other at any level. Experiments have found that centralized networks are faster and more accurate than decentralized networks for simple tasks, while for complex tasks decentralized channels are quicker and more accurate. The most central person is most satisfied in centralized networks, while group members' satisfaction is higher in decentralized networks.

Vertical communication is communication that moves up and down the organization's chain of command. Status and power differences between manager and subordinates, a subordinate's desire for upward mobility, and a lack of trust between manager and subordinates interfere with accurate and complete vertical communication.

Lateral communication improves coordination and problem solving and fosters employee satisfaction. Informal communication occurs outside the organization's formal channels. A particularly quick and pervasive type of informal communication is the grapevine.

Overcoming the barriers to effective organizational communication requires that individual managers acknowledge the difficulties inherent in the communication process. Making relevant information explicit and remaining sensitive to how a particular communication will affect its receiver can minimize some of these difficulties. Effectively implementing MBO programs and OD can improve communication throughout an organization.

The recent developments in information technology have dramatically altered many aspects of organizational activity, especially interpersonal relationships. Managers should attempt to compensate in the work environment for the isolation of those who work at computer terminals.

1. Why is effective communication important to the manager?

2. What part does communication play in enabling managers to fulfill the three roles identified by Mintzberg?

3. List the eight elements in the expanded communication model.

4. What are some of the considerations involved in choosing the correct channel for one's message?

5. What is "noise" in a communication system?

6. Describe the common barriers to effective interpersonal communication. How may these barriers be overcome?

7. How does Gibb describe the behaviors leading to effective communication? What behaviors lead to open communication?

8. What four factors influence the effectiveness of organizational communication? How do they exert this influence?

9. What are the functions of vertical communication? How is accurate and complete vertical communication hindered?

10. What is the function of the grapevine? Why do managers sometimes use the grapevine to convey information? What are some possible grapevine chains according to Keith Davis? Which chain is most likely to be used in organizations?

11. How may the barriers to organizational communication be overcome?

12. What are some of the consequences of the use of computer communications technology in the workplace?

Notes

1. Peter C. Gronn, "Talk as Work: The Accomplishment of School Administration," *Administrative Science Quarterly* 28, no. 1 (March 1983):1–21.

2. Rosemary Stewart, *Managers and Their Jobs* (London: Macmillan, 1967), pp. 72–73.

3. Henry Mintzberg, "The Manager's Job: Folklore and Fact," *Harvard Business Review* 53, no. 4 (July–August 1975):49–61. See also Henry Mintzberg, *The Nature of Managerial Work* (New York: Harper & Row, 1973).

4. F. E. X. Dance, "The 'Concept' of Communication," *Journal of Communication* 20, no. 2 (June 1970):201–210.

5. Lyman W. Porter and Karlene H. Roberts, "Communication in Organizations," in Marvin D. Dunnette, ed., *Handbook of Industrial and Occupational Psychology*, 2d ed. (New York: Wiley, 1983), pp. 1553–1589.

6. Our discussion is based on Linda M. Micheli, Frank V. Cespedes, Donald Byker, and Thomas J. C. Raymond, *Managerial Communication* (Glenview, Ill.: Scott, Foresman, 1984), pp. 186–201; and Judson Smith and Janice Orr, *Designing and Developing Business Communications Programs That Work* (Glenview, Ill.: Scott, Foresman, 1985), pp. 4–6. See also Norman B. Sigband and Arthur H. Bell, *Communication for Management and Business* (Glenview, Ill.: Scott, Foresman, 1986); Courtland L. Bovee and John V. Thill, *Business Communications Today* (New York: Random House, 1986); and Robert W. Rasberry and Laura F. Lemoine, *Managerial Communications* (Boston: Kent, 1986).

7. See Paul R. Timm and Christopher G. Jones, *Business Communication: Getting Results* (Englewood Cliffs, N.J.: Prentice-Hall, 1983), p. 5.

8. Larry R. Smeltzer and John L. Waltman, *Managerial Communication: A Strategic Approach* (New York: Wiley, 1984), p. 4.

9. Ibid., p. 41.

10. Ibid., p. 5.

11. Ibid.

12. See James L. Gibson, John M. Ivancevich, and James H. Donnelly, Jr., *Organizations: Behavior, Structure, Processes*, 5th ed. (Dallas: Business Publications, 1985), p. 535.

13. Smeltzer and Waltman, *Managerial Communication*, p. 189.

14. Harold J. Leavitt and Ronald A. H. Mueller, "Some Effects of Feedback on Communicating," *Human Relations* 4, no. 4 (November 1951):401–410.

15. Harold J. Leavitt, *Managerial Psychology*, 4th ed. (Chicago: University of Chicago Press, 1978),

pp. 117–126. See also John T. Samaras, "Two-Way Communication Practices for Managers," *Personnel Journal* 59, no. 8 (August 1980):645–648.

16. C. Glenn Pearce, Ross Figgins, and Steven P. Golen, *Principles of Business Communication: Theory, Application, and Technology* (New York: Wiley, 1984), p. 516.

17. Ibid., p. 516.

18. Ibid., p. 524.

19. See Robert Rosenthal, *Experimenter Effects in Behavioral Research* (New York: Appleton-Century-Crofts, 1966); Robert Rosenthal and Donald B. Rubin, "Interpersonal Expectancy Effects: The First 345 Studies," *Behavioral and Brain Sciences* 1, no. 3 (September 1978):377–415; Dov Eden, "Self-Fulfilling Prophecy as a Management Tool: Harnessing Pygmalion," *Academy of Management Review* 9, no. 1 (January 1984):64–73. For a critique challenging this series of studies, see Harry L. Miller, "Hard Realities and Soft Social Science," *Public Interest*, no. 59 (Spring 1980):67–82.

20. Pearce et al., *Principles of Business Communication*, pp. 529, 533–534.

21. W. Charles Redding, *The Corporate Manager's Guide to Better Communication* (Glenview, Ill.: Scott, Foresman, 1984), pp. 74–75.

22. Pearce et al., *Principles of Business Communication*, p. 538.

23. Ibid., pp. 522–523.

24. Ibid., pp. 522, 524.

25. David V. Gibson and Barbara E. Mendleson, "Redundancy," *Journal of Business Communication* 21, no. 1 (Winter 1984):43–61, especially 52.

26. Micheli, Cespedes, Byker, and Raymond, *Managerial Communication,* p. 107.

27. Richard L. Weaver II, *Understanding Business Communication* (Englewood Cliffs, N.J.: Prentice-Hall, 1985), p. 108.

28. Jack R. Gibb, "Defensive Communication," *Journal of Communication* 11, no. 13 (September 1961):141–148.

29. Carl R. Rogers and F. J. Roethlisberger, "Barriers and Gateways to Communication," *Harvard Business Review* 30, no. 4 (July–August 1952):48.

30. See Raymond V. Lesikar, "A General Semantics Approach to Communication Barriers in Organizations," in Keith Davis, ed., *Organizational Behavior: A Book of Readings,* 5th ed. (New York: McGraw-Hill, 1977), pp. 336–337.

31. See Harold J. Leavitt, "Some Effects of Certain Communication Patterns on Group Performance," *Journal of Abnormal and Social Psychology* 46, no. 1 (January 1951):38–50. Our discussion is also based on H. Joseph Reitz, *Behavior in Organizations*, rev. ed. (Homewood, Ill.: Irwin, 1981); Gibson et al., *Organizations: Behavior, Structure, Processes*, pp. 544–545; Leavitt, *Managerial Psychology;* and Marvin E. Shaw, "Communication Networks," in Leonard Berkowitz, ed., *Advances in Experimental Social Psychology*, Vol. 1 (New York: Academic Press, 1964), pp. 111–147. See also Karlene H. Roberts and Charles O'Reilly III, "Some Correlations of Communication Roles in Organizations," *Academy of Management Journal* 22, no. 1 (March 1979):42–57.

32. Kenneth N. Wexley and Gary A. Yukl, *Organizational Behavior and Personnel Psychology,* rev. ed. (Homewood, Ill.: Irwin, 1984), pp. 80–83.

33. Michael J. Glauser, "Upward Information Flow in Organizations: Review and Conceptual Analysis," *Human Relations* 37, no. 8 (August 1984):613–643.

34. Porter and Roberts, "Communication in Organizations," pp. 1573–1574. See also Robert A. Snyder and James H. Morris, "Organizational Communication and Performance," *Journal of Applied Psychology* 69, no. 3 (August 1984):461–465.

35. Wexley and Yukl, *Organizational Behavior and Personnel Psychology*, pp. 82–83.

36. See also Robert E. Kaplan, "Trade Routes: The Manager's Network of Relationships," *Organizational Dynamics* 12, no. 4 (Spring 1984):37–52; and Eric M. Eisenberg, Peter R. Monge, and Katherine I. Miller, "Involvement in Communication Networks as a Predictor of Organizational Commitment," *Human Communication Research* 10, no. 2 (Winter 1983):179–201.

37. See Richard L. Simpson, "Vertical and Horizontal Communication in Formal Organizations," *Administrative Science Quarterly* 4, no. 2 (September 1959):188–196.

38. Keith Davis, "Grapevine Communication among Lower and Middle Managers," *Personnel Journal* 48, no. 4 (April 1969), pp. 269–272.

39. See Keith Davis, "Management Communication and the Grapevine," *Harvard Business Review* 31, no. 5 (September–October 1953):43–49; "Communication *within* Management," *Personnel* 31, no. 3 (November 1954):212–218; and "Cut Those Rumors Down to Size," *Supervisory Management,* June 1975, pp. 2–6.

40. Raymond V. Lesikar, *Business Communication: Theory and Application*, 5th ed. (Homewood, Ill.: Irwin, 1984), pp. 20–22.

41. Fritz Steele, "The Ecology of Executive Teams: A New View of the Top," *Organizational Dynamics* 11, no. 4 (Spring 1983):65–78.

42. See Elaine B. Kerr and Starr Roxanne Hiltz, *Computer-Mediated Communication Systems* (New York: Academic Press, 1982); and Robert Johansen and Christine Bullen, "What to Expect from Teleconferencing," *Harvard Business Review* 62, no. 2 (March–April 1984):164–174.

43. J. F. Rockart and M. S. Scott Morton, "Implications of Changes in Information Technology for Corporate Strategy," *Interfaces* 14, no. 1 (January–February 1984):87.

44. Steve Lambert, *Online: A Guide to America's Leading Information Services* (Bellevue, Wash.: Microsoft Press, 1985); and Rockart and Morton, "Implications of Changes in Information Technology for Corporate Strategy," pp. 87–88.

45. Rockart and Morton, "Implications of Changes in Information Technology for Corporate Strategy," pp. 92–93.

46. Ilan Salomon and Meira Salomon, "Telecommuting: The Employee's Perspective," *Technological Forecasting and Social Change* 25, no. 1 (February 1984):15–28; and Reagan M. Ramsower, *Telecommuting: The Organizational and Behavioral Effects of Working at Home* (Ann Arbor: UMI Research Press, 1985).

47. F. Warren Benton, *Execucomp: Maximum Management with the New Computers* (New York: Wiley, 1983), pp. 216–217.

48. E. More and R. K. Laird, "Modern Technology and Organizational Communication Implications for Management," *Journal of Information Science* 7, nos. 4–5 (1983):182.

CASE STUDY: The President and the Personnel Manager

Molecular Membranes is a small high-tech firm owned by its president, Ross Ellenshaw, and his family. It manufactures delicate osmotic membranes that perform crucial functions in sophisticated sensing instruments. The personnel manager, Anita Weiss, was, at the time of this case, the only woman holding a supervisory or managerial position in the company. She had been with Molecular Membranes since its founding, and she and her husband had been close friends of Ellenshaw and his wife for many years.

However, for about the last two years, Weiss and Ellenshaw had found themselves drifting apart. Their socializing off the job had virtually ended, and job-related conferences between the two of them—formerly a frequent occurrence—had become a rare event. This state of affairs began when Ellenshaw, after prolonged soul-searching and study of contemporary management literature, had decided to effect a drastic change in management philosophy. With the active intervention of an academic counselor, the president had made strenuous efforts to convert the company from a paternalistic to a participative managerial style, extending to all levels of supervisors and employees. A central device for inducing this change was a program of high-level management conferences. These meetings, conducted by Ellenshaw with the academic consultant always present as a dominant contributor, were both frequent and lengthy. The basic theme was an effort to apply McGregor's famous Theory Y view of management.

During all this time, Weiss felt more and more alienated, in fact almost isolated, from the president and the other managers. No longer was Ellenshaw available for the cozy and frank conversations the two of them had enjoyed for years. On many occasions, Weiss felt like an outsider at management meetings. The other participants would spring "surprises" upon her and (allegedly) put her down as an old fogy ignorant of the latest management thinking. At the same time, however, it was her obligation as personnel manager to administer the old policies, since they were still incorporated in the company "bible"—the employees' manual. In short, Weiss perceived herself as occupying an impossible role, caught between conflicting demands and subjected to confusing or contradictory messages from the president.

At the joint request of Ellenshaw and Weiss, and with the consent of the academic consultant, a specialist in organizational communication was brought in to assist them in finding ways to reestablish "open" communication. One important technique introduced by the specialist was having them exchange detailed written documents setting forth with complete candor their perceptions of all the factors leading up to the present difficulty.

In these documents, explained the specialist, brutal honesty was essential. The "criss-cross" comparison of perceptions was, understandably, a nerve-racking experience for both Weiss and Ellenshaw. Below are excerpts from Weiss's statement. Keep in mind that these represent only her perceptions; those of Ellenshaw were different.

> During the time when we've *both* been working toward a participatory method of management, we have been saddled with an authoritarian Policy Manual—one that dictates that the Personnel Manager has many requirements and responsibilities—in conflict with participatory management. A manual that *I* have had to administer until it can be replaced. This has created a credibility gap for me.
>
> Since I was administering things, and still making a lot of authoritarian decisions as decreed by the Policy Manual, I was perceived as "inflexible." It's been a long and difficult experience for me, with no recognized structure for determining who makes which inputs.
>
> Perhaps I was wrong in declining the opportunity to attend those meetings with you. . . . But at the time I was trying to be sensitive to your efforts to establish a new role of leadership for yourself.
>
> Uncertainty and ambiguity concerning my role were a problem for me. Sometimes I was only a sounding board, but at other times I was providing the inputs and making specific recommendations. I felt that the resolution of *top-level* people-relations problems were beyond my expertise. . . . How do I keep communication lines "open" without becoming a tattletale in the middle (right now I'm the one both sides are talking to)?
>
> I resented having my research, my ideas . . . filtered through someone else to you, when I used to work directly with you before. I now perceive conflict in almost every aspect of those working relationships—generated, no doubt, by the total *system* as much as by any *individuals*.

Source: From *The Corporate Manager's Guide to Better Communicating* by W. Charles Redding. Copyright © 1984 by Scott, Foresman and Company. Reprinted by permission.

Case Questions
1. Why had communication broken down between Weiss and Ellenshaw?
2. How could Ellenshaw have prevented problems with Weiss? How could Weiss have better adapted to the new managerial climate?
3. How might the written documents overcome the barriers to communication between them?
4. Has Weiss's credibility been irretrievably damaged?
5. What do you think is the ultimate solution to this communication problem?

19 ORGANIZATIONAL CAREERS AND INDIVIDUAL DEVELOPMENT

Upon completing this chapter you should be able to:

1. Describe early career experiences and dilemmas that can influence adjustment to an organization and later career success.
2. Discuss some causes of stress in organizations and explain how stress can be managed.
3. Explain the relationship between the life cycle and the evolution of careers over time.
4. Explain what is meant by the terms "career concepts" and "career anchors."
5. Describe how an individual's position within the organization can change over time.
6. Explain what is meant by a "career plateau."
7. Discuss the various strategies and techniques that can be used to manage one's career.
8. Discuss mentoring and the special problems faced by dual career couples and women in management.

In recent years there has been a growing interest in the study of managerial careers and in helping individuals understand how their careers will evolve. It has become apparent that many individuals experience similar events and problems at particular times during their careers—for example, when deciding which organization to join, starting work, changing jobs, and so on. Because these events and problems are somewhat predictable, it is possible for individuals to prepare for them beforehand. Thus, individuals who are knowledgeable about what they can expect may be in a better position than others to take an active role in managing their own careers.

In the other chapters of this book (particularly chapter 12), we have been concerned with how individuals manage *other people's* careers or the organization's resources. In this chapter, the emphasis is on the *reader's* own career. We will describe the influence of early organizational experiences on the individual's future performance and satisfaction; the early career dilemmas a young manager is likely to encounter; the stages through which careers evolve; and, finally, how individuals can take an active role in managing their careers so that they can realize their career goals.

Early Organizational Career Experiences

The Formation of Expectations

Many young people are challenged and excited by their first weeks on a new job. For others, this early period is frustrating and disappointing. Some difficulties may be due to the individual's lack of information and preparation. Often, unpleasant surprises result from the unrealistic expectations aroused during the recruiting process. (See chapter 12.) Recruiters and interviewers inflate the attractiveness of a job to secure a sufficient number of candidates in the applicant pool. Applicants overstate their abilities and understate their needs to improve their chances of getting the job; in addition, they may fail to research the organization to which they are applying. Thus, each side offers a mixed bag of truths, half truths, and concealments—all likely to create problems when those hired begin to work. New employees may soon learn that the initial job is not as challenging as they had expected, that their treatment will not be special after all, and that their ability to affect the organization is nowhere near what they had been led to believe.

The problem of inflated expectations can exist for anyone, but it may be especially severe for those young MBAs who have done particularly well in their studies and/or have graduated from prestigious business schools. They have become accustomed to fast, regular (and usually favorable) feedback on their performance and to the challenging atmosphere of the university. They expect to find the same conditions on their new job. But once on the job, they perceive themselves as just additional cogs in a wheel—their skills and abilities unused and unsought.[1]

An individual whose expectations are inconsistent with the realities of a new job is not likely to develop an effective and satisfying work role in the organization.

Edgar Schein found that almost 75 percent of one sample of MBA graduates changed jobs at least once over a five-year period.[2] He also found that within five years most companies lose over half of the college graduates they hire. Schein attributes this high turnover to the clash between the graduates' expectations and the realities of the organization. Similarly, in their study of a small group of American business school graduates working in South America, John D. Aram and James A. F. Stoner found that job continuation and satisfaction were related to how closely the graduates' initial expectations matched the realities of their jobs.[3]

The Reality Shock Syndrome. Apparently, for many individuals the disparity between initial job expectations and the hard realities of the job can be unpleasant and disconcerting. This clash between high expectations and frustrating on-the-job experiences has been characterized by Douglas T. Hall as "reality shock."[4] Hall suggests that reality shock produces a *syndrome of unused potential* in new job recruits. Six factors contribute to this *reality shock syndrome*, according to Hall:

1. *Low initial challenge.* Recruiters often overstate the promise and challenge of the first job in order to attract the most promising candidates. Most organizations, however, start new employees on comparatively easy projects and only gradually increase the difficulty of the projects as the recruits gain training and experience. Thus, the new employees' expectations of early job challenge are not fulfilled.
2. *Low self-actualization satisfaction.* The recruiter may promise growth and self-fulfillment on the job; often, however, the organization rewards conformity to its customs and ways of doing things. Recruits who desire more independence may choose to look for another opportunity soon.
3. *Lack of performance appraisal.* Most organizations promise new recruits regular feedback on their performance. Most managers favor such feedback and believe that performance appraisal is necessary to motivate and train new employees. However, many managers perform the appraisal task poorly or neglect it entirely. Young recruits are left in a state of confusion about how well they are doing and what they need to do to improve.
4. *Unrealistically high aspirations.* New college graduates and MBAs begin work eager to apply the modern skills and techniques they have been taught. Many such graduates believe that they already have the ability to perform at managerial levels well above their entry position. In fact, they are generally unskilled in the practical applications of the techniques they have learned in school, and their high aspirations and "classroom theories" are often resented by others in the organization. Superiors will generally not appreciate learning that a skill they have been using is outdated. The fact that others do not rate them quite as highly as they rate themselves comes as a rude awakening to many young employees.
5. *Inability to create challenge.* When experienced individuals are given unchallenging jobs, they can often create challenge for themselves—by doing the job in a new and better way, for example, or by asking for additional assignments. Recent graduates, however, accustomed to having challenging assignments presented to them, may have little or no experience in creating challenge on their own; they may therefore accept dull assignments passively.
6. *Threats to superiors.* Often, newcomers fresh out of college or graduate school bring more technical expertise to a job than their superiors possess and may also

be entering the organization at a much higher salary than the superior initially received. For these reasons, the young recruits may be regarded as threats, and the relationship between superiors and the new employees can become somewhat strained.

A particularly powerful cause of the reality shock syndrome is the realization by young employees that they must conform to the established procedures and practices of the organization far more than they had anticipated. Each organization attempts to "socialize" its new employees to its values, norms, and behavior patterns. A conservative organization, for example, may have fairly strict dress codes; an aggressively managed organization may have comparatively high sales quotas; a rigidly structured organization may limit the amount of communication between departments. To get ahead in the organization, or even to fit comfortably within it, new employees soon discover they must conform to these previously established patterns. New entrants may also discover that many of their ideas and innovations are strongly resisted. Organizations are usually much slower to change than young recruits expect, and even good suggestions are frequently ignored. Given these realities, it is hardly surprising that so many newcomers leave their first jobs a few months or a few years after they have been hired.[5]

The Realistic Job Preview. To create more realistic expectations, some organizations give applicants and new employees a *realistic job preview (RJP)*, which describes positive *and* negative aspects of the position. For example, recruits might be told that they will be supervised quite closely in their first job, rather than being given a large amount of independence, or that some aspects of their jobs will be boring. James A. Breaugh has described four ways that RJPs may improve performance and reduce the turnover caused by reality shock:[6]

1. By creating more realistic expectations, RJPs reduce the chances that employees will later be disappointed.
2. By letting candidates know what types of problems are expected, RJPs may improve their ability to resolve the problems.
3. By creating an atmosphere of honesty, RJPs may improve employees' commitment to the organization because they feel that they made informed decisions, rather than being tricked or misled.
4. By describing jobs realistically, RJPs increase the chances that inappropriate candidates will turn down jobs that would not meet their needs.

Studies of the effectiveness of RJPs have yielded mixed results. Some indicate that RJPs produce more realistic job expectations and decreased job turnover,[7] while others find that they have no significant impact.[8] This lack of clarity results in part from the difficulty of conducting such research in organizational settings and also from variations in the ways RJPs are actually conducted. Whether or not formal previews produce the benefits claimed in some research, it is probably desirable for recruiters and interviewers to try to give a balanced picture of the job and the organization when they are negotiating with potential recruits.

Early Job Experiences

Three aspects of the individual's early job experiences seem especially relevant to subsequent career success: the amount of challenge in the first assignment, the

"Welcome aboard, Mr. Ryker. For a while you'll be a little frog in a big pond, but we need little frogs."

Drawing by Weber; © 1981 The New Yorker Magazine, Inc.

actions of the first supervisor, and how well the individual fits into the organizational culture.

Initial Job Assignment. The importance of the initial job assignment has been affirmed by a number of research studies. One study of 1,000 recent college graduates hired by a large manufacturing company found that about half had left the company within a three-year period. Those graduates who had left the company, as well as those who had remained, cited the lack of job challenge as the major cause of disenchantment with the firm.[9] In the study discussed in chapter 12, David E. Berlew and Douglas T. Hall followed the careers of 62 junior executives over the first five years of employment.[10] The researchers found that the degree of challenge the junior executives were given in their first jobs correlated closely with how successfully they performed subsequent assignments and with how rapidly their careers advanced.

Berlew and Hall suggest that the successful accomplishment of challenging tasks causes individuals to internalize high performance standards, which are then applied to future work tasks. In addition, successful task accomplishment causes the organization's expectations to increase so that individuals are given more difficult and challenging assignments. Those who are given unchallenging jobs, on the other hand, neither internalize high standards nor receive as much recognition for their work. Yet, despite the evident importance of challenging job assignments, many organizations continue to provide their new employees with relatively routine initial assignments.

Actions of the First Supervisor. The influence of the first supervisor on a new employee's subsequent performance has also been noted by a number of researchers.[11] For the newcomer, the first supervisor embodies the virtues and defects of the organization itself. If the supervisor is found wanting by the new employee, the organization may be regarded as an undesirable place to work. Nevertheless, many companies often entrust the handling of incoming graduates to men and women who have not been trained for the task and who are not especially good managers.

Special training, patience, and insight are required by supervisors of new employees for a number of reasons. First, new employees are likely to make a higher-than-average number of mistakes; impatient supervisors may overreact to these mistakes and weaken the new employees' self-image and enthusiasm. Second, insecure supervisors often control new employees too closely—either to keep them from making mistakes or to keep them from appearing too successful or knowledgeable. The result is that the employees are not permitted to learn from their mistakes and may not achieve recognition for their successes.

Finally, and most important, the expectations of supervisors affect new employee's attitudes and performance, since the employees will tend to fulfill those expectations regardless of their actual ability.[12] If, for example, the supervisor looks upon the newcomers as potentially outstanding performers, he or she will treat them accordingly, thereby motivating them to do their best—and the supervisor's expectation will tend to be confirmed. Conversely, a supervisor who expects newcomers to perform poorly will communicate these expectations directly or indirectly, thereby triggering the indifferent performance that fulfills the negative expectations. For these reasons, supervisors play a major role in influencing the early performance and future career progress of new employees.

How Individuals Fit in the Organizational Culture. As noted in earlier chapters, every organization has a culture—a set of shared understandings that determine the organization's style of work, attitude toward employees, and approach to how tasks should be accomplished. In one job, a newcomer may feel comfortable from the outset; he or she speaks the same language co-workers do and gets good responses to early efforts and initiatives. In another job, a clash of styles is evident from the beginning or soon emerges. The congruence between individual style and an organization's culture has an early impact that may color the individual's whole experience with the organization. It helps determine how well employees are likely to perform, how much they will enjoy working in the organization, and whether they are likely to want to stay.

A fit that is initially less than perfect does not necessarily mean that a person is in the wrong job. The individual will make adjustments as he or she is socialized into the organization's practices. Indeed, adjustments of this sort are likely even when the employee and the organization are very compatible. If the initial fit is good, these adjustments will tend to be small and painless for both the individual and his or her co-workers. On the other hand, attempts to make major changes can be traumatic and are relatively unlikely to be successful. Of course, the organization may also make adjustments to accommodate the individual, but such adjustments are normally small in magnitude and slow in coming.[13]

Early Career Dilemmas

Based on a review of the literature and on an analysis of his own interviews with hundreds of young managers, Ross A. Webber has pinpointed three classes of career problems that typically plague managers early in their working lives: political insensitivity and passivity, loyalty dilemmas, and personal anxiety.[14] Webber suggests that awareness of these problems may keep their potentially damaging consequences to a minimum.

Political Insensitivity and Passivity

As we saw in chapter 11, the struggle for and exercise of power are inevitable and probably essential parts of organizational life. Managers *seek* power because with power they can more easily achieve personal and organizational goals. Managers *exercise* power in order to influence their subordinates to perform effectively and in order to protect the integrity of their units.

Forming political alliances is also an integral part of organizational life. Managers who "play politics" well—that is, who skillfully gain the cooperation of their peers and superiors and who utilize that cooperation to achieve organizational objectives—help their units and the total organization perform well. People who belong to powerful political alliances can focus their energies and make decisions more effectively. A politically allied manager, for example, can get information quickly from the informal network of colleagues and can speed up the decision-making process. The use of such options helps managers do their jobs better.

Like other sources of power, however, political alliances can be used destructively. Forming a political alliance to gain dominance over another person and thereby diminish his or her influence is unlikely to benefit the manager or the organization in the long run. Using people as pawns is self-defeating because it produces resistance or passivity.[15] As our discussion of McClelland and Burnham's work in chapter 11 indicated, successful managers influence others in the interests of the organization, not for self-aggrandizement.[16]

When used appropriately, organizational politics produces benefits and should not be avoided. But young business school graduates are often insensitive to this aspect of the organization. They may not distinguish between healthy organizational politics and the unhealthy manipulation of power. Furthermore, the texts, lectures, and case studies on which their education is based often create the impression that organizational problems are always solved *rationally*—that objectively sound solutions, for example, are always accepted on the basis of their merits. In reality, supervisors may ignore the suggestions of newcomers because they have not had time to gain confidence in the subordinate's judgment or because they see such suggestions as threats to their position.

Confronted with these realities, according to Webber, new employees frequently become passive or withdrawn. Instead of seeking to understand their surroundings, forming their own political connections, and beginning to build a power base, young managers often concentrate on their narrow specialties and permit their careers to drift.

As new employees begin to develop their political awareness and contacts, they should build effective working relationships with a broad base of people who will help them do their jobs, rather than commit themselves to a single alliance or powerful individual. Young managers who learn to accept organizational realities as they are, says Webber, can adapt more quickly to the organization and begin to manage their own careers early.

Loyalty Dilemmas

When new employees enter the organization, they are confronted with various demands on their loyalty from their superiors. Demands for loyalty are legitimate, because a certain amount of compliance is necessary to keep the organization functioning. However, definitions of loyalty differ and loyalty demands often conflict with reality as perceived by a young subordinate; moreover, if taken to an extreme, meeting some definitions of loyalty can damage both the subordinate and the organization. Webber describes five common ways that loyalty can be defined by a superior:

1. *"Obey me."* Managers have a right to expect that their legitimate directives will be carried out. Disobedience if carried too far will prevent the organization from reaching its objectives. However, unquestioning obedience on the part of subordinates can lead to ineffective actions. Subordinates who know, for example, that a superior's instructions are inappropriate but who proceed to obey them out of loyalty are doing their superior and organization more harm than good. Sometimes, loyalty may even call for disobedience of an order that is unethical, or made in haste or anger. To a large extent, the Watergate break-in and cover-up occurred because subordinates were excessively obedient to illegitimate higher-level directives.

2. *"Protect me and don't make me look bad."* Managers are responsible for and ultimately judged by the actions of their subordinates. They therefore have a right to expect that subordinates consider their superiors' reputation as they carry out their work activities and interact with those outside their organizational units. Sometimes, however, this loyalty demand leads subordinates to avoid taking necessary risks or to cover up mistakes.

3. *"Work hard."* In the eyes of many managers, the best proof of loyalty to the organization is the willingness to work long and hard. However, if unrealistic standards of performance are demanded, morale may drop and subordinates may feel overburdened.

4. *"Be successful."* "Get the job done no matter what" and "I don't care what you do as long as the bottom line shows a profit" are often implicit (if not explicit) in managers' instructions to their subordinates. This may cause subordinates to feel a conflict between organizational loyalty and their own ethical codes. If they disobey instructions, their careers might suffer; if they violate their ethics (or the law), guilt or scandal might result.

5. *"Tell me the truth."* It is obviously important for superiors to be told about problems in their units—not only so they can take steps to deal with the problems, but also so they can prepare to deal with their own superiors. All too often, however, reporting a problem—especially when it is in the subordinate's area of responsibility—may cause the subordinate to be blamed or punished. In such situations, newcomers often learn to apply their loyalty selectively, putting self-protection before the needs of their superiors or the organization. As a consequence, failures may not be reported until it is too late to minimize their consequences.

Personal Anxiety

As their assignments grow more challenging, and salary increases and promotions signal recognition of their efforts, young managers derive greater satisfaction from their jobs. Webber suggests that, paradoxically, they also begin to feel anxiety about their growing commitment to the organization. The independence and integrity they valued as students and young managers sometimes conflict with the increasing demands made on them in higher-level positions. The manner in which they resolve this conflict will play an important role in determining how their careers unfold.

Edgar Schein has described three ways in which an individual can respond to the organization's efforts to enforce compliance with its values and expectations:[17]

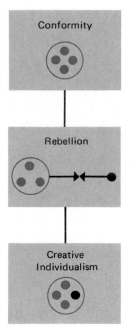

1. *Conformity:* The individual completely accepts all the organization's norms and values. Total conformity represents a loss for both the individual and the organization. The individual loses his or her sense of identity and initiative, while the organization loses access to the diversity of opinion and ideas that its long-term health requires.

2. *Rebellion:* The individual completely rejects the organization's values and expectations. The rebellious, extremely individualistic person either causes the organization to change or, more likely, voluntarily leaves the organization or is dismissed.

3. *Creative individualism:* The individual accepts the organization's important, constructive values and neglects those that are trivial or inappropriate. Obviously, this distinction is difficult to make. The individual's decision about which norms are important may not be accurate, and the individual may be criticized for violating even unimportant norms. Moreover, with each lateral transfer or promotion, new norms come into play while others lose their relevance. (The values of one's superior in a research department, for example, are likely to be somewhat different from those of one's superior in the sales department.) An individual will therefore have to make many choices about which values to accept over the course of his or her career. Nevertheless, the benefits of creative individualism are high: The individual maintains his or her integrity, independence, and personal sense of satisfaction; and the organization has access to the fresh ideas and objective viewpoints it needs.

Role Conflict

Daniel Katz and Robert L. Kahn have discussed the *role conflict* individuals experience when they are confronted with two or more incompatible demands. Katz and Kahn have identified six types of role conflict that they believe are fairly common in organizations.[18]

1. *Intrasender conflict* occurs when a single supervisor presents a subordinate with a set of incompatible orders or expectations. For example, a division manager orders a purchasing agent to buy materials immediately at a price that requires prior home office authorization and then warns the agent not to violate the rulebook regulations.

2. *Intersender conflict* arises when orders or expectations from one person or group clash with the expectations or orders from other persons or groups—for example, when a superior orders a supervisor to speed up production, and the work crew makes clear that any attempt to comply with this order will lead to serious trouble in the ranks.

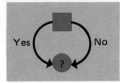

Intrasender

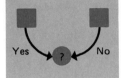

Intersender

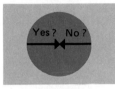

Inter-role

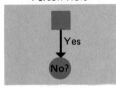

Person-Role

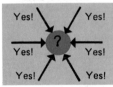

Role Overload

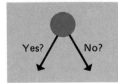

Role Ambiguity

3. *Inter-role conflict* occurs when the different roles played by the same person give rise to conflicting demands. In their roles as spouse and parent, for example, workers may be pressed to share child-care activities at home; but in their roles as loyal workers, the same individuals may have to put in a considerable amount of overtime to get their work done. This particular type of inter-role conflict is extremely common and often creates great tension both on the job and at home, especially in two-career families.[19]

4. *Person-role conflict* occurs when on-the-job role requirements run counter to the individual's needs or values. An executive ordered to bribe a domestic or foreign official, for example, might find the assignment completely unethical. Yet his or her desire for career success might make it difficult to refuse to carry out the order.

5. In *role overload conflict,* the individual is confronted with orders and expectations from a number of sources that cannot be completed within the given time and quality limits. Should quality be sacrificed in the interests of time? Should some tasks be carried out and others ignored? If so, which tasks should get priority? Dilemmas like these are a constant part of the manager's job.

6. *Role ambiguity* occurs when the individual is provided with insufficient or unclear information about his or her responsibilities. The individual is therefore uncertain about what he or she is supposed to do. Role ambiguity is often experienced by new managers who are given a set of duties and responsibilities without being told exactly how to carry them out.

Stress

Stress is created for many organization members by the conflicts they feel between their independence and their commitment to the organization, organizational pressures for conformity, day-to-day demands of the workplace, and various forms of role conflict. Young managers may be particularly at risk—some evidence indicates that young people in general are more vulnerable to stress than older employees.[20] For everyone, however, stress is simply a fact of organizational life. Fortunately, many of the causes and effects of stress are subject to change when they are appropriately managed.[21]

Causes of Stress. What exactly do we mean by *stress*? One widely accepted definition is offered by McGrath: " . . . there is a potential for stress when an environmental situation is perceived as presenting a demand which threatens to exceed the person's capabilities and resources for meeting it."[22] The sources of pressure and tension that cause stress are known as *stressors.*

Different jobs vary greatly in the amount of stress they generate. Physicians, office managers, and supervisors, for example, must endure a good deal of stress. Craft workers, farm laborers, and college professors, on the other hand, face relatively little stress.[23] People also differ in what causes them to experience stress, how severely they feel it, and how they react to it. Before a major exam, many students feel some stress, but some feel virtually none. Of those who feel stress, some will feel it only slightly, whereas others may be nearly incapacitated by it. Of those who feel it severely, some will be able to calm themselves using various kinds of relaxation techniques, but others will be unable to control it.

When most of us imagine a stressful environment, we envision a harried office worker, the in-box overflowing with work to be done, trying simultaneously to answer the phone, explain to the boss why everything is late, and write a report. This picture is not inaccurate—role overload is a major cause of stress at work. There are two kinds of overload. *Quantitative overloading* occurs when a person has more work than he or she can complete in a given time. *Qualitative overloading* occurs when the employee lacks the skills or abilities needed to complete the job satisfactorily. *Underloading* can also be a problem—a person who does not have enough to do faces boredom and monotony, which are also quite stressful.

In addition to role conflicts and over- and underloading, a variety of aspects of the work environment can cause stress. These include:

· *Responsibility for others.* **Those who must work with other people, motivate them, and make decisions that will affect their careers experience more stress than those who do not have such responsibilities.**

· *Lack of participation in decisions.* **People who feel that they are not involved in decisions that influence their jobs experience relatively high levels of stress.**

· *Performance evaluations or appraisals.* **Having one's performance evaluated can be very stressful, especially when it affects one's job and income.**

· *Working conditions.* **Crowded, noisy, or otherwise uncomfortable working conditions can be a source of stress.**

· *Change within an organization.* **Stress can result from any major change within an organization—an alteration in company policy, a reorganization, or a change in leadership, for example.**

Effects of Stress. Stress can have serious consequences for both our health and our work performance. In terms of health, the current belief among many medical practitioners is that 50 to 70 percent of all physical illnesses are related to stress. The link between stress and heart disease is well known. High levels of stress are also associated with diabetes, ulcers, high blood pressure, and arteriosclerosis. Stress can cause depression, irritation, anxiety, fatigue, lowered self-esteem, and reduced job satisfaction. Sustained over a long enough period, stress can lead to attempts to escape through the use of drugs or alcohol, which can lead, in turn, to deterioration of job performance. It may also lead to *burnout,* which has been defined as a state of mind resulting from prolonged exposure to intense emotional stress and involving three major components: physical, emotional, and mental exhaustion.[24]

Although these potentially debilitating aspects of stress have been thoroughly and repeatedly demonstrated in many research studies, it has also been observed that not everyone experiences them. Salvatore R. Maddi and Suzanne C. Kobasa investigated the factors causing some people to be exhausted and drained by stressful events and others to be stimulated and challenged by them.[25] The ability to handle stress, they found, was a function of four characteristics:

· **Personal style and personality (how one tended to perceive, interpret, and respond to stressful events).**

· **Social supports (the extent to which family, friends, co-workers, and others provided encouragement and emotional support during stressful events).**

· **Constitutional predisposition (how robust and healthy one's body seemed to be in terms of in-born physical construction).**

· **Health practices (the extent to which one stayed in good physical condition through exercise and avoiding destructive behaviors like smoking).**

In their research, the most important factor by far was a personality dimension they called "hardiness." Individuals high in hardiness were *committed* to their work and life rather than being alienated from them, had a sense of control rather than powerlessness when confronted with problems, and interpreted change and problems as challenges rather than as threats.

These three characteristics of commitment, control, and challenge led the individuals high in hardiness to think about stressful events in optimistic ways and to act decisively toward them—thus changing them in a less stressful direction. This *transformational coping* process served them well in managing their organizations and at the same time reduced the likelihood of illness in both the short and long run. Individuals low in hardiness, on the other hand, tended to think pessimistically about stressful events and took evasive action to avoid contact with them. In doing so, they were less effective managerially and much more likely to experience health problems.

Managing Stress. Effective management of stress occurs on two levels: the organizational and the individual. On the organizational level, good management helps reduce stressors to reasonable levels, while poor management often increases them. Changes can also be made in organizational structure and the nature of specific jobs. Benefits may result from:

· **Decentralization of authority, which reduces feelings of helplessness among employees**
· **Adjusting reward systems so that performance appraisals are viewed as fair and reasonable**
· **Allowing employees to participate in making decisions that will affect them**[26]
· **Improving and broadening lines of communication**
· **Enlarging jobs so that they include more varied activities**
· **Enriching jobs by giving employees more responsibility for planning and directing their own work**

On an individual basis, stress can often be reduced by managing one's own job and work situation so one does not get overwhelmed. Some managers, for example, feel obliged to accept every task that is offered to them, even when other people in the organization could do some of them just as effectively. Other managers dislike delegating authority, assuming enormous burdens while their subordinates have trouble keeping busy. To be most productive, however, managers should take advantage of all available resources and avoid undertaking more work than they can handle. Careful planning for periods of peak work load is also valuable.

In addition to reducing the number of stressors in one's work, one can also seek to reduce the effects of the stressors that remain. Probably the most important way to reduce the negative effects of stress is to develop the habit of viewing problems optimistically and acting decisively toward them—experiencing commitment, control, and challenge rather than alienation, powerlessness, and threat. Although Maddi and Kobasa refer to hardiness as a "personality" characteristic—and personality is notoriously difficult to change—they are optimistic about people's ability to increase their hardiness and offer some specific suggestions for doing so. Similar approaches are used in *coping skills training*, programs in which people learn to recognize and cope with situations that cause them to feel helpless.[27]

Improving physical fitness is one step in handling stress. People who exercise and strengthen their cardiovascular systems and increase their endurance are less susceptible to illnesses caused by stress. As the connection between health and physical fitness has become clear, many companies have added exercise rooms or entire gymnasiums to their facilities.

Training in relaxation techniques can also diminish the effects of stress. *Relaxation training* is a popular method in which people learn how to relax their muscles—for example, starting with the feet and working toward the head. Deep breathing can also lower tension. Another technique is *meditation,* in which individuals assume a comfortable position, close their eyes, and attempt to clear all disturbing thoughts from their minds. Finally, *biofeedback* techniques help people learn how to detect and control physical changes (such as high blood pressure) that may be linked to stress. Occupational stress management programs using techniques such as these hold a good deal of promise for helping people handle stress on the job.

Careers Over Time

In this section we will help readers look ahead to future events in their careers. For at least two reasons, students and managers are often intrigued by theories, books, and articles on the evolution of careers over time. First, each of us has a career, and we can place ourselves at some stage or point in the various career models. We can consider how well the particular model describes our past experiences and behaviors and contemplate what the model implies for our future. If we accept the model, we can utilize it as a tool in planning our future. If we reject it, we can use it as a springboard for creating our own perspective, one that better corresponds to our own past experiences and our view of ourselves and the world. Second, the models can help us to understand others in our lives—bosses, co-workers, subordinates, parents, siblings, spouses, friends, and so on—and to manage our relationships with them.

In this section, we consider first how lives and careers evolve over time. We focus on the predictable life and career events experienced by most (but not all) individuals. Then we examine the themes and patterns that may emerge in our careers and that can help us manage our working lives. Finally, we consider the career-related roles and events that occur within organizations. Thus, as we move through this section, we gradually narrow our focus from broad life-stage issues to career patterns that may or may not be organizationally based to events that are determined by factors within organizations.[28]

Careers and the Life Cycle

There are a number of ways of looking at careers and the relationship between careers and the life cycle. Many theorists base their analysis of career events on psychoanalyst Erik Erikson's famous theory of life stages.[29] Erikson has divided the individual's life into eight stages, four in childhood and four in adulthood. In each stage the individual must successfully complete a "developmental task" before going on to the next stage.

Erikson's four adult stages are adolescence, young adulthood, adulthood, and maturity. (The childhood stages are not important for our discussion.) In *adolescence,* the individual's developmental task is to achieve an ego identity. The individual tries to reconcile the differences between his or her self-perception and how he or she is perceived by others. Also, the individual attempts to select an occupation in which his or her skills and interests can be utilized. In *young adulthood,* the individual attempts to develop satisfactory relationships or intimacy with others. This intimacy may involve a mate, a work group, or members of a common cause. In *adulthood,* the individual is concerned with what Erikson calls generativity—the guiding of the next generation. For example, the person passes on his or her knowledge and values to children or students, or sponsors younger colleagues in the workplace. Finally, in *maturity,* the person attempts to achieve ego integrity—the feeling that life has been satisfying and meaningful.[30]

The Levinson Model. An especially interesting perspective on the evolution of careers has been provided by Daniel Levinson and his colleagues.[31] Levinson studied a group of 40 men in four occupational groups (hourly workers in industry, business executives, university biologists, and novelists) between the ages of 35 and 45. The model that he derived from his study suggests that adult life involves a series of personal and career-related crises or transitions that occur in a fairly predictable sequence every five to seven years. (See fig. 19–1.)

· *Age 17–22: Early Adult Transition.* The individual must successfully manage to break away from family ties and become his or her own person. Individuals in this stage may still be at least partially dependent financially and emotionally on their parents. Those who gradually assert their independence can embark on their careers with some measure of self-sufficiency and confidence. Those who prolong parental ties, according to Levinson, often underperform in their careers.

· *Age 22–28: Entering the Adult World.* The individual has completed his or her education and begins to make commitments for the future. A life-style and career are selected. The individual becomes preoccupied, in Levinson's terms, with getting into the adult world. For those who are uncertain about the course they wish to follow, these years may be characterized by a dogged search for satisfactory career goals.

· *Age 28–33: Age-30 Transition.* Sometime during this period the individual reviews his or her progress toward previously established personal and career goals. If progress has been satisfactory, the individual may continue on the same track. If not, radical changes and turmoil may result. Moves to a new geographic location, job or career changes, or divorces are comparatively common during this stage. Even seemingly successful individuals may feel that they have only one last chance to break out of their established pattern and to do what they really want to do with their lives.

· *Age 33–40: Settling Down.* In these years, everything else is subordinated to job and career advancement. The individual strives toward becoming his or her own person. Social contacts and friendships are cut or minimized to enable the individual to concentrate on getting ahead on the job. In place of friends, a young manager may seek a "sponsor" in the company who will help steer him or her toward the top. Those individuals who are uncomfortable with authority figures may have a particularly difficult time searching for and relating to a higher-level sponsor.

- *Age 40–45: Mid-life Transition.* These years represent a second transitional period in which the individual again reviews career progress. The manager who is satisfied with the way his or her career has developed will continue to work effectively. In fact, a certain pride in one's achievements and experience begins to develop. But if progress has not lived up to early dreams and expectations, a "mid-life crisis" may result. Feelings of resentment, sadness, or frustration may cause an individual to lose his or her emotional equilibrium. The crisis may manifest itself in excessive drinking, in quitting the job and possibly wrecking one's managerial career, in flaunting a "middle-aged hippie" life-style, or in some other spectacular break with past behavior.
- *Age 45–50: Entering Middle Adulthood.* During this period, the reassessments conducted during the mid-life transition are consolidated. Individuals settle into their new or reconfirmed perspectives on their careers. They devote increased attention to old relationships and develop new ones more consciously. For some, this is a period of increased concern about decline and constraints at work and in their personal lives. For others this can be a highly satisfying period—with a sense of fulfillment and mature creativity.
- *Age 50–55: Age-50 Transition.* In this period, issues and tasks that were not satisfactorily handled in the earlier age-30 or mid-life transitions come up. Individuals who changed too little in the mid-life transition and built unsatisfactory life structures may experience crises. Levinson believes at least a moderate crisis will occur in either the mid-life or age-50 transition.
- *Age 55–60: Culmination of Middle Adulthood.* This period is a relatively stable one, similar to the settling down period of early adulthood. Whether or not their ambitions have been satisfied, individuals must accept the fact that their careers are coming to an end and begin to prepare for retirement. Individuals who have been able to rejuvenate themselves and enrich their lives can find great fulfillment in this period.
- *Age 60–65: Late Adult Transition.* During this period, most people retire, and retirement often has a significant effect on how one views oneself and is viewed by others. For many it is a period of deep reflection. Some people are only too happy to leave their careers, even when they enjoyed and felt successful in them. Others find the transition painful and attempt to avoid coming to grips with it.
- *Age 65 and older: Late Adulthood.* This is a period of evaluation and summing up. Freed of the responsibility of going to work, many people thoroughly enjoy their leisure and devote themselves to pursuits that they had to neglect when they were younger. Others are troubled by financial difficulties and health problems. Much remains to be learned about this period.

Levinson's work provides a valuable foundation for subsequent efforts to understand how people's lives and careers change as they get older. However, his career stages need to be carefully interpreted. He conducted his interviews in the late 1960s and early 1970s, and since that time the work force and the typical career pattern have changed considerably. For one thing, Levinson and his colleagues based their stages on a sample consisting entirely of men, so it is not known how accurately these stages reflect the career development of women. In his sample, the husband tended to be the sole breadwinner and the wife was a full-time homemaker and

FIGURE 19-1 CAREERS AND THE LIFE CYCLE

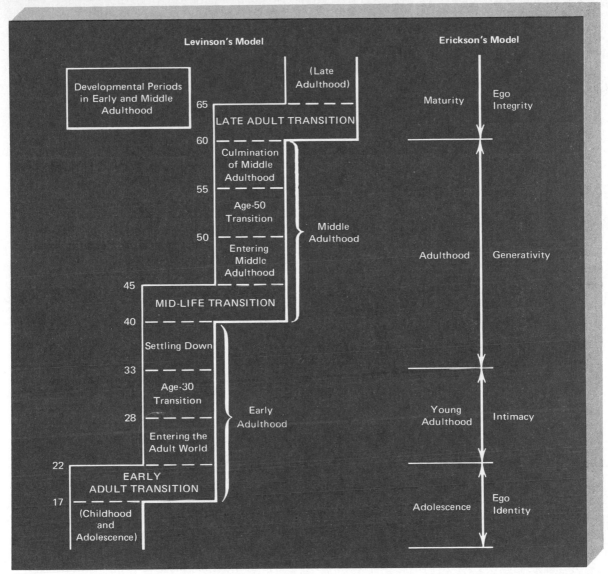

Sources: Levinson's Model from *The Seasons of a Man's Life*, by Daniel J. Levinson. Copyright © 1978 by Daniel J. Levinson. Reprinted by permission of The Sterling Lord Agency, Inc. Erickson's Model adapted from Erik H. Erikson, *Childhood and Society*, 2nd ed. (New York: Norton, 1963).

child-raiser. Therefore, it is not clear how well the career and life stages will fit even men in the future—as progressively more of them become members of dual-career couples.

Future research may show that the career patterns of men and women in dual-career couples will more closely resemble each other than they will those of men or women in one-earner families.

Career Patterns and Themes

Levinson's work presents a model of the career and life tasks to be addressed in different chronological periods in one's life. Michael J. Driver[32] and Edgar H. Schein[33] have suggested that careers can also be looked at in terms of broad *themes* or *patterns* that emerge over time. Their perspectives are concerned with how individuals' abilities, interests, and desires influence their subsequent career patterns.

Driver's Career Concepts. Many of us share certain assumptions about the nature of careers. We assume, first, that careers involve working in an organization; second, that an individual will attempt to move up in the organization, acquiring more influence and a larger income; and third, that the person's ultimate goal is to head the organization.

This stereotypical view of the most common type of career does have some validity. It is true that many people hope to climb the organizational ladder and that many would love to keep climbing until they reach the top. But this view does not encompass all of the career patterns that people follow. Many people—even many people who have undergraduate and graduate degrees in management—do not want to become presidents of their organizations. Some do not wish to be promoted, and some wish to avoid working for an organization altogether. Driver's career concepts offer several alternative ways people may perceive their careers.

Driver describes four basic *career concepts,* which are shown (along with two additional patterns) in figure 19–2. The first, or *linear concept,* most closely resembles the stereotypical view of careers we have just discussed. The individual chooses a field early in life, develops a plan for upward movement in the field, and executes it. The movement may be up an organizational hierarchy, within a professional association, or within some similar reference group.

A person who has a *steady state* career concept also selects a job or field early in life and stays with it. Although the person may continue to improve professional skills and seek a higher income, he or she does not attempt to move up the organizational hierarchy.

Driver believes that individuals with linear career concepts are motivated by the need for achievement—"to move up and score according to established 'rules of the game' "—and steady staters are motivated by security.[34] *Spiral* career concept individuals, on the other hand, are motivated by the desire for personal growth. They tend to plunge into a new job or field, work hard, and frequently perform very well—moving up in status and rank. Then, after about five to seven years, they move into another type of work or an entirely new field that offers new challenges and opportunities to grow.

The last group, the *transitories,* drift with no particular pattern from one job to another, never choosing a particular field and only occasionally and temporarily moving up in an organization. Driver suggests that they are driven by the need for independence and perhaps by the fear of commitment.

Although there is no necessary connection between a person's chosen field and a particular career concept, certain fields may tend to be associated with a certain concept. Semiskilled laborers and actors, for example, may tend to follow the transitory concept, seeking work where they can find it but rarely rising to higher

FIGURE 19–2 CAREER CONCEPTS AND PATTERNS

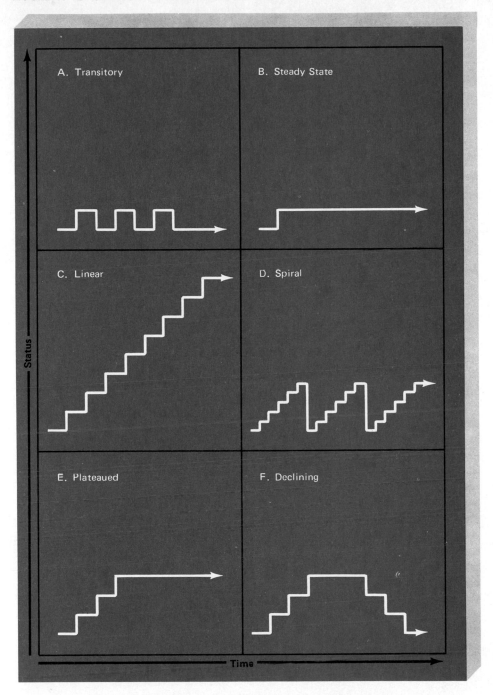

Source: Adapted from James G. Clawson, John P. Kotter, Victor A. Faux, and Charles C. McArthur, *Self-Assessment and Career Development*, 2nd ed. (Englewood Cliffs, N.J.: Prentice-Hall, 1985), p. 166.

levels. The steady-state career concept seems to be most common in the established professions (for example, medicine) and skilled trades (for example, carpentry). Individuals in these fields, after completing training, may become better at what they do and receive higher fees, but their day-to-day work changes relatively little. The linear concept may be most common for corporate managers and professors, among others; they begin at the bottom rung of the organization and gradually acquire more responsibility and higher status and income. The spiral concept might predominate among consultants and writers, who may apply their skills in one area and then in another. Of course, in all of these fields, there are many exceptions to the single most common career pattern.

In addition to Driver's four career concepts, two other patterns are common in careers. A *plateaued* individual has risen to a certain level and then remains at that level (this pattern is discussed later in the chapter). In a *declining* career, a person rises to a certain level, remains there for a time, and then begins a descent back to lower levels. These two patterns are also illustrated in figure 19–2.

Schein's Career Anchors. A *career anchor* is an occupational self-concept—a personal sense of the type of work an individual wants to pursue and what that work implies about the individual. According to Schein, people's career anchors begin to develop early in their careers, when they are going through a period of mutual discovery with their organizations. New employees gradually come to understand how they fit into the organization and how they contribute to it. They also come to understand how the organization meets their needs, interacts with them, and gives them feedback. As employees go through this process of adaptation, they develop an occupational self-concept. Schein sees this self-concept as having three components: (1) self-perception of talents and abilities based on one's performance in a variety of work settings; (2) self-perceived motives and needs based on both self-diagnosis and on feedback from others; and (3) self-perceived attitudes and values based on interactions with the norms and values implicit in the organization and the work setting.[35] People need to work in an organization for a few years, Schein says, before they can develop an accurate sense of what they really want and where it can be achieved. On the basis of his research, he concluded that many people were motivated by one of five factors:

1. *Technical/Functional Competence.* Some individuals "fall in love" with a particular field or function. They want to be outstanding financial analysts or first-rate market researchers. Although they may become managers, they are attracted and challenged by their field or the functional area of their work, not by the process of managing per se. Their self-concepts are associated with their skills in their area of interest and training.
2. *Managerial Competence.* Some individuals simply want to manage—and the larger the operation to be managed, the more attractive it is to them. They believe their abilities lie in the area of analyzing problems, making decisions, remaining emotionally stable, and being interpersonally competent. Their early career experiences indicate to them that they will be able to rise in the management hierarchy.
3. *Security.* Some individuals seek a secure work environment and career by tying themselves to a particular organization or geographic location. If their commitment is to a particular organization, they accept the organization's values,

norms, and definition of their career path—for example, moving geographically if they are transferred or promoted. If their commitment is to a specific geographic location, they will change employers rather than move away from the preferred location.

4. *Creativity.* Some individuals want to create something new. Their fundamental need is to start something and make it a success. They tend to take leadership roles on new projects and to become entrepreneurs.

5. *Autonomy.* Some individuals simply do not want to be in an organization. They find organizational life unpleasant or difficult in some way, and they are primarily concerned with maintaining their freedom. They seek work in realms where there will be few restrictions on their ability to pursue their interests.

Individuals with security, technical/functional, or managerial career anchors are likely to have a comfortable relationship with the organization they work for. However, those with autonomy anchors, and some with creativity anchors, are likely to be uncomfortable in any organization.

Although many individuals seem to feel that one or perhaps two of the career anchors fit their own self-perceptions fairly accurately, the five career anchors should not be considered a definitive list. Schein developed his concepts by studying the careers of 44 graduate management school alumni, and he and other researchers have described other possible career anchors.[36]

Careers Within Organizations

Thus far, we have discussed broad models of career and life development (Erikson, Levinson) and perspectives on the interaction between individual factors and career development (Driver, Schein). In this section we focus on how careers may develop *within* organizations. We will consider two perspectives, Edgar Schein's conical model and the sequential roles and relationships model of Gene W. Dalton, Paul H. Thompson, and Raymond L. Price.

Schein's Conical Model. Schein has offered a distinctive perspective on careers, emphasizing not only how the individual's behavior changes in the course of a career but also how the individual's positions and relationships within the organization change over time.[37] Schein focuses particularly on how individuals' movements through the various parts of the organization affect their actions and the way they are perceived by the organization.

According to Schein, the organization can be viewed more usefully as a cone, rather than as the traditional hierarchical triangle. (See fig. 19–3.) The three dimensions of the cone represent the ways an individual can move through the various parts of the organization. *Vertical* movement is hierarchical change in one's formal rank or management level. *Radial* movement is movement toward or away from the organization's "central core" or "inner circle" of power. *Circumferential* movement is a transfer to a different division, function, or department.

Each type of movement, according to Schein, involves passage through appropriate boundaries. *Hierarchical* boundaries separate one management level from another; *inclusion* boundaries separate groups closer to the center of power from those farther away; and *circumferential* boundaries separate one division or depart-

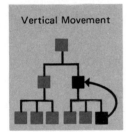

Vertical Movement

Radial Movement

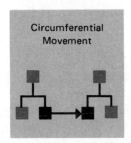

Circumferential Movement

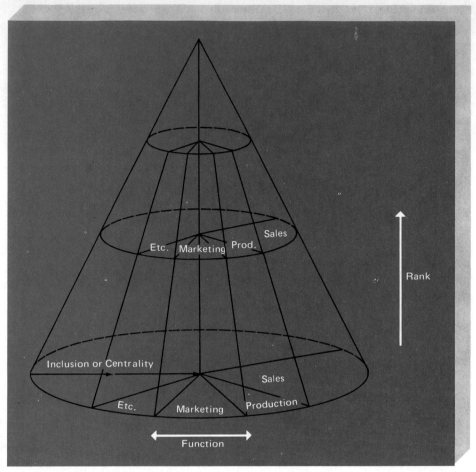

FIGURE 19–3
A THREE-
DIMENSIONAL
MODEL
OF AN
ORGANIZATION

Source: Edgar H. Schein, "The Individual, the Organization, and the Career: A Conceptual Scheme," *Journal of Applied Behavioral Science* 7, no. 4 (October–November–December 1971): 404. Copyright 1971 NTL Institute for Applied Behavioral Science. Reproduced by special permission.

ment from another. A central concept in this model is that for individuals to cross these boundaries, they must first be accepted by the members of the group they are trying to join.

Schein describes how different individuals within the organization might move through the organization in one or all of the three possible directions. An outstanding scientist, for example, might be promoted to ever higher levels (to keep him or her from leaving for a better job) without ever coming an inch closer to the core of administrative power. Conversely, a supervisor of long standing who has moved radially toward the center of power by building good relationships with the production manager and other important managers may wield more influence within the organization than the higher-ranking scientist. Those destined for the upper levels of management may first move across a number of functional boundaries (such as production, sales, and finance) to acquire a generalist's background before they are promoted to a higher rank and allowed greater influence. Continued circumferential movement, without an upward passage through the boundaries of rank, may be the mark of an individual who is needed by the organization but who is not considered suitable for promotion.

To Schein, a person's career within the organization involves a series of passages or steps from one position in the cone to another. With each passage, the organization will attempt to influence the individual, and the individual will attempt to influence the organization in return. If, for example, the individual moves radially or vertically, the members of the individual's new department or power alliance will attempt to *socialize* the individual to their way of doing things. Acquiring the proper values and attitudes is considered an important part of a move to a higher level or a more powerful position. If the individual moves circumferentially, members of the new division or department will emphasize the *training* of the individual. Such a move requires that the individual be taught new skills more than new attitudes and values. Successful socialization or training will cause the individual to become accepted and prepared for a move to the next position. (See table 19–1.)

The individual's attempt to influence the organization is termed *innovation* by Schein. Innovation, Schein believes, will most likely occur when the individual is in the middle of a given career stage, rather than having just entered or preparing to leave that stage. New arrivals, obviously, have still not become fully accepted, so they therefore are comparatively powerless to induce change. People who are about to move to another position have lame duck status and therefore less influence. At the middle of a stage, the individual is fully involved in his or her present job and can recommend changes with some confidence and authority.

Schein also suggests that socialization, training, and innovation continue throughout a career. He believes, however, that socialization and training are more prevalent during early career stages, when the individual has not yet been fully acclimated to the organization, and that innovation is more prevalent at later career stages, when the individual has more experience and status.

Four Career Roles and Relationships. Dalton, Thompson, and Price have emphasized a different dimension of organizational activity, focusing on the sequence of roles and relationships an individual may experience.[38] (See table 19–2.) When individuals start their careers, they function in the role of *apprentices*. They do mostly routine work, ideally under the supervision of mentors who will help them learn. Since they are in subordinate roles, they must accommodate themselves to a certain measure of dependence. The employee next comes to be considered a *colleague* who makes an independent contribution to the activities of the organization. Colleagues are still someone's subordinate, but they rely less on their superiors for advice and direction. Some people have trouble developing the confidence necessary for independence. At the third level, employees become *mentors* themselves. Mentors function in a number of roles. They develop ideas and manage others, and they must learn to assume some responsibility for their subordinates' work. Finally, if they continue to progress in the organization, they become *sponsors,* upper-level managers who define the direction of the entire organization or some major segment of it. Part of their influence lies in their ability to choose key people in the organization. At this level, managers must broaden their perspectives and lengthen their time horizon. Thus, at each stage, tasks change and different relationships and personal adjustments are required.[39]

TABLE 19–1 BASIC STAGES, POSITIONS, AND PROCESSES INVOLVED IN A CAREER

Basic Stages and Transitions	Statuses or Positions	Psychological and Organizational Processes: Transactions between Individual and Organization
1. Pre-entry	Aspirant, applicant, rushee	Preparation, education, anticipatory socialization
Entry (transition)	Entrant, postulant, recruit	Recruitment, rushing, testing, screening, selection, acceptance ("hiring"); passage through external inclusion boundary; rites of entry; induction and orientation
2. Basic training, novitiate	Trainee, novice, pledge	Training, indoctrination, socialization, testing of the person by the organization, tentative acceptance into group
Initiation, first vows (transition)	Initiate, graduate	Passage through first inner inclusion boundary, acceptance as member and conferring of organizational status, rite of passage and acceptance
3. First regular assignment	New member	First testing by the person of his or her own capacity to function; granting of real responsibility (playing for keeps); passage through functional boundary with assignment to specific job or department
Substages a. Learning the job b. Maximum performance c. Becoming obsolete d. Learning new skills, etc.		Indoctrination and testing of person by immediate work group leading to acceptance or rejection; if accepted, further education and socialization (learning the ropes); preparation for higher status through coaching, seeking visibility, finding sponsors
Promotion or leveling off (transition)		Preparation, testing, passage through hierarchical boundary, rite of passage; may involve passage through functional boundary as well (rotation)
4. Second assignment	Legitimate member (fully accepted)	Processes under no. 3 repeat
5. Granting of tenure	Permanent member	Passage through another inner inclusion boundary
Termination and exit (transition)	Old-timer, senior citizen	Preparation for exit ... rites of exit (testimonial dinners, and so on)
6. Post exit	Alumnus, emeritus, retired	Granting of peripheral status, consultant or senior adviser

Source: Edgar H. Schein, "The Individual, the Organization, and the Career: A Conceptual Scheme," *Journal of Applied Behavioral Science* 7 no. 4 (October–November–December 1971): 415–416. Copyright 1971 NTL Institute for Applied Behavioral Science. Reproduced by special permission.

TABLE 19–2 FOUR CAREER ROLES AND RELATIONSHIPS

	Role I	Role II	Role III	Role IV
Central activities	Helping Learning Following directions	Independent contributor	Training Interfacing	Shaping the direction of the organization
Primary relationship	Apprentice	Colleague	Mentor	Sponsor
Major psychological issues	Dependence	Independence	Assuming responsibility for others	Exercising power

The Career Plateau

The *career plateau* may be defined as "the point in a career where the likelihood of additional hierarchical promotion is very low."[40] The term has a negative connotation, because it seems to imply that the individual is no longer promotable because of lack of ability or some other flaw. This negative connotation, however, is derived in part from the widespread acceptance of the *linear* career concept as the only model for a successful career.

Rather than always being a sign of a personal shortcoming, reaching a career plateau is a normal organizational occurrence—it happens to just about everyone. Lack of ability, lack of skill in organizational politics, or inaccurate assessment by a superior is sometimes responsible. Usually, however, individuals reach a plateau simply because there are far more candidates for higher-level positions than there are positions available. Since job openings become progressively more scarce as one ascends the organizational hierarchy, even highly successful managers eventually reach a career plateau.

In recent years, organizational growth has slowed but the number of management candidates has increased. This has caused more attention to be given to the problems faced by individuals and their organizations when a career plateau is reached. Before we discuss these problems, we should note that for the individual manager a career plateau is frequently reached at the same time as a mid-life crisis.[41] For the organization, the way in which career plateaus are managed is likely to have a strong influence on how well the organization functions.

Management Career States. Two variables are useful in defining an individual's current career state: the organization's evaluation of how promotable the individual is and the organization's perception of how well the individual is performing at present. Based on these variables, four basic stages in management careers can be identified (see fig. 19–4):

1. *Learners or comers.* These individuals, considered to have advancement potential, are not performing up to par at present. Not many individuals are likely to be in this category, but members of training programs and recently promoted

managers who have not yet fully learned their new jobs could be included in it.

2. *Stars.* These individuals are seen as doing high-quality work and are considered to have high advancement potential. They are sometimes placed on "fast-track" career paths and usually receive the greatest exposure to management development activities.

3. *Solid citizens.* These managers, seen as doing good or even outstanding work, have for one reason or another little, if any, chance for further advancement. They may constitute the largest group of managers in most organizations and accomplish most of their organization's work.

4. *Deadwood.* These individuals are seen as having little or no chance for advancement, and their current performance is seen as marginal or inadequate. Often they are shunted aside to minor, dead-end posts and then forgotten, but sometimes attempts are made to rehabilitate them so that they become solid citizens once again.

The solid citizens and deadwood have reached career plateaus, while the comers and stars are still on an upward track. Since the solid citizens are effective, it might seem that the only problems for management are how to speed up the development

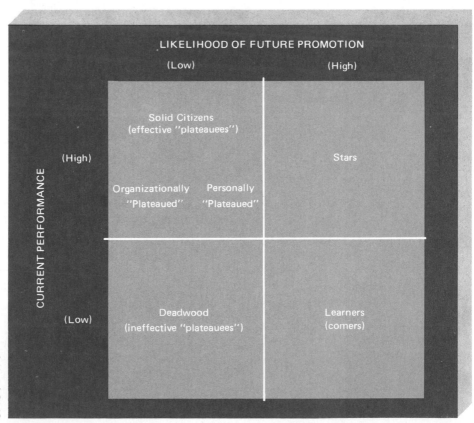

FIGURE 19–4
A MODEL OF MANAGERIAL CAREER STATES

Source: Thomas P. Ference, James A. F. Stoner, and E. Kirby Warren, "Managing the Career Plateau," *Academy of Management Review*, 2, no. 4 (October 1977). Used by permission.

of the learners and how to "turn around" the deadwood. And the learners do receive additional training help while deadwood frequently receive special attention as candidates for rehabilitation or outright dismissal. Yet the solid citizens present management with a greater challenge than is usually recognized. Once they realize they have reached a career plateau, the solid citizens may lose motivation and gradually drift into the deadwood category—unless management takes steps to prevent this decline. The dangers of lost motivation may be particularly great for individuals who think of their careers in *linear* terms or whose career anchor is *managerial competence.*

As our discussion implies, these career stages change over time. Newcomers usually enter the organization as learners. If they perform well, they move into the "star" category and become active candidates for promotion. With each promotion they temporarily move again into the "learner" category; as they take command in their new jobs they again become "stars." As the years pass, however, increasing numbers of individuals reach career plateaus. This may happen for *organizational* reasons—fewer job openings exist at higher levels; younger or more qualified candidates may be sought by the organization for the higher-level jobs available; or the individuals may be regarded as too valuable in their present positions to be promoted. Individuals may also reach plateaus for *personal* reasons—they may lack the technical or career skills needed to move to a higher position, or they may simply lack the desire for further promotion. Regardless of the reason for reaching a plateau, they now become "solid citizens." They may remain effective until they retire, or until such factors as age, lack of motivation, or lack of new training cause their performance to decline.[42]

Solid citizens can be productive and successful for many years, maintaining a sense of growth and achievement by seeking new challenges or by obtaining transfers to other jobs at the same organizational level. In addition, there are options available if the plateau is unsatisfying—for instance, one can acquire additional training to become eligible again for promotion, or one can move to another organization that offers greater opportunity.

It is important to remember that one's bosses, co-workers, and subordinates will also be passing through the various career states. Understanding the process by which careers develop and plateaus are reached is useful in helping others deal with the experience.

Individual Career Management

While organizations can help individuals manage their careers,[43] career management is ultimately the individual's responsibility. Conscious career management by the individual can have many advantages. Like organizations, individuals who develop plans for the future are more likely to achieve their goals. They can focus their energies on the career goals they have selected, rather than drifting from job to job. In addition, they are less vulnerable to chance events and to having undesirable career decisions made for them by others. Finally, individuals who are competent in managing their own careers and who have well-thought-out goals and plans for reaching them tend to be more motivated and purposeful than others; thus, they are often more useful to their organizations and more likely to be successful within them.

In discussing the elements of effective individual career management, we will focus on methods of career planning, managing the day-to-day work situation effectively, and handling special issues relevant to one's own career. A well-thought-out career strategy can help one do the right things; it can also help one do things right in the important day-to-day actions that translate the plan into reality.

Individual Career Planning

The starting point for individual career planning is to understand what one wants from one's work, career, and life. (Various career planning approaches offer assistance in gaining insight into these matters.) To many people, career planning means developing a program for moving toward the top of the organization. As we explained in our discussion of Driver's career concepts and Schein's career anchors, however, planning for a linear career of this sort is inappropriate for many other individuals.

Realistic Career Strategies. Individual career planning can be approached like any other type of planning, although it resembles strategic planning most closely.[44] Alan N. Schoonmaker has offered a nine-step career strategy that includes systematic career planning.[45] Some of his steps sound rather harsh—in the first two steps, for example, he reminds us of certain unpleasant facts about organizational careers. Nevertheless, his strategy is basically realistic. The steps are:

1. *Accept the fact that there are some inescapable and irreconcilable conflicts between you and your organization.* In short, what is good for the organization is not always good for you. So, being careful not to be disloyal, you must always recognize the need to look out for your own interests.

2. *Accept the fact that your superiors are essentially indifferent to your career ambitions.* Your superiors are ultimately responsible only for themselves and their units; you should assume they will help you only if doing so helps them achieve their own objectives. As Schoonmaker has noted, the responsibility of your superiors to themselves and the organization would make any other attitude improper for them. Realizing this will help you avoid being manipulated by false promises and unrealistic expectations.

3. *Analyze your own goals.* Many people act to fulfill goals they have been taught should be important to them rather than those that really are. They therefore may spend their entire lives searching for an unattainable satisfaction. To get what you want, you first have to *know* what you want. Career management does not mean simply charting a series of promotions that end in an executive suite—it means planning to achieve *any* career goal that is meaningful to *you*.

4. *Analyze your assets and liabilities.* It is unrealistic to pursue goals that require abilities you do not have; it is foolish not to take advantage of those abilities you do have. Your career goals should allow you to maximize your assets and minimize your liabilities.

5. *Analyze your opportunities.* Determine what your options are inside and outside of the organization. Systematically assess the positions available in your own and other firms. Personal observations, tips from colleagues, and published information may be useful in this process.

6. *Learn the rules of company politics.* Note what your company values and rewards and how those who are rewarded behave. Learn which people are the most

crucial in accomplishing various kinds of tasks. ("Keep up a good relationship with the parts department manager and he'll help you meet your production schedule.")

7. *Plan your career.* A goal without a plan is no better than a daydream. Many managers select goals without any idea of how they are going to reach them; often, they fail to attain those goals because they drift indecisively from job to job or stay too long in one position. Planning will help you to make better decisions at each step of your career.

8. *Carry out your plan.* The best plan is useless if it is not carried out. If your plan calls for you to ask for a raise, request a transfer, find another job, or turn down a job offer—*do it!*

9. *Chart your progress.* Very rarely does a career progress without a hitch—a sponsor takes early retirement, the job market changes, a new colleague in the same department proves to be a "star." Your goals are also likely to change somewhat over time—a new opportunity, for example, may not seem attractive if you are highly satisfied in your present job. Like organizational plans, career plans have to be revised periodically to keep up with current realities.

Managing the Work Situation. Once you have developed a career plan and have a job in your field, you can use a number of tactics to further your career. First and most important, you can *do excellent work.*[46] High performance and work excellence are the foundation of a career strategy. The better you are at helping your organization meet its goals, the more likely the organization is to reward you. But doing good work produces more personal benefits as well. It is more satisfying to do good work than to do mediocre work. To keep doing excellent work, you must keep learning and growing. Superior work usually garners more acknowledgment, respect, and support from bosses, peers, and subordinates. It leads to more exciting and challenging opportunities within and outside the organization. Furthermore, those who have proved their ability to do first-rate work are likely to be given more autonomy. The list could be extended almost indefinitely. Of course, excellent work alone does not *inevitably* lead to career success—your efforts may be ignored, or they may arouse the jealousy of your colleagues—but as a general rule, it is the best possible basis for attempts to realize your career ambitions.

First-rate work cannot be done in isolation. A person who performs brilliantly in some areas but doesn't get along with colleagues is unlikely to go very far. This suggests two other tactics for succeeding in the organization: *develop good working relationships* and *help your boss succeed.* It is difficult to imagine how one could truly be doing excellent work without being effective in these two areas.

Developing good working relationships is crucial to success because organizations are by their nature cooperative efforts. Ronald J. Burke notes that it's *both* what you know *and* who you know that counts.[47] To accomplish tasks, you must establish a network of co-workers—superiors, peers, and subordinates—who are able and willing to help you meet your objectives. It is easier to do excellent work if you are part of such a network (and it is easier to become part of such a network if you do excellent work). Building good relationships begins early in your career. At times it may be tempting to disagree publicly with your boss, go over your supervisor's head to a superior, engage in personal criticism, hold grudges, express hostility, or seek revenge, but such actions do not advance careers. Every bad working relationship is a lost opportunity.

Helping your boss succeed is a good way to help yourself succeed. The more you help your boss—by doing good work, suggesting new approaches to problems, and keeping him or her informed—the more valuable to your boss you will be. In fact, becoming indispensable to an upwardly mobile boss can help you become part of an "advancement sandwich," in which your boss, you, and the subordinate that you train move up in the organization together. Other bosses are also likely to find you an attractive subordinate if you have helped your supervisor become more successful.[48]

Other techniques that may be less important than those we have just described but can still be valuable include:

· *Be mobile.* For those who aspire to top management, movement within the organization is highly desirable. Experience across the functional lines of an organization for example, will help you develop the variety of skills you will need as a general manager. Experience at different geographic locations will give you an understanding of the organization as a whole and may bring you to the attention of those at the very top. You should be aware, however, that high geographic mobility usually costs a great deal in terms of one's social and family relationships. You must weigh the sacrifices that repeated moves require against the growth potential they may afford.[49]

If you are growing as much and as fast as you desire and are being appropriately recognized, then movement outside your organization is not an effective strategy. Joining another organization normally will require a whole new set of alliances and relationships. But if you are not gaining the experience and training necessary for advancement, if you have been placed in a dead-end job, or if you are not progressing as fast in responsibility and recognition as you desire, then leaving for a more challenging opportunity elsewhere is usually a better idea than waiting for things to improve where you are.

· *Find a sponsor.* A higher-level sponsor is an organizational ally who can pass on the knowledge he or she has gained to younger employees. Later in this chapter we discuss this topic at some length.

· *Become visible.* It can be very frustrating to know you are doing good work but not being rewarded for it. To receive recognition for your performance, you have to make sure your superiors are aware of it. This can be done in a number of tactful ways. These include sending memos to a superior when projects have been completed, submitting short progress reports, and seeking evaluation and advice directly from a superior or from colleagues. Making it known that you have received and rejected another job offer is, according to Schoonmaker, a particularly effective way of getting noticed.

· *Present the right image.* When you become visible, it is important to give the right impression. Hardworking individuals who appear slow or uncertain may be perceived as lazy or indifferent, regardless of actual performance. Individuals who are eager to "belong" to the organization but dress or behave in ways that are contrary to the organization's "style" may be regarded as nonconformists or outsiders. Clothing, posture, tone of voice, and demeanor all contribute to how individuals are perceived. Some people find it phony and distasteful to try to fit the mold of the organization. However, if you select an organization whose norms and values are compatible with yours, you should have relatively few problems adjusting to its style.[50]

Handling Specific Career Issues

We have been discussing general strategies for meeting career goals. Three additional topics are also of interest to young managers in considering their own lives and careers. First, many young managers will be members of dual-career couples. Such couples must cooperatively plan their careers and their personal relationship more carefully than either single people or spouses in traditional marriages. Second, managers need to understand mentoring relationships. A relationship with a mentor can be a valuable career asset, but it can be a liability as well. Third, women's careers in management may require especially careful planning because women have often faced special barriers in managerial situations, and the events of their lives make some career issues more acute for them than for men. Familiarity with these issues is valuable for one's own career and to help others manage these issues effectively.

Dual-Career Couples

Couples in which both spouses are employed full time must work hard to integrate and balance the demands and opportunities of two separate careers. Mutual accommodation is constantly necessary on small matters. When both spouses return from work tired, who will make dinner? Who stays home to take care of a child with an upset stomach? Major conflicts also arise. Suppose that one spouse receives a very attractive job offer in another part of the country and the other spouse is reluctant to leave his or her current job. Which one gives in? Flexibility and willingness to compromise are imperative for both the career and the relationship, but choices can still be difficult.

   Francine Hall and Douglas T. Hall have identified four general styles of effectively managing two careers.[51] Each is based on the spouses' differing (or similar) degrees of commitment to home or to career.

· *Accommodators.* Couples of this type most closely resemble the traditional family. One spouse assumes major (but not total) responsibility for career roles and the other assumes major responsibility for family roles.
· *Adversaries.* This type occurs when both spouses are highly involved in their careers but also value having someone take responsibility for home-related roles. There are likely to be conflicts because neither is willing or able to make the career sacrifices necessary to maintain the home.
· *Allies.* In this type, the two spouses are both highly involved in either their career or home roles and place little emphasis on the other area. If both are highly involved in their career roles, for example, they are likely to forgo having children and devote little attention to maintaining a well-ordered home.
· *Acrobats.* Couples of this sort are highly involved in all their roles. They give equal weight to both family and career, but rather than attempting to get their spouses to take over, they attempt to perform both roles themselves.

As dual-career couples have become more common, organizations have become more responsive to their special needs. This may involve such changes as providing flexible work environments, revising transfer policies, offering couples career management assistance, and providing local support services, such as day care and after-school centers for children.[52]

Mentors and Mentoring Relationships

As recounted by Homer in *The Odyssey,* Mentor was the servant of Odysseus entrusted with a wide range of responsibilities in the care and training of Odysseus' son, Telemachus.[53] Today, as we mentioned in the section on finding a sponsor, mentors are still seen as older, more experienced individuals who pass on the benefits of their experience to younger persons. Some observers believe that mentor relationships play a key role in assisting those who have successful careers. Others contend that they are less important and that the relationships are more complex than Homer suggests.

According to Kathy E. Kram,[54] the interactions that occur in a mentoring relationship can certainly be helpful in a person's career. She divides the functions of mentoring into two broad categories: career functions and psychosocial functions. *Career functions* are the aspects of the relationship that help the younger person learn the ropes and prepare for advancement. Included in this realm are such activities as sponsoring the younger person's career through public support, helping the junior person gain exposure and visibility in the organization, coaching the younger colleague in specific strategies, protecting him or her from negative contacts, and seeing that he or she is assigned challenging, constructive work.

Psychosocial functions are the aspects of the relationship that "enhance a sense of competence, clarity of identity, and effectiveness in a professional role."[55] The mentor's attitudes, values, and behavior provide a model for the younger person to emulate. The older person also provides support and encouragement for the younger colleague and helps him or her explore personal concerns that may interfere with productivity at work. Finally, the two colleagues are often friends who like and understand each other and enjoy each other's company.

Kram's studies indicate that the mentor relationship is not one-sided. In addition to the satisfaction of passing on the benefits of experience, the mentor receives technical and psychological support from a loyal subordinate and is recognized by others as effectively developing talent. The relationship can also take a number of different forms—it is not restricted to a single older person dispensing wisdom to a younger colleague. Mentor roles can be filled by a number of persons, both within the organization and outside it—one's boss, other individuals higher in the organization, co-workers, friends outside work, a spouse, and even subordinates. Attempts to identify a single individual and form a mentor relationship with him or her are frequently misdirected and unsuccessful. If one happens to find a single person with whom one feels compatible and who fulfills a variety of mentoring roles, so much the better. However, Kram says it is more important to develop a *network* of mutually supportive relationships in which a number of individuals provide a variety of mentoring functions.[56]

Women's Careers in Management

Women managers must confront the same challenges and issues as men in management, and they must deal with additional issues as well. For example, discrimination, sexual stereotyping, the conflicting demands of marriage and work life, and increased social isolation and loneliness are more likely to affect managerial women than men.[57] These factors can prevent women from entering management and may make it harder for them to do their best work when they do become managers. The problems women may face in pursuing managerial careers stem from at least three sources: (1) the woman's attitudes toward herself and her career; (2) the attitudes of the men and women with whom she works, and (3) broad organizational policies and procedures. Each source may create barriers to women's career progress and success. Circumstances in all three areas are changing, however, and in general the trend is for barriers to be reduced.

Women's Attitudes. Until recently, most females who were old enough to consider becoming managers had not been socialized to see themselves in managerial roles. This factor, in combination with organizational and societal barriers to professional and managerial careers, led many women to choose other alternatives. The changes in this area have been dramatic. In 1972 and 1973, for example, less than 5 percent of all MBA graduates were female; by 1981 and 1982, the figure had risen to approximately 30 percent.[58] Nevertheless, many women's expectations remain relatively low. A study of Stanford MBAs found that women graduates had lower ultimate salary hopes and expectations. In fact, on the average, women's peak salary expectations were less than 40 percent of men's.[59] These expectations may be realistic to the extent that women's careers may be disrupted by child rearing, organizational barriers, and other factors. However, lower expectations may also function as a self-fulfilling prophecy, discouraging women from progressing as far as they might in their careers.

Attitudes of Co-workers. It has long been recognized that some workers are prejudiced against female professionals and managers. This prejudice is not based on the performance of women managers and professionals as a group. Research shows that men and women managers are very similar in terms of attitudes, behavior, and performance.[60] Other research indicates that the biases against women found in earlier studies are diminishing. Hazel F. Ezell, Charles A. Odewahn, and J. Daniel Sherman, for example, report that men who have been subordinates of women managers are more favorably disposed toward them than men who have not.[61] As women become more common at all levels of management, we can expect further changes and greater acceptance.

Organizational Policies and Procedures. Although the Reagan administration has not been as aggressive as some previous administrations in enforcing legislation for equal opportunity and affirmative action for women and minorities, there have still been dramatic reductions in the barriers to women and minorities in education and organizational careers since the passage of the 1964 Civil Rights Act.

Just as some men face special career barriers and members of minorities face even greater barriers, many women managers will face gender-related barriers. This is not to say that such barriers cannot be overcome with creativity and persistence—some can and some cannot. Nor is it true that being a women is never advantageous—in some circumstances it is. However, many women have to devote time and energy to dealing with issues, problems, and barriers that most men never encounter, and dealing with these issues detracts from "getting the job done."

Since the situation is changing so rapidly, it seems likely that models of women's careers and career success based on even recent experiences may prove to be poor predictors of the future. How, then, can a woman manage her own career most effectively? If we assume that most career tasks are reasonably similar for men and women but that a few are quite different, the most fruitful approach may be to work hard at doing the best possible job with the many "general" issues and use the existing models and guidelines for handling gender-related tasks.[62]

Summary   Certain events occur with relative predictability over the course of a person's career. Understanding these events enables us to prepare for them and to take an active role in managing our own careers.

Early career experiences commonly include the formation of unrealistic expectations and reality shock when these expectations clash with frustrating on-the-job experiences. Low initial challenge, low self-actualization satisfaction, and lack of performance appraisal are some organizational factors that contribute to reality shock. Realistic job previews may help prevent reality shock, but research has yielded inconsistent results on this point.

The amount of challenge in the initial job assignment, the actions of one's first supervisor, and the new employee's fit with the organizational culture are particularly important career influences. Dilemmas that arise early in one's career relate to political insensitivity and passivity, loyalty demands, and personal anxiety about one's growing commitment to the organization. The latter can sometimes be resolved through "creative individualism," which permits the individual to accept only the most important values of the organization.

Stress is part of organizational life. It is often caused by overload. There are two kinds of overloading: quantitative, in which a person has more work than he or she has time for, and qualitative, in which the person lacks the skills to do a job. Underloading may also be a problem. Stress can have serious health consequences. A variety of techniques can be used to reduce stressful factors in the environment and to help people deal with the stress that does occur.

Several models of the career stages through which many individuals must pass have been developed. Levinson and his colleagues, for example, have devised a model that describes adult life as a series of predictable events that occur every five to seven years. The stages are called the early adult transition, entering the adult world, the age-30 transition, settling down, the mid-life transition, the beginning of middle adulthood, the age-50 transition, the second middle adult structure, the late adult transition, and the late adult era.

Driver and Schein have developed two perspectives on the patterns that careers follow. Driver has suggested that most careers follow one of four basic career concepts: transitory, steady state, linear, or spiral. Schein developed the concept of the career anchor, a form of self-concept that develops through one's experiences in the workplace and that functions as a guide for one's entire career. Schein described five career anchors—security, technical or functional competence, managerial competence, creativity, and autonomy.

Schein has also devised a model that describes how the individual's positions within the organization change over time. The organization appears as a cone in which vertical, radial, and circumferential movement can take place across various boundaries. With each movement, the individual is socialized or trained to fit into the new position. Schein believes individuals are most likely to be innovative at the midpoint of their tenure in a position.

Individuals reach a career plateau when they are no longer candidates for promotion. Stars and learners are considered eligible for promotion; solid citizens and deadwood, however, are considered no longer promotable. Almost everyone in an organization eventually reaches a plateau, frequently because of the scarcity of positions available at higher levels of the hierarchy.

The starting point for individual career planning is to understand what one wants from one's work, career, and life. Schoonmaker has offered a nine-step career strategy that involves systematic career planning. Once one has mounted a successful job campaign and gotten a job in one's chosen field, much can be done to manage the work situation to one's advantage. The most important tasks are to do excellent work, develop good working relationships, and help your boss succeed.

Dual-career couples must work hard to integrate and balance the demands and opportunities of two separate careers. Mentors serve a variety of functions, some of them directly related to one's career, others more psychosocial in nature. Mentor roles can be filled by a variety of persons within and outside the organization; the employee need not attempt to form a relationship with a single individual.

Women face a number of barriers to successful careers. Three major sources of barriers are women's attitudes toward themselves and their careers, the attitudes of co-workers, and organizational policies and procedures. Although barriers have been reduced in recent years and will probably diminish further, women in management will face greater pressures than men for some time.

Review Questions

1. Why do you think individuals develop unrealistic expectations about their first jobs? Why is this tendency especially severe among business school graduates?

2. What is reality shock? What factors contribute to it?

3. What three factors in an individual's early job experiences have an especially strong influence on subsequent job success? Why are these factors so influential?

4. Why are young business school graduates often insensitive to the political dimension of organizational life? What is the proper function of political alliances in an organization?

5. Webber describes five common ways by which loyalty may be defined by a superior. What are these five ways? What ethical and other conflicts arise sometimes for subordinates in applying these directives?

6. In what three ways can people respond to the organization's efforts to enforce compliance with its expectations? Which way do you think is best? Why?

7. What are the six types of role conflict identified by Katz and Kahn?

8. What are the most common causes of stress? How can stress affect health? Describe the various procedures that can be used to reduce stress and help people deal with it.

9. What are the ten stages in Levinson's model of adult development?

10. Compare Driver's career concepts notion with Schein's idea of career anchors.

11. Identify individuals you know who work for organizations and try to fit them into the career stages or states of the various models presented in the chapter. Can they be accurately placed?

12. According to Schein, what three types of movement are possible within organizations? What three types of organizational boundaries exist? How does the organization attempt to influence the individual who is making a position change? When can the individual most effectively influence the organization?

13. List the nine steps in Schoonmaker's career strategy. How reasonable do they sound to you?

14. What are the three most important steps one can take in the work situation to further one's career?

15. What are the special issues that must be confronted by dual-career couples? Discuss the four general styles of managing two careers.

16. According to Kram, what are the two categories of functions served by mentors? Should one assume that it is imperative to find an individual to serve as one's mentor? Why or why not?

17. What are some of the special problems faced by women in management?

Notes

1. See Lyman W. Porter, Edward E. Lawler III, and J. Richard Hackman, *Behavior in Organizations* (New York: McGraw-Hill, 1975), pp. 131–136, 172–178.

2. Edgar H. Schein, "The First Job Dilemma," *Psychology Today,* March 1968, pp. 22–37.

3. John D. Aram and James A. F. Stoner, "Development of an Organizational Change Role," *Journal of Applied Behavioral Science* 8, no. 4 (October–November–December 1972):438–449. See also John Paul Kotter, "The Psychological Contract: Managing the Joining-Up Process," *California Management Review* 15, no. 3 (Spring 1973):91–99. For a thorough discussion of the process of entering an organization, see John P. Wanous, *Organizational Entry: Recruitment, Selection, and Socialization of Newcomers* (Reading, Mass.: Addison-Wesley, 1980).

4. Douglas T. Hall, *Careers in Organizations* (Pacific Palisades, Calif.: Goodyear, 1976).

5. John Van Maanen and Edgar H. Schein, "Toward a Theory of Organizational Socialization," in Barry M. Staw, ed., *Research in Organizational Behavior,* vol. 1 (Greenwich, Conn.: JAI Press, 1979), pp. 209–264; and Wanous, *Organizational Entry,* pp. 167–198.

6. James A. Breaugh, "Realistic Job Previews: A Critical Appraisal and Future Research Directions," *Academy of Management Review* 8, no. 4 (October 1983):613.

7. See, for example, John P. Wanous, "Effects of a Realistic Job Review on Job Acceptance, Job Attitudes, and Job Survival," *Journal of Applied Psychology* 58, no. 3 (December 1973):327–337; Wanous, *Organizational Entry,* pp. 37–84; and Bernard L. Dugoni and Daniel R. Ilgen, "Realistic Job Previews and the Adjustment of New Employees," *Academy of Management Journal* 24, no. 3 (September 1981):579–591.

8. See Donald P. Schwab, "Review of Wanous, *Organizational Entry,*" *Personnel Psychology* 34 no. 1 (Spring 1981):167–170; and Breaugh, "Realistic Job Previews," p. 612.

9. Marvin D. Dunnette, Richard D. Arvey, and Paul A. Banas, "Why Do They Leave?" *Personnel* 50, no. 3 (May–June 1973):25–39.

10. David E. Berlew and Douglas T. Hall, "The Socialization of Managers: Effects of Expectations on Performance," *Administrative Science Quarterly* 11, no. 2 (September 1966):207–223.

11. See, for example, Schein, "The First Job Dilemma"; J. Sterling Livingston, "Pygmalion in Management," *Harvard Business Review* 47, no. 4 (July–August 1969):81–89; and Douglas W. Bray, Richard J. Campbell, and Donald Grant, *Formative Years in Business* (New York: Wiley, 1974), p. 73.

12. The powerful impact of expectations on performance has been demonstrated experimentally in research reviewed by Robert Rosenthal and Donald B. Rubin, "Interpersonal Expectancy Effects: The First 345 Studies," *Behavioral and Brain Sciences* 1, no. 3 (September 1978):377–415. See also Dov Eden, "Self-Fulfilling Prophecy as a Management Tool: Harnessing Pygmalion," *Academy of Management Review* 9, no. 1 (January 1984):64–73.

13. For an exercise that simulates how one might assess one's fit with an organization, see James G. Clawson, John P. Kotter, Victor A. Faux, and Charles C. McArthur, *Self-Assessment and Career Development,* 2nd ed. (Englewood Cliffs, N.J.: Prentice-Hall, 1985), pp. 277–287.

14. Ross A. Webber, "The Three Dilemmas of Career Growth," *MBA* 9, no. 5 (May 1975):41–48.

15. David C. McClelland, "The Two Faces of Power," *Journal of International Affairs* 24, no. 1 (1970):29–47.

16. David C. McClelland and David H. Burnham, "Power Is the Great Motivator," *Harvard Business Review* 54, no. 2 (March–April 1976):100–110.

17. Edgar H. Schein, "Organizational Socialization and the Profession of Management," *Industrial Management Review* 9, no. 2 (Winter 1968):1–16.

18. Daniel Katz and Robert L. Kahn, *The Social Psychology of Organizations,* 2nd ed. (New York: Wiley, 1978). See also Robert L. Kahn, D. M. Wolfe, R. P. Quinn, J. D. Snock, and R. A. Rosenthal, *Organizational Stress: Studies in Role Conflict and Ambiguity* (New York: Wiley, 1964); and Andrew J. DuBrin, *Fundamentals of Organizational Behavior: An Applied Perspective,* 2nd ed. (Elmsford, N.Y.: Pergamon Press, 1978), chapter 4.

19. Francine Hall and Douglas T. Hall, *The Two-Career Couple* (Reading, Mass.: Addison-Wesley, 1978).

20. Saroj Parasuraman and Joseph A. Alutto, "Sources and Outcomes of Stress in Organizational Settings: Toward the Development of a Structural Model," *Academy of Management Journal* 27, no. 2 (June 1984):330–350.

21. Our discussion is based largely on Robert A. Baron, *Understanding Human Relations: A Practical Guide to People at Work* (Boston: Allyn and Bacon, 1985), pp. 272–302. Other general sources on stress are Leonard Moss, *Management Stress* (Reading, Mass.: Addison-Wesley, 1981); James C. Quick and Jonathan D. Quick, *Organizational Stress and Preventive Management* (New York: McGraw-Hill, 1984); and Jere E. Yates, *Managing Stress: A Businessperson's Guide* (New York: AMACOM, 1979).

22. Joseph E. McGrath, "Stress and Behavior in Organizations," in Marvin D. Dunnette, ed., *Handbook of Industrial and Organizational Psychology* (New York: Wiley, 1983), p. 1352.

23. Based on information gathered by the National Institute for Occupational Safety and Health, U.S. Department of Health, Education, and Welfare, 1978. See Baron, *Understanding Human Relations,* p. 301.

24. A. M. Pines, E. Aronson, and D. Kafrey, *Burnout: From Tedium to Personal Growth* (New York: Free Press, 1981).

25. Salvatore R. Maddi and Suzanne C. Kobasa, *The Hardy Executive: Health and Stress* (Homewood, Ill.: Dow Jones-Irwin, 1984), especially pp. 59–87.

26. Susan E. Jackson, "Participation in Decision Making as a Strategy for Reducing Job-Related Strain," *Journal of Applied Psychology* 68, no. 1 (1983):3–19.

27. Lawrence R. Murphy, "Occupational Stress Management: A Review and Appraisal," *Journal of Occupational Psychology* 57, no. 1 (1984):1–15. See also Addison W. Somerville, Agnes R. Allen, Barbara A. Noble, and D. L. Sedgwick, "Effect of a Stress Management Class: One Year Later," *Teaching of Psychology* 11, no. 2 (April 1984):82–85.

28. Much of our discussion is based on Hall, *Careers in Organizations*, pp. 47–64.

29. See Erik H. Erikson, *Childhood and Society*, 2nd ed. (New York: Norton, 1963), pp. 247–274.

30. Donald Super and his colleagues have divided vocational life into five stages: *growth* (birth–14), *exploration* (15–24), *establishment* (25–44), *maintenance* (45–64), and *decline* (65 and older). See Donald E. Super, John O. Crites, Raymond C. Hummel, Helen P. Moser, Phoebe L. Overstreet, and Charles F. Warnath, *Vocational Development: A Framework for Research* (New York: Teachers College Press, 1957), pp. 40–41.

31. Daniel J. Levinson, Charlotte N. Darrow, Edward B. Klein, Maria H. Levinson, and Braxton McKee, *The Seasons of a Man's Life* (New York: Knopf, 1978). This discussion and many other parts of this chapter have benefited greatly from a review by James G. Clawson. See Clawson et al., *Self-Assessment and Career Development*, pp. 386–387; Gail Sheehy, *Passages* (New York: Dutton, 1976); and Roger L. Gould, *Transformations: Growth and Change in Adult Life* (New York: Simon & Schuster, 1978).

32. Michael J. Driver, "Career Concepts—A New Approach to Career Research," in Ralph Katz, ed., *Career Issues in Human Resource Management* (Englewood Cliffs, N.J.: Prentice-Hall, 1982), pp. 23–32; and "Career Concepts and Career Management in Organizations," in Cary L. Cooper, ed., *Behavioral Problems in Organizations* (Englewood Cliffs, N.J.: Prentice-Hall, 1979), pp. 79–139.

33. Edgar H. Schein, *Career Dynamics: Matching Individual and Organizational Needs* (Reading, Mass.: Addison-Wesley, 1978), pp. 124–171. For a summary of these concepts, see Thomas J. DeLong, "The Career Orientations of MBA Alumni: A Multidimensional Model," in Katz, *Career Issues*, pp. 50–64.

34. Driver, "Career Concepts—A New Approach to Career Research," p. 27.

35. Schein, *Career Dynamics*, p. 125.

36. DeLong, "The Career Orientations of MBA Alumni," in Katz, *Career Issues*, p. 53. DeLong has noted three plausible possibilities: *identity*, the anchor for those who seek the status of belonging to certain companies and organizations; *service*, the anchor for those who want to use their skills to help others; and *variety*, the anchor for those who seek novelty and freshness in their work projects.

37. Edgar H. Schein, "The Individual, the Organization, and the Career: A Conceptual Scheme," *Journal of Applied Behavioral Science* 7, no. 4 (October–November–December 1971):401–426.

38. Gene W. Dalton, Paul H. Thompson, and Raymond L. Price, "The Four Stages of Professional Careers—A New Look at Performance by Professionals," *Organizational Dynamics* 6, no. 1 (Summer 1977):19–42.

39. The relationship of professional and private lives of managers is dealt with by Paul Evans and Fernando Bartolomé in *Must Success Cost So Much?* (New York: Basic Books, 1980), pp. 27–41.

40. Thomas P. Ference, James A. F. Stoner, and E. Kirby Warren, "Managing the Career Plateau," *Academy of Management Review* 2, no. 4 (October 1977):602–612. Our discussion is based on these sources: Stoner, Ference, Warren, and H. Kurt Christensen, *Managerial Career Plateaus—An Exploratory Study* (New York: Center for Research in Career Development, Columbia University, 1980); and Warren, Ference, and Stoner, "Case of the Plateaued Performer," *Harvard Business Review* 53, no. 1 (January–February 1975):30–38ff. See also John W. Slocum, Jr., William L. Cron, Richard W. Hansen, and Sallie Rawlings, "Business Strategy and the Management of Plateaued Employees," *Academy of Management Journal* 28, no. 1 (March 1985):133–154.

41. See Harry Levinson, "On Being a Middle-Aged Manager," *Harvard Business Review* 47, no. 4 (July–August 1969):51–60.

42. See Laurence J. Peter and Raymond Hull, *The Peter Principle* (New York: Morrow, 1969). Peter and Hull suggest that the managerial career cycle ends when managers are promoted to their "level of incompetence": a job beyond their ability. This certainly does happen, but managers probably reach plateaus more frequently while they are still performing effectively and when they then can still develop and grow.

43. Many organizations have developed programs to assist individuals in managing their careers. For

example, under the guidance of Walter D. Storey, General Electric has developed career planning programs and a manual entitled *Career Action Planning*. Arthur D. Little uses a manual entitled *Effective Career Management*. The point at which organizations should work with individuals to develop and manage their careers is discussed thoroughly by Manuel L. London and Stephen A. Stumpf in *Managing Careers* (Reading, Mass.: Addison-Wesley, 1982).

44. For information on developing individual career plans, see Alan N. Schoonmaker, *Executive Career Strategy* (New York: American Management Associations, 1971); Andrew H. Souerwine, *Career Strategies: Planning for Personal Achievement* (New York: AMACOM, 1978); Richard Nelson Bolles, *What Color Is Your Parachute?* [revised annually] (Berkeley, Calif.: Ten Speed Press, 1986); and Nicholas N. Weiler, *Reality and Career Planning: A Guide to Personal Growth* (Reading, Mass.: Addison-Wesley, 1977). Detailed guidance on individual career planning can be found in London and Stumpf, *Managing Careers*. The Clawson et al. text (*Self-Assessment and Career Development*) provides detailed guidance on developing a career strategy that is especially appropriate for MBA students, but many other students have also found it useful. In addition, a growing number of college and graduate schools of business offer full-credit courses in career planning and development for their management students. Schools that have offered such courses for a number of years include the Harvard Business School, Fordham Graduate School of Business Administration, and Northeastern University.

45. Schoonmaker, *Executive Career Strategy*, pp. 6–11.

46. This section is based in part on Schoonmaker, *Executive Career Strategy*, and DuBrin, *Fundamentals of Organizational Behavior*, chapter 5.

47. Ronald J. Burke, "Relationships In and Around Organizations: It's *Both* Who You Know and What You Know that Counts," *Psychological Reports* 55, no. 1 (August 1984):293–307.

48. See John J. Gabarro and John P. Kotter, "Managing Your Boss," *Harvard Business Review* 58, no. 1 (January–February 1980):92–100; and Lloyd Baird and Kathy Kram, "Career Dynamics: Managing the Superior/Subordinate Relationship," *Organizational Dynamics* 11, no. 4 (Spring 1983):46–64.

49. See John F. Veiga, "The Mobile Manager at Mid-Career," *Harvard Business Review* 51, no. 1 (January–February 1973):115–119; and "Do Managers on the Move Get Anywhere?" *Harvard Business Review* 59, no. 2 (March–April 1981):20–36.

50. Schoonmaker, in *Executive Career Strategy*, adds that incompetent superiors can also hinder your career. Requesting a transfer from such a superior is likely to be viewed as disloyalty. Schoonmaker suggests as an alternative that you let a superior in another department know of your competence and availability so that that person can arrange a transfer.

51. Hall and Hall, *The Two-Career Couple*, pp. 22–25.

52. Ibid., pp. 232–235.

53. We were reminded of this fact by James G. Clawson, "Is Mentoring Necessary?" *Training and Development Journal* 39, no. 4 (April 1985):36.

54. Kathy E. Kram, *Mentoring at Work: Developmental Relationships in Organizational Life* (Glenview, Ill.: Scott, Foresman, 1985), chapters 2 and 3.

55. Ibid., p. 22.

56. See also Kathy E. Kram and Lynn A. Isabella, "Mentoring Alternatives: The Role of Peer Relationships in Career Development," *Academy of Management Journal* 28, no. 1 (March 1985):110–132.

57. Debra L. Nelson and James C. Quick, "Professional Women: Are Distress and Disease Inevitable?" *Academy of Management Review* 10, no. 2 (April 1985):206–218. See also Cary L. Cooper and Marilyn J. Davidson, "The High Cost of Stress on Women Managers," *Organizational Dynamics* 10, no. 4 (Spring 1982):44–53.

58. Ruth B. Ekstrom, "Women in Management: Factors Affecting Career Entrance and Advancement," *Selections* 2, no. 1 (Spring 1985):29–32.

59. Ibid.

60. Susan M. Donnell and Jay Hall, "Men and Women as Managers: A Significant Case of No Significant Difference," *Organizational Dynamics* 8, no. 4 (Spring 1980):60–77.

61. See, for example, Hazel F. Ezell, Charles A. Odewahn, and J. Daniel Sherman, "Women Entering Management: Differences in Perceptions of Factors Influencing Integration," *Group and Organizational Studies* 7, no. 2 (June 1982):243–253.

62. See Eliza G. C. Collins, *"Dearest Amanda . . ." An Executive's Advice to Her Daughter* (New York: Harper & Row, 1984); and Betty Lehan Harragan, *Games Mother Never Taught You: Corporate Gamesmanship for Women* (New York: Rawson, 1977).

CASE STUDY: A Talk with Kirkeby's Son

"Did you want to see me?" Brad Kirkeby poked his head into the open doorway of his boss's office.

"Sure did, Brad. Come on in. I'll be finished with these overtime authorizations in a minute." Anthony Carboni continued initialing time cards while Kirkeby came in and sat down. Putting the cards to one side of his desk, Carboni looked up and smiled.

"Well, Brad, how's it going?"

"Boring as hell!"

Carboni retained his composure. He cared little for the disrespectfulness of so many young people and their total lack of tact. But Carboni had two reasons for restraint in this case. First, Brad Kirkeby was recently out of college and on an 18-month company rotational training program. He would be in Carboni's section for only another 45 days. Second, Brad was the son of Lawrence Kirkeby, one of Lockport Aircraft's most capable designers.

"I'm sorry to hear that," replied Carboni. "What seems to be the problem?"

"I'm going out of my mind with blueprint check." Kirkeby's response was emphatic but not hostile.

"Well," said Carboni, "someone has to check blueprints."

"But why me?" replied Kirkeby. "Can't a draftsman or a clerk do it?"

"Oh, I suppose he could," said Carboni, "but this is the way we've always developed potential structure designers . . . by having them learn all phases of the business from the bottom up."

"No disrespect intended, Mr. Carboni, but that argument escapes me. It's like saying that if you want to be an actor, you have to have experience as a stagehand. I joined Lockport Aircraft to design airplanes, not to check blueprints."

"And so you will, Brad . . . eventually."

Kirkeby laughed. "Eventually . . . in time, Brad . . . wait your turn, Brad. In the long run it will all work out. Mr. Carboni, do you know what Lord Keynes, the famous British economist, said about the long run?"

"No," replied Carboni, growing less patient each moment.

"Lord Keynes said, 'In the long run we'll all be dead!' "

"Meaning?"

"Meaning that I don't want to die or retire before I'm given a meaningful job to do."

Carboni lit a cigar and puffed several times while looking directly at Kirkeby.

"I'm trying to understand you, Brad," he replied at last. "But you are simply going to have to adjust to the fact that you are out of college and in the real world now. It takes years of experience before you assume major structural design responsibility."

"That's because what they call experience in the Lockport Aircraft training program is merely a succession of routine tasks that could be done as well by a moron. Experience is learning and I'm not learning anything!"

"Look, Brad. I know you get all those aeronautical design theory courses in college and you expect to design planes your first week out of college. Face it, there's a certain amount of routine work in any job. Every day can't be a learning experience like it was in college."

"I don't see why not," replied Kirkeby. "If I was hired to eventually design planes, shouldn't I be working next to designers instead of piddling around with trivia?"

"The work in this section is hardly trivia!" Carboni was angry now but forced himself to keep from shouting. "But the work in this section is not the issue. You want to design airplanes like your father . . . right?"

"Right."

"Well," said Carboni, "your father has been with Lockport Aircraft for 25 years . . . eight years longer than I have. He started at the bottom and worked himself up step by step until, now, he's one of the most respected designers in the industry."

"My father is living proof of how ridiculous the system is. He had models at home when I was a boy . . . models he built in his spare time of wing and fuselage structures for as yet undreamed-of Mach 1 and Mach 1.5 power plants."

"Lawrence Kirkeby was always considered to be a very talented person," replied Carboni calmly.

Brad Kirkeby continued, "He was way ahead of his time. And what did this company have him doing for most of those years? Did they use his creative talents to design planes, or on research to advance the state of the art? No. That would have been too obvious. They made him waste nearly 20 potentially creative years on trivial assignments before he became a designer with the authority to control technical considerations."

"How naive can you be, Brad Kirkeby? Do you really believe that your father alone came upon this advanced design information and was frustrated for years by a repressive and unresponsive management?" Carboni was angry now and let it show as he continued.

"Sure your father was talented. That's how he got to be chief designer at Lockport Aircraft. But he was and is still a mortal like the rest of us. Lawrence Kirkeby made his share of mistakes along the line. It was only after years of detailing and understudy with our top designers that his own ideas began to evolve and his real talents began to show. That's when he was moved to a responsible design position."

Brad Kirkeby started to reply, but Carboni cut him off.

"That's the trouble with you kids nowadays. You want everything in life without having to pay the price for it. You tell me you're bored with your job and ought to be designing planes instead. For your information, there are at least 30 bright young men currently in the company who have already passed this apprenticeship that you consider so useless and are now on detailing and limited design activity. Do you suggest I pass them up and promote you to the head of the class, simply because you're bored with your present assignment?"

"Of course not, but . . . " Brad Kirkeby made an attempt to intervene.

"You're damned right I won't," shouted Carboni, answering his own question. "You've been in my section two months now and have turned in only mediocre work at best. You probably can justify that to yourself on the grounds that the work doesn't turn you on. Well, let me tell you something, Brad Kirkeby, talent is one hell of a lot more than just saying you have it. Talent is proving it in the work you do *now* . . . not the work you say you'll do next year or the year after! For all of your big talk about how great you are and how dull the work is, you have yet to prove to me you're anything but a phony!"

Source: Case from Robert D. Joyce, *Encounters in Organizational Behavior* (Elmsford, N.Y.: Pergamon Press, 1972), pp. 151–154. Reprinted with permission of the publisher.

Case Questions
1. What are the issues involved in this case?
2. To what extent do you agree with the basic position(s) taken by Kirkeby?
3. To what extent do you agree with the basic position(s) taken by Carboni?
4. How can you explain Kirkeby's behavior?
5. How important is Carboni's behavior in determining Kirkeby's career at Lockport?

CASE ON LEADING

Cookie Wars

David Liederman makes a remarkable soft-and-chewy chocolate-chip cookie. So does Debbi Fields. Some people prefer one to the other.

Cookie eaters who enjoy large chunks of chocolate in a thin, very buttery cookie with just a hint of crispiness at the edges will buy theirs at Liederman's David's Cookies stores. Connoisseurs who prefer a more traditional chip in a thicker cookie—still a bit doughy on the inside—will patronize a Mrs. Fields Chocolate Chippery store. At Mrs. Fields you are encouraged to buy cookies still warm from the oven. At David's they won't sell a cookie until it cools.

This year, American snackers will spend at least $200 million on fresh-baked, soft-and-chewy, over-the-counter cookies, twice what they spent just two years ago and half what cookie makers expect them to spend next year. Liederman and Fields are both baking big batches of this business, but that is about all they have in common. For in addition to having distinctly different tastes in cookies, they have radically different notions of how to grow a cookie company.

Wheeler-dealer entrepreneurs will admire Liederman's franchising and licensing strategy. Apostles of corporate culture will applaud Fields's insistence on company-owned-and-operated stores. Automation fans will marvel at David's cookie production system, while the more idiosyncratic will appreciate the flexibility that Mrs. Fields gives its employees. People who appreciate cute corporate aphorisms, such as "Good enough never is," will love Mrs. Fields. People who are embarrassed by them can take refuge at David's.

After a point, greatness in a cookie simply comes down to individual taste. Maybe that is true of cookie companies, too. Debbi Fields couldn't run David Liederman's company for a day; but neither could he run hers. Their companies, like their cookies, reflect the individuals.

Walk toward the river on East 50th Street in Manhattan to a gray, four-story townhouse. In front, double-parked, is a chauffeured Cadillac limousine. Within the house is one of midtown's rare private garages. Ring the bell, and when you have passed inspection over the hidden TV camera, walk through the garage to a two-room office area. The larger room is filled with 35-year-old David Liederman—you can recognize him by his bulk—who is likely to be shouting shorthand into a telephone that beeps more or less continuously through the day. A typical Liederman conversation might be: "What . . . Yeah. . . . No. . . . Tell him Toronto is gone. . . . Yeah."

From here Liederman presides over the growth of his cookie empire. At the moment it consists of a management office on 42nd Street and a plant in Long Island City that manufactures and ships cookie dough to roughly 150 (and growing)

David's Cookies stores. Of the 150 stores, 31 are in Manhattan and are company-owned. The rest, spread unevenly across the country, either are owned by territorial franchisees or are operated by department store employees in such places as Macy's. Four (and also growing) Japanese stores are operated by Liederman's joint-venture partner, Nissho Iwai Corporation.

There is a reason why the empire looks that way, and it reflects Liederman's view of how the business works. It has, as he sees it, two parts: First you have to make the cookie, and then you have to sell it. In both parts you want to minimize the probability of error. In Liederman's mind, that means either minimizing the number of people involved or, when that is not practical, supervising them as closely as possible.

In part one, you minimize the number of people involved. You do that by making all the cookie dough in a single nearby plant where you can keep an eye on the process. Then you chill it and ship it to the stores, where all an employee must do is put the dough on a baking tray, put the tray into an automatic oven, and collect it when the finished cookies emerge 7½ minutes later.

Part two of the business—selling the freshly baked cookies—still requires lots of people, and you can't easily manage hourly counter help in Tennessee, for example, from a Manhattan townhouse. So you turn the retailing end of the business over to someone in Tennessee, a franchisee or licensee, whose livelihood depends on how well he or she manages.

"Anybody who tells you that the retail business is wonderful and exciting," says Liederman, "is out of his mind. . . . The realities of the retail business in any typical urban environment are not wonderful: the external robberies, the internal robberies, the motivation. . . . A very close friend of mine is executive vice-president in charge of operations for The Horn & Hardart Company. . . . I said to him, 'Define your job for me.' He said, 'My job is to keep my employees stealing as little as possible.'

"People problems. That's why I look for guys like [Cambridge, Massachusetts, franchisee Jim] Bildner all over the country. Because if they're young and aggressive and they want to kill for the business, they'll be standing there, and that's much better than me trying to run a Cambridge cookie store out of 42nd Street, New York City.

"You have to think at the lowest common denominator. One of the reasons we do so well in the cookie business is that a chimpanzee could take cookies out of that bag and more often than not put them on the tray properly.

"One thing we talked about in Japan with my partners over there would be having a totally automatic cookie store. Do you realize there are totally automatic French-fry machines now?"

"We're a people company," chirps Debbi Fields, "and what we're really selling a customer is a feel-good feeling." Liederman would gag on the phrase.

Fields is a wasp-waisted, clear-skinned, 27-year-old, three-time mother with the kind of irrepressible California cheeriness that gives the average New Yorker—David Liederman, for example—a migraine. "That airhead," he calls her when he is especially riled. "She," Liederman maintains, "is really he. Randy Fields [Debbi's husband] runs Mrs. Fields Cookies. Debbi Fields is a nice, good-looking blonde who doesn't make any business decisions at all." Debbi Fields, for her part, wouldn't dream of calling Liederman a name—not publicly, anyway.

At Mrs. Fields's corporate offices in Park City, Utah, high in the ski country 40 minutes east of Salt Lake City, the same phrases keep popping up. "Good enough never is," a half-dozen people will say. "Having a Mrs. Fields experience" is what people there say when they mean eating a cookie. Even chief operating officer Taylor Devine, a mature, dignified New Englander, a veteran of strategic-planning consulting at Arthur D. Little in Cambridge, Massachusetts, discussed "feel-good feelings" over dinner—sober, in a public dining room. The marketing manager was the first of several Debbi Fields executives who said, "We're all high on energy here."

Even for a non-New Yorker, all this happy talk takes a little getting used to, but there is no doubt of its source. "I'm the heart and soul of the company. That's my job," explains Debbi Fields, a woman whose apparent niceness would trouble even the credulous. "Sometimes," she says, "when I'm frustrated or disappointed I think, well, maybe I haven't done enough good things. . . . So I do something nice for somebody and I snap right out of it."

"This sounds stupid," says Randy Fields, 36, a businessman who has made a lot of money in oil, venture capital, and financial consulting to *Fortune* 500 companies, "especially to a businessperson, but she succeeds because she is a good person. I've seen her stop her car and help a little old lady carry her groceries. . . . I absolutely swear that she is exactly what she appears to be."

She appears to be in charge of a company that started in 1977 with a single cookie store in Palo Alto, California, south of San Francisco, capitalized with $50,000 borrowed from Randy. In 1985, the company will by year end have generated sales of at least $45 million from 300 cookie stores across the country and in Singapore; Sydney, Australia; and Hong Kong. Each one of the stores is company-owned, and every cookie is sold by a Mrs. Fields employee.

Mrs. Fields, unlike David's, doesn't mix its cookie dough in a central plant. Instead, store employees combine ingredients (some in proportioned containers) that are shipped to the store by independent distributors under contract with the company. Nor are the store ovens automatic. Employees must put the raw dough in to bake and remember to take the finished cookies out. "I don't know how long they bake," says Colleen Clifford, who works at a Salt Lake City Mrs. Fields store. "You just *know* when they're done."

Two vice-presidents for operations at the corporate level oversee six (eventually ten) regional operations managers, each of whom is responsible for about 30 stores. Store managers, some of whom may manage two or three stores, get help from team leaders, selected from among the hourly employees. Everyone but hourly employees attends training school in Park City. Everyone in the company, even secretaries at the corporate offices, gets working experience in a cookie store, and not just at the counter. Stan Slap, one of the vice-presidents for operations, went with Debbi Fields to visit a San Francisco store soon after he joined the company. "We went in. Everything looked fine, but people were really busy, so Debbi said, 'What can I do to help?' The manager said, 'Well, the back room is a mess.' So Debbi and I spent the next two hours on our hands and knees cleaning the back room."

Before being hired by Mrs. Fields, candidates get the customary interview. In addition, they frequently get auditions before audiences of other candidates and employees. Natural hams have a leg up on competing job applicants. "We want people to be outrageous," Fields says. "We want people to be themselves. . . . We don't tell people that they have to be pleasant. We tell them that we want them to have fun. We tell them that they have to greet customers. We don't tell them how they have to greet customers." At a San Francisco Mrs. Fields, Chrissy Woodward sometimes attracts people by tossing out free cookies, then leading the assembled crowd in Mrs. Fields cheers.

Chrissy: "And how MANY do you buy?"
Crowd: "A DOZEN!"
Chrissy: "Oooh-wee."
Crowd: "OOOH-WEE!"

A daily profit-and-loss statement is generated for every store, but store managers don't see them. "Store managers can't be profit-driven," says Randy Fields. "They have to be driven by sales and by making people happy. If they had access to the P&L, would they take the cookies off the rack after two hours?" Two hours is as long as a Mrs. Fields cookie is supposed to remain unsold. (At David's the advertised limit is 12 hours, but while Mrs. Fields promotes its warm cookies, recall that a David's cookie is a cool cookie.)

"Mrs. Fields cookies," says Debbi Fields, "is an extension of how I see the world. I believe people will do their very best, I really do, provided that they are getting proper support. . . . Sometimes I've gone into a store, and we haven't had soft-and-chewy cookies, and I've shut the store down. I'm known for doing that. They have to be perfect. There's no word at Mrs. Fields for 'it's good enough.' I'll go in and throw away $600 worth of product. I don't think about what I'm throwing away. . . . I just assume that there's been some reason why the people were not taught what the standards of the company are.

"The reason why I know when a cookie is overbaked is because I've overbaked them. I know when one is underbaked because I've underbaked them. I've been there. I understand these things. And therefore I'm there to teach [the employees]. I'm their support system. We do it together, and we start feeling good about what we're doing.

"It's a people company. That's what it's all about. . . . Mrs. Fields is in the business of selling cookies, but that's just what the customer believes. What we really do is . . . we take care of people.

"You say that people come to work for money, and I disagree with that. Money is part of a whole picture. People come to work because they need to be productive. They need to feel like they are successful in whatever they do. . . . Money is not the issue. I don't know if giving them stock in the company would change anything.

"I'm not brilliant. I am *not* brilliant. But I do understand one thing, and that is feelings, and emotion, and caring. You know, everybody likes to be made to feel special and important. They like to be acknowledged. That's my real role. To make people feel important and to create an opportunity for them. That's really my role as the cookie president, the cookie person.

"I knew what I was really good at. I make great cookies; that I really do well. And I'm really good at dealing with people. So I fulfill my needs every day, because I do what I like to do. But there are some things that I am just not a whiz kid at. I am not great with numbers. And so I thought, well, understanding my limitations, I need superstars. . . . I have surrounded myself with superstars. And they know it. . . . I do rely on Randy's expertise with numbers because he's so good at it. . . . I would be foolish not to."

David's and Mrs. Fields compete, but not head-to-head yet. The market for high-quality, premium-price, over-the-counter, hand-dropped, soft-and-chewy cookies is too big and growing too fast. "We're in a race," Liederman says, "but we're both going to win. It's comical to me that all we're both doing is selling pretty good cookies—in my case very good cookies, in her case pretty good cookies. . . .

"The problem with the cookie business is that there are four companies that are all trying to be the McDonald's. Which is not to say that Wendy's and Burger King don't make a living, but to be the clear-cut leader you have to have stores, outlets, and there's not a cookie company in the United States that has more than 160 now. By way of comparison, Baskin-Robbins has 3,200 stores. There are nine domestic ice cream companies that have more than 300 stores. The cookie business is just starting, and we're all running around like chickens with our heads cut off picking up one location at a time. At the rate we're going, it's highly conceivable that [David's] could have more stores in Japan than in the United States, which doesn't mean we won't be doing well in the United States, but it does mean that we will not have been able to get the big deal. We're talking about 7-Eleven or maybe a supermarket chain that can open up 300, 400, 500 outlets at once."

"Oh," says Debbi Fields, "you're going to ask me those questions like . . . See, that's one of the reasons I don't read those corporate-strategy books. Most people will ask me, 'Aren't cookies a fad? Isn't there a saturation point? Isn't there a product life cycle?' I think that's all baloney. My view of the market is quite simply: Are our cookies incredibly fabulous? Yes. Do they make people happy? Yes. Are they as good as homemade? In my opinion, yes. Do people love to eat them? Yes. Are they going to give up the things they love to eat? I think that's very doubtful. . . . I mean, really, if something is fresh, warm, and wonderful and it makes you feel good, are you going to stop buying cookies? You grew up with cookies. Your mom made you cookies."

Both companies are opening more stores. Each expects to have twice as many outlets by the end of 1985 as it did in early 1984, even without Liederman's "big deal." Unlike American steel and automobiles, American cookies sell well overseas. David's, says Liederman, will be in ten more countries by December 1985. "My Japanese partner wants the whole Far East perimeter. They want to buy a few franchises in Oregon, open up western Canada. 'And while we're at it,' they say, 'why not sell us a couple of stores in New York.' You don't have to be a brain surgeon to see that sooner or later I'll be learning to speak Japanese, and I'm not sure I want that right now.

"You know what? There's still no plan. The plan is I want to get hundreds of stores open . . . and to maintain controlling interest in the company. How do we get there? I don't have the answer to that. Maybe I should marry Debbi Fields."

Source: Reprinted with permission, *Inc.* magazine, July 1984. Copyright © 1984 by Inc. Publishing Company, 38 Commercial Wharf, Boston, Mass. 02110.

Questions

1. What are the main differences in leadership style between David Liederman and Debbi Fields?
2. What is the relationship between leadership style and organizational structure in the two companies?
3. How are employees motivated in Liederman's company? In Fields's?
4. How are interpersonal and organizational communications handled in each company?
5. Is Debbi Fields really the leader of her company? Does Liederman face threats to his business that Fields does not? Why?
6. In your opinion, which company will ultimately be more successful?

PART FIVE
CONTROLLING, INFORMATION SYSTEMS, AND INTERNATIONAL MANAGEMENT

20 EFFECTIVE CONTROL

Upon completing this chapter you should be able to:

1. Explain why the control function is necessary.
2. Describe the link between planning and controlling.
3. State why managers need to find the right degree of control.
4. Describe the four different types of control methods.
5. Describe the steps in the control process.
6. Summarize the issues that managers have to deal with in designing a control system.
7. Explain the importance of "key performance areas" and "strategic control points."
8. Describe the characteristics of effective control systems.

As sales manager of Data Peripherals, Inc., it is your responsibility to see that each division meets its sales quota. At the quarterly sales conference, Marsha Shore, regional sales manager of the western division, reports that her division "missed our total sales objective by 8 percent but expect[s] to make that up when we surpass our objective for the next quarter."

Then you hear from Bruce Conacher of the eastern division: "Our figures for the quarter show that we exceeded our sales objective by almost 12 percent."

In evaluating the situation, you first consider the western division. Ms. Shore has an excellent record with the company and a proven record of reliability and accuracy in predicting future performance for her division. Mr. Conacher, although new to the job, more than met his objective this time; and it seems reasonable to assume he should be able to repeat his success. You therefore decide that no special action is needed.

Sometime later you receive the divisional profit and loss figures. You are more than a little surprised to find that the western division, in spite of missing its sales objective, shows a higher contribution to profits than the eastern division, which more than met its objective.

Naturally, you investigate. And you find the answer: Mr. Conacher, in order to meet his sales objective, concentrated his division's efforts on large, established accounts, persuading them to place large orders and thus qualify for substantial quantity discounts. Result? High sales, minimum profits.

The situation is reflected in the next quarter's results when the eastern division, with most of its big accounts already overstocked, falls 18 percent below its quota. The western division, on the other hand, having spent a significant portion of its effort in the previous quarter on opening new accounts, is now reaping the benefit and, true to Ms. Shore's prediction, surpasses its objective by over 15 percent.

As in the situation just described, control factors are often key in achieving organizational effectiveness. In this final part of the book we will describe the process of control, the various control methods that managers can use, and the ways in which the control process can be made more effective. We will also discuss the role of information systems and computerized information processing aids, such as decision support systems and expert systems, in helping managers manage and control their organizations. Finally, in the last chapter of the book, we will discuss the managerial processes and challenges involved in managing in a progressively more integrated and competitive global environment.

The Meaning of Control

Earl P. Strong and Robert D. Smith have described the need for control this way:

> There are a number of conflicting viewpoints regarding the best manner in which to manage an organization. However, theorists as well as practicing executives agree that *good management requires effective control*. A combination of well-planned objectives, strong organization, capable

direction, and motivation have little probability for success unless there exists an adequate system of control.[1]

In other words, the information in the other parts of this book on planning, organizing, and leading, even if it were effectively applied, is not likely to help managers achieve their goals unless the information on control is also applied effectively.

The Link between Planning and Controlling

A good definition of management *control* is "the process through which managers assure that actual activities conform to planned activities." In the planning of an organization's activities, the fundamental goals and objectives and the methods for attaining them are established. The control process measures progress toward those goals and enables managers to detect deviations from the plan in time to take corrective action before it is too late.[2] Often, different individuals fulfill the planning and control roles, but they must communicate in order for both functions to work effectively.[3]

Our example at the start of this chapter illustrates the link between planning and controlling. The sales quotas represented the goals agreed to by upper management and the sales department; the quarterly sales conferences, during which sales managers reported on their progress toward those quotas, represented one of the company's control devices. In the example, short-term objectives were being met at the expense of long-term organizational goals. Data Peripheral's control system did not detect that trade-off—a common fault in the controls set up by many firms.[4] Additional controls might have required that a certain percentage of the sales target be made up of new business. Then, Conacher's concentration on established accounts would have been detected, and corrective action could have been taken.

What Is Control?

The definition of control used above suggests what control is intended to accomplish. It does not indicate what control *is*. Robert J. Mockler's definition of control points out the essential elements of the control process:

> **Management control is a systematic effort to set performance standards with planning objectives, to design information feedback systems, to compare actual performance with these predetermined standards, to determine whether there are any deviations and to measure their significance, and to take any action required to assure that all corporate resources are being used in the most effective and efficient way possible in achieving corporate objectives.[5]**

Steps in the Control Process. Mockler's definition divides control into four steps. (See fig. 20–1.) The first step is to *establish standards and methods for measuring performance*. This step might involve standards and measurements for everything from sales and production targets to worker attendance and safety records. For this step to be effective, the standards must be specified in meaningful terms and accepted by the individuals involved. The methods of measurement should also be accepted as accurate. An organization may set an objective to become the "leader in its field," but this standard is little more than verbal inspiration if it is not defined and if a system of measurement is not established.

FIGURE 20-1 BASIC STEPS IN THE CONTROL PROCESS

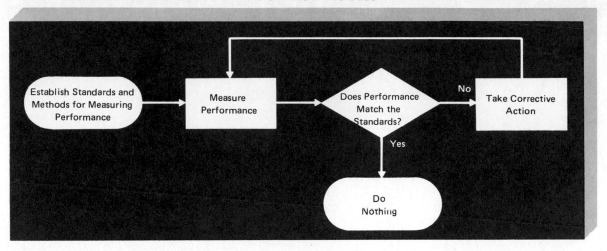

The second step is to *measure the performance*. Like all aspects of control, this is an ongoing, repetitive process, with the actual frequency dependent on the type of activity being measured. Safe levels of gas particles in the air, for example, may be continuously monitored in a manufacturing plant, whereas progress on long-term expansion objectives may need to be reviewed by top management only once or twice a year. A fault to be avoided, however, is to allow too long a period of time to pass between performance measurements.

Does performance match the standards? In many ways, this is the easiest step in the control process. The complexities presumably have been dealt with in the first two steps; now it is a matter of comparing measured results with the targets or standards previously set. If performance matches the standards, managers may assume that "everything is under control"; and, as figure 20–1 shows, they do not have to intervene actively in the organization's operations.

The final step is to *take corrective action* if performance falls short of standards and the analysis indicates action is required. This corrective action may involve a change in one or more activities of the organization's operations, or it may involve a change in the standards originally established. Unless managers see the control process through to its conclusion, they are merely monitoring performance rather than exercising control. The emphasis should always be on devising constructive ways to bring performance up to standard, rather than merely identifying past failures.

The control process must be carried out by managers throughout the organization. Because of the prominence of financial controls, some people assume that control responsibility can be left largely in the hands of accountants and controllers. Financial controls often do set the resource limits within which managers must operate; and many control methods involve budgets, profit and loss statements, and other financial tools. However, *all* managers need to exercise control to carry out their activities successfully.[6]

The control devices that managers use are often nonfinancial in nature. For example, such factors as absenteeism, employee turnover, sales force performance, new-product development, plant safety, employee productivity, public relations, market share, and product quality—all important activities at every level of the organization—must be controlled, at least partially, through nonfinancial means. Product quality, for example, will usually be controlled through statistical quality control methods, periodic inspections, and product testing.

The Importance of Control

It is impossible to imagine any organization completely devoid of control in the broadest sense of the term. Control is necessary for an organization to achieve its objectives. What factors make control important for managers and their organizations? How much control do managers need to exercise?

Organizational Factors Creating the Need for Control

There are many factors that make control a necessity in today's organizations. They include the changing environment of organizations, the increasing complexity of organizations, the fallibility of organization members, and the need of managers to delegate authority. We will discuss these factors here.

Change. Suppose the Fanfold Paper Corporation, a supplier to Data Peripherals, Inc., operated in a static market. Every year the company would make and sell the same amount of computer paper to the same customers. Manufacturing and labor costs would never vary, nor would availability and costs of materials. In other words, last year's results would govern this year's production. Planning and controlling for this company would quickly become automatic.

Even in the most stable industries, however, such a situation does not exist. Change is an inevitable part of any organization's environment: Markets shift; new products emerge; new materials are discovered; new regulations are passed. Through the control function, managers detect changes that are affecting their organization's products or services. They can then move to cope with the threats or opportunities these changes create.

Complexity. The one-room schoolhouse and the small family business could be controlled on a relatively informal, unplanned basis. Today's vast organizations, however, require a much more formal and careful approach. Diversified product lines must be watched closely to ensure that quality and profitability are maintained; sales in retail outlets need to be recorded accurately and analyzed; the organization's various markets, foreign and domestic, require close monitoring.

Adding to the complexity of today's organizations is decentralization. Many organizations now have regional sales and marketing offices, widely distributed research facilities, or geographically separated plants. Decentralization can simplify an organization's control efforts, since not all the organization's operations any longer require control by central headquarters. Paradoxically, in order for decentralization to be effective, each decentralized unit's control activities must be especially precise. Performance against established standards has to be watched closely so that general managers can appraise the effectiveness of the unit for which they are responsible and so that corporate management can, in turn, appraise the effectiveness of the general managers.

Mistakes. If they or their subordinates never made mistakes, managers could simply establish performance standards and note significant and unexpected changes in the environment. But organization members do make mistakes—wrong parts are ordered, wrong pricing decisions are made, problems are diagnosed incorrectly. A control system allows managers to detect these mistakes before they become critical.

Delegation. As we discussed in chapter 11, when managers delegate authority to subordinates, their responsibility to their own superiors is not diminished. The only way managers can determine if their subordinates are accomplishing the tasks that have been delegated to them is by implementing a system of control. Without such a system, managers are unable to check on subordinates' progress.

Finding the Right Degree of Control

The word "control" often has unpleasant connotations because it seems to threaten personal freedom and autonomy.[7] At a time when the legitimacy of authority is being sharply questioned, and when there is a growing movement toward greater independence and self-actualization for individuals, the concept of organizational control makes many people uncomfortable. Yet control is necessary in organizations. Today, however, organizational control methods have become more precise and sophisticated than ever, in part as a result of the widespread use of computer data processing. How can managers deal with the potential conflict between the needs for personal autonomy and for organizational control?

One way to deal with the seeming disparity between these two needs is to recognize that excessive control will harm the organization as well as the individuals within it. Controls that bog down organization members in red tape or limit too many types of behavior will kill motivation, inhibit creativity, and ultimately damage organizational performance. For example, in the episode that begins this chapter, Mr. Conacher's problem could be avoided by establishing a standard for a minimum percentage of sales to come from new accounts. Alternatively, Data Peripherals might decide that this situation was basically the result of his inexperience in his new position and should be dealt with by more careful coaching and training of new regional sales managers, instead of by adding one more standard to the existing control system.

The degree of control that is considered extreme or harmful will vary from one situation to another. An advertising agency, for example, may require much looser controls than a medical testing lab. The economic climate may also affect the degree of control acceptable to organization members. In a recession, most people will accept tighter controls and restrictions; when things are booming, rules and restrictions will often seem less appropriate.

Inadequate controls, of course, will also harm the organization by wasting resources and by making it more difficult to attain goals. Individuals may be harmed by inadequate controls as well; a decrease in control does not necessarily lead to an increase in personal autonomy. In fact, individuals may have even less personal freedom and autonomy because they may not be able to predict or depend on what their co-workers will do. (Anarchy, the lack of any social or organizational controls, is not a situation of great personal freedom but one of massive uncertainty and unpredictability.) In addition, if the lack of an effective system of organizational

"Right, Chief, you told me to go to New Jersey to inspect our plant, and I went to a revival of 'Singin' in the Rain' instead. What can I say?"

Drawing by C. Barsotti; © 1983 The New Yorker Magazine, Inc.

controls causes individual managers to supervise their subordinates more closely, the freedom of those subordinates will be further reduced.

In establishing controls, then, the task for managers is to find the proper balance between appropriate organizational control and individual freedom. With too much control, organizations become stifling, inhibiting, and unsatisfying places to work. With too little control, organizations become chaotic, inefficient, and ineffective in achieving their goals.

Because organizations, people, environments, and technology keep changing, an effective control system requires continuing review and modification. For example, if an organization's manufacturing or service divisions employ relatively unskilled individuals who are not very interested in their work, its control system might require frequent and detailed quality and productivity checks. But if the organization were to produce the same product or service in a different location with workers who are more skilled or more interested in the work, the control system might require fewer points of measurement, and the workers could be given more autonomy and more responsibility to monitor and correct their own performance.[8]

Types of Control Methods

Most methods of control can be grouped into one of four basic types: pre-action controls, steering controls, screening or yes/no controls, and post-action controls.[9] We will discuss these control types here. In the next chapter, we will describe actual control techniques.

Pre-action Controls

Pre-action controls (sometimes called *precontrols*) ensure that before an action is undertaken the necessary human, material, and financial resources have been budgeted. When the time for action occurs, budgets (discussed in chapter 21) make sure the requisite resources will be available in the types, quality, quantities, and locations needed. Budgets may call for the hiring and training of new employees, the purchase of new equipment and supplies, and the design and engineering of new materials or products. The sales budgets allocated to Shore and Conacher in the opening example are examples of pre-action controls.

Steering Controls

Steering controls, or "feedforward controls," are designed to detect deviations from some standard or goal and to allow corrections to be made before a particular sequence of actions is completed.[10] The term "steering controls" is derived from the driving of an automobile. The driver steers the car to prevent it from going off the road or in a wrong direction so the proper destination will be reached. For example, if the Data Peripherals sales manager had been aware that Conacher was overloading his prime accounts in order to reach his sales quota, he or she could have instituted corrective action during the quarter in order to put him back on target. Steering controls are effective only if the manager is able to obtain timely and accurate information about changes in the environment or about progress toward the desired goal.

Yes/No or Screening Controls

Yes/no control provides a screening process in which specific aspects of a procedure must be approved or specific conditions met before operations may continue. If Conacher had been required to have all discounts over a specified amount approved by upper management, that requirement would have been a yes/no control.

Because steering controls provide a means for taking corrective action while a program is still viable, they are usually more important and more widely used than other types of control. However, steering controls are rarely perfect, and so yes/no controls become particularly useful as "double-check" devices. Where safety is a key factor, as in aircraft design, or where large expenditures are involved, as in construction programs, yes/no controls provide managers with an extra margin of security.

Post-action Controls

As the term suggests, *post-action controls* measure the results of a completed action. The causes of any deviation from the plan or standard are determined, and the findings are applied to similar future activities. In our Data Peripherals example, we would be exercising a form of post-action control by stipulating for our next quarter's objectives that 10 percent of the sales quota must come from new business. Post-action controls are also used as a basis for rewarding or encouraging employees (for example, meeting a standard may result in a bonus).

The flow of information and corrective action for all four types of control is shown in figure 20–2. Speed of information flow is a vital factor in efficient control, since the sooner deviations are discovered, the sooner corrective action can be taken. Accuracy is also vital, since corrective actions are based on the information obtained from reports, computer printouts, and other sources. (We will discuss management information systems in chapter 22.)

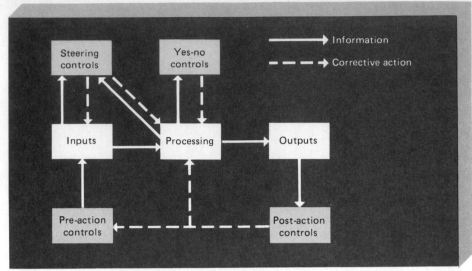

FIGURE 2C–2
FLOW OF
INFORMATION
AND CORRECTIVE
ACTION FOR THREE
TYPES OF
CONTROL

The Importance of Steering Controls

The four types of control we have discussed—pre-action, steering, yes/no, and post-action—are not alternatives for one another. Most organizations will use a combination of all four in attaining their goals. Steering controls are, however, particularly important. Just as outfielders cannot wait until a fly ball lands to see where they should have been standing, managers cannot afford to wait until all results are in before they begin to evaluate performance.

In addition to allowing managers to correct miscalculations, steering controls allow managers to take advantage of unexpected opportunities. Deviations from a standard or plan may, after all, take place in a positive direction; by becoming aware of these deviations before it is too late, managers can shift their organization's resources to where they will do the most good.

Design of the Control Process

In this section we will expand our description of the steps in the control process. Although much of our discussion will be appropriate to yes/no and post-action controls, our primary focus will be on the development of effective steering controls.

The Control Process

William H. Newman has provided a rich discussion of the procedures for establishing a *control system*.[11] We will describe his approach in terms of five basic steps that can be applied to all types of control activities—from monitoring the frequency with which articles are published by professors at a university to checking how often a shipping department meets its delivery dates:

Define desired results. The results that managers desire to obtain (or maintain) should be defined as specifically as possible. Goals expressed in vague or general terms, such as "cut overhead costs" or "fill orders faster," are not nearly as constructive as "cut overhead by 12 percent" or "ship all orders within three working days." The latter phrasing not only provides managers with a basis for working out ways to estimate and implement necessary procedures, but it also includes a yardstick by which they can measure their success or failure in achieving their objectives.

Desired results, according to Newman, should also be linked to the individual responsible for achieving them. If the objective is "reduce shipping time by 10 percent," one person (such as the manager in charge of order processing) should be given the responsibility and authority to meet that objective. If successful, that person should be given credit.

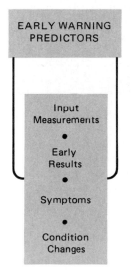

EARLY WARNING PREDICTORS

Input Measurements

•

Early Results

•

Symptoms

•

Condition Changes

Establish predictors of results. The purpose of steering controls is to allow managers to correct deviations before a set of activities is completed. The deviations detected by steering controls must therefore be predictors of results; they must reliably indicate to managers whether corrective action needs to be taken. An important task of managers who are designing the control program is to find a number of reliable indicators or predictors for each of their goals.

Newman has identified several early warning predictors that can help managers estimate whether desired results will be achieved. Among these are:

Input measurements. A change in key inputs will suggest to managers that they need to change their plans or to take some corrective action. For example, incoming orders will determine the number of items to be manufactured; raw material costs will directly affect future product prices; a worsening in economic conditions will very likely cause a decline in consumer demand.

Results of early steps. If early results are better or worse than expected, a reevaluation may be called for and appropriate action taken. The first month's sales of a new ice cream flavor, for example, may provide a useful indication of its future popularity.

Symptoms. These are conditions that seem to be associated with final results, but they do not directly affect those results. For example, whenever sales representatives get their sales reports in late, the sales manager may assume that quotas have not been met. The difficulty is that symptoms are susceptible to very wrong or misleading interpretations.

Changes in assumed conditions. Original estimates are based on the assumption that "normal" conditions will prevail. Any unexpected changes, such as new developments by competitors or material shortages, will indicate the need for a reevaluation of tactics and goals.

Managers may also use past results to help them make estimates of future performance. In this type of post-action control, performance on a previous cycle is used to make predictions and adjustments for the next cycle. As a general rule, the greater the number of reliable and timely predictors, the more confident the manager can be in making performance predictions.

Establish standards for predictors and results. Establishing standards, or pars, for predictors and final results is an important part of designing the control process. Without established pars, managers may overreact to minor deviations or fail to react when deviations are significant.

A par or standard has two basic aims: (1) to motivate and (2) to serve as a benchmark against which actual performance can be compared. Obviously, a control system is most effective when it motivates people to high performance. Since most people respond to a challenge, their success in meeting a tough standard may well provide a greater sense of accomplishment than meeting an easy one. However, if a par is so tough that it seems impossible to meet, it will be more likely to discourage than to motivate effort. Standards that are too difficult may, therefore, actually cause performance to decline.

Newman has argued that very tough but potentially attainable standards should be established so that high performance will be encouraged even if the actual goals are missed. Peters and Waterman have noted that the excellently managed companies they studied tended to accomplish a similar objective by setting goals that are normally achievable and by establishing the expectation that many individuals will exceed the goals by considerable margins.[12] Both these approaches to setting standards seem to work—*provided they are well understood and accepted by everyone concerned.*[13]

Establish the information and feedback network. The fourth step in the design of a control cycle is to establish the means for collecting information on the predictors and for comparing the predictors against their pars. As we shall see, the communication network works best when it flows not only upward but also downward to those who must take corrective action. In addition, it must be efficient enough to feed the relevant information back to key personnel in time for them to act on it.

To keep managers from getting bogged down in communications about how matters are progressing, control communications are often based on the *management by exception* principle. This principle suggests that the controlling manager should be informed about an operation's progress only if there is a significant deviation from the plan or standard. The manager can then concentrate fully on the problem situation.

Evaluate information and take corrective action. This final step involves comparing predictors to pars, deciding what action (if any) to take, and then taking that action. (See figure 20–3 for the elements in a control cycle.)

Information about a deviation from a par must first be evaluated; as we suggested earlier, some deviations are due to local or temporary circumstances and will not really affect the final result. Alternative corrective actions, if they are required, are then developed, evaluated, and implemented.

Key Considerations in Establishing a Control System

Jerome E. Schnee and Thomas P. Ference have described a number of important considerations for establishing a control system.[14] Six of these issues will be presented in the following discussion.

Types of Measurement. Most types of measurement are based on some form of established standards.[15] Such standards may be historical—that is, based on records and information concerning the organization's past experiences. Sales standards, for example, are often historical in nature—the salespeople are expected to increase sales by a certain amount each year. A problem with historical standards is that past performance may have been poor; in addition, circumstances may have changed since past data were compiled.

External standards are those derived from other organizations or other units of the same organization (such as the company's various sales offices). The difficulty here is finding organizations or units that are similar enough to make the external

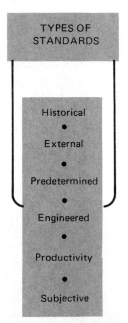

TYPES OF
STANDARDS

Historical
•
External
•
Predetermined
•
Engineered
•
Productivity
•
Subjective

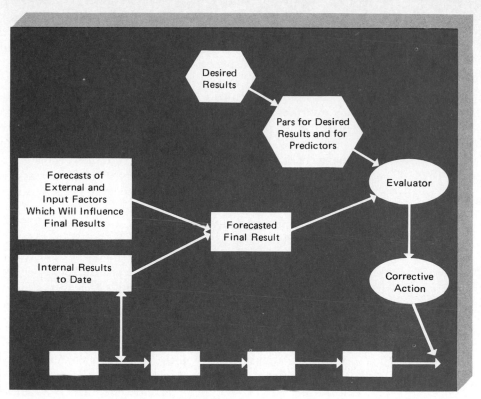

Source: William H. Newman, *Constructive Control: Design and Use of Control Systems*, p. 13. © 1975. Adapted by permission of Prentice-Hall, Inc., Englewood Cliffs, N.J.

FIGURE 20–3 ELEMENTS IN A CONTROL CYCLE

standards meaningful. Wherever possible, *predetermined* standards should be used. These standards (or budgets) are developed in the planning process; they are based on careful study and analysis of the organizational units' internal and external environments.

Engineered standards, concerned with machine capabilities, are often supplied by machine manufacturers. Time and motion studies are useful in setting *assembly-line productivity* standards, if the cost of the engineer who will perform these studies will be offset by increases in efficiency, *and* if employees are willing to accept the new standards. Even professional tasks that are repetitive in nature, such as some surgical procedures or the drafting of simple wills, may have reasonable time standards set for them. For other types of tasks, *subjective* standards, which are based on a manager's discretion, may be established. Such subjective standards become more appropriate as the complexity of a task increases.

The Number of Measurements. The number of measurements must be limited. As the number of controls applied to an individual's work increases, the individual loses autonomy and freedom in how and when the work is to be performed. At some point, the individual may see the number of controls as so constraining and threatening, he or she will start thinking more in terms of self-defense than of performance. Rather than developing new and more effective ways to get the work done, and rather than seeking new responsibilities, the individual will attempt to "look good" on those dimensions of the work that are being monitored. The resulting defensive maneuvers will frequently be at the expense of other aspects of work that are not as subject to detailed measurement and control. Managers who do not realize this may well respond to this situation by adding additional controls for the specific areas that are being neglected.

The problem of "overcontrol" can be tackled in three ways. First, controls should be focused on the major objectives to be achieved, rather than on minor or unimportant matters. This approach is, in part, the point Peters and Waterman make when they observe that excellently managed companies tend to have "simultaneous loose-tight properties."[16] Those companies tightly control performance on a few "core values they hold dear" and allow a great deal of autonomy, independence, and innovation in seeking the objectives associated with those values. Focusing on major objectives eliminates much of the waste and unnecessary pressures of "control for the sake of control." Second, minor targets can be stated in general terms rather than quantified absolutes. For example, instead of targeting personnel turnover at some definite percentage, the criterion could be to "maintain staff at a satisfactory level." Finally, as in the excellently managed companies, organization members should be allowed considerable leeway in terms of how they achieve their control objectives. For example, managers should have the authority to train their subordinates in their own way, so long as the desired results are achieved.

Authority for Setting Measures and Standards. Performance standards can be set with or without the participation of the people whose performance is being controlled. We have discussed the advantages of subordinate participation in the standard-setting process in a number of places throughout our text. When standards are set unilaterally by upper-level managers, there is a danger that employees will regard those standards as unreasonable or unrealistic; they may then not put forth their best efforts to meet them.

Flexibility of Standards. Managers need to determine whether standards should be uniform throughout the similar units of the organization. Sales territories, for example, may be considered roughly equivalent, and so the performance of salespeople may be measured against a uniform standard. Often, however, allowances must be made for the varied circumstances each organizational unit or member must face. For instance, when sales territories are not comparable, a salesperson's performance may be judged by the past sales history of his or her specific territory.

Managers need to make a similar decision about the extent to which qualitative versus quantitative measures will be used in the control system. For some tasks (such as envelope stuffing), performance may be accurately and easily measured in quantitative terms. For other tasks (such as research and development activities), both qualitative and quantitative measures will have to be used.

Frequency of Measurement. Frequency and timing of measurement depend on the nature of the task being controlled. Quality control inspection of items coming off an assembly line often requires hourly monitoring. The use of statistical quality control (which is increasing in the United States) requires the establishment of sample size and the setting of an interval between sample testing. Product development, on the other hand, may be measured on a monthly basis, since significant changes are unlikely to take place on a daily basis.

Managers are often tempted to measure performance at a time convenient for themselves. For example, they may wish to check product quality at the end of the workday or to evaluate employees only during an annual review period. Such a temptation should be avoided, since nonrepresentative measurements may result. For example, assembly-line employees may be especially careful with the last run of items on the assembly line if they know a quality inspection will take place at the end of the day. Random inspection during the workday would probably provide more realistic measures of product quality.

Direction of Feedback. The purpose of control is to ensure that present plans are being implemented and that future plans will be developed more effectively. A well-designed control system will usually include feedback of control information to the individual or group performing the controlled activity. If the control system merely provides information for superiors to check up on their subordinates, the effectiveness of the system is lost: The people whose actions are being controlled may never find out what they need to do to perform more effectively and will view the control system as punitive. The individuals whose actions are being monitored are usually in the best position to take whatever corrective action is necessary, because they are closest to the activities being controlled.

Key Performance Areas

In order for upper-level managers to establish effective control systems, they must first identify the key performance areas of their organization or unit. *Key performance* or *key result areas* are those aspects of the unit or organization that have to function effectively in order for the entire unit or organization to succeed. These areas usually involve major organizational activities or groups of related activities that occur throughout the organization or unit—for example, its financial transactions, its manager-subordinate relations, or its manufacturing operations. The broad controls that upper managers establish for these key performance areas will help define the more detailed control systems and standards of lower-level managers.[17]

Strategic Control Points

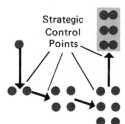

Strategic Control Points

In addition to key performance areas, it is also important to determine the critical points in the system where monitoring or information collecting should occur. If such *strategic control points* can be located, then the amount of information that has to be gathered and evaluated can be reduced considerably.

The most important and useful method of selecting strategic control points is to focus on the most significant elements in a given operation. Usually only a small percentage of the activities, events, individuals, or objects in a given operation will account for a high proportion of the expense or problems that managers will have to face. For example, 10 percent of a manufacturer's products may well yield 60 percent of its sales; 2 percent of an organization's employees may account for 80 percent of its employee grievances; and 20 percent of the police precincts in a city may account for 70 percent of the city's violent crimes.

Another useful consideration in selecting an operation's strategic control points is the location of those areas of the operation in which change occurs. For example, in an organization's system for filling customer orders, a change occurs when the purchase order becomes an invoice, when an inventory item becomes an item to be shipped, or when the item to be shipped becomes part of a truckload. Since errors are more likely to be made when such changes occur, monitoring change points is usually a highly effective way to control an operation.

Characteristics of Effective Control Systems

Reliable and effective control systems have certain characteristics in common. The relative importance of these characteristics varies with individual circumstances, but most control systems are strengthened by their presence.[18]

1. *Accurate.* Information on performance must be accurate. Inaccurate data from a control system can cause the organization to take action that will either fail to correct a problem or create a problem where none exists. Evaluating the accuracy of the information they receive is one of the most important control tasks that managers face.

2. *Timely.* Information must be collected, routed, and evaluated quickly if action is to be taken in time to produce improvements. In our chapter opening example, the relevant information about sales in Conacher's division reached the sales manager too late to take action during the quarter.

3. *Objective and Comprehensible.* The information in a control system should be understandable and be seen as objective by the individuals who use it. The less subjective or ambiguous the control system is, the greater the likelihood that individuals will react knowledgeably and efficiently to the information they receive. A difficult-to-understand control system will cause unnecessary mistakes and confusion or frustration among employees.

4. *Focused on Strategic Control Points.* As we mentioned earlier, the control system should be focused on those areas where deviations from the standards are most likely to take place or where deviations would lead to the greatest harm. The system should also be focused on those points where corrective action can be most effectively applied. For example, it would do little good to control parts quality after the parts have already been shipped to customers. Parts quality is most logically checked while they are being produced and immediately after the parts come off the assembly line.

5. *Economically Realistic.* The cost of implementing a control system should be less than, or at most equal to, the benefits derived from the control system. The best way to minimize waste or unnecessary expenditure in a control system is to do the minimum amount necessary to ensure that the monitored activity will reach the desired goal. For example, in most situations it would be wasteful for a sales manager to receive daily sales reports. Weekly or monthly sales reports are usually sufficient.

6. *Organizationally Realistic.* The control system has to be compatible with organizational realities. For example, individuals have to be able to see a relationship between performance levels they are asked to achieve and rewards that will follow. Furthermore, all standards for performance must be realistic. Status differences between individuals also have to be recognized. Individuals who have to report deviations to someone they perceive as a lower-level staff member may stop taking the control system seriously.

7. *Coordinated with the Organization's Work Flow.* Control information needs to be coordinated with the flow of work through the organization for two

reasons. First, each step in the work process may affect the success or failure of the entire operation. Second, the control information must get to all the people who need to receive it. For example, an appliance company that receives parts from several of its manufacturing plants and assembles them in one central location needs to be sure that all parts plants are performing up to par. Plant managers also need to know when a serious problem develops in one of the other plants, since the work pace in their own plants may have to be adjusted.

8. *Flexible.* As we suggested earlier, few organizations today are in such a stable environment that they do not have to worry about the possibility of change. For almost all organizations, controls must have flexibility built into them so that the organizations can react quickly to overcome adverse changes or to take advantage of new opportunities.

9. *Prescriptive and Operational.* Effective control systems ought to indicate, upon the detection of a deviation from standards, what corrective action should be taken. The information should be in a usable form when it reaches the person responsible for taking the necessary action.

10. *Accepted by Organization Members.* For a control system to be accepted by organization members, the controls must be related to meaningful and accepted goals. Such goals must reflect the language and activities of the individuals to whom they pertain. Top managers, for example, are concerned with financial performance. At their level, it would be meaningful to relate at least some controls to quarterly financial results and budgets. For first-line supervisors, however, control should relate to such tangible things as hours of work, number of products produced, percentages of rejects, downtime, and material wastage. In their eyes, controls are meaningful if they provide timely and accurate data on operational, day-to-day activities.

For a control standard to work as intended, suggests Newman, it must also be accepted by organization members as an integral and fair part of their jobs. For example, the necessity to keep costs under budget should be accepted as both normal and desirable. As you will recall from our discussion of joint goal setting in chapters 4 and 6, when the people who must meet standards have a role in setting them, they are more likely to be committed to those standards. The control system must also be consistent with the organization's culture, or it will likely be ineffective.

Problems in Establishing Effective Control Systems. Most individuals experience at least some discomfort at the prospect of having their performance monitored and reported to others. As we have noted, when controls are of the "steering" kind and when progress toward goals is fed back to the individual whose actions are being controlled, resentment can often be reduced or entirely eliminated.[19] Nevertheless, a number of problems that hinder the effectiveness of control systems seem to recur.

Easily measured factors receive too much weight, while difficult-to-measure items are not given enough attention. This problem arises because it is quicker and easier to measure the performance of those factors that can be quantified. For example, personnel turnover figures are often carefully checked, but little or no control may be exercised over whether or not the most qualified employees are being retained. As a result, the control system may concentrate on comparatively minor matters at the expense of more important organizational goals.

Short-run factors may be overemphasized at the expense of long-run factors.

Long-run results are more unpredictable than short-run achievements. In addition, it is often difficult, if not impossible, to design measurements that can relate long-term results to specific current actions. Customer goodwill, for example, may be an important determinant of long-term growth, but managers have a hard time fitting it into a control system. The long-term growth and survival of the organization may therefore not be given the attention they need by the control system.

The control system may not be adjusted to reflect shifts in importance of various activities and goals over time. No organization can afford to neglect such things as dependable quality, assured delivery, new product development, and the control of manufacturing and selling expenses. But at various stages of the company's growth, a shift in emphasis may be essential as one or another of these factors assumes a higher priority in the struggle for survival. In practice, many managers accept the usefulness of existing controls, rather than adjusting them as situations change and new objectives emerge.

Summary

Control is the vitally important process through which managers assure that actual activities conform to planned activities. It involves four basic steps: (1) the establishment of standards and methods for measuring performance; (2) the measurement of performance; (3) the comparison of performance against the standards; and (4) the taking of corrective action.

The changing environment of organizations, the increasing complexity of organizations, the fact that organization members make mistakes, and the fact that managers must delegate authority are among the factors that make control necessary.

Most control methods can be grouped into four basic categories: pre-action controls, which ensure that the necessary human, material, and financial resources are available for the operation; steering controls, which detect performance deviations before a given operation is completed; yes/no or screening controls, which ensure that specific conditions are met before an operation proceeds further; and post-action controls, in which past experience is applied to future operations. While all four are important, steering controls are particularly critical since they allow corrective action to be applied early enough to prevent failure or to take advantage of unexpected opportunities.

Establishing a control system using steering controls involves (1) defining desired results; (2) establishing predictors of results; (3) establishing standards for predictors and results; (4) establishing the information and feedback network; and (5) evaluating the information and taking corrective action.

In designing a control system, managers must decide on the types and number of measurements to be used, who will set the standards, how flexible the standards will be, the frequency of measurement, and the direction that feedback will take.

For a control system to be effective, it must be accurate, timely, objective, focused on key performance areas and strategic control points, economically realistic, organizationally realistic, coordinated with the organization's work flow, flexible, prescriptive, and acceptable to organization members. These characteristics can be applied to controls at all levels of the organization.

Review Questions

1. What is the importance of the control function?
2. How are planning and controlling linked?
3. List the four basic steps in the control process. What are the key elements in each of these steps?
4. What organizational factors create the need for control?
5. What are the four main types of control? How is each type used? Which is most important? Why?

6. According to William Newman, what are the five steps in designing a control system? How do managers go about carrying out these steps?

7. With what six issues do Jerome Schnee and Thomas Ference suggest managers must be concerned in designing a control system? How might managers resolve these issues?

8. What are key performance areas?

9. What is the "management by exception" principle?

10. What are strategic control points? How may managers locate them?

11. What are the characteristics of effective control systems? Which of these characteristics is most important?

Notes

1. Earl P. Strong and Robert D. Smith, *Management Control Models* (New York: Holt, Rinehart, 1968), pp. 1–2.

2. Richard L. Daft and Norman B. Macintosh, "The Nature and Use of Formal Control Systems for Management Control and Strategy Implementation," *Journal of Management* 10, no. 1 (Fall 1984):43–66.

3. Vijay Sathe, "The Controller's Role in Management," *Organizational Dynamics* 11, 3 (Winter 1983):31–48.

4. J. H. Horovitz, "Strategic Control: A New Task for Top Management," *Long Range Planning* 12, no. 3 (June 1979):28–37.

5. Robert J. Mockler, *The Management Control Process* (Englewood Cliffs, N.J.: Prentice-Hall, 1972), p. 2.

6. Donald J. Cockburn, "Another Way of Looking at Internal Control," *CA Magazine* 117, no. 11 (November 1984):75–77.

7. See Peter F. Drucker, *Management: Tasks, Practices, Responsibilities,* abridged and rev. ed. (New York: Harper & Row, 1985).

8. See Giorgio Inzerilli and Michael Rosen, "Culture and Organizational Control," *Journal of Business Research* 11, no. 3 (September 1983):281–292.

9. Our discussion is based on William H. Newman, *Constructive Control* (Englewood Cliffs, N.J.: Prentice-Hall, 1975), pp. 6–9.

10. See Harold Koontz and Robert W. Bradspies, "Managing through Feedforward Control," *Business Horizons* 4, no. 3 (June 1972):25–36.

11. Newman, *Constructive Control,* pp. 12–25.

12. Thomas J. Peters and Robert H. Waterman, *In Search of Excellence* (New York: Harper & Row, 1982), pp. 57–59.

13. For a discussion of the relationship between goal difficulty and performance, see Edwin A. Locke and Gary T. Latham, *Goal Setting: A Motivational Technique That Works!* (Englewood Cliffs, N.J.: Prentice-Hall, 1984), especially pp. 21–26.

14. Our discussion of these issues is based largely on Schnee and Ference's lecture notes and Newman's *Constructive Control,* supplemented by the authors' experiences; thus, it may not reflect their perspectives with complete accuracy.

15. See Robert N. Anthony, John Dearden, and Norton M. Bedford, *Management Control Systems,* 5th ed. (Homewood, Ill.: Irwin, 1984), pp. 158–159.

16. Peters and Waterman, *In Search of Excellence,* pp. 15–16 and 318–325.

17. See Paul M. Stokes, *A Total Systems Approach to Management Control* (New York: American Management Associations, 1968).

18. Our discussion in this section is based on Newman, *Constructive Control;* William H. Sihler, "Toward Better Management Control Systems," *California Management Review* 14, no. 2 (Winter 1971):33–39; John R. Curley, "A Tool for Management Control," *Harvard Business Review* 29, no. 2 (March–April 1951):45–49; and Strong and Smith, *Management Control Models,* pp. 17–18. See also Peter Lorange and Declan Murphy, "Considerations in Implementing Strategic Control," *Journal of Business Strategy* 4, no. 4 (Spring 1984):27–35; and M. Lynne Markus and Jeffrey Pfeffer, "Power and the Design and Implementation of Accounting and Control Systems," *Accounting, Organizations and Society* 8, no. 2/3 (1983):205–218.

19. The problems of establishing effective control systems have many similarities to the dysfunctional reactions to budgets to be discussed in chapter 21.

CASE STUDY: Taking the Pulse of Trucking

"You just can't get on the road and run a truck anymore," Kenny Benoit, a driver for 18 years, said as he finished his run at the terminal of the Kimberly-Clark Corporation in New Milford, Connecticut.

Mr. Benoit's truck, like all 50 new tractors leased from Ryder System Inc., is equipped with electronic devices that monitor the driver. An electronic engine control system by TRW Inc. sets the top speed at 58 miles per hour and the minimum at 53, taking most control of cruising speed out of the driver's hands. Another TRW system records a vast variety of details about each trip, from the number of revolutions per minute—an important measure of fuel economy—to the length of time the truck runs at a particular speed and the duration of the unloading period.

After the 1973 fuel crisis, truck manufacturers introduced modifications that brought down the maximum speed—to 60 m.p.h., from 70 or 75—and thus improved fuel mileage. Most of the changes were mechanical, however. Now, hundreds of trucking companies are testing and installing sophisticated electronic devices capable of controlling and monitoring the driver much more closely. And they report savings well into the millions of dollars.

Besides TRW, the other major developers and manufacturers of electronic devices for trucking are Engler Instruments, Rockwell International Automotive Electronics, and Argo Instruments. Many are developing still more sophisticated devices.

"In the next three to five years there will be a lot of microcomputers put on the truck," said James R. Barr, environmental specialist at the American Trucking Association. The trend will probably be "to take more and more control away from the driver," he said.

Drivers, predictably, are unhappy with the new controls. They complain that it is often impossible to overtake cars. And when they finish their trip, they must take the device out of the cab and into the driver check-in room, where it is plugged into a computer and prints out an electronic history of the trip. "It's like someone riding with you and writing down everything you did," Mr. Benoit said.

"It bores you to death," said Gus Moffie, a driver with the Kimberly-Clark Integrated Service Corporation, a subsidiary that runs the company's fleet of 200 trucks. Mr. Moffie said that "on long stretches of road you don't have a lot to do to keep your eyes open." He added, "The other problem is that when you get in delays you can't make up the time."

But to Ralph Schatz, the fleet manager for Kimberly-Clark, which is the largest user of these devices, they have been a blessing. He said that fuel economy with the new devices, which became available to the fleet in July, has gone from an average of 5.99 miles a gallon to 7.1. He calculated that for each tenth of a mile per gallon the company saved $85,000 a year in fuel costs.

Jerry Weeks, president of the Kimberly-Clark subsidiary, estimated that a saving of one mile per gallon represents a cut of about 22 percent in fuel costs. Thus, the company, which has an annual fuel bill of $5 million, expects to offset quickly the cost of the devices—$1,400 per tractor.

At Kimberly-Clark, the recording device has not yet been used to confront drivers whose habits may interfere with top fuel efficiency. But the company is using the information on when a truck stops and backs into a customer's loading dock as a means of charging customers who delay a driver. It has been able to collect a fee of $25 an hour for delays. Customers cannot challenge the tamper-proof recorders, Kaspar Tucci, director of United States operations for the subsidiary, said, while they would often challenge the drivers' logs.

Other companies have used the computer printouts to confront their drivers with errant driving patterns. Al Bodo, transportation manager of Royal Foods Distributors in Woodbridge, N.J., one of the Fleming Companies, said the company had set up performance parameters for drivers. After a trip, each of the company's 105 drivers brings in his cartridge, which provides a quick readout on such information as how long he idled and whether he was speeding or going over the revolutions-per-minute limit for each gear.

If a driver has far exceeded the limits, he is given counseling on his driving habits. If a driver still does not change, Mr. Bodo said, "we have taken disciplinary action." These may be warnings at first but can lead to a temporary suspension.

The system has enabled Royal Foods to get a 6 percent increase in fuel economy, from 5.4 miles a gallon last year to 5.69 this year, he said.

Technology of the Future Trevor O. Jones, vice-president and general manager of TRW's transportation electronics group, said that the company has plans for devices that could improve the driver's comfort and safety as well as efficiency.

The technology is already here for systems that could control the climate in the cab and adjust the seat to lessen shock and vibration. A power steering assist would also allow a driver to select a steering "feel" from light to heavy, depending on preference.

Other possibilities for which the technology is in place include an engine protection system that could warn drivers to shut off the engine if it faced damage from a malfunction, a radar unit that could warn drivers if they are on a collision course with another vehicle or object, and a device that could warn drivers when they became drowsy.

All these devices, Mr. Jones said, could someday be tied into one system that could feed information continuously to a computer monitored by the fleet manager. The manager could correct inefficiencies, record road speeds, idle times, and fuel consumption, and monitor other data to improve efficiency. However, he added, the costs of such systems, which derive from aerospace technology, may delay their introduction into the trucking industry by five to 10 years.

Source: Adapted from Agis Salpukas, "Taking the Pulse of Trucking," *New York Times,* September 8, 1984, pp. 31–33. Copyright © 1984 by The New York Times Company. Reprinted by permission.

Case Questions 1. Why has the trucking industry found it profitable to install computerized controls in its vehicles?
2. Describe the monitoring and controlling systems in terms of the four basic categories of control methods.
3. If you were a truck driver, how would you feel about such devices? Would they make the job more, or less, attractive?
4. Do you think organizations should rely on self-monitoring by employees in situations like this one? In other types of situations? Why?
5. As the manager of a trucking firm, how would you explain to your drivers why installation of devices to improve driver safety and comfort is lagging behind the use of devices to improve driver productivity?

21 FINANCIAL CONTROL METHODS

Upon completing this chapter you should be able to:

1. State why financial control methods are important to managers.
2. Describe various types of financial control methods, including financial statements, ratio analysis, and break-even analysis.
3. Explain why budgets are one of the most important control devices that managers use.
4. Identify the various types of budgets an organization can use.
5. Describe the potentially functional and dysfunctional aspects of budgets and how the dysfunctional aspects might be overcome.
6. Describe the two types of auditing.

N o single, unified method of control has ever been devised for all of an organization's activities. There are simply too many kinds of activities in an organization for any one control system to be effective. Instead, managers use a series of control methods and systems to deal with the differing problems and elements of their organization. These control systems are, however, interrelated sufficiently to allow managers to coordinate the organization's activities and to keep them focused on the organization's major goals.[1]

In this chapter, we will discuss various financial methods of control that managers can use, including budgets, financial statements, ratio analysis, break-even analysis, and audits.

Financial Controls

The financial control methods we will discuss are financial statements, ratio analysis, and break-even analysis. These methods are used to evaluate an organization's performance in dimensions that are crucial to its health and survival.

Financial Statements

Financial statements are analyses in monetary terms of the flow of goods and services to, within, and from the organization. They are prepared by accountants and are the key summaries of the firm's accounting records. Financial statements provide a means for controlling three major conditions of an organization: its *liquidity*—the ability to convert assets into cash in order to meet current financial needs and obligations; its *general financial condition*—the long-term balance between debt and equity (the assets of the firm after its liabilities have been deducted); and its *profitability*—the ability to earn profits steadily and over an extended period of time.[2]

Financial statements are usually prepared *ex post* (in retrospect) to indicate what financial events have occurred since the last statement. Depending on the company, the period covered by a financial statement might be the previous year, the previous quarter, or the previous month. As we suggested in chapter 20, the usefulness of financial statements for applying control measures is limited by the fact that they cover only past events and cannot, obviously, be used to influence those events. A quarterly or monthly statement often can, however, provide managers with useful information about trends or events in time to allow them to take corrective action in the coming months.

The financial statements most often used on a regular basis by organizations are balance sheets and income statements. We will describe them along with cash flow statements and statements of the sources and uses of funds, which are also widely used.[3]

The use of computer software for the collection and analysis of accounting and financial data is now nearly universal. About a dozen accounting software packages have achieved national prominence. When evaluating such programs for possible purchase and implementation, financial managers should make sure that they

FIGURE 21–1 THE BALANCE SHEET

CHAPNER METALS
Consolidated Balance Sheet
As of December 31, 1987

ASSETS			LIABILITIES AND NET WORTH		
Current Assets	950,000		Current Liabilities	$ 600,000	
Cash		50,000	Accounts Payable		475,000
Marketable Securities		350,000	Accrued Expenses		
Accounts Receivable		250,000	Payable		125,000
Inventories		300,000	Long-Term Liabilities	600,000	
			Total Liabilities	1,200,000	
Fixed Assets	1,250,000				
Land		50,000	Net Worth	1,070,000	
Plant and Equipment		1,500,000	Common Stock at Par		850,000
Less Accumulated			Accumulated Retained		
Depreciation		300,000	Earnings		220,000
Other Assets					
Patents and Goodwill	70,000				
			Total Liabilities		
Total Assets	$2,270,000		and Net Worth	$2,270,000	

comply with the guidelines of the IRS, the FASB (Financial Accounting Standards Board), and other regulatory agencies, and that the software vendor will continue to supply updated versions as the rules change.[4]

Balance Sheet. The message of a *balance sheet* is, "Here's how this organization stacks up financially *at this particular point in time*." The point in time covered by our sample balance sheet, figure 21–1, is indicated by the line "As of December 31, 1987."

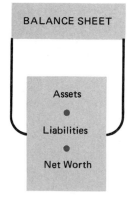

BALANCE SHEET

Assets
•
Liabilities
•
Net Worth

In its simplest form, the balance sheet describes the company in terms of its *assets, liabilities,* and *net worth*. A company's assets range from money in the bank to the goodwill value of its name in the marketplace. The left side of the balance sheet lists these assets in descending order of liquidity. A distinction is made between current assets and fixed assets. *Current assets* cover items such as cash, accounts receivable, marketable securities, and inventories—assets that could be turned into cash at a reasonably predictable value within a relatively short time period (typically, one year). *Fixed assets* show the monetary value of the company's plant, equipment, property, patents, and other items used on a continuing basis to produce its goods or services.

Liabilities are also made up of two groups, current liabilities and long-term liabilities. *Current liabilities* are debts, such as accounts payable, short-term loans, and unpaid taxes, that will have to be paid off during the current fiscal period. *Long-term liabilities* include mortgages, bonds, and other debts that are being paid off gradually. The company's *net worth* is the residual value remaining after total liabilities have been subtracted from total assets. The widespread use of electronic spreadsheets, such as *VisiCalc, SuperCalc, Lotus 1-2-3*, and *MultiPlan*, has made the preparation of balance sheets much easier in the 1980s.

Income Statement. While the balance sheet describes a company's financial condition at a given *point* in time, the *income statement* summarizes the company's financial performance over a given *interval* of time. The income statement, then, says, "Here's how much money we're making" instead of "Here's how much money we're worth."

Income statements, such as figure 21–2, start with a figure for gross receipts or sales and then subtract all the costs involved in realizing those sales, such as the cost of goods sold, administrative expenses, taxes, interest, and other operating expenses. What is left is the net income available for stockholders' dividends or reinvestment in the business.

Cash Flow and Sources and Uses of Funds Statements. In addition to the standard balance sheet and income statement, many companies report financial data in the form of a statement of cash flow or a statement of sources and uses of funds. These statements show where cash or funds came from during the year (from operations, reducing accounts receivable, and sale of investments, for example) and where they were applied (purchase of equipment, payment of dividends, and reducing accounts payable, for example). They should not be confused with income statements; cash flow statements show how cash or funds were used rather than how much profit or loss was achieved.

Financial statements are also used by managers, stakeholders, and others to evaluate the organization's performance. Within the company, managers will com-

CHAPNER METALS
Statement of Income
For the Year Ended December 31, 1987

Gross Sales		$4,298,000
Less Returns	$ 798,000	
Net Sales		3,500,000
Less Cost of Sales and Operating Expenses		
Cost of Goods Sold	2,775,000	
Depreciation	100,000	
Selling and Administrative Expenses	75,000	2,950,000
Operating Profit		550,000
Other Income		15,000
Gross Income		565,000
Less Interest Expense	75,000	
Income before Taxes		490,000
Less Taxes	196,000	
Income after Taxes		$ 294,000

FIGURE 21–2
THE INCOME STATEMENT

pare the current statements of their organization with earlier statements and with those of competitors. People outside the company will use the statements to gauge the organization's strengths, weaknesses, and potential. For example, managers may go outside the company to borrow funds from bankers or to sell new stock to investors. The bankers or investors will analyze the financial statements and will be influenced by what they see in them.

Several types of key information for the evaluation of a firm are not provided by financial statements, and thus the usefulness of statements is limited. For example, recent technological or scientific breakthroughs made by the company are unlikely to be reported. Likewise, financial statements may not reflect changes in the external environment—for example, abrupt shifts in the desires or real income of consumers—that may be key to the organization's success or failure.[5]

Ratio Analysis

For organizations as well as for individuals, financial performance is relative. An annual salary of $30,000 will be seen as high if the average salary in the individual's field or industry is $20,000, and low if the average salary is $40,000. Similarly, company profits of $1 million might be very high for a restaurant but very low for an oil company. For the "bottom line" on a financial statement to be meaningful, it must ultimately be compared with something else. In *ratio analysis,* key summary figures from the firm's financial statements or records are reported as percentages or fractions of one another. Such ratios can provide quick assessments of financial performance or condition. Today, as opposed to the recent past, ratios are easily and inexpensively developed by computer from the firm's electronic records for timely use by managers.[6]

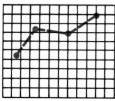

RATIO ANALYSIS COMPARISONS

1. Over Time

The ratio analysis comparisons can be made in one of two ways: (1) comparison over a time period—the present ratio compared with the same organization's ratio in the past (or with a future projection); and (2) comparison with other, similar organizations or with the industry as a whole. The first type of comparison will indicate how the organization's performance or condition has changed; the second type will suggest how well the organization is doing relative to its competitors.

There are many kinds of ratio categories and many kinds of ratios. The ratios most commonly used by organizations are profitability, liquidity, activity, and leverage; these are listed in table 21–1. Return on investment (under profitability) is generally seen as the most important and encompassing ratio in general use; it reveals the success of the firm in employing its resources. The current ratio (under liquidity) indicates the ability of the firm to repay its present short-term debt. Inventory turnover (under activity) is often compared to industry averages and figures from previous years to assess efficiency. Debt ratios (under leverage) are computed to assess a firm's ability to meet its long-term commitments.[7]

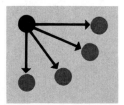

2. With Other Organizations

Break-Even Analysis

Let us assume that the Biocraft Corporation makes only one product, a genetically tailored bacteria for coating plant seeds, which it sells to distributors for $20 per unit. The variable cost of producing the bacteria is $10 per unit. In addition, the company has annual fixed costs of $100,000. (See the discussion of fixed and variable costs later in this chapter.) At what precise point will the company's sales cover its costs?

TABLE 21–1 CATEGORIES OF RATIOS FOR ANALYSIS

Category	Typical Ratio	Calculation	Measures
Profitability	Return on investment	$\dfrac{\text{Profits after taxes}}{\text{Total assets}}$	The productivity of assets
Liquidity	Current ratio	$\dfrac{\text{Current assets}}{\text{Current liabilities}}$	Short-term solvency
Activity	Inventory turnover	$\dfrac{\text{Sales}}{\text{Inventory}}$	The efficiency of inventory management
Leverage	Debt ratio	$\dfrac{\text{Total debt}}{\text{Total assets}}$	The proportion of financing supplied by creditors

Helping managers to find that point and apply the information gained from it is the purpose of *break-even analysis* (also called cost-volume-profit analysis). Through break-even analysis, managers can study the relationship between costs, sales volume, and profits. They can specifically determine how changes in costs and volume will affect profits.

The relationship between fixed costs, variable costs, units sold, and profit can be seen in a diagram sometimes referred to as a break-even chart or a profitgraph. Figure 21–3 illustrates such a graph for our company, covering a sales period of one year. The graph shows that a net loss will result on sales of fewer than 10,000 units but that any sales above that figure will produce a profit. Our break-even point, then, is 10,000 units.

Break-even analysis gives managers a rough profit and loss estimate for different sales volumes. Managers obtain this estimate by selecting the given volume along the horizontal axis and moving up vertically to discover the projected revenue and total costs for that volume. The graph can also be used to estimate the effect of changes in expenses and sales price. In our example, if fixed costs increase by $40,000, the break-even level would increase to 14,000 units. Alternatively, if the unit price of tailored bacteria drops to $15, the break-even point will move up to 20,000 units.

Break-even analysis can also be used to identify the minimum sales volume necessary to meet established profit objectives and to provide data helpful in decisions to drop or add product lines.[8] As a control device, break-even analysis provides one more yardstick by which to evaluate company performance and provides a basis for corrective action to improve performance in the future. ("Our sales reached $5 million this month; for that sales volume we had projected profits of $600,000, but our reported profits are only $500,000. We will need to find the causes of the difference.")

Limitations of Break-Even Analysis. One of the virtues of break-even analysis as an operational tool is its simplicity. Unfortunately, the simple assumptions upon which break-even analysis is based may affect the accuracy of the results. Among the more questionable of these assumptions are the following:

1. *That variable costs per unit are constant.* If production facilities approach capacity, bottlenecks and equipment problems may require large increases in vari-

FIGURE 21–3 A PROFITGRAPH FOR BIOCRAFT CORPORATION

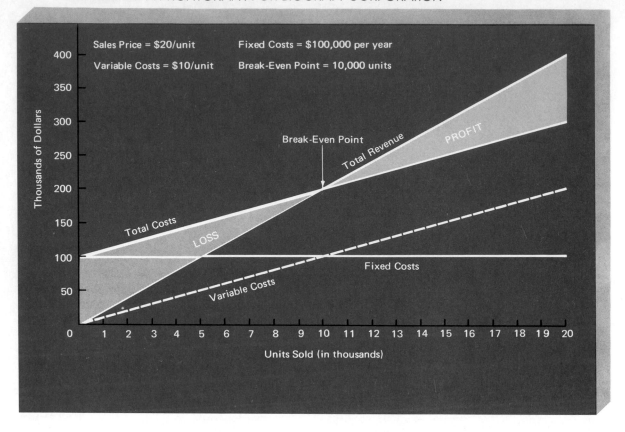

able labor costs to keep the equipment performing. Raw material costs may also rise because of increased production defects.

2. *That fixed costs are constant.* Costs that appear fixed may change in ways that are difficult to predict. For example, as volume rises, new equipment may have to be purchased to alleviate bottlenecks, additional clerical staff may be required to process orders, and additional staff people may be needed to improve coordination.

3. *That prices are constant.* Increased sales may be concentrated in a few customers who receive large-quantity discounts; or sales may be made at greater distances, with the selling company deducting the additional transportation costs from revenues.

4. *That costs can be classified as fixed or variable.* In practice, many costs are quite difficult to classify. For example, if inventories increase to support the higher production levels and an additional warehouse must be leased, is that a fixed cost, since it will not increase or decrease with subsequent volume changes, or is it a variable cost brought about by the higher volume of production?

In spite of its weaknesses, break-even analysis has many positive uses. The information it provides may not be precisely accurate, but it is usually accurate enough to justify its use as a decision-making aid and as a control device. In addition, the advent of electronic spreadsheets, such as *Lotus 1-2-3* and *VisiCalc,* has made break-even analysis easier for managers to use.[9]

Budgetary Control Methods

Budgets are formal quantitative statements of the resources set aside for carrying out planned activities over given periods of time. They are the most widely used means for planning and controlling activities at every level of an organization. A budget indicates the expenditures, revenues, or profits planned for some future date. The planned figures become the standard by which future performance is measured.

Budgets are a fundamental part of organizations' control programs.[10] They are widely used because they are stated in monetary terms. Dollar figures are easily used as a common denominator for a wide variety of organizational activities—hiring and training personnel, purchasing equipment, manufacturing, advertising, and selling—and so they can be used by the organization's existing accounting system to cover all departments. In addition, the monetary aspect of budgets means that they can directly convey information on a key organizational resource—capital—and on a key organizational goal—profit. They are, therefore, heavily favored by profit-oriented companies.

Another reason why budgets are the most widely used control tool is that they establish clear and unambiguous standards of performance. Budgets cover a set time period—usually a year. At stated intervals during that time period, actual performance will be compared directly with the budget. Frequently, deviations can quickly be detected and acted upon.

In addition to being a major control device, budgets are also one of the major means of coordinating the activities of the organization. The interaction between managers and subordinates that takes place during the budget development process will help define and integrate the activities of organization members.

In this section we will describe the role of budgets in a control system, the budgeting process itself, the types of budgets that managers have available, the benefits and drawbacks of budgets, and how those drawbacks can be overcome.

Budgetary Control and Responsibility Centers

Control systems can be devised to monitor organizational *functions* or organizational *projects*. Controlling a function involves making sure that a specified activity (such as production or sales) is properly carried out. Controlling a project involves making sure that a specified end result is achieved (such as the development of a new product or the completion of a building). Budgets can be used for both types of systems; our discussion will emphasize the use of budgets to control functions.

Responsibility Centers. Any organizational or functional unit headed by a manager who is responsible for the activities of that unit is called a *responsibility center*. All responsibility centers use resources (inputs or costs) to produce something else (outputs or revenues). Depending on how these inputs and outputs are measured by the control system, there are four major types of responsibility centers: revenue centers, expense centers, profit centers, and investment centers. We will describe these briefly here; the types of budgets used in these centers will be described more fully later.

Revenue centers are those organizational units in which outputs are measured in monetary terms but are not directly compared to input costs. A sales department is an example of such a unit. The effectiveness of the center is not judged by how much

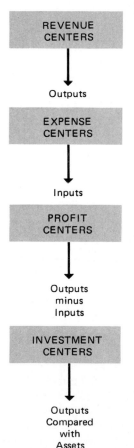

REVENUE
CENTERS

↓

Outputs

EXPENSE
CENTERS

↓

Inputs

PROFIT
CENTERS

↓

Outputs
minus
Inputs

INVESTMENT
CENTERS

↓

Outputs
Compared
with
Assets

revenue (in the form of sales) exceeds the costs of the center (in salaries or rent, for example). Rather, budgets, or sales quotas, are prepared for the revenue center, and the figures are compared with sales orders or actual sales. In this way, a useful picture of the effectiveness of individual salespeople or of the center itself can be determined.

In *expense centers,* inputs are measured by the control system in monetary terms, but outputs are not. So budgets will be devised only for the input portion of these centers' operations. Organizational units commonly considered expense centers include administrative, service, and research departments.

There are two categories of expense centers: engineered and discretionary. *Engineered* expenses are those for which costs can be calculated or estimated with high reliability—for example, the costs of direct labor or raw materials. *Discretionary* expenses are those for which costs cannot be reliably estimated beforehand (research costs, for example) and must depend to a large extent on the manager's judgment (or discretion). At review time, actual input expenses will be measured against budgeted input expenses.

In a *profit center,* performance is measured by the numerical difference between revenues (outputs) and expenditures (inputs). Such a measure is used to determine how well the center is doing economically and how well the manager in charge of the center is performing.

A profit center is created whenever an organizational unit is given responsibility for earning a profit. In a divisionalized organization, in which each of a number of divisions is completely responsible for its own product line, the separate divisions are considered profit centers. The expenditures of all a division's subunits are totaled and then subtracted from the revenues derived from that division's products or services. The net result is the measure of that division's profitability.

In nondivisionalized organizations, or *within* a division, individual departments may also be made into profit centers by crediting them for revenues and charging them for expenses. A manufacturing department, for example, would normally be considered an expense center. Allowing the manufacturing department to "sell" its products at an agreed-upon price (called a *transfer price*) to the sales department would be one way to turn that department into a profit center. The difference between the transfer price and the manufacturing cost per unit would represent the manufacturing department's "profit."

In an *investment center,* the control system does not measure only the monetary value of inputs and outputs, but it also assesses how those outputs compare with the assets employed in producing them. Assume, for example, that a new hospital requires a capital investment of $20 million in property, buildings, equipment, and working capital. In its first year, the hospital has $2 million in labor and other input expenses and $4 million in revenue. The hospital would *not* be considered to have earned a $2 million profit for two reasons: a deduction from revenues would have to be made to allow for depreciation of buildings and equipment; and the cost of that investment, in terms of what *could* have been earned if the funds had been invested elsewhere, would have to be taken into account. In this way, a much more accurate picture of profitability would be obtained. Any profit center can, in fact, be considered an investment center as well, because its activities will require some form of capital investment. However, if a center's capital investment is minor (as in a consulting firm) or if its managers have no control over capital investment, it may be more appropriately treated as a profit center.

"At the moment, there's $413,874,691.03 in the kitty."
Drawing by Weber; © 1982 The New Yorker Magazine, Inc.

The Budgeting Process

In this section, we will focus on four key areas of the budgeting process: the ways in which budgets are drawn up and approved; the role played by the budget department and budget committees; the ways in which budgets are revised; and problems that commonly occur when budgets are being developed.[11]

How Budgets Are Drawn Up and Approved

The budgeting process usually begins when managers receive top management's economic forecasts and sales and profit objectives for the coming year. These will usually be accompanied by a timetable stating when budgets must be completed. The forecasts and objectives provided by top management represent guidelines within which other managers' budgets will be developed.

In a few organizations, budgets are imposed by top managers with little or no consultation with lower-level managers.[12] In most companies, however, budgets are prepared, at least initially, by those who must implement them. The budgets are then sent up for approval by superiors. This type of "bottom-up" budgeting has many advantages for the organizations. Supervisors and lower-level department heads have a more intimate view of their needs than do managers at the top, and they can provide more realistic breakdowns to support their proposals. They are also less likely to overlook some vital ingredient or hidden flaw that might subsequently impede implementation efforts. Managers will also be more strongly motivated to accept and meet budgets that they have had a hand in shaping. Finally, morale and satisfaction are usually higher when individuals participate actively in making decisions that affect them. The box above lists the best aspects of top-down and bottom-up budgeting.

The process by which lower-level managers participate in developing budgets is similar to the multilevel planning process described in chapter 4. Supervisors prepare their budget proposals using the guidelines drawn up by upper management. The lower-level budgets are reviewed, finalized, and used by department heads to draw up department budgets. These budgets are then submitted to higher-level managers for approval. The process continues until all budgets are completed, assembled by the controller or budget director, and submitted to the president (or budget committee) for further review. At last, the master budget is sent to the board of directors for approval.

The Role of Budget Personnel

Developing budgets is the responsibility of line managers. They may receive information and technical assistance from the staff of a planning group or budget department. (Managers of staff departments will, of course, be responsible for their own department budgets.) Many organizations have formal budget departments and committees. These groups are likely to exist in large, divisionalized organizations in which the division budget plays a key role in planning, coordinating, and controlling activities.[13]

The *budget department,* which generally reports to the corporate controller, provides budget information and assistance to organizational units, designs budget systems and forms, integrates the various departmental proposals into a master budget for the organization as a whole, and reports on actual performance relative to the budget.

The *budget committee,* made up of senior executives from all functional areas, reviews the individual budgets, reconciles divergent views, alters or approves the budget proposals, and then refers the integrated package to the board of directors. Later, when the plans have been put into practice, the committee reviews the control reports that monitor progress. In most cases, the budget committee must approve any revisions made during the budget period.

How Budgets Are Revised

Budgets cannot be revised whenever managers please. Still, because budgets are based on forecasts that can be rapidly overtaken by reality, provision should be made for necessary revisions. In cases where the budget is used primarily as a planning tool, formal updating periods may be established at stated intervals. Where the budget is a main part of the control and evaluation mechanism, revisions are limited to cases where deviations have become so great as to make the approved budget unrealistic. The aim is to build reasonable stability and firmness into the budget without being excessively rigid.[14]

Comparisons of actual performance with budgets are known as reviews or *audits*, and are now often done electronically. To be effective, audits depend on a regular, accurate flow of data from organizational units. Unit managers will regularly submit monthly or weekly progress reports that are audited on a monthly basis by those individuals with control responsibility or automatically by computer. If deviations are detected, the appropriate managers will be asked to explain them and to specify the corrective action they plan to take. Serious deviations may require that the budget be revised.[15] Types of audits and their uses will be discussed in greater detail later in the chapter.

Some Problems in Budget Development

During the budget development process, the organization's limited resources are allocated, and managers may fear that they will not be given their fair share. Tension will heighten as competition with other managers increases. Anxieties may also arise because managers know they will be judged by their ability to meet or beat budgeted standards, and so are concerned about what those standards will be. Conversely, their superiors are concerned with establishing aggressive budget objectives, and so will often try to trim their subordinates' expenditure requests or raise their revenue targets.

Henry L. Tosi has described four important reactions to these budget development anxieties:[16]

1. *Political Behavior.* Political activity may increase sharply as managers try to influence resource allocations. Managers may withhold information until the last minute in order to magnify its importance, ingratiate themselves with superiors, or attempt to gain influence in other ways.
2. *Dysfunctional Reactions to Budget Units.* Supervisors who are unhappy with resource allocations are not really in a position to vent their anger on their superiors. Instead, they will usually take out their hostility on the staff personnel who compile the budget data and assemble the final budget figures.
3. *Overstatement of Needs.* Slack is often built into budgets as a legitimate hedge against unforeseen events and inflation. Some managers, however, pad their budget estimates to protect themselves in the struggle for resources and to compensate for the fact that cuts are often made in requested amounts. Managers who submit requests based only on their actual needs will then suffer if their requests are automatically cut along with those of other managers.
4. *Covert Information Systems.* When budgets are kept secret, managers will often try to find out how their allocations compare with others by developing covert or informal information sources—secretaries, budget staff members, or col-

leagues. The danger for the organization lies in the possibility that inaccurate information will be spread through the grapevine, unnecessarily increasing the rivalry and tension between organizational units.

Organization-wide participation in the budgeting process, as in the examples provided earlier, often minimizes these types of anxiety reactions. When all managers are involved in budget development, they are more likely to be satisfied with their resource allocations.[17]

Types of Budgets

Organization budgets are of two kinds: operating budgets and financial budgets. The *operating budgets* indicate the goods and services the organization expects to consume in the budget period; they usually list both physical quantities (such as barrels of oil) and cost figures. The *financial budgets* spell out in detail the money the organization intends to spend in the same period and where that money will come from. Figure 21–4 shows the operating and financial components of a manufacturing firm's comprehensive budget. Each rectangle in the diagram represents one or more of the types of budgets we describe below. These different types of budgets make up the firm's overall budgetary plan.[18]

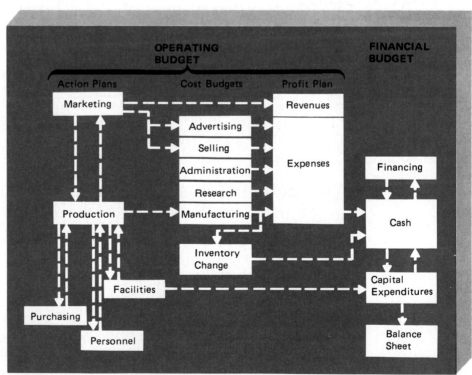

FIGURE 21–4
BUDGET
COMPONENTS

Source: Gordon Shillinglaw, *Managerial Cost Accounting*, 5th ed., p. 210. Copyright © 1982. Reproduced with permission of Richard D. Irwin, Inc.

Operating Budgets

The most common types of operating budgets parallel three of the responsibility centers discussed earlier—expense, revenue, and profit.[19]

Expense Budgets. As mentioned earlier, there are two types of expense budgets, one for each of the two types of expense centers—engineered cost budgets and discretionary cost budgets.

Engineered cost budgets are typically used in manufacturing plants but can be used by any organizational unit in which output can be accurately measured. These budgets usually describe the material and labor costs involved in each production item, as well as the estimated overhead costs.[20] Engineered cost budgets are designed to measure efficiency: exceeding the budget will mean that operating costs were higher than they should have been.

Discretionary cost budgets are typically used for administrative, legal, accounting, research, and other such departments in which output cannot be accurately measured. Discretionary cost budgets are not used to assess efficiency, because performance standards for discretionary expenses are difficult to devise. For example, if the market research department exceeds its budget, it will often be difficult for managers to determine how that department's work could have been performed more efficiently.

Revenue Budgets. *Revenue budgets* are meant to measure marketing and sales effectiveness. They consist of the expected quantity of sales multiplied by the expected unit selling price of each product. The revenue budget is the most critical part of a profit budget, yet it is also one of the most uncertain, because it is based on projected future sales. Companies with a large volume of back orders or where sales volume is limited only by the companies' productive capacity can make firmer revenue forecasts than companies that must reckon with the swings of an unstable or unpredictable market. However, marketing and sales managers of even these latter companies can control the quality and quantity of their advertising, service, personnel training, and other factors that affect sales. This control gives them some influence over sales volume and frequently enables them to make reasonably accurate sales estimates.

Profit Budgets. A *profit budget* combines cost and revenue budgets in one statement. It is used by managers who have responsibility for both the expenses and revenues of their units. Such managers frequently head an entire division or company. The profit budgets, which are sometimes called *master budgets,* consist of a set of projected financial statements and schedules for the coming year. Thus, they serve as annual profit plans.

Profit budgets have three main uses:

1. **They plan and coordinate overall corporate activities. For example, they make it possible to integrate the use of manufacturing facilities with sales forecasts.**
2. **They provide benchmarks that are useful in judging the adequacy of expense budgets. For example, if the budget indicates that profits will be low, the expense budget might be revised downward.**
3. **They help assign responsibility to each manager for his or her share of the overall organization's performance.**

Financial Budgets

The *capital expenditure, cash, financing,* and *balance sheet budgets* integrate the financial planning of the organization with its operational planning. These budgets, prepared with information developed from the revenue, expense, and operating budgets, serve three major purposes. First, they verify the viability of the operating budgets ("Will we generate enough cash to do what we are planning to do?"). Second, their preparation reveals financial actions that the organization must take to make execution of its operating budgets possible ("If events conform to plans, we'll be short of cash in October and November; we'd better talk to our bankers this month about a line of credit to cover that period"). Third, they indicate how the organization's operating plans will affect its future financial actions. If these actions will be difficult or undesirable, appropriate changes in the operating plans may be required. ("In order to make our planned capital expenditures, we will have to arrange major borrowings in the capital markets in the next 12 months. But our economists say that will be poor timing; we had better rethink the expansion of our unit in Texas.") Recent research has found that industry is adopting increasingly sophisticated financial budgeting techniques. Most of these have been developed by academics.[21]

Capital Expenditure Budgets. *Capital expenditure budgets* indicate the future investments in new buildings, property, equipment, and other physical assets the organization is planning in order to renew and expand its productive capacity. Formulation of the capital expenditure budget reveals important projects the organization will undertake and significant cash requirements the organization will face in the future. Because of the long useful life of buildings and equipment and their relative inflexibility, the choices made on new capital expenditures are not easily altered. Thus, the decisions in the capital expenditure budget are frequently among the more important ones for the organization.

Cash Budgets. *Cash budgets* bring together the organization's budgeted estimates for revenues, expenses, and new capital expenditures. The development of the cash budget will frequently reveal information about the *level* of funds flowing through the organization and about the *pattern* of cash disbursements and receipts. For example, preparation of the cash budget may show that the firm will be generating a great deal more cash than it will be using during the next year. This information may encourage management to move more aggressively on its capital expenditure program or even to consider additional areas of investment.

Financing Budgets. *Financing budgets* are developed to assure the organization of the availability of funds to meet the shortfalls of revenues relative to expenses in the short run and to schedule medium- and longer-term borrowing or financing. These budgets are developed in conjunction with the cash budget to provide the organization with the funds it needs at the times it needs them.

Balance Sheet Budgets. The *balance sheet budget* brings together all of the other budgets to project how the balance sheet will look at the end of the period if actual results conform to planned results. This budget, also called a *pro forma* balance sheet, can be thought of as a final check on the organization's planned programs and activities. Analysis of the balance sheet budget may suggest problems or opportunities that will require managers to alter some of the other budgets. For example, the balance sheet budget may indicate that the company has planned to borrow more heavily than is prudent. This information might lead to a reduction in planned borrowing and reduced capital expenditures or—alternatively—to the decision to issue additional stock to obtain some of the desired financing.

Variable versus Fixed Budgets

One difficulty with budgets is that they are often inflexible. Thus, they may be seen as inappropriate for situations that change in ways beyond the control of those responsible for achieving the budgeted objectives. For example, an expense budget based on annual sales of $12 million may be completely off track if sales of $15 million are achieved. The expense of manufacturing will almost always increase if more items are produced to meet the larger demand. It would therefore be unreasonable to expect managers to keep to the original expense budget.

To deal with this difficulty, many managers resort to a *variable* budget. (This type of budget is referred to by a variety of names, such as flexible budget, sliding-scale budget, and step budget.) Whereas *fixed* budgets express what individual costs should be at *one* specified volume, variable budgets are cost *schedules* that show how each cost should vary as the level of activity or output varies. Variable budgets are, therefore, useful in identifying in a fair and realistic manner how costs are affected by the amount of work being done.

Fixed, Variable, and Semivariable Costs. There are three types of costs that must be considered when variable budgets are being developed: fixed, variable, and semivariable costs.[22]

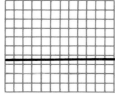

FIXED COSTS

Fixed costs are those that are unaffected by the amount of work being done in the responsibility center. These costs accumulate only with the passage of time. For example, for many organizational units, monthly salaries, insurance payments, rent, and research expenditures will not vary significantly for moderate ranges of activity. (See fig. 21–5.)

Variable costs are expenses that vary directly with the quantity of work being performed. An example is raw materials—the more goods produced, the greater the quantity (and cost) of raw materials required.

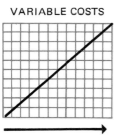

VARIABLE COSTS

Quantity of Work

Semivariable costs are those that vary with the volume of work performed but *not* in a directly proportional way. Semivariable costs often represent a major part of an organization's expenses. For example, short-term labor costs are usually semivariable—the number of personnel hired (or laid off) will rarely be based directly on day-to-day changes in production. Similarly, the cost of the total sales effort often does not vary directly with the number of products sold.

Devising Variable Budgets. In devising their budgets, managers must try to break down their total costs into fixed and variable elements. The result will be more accurate and useful budgets.

The problem in devising variable budgets is that cost variability is often difficult to determine. Usually managers will use one or more of the following three methods to determine their variable costs:

1. *Direct estimates.* **Managers estimate which components of their expenses are variable, either by exercising their judgment based on experience or by relying on studies performed by industrial engineers.**

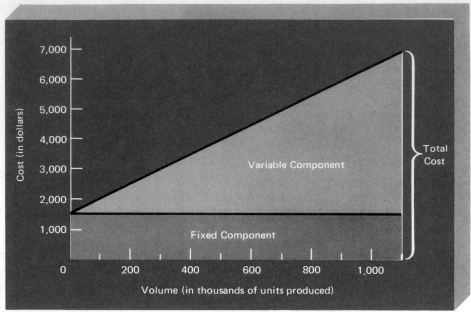

FIGURE 21–5
THE VARIABLE AND
FIXED
COMPONENTS OF
TOTAL COST

2. *High and low point method.* Two budgets are developed—one for maximum assumed output and one for minimum assumed output. The difference in cost between these two budgets divided by the difference in volume will yield the variable rate.

3. *Correlation method.* Monthly data on the organization's past output and cost variability are assembled. Projections based on these data and on conditions in the present are made to estimate future cost variability.

Variable budgets are used most appropriately in responsibility centers, where operations are repetitive, where there are a large number of different expenses, and where these expenses can be accurately estimated. The main disadvantage of variable budgets is that they are often quite expensive to prepare.

Zero-Base Budgeting

In the normal budgeting process, the previous year's level of expenditure is often assumed to have been appropriate. The task of individuals preparing the budget is to decide what activities and funds should be dropped and, more often, what activities and funds should be added. Such a process builds into an organization a bias toward continuing the same activities year after year—well after their relevance and usefulness may have been lost because of environmental changes or changes in the organization's objectives.

Zero-base budgeting (ZBB), in contrast, enables the organization to look at its activities and priorities afresh. The previous year's resource allocations are not automatically considered the basis of this year's resource allocations. Instead, each manager has to justify anew his or her entire budget request.

ZBB involves allocating an organization's funds on the basis of a cost-benefit analysis of each of the organization's major activities.[23] The process involves three major steps:

1. *Break down each of an organization's activities into "decision packages."* A decision package includes all the information about an activity that managers need to evaluate that activity and compare its costs and benefits to other activities, *plus* the consequences expected if the activity is not approved and the alternative activities that are available to meet the same purpose.
2. *Evaluate the various activities and rank them in order of decreasing benefit to the organization.* Usually each manager will rank the activities for which he or she is responsible. Rankings for all organizational activities are reviewed and selected by top managers.
3. *Allocate resources.* The organization's resources are budgeted according to the final ranking that has been established.

ZBB includes these benefits: managers must quantify each alternative and thereby provide the measures needed for comparisons; low-priority programs can be cut or eliminated with more confidence; and alternative programs and their advantages are presented with greater clarity for periodic review. However, the approach does have some drawbacks as well. One major problem is that managers are often very reluctant to submit their programs to such intense scrutiny. Or they may inflate the importance of the activities they control. In addition, managers often inadequately understand the aims, strengths, and weaknesses of ZBB. Further, their lack of understanding may prevent them from marshaling appropriate data for its implementation.[24] A less critical problem, but one that must be considered, is the increased information processing required by ZBB.[25] These problems can be overcome, however, through proper training of managers and foresighted administration of the entire program.[26]

Functional and Dysfunctional Aspects of Budget Systems

Like other control methods, budgets have the potential to help organizations and their members reach their goals. How useful budgets are in practice depends on how effectively they are conceived and carried out. It is particularly important that the budgeting process, like other types of control, be clear and acceptable to the people whose activities it controls.

Potentially Functional Aspects of Budgets.   V. Bruce Irvine has described some of the potentially functional aspects of budgets:[27]

1. *Budgets can have a positive impact on motivation and morale.* Most individuals need to achieve things they are committed to and desire to be accepted by groups to which they belong. Budgets can activate these motivational factors by creating common goals and the feeling that everyone is working toward them.

2. *Budgets make it possible to coordinate the work of the entire organization.* Since a comprehensive budget is a blueprint of all the firm's plans for the coming year, top management can tie together the activities of every unit.

3. *Budgets can be used as a signaling device for taking corrective action.* One of the main purposes of any control system is to alert the appropriate organization members that a standard has been violated. If, for example, the expenses incurred

exceed the budgeted ones by a significant margin, then managers know that some corrective action is probably needed.

4. *The budget system helps people learn from experience.* Once the budget period is over, managers can analyze what occurred, isolate errors and their causes, and take steps to avoid those errors in the next budget period.

5. *Budgets improve resource allocation.* In the budgeting process, all requests for resources should be clarified and logically supported. The need to quantify their plans forces managers to examine their available resources more carefully when considering how to allocate them.

6. *Budgets improve communication.* A plan cannot be put into effect unless it is communicated to those who must carry it out. In the process of developing the budget with those responsible for its implementation, managers can communicate their own objectives and plans more effectively.

7. *Budgets help lower-level managers see where they fit in the organization.* The budget gives these managers goals around which to organize their activities. In addition, it indicates what organizational resources will be made available to them.

8. *Budgets let new people see where the organization is going.* This aspect of budgets can enhance the morale of junior managers because it helps them become acclimated to the organization's goals and priorities.

9. *Budgets serve as a means of evaluation.* Performance can more easily (and often more fairly) be measured against previously approved benchmarks.

Potentially Dysfunctional Aspects of Budgets. Managers often find that unintended and unanticipated consequences arise from their budget systems. These dysfunctional aspects of their budget systems may interfere with the attainment of the organization's goals.[28] In this section we will describe some of the dysfunctional aspects of the budgeting process that commonly develop.

1. *Differing perceptions of budgets by organization members.* Irvine identified a number of reasons why budgets are often perceived as dysfunctional. Supervisors may view budgets as unfair because others use them to evaluate results without follow-up investigations into the reasons for success or failure. Budgets would be considered more fair if reasons for budget deviations and mitigating circumstances were taken into account. Supervisors may also find budgets unhelpful in handling their current problems. Another problem is that managers find it difficult to understand the jargon and specialized formats of performance reports prepared by the budget department and so cannot adequately respond to the criticism the reports may contain.

2. *Mechanical considerations.* Certain potentially negative effects of budgets can be traced to the mechanics of budgets and the budgeting process. For instance, there are expenses involved in installing and operating a budget system; if these costs outweigh the benefits obtained by the system, the organization's goals are not being effectively achieved.

3. *Communication and budgets.* Often, employees whose performance is being controlled may not know whether they have conformed to the budget until their superiors call them in about a problem or perhaps not even until a performance appraisal takes place. In addition, deviations may not be communicated to them until the budget period is over; as a result, employees never get the opportunity to learn from their mistakes and to take corrective action on their own. This may lead them to regard budgets as a rating tool or as a device for catching their mistakes.

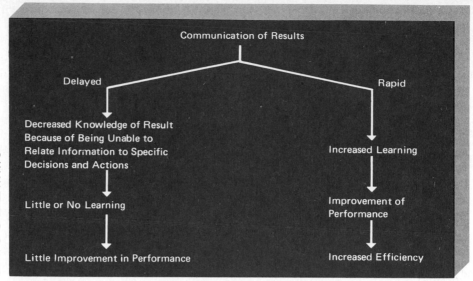

FIGURE 21–6
THE IMPORTANCE
OF THE
COMMUNICATION
FACTOR WHEN
USING BUDGETS TO
CONTROL AND
MOTIVATE
EMPLOYEES

Source: Reprinted from the March–April 1970 issue of *Cost and Management* by permission of The Society of Management Accountants of Canada.

However, when actual results are communicated immediately and directly, employees whose performance is being controlled can then act to correct errors or at least avoid repeating them in the future. In addition, they can rely more confidently on the budget for guidance in their daily activities. (See fig. 21–6.)

4. *The motivational impact of budgets*. Most managers believe budgets are effective motivational devices. When budgeted standards are not met, it is assumed that people will be motivated to work harder next time around. When high standards are set and made known to employees, most managers believe the employees will be more motivated to attain those standards.

In Kurt Lewin's *force field* concept[29] discussed in chapter 13 (see p. 356), behavior is seen as the result of an equilibrium between opposing *driving* and *restraining* forces. Managers often try to motivate employees to high performance by promising more rewards or applying verbal pressure. The budgeting process also increases the pressure on employees. As Irvine has noted, managers will use budgets to raise their subordinates' performance in a number of specific ways, including budget pep talks, red circles around poor showings, production and sales drives built around the budget, threats of reprimand, and inducing feelings of failure if budgets are not met.

These pressures for increased efficiency are felt by employees, who may begin to resist and resent them. The employees will often find ways to minimize their growing work load and protect themselves from censure. Interdepartmental strife may increase, with every supervisor trying to blame budget deviations on someone else. Scapegoating may increase, as line people blame staff members for budget deviations or production department members blame salespeople for a poor sales record.

To blunt the dysfunctional impact on motivation, Irvine suggests that management would do better if it reduced the forces that decrease performance rather than increasing the pressures for greater performance. For example, the resentment that budget pressures generate can often be reduced when managers and subordinates meet, develop, and agree on budget standards together. Meetings can also be held to discuss any problems that employees anticipate with a particular budget and ways the budget can be improved. The budgets can also be used more openly as a positive rating device; budget staff members should be encouraged to credit publicly individuals who are coming in under budget, instead of just publicizing poor showings. As Peters and Waterman have noted, excellently managed companies tend to be particularly good at celebrating success in meeting the objectives that are frequently included in budgets.

5. *Goal difficulty and goal achievement.* Much of what management writers have noted about negative reactions to budgets is related to two common perceptions. The first is that budget goals may be seen as too high. For example, a very high sales or production level may have been set. Second, the amount of resources allocated to attain the budgeted goals may be perceived as inadequate. For example, the expense budget may be too restrictive for the goals to be accomplished.

One generally accepted guideline for effective budgeting is to establish goals that are difficult but attainable. If such goals are set, as Peters and Waterman and other researchers have observed, employees will often be challenged and inspired to improve their performance and meet or exceed the budgeted goals.[30]

Roger Dunbar has analyzed some of the research on goal setting.[31] He suggests that setting high goals will improve performance up to a certain point; eventually, however, the goals become unacceptable to employees, and their performance drops off sharply. Also, there is a point at which even increased performance becomes less profitable for the organization—as goals become more difficult to attain and are consistently missed, the cost of coordination increases. When the added cost of coordination nullifies the benefits achieved by higher performance, says Dunbar, then that higher performance is no longer profitable for the organization.

Auditing

To much of the general public, the term *auditing* conjures up scenes of stern-faced individuals scrutinizing a company's books in order to find out who is cheating the company, how they are juggling the figures to cover it up, and how much they have already embezzled. While the discovery of fraud is, in fact, one important facet of auditing, it is far from being the only one. Auditing has many important uses, from validating the honesty and fairness of financial statements to providing a critical basis for management decisions. In this section, we will discuss two types of auditing: *external auditing* and *internal auditing.*[32]

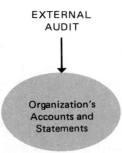

EXTERNAL
AUDIT

Organization's
Accounts and
Statements

External Auditing

The traditional external audit is largely a verification process involving the independent appraisal of the organization's financial accounts and statements. Assets and liabilities are verified, and financial reports are checked for completeness and accuracy. The audit is conducted by accounting personnel employed by an outside CPA firm or by chartered accountants. The auditors' purpose is *not* to prepare the company's financial reports; their job is to verify that the company, in preparing its own financial statements and valuing its assets and liabilities, has followed generally accepted accounting principles and applied them correctly.

The external audit plays a significant role in encouraging honesty not only in the preparation of statements but also in the actual operation of the organization. It is, in fact, a major systematic check against fraud within the organization. For people outside the organization, such as bankers and potential investors, the external audit provides the major assurance that publicly available financial statements are accurate.

The external audit takes place after the organization's operating period is finished and its financial statements are completed. For this reason, and also because it generally focuses on a comparatively limited set of financial statements and transactions, the external audit does not usually make a major contribution to control of the ongoing operations of the organization. However, knowing that the audit will inevitably occur is a strong deterrent against actions that may lead to embarrassment (or an uncomfortable prison term) if they are discovered during or after the audit. Failure to act on the warnings of external auditors can be costly. In June 1985, officials of New York's Transit Authority announced that they would have to write off $100 million of government reimbursement funds because of haphazard documentation of expenses. They had been made aware of the problem by the accounting firm of Ernst & Whinney in 1982, but no action was taken.[33]

Internal Auditing

INTERNAL AUDIT

Organization's Financial System

The internal audit is carried out by members of the organization. Its objectives are to provide reasonable assurance that the assets of the organization are being properly safeguarded and that financial records are being kept reliably and accurately enough for the preparation of financial statements. Internal audits also assist managers in appraising the organization's operational efficiency.

The internal audit will evaluate how adequately the organization's control system is working toward realizing organizational objectives. It will evaluate several of the organization's reports for accuracy and usefulness and will lead to recommendations for improvements in the control system. Because of the concentration on the operations of the organization, this process is also known as "operational auditing."

The internal audit may be carried out as a separate project by assigned members of the financial department or, in larger organizations, by a full-time internal auditing staff. The range and depth of the audit will also vary greatly, depending on company size and policy, from a relatively narrow survey to a broad, comprehensive analysis. This more complete internal audit will provide an appraisal not only of the organization's control system but also of its policies, procedures, and use of authority. It may also evaluate the quality and effectiveness of the managerial methods being used.

Although the internal audit does provide management with useful information, it does have some limitations:

1. *Cost.* Internal audits can be expensive, particularly if they are carried out in depth.
2. *Skill.* Internal auditing involves more than simply gathering facts. Well-trained personnel are needed if the results are to be useful to managers.
3. *Tact.* Even if the auditors are skilled, many employees may still regard auditing as a form of "snooping" or "checking up." If the auditors are not tactful and experienced in interpersonal communication, the audit may even have a negative effect on the employees' motivation.

Computers and Auditing

The changeover from traditional manual processing of information (now rarely done even in small firms) to the computerization of company records has brought about changes in the way data are handled that auditors, and indeed all managers, should be aware of. For example, uniformity in the way a computer is fed data has been found to cut down on many types of clerical errors. However, this same uniformity can also result in whole categories of transactions being incorrectly handled because of errors in programming. In other cases, the very ease of use of spreadsheet, budgeting, and other programs can lull users into abandoning traditional checking procedures; data are assumed to be accurate simply because they have come out of a computer.[34]

Care must also be taken with computer systems to avoid having one individual assume too much control over functions normally divided up among several individuals under manual processing. The availability of passwords or key-locked systems to limit access to data bases is one advantage that electronic record-keeping has over traditional manual practice.

Currently available auditing software is designed to meet the specific needs of computer-assisted audits. These include *Panaudit, EDP Auditor, Mark IV, DYL-Audit,* and *Auditape,* among others. With this software, an auditor would typically be able to check such information as whether or not a person receiving an employee discount is properly listed in the information system and has not been terminated or otherwise made ineligible. Another possible problem area easily checked with these programs is the issuance of duplicate checks.[35]

A recent conference held by the California Society of CPAs foresaw important auditing uses of forthcoming computers with artificial intelligence capabilities and financial expert systems. According to Robert K. Elliot of the Peat, Marwick, Mitchell & Co. accounting firm, the auditor of the future will not only need to possess a general knowledge of budgeting, cost control, profit planning, financial forecasting, and behavioral science, but will also need to be familiar with computer modeling and artificial intelligence.[36]

Summary

Financial control methods include budgets, financial statements, ratio analysis, break-even analysis, and audits. Commonly used financial statements are balance sheets, income statements, and cash flow and sources and uses of funds statements. These statements are used by managers to control their organization's activities and by individuals outside the organization to evaluate its effectiveness. Common types of ratio analysis are profitability, liquidity, activity, and leverage. These ratios may be used to compare the organization's performance against that of competitors or against its own performance in the past. Break-even analysis is designed to reveal the relationship between costs, sales volume, and profits.

Budgets are among the most widely used devices for controlling and coordinating the activities of an organization. The four major types of responsibility centers that budgets may control are revenue, expense, profit, and investment centers. The budgeting process begins when top management sets the strategies and goals for the organization. The creation of the budget involves many levels of management, with the budget's final approval coming from the board of directors.

The budget development process typically arouses anxiety among managers, who may react with behavior adverse to the best interests of the organization. Effective participation in the budgeting process usually reduces these reactions.

Overall organizational budgets may be operating or financial. Specific types of budgets include expense (engineered and discretionary), revenue, profit, cash, capital expenditure, and balance sheet budgets. Budgets may also be fixed, variable, or semivariable. Zero-base budgeting is a special budgeting approach that attempts to base resource allocations on current rather than historical needs.

Budgets have potentially functional and dysfunctional aspects. Potentially functional aspects include improved coordination and communication, higher motivation and morale, and increased learning by lower-level managers. Potentially dysfunctional aspects include differing perceptions by line and staff members, mechanical problems, and unnecessary and harmful pressures on organization members. Some of these pressures may be reduced if high but attainable budget goals are set.

Auditing serves many important functions in the organization, from validating the accuracy of financial statements and uncovering fraud to providing a critical basis for management decisions. External auditing is an independent appraisal of a firm's financial accounts and statements. Internal audits are carried out within the organization to assure proper safeguards for company assets exist, to confirm that records are being accurately kept, and to seek ways of improving organizational efficiency.

Auditing, like other financial functions, is now being computerized. Today's managers can make use of specialized software for preparing everything from financial statements to budgets.

Review Questions

1. Financial statements are used to control what three major conditions of an organization?

2. What are the major types of financial statements? What information does each type provide?

3. What is ratio analysis? How may comparisons of ratios be made? What are the major types of ratios used by organizations? What information is each type expected to provide?

4. What is the purpose of break-even analysis? What are the steps involved in creating a profitgraph? What is the break-even point? What are the advantages and disadvantages of break-even analysis?

5. Why are budgets so widely used in organizations?

6. What are four major types of responsibility centers? What organizational units are commonly considered as belonging to each type of center? How is the performance of each center measured?

7. How are budgets prepared, approved, and revised? What are the advantages of lower-level participation in the budgeting process?

8. What four reactions has Henry Tosi described concerning the anxieties of budget development?

9. What types of budgets are used for three of the responsibility centers described in the chapter? Describe each budget. What is the purpose of each budget?

10. What are cash, expenditure, and balance sheet budgets? Why are they used?

11. What are variable budgets? What types of costs must managers consider when devising variable budgets? Why? How may variable costs be determined?

12. What are the basic steps in zero-base budgeting? What are some benefits as well as problems to this approach?

13. What are the potentially functional and dysfunctional aspects of budgets?

14. What are the two basic types of audits? What is the purpose of each type?

15. How has computerization affected financial control?

Notes   1. See William H. Newman, *Constructive Control: Design and Use of Control Systems* (Englewood Cliffs, N.J.: Prentice-Hall, 1975), pp. 6–9, 128–129.

2. See Earl P. Strong and Robert D. Smith, *Management Control Models* (New York: Holt, Rinehart & Winston, 1968), p. 55.

3. See Strong and Smith, *Management Control Models*, pp. 56–61; and J. Fred Weston and Thomas E. Copeland, *Managerial Finance*, 8th ed. (Hinsdale, Ill.: Dryden Press, 1986).

4. See G. William Dauphinais and Michael A. Yesko, "Business Accounting Software Comes of Age?" *PC*, June 25, 1985, pp. 146–148; Eldon Ladd, "How to Evaluate Financial Software," *Management Accounting* 66, no. 7 (January 1985):39–42; and Erik Sandberg-Diment, "When Accounting Goes Electronic," *New York Times*, July 7, 1985, p. Fl7.

5. Michael H. Granof, *Financial Accounting*, 3d ed., (Englewood Cliffs, N.J.: Prentice-Hall, 1985).

6. Weston and Copeland, *Managerial Finance*.

7. Granof, *Financial Accounting*. See also Gordon Shillinglaw, *Managerial Cost Accounting: Analysis and Control*, 5th ed., (Homewood, Ill.: Irwin, 1982), pp. 787–792.

8. R. M. S. Wilson, *Financial Control: A Systems Approach* (New York: McGraw-Hill, 1974), pp. 137–138.

9. For an article on how to set up break-even charts using *Lotus 1-2-3* and *Symphony* software, see Charles W. Kidd, "Using the Power of Break-even Analysis," *Lotus* 1, no. 2 (June 1985):29–30ff.

10. This discussion of budgets is based on Robert N. Anthony, John Dearden, and Norton M. Bedford, *Management Control Systems*, 5th ed. (Homewood, Ill.: Irwin, 1984), especially chapters 5, 6, and 7.

11. See Shillinglaw, *Managerial Cost Accounting*, pp. 209–234; Anthony, Dearden, and Bedford, *Management Control Systems*, p. 444; and Jeremy Bacon, *Managing the Budget Function* (New York: National Industrial Conference Board, 1970).

12. For a good description of this budget process, see Chris Argyris, "Human Problems with Budgets," *Harvard Business Review* 31, no. 1 (January 1953):97–110. See also Peter Brownell, "Leadership Style, Budgetary Participation and Managerial Behavior," *Accounting, Organizations and Society* 8, no. 4 (1983):307–321.

13. Kenneth A. Merchant, "Influence on Departmental Budgeting: An Empirical Examination of a Contingency Model," *Accounting, Organizations and Society* 9, nos. 3/4 (1984):291–307.

14. Paul J. Carruth and Thurrell O. McClendon, "How Supervisors React to 'Meeting the Budget' Pressure," *Management Accounting* 66, no. 5 (November 1984):50–54.

15. Jerry A. Viscione, "Small Company Budgets: Targets Are Key," *Harvard Business Review* 62, no. 3 (May–June 1984):42–50.

16. Henry L. Tosi, Jr., "The Human Effects of Budgeting Systems on Management," *MSU Business Topics* 22, no. 4 (Autumn 1974):53–63.

17. For a discussion of the successful use of a rational budget decision-making model by Stanford University, see Ellen Earle Chaffee, "The Role of Rationality in University Budgeting," *Research in Higher Education* 19, no. 4 (1983):387–406.

18. See Shillinglaw, *Managerial Cost Accounting*, pp. 209–210.

19. Anthony, Dearden, and Bedford, *Management Control Systems*, pp. 198–202, 443–448.

20. For a discussion of the use of one such budgeting technique in military acquisitions, see H. W. Lanford and T. M. McCann, "Effective Planning and Control of Large Projects—Using Work Breakdown Structure," *Long Range Planning* 16, no. 2 (April 1983):38–50.

21. Thomas P. Klammer and Michael C. Walker, "The Continuing Increase in the Use of Sophisticated Capital Budgeting Techniques," *California Management Review* 27, no. 1 (Fall 1984):137–148.

22. We are indebted to Glenn A. Welsch, *Budgeting: Profit Planning and Control*, 4th ed. (Englewood Cliffs, N.J.: Prentice-Hall, 1976), for our treatment of this topic.

23. See Peter A. Pyhrr, "Zero-Base Budgeting," *Harvard Business Review* 48, no. 6 (November–December 1970):111–121.

24. Stanton C. Lindquist and K. Bryant Mills, "Whatever Happened to Zero-Base Budgeting?" *Managerial Planning* 28, no. 4 (January–February 1981):31–35.

25. Lawrence A. Gordon, Susan Haka, and Allen G. Schick, "Strategies for Information Systems Implementation: The Case of Zero Base Budgeting," *Accounting, Organizations and Society* 9, no. 2 (1984):111–123.

26. For a recent book on the use of ZBB in data processing departments, see Thomas J. Francl, W. Thomas Lin, and Miklos A. Vasarhelyi, *Planning, Budgeting, and Control for Data Processing: How to Make Zero Base Budgeting Work for You* (New York: Van Nostrand Reinhold, 1984).

27. V. Bruce Irvine, "Budgeting: Functional Analysis and Behavioral Implications," *Cost and Management* 44, no. 2 (March–April 1970):6–16.

28. Our discussion is based on Irvine, "Budgeting: Functional Analysis and Behavioral Implications," and Argyris, "Human Problems with Budgets."

29. Kurt Lewin, "Group Decision and Social Change," in Eleanor E. Maccoby, Theodore M. Newcomb, and Eugene L. Hartley, eds., *Readings in Social Psychology,* 3d ed. (New York: Holt, Rinehart & Winston, 1958), pp. 197–211. See also Edgar F. Huse and Thomas G. Cummings, *Organization Development,* 3d ed. (St. Paul, Minn.: West Publishing, 1985), pp. 72–73.

30. See Neil C. Churchill, "Budget Choice: Planning vs. Control," *Harvard Business Review* 62, no. 4 (July–August 1984):150–166.

31. Roger L. M. Dunbar, "Budgeting for Control," *Administrative Science Quarterly* 16, no. 1 (March 1971):88–96.

32. See Wayne S. Boutell, *Contemporary Auditing* (Belmont, Calif.: Dickenson Publishing, 1970); and Arthur W. Holmes and Wayne S. Overmyer, *Basic Auditing,* 5th ed. (Homewood, Ill.: Irwin, 1976).

33. Suzanne Daley, "Billing Errors Cost Transit Authority Millions," *New York Times,* June 20, 1985, pp. Al, B16.

34. See "How Personal Computers Can Trip Up Executives," *Business Week,* September 24, 1984, pp. 94–102; and Michael Sobol, "Microcomputers and Auditing: Don't Make the Same Mistake Four Times," *EDP Journal,* no. 1 (1985): 36–41.

35. Joseph R. Pleier, "Computer-Assisted Auditing," *EDP Journal,* no. 2 (1984):12–21.

36. "Educational Conference Views Changing Role of Auditor in Next Decade," *Journal of Accountancy* 157, no. 1 (January 1984):10, 12.

CASE STUDY: False Reports

Max Baxter, sales manager of the Blue Ridge Furniture Manufacturing Company, had just completed a two-week trip auditing customer accounts and prospective accounts in the southeastern states. His primary intention was to do follow-up work on prospective accounts contacted by sales staff members during the past six months. Prospective clients were usually furniture dealers or large department stores with furniture departments.

To his amazement, Baxter discovered that almost all the so-called prospective accounts were fictitious. The people had obviously turned in falsely documented field reports and expense statements. Company salespeople had actually called upon only 3 of 22 reported furniture stores or department stores. Thus Baxter surmised that salespeople had falsely claimed approximately 85 percent of the goodwill contacts. Further study showed that all salespeople had followed this general practice and that not one had a clean record.

Baxter decided that immediate action was mandatory, although the salespeople were experienced senior individuals. Angry as he was, he would have preferred firing them. But he was responsible for sales and realized that replacing the staff would seriously cripple the sales program for the coming year.

Source: Case from John M. Champion and John H. James, *Critical Incidents in Management,* 4th ed., p. 107. Copyright © 1980. Used by permission of Richard D. Irwin, Inc.

Case Questions **1.** As Max Baxter, what would you do now to resolve the problem of the false reports?

2. What could Baxter have done to prevent this problem?

22 INFORMATION SYSTEMS AND CONTROL

Upon completing this chapter you should be able to:

1. State why an information system is an important part of management planning, decision making, and control.
2. Describe how managers can evaluate the value and cost of information.
3. Explain why managers at different levels of the organization have different information needs.
4. Describe how a management information system (MIS) can be implemented effectively.
5. Identify the problems that can develop when a computer-based MIS is being implemented, and state the ways these problems can be overcome.
6. Describe the different types of management information and decision systems—MISs, decision support systems (DSSs), and expert systems (ESs)—and their relationship to each other.
7. Describe the uses and impacts of decision support and expert systems on managers and organizations.

All the managerial functions—planning, organizing, leading, and controlling—are necessary for successful organizational performance. To support these functions, especially planning and controlling, systems for supplying information to managers are of special importance. Only with accurate and timely information can managers monitor progress toward their goals and turn plans into reality. If managers cannot stay "on track," making appropriate corrections and adjustments as they progress, their work will be fruitless.

In this chapter we will examine the ways in which organizational information systems help provide the information required for effective control. We will discuss the workings of three forms of computer-based systems for utilizing information—management information systems (MISs), decision support systems (DSSs), and expert systems (ESs), an application of artificial intelligence. We will also discuss the current use of computers by, and the impact of computerization on, organizations and managers' jobs, and will briefly review future developments.[1]

We emphasize computer-based information and decision support systems throughout this chapter for two reasons. First, these systems are rapidly becoming indispensable for planning, decision making, and control. How quickly and accurately managers receive information about what is going right and what is going wrong—how well the information system functions—determines, to a large extent, how effective the control system will be.[2] Second, organizational information and decision support systems are undergoing major changes as a result of dramatic increases in computer capabilities and use. For example, as we discuss later in this chapter, in less than a decade MIS has evolved into DSS, and DSS in turn has begun to evolve toward expert systems. Computer-based information systems offer managers ever-increasing opportunities for improving their control systems. Thus, it has become crucial for managers to understand how these systems should be designed, implemented, and managed.

Information and Control

To appreciate the central role played by information in making control effective, consider a modest-size manufacturer of automobile replacement parts with annual sales of $10 million. Every year the firm's 350 employees service 20,000 customer orders. These orders must be processed, billed, assembled, packed, and shipped—adding up to some 400,000 transactions that must be controlled.

And that is only the beginning. The firm writes 25,000 checks annually. Half of these cover wages; most of the others pay for the 5,000 purchase orders issued every year. Costs are assembled from 17,000 time cards, 6,000 job orders, and 20,000 materials requisitions. Each year, that small $10 million firm is processing almost a million pieces of information related to its activities—and that figure does not include all the other pieces of control information being processed, such as those related to inventory and quality control.

The Computer Revolution

Before the widespread use of computers, managers could not effectively make use of large amounts of valuable information about an organization's activities. The information either reached managers too late or was simply too expensive to gather in usable form.[3] Today, managers have at their command a wide range of data processing and information tools. In place of a few financial controls, managers can draw on computer-based information systems to control activities in every area of their organization. On any number of performance measures, the information provided by these systems helps managers compare standards with actual results, detect deviations, and take corrective action before it is too late to make changes.

The introduction of computerized information systems has sharply changed management control in many organizations. Even a neighborhood retailer may now use computers to control inventory, sales, billing, and other activities. In large organizations, complex electronic data processing (EDP) systems monitor entire projects and sets of operations. It is not unusual to find that computers have replaced bookkeepers and that accountants and controllers routinely perform broader management functions than they ever did in the past.[4]

Contemporary managers need to be effective at, and comfortable with, using computers, since managerial dependence on them is growing rapidly. There are approximately 12 million microcomputers now in use in the United States—one for every 20 citizens.[5] One projection estimates that by 1990, 51 percent of American managers will be using some sort of electronic work station.[6] In order for managers to be sure that the computer-based information they are receiving is accurate and applicable, they need to understand the processes by which *data* are fed to, analyzed, and delivered by computers. However, in most cases they do not need to learn how to program computers. Rather, managers should understand how computerized information systems work; how they are developed; their applications, capabilities, limitations, and costs; and the manner in which information systems may be used.[7] Such an understanding is not difficult to achieve. One survey found that business firms were more successful in teaching basic information about computers to business graduates than they were in teaching basic business subjects to computer science graduates.[8]

The Value and Cost of Information

In designing or improving an information system for management, one of the issues that managers need to consider is whether the benefits of the proposed system justify the cost. The purpose of an MIS is to provide managers with the right information at the right time. Yet, if the potential savings from the information are outweighed by the cost of the information system, then the system under consideration is not cost-effective. Cost-effectiveness of an information system, however, can be difficult to determine, because the value of the information is difficult to quantify.[9] Robert H. Gregory and Richard L. Van Horn have suggested that the value of information depends on four factors: its quality, timeliness, quantity, and relevance to management's ability to take action.[10]

Information quality. To judge the quality of information, managers should compare the reported facts to reality. The more accurate the information, the higher its quality and the more securely managers can rely on it when making decisions. In general, however, the cost of obtaining information increases as the quality of the desired information becomes higher. For example, double- or triple-checking recently obtained information against other records obviously verifies its reliability, but the extra checking steps may be costly in person- or computer-hours. The degree of accuracy needed will vary with the situation: Inventory in the auto-parts manufacturer's supply facility will need to be updated more frequently, and probably checked more carefully, than inventory in a neighborhood hardware store. If information of a higher quality does not add materially to a manager's decision-making capability, it is not worth the added cost.

EVALUATING
INFORMATION

Information timeliness. For effective control, corrective action must be applied before too great a deviation from the plan or standard has taken place. Thus, the information provided by an information system must be available in time for action to be taken. Just when information will be considered timely, however, will depend on the situation. For example, information destined for top-level managers to monitor progress on long-range objectives may be considered timely if it arrives at quarterly intervals. However, middle- and lower-level managers responsible for ongoing operations and activities need more frequent control information. A shop superintendent, for example, needs a daily report on machine downtime if delays are to be minimized. Quality-control managers must get a daily or weekly report on all customer rejections. On a monthly or quarterly basis, such information would be ancient history and of no value.

Information quantity. Managers can hardly make accurate and timely decisions without sufficient information. However, managers are often inundated with irrelevant and useless information. If they receive more information than they can productively use, they may overlook information on serious problems.

Information relevance. Similarly, the information that managers receive must have relevance to their responsibilities and tasks. The personnel manager does not need to know inventory levels—and the manager in charge of reordering inventory does not need to know about the status of staff members in other departments.

What Information Is Needed? In deciding what information a given manager needs, it is helpful to distinguish between data, information, and management information. *Data* are raw, unanalyzed facts, figures, and events from which information *can* be developed—for example, the inventory records for welding rods at a factory in Spokane. *Information* is analyzed or processed data that informs a recipient about a situation—the inventory of welding rods at the Spokane plant is a 12 days' supply whereas the desired minimum inventory is a 30 days' supply. *Management information* is information that has action implications; that is, because it is accurate, timely, and relevant and because it represents the key features of a situation, managers can determine from it what they must do about the situation. The inventory information above is management information because it implies the need for immediate action (increasing the inventory and determining how and why the inventory was allowed to fall to such a low level).

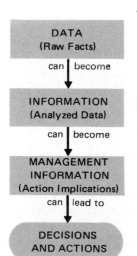

In early applications of EDP systems, many managers became swamped by potentially interesting but basically unhelpful data and information. However, this difficulty is not an inevitable part of computer use in organizations. In fact, the capabilities of computers make it possible to *condense* information to only the most relevant, useful, and timely essentials. Computers can be programmed to report only those situations that require managerial attention, or information can be selectively accessed and analyzed from the raw data in order to guide decisions.

Management Information Systems

One of the difficulties associated with discussing *management information systems* (*MIS*) is the fact that there are many definitions of them.[11] For our purposes, we will define an MIS as *a formal method of making available to management the accurate and timely information necessary to facilitate the decision-making process and enable the organization's planning, control, and operational functions to be carried out effectively*. The system provides information on the past, present, and projected future and on relevant events inside and outside the organization.[12]

The use of the word "formal" in our definition is not intended to negate the importance of the informal communication network in the organization's control mechanisms. In fact, managers often detect problems *before* they show up in formal control reports because they are tuned in to the grapevine. The ability of managers to maintain effective informal communication channels, to sense the implications of the information those channels transmit, and to evaluate, decide, and act quickly on such information extends enormously the usefulness of the MIS.

The Evolution of MIS

Organizations have always had some kind of management information system, even if it was not recognized as such. In the past, these systems were of a highly informal nature in their setup and utilization. Not until the advent of computers, with their ability to process and condense large quantities of data, did the design of management information systems become a formal process and field of study. Attempts to use computers effectively led to the identification and study of information systems and to the planning, implementation, and review of new ones.

EDP. When computers were first introduced into organizations, they were used mainly to process data for a few organizational functions—usually accounting and billing. Because of the specialized skills required to operate the expensive, complex, and sometimes temperamental equipment, computers were located in electronic data processing (EDP) departments. As the speed and ease of processing data grew, other data processing and information-management tasks were computerized. To cope with these new tasks, EDP departments developed standardized reports for the use of operating managers. These reports became important points of many organizations' management information systems.

MIS. The growth of EDP departments spurred managers to plan their organizations' information systems more rationally. These efforts led to the emergence of the concept of computer-based information systems (CBIS), which became better known as computer-based MIS—or simply MIS. As the EDP departments' functions expanded beyond routine processing of masses of standardized data, they began to be called MIS departments.

DSS. Recent advances in computer hardware and software have made it possible for EDP/MIS experts, and then for managers, to gain "on-line" or "real-time" access to the data bases in CBISs. The widespread use of microcomputers has enabled managers to create their own data bases and electronically manipulate information as needed rather than waiting for reports to be issued by the EDP/MIS department. While MIS reports are still necessary for monitoring ongoing operations, DSS permits less structured use of data bases as special decision needs arise.[14]

Expert Systems. The near future will witness the widespread use of *expert systems (ESs)*. Expert systems use artificial intelligence to diagnose problems, recommend strategies to avert or solve these problems, offer a rationale for these recommendations, and "learn" from each experience or situation. In effect, the expert system acts like a human "expert" in analyzing unstructured situations. (We discuss artificial intelligence and expert systems in more detail later in this chapter.)

Differing Information for Different Management Levels

G. Anthony Gorry and M. S. Scott Morton have pointed out that an organization's information system must provide information to managers with three levels of responsibilities: operational control, management control, and strategic planning.[15] We can think of these three categories in terms of the activities that take place at different levels of the managerial hierarchy (first-line, middle, and top). The design of the MIS must take into account the information needs of the various managerial levels. For example, as shown in table 22–1, the information sources for operational control are based largely within the organization, while the information sources for strategic planning tend to be outside the organization.

Operational Control. An MIS for operational control must provide highly accurate and detailed information on a daily or weekly basis. A production supervisor has to know if materials wastage is excessive, if costly overruns are about to occur, or if the machine time for a job has expired. A sales manager may need to know the number

TABLE 22–1 INFORMATION REQUIREMENTS BY DECISION CATEGORY			

Characteristics of Information	Operational Control (First Line)	Management Control (Top and Middle Level)	Strategic Planning (Top Level)
Source	Largely internal	←——————→	Largely external
Scope	Well defined, narrow	←——————→	Very wide
Level of Aggregation	Detailed	←——————→	Aggregate
Time Horizon	Historical	←——————→	Future
Currency	Highly current	←——————→	Fairly old
Required Accuracy	High	←——————→	Low
Frequency of Use	Very frequent	←——————→	Infrequent

Source: Adapted from G. Anthony Gorry and Michael S. Scott Morton, "A Framework for Management Information Systems," *Sloan Management Review* 13, no. 1 (Fall 1971): 59. Copyright © 1971 by the Sloan Management Review Association. All rights reserved.

of customer calls made by sales representatives each week. Obviously, accuracy and timeliness of information are particularly important at this level, since the manager will frequently be required to take on-the-spot corrective action.

Middle Management. Middle-level managers, such as division heads, will be concerned with the current and future performance of their units. They will therefore need information on important matters that will affect those units—large-scale problems with suppliers, abrupt sales declines, or increased consumer demand for a particular product line. Thus, the type of information middle-level managers will require falls somewhere between the extremes required by lower- and top-level managers. For example, in devising and using break-even charts (see chapter 21), middle-level managers will need to know about plant costs in some detail; they will also need broader-based information on economic conditions and expected market demand.

Top Management. For top managers, the MIS must provide information for strategic planning and management control. For strategic planning, the external sources of information—on economic conditions, technological developments, the actions of competitors—assume paramount importance.[16] This information should possess sufficient accuracy to indicate trends and reflect current forecasts. Because strategic plans are broad and long range, they require approximate indications of future conditions rather than exact statements about the past or present.

For the *management control* functions of top managers, however, the sources of information must be both internal and external. Top managers are typically concerned about the overall financial performance of their organizations. They therefore need information on quarterly sales and profits, as well as on the performance of competitors. Internal control reports for top managers come in at monthly, quarterly, and sometimes even annual intervals. Such a slow-paced information flow is possible because top managers will not be concerned with day-to-day operating control but with longer-range problems, plans, and performance.

How may the various needs of different managerial levels be translated into a management information system? One major company designed the manufacturing component of its MIS this way: *Supervisors* receive daily reports on direct and indirect labor, materials usage, scrap, production counts, and machine downtime; *superintendents* and *department heads* receive weekly departmental cost summaries and product cost reports; *plant managers* receive weekly and monthly financial statements and analyses, analyses of important costs, and summarized product cost reports; *divisional managers* receive monthly plant comparisons, financial planning reports, product cost summaries, and plant cost control reports; and, finally, *top managers* receive overall monthly and quarterly financial reviews, financial analyses, and summarized comparisons of divisional performance.

Designing a Computer-Based MIS

Many articles and books have described the systematic steps that should be followed in designing and implementing an MIS.[17] Robert G. Murdick reviewed a number of these sources and adapted them to form his own model of how an MIS should be developed.[18] (See fig. 22–1.) This flow chart indicates the complexity and amount of work required for MIS development. For the sake of simplicity, we may break down Murdick's model into the four following stages.

1. *A preliminary survey and problem definition stage.* With the formation of a task force charged with the design of an MIS, there should be a thorough assessment of the organization's capabilities and strategic goals, as well as an assessment of any external factors relevant to the organization's functions. From this assessment a definition of the information system the organization needs can be decided upon, and the determination of informational, operational, and functional objectives can be accomplished.

2. *A conceptual design stage.* Through an analysis of the current information system, alternative MIS designs with specific performance requirements can be developed. These alternatives are then weighed against organization objectives, capabilities, and needs. This examination leads to an initial selected project plan. At this point, tasks are delegated, information on the task force's study communicated to employees, and the plan for a training program conceived.

3. *A detailed design stage.* Once the conceptual plan is decided upon, performance specifications of the new MIS can be established. Components, programming, flow charting, and data bases (including specifications for personnel interaction with the system) can be designed. A model of the system is created, tested, refined, and reviewed until it meets the specified level of performance.

4. *A final implementation stage.* The formal requirements for the new MIS are determined. The logistics of space allocations, equipment additions, and forms design are worked out and enacted. The training program commences. Design and testing of software for the MIS are completed, and the organization's data bases are entered into the system. After a series of final checks, the MIS is ready for implementation.

It should be emphasized that creation of an MIS is a long-term task that requires the skills of a variety of specialists. In fact, the design and implementation of an MIS such as that shown in Murdick's model might well require a major team effort by managers and information systems analysts over a period of two or three years.

Guidelines for Effective Design

How can these steps in the MIS development process be carried out effectively? For our purposes, we can focus on five guidelines for effective MIS design: (1) make users part of the design team; (2) carefully consider the costs of the system; (3) favor relevance and selectivity of information over sheer quantity; (4) pretest the system before installation; and (5) train the operators and users of the system carefully.

1. *Include users on the design team.* It is widely agreed that cooperation between the operating managers (who use the information) and systems designers is not only desirable but necessary. Users know what information they need, when it is needed, and how it will be used for managerial action and decision making. Management scientists and systems designers often do not think like managers and may be unaware of the key factors that enter into an operational decision. Unless operating managers have a decisive voice in the design of the MIS, the information system may fail to provide needed information while simultaneously overloading them with useless information.[19]

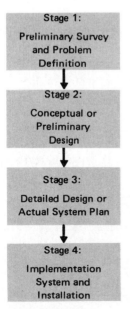

Stage 1:
Preliminary Survey and Problem Definition

Stage 2:
Conceptual or Preliminary Design

Stage 3:
Detailed Design or Actual System Plan

Stage 4:
Implementation System and Installation

FIGURE 22–1
MIS DEVELOPMENT

Source: Adapted from
Robert G. Murdick, "MIS
Development Procedures,"
*Journal of Systems
Management* 21, no. 12
(December 1970):24–25.
Reprinted by permission.

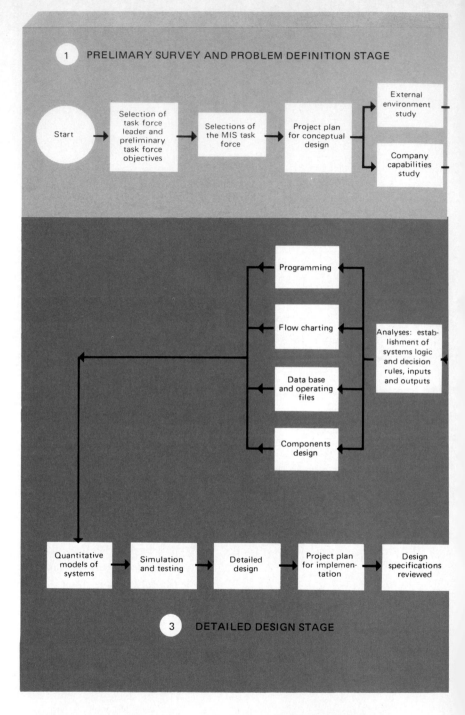

2. *Weigh the money and time costs of the system.* To keep the MIS on track and on budget, designers need to specify how the system will be developed—and this includes schedules of time required for different steps, milestones to be reached, and budgeted costs. This component of the design stage is often neglected, particularly

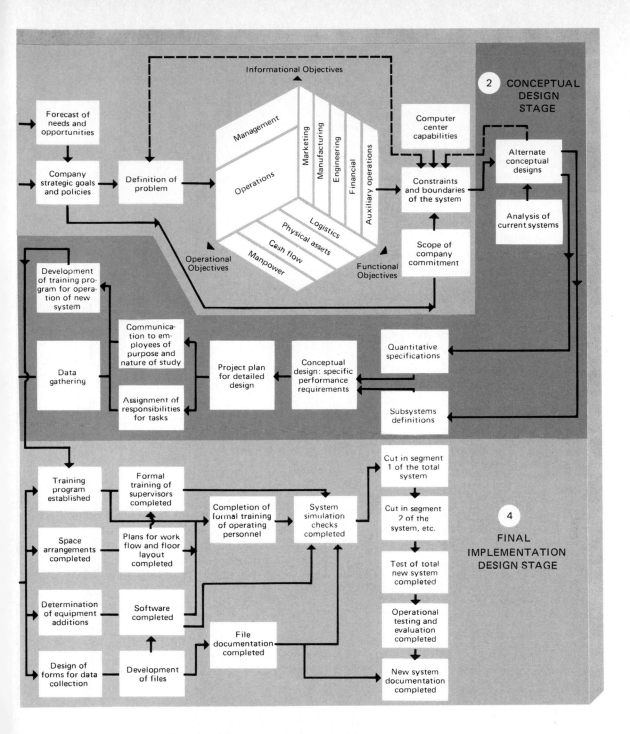

in nonprofit organizations, because managers tend to justify MIS on cost-saving grounds and may fear that documentation of the system's actual installation costs will discredit their original estimates. As a result, an unnecessarily expensive system may be implemented. If managers justify the design and installation of a new system on a cost-benefit basis, cost overruns are less likely to occur. In addition, the system design should specify which units of the organization will be responsible for installing and operating the system. In this way, the appropriate managers can be held accountable for costs.[20] It should be noted that the greater portion of MIS operating costs go for the maintenance of existing software.[21]

3. *Favor relevance and selectivity over sheer quantity.* As we have seen, a manager needs *enough* information for an informed decision; *more* information is not necessarily better, although many managers prefer to have too much rather than too little information.[22] In one study, decision makers who perceived themselves as experiencing information overload had lower performance levels but a higher satisfaction level than those decision makers who perceived information underload.[23] A properly designed MIS does not supply middle- or top-level managers with the routine details of an organization's daily activities. For example, instead of supplying sales management with voluminous monthly printouts of sales results, the MIS department can supply information on all salespeople who exceed 10 percent plus or minus the sales quota.[24] The MIS *filters* or evaluates information so that only the most relevant information will be supplied to the appropriate manager. In addition, the effective MIS *condenses* information, so what is relevant can be absorbed quickly. The information system should also provide top-level managers with data on critical factors and changes related to organizational effectiveness.[25]

4. *Pretest the system before installation.* This important step has too often been neglected by MIS designers. Even when managers and system designers cooperate in the system's development, important factors may be overlooked. Omissions and bugs will show up during the test period. If they do not become apparent until the system is finally implemented, costly problems may arise and expensive changes may be necessary.

There are four basic approaches to installing a new MIS that have some bearing on the length and extensiveness of the pretest stage.[26] In *crash* or *direct installation,* the new system replaces the old one entirely. The switch is effected all at once, and there is total dependence on the new system. In this case, extensive pretest should be done, since the organization will not be able to fall back on the old system if the new system fails or reveals major operational bugs.[27]

With *parallel installation,* the new system is implemented and operated side by side with the old system. This approach allows comparison of outputs between systems so that adjustments can be made before the old system is removed. While cutting down on the amount of pretesting needed in crash installation, parallel installation can be costly since the organization is maintaining two information systems.

Pilot installation offers the organization the ability to test the new MIS in operation as it is used by a small part of the organization—for example, by the sales management of one division. Problems can then be discovered and corrected before total installation.

Phased installation offers the organization the ability to implement the new MIS segment by segment, allowing for operational testing and debugging before moving on to the next segment. However, this approach requires particular attention in the design stage since old and new systems must be able to work together during the installation process.

5. Provide adequate training and written documentation for the operators and users of the system. A training program for managers and MIS operators is important for two major reasons. Without training and written instructions for the operation and use of the MIS, the organization will be at a loss when experienced personnel leave. Also, operators must understand the information needs of managers at different levels so that they know what they are doing, for whom they are doing it, and why. Perhaps most important, managers need to understand how the MIS operates so they can control it, rather than letting it control them. EDP/MIS technicians often gain power at the expense of managers when they are the only ones who understand how a system works.

Even with great care in design and implementation, an MIS may not fit the needs of users as closely as desired, either because it is difficult to use (not sufficiently user-friendly) or because it does not supply all the information asked for. In these cases, attempts are then made to fit the users to the system. Such attempts are unlikely to be successful if users are not "DP-friendly."[28] To help users become DP-friendly, there should be a general orientation to the new system so that employees can become familiar with the hardware, applications software, and available organizational support from the MIS department. It should be made plain how the new MIS will change the organizational structure and task responsibilities and how the job of each employee will be affected by the new MIS.[29]

Implementing a Computer-Based MIS

Use of computers for the solution of many organizational problems has grown rapidly, despite the problems involved in implementing a computerized MIS. Managers should be aware of the systems and technological problems of systems design and installation, although these are, strictly speaking, the concern of information system and data processing personnel and are obviously beyond the scope of an introductory management text. Our discussion, therefore, focuses on the "people problems," which are more important for most managers to understand, are at least as difficult to solve, and are no less likely to inhibit successful implementation of a computerized information system. The primary responsibility for their solution will fall upon managers.[30]

Problems in Implementing a Computer-Based MIS

G. W. Dickson and John K. Simmons have indicated five major factors that determine whether and to what extent the implementation of a new MIS will be resisted.

1. *Disruption of established departmental boundaries.* The establishment of a new MIS often results in changes in several organizational units. For example, inventory and purchasing departments may be merged to make use of the MIS more efficient. Such changes may be resisted by department members, who may resent having to change the way they do things or the people with whom they work.

2. *Disruption of the informal system.* The informal communication network may be disrupted as a new MIS alters communication patterns. If organization members prefer some of the earlier, informal mechanisms for gathering and dis-

tributing information, they may resist the more formal channels set up for the new system.

3. *Specific individual characteristics.* People with many years of service with the organization have "learned the ropes" and know how to get things done in the existing system. They may tend to resist change more tenaciously than newer people who have been with the organization for a comparatively short period of time and who do not have as large an investment in organizational know-how and relationships.

4. *The organizational culture.* If top management maintains open communication, deals with grievances, and, in general, establishes a culture with high trust throughout the organization, there is likely to be less resistance to the installation of a new MIS. However, if top managers are isolated or aloof from other organization members, or if the organizational culture supports inflexible behavior, then effective implementation of the MIS is likely to be hindered.

5. *How the change is implemented.* As we have seen repeatedly in earlier chapters, the manner in which changes are designed and implemented affects the amount of resistance the changes will encounter. In general, when managers and subordinates make change decisions together, there is greater likelihood that the changes will be accepted.

Dickson and Simmons have observed that the frustrations associated with the implementation of a new MIS can manifest themselves in three ways: *Aggression* is manifested when individuals hit back at the object (or person) frustrating them. Aggression against a computer-based MIS has gone as far as sabotage—by using equipment incorrectly, by putting incomplete or inadequate information into the system, or by actual destruction of hardware or software. *Projection* is the psychological mechanism of blaming difficulties on someone or something else. When managers (or other individuals) blame the computer system for problems caused by human error or other factors unrelated to the system itself, projection is taking place. *Avoidance* is manifested when individuals defend themselves by withdrawing from or avoiding a frustrating situation. Managers may exhibit avoidance behavior when they ignore the output of an MIS in favor of their own information sources.

Because people at different levels of the organization are affected by a computer-based MIS in different ways, the frequency with which each type of behavior is manifested will depend on the hierarchical level of the individuals and managers affected by the MIS change. (See table 22–2.) Among lower-level nonclerical personnel, for example, the installation of a new MIS may cause an increase in job complexity. Clerical workers (like key punchers) who will be working directly with the new system are less likely to manifest aggression toward it: the MIS represents a major part of their job. They may, however, resist changes in the system through projection—for example, by making remarks about the new system's failings and inadequacies relative to the old system.

Operating management—including both first-line and middle managers—generally experiences the greatest impact from a new MIS. The information supplied by the MIS to top managers will, after all, help determine how the operating managers are evaluated. The problem for operating managers is that they have less control over how and when this information is filtered, interpreted, and presented to their superiors; instead of supplying it directly to top managers, they supply it to the MIS, which is operated by staff specialists. This loss of control is a source of anxiety to operating managers.

TABLE 22–2 WORK GROUPS, THEIR RELATION TO MIS, AND THEIR POSSIBLE DYSFUNCTIONAL BEHAVIORS

Organizational Subgroup	Relation to MIS	Dysfunctional Behavior
Top Management	Generally unaffected and unconcerned with systems	Avoidance
Technical Staff	Systems designers and agents of systems change	None
Operating Management	Controlled from above by systems; job content and context modified by new systems	Aggression, avoidance, and projection
Operating Personnel: Clerical	Particularly affected by clerical systems; jobs eliminated; job patterns changed	Projection
Nonclerical	Provide system inputs	Aggression

Source: Adapted from G. W. Dickson and John K. Simmons, "The Behavioral Side of MIS," *Business Horizons* 13, no. 4 (August 1970): 63.

Other sources of anxiety for managers include the fact that a computerized MIS tends to allow more centralized decision making, which makes it easier for top managers to increase their control over operating managers. In addition, there is always the possibility that a computer-based MIS will eliminate or substantially alter some first-line and middle management jobs. Thus, the resistance of operating managers to the MIS may encompass all three types of psychological reactions: They may fight the system (aggression); they may ignore it, sticking to their old communication channels (avoidance); or they may blame the system for failures caused by other factors (projection). Table 22–3 illustrates the reasons why operating managers are especially likely to resist a computer-based MIS.

TABLE 22–3 REASONS FOR RESISTANCE TO MIS (BY WORKING GROUP)

	Top Management	Operating Management	Operating (Clerical)	Operating (Nonclerical)
Threats to economic security		X	X	
Threats to status or power		X	X*	
Increased job complexity	X		X	X
Uncertainty or unfamiliarity	X	X	X	X
Changed interpersonal relations or work patterns		X*	X	
Changed superior-subordinate relationships		X*	X	
Increased rigidity or time pressure	X	X	X	
Role ambiguity		X	X*	X
Feelings of insecurity		X	X*	X*

X = The reason is possibly the cause of resistance to MIS development.
X* = The reason has a strong possibility of being the cause of resistance.

Source: G. W. Dickson and John K. Simmons, "The Behavioral Side of MIS," *Business Horizons* 13, no. 4 (August 1970): 68. Copyright © 1970 by the Foundation for the School of Business at Indiana University. Reprinted by permission.

TABLE 22–4 COMPUTER SECURITY CONCERNS

Concern	Mainframe Computers	Microcomputers
Physical Security —Fire damage —Water damage —Deliberate destruction —Wind damage	Greater exposure per occurrence because of cost factors.	Possibility of more frequent occurrence because of the working environment.
—Theft of computer	Not a concern due to size of the central processing unit (CPU).	Greater concern due to size and locations.
—Theft of terminals, other peripherals	Size, location, general building security and other factors are similar for both.	
—Loss or destruction of storage media.	Maximum exposure, but mitigated by hardware/software controls, better storage facilities, tighter security.	Maximum exposure due to physical characteristics of media (floppy disk) and physical location of computers, lack of secure storage areas.
Software Security —Theft of licensed software	Some exposure, but less likely due to limited market for material.	Significant exposure due to open market for pirated material.
Programs Written In-house —Accuracy of new programs	Considerable exposure, but mitigated by quality of data processing personnel and by testing requirements.	Greater exposure because: —Users are not programmers —Incomplete testing and review
—Program changes	Considerable exposure in either case, but there are generally tighter controls in large installations. Micro users are not subject to the same constraints.	
—Program loss or destruction	Exposure mitigated by software controls and by backup/recovery procedures generally in place.	Greater exposure for some configurations; may not have adequate facilities for making backup copies.

The top management in many organizations is, in the main, unaffected by and comparatively unconcerned with the implementation of an MIS. Top managers have much to gain from such a system, because it will enable them to make more informed decisions. However, they tend to avoid active involvement with it, perhaps out of unfamiliarity with or feelings of insecurity about computers. This lack of direction and support from top managers often exacerbates the difficulties other organization members have with the MIS.

In other cases, top and middle management are greatly involved in the design process for an MIS. The design takes place within the political system of the organization, and nonrational considerations of MIS designers and subgroups of users can have an impact on the eventual design, implementation, use, and organizational reaction and behavior to the new MIS.[31] For example, divisional requirements for information by middle management might differ from the overall organizational requirements for information by top management. The information most useful to top managers might also facilitate the evaluation of divisional

Concern	Mainframe Computers	Microcomputers
Programs Written In-house		
—Inability to continue processing due to lack of documentation	Minimal exposure; runs generally not dependent upon documentation. Also, mitigated by quality assurance reviews and turnover requirements.	Greater exposure (if the person running the job leaves, the job may have to be reprogrammed) due to user independence, lack of documentation requirements.
—Data security (integrity)	Moderate exposure, but mitigated by run-to-run balancing capabilities, machine/software checks.	Greater exposure to loss due to ease of erasing files. If data are down-loaded from mainframe, some may not be received. Also, if similar data are down-loaded to various micros and processed independently, the data can lose integrity.
—Release of privileged data	Considerable exposure, but mitigated by locking devices and/or password protection, personnel controls.	Greater exposure due to lack of separation of duties, user-controlled security.
Inappropriate Use Of Corporate Assets		
—Initial justification for installation	Minor exposure due to required review and approval procedures.	Greater exposure, cost not considered substantial.
—Processing data not required by business (game playing, use of facilities for moonlighting, duplication of effort, and so on)	Some exposure, but mitigated by console logs, review capabilities, and monitoring by management. Chargeback systems also tend to reduce exposure.	Greater exposure due to lack of the controls listed under Mainframe heading.

Source: Adapted from Edwin B. Opliger, "Identifying Microcomputer Concerns," *EDP Journal* 1 (1985): 43–44.

performance; this might be perceived by middle managers as a threat to their security. Both groups will jockey for position and try to protect their interests. After the design is completed, winners and losers of the political battle may take different stances toward the new MIS.

Security. Security of the new system is a control issue that must be addressed in design and implementation stages—for example, by placing equipment in safe and supervised areas and by the construction of password and read-only files. Table 22–4 outlines some important security concerns and the degree of risk associated with two major MIS configurations—mainframe computers and micro- or personal computers. While the protection of mainframe configurations is usually adequate, security for microcomputer systems is sorely lacking in many organizations, which tend to be ignorant of the risks involved and often neglect appropriate security measures.[32]

Organizations using microcomputer-based information systems have experi-

"Here's the story, gentlemen. Sometime last night, an 11-year-old kid in Akron, Ohio, got into our computer and transferred all our assets to a bank in Zurich."

Drawing by Stevenson; © 1983 The New Yorker Magazine, Inc.

enced increased control problems, such as theft and vandalism, the destruction or alteration of data, and the unauthorized dissemination of restricted or sensitive information.[33] Problems with theft and vandalism can be limited by placing equipment in secure areas or by making existing facilities more secure. Software or program piracy can be prevented by copyguarding important programs and by securely storing authorized originals and backup copies. Data can be protected by making alterations to on-line data files possible only with the correct password, or by making backup copies of disks to preserve originals from intentional or accidental erasure. (However, duplicating software and data files creates more copies to be stolen.) Those managers who need the data files on a timely basis can each be issued a disk copy under tight reporting procedures and schedules.

Overcoming the Implementation Problems

No single approach will overcome all the implementation problems we have identified. Each situation must be separately diagnosed and its own individual "cure" prescribed. However, some implementation problems can be mitigated if the MIS design process follows the guidelines we mentioned above. Dickson and Simmons have described a number of factors that they consider important in helping managers overcome implementation problems:

1. *User orientation.* Perhaps the most critical step in overcoming implementation problems is to ensure that the MIS is user-oriented in both design and implementation. If the system's output fails to meet the users' needs with a minimum of adjustment and new learning, users will stick firmly, and logically, to their own systems, thereby reducing the chances that the MIS will eventually become useful to them. Such problems will be less likely to arise if, as recommended above, users are included in the MIS team from the inception of the project. MIS design staff should be rewarded for fulfilling user needs as well as for meeting project deadlines.[34]

2. *Participation.* Many implementation problems can be overcome (or avoided) if future users are made members of the MIS team. Operating managers in particular should have a major say in the items to be included, the disposition of information, and possible job modifications. Participation by all levels of management and staff who will be using the MIS will ensure that the system will reflect users' needs. Employees who have a say in any changes in their job relationships and tasks caused by the new MIS will have more confidence in the quality and usability of the new system. It is also important to establish effective lines of communication for implementing, training, and debugging processes for the system. If the entire design and implementation process is taken over by technologists, serious line–staff conflicts may develop.[35]

3. *Communication.* The aims and characteristics of the system should be clearly defined and communicated to all members of the MIS team as well as to users. This task is particularly difficult because the character of an MIS evolves as it is being designed and implemented, and therefore the final nature of the MIS cannot be known with precision at the outset. But without a clear understanding of the system's basic objectives and characteristics, team members and users will have constant differences of opinion, and the installed MIS is unlikely to satisfy the needs of users. A key to knowing user needs, determining possible political ramifications, and ensuring that all affected employees feel that they are participating is the establishment of clear and working lines of communication.

4. *Redefinition of performance measurements.* A new MIS may modify a manager's job to the point where old methods of performance evaluation no longer apply. For this reason, an MIS that calls for new evaluation procedures and/or criteria must be accompanied by incentives to encourage both high performance and acceptance of the system. The new methods must also be clearly explained so that managers will know how their accomplishments will be measured and rewarded.

5. *New challenges.* The notion that a computer can do many of the things that a manager can do—and do them faster and perhaps more thoroughly—has a lot to do with the feelings of insecurity a computer-based MIS may arouse. One way to reduce this sense of insecurity is to publicize the challenges made possible by the computer system. A new MIS may liberate middle managers from many boring and routine tasks. Thus, they may have an opportunity to take a larger role in activities like long-range planning that have tended to be the exclusive prerogative of upper-level managers. It may also give them the opportunity to use information provided by the system in more creative and productive ways.

Decision Support Systems, Networking, and Expert Systems

Decision support systems (DSSs) and expert systems (ESs) are becoming more useful to managers. As with MIS, DSS and expert systems offer managers the ability to receive filtered, condensed, and analyzed information that can enhance their job performance, and, in the case of expert systems, can provide managers with an information system that can keep pace with their own knowledge and sophistication.

Decision Support Systems

A decision support system is *an interactive computer system that is easily accessible to, and operated by, noncomputer specialists to assist them in planning and decision-making functions.* While DSSs may differ in their emphases on data access and modeling functions, there is an overriding emphasis in all such systems on user accessibility to data for decision making.[36] This decision-making applicability permits managers to simulate problems using formal mathematical models and to test the outcomes of various alternatives for reaching the best possible decisions.[37]

Differences between DSS and MIS. Since the DSS is an outgrowth of the MIS, there are basic similarities between them: They are both computer-based and designed to supply information to managers. However, there are some important advantages to a DSS. First of all, a DSS is geared to information *manipulation* and not essentially to data storage and retrieval as are many MISs.[38] A DSS is operated directly by its users; when they need access to information, they can immediately consult their own on-line system without having to wait days or weeks for results from the MIS department. Once managers call up the required data through a DSS, they can manipulate it directly, asking questions and reformatting the data to meet their specific needs without having to explain what they want to EDP/MIS staff.[39] Managers can thus be certain that they will get the information they need when they need it. In addition, direct manipulation of data has the advantage of greater security for sensitive information.

Another key difference between an MIS and a DSS is that a DSS helps managers make nonroutine decisions in unstructured situations.[40] An MIS, on the other hand, emphasizes standard, periodical reports and cannot respond well to nonroutine, unstructured, or *ad hoc* situations.[41] MIS departments may be unfamiliar with the decisions made in such situations; because they often have a tremendous backlog of requests for data, they may be unable to respond quickly to additional special requests. Conversely, some managers who have no difficulty manipulating the data themselves may have difficulty explaining their information requirements to MIS staff.

The ability of DSS users to access data directly and perform some of their own data management chores has reduced one kind of intraorganizational conflict. In the early stages of computer-based MIS development, conflicts and stresses between MIS users—managers and others—and EDP/MIS department personnel arose from a variety of issues. These included the dependence of users on DP experts; the differing personal styles, backgrounds, values, and objectives of users and experts; and the evolving nature of information systems as new technologies and concepts appeared almost overnight.[42] The introduction of DSSs and on-line access to data has led to a reduction in friction between individuals from various organizational subcultures and EDP/MIS staff, who often constitute a subculture of their own.

Using DSS. At Pet Foods in St. Louis, the sales forecasting department performs a large percentage of its own data processing tasks. Using readily available DSS applications software, users can project sales demand by units per territory and region and translate that information into a financial forecast. Through this process, the department can determine the effects of closing a particular warehouse in a matter of days where the same task might take the MIS department weeks or months.[43] This is but one example of the successful application of DSS.

The ideal DSS solicits input data needed from the user and then prompts the user to consider all key decision points.[44] Many software applications on the market can perform these functions. Among the more popular DSS applications software are spreadsheet packages such as *Lotus 1-2-3* and *VisiCalc*, data management packages such as *dBase III* and *Powerbase*, project management software such as *Total Project Manager*, integrated software packages such as *Symphony, Framework*, and *Jazz*, and assorted financial analysis and planning packages. DSS software can support such organizational functions as marketing, production, and finance as well as many other decision-making areas.[45]

DSS vs. EDP/MIS. The increasing use of DSSs, especially those connected to a central host computer, raises doubts about the continued need for separate EDP/MIS departments.[46] The proliferation of microcomputers, off-the-shelf DSS software, and fourth-generation programming languages that boost programmer productivity has reduced the demand for MIS programmers, who generally specialize in the writing of programs for minicomputers and mainframes.[47] User-MIS department conflicts, which were reduced through the introduction of a DSS, may be replaced by the fears of EDP/MIS staff that they may be made irrelevant in a totally DSS-oriented organization. However, use of a DSS may not necessarily supplant EDP/MIS departments. Rather, many companies still need the massive data processing and storage capacities of mainframes computers, and mainframes require EDP/MIS staff to operate and maintain them. Such companies are best served by an information system that integrates both DSS and MIS functions and activities.[48]

Another concern of EDP/MIS staff is that with every manager using his or her own DSS there will be a proliferation of unauthorized and incompatible private files.[49] Some MIS staff may fear that data will become an individual resource rather than an organizational one—data becoming the proprietary concern of individuals who might hold it for "ransom"—or that confusion will be created as to which data files are correct. However, this possible problem is more than compensated for by the real advantages of a DSS, which are, on the whole, advantages to the organization as well. The extra cost and duplication of computing resources and the lack of control over data in DSSs are outweighed by the more effective decisions that they make possible.[50] Centralized control of data, the aim of an MIS, should be supplanted by decentralized controls for the sharing of accurate DSS data.[51]

The use of DSS involves many new things for managers to learn. For example, users of DSSs are learning that with this *unstructured* decision-making tool, the models created for decision making often contain assumptions relevant only to one specific situation.[52] Assumptions made for an older model might not be appropriate for a new situation and might render the new information and decision erroneous. And since a DSS can speed the information-decision process to a matter of days or hours, documentation of models and their underlying assumptions are likely to lag far behind. In many situations, it will be necessary to scrap preexisting models. In others, special care must be taken to retain and document models for situations that are apt to recur.

GDSS. As we discussed in chapter 6 in the section on group decision making, a DSS can be configured to serve as a group decision-making tool.[53] A *group decision support system (GDSS)* is a computer-based system for managers to share and manipulate information in a decision-oriented meeting. Managers assembled at a common meeting site, or in many separate locations, share and manipulate data on individual terminals hooked up to a central computer. Information from one terminal may be sent to the main computer for display to all group members. In this way, individual decision makers can interact with each other, and with each other's data and analyses, on a group level. Information is stored, manipulated, and analyzed by the group to achieve the most effective group decision, and thus to increase group decision-making ability.

Networking

The GDSS is one specialized form of *networking*. Networks are simply groups of computers that can communicate with each other and share common resources, data bases, hardware, and so on. Paralleling the growth of microcomputer DSSs, there has been a similar, rapid growth in ways to link microcomputers, terminals, and systems in networks. These networks can be formed either *intraorganizationally,* linking groups of users or various departments, or *interorganizationally,* linking the organization to outside data bases. One estimate projects that by 1987 at least 110,000 microcomputer networks will be in use.[54]

Intraorganizational Networking. The two major ways to form *intraorganizational* networks are to link together microcomputers into local networks to share data and results and to link networked microcomputers with a mainframe computer.[55] More and more companies are linking single-user microcomputers with large mainframes through such programs as Cullinet Software's Information Database.[56]

Networks can be configured as stars or rings. (See fig. 22–2.) In a *star network,* individual microcomputers are connected to a central host—a minicomputer or a mainframe.[57] The individual computers do not communicate directly with each other, but go through the central host. The *ring network* has no central controlling computer. Instead, the microcomputers are linked to each other in a ring or circle; information travels the circumference of the ring in either direction. The *local area network* (LAN) is an intraorganizational, user-oriented network. Its configuration may be either a star or a ring. The LAN permits users to share data storage facilities and to communicate with each other. In a LAN it is not unusual to have several terminals working from files stored in a common data base. In some instances, a LAN may be linked to an intercity network, thus permitting users access to a greater range of information.

Interorganizational Networking. Interorganizational networks, a dramatic and powerful use of information system technology, link the information systems of two

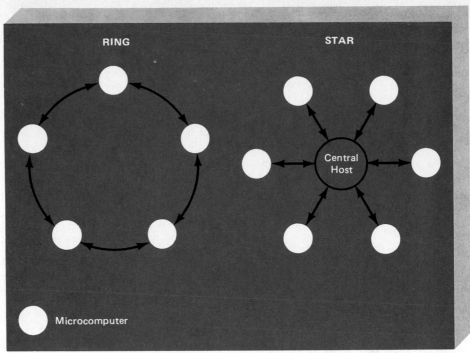

FIGURE 22–2
MICROCOMPUTER
NETWORKS

or more organizations. This direct access to external information can increase an organization's efficiency of information transfer and increase the effective use of internal information. For example, to facilitate computer links for just-in-time inventory systems, GM requires its major suppliers to use the same Automotive Industry Action Group-endorsed computer hardware standards and communication protocols that it uses.[58] American Hospital Supply (AHS) installed its own terminals in hospitals for the direct ordering of its supplies and medicines, thereby outflanking its competitors. AHS also offers the hospitals software enhancements for their own use with the terminals, thus "locking in" these customers. One controversial example of vendor "lock-in" was associated with American Airlines' Sabre computer reservation system. Sabre, used by many independent travel agents, initially displayed American Airlines' flights first, and most agents tended to book them heavily because of this. In a court decision, this practice was held to be an unfair competitive advantage.

Some companies provide informational services or products electronically via interorganizational networks. For example, Prentice-Hall supplies an on-line tax information update service that can be delivered directly to the information systems of organizations' tax and legal departments.[59] In general, the availability and diversity of external data bases have grown rapidly. According to one estimate, in 1979 there were 221 companies marketing 400 data bases worldwide; by 1985, there were 1,316 companies marketing 2,764 data bases.[60]

Problems associated with interorganizational information systems include their high cost and vulnerability to misuse or security penetration. Complications may also ensue if there are any internal systems changes by supplier or receiver.[61]

Expert Systems

Even though DSSs are currently being widely adopted, expert systems (ESs) may well take their place in the near future as tools for improving organizational decision making and control.[62] Expert systems are also called "knowledge-based" systems since they are built on a framework of known facts and responses to situations; they may also be called *artificial intelligence (AI)*.[63] Although the exact terminology for this new technology has not been totally agreed upon, we have used the term *expert systems* in our discussion to differentiate such systems from AI, of which they are more appropriately considered an application.[64]

The potential importance to managers of artificial intelligence research—the effort to make machines smarter—cannot be overstated. According to Patrick H. Winston and Karen A. Prendergast, "Some people believe artificial intelligence is the most exciting scientific and commercial enterprise of the century."[65] Sales of AI technology exceeded $700 million in 1985, an increase of 60 percent over 1984. Hundreds of small companies, many bankrolled by industrial giants such as Lockheed, GM, and Control Data, are entering the field with specialized AI software and expert systems.[66] Expert systems are designed to apply the fruits of AI research to scientific, technological, and business problems by emulating the abilities and judgments of human experts.

Typically, a human expert has specialized knowledge that he or she uses to solve specific problems. This knowledge is continually being expanded and corrected from experience—that is, the expert possesses an ability to learn from mistakes. Up to now, computer systems have not possessed that capability. Human experts can also change their approaches to suit particular problems and can transfer and apply knowledge from one field to another.

Expert systems perform similarly to human experts by melding AI software with certain DSS features. Like a DSS, expert systems retrieve and store data, are interactive and user-oriented, are on-line, can manipulate data, and can create models. However, unlike a DSS, they can also diagnose problems, recommend alternative solutions and strategies, offer rationales for their diagnoses and recommendations, and learn from previous experiences by adding information developed in solving problems to their current base of knowledge.[67]

An expert system guides users through problems by asking them an orderly set of questions about the situation and drawing conclusions based on the answers it has been given. Its problem-solving abilities are guided by a set of programmed rules modeled on the actual reasoning processes of human experts in the field.[68]

Because of their advanced capabilities, expert systems may supplant many kinds of DSSs. Users will no longer have to develop alternatives from information supplied by a DSS, but instead will be readily able to evaluate the alternatives and explanations offered by expert systems. Expert systems can provide expertise when human experts are not available, and in many cases reach conclusions more rapidly even when they are. Human experts may find expert systems useful when making decisions involving complex, interdependent elements.

Uses of Expert Systems. The end of the last decade and the beginning of the 1980s saw the implementation of the first expert systems. Some initial applications were for determining medical diagnoses and treatment and for mineral prospecting. One of the first business applications of expert systems was developed by Schlumberger,

Ltd.; its system evaluates potential oil sites using an amount of data far exceeding that which human experts could interpret in a timely fashion.[69]

There are four broad categories of management information tasks where expert systems are now being applied and will continue to be applied in the near future.

1. *Resource allocation.* Expert systems are used for such tasks as portfolio management and capital budgeting.
2. *Problem diagnosis.* Financial statements, accounts receivable reports, and other kinds of reports can be reviewed for possible problems, divergences, and inconsistencies.
3. *Scheduling and assignment.* Expert systems can, for example, be applied to office scheduling and personnel assignment tasks.
4. *Information management.* Information sources contained in data files and produced by decision modeling can be managed through expert systems. For example, an expert system might question a manager about changes in market demand or inventory levels, offer hypotheses about probable causes, and then determine and explain alternative responses and solutions to the problem. Or, the expert system might make recommendations on information fed to it on proposed financial or operating decisions such as closing a particular plant or developing a new product line.

Some business-oriented expert system software is already available. Odyssey is a scheduling system that permits users to resolve any conflicts in scheduling business trips. Nudge helps users schedule business meetings. And Omega performs personnel assignment functions by matching job requirements to personnel characteristics.[70]

Design and Implementation of Expert Systems. Robert W. Blanning has identified five characteristics of managerial decision making that may have implications in expert system design, implementation, acceptance, and use:[71]

1. The majority of management problems are unstructured.
2. A manager's time and attention are limited resources.
3. Managers have different problem-solving styles.
4. Managers frequently work in groups on both formal and informal bases.
5. Many managers already have access to an array of computer-based tools.

Given these characteristics, it can be seen that imparting managerial knowledge to an expert system is no mean task; many problems are open-ended and unstructured, and managers solve them in very different ways. The expert system should be designed to begin with partially structured problems, such as resource allocation alternatives, and then move to more unstructured problems, such as strategic planning. Existing and new expert system *software* may have to contain elements already in DSS with which managers are familiar and comfortable in order to gain acceptance. In particular, the expert system's evaluations and rationales and the way it requests data input should be in formats and language that managers understand. Expert systems should be carefully evaluated by comparing their results against the results of human problem solving to determine the system's accuracy and clarity of presentation. Finally, expert systems should be developed incrementally, with each step built on an analysis of current performance and future needs.

The Future of Expert Systems. The end of this decade and the beginning of the next should witness a great increase in the use of artificial intelligence in business. As was mentioned earlier, American organizations are currently investing much effort and resources in the development of artificial intelligence for expert systems and other applications.[72] The Japanese are also devoting a great deal of energy to AI in their "fifth-generation" computer project; the expectation is that a qualitative advantage in computer technology will translate into a national economic advantage.[73] New expert systems will be developed rapidly as a result of these efforts, although these systems may be very expensive for some time to come.[74]

Impact of Computers and MIS on Managers and Organizations

The application of computer technology to management information and decision support systems has certainly had an effect on how managers perform their tasks and on how organizations behave. The widespread use of expert systems will undoubtedly bring further changes in managerial and organizational behavior. In this section we will discuss a prediction from the late 1950s on how computers would change business in the light of what has happened since.

An Early Prediction

In 1958, Harold J. Leavitt and Thomas L. Whisler assessed the impact of the nascent computer revolution in its application to information management and offered their predictions as to how management would appear in the 1980s.[75] They believed that the revolution in what they called *information technology* would have a significant impact on middle and top management and the structure and behavior of organizations. These changes were in the four following areas:

1. *Increased structuring of middle management.* Just as adaptation of Frederick W. Taylor's scientific management principles led to more routine and highly structured jobs for workers, Leavitt and Whisler contended that computers would enable most middle management decisions to be programmed and standardized decisions; middle managers would require less autonomy and skill, and middle management positions would become highly routinized.
2. *Increased status for some middle management positions.* The standardization of most middle management positions would create two different classes of middle managers: the majority, whose tasks and positions would be programmed and made routine, and a minority to codify and program the tasks and decisions for the others, plus those managers still involved directly in research, development, and planning. The nonstandardized management class would move toward top management status.
3. *More distinct differences between top and middle management.* As the role of most middle managers would tend toward performing within highly structured norms, the differences in function and role between top management would become more and more clear.

4. *Recentralization of the organization.* With increased information flow to top management and with a large corps of middle managers performing relatively routine tasks, there would be an augmented ability for top management to control the organization from above.

What Has Been Happening

Plainly, the effect of computer-based information systems on management and organizations has not turned out exactly as Leavitt and Whisler foresaw. The changes brought on by the computer revolution of the past 30 years have not been nearly so pervasive and radical as they envisioned. The chief effect of computerization has been the ability of organizations to process (and create) paperwork with ever greater accuracy and speed; there has been little effect on the roles of managers and the structure of organizations.[76] The segregation of middle managers into "functionary" and "programmer" roles has just not taken place. In fact, Paul Attewell and James Rule cite evidence that computerization may lead to an increase in the number of management levels.[77] They have also found that access to information can strengthen the positions of subordinates.

The formation of an elite and aloof top level of management has also not come to pass. The amount of use that top managers make of computer-based information and computers themselves varies from organization to organization and is a matter of contention among management authors.[78] And top management is not necessarily in control of the computerization of the organization. For example, individual departments can often purchase microcomputers and powerful DSS software directly without having a corporate EDP/MIS decision on its purchase.[79] In this way, middle managers are determining their information and systems needs for themselves and not having systems imposed on them from above. At the same time, information systems departments in organizations are undergoing changes. Many organizations are considering combining office automation, data processing, and information communication functions into one department.[80] What the effects of this change will be remains to be seen.

The results on the recentralization of organizations are not conclusive. In their review of the literature on the effects of computers, Attewell and Rule found that computer-based information systems either do not greatly affect organizational structure or, at most, reinforce existing structures.[81] On the one hand, they found that computerization increased "top-down" communication and top-level monitoring of operational activities—steps toward centralization. However, they also noted that the effective use of MIS data by middle managers may lead to decentralization. In cases where changes did occur, centralization occurred more often than decentralization. Other studies claim that intraorganizational networking and use of DSSs can lead to greater delegation and decentralization.[82]

The Continuing Computer Revolution

To say that we are rapidly moving from an industrial-based society to an information-based one is not an overstatement. For the foreseeable future, managers will have to keep abreast of, and anticipate, further advancements and applications from

FIGURE 22-3 WHAT PACKING MORE POWER ON A CHIP WILL BRING

	1980	1985	1987	1990	1995
Circuit Size:	4 Microns	2 Microns	1 Micron	0.5 Micron	0.25 Micron
Memory Capacity:	64K	256K	1,024K	4,096K	16,384K
Power Range:	Desktop Microcomputer	Minicomputer	Mainframe Computer	Supercomputer	Ultracomputer
Applications:	Digital watches, video games, personal computers	Lap computers, engineering work stations, programmable appliances	Pocket computers, electronic map-navigators, high-resolution TVs	Robot that can see, freeze-frame TVs, computers that recognize and use natural languages	Star Wars systems, personal robots, computers with humanlike logic

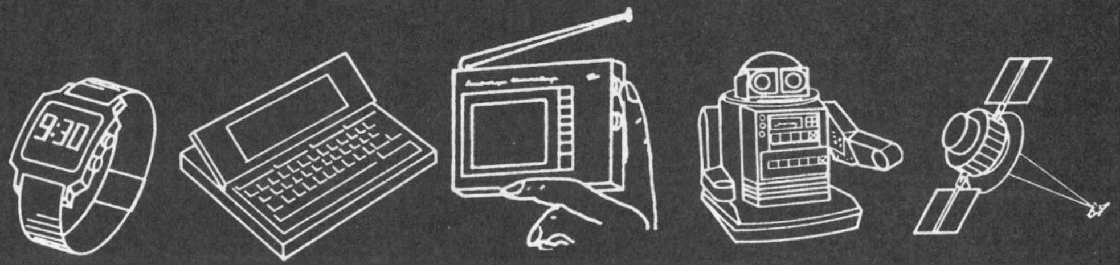

Source: Reprinted from the June 10, 1985 issue of *Business Week* by special permission. Copyright © 1985 by McGraw-Hill, Inc.

the continuing computer revolution. In addition, managers will need to evaluate new developments and determine their effects on their organizations.

The expansion of computer capabilities and further developments in artificial intelligence may prompt major adjustments in the way managers work and in the way organizations act. In mid-1985, some 30 U.S., Japanese, and European semiconductor manufacturers were developing new integrated circuits with greatly increased memory capability.[83] Figure 22-3 shows the projected increase in memory for these new chips and presents some of their technological applications. By 1995, a few hundred dollars might buy as much computing power in one chip as $48 million would have bought in 1985 supercomputers. Such fifth-generation computers will provide the computing power necessary for advanced AI applications. It might not be unusual to see, for example, a manager carrying on a dialog with a pocket computer that can organize messages, schedule meetings, and offer business advice. Robots and robot vision systems for manufacturing control will become normal parts of the production process. One day we may truly create an information-based society whose members will have the leisure time to enjoy the fruits of its key industries: knowledge, communications, and computer-based consumer products.[84]

Summary   Effective planning, decision making, and control are based on the effective management of information. All organizations have both an informal and a formal information system; today, a formal information system is usually computer-based. There are three forms of computer-based information systems—management information systems (MIS), decision support systems (DSS), and expert systems. Over the years, MIS has been evolving into DSS and from there to expert systems.

An MIS may be defined as a formal method for providing managers with the information they need to carry out their tasks effectively. The value of information supplied by an MIS depends on the information's quality, quantity, timeliness, and relevance to management action. The cost of obtaining the information must be balanced against the information's benefits.

The information needs of managers differ with their hierarchical level. Top managers require information on strategic planning. Thus, their information sources will be largely external. Middle-level managers require information sources that will be both external and internal. In addition, they will require a more rapid information flow. Lower-level managers, who are concerned with operational control, will require frequent, highly detailed, and accurate information—predominantly from internal sources.

Guidelines for an effective MIS include: (1) making users part of the design team; (2) carefully considering the costs of the system; (3) favoring relevance and selectivity over sheer quantity; (4) pretesting the system before installation; and (5) training the operators and users of the system carefully.

There are a number of people problems that can arise when a computer-based MIS is being implemented. These problems are likely to develop if the MIS disrupts established departmental boundaries, if it disrupts the informal communication system, if individuals resist the system, if the organizational culture is not supportive, and if the change is implemented without manager–subordinate participation. The reactions of organization members to a computer-based MIS may include aggression, projection, and avoidance, depending on their organizational level and how the MIS will affect them.

A DSS is a direct user-access information system that permits managers to manipulate data and create models in order to assist them in making unstructured decisions. A DSS differs from an MIS because it involves the direct interaction of users with data. A DSS can be used by groups to form a group decision support system (GDSS), which permits managers to meet and interact with the data and with each other to achieve group decisions.

Managers can now be linked with each other in computer networks so that they can share computing resources and exchange information. Two major types of networking are intra-organizational—linking users within a department or across divisions—and interorganizational—linking the organization to external data bases.

Expert systems are a form of artificial intelligence that exhibit many features of human experts. These systems are distinctly user-oriented and, through prompting and questioning the user, can diagnose problems, recommend solutions, and offer explanations for their diagnoses. Expert systems are currently being applied to resource allocations, problem diagnosis, scheduling and personnel assignments, and information management.

The impact of computers and MISs on managers and organizations is still being debated. Early predictions of increased routinization of middle management tasks and the creation of different classes of middle managers have not been borne out. But AI applications in organizations may yet bring fundamental changes to managing.

Review Questions

1. Why is an effective information system a key part of effective managerial planning, decision making, and control?

2. On what four factors does the value of information depend? How do managers weigh these factors against the cost of a management information system (MIS)?

3. How might MIS be defined?

4. What are the differences between data, information, and management information? Which is most desirable for managers? Why?

5. What are the differing information needs at different management levels? How may an MIS be designed to meet these different needs?

6. What are the four major stages in developing an MIS? How may these stages be carried out effectively?

7. According to Dickson and Simmons, what five factors determine whether and to what extent the implementation of a new MIS will be resisted?

8. What are the major security concerns associated with computer-based information systems? How may they be solved?

9. In what three ways may individuals show the frustrations associated with the implementation of a computer-based MIS?

10. What is a decision support system (DSS)? How does it differ from an MIS?

11. How can a DSS be used?

12. How can networking improve the effectiveness of an organization?

13. What is an expert system? How does it differ from an MIS and a DSS?

14. To what kinds of tasks can expert systems be applied?

15. How will future developments in computer technology have an impact on managers, organizations, and their use of information?

Notes

1. For an account of the rise of the computer age, see G. Harry Stine, *The Untold Story of the Computer Revolution* (New York: Arbor House, 1985).

2. Information systems are also important for effective planning. See Kweku Ewusi-Mensah, "Information Systems for Planning," *Long Range Planning* 17, no. 5 (October 1984):111–117.

3. Earl P. Strong and Robert D. Smith, *Management Control Models* (New York: Holt, Rinehart & Winston, 1968), pp. 119–120.

4. Robert J. Mockler, *The Management Control Process* (Englewood Cliffs, N.J.: Prentice-Hall, 1972), pp. vii, 73.

5. F. Warren Benton, *Execucomp: Maximum Management with the New Computers* (New York: Wiley, 1983), p. 243.

6. Peggy Schmidt, "What's New in Computer Psychology," *New York Times*, January 20, 1985, p. F15.

7. For a description of 12 computer-related competence standards for managers, see Benton, *Execucomp*, pp. 9–16.

8. Hirohide Hinomoto, "Education in Information Systems," *Academy of Management Journal* 18, no. 2 (June 1975):402–407.

9. Gilbert W. Fairholm, "A Reality Basis for Management Information System Decisions," *Public Administration Review* 39, no. 2 (March–April 1979):176–179; and Fred R. McFadden and James D. Suver, "Costs and Benefits of a Data Base System," *Harvard Business Review* 56, no. 1 (January–February 1978):131–139.

10. Robert H. Gregory and Richard L. Van Horn, "Value and Cost of Information," in J. Daniel Couger and Robert W. Knapp, *Systems Analysis Techniques* (New York: Wiley, 1974), pp. 473–489. See also Barry J. Epstein and William R. King, "An Experimental Study of the Value of Information," *Omega* 10, no. 3 (1982):249–258.

11. John Dearden, in "MIS Is a Mirage," *Harvard Business Review* 50, no. 1 (January–February 1972):90, even suggested that the concept of MIS "is embedded in a mishmash of fuzzy thinking and incomprehensible jargon." Since then, however, managers have become more comfortable with the concept, and there is greater agreement about it; see Paul H. Cheney and Norman R. Lyons, "MIS Update," *Data Management* 19, no. 10 (October 1980):26–32.

12. See Walter J. Kennevan, "Management Information Systems," *Data Management* 8, no. 9 (September 1970):62–64.

13. This discussion is drawn, in part, from Michael S. Scott Morton and John F. Rockart,

"Implications of Changes in Information Technology for Corporate Strategy," *Interfaces* 14, no. 1 (January–February 1984):84–95.

14. For further discussion of the differences between and evolution of MIS and DSS, see Ralph H. Sprague, Jr., "A Framework for the Development of Decision Support Systems," in Hugh J. Watson and Archie B. Carroll, eds., *Computers for Business* (Plano, Texas: Business Publications, 1984), pp. 197–226.

15. G. Anthony Gorry and Michael S. Scott Morton, "A Framework for Management Information Systems," *Sloan Management Review* 13, no. 1 (Fall 1971):55–70. Gorry and Scott Morton based their framework on the three-part division of managerial activities described by Robert N. Anthony in *Planning and Control Systems* (Boston: Harvard University Graduate School of Business Administration, 1965), pp. 15–21.

16. Charles R. Litecky, "Corporate Strategy and MIS Planning," *Journal of Systems Management* 32, no. 1 (January 1981):36–39.

17. See, for example, John C. Carter and Fred N. Silverman, "Establishing an MIS," *Journal of Systems Management* 31, no. 1 (January 1980):15–21.

18. Robert G. Murdick, "MIS Development Procedures," *Journal of Systems Management* 21, no. 12 (December 1970):22–26.

19. See Arnold Barnett, "Preparing Management for MIS," *Journal of Systems Management* 23, no. 1 (January 1972): 40–43.

20. Regina Herzlinger, "Why Data Systems in Nonprofit Organizations Fail," *Harvard Business Review* 55, no. 1 (January–February 1977):81–86.

21. Michael Potter and Robin McNeill, "The New Programmer—The Next Wave of Computer Innovation in North American Business," *Business Quarterly* 48, no. 4 (Winter 1983):132–134.

22. See Russell L. Ackoff, "Management Misinformation Systems," *Management Science*, December 1967, pp. 147–156.

23. Charles A. O'Reilly III, "Individuals and Information Overload in Organizations: Is More Necessarily Better?" *Academy of Management Journal* 23, no. 4 (December 1980):684–696.

24. John P. Murray, *Managing Information Systems as a Corporate Resource* (Homewood, Ill.: Dow Jones-Irwin, 1984).

25. John F. Rockart, "Chief Executives Define Their Own Data Needs," *Harvard Business Review* 57, no. 2 (March–April 1979):81–93, describes a process for determining the factors CEOs consider critical for their organizations' success ("critical success factors").

26. See H. L. Capron and Brian K. Williams, *Computers and Data Processing*, 2nd ed. (Menlo Park, Calif.: Benjamin/Cummings Publishing, 1984), chapter 9; and Steven L. Mandell, *Computers and Data Processing: Concepts and Applications*, 2nd ed. (St. Paul, Minn.: West Publishing, 1982), p. 34.

27. A case study from the Harvard Business School, "First National City Bank Operating Group (A), 474–165, 1975, and (B), 474–166, 1975," describes the direct installation approach used by John Reed—currently CEO of Citicorp—to mechanize the "back office" operations (routine check and other paper processing) of Citibank when he was senior vice-president of the Operating Group in 1970. This mechanization effort was not a purely MIS installation. However, it is an example of the direct approach to a complex operations systems conversion that used computers and related equipment and that contained facets of Citibank's MIS.

28. Jennifer E. Beaver, "Bend or Be Broken," *Computer Decisions* 16, no. 16 (December 1984):131–133, 136–138. See also M. Lynne Markus and Daniel Robey, "The Organizational Validity of Management Information Systems," *Human Relations* 36, no. 3 (March 1983):203–226.

29. Benton, *Execucomp*, p. 238.

30. Our discussion in this section is based on G. W. Dickson and John K. Simmons, "The Behavioral Side of MIS," *Business Horizons* 13, no. 4 (August 1970):59–71.

31. Daniel Robey and M. Lynne Markus, "Rituals in Information System Design," *MIS Quarterly* 8, no. 1 (March 1984):5–15.

32. Edwin B. Opliger, "Identifying Microcomputer Concerns," *EDP Journal*, no. 1 (1985):42–67.

33. Paul E. Dascher and W. Ken Harmon, "The Dark Side of Small Business Computers," *Management Accounting* 65, no. 11 (May 1984):62–67.

34. Michael Newman, "User Involvement—Does It Exist, Is It Enough?" *Journal of Systems Management* 35, no. 5 (1984):34–38.

35. Blake Ives and Margrethe H. Olson, "User Involvement and MIS Success: A Review of Research," *Management Science* 30, no. 5 (May 1984):586–603. Ives and Olson note the lack of research demonstrating the benefits of user participation, but they do suggest that participation is useful for unstructured situations and also for situations where user acceptance is important for MIS success.

36. Steven Alter, in "A Taxonomy of Decision Support Systems," *Sloan Management Review* 19, no. 1 (Fall 1977):39–59, describes seven different types of DSS from systems that are heavily data-oriented to those that are heavily model-oriented. His taxonomy is based on the extent to which the system's outputs bear on decision making.

37. Bernard C. Reimann and Allan D. Waren, "User-Oriented Criteria for the Selection of DSS Software," *Communications of the ACM* 28, no. 2 (February 1985):166–179.

38. "Fourth-Generation Languages Make DSS Feasible for All Managers," *Management Review* 73, no. 4 (April 1984):4–5.

39. Donald R. Wood, "The Personal Computer: How It Can Increase Management Productivity," *Financial Executive* 52, no. 2 (February 1984):15.

40. Andrew T. Masland, "Integrators and Decision Support System Success in Higher Education," *Research in Higher Education* 20, no. 2 (1984):211–233.

41. Hugh J. Watson and Marianne M. Hill, "Decision Support Systems or What Didn't Happen with MIS," *Interfaces* 13, no. 5 (October 1983):81–88.

42. These initial conflicts and stresses are described in Chris Argyris, "Management Information Systems: The Challenge to Rationality and Emotionality," *Management Science* 17, no. 6 (February 1971):B–275–292.

43. Beaver, "Bend or Be Broken," p. 43.

44. Andrew P. Sage, Bernard Galing, and Adolpho Langomasi, "The Methodologies for Determination of Information Requirements for Decision Support Systems," *Large Scale Systems* 5, no. 2 (October 1983):158.

45. "What's Happening with DSS?" *EDP Analyzer* 22, no. 7 (July 1984):1–16.

46. John Child, "New Technology and Developments in Management Organization," *Omega* 12, no. 3 (1984):211–223.

47. Potter and McNeill, "The New Programmer—The Next Wave of Computer Innovation in North American Business," p. 132.

48. See Harry Katzan, Jr., *Management Support Systems: A Pragmatic Approach* (New York: Van Nostrand Reinhold, 1984), pp. 2–3.

49. Beaver, "Bend or Be Broken," p. 132.

50. "What's Happening with DSS?" *EDP Analyzer,* pp. 1–16.

51. Wood, "The Personal Computer: How It Can Increase Management Productivity," pp. 17–18.

52. "What's Happening with DSS?" *EDP Analyzer.*

53. George P. Huber, "Issues in the Design of Group Decision Support Systems," *MIS Quarterly* 8, no. 3 (September 1984):195–204.

54. Bro Uttal, "Linking Computers to Help Managers," *Fortune,* December 26, 1983, p. 145.

55. Opliger, "Identifying Microcomputer Concerns," p. 55.

56. Bill Catchings, "A Bridge Between Mainframes and Micros," *PC,* November 13, 1984, pp. 143–145.

57. This discussion is drawn from Marvin R. Gore and John W. Stubbe, *Computers and Information Systems,* 2nd ed. (New York: McGraw-Hill, 1984), pp. 142–143.

58. James I. Cash, Jr., and Benn R. Konsynski, "IS Redraws Competitive Boundaries," *Harvard Business Review* 63, no. 2 (March–April 1985):134–142.

59. The American Hospital Supply and Prentice-Hall examples are from John Diebold, *Business in the Age of Information* (New York: AMACOM, 1985), pp. 117–120, 122–123.

60. Laura Gardner, "Now the Hard Part: Getting Customers On Line," *Venture* 7, no. 7 (July 1985):70.

61. F. Warren McFarlan, "Information Technology Changes the Way You Compete," *Harvard Business Review* 62, no. 3 (May–June 1984):98–103.

62. "What's Happening with DSS?" *EDP Analyzer.*

63. The discussion of expert systems is drawn mainly from Robert W. Blanning, "Knowledge Acquisition and System Validation in Expert Systems for Management," *Human Systems Management* 4, no. 4 (Autumn 1984):280–285; Robert W. Blanning, "Expert Systems for Management: Possible Application Areas," *Institute for Advancement of Decision Support Systems DSS-84 Transactions* (1984):69–77; and Robert W. Blanning, "Issues in the Design of Expert Systems for Management," *Proceedings of the National Computer Conference* (1984): 489–495.

64. Walter Reitman, "Artificial Intelligence Applications for Business: Getting Acquainted," in Walter Reitman, ed., *Artificial Intelligence Applications for Business* (Norwood, N.J.: Ablex Publishing, 1984), pp. 1–9. For an excellent discussion of AI, see Jeffrey Rothfelder, *Minds Over Matter: A New Look at Artificial Intelligence* (New York: Simon & Schuster, 1985).

65. Patrick H. Winston and Karen A. Prendergast, eds., *The AI Business: The Commercial Uses of Artificial Intelligence* (Cambridge, Mass.: MIT Press, 1985), preface.

66. See Emily T. Smith, "A High-Tech Market That's Not Feeling the Pinch," *Business Week,* July 1, 1985, p. 78.

67. Michael W. Davis, "Anatomy of Decision Support," *Datamation,* June 15, 1985, pp. 201ff.

68. Robert C. Schank with Peter G. Childers, *The Cognitive Computer: On Language, Learning, and Artificial Intelligence* (Reading, Mass.: Addison-Wesley, 1985), p. 33.

69. Howard Austin, "Market Trends in Artificial Intelligence," in Reitman, ed., *Artificial Intelligence Applications for Business,* pp. 267–286.

70. Blanning, "Knowledge Acquisition and System Validation in Expert Systems for Management," p. 282.

71. Blanning, "Issues in the Design of Expert Systems for Management," p. 493.

72. "What's Happening with DSS?" *EDP Analyzer.*

73. Winston and Prendergast, eds., *The AI Business.* For discussions of Japanese and American efforts in AI, see also Edward A. Feigenbaum and Pamela McCorduck, *The Fifth Generation: Artificial Intelligence and Japan's Computer Challenge to the World* (New York: New American Library, 1984); and Frank Rose, *Into the Heart of the Mind: An American Quest for Artificial Intelligence* (New York: Harper & Row, 1984).

74. Beaver, "Bend or Be Broken," p. 138.

75. Harold J. Leavitt and Thomas L. Whisler, "Management in the 1980's," *Harvard Business Review* 36, no. 6 (November–December 1958):41–48. See also Jerome Kanter, *Management Information Systems* (Englewood Cliffs, N.J.: Prentice-Hall, 1984), pp. 289–316.

76. Scott Morton and Rockart, "Implications of Changes in Information Technology for Corporate Strategy," pp. 84–95.

77. Paul Attewell and James Rule, "Computing and Organizations: What We Know and What We Don't Know," *Communications of the ACM* 27, no. 12 (December 1984):1184–1192.

78. For a lively debate on the use and impact of computers on top management, see John Dearden, "Will the Computer Change the Job of Top Management?" *Sloan Management Review* 25, no. 1 (Fall 1983):57–60; and David Davis, "Computers and Top Management," *Sloan Management Review* 25, no. 3 (Spring 1984):63–67.

79. Erik Sandberg-Diment, "Macintosh Marketing Overcomes Its Drawbacks," *New York Times,* March 26, 1985, p. C4.

80. Scott Morton and Rockart, "Implications of Changes in Information Technology for Corporate Strategy," pp. 84–95.

81. Attewell and Rule, "Computing and Organizations," pp. 1188–1189.

82. Child, "New Technology and Developments in Management Organization," p. 220.

83. John Wilson with Scott Ticer, "Superchips: The New Frontier," *Business Week,* June 10, 1985, pp. 82–85, summarizes the directions where this new superchip technology might lead.

84. Gore and Stubbe, *Computers and Information Systems,* pp. 386–387.

CASE STUDY: Electronic Advisers

Gary Chapman ordinarily suffers fools patiently, if not gladly. But today, when a fellow employee at EEV Inc., an electronic-parts manufacturer in Elmsford, New York, pokes his head into Chapman's office, interrupting the sales manager's telephone conversation for the third time, Chapman says firmly, "I'm busy. I'm on the phone."

The tactic works. His colleague retreats—once and for all.

Chapman is both surprised and delighted by the outcome. To learn how best to handle his nettlesome co-worker, he sought advice from neither friend, how-to book, consultant, nor shrink. Instead he turned to The Management Edge, a software package from Human Edge Software Corporation in Palo Alto, California, a new company whose computer programs promise frazzled managers sound advice on handling subordinates, superiors, customers—indeed, anyone they might encounter during the business day.

Although using the computer to juggle people—rather than words or numbers—may have the ring of Orwellian fantasy, the concept is catching on among software developers. Resource 1 Inc., in San Diego, for example, is introducing computer programs based on the works of noted management experts and best-selling authors, such as Alec Mackenzie (*The Time Trap*) and Kenneth Blanchard and Robert Lorber (*Putting The One Minute Manager to Work,* their sequel to *The One Minute Manager*). The software, claims Mona Williams, a company spokeswoman, will help managers change their behavior while simultaneously teaching them computer skills.

Human Edge's business-strategy software is by far the most sophisticated attempt yet to tackle the vagaries of human behavior. Founded by psychologist Jim Johnson, who also started Psych Systems Inc., developer and seller of the first on-line automated psychological testing service, the company has five products—*The Sales Edge, The Management Edge, The Negotiation Edge, The Communications Edge,* and *The Leadership Edge*—that are all expert, or knowledge-based, systems, a type of artificial intelligence.

Writing this kind of software requires collecting a number of "rules" that are culled either from experts or from the existing research on a subject. Using the rules, a computer can then figure out what the best course of action is in any given situation. To develop *The Sales Edge*, for example, Johnson and his staff went through stacks of sales-oriented business literature, gleaning, he says, "every piece of advice that any expert has ever offered." Then they structured the recommendations according to their appropriateness for individual personality types.

All the programs work similarly: First you agree or disagree with 70 to 100 statements, such as, "I often have trouble going to sleep because of worries about the job," "I like to attend parties related to my job," and "A good manager has total control." From your responses the computer develops a personality profile.

Then, whenever you need tips on dealing with a specific individual, you assess his or her character by checking off adjectives: "self-protecting," "simple-minded," "smart," or "prestige-oriented," for instance. (With *The Management Edge* you also describe the work environment; *The Negotiation Edge*, which used decision-making theory based on mathematical formulas, requires that you enter your expectations.)

With the profiles loaded, the computer will search through its huge store of information—the packages contain 300,000 to 400,000 words of text on two or three disks—and produce a report giving you specific pointers on how to act most effectively with the targeted individual. *The Sales Edge*, which walks you through preparation, presentation, and opening and closing ploys, tells you what to expect from your quarry and how to succeed. *The Management Edge* covers such areas as motivating employees, finding the right niche for a worker, firing, and improving communications.

When Gary Chapman plugged in *The Management Edge*, he was told that his co-worker, whose irritating habits he had chalked up to overenthusiasm, belongs to that troublesome class of individuals who don't recognize other people's responsibilities and obligations. And, the report admonished Chapman, "you too easily forgive those things." On the second or third occasion, point your view out to him, the report continued, then go about your business—advice which Chapman followed with good effect.

Chapman has also tried *The Management Edge* with customers and managers of the corporation's parent company in England. As a technical person, he says, he tends to be "very meticulous about numbers" and usually gets "right down to the details." But the computer informed him that several of his frequent business contacts become overwhelmed by too many specifics. So Chapman forced himself to concentrate on the larger picture by putting a big sign on his desk that read, "No details." "It was fantastic," he says. "People were more receptive to the things I wanted to do."

"I hope nobody else gets [*The Management Edge*]," Chapman adds, "because it's like a secret weapon, like being able to hear somebody's dreams. You can plan the whole strategy before you go see [anyone], and you know you're right."

Although some users consider the programs the next best thing to an ever-vigilant personal consultant, detractors argue that this type of software is, by its nature, limited. "It's a nice game, and it might be reasonably accurate," says Murray Weiner, a consultant with Rohrer, Hibler & Replogle Inc., an international industrial psychology and management consulting firm. "But it can't possibly get into all of the conceivable interactions."

Even Johnson admits that strategy software isn't a total solution to life's tribulations. When Johnson wanted to fire an employee of his Palo Alto firm who had become a morale problem, he ran the outplacement section of *The Management Edge* on him. Proceed with caution, the report advised, this employee tends to be litigious. So Johnson hired a labor lawyer to ensure that the procedure was carried out in strict accordance with California law. "Sure enough," says Johnson, "he sued."

Source: Reprinted with permission, *Inc.* magazine, March 1984. Copyright © 1984 by Inc. Publishing Company, 38 Commercial Wharf, Boston, Mass. 02110.

Case Questions

1. How is Gary Chapman using *The Management* Edge to make decisions?

2. What are the limitations of the program? What are the advantages?

3. Do you agree with Murray Weiner that *The Management Edge* and other such programs are no more than "games"?

4. In your opinion, will most managers be using an information system like *The Management Edge* in the future? Explain. Would you be comfortable with such a system? Discuss why or why not.

23

INTERNATIONAL MANAGEMENT

Upon completing this chapter you should be able to:

1. Describe the process by which a company goes international.
2. Define a multinational enterprise (MNE).
3. Discuss the positive and negative impacts that MNEs have on their home and host countries.
4. List and discuss the managerial challenges of operating in the international environment.
5. Describe the managerial approaches MNEs may select to apply abroad.

Mattel Toys, one of the best-known and most successful toymakers in the United States, was confident that its introduction into the Japanese market of the Barbie Doll, for years America's favorite doll, would be a resounding success. Instead, the effort fell resoundingly flat—the Japanese simply would not buy it. Why did this happen?

The doll that Mattel introduced to the Japanese early in the 1970s was exactly the same as the one sold in the United States: adult, sophisticated, and elaborately made-up and clothed. But Mattel had fallen into one of the most common pitfalls of international business: the failure to account for cultural differences between nations. Japanese children were accustomed to playing with much more childlike dolls and could not relate to the American newcomer. As a result, Barbie's sales in Japan were abysmal.

In 1981, Mattel introduced a modified Barbie in Japan. Although still somewhat American in appearance, the new Barbie had slightly Oriental eyes and a more girlish figure. By 1983, Japan accounted for a respectable 12.7 percent of Barbie's international sales, testimony to the extent that the Japanese accepted the "culturally modified" Barbie.[1]

This example illustrates how important it is for managers to understand the implications of international business. So many companies have chosen to do business in and with other countries that managers must expand their own horizons to encompass the unique opportunities and problems this situation creates. In this chapter, we will begin by examining the increasing internationalization of the world economy and by describing the process a company goes through in becoming international. Then we will focus on the perceptions associated with the multinational enterprise as an institution. Finally, we will look at some of the challenges encountered by multinational enterprises in managing both the human resources of an organization and the relationship of the organization to its environment.

The Increasing Internationalization of the World Economy

Before looking at the characteristics of international business, it is helpful to realize the ways in which the world economy has become more and more international. Our focus in this chapter will be on the increasingly multinational character of business, but many nonbusiness activities have also become more international. For example, the enrollment of foreign students in United States universities has become quite common. International tourism is increasing, as are joint space ventures and the spread of international telecommunications. Even national cuisines are taking on an international flavor; the hamburger, as defined by McDonald's, has become a universally recognized food. (See box.)

Why Companies Go International

Although there are a variety of reasons why a company might decide to go international, according to Donald Ball and Wendell McCulloch, all of them can be categorized as aggressive or defensive.[2]

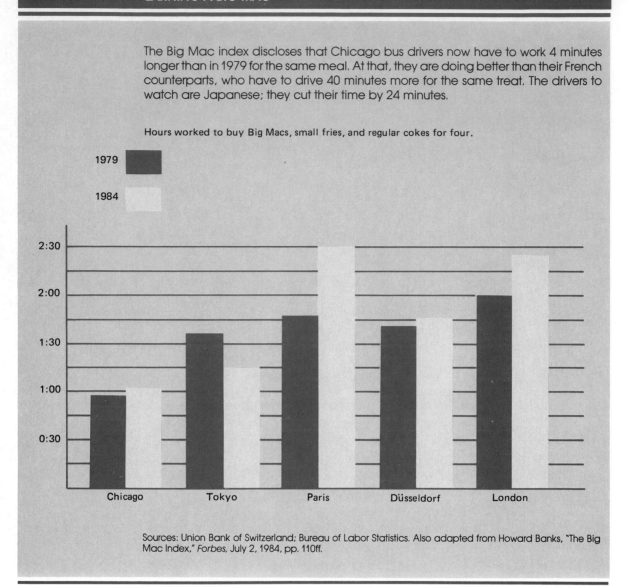

The Big Mac index discloses that Chicago bus drivers now have to work 4 minutes longer than in 1979 for the same meal. At that, they are doing better than their French counterparts, who have to drive 40 minutes more for the same treat. The drivers to watch are Japanese; they cut their time by 24 minutes.

Hours worked to buy Big Macs, small fries, and regular cokes for four.

1979
1984

2:30
2:00
1:30
1:00
0:30

Chicago   Tokyo   Paris   Düsseldorf   London

Sources: Union Bank of Switzerland; Bureau of Labor Statistics. Also adapted from Howard Banks, "The Big Mac Index," *Forbes,* July 2, 1984, pp. 110ff.

Aggressive reasons are those which support an attempt to increase profits, sales, and markets. A few examples would be the desire to:

1. **Open new markets.**
2. **Obtain greater profits.**
3. **Acquire products for the home market (or *other* foreign markets).**
4. **Satisfy management's desire for expansion.**

Defensive reasons for opening international markets include the wish to protect profits, sales, and markets. All of the following aims fit into this category:

1. **Protect domestic markets.**
2. **Protect foreign markets.**
3. **Guarantee a supply of raw materials.**
4. **Acquire technology.**
5. **Achieve geographic diversification.**
6. **Seek politically stable bases for new operations.**

The reasons for going international vary according to some factors, such as time. During the 1950s, the U.S. companies that went overseas acted for reasons that were primarily defensive. Many of the moves at that time were attempts to overcome the trade barriers imposed against U.S. goods by dollar-short countries.

By the time the 1960s arrived, these barriers had begun to disappear, and U.S. companies were taking a more aggressive stance toward internationalization. Many of them saw opportunities to take advantage of their superiority over foreign companies in technology, management, and marketing by tapping the inexpensive labor market to be found in many countries.[3]

The reasons for going abroad may also vary by industry. Companies in raw-materials-based industries, such as oil or mining, frequently go international in order to obtain a guaranteed and/or cheaper source of the needed raw material. Manufacturing companies, on the other hand, have in the past frequently ventured overseas to protect old markets or to seek new ones. More recently, they have done so in an attempt to find a cheap source of labor.

The nationality of a company will also affect its motives in going international. While some non-U.S.-based companies may choose to come to the United States for its political stability, it is unlikely that a U.S. firm would go overseas for that reason (although political *instability* may be a major barrier to investing in one country versus another). Similarly, it has been much more common for foreign companies to come to the United States to acquire technology and managerial knowledge than vice versa.[4] Recently, however, U.S. companies have begun to look to Japan for new ideas in management, as we will see later in this chapter.

How Companies Go International

The process of an organization's internationalization has been broken down into four general degrees or stages by Christopher Korth.[5] Table 23–1 illustrates these four degrees and their relationship to one another. The degrees described apply equally well to companies that deal in services as to those that deal in the production of goods.

Firms often proceed through the stages in sequence, although some will settle permanently at an intermediate stage. A few will return to an earlier stage, as Chrysler did during the early 1980s, by selling off much of its overseas operations to generate cash and cut losses.

First-degree internationalization occurs when a company has only indirect or passive international dealings. This low level of involvement is often accomplished

TABLE 23-1 FOUR DEGREES OF INTERNATIONALIZATION

	First-Degree Internationalization	Second-Degree Internationalization	Third-Degree Internationalization	Fourth-Degree Internationalization
Nature of contact with foreign markets	Indirect, passive	Direct, active	Direct, active	Direct, active
Locus of international operations	Domestic	Domestic	Domestic and international	Domestic and international
Orientation of company	Domestic	Domestic	Primarily domestic	Multinational (domestic operations viewed as part of the whole)
Type of international activity	Foreign trade of goods and services	Foreign trade of goods and services	Foreign trade, foreign assistance contracts, foreign direct investment	Foreign trade, foreign assistance contracts, foreign direct investment
Organizational structure	Traditional domestic	International department	International division	Global structure

Source: Christopher M. Korth, *International Business, Environment and Management,* 2nd ed., p. 7. Copyright 1985. Reprinted by permission of Prentice-Hall, Inc., Englewood Cliffs, N.J.

with the assistance of a third company that acts as a go-between with foreign customers and suppliers. (See the box for the various types of international activities in which a company might engage.) Another characteristic of first-degree internationalization is that an existing department within the organization will most likely handle the international activities. These are usually not weighty enough to require their own specialized department.

In *second-degree internationalization,* a company deals directly with its overseas concerns. Although it retains some of the foreign trade agents mentioned above, the company starts to seek out foreign customers and suppliers in an active rather than passive manner.

At this level of involvement, the company will probably create an import or export department. In addition, although there are no company workers permanently based abroad, some managers will travel regularly to the countries with which the company deals. This is important for improving customer and/or supplier relationships and becoming familiar with the company's foreign markets.

INTERNATIONAL CORPORATE ACTIVITIES

- Export/import of goods and services
- Licenses/franchising
- Management contracts
- Joint ventures
- Foreign subsidiaries or branches

Third-degree internationalization is reached when the international concerns of a company are of a much higher importance to its overall makeup. Although the firm is still basically domestically oriented, it has a direct hand in importing, exporting, and/or producing its goods or services abroad. In this stage some management has been permanently placed overseas. In addition, the organization probably possesses an entire international division, instead of only a department.

Fourth-degree internationalization is the last stage in the process. A company reaches this level when its management sees the company orientation as being primarily multinational, as opposed to domestic. In other words, the company's domestic concerns are no longer seen as having a greater priority than its international ones.

Managerial Attitudes toward Internationalization

The attitudes of a company's managers are very important in guiding the company's progressive internationalization. These attitudes remain important when a company reaches the multinational stage. Howard Perlmutter has identified three primary attitudes among the managers of international companies: ethnocentric, polycentric, and geocentric.[6]

He describes the *ethnocentric* attitude as one that sees foreign countries and their peoples as inferior to the home country. Managers with this attitude believe home-country approaches are the best and apply them around the world. Managers with *polycentric* attitudes see all countries as being different and difficult to understand. They tend to let their foreign offices make their own decisions, believing that "they must know what works best in their own countries." The third view, the *geocentric* attitude, recognizes both similarities and differences among countries and attempts to draw the most effective individuals and methods from anyplace in the world and to utilize them in any appropriate part of the world.

All firms contain varying degrees of each of these attitudes. In other words, one group of managers in a particular firm might tend toward geocentrism, while another group might lean toward ethnocentricity. In Perlmutter's view, it is most beneficial for managers of multinational enterprises to adopt geocentric attitudes.

The Multinational Enterprise

Although it does not necessarily follow that a company will progress through all four degrees once it begins the process of internationalization, some companies do grow to the point where they become *multinational enterprises (MNEs)*. The study of such companies is relatively new, and there is a lack of consensus as to the exact definition of an MNE. We will define an MNE as a cluster of corporations controlled by one headquarters but with operations spread over many countries.[7]

In this section we will examine the growth of MNEs both in size and in number, and discuss their spread both geographically and in the types of activities in which they are involved. We will also examine the economic and noneconomic impacts that MNEs have on their home countries (where they originate) and their host countries (where they operate).

The Rise and Spread of Multinational Enterprises

International business has existed in some sense since prehistory, when such products as flint blanks and ceramics were traded across great distances. At the time of the Roman Empire, it was possible in many lands to buy the goods of distant foreign producers. The first American company to operate a foreign production plant successfully was the Singer Sewing Machine Company, whose Scottish factory opened in 1868.[8]

In the last two decades, many studies of the multinational firm have been undertaken. This research interest is primarily a result of the tremendous growth that has occurred in the last 25 years in both the size and the number of MNEs. An obvious companion to this growth has been an increase in the influence of MNEs, accompanied by much debate, concern, and study on the part of governments and organizations such as the United Nations.

Table 23–2 gives an idea of just how large some multinational firms have grown. It shows the 1984 ranking of the world's nations and MNEs, according to gross national product or total sales, respectively. Although the United States, with monoliths like Exxon, General Motors, ITT, IBM, and Union Carbide, accounts for more than half of the world's direct foreign investment, it does not have a monopoly on the world's largest MNEs.[9] Many of them are European, such as the Royal Dutch/Shell group, British Petroleum, and ENI (Italy). They are being joined by an increasing number of Japanese firms, including Mitsubishi, Toyota, and Hitachi.

The Impacts of MNE Operations

Some studies of the impacts of MNEs on host or home countries have shown the overall impact to be solidly favorable, but others have reached the opposite conclusion.[10] It is fair to say that most studies indicate the effects are *relatively* favorable. However, these studies are usually heavily dependent on key assumptions made by the researchers. And, because there may be a mix of positive and negative impacts, how the impacts are weighted can influence the overall conclusion. For example, if an MNE had only two impacts—creating jobs and bribing government officials—its overall impact is favorable if we care a great deal about jobs and don't mind bribery. Its impact is negative if our preferences (weighting) are reversed.

Impacts of MNEs on Host Countries. Christopher Korth has identified some of the potential benefits and costs that the operations of an MNE may have on a host country.[11] Note that these benefits and costs, listed below, are only potential. Whether they actually occur in a specific situation depends on the environment, including government actions, and the actual behavior of the MNE involved. Among the major potential benefits are:

· Transfer of capital, technology, and entrepreneurship to the host country
· Improvement of the host country's balance of payments
· Creation of local job and career opportunities
· Improved competition in the local economy
· Greater availability of products for local consumers

TABLE 23–2
RANKING OF MNEs
AND NATIONS
ACCORDING TO
GNP OR TOTAL
SALES

Ranking	Nation or Firm	GNP or Total Sales for 1982 ($ billions)
22	Belgium	$106.5
23	*Exxon*	97.2
24	Indonesia	88.5
25	*Shell*	83.8
26	South Africa	81.2
27	Nigeria	77.9
28	Austria	75.1
28	South Korea	75.1
30	Argentina	71.6
31	Hungary	69.1
31	Venezuela	69.1
33	Turkey	63.7
34	Denmark	63.6
35	Yugoslavia	63.3
36	*General Motors*	60.0
37	*Mobil Oil*	59.9
38	Norway	58.5
39	Romania	57.6
40	Finland	52.2
41	*British Petroleum*	51.3
42	Taiwan	48.9
43	*Texaco*	47.0
44	Algeria	46.8
45	Greece	42.0
46	Philippines	41.6
47	Colombia	39.4
48	Thailand	38.3
49	Bulgaria	37.5
50	*Ford*	37.1
51	*IBM*	34.4
51	*Standard Oil of California*	34.4
53	*Du Pont*	33.3
54	Pakistan	33.1
55	Kuwait	31.8
56	Egypt	30.6
57	*Gulf Oil*	28.4
58	*Standard Oil (Indiana)*	28.1
59	Hong Kong	27.8
60	*ENI (Italy)*	27.5
61	Malaysia	27.0
62	*General Electric*	26.5
62	*Atlantic Richfield*	26.5
64	United Arab Emirates	26.1

Note: Belgium is ranked 22 because it is 22nd in GNP among nations; the United States is ranked number 1.

Sources: World Bank, *World Development Report 1984*, (Washington, D.C., 1984), and "International 500," *Fortune*, August 22, 1983, p. 170. Eastern bloc and Taiwan data from *Handbook of Economic Statistics, 1983*, published by the Central Intelligence Agency, September 1983.

These benefits may occur in any given situation, and many MNE managers and some analysts believe that they usually do. It is possible, though, that in each area of potential benefit the opposite can in fact occur. For example, the MNE may use local financing, thereby absorbing capital that might have financed indigenous companies; or a few well-advertised, standardized consumer products may drive many locally produced products from the market, thereby reducing consumer choice.

Not all costs have analogous benefits, however. Generally, the potential negative impacts, which are very emotional issues with some observers, can be placed into three broad categories:

· **Political interference on the part of the MNE**
· **Social/cultural disruptions and changes (which are bound to have both advocates and opponents)**
· **Local economic dependence on decisions made outside of the country**

There have clearly been abuses on the part of some MNEs in the past. United Fruit, for example, is generally acknowledged to have engaged in extensive political and economic interference in Latin America between the two world wars. More recently, officials of ITT have been accused of conspiring with the CIA to prevent the election of Salvador Allende Gossens, a Marxist, to the presidency of Chile.[12] And the Japanese electronics giant, Hitachi, has admitted stealing proprietary technology from IBM.

Generally, though, the ethics of MNEs are kept on a par with or above those of local companies. Today, MNEs have high political visibility and, despite their size and power, are vulnerable to punitive actions by local governments. Under such conditions, few companies are likely to risk even the appearance of unethical behavior.

It is worth noting that although MNEs are viewed with caution and suspicion by some host country government officials, they are actively courted by most countries rather than denied entry.

Impacts of MNEs on Home Countries. The debate over the benefits and costs of MNEs to their home countries is less intense than that over the effects on host countries. This is probably due to the absence of highly charged emotional issues, such as political interference, cultural disruption, and economic dependence. The benefits to a home country may include:[13]

· **The acquisition of raw materials from abroad, often from a steadier supply and at lower prices than can be found domestically**
· **Technology and management expertise acquired from competing in foreign markets**
· **The export of components and finished goods for assembly or distribution in foreign markets**
· **An inflow of income from overseas profits (dividends), licensing fees, and management contracts**
· **Job and career opportunities at home and abroad in connection with overseas operations**

One potential negative impact on home countries that MNE critics point to is a weakening in the national balance of payments, caused by the outflow of capital from investments made overseas and a reduction in exports as products are manufactured overseas rather than at home. In the long run, these losses may be more than compensated for by the flow of income from dividends, licensing fees, royalties, and sales of components for foreign assembly. Another risk, however, is the chance that the home country could suffer the lessening or loss of technological advantage.[14]

The most volatile issue on the home front is whether foreign investment (most obviously in manufacturing) by an MNE causes the loss of domestic jobs. If a company's factory production is moved overseas, on the surface it would certainly seem to cause job loss at home. Some observers feel that this job displacement is inevitable whether or not MNEs decide to invest overseas. They contend that even if one organization ignores the possible cost benefits of moving its production overseas, some of its competitors will take advantage of the opportunity. This will put the stay-at-home company at a competitive disadvantage with a consequent loss of business and reduction of work force. Hence, the job loss will take place anyway.[15] Other observers note, however, that such a conclusion is heavily dependent on assumptions about what would happen if all local companies were prohibited from investing in overseas manufacturing. Those observers go on to note that many government tax, political, and insurance policies and programs actually encourage companies to manufacture abroad rather than at home.

The actions of MNEs abroad may also have possible political impacts on their home countries. Examples would be the continuing protests by some segments of U.S. society over the involvement and investment in South African business by American MNEs and the move to effect more governmental regulation of the American chemical industry following the Bhopal disaster of 1984 (see the case study for chapter 3).

The Challenges of Multinational Management

As Mattel Toys' marketing executives learned, the task of managing in a multinational environment is one that involves coping with a unique set of circumstances and challenges. In this section, we will look at the economic, political-legal, sociocultural, and technical dimensions of the international environment and some of the ways that MNEs can adjust to them. In addition, we will examine how the tasks, problems, and opportunities of operating in multiple environments influence the ways that the basic management functions—planning, organizing, leading, and controlling—are performed in an MNE.

Finally, we will return to and extend our discussion on the evolution of management thought begun in chapter 2. The rise in prominence of MNEs has raised many questions in this area. For example, how effective have the responses of MNEs been to the multiple environments they face? How applicable are concepts of management largely developed in Western countries to environments around the world?

Managing in a Multinational Environment

As we discussed in chapter 3, organizations must be alert to the political-legal, sociocultural, economic, and technological aspects in the international dimension of their environment as well as in the domestic. Particular attention must be paid to the international environment because differences and changes are often much greater in magnitude in foreign countries than in the home country. Unexpected conditions or events can have a major impact on overseas operations, markets, and investments, as was the case with the Iranian revolution, and its virtually complete destruction of substantial U.S. business operations in Iran.

Monitoring and coping with problems in the international environment are more difficult than uncovering and dealing with problems in the domestic environment. Each foreign country will be different from the home country and from other foreign countries, sometimes drastically so. As the MNE progressively becomes involved with more and more countries, the sheer number of situations strains the organization's ability to pay attention to any single problem. Another difficulty is that managers instinctively understand the basic situation and emerging trends of their domestic environment, but may take a long time to develop a "gut feel" for a foreign environment. Some managers never achieve such an understanding, as was the case in Iran, where the revolution took most American managers completely by surprise.

In both the domestic and international environments, it is important to understand the current state of the environment and to monitor and predict changes. In a domestic company of reasonable size, the primary focus is usually on the elements of the environment that involve *change*. Over the long run, this is also true of the international realm. In the short run, however, when a company is first getting established in a foreign country, it is the environment's *current state*—the reality of the situation at the moment—that gets the most attention. This is understandable. When a company is setting up in a new location, it puts great emphasis on learning local customs, laws, values, and so on. Otherwise, it runs such risks as unwittingly breaking the law, alienating its new workers, or offending local officials. For example, the laws relating to the seizure of company bank deposits differ greatly among countries. In Holland, an aggrieved party can ask a court to impound over $1 million of a company's deposits to insure eventual payment of a $50,000 claim. The court is not required to inform the company of this; the first the company might know of the action could be when its checks start bouncing. Obviously, MNEs need to know about such current environmental factors. Later, as managers gain experience in the host country, increasing attention can be paid to changes in the environment.

Below are four major areas of the international environment and some of the major differences between them and their domestic counterparts. Where the foreign branch and the home office are located will determine how strong the differences are. A U.S. firm that opens a branch in the United Kingdom will make fewer adjustments than a U.S. firm that opens a branch in Morocco.

Economic. The main economic concerns that face a domestic company are the national patterns in economic growth, investment, and inflation. The international organization, however, must also be concerned with various aspects of international trade, such as the extent of controls on imports and exports, on foreign investors, and the repatriation of earnings. In addition, the value of the country's currency—the "foreign exchange rate"—and the overall balance of payments situation are important factors to monitor.

Political-Legal. When contemplating involvement with a foreign country, MNEs are primarily concerned with the stability of its political system, the economic and political philosophy of the group in office, the attitudes of powerful opposition groups, and the efficiency of the country's government bureaucracy. Naturally, any government policy specifically directed toward encouraging or discouraging foreign and domestic enterprises is an important factor. A country's international affairs are also important, since external conflicts—due either to the country's own problems or to treaty obligations—can affect the national political system.

The legal elements that affect those dealing in the international dimension are many and varied. Among the things that the multitude of laws and regulations cover are taxation, trade tariffs and quotas, copyright laws, and currency exchange.[16] Laws in the home country may also affect operations abroad. The Foreign Corrupt Practices Act of 1977 prohibits U.S. firms from the payment of bribes or fees to representatives of foreign businesses (an accepted practice in some countries). Critics claim that the act hampers U.S. business unfairly, as the United States is the only industrialized nation to have such a law.

Sociocultural. To be successful, the business manager who deals in the international dimension must learn to be aware of and adapt to a potentially large number of diverse societies. Different cultures have different concepts of formality or courtesy, which may extend even to what time a 10 o'clock meeting actually starts.[17] (See

---

WHAT AMERICANS ARE LIKE

- Citizens of the United States call themselves "Americans." Other "Americans"—citizens of Mexico, Central and South America—often find the term inappropriate. However, Americans have been calling themselves "Americans" for the more than 200 years of their brief history, and you will hear the term often.
- Americans are very informal. They like to dress informally, entertain informally, and they treat each other in a very informal way, even when there is a great difference in age or social standing. Foreign students may consider this informality disrespectful, even rude, but it is a part of U.S. culture.
- Americans are generally competitive. The American style of friendly joking or banter, of "getting the last word in," and the quick witty reply are subtle forms of competition. Although such behavior is natural to Americans, you may find it overbearing or disagreeable.
- Americans are achievers. They are obsessed with records of achievement in sports and they keep business achievement charts on their office walls and sports awards displayed in their homes.
- Americans ask a lot of questions, some of which may to you seem pointless, uninformed, or elementary. You may be asked very personal questions by someone you have just met. No impertinence is intended; the questions usually grow out of genuine interest.
- Americans value punctuality. They keep appointment calendars and live according to schedules. To foreign students, Americans seem "always in a hurry," and this often makes them appear brusque. Americans are generally efficient and get a great many things done, simply by rushing around.
- Silence makes Americans nervous. They would rather talk about the weather than deal with silence in a conversation.

Source: Excerpts from Margo Ernest, ed., *Predeparture Orientation Handbook: For Foreign Students and Scholars Planning to Study in the United States* (Washington, D.C.: U.S. Information Agency, Bureau of Educational and Cultural Affairs, 1984), pp. 103–105, as cited in "What Americans Are Like," *New York Times*, April 16, 1985.

---

the box, which contains excerpts from a pamphlet for people about to encounter Americans for the first time.) Miscalculation in any of the many day-to-day operating aspects of a culture can lead to serious gaffes, such as ineffective, or even offensive, marketing and the alienation of workers or suppliers.

In addition to everyday cultural characteristics, it is helpful to be familiar with a country's social structure. Specifically, this involves being aware of such factors as divisions in the population based on religion, ethnicity, language, and/or class, and the general psychology (work ethic, level of social unrest, and political activism) of the population.

Technological. With respect to the technological environment, managers must be aware that the level of technological advancement varies among countries. When a company injects new technology into a nation that is less technologically advanced than its home country, it is forcing change upon the host. Instituting this change can often be difficult, especially if it runs contrary to the wishes of the host government. Even with the enthusiastic backing of the host government, the introduction of new technology may not always be immediately successful. The People's Republic of China has recently embarked on a program of extensive computerization throughout the country, but widespread lack of experience with electronics led initially to underuse and even abandonment of equipment.

Handling the Differences

Managers pay particular attention to the environmental factors discussed above when they are assessing the attractiveness of entering or remaining in a particular country and are considering how to reduce the risks of doing so. Managers also need to keep these factors in mind in day-to-day operations to perform effectively in the country. Having examined some of the characteristics of the different realms of the international environment, we will now look at some of the possible ways managers can cope with them.

Economic. One thing that MNEs do is work hard at forecasting economic conditions in the countries they operate in, sell to, or purchase from. Companies that are large enough will have their own economic staff and use the services of outside forecasting consultants. Smaller companies tend to rely on the general knowledge of nonspecialized line managers and forecasts supplied by private companies, banks, and governments.

MNEs are also likely to forecast the future value of foreign currencies relative to their home country currency. When a company enters into a transaction with an overseas customer or supplier for which the terms of payment are not immediate, there is a certain amount of foreign exchange risk involved. As an example, consider a U.S. firm that agrees to buy 100,000 francs worth of raw materials from a French supplier for its Swiss factory. The terms of the agreement state that the U.S. firm will pay within 90 days in French francs. If the rate of exchange happens to shift from 10 francs to the dollar at the time of the sale to 9 francs to the dollar 90 days later, the American company will end up paying the equivalent of $11,111 instead of $10,000. On the other hand, if a shift occurs in the other direction, the U.S. firm will gain.

When dealing in million of dollars, this fluctuation can be quite significant. Hence many MNEs engage in *hedging* and *covering* their international financial transactions; these terms refer to methods used to protect against possible fluctuations in currency exchange rates.[18] Among the various types of hedging and covering methods are negotiating which currency will be used as payment in contracts and taking or making loans in foreign currencies. Foreign exchange-rate forecasting, hedging, and covering methods have become very sophisticated activities.

Political-Legal. Political risk forecasting has likewise developed into a sophisticated activity.[19] *Political risk* can be defined as the probability that political forces will cause upheavals in a country's business environment, which will then affect the profit and other goals of a particular business enterprise.[20] One form of such forecasting tries to predict abrupt or drastic changes; others model more gradual changes over longer periods. MNEs also pay particular attention to the forecasting of governmental controls. This includes trying to anticipate the changes in national controls that host countries often make in order to increase the national benefits from foreign investment.

Operations within a foreign country can be conducted so as to minimize the dangers of creating political problems. One common practice is to employ local citizens, especially politically well-connected ones, in key positions in upper management. This provides local expertise and reduces concern about foreigners controlling organizations that operate locally.

Sociocultural. The use of local nationals in key management positions can also help ease social and cultural friction. The desire to reduce sociocultural trauma for individuals has led more and more organizations to adopt formal orientation programs for managers who are being sent abroad.[21] In addition, managers are being encouraged to learn as much as possible about the host country's history, customs, and especially language, the most direct route to the heart of any culture.

Technological. One challenge that MNEs have responded to poorly, according to some observers, is the need to adjust methods of production to the varying levels of technological sophistication found throughout the world. For example, the introduction of automated production techniques to a culture whose technology still depends on manual labor may be both inappropriate and unsuccessful. Other observers, however, praise MNEs for using advanced technology in less-developed countries because this may result in a broadening of the host's own technology base.

Adjusting the Management Process

Operating in the international environment also affects the ways in which the basic management functions of planning, organizing, leading, and controlling are carried out. Our focus here, as in the previous discussion, will be on management actions at the "macro" level: What special steps are needed in the planning and control systems of MNEs? Should organizations be structured and coordinated differently in different countries? Should performance appraisal and reward systems differ among countries? In addition, there are decisions to be made on the "micro" level: How should one individual interact with another from a different country? Should people in one country be managed differently from people in another?

The discussion below covers some of the differences between purely domestic and international management processes, but obviously not all of them.

Planning. In chapter 5, we noted some of the reasons that companies were likely to engage in strategic planning: the increasing rate of technological change, the growing complexity of both the managerial job and the external environment, and the longer lead time between current decisions and their future results. When a company is multinational, there are at least three additional factors that make strategic planning essential:[22]

1. **The scope of the multinational management task**—the many and varied tasks required to run a global organization.
2. **The increase in the internationalization of the company**—the greater distances between the firm's subsidiaries, the differences between their environments, and their complex interrelationships.
3. **The necessity for greater efficiency due to increased and more varied competition.** This desire for efficiency has led many organizations to institute worldwide marketing and production standards in an effort to reduce costs.

Rather than merely supplementing their domestic strategy with a separate international one, MNEs are likely to adopt a *global* strategic plan that incorporates both areas—often a difficult task given the firm's complex structure, multiple environments, and so on. One of the most difficult tasks of multinational strategic planning is balancing the autonomy and initiative of individual subsidiaries against the consistency and predictability of the total system.

The strategic planning process for an MNE goes beyond merely developing a strategy. It also places emphasis on improving the management practices of the organization. One study on the long-term planning of U.S. and Australian companies with significant international operations showed that three of the four activities that received relatively high effort were: (1) aiding corporate management in the formulation of strategy, goals, and objectives; (2) integrating operational and strategic planning; and (3) improving the quality of thinking of corporate management.[23] Another study, an informal inquiry conducted by Jacques Horovitz in the early 1980s, produced similar results. He found that large European MNEs were focusing their attention on improving the strategic thinking of their managers.[24] Thus, companies appear to be putting a high priority on learning to behave more strategically.

Organizing. Like any other company, an MNE must accomplish the basic organizing functions we discussed in chapter 9. It is especially important for MNEs to strike an optimum balance between two basic organizational tasks that tend to inhibit one another. The first of these tasks is finding the most efficient manner to combine work into units (departmentalization). This must be balanced against the second task, the coordination of the work so that the organization's overall objectives can be met.[25]

Most MNEs have moved in an evolutionary manner from being domestic to being somewhat international to being multinational. Because of this, many of them create an international division early on. Later, however, they dismantle this division and opt for global thinking, in which no distinction is made between domestic and international business. This process involves frequent reorganization and experimentation with different organizational structures as the company seeks to balance the requirements of changing strategies, capabilities, and environments.[26]

Even when the company has achieved a global orientation, its operations in many different environments make it difficult to decide which departmentalization method will work the best. Most commonly, operations are partitioned according to either products or geography. Less frequently, departments will be created according to types of customers or organizational function (production, finance, personnel, marketing, and so on). No matter which form is chosen, there are going to be tough trade-offs.

Because of these trade-offs, many MNEs adopt some form of matrix structure (see chapter 9). Although matrix structures may be necessary in these cases, substantial managerial skill is required to make them work well and to be able to work within them. Furthermore, they are viewed as problematic by those who subscribe to Peters and Waterman's observations about the desirability of simple form (see chapter 1).[27]

Staffing. With regard to staffing, there are both advantages and disadvantages to being a multinational firm. On the one hand, finding the right people for organizational positions is often more difficult for MNEs than for domestic companies. Talented employees are often unwilling to relocate to another country. On the other hand, an MNE literally has a whole world of talent to draw on.

Of particular importance to MNEs is effective selection and training of any personnel who will have a high level of international involvement, either by being stationed abroad or by interacting frequently with managers and other individuals from overseas. Rosalie Tung has reported that Japanese MNEs have better success rates with managers they send overseas than do U.S. MNEs. She attributes this success to more effective selection and training of managers and offers several recommendations to American MNEs seeking to improve their performance in this area. These include sponsoring training programs for managers and their families going abroad and developing a longer-term orientation toward overseas operations. This longer-term orientation would involve longer tenures abroad for managers and more consistent support for them from corporate headquarters.[28]

Many men (and some women) used to assume that women were unsuitable for or uninterested in international jobs, particularly in countries with patriarchal social structures. The fallacy of this viewpoint is now generally recognized, although even today less than 3 percent of all international managers are women.[29]

International compensation is frequently be a tricky area for MNEs. Often there are conflicts within the organization between attempts to adapt to differences among countries and pressures to maintain uniform compensation policies and procedures throughout the organization as a whole. If an organization adopts inconsistent salary scales, it will probably have difficulty in moving managers from high-paying countries to low-paying ones. In addition, jealousy may arise among managers who receive different compensation for comparable jobs. Yet if company-wide uniform pay scales are decided on, the MNE may find itself paying well above the market level in some countries, which can be considered an unnecessary expense. In other countries, its salary scales may be below the country's norm, and the MNE may have trouble attracting and retaining skilled managers. One solution that many companies have adopted is to pay a similar base salary and then add on various bonuses and allowances according to individual situations.[30]

An organization composed of individuals with a wide variety of backgrounds, nationalities, and cultures obviously offers many possibilities for conflict and disagreement. Based on the theories of conflict management and its relationship to

"It doesn't look good. Some of our nationals are at war with some of our other nationals."

Drawing by S. Harris; © 1983 The New Yorker Magazine, Inc.

creativity discussed in chapter 14, an MNE has a great opportunity to capitalize on its diversity. Although poor resolution of conflict will hurt organizational performance, effective resolution has the potential to open up higher levels of creativity and performance.

Leading. The topic of leading in an MNE is currently a source of much debate. Because of its importance, we will devote special attention to it in the section on Selecting a Managerial Approach.

Controlling. Theoretically, an MNE could centralize all aspects of control and organizational decision making at its headquarters. As we saw in our discussion of delegation (chapter 11), however, this would be extremely inefficient and impractical. The same can be said of allowing all decisions to be made at the business-unit level.

Generally, the decision-making and control processes are distributed between the company headquarters and its subsidiaries in each nation. Five factors that influence where decisions will be made are:[31]

1. **Trade-offs between the benefits of standardization and the tailoring of products and equipment to local conditions.**
2. **The proficiency of overseas business-unit management and the degree of reliance on that management at corporate headquarters.**

3. The size of the MNE and the length of time it has been an MNE.
4. The need for individual units to make sacrifices for the benefit of the international enterprise as a whole.
5. The need to motivate unit management through involvement in the decision-making process.

The two prevailing control models used by MNEs today are bureaucratic control and culture control. *Bureaucratic control* employs explicit rules and regulations that outline desired output and behavior. *Culture control,* which is characteristic of many large Japanese firms, utilizes implicit and informal direction based on a broad company culture.[32] Bureaucratic companies usually spell out operational procedures for their foreign managers in the form of manuals and keep close tabs on those managers' actions. Culture control firms, on the other hand, tend to train their managers extensively before they send them overseas and then give them more authority and autonomy and require fewer formal reports.

All MNEs need to have their affiliates report regularly on new technology, market developments, and competitors' actions. These and other reports can aid headquarters in the vital task of developing and implementing an effective management evaluation system. The tasks of tracking events in the international environment and developing effective systems for evaluating local management can be quite complex due to the variety of circumstances under which each subsidiary and its management operate.

Selecting a Managerial Approach

As was mentioned above, the issue of leadership in MNEs is currently the focus of lively inquiry and debate. The issues involved go beyond the question of which managerial approach should be favored by top management for the total system and for each host country operation. Also raised is the question of which managerial approach is likely to work best in the *home* country.

Our discussion will be built on three possibilities:

1. The possibility that no single approach to management—including the Western or Japanese ones—will be effective and appropriate in all the world's diverse societies.
2. The possibility that Japanese management procedures offer some insights and broad guidelines for effective management in general—even if they are not the universally best way to manage in all environments.
3. The possibility that a new synthesis of management theories may be emerging, building on the earlier successes of U.S./Western management approaches in the 1950s and 1960s and the present success of many companies like the ones studied by Peters and Waterman—companies with some practices quite similar to those of well-managed Japanese companies.

Applying U.S. Approaches Abroad

How well do U.S. approaches work abroad? There are at least two ways to view this question. Plainly, on the one hand, U.S. companies have a long record of successful overseas operations following the types of practices supported by U.S./Western-based theory. It was not too long ago, in fact, that some writers feared that U.S. MNEs would completely dominate world business.[33] And their management skills were seen as their key competitive advantage.

On the other hand, management theory states that what works managerially in a given situation depends on a number of factors. (Recall the contingency theories of leadership that were presented in chapter 16 and the various influences that can enter into motivation as explained in chapter 15.) Therefore, it is logical to assume that, in the international arena, what works with some people won't work with others. An organization needs to plan wherever it has operations but the best way to go about planning might be quite different in India and in the United States.

The Hofstede Studies. Geert Hofstede has conducted a series of studies in 40 countries on variations in national character.[34] He came to the conclusion that not only do people vary a lot, but those variations seriously challenge the rules of effective managerial practice based on Western theories and peoples.

Hofstede cites four dimensions that he feels describe important aspects of a national culture:

1. **The first dimension he calls *individualism versus collectivism.* This measures an individual's relationship with other people and the degree to which the desire for personal freedom is played off against the need for social ties.**
2. **The dimension called *power distance* evaluates the way a particular society handles the inequality among people. On one end of the scale are countries and peoples that try to play down inequality as much as possible. At the other end are cultures that accept and support large imbalances in power, status, and wealth.**
3. **The *uncertainty avoidance* dimension measures how a society deals with the uncertainty of the future. A weak-uncertainty-avoidance society is one that does not feel threatened by this uncertainty and is generally tolerant and secure about the future. Strong uncertainty-avoidance cultures, on the other hand, try to overcome future uncertainties by developing institutions that create security and avoid risk. These include legal, technological, and religious institutions.**
4. **The last dimension Hofstede calls *masculinity versus femininity.* Hofstede defines a society as masculine if there are extensive divisions of social roles by sex and as feminine if these divisions are relatively small.**

In light of the differences between nations that he found in these dimensions, Hofstede feels that it is unrealistic to expect any single management approach to be applicable worldwide. For example, he notes that U.S. theories on leadership are theories for leading people in a culture that is extremely high in individualism. Applying these theories to countries that are collectivist in nature—most Third World nations, for example—is likely to yield an ineffective employer-employee relationship.

Western theories of motivation, he feels, are likewise flawed by a high individualism bias. In the United States, the strongest form of motivation is regarded as an internal need to gain self-respect or achieve personal goals. In collectivist societies, motivation is more externally directed. People feel obligations to the groups to which they belong, such as their family, enterprise, or country, and are driven to seek more "status" within these groups than to gain self-realization.

Hofstede sees organizational structure and policies as ways to distribute power and avoid uncertainty. As such, it is affected by power distance and uncertainty avoidance. The United States placed very close to the middle of the scale in both these aspects in Hofstede's studies. This fact may account for some of the success of U.S. MNEs—organizational practices favored by U.S. managers may be reasonably acceptable to people from cultures at other ends of the scale.

Applying Japanese Approaches Abroad and Synthesizing Differing Approaches

Although Hofstede has expressed serious doubts about the applicability of American/Western management practices in other countries, some observers have become very excited about the effectiveness of Japanese practices. The study of Japanese management has become such a fad, in fact, that stories like the following have been heard in many a boardroom:

> A Frenchman, a Japanese, and an American are to be executed by a firing squad. As the executioner leads them into the courtyard, he offers each the traditional last request. "I wish," responds the Frenchman, "to sing La Marseillaise one last time." "Granted," replies the executioner. "I would like to give a lecture on Japanese management one last time," says the Japanese. "Granted," says the executioner, who then looks at the American. "Please," implores the American, "shoot me first so I won't have to listen to any more lectures on Japanese management!"

It should be noted that what most people refer to as "Japanese management practices" are drawn from a select group of companies, responsible for perhaps as little as one-third of employment within Japan.

William G. Ouchi is among those who have studied Japanese business with the hope that it might provide solutions to some American problems.[35] Table 23–3 lists some of the characteristics noted by Ouchi that distinguish Japanese organizations from American ones.

TABLE 23–3
CHARACTERISTICS OF JAPANESE AND AMERICAN ORGANIZATIONS

Japanese Organizations	American Organizations
Lifetime Employment	Short-term Employment
Slow Evaluation and Promotion	Rapid Evaluation and Promotion
Non-Specialized Career Paths	Specialized Career Paths
Implicit Control Mechanisms	Explicit Control Mechanisms
Collective Decision Making	Individual Decision Making
Collective Responsibility	Individual Responsibility
Wholistic Concern	Segmented Concern

Source: William G. Ouchi, *Theory Z: How American Business Can Meet the Japanese Challenge* (Reading, Mass.: Addison-Wesley, 1981), p. 58.

These differences in organizational characteristics are associated with differences in managerial behavior. Naturally, there are wide variations in how individual Japanese managers act, as is the case in all countries. Yet, there are a number of ways in which Japanese managers *appear*, on the average, to differ from American managers. Overall, Japanese managers appear to be more concerned with the longer-term implications of decisions and actions and more willing to make current sacrifices for future benefits. They are more likely to encourage subordinates to participate in decision making and to welcome and acknowledge suggestions from subordinates. Partly because of this participation, they are also less likely to make quick, unilateral decisions; communication between managers and subordinates is also more indirect and subtle. Managers try hard to avoid embarrassing co-workers in public or in private. They get to know their co-workers well as individuals and show concern for their welfare, even helping to resolve personal problems outside the workplace.

There is much controversy over Japanese management style. Some observers doubt that management is the key to the success of "Japan, Inc." Others challenge the "one big happy family" image of Japanese companies and argue that employee fear of punishment is a major factor in Japanese success. They also point out the restricted nature of some of the supposed employee benefits in Japanese firms. For example, "lifetime employment" is essentially restricted to males, since it is assumed that women will work for a few years, get married, and then leave the company. In addition, guaranteed lifetime employment terminates at age 55. Most individuals are then forced to seek other, lower-paying jobs because of relatively modest pension benefits.[36]

In the overall analysis, however, Japanese companies do seem to do many things well. Several studies offer evidence that Japanese management practices work well for Japanese subsidiaries operating in the United States and the United Kingdom.[37] In fact, Pascale and Athos, among other observers, have noted that there is much similarity between well-managed Japanese firms and well-managed U.S. firms.[38]

This similarity between well-managed Japanese and U.S. firms should not come as too much of a surprise. And it contains a unique irony. When they studied American management theories during the 1950s, the Japanese accepted them as genuine practices of American companies, not realizing that in actuality few U.S. companies followed them.[39] When American managers were interviewed by those visitors from overseas, they frequently described what they felt they should be doing rather than what they were doing. In addition, the Japanese listened carefully to some American experts who were largely ignored at home, like W. Edwards Deming, whose concepts of quality control profoundly influenced the Japanese drive to move from a country known for shoddy products to a world leader in manufacturing quality.[40] These theories and apparent management practices were then adapted to the Japanese situation and put into practice. A high commitment was made to refining and improving them over time according to feedback gathered from their usage. Honda is one example of a Japanese company that used this approach successfully in designing its products for the U.S. market.[41]

The same "try it, find out what happens, try to improve it, and try again" approach may well be the "secret" to management excellence in any country or organization in the future. Fayol's perspective that organizations require planning, organizing, leading, and controlling is likely to remain valid, but how this general framework will be best applied in any given country will depend on many contingencies. As managers "try, observe, adjust, and try again," the resulting practices around the world should acquire many similarities to each other, and the differences may look like "commonsense" differences once they are uncovered. And those practices that do work will continue to change and evolve over time.[42]

Summary

Companies go international for a variety of reasons, all of which can be categorized as either aggressive, such as opening new markets, or defensive, such as protecting the supply of an important raw material.

The extent of a company's internationalization is defined by such factors as the directness of the company's international involvement, the company's organizational structure, and the importance of the company's international concerns relative to its domestic ones. The way an organization's management perceives the international realm can generally be categorized as either ethnocentric, polycentric, or geocentric.

On balance, it would seem that multinational enterprises (MNEs) do have a positive effect on their host countries. Potential benefits would include technology and capital transfer, improvement of the host country's balance of payments, and the creation of local job and career opportunities. The most debated issue surrounding the effect of MNEs on their home countries is whether foreign investment, particularly in manufacturing, causes the loss of domestic jobs.

A manager dealing in the international environment faces a unique set of challenges and problems. For one thing, international managers must cope with a variety of environments that are all quite different from one another. In addition, there are often conflicts within an MNE between attempts to adapt to differences among countries and pressures to maintain uniform policies throughout the MNE as a whole.

There is currently much debate over selecting a managerial approach for an MNE. Although U.S. firms have attained a fair amount of success operating abroad, Geert Hofstede's research indicates that any single approach is likely to be ineffective in many of the diverse societies around the world. The success of Japanese companies, however, suggests that Japanese management practices may offer some guidelines toward effective management in general.

Review Questions

1. Why do companies become internationalized?

2. Describe the four degrees of corporate internationalization identified by Christopher Korth.

3. What are some international activities in which a company might engage?

4. List the three attitudes toward internationalization that managers may adopt.

5. Define a multinational enterprise (MNE).

6. What are the possible impacts of MNEs on their host countries? On their home countries?

7. What aspects of the international environment must managers be aware of?

8. How can familiarity with and responsiveness to foreign sociocultural characteristics aid international managers?

9. How should managers adjust management practices when planning for the international environment?

10. What special problems do the managers of MNEs face when organizing international operations?

11. According to Rosalie Tung, how can the managers of American MNEs learn from the human resource management practices of Japanese MNEs?

12. Discuss Hofstede's findings on variations in national character. How might these be relevant to managers?

13. How does Japanese management style differ from U.S. management style?

Notes
1. Walecia Konrad, "Made in America," *Madison Avenue* 26, no. 3 (March 1984):42.

2. Donald A. Ball and Wendell H. McCulloch, Jr., *International Business: Introduction and Essentials,* 2nd ed. (Plano, Texas: Business Publications, 1985), pp. 39–48. The authors have drawn frequently on this source throughout this chapter.

3. Ibid., p. 39 (originally from Sanford Rose, "Why the Multinational Tide Is Ebbing," *Fortune,* August 1977, pp. 110–114ff.

4. Stefan H. Robock and Kenneth Simmonds use similar classifications for the motivation behind a company's decision to go international: (1) market seeking; (2) resource seeking; (3) production-efficiency seeking; (4) technology seeking; (5) risk avoidance (companies looking, through diversification, to lower the chances of production interruption, stabilize demand, and generally lower the political risk to the system); (6) defensive or exchange of threat (when companies in oligopolistic industries decide to follow one another into overseas markets in order to have the capability to react to each other's price cuts or any other resulting competitive action). For more information, see Stefan H. Robock and Kenneth Simmonds, *International Business and Multinational Enterprises,* 3d ed. (Homewood, Ill.: Irwin, 1983), pp. 54–55.

5. Christopher M. Korth, *International Business, Environment, and Management,* 2nd ed. (Englewood Cliffs, N.J.: Prentice-Hall, 1985), pp. 6–10.

6. Howard Perlmutter, "The Tortuous Evolution of the Multinational Corporation," *Columbia Journal of World Business* 4, no. 1 (January–February 1969):9–18.

7. Robock and Simmonds, *International Business and Multinational Enterprises,* p. 7. See also Yair Aharoni, "The Issue of Defining Transnational Corporations," in *Transnational Corporations in World Development; A Re-examination* (New York: United Nations, 1978), pp. 158–161, and "On the Definition of a Multinational Corporation," *Quarterly Review of Economics and Business* 11, no. 3 (Autumn 1971):27–37.

8. Myra Wilkens, *The Emergence of Multinational Enterprise* (Cambridge, Mass.:" Harvard University Press, 1970)

9. Reed Moyer, ed., *International Business: Issues and Concepts* (New York: Wiley, 1984), p. 137.

10. See, for example, Richard J. Barnet and Ronald E. Müller, *Global Reach: The Power of the Multinational Corporations* (New York: Simon & Schuster, 1974) for a popular critique of MNEs, widely cited by critics of MNEs in the 1970s. See also Joseph S. Nye, Jr., "Multinational Corporations in World Politics," *Foreign Affairs* 53, no. 1 (October 1974):153–175; and Peter F. Drucker, "Multinationals and Developing Countries: Myths and Realities," *Foreign Affairs* 43, no. 1 (October 1974):121–143 (both reprinted in Moyer, *International Business*).

11. This discussion is based on Korth, *International Business, Environment, and Management,* pp. 277–297, 308–326.

12. Robock and Simmonds, *International Business and Multinational Enterprises,* p. 233 (originally from "Dollar Diplomacy, 1972 Style," *Newsweek,* April 10, 1972).

13. Korth, *International Business, Environment, and Management,* pp. 297–301.

14. Lawrence G. Franko, "Foreign Direct Investment in Less Developed Countries; Impact on Home Countries," *Journal of International Business Studies* 9, no. 2 (Winter 1978): 55–65; and Robert G. Hawkins and Bertram Finn, "Regulation of Multinational Firms' Foreign Activities: Home Country Policies and Concerns," *Journal of Contemporary Business* 6, no. 4 (Autumn 1977):14–30 (both reprinted in Moyer, *International Business*).

15. Moyer, *International Business,* p. 138. For a discussion of the types of jobs U.S. MNEs might move overseas and the impacts of doing so on the U.S. economy and work force, see Robert A. Reich, *The New American Frontier* (New York: Times Books, 1983).

16. Ball and McCulloch, *International Business,* pp. 242–267.

17. For an interesting early book that called managers' attention to these kinds of cultural differences, see Edward T. Hall, *The Silent Language* (New York: Doubleday, 1959).

18. See Carl R. Beidleman, John L. Hilley, and James A. Greenleaf, "Alternatives in Hedging Long-Date Contractual Foreign Exchange Exposure," *Sloan Management Review* 24, no. 4 (Summer 1983):45–54.

19. See, for example, Brian Leavy, "Assessing Country Risk for Foreign Investment Decisions," *Long Range Planning* 17, no. 3 (June 1984):141–150; and Thomas W. Shreeve, "Be Prepared for Political Risks Abroad," *Harvard Business Reivew* 62, no. 4 (July-August 1984):111–118.

20. Robock and Simmonds, *International Business and Multinational Enterprises*, p. 342.

21. See Chris Lee, "Cross-cultural Training: Don't Leave Home Without It," *Training* 20, no. 7 (July 1983):20–21ff.; and Philip S. Gutis, "Bridging the Cultural Gap," *New York Times,* October 7, 1984, p. 15.

22. Ball and McCulloch, *International Business,* pp. 611–612. See also David C. Shanks, "Strategic Planning for Global Competition," *Journal of Business Strategy* 5, no. 3 (Winter 1985):80–89.

23. The fourth high-effort activity was associated with the mechanics of basic planning: defining guidelines, formats, and timetables. See Noel Capon, Chris Christodoulou, John U. Farley, and James Hulbert, "A Comparison of Corporate Planning Practice in American and Australian Manufacturing Companies," *Journal of International Business Studies* 15, no. 2 (Winter 1984):41–54.

24. Jacques Horovitz, "New Perspectives on Strategic Management," *Journal of Business Strategy* 4, no. 3 (Winter 1984):19–33.

25. Ball and McCulloch, *International Business,* p. 613.

26. For suggestions on how excessive reorganizations have been avoided by such companies as Corning, Timken, and Eli Lilly, see Christopher A. Bartlett, "MNCs: Get Off the Reorganization Merry-Go-Round," *Harvard Business Review* 61, no. 2 (March–April 1983):138–146, and "How Multinational Organizations Evolve," *Journal of Business Strategy* 3, no. 1 (Summer 1983):20–32.

27. Ball and McCulloch, *International Business,* pp. 613–623.

28. Rosalie L. Tung, "Human Resource Planning in Japanese Multinationals: A Model for U.S. Firms?" *Journal of International Business Studies* 15, no. 2 (Fall 1984):139–149.

29. Nancy J. Adler, "Women in International Management: Where Are They?" *California Management Review* 26, no. 4 (Summer 1984):81.

30. Ball and McCulloch, *International Business,* p. 644; *Worldwide Executive Compensation: New Problems and Solutions* (New York: Business International Corp., 1974).

31. Ibid., p. 632.

32. B. R. Baliga and Alfred M. Jaeger, "Multinational Corporations: Control Systems and Delegation Issues," *Journal of International Business Studies* 15, no. 2 (Fall 1984):26–28. See also Alfred M. Jaeger, "The Transfer of Organizational Culture Overseas: An Approach to Control in the Multinational Corporation," *Journal of International Business Studies* 14, no. 2 (Fall 1983):101.

33. See, for example, Jean-Jacques Servan-Schreiber, *The American Challenge* (New York: Atheneum, 1968).

34. Geert Hofstede, "The Cultural Relativity of Organizational Practices and Theories," *Journal of International Business Studies* 14, no. 1 (Fall 1983):78–85, and *Culture's Consequences: International Differences in Work-Related Values* (Beverly Hills, Calif.: Sage, 1980). For a rich debate on the applicability of Western management in other cultures, see Geert Hofstede, "Motivation, Leadership, and Organization: Do American Theories Apply Abroad?" *Organizational Dynamics* 9, no. 1 (Summer 1980):42–63, and "Do American Theories Apply Abroad?: A Reply to Goodstein and Hunt," *Organizational Dynamics* 10, no. 1 (Summer 1981):63–68; and John W. Hunt, "Applying American Behavioral Science: Some Cross-Cultural Problems," *Organizational Dynamics* 10, no. 1 (Summer 1981):55–62.

35. William G. Ouchi, *Theory Z: How American Business Can Meet the Japanese Challenge* (Reading, Mass.: Addison-Wesley, 1981). Other studies of note are Richard Pascale and Anthony Athos, *The Art of Japanese Management* (New York: Simon & Schuster, 1981); and N. Hatvany and V. Pucik, "An Integrated Management System: Lessons from the Japanese Experience," *Academy of Management Review* 6, no. 3 (July 1981):469–480.

36. S. Prakash Sethi, Nobuaki Namiki, and Carl L. Swanson, *The Attack on Theory Z: The False Promise of the Japanese Miracle* (Marshfield, Mass.: Pitman, 1984).

37. See Martin K. Starr and Nancy E. Bloom, *The Performance of Japanese-Owned Firms in America: Survey Report* (New York: Center for Operations, Graduate School of Business, Columbia University, 1985); Malcolm Trevor, "Does Japanese Management Work in Britain?" *Journal of General Management* 8, no. 4 (Summer 1983):28–43; and Satoshi Kamata, *Japan in the Passing Lane: An Insider's Account of Life in a Japanese Auto Factory* (New York: Pantheon, 1983). For a discussion of the extent to which some Japanese companies have introduced these techniques in U.S. subsidiaries, see Richard D. Robinson, *The Japan Syndrome: Is There One?* (Atlanta: Georgia State University, 1985).

38. See also Pascale and Athos, *The Art of Japanese Management;* and J. Bernard Keys and Thomas

R. Miller, "The Japanese Management Theory Jungle," *Academy of Management Review* 9, no. 2 (April 1984):345–346.

    39. Raymond G. Hunt, "Taking Mayo and McGregor Seriously," *California Management Review* 27, no. 1 (Fall 1984): 173–176; and Ryuji Fukada, *Managerial Engineering: Techniques for Improving Quality and Productivity in the Workplace* (Stamford, Conn.: Productivity, Inc., 1983).

    40. W. Edwards Deming, "The Roots of Quality Control," *Pacific Basin Quarterly*, no. 12 (Spring–Summer 1985):1–4.

    41. Richard T. Pascale, "Perspectives on Strategy: The Real Story Behind Honda's Success," *California Management Review* 26, no. 3 (Spring 1984):47–72.

    42. Modesto A. Maidique, "Point of View: The New Management Thinkers," *California Management Review* 26, no. 1 (Fall 1983):151–161.

CASE STUDY: Management, Korean Style

When Japanese companies first began manufacturing in the United States, many people smiled at oddities like prework exercise, but analysts were struck with the efficiency of the Japanese management style. Now, the Koreans are coming, setting up their own factories and bringing their version of management "harmony."

Dozens of South Korean corporations have already opened offices in the United States, and two have begun manufacturing operations. The Lucky-Goldstar Group opened a color television factory in Huntsville, Alabama two and a half years ago, and is now bustling with expansion plans. Last fall the Samsung Group also began producing color televisions, at a factory in Roxbury Township, N.J.

In gambling that they can manufacture profitably in America, just when American manufacturers are bitterly complaining and even going abroad because of foreign competition, the Koreans are counting on a blend of their own traditional management style with American business methods.

The Korean style is similar to the much better known Japanese approach, although experts say the Koreans are often more willing to blend their techniques with American methods. Korean management aims to foster a family atmosphere, in which employees interact freely with executives and share a strong commitment to the company's success.

Acting more as a gentle patriarch than as president of the Gold Star of America plant, P. W. Suh has taken charge of the delicate task of grafting Korean management principles onto Dixie. Mr. Suh concedes that there have been awkward moments—such as the reluctance of some American workers to wear uniforms—but in general employees and management alike appear to appreciate the result.

"You wouldn't believe what Gold Star does for us," said Rachel Cothren, pausing from her job on the assembly line. "My husband was in the hospital for major surgery, and some of the management came and sat with me through that. Mr. Suh came and stayed with me in intensive care, and brought books and magazines."

This carefully cultivated image of a friendly, caring company of one happy family typifies the Korean management style. But the friendship is not for nothing. It is intended to keep unions at bay and to foster a loyalty and enthusiasm in the work force that will generate more televisions per hour than American management can. One measure of its success is a daily absenteeism rate at Gold Star that averages 1 percent, compared with 5 percent in American companies.

The idea is to import not Korean televisions but Korean management methods.

These methods are associated with an economic miracle that produced even faster economic growth in South Korea over the last 25 years than in Japan. The Korean growth was three times faster than that in the United States.

The principal weapon in the Korean armory is its management philosophy, what the Koreans call *inhwa,* or harmony. Even in South Korea, Lucky-Goldstar is an exemplar of this philosophy.

"If we are in a hurry, we may ask employees for special consideration to do things differently," said D. H. Koo, president of overseas operations for the Lucky-Goldstar Group, explaining the Korean approach. "And they will oblige. But in the United States maybe they do not care that there is a hurry."

Mr. Koo and his colleagues in the Lucky-Goldstar boardrooms want employees at the Huntsville plant to care, and so they are trying to transplant *inhwa.* "I expect dedication and loyalty in the future, if we help our family," Mr. Suh said, using "family" to refer to his work force.

Telling employees about company goals, and even asking for help, are cardinal principles of Gold Star. "Family meetings," for all of the staff, are held monthly, and quality discussions are scheduled for every two weeks. In addition, bonuses are used to build enthusiasm. About three days a week, workers get a bonus—an hour of overtime pay—if their assembly line has increased output while maintaining quality levels. Employees also get $50 in cash if they do not miss a day of work for three months.

Similar management methods are used at the other Korean manufacturing plant in the United States, Samsung's in Roxbury Township. The employees are also called a family, and interaction between workers and executives is stressed.

Like the Japanese, the Koreans are coming to the United States largely because of fear that protectionist rules could keep out their exports. In February 1984, the Commerce Department ruled that Korean electronics companies were dumping—or selling for less than fair value—color television sets in the United States. Gold Star is now required to post cash deposits of 7.4 percent of the value of its shipments, although the final assessments may vary from that.

But in coming to America, the Koreans are also facing tough price competition. Although 1983 and 1984 were boom years for color televisions, with about 16 million units sold last year, price competition has been severe.

Although imports have been a major reason for the price competition, three out of four television sets sold in the United States are still made in this country. About two dozen manufacturers continue to produce sets in the United States.

Charles K. Ryan, an analyst at Merrill Lynch & Company, said that Korean companies operating in South Korea and in the United States might come to dominate the lower level of the color television market, for 13-inch and low-priced 19-inch models, while more established companies produce larger, more complex televisions where the markup is higher.

One frustration for Gold Star is that because it lacks name recognition and a reputation, it has to sell at lower prices than its competition. Gold Star sells its televisions under its own name and under private brand names like Montgomery Ward, General Electric, and K mart.

Notwithstanding the competition, Gold Star seems to be happy with its American experience. Since opening the factory in Huntsville, Gold Star has doubled its capacity and plans soon to add microwave ovens, computers, and videocassette recorders. Gold Star executives are buoyed by the finding that televisions produced in Huntsville can compete in price with sets produced in South Korea.

The basic wage in the Huntsville plant is $4.56 an hour, although bonuses and benefits add significantly to that. The comparable South Korean wage is $1.30. But mechanization has reduced the role of labor in the Alabama plant, so that it costs only about $7 more to produce a television set in Huntsville than to build it in South Korea and ship it to the United States. The anti-dumping duty on Korean sets more than makes up that gap, Gold Star said.

Source: Nicholas D. Kristof, "Management, Korean Style," *New York Times,* April 11, 1985, pp. Dlff. Copyright © 1985 by The New York Times Company. Reprinted by permission.

Case Questions
1. Describe the Korean method of management. What advantages and disadvantages does it have over U.S. methods? How has it borrowed from U.S. methods?
2. Why are Korean manufacturers setting up manufacturing operations in the United States?
3. In your opinion, will the entry of foreign electronics manufacturers have a positive or negative impact on the domestic electronics industry? Explain.
4. Can the recent success of Japanese and Korean MNEs be best explained by political, economic, or cultural factors?

CASE ON CONTROLLING, INFORMATION SYSTEMS, AND INTERNATIONAL MANAGEMENT

Controlling a Multinational: ITT

International Telephone and Telegraph (ITT) was founded in 1920 by Colonel Sosthenes Behn. Beginning with a small telephone company in Cuba, Behn built ITT into a multinational empire that, after World War II, included subsidiaries in the major Latin American and European countries, Japan, and South Africa. Based in the United States, the company manufactured communications equipment, operated telephone networks, and was a major contractor for the U.S. Department of Defense. But in the late 1950s, at the time of Behn's death, ITT lacked leadership and direction; earnings were a meager $29 million on sales of $765.6 million—less than 4 percent.

In 1959, Harold S. Geneen was hired as president and chief executive officer of ITT, where he remained until 1977. In his first few months on the job, Geneen immediately faced serious problems with the proper control of ITT's European subsidiaries. His approach to solving these problems, as can be seen from the following selections, was highly personal, labor-intensive, and numerical—and also quite effective. Later, in 1968, when ITT had become the largest and most stable conglomerate of its time, the company encountered control problems of a different kind with its Rayonier subsidiary.

1. "The first week or so after joining the company, I devoted most of my time to studying the company's financial statements and reports, division by division, unit by unit. As an accountant by profession and an old-fashioned bookkeeper at heart, I had always believed that the numbers were the bare bones of a corporation. The numbers, coming in from units of the company all over the world, identified the assets of ITT, the sources of its income, the cash flow, where the money was going. More than that, the relationship among the numbers was for me like reading between the lines of a book. I could visualize the operations from unit to unit, the thrust or lack of thrust of the divisions. In my mind's eye, I could see the men writing the reports I read. I got a sense of the general health of the company, the performers and nonperformers, the problem areas. Then I started asking questions. I called in various executives in the home office and went over with them the various financial statements. Little by little I came to know the men involved in this company that Sosthenes Behn had fashioned over the years in his highly individualistic way.

"In that first year, there was the expected jolt to the company of having a new man come in from the outside and take charge. There was the usual politicking for position with the new boss. There were two or three top executives who were very unhappy that one of them had not been chosen to lead. There were some immediate decisions to be made. But, above all, it was the internal financial reports that were important and, to me, something of a shock.

"ITT was not what I had expected from reading the various Wall Street reports of security analysts. I had been led to believe, as had most of the public, that ITT was doing very well domestically, particularly with military electronics. Shortly before I came upon the scene, it had been announced that ITT had been awarded a major, multimillion-dollar contract on the communications system connecting all Army bases worldwide. That was in addition to the well-known work of ITT in building the global communications systems for the Air Force, the Strategic Air Command, and other military uses. Nevertheless, ITT had a very low return on its overall sales and assets, which led security analysts to believe that ITT must be losing money on its overseas operations.

"Exactly the opposite was true. I was surprised to learn that even with all those military contracts, which added up to three quarters of all ITT's domestic sales, the domestic operations were yielding only about 15 percent of the company's profits. Eighty-five percent of our earnings came from the telephone and telegraph operations in 24 foreign countries, most of it from Western Europe. Not that those earnings were so great either. Net profits hovered at the 3 percent mark.

"The company was lopsided. It was an American company with 113,000 employees abroad and only 23,000 in the United States. Worse, virtually our whole management team was at home and not where the work was being done: fifteen vice-presidents with offices in Manhattan and one, only one, coordinating all the work abroad.

"That one man was Henry Scudder, a tall, distinguished, soft-spoken fellow who dressed and acted like an international diplomat and spoke with a trace of a British accent. He was a tireless, dogged worker. Over the next six months, Hank Scudder was to lead me on a tour of all, or almost all, of ITT facilities in Western Europe, South America, Australia, and the Far East.

"Returning to America only for the monthly board of directors meetings, I spent most of those first six months visiting the company's plants, meeting the managing directors, their top staffs, walking through the factories, seeing and touching the products we produced, lunching with bankers, some customers, some government officials. They all wanted to get a look at the new man running ITT as much as I wanted to blend together impressions of the men running the companies with the reports they had turned in to headquarters. It was the age before the jet plane and, among other impressions, I gained a healthy respect for the job Sosthenes Behn had done traveling by ship and train to the outposts of the ITT empire. I also sensed the deep loyalty that these managing directors in England, Germany, France, and elsewhere felt toward Colonel Behn and toward ITT. After all, each of these companies was run entirely by men who were native to the countries in which they were located and yet they were all working for American stockholders.

"It took a while, as we toured the ITT plants in Europe, before Hank Scudder opened up to me. In his most diplomatic fashion, he acknowledged honestly that he felt that his major contribution to the company over the past several years had been to keep the various cardboard vice-presidents who occupied the New York office from upsetting the European operations. He maintained a staff of about 20 people in New York to accomplish just that: to arrange things so that certain vice-presidents in New York never had to go to Europe on other than ceremonial or social visits. Not one office or even one desk was assigned in any of the European companies to a New York executive. Hank Scudder traveled from country to country, from company to company, meeting with managing directors in hotel rooms. He and he alone went over their problems, approved or disapproved their budgets, their plans, their capital expenditures, and whatever. The foreign managing directors liked it that way. They conducted their own businesses virtually as they wished; they worked through Hank Scudder and sent their earnings and reports back to America.

"While I could appreciate the appeal of such an arrangement, it certainly was no way to run a company. One of the most obvious drawbacks was that such independence from the home office allowed the European companies the freedom to compete more fiercely with one another than they competed with rival companies. As I visited and talked with the managers, it became evident that the personal and emotional hostilities of World War II had carried over well into peacetime. These men shared nothing with one another. Each company had its own elaborate research and development facilities, and they were all doing essentially the same work. It was as if each one was inventing the wheel over and over again. Worse, they designed their telephone switching and other equipment so that they were not interchangeable. They each made the same kinds of consumer products and competed throughout the European market with one another. It was waste on a terrible scale.

"As the months went on, I discovered there were many things that had to be ironed out between the European and American managements. They had different products, different kinds of markets, and a wholly different attitude toward competition than we did in America. I felt that there was room for higher markups and profits in Europe than our companies were getting. I tried to convince them of the need for a higher turnover of inventories and receivables and better use of their available assets. But traditions and habits, even in professional management, are hard to break.

"At least some of them are. At our very first European General Managers Meeting, held in an overcrowded Paris hotel meeting room, I made a long, detailed presentation of the need to introduce certain modern American management methods into the European companies. At the end, I asked for questions. Not one man there raised his hand. At lunch afterwards, I asked about that and it was explained to me that at the last such meeting, chaired by Colonel Behn more than two years ago, one man had questioned the old colonel and not long afterwards he had been fired. No one had dared to ask a question since then.

"Another director confided to me that perhaps in my ignorance as an American I had committed a social faux pas in addressing them by their first names. That, he explained, was simply not done in Europe until one was invited to such familiarity. After lunch, I told the group firmly that this was an American company, that we were all of one family, and that we would follow the American custom of using first names, and that, furthermore, as one family we would henceforth be open and candid with one another. Questions were always welcome, and answers were always to be candid and honest.

"One of the earliest decisions made was to create an ITT-Europe, which would serve as a headquarters for all those operations. There were many problems. They did not involve business management so much as they did national attitudes and different personality quirks of the managers in Germany, France, England, Belgium, the Netherlands, and elsewhere. We chose to put our headquarters in Belgium, not because of its central location in Europe or because Brussels was the seat of the Common Market. We chose Belgium because it was neutral ground. Frenchmen and Englishmen who would not agree to be ruled from an ITT headquarters in Germany would go to Belgium. Germans who would not go to Paris or London would agree to meet in Brussels.

"One of the most difficult problems to solve in postwar Europe was how to persuade managers of the French or British companies to follow the lead of the Germans or Italians, or vice versa, and how to convince the companies in the smaller nations to go along with the decisions made by the bigger companies without feeling dominated. Our early meetings sounded something like United Nations meetings of have and have-not nations. We solved this one with the idea of establishing what we called our Strategy and Action Boards. They were set up along product lines, consisting of the leading producers of a given product along with one or two of the smaller producers. The decision of the Strategy and Action Board on any one product line was binding upon all other European companies.

"Since most of the smaller companies depended one way or another on one or more of the larger companies for parts and other products, this seemed to solve the rivalry problems. Decisions were made by three or four persons rather than eight or nine, and since different national companies served on different product strategy boards, national rivalries were assuaged. These Strategy and Action Board decisions finally worked their way down the ranks and served as a working start to unified European operations. Over the years that I was at the helm of ITT (from 1959 to 1977), it accomplished its goal of becoming a unified organization with pride in its combined accomplishments. During that period, ITT-Europe increased its sales from some $300 million to more than $7 billion."

2. "One of our basic policies at ITT, which grew out of our monthly General Managers Meetings, was: *No surprises!*

"Ninety-nine percent of all surprises in business are negative. No matter how adept we were as a management team, mistakes would be made, the unexpected would happen, problems would arise. But the earlier we discovered and dealt with the unexpected problem, the easier it would be to solve. We might not catch all of them at an early stage, but if we dealt with 95 percent of these situations early enough, we would have the time and energy to handle the few big problems that got through our net.

"So, very early on, I demanded that all our company managers put all their significant problems into their monthly reports. I wanted no cover-ups, no surprises. Then one day a company manager told us of a massive strike he had on his hands. How long had the strike been threatened? Three months. Why hadn't he warned us in his monthly report? He had. Where? On page 18, hidden in one line of a paragraph in the middle of the page. So I amended the policy. Managers were to put all their significant problems in their monthly reports on a 'red flag' page at the beginning of the report, and *keep putting them in* with 'red flags' until the problems were solved.

"In my first few years at ITT, I read so many wishy-washy, equivocating, vague reports that I became exasperated in my search for the meaning of what I was reading. I lectured interminably to executives on the line and on the staff on how important it was for headquarters to understand what was being recommended to us for a decision and also *why* the recommendation was being made and also *who* was responsible for the recommendation. So, in no uncertain terms, I sent out a memo on what I expected in a report:

> **Effective immediately, I want every report specifically, directly and bluntly to state at the beginning a summary containing the following facts in this order.**
>
> **1. A clear short statement of the action recommended.**
>
> **2. A brief summary of what the problem really is.**
>
> **3. The reasoning and the figures where necessary for clarity and perspective to understand the basis of the reasoning and judgment areas leading to this recommendation.**
>
> **4. A brief personal statement by the writer expressing any further personal opinion, his degree of confidence and any other questions that he has in this respect.**
>
> **Obviously, to make this kind of direct, clear-judgment statement, one must first do hard 'crisp' thinking and adequate homework. Otherwise, we will get a continuation of vague, general statements and reports which indicate no clear position, or basis for any taken by the writer. In the future this kind of 'indefinite' statement and report will be subject to review with the author, and action will be taken on this point alone.**

"Indeed, in the early years as the executives in the company came to know one another better and better, a great deal of time was spent in my reading a line or two of a report and demanding to know what the writer of those lines meant. If the man knew and was reluctant to put the facts out in the open, my questions would force him to admit what he was trying to hide. If the man did not know or understand his own lines (which was often true because he had not written them), then my questions, doubly embarrassing, would force him to do his own homework.

"It took me a while to convince our managers that I was sincere in telling them that there was no shame or humiliation in being wrong or making an occasional mistake. Mistakes are a facet of business, and should be treated as such. The important thing was to face up to one's mistakes, examine them, learn from them, and go on about one's business. The only real mistake was being afraid to make a mistake."

3. "A new president, as his first priority, will carefully go over the figures of his company, looking not at individual numbers but at the overall numbers in relation to one another. He is searching for trends and currents that tell him what is happening: numbers have a way of synthesizing the mass effects of many, many individual items that make up the whole. Once he has that mainstream in mind, however, he will begin to look into the detailed figures behind the overall averages, and he will focus on the numbers that interest him the most: sales, costs, earnings, margins, marketing, assets investment, debt and interest, whatever.

"Suppose he comes up with the number 4 (which can represent $4 million, $40 million, or $400 million) for one element of one division. Breaking down that 4, he may find it does not represent $2 + 2$ or $3 + 1$. Very frequently in business a total of 4 can mean $+12$ and -8. Maybe the $+12$ should be higher, he thinks, but he focuses upon the -8 and he finds that consists of $+5$ and -13. So he delves into the -13 and perhaps he finds that represents the losses on a series of products that are terribly outmoded and not selling. By stopping production on that one line of products, he saves that loss of 13, and when he applies that saving to the bottom line of that division, the total of $+4$ rises to $+17$, a healthy gain for the new regime. Remember, he did not change the numbers; he changed what was behind the numbers.

"As he moves on, reading the books of the company, he probably will find gaps in the information he needs and wants. He will then call for figures that had never been collected before, and those figures will enable him to maintain a tighter control on the varied operations of the company. Obviously, the head of a company, a division, or a department wants the figures on only the elements in which he has an interest. He may want to know how many tons of coal Plant A is burning every month, but he does not care about the amount of fly ash that is coming out of the chimney. But then one day the Environmental Protection Agency imposes a fine of $1,000 for every day a company's fly ash exceeds 2 percent of the coal burned. When he finds his company is paying $30,000 a month in fines, he becomes interested in a monthly figure on fly ash. Now it is important to him.

"Sometimes, however, outside events beyond the control of any individual company overtake the usual early-warning system that even good numbers provide. A sudden rise in the cost of energy, an international event of significant proportions, a plunge into recession of a whole national economy can wreak havoc with the best-laid plans. It has happened to the auto industry, the oil industry, the steel industry, and to segments of ITT.

"Consider, for example, one company with $40 million in annual sales and reaping a handsome profit. It expands to $60 million in annual sales, earning even more money. It builds its sales volume to $80 million a year, and profits rise proportionally. Then the cycles change, the economy slumps, customers suddenly stop buying, annual sales slide back down to old level of $40 million a year. But now the company is losing money on that volume. What happened? What can you do about it? No mere snipping at costs here and there will save the situation. Some men will sit back and say, 'We're waiting for the volume to come back. Look, we made lots of money at $80 million and we'll make it again. We just have to wait for the economy to turn around.' That's hope. Others might say, 'Hell, we're in all kinds of trouble and it's hopeless. Let's sell the thing and get out from under.'

"At ITT, when outside events overtook us and there was nothing else we could do, we 'restructured' the company so that it could cope with its new environment. To sit back and wait for the vicissitudes of the economy to help us was unacceptable as a solution. To sell off a company in times of distress ran against our grain. The numbers, which told us what was going on within that company, played a big part. We went over every relevant figure of every operation and scaled the company back down to the size it was when it was making money on annual sales of $40 million. It is simply amazing how many expenses once deemed necessary become luxuries when your company is operating at a loss. Restructuring also involved cutting back on plant and employees so that the company once again resembled its old $40 million self. At the same time, while restructuring we adopted the practice of putting forth a tremendous effort to try to increase sales a little bit, even 5 or 10 percent. We cut the company back to the $40 million structure and then tried to do $42 or $44 million in business. We called it our 'one-two punch.' Cannon Electric, which makes heavy-industry electrical connectors, was one ITT subsidiary that went through restructuring during an economic recession and then was built up to a point where it is now three times as big and as successful as it had ever been before. We could not have done it without a firm grasp on its numbers."

4. "Few things to my mind were more important in managing than checking the facts, bearing in mind the Law of Inverse Time-to-Veracity. Management seldom makes the wrong decisions per se. Things go wrong, and sometimes seriously wrong, when management makes the 'right' decision based upon 'facts' that are mistaken, misleading, or overlooked.

"The most costly management mistake we made at ITT was in building a giant wood-cellulose-processing plant in Port-Cartier, Quebec, as part of our expansion plans for Rayonier, a forest-products company we acquired in 1968. In our usual exploring to develop the future potential of this new company, Rayonier's management suggested that it had long sought to build such a plant. Only the need for capital had prevented it from going ahead. Millions of acres of virgin timberland—about the size of the state of Tennessee—could be leased in Quebec Province from the Canadian government for very little money, and new technology made it feasible to build a processing plant at the edge of the timberland that could convert the wood to cellulose. The cost of the plant was estimated at $120 million. Once completed, the new modern plant would make Rayonier, which we had acquired for $293 million in ITT common and preferred stock, into the largest cellulose manufacturer in the nation.

"Rayonier's plans were checked and rechecked, the risks and rewards were carefully analyzed, and we decided to go ahead. The usual gauntlet of problems showed up, but they were more or less anticipated. Then we encountered unexpected union problems at the project. To make matters worse, the new technology to recycle chemicals used to process the wood developed serious flaws. But these problems could have been managed in time, I thought. What stumped us was a fundamental miscalculation made at the outset of the project: All those lovely trees out there in the wilderness of Canada's Far North grew to no more than three inches in diameter, because of the extreme cold. The cost of harvesting and transporting them to the plant precluded the possibility of a profitable venture. We could not 'manage' the size of the trees. Ten years after we had started, we had to abandon the project and take a loss of approximately $320 million. A good part of that loss was recouped when we sold off the entire Canadian subsidiary of Rayonier for $355 million. But that $320 million loss could have been averted if someone had actually gone up and looked at those trees before we had begun."

Source: Adaptation from *Managing* by Harold Geneen and Alvin Moscow. Copyright © 1984 by Harold Geneen and Alvin Moscow, Inc. Reprinted by permission of Doubleday & Company, Inc.

Questions

1. What were the control problems ITT faced in Europe?

2. Describe ITT's European structure. Why do you think it evolved that way? Who do you think was responsible: Behn, Scudder, the European managers, or the American managers?

3. What steps did Geneen take to increase his control over the European subsidiaries? Over the corporation as a whole? Classify these according to the four methods of control.

4. What function did the ITT managers' monthly reports serve?

5. What, according to Geneen, was the mistake ITT made with the Rayonier plant? Do you think such problems are common to multinationals?

6. Referring to his style of management, Geneen has written, "It's the numbers straight and clear that matter." Is this management style old-fashioned? Would you expect that ITT still abides by that principle today?

GLOSSARY

Accountability   The requirement that organization members to whom responsibility and authority are delegated be held answerable for results. (p. 307)

Action research   The method through which organizational-development change agents learn what improvements are needed and how the organization can best be aided in making improvements. (p. 364)

Arbitration   A form of compromise in which opposing parties agree to submit to the decision of a third party. (p. 391)

Artificial intelligence (AI)   A computer technology that enables computers to emulate the problem-solving, linguistic, and other capabilities of human beings. (p. 640)

Assembly-line production   A technology in which the product moves through stations where workers or robots complete specific components of its manufacture. (p. 201)

Auditing   The process of verifying the validity of an organization's financial statements and records by outsiders or by members of the organization. (p. 612)

Avoidance learning   Learning to behave in such a way so as to avoid or escape from unpleasant consequences. (p. 430)

Balance sheet   A statement showing a company's assets, liabilities, and net worth at a given time. (p. 594)

BCG matrix   A corporate portfolio management approach that examines the rate of market growth and market share of each of a corporation's business units to help top management develop a balance between those business units that absorb cash and those that provide it. (p. 121)

Behavior modification   An approach to motivation based on the "law of effect"—that behavior which leads to rewarding consequences tends to be repeated, and behavior with negative consequences tends not to be repeated. Thus, managers can change behavior by changing the consequences of that behavior. (p. 422)

Behavioral school   A group of management scholars trained in sociology, psychology, and related fields, who use their diverse knowledge to understand and improve the way organizations are managed. (p. 37)

Board of directors   A group elected or appointed to oversee the management of an organization. (p. 57)

Boundary-spanning roles   Jobs in which individuals acts as liaisons between departments or organizations that are in frequent contact. (p. 267)

Bounded rationality   The concept that managers make the most logical decisions they can within the constraints of limited information and ability. (p. 157)

Break-even analysis   A mathematical procedure for studying the relationships between cost, sales volume, and profit. Also called cost-volume-profit analysis. (p. 597)

Budgets   Formal quantitative statements of the resources allocated to specific programs or projects for a given period. (pp. 90, 599)

Bureaucratic control   A method of control that employs strict rules and regulations to help ensure desired behavior by organizational units—often used by multinational enterprises to control subsidiaries. (p. 669)

Burnout   A state of emotional, mental, and physical exhaustion that results from continued exposure to high stress. (p. 536)

Business unit strategy   The level of strategy that concerns a portion of a company large and distinct enough to be considered a separate business. (p. 120)

Capacity planning   The determination of the amount of products or services that an operations system should be capable of producing. (p. 203)

Career anchor   According to Edgar H. Schein, an

687

occupational self-concept—an individual's sense of the kind of work he or she seeks to pursue and what that type of work implies about the individual. (p. 544)

Career concepts Four basic career patterns—linear, steady state, spiral, and transitory—described by Michael J. Driver. (p. 542)

Career plateau A career stage in which the likelihood of additional hierarchical promotion is very low. (p. 549)

Centralization The extent to which authority is concentrated at the top of the organization. (p. 311)

Chain of command The hierarchy of authority, encompassing all organization members, that extends from top to bottom of the organization. (pp. 73, 246)

Change agent The individual leading or guiding the process of a change in an organizational situation. (p. 355)

Channel The medium of communication between a sender and a receiver. (p. 502)

Charismatic leaders Leaders who, through their personal vision and energy, inspire followers and have a major impact on their organizations. Also called "transformational leaders." (p. 463)

Classical organization theory An early attempt, pioneered by Henri Fayol, to identify the principles and skills that underlie effective management. (p. 33)

Client system The individual, group, or organization that is the target of a planned change. (p. 355)

Closed system A system that does not interact with its environment. (p. 44)

Coercive power The negative side of reward power, based on the influencer's ability to punish the influencee. (pp. 300, 446)

Collaborative management Management through power sharing and subordinate participation; the opposite of hierarchical imposition of authority. (p. 364)

Collective bargaining The process of negotiating and administering agreements between labor and management concerning wages, working conditions, and other aspects of the work environment. (p. 55)

Command group A group composed of a manager and his or her subordinates who interact with each other toward a common objective. (p. 473)

Commissions Groups, whose members are usually appointed by government officials, charged with administrative, regulatory, or legislative tasks. (p. 484)

Committee A formal organizational group, usually relatively long-lived, created to carry out specific organizational tasks. (p. 485)

Communication network A set of channels within an organization or group through which communication travels. (p. 513)

Competition The situation in which two or more parties are striving toward mutually incompatible goals and cannot interfere with each other. (p. 380)

Computer-aided design (CAD) The process of designing products interactively with computers. (p. 202)

Computer-aided manufacturing (CAM) The use of computers to aid in setting up, monitoring, and controlling production equipment. (p. 205)

Computer-assisted instruction (CAI) A training technique in which computers are used to lessen the time necessary for training by instructors and to provide additional help to individual trainees. (p. 338)

Computer-based information system (CBIS) A formal system for providing various levels of management with information through the use of computers. (p. 622)

Computer-integrated manufacturing (CIM) The use of computers to design products, plan how they will be produced, and monitor and control the actual production. Also called CAD/CAM. (p. 205)

Conceptual skill The mental ability to guide and coordinate the organization's activities through the comprehension of the organization as a whole and an understanding of the interdependence of its parts. (p. 15)

Conflict See organizational conflict. See also dysfunctional conflict and functional conflict.

Consensus A method of conflict resolution in which the parties attempt to find the best solution rather than attempting to achieve a victory over each other. (p. 391)

Contingency approach The view that the management technique that best contributes to the attainment of organizational goals might vary in different types of situations or circumstances. (p. 45)

Continuous-process production A production technology that yields long flows of homogeneous materials, such as oil refining. (p. 201)

Continuous reinforcement In behavior modification, a reinforcement schedule in which individuals are immediately and dependably rewarded after a specific behavior. (p. 431)

Controllable variable A part of a problem situation that can be manipulated to achieve a solution. (p. 172)

Controlling The process of monitoring actual organizational activities to see that they conform to planned activities and correcting flaws or deviations. (p. 574)

Cooperation The process of working together to attain mutual objectives. (p. 380)

Coordination The integration of the activities of the separate parts of an organization to accomplish organizational goals. (p. 263)

Corporate-level strategy The strategy created by top management to achieve the entire organization's objectives and to provide a framework for strategy and operations at lower levels of the company. (p. 119)

Corporate portfolio management The process through which the top management of a multi-business company determines the strategic role each of the separate business units will play in the total company's strategy. (p. 120)

Corporate social responsibility The concept that corporations have an obligation to act for the good of society. (p. 53)

Critical path method (CPM) A network analysis technique used to schedule and control work on projects for which the time required to complete tasks is known fairly precisely. (p. 187)

Culture See organizational culture.

Culture control A method of control that emphasizes implicit and informal direction based on a broad company culture; associated with many large Japanese companies. (p. 669)

Data Raw, unanalyzed facts, figures, and events. (p. 620)

Decentralization The delegation of power and authority from higher to lower levels of the organization, often accomplished by the creation of small, self-contained organizational units. (pp. 311, 361)

Decision making The process of identifying and selecting a course of action to solve a specific problem. (pp. 87, 141)

Decision support system (DSS) An easily accessible microcomputer-based information system that aids individual managers in planning and decision making. (pp. 144, 623)

Decoding The interpretation and translation of a message into meaningful information. (p. 503)

Delegation The act of assigning formal authority and responsibility for completion of specific activities to a subordinate. (p. 306)

Delphi method A survey of expert opinion that includes each expert's review of the others' ideas. (p. 184)

Departmentalization The grouping into departments of work activities that are similar and logically connected. (p. 234)

Descriptive model A management science model that provides information on relationships between variables but does not supply solutions to problems. See normative model. (p. 174)

Dialectical inquiry method A method of analysis in which a decision maker determines and negates his or her assumptions, and then creates "counter solutions" based on the negative assumptions. (p. 149)

Differential rate system Frederick W. Taylor's compensation system involving the payment of higher wages to more efficient workers. (p. 29)

Direct-action environment Elements of the environment that directly influence the organization. (p. 54)

Dissatisfiers Factors that do not cause job satisfaction but may result in dissatisfaction, including working conditions, salaries, and company policy. (p. 426)

Division of work The breakdown of a complex task into components so that individuals are responsible for a limited set of activities instead of the task as a whole. (p. 234)

Dysfunctional conflict Any conflict that results in decreased efficiency and greater factionalism within the organization. (p. 387)

Effectiveness The ability to determine appropriate objectives: "doing the right things." (p. 9)

Efficiency The ability to minimize the use of resources in achieving organizational objectives: "doing things right." (p. 9)

Electronic data processing (EDP) Storage and analysis of data using computers. (p. 622)

Electronic mail Data and text circulated through interlinked computers. (p. 520)

Encoding The translation of information into a series of symbols for communication. (p. 502)

Entrepreneur The originator of a new business venture. Also, as described by Henry Mintzberg, a decisional role in which managers attempt to improve their units by initiating productive change voluntarily. (p. 17)

Equity theory A theory of job motivation emphasizing the role played by an individual's belief in the equity or fairness of rewards and punishments in determining his or her performance and satisfaction. Also called inequity theory. (p. 437)

Ethnocentric The attitude that the home country is superior to other countries and that methods which work at home will work elsewhere. (p. 657)

Expectancy approach   A model of motivation specifying that effort to achieve high performance is a function of the perceived likelihood that high performance can be achieved and will be rewarded if achieved, and that the reward will be worth the effort expended. (p. 433)

Expert power   Power based on the belief or understanding that the influencer has specific knowledge or relevant expertise which the influencee does not. (pp. 300, 446)

Expert system (ES)   An advanced computer program that emulates the problem-solving abilities of human experts through the use of artificial intelligence. (pp. 170, 623)

External audit   The check of a firm's financial statements and records for validity, accuracy, and completeness by accounting personnel from outside the organization. (p. 612)

External environment   The environment outside the organization (p. 54)

Extinction   In behavior modification, withholding reinforcement following an undesired behavior in the belief that such behavior will eventually disappear if not reinforced. (p. 430)

Fear of failure   The fear of not reaching organizational or personal goals and of potential public embarrassment if such failures are recognized. (p. 425)

Fear of success   Fear of the burden and stress that may accompany success and the envy and dislike it may generate in others. (p. 425)

Feedback (interpersonal)   The reversal of the communication process that occurs when the receiver expresses his or her reaction to the sender's message. (p. 504)

Feedback (job-based)   The part of system control in which the results of actions are returned to the individual, allowing work procedures to be analyzed and corrected. (p. 45)

Financial budgets   Budgets that detail how the organization intends to spend money in the budget period and where that money will come from. (p. 604)

Financial statements   Statements showing, in monetary terms, flow of resources, goods, and services to, within, and from the organization. (p. 593)

First-line managers   Managers who are responsible for the work of operating employees only and do not supervise other managers. They are the "first" or lowest level of managers in the organizational hierarchy. (p. 11)

Forecasting   The attempt, using specific techniques, to predict outcomes and project future trends. (p. 62)

Formal authority   Power rooted in the general understanding that specific individuals or groups have the right to exert influence within certain limits by virtue of their position within the organization. Also called legitimate power. (pp. 298, 459)

Formal groups   Any group created by organizational management that is directed toward achieving specific objectives. (p. 472)

Function layout   The organizing of physical production arrangements to foster a specific purpose, such as storage or sales. (p. 207)

Functional conflict   Any conflict that has positive, constructive, and nondivisive results. (p. 387)

Functional-level strategy   The level of strategy that establishes a framework for the management of organizational functions, such as marketing or production, so that they conform to the business-unit-level strategy. (p. 120)

Functional manager   A manager responsible for just one organizational activity, such as finance or human resource management. (p. 11)

Functional organization   A form of departmentalization in which everyone engaged in one functional activity, such as marketing or finance, is grouped into one unit. (p. 248)

Game theory   A method of analyzing and predicting the behavior of rational people in competitive and conflict situations. (p. 175)

Gantt chart   A graphic method of planning and control that allows a manager to view the starting and ending dates for various tasks. (p. 186)

General manager   The individual responsible for all activities, such as production, sales, marketing, and finance, for a complex unit like a company or subsidiary. (p. 11)

Geocentric   The attitude that accepts both similarities and differences among countries, and takes a balanced view toward the management of operations in every nation. (p. 657)

Goal   The basic direction of an organization—its purpose, mission, and objectives. (pp. 3, 111)

Grapevine chain   The various paths through which informal communication is passed through an organization; includes the "single-strand," "gossip," "probability," and "cluster" chains. (p. 516)

Group cohesiveness   The degree of solidarity and positive feeling held by individuals toward their group. (p. 477)

Group decision support system (GDSS)   The use of a computerized information system in a group meeting to make more efficient use of information for group decisions. (pp. 145, 638)

Hawthorne effect   The possibility that workers who receive special attention will perform better simply because they received that attention: one interpretation of Elton Mayo and his colleagues' studies. (p. 39)

Human resource audit   The analysis and appraisal of the organization's current human resources. (p. 323)

Human resource information system (HRIS)   A system, frequently computerized, for collecting, storing, maintaining, retrieving, and validating data concerning an organization's personnel. (p. 346)

Human resource planning   Planning for the future personnel needs of an organization, taking into account both internal activities and factors in the external environment. (p. 319)

Human skill   The ability to work with, communicate with, and motivate individuals or groups. (p. 15)

Implementation (in MS)   The use of methods or concepts developed in a management science effort to solve problems. Also see installation and internalization (in MS). (p. 178)

Income statement   A summary of the financial performance of a company over a certain interval, such as a quarter or year. (p. 595)

Incremental adjustment   A method of managerial problem solving in which each successive action represents only a small change from existing activities. (p. 156)

Indirect-action environment   Those elements of the external environment that affect the climate in which the operations of the organization take place, including the economy and the political situation, but which do not affect the organization directly. (p. 54)

Induction and orientation   Activities intended to ease an individual's entrance into an organization through introducing the individual to the organization and providing information on the organization. (p. 320)

Influence   Any actions or examples of behavior that cause a change in attitude or behavior of another person or group. (p. 298)

Informal communication   The grapevine, or any communication within the organization that is not officially sanctioned. (p. 516)

Informal groups   Unofficial groups that are created by members of an organization without the express encouragement of managers. (p. 472)

Informal organization   The undocumented and officially unrecognized relationships between members of an organization that inevitably emerge out of the personal and group needs of employees. (p. 255)

Information ownership   The possession by certain individuals of unique information and knowledge concerning their work. (p. 513)

Inputs   Resources from the environment that enter any system, such as an organization. (p. 54)

Installation (in MS)   The part of a management science effort in which a mathematical model is developed and used with actual data. See also implementation and internalization (in MS). (p. 178)

Integration   The degree to which employees of various departments work together in a unified way. (p. 265)

Internal audit   The monitoring from within an organization of the validity, accuracy, and completeness of its financial statements and records. (p. 613)

Internal environment   Everything within the organization, including its workers, managers, working conditions, and culture. (p. 53)

Internalization (in MS)   The third dimension of a management science effort in which the concepts and methodology of management science become part of the thinking of managers, allowing them to recognize appropriate times to use these techniques. Also see implementation and installation (in MS). (p. 178)

Job depth   The amount of autonomy an individual possesses in performing his or her work. (p. 237)

Job enlargement   The combining of various operations at a similar level into one job to provide more variety for workers and thus increase motivation and satisfaction. An increase in job scope. (p. 240)

Job enrichment   The combining of several activities from a vertical cross section of the organization into one job to provide the worker with more autonomy and responsibility. An increase in job depth. (p. 241)

Job scope   The number of separate operations a particular job requires and the frequency with which the job cycle must be repeated. (p. 237)

Job-shop production   The production of small batches of custom-made products. (p. 201)

Job specialization   The division of work into standardized, simplified tasks. (p. 235)

Judgmental forecasting   A forecasting technique that utilizes intentions and opinions as its raw data. (p. 182)

Just-in-time (JIT) inventory   A production system that eliminates inactive production inventory through delivery to the production line of parts and supplies exactly when they are needed. Also called *kanban*. (p. 212)

Large batch/mass production   The production of large quantities of similar items, often on an assembly line. (p. 281)

Lateral communication   Communication between departments of an organization that generally follows the work flow, thus providing a direct channel for coordination and problem solving. (p. 516)

Lateral relationship   A relationship that cuts across the chain of command, allowing direct contact between members of different departments. Examples include some committees, liaison roles, and integrating roles. (p. 267)

Leader-member relations   The quality of the interaction between a leader and his or her subordinates; according to Fred Fiedler, the most important influence on the manager's power. (p. 456)

Leadership   The process of directing and inspiring workers to perform the task-related activities of the group. (p. 445)

Leadership functions   The group maintenance and task-related activities that must be performed by the leader, or someone else, for a group to perform effectively. (p. 448)

Leadership styles   The various patterns of behavior favored by leaders during the process of directing and influencing workers. (p. 448)

Leading   The process of directing and influencing task-related activities of organization members. (p. 4)

Legitimate power   See formal authority.

Line   Those managers and workers directly responsible, throughout the chain of command, for achieving organizational goals. (p. 303)

Linear programming model   A mathematical model used to determine the optimum allocation of limited resources to attain a goal. (p. 174)

Local area network (LAN)   An intraorganizational, user-oriented computer network that allows users to communicate with each other and to share facilities for data storage. (p. 638)

Logical incrementalism   A synthesis of the planning, adaptive, and entrepreneurial modes of strategy making in which top management makes small, successive changes in organizational strategy using the strategy mode best suited to each situation. (p. 114)

Management   The process of planning, organizing, leading, and controlling the work of organization members and of using all available organizational resources to reach stated organizational goals. (p. 4)

Management by objectives (MBO)   A formal set of procedures that establishes and reviews progress toward common goals for managers and subordinates. (p. 95)

Management information system (MIS)   A formal, usually computerized, structure for providing management with information, often through an MIS department. (pp. 144, 622)

Management science (MS)   Mathematical techniques for modeling, analysis, and solution of management problems. Also called operations research. (p. 169)

Management science school   A group of management scholars trained in quantitative methods who develop mathematical techniques for analyzing and solving organizational problems. (p. 42)

Managerial performance   The measure of how efficient and effective a manager is; how well he or she determines and achieves appropriate objectives. (p. 9)

Managers   Individuals who plan, organize, lead, and control other individuals in the process of pursuing organizational goals. (p. 6)

Matrix organization   An organizational structure in which each employee reports to both a functional or divisional manager and to a project or group manager. (p. 252)

Mentors   Individuals who pass on the benefits of their knowledge to other individuals who are usually younger and less experienced. (p. 547)

Message   The encoded information sent by the sender to the receiver. (p. 502)

Middle managers   Managers in the midrange of the organizational hierarchy; they are responsible for other managers and sometimes for some operating employees. (p. 11)

Milestone scheduling   A technique that adds detail and precision to the Gantt Chart by marking particular dates by which the various phases of the entire project are to be completed. (p. 186)

Mission   The unique reason for an organization's existence that makes it different from all others. (p. 111)

Motivation   The factors that cause, channel, and sustain an individual's behavior. (p. 417)

Multinational enterprise (MNE)   A large corporation with operations and divisions spread over many countries but controlled by one headquarters. (p. 657)

Network analysis   A technique used for scheduling

complex projects that contain interrelationships between activities or events. (p. 187)

Networking   The linking of groups of computers, either intraorganizationally or interorganizationally, so that they can communicate with each other and share common data bases and resources. (p. 638)

Noise   Anything that confuses, disturbs, diminishes, or interferes with communication. (p. 503)

Nonprogrammed decisions   Specific solutions created through an unstructured process to deal with non-routine problems. (p. 143)

Normative model   A model that prescribes a solution to a problem. (p. 174)

Objectives   The targeted goals of an organization toward which resources and efforts are channeled. (p. 98)

One-way communication   Any communication from the sender without feedback from the receiver. (p. 504)

Open system   A system that interacts with its environment. (p. 44)

Operating budgets   Budgets that indicate expected consumption of resources over the budget period, usually listing both physical quantities and costs. (p. 604)

Operational plans   Plans that detail the implementation of strategic plans. (p. 89)

Operations   The production activities of an organization. (p. 197)

Operations management   The planning, organizing, directing, and controlling of an organization's production/operations system. (p. 198)

Operations research   See management science.

Operations system   The organizational system or subsystem whose function is to transform inputs into desired outputs. (p. 199)

Organizational conflict   Disagreement between individuals or groups within the organization stemming from the need to share scarce resources or engage in interdependent work activities, or from differing statuses, goals, or cultures. See also dysfunctional and functional conflict. (p. 379)

Organizational culture   The set of important understandings, such as norms, values, attitudes, and beliefs, shared by organizational members. (p. 371)

Organizational design   The determination of the organizational structure that is most appropriate for the strategy, people, technology, and tasks of the organization. (p. 272)

Organizational development   A long-range effort supported by top management to increase an organi-zation's problem-solving and renewal processes through effective management of organizational culture. (p. 363)

Organizational goals   The purpose, mission, and objectives that are the reason for an organization's existence and that form the basis of its strategy. (p. 111)

Organizational life cycle   The pattern of developmental changes that typically occurs in organizations. (p. 285)

Organizational structure   The arrangement and interrelationship of the various component parts and positions of a company. (p. 243)

Organization chart   A diagram of an organization's structure, showing the functions, departments, or positions of the organization and how they are related. (p. 246)

Organizing   The process of arranging an organization's structure and coordinating its managerial practices and use of resources to achieve its goals. (p. 4)

Orientation   See induction and orientation.

Outputs   Transformed inputs that are returned to the external environment as products or services. (p. 54)

Overload   The condition of being unable to meet all of the various performance expectations held by oneself and others. See qualitative overload and quantitative overload. (p. 536)

Partial reinforcement   In behavior modification, a schedule of reinforcement in which rewards are given intermittently. (p. 431)

Path-goal model of leadership   A leadership theory emphasizing the leader's role in clarifying for subordinates how they can achieve high performance and its associated rewards. (p. 458)

Performance   The quantity and quality of the work accomplished by an individual, group, or organization. (p. 477)

Performance appraisal   The process of evaluating an individual's performance by comparing it to existing standards or objectives. (p. 321)

Personal staff   Assistants who aid managers in performing their work. (p. 304)

Persuasion   A process by which individuals or groups attempt to get others to accept their fixed point of view. (p. 482)

Planning   The process of establishing objectives and suitable courses of action before taking action. (p. 4)

Policy   A standing plan that establishes general guidelines for decision making. (p. 91)

Polycentric   The attitude that all countries are different and difficult to understand; therefore, foreign offices must be relied on to know what works best in their own countries. (p. 657)

Position power The power, according to Fred Fiedler, that is inherent in the formal position the leader holds. This power may be great or small, depending upon the specific position. (p. 457)

Positive reinforcement In behavior modification, any consequence that results in the repetition of a given behavior. (p. 430)

Post-action control A control method that uses the results of a completed action to guide changes in future activities. (p. 549)

Power The ability to exert influence; that is, the ability to change the attitudes or behavior of individuals or groups. (p. 298)

Pre-action controls A control method that budgets for all necessary material, financial, and human resources before an action is begun. (p. 578)

Procedure A standing plan of detailed guidelines for handling organizational actions that occur regularly. (p. 91)

Process consultation A technique by which consultants help organization members understand and change the ways they work together. (p. 366)

Process production The continuous manufacture of products that are sold by volume or weight, such as chemicals. (p. 281)

Production The transformation of organizational resources into finished goods and services. (p. 197)

Productivity A measure of the performance of a worker or an operations system relative to resource utilization: output divided by input. (p. 215)

Product or market organizational structure The organization of a company by divisions that brings together all those involved with a certain type of product or customer. (p. 247)

Program A single-use plan that covers a relatively large set of organizational activities and specifies major steps, their order and timing, and unit responsible for each step. (p. 90)

Program evaluation and review technique (PERT) A network analysis technique, using estimates of the time required to complete tasks, which is used to schedule and control projects for which task completion times cannot be predicted fairly precisely. (p. 187)

Programmed decisions Solutions to routine problems determined by rule, procedure, or habit. (p. 142)

Purpose The primary role of an organization in society; the broad aim to produce a good or service. (p. 111)

Qualitative forecasting A judgment-based forecasting technique used when hard data are scarce or difficult to use. (p. 182)

Qualitative overload The situation that occurs when an individual does not have the abilities or skills necessary for the satisfactory completion of a task. (p. 536)

Quality circle Periodic meetings of labor and management personnel to solve quality-control and productivity problems. (p. 214)

Quality control The process of ensuring that goods and services meet predetermined standards. (p. 213)

Quantitative forecasting Forecasting techniques used when enough hard data exist to specify relationships between variables. (p. 183)

Quantitative overloading The situation that occurs when an individual is given more tasks than he or she can accomplish in a given time. (p. 536)

Ratio analysis The process of stating key figures from an organization's financial statements as fractions or percentages of one another to assist in the assessment of its financial performance or condition. (p. 596)

Realistic job preview (RJP) A description provided by the organization to applicants and new employees that gives both the positive and negative aspects of the job. (p. 529)

Reality shock syndrome An individual's reaction to the difference between high job expectations and the frustrating day-to-day realities of the workplace. (p. 528)

Receiver The individual whose senses perceive the sender's message. (p. 503)

Recruitment The development of a pool of job candidates in accordance with a human resource plan. (p. 320)

Redundancy Repeating or restating a message to ensure its reception or to reinforce its impact. (p. 510)

Reference group A group with whom individuals identify and compare themselves. (p. 472)

Referent power Power based on the desire of the influencee to be like or identify with the influencer. (pp. 300, 446)

Refreezing Transforming a new behavior pattern into the norm through reinforcement and supporting mechanisms. (p. 357)

Replacement chart A chart that diagrams an organization's positions, showing the incumbents, likely future candidates, and readiness of candidates to enter those positions. (p. 303)

Responsibility center   Any organizational unit that is headed by a manager responsible for the unit's activities; major types include revenue, expense, profit, and investment centers. (p. 599)

Reward system   System of performance motivation through wage increases, bonuses, promotions, and so on. (p. 427)

Role conflict   Situation in which an individual is confronted by two or more incompatible demands. (p. 534)

Role perception   The individual's understanding of the behaviors needed to accomplish a task or perform a job. (p. 417)

Rules   Standing plans that detail specific actions to be taken in a given situation. (p. 91)

Satisfiers   Positive motivating factors in the work environment, including achievement, responsibility, recognition, and advancement. (p. 426)

Scalar principle   The concept that a clear line of authority through the organization must exist if delegation is to work successfully. (p. 307)

Scenario construction   The building of a logical, hypothetical description of sequences of events so as to examine the dynamics of alternative sets of conditions. (p. 184)

Scientific management   A management approach, formulated by Frederick Taylor and others between 1890 and 1930, that sought to determine scientifically the best methods for performing any task and for selecting, training, and motivating workers. (p. 28)

Sender   The initiator of a communication. (p. 502)

Sensitivity training   An early personal growth technique, at one time fairly widespread in organizational development efforts, that emphasizes increased sensitivity in interpersonal relationships. (p. 366)

Separation (in organizational conflict)   A conflict resolution technique in which parties on opposite sides of a conflict are kept apart until they agree to a solution. (p. 391)

Simulation models   Models (usually computerized) of situations that are too complex for standard mathematical equations to describe effectively. (p. 175)

Single-use plans   Detailed courses of action used once or only occasionally to solve problems that do not occur repeatedly. (p. 90)

Situational leadership theory   An approach to leadership developed by Paul Hersey and Kenneth H. Blanchard that describes how leaders should adjust their leadership style in response to their subordinates' evolving desire for achievement, experience, ability, and willingness to accept responsibility. (p. 460)

Small batch production   The manufacture of products in small quantities and in various stages. (p. 281)

Span of management   The number of subordinates who report to a given manager. (p. 269)

Sponsor   A higher-level organizational ally who can help a manager achieve success in the organization. (p. 547)

Staff   The individuals or groups who provide line managers with advice and services. (p. 304)

Staffing   The process of recruiting, placing, training, and developing personnel. (p. 319)

Stakeholders   Those groups or individuals who are directly or indirectly affected by the organization's pursuit of its goals. (p. 53)

Standing committees   Permanent committees that exist to respond to a continuing organizational need. (p. 484)

Standing plans   An established set of decisions used by managers to deal with recurring or organizational activities; major types are policies, procedures, and rules. (p. 90)

Steering controls   Controls designed to detect any deviation from a predetermined standard and to allow corrections to be made prior to the completion of a specific sequence of actions. Also known as feedforward controls. (p. 579)

Stockholders   Owners of corporate stocks. Also called shareholders. (p. 53)

Strategic business unit (SBU)   A grouping of business activities within a multibusiness corporation that generate closely related products or services; equivalent to a single-business company. (p. 120)

Strategic control   The process of checking strategy implementation progress against the strategic plan at periodic or critical intervals to determine if the corporation is moving toward its strategic objectives. (p. 128)

Strategic planning   The active formulation by top management of an organization's objectives and the definition of strategies for achieving them. (p. 115)

Strategic plans   Comprehensive plans designed to define and achieve the long-term objectives of the organization. (p. 89)

Strategy   The broad program for defining and achieving an organization's objectives; the organization's response to its environment over time. (p. 111)

Stress   The tension and pressure that result when an

individual views a situation as presenting a demand that threatens to exceed his or her capabilities and resources. (p. 535)

Stressors   The sources of tension and pressure that create stress. (p. 535)

Structure   The arrangement and interrelationships of the components of an organization. (p. 243)

Subsystems   Those parts comprising the whole system. (p. 44)

Superordinate goals   Higher-level goals that encompass lower-level goals; also the significant meanings or guiding concepts that an organization imbues in its members. (p. 391)

Synergy   The situation in which the whole is greater than its parts. In organizational terms, the fact that departments that interact cooperatively can be more productive than if they operate in isolation. (p. 44)

System boundary   The boundary that separates each system from its environment. It is rigid in a closed system, flexible in an open system. (p. 45)

Systems approach   View of the organization as a unified, directed system of interrelated parts. (p. 44)

Task force   A temporary group formed to address a specific problem. (p. 483)

Task structure   A work situation variable that, according to Fred Fiedler, helps determine a manager's power. In structured tasks, managers automatically have high power; in unstructured tasks, the manager's power is diminished. (p. 456)

Team building   A method of improving organizational effectiveness at the team level by diagnosing barriers to team performance and improving interteam relationships and task accomplishment. (p. 367)

Telecommuting   The use of computers to enable individuals to work at home, sending only the work (via telephone or data network) to the workplace. (p. 520)

Theory X   The assumptions that the average employee dislikes work, is lazy, has little ambition, and must be directed, coerced, or threatened with punishment to perform adequately. (p. 105)

Theory Y   The assumption that the average person can enjoy work, be committed to objectives, and seek responsibility. (p. 104)

Theory Z   According to William Ouchi, the management belief that the key to productivity and quality is the development and participation of all employees. (p. 220)

Three-position plan   A scientific management concept developed by Frank and Lillian Gilbreth in which each worker would simultaneously do his or her job, prepare for the next job, and train his or her future replacement. (p. 31)

Transactional analysis   An approach to improving interpersonal effectiveness, sometimes used in organizational development efforts, that concentrates on the styles and content of communication. (p. 366)

Transformational leaders   See charismatic leaders.

Uncontrollable variable   A part of a problem situation that cannot be manipulated in the short run and thus constrains the set of feasible solutions. (p. 172)

Underloading   Stress caused when a worker does not have enough work to do, resulting in boredom and monotony. (p. 536)

Unfreezing   Making the need for change so obvious that the individual, group, or organization can readily see and accept that change must occur. (p. 357)

Unit production   The production of individual goods or services that are tailored to a customer's specifications. (p. 281)

Valence   The value or motivating strength of a reward to the individual. (p. 434)

Vertical communication   Any communication that moves up or down the chain of command. (p. 515)

Vertical information system   Means through which data are transmitted up and down the managerial hierarchy. (p. 267)

Video conferencing   Meetings held via telecommunications, usually by satellite television transmission, rather than by face-to-face contact. (p. 520)

Waiting-line model (queuing)   A management science technique for determining the most appropriate number of servicing units in situations with waiting lines. (p. 174)

Work-flow layout   Spatial arrangement of production facilities. (p. 207)

Yes/no control   Control method involving a screening process in which approval of specific aspects of a procedure must be granted before operations are allowed to continue. (p. 579)

Zero-base budgeting (ZBB)   A budgeting approach in which all of the organization's activities, existing ones and proposed new ones, are considered on an equal footing in resource allocation decisions, rather than using the previous year's budget as a starting point. (p. 608)

COMPANY INDEX

NAME INDEX

698

SUBJECT INDEX

Abilities: career planning analysis, 552; of managers, 34; and motivation, 417. *See also* Skills

Absenteeism: after job redesign, 242; under Korean management, 676; and leadership style, 450

Acceptance: of authority, 299; of control system, 587; criterion for effective decisions, 155, 157–58; of group solution, 480

Acceptance sampling, 214

Access discrimination, 330

Accommodation: in dual-career couples, 555; in management-labor relations, 394, 395

Accountability: and conflict reduction, 393; and delegation of authority, 307

Accuracy: control system characteristic, 586; of vertical communication, 515

Achievement: American obsession with, 663; and linear career concept, 542; as satisfier, 426

Achievement need, and entrepreneurial behavior, 424–25

Action research, 364–65

Adaptability, of organizational structure, 256. *See also* Flexibility

Adaptive mode, of strategy making, 113, 114

Ad hoc groups, 480–83

Adulthood, transitions and crises, 539–40

Aerospace industry: computer simulation training, 175; international ventures, 653; matrix organizations, 252; use of PERT, 187

Affiliation: need for, 424–25; union benefit, 394

Affirmative action (AA), 329, 330, 345; for women, 557

Africa, 72

Age discrimination, 329, 345

Age Discrimination in Employment Act of 1967, 329, 343

Aggression: and international expansion, 653–54; response to MIS implementation, 630, 631

Agreement: to overcome resistance to change, 359 *tab.*, premature, in committees, 487

AI. *See* Artificial intelligence

Airline industry: computerized reservation systems, 639; productivity problems, 216

Alcohol abuse. *See* Substance abuse

Algonkian tribes, 297

Alienation: due to division of work, 236–37; and job scope, 240

Allocation problems, applying MS to, 176. *See also* Resource allocation

Alternatives: capacity planning, 202; comparing with PERT and CPM, 191; in problem solving, 153–54, 158, 481; process selection, 204; strategic, 127

Alternative work schedules, 241

Ambiguity: as barrier to exposing unethical behavior, 73–74; as source of conflict, 384–85

American Management Associations (AMA), 340, 518

Americans, guidelines on, for foreigners, 663

American Tobacco v. *Patterson*, 349 *n.* 15

American Trucking Association, 590

Analysis: emphasis of management education, 20; as function of managers, 7–8; in MS, 173; in strategic planning, 124–25, 126; of undesirable behavior, 432

Antidiscrimination laws, 60, 327–31

Antipollution laws, 60, 279, 354

Anxiety: over budget development, 603–4; in early career, 534; due to MIS implementation, 630–31; of new employees, 337. *See also* Stress

Application form, 332

Apprentices: career role, 547; training of, 338. *See also* New employees

Arbitration, 391

Artificial intelligence (AI): auditing applications, 614; and expert systems, 623, 640; future of, 642, 644. *See also* Expert systems

Assembly-line production, 201–2; effect on motivation, 426; productivity standards, 583; scientific management contributions, 28, 32; span of management concerns, 283; as technological choice, 204; and worker alienation, 237

Assessment centers, 336

Assumptions: about behavior in organizations, 434; in break-even analysis, 597–98; in motivation theories, 420 *tab.*; of OD practitioners, 365–66

Attitudes: approaches to changing, 362; effect on productivity, 217, 219; as force for change, 354; toward internationalization, 657; toward women, 557

Auditape, 614

Auditing, 612–14; and budget revision, 603; computer software, 614; of corporate social performance, 67–69; external, 612–13; and functional staff authority, 305; of human resources, 323–24; internal, 613

Australia, 666, 680

Authoritarian management: decision-making style, 159, 162; effectiveness factors, 458; and manager characteristics, 454; on Managerial Grid, 450; in the military, 449; and motivation, 276; removing, to stimulate conflict, 388; and subordinate preferences, 459; use in emergencies, 452

Authority: in Algonkian culture, 297; basis of, 298–99; changing attitudes toward, 354; of committees, 488; and conformity, 476–77; and control, 577, 584; decentralization of, 311–14; defined, 298; delegation of, 306–11; dispersion of, in committees, 487; dual, in matrix organizations, 252; functional, of staff, 305; and legitimate power, 300; in line and staff positions, 302–5, 392; of linking manager, 268; need for, 297; principle of, 35; response of creative people to, 398

Authority structure: and communication, 512–13; and leadership style, 459. *See also* Chain of command; Management hier-archy

Automated Guided Vehicle Systems (AGVS), 205

Automation: of information systems, 643 (*see also* Computer-based information systems); and human resource planning, 322; inappropriate use by MNEs, 665; and motivation, 438; robotization, 205, 644; as source of organizational change, 353–54. *See also* Computers; Technological advances

Automobile industry: CAD techniques, 202; competition, 56; failure to respond to change, 116–17; use of robots, 205

Automotive Industry Action Group, 639

Autonomy: as career anchor, 545; as core job dimension, 237–38, 239; in excellently managed companies, 10; in implementation of MBO, 99; increasing through job enrichment, 241, 242 *tab.*; vs. need for control, 577–78; in self-managed groups, 463; and supervisory behavior, 238

Avoidance: as barrier to problem solving, 155, 156; to resolve conflict, 390; response to MIS implementation, 630, 631; of uncertainty, 670, 671

Avoidance learning, 430

Background investigation, 332

Balance sheet, 594–95

Balance sheet budgets, 606–7

Banking industry: deregulation of, 373; process selection, 205

BCG matrix, 121–22, 136 *n.* 26

Behavior: changes due to intergroup conflict, 385; in defensive vs. supportive communication, 510–12; driving and restraining forces, 356; expectancy view, 434; impact of past consequences on, 428–32; of leaders, 446, 448–52; modeling, 339; "phony," in employment interview, 334; rules for modifying, 431–32; three-step change process, 327

Behavioral modification theory: of leadership, 462–63; of motivation, 422, 429–32

Behavioral rating, 343

Behavioral school, 37–41; contributions and limitations, 41; evolution of theories, 37–38; human relations movement, 38–39; industrial psychology, 38; present-day importance, 42–43; view of bureaucracy, 274; view of conflict, 380

Belgium, 682

Bhopal, India, disaster, 77–78, 353, 661

Bias, in performance appraisal, 344. *See also* Discrimination

Big bang approaches, 216

Bill of Rights, 301

Biofeedback, for stress reduction, 538

Blacks. *See* Minorities

Boards, 484–85; of directors, 57, 484

Bonuses: for international managers, 667; in Korean management, 677; as motivators, 427

Bootstrapping forecasting methods, 182 *tab.*

703

management-labor negotiations, 396; in matrix organizations, 255; planning need, 87

Flextime, 241

Food and Drug Administration (FDA), 55, 72

Forced-distribution system, for performance appraisal, 343

Force-field theory, 356, 357 *fig.*, 611

Fordham Graduate School of Business Administration, 562 *n.* 44

Forecasting: and budgeting, 601; and capacity planning, 202; choosing appropriate techniques, 185; with DSS, 637; of economic and sales information, 181–83; of environmental trends, 62; in human resource planning, 323; by MNEs, 664–65; and operations planning, 210–11; purposes, 180–81; and strategic planning, 125; of technological change, 183–85

Foreign competition, influence on staffing, 319

Foreign Corrupt Practices Act of 1977, 61, 663

Foreign currency rates, forecasting, 662, 664–65

Foreign trade agents, 656

Formal appraisal, 342–43. *See also* Performance appraisal

Formal authority: basis of, 298–99; defined, 298; delegation of, 306–11; in line and staff position, 302–5; of linking manager, 268. *See also* Authority

Formal groups: guidelines for effectiveness, 488–91; types, 472, 473, 483–84

Formalization stage, in organizational life cycle, 285, 286 *tab.*

Formal organization: communication channels, 512; structure, 247

Fortune, 413

Fortune 500, 136 *n.* 24, 567

Fortune 1000, 136 *n.* 24

Framework, 637

France, 60, 680, 682

Functional authority, 305

Functional competence, career anchor, 544, 545

Functional conflict, 381, 386

Functional-level strategy, 128

Functional managers, 11

Functional organizational structure, 247, 248–49

Fundamental attribution error, 431

Gallup polls, 67, 77 *n.* 36

Game theory, 175, 177

Gantt chart, 31, 186, 187 *fig.*

General managers, 11–12

General recruiting, 324

General systems theory, 44–45

Geocentric attitudes 657

Geography: division by, 249, 250 *fig.*; and pressure group influence, 60; and span of management, 271–72

Germany, 680, 682

Global strategic planning, 666

Goal achievement: and budgeting, 612; in Grid OD, 370; as management aim, 4; in MBO, 103

Goals: and achievement need, 425; career planning analysis, 552; of committees, 488; conflicting, 383; as coordination mechanism, 267; helping individuals to establish, 94; organizing to attain, 233; planning steps, 88; prioritizing, 7; reluctance to establish, 93–94; strategic, 111–12; superordinate, 389, 391; transcendent, 464

Goal setting: and budgeting, 612; effect on performance, 100, 107 *n.* 23; in Grid OD, 370; in MBO, 98–99, 100; planning step, 88; in strategic planning, 123

Government, external environment component, 60. *See also* Federal government; Government regulation

Government agencies, 56–57

Government regulation: and AT&T breakup, 409, 413; business opposition to, 56–57, 62; cost of resisting, 354; as ethical guideline, 72; in foreign countries, 665; Friedman's view, 64; historical trends, 60; and human resource management, 323, 327–31, 346; of interorganizational conflict, 383; and job design, 208; of MNEs, 663; of monopolies, 56; productivity effects, 219. *See also* Deregulation

Grapevine, 475, 516–17, 622

Graphic rating, in performance appraisal, 343

Gratification, as output, 199

Great Britain. *See* United Kingdom

Grid OD, 367, 369–70, 375 *n.* 23

Gross national product (GNP), of various nations compared to large MNEs, 659 *tab.*

Group cohesiveness: effect on members, 477; and group performance, 477–78

Group decision support systems (GDSS), 145, 638

Group goals, 301

Group maintenance function, 448, 476

Group norms: conformity to, 476–77; and performance, 478

Groups, 471–92; characteristics of, 475–77; in collectivist societies, 670; committees and task forces, 483–88; communication structures, 513–15; conflict between, 382; conflict with individuals, 382; defined, 472; effective and ineffective, 483 *tab.*; Follett's view, 36–37; formal, 473; guidelines for effectiveness, 488–90; informal, 255, 473–75; loyalty to, as barrier to exposing unethical behavior, 73; OD assumptions, 365; OD techniques, 366; performance appraisal by, 342; performance of, 477–79; problem solving in, 479–83; self-managed, 463; stimulating creativity in, 399–400; team-building techniques, 367–69; types, 472. *See also* Committees; Task forces; Work groups

Groupthink, 405 *n.* 13, 487

Growth. *See* Organizational growth; Personal growth

Halo effect, 344

Handicapped persons, employment rights, 329

Harvard Business School, 562 *n.* 44

Harvard University, 39, 213

Hawthorne effect, 38–39, 49 *n.* 16

Health: physical examination of candidates, 333; stress effects, 536, 537, 538

Hedging, in foreign exchange rates, 664–65

Hierarchical boundaries, 545

Hierarchy: of business activism, 65; of human needs, 40–41, 423–24; of organizational plans, 89; principle of, 35. *See also* Management hierarchy

High technology: advantages of self-managed groups, 463; staffing for, 319. *See also* Computer revolution; Expert systems; Technological advances

Hiring. *See* Selection

Hiring specification, 324

Hispanics. *See* Minorities

Honesty: and loyalty, 533; in realistic job preview, 529. *See also* Ethics

Horizontal decentralization, 244

Hospitals: conflict in, 387; effect of Medicaid, 279; interorganizational networking, 639; use of MBO, 98

HRIS. *See* Human resource information systems

Human needs: effect of transformational leaders on, 464; hierarchy of, 40–41, 423–24; and motivation, 419–21, 434

Human relations movement, 38–40; contributions and limitations, 39–40; criticism of bureaucracy, 274; Hawthorne experiments, 38–39; motivation model, 418–19, 420 *tab.*

Human resources department: evaluating effectiveness of, 346–47; involvement in OD, 371; responsibility for complying with EEO regulations, 330

Human resource information systems (HRIS), 346–47

Human resource planning, 322–24; forecasting element, 323; human resource audit element, 323–24; need for, 322; in rapidly growing organizations, 287; and staffing process, 319–20; steps, 322–23; surveys to determine training needs, 338

Human resources model of motivation, 418, 420 *tab.*

Human skills: defined, 15, 16; difficulty in teaching, 20. *See also* Interpersonal skills

Ideas: clarifying for communication, 519; generating and developing, 400–401, 402; resistance to, 392

Identity, as career anchor, 561 *n.* 36

Image, and career development, 554

Immersion, step in creative process, 398

Implementation: of decisions, 154, 158; of expert systems, 641; and group acceptance, 479, 480; of MBO plans, 99; of MIS, 625, 629–35; of MS efforts, 173–74, 178–79, 193 *n.* 16; reducing resistance to change, 95; step in creative process, 401–2; of strategy, 128, 132

Impoverished management, 450

In-basket exercise, 336

Incentives: promotion as, 345; types of, 428. *See also* Financial incentives; Rewards

Incentive systems, in scientific management, 29, 31

Inclusion boundaries, 545

Income statement, 595

Incremental adjustment: problem-solving approach, 156; for productivity improvement, 216

Incubation, step in creative process, 398

In-depth interviews, for selection, 333, 334

India, 77–78, 353, 502, 661

Indirect-action environment, 54–55, 58–61; forecasting, 62

Individual characteristics: influence on motivation, 422, 423–25; and response to MIS, 630; and response to stress, 536–37

Individualism: vs. collectivism, 670; creative, of new employees, 534

Individuals: barriers to planning, 94; brainstorming by, 399; conflict between, 382; conflict with groups, 382; conflict within, 382; creative, 398; domination of group by, 480–81, 487–88; matching to job, 425; and MBO, 98–99, 101; and OD, 365, 366; problem solving by, 155–58, 478–79; resistance to change, 356, 358; subordination to common good, 35

Individual style: fit with organizational culture, 531; line–staff differences, 393; and response to stress, 536; screening for, in selection process, 336; as source of conflict, 384

Individual values, person-role conflict, 535

Induction, 320, 336–37

Industrial Engineering, 31

Industrial psychology, 38

Industrial revolution, 27, 269

Industry level: barriers to improved social performance, 69–70; ethical codes, 72

Inequity theory of motivation, 437

Inflation: effect on productivity, 219; recent trends, 59

Influence: and formal authority, 299; defined, 298; and leadership, 445, 458

Informal appraisal, 342
Informal communication, 516–17; and MIS, 622, 629–30; and problem finding, 148
Informal groups, 472; advantages and disadvantages, 255, 473–75
Informal leadership, 475–76
Informal organization, 37, 255
Informal power, 302
Information: access to, as source of power, 515; acquiring for decision making, 157–58; advanced technologies, 520–21; available in groups, 480; and control, 579, 580 *fig.*, 586–87; and coordination, 264, 266; defined, 621; encoding, 502; preceptive and receptive methods of gathering, 179; providing access to, to stimulate conflict, 388; types, 621–22; types provided in induction and orientation programs, 336–37; value and cost factors, 620–22
Informational roles, 17, 500
Informational transformation processes, 199
Information Database, 638
Information ownership, 512, 513
Information systems, 619–45; and control, 619–22; and coordination, 269; covert, and budget development, 603–4; DSS, 636–38 (*see also* Decision support systems); expert systems, 640–42 (*see also* Expert systems); for human resources, 346–47; MIS, 622–35 (*see also* Management information systems); networking, 638–39; vertical, 267. *See also* Computer-based information systems
Information technology: early predictions, 642–43; new advances, 520–21, 643–44
In-house education, 340–41
Inhwa (harmony), 676–77
Initiating structure, 449
Initiative, principle of, 35
Innovation: and career development, 547; and conflict, 381; and creativity, 397; organizational, 400–402. *See also* New-product development; Organizational change; Technological advances
Inputs: from external environment, 54; to operations system, 199
Insecurity, as barrier to delegation, 309, 310
Installation: of MIS, 628; of MS efforts, 178–79
Integrating roles, 268
Integration: for implementation of ideas, 402; and stability of external environment, 280; of staff and line activities, 393; of various departments, 265. *See also* Coordination
Integrative problem solving, 391, 401
Interaction, to encourage creativity, 402
Interactionist view of conflict, 380
Interactive strategic planning, 128
Interdependence: of organizational elements, 360–61; as source of conflict, 383; three types, 264
Intergroup cohesiveness, 391
Intergroup conflict, 382; behavior changes due to, 385; reduction methods, 389; resolution methods, 391; sources, 383–85
Intergroup development, OD techniques, 366, 370
Internal auditing, 613
Internal environment: and employee preferences for leadership style, 459; focus of older management theories, 53; forces for organizational change, 353–54; and human resource planning, 323. *See also* Organizational culture; Work environment
Internalization: of change agent's values, 357; of MS effort, 178–79
Internal Revenue Service (IRS), 594
International division, 657, 666
International environment, 61, 661–69
Internationalization: degrees of, 655–67; managerial attitudes toward, 657; reasons

for, 653–54, 674 *n.* 4
International management, 652–73; challenges, 661–69; selecting a managerial approach, 669–72; world economic trends, 653–57. *See also* Multinational enterprises
Internships: recruitment for, 324; training method, 338
Interpersonal communication, 501–12; with advanced information technology, 520; barriers to, 505–12; one- and two-way, 504–5; process, 501–4
Interpersonal orientation, differences between organizational units, 265
Interpersonal relationships, informal, 255
Interpersonal roles, 16–17, 500
Interpersonal skills: assessment of, in selection process, 335, 336; for MBO, 102. *See also* Human skills
Inter-role conflict, 535
Interviewing, in selection process, 332, 333, 334, 335
Intraorganizational networking, 638; effect on organizational structure, 643
Intrinsic outcomes, 435, 436
Intuition, 23 *n.* 23; and problem finding, 148; and problem solving, 179
Inventory planning and control systems, 212–14
Inventory problems, MS application, 176
Inventory turnover ratio, 596, 597 *tab.*
Investment centers, 600
Involvement, to overcome resistance to change, 358
Iran, 662
Israel, 245–46

Japan: attention to AI, 642, 644; U.S. businesses in, 566, 570, 653, 657, 679; U.S. car imports from, 229
Japanese firms: GE competitors, 224–25; just-in-time inventory system, 212–13, 223 *n.* 19; MNEs, 658, 660–61, 667; operating systems, 201; organizational structure, 60; productivity, 219–20; quality control procedures, 214; values-based strategy, 120
Japanese management: culture control model, 669; motivation research, 431; use by MNEs, 669, 671–72; U.S. interest in, 655; value placed on cooperativeness, 266
Jargon: in behavioral science, 41; communication barrier, 507; dysfunctional aspect of budgets, 610
Jazz, 637
JIT. *See* Just-in-time inventory
Job applicants, selection of, 331–36
Job characteristics, 237–38; analysis to determine training needs, 338; and motivation, 238, 239 *tab.*, 422–23, 426
Job depth, defined, 237
Job description: in MBO, 102; and recruitment, 324
Job design, 208–9, 237–39
Job dissatisfaction. *See* Dissatisfaction
Job enlargement: defined, 240–41; effective use of, 242–43; to meet individual needs, 284; and stress management, 537; as technostructural approach to change, 362
Job enrichment: defined, 241; effective use of, 242–43; guidelines, 242 *tab.*; to meet individual needs, 284; and motivation, 426, 437; and stress management, 537; as technostructural approach to change, 362
Job redesign, 240–42. *See also* Job enlargement; Job enrichment
Job rotation, 240–41; in management development program, 340; for training, 338
Jobs: danger of eliminating due to MIS implementation, 631; intrinsically rewarding, 436–37; matching individual to, 425; MNE influences, 658, 660, 661
Job scope, defined, 237

Job security: after AT&T breakup, 412; in Japan, 672; union benefit, 394
Job-shop production, 201, 202; process layout, 207; technological choice, 204
Job specialization: advantages, 235–36; concerns about, 236–37; influence on communication, 513; trade-offs with satisfaction and productivity, 239–40
Job titles, nonsexist, 330
Judgmental forecasting methods, 182 *tab.*
Just-in-time inventory (JIT), 212–13, 639

Kanban. See Just-in-time inventory
Key performance areas, 585
Knowledge: available in groups, 480; lack of, as barrier to planning, 93; management as a field of, 18; preservation of, in organizations, 5. *See also* Information
Knowledge-based systems, 640. *See also* Expert systems
Korean management, 676–77

Labor, division of. *See* Division of labor; Division of work
Labor market: external environment component, 55; international, 655; recruitment from, 324–25
Labor productivity index, 215
Labor unions: contract negotiations, 393–97; growth of, 32; reasons for joining, 393; as stakeholders, 55
Laissez-faire management, 450
LAN. *See* Local area network
Language, communication problems, 506–7, 509, 517
Large batch production, 281
Large organizations: role of planning staffs, 129; structure, 245. *See also* Organizational size
Lateral communication, 516–17
Lateral relationships, 267–68
Lateral transfers, 321
Latin America, 72, 660, 679
Law of effect, 429
Law of the instrument, 50 *n.* 34
Laws: concerns of MNEs, 662–63, 665; to ensure equal employment opportunities, 329–31; factor in ethical decision making, 72; obedience to, and business activism, 64
Lawsuits: over background investigations, 333; over fair employment and comparable worth issues, 331
Layoffs, 321; planning for, 322
Layout planning, 207–8, 209
Leaderless group discussion, 336
Leader-member relations, 456
Leader role, 17
Leaders: in conflict situations, 385, 386, 389; domination of group by, 480–81, 487–88; guidelines for making groups effective, 489; influence of communication network on emergence of, 514–15; OD involvement, 371; problem-solving techniques, 481, 482; of synectics group, 399–400; two basic functions, 448, 476
Leadership, 445–65; based on negative power, 301; behavior associated with, 446, 448–52; contingency approaches, 455–64; defined, 445; effectiveness factors, 452–55; Follett's view, 37; functions, 448; and group problem-solving, 482–83; in individualist vs. collectivist societies, 670; informal, 475–76; in MNEs, 669–72; and motivation, 417; nature of, 445–46; path-goal approach, 458–59; and power, 445, 446; in self-managed groups, 463; situational theories, 446, 460–61; social-learning/behavior modification theories, 462–63; trait approach, 446–47; transformational and charismatic, 300, 463–64
Leadership Edge, The, 650
Leadership styles, 448–52; authoritarian (*see*

Authoritarian management); classification of, 450, 467 *n.* 10; Fiedler model, 456–58; flexibility of, 461–62; influences on choice of, 451–52; on Managerial Grid, 450; in Systems 1–4, 450–51; task- vs. employee-oriented, 448–49; transactional and transformational, 463; university studies, 449–50; and work situation, 456–58

Leading: as management function, 4, 13; in MNEs, 668

Learners, career state, 549–50, 551

Learning theory, 429–32

Least-preferred co-worker (LPC), in leadership studies, 456

Legitimate power: defined, 300; delegation of, 306; and leadership, 446. *See also* Authority

Leverage, debt ratio, 596, 597 *tab.*

Liabilities, on balance sheet, 594

Liaison role, 17, 517

Life-cycle models: of individuals and their careers, 538–41, 561 *n.* 30; of organizations, 285–90; of supervisor-subordinate relationships, 460–61

Lifetime employment: at AT&T, 410; in Japan, 672

Linear career concept, 542, 544; and career plateaus, 549, 551

Linear programming models, 174, 176, 177

Line management, 303–4; budget preparation, 602; conflict with staff, 392–93, 635

Liquidity, 593; current ratio, 596, 597 *tab.*

Local area network (LAN), 638

Locational transformation processes, 199

Location planning, 206–7, 223 *n.* 16

Logical incrementalism, 114

Long-range planning, 87, 115, 118. *See also* Strategic planning

Long-term liabilities, 594

Lotus 1-2-3, 595, 598, 637

Love Canal, 60

Loyalty: as barrier to exposing unethical behavior, 73; early career dilemmas, 533

LPC. *See* Least-preferred co-worker

Mainframe computers: false expectations of manufacturers, 148; in intraorganizational networking, 638; security concerns, 632–33. *See also* Computers

Majority rule, to resolve conflict, 390

Management: as art and science, 18–19; attributes contributing to excellence, 9–11; collaborative, 364; of conflict, 387–91; defined, 3–4, 18; Japanese (*see* Japanese management); Korean, 676–77; philosophy of, 37; principles of, 34–35; as profession, 19; of stress, 537–38; theories of (*see* Management theories)

Management by exception, 582

Management by objectives (MBO), 95–105; applications, 97–98; assumptions about human nature, 96; communication improvements due to, 518; description, 97; evaluation of, 100–101; formal system, 99; and performance appraisal, 343; requirements for effectiveness, 103–5; strengths and weaknesses, 101–3; use of coaching, 339–40

Management consultants. *See* Consultants

Management development. *See* Management training and development programs

Management Edge, The, 649–51

Management education, criticism of, 20–21. *See also* Management training and development programs

Management hierarchy: in bureaucracy, 274–75; career concepts, 542; and coordination, 266, 267. *See also* Chain of command; Management levels

Management information, defined, 621

Management information systems (MIS), 622–35; as aid to idea development, 401;

compared to DSS, 144, 619, 623, 636, 637–38; as coordination mechanism, 267; cost effectiveness, 620; defined, 622; design stages, 624–25; evolution of, 622–23; guidelines for effective design, 625–29; impact on managers, 436, 642–44; implementation of, 629–35; requirements of different management levels, 623–25; security concerns, 633–34

Management-labor conflict, 393–97; Follett's view, 36–37; scientific management view, 380

Management levels, 11; and committee membership, 486 *fig.*; and control system requirements, 587; and information requirements, 621, 623–24; number of, and complexity of technology, 282–83; on organization chart, 246; and time allocated to planning, 86; types of skills required, 15–16, 34. *See also* First-line management; Middle management; Top Management

Management principles, 19, 34–35

Management process, 4; functions, 12–14; in international environment, 665–69; planning and, 85–88; theory, 43, 50 *n.* 26

Management science (MS), 169–80; advantages and limitations, 178; applications, 49 *n.* 21, 175–77; basic steps, 172–74; characteristics, 171–72; effect of management styles on, 179; forecasting models, 180–85; historical perspectives, 170; keys to effective use, 179–80; for problem finding, 148; three dimensions, 178–79; types of models, 174–75

Management science school, 42

Management style: and decision making, 159–62; effect on MS, 179; of excellently managed companies, 9–10; and formal planning, 132; and implementation of MBO, 102; on Managerial Grid, 450; and strategy making, 113–14. *See also* Individual style; Leadership style

Management theory, 27–48; behavioral school, 27, 37–41; classical school, 27–36; contingency approach, 45–46; eclectic approach, 47; evolution of, 27, 42–44; quantitative school, 27, 41–42; systems approach, 44–45; transitional theories, 36–37

Management training and development programs, 19–22, 338–41; as aid to establishing goals, 94; at assessment centers, 336; in business ethics, 547; and career development, 547; committees as vehicles for, 487; common mistakes, 341; criticism of, 20–21; in Grid OD, 370; for international managers, 667; in leadership, 458, 462; for MBO, 103; methods, 339–41; for MIS users, 628–29; recommended by Fayol, 34; recruitment for, 324; in use of computers, 620

Managerial competence, as career anchor, 544, 545, 551

Managerial Grid, 369–70, 450

Managerial linking roles, 268

Managerial performance: assessing potential for, 335–36; evaluation criteria, 8–9

Managerial roles, 6–8, 16–18; in communication, 500; coordination-promoting, 267, 268; at different career stages, 547; of leaders, 276

Managerial skills, 14–16; Fayol's view, 33; teaching to managers, 19–20

Managerial values: and ethical behavior, 71–73; influence of—on organizational structure, 283; on problem finding, 146; on strategy development, 120, 123

Managers: abilities, 34; accountability of, 307; attitudes toward internationalization, 657; barriers to delegation, 309–10; barriers to improved social performance, 69; conflict-stimulating, 388; credibility of,

508; as determinants of organizational structure, 283–84; female, 556–57; forces in, and leadership style, 451; functions and roles, 6–8, 33–34; impact of computers and MIS on, 642–44; implications of motivation theories, 436, 438; as linking pins, 473; on-the-job training roles, 339–41; outside recruitment, 326; of project teams, 252; reactive and proactive, 76 *n.* 18; reference groups, 472; response to pressures for change, 354–55; selection of, 336; sources of power, 300; training of, 19–22 (*see also* Management training and development programs); types of, 11–12. *See also* Supervisors

Manufacturing companies: MNEs, 661; reasons for going international, 655; span of management studies, 271–72; task-technology and structure, 291–83

Manufacturing management, 197, 198. *See also* Operations management

Market, organization by, 247, 249–51, 252

Mark IV, 614

Massachusetts Institute of Technology (MIT), 45, 340

Mass production, 281; and span of management, 282, 283

Master budgets, 605

Materials requirements planning (MRP), 212

Maternity leaves, 329

Matrix organizations, 247, 251–43; advantages and disadvantages, 254–55; and coordination, 268; evolution of, 252–54; functional authority relationships, 305; MNEs, 667; project teams, 252–53, 254, 494 *n.* 33; suitability for innovation, 402; violation of unity of command principle, 48 *n.* 10, 308

Maturity: and developmental tasks, 539; of employee, 460–61

MBA graduates: expectations of first job, 527, 528; female, 557; recruitment of, 324; turnover rates, 528

MBO. *See* Management by objectives

Measurement: in control process, 574–75, 582–85, 587; of OD results, 371; of undesirable behavior, 431

Mechanistic systems, 280, 281

Mediator role, 8

Medicaid, 279

Meditation, to reduce stress, 538

Mentors, 547, 556

Messages: in communication process, 502; effect on, of advanced information technology, 520; overtones, 519; redundant, 510; restatement of, 509

Mess management, 193, *n.* 11

Mexico, 61

Microcomputers: demand for, 148; for DSS, 144, 623, 637; effect on leadership roles, 463; and networks, 638, 639 *fig.*; for PERT and CPM, 188; prevalence, 620, 643; production applications, 212, 213, 217. *See also* Computers

Middle management: competition for personnel, 326; defined, 11; impact on—of computers, 642–43; of MIS, 630–31, 632–33; of technology, 59; information requirements, 624; transfers, 346; type of skills needed, 15, 16; university-sponsored development programs, 340. *See also* Management levels

Middle-of-the-road management, 450

Mid-life crisis, 540, 549

Milestone scheduling, 186–87

Mining industry: effects of planned technological change, 362; safety problems, 65

Minorities, EEO concerns, 345, 557

MIS. *See* Management information systems

Mission, of organization, 111, 123

MNEs. *See* Multinational enterprises

Mobility, as career tactic, 554

Modeling, of behavior, 339, 428
Models: of change process, 355–57; of communication process, 501; of conflict dynamic, 386; for forecasting, 180–85; of leadership, 456–59; of life-cycle tasks, 538–40; for location planning, 207; of management process, 12–14; of motivation, 418–19; of operations system, 199; of organizational design, 276; of organizational life cycle, 285–86; of problem-solving process, 151–54, 159–62; of task design process, 238; use in MS, 42, 171, 173, 174–75
Modern Times, 247
Monitor role, 17
Mopping-up stage, in management-labor negotiations, 395
Morale, effect of budgets on, 609. *See also* Satisfaction
Motivation, 417–39; and behavior modification, 429–32; career anchors, 544–45; content theories, 419–21; of creative people, 398; effect of budgets on, 609, 611; equity theory, 437; expectancy theory, 422, 433–37; financial incentives, 218, 428, 431; guidelines for managers, 438; human relations model, 418–19, 420 *tab.*; human resources model, 419, 420 *tab.*; importance of, 417; in individualist vs. collectivist societies, 670; and individual needs, 423–25; and job characteristics, 238, 239 *tab.*, 426; maintaining with transfer, 346; Maslow's theory, 40–41; process theories, 421–22; and productivity, 219; reinforcement theories, 422; under System 4 leadership, 450; systems view, 422–23; Theory X and Theory Y assumptions, 96, 275, 276; traditional model, 418, 420 *tab.*; and work situation characteristics, 426–28
MRP. *See* Materials requirements planning
Multinational enterprises (MNEs), 652–73; defined, 657; economic concerns, 662, 664–65; impact on home countries, 660–61; impact on host countries, 658–60; and international environment, 661–65; managerial attitudes, 657; political-legal concerns, 662–63, 665; reasons for going international, 653–55, 674 *n.* 4; rise and spread of, 658; sociocultural concerns, 663–64, 665 stages in internationalization process, 655–57; technological concerns, 664, 665
Multiplan, 595
"Myth of the Well-Educated Manager, The" (Livingston), 20

National Technical University, 341
Needs: to manage, 20; Maslow's hierarchy, 40–41, 423–24; overstatement of, in budget development, 603; for power, 21; scientific management view, 32; of successful managers, 20–21. *See also* Human needs
Needs analysis: for management development programs, 339; overly hasty, 341
Negotiation: of management-labor conflicts, 395–97; to overcome resistance to change, 359 *tab.*, 360
Negotiation Edge, The, 650
Negotiator role, 17
Neoclassical approach to organizational design, 274–76
Netherlands, 662, 682
Network-based scheduling techniques, 186–91 *See also* Critical path method; Program evaluation review technique
Networking (computer-based), 638–39; for idea development, 401
Networking (interpersonal): and career planning, 326; with co-workers, 553; and mentoring, 556; for task accomplishment, 553. *See also* Communication networks
Neutrality, communication behavior, 511

New employees: career roles, 547; career state, 551; development of self-concept, 544; function of budgets for, 610; induction and orientation, 336–37; inflated expectations, 527–29; initial job assignment, 530–31; leadership requirements, 460; role in generation of ideas, 400; training and development programs, 337–38
New Lanark, Scotland, cotton mills, 28
New-product development: advantages of group decision making, 479; and creativity, 399–400, 402; leadership requirements, 455, 463; and organizational structure, 277, 312; with self-managed groups, 463. *See also* Innovation
New York Transit Authority, 613
1984 (Orwell), 487
Noise, in communication process, 503–4, 507, 509
Nominal group process, 399
Nonproductive facilities, 207
Nonprogrammed decisions, 143, 144
Nonverbal communication, 502, 508, 509, 510
Normative models, 174
Normative view of authority, 298
Norms, of group. *See* Group norms
Northeastern University, 562 *n.* 44
Not-for-profit organizations: characteristics, 130; strategic planning, 130–131
Nudge, 641

Obedience: and authority, 298–99; demanded by supervisor, 533; malicious, 390
Objective quality, criterion for effective decisions, 155, 158
Objectives: accomplishing through organizations, 5; choice of, and effectiveness, 9; as direction for creativity, 403; vs. drives, 97; identification of, 123, 152–53; in MBO, 98–99, 103–4; negotiating guidelines, 396 *tab.*; in operations planning and control, 211; and performance appraisal, 343; and strategy, 111, 112
Occupational Safety and Health Administration, (OSHA), 55, 56, 208
OD. *See* Organizational development
Odyssey, 641
Odyssey, The (Homer), 556
Office of Economic Opportunity (OEO), 60
Office of Strategic Services (OSS), 336
Off-the-job training, 338, 340–41
Ohio State University, 449
Omega, 641
One-Minute Manager, The (Blanchard and Johnson), 463, 650
One-way communictaion, 504–5
On-the-job training, 338, 339–40, 341
Open system, defined, 44
Operant conditioning: and leadership, 462–63, 468 *n.* 30; and motivation, 422, 429
Operating budgets, 604, 605
Operating management, and MIS implementation, 630, 631 *tabs.*, 635
Operational approach, 43, 50 *n.* 26
Operational auditing, 613
Operational control, MIS information requirements, 623–24
Operational plans, 89–91
Operations management: elements of, 198; planning and control, 201–12; recent trends, 197–98; and strategic planning, 200; types of decisions required, 200. *See also* Operations systems
Operations research (OR), 41–42, 143. *See also* Management science
Operations systems: capacity planning, 203; characteristics, 199–202; continuous and assembly-line vs. job-shop production, 201–2; facility location planning, 206–7;

job design, 208–9; layout planning, 207–8, 209 *fig.*; model, 199–200; organizational strategy, 200–201; process selection, 204–5; product/service planning and design, 202–3. *See also* Operations management
Opportunities: career planning analysis, 552; vs. problems, 148–50; strategic, 126; unexpected, 580
Opportunity finding, 148–50; education for, 20; influences on, 146–47
OR. *See* Operations research
Order, principle of, 35
Organic systems, 280, 281
Organization: definitions, 233; informal, 255. *See also* Organizations
Organizational analysis, to determine training needs, 338
Organizational change, 353–74; approaches to planning, 360–63; forces for, 353–54; managerial response to pressures for, 354–55; models of, 355–57; OD approach, 363–71 (*see also* Organizational development); in organizational culture, 371–73; readiness of system for, 357–58; required for MBO, 102; resistance to, 358–60; stress due to, 356
Organizational characteristics: and decentralization, 312, 313; U.S. vs. Japanese, 671–72
Organizational climate: for creativity, 402–3; and communication, 519; effect of indirect-action environment, 58; for ethical behavior, 74. *See also* Organizational culture
Organizational communication: and advanced information technology, 520–21; influences on, 512–13; lateral and informal, 516–17; networks, 513–15; overcoming barriers to, 517–20; vertical, 515–16
Organizational conflict, 379–97; behavioral effects, 385; consequences of, 386–87; defined, 379–80; dynamic intensification of, 385–86; functional and dysfunctional, 381–82, 387; level of, 387; between line and staff, 392–93; between management and labor, 393–97; methods of managing, 387–91; sources, 383–85; suppression of, 379, 390; traditional vs. interactionist view, 380–81; types, 382
Organizational culture, 371–73; at AT&T, 410; changes in, 373; and conflict results, 387; and creativity, 400–401; and degree of centralization, 313; of excellently managed companies, 10; feedback-supporting, 510; fit of new employee to, 531; influence on leadership style, 455; and MIS implementation, 630; and motivation, 427–28, 438; in rapidly growing organizations, 287; role of performance appraisal, 342, 344
Organizational decline, 285, 287–89
Organizational design, 263, 272–90; to adjust to external environment, 63; classical approach, 273–74, 361; contingency approaches, 276–84; neoclassical approach, 274–76. *See also* Organizational change; Organizational structure
Organizational development (OD), 363–71; assumptions and values, 365–66; communication improvements due to, 518; conditions for successful programs, 370–71; defined, 363–64; evaluation of, 370; Grid technique, 369–70; survey feedback technique, 367; team-building techniques, 367–69; types of activities, 366–67
Organizational goals, 111–12. *See also* Goals
Organizational growth: and decentralization, 312, 313; effect on organizational structure, 277, 285, 287; very rapid, 287
Organizational life cycle, 285–90
Organizational performance: and conflict, 381; evaluation of, 8–9, 597; of social responsibilities, 67–70

Organizational politics: and budget development, 603; career planning analysis, 552–53; in committees, 487; insensitivities of new employee, 332–33; management roles, 8, 22, *n.* 2

Organizational responsibility, 63–70. *See also* Corporate social responsibility

Organizational size: and decentralization, 312; of MNEs, 658, 659 *tab.*; and organizational structure, 245, 283. *See also* Large organizations; Small organizations

Organizational structure, 243–56; CBIS impact, 643; changing to stimulate conflict, 388; and command groups, 473; and communication, 514–15; and conflict results, 387; and creativity, 401, 402; criteria for selection of, 256; defined, 243; determinants of, 244–45; and division of work, 234–43; elements of, 243–44; employees' influence on, 284; of excellently managed companies, 10; and external environment, 279–81; forms, 247; functional, 248–49; and informal organization, 255; managers' influence on, 283–84; matrix organization, 251–55; of MNEs, 666–67; organizational life-cycle changes, 285–86; on organization chart, 246–47; planned change in, 360, 361; product/market organization, 249–51; responses to decline, 289; and span of management, 270; and strategy, 277–79; in Systems 1–4, 276; and task-technology, 281–83

Organizational systems, 199; mechanistic vs. organic, 280, 281; readiness for change, 357–58

Organizational units: coordination of (*see* Coordination); disruption by MIS, 629; independent, 268; interdependence, 264; strategic (SBUs), 122–28

Organizational values: as basis for strategy, 120, 123; individual responses to, 534; influence on, of OD change agents, 365–66

Organization chart, 246–47, 324

Organizations: barriers to improved social performance 69; career development in, 545–47; characteristics of groups in, 475–76; common elements, 3; communication in, 512–21; conflict between 382–83; creation of, 286; declining, 287–89; functions, 4–5; impact of computer technology on, 642–44; implications of expectancy theory for, 436–37; improving productivity in, 216–17; mission, 111–12, 123; OD techniques for, 366–67; power in, 301–2; purpose, 111, 136 *n.* 30; rapidly growing, 287; restructuring to stimulate conflict, 388; survival rates, 286, 290; as systems, 199; value-driven, 123

Organizing: defined, 33, 243; departmentalization, 245–56; division of work, 235–43; as management function, 4, 13; in MNEs, 666–67; multistep process, 233–34; and organizational structure, 243–45; for stability and change, 233

Orientation: differences between organizational units, 265; for international managers, 667; to MIS, 635; of new employees, 320, 336–37

OSHA. *See* Occupational Safety and Health Administration

Outplacement services, 346

Outputs: to external environment, 54; from operations system, 199

Overcontrol, 577, 584

Panaudit, 614

Panic, as barrier to problem solving, 156

Parallel installation, of MIS, 628

Partial productivity, 215

Partial reinforcement, 431

Participative management. *See* Employee participation

Passivity, in early career, 532–33

Past experience: deviation from, and problem solving, 147; impact on behavior, 428–32; problem of evaluating job candidate's record, 335

Path-goal model of leadership, 458–59

Pay. *See* Bonuses; Rewards; Salaries

Peers: appraisal by, 342; influence on leadership style, 455; influence on motivation, 428. *See also* Co-workers; Work groups

People: and communication, 501; concern for, on Managerial Grid, 369–70; and leadership, 445; manager's interaction with, 6–7; OD assumptions, 365; and organizational structure, 244, 283–84; planned change in, 360, 361, 362; productivity through, 217–21. *See also* Employees; Human resource planning; Individuals; Managers

Perceptions: of budgets, 610; and communication, 506, 508–9, 518; consistency of, and cohesion, 405 *n.* 6; distorted, due to conflict, 385; effect on leadership style, 453; of role, 41; as source of conflict, 383

Performance: and achievement need, 425; of competitors, and problem finding, 148; and control, 13, 575, 585–86; effect on—of behavior modification, 432; of early job experience, 337; of first supervisor, 531; of information overload, 628; of MBO, 100–101; of performance appraisal, 343; of planned change approaches, 362; of praise, 431; of stress, 536; efficiency and effectiveness criteria, 9; equity theory, 437; expectancy theory, 434–36; and expression of feelings, 365; factors influencing, 417; gaps, 127; of groups, 477–79; information, 158; linking pay to, 428; outcome expectancy, 434; potential, 342; problems in evaluating candidate's past record, 335; and professional status, 19; profitability concerns, 612; and satisfaction, 419; of women managers, 557. *See also* Managerial performance; Organizational performance

Performance appraisal, 341–45; to determine training needs, 338; formal (systematic) and informal, 342–43; impact of budgets on, 610–11; lack of, for new recruits, 528; in MBO, 97, 102; Owen's reforms, 82; problems, 343–45; step in staffing process, 321; and stress management, 536, 537

Performance review, in MBO, 99, 100

Performance standards: for MIS, 635; in System 4 leadership style, 451

Permanent groups, 473, 485

Personal growth: need for, and job satisfaction, 240; spiral career concept, 542

Personality: and leadership effectiveness, 452–53; problem of trying to modify through training program, 341; and response to stress, 536–37. *See also* Individual characteristics

Personal staff, 304–5

Personnel assignment, with expert systems, 641

Personnel department. *See* Human resouces department

Personnel policies, and motivation, 426–27

Person-role conflict, 534

Persuasion, vs. problem-solving activity, 482, 483 *tab.*

PERT. *See* Program evaluation and review technique

Physical transformation processes, 199

Planned change: vs. reactive change, 354–55; three approaches, 360–62. *See also* Organizational change

Planned work activities, for management development, 340

Planning, 84–105; to adjust to external environment, 62–63; aids to, 169–92 (*see also* Critical path method; Management science; Program evaluation and review technique); allocation of time to, 86; barriers to, 93–95; basic steps, 87–88; and controlling, 92, 574; and decision making, 87, 141; defined, 33; forecasts as premises for, 181; gaps, 181; for human resources, 319–20, 322–24 (*see also* Human resource planning); of individual careers, 552–54; in international environment, 665–66; long-range and short-range, 86–87; as management function, 4, 12–13; and the management process, 85–88; MBO approach, 95–105 (*see also* Management by objectives); need for flexibility, 87; operational, 89–91; and operations management, 210–12; via profit budgets, 605; significance of, 85. *See also* Strategic planning

Planning mode, of strategy making, 113–14

Planning staffs: improper use of, 117, 132; role in large organizations, 129

Plans: as coordination mechanism, 267; deviation from, and problem finding, 147–48; operational, 89–91

Plant managers, information needs, 624

Polaris missile program, 187

Policies: changes at AT&T, 410; as dissatisfier, 426; to encourage ethical behavior, 74; influence on leadership style, 455; and motivation, 420 *tab.*, 426–27; as standing plans, 91; toward women, 557

Political insensitivity, in early career, 532–33

Political-legal variables: external environment component, 60; MNE concerns, 660, 661, 662–63, 665

Political risk, of MNEs, 665

Politicians, managers as, 8, 22 *n.* 2

Politics, organizational. *See* Organizational politics

Pollution controls, 60, 279, 354

Polycentric attitudes, 657

Pooled interdependence, 264

Position power, 457

Positive reinforcement, 430, 432

Post-action controls, 579, 581

Power: access to information as source of, 515; American ambivalence about, 301; characteristics of successful users, 301–2; defined, 298; effect on communication, 515; dispersion of, in committees, 487; equalization of, as goal of OD, 365–66; imbalance of, in employment interview, 335; and leadership, 445, 446, 457–58; in line and staff positions, 304; at lower levels of the organization, 302; need for, 21, 424, 425; political insensitivity to, 532–33; sources of, 299–300; two faces of, 301; unified theory of, 315 *n.* 14

Power bargaining, management-labor, 394

Powerbase, 637

Power distance, national characteristic, 670, 671

Practice of Management, The (Drucker), 95, 97

Praise, effect on performance, 431

Pre-action controls, 578–79

Preceptive information gathering, 179

Predetermined standards, 583

Predictors, in control process, 581–82

Pregnancy Discrimination Act of 1978, 329

Prices, assumptions in break-even analysis, 598

Principles: of management, 34–35; professional, 19

Principles of Scientific Management, The (Taylor), 30

Priority setting: ambiguous, as barrier to exposing unethical behavior, 73–74; and decision making, 157; as management role, 7; in zero-base budgeting, 608–9

Satisfiers, 426
SBUs. *See* Strategic business units
Scalar principle of delegation, 307–8
Scenario construction, 184
Scheduling: detailed, 211–12; with expert systems, 641; MS application, 177
Science, management as, 18–19
Scientific management theory, 28–32; of conflict, 380; contributions and limitations, 32; forerunners, 28; Gantt, 31; the Gilbreths, 31; of motivation, 418; of planned technological change, 362; Taylor, 28–31; of work simplification, 238
Screening controls, 579
Screening interview, 332
Securities and Exchange Commission (SEC), 57, 484
Security: behavioral variations, 421; as career anchor, 545; MIS concerns, 633–34; on needs hierarchy, 423, 424; provided by informal groups, 474; and steady state career concept, 542. *See also* Job security
Selection, 331–36; assessment centers, 336; interviewing, 334; of managers, 334–36; planning for, 322; in rapidly growing organizations, 287; substituting training for, 341; scientific management theory, 30, 32; and staffing process, 320; steps in process, 331–33
Self-actualization: encouraged by transformational leader, 463; need for, 423, 424; problems of new recruits, 528
Self-actualizing man, 40–41
Self-concept, occupational, 544
Self-confidence: and domination of group, 481; leadership trait, 446, 447, 464; screening for, in selection process, 335
Self-fulfilling prophecies: due to labeling, 507; and leadership expectations, 454; and women's lower expectations, 557
Self-managed groups, 463
Semivariable costs, 607
Senders: in communication process, 502, 505, 508, 510; role conflicts, 534
Separation: as form of compromise, 391; from organization, 321, 346
Service, as career anchor, 561 *n.* 36
Service organizations, strategic planning, 118, 135 *n.* 20
Services: design of, 202; informational, 639; location planning, 207; process selection, 205
Service sector, productivity, 218–19
Sexism, in job titles, 330
Sexual harassment, 329
Sexual stereotyping, 447
Shareholders, 57, 484
Shop Management (Taylor), 30
Simulation: assessment center exercises, 337; MS models, 175, 176, 177
Single-use plans, 89, 90
Skills: Babbage's view, 28; for internal audit, 613; human resource audit of, 323. *See also* Managerial skills
Skill variety: as job characteristic, 237–38, 239; in turbulent vs. stable environments, 280
Slack resources, 268
Small batch production, 281
Small organizations: characteristics, 129; strategic planning in, 129–30. *See also* Organizational size
Social activism, and criticism of business, 57, 60, 63. *See also* Business activism
Socialization: and career development, 547; of new employee, 529, 531
Social-learning theory of leadership, 462–63
Social man concept, 39, 40
Social needs: in Maslow's hierarchy, 423; and motivation, 418
Social performance, 67–70. *See also* Corporate social responsibility

Social Responsibilities of Business Corporations (CED), 63
Social values: in indirect-action environment, 59–60; of informal groups, 474, 475
Sociocultural variables: external environment component, 59–60; MNE concerns, 663–64, 665
Software. *See* Computer software
South Africa, 53, 57, 59, 661, 679
South America, 680
South Essex studies, 281
South Korea, 677
Span of management, 269–72; and coordination, 263; and production technology, 381–83
Specialization: and conflict over goals, 383; in leadership functions, 448; and organizational size, 245; and organizational structure, 243. *See also* Job specialization
Specialized staff, 304–5
Spiral career concept, 542, 544
Spokesperson role, 17
Sponsors: career role, 547; search for, 539, 554. *See also* Mentors
Spontaneity, communication behavior, 511
Stability: environmental, 279, 280; forces for, 356; and organizational structure, 233, 256; of staff, principle of, 35
Staff: conflict with line, 392–93; functional authority, 305; personal vs. specialized, 304–5; role in management development programs, 341; stability of, 35
Staffing: defined, 319; in MNEs, 667; and organizing, 13; process, 319–21; in rapidly growing organizations, 287; recent emphasis on, 283
Staff positions, 304
Stakeholders: influence of, 75 *n.* 1, 298; internal and external, 53, 54 *fig.*, 55; strategic planning considerations, 125
Standardization: and organizational size, 245; and organizational structure, 243–44
Standard procedures, 91
Standards: budgets as, 599; and control process, 13–14, 574, 581–83; differences between organizational units, 264; shifting, problem in performance appraisal, 344
Standing plans, 89, 90–91
Stanford Research Institute, 130
Stanford University, 340, 557, 616 *n.* 17
Stars: in BCG matrix, 121, 122; career state, 550, 551
Status: effect of differences on communication, 515; need for, 424; provided by informal groups, 474; union benefit, 394
Steady state career concept, 542, 544
Steering controls, 579, 580, 581
Stereotypes: of career, 542; negative, increase due to conflict, 385, 386; sexual, 447
Stockholders, 57, 484
Strategic Air Command, 680
Strategic alternatives, 127
Strategic business units (SBUs), 120, 122–28
Strategic control, 128; points, 585–86
Strategic decisions, in quality control, 214
Strategic planning, 111–34; advantages and disadvantages, 117–18; basic approaches, 128; characteristics, 115; defined, 114–15; effectiveness of, 118; formal process, 118–28; global, of MNEs, 666; and human resource planning, 322; importance of, 116–17; information requirement, 624; in large organizations, 129; in not-for-profit organizations, 130–31; vs. operational planning, 89, 115; and operations management, 200–201; overcoming barriers to, 131–33; in small businesses, 129–30
Strategy: approaches to developing, 112–14; for behavior modification, 432; characteristics of, 112; and communication behavior, 511; current, identification of, 123–24; and decentralization, 312; defined, 111;

implementation of, 128, 132; for individual career management, 552–53; and organizational goals, 111–12; and organizational structure, 244, 277–79; three levels of, 119–28
Stress, 535–38; after AT&T breakup, 410–12; causes, 535–36; effects, 336–37; management of, 337–38; due to organizational decline, 228; due to panic over problem solving, 156
Stressors, 535, 537
Strikes, 396–97
Structure. *See* Organizational structure
Subordinates: appraisal of superiors by, 342–43; delegation to, 309, 310; emotional reactions in, 508; formal appraisal of, 342, 344; and leadership style, 445, 451, 454–55, 459; loyalty dilemmas, 333; maturity of, 460–61; on organization chart, 245; participation in MBO, 99, 100, 104; relationship to organization, 6; Theory X and Theory Y assumptions, 275; upwardly mobile, communication effects, 515; when to involve in decision making, 159–62. *See also* Supervisor-subordinate relationship
Substance abuse: effect on productivity, 219; preemployment testing, 333; due to stress, 536
Subsystems: defined, 44; operations as, 199
Success: fear of, 425; fundamental attribution error, 431; and loyalty, 533
SuperCalc, 595
Superchips, 644
Superiority, communication behavior, 511–12
Superiors: appraisal of, 342–43; authority of, 298–99; career planning considerations, 552, 553–54; formal appraisal by, 342; influence on leadership style, 454; threat of new recruits to, 528–29; when to refer decision making to, 150–51. *See also* Supervisors; Top management
Superordinate goals, 389, 391
Supervisors: as behavioral models, 339; and budgeting process, 601–2, 610; first, influence on subsequent performance, 531; Gantt's bonuses, 31; helping him/her to succeed, as career strategy, 553, 544; implications for, of computer revolution in communication, 520–21; influence on employee motivation, 428, 437; information requirements, 624; loyalty demands, 533; roles in training and development programs, 339–40, 341. *See also* Managers
Supervisor-subordinate relationship: advantages of group meetings, 488; authority issues, 298–99; coaching, 339–40; delegation problems, 310; under different leadership styles, 450–51; life cycle, 460–61; loyalty issues, 533; neoclassical views, 274–76; role conflicts, 534; sociocultural variables, 59; in Systems 1–4, 276; vertical communication, 515–16
Survey feedback technique, 366–67, 368 *fig.*
Survival-of-the-fittest model, 298
Swiss watch industry, 402
Symbols: in communication, 501, 502, 517; managers as, 8; of organizational culture, 372, 373
Symphony, 637
Synectics, 399–400
Synergy: defined, 44; in groups, 490
Systematic problem-solving style, 179
System boundary, 45
Systems: general theory, 44–45; mechanistic and organic, 280; open and closed, 44; the organization as, 199; of problems, 193 *n.* 11; readiness for change, 357–58. *See also* Control systems; Information systems; Operations systems
Systems approach: to external environment, 53; to management, 44–45; to motivation, 422–23; in MS, 171–72